AMERICAN
DECADES
1930-1939

AMERICAN DECADES
1930-1939

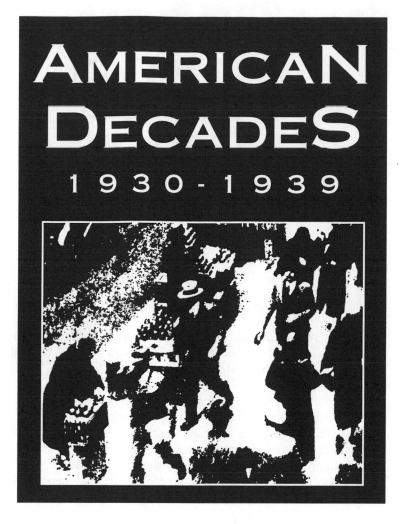

EDITED BY
VICTOR BONDI

A MANLY, INC. BOOK

 **Gale Research Inc.**

An International Thomson Publishing Company

I(T)P
Changing the Way the World Learns

NEW YORK • LONDON • BONN • BOSTON • DETROIT • MADRID
MELBOURNE • MEXICO CITY • PARIS • SINGAPORE • TOKYO
TORONTO • WASHINGTON • ALBANY NY • BELMONT CA • CINCINNATI OH

AMERICAN DECADES
1930-1939

Matthew J. Bruccoli and Richard Layman, *Editorial Directors*

Karen L. Rood, *Senior Editor*

Printed in the United States of America

Library of Congress Catalog Card Number 95-078320
ISBN 0-8103-5725-9

I(T)P™

The trademark **ITP** is used under license.
10 9 8 7

CONTENTS

INTRODUCTION

On the Road. In the summer of 1935 a gangling, fourteen-year-old Arkansas farm boy named Lee Webster hiked twenty miles from his home in Landis to the nearest paved highway, caught a ride, and went looking for work. Over the next six years Webster — this writer's grandfather — threshed wheat in Kansas; worked in a carnival in Nebraska; harvested corn in Minnesota; gambled in Kansas City; trucked melons in Missouri, stave bolts in Illinois, and lettuce in Colorado; surveyed the Wisconsin woods with the Civilian Conservation Corps; married; divorced; joined the U.S. Army Air Corps; and arrived in Hawaii just in time for the Japanese attack at Pearl Harbor on 7 December 1941. His restlessness and wandering were typical: millions of Americans, both men and women, hopped freight trains and hitched rides just about anywhere trying to make ends meet during the Depression. No single locale defined America in the 1930s the way Chicago did in the 1920s or New York did in the 1940s. America was on the road in the 1930s. People clogged the highways looking for work, met strangers on back stoops and shared food, slept in jails overnight to keep from freezing. Jazz bands crisscrossed the nation and egged on jitterbuggers in dance halls. Aviators chased each other across the continent, setting and breaking records with their new and improved flying machines. Families took new parkways to new national parks, and streamlined Zephyr trains sped businessmen across the prairies. Writers such as John Steinbeck, Jack Conroy, and Nelson Algren and folksingers such as Woody Guthrie hit the pavement and rails by the dozens, writing stories, essays, songs, exposés, and travelogues of Depression-era America. Their accounts provide a rich portrait of a nation on the road and in search of itself. America in the 1930s had lost direction, and it was filled with restless, ceaseless, and unfocused energy.

Getting By. It was an energy born, for the most part, of desperation. Hard times, drifting — even hunger — were nothing new in American life. What made the Great Depression unusual was the scale of suffering and the almost apocalyptic sense that nothing would make it go away. The suicide rate rose 30 percent between 1928 and 1930. In 1930 a Pennsylvania man caught stealing a loaf of bread for his four hungry children was so overcome with shame that he returned home and hanged himself in his cellar. For the writers or a young man like Lee Webster, the rootless character of the decade spelled adventure; for most families, hard times meant misery and tough choices. Savings ran out; pensions disappeared; banks closed; charity funds were exhausted. Hungry children were sent to live with wealthier relatives. Mothers chose between buying bread or buying coal. Family farms were sold, and cars were junked for scrap. Bitter men wallpapered the walls of their houses with worthless stock certificates. Everyone stretched what they had to get by. Dandelions and catsup made passable soups. Darning clothes when one could find thread, fixing radios with scrap metal, and plugging cracks in walls with old newspaper became necessities for millions. The elderly suffered terribly. Too old to work, many lost their life savings to bank closures. Lacking shoes and clothes, children stayed home from school, ashamed of their poverty. In many places it did not matter: short of operating funds, schools closed by the thousands. Extreme actions were not unusual. In Washington State homeless men set forest fires so they would be hired to put them out. People ate grass and weeds in Arkansas and huddled together in cars to keep warm in North Dakota. Grocers went broke extending lines of credit to their neighbors. Teachers were paid in scrip that often could not be redeemed. Many teachers worked for room and board, as did millions of others desperate for work of any kind. Farmers saw their lands dry up and blow away. The dust storms were so severe that western Kansas and eastern Colorado were virtually depopulated. In the South sharecroppers and tenants were thrown off their lands by the thousands; objections to the evictions were dealt with by Klansmen and lynching. Desperation fueled intolerance; intolerance fueled desperation. The expert advice for resolving the Depression, from President Herbert Hoover's millionaire secretary of the treasury Andrew Mellon, was brutal: "Liquidate labor, liquidate stocks, liquidate the farmers, liquidate real estate."

Two Nations. Mellon's advice sat poorly with the nearly thirteen million unemployed Americans, as well as with the millions working reduced hours for lower wages and the millions whose jobs were threatened. The Depression opened a class division in American life that would not be healed until after World War II. Despite hyperbolic reports about the impact of the Depression on the rich, America in the Depression was, as John Dos Passos noted in *The Big Money* (1936), two nations: a rich America and a poor America. The Depression wiped out the many in between. There were also an urban America and a rural America; an Anglo-Saxon America and an ethnic America; a wet America and a dry America. The country was divided into opposites as at no time since the Civil War, and the sense of anger and danger was akin to that of Abraham Lincoln's day. The deeper the Depression sank, the tighter the divisions became. "Brother Can You Spare a Dime" gave way to "Which Side Are You On?" as the representative song of the decade. At middecade the social divisions in the country overlay each other and the distinctions became acute. In the presidential election of 1936, it was rich, WASP, dry America versus poor, ethnic, wet America — the Liberty League versus the New Deal. The Liberty League lost, resoundingly. Yet it lost in an election, and that was significant. Despite the often strident rhetoric of the decade, no Bolshevik coup, no Nazi takeover, occurred in America. As adrift as America seemed during the Depression, it was guided by a surer sense of destiny than that which governed Europe.

New Deal Democracy. Much of the credit for stability in the United States belonged to the New Deal. Despite President Franklin D. Roosevelt's penchant for ill-considered experiment, for deployment of contradictory programs, for political vacillation, the New Deal he built consistently advanced democracy and the reform of capitalism. It also created the largest federal government ever; the postwar Democratic Party coalition of finance capital, big labor, African Americans, Southerners, and liberals; and the beginnings of a Supreme Court that would broadly extend civil liberties after World War II. Many found the creation of a large federal bureaucracy fascistic and the New Deal welfare programs communistic, but Roosevelt and his associates hewed closely to a democratic center. There was no confiscation of private property, no dissolution of Congress. Even the most reckless New Deal measure, the 1937 attempt to pack the Supreme Court, was within the realm of constitutional interpretation. In retrospect Roosevelt's support for civil rights for African Americans seems half-hearted — there was no antilynching law passed during the decade, despite sensational crimes such as the lynching of Claude Neal in 1934 — but it reflected Roosevelt's understanding of his own political and constitutional limitations. Often Roosevelt worked within those limitations in surprisingly effective ways, a testament to his ability as a leader. He appointed prominent blacks to positions in the New Deal and nominated the first African American federal judge, William Hastie. Another example of Roosevelt's ability to pursue his objectives within constitutional limitations was in education. As the Depression struck American schools, reformers demanded federal financing of education, a radical break with the tradition of local control of schools. The New Dealers refused to take this step, but

by threatening to withhold funding for more politically viable projects such as roads and dams, the New Dealers forced states to systematize their school-financing programs. New Dealers also provided education for children through agencies such as the National Youth Administration and the Civilian Conservation Corps. In this often indirect manner, the New Deal constructed a large federal government that responded to the needs of the common man in ways in which later federal bureaucracies failed. The New Deal succeeded in expanding the power of the federal government even as it kept strictly to government of, by, and for the people.

New Deal Capitalism. The New Deal also forced American capitalism to modernize and to act in a more socially responsible fashion. Government regulation imposed order, discipline, and honesty on chaotic markets — an order for which many businessmen clamored. It was Gerald Swope of General Electric who proposed the industrial cartels that would become part of the National Industrial Recovery Act; oilmen themselves drafted the Connelly Hot Oil Act; securities experts and investors clamored for the Securities and Exchange Commission; bankers suggested federal insurance as a way of reassuring depositors. Those who view the history of the 1930s as a contest between business and government — who view the New Deal as antibusiness — profoundly misunderstand the history of American industry during the decade. The New Deal was part of an evolution in American capitalism, the natural expression of a shift from industrial manufacturing to consumer production. The New Deal's support for big labor, Social Security, public-works programs, progressive taxation, and other measures to redistribute wealth lay the foundation for the consumer economy of the postwar era by raising wages and improving working conditions. Granted, much of the New Deal's success was due to good fortune. New Deal economists such as Raymond Morley or Rexford Tugwell had no more sophisticated grasp of the causes of the Depression than Hoover or Mellon. Countercyclical spending and Keynesian economics were doctrines they stumbled on rather than developed. The prosperity of the postwar era owed as much to the preeminent position of the United States in global trade as it did to New Deal planning. Yet it was important that the New Deal represented the interests of a growing consumer sector in American business and that it worked toward a solution to the Depression. The many critics of the New Deal never understood that it was popular because it tried to solve the Depression. That energy and activism, coupled with the ebullient confidence Roosevelt exuded throughout his life, stood in marked contrast to the standpatters in the Hoover administration and the Liberty League. It also exhibited a realism Hoover and his associates could never accept. Throughout the 1930s they called for a return to the business ethics and economic principles of the Roaring Twenties, never quite grasping that those ethics and principles had caused the Depression in the first place. There was no going back. America in the 1930s was entering a new age.

Decline of WASP culture. Part of the success of the New Deal in politics and economics came from its embrace of the cultural transformation of the 1930s. American culture was becoming more plural, more populist, more modern. The white, Anglo-Saxon, 100 percent Americanism of the 1920s changed. American society became more inclusive, in part because the Nazis became so obsessively exclusive, in part because the WASPs of the 1920s discredited themselves, and in part because ethnic Americans manned the New Deal and the new consumer and communications industries ushering in the new age. America before the Depression had been culturally monochromatic, so given to notions of Anglo-Saxon racial superiority that it disenfranchised African Americans and created the eugenics movement. Nativist Protestant groups succeeding in winning the prohibition of the sale and distribution of alcohol, fundamentally an antiimmigrant measure stripping the urban poor of beer gardens and saloons that had been at the center of their social life. Evangelists such as Billy Sunday, Bishop James Cannon, and Aimee Semple McPherson were national celebrities. But times were changing. Anthropologists such as Franz Boas and Ruth Benedict undermined the quasiscientific basis of white racism and the eugenics movement, and the Nazi embrace of racism and eugenics repelled many. WASP paragons of respectability were the subjects of scandals in the 1930s. Congressional investigations disclosed unethical and illegal business dealings by big businessmen such as J. P. Morgan, Samuel Insull, Mellon, Richard Whitney, and Charles E. Mitchell. Bishop Cannon and McPherson displayed less-than-saintly moral behavior. Henry Ford and Charles Lindbergh became known more for their intolerance than their achievements. The straight-laced moral code of WASP culture was so irredeemably tarnished that even Sinclair Lewis and H. L. Mencken stopped mocking it during the 1930s. The repeal of Prohibition in 1933, the first repeal of a constitutional amendment in American history, represented the eclipse of the old Anglo-Saxon, nativist, puritanical, rural American culture. As surely as the old economic order had fallen, so had the old cultural order. And a culture liberated from Anthony Comstock, Bishop Cannon, Lothrop Stoddard, the *Literary Digest,* and William Jennings Bryan was a culture full of possibilities.

Rise of Ethnic America. In the 1930s ethnic Americans refused to take a subordinate role in culture and society any longer. The great waves of European migration had peaked at the turn of the century; by the 1930s the first generation of Americans born to these immigrants was reaching its maturity. For most of their lives they had been burdened with slights, discriminations, and outright prejudice against them and their family traditions. In the 1930s they asserted themselves. Ethnic Americans shut out of WASP-dominated businesses such as banking, automobile manufacturing, and railroading moved into retailing, radio, and motion pictures. Although the distinction between WASP, Republican industrialists and ethnic, Democratic businessmen was not absolute, the New Deal depended on the financial support of new, ethnic businessmen such as Joseph Kennedy, Jack Warner, and David Sarnoff. These men often backed New Deal policies that had the indirect effect of punishing their business antagonists. More important, their financial future depended on the success of the New Deal in building a consumer economy and on their ability to produce goods desired by millions of ethnic Americans. The popular culture of the decade — pulp fiction, comic books, radio comedy, soap operas, and to a great extent the Hollywood movie — owed much to immigrant, ethnic experience. African Americans and poor white farmers, equally marginalized and ignored by society and culture before the Depression, also asserted themselves, their condition analogous to that of the children of immigrants. They too made their contribution to the new culture, especially in the realms of music and sports. The new culture thus brought people heretofore beneath the bar of respectability to the fore. Symbols of the success of these Americans were easy to spot: James Cagney, Paul Robeson, Louis Armstrong, Joe Louis, Eddie Cantor, Ella Fitzgerald, Joe DiMaggio, and the Marx Brothers. The success of this new culture, however, was only partial. All-American Shirley Temple was a bigger movie star during the decade than Al Jolson or Robeson. While Italian American boys in the Bronx might thrill to radio programs with scripts by Jewish writers or pulp fiction written by Irish authors, it was equally significant that the protagonists of those pieces were WASPs of the old school.

The New National Culture. The culture of the 1930s was nonetheless distinctive in its search for a more inclusive, plural definition of America. These searches were conducted in two ways: by exploring new mass-media formats such as radio and jazz and by broadening the content of high culture. Mass media and lowbrow culture appropriated the WASP standards of the 1920s and supplemented them, adding ethnic sidekicks to WASP heroes or fusing vaudevillian comedy routines to classical standards of music, as in Marx Brothers films. By the end of the decade high culture was working in the opposite direction, embracing the new media, creating ethnic protagonists, or fusing high and low culture into something distinctly American. James T. Farrell made the ethnic experience the center of his Studs Lonigan trilogy (1932–1935), and John Dos Passos portrayed the new ethnic Americans as the heroes of his *U.S.A.* trilogy (1938), as well as integrating newspaper stories and popular music of the day into his text. Often this fusion of high and low culture was midwifed by New Deal–sponsored programs such as the Federal Theatre Project, the Federal Art Project, the Federal Music Project, and the Federal Writers' Project, which carried artists through the lean days of the Depression. The Federal Art Project created a distinctive style of public art, adorning public buildings around the country with bold, nationalist murals. Painters such as Thomas Hart Benton, Grant Wood, Georgia O'Keeffe, Stuart Davis, Arthur Dove, and Charles Sheeler searched for American icons in the landscapes, the cities, and the factories, and put them on canvas. John Houseman, Burgess Meredith, and Orson Welles took their classical training from the private stage to the Federal Theatre Project; from there they took their sense of the dramatic to the people on radio and in movies. Welles's *Citizen Kane* (1941) was the natural outcome of this experience — a Faustian tale of wealth and betrayal set in contemporary America and executed in a popular medium. Similarly, filmmaker John Ford tried to give a classical, epic scope to the western, heretofore a pulp-fiction favorite. Choreographers Martha Graham and Doris Humphrey gave dance a populist, accessible gloss and explored the meaning of America in pieces such as *American Holiday* and *American Document*. Classical composers such as Aaron Copland, Marc Blitzstein, and George Gershwin fused jazz to classicism and also explored the meaning of America in pieces such as *Billy the Kid* (1938), *The Cradle Will Rock* (1937), and *Porgy and Bess* (1935). The Federal Music Project had a hit with *Swing Mikado* (1939), a Gilbert and Sullivan piece set to contemporary rhythms. A host of classically trained musicologists, including Alan Lomax and Howard Odum, combed the rural South searching for blues and country music to archive and record. Jazz music, the most popular form of music during the decade, effortlessly synthesized African American music and European instrumentalism. It perfectly embodied the distinctly American art form so many artists were working toward: reflective and energetic, complex but accessible, dynamic yet simple. No surprise that artist Stuart Davis would be inspired by jazz to create a series of abstract paintings probing the meaning of America. Jazz was characteristically and unmistakably American.

Solidarity. The new national culture made an important but almost intangible contribution to Americans' sense of themselves within the broader society. Certainly African Americans identified their struggles with the career of boxer Joe Louis; Jews saw their story in the success of Jolson or Cantor; the Irish and Italians recognized the similarities between their lives and those of the Dead-End kids in *Angels With Dirty Faces* (1938); and poor whites heard their plight in Jimmie Rodgers's lonesome songs. The culture, in other words, built something like class consciousness, contributing to a deep sense of community. During the 1930s individual Americans tended to see themselves as part of a group, and a sense of community and solidarity often determined individual behavior. This communal consciousness manifested itself in a variety of ways, especially in identification with sports heroes, movie stars, and musicians. In the early 1930s it was reflected in public support for the National

Recovery Administration (NRA) and the NRA slogan "We Do Our Part." Suffering disproportionately from the Depression, African Americans dedicated their efforts to improving their communities, especially in northern cities such as New York, where Harlem residents mounted the "DON'T SHOP WHERE YOU CAN'T WORK" campaign, or in Philadelphia, where African Americans succeeded in desegregating the city schools. Tribal authority and the right to own land were restored to Native Americans with the passage of the Indian Reorganization Act in 1934. Dedication to the group took exceptional form among left-wing political activists, especially the Communists, who sacrificed their own desires (and sometimes their own good sense) for the good of the greater cause. A sense of shared destiny, of common culture and values, held labor unions together through this difficult decade. Solidarity was the key to winning strikes. At every major labor protest of the decade — the Harlan County strike, the San Francisco general strike, the sit-down strikes of 1936 and 1937 — strikers pooled money and resources, and families supported their men on the picket lines or locked into factories. Helped by New Deal policymakers, workers won unemployment insurance, pension plans, grievance committees, higher wages, the forty-hour workweek, overtime pay, and the abolition of child labor. Solidarity was far from universal, of course. The labor unions, after all, struggled bitterly against each other for membership. But the pluralism and inclusiveness of labor unions set an admirable example for the rest of the nation. Many unions integrated during the course of the decade, setting aside years of racism. Women rose to levels of authority in unions far more often than they did in business. Union members overcame linguistic differences and conflicts of custom to work together for the good of the group.

Progress. Even during the bleakest days of the Depression, Americans maintained a sense of possibility. The belief in the ultimate success of the American experiment — in inevitable, gradual progress toward elimination of disease, poverty, and ignorance — was so profoundly embraced throughout American history that the period before the 1920s was known for its "progressivism." During the 1920s Americans focused much of their progressive idealism on the pursuit of wealth. The Depression dealt progressivism a harsh blow, as many of the "progressive" improvements of earlier decades, such as expansion of education, improvement of nutrition, and construction of good housing, came under the budget cutter's ax. New Deal economists talked of planning the economy. Yet they believed that once certain sectors of the economy were planned and maintained, the economy would resume its upward path, and there were other reassuring signs of progress during the decade. Although most Americans still lived in fear of diseases such as polio, syphilis, and tuberculosis, medicine was improving. Scientists discovered sulfa drugs, the first of the formidable chemical weapons against infectious diseases. Neocaine and other new anesthetics, blood typing, and transfusions revolutionized surgery. Despite the Depression public health improved with the introduction of highspeed X-ray machines to diagnose tuberculosis. The use of contraception increased. Technological advances led to new, faster airplanes that surmounted old barriers of distance. There were extraordinary feats of engineering: the Boulder Dam, the Grand Coulee Dam, the Golden Gate Bridge, and the Empire State Building. Astronomers probed the outer reaches of the galaxy. Physicists probed the inner mysteries of the atom. Biologists investigated the structure of the gene. The development of plastics, nylon, and other synthetic materials promised to revolutionize daily life. Radio linked the nation. Television was introduced. Americans' confidence in progress was apparent in the vogue of "streamline" design, a style derived from aerodynamics and aviation that imparted to such prosaic items as vacuum cleaners, toasters, and pencil sharpeners a sense of curved speed and shiny futuristic progress. A sense of progress was also evident in the World's Fairs of the decade: the Chicago Century of Progress Exhibition of 1933–1934 and the New York World of Tomorrow Fair of 1939–1940. The New York fair was especially given to visions of a future of luxury, ease, and efficiency, where illness was unthinkable, amusement was televised, and work was performed by robots.

Restoration and War. The 1939 fair offered proof of a restoration of Americans' faith in progress and confidence in the future. By 1939, although many sectors of the economy remained in the doldrums, economic prosperity had begun to return; political democracy seemed healthy. Yet the status quo in 1939 was much changed from the status quo in 1929. Americans were more sensitive to the social injustices that they had once ignored. Politics was governed by a much greater sense of distinct interest groups and partisanship and by a greater sense of responsibility for the welfare of the nation. The authority of the federal government had vastly increased. Though nine million people remained unemployed, the economic theories of the New Deal had been refined and improved, and they governed the prosperity of the 1940s. In every area of American life, the theories, attitudes, coalitions, and movements formed in the 1930s were responsible for the commanding power and prosperity of the nation in the 1940s. The experiment of the New Deal was the key to the successful war economy. Roosevelt's political acumen made the United States an international political power vital to the victory of the Allies in World War II. The new national culture offered Americans a sense of solidarity crucial to war morale. Lee Webster's road led to Pearl Harbor, and after the war, to prosperity and upward mobility using the engineering skills taught to him by the U.S. Army Air Corps. By the end of the 1930s the wandering of the nation had fixed on a path that led to prosperity, the gradual expansion of civil liberties, and a commanding position in world affairs.

ACKNOWLEDGMENTS

This book was produced by Manly, Inc. Karen L. Rood and Darren Harris-Fain were the in-house editors.

Production coordinator is James W. Hipp. Photography editor is Bruce Andrew Bowlin. Photographic copy work was performed by Joseph M. Bruccoli. Layout and graphics supervisor is Penney L. Haughton. Copyediting supervisor is Laurel M. Gladden. Typesetting supervisor is Kathleen M. Flanagan. Systems manager is George F. Dodge. Julie E. Frick is editorial associate. The production staff includes Phyllis A. Avant, Ann M. Cheschi, Melody W. Clegg, Patricia Coate, Joyce Fowler, Stephanie C. Hatchell, Jyll Johnston, Margaret Meriwether, Kathy Lawler Merlette, Jeff Miller, Pamela D. Norton, Laura S. Pleicones, Emily R. Sharpe, William L. Thomas Jr., and Allison Trussell.

Walter W. Ross and Robert S. McConnell did library research. They were assisted by the following librarians at the Thomas Cooper Library of the University of South Carolina: Linda Holderfield and the interlibrary-loan staff; reference-department head Virginia Weathers; reference librarians Marilee Birchfield, Stefanie Buck, Cathy Eckman, Rebecca Feind, Jill Holman, Karen Joseph, Jean Rhyne, Kwamine Washington, and Connie Widney; circulation-department head Caroline Taylor; and acquisitions-searching supervisor David Haggard.

AMERICAN DECADES

1930-1939

WORLD EVENTS: SELECTED OCCURRENCES OUTSIDE THE UNITED STATES

1930

- Max Beckmann paints *Self-Portrait with Saxophone*.

- Luis Buñuel's movie *L'Age d'or* (The Golden Age) is released.

- Agatha Christie's mystery novel *The Murder at the Vicarage* is published.

- Sigmund Freud's *Das Unbehagen in der Kultur* (Civilization and Its Discontents), a study of the political consequences of neurosis, is published.

- Alfred Hitchcock's movie *Murder* is released.

- Wyndham Lewis's novel *The Apes of God* is published.

- The Villa Savoye, designed by Le Corbusier, is completed in Poissy-sur-Seine, France.

- José Ortega y Gasset's *La rebelion de las masas* (The Revolt of the Masses), a study of political authoritarianism, is published.

- Ezra Pound's *A Draft of XXX Cantos*, the first collected edition of Cantos 1–30 in his ongoing epic poem *The Cantos*, is published.

- Diego Rivera's murals *Fall of Cuernavaca* and *Cortez and his Mercenaries* are unveiled at the Palacio de Cortez in Mexico City.

- Stephen Spender's *Twenty Poems* is published.

- Tristan Tzara's *L'Homme approximatif* (Approximate Man), a Dadaist prose poem, is published.

- Uruguay wins the first World Cup soccer championship.

- British Arctic explorer H. G. Watkins continues to explore Greenland.

- Dr. Alfred Wegener leads a German scientific expedition to Greenland.

- Sir Douglas Mawson of Great Britain and Hjalmar Riiser-Larsen continue independent investigations of Antarctica.

1 Jan.   The Indian National Congress, meeting at Lahore, votes for the complete independence of India from Great Britain.

21 Jan.–
22 Apr. The world's major naval powers meet in London to discuss limiting the tonnage and armaments of their navies. The conference concludes with the signing of a treaty by Great Britain, Italy, France, Japan, and the United States.

28 Jan. Spanish strongman Miguel Primo de Rivera resigns as prime minister because of ill health. He dies on 16 March.

3 Feb. France passes a national workman's compensation law.

12 Mar. Authorized by the All-India Trade Congress, Mohandas Gandhi begins a civil disobedience campaign against British rule by leading a 165-mile march to extract salt from the sea.

5 May Gandhi is arrested by British authorities.

19 May The Union of South Africa gives white women the right to vote. Blacks of both sexes remain disenfranchised.

30 June In accordance with the Treaty of Versailles, Allied troops leave the Rhineland.

30 July The fascistic National Union Party is formed in Portugal.

2 Sept. French aviators Dieudonné Coste and Maurice Bellonte make the first nonstop flight from Paris to New York.

8 Sept. A joint U.S.–League of Nations commission reports that slavery is still practiced in Liberia.

14 Sept. In German national elections Adolf Hitler's National Socialist (Nazi) Party wins ninety-five seats in the Reichstag.

24 Sept. Noël Coward's play *Private Lives* premieres at the Phoenix Theatre in London.

13 Oct. Newly elected Nazi delegates arrive in uniform at the German Reichstag, a violation of parliamentary rules.

20 Oct. The British government issues the Passfield White Paper, which suggests that the immigration of Jews to Palestine be halted until the problem of unemployment among the Palestinian Arabs can be addressed.

26 Oct. The ballet *Zoloty Vek* (The Age of Gold), with music by Dmitry Shostakovich, premieres in Leningrad.

30 Oct. Greece and Turkey sign an agreement accepting the status quo in the eastern Mediterranean.

2 Nov. Thirty-nine-year-old Ras (Prince) Tafari takes the name Haile Selassie and is crowned emperor of Ethiopia. He will reign until 1974.

5 Nov. Chinese Nationalist troops begin an offensive against Communist forces in Hunan, Hupeh, and Kiangsi provinces.

14 Nov. Japanese prime minister Hamaguchi Osachi is shot by a right-wing militant. He dies several months later.

12 Dec. In accordance with the Treaty of Versailles, Allied troops leave the Saarland.

15 Dec. In response to increased Republican activity, martial law is declared in Spain.

1931

24 Dec.	Federico García Lorca's play *La zapatera prodigiosa* (The Shoemaker's Prodigious Wife) premieres at the Teatro Español in Madrid.
31 Dec.	In the encyclical *Casti connubi* Pope Pius XI condemns contraception as an "offense against the law of God and of nature."

- Salvador Dalí paints *The Persistence of Memory.*
- Frida Kahlo paints *Portrait of Frida and Diego,* a self-portrait of the artist with her husband, muralist Diego Rivera.
- Paul Klee paints *The Ghost Vanishes.*
- Fritz Lang's movie *M* is released.
- The planned capital of New Delhi, India, designed by British architects Edwin L. Lutyens and Herbert Baker, is formally opened.
- Paul Maximilian Landowski's statue *Christ the Redeemer* is dedicated atop a mountain overlooking Rio de Janeiro.
- Anthony Powell's novel *Afternoon Men* is published.
- Jean Renoir's movie *La Chienne* (The Bitch) is released.
- George Seferis's *Strophe,* a volume of poetry, is published.
- Virginia Woolf's novel *The Waves* is published.
- Professor Auguste Picard becomes the first human to venture into the stratosphere, ascending to a height of fifty-two thousand feet in a balloon.

26 Jan.	British authorities release Gandhi from prison.
8 Feb.	The Spanish monarchy restores the constitution and sets March as the date for parliamentary elections.
4 Mar.	Indian nationalists agree to end civil disobedience in India in return for the release of political prisoners.
12 Apr.	Municipal elections in Spain result in victory for those favoring the establishment of a republic. Republican leader Niceta Alcalá Zamora will become president of a new provisional government.
14 Apr.	King Alfonso XIII leaves Spain after a forty-five-year reign, paving the way for the creation of a republic.
26 Apr.	Frederick Ashton's ballet *Façade* premieres at Cambridge Theatre in London.
30 Apr.	Troops led by rebel general Chen Jitang seize control of Canton from forces loyal to Chiang Kai-shek.
11 May	The failure of the Austrian bank Kreditanstalt precipitates a financial panic in Germany and eastern Europe.
17 June	Vietnamese nationalist leader Ho Chi Minh is arrested by British authorities in China.
18 June	Canada raises tariffs against the United States.

1 July	The Benguela-Katanga Railway, the last link in the trans-African railway, is finished.
13 July	Danatbank of Germany goes into bankruptcy.
3 Aug.	A dam bursts on Yangtze River in China, flooding forty thousand square miles, killing hundreds, and precipitating widespread famine.
24 Aug.	Amid disputes over the financial crisis in Great Britain, the Labour government collapses, but Prime Minister Ramsay MacDonald is able to assemble a new coalition that governs until 1935.
10 Sept.	Economic austerity measures provoke riots in London, Liverpool, and Glasgow.
15 Sept.	Great Britain devalues the pound sterling.
18 Sept.	Attributing the explosion to Chinese terrorists, Japanese officers bomb a section of the South Manchurian Railway and use the blast as a pretext to attack all of Manchuria.
21 Sept.	In response to a financial panic, the Bank of England suspends the gold convertibility of British currency.
4 Nov.	Jean Giraudoux's play *Judith* premieres at the Comédie des Champs-Elysées in Paris.
12 Nov.	The republican government of Spain finds King Alfonso XIII guilty of treason in absentia, preventing his return from exile.
9 Dec.	Spain adopts a republican constitution. Alcalá Zamora becomes the first president.
11 Dec.	Japan abandons the gold standard.

1932

- Jean de Brunhoff's *L'Histoire de Babar* (The Story of Babar), the first of a popular series of children's books featuring Babar the Elephant, is published.
- Aldous Huxley's novel *Brave New World* is published.
- Henri Matisse completes his painting *Danse* I.
- François Mauriac's novel *Le Nœud de vipères* (Vipers' Tangle) is published.
- Pablo Picasso paints *Girl Before a Mirror*.
- Joseph Roth's novel *Radetzkymarsch: Roman* (Radetzky March) is published.
- Georges Rouault paints *Christ Mocked by Soldiers*.
- Chemists at Imperial Chemical Industries in Great Britain synthesize the first plastic.
- German biochemist Gerhard Domagk discovers sulfa drugs, revolutionizing the treatment of infectious diseases.
- Civil war rages in El Salvador, where Communist insurgents attack a military oligarchy.
- Labour Party M.P. Oswald Mosley establishes the British Union of Fascists.

- Severe famine sweeps through Russia, owing in part to Soviet agricultural policy.

4 Jan.   Mohandas Gandhi is arrested following the resumption of civil disobedience to protest British rule. The Indian National Congress is outlawed, but after a six-day fast Gandhi succeeds in bringing about changes in the law that governs the treatment of the untouchables, the lowest of the rigidly defined castes in India.

4 Jan.   The Japanese occupation of Shanhaikwan, Manchuria, effectively solidifies Japan's control over southern Manchuria.

7 Jan.   The U. S. government formally protests the Japanese occupation of Manchuria.

28 Jan.–
4 Mar.   Japanese forces attack the Chinese city of Shanghai.

2 Feb.   A sixty-nation disarmament conference begins in Geneva, Switzerland.

18 Feb.   Acting for Japanese authorities, Chinese officials in Manchuria proclaim that province the independent nation of Manchukuo.

21 Feb.   Arnold Schoenberg's Four Orchestral Songs premieres at Frankfurt-am-Main.

18 Mar.   The Harbor Bridge, the largest arch bridge in the world, opens in Sydney, Australia.

4 Apr.   The Ballets Russes de Monte Carlo stages *Cotillon* at the Théâtre de Monte Carlo.

6 May   French president Paul Doumer is assassinated by a deranged Russian émigré. He is succeeded by Albert Lebrun.

15 May   Japanese prime minister Inukai Tsuyoshi is assassinated by military reactionaries.

20 May   Austrian minister of agriculture Engelbert Dollfuss forms a new government.

28 May   The Dutch complete nine years of work on a dike that reclaims millions of acres of farmland from the Zuider Zee.

30 May   Heinrich Brüning resigns as head of the German government. A political crisis arises after no German party polls a majority of votes. Franz von Papen forms a government responsible to German president Paul Hindenburg alone.

5 July   António de Oliveira Salazar becomes premier of Portugal. He will be dictator of the country for nearly thirty-eight years.

9 July   At a meeting in Lausanne, Switzerland, representatives of Germany, France, Belgium, Great Britain, and Italy sign a pact that will allow Germany to substitute a bond issue for its reparation debt from World War I. Because of opposition in the U. S. Congress, the agreement is not ratified, but Germany never resumes reparation payments.

31 July   After the German elections the Nazis have 230 seats in the Reichstag; socialists have 133; centrists have 97; and Communists have 89. No party has secured a majority, and no coalition is formed.

10 Aug.   Military leaders in Seville launch a revolt against the Republican government of Spain. The revolt is suppressed by troops loyal to the government.

13 Aug.   Hitler refuses German president Hindenburg's request to serve as vice chancellor under Franz von Papen.

30 Aug.	Nazi leader Hermann Göring is elected president of the German Reichstag.
12 Sept.	The German Reichstag is dissolved, and new elections are called.
16 Sept.	In Geneva, Germany leaves an international conference on land armaments after the French refuse to disarm prior to the signing of security arrangements.
25 Sept.	Catalonia secures a charter for political autonomy from the government of Spain.
3 Oct.	Iraq is admitted to the League of Nations.
6 Nov.	Although the Nazis lose and the Communists gain seats in the German national election, no party is able to break the Reichstag political deadlock.
17 Nov.	Von Papen resigns as chancellor of Germany. Adolf Hitler rejects the position after President Hindenburg refuses to increase the powers of the chancellor.
2 Dec.	Gen. Kurt von Schleicher forms a new German cabinet.
27 Dec.	The Union of South Africa goes off the gold standard.

1933

- Colette's novel *La Chatte* (The Cat) is published.
- Dazai Osamu's novel *Gyofukuki* is published.
- Alberto Giacometti sculpts *The Palace at Four A.M.*
- André Malraux's novel of Asian imperialism, *La Condition humaine* (Man's Fate), is published.
- Henri Matisse completes his painting *Danse* II.
- Chilean poet Pablo Neruda's *Residencia en la tierra* (Residence on Earth) is published.
- George Orwell's autobiography *Down and Out in Paris and London* is published.
- Diego Rivera's controversial mural *Man at the Crossroads* at Rockefeller Center in New York is destroyed because it includes a portrait of Lenin.
- Ignazio Silone's antifascist novel *Fontamara* is published.
- Gertrude Stein's memoir *The Autobiography of Alice B. Toklas* is published.
- Franz Werfel's novel *Die vierzig Tage des Musa Dagh* (The Forty Days of Musa Dagh) is published.
- The Soviet Union completes two massive public works projects: the Dnieper River Dam (construction overseen by American engineer Hugh Lincoln Cooper) and the Baltic–White Sea Stalin Ship Canal.

8 Jan.	Anarchists and syndicalists in Barcelona foment a rebellion against the Spanish government. The uprising is suppressed.
28 Jan.	Kurt von Schleicher's government in Germany collapses.
30 Jan.	Nazi leader Adolf Hitler becomes chancellor of Germany. In the absence of a political majority, elections are set for 5 March.
2 Feb.	German delegates return to the Geneva conference on international land disarmament.

3 Feb.	Hitler issues a memorandum informing German naval officers that he intends to commit Germany to a massive rearmament campaign.
24 Feb.	The League of Nations Assembly formally adopts a policy of not recognizing the Japanese protectorate of Manchukuo.
27 Feb.	The German Reichstag is destroyed by a fire likely set by the Nazis. Hitler denounces the fire as a Communist plot and secures from President Hindenburg emergency decrees suspending constitutional guarantees, allowing Nazi storm troopers to attack political enemies with impunity. The Communist Party will be outlawed in Germany.
4 Mar.	Responding to growing political confusion in Austria, Chancellor Dollfuss suspends parliament and constitutional rights. "Austria's Parliament has destroyed itself," he explains, "and nobody can say when it will be allowed to take up its dubious activities again."
5 Mar.	In the German national elections the Nazis win 44 percent of the vote.
17 Mar.	Nazi sympathizer Hjalmar Schacht is appointed president of the Reichsbank, the central bank of Germany.
20 Mar.	In Dachau, Germany, near Munich, the Nazis establish their first concentration camp for party enemies.
23 Mar.	The German Reichstag passes the Enabling Act, giving the Nazi government dictatorial powers until 1 April 1937. The ninety-four votes against the bill are all cast by Social Democrats.
1 Apr.	The Nazis inaugurate a national boycott of all Jewish-owned businesses and professions in Germany.
8 Apr.	France dispatches a military envoy to Moscow for the first time since World War I.
1 May	Argentina and Great Britain sign a reciprocal trade agreement.
17 May	The Spanish government nationalizes church property and abolishes religious education.
26 May	Australia assumes control of almost one-third of Antarctica.
27 May	Japan announces its withdrawal from the League of Nations, to go into effect in two years.
19 June	The Austrian government dissolves the Austrian Nazi Party.
21 June– 27 July	At an international economic conference in London the participants fail to agree on methods of stabilizing exchange rates for currency transactions.
1 July	Despite Nazi opposition to the performance of works by Jews, Richard Strauss's opera *Arabella*, with a libretto by part-Jewish Austrian writer Hugo von Hofmannsthal, is performed at the Staatsoper in Dresden.
14 July	The Nazi Party is declared the sole political party in Germany.
20 July	The Vatican signs a concordat with the Nazi government of Germany. The Nazis will tolerate Catholic religion and education in return for political neutrality from Catholic officials in Germany.

1 Aug.	Gandhi is arrested again in India, but he is released after a few days because his health is deteriorating from the effects of a hunger strike.
12 Sept.	Fulgencio Batista y Zalívar leads a successful military coup against the government of Cuba.
14 Oct.	Germany withdraws simultaneously from the Geneva disarmament conference and the League of Nations.
15 Oct.	Dmitry Shostakovich's Concerto for Piano, Trumpet, and String Orchestra premieres in Leningrad.
12 Nov.	Hitler wins a 90 percent vote of confidence from German voters in a plebiscite on Nazi policy. No electoral opposition was permitted.
16 Nov.	The United States and the Soviet Union establish diplomatic relations.
19 Nov.	Spanish elections result in gains for right-wing groups, who occupy 44 percent of the seats in the Córtes.
28 Nov.	The Moroccan-Tunisian railway opens.
29 Dec.	Romanian premier Ion Duca is assassinated by members of the fascist Iron Guard. Gheorghe Tatarescu assumes premiership.

1934

- Morley Callaghan's novel *Such Is My Beloved* is published.
- Isak Dinesen's *Seven Gothic Tales* is published.
- German geographer Karl Haushoker's *Macht und Erde* (Power and Earth), is published. The Nazis subsequently use this geopolitical study, based on work by British strategist Halfor John Mackinder, to provide a justification for their policy of seeking lebensraum (living space).
- René Magritte's painting *Homage to Mack Sennett* is unveiled.
- Pablo Picasso paints *The Bullfight*.
- Christina Stead's *The Salzburg Tales*, a collection of short stories, is published.
- P. Pamela Travers's children's book *Mary Poppins* is published.
- T'sao Yu's play *Thunderstorm*, an attack on Chinese traditionalism, premieres in Peking.
- Jean Vigo's movie *L'Atalante* is released.
- Evelyn Waugh's *A Handful of Dust* is published.
- Many European countries and the United States sign the Warsaw Convention, establishing international liabilities in transportation.
- The British conduct two Arctic expeditions to Greenland, Baffin Island, and outlying islands.
- Australian John Rymill leads a two-year exploratory expedition to the Antarctic.
- American aviator Adm. Richard Byrd begins his second large Antarctic expedition.

22 Jan. Dmitry Shostakovich's opera *Lady Macbeth of the Mzensk District* premieres at the Maly Opera House in Leningrad. The opera is a popular success, but *Pravda,* the official government newspaper, calls it an "ugly flood of confusing sound," and another critic condemns it as "un-Soviet."

26 Jan. Germany and Poland sign a ten-year nonaggression pact.

6–9 Feb. Street riots erupt in France following revelations of government corruption and cover-ups of the illegal activities of Serge-Alexandre Stavisky, a Russian-born con man who committed suicide on 8 January.

9 Feb. Turkey, Greece, Romania, and Yugoslavia sign the Balkan Pact, designed to protect their territorial integrity against invasion by Bulgaria.

11–15 Feb. Austrian chancellor Engelbert Dollfuss ruthlessly suppresses the Socialist Party. Fighting breaks out in the streets of Vienna as police raid the party headquarters and bombard a Socialist housing unit.

21 Feb. Nicaraguan strongman Gen. Anastasio Somoza García invites guerrilla leader Gen. Augusto César Sandino to a peace conference and then has him murdered.

7 Mar. Germany and Poland agree to lower trade barriers between their two countries.

12 Mar. Members of the Estonian military establish Konstantin Päts as dictator.

20 Mar. The world's first practical radar tests are conducted by German naval scientist Rudolf Kuhnold in Kiel.

30 Apr. A new Austrian constitution grants Chancellor Engelbert Dollfuss near-dictatorial powers.

15 May Following a military coup in Latvia, Karlis Ulmanis becomes virtual dictator.

19 May With the aid of Bulgarian ruler Boris III, fascists in that nation overthrow the constitutional government. Boris becomes dictator. On 12 June all political parties are abolished.

24 May Tomás Masaryk is reelected president of Czechoslovakia.

29 May The United States accedes to the removal from the Cuban constitution of the Platt Amendment of 1902, which gave the United States the right to intervene in the internal affairs of Cuba.

30 June In what becomes known as the Night of Long Knives, German Nazis conduct a political purge of their own membership, executing seventy-seven people, including leaders Ernst Röhm and Gregor Strasser.

2 July Gen. Lárzaro Cárdenas is elected president of Mexico. Mexican muralists Diego Rivera, José Clemente Orozco, and David Alfaro Siqueiros subsequently return to that country as Cárdenas begins a program of land reform and socialization of industry.

13 July Nazi leader Heinrich Himmler is appointed head of German concentration camps.

25 July Nazi leaders in Austria assassinate Chancellor Engelbert Dollfuss in an attempt to overthrow the government.

30 July Following the collapse of the Nazi coup in Austria, Dollfuss's associate Kurt von Schuschnigg forms a new cabinet in Austria.

19 Aug. Following the death of German president Paul Hindenburg on 2 August, Adolf Hitler becomes president, although he prefers the title Führer (leader).

18 Sept. The Soviet Union joins the League of Nations.

27 Sept. Effectively sabotaging French efforts to promote eastern European security arrangements, Poland announces that it will not allow Soviet troops to cross Poland to fulfill treaty obligations.

Oct. Mao Tse-tung's Chinese Communist troops begin their famous Long March, with Nationalist Chinese forces in pursuit. Mao leads his troops six thousand miles, over eighteen mountain ranges and six major rivers, saving the majority of his army.

6 Oct. Catalonia declares independence from Spain. The Spanish government will successfully suppress the independence movement as well as a rebellion of miners in Asturias.

9 Oct. King Alexander of Yugoslavia and French foreign minister Louis Barthou are assassinated in Marsailles by a Macedonian terrorist.

1 Dec. Sergey M. Kirov, one of Joseph Stalin's most trusted aides, is assassinated in Leningrad. Stalin uses the assassination as justification for a major purge of the Soviet Communist Party.

5 Dec. Italian and Ethiopian troops clash on the border between Ethiopia and Italian Somaliland.

14 Dec. Turkish women secure the right to vote and to sit in the national assembly.

29 Dec. Federico García Lorca's play *Yerma* premieres at the Teatro Español in Madrid.

1935

- Alfred Hitchcock's movie *The 39 Steps* is released.

- Afrikaans poet N. P. van Wyk Louw's *Alleenspraak* (Monologue) is published.

- Nazi propagandist Leni Riefenstahl's *Triumph of the Will*, a documentary on her party's Nuremberg rallies, is released.

- German radio bans jazz music of black or Jewish origin.

- American Lincoln Ellsworth successfully flies twenty-three hundred miles across the Antarctic.

7 Jan. France and Italy announce diplomatic agreements regarding conflicting interests in Africa.

13 Jan. A plebiscite in the Saarland results in the return of that territory to Germany, effective 1 March.

14 Jan. The Lower Zambezi railroad bridge is completed and is the world's longest until the completion of the Huey P. Long Bridge in Metairie, Louisiana, on 10 December.

15–17 Jan. Soviet Communists Grigory Zinovyev, Lev Kamenev, and others are tried for treason in connection with their alleged complicity in the murder of Sergey Kirov and are sent to prison for terms of five to ten years.

8 Mar.	Hitler reveals the existence of a German air force and announces plans to expand the size and strength of German armed forces.
16 Mar.	Germany formally denounces the disarmament clauses of the Treaty of Versailles. Hitler announces the reintroduction of universal military conscription in Germany.
24 Mar.	Persia officially changes its name to Iran.
11–14 Apr.	French, British, and Italian representatives meet in the Italian resort city of Stresa to negotiate common responses to German rearmament.
17 Apr.	The League of Nations formally condemns Germany's repudiation of the Treaty of Versailles.
23 Apr.	Poland adopts a new, authoritarian constitution.
2 May	France and the Soviet Union conclude a pact of mutual military assistance.
16 May	The Soviet Union and Czechoslovakia conclude a pact of mutual military assistance.
31 May	Emlyn Williams's play *Night Must Fall* premieres at the Duchess Theatre in London.
7 June	Stanley Baldwin replaces Ramsay MacDonald as British prime minister.
12 June	Bolivia and Paraguay end a three-year war over the disputed Chaco region but do not sign a peace treaty until 1938.
15 June	T. S. Eliot's play *Murder in the Cathedral* premieres at the Canterbury Festival; on 1 November it opens at the Mercury Theatre in London.
18 June	An Anglo-German naval agreement is announced, allowing Germany to exceed limits on naval tonnage placed on it by the Treaty of Versailles, so long as German tonnage does not exceed 35 percent of the combined fleets of the British Commonwealth.
25 July– 20 Aug.	At the meeting of the Third International in the Soviet Union, the Communist Party announces the strategy of creating Popular Front coalitions of liberals, Communists, and other leftists to combat the spread of fascism.
2 Aug.	The British parliament approves the Government of India Act, radically restructuring the administration of British possessions in Asia.
30 Aug.	Soviet coal miner Aleksey Grigorievich Stakhanov and his crew bring in a record tonnage of coal mined in a single night, becoming the symbol of Stalin's Stakhanov movement to increase industrial productivity.
15 Sept.	The Nuremberg Laws, depriving Jews of the rights of citizenship and forbidding intermarriage between Gentiles and Jews, are decreed in Germany.
25 Sept.	The Nazi government places the German Protestant churches under state control.
3 Oct.	Italian troops invade Ethiopia.
3 Nov.	Radical, socialist, and Communist Parties in France unite to form an antifascist Popular Front coalition.

18 Nov.	The League of Nations votes to impose economic sanctions on Italy because of its invasion of Ethiopia.
21 Nov.	Jean Giraudoux's play *La Guerre de Troie n'aura pas lieu* (The Trojan War Will Not Take Place) premieres at the Théâtre de l'Athénée in Paris.
13 Dec.	Tómas Masaryk resigns as president of Czechoslovakia and is succeeded by foreign minister Edvard Benes.

1936

- T. S. Eliot's *Collected Poems 1909–1935* is published.
- Max Ernst paints *La Ville Entière.*
- Aldous Huxley's novel *Eyeless in Gaza* is published.
- Robin Hyde's novel *Passport to Hell* is published.
- Piet Mondrian paints *Composition in Yellow and Black.*
- Meret Oppenheim produces her *Fur Breakfast,* a fur-covered teacup, saucer, and spoon.
- Leni Riefenstahl's documentary movie *Olympia* is released.
- Georges Rouault paints *The Old King.*
- Simon Vestdijk's novel *Meer Visser's hellevaarb* (Mr. Visser's Descent into Hell) is published.
- The Soviet Communist Party begins its Great Purge. By 1938 an estimated ten million people will have died.

9 Jan.	Noël Coward's plays *The Astonished Heart* and *Red Peppers* are staged at the Phoenix Theatre in London.
30 Jan.	American president Franklin D. Roosevelt proposes an inter-American conference on Western Hemispheric security.
4 Feb.	Switzerland forbids political organizing by National Socialists.
6 Feb.	Lithuania abolishes all political parties except the fascist Nationalist Union.
14 Feb.	Ramón María del Valle-Inclán's play *Los cuernos de don Friolera* (The Horns of Don Friolera) is staged at the Teatro de la Zarzuela in Madrid.
16 Feb.	A left-liberal Popular Front coalition wins a decisive victory over right-wing parties in Spanish elections.
26 Feb.	Prominent Japanese officials, including Keeper of the Privy Seal Saito Makoto and Finance Minister Takahashi Korekiyo, are assassinated in an uprising of young army officers.
27 Feb.	The French Chamber of Deputies ratifies the Franco-Soviet Pact, a mutual-defense agreement.
7 Mar.	Battalions of German infantry move into the demilitarized zone of the Rhineland in violation of the Versailles and Locarno Treaties.
12 Mar.	Great Britain, France, Belgium, and Italy denounce German militarization of the Rhineland.

1 Apr.	Austria resumes military conscription.
30 Apr.	Great Britain announces the construction of thirty-eight new warships.
2 May	Serge Prokofiev's *Peter and the Wolf* premieres in Moscow.
5 May	Italian troops occupy Addis Ababa, completing their invasion of Ethiopia. In a 30 June address to the League of Nations, Ethiopian emperor Haile Selassie warns, "It is us today. It will be you tomorrow."
10 May	Manuel Azaña y Díaz is elected the new president of Spain.
24 May	In Belgian parliamentary elections the Rexists, a fascist party led by Léon Degrelle, win twenty-one seats.
2 June	The government of Nicaragua is overthrown by Gen. Anastasio Somoza García, head of the National Guard, who installs himself as dictator.
5 June	In France the first Popular Front government is formed by Socialist Party leader Léon Blum.
12 June	France establishes the forty-hour workweek.
11 July	Rome and Berlin conclude a secret agreement wherein Italy acquiesces to German ambitions in Austria.
18 July	Spanish military officers in Morocco rise up against the Republican government of Spain, beginning the Spanish Civil War.
4 Aug.	Greek premier Ioannis Metaxas declares himself dictator, proclaims martial law, and dissolves the parliament.
19 Aug.	Spanish poet Federico García Lorca, a supporter of the Spanish Republic, is killed by Falangists.
19–23 Aug.	In the Soviet Union Grigory Zinovyev, Lev Kamenev, and sixteen others are once again put on trial by Stalinists, found guilty of treason, and executed.
10 Sept.	Joseph Goebbels, German minister of propaganda, accuses Czechoslovakia of harboring Soviet air forces.
26 Sept.	Switzerland devalues the Swiss franc.
27 Sept.	France, Switzerland, and the Netherlands abandon the gold standard.
1 Oct.	Gen. Francisco Franco assumes command of the fascist rebels in Spain.
2 Oct.	France devalues the franc.
4 Oct.	Italy devalues the lira.
12 Oct.	British fascist leader Oswald Mosley leads an anti-Jewish march in London.
19 Oct.	The German government announces the beginning of the Four-Year Plan, a program to develop economic self-sufficiency in strategic materials.
25 Oct.	Germany and Italy form the Rome-Berlin Axis.
1–23 Nov.	In Buenos Aires Western Hemispheric nations at the first Pan-American conference agree to consult each other on security issues.

6 Nov. Fascist forces lay siege to Madrid. Gen. Emilio Mola claims a "fifth column" of fascist supporters within the city will deliver it to his troops. The Republican government begins executing rightists in response.

18 Nov. Germany and Italy recognize Francisco Franco's new government in Spain.

25 Nov. Germany and Japan sign the Anti-Comintern Pact, a security accord aimed at mutual protection from the Soviet Union.

10 Dec. King Edward VIII of Great Britain voluntarily abdicates the throne to marry an American-born divorcée, Wallis Warfield Simpson. The first British king to give up the crown of his own accord, Edward VIII is succeeded by his brother, George VI.

25 Dec. Eighty-two Americans sail from New York to join the International Brigades of antifascists fighting for the Spanish Republic.

1937

- André Breton's Surrealist novel *L'Amour fou* (Mad Love) is published.

- Kawabata Yasunari's novel *Yukiguni* (The Snow Country) is published.

- Paul Klee paints *Revolutions of the Viaducts.*

- Arthur Koestler's *Spanish Testament*, a pro-Republican account of the Spanish Civil War, is published.

- René Magritte paints *The Pleasure Principle.*

- Joan Miró paints *Still Life with Old Shoe.*

- George Orwell's *The Road to Wigan Pier*, a study of the British unemployed, is published.

- J. R. R. Tolkien's novel *The Hobbit* is published.

- Leon Trotsky's *The Revolution Betrayed*, an indictment of Stalinism, is published.

- The Nazis open their first exhibition of "degenerate art," mostly abstract works that they consider decadent.

- The Soviet Union establishes a research station near the North Pole.

- The Soviet Union opens the Moscow-Volga ship canal.

- Frozen foods are introduced in Great Britain.

23–30 Jan. In Moscow the show trials of Communist leaders result in long prison terms or death sentences for treason. Assistant commissar for heavy industry Grigory Pyatakov is executed on 31 January. Karl Radek, formerly on the editorial board of *Izvestiya*, is sentenced to ten years in prison, where he dies under mysterious circumstances in 1939.

24 Jan. Bulgaria and Yugoslavia conclude a nonaggression pact.

28 Jan. The Communists and Nationalists in the Chinese Civil War declare a truce to join in opposition to Japanese military and political pressure.

26 Feb. Christopher Isherwood and W. H. Auden's play *The Ascent of F6* opens at the Mercury Theatre in London.

18 Mar.	Spanish Republicans defeat Italian troops at Brihuega.
25 Mar.	Italy and Yugoslavia conclude a nonaggression pact.
26 Apr.	German warplanes destroy the defenseless Basque town of Guernica. Pablo Picasso's 1937 painting *Guernica* is his outraged protest against this bombing and war in general.
13 May	Jean Giraudoux's play *Electre* is staged at the Théâtre de l'Athénée in Paris.
28 May	Following the retirement of Stanley Baldwin, Chancellor of the Exchequer Neville Chamberlain becomes British prime minister.
31 May	German warships bombard Almería, Spain.
2 June	Alban Berg's opera *Lulu* is performed at the Municipal Theater in Zurich.
12 June	Stalin's government executes Soviet military leaders who allegedly conspired with Germany and Japan.
17 June	Soviet fliers Valeri P. Chkalov, Georgi P. Baidukov, and Alexander V. Beliakov fly nonstop over the North Pole from Moscow to Vancouver.
19 June	The French Popular Front government of Léon Blum falls after failing to gain emergency fiscal powers. Radical socialist leader Camille Chautemps forms a new government.
7 July	The Japanese launch full-scale military operations against China.
8 July	The Peel Report, recommending the division of Palestine into Arab and Jewish states, is published in London. Parliament rejects the proposal.
9 July	Turkey signs a nonaggression pact with Iraq, Iran, and Afghanistan.
14 July	Russian aviator Mikhail Gromov and two companions fly nonstop over the North Pole from Moscow to Riverside, California, setting a new nonstop distance record.
16 July	The Nazis open a concentration camp for political prisoners at Buchenwald, near Weimar.
28 July	Peking falls to the Japanese.
8 Aug.– **8 Nov.**	Fierce fighting between Japanese and Chinese troops results in the Japanese occupation of Shanghai. Japan earns worldwide condemnation for its bombing of Chinese cities.
25 Aug.	The Japanese navy begins a blockade of all but European possessions on the South China Sea coast.
27 Aug.	Pope Pius XI recognizes the fascist government of Spain.
29 Aug.	China and the Soviet Union conclude a nonaggression pact, opening the sale of military aircraft to China.
8 Sept.	A Pan-Arab Congress meeting at Bludan, Syria, rejects the Peel plan for the division of Palestine.
5–6 Oct.	The League of Nations and the United States formally condemn Japanese actions in China.

13 Oct.	In a diplomatic message the German government promises not to violate Belgian borders so long as Belgium abstains from military action against Germany.
16 Oct.	Czech police suppress a meeting of the Sudeten German Party in Teplitz, where the party is demanding political autonomy for Sudeten Germans.
6 Nov.	Italy signs the Anti-Comintern Pact.
10 Nov.	Brazilian president Getúlio Vargas proclaims a new constitution and assumes dictatorial powers, which he will exercise for the next fifteen years.
20 Nov.	The Chinese capital is moved from Nanking to Chungking.
21 Nov.	Dmitry Shostakovich's Symphony No. 5 premieres to acclaim in Leningrad.
26 Nov.	Robert Schumann's Concerto for Violin and Orchestra in D minor, written in 1853, is performed for the first time, at the Deutsches Opernhaus in Berlin.
28 Nov.	Naval forces loyal to Francisco Franco blockade Spain.
11 Dec.	Italy withdraws from the League of Nations.
12 Dec.	Japanese bombers attack American and British ships near Nanking, provoking a serious diplomatic confrontation.
13 Dec.	After serious fighting, Nanking falls to the Japanese.
24 Dec.	Hangchow falls to the Japanese.
28 Dec.	King Carol of Romania appoints fascist leader Octavian Goga prime minister. Goga immediately embarks on a program of anti-Semitic legislation.

1938

- Isak Dinesen's novel *Out of Africa* is published.
- Sergey Eisenstein's movie *Aleksandr Nevsky* is released.
- Daniel O. Fagunwa's novel *Ogboju ode iinn igbo irummale* (The Forest of a Thousand Demons) is published.
- Alfred Hitchcock's movie *The Lady Vanishes* is released.
- George Orwell's *Homage to Catalonia*, about his experiences while fighting for the Republic in the Spanish Civil War, is published.
- Marcel Pagnol's movie *La Femme du boulanger* (The Baker's Wife) is released.
- Jean-Paul Sartre's novel *La Nausée* (Nausea) is published.
- Violence escalates between Jews and Arabs in British-controlled Palestine.

10 Jan.	The Japanese occupy Tsingtao.
	Jean Anouilh 's play *La Sauvage* (The Restless Heart) is staged at the Théâtre de Mathurius in Paris.
4 Feb.	British engineer John L. Baird demonstrates mechanically based high-definition color television in London.
10 Feb.	King Carol of Romania dismisses Prime Minister Octavian Goga, suspends the constitution, and abolishes all political parties.

12 Feb.	At Berchtesgaden, Adolf Hitler demands that Austrian chancellor Kurt Schuschnigg accede to increased participation of Austrian Nazis in the Austrian government or face German military occupation.
20 Feb.	British foreign secretary Anthony Eden resigns his post in protest over the British government's negotiations with Italy over spheres of influence in the Mediterranean. He is succeeded by Edward F. L. Wood, Baron Irwin (later Earl of Halifax).
	Hitler declares that he will protect ethnic Germans living outside the Reich by military force if necessary.
2–15 Mar.	Soviet authorities try, convict, and execute Bolshevik leaders Nikolay Bukharin, Aleksey Rykov, and others considered to be enemies of Stalin.
9 Mar.	Responding to increasing political turmoil, Chancellor Kurt Schuschnigg announces a plebiscite on Austrian independence to be held the following Sunday; only "Yes" ballots are to be provided.
11 Mar.	Germany demands postponement of the Austrian independence plebiscite and the resignation of Chancellor Schuschnigg.
12 Mar.	German troops cross the Austrian border to enforce the German *Anschluss* of Austria. Austrian Nazi Arthur Seyss-Inquart becomes chancellor.
14 Mar.	Hitler arrives in Vienna to take formal possession of Austria.
18 Mar.	The Mexican government nationalizes $450 million worth of American and British oil properties.
28 Mar.	The Japanese install a puppet government in occupied areas of China.
10 Apr.	A rigged plebiscite in Austria results in overwhelming approval of the German *Anschluss.*
	Following the 10 March collapse of Camille Chautemps's government in France, Edouard Daladier reorganizes the French cabinet.
16 Apr.	England and Italy arrive at diplomatic agreements regarding spheres of influence in the Mediterranean.
24 Apr.	Sudeten German leader Konrad Henlein issues his Karlsbad program, demanding complete autonomy for German Czechs.
25 Apr.	Great Britain and Ireland conclude diplomatic agreements designed to reduce tensions over tariff barriers and the disposition of Northern Ireland.
3–9 May	Hitler pays a state visit to Rome.
26 May	The Volkswagen (people's car) factory is dedicated in Wolfsburg, Germany. The low-cost "beetle" automobile is designed by engineer Ferdinand Porsche on commission from Hitler. Despite the dedication of the car plant, mass production of the Volkswagen will not occur for ten years.
11 July– 10 Aug.	Soviet and Japanese troops clash along the border between Siberia and China.
21 July	The ballet *St. Francis,* with choreography by Léonide Massine and music by Paul Hindemith, is performed at Drury Lane Theatre in London.

31 July	Greece and Bulgaria conclude diplomatic agreements allowing Bulgaria to rearm with German help.
3 Aug.	Italy introduces race laws governing the conduct of the Italian Jews.
10 Aug.	William Butler Yeats's play *Purgatory* premieres at the Abbey Theatre in Dublin.
7 Sept.	France calls up its military reservists.
15 Sept.	British prime minister Neville Chamberlain flies to Berchtesgaden to negotiate a resolution of the Czech crisis with Hitler.
22 Sept.	Prime Minister Chamberlain flies to the German city of Godesberg for further negotiations with Hitler over the Czech crisis.
24 Sept.	As British and French peace negotiations with the Germans deadlock, Czechoslovakia mobilizes its armed forces for war with Germany.
27 Sept.	In response to the Czech crisis, Britain and France mobilize their armed forces.
29 Sept.	Representatives of Great Britain, France, Italy, and Germany meet in Munich in a last-ditch effort to avert war over Czechoslovakia.
1 Oct.	The Munich conference ends with an agreement that cedes the Sudetenland to Germany while leaving the rest of Czechoslovakia outside the German Reich.
2 Oct.	Poland occupies the Teschen region of Czechoslovakia.
4 Oct.	Following Socialist and Communist objections to the Munich Pact, the French Popular Front collapses. The Daladier government turns right in search of political support.
5 Oct.	Edvard Benes resigns as president of Czechoslovakia.
6–8 Oct.	Slovakia and Ruthenia are separated from Czechoslovakia as autonomous states.
10 Oct.	British troops retake Bethlehem, Palestine, from Arab extremists. In Tiberias twenty Jews are murdered in continuing violence between Jews and Arabs.
18 Oct.	British troops retake the old city of Jerusalem, which has been occupied by Arab extremists.
21 Oct.	Following a ruthless bombing campaign, Japanese troops occupy Canton.
2 Nov.	Hungary acquires parts of southern Slovakia.
9 Nov.	The Kristallnacht (Crystal Night): following the assassination of a Nazi official by a German-born Polish Jew, Nazis conduct the worst pogrom in German history, destroying Jewish homes, synagogues, and shops and sending twenty thousand to thirty thousand Jews to concentration camps.
10 Nov.	The founder of the Turkish republic, Kemal Atatürk, dies. He is succeeded as president by Ismet Inönü.
12 Nov.	The Daladier government of France modifies the forty-hour workweek, provoking widespread labor unrest.
17 Nov.	Great Britain, Canada, and the United States sign a trade pact.
26 Nov.	Poland and Russia sign a nonaggression pact.
1 Dec.	Great Britain begins voluntary registration for the draft.

6 Dec. Germany and France sign a diplomatic accord guaranteeing the inviolability of existing frontiers.

10 Dec. Germany and Romania sign an economic agreement providing Germany access to Romanian oil.

18 Dec. German physicists led by Otto Hahn produce the first nuclear fission of uranium.

24 Dec. Twenty-one American republics adopt the Declaration of Lima, an affirmation of their intention to resist attacks on their sovereignty from outside the Western Hemisphere.

1939

- Marcel Carné's movie *Le Jour se lève* (Daybreak) is released.
- Aimé Césaire's long anticolonial poem *Cahier de retour au pays natal* (Return to My Native Land) is published in the French journal *Volontés*.
- C. S. Forester's novel *Captain Horatio Hornblower* is published.
- James Joyce's novel *Finnegans Wake* is published.
- Ernst Jünger's allegorical anti-Nazi novel *Auf den Marmorklippen* (On the Marble Cliffs) is published.
- Richard Llewellyn's novel *How Green Was My Valley* is published.
- Jean Renoir's movie *La Règle du jeu* (The Rules of the Game) is released.
- Italian political theorist Bruno Rizzi's *The Bureaucratization of the World,* a study of authoritarianism, is published.
- Jan Struther's novel *Mrs. Miniver* is published.
- César Vallejo's *Poemas humanos* (Human Poems) are published.

14 Jan. Norway claims approximately one million square miles of territory in Antarctica.

26 Jan. Franco's troops take Barcelona.

10 Feb. Pope Pius XI dies.

24 Feb. Hungary joins the Anti-Comintern pact.

27 Feb. Great Britain and France recognize Francisco Franco's regime as the government of Spain.

2 Mar. Papal diplomat Eugenio Pacelli becomes Pope Pius XII.

15 Mar. German troops occupy Bohemia and Moravia in violation of the 1938 Munich agreement. Hungary occupies Carpatho-Ukraine. Czechoslovakia ceases to exist.

18 Mar. Great Britain and France send envoys to the Soviet Union, Poland, Romania, Yugoslavia, Greece, and Turkey in an effort to form a military coalition against Germany.

23 Mar. Germany absorbs Memel, Lithuania.

23 Mar. Arabs and Jews in Palestine reject a British plan to turn Palestine over to both groups gradually.

28 Mar.	Madrid and Valencia surrender to the fascists, ending the Spanish Civil War. Estimates place the number of dead at close to one million.
31 Mar.	The governments of Great Britain and France pledge to protect Poland from German territorial ambitions.
7 Apr.	Spain joins Germany, Italy, and Japan in the Anti-Comintern Pact.
	Italy invades Albania.
11 Apr.	Hungary withdraws from the League of Nations.
12 Apr.	Italy formally absorbs Albania.
13 Apr.	Britain and France provide diplomatic guarantees of independence to Greece and Romania.
17 Apr.	Stalin authorizes simultaneous Soviet diplomatic negotiations to form military alliances with either Great Britain and France or Germany.
23 Apr.	Béla Bartók's Concerto No. 2 for Violin and Orchestra is performed in Amsterdam.
27 Apr.	The British government begins universal military conscription.
28 Apr.	In an address to the Reichstag, Hitler denounces the 1935 Anglo-German naval agreement and the 1934 German nonaggression pact with Poland.
3 May	Soviet foreign minister Maksim Litvinov is replaced by Vyacheslav Molotov.
	Hungary passes a series of drastic anti-Semitic laws.
17 May	A British white paper repudiates the Balfour Declaration of 1917 and limits Jewish immigration to Palestine.
20 May	Following a victory parade in Madrid, German and Italian troops begin to withdraw from Spain.
22 May	Germany and Italy announce a military alliance they call the "Pact of Steel."
23 May	The SS *St. Louis* leaves Hamburg with 937 Jewish refugees. After its passengers are denied entry into Cuba and the United States, the ship will return to Hamburg, and most of those aboard will die in the Holocaust.
8–11 June	King George and Queen Elizabeth of Great Britain visit the United States.
25 July	Britain and France dispatch envoys to Moscow to pursue negotiations for a military alliance with the Soviet Union.
26 July	The United States notifies Japan that it intends to abrogate the commercial agreement of 1911, opening the way to American trade restrictions.
23 Aug.	The Soviet Union and Nazi Germany agree to two treaties: one to maintain military neutrality toward one another; the other to divide Poland and the Baltic states following an anticipated German attack on Poland in the autumn. The Anti-Comintern Pact is rendered null and void.
24 Aug.	The Luftwaffe's new turbojet aircraft is tested at Rostock-Marienehe.
1 Sept.	Following a fabricated border clash, German troops invade Poland.
3 Sept.	Great Britain and France declare war on Germany, beginning World War II.

17 Sept.	Soviet troops invade Poland from the east.
21 Sept.	Romanian premier Armand Calinescu is assassinated by the fascist Iron Guard.
23 Sept.– **3 Oct.**	Representatives of Western Hemisphere nations meet in Panama to plan a Pan-American response to the war in Europe.
27 Sept.	Warsaw surrenders to German troops.
28 Sept.	Germany and the Soviet Union partition Poland.
30 Nov.	The Soviet Union invades Finland.

CHAPTER TWO

THE ARTS

by LAURA BROWDER and DAVID MCLEAN

CONTENTS

Sidebars and tables are listed in italics.

1930

Movies
Abraham Lincoln, directed by D. W. Griffith and starring Walter Huston and Una Merkel; *All Quiet on the Western Front,* directed by Lewis Milestone and starring Lew Ayres; *Anna Christie,* directed by Clarence Brown and starring Greta Garbo; *The Big House,* directed by George Hill and starring Wallace Beery; *The Big Trail,* directed by Raoul Walsh and starring John Wayne (in his first role); *The Dawn Patrol,* directed by Howard Hawks and starring Richard Barthelmess and Douglas Fairbanks Jr.; *Hell's Angels,* directed by Howard Hughes and starring Ben Lyon and Jean Harlow; *Lightnin',* directed by Henry King and starring Will Rogers, Louise Dresser, and Joel McCrea; *Little Caesar,* directed by Mervyn LeRoy and starring Edward G. Robinson; *The Royal Family of Broadway,* directed by George Cukor and Cyril Gardner and starring Frederic March and Ina Claire; *Tom Sawyer,* directed by John Cromwell and starring Jackie Coogan and Mitzie Green.

Fiction
Max Brand, *Destry Rides Again;* Pearl Buck, *East Wind, West Wind;* Edward Dahlberg, *Bottom Dogs;* John Dos Passos, *The 42nd Parallel;* William Faulkner, *As I Lay Dying;* Edna Ferber, *Cimarron;* Michael Gold, *Jews Without Money;* Dashiell Hammett, *The Maltese Falcon;* Oliver La Farge, *Laughing Boy;* Katherine Anne Porter, *Flowering Judas.*

Popular Songs
"Beyond the Blue Horizon," by Richard A. Whiting and W. Franke Harling, lyrics by Leo Robin; "Georgia on My Mind," by Hoagy Carmichael, lyrics by Stuart Gorrell; "It Happened in Monterey," by Mabel Wayne, lyrics by Billy Rose; "My Baby Just Cares for Me," by Gus Kahn and Walter Donaldson; "Sing You Sinners," by W. Franke Harling, lyrics by Sam Coslow; "Three Little Words," by Harry Ruby, lyrics by Bert Kalmar.

- Americans go to the movies in unprecedented numbers as the Vitascope widens screens and the new talkies provide an added dimension to the viewing experience.

- Grant Wood's painting *American Gothic,* in which he portrays his sister and his dentist as rural farmers, helps launch American Regionalism.

7 Jan.
Children of Darkness, by Edwin Justus Mayer, opens at New York's Biltmore Theater.

14 Jan.
Bobby Clark and Red Nichols's Band — including Benny Goodman, Glenn Miller, Jimmy Dorsey, and Jack Teagarden — perform songs by George and Ira Gershwin, such as "I've Got a Crush on You," in *Strike Up the Band,* which opens at New York's Times Square Theater. The musical is based on the book by George S. Kaufman.

18 Feb.
Simple Simon, with music by Richard Rodgers and lyrics by Lorenz Hart, opens at New York's Ziegfeld Theater. Songs include "Ten Cents a Dance" and "I Still Believe in You."

21 Feb.
Marc Connelly's play *Green Pastures,* an adaptation of a 1928 collection of tales by Roark Bradford depicting God and heaven as envisioned by a black country preacher, opens at New York's Mansfield Theater and runs for 640 performances.

28 Mar.
Walter Piston's Suite for Orchestra is first performed at Boston's Symphony Hall.

14 Apr.   Philip Barry's *Hotel Universe*, starring Ruth Ford, Glenn Anders, Earle Larimore, and Morris Carnovsky, opens at New York's Martin Beck Theater.

3 May   Ogden Nash publishes his poem "Spring Comes to Murray Hill" in *The New Yorker*. Shortly thereafter he joins the magazine's staff and becomes famous for his light verse.

24 Sept.   The play *Once in a Lifetime*, by George S. Kaufman and Moss Hart and starring Spring Byington, opens at New York's Music Box Theater and runs for 401 performances.

14 Oct.   *Girl Crazy*, starring Ethel Merman, with music by George Gershwin and lyrics by Walter Donaldson and Ira Gershwin, opens at New York's Alvin Theater and runs for 272 performances. Songs include "I Got Rhythm," "Embraceable You," and "Little White Lies."

16 Oct.   *The Garrick Gaieties*, starring Sterling Holloway, Rosalind Russell, and Imogene Coca, opens at New York's Guild Theater. Songs include "I'm Only Human After All," by Vernon Duke with lyrics by E. Y. Harburg and Ira Gershwin.

22 Oct.   Ethel Waters and Cecil Mack's Choir perform songs such as Eubie Blake's "Memories of You" in *Lew Leslie's Blackbirds of 1930*, which opens at New York's Royale Theater.

13 Nov.   W. A. Drake's play adaptation of the Vicki Baum novel *Grand Hotel*, starring Henry Hull and Sam Jaffe, opens at New York's National Theater and runs for 459 performances.

18 Nov.   Bob Hope, Marilyn Miller, Eddie Foy, and Fred and Adele Astaire star in the musical *Smiles*, which opens at New York's Ziegfeld Theater.

8 Dec.   *The New Yorkers*, starring Hope Williams, Ann Pennington, Jimmy Durante, Lew Clayton, and Eddie Jackson, and with music and lyrics by Cole Porter, opens at New York's Broadway Theater. Songs include "Love for Sale."

1931

Movies   *An American Tragedy*, directed by Josef von Sternberg and starring Sylvia Sidney, Phillips Holmes, and Frances Dee; *City Lights*, directed by and starring Charlie Chaplin; *Dishonored*, directed by Josef von Sternberg and starring Marlene Dietrich; *Dracula*, directed by Tod Browning and starring Bela Lugosi; *Frankenstein*, directed by James Whale and starring Boris Karloff; *Monkey Business*, directed by Norman Z. McLeod and starring the Marx Brothers; *Public Enemy*, directed by William Wellman and starring James Cagney, Jean Harlow, and Mae Clarke; *Scarface*, directed by Howard Hawks and starring Paul Muni and Ann Dvorak; *Skippy*, directed by Norman Taurog and starring Jackie Cooper; *Street Scene*, directed by King Vidor and starring Sylvia Sidney and William Collier Jr.; *Svengali*, directed by Archie Mayo and starring John Barrymore.

Fiction   Pearl Buck, *The Good Earth*; Louis Colman, *Lumber*; James Gould Cozzens, *S.S. San Pedro*; William Faulkner, *Sanctuary*; Dashiell Hammett, *The Glass Key*; Henry Miller, *Tropic of Cancer*; Nathanael West, *The Dream Life of Balso Snell*.

Popular Songs

"All of Me," by Seymour Simons and Gerald Marks; "Dream a Little Dream of Me," by Fabian Andre and Wilbur Schwandt, lyrics by Gus Kahn; "Heartaches," by Al Hoffman, lyrics by John Klenner; "I Don't Know Why (I Just Do)" by Fred E. Ahlert, lyrics by Roy Turk; "I Love a Parade," by Harold Arlen, lyrics by Ted Koehler; "I Surrender, Dear," by Harry Barris of the Rhythm Boys, lyrics by Gordon Clifford; "(I'll Be Glad When You're Dead) You Rascal You," by Sam Theard; "Lazy River," by Hoagy Carmichael and Sidney Arodin; "Love Letters in the Sand," by J. Fred Coots, lyrics by Nick and Charles Kenny; "Mood Indigo," by Duke Ellington, lyrics by Albany "Barney" Bigard and Irving Mills; "Out of Nowhere," by Edward Heyman and John Green; "Sweet and Lovely," by Gus Arnheim, Harry Tobias, and Jules Lemare; "When It's Sleepy Time Down South," by Leon Rene, Otis Rene, and Clarence Muse; "When I Take My Sugar to Tea," by Sammy Fain, lyrics by Irving Kahal and Pierre Norman Connor; "Where the Blue of the Night (Meets the Gold of the Day)" by Fred E. Ahlert with lyrics by Roy Turk, performed by Bing Crosby.

- U.S. movie theaters begin showing double features to increase business. Many unemployed workers spend their afternoons at the movies.

- The Whitney Museum of American Art is founded by railroad heiress–sculptor Gertrude Vanderbilt Whitney.

26 Jan. *Green Grow the Lilacs,* by Lynn Riggs and starring Helen Westley, Lee Strasberg, and Franchot Tone, opens at New York's Guild Theater.

3 Mar. Congress votes to designate "The Star Spangled Banner" the national anthem.

3 Apr. In a concert celebrating the Boston Symphony's fiftieth anniversary, Paul Hindemith's *Concert Music for String Orchestra and Brass Instruments* is first performed at the Symphony Hall.

1 May Kathryn Elizabeth "Kate" Smith, who has played comic fat-girl roles on Broadway and performs in a singing role at New York's Palace Theater, makes her radio debut singing "When the Moon Comes over the Mountain."

19 May *Billy Rose's Crazy Quilt,* starring Rose's wife, Fanny Brice, with music by Harry Warren and lyrics by Rose and Mort Dixon, opens at New York's Forty-fourth Street Theater.

3 June Fred and Adele Astaire make their final appearance together on the first revolving stage to be used in a musical in *The Band Wagon,* which opens at the New Amsterdam Theater.

1 July *The Ziegfeld Follies,* starring Helen Morgan, Ruth Etting, and Harry Richman, with music by Walter Donaldson, Dave Stamper, and others, and lyrics by E. Y. Harburg and others, opens at New York's Ziegfeld Theater.

27 July Naked chorus girls are a part of the lineup for *Earl Carroll's Vanities,* which opens at the new three-thousand-seat Earl Carroll Theater on Seventh Avenue at Fiftieth Street in New York City. In 1932 the show is modified and moved to the Broadway Theater, starring Milton Berle and Helen Broderick.

5 Oct. *The House of Connelly,* by Paul Green and starring Stella Adler, Franchot Tone, Clifford Odets, and Rose McClendon, opens at New York's Martin Beck Theater.

13 Oct. *Everybody's Welcome,* starring Tommy and Jimmy Dorsey, Ann Pennington, and Harriet Lake (Georgia Sothern), opens at New York's Shubert Theater. Songs include Herman Hupfeld's "As Time Goes By."

26 Oct. Eugene O'Neill's *Mourning Becomes Electra*, starring Alla Nazimova and Alice Brady, opens at New York's Guild Theater, where it runs for 150 performances.

22 Nov. Ferde Grofe's "Grand Canyon Suite" is first performed at Chicago's Studebaker Hall in a concert by Paul Whitman and His Orchestra.

26 Dec. With music by George Gershwin and lyrics by Ira Gershwin, *Of Thee I Sing*, starring Victor Moore and William Gaxton, opens at New York's Music Box Theater and runs for 441 performances. Songs include "Love is Sweeping the Country" and the title song.

1932

Movies *The Big Broadcast*, musical directed by Frank Tuttle and starring Kate Smith, George Burns, Gracie Allen, Cab Calloway, Bing Crosby, the Mills Brothers, and the Boswell Sisters; *A Bill of Divorcement*, directed by George Cukor and starring John Barrymore and Katharine Hepburn; *Blonde Venus*, directed by Josef von Sternberg and starring Marlene Dietrich, Herbert Marshall, and Cary Grant; *Grand Hotel*, directed by Edmund Goulding and starring Greta Garbo, Joan Crawford, John and Lionel Barrymore, Lewis Stone, Wallace Beery, and Jean Hersholt; *Horse Feathers*, directed by Norman Z. McLeod and starring the Marx Brothers; *I Am a Fugitive from a Chain Gang*, directed by Mervyn LeRoy and starring Paul Muni; *Million Dollar Legs*, directed by Edward Cline and starring W. C. Fields and Jack Oakie; *Trouble in Paradise*, directed by Ernst Lubitsch and starring Miriam Hopkins, Kay Francis, and Herbert Marshall.

Fiction Sherwood Anderson, *Beyond Desire*; Fielding Burke, *Call Home the Heart*; Edward Dahlberg, *From Flushing to Calvary*; John Dos Passos, *1919*; James T. Farrell, *Young Lonigan: A Boyhood in Chicago Streets*; William Faulkner, *Light in August*; Erle Stanley Gardner, *The Case of the Velvet Claws* (first Perry Mason detective novel); Grace Lumpkin, *To Make My Bread*; Laura Ingalls Wilder, *Little House in the Big Woods*.

Popular Songs "How Deep is the Ocean?," by Irving Berlin; "I'm Gettin' Sentimental over You," by George Bassman, lyrics by Ned Washington; "(I Don't Stand) A Ghost of a Chance (with You)," by Victor Young, lyrics by Bing Crosby and Ned Washington; "(I'd Love to Spend) One Hour with You," by Richard A. Whiting, lyrics by Leo Robin; "It Don't Mean a Thing (If It Ain't Got that Swing)" by Duke Ellington, lyrics by Irving Mills; "I Wanna Be Loved," by John Green, lyrics by Billy Rose and Edward Heyman; "Minnie the Moocher," by Cab Calloway with lyrics by Irving Mills & Clarence Gaskill; "Say It Isn't So," by Irving Berlin; "Shuffle Off to Buffalo," by Al Dubin and Harry Warren; "That Silver Haired Daddy of Mine," by Gene Autry and Jimmy Long; "Willow Weep for Me," by Ann Ronell.

- *Death in the Afternoon*, Ernest Hemingway's extended essay on bullfighting, is published.

- Painter Ben Shahn produces *Sacco and Vanzetti*, the first of twenty-three gouaches inspired by the 1927 execution.

- Polaroid film, the first synthetic light-polarizing film, is invented by Harvard College dropout Edwin Herbert Land.

- Sculptor and painter Alexander Calder's motorized and hand-cranked "stabiles" are exhibited in Paris.

- Sculptor Joseph Cornell exhibits his first boxes containing found objects in New York City.

- Washington's Folger Library opens. Its vast William Shakespeare collection is funded by the late Standard Oil chairman Henry Clay Folger.

Feb.   Weston Electrical Instruments commercially introduces the Photronic Photoelectric Cell, the first exposure meter for cameras, developed by William Nelson Goodwin Jr.

4 Apr.   George Bernard Shaw's *Too True to Be Good*, starring Beatrice G. Lilly, Hope Williams, and Claude Rains, opens at New York's Guild Theater.

30 Apr.   Walter Piston's Suite for Flute and Piano is first performed at the artists' colony Yaddo, outside Saratoga Springs, New York.

22 Oct.   *Dinner at Eight* by George S. Kaufman and Edna Ferber, and starring Constance Collier, opens at New York's Music Box Theater and runs for 232 performances. The next year the play is made into a movie, directed by George Cukor and starring John Barrymore and Jean Harlow.

8 Nov.   *Music in the Air*, starring Al Shean and Walter Slezak, with music by Jerome Kern and lyrics by Oscar Hammerstein II, opens at New York's Alvin Theater.

29 Nov.   Fred Astaire and Claire Luce star in *Gay Divorce*, with music and lyrics by Cole Porter, which opens at New York's Ethel Barrymore Theater and runs for 248 performances.

12 Dec.   *Biography*, by S. N. Behrman, starring Earle Larimore and Ina Claire, opens at New York's Guild Theater and runs for 283 performances.

27 Dec.   Radio City Music Hall opens in New York City's Rockefeller Center.

29 Dec.   Composer Roy Harris's *From the Gayety and Sadness of the American Scene* is first performed in Los Angeles.

1933

Movies   *42nd Street*, musical directed by Lloyd Bacon and starring Warner Baxter, Bebe Daniels, and Dick Powell; *Counsellor-at-Law*, directed by William Wyler and starring John Barrymore and Bebe Daniels; *Duck Soup*, directed by Leo McCarey and starring the Marx Brothers; *Flying Down to Rio*, musical directed by Thornton Freeland and starring Dolores Del Rio, Ginger Rogers, and Fred Astaire; *Footlight Parade*, musical directed by Lloyd Bacon and starring James Cagney and Joan Blondell; *Gold Diggers of 1933*, musical directed by Mervyn LeRoy and starring Ginger Rogers, Joan Blondell, and Dick Powell, with songs including "We're in the Money," by Al Dubin and Harry Warren; *International House*, directed by A. Edward Sutherland and starring W. C. Fields, George Burns, and Gracie Allen; *King Kong*, directed by Ernest Schoedsack and starring Fay Wray and Bruce Cabot; *Little Women*, directed by George Cukor and starring Katharine Hepburn and Joan Bennett; *Man's Castle*, directed by Frank Borzage and starring Spencer Tracy and Loretta Young; *Penthouse*, directed by W. S. Van Dyke and starring Warner Baxter and Myrna Loy; *Queen Christina*, directed by Rouben Mamoulian and starring Greta Garbo and John Gilbert; *She Done Him Wrong*, directed by Lowell Sherman and starring Cary Grant and Mae West (as Diamond Lil, who speaks the line "Come up and see me sometime"); *Sons of the Desert*, directed by William A. Seiter and starring Laurel and Hardy.

Fiction   Erskine Caldwell, *God's Little Acre;* Jack Conroy, *The Disinherited;* James Gould Cozzens, *The Last Adam;* Josephine Herbst, *Pity Is Not Enough;* Meyer Levin, *The New Bridge;* Nathanael West, *Miss Lonelyhearts.*

Popular
Songs   "Did You Ever See a Dream Walking?," by Harry Revel and Mack Gordon; "Everything I Have Is Yours," by Burton Lane, lyrics by Harold Adamson; "I Like Mountain Music," by Frank Weldon, lyrics by James Cavanaugh; "Lazybones," by Hoagy Carmichael, lyrics by Johnny Mercer; "Let's Fall in Love," by Harold Arlen, lyrics by Ted Koehler; "Love Is the Sweetest Thing," by Ray Noble; "It's only a Paper Moon," by Harold Arlen, lyrics by E. Y. Harburg and Billy Rose; "Sophisticated Lady," by Duke Ellington, lyrics by Irving Mills and Mitchell Parish; "Stormy Weather," by Harold Arlen, lyrics by Ted Koehler.

- Justice John M. Woolsey of the U.S. District Court in New York rules that James Joyce's *Ulysses,* previously banned for reasons of obscenity, is acceptable for publication in the United States.

- Diego Rivera produces the mural *Man at the Crossroads,* which is destroyed because it portrays Russian Communist leader Vladimir Ilyich Lenin, for New York's Radio City Music Hall.

- Darryl Zanuck of Warner Bros. and other Hollywood executives organize 20th Century Pictures.

- An animated feature by Walt Disney, *The Three Little Pigs,* with songs such as "Who's Afraid of the Big Bad Wolf," by Frank E. Churchill, captures the imagination of children and adults.

24 Jan.   Noël Coward's *Design for Living,* starring Coward, Alfred Lunt, and Lynn Fontanne, opens at New York's Ethel Barrymore Theater and runs for 135 performances. That year the play is made into a film directed by Ernst Lubitsch and stars Gary Cooper, Fredric March, and Miriam Hopkins.

27 May   To celebrate the Century of Progress, fan dancer Sally Rand appears at the Chicago World's Fair, attracting thousands.

30 Aug.   Samuel Barber's *School for Scandal* Overture is first performed at Philadelphia's Robin Hood Dell.

26 Sept.   The Group Theatre production of Sidney Kingsley's *Men in White,* starring Morris Carnovsky, Luther Adler, and Elia Kazan, opens at New York's Broadhurst Theater, where it runs for 367 performances.

30 Sept.   Based on the book by Irving Berlin and Moss Hart, the musical *As Thousands Cheer,* with music and lyrics by Berlin, Edward Heyman, and Richard Myers, opens at New York's Music Box Theater on Broadway. The show, starring Marilyn Miller, Clifton Webb, and Ethel Waters, runs for 400 performances.

2 Oct.   Eugene O'Neill's only comedy, *Ah, Wilderness,* opens at New York's Guild Theater and stars George M. Cohan, William Post Jr., Elisha Cook Jr., and Gene Lockhart. The play runs for 289 performances.

24 Oct.   *Mulatto,* by Langston Hughes, opens at New York's Vanderbilt Theater and stars Rose McClendon.

18 Nov.   Ray Middleton, George Murphy, Bob Hope, and Fay Templeton star in *Roberta*, which opens at New York's New Ambassador Theater. With music by Jerome Kern and lyrics by Otto Harbach, songs include "Smoke Gets in Your Eyes" and "The Touch of Your Hand."

4 Dec.   Jack Kirkland's adaptation of Erskine Caldwell's 1933 novel *Tobacco Road*, starring Henry Hull, opens at New York's Masque Theater and runs for 3,182 performances.

1934

Movies   *Babes in Toyland*, directed by Gus Meins and Charles R. Rogers and starring Laurel and Hardy; *Bright Eyes*, musical directed by David Butler and starring Shirley Temple, who sings "On the Good Ship Lollipop"; *It Happened One Night*, directed by Frank Capra and starring Clark Gable and Claudette Colbert; *It's A Gift*, directed by Norman Z. McLeod and starring W. C. Fields; *The Lost Patrol*, directed by John Ford and starring Victor McLaglen and Boris Karloff; *Man of Aran*, documentary by Robert Flaherty; *She Loves Me Not*, musical directed by Elliott Nugent and starring Bing Crosby, Miriam Hopkins, and Kitty Carlisle; *Stand Up and Cheer*, musical directed by Hamilton McFadden and starring Shirley Temple, who sings "Baby Take a Bow"; *Tarzan and His Mate*, directed by Cedric Gibbons and Jack Conway and starring Johnny Weissmuller and Maureen O'Sullivan; *Treasure Island*, directed by Victor Fleming and starring Wallace Beery and Jackie Cooper; *Twentieth Century*, directed by Howard Hawks and starring John Barrymore and Carole Lombard; *What Every Woman Knows*, directed by Gregory La Cava and starring Helen Hayes and Brian Aherne.

Fiction   James M. Cain, *The Postman Always Rings Twice;* Robert Cantwell, *The Land of Plenty;* Edward Dahlberg, *Those Who Perish;* James T. Farrell, *The Young Manhood of Studs Lonigan;* F. Scott Fitzgerald, *Tender Is the Night;* Waldo Frank, *The Death and Birth of David Markand: An American Story;* Daniel Fuchs, *Summer in Williamsburg;* Dashiell Hammett, *The Thin Man;* Josephine Herbst, *The Executioner Waits;* Edward Newhouse, *You Can't Sleep Here;* John O'Hara, *Appointment in Samarra;* Henry Roth, *Call It Sleep;* William Saroyan, *Daring Young Man;* Tess Slesinger, *The Unpossessed;* Irving Stone, *Lust for Life;* Rex Stout, *Ferde-lance;* Jerome Weidman, *I Can Get It for You Wholesale;* Nathanael West, *A Cool Million.*

Popular Songs   "The Beer Barrel Polka," (Roll Out the Barrel) by Czech songwriters Jaromir Vejvoda, Wladimir A. Timm, and Vasek Zeman; "Blue Moon," by Richard Rodgers, lyrics by Lorenz Hart; "Deep Purple," by Peter De Rose, lyrics by Mitchell Parish; "I Only Have Eyes for You," by Harry Warren, lyrics by Al Dubin; "Little Man, You've Had a Busy Day," by Mabel Wayne, lyrics by Maurice Sigler and Al Hoffman; "Love Thy Neighbor," by Harry Revel, lyrics by Mack Gordon; "Miss Otis Regrets," "The Object of My Affection," by Pinky Tomlin, Coy Poe, and Jimmy Grier; "On the Good Ship Lollipop," by Richard A. Whiting, lyrics by Sidney Clare; "Solitude," by Duke Ellington, lyrics by Eddie De Lange and Irving Mills; "Stars Fell on Alabama," by Frank Perkins, lyrics by Mitchell Parish; "Tumbling Tumbleweeds," by Bob Nolan; "The Very Thought of You," by Ray Noble; "Winter Wonderland," by Felix Bernard, lyrics by Richard B. Smith; "You Oughta Be in Pictures," by Dana Suesse, lyrics by Edward Heyman.

- The Berkshire Music Festival has its first season in Lenox, Massachusetts, on the 210-acre Tappan family estate, which accomodates fourteen thousand concertgoers.

- Thomas Hart Benton produces several paintings, including *Lord, Heal the Child; Homestead; Ploughing It Under;* and *Going Home.*

- Chicago clock maker Laurens Hammond patents the Hammond organ, the world's first pipeless organ — an invention that leads to a whole generation of electrically amplified instruments.

- Harlem's Apollo Theater is opened by Leo Brecher and Frank Schiffman, who allow black patrons and book blues singer Bessie Smith, making the Apollo the leading showcase for black performers.

- Fritz Lang, director of the acclaimed films *Metropolis* (1926) and *M* (1931), continues his career in the United States after fleeing Germany to avoid collaboration with the Nazi government.

4 Jan. — *The New Ziegfeld Follies,* starring Fanny Brice, Jane Froman, Vilma and Buddy Ebsen, and Eugene and Willie Howard, opens at New York's Winter Garden Theater and runs for 182 performances.

18 Jan. — Eugene O'Neill's *Days Without End,* starring Earle Larimore, Stanley Ridges, and Ilka Chase, premieres at Henry Miller's Theater in New York City and runs for only fifty-seven performances.

26 Jan. — *Symphony–1933* by Roy Harris is first performed at Boston's Symphony Hall.

20 Feb. — Gertrude Stein's opera, *Four Saints in Three Acts,* with music by Virgil Thomson, opens at New York's Forty-fourth Street Theater, adding to Stein's popularity with her use of bewildering lines.

1 July — The Hays Office, created by the U.S. film industry's Motion Picture Producers and Distributors of America (MPPDA), hires former postmaster general Will H. Hays to administer an industrywide production code that will curtail on-screen displays of sexuality.

7 Nov. — Sergei Rachmaninoff's *Rhapsody on a Theme of Paganini* for piano and orchestra is first performed in Baltimore in a concert by the Philadelphia Orchestra.

20 Nov. — *The Children's Hour,* by Lillian Hellman, premieres at Maxine Elliott's Theater in New York City, disturbing audiences with its references to a lesbian relationship.

21 Nov. — *Anything Goes,* by Guy Bolton, P. G. Wodehouse, Howard Lindsay, and Russel Crouse, with music and lyrics by Cole Porter, and starring William Gaxton, Ethel Merman, and Victor Moore, opens at New York's Alvin Theater and runs for 420 performances. Songs include "The Gypsy in Me" and "I Get a Kick Out of You."

24 Nov. — S. N. Behrman protests Nazi treatment of German Jews in *Rain from Heaven,* which opens at New York's Golden Theater.

25 Dec. — Samson Raphaelson's *Accent on Youth,* starring Constance Cummings, premieres at New York's Plymouth Theater.

1935

Movies

Anna Karenina, directed by Clarence Brown and starring Greta Garbo and Fredric March; *The Bride of Frankenstein,* directed by James Whale and starring Elsa Lanchester and Boris Karloff; *David Copperfield,* directed by George Cukor and starring Freddie Bartholomew, W. C. Fields, and Lionel Barrymore; *Gold Diggers of 1935,* musical directed by Busby Berkeley and starring Dick Powell, with music by Henry Warren and lyrics by Al Dubin, including "Lullaby of Broadway"; *The Good Fairy,* directed by William Wyler and starring Margaret Sullavan and Herbert Marshall; *The Informer,* directed by John Ford and starring Victor McLaglen; *Lives of a Bengal Lancer,* directed by Henry Hathaway and starring Gary Cooper and Franchot Tone; *The Man on the Flying Trapeze,* directed by Clyde Bruckman and starring W. C. Fields; *Mississippi,* musical directed by A. Edward Sutherland and starring Bing Crosby, W. C. Fields, and Joan Bennett, with music by Richard Rodgers and lyrics by Lorenz Hart; *Mutiny on the Bounty,* directed by Frank Lloyd and starring Charles Laughton, Clark Gable, and Franchot Tone; *A Night at the Opera,* directed by Sam Wood and starring the Marx Brothers; *Ruggles of Red Gap,* directed by Leo McCarey and starring Charles Laughton, Mary Boland, and Charles Ruggles; *The Story of Louis Pasteur,* directed by William Dieterle and starring Paul Muni; *Top Hat,* musical directed by Mark Sandrich and starring Fred Astaire and Ginger Rogers, with music by Irving Berlin, including "Cheek to Cheek."

Fiction

Nelson Algren, *Somebody in Boots;* James T. Farrell, *Judgment Day;* Tom Kromer, *Waiting For Nothing;* Sinclair Lewis, *It Can't Happen Here;* Horace McCoy, *They Shoot Horses, Don't They?;* John Steinbeck, *Tortilla Flat;* Clara Weatherwax, *Marching! Marching!;* Thomas Wolfe, *Of Time and the River* and *From Death to Morning.*

Popular Songs

"About a Quarter to Nine," lyrics by Al Dubin, music by Harry Warren; "I'm Gonna Sit Right Down and Write Myself a Letter," by Fred E. Ahlert, lyrics by Joe Young; "I'm in the Mood for Love," by Jimmy McHugh and Dorothy Fields; "I Won't Dance," by Jerome Kern, lyrics by Otto Harbach and Oscar Hammerstein II; "In a Sentimental Mood," by Duke Ellington; "(Lookie, Lookie, Lookie) Here Comes Cookie," by Mack Gordon; "Moon Over Miami," by Joe Burke, lyrics by Edgar Leslie; "The Music Goes Round and 'Round," by Edward Farley and Michael Riley, lyrics by "Red" Hodgson; "Red Sails in the Sunset," by Hugh Williams, lyrics by Jimmy Kennedy; "She's a Latin from Manhattan," lyrics by Al Dubin, lyrics by Harry Warren; "When I Grow Too Old to Dream," by Sigmund Romberg, lyrics by Oscar Hammerstein II.

- The Works Progress Administration (WPA) Federal Arts Projects are created, giving artists jobs to decorate post offices and other federal buildings.

5 Jan.

Waiting for Lefty, by Clifford Odets, premieres at New York's Civic Repertory Theater and runs for 168 performances. On 26 March the play is moved to Longacre Theater in a Group Theatre production, with the top price of $1.50 per seat.

19 Feb.

Clifford Odets's *Awake and Sing!* premieres at the Belasco Theater, starring Stella Adler, Morris Carnovsky, and John Garfield. The show will run for 209 performances.

Apr.

The radio show *Your Hit Parade* debuts with a lineup of top song hits.

17 July

The show-business newspaper *Variety* headlines its issue with a report that rural audiences do not support movies that portray country folk and bucolic settings.

21 Aug.	Bandleader Benny Goodman's career takes a dramatic turn for the better when he opens at the Palomar Ballroom in Los Angeles, where he is dubbed the "King of Swing."
25 Sept.	Maxwell Anderson's *Winterset,* starring Burgess Meredith and Richard Bennett, opens at New York's Martin Beck Theater. The play is based on the Sacco-Vanzetti case.
10 Oct.	The opera *Porgy and Bess,* with music by George Gershwin and lyrics by Ira Gershwin and DuBose Heyward, opens at the Alvin Theater in New York, where it runs for 124 performances. Songs include "It Ain't Necessarily So," "Bess, You Is My Woman Now," and "Summertime."
12 Oct.	With music and lyrics by Cole Porter and songs that include "Begin the Beguine" and "Just One of Those Things," *Jubilee,* starring Melville Cooper, Mary Boland, and Montgomery Clift, opens at New York's Imperial Theater.
16 Nov.	Jimmy Durante stars in *Jumbo* with a live elephant at the New York Hippodrome. With music by Richard Rodgers and lyrics by Lorenz Hart, songs include "The Most Beautiful Girl in the World."
27 Nov.	*Boy Meets Girl,* by Bella (Cohen) and Samuel Spewack, and starring Jerome Cowan, Garson Kanin, and Everett Sloane, opens at New York's Cort Theater and runs for 669 performances.

1936

Movies	*Born to Dance,* musical directed by Roy Del Ruth and starring James Stewart and tap dancer Eleanor Powell, with songs by Cole Porter including "I've Got You Under My Skin"; *Camille,* directed by George Cukor and starring Greta Garbo, Robert Taylor, and Lionel Barrymore; *Dodsworth,* directed by William Wyler and starring Walter Huston and Paul Lukas; *Follow the Fleet,* musical directed by Mark Sandrich and starring Fred Astaire, Ginger Rogers, Randolph Scott, and Betty Grable, with songs by Irving Berlin including "Let's Face the Music"; *Fury,* directed by Fritz Lang and starring Sylvia Sidney and Spencer Tracy; *The Great Ziegfeld,* directed by Robert Z. Leonard and starring William Powell and Myrna Loy; *Mr. Deeds Goes to Town,* directed by Frank Capra and starring Gary Cooper and Jean Arthur; *Modern Times,* directed by and starring Charlie Chaplin; *My Man Godfrey,* directed by Gregory La Cava and starring Carole Lombard and William Powell; *Petrified Forest,* directed by Archie Mayo and starring Leslie Howard and Humphrey Bogart; *The Prisoner of Shark Island,* directed by John Ford and starring Warner Baxter; *San Francisco,* musical directed by W. S. Van Dyke and starring Clark Gable, Jeanette MacDonald, and Spencer Tracy; *Show Boat,* musical directed by James Whale and starring Paul Robeson, Irene Dunne, and Helen Morgan; *Swing Time,* musical directed by George Stevens and starring Ginger Rogers and Fred Astaire, with music by Jerome Kern and lyrics by Dorothy Fields, including "The Way You Look Tonight"; *Theodora Goes Wild,* directed by Richard Boleslawski and starring Irene Dunne and Melvyn Douglas.
Fiction	Djuna Barnes, *Nightwood;* Thomas Bell, *All Brides Are Beautiful;* James M. Cain, *Double Indemnity;* John Dos Passos, *The Big Money;* Walter D. Edmonds, *Drums Along the Mohawk;* James T. Farrell, *A World I Never Made;* William Faulkner, *Absalom, Absalom!;* Munro Leaf, *The Story of Ferdinand;* Henry Miller, *Black Spring;* Margaret Mitchell, *Gone With the Wind;* John Steinbeck, *In Dubious Battle.*

Popular Songs

"Cool Water," by Bob Nolan; "Goody — Goody," by Matt Malneck and Johnny Mercer; "I'm an Old Cowhand (from the Rio Grande)," by Johnny Mercer; "Moonlight and Shadows," by Frederick Hollander and Leo Robin;"The Night Is Young and You're So Beautiful," by Dana Suesse, lyrics by Billy Rose and Irving Kahal; "Pennies From Heaven," by Arthur Johnston and Johnny Burke; "Ramblings on My Mind," by Robert Johnson; "Sing, Sing, Sing," by Louis Prima; "Stompin' at the Savoy," by Benny Goodman, Edgar Sampson, and Chick Webb, lyrics by Andy Razaf; "Walkin' Blues," by Robert Johnson.

- *The Flowering of New England,* a study of U.S. literary history by Van Wyck Brooks, is published.

- Public-speaking teacher Dale Carnegie's book *How to Win Friends and Influence People* is published.

- Carl Sandburg's poem "The People, Yes" is published.

- Songs such as "Good Night, Irene" by traveling blues singer Huddie "Leadbelly" Ledbetter are collected by Alan and John Avery Lomax and published in *Negro Folk Songs as Sung by Leadbelly.*

- Folksinger Woodrow Wilson "Woody" Guthrie is hired by the Department of the Interior to promote nationalistic feeling in the Northwest by traveling and performing his songs such as "Roll On, Columbia" and "Those Oklahoma Hills." Instead of his usual hitchhiking, he is chauffeured through several states and writes twenty-six songs in twenty-six days.

17 Feb. S. N. Behrman's *End of Summer,* starring Ina Claire, Osgood Perkins, Mildred Natwick, Van Heflin, and Sheppard Strudwick, opens at New York's Guild Theater.

14 Mar. *Triple-A Plowed Under,* a Living Newspaper written for the WPA Federal Theatre Project by the Living Newspaper staff, opens in New York at the Biltmore Theater.

29 Mar. Robert Sherwood's antiwar *Idiot's Delight* opens at New York's Shubert Theater and runs for three hundred performances.

11 Apr. Richard Rodgers and Oscar Hammerstein II collaborate on music and lyrics for *On Your Toes,* which opens at New York's Imperial Theater, starring Ray Bolger, Tamara Geva, and George Church.

9 July *The Women,* by Clare Boothe Luce and starring Ilka Chase, Jane Seymour, Arlene Francis, Doris Day, and Marjorie Main, opens at New York's Ethel Barrymore Theater and runs for 657 performances.

21 Sept. George Kelly's *Reflected Glory,* starring Tallulah Bankhead, opens at New York's Morosco Theater.

22 Oct. *Stage Door,* by George S. Kaufman and Edna Ferber, and starring Margaret Sullavan and Tom Ewell, opens at New York's Music Box Theater and runs for 169 performances. The next year it is made into a movie directed by Gregory La Cava and starring Katharine Hepburn, Adolphe Menjou, Lucille Ball, and Ginger Rogers.

27 Oct.   *It Can't Happen Here,* by Sinclair Lewis and John C. Moffitt, produced under the auspices of the Federal Theatre Project, opens simultaneously in seventeen cities across the nation.

29 Oct.   Songs such as "De-Lovely" highlight Cole Porter's music and lyrics for *Red, Hot and Blue,* which opens at New York's Alvin Theater and stars Ethel Merman, Jimmy Durante, Grace and Paul Hartman, and Bob Hope.

6 Nov.   Symphony No. 3 in A minor by Sergei Rachmaninoff premieres at Philadelphia's Academy of Music.

14 Dec.   George S. Kaufman and Moss Hart's *You Can't Take It With You* opens at New York's Booth Theater, where it runs for 837 performances.

16 Dec.   *Brother Rat,* by John Monks Jr. and Fred F. Finklehoff, and starring Eddie Albert, Frank Albertson, Ezra Stone, and José Ferrer, opens at New York's Biltmore Theater and runs for 577 performances.

1937

Movies   *The Awful Truth,* directed by Leo McCarey and starring Irene Dunne and Cary Grant; *Captains Courageous,* directed by Victor Fleming and starring Spencer Tracy and Freddie Bartholomew; *A Day at the Races,* directed by Sam Wood and starring the Marx Brothers; *History is Made at Night,* directed by Frank Borzage and starring Charles Boyer and Jean Arthur; *The Hurricane,* directed by John Ford and starring Dorothy Lamour, Jon Hall, and Raymond Massey; *The Life of Emile Zola,* directed by William Dieterle and starring Paul Muni; *Lost Horizon,* directed by Frank Capra and starring Ronald Colman, Sam Jaffe, and Thomas Mitchell; *Make Way for Tomorrow,* directed by Leo McCarey and starring Victor Moore and Beulah Bondi; *The Prisoner of Zenda,* directed by John Cromwell and starring Ronald Colman, Madeleine Carroll, and Douglas Fairbanks Jr.; *Shall We Dance,* musical directed by Mark Sandrich and starring Ginger Rogers and Fred Astaire, with music by George Gershwin and lyrics by Ira Gershwin, including "They Can't Take That Away from Me"; *Snow White and the Seven Dwarfs,* the first full-length animated feature by Walt Disney, with music by Frank Churchill and lyrics by Larry Mose, including "Heigh-Ho," "Some Day My Prince Will Come," and "Whistle While You Work"; *A Star Is Born,* directed by William A. Wellman and starring Fredric March and Janet Gaynor; *They Won't Forget,* directed by Mervyn LeRoy and starring Claude Rains and Lana Turner; *Topper,* directed by Norman Z. McLeod and starring Constance Bennett, Cary Grant, and Roland Young.

Fiction   James M. Cain, *Serenade;* Daniel Fuchs, *Low Company;* Ernest Hemingway, *To Have and Have Not;* Zora Neale Hurston, *Their Eyes Were Watching God;* Meyer Levin, *The Old Bunch;* John Phillips Marquand, *The Late George Apley;* Wallace Stegner, *Remembering Laughter;* John Steinbeck, *Of Mice and Men.*

Popular Songs

"Blue Hawaii," by Leo Robin and Ralph Rainger; "The Dipsy Doodle," by Larry Clinton; "A Foggy Day" by George Gershwin, lyrics by Ira Gershwin; "Good Mornin'," by Sam Coslow; "Harbor Lights," by Jimmy Kennedy and Hugh Williams; "Hell Hound on My Trail," by Robert Johnson; "I've Got My Love To Keep Me Warm," by Irving Berlin; "In the Still of the Night," by Cole Porter; "I Can Dream, Can't I?" by Sammy Fain, lyrics by Irving Kahal; "The Joint Is Jumpin'," by Thomas "Fats" Waller, Andy Razaf, and James C. Johnson; "Me and the Devil Blues," by Robert Johnson; "The Moon of Manakoora," by Alfred Newman, lyrics by Frank Loesser; "Nice Work If You Can Get It," by George Gershwin, lyrics by Ira Gershwin; "Once in a While," by Michael Edwards, lyrics by Bud Green; "Rosalie," by Cole Porter; "Sweet Leilani," by Harry Owens; "That Old Feeling," by Sammy Fain and Lew Brown; "Too Marvelous For Words," by Richard A. Whiting, lyrics by Johnny Mercer.

- The Academy of Motion Picture Arts and Sciences awards the newly inaugurated Thalberg Memorial Award to the late M-G-M producer Irving Grant Thalberg.

- Dr. Seuss (Theodore Seuss Geisel) wins popularity with children learning to read with his imaginative rhyming and illustrations in *And to Think That I Saw It on Mulberry Street*.

- The six-and-a-half-minute *Porky's Hare Hunt*, the first Bugs Bunny cartoon, is released by Warner Bros. and features the voice of Mel Blanc as both Bugs Bunny and Porky Pig.

- Arturo Toscanini, seventy years old, is replaced as conductor of the New York Philharmonic but is hired by the National Broadcasting Company to conduct the NBC Symphony.

- Wallace Stevens's collection of poetry *The Man with the Blue Guitar* is published.

9 Jan.   Maxwell Anderson's *High Tor*, starring Burgess Meredith and Peggy Ashcroft, opens at New York's Martin Beck Theater.

21 Jan.   Ernest Bloch's *Voice in the Wilderness* Symphonic Poem for Orchestra and Cello Obligato is premiered in Los Angeles.

20 Feb.   *"Having a Wonderful Time,"* by Austrian American playwright Arthur Kober, premieres at New York's Lyceum Theater.

14 Apr.   Songs such as "My Funny Valentine" and "The Lady Is a Tramp," by Richard Rodgers and Lorenz Hart, are showcased in *Babes in Arms*, which premieres at New York's Shubert Theater.

19 May   John Murray and Allen Boretz's *Room Service*, starring Sam Levine, Eddie Albert, and Betty Field, opens at New York's Cort Theater and runs for five hundred performances.

20 June   Walter Piston's Concertino is premiered in a CBS radio broadcast from New York.

23 Nov.   *Golden Boy*, by Clifford Odets, opens at New York's Belasco Theater. Starring Jules Garfield, Lee J. Cobb, Karl Malden, and Elia Kazan, the play runs for 250 performances.

1938

23 Nov.   John Steinbeck's stage version of his new novel *Of Mice and Men* is polished by director George S. Kaufman and premieres at New York's Music Box Theater while Steinbeck gathers material for his next novel, *The Grapes of Wrath. Of Mice and Men* is made into a movie released in 1939, directed by Lewis Milestone and starring Burgess Meredith and Lon Chaney Jr.

27 Nov.   *Pins and Needles,* with music and lyrics by Harold Rome and sponsored by the International Ladies Garment Workers Union (ILGWU), opens at New York's Labor Stage Theater and runs for 1,108 performances.

Movies   *The Adventures of Robin Hood,* directed by Michael Curtiz and starring Errol Flynn; *The Adventures of Tom Sawyer,* directed by Norman Taurog and starring Tommy Kelly and Jackie Moran; *Bringing Up Baby,* directed by Howard Hawks and starring Katharine Hepburn and Cary Grant; *The Dawn Patrol,* directed by Edmund Goulding and starring Errol Flynn, Basil Rathbone, and David Niven; *Hard To Get,* musical directed by Ray Enright and starring Dick Powell and Olivia de Havilland, with music by Harry Warren and lyrics by Johnny Mercer, including "You Must Have Been a Beautiful Baby"; *Holiday,* directed by George Cukor and starring Katharine Hepburn and Cary Grant; *In Old Chicago,* directed by Henry King and starring Tyrone Power and Alice Faye; *Jezebel,* directed by William Wyler and starring Bette Davis, Henry Fonda, and George Brent; *Pygmalion,* directed by Anthony Asquith and Leslie Howard and starring Howard and Wendy Hiller; *Sing You Sinners,* musical directed by Wesley Ruggles and starring Bing Crosby, Fred MacMurray, and Donald O'Connor; *A Slight Case of Murder,* directed by Lloyd Bacon and starring Edward G. Robinson; *Three Comrades,* directed by Frank Borzage and starring Margaret Sullavan, Robert Taylor, and Franchot Tone; *You Can't Take It With You,* directed by Frank Capra and starring Jean Arthur, James Stewart, and Lionel Barrymore.

Fiction   Taylor Caldwell, *Dynasty of Death;* John Dos Passos, *U. S. A.;* James T. Farrell, *No Star Is Lost;* Albert Maltz, *The Way Things Are and Other Stories;* Kenneth Robeson (Lester Dent), *The Man of Bronze;* Wallace Stegner, *The Big Rock Candy Mountain;* Allen Tate, *The Fathers;* Richard Wright, *Uncle Tom's Children;* Leane Zugsmith, *The Summer Children.*

Popular Songs   "A-Tisket, A-Tasket," by Ella Fitzgerald and Al Feldman; "Camel Hop," by Mary Lou Williams; "Cherokee," by Ray Noble; "F. D. R. Jones," by Harold Rome; "The Flat Foot Floogie," by Slim Gaillard, Slam Stewart, and Bud Green (who were forced to change the word "floozie" to "floogie" to gain radio airplay); "I Let a Song Go Out of My Heart," by Duke Ellington, lyrics by Irving Mills, Henry Nemo, and John Redmond; "Jeepers Creepers," by Harry Warren, lyrics by Johnny Mercer; "Love Walked In," by George Gershwin, lyrics by Ira Gershwin; "One O'Clock Jump," by William "Count" Basie; "Thanks for the Memory," by Ralph Rainger and Leo Robin (title song for a film starring Bob Hope, who makes it his theme song); "That Old Feeling," by Sammy Fain and Lew Brown.

- Thomas Hart Benton exhibits his painting *Cradling Wheat.*

- The Cloisters, a medieval European nunnery filled with priceless art donated by the Rockefeller family to the Metropolitan Museum of Art, opens in New York's Tryon Park.

- Woody Guthrie releases his *Talking Union* album and makes appearances to support labor unions.

- Glenn Miller forms his own big band and begins touring after breaking from playing trombone and arranging music for Tommy and Jimmy Dorsey and Ray Noble.

- Cole Porter is injured in a fall from a horse and is left crippled.

- The samba and the conga are introduced to U.S. dance floors.

- Delmore Schwartz's first collection of poems, *In Dreams Begin Responsibilities,* is published.

17 Jan. Benny Goodman and His Orchestra, along with Duke Ellington, Count Basie, and members of their orchestras, give the first jazz performance in Carnegie Hall.

25 Jan. Ian Hay's *Bachelor Born* opens at New York's Morosco Theater and runs for four hundred performances.

26 Jan. Paul Vincent Carroll's *Shadow and Substance*, starring Cedric Hardwicke, Sara Allgood, and Julie Haydon, opens at New York's Golden Theater.

3 Feb. *On Borrowed Time,* by Paul Osborn and starring Dorothy Stickney, Dudley Digges, and Dickie Van Patten, premieres at New York's Longacre Theater.

4 Feb. *Our Town,* by Thornton Wilder, opens at Henry Miller's Theater in New York and runs for 336 performances.

26 Mar. Howard Hanson's Symphony No. 3 is first performed in an NBC Orchestra radio concert.

30 Mar. Walter Piston's *The Incredible Flutist* is premiered at Boston's Symphony Hall.

22 Sept. Ole Olsen and Chic Johnson delight audiences with their slapstick comedy in the musical *Hellzapoppin',* which opens at New York's Forty-sixth Street Theater and runs for 1,404 performances.

9 Oct. The ballet *Billy the Kid,* with music by Aaron Copland and choreography by Eugene Loring, opens at the Chicago Civic Opera House.

15 Oct. Robert Sherwood's *Abe Lincoln in Illinois,* starring Raymond Massey, opens at the Plymouth Theater and runs for 472 performances.

9 Nov. Mary Martin simulates a striptease to Cole Porter's "My Heart Belongs to Daddy" in *Leave It to Me,* which premieres at New York's Imperial Theater.

11 Nov. On Armistice Day, Kate Smith sings Irving Berlin's "God Bless America" in a radio broadcast and later acquires exclusive air rights to the song, which Berlin originally wrote for his 1918 show *Yip-Yip Yaphank* but put aside.

7 Dec. Philip Barry's *Here Come the Clowns,* starring Eddie Dowling, Madge Evans, and Russell Collins, premieres at New York's Booth Theater.

1939

Movies

Dark Victory, directed by Edmund Goulding and starring Bette Davis; *Destry Rides Again*, directed by George Marshall and starring James Stewart and Marlene Dietrich; *Drums Along the Mohawk*, directed by John Ford and starring Henry Fonda and Claudette Colbert; *Goodbye, Mr. Chips*, directed by Sam Wood and starring Robert Donat and Greer Garson; *Gone With the Wind*, directed by Victor Fleming and starring Vivien Leigh, Clark Gable, Leslie Howard, and Olivia de Havilland; *Gunga Din*, directed by George Stevens and starring Cary Grant, Victor McLaglen, Douglas Fairbanks Jr., Joan Fontaine, and Sam Jaffe; *The Hound of the Baskervilles*, directed by Sidney Lanfield and starring Basil Rathbone and Nigel Bruce; *The Hunchback of Notre Dame*, directed by William Dieterle and starring Charles Laughton; *Love Affair*, directed by Leo McCarey and starring Irene Dunne and Charles Boyer; *Mr. Smith Goes to Washington*, directed by Frank Capra and starring James Stewart and Jean Arthur; *Only Angels Have Wings*, directed by Howard Hawks and starring Cary Grant, Jean Arthur, and Richard Barthelmess; *Stagecoach*, directed by John Ford and starring John Wayne and Claire Trevor; *The Stars Look Down*, directed by Carol Reed and starring Michael Redgrave and Margaret Lockwood; *The Wizard of Oz*, musical directed by Victor Fleming and starring Judy Garland, Ray Bolger, Bert Lahr, Jack Haley, Frank Morgan, and Margaret Hamilton, with music by Harold Arlen and lyrics by E. Y. Harburg, including "Somewhere Over the Rainbow," "Follow the Yellow Brick Road," and "We're Off to See the Wizard"; *Wuthering Heights*, directed by William Wyler and starring Laurence Olivier and Merle Oberon.

Fiction

Sholem Asch, *The Nazarene*; Raymond Chandler, *The Big Sleep*; Josephine Herbst, *Rope of Gold*; Norman MacLeod, *You Get What You Ask For*; John P. Marquand, *Wickford Point*; Henry Miller, *Tropic of Capricorn*; Katherine Anne Porter, *Pale Horse, Pale Rider*; John Steinbeck, *The Grapes of Wrath*; Dalton Trumbo, *Johnny Got His Gun*; Robert Penn Warren, *Night Rider*; Nathanael West, *The Day of the Locust*; Thomas Wolfe, *The Web and the Rock*.

Popular Songs

"And the Angels Sing," by Ziggy Elman, lyrics by Johnny Mercer; "Ciribiribin (They're So in Love)" by composer A. Pestalozza, lyrics by Harry James and Jack Lawrence; "Heaven Can Wait," by Jimmy Van Heusen, lyrics by Eddie De Lange; "I'll Never Smile Again," by Ruth Lowe; "I Get Along without You Very Well (except Sometimes)," by Hoagy Carmichael, lyrics by Jane Brown Thompson; "In the Mood," by Joe Garland, lyrics by Andy Razaf; "The Lady's in Love with You," by Burton Lane, lyrics by Frank Loesser; "Moonlight Serenade," by Glenn Miller, lyrics by Mitchell Parish; "Scatterbrain," by Kahn Keene, Carl Bean, Frankie Masters, and Johnny Burke; "Sent for You Yesterday (and Here You Come Today)," by Ed Durham, William "Count" Basie, and Jimmy Rushing; "South of the Border (Down Mexico Way)," by Jimmy Kennedy and Michael Carr; "Three Little Fishies (Itty Bitty Poo)" by Saxie Dowell; "Undecided," by Charles Shavers, lyrics by Sid Robin.

- Austrian American Ludwig Bemelmans's new novel *Hotel Splendide* is soon overshadowed by the release of his children's book *Madeline*, which he has illustrated himself.

- Thomas Hart Benton exhibits several paintings, including *Persephone*, *Threshing Wheat*, *Weighing Cotton*, and *Susannah and the Elders*.

- Virginia Lee Burton's children's book *Mike Mulligan and His Steam Shovel* is published.

- Dutch American painter Willem de Kooning exhibits his *Seated Man*.

- Grandma Moses (Anna Mary Robertson Moses) gains overnight fame for her primitivist paintings when art collector Louis Caldor buys her work and exhibits it at the Museum of Modern Art (MOMA) in New York City.

- The MOMA in New York City moves to a new building at 11 West Fifty-third Street.

- New Jersey roadhouse singer Frank Sinatra joins a new band formed by Harry James but leaves within a year to join the Tommy Dorsey band.

10 Jan.   Paul Vincent Carroll's *The White Steed,* starring Barry Fitzgerald and Jessica Tandy, opens at New York's Cort Theater.

20 Jan.   Sonata No. 1 for piano and orchestra, by Charles Ives, is first performed at New York's Town Hall.

21 Jan.   *The American Way,* by George S. Kaufman and Moss Hart and starring Fredric March and Florence Eldredge, opens at New York's Center Theater in Rockefeller Center.

15 Feb.   Lillian Hellman's *The Little Foxes,* starring Tallulah Bankhead, Carl Benton Reid, Dan Duryea, and Patricia Collinge, opens at New York's National Theater and runs for 191 performances.

24 Feb.   Roy Harris's Symphony Number 3 premieres at Boston's Symphony Hall.

18 Mar.   *The New Yorker* publishes "The Secret Life of Walter Mitty," by James Thurber.

28 Mar.   Katharine Hepburn, Lenore Lonergan, Shirley Booth, Van Heflin, and Joseph Cotten star in Philip Booth's *The Philadelphia Story,* which opens at New York's Shubert Theater.

13 Apr.   William Saroyan's *My Heart's in the Highlands* premieres at New York's Guild Theater and has a short run of forty-three performances.

19 June   *The Streets of Paris,* starring Brazilian Carmen Miranda singing "South American Way," opens at New York's Broadhurst Theater.

28 Aug.   The Three Stooges appear in the thirteenth and final version of *George White's Scandals* at New York's Alvin Theater. With music by Sammy Fain and lyrics by Jack Yellen, songs include "Are You Having Any Fun."

18 Oct.   Desi Arnaz costars with Eddie Bracken, Van Johnson, Richard Kollmar, and Marcy Wescott in the New York Imperial Theater premiere of *Too Many Girls.* Richard Rodgers and Lorenz Hart's songs include "I Didn't Know What Time It Was."

25 Oct.   *The Man Who Came to Dinner,* by George S. Kaufman and Moss Hart, opens at New York's Music Box Theater and runs for 739 performances.

          William Saroyan's *The Time of Your Life,* starring Eddie Dowling, Julie Haydon, Gene Kelly, and Celeste Holm, opens at New York's Booth Theater.

3 Nov.   Clare Boothe Luce's *Margin for Error,* starring Otto Preminger, premieres at New York's Plymouth Theater.

8 Nov.   *Life With Father,* a comedy by Howard Lindsay and Russel Crouse based on the book by Clarence Day, opens a run of 3,244 performances at New York's Empire Theater.

27 Nov.   Maxwell Anderson's *Key Largo,* starring José Ferrer, Paul Muni, and Uta Hagen, opens at New York's Ethel Barrymore Theater.

6 Dec.   *Du Barry Was a Lady,* starring Bert Lahr, Ethel Merman, and Betty Grable, with music and lyrics by Cole Porter, opens at New York's Forty-sixth Street Theater.

OVERVIEW

A Vital Decade. Despite the Depression the 1930s were a rich and vibrant decade for the arts. They were certainly a golden age for American letters, as writers produced works that have since been acknowledged as classics: William Faulkner's *Light in August* (1932) and *Absalom, Absalom!* (1936), Zora Neale Hurston's *Their Eyes Were Watching God* (1937), John Steinbeck's *The Grapes of Wrath* (1939), John Dos Passos's *U.S.A.* trilogy (1938), James T. Farrell's *Studs Lonigan* trilogy (1932–1935), F. Scott Fitzgerald's *Tender Is the Night* (1934), and Eugene O'Neill's *Mourning Becomes Electra* (1931). It was a revolutionary decade in American dance, as Martha Graham and Doris Humphrey choreographed their first fusions of ballet, expressionism, and jazz — a synthesis that defined the term *modern dance*. Artists of the decade produced vibrant portraits of the rural countryside, politically charged murals, and the first explorations of Abstract Expressionism. Hollywood developed the "American Style" of filmmaking, a type of seamless narrative that lifted the burden of the Depression for millions. Musicologists such as Alan Lomax and Howard Odum introduced blues and country music to a broad audience for the first time; and swing jazz swept the nation, providing a lively soundtrack that belied the miseries of the time.

Modernism and the Depression. The Depression affected artists as profoundly as it did other Americans. It compounded the difficulties of artists struggling to earn a living with their craft. Established artists turned their attention to the economic calamity or risked becoming irrelevant. At the same time artists were still assimilating the revolutionary aesthetic innovations of modernism introduced in preceding decades. During the 1930s their experiments with modernism were influenced by their encounters with the Depression, resulting in distinctly national art — one that employed the innovations of modernism to explore the effects of the Depression on the common man. It was, in a sense, a decade of documentary expression, one in which artists explored a myriad of representational forms, all oriented toward revealing an often desperate reality.

Documentary Expression. Since World War I some of the finest American writing, such as the novels of Fitzgerald and Sinclair Lewis, had been oriented toward exposing the hypocrisy and falseness of American culture. The Depression convinced many that this situation was getting worse. The term *depression* was suggested by President Herbert Hoover as a substitute for *panic* or *crisis* — terms that Americans had formerly used to describe economic downturns. Hoover and other businessmen consistently argued that the Depression was psychological, not structural, and that "confidence" and proper thinking could resolve the emergency. Advertising experts such as Albert Lasker did their best to provide diversions, confidence, and good thoughts, but by 1932 the divide between official pronouncements and the reality of common experience was so profound that Hoover was voted out of office. Artists used documentary expression in works designed to combat the insincerity of men like Lasker. Many novelists turned to journalism in the early part of the decade. In 1931 Theodore Dreiser and Dos Passos traveled to Harlan County, Kentucky, to report on the coal strike there. Sherwood Anderson, Edward Dahlberg, Jack Conroy, and Nelson Algren wrote about the sufferings of common people in travelogues and exposés. Later in the decade photographers such as Dorothea Lange, Walker Evans, and Margaret Bourke-White portrayed rootlessness and depression, often under commission by the federal Farm Security Administration.

Discovering the Common Man. By the time Franklin Roosevelt was elected, many artists had discovered a fascinating society on the farms and roads and in the factory yards of the nation. In contrast to the insular, European-derived art of the Eastern Seaboard, the folk practices and native art of the American interior were guileless, accessible, and quite often profound. A vogue for "folk" art — for genuine, unaffected expression — seized many artists and critics. The writer Constance Rourke made a career compiling folktales and humor. A similar admiration for folk culture infused Marc Connelly's play *Green Pastures* (1930) and Lynn Riggs's "folk drama" *Green Grow the Lilacs* (1931), which Richard Rodgers and Oscar Hammerstein adapted into the smash Broadway musical *Oklahoma!* in 1943. Musicologists such as Lomax and Odum, recorded, archived, and disseminated blues and country music for the nation at large. Southern and western musicians such as the Carter Family, Jimmie

Rodgers, Huddie "Leadbelly" Ledbetter, and Woody Guthrie became nationally known folk musicians. Other musicians of the 1930s, such as bluesmen Robert Johnson and Son House, were less popular during that decade but became legendary in subsequent years.

Regionalism. Regionalism — an artistic or literary style tied to the American landscape — was ascendant in American art of the 1930s. Regionalist painters such as Grant Wood, John Steuart Curry, Charles Burchfield, and Thomas Hart Benton tried to document the experience of rural America and give expression to its spirit. Other artists, such as Edward Hopper, Charles Sheeler, and Georgia O'Keeffe, found inspiration for their paintings in the American countryside. Many writers sought to give expression to the spirit of a particular region: Steinbeck, California; Farrell, Chicago; Wallace Stegner, the West.

The South. The nation took a romantic interest in the South during the 1930s, in part because of the position of that region in Roosevelt's New Deal coalition and also because of the strong sense of tradition identified with the southern sensibility. Few areas suffered as greatly as the South during the Depression. John Crowe Ransom, Robert Penn Warren, Donald Davidson, and Allen Tate were members of the Agrarians, a group of southerners who argued that modern urban life was destroying the traditions and vitality of the agriculturally based South. New Orleans–born Lillian Hellman explored southern decay in her play *The Little Foxes* (1939). Faulkner's novels of the South, set in the imaginary Mississippi county of Yoknapatawpha, combined an obsession with history and tradition with a striking modernist style. Others took a critical attitude toward the South. Erskine Caldwell's novel *Tobacco Road* (1932) was a best-selling critique of sharecropping, while Richard Wright's *Uncle Tom's Children* (1938) explored the Jim Crow racism of the South.

Federal Projects. At the center of efforts to document the distinctive culture of different American regions and to expose political oppression and suggest reforms were the host of federally funded projects for artists, musicians, dancers, and writers. Administered by the Works Progress Administration (WPA), these projects kept many struggling artists employed during the decade, giving writers such as Wright and painters such as Jackson Pollock and Mark Rothko relief from financial pressure so that they could develop their innovative styles of the 1940s. The WPA programs also carried on the search for folk and regional expression, especially through the Federal Writers' Project's famous American Guide series, for which writers were hired to collect and document the history and folktales of individual states and locales. The WPA also compiled the memories of African Americans who had been born slaves (they would be published in 1947 as *Lay My Burden Down*). The Federal Music Project funded an index of American folk music and composers. WPA programs also carried forward the documentary experiments of the early 1930s. No longer debunking

official government pronouncements, WPA-sponsored documentaries took aim at specific oppression, especially through the Federal Theatre Project (FTP) Living Newspaper series. The Living Newspapers attempted to put the political struggles of the 1930s on the stage, with plays often highly critical of big business, landowners, and bigots. Lewis's antifascist drama, *It Can't Happen Here* (1936), was performed by the FTP around the country; Marc Blitzstein's prounion opera, *The Cradle Will Rock* (1937), was so controversial that the WPA canceled funding for it. The Federal Art Project commissioned murals for public buildings from artists who, working in a radical tradition derived from Mexican muralist Diego Rivera, often chose themes highly critical of contemporary America. Other WPA-sponsored documentary projects were less specific, focusing attention on the roots of the Depression in particular regions, as in filmmaker Pare Lorentz's WPA-sponsored documentaries about the West, *The Plow that Broke the Plains* (1936) and *The River* (1938). Helen Tamiris of the FTP choreographed dances such as *Salut au Monde* (1936) — after Walt Whitman — on broadly American themes and the civil rights piece *How Long Brethren* (1937). Robert Sherwood's *Abe Lincoln in Illinois* was performed by the FTP in 1938 and won a Pulitzer Prize in 1939. These and other, more overtly political experiments, had a significant influence on how Americans identified with their history and their socio-economic group. The WPA experiments, in other words, contributed something like "class consciousness" to millions of Americans — a sense of shared oppression vital in sustaining New Deal reforms.

Ideological Conflicts. The WPA programs were opposed by conservatives, who often considered them propaganda for the New Deal. T. S. Eliot's social conservatism is basic to his poetic expression. Poet Ezra Pound ardently embraced fascism. Less extreme was the anti-Roosevelt satire of Broadway playwright George S. Kaufman. Robert Frost wrote anti–New Deal poems. Yet many more artists embraced communism or socialism. The 1930s were the decade of the artist as radical, and many hoped their work would lead to a sweeping alteration, if not outright overthrow, of the capitalist system. Writers such as Mike Gold joined the Communist Party, collapsed any distinction between art and propaganda, and sought to inspire the masses to political action and revolution. Fiction writer Josephine Herbst documented the difficulties facing women radicals in a trilogy of well-received novels. Ruth McKenney dispassionately documented the effect of the Depression on Akron, Ohio, for her left-wing *Industrial Valley* (1939). Poets Archibald MacLeish and Edna St. Vincent Millay wrote antifascist works. Artist Peter Blume painted a surreal antifascist canvas, *The Eternal City* (1934–1937). The most widely produced and influential play of the decade was Clifford Odets's *Waiting for Lefty* (1935), about a New York City cabdrivers' strike.

Hollywood. Not all art of the 1930s was committed to the ideological disputes of the period. The movies were primarily an entertainment business, and the foremost development in American cinema was the deathblow the Depression dealt to independent filmmakers and independent theaters. Small theaters could not sustain the downturn and were soon absorbed by the major studios. Economic pressure early in the decade also forced filmmakers to focus on the source of their bread and butter, entertainment. Lavish musicals such as *Gold Diggers of 1933* and extravaganzas such as *Cleopatra* (1934) amused many weary Americans, and taut gangster thrillers such as *Public Enemy* (1931) and monster movies such as *Frankenstein* (1931) kept millions on the edge of their seats and away from the miseries of economic necessity, if only for a few hours. In contrast to European experiments in cinema, the "American style" of direction, a type of seamless narrative, was developed to meet the appetite of the public for entertainment. Perky child actor Shirley Temple was the foremost star of the decade. *Gone With the Wind* (1939), almost a Gothic soap opera, was the biggest picture of the time. Yet there were gripping films produced in the 1930s that were both entertaining and edifying: *All Quiet on the Western Front* (1930); *I Am a Fugitive from a Chain Gang* (1932), starring Paul Muni; *Emperor Jones* (1933), with Paul Robeson; John Ford's brooding *The Informer* (1935); the antilynching movie *They Won't Forget* (1937); and the superb *Petrified Forest* (1936).

Swing. Jazz and swing music were also extremely popular forms of entertainment. By the end of the decade, hot jazz orchestras such as those led by Chick Webb, Earl Hines, Duke Ellington, Count Basie, Benny Goodman, Tommy Dorsey, and Artie Shaw crisscrossed the nation playing to packed urban, interracial ballrooms filled with jitterbugging dancers. These bands also played live on the radio, and records by jazz musicians such as Louis Armstrong and Ella Fitzgerald were best-sellers. Big-band jazz and swing were energetic, exciting, and visceral. The music was also deceptively simple, its frenetic rhythms obscuring complex arrangements and instrumental skill. Swing proved that popular art could hold its own with high art. Jazz was certainly the most popular music in the United States, definitively American — and the equal in emotional range and orchestrated complexity to European-style classical music.

New Syntheses. During the 1930s many writers reconsidered their attitudes toward popular media such as movies, radio, and pulp fiction. In part their attention to these media was a function of the Depression. Fitzgerald, Faulkner, Dorothy Parker, and Nathanael West worked as screenwriters. Playwrights and theater actors such as John Houseman, Orson Welles, and Burgess Meredith found work in radio. James M. Cain, Horace McCoy, and Raymond Chandler were among the writers who took pulp fiction to new realms of expression. Whatever the economic need, however, the new mass media were popular, and artists struggling to reach a mass audience soon realized that many techniques of the popular media could be used in high art. Artist Stuart Davis incorporated the graphic techniques of advertising in his paintings and sought to give visual expression to jazz. Dos Passos had been a partisan of the art-for-art's sake position earlier in his career and then abandoned it for radical engagement. Fusing the modernist novel to the documentary, *U.S.A.* featured everyman heroes and heroines and literally transcribed newspaper accounts, radio broadcasts, and popular songs. The trilogy was a spectacular example of the new synthesis.

The New National Act. By the end of the 1930s modernist innovations, the conventions of documentary expression, a concern with the common man and his history, and a growing admiration for popular culture led artists to produce distinctive works exemplifying a new national culture — one both populist and modernist, sophisticated and simple. Poet Carl Sandburg completed his biography of Abraham Lincoln in 1939, and in 1936 he produced a volume of poems whose title exemplifies the new national culture: *The People, Yes.* Graham and Humphrey took modern dance from probing psychological studies, such as Graham's *Primitive Mysteries* (1931), to celebrations of Americanism, such as Graham's *American Document* (which used readings from Jonathan Edwards and the Declaration of Independence) and Humphrey's *American Holiday.* Lincoln Kirstein's American Ballet Caravan performed dances with American themes, including *Pocahontas* and *Filling Station.* Classical composer Aaron Copland drew on folk songs and western tales for his ballet *Billy the Kid* (1938), and George Gershwin combined jazz and folk tales to produce the opera *Porgy and Bess* (1935). Director John Ford expressed the new national culture in his movies *Drums Along the Mohawk* (1939) and *Young Mr. Lincoln* (1939).

The New International Art. By the end of the 1930s native American artists had been joined by a host of European exiles, such as novelist Thomas Mann; painters Hans Hofmann, Josef Albers, and George Grosz; architect Walter Gropius; and composers Arnold Schoenberg and Paul Hindemith. All continued explorations in fusing high and low culture, American populism and European sophistication. The Depression decade became the catalyst for the extraordinary explosion of fine arts and letters after World War II that resulted in a new international art.

TOPICS IN THE NEWS

ART IN THE 1930S

The Great Debate. Although the now legendary Armory show had brought modern art to America in 1913, as the 1930s opened, the merits of modernism versus traditional figure painting were still being fervently debated. The social activism and mass political movements of the 1930s demanded a public and useful art. The modern movements — Dadaism, Cubism, Fauvism, and Surrealism — seemed private and effete. As the Depression took hold in America and war brewed in Europe, Americans drew inward, concerned with domestic problems and injustice. This isolationism led not simply to art in search of an American idiom, but anti-European sentiment espoused by the American Regionalists. Thomas Hart Benton, once a student in Paris, led the charge to rid America of what he called the "dirt" of European influence. On the other side of the debate were a small number of young American artists, mostly living in New York City, who embraced the aesthetic pursuit of painting instead of social relevance. They were a triply blessed group: they had financial support in the form of the Works Progress Administration (WPA)/Federal Art Project (FAP), which brought the painters into a community and allowed them the freedom to work; they had many of the masters of European modernism coming to New York from an increasingly distressing situation in Europe, bringing their ideas and skill with them; and they were talented. Painters who would triumph in the 1950s under the inclusive banner of Abstract Expressionism included Jackson Pollock, Mark Rothko, Arshile Gorky, Willem de Kooning, and Robert Motherwell. They were all in New York in the 1930s. America was a rapidly changing country, and the debate in art seemed to mirror the debate in society at large. A rural country was becoming an urban industrial nation. Capital was combating with labor, and traditional values were debating with modern sensibilities. In effect, with their huge popularity, the American Regionalists won the battle, but the abstract artists and the modernists eventually won the war.

Two Views of Industry. The conflicts that defined art in the 1930s were evident from the industrial explosion of the previous decade. Charles Sheeler, a Cubist-influ-

Grant Wood's *American Gothic*, 1930

enced painter and commercial photographer, was among the first to respond to the growing influence of the machine age. His 1927 photographs of Henry Ford's new Model A plant at River Rouge, Michigan, had redefined advertising and commercial photography. The photographs showed an obsessive interest in the beauty, form, and size of this new industrial development. Sheeler followed up the photographs with paintings that provide a glimpse into the modern mind. His *American Landscape* (1930) and *Classic Landscape* (1931) portrayed the River Rouge plant in the same idiom as his photographs. They are natureless landscapes, aesthetic instead of realistic portrayals of industry. They are devoid of workingmen and the assembly line. They seem to represent coldly a brave new world. Ironically, the other view of industry that influenced art in the 1930s was sponsored by the same automobile company. The famous Mexican

Photographer Alfred Stieglitz's New York gallery, which he opened in 1906, became a locus for several major 1930s painters. The modern art that Stieglitz exhibited as early as 1907, as well as his sponsorship of young artists such as Max Weber, Marsden Hartley, Arthur Dove, Stanton MacDonald-Wright, Georgia O'Keeffe, and John Marin, deeply influenced the direction American painting would take in the decades to come. Marsden Hartley (1877–1943), in his directness and his unmediated love of the sea and of nature, can trace his artistic lineage to Winslow Homer as well as to the German Expressionism from which he learned. Georgia O'Keeffe (1887–1986), whom Stieglitz married, provides an interesting bridge between the European-influenced modernists of the 1920s and the Regionalists of the 1930s: the Texan art teacher painted brightly colored abstractions based on the wildflowers of her Texas childhood and later the bleached skulls and endless skies of her adopted New Mexico home: O'Keeffe, more than anyone, remythologized the western landscape and gave its images to a new generation.

muralist and avowed Marxist Diego Rivera painted murals for the Ford Motor Company in Detroit. Rivera's murals burst with the energy of work and the worker, depicting a furious chaos of man working with machine industry. The public mural, especially those of the social realist bent, became commonplace in the 1930s. Rivera traveled to New York in 1932 at the request of the capitalist John D. Rockefeller and painted the controversial mural at the RCA building, *Man at the Crossroads Looking with Hope and High Vision to the Choosing of a New and Better Future*. His inclusion of Lenin angered many, but the mural made its point: art was a social force, not simply an aesthetic exercise.

Regionalism. By far the most popular painters with the 1930s public were the American Regionalists, or American Scene painters. Regionalism was a reaction against Europe, a nostalgic look back toward traditional forms in order to find traditional American scenes and values. European ideas were a foreign invasion of sorts, effete and unfathomable to most people. The Regionalists were led by Benton, who believed that art was democratic, to be seen by all and understood by all. He was a staunch individualist throwing off the intrusive theories of Europe. Benton, along with Grant Wood and John Steuart Curry, was the core of the movement that dominated 1930s style in public art. The movement grew out of *Time* magazine's 1934 Christmas issue, which had promoted the Regionalists' reactionary art. A movement was born. Regionalism had roots in and was closely tied

to magazine and book illustration. The subjects of Curry's work were often American folk legends and history. Benton painted nostalgic rural scenes of real people at work in the fields, or archetypes of industrial work and scenes from the town. His New School murals of 1930 present stylized American scenes, work that has some likeness in propaganda terms to the official Soviet art of the same period. Wood displayed more wit than his counterparts but was a full-fledged member of the movement. His *American Gothic* is an oft-quoted American classic, and his *Parson Weems' Fable* displays playfulness missing from other Regionalists. An outgrowth of the popular Regionalism was Social Realism. The Social Realists were American Scene painters but more politically astute and socially motivated than Regionalists. Like the Social Realist novelists of the era, they specialized in revealing the dehumanizing effects of urban life and believed in engagement with the world. They were active in reform movements. Among the members of this school were Ben Shahn, Moses Soyer, Reginald Marsh, Peter Blume, and Philip Evergood. They were associated with the WPA to produce public art for the public good.

Bridges. Two artists bridged the gap between realism and the coming explosion of modernism. Both Edward Hopper and Stuart Davis had been students of realist painter and teacher Robert Henri. Both had shown paintings at the famous Armory show but afterward had taken different paths. Davis was among the first Americans to embrace the modernism of Europe. He experimented with Cubist ideas and in 1927, with *Egg Beater*, began to paint full-fledged abstractions. More than with his painting, however, Davis influenced the move toward abstraction through his work as the editor of *Art Front*, the magazine of the Artists' Congress. Through the 1930s he painted less while writing, editing, and arranging exhibitions more. He did manage to paint four major murals, including the *History of Communication* for the 1939 New York World's Fair. His friendship with and influence on the young Surrealist Gorky was a key step toward passing modernist ideas to the generation that would become the Abstract Expressionists. While Davis embraced and nurtured modernism, Hopper moved in another direction. Hopper, often called an American Scene painter, is done a disservice with the title. He was an isolated figure in the 1930s — painting realistic scenes, but in his own way, with some of the influence of modernism. Hopper, like the French Impressionists, was mainly interested in light and the way it functioned on objects and architecture. His other great theme, however, was loneliness. Whether painting his oddly silent urban scenes such as *Early Sunday Morning* (1930), or more-rural scenes, as in *Gas* (1940), Hopper reveals human isolation. Even in paintings devoid of Hopper's typical, introspective human figures, the loneliness is present in tone, color, and composition. Neither abstract artist nor nostalgic Regionalist, Hopper's work is considered among the strongest of the 1930s.

Triumph of the Modern. The triumph of abstract art in 1930s New York can be seen only in retrospect. At the time abstract artists were poor, unknown, and working on the fringe. Their public triumph occurred in the 1940s. But the movement that exploded into prominence in the 1940s was nurtured in the 1930s in New York City. The forces were largely political. First, the growing tension in Europe and the rise of Nazism began forcing artists into exile as early as 1932 when the legendary teacher and painter Hans Hofmann arrived in New York. French Purist Jean Helion, Fernand Léger, and Josef Albers also arrived. Albers began teaching at the experimental and influential Black Mountain College in North Carolina in 1933. Hofman's school on Eighth Street became a place where the new ideas from Europe were demonstrated and explained to the young American artists in New York because of the WPA/FAP. The Depression had caused the art market to bottom out, and artists, like other workers in America, required federal support in order to survive. The WPA/FAP began in 1933 as the Public Works of Art Project. Abandoned in 1934 the FAP was started again in 1935. It gave painters a monthly stipend and asked that a painting be produced about every eight weeks. The paintings were then given to public buildings. Besides financial support the WPA brought painters together in a community of talent and ideas. It gave painters time to paint and generally made no demands on style, thus fostering abstract work as well as the more prevalent Regionalism. Davis, Kooning, Gorky, Pollock, Adolph Gottlieb, Rothko, and Ad Reinhardt were among the painters on the WPA rolls. By the time the WPA was disbanded in 1943, more than five thousand artists in more than a thousand American cities had benefited, and abstraction was still an underground movement. In 1936 the American Abstract Artists (AAA) group formed. Their stated goal was to make New York the world center of abstract art. They began sponsoring abstract exhibits. Although the Museum of Modern Art had held a "Cubism and Abstract Art" exhibit in 1936, it generally did not support American abstract art. As late as 1940 AAA members were picketing MOMA demanding more American abstract exhibits. In the meantime galleries such as Solomon R. Guggenheim's Museum of Non-objective Art (opened in 1937) and A. E. Gallatin's Museum of Living Art became the centers of abstract exhibits, while journals such as *Cahiers d'Art, Minotaure, Verve,* and *Plastique* kept modern ideas circulating.

Sculpture. As in painting, the 1930s were a decade of crossover for American sculpture, which led to a more American idiom in the 1940s. The influence of modern ideas was strong but debated against the romanticism of traditional figure sculpting. Sculptors' interest in the modern transcended mere form. Like the European Cubists and Dadaists, American sculptors grew intensely interested in the machine and the objects of industrial culture. Three-dimensional space and the use of metals allowed for a more direct address to the machine age.

Constructivism, with its emphasis on combining materials and pieces rather than simply carving direct from a material, dominated the American scene. Welding technique, learned literally in the factory by David Smith and Theodore Roszak, was applied to sculpture. Alexander Calder was the first American sculptor to gain recognition in Europe. Calder was a Surrealist and constructivist whose miniature circus productions had gained the attention of the Paris art world in the 1920s. In 1930 he began to truly pay attention to modern movements. His experimentation came in the creation of mechanized, movable sculpture that seemed to reproduce Cubist painting in three dimensions. Later, he abandoned the use of motors to drive his mobiles and created windblown mobiles that produced random movement. Like Calder, Isamu Noguchi was aligned with European theories. Trained by Constantin Brancusi, Noguchi was a carver in sensibility. His Japanese roots prevented his receiving WPA funding, and he supported himself on portraits and public sculpture. He was an early innovator in large "environmental" sculpture and deeply committed to the social movements of the time. His political beliefs led him to experiment in city development and planning techniques. He also explored his oriental roots in terra-cotta sculpture. The bridges between Calder and Noguchi and the flowering of the 1940s were Smith, Roszak, and Ibram Lassaw. Smith is arguably America's most accomplished sculptor. His Surrealist/Cubist form and his direct welding applications (begun in 1932) were direct statements of the machine age. Smith described metal sculpture as "of this century: power, structure, movement, progress, suspension, destruction, and brutality." Roszak, like Smith, had begun as a painter but found his form in metal, especially in machinelike pieces such as *Air-port Structure* (1932), based on an airplane engine. Lassaw was the last of the pioneer abstractionists in the 1930s. He worked in plaster as well as in combinations of traditional and contemporary metal sculpture. Lassaw was also a major force behind AAA.

Sources:

Wayne Anderson, *American Sculpture in Progress* (New York: New York Graphic Society, 1975);

Robert Hughes, *Nothing If Not Critical* (New York: Penguin, 1990);

Barbara Rose, *American Art Since 1900: Revised and Expanded* (New York: Praeger, 1975);

Terry Smith, *Making the Modern: Industry, Art, and Design in America* (Chicago: University of Chicago Press, 1993).

DANCE

Dance Overview. The 1930s were a period during which America shook off European influences in order to develop its own ballet and its own modern dance, both with distinctly American themes. While Martha Graham experimented with mystical imagery, Helen Tamiris created dances based on Walt Whitman's poetry, and across the nation jitterbugs created an interracial swing subculture whose frenetic signature dance alarmed moralists.

Martha Graham shaking hands with a new student at the
School of Contemporary Dance at
Bennington College

Duncan and St. Denis. Until Ruth St. Denis and her husband, Ted Shawn, formed their Denishawn dance company in 1915 in Los Angeles, Americans had to rely on European touring companies for their dance. In fact, both St. Denis and Isadora Duncan got their starts in theatrical productions and danced extensively in Europe before coming back to the United States. Duncan's influence sprang in large part from her image, which was one of unfettered sexuality. She derived her plots from classical sources, but she appeared on stage barefoot and in loose clothing. St. Denis and Shawn, along with Duncan, appealed to those progressives who wished to break loose from the shackles of Puritanism: their ambiguous sexuality and their combining of orientalist and athletic traditions helped them to create a dance that was distinctly American. By stretching the rules of ballet until they were close to breaking, St. Denis and Shawn helped create what became known as modern dance. Moreover, St. Denis and Shawn are important not only for what they themselves did but for the dancers they spawned.

Passing the Torch. Although Martha Graham did not even begin her dance training until 1916, when she was twenty-two, by the mid 1930s she had become perhaps the most influential choreographer in America, a position she retained throughout her lifetime. Indeed, three-quarters of her company members since the early 1930s have become choreographers. Inspired by the self-consciously exotic performance of St. Denis, whose pieces bore titles such as *The Veil of Isis, Incense, Radha,* and *Yogi,* Graham began her formal dance training at the Denishawn academy. Her first star performance was in *Xochitl* (1920), a ballet set centuries in the past, concerning a Toltec girl, written for her by Shawn. It was also here that she would forge a lasting romantic and professional link with Louis Horst, the married composer and musical director of the Denishawn dance company, who was to remain one of her greatest artistic influences. Although she had broken

from St. Denis and Shawn and was beginning to shed the exotic, romantic style promoted by Denishawn, Graham's first pieces still bore titles such as *Flute of Krishna* (1926) and *Three Gopi Maidens* (1926). Many works choreographed in the period from 1926 to the mid 1930s resembled those in the repertory of the more innovative ballet companies of the time; the group dance *Primitive Mysteries* (1931) is still hailed as a masterpiece. By this point she had already developed her signature spiral movements and linear stage patterns.

The Dance Repertory Theatre. In 1930 Graham, Tamiris, Doris Humphrey, and Charles Weldman formed the Dance Repertory Theatre, whose stated goal was to develop dance as an American art, one that would have a less polished texture than European ballet, one that would express the raw energy of the nation. As Graham said, "A new vitality is possessing us. No art can live and pass untouched through such a vital period as we are now experiencing." Gone would be the lavish costumes, fancy scenery, and timeless, storybook themes favored by Anna Pavlova and Duncan; instead, the work would take place on a bare stage and would center on themes of modern life, social injustice, nature, and relationships between the sexes. This new dance, called "modern dance," would be punctuated by "America's great gift to the arts . . . rhythm: rich, full, unabashed, virile." Starting in 1934 this collaboration would be furthered by the participation of Graham, Doris Weidman, and Charles Humphrey, and choreographer Hanya Holm, in five summers at Bennington College's School of the Dance, which enabled the pioneers to teach their method to a new generation of dancers. Dance Repertory Theatre pieces tended to emphasize the country's past as well as to describe the current scene, as witnessed by such productions as Humphrey's *American Holiday*; Weidman's *American Saga,* a dramatization of the Paul Bunyan legend; and Graham's *American Document.*

From Mysticism to Social Consciousness. While Graham experimented with orientalist and Jungian imagery, choreographer Tamiris focused on social problems in her dance pieces. As the head of the Federal Theatre Project's New York–based Dance Project, Tamiris was responsible for a wide range of productions on American themes, including Walt Whitman's *Salut au Monde* (1936), the Living Newspaper *One-Third of a Nation* (1937), and perhaps her most famous piece, *How Long Brethren* (1937), her dance dramatization of Lawrence Gelert's African American *Songs of Protest.* Tamiris combined elements of modernism and popular culture to create dance pieces that would be accessible to a mass audience and pack a political wallop.

Americanism. As Horst said, "The artist is always a radical. If he is an artist he is progressive and if he is progressive he must break with tradition. All great art contains an element of social criticism, for it expresses the life of its time." This attitude was reflected in Graham's more-documentary work in the late 1930s. While her work in the 1920s and early 1930s was far from political, with her pre-1934 pieces typically bearing titles such as "Adolescence," "Ekstasis," and "Four Insincerities," in the period from 1935 to 1940 fully three-quarters of her work was based on American themes or dealt with the political situation abroad. Perhaps her most representative work of this period was the highly acclaimed *American Document,* a ballet that reviewed the country's past, incorporating such documents as the Preamble to the Declaration of Independence. One of the ballet's five sections, titled *Puritan Episode,* used the modernist technique of collage in its juxtaposition of readings from Jonathan Edwards and the *Song of Songs.* Other Graham works of the 1930s included *American Provincials* (1934), the anti-fascist *Deep Song* (1937), and *American Lyric* (1938). Although from a slightly later period, one of Graham's most acclaimed works, *Appalachian Spring* (1944), with music composed by Aaron Copland, belongs to this group of dances.

The New Ballet. Although many critics, including the influential John Martin of *The New York Times,* rejected ballet as being academic and, worse, representing European cultural dominance, ballet in the 1930s was given a distinctively American slant by a young department-store heir named Lincoln Kirstein, creator of the American Ballet Company. The company, founded in 1934, had as its aim the development of a uniquely American form of ballet, one which incorporated both traditional elements and popular music, notably ragtime and swing. The success of its early productions moved the Metropolitan Opera to adopt the American Ballet Company as its official ballet. Although that connection was broken in 1938, and although the company had practically ceased to exist by 1940, Kirstein had by that point founded the Ballet Caravan, which performed such American-themed works as *Pocahontas* (1936) and *Filling Station* (1938).

Jitterbugging. With the swing craze that swept the nation in the 1930s came the advent of a new dance, the jitterbug. Swing fans themselves became known as jitterbugs, or alligators, and their dance inspired the condemnation of moralists and jazz musicians. As Benny Goodman recalled, "The bugs, literally glued to the music, would shake like St. Vitus with the itch. Their eyes popped, their heads pecked, their feet tapped out the time, arms jerked to the rhythm." Psychiatrists worried about the appearance of mass hysteria and the resulting loss of inhibitions: jitterbugging was banned in some midwestern dance halls by 1939. Jitterbugging was an interracial phenomenon, though the skilled dancers whose intricate and innovative steps incorporated more acrobatic variations with each passing year tended to be black and to congregate in urban ballrooms. By contrast, the high-school- and college-aged white jitterbugs often demonstrated more enthusiasm than skill and annoyed musicians by applauding at the wrong moments: these belonged to the group dismissed as "ickies." With the end of Prohibition, dance clubs, at least in large cities, became

Jitterbuggers in New York City, 1938

more respectable, were more racially integrated, and began to attract a wider range of classes and ages. At the height of the swing craze, in 1938, it sometimes seemed as though all America was dancing — frenetically, energetically, intricately — in a style that an earlier generation found virtually unrecognizable.

Sources:

Charles C. Alexander, *Here the Country Lies* (Bloomington: Indiana University Press, 1980);

Merle Armitage, ed., *Martha Graham: The Early Years* (New York: Da Capo Press, 1978);

Hallie Flanagan, *Arena: The Story of the Federal Theatre* (New York: Duell, Sloan & Pearce, 1940);

Ernestine Stodelle, *Deep Song: The Dance Story of Martha Graham* (New York: Macmillan, 1984);

William Stott, *Documentary Expression and Thirties America* (Chicago: University of Chicago Press, 1973);

David W. Stowe, *Swing Changes* (Cambridge, Mass.: Harvard University Press, 1994).

THE FEDERAL THEATRE PROJECT

A National Theater. In 1935 Works Progress Administration director Harry Hopkins tapped respected Vassar College drama director Hallie Flanagan to head the Federal Theatre Project (FTP), whose purpose would not only be to provide employment to thousands of unemployed actors, directors, set designers, and costume designers, but also to create a theater that would be affordable and accessible to all. Each state was to have its own FTP chapter, from which it would develop productions

Scene from the WPA Theatre production of *The Swing Mikado* at the New York Theatre, 1939

suitable for that state. Between its founding in 1935 and its loss of funding in 1939 at the hands of the House Un-American Activities Committee, the FTP produced farces; marionette shows; children's plays; modern dramas such as T. S. Eliot's *Murder in the Cathedral* and Sinclair Lewis and John C. Moffitt's *It Can't Happen Here* (which opened simultaneously in seventeen cities, including Yiddish- and Spanish-language productions); productions of William Shakespeare and Christopher Marlowe; theater by and for the blind; radio plays; pageants; and dramas in a range of languages, including Yiddish, Spanish, Italian, German, and French. Audiences for FTP productions ultimately numbered twenty-five million.

Controversy. Although Federal Theatre Project productions tended to be both popular and well reviewed, they were not without their detractors. The children's play *The Revolt of the Beavers*, for instance, generated a great deal of controversy over its depiction of a revolution in Beaverland, in which The Chief and his cohorts force the other beavers to supply the bark for a wheel that produces clothes and food. The chief and his pals are the only ones with blue sweaters, roller skates, and ice cream. The working beavers' objections lead to their replacement by "barkless" beavers. Finally, Oakleaf, an exiled beaver, a beaver professor, and two children organize a beaver club and establish a new order where all things are shared by all. Unsurprisingly, this production was denounced by

conservative legislators for its leftist slant. By 1938 the FTP was increasingly embattled.

The Negro Theatre Project. Headed by John Houseman and Orson Welles (who shortly afterward became famous as the director and star of *Citizen Kane* in 1941), the Negro Theatre Project, based in New York and with chapters located in cities across the country, produced several innovative dramas, including an all-black *Macbeth*, set in Haiti; *Turpentine*, a social drama exposing the tyranny and injustice of the southern labor-camp system; Frank Wilson's *Walk Together Chillun;* Theodore Ward's *Big White Fog*, which dealt with Marcus Garvey's Back-to-Africa movement; and *The Swing Mikado*, a black version of the Gilbert and Sullivan operetta, which was seen by 250,000 people in Chicago alone. The Negro Theatre Project provided a means for black theater artists to acquire training in areas such as lighting and set design, from which they had previously been barred by white unions. Black playwrights were offered an opportunity to hone their craft, and African American actors were given the chance to play noncaricatured roles.

The Living Newspapers. Perhaps the most acclaimed productions of the Federal Theatre Project, the Living Newspapers were dramas that dealt with contemporary issues: *One-Third of a Nation* (the dearth of safe, affordable housing), *Power* (the problems caused by electrical monopolies), *Triple-A Plowed Under* (a recent Supreme Court decision that had adversely affected farmers). As formally innovative as they were topical, Living Newspapers were heavily researched, historically grounded, collaboratively written documentary dramas that incorporated such elements as snippets from the *Congressional Record*, items from police blotters, *New York Times* articles, and popular songs and speeches by Communist leaders in a modernist pastiche. Acclaimed by reviewers, attacked by conservative congressmen, the Living Newspapers blended song, dance, film, sermons, pageantry, and skits to create theater whose purpose was not only to entertain but to stir audiences to civic action: the Chicago production of *Spirochete,* a drama about the history of syphilis, featured a blood-testing lab in the theater lobby, in order that patrons might make sure that they themselves were not infected. (A priest and the governor's daughter were the first volunteers.) Some Living Newspapers were written and even rehearsed, though they could not be produced for political reasons. The most notable of these was *Liberty Deferred,* a Living Newspaper reexamination of southern history written by two young African American playwrights, Abram Hill and John Silvera, which includes not only documentary evidence detailing the growth of slavery in Virginia but spoken commentary from James Weldon Johnson, Thomas Jefferson, Frederick Douglass, and A. Philip Randolph. In addition to directly quoted speeches from historical figures, characters include such mythological figures as Jim Crow and Jim Lily White. This blend of fact and fiction is effectively used in what is perhaps the most striking scene, a portrayal of a "Lynchotopia" — the fabled land where all lynch victims go. Southern senators at this time were successfully blocking the passage of an antilynching bill; the play was destined to remain unproduced.

Sources:

Lorraine Brown, ed., *Liberty Deferred and Other Living Newspapers of the 1930s* (Fairfax, Va.: George Mason University Press, 1989);

Brown and John O'Connor, *Free, Adult, Uncensored: The Living History of the Federal Theatre Project* (Washington, D.C.: New Republic Books, 1978);

Hallie Flanagan, *Arena: The Story of the Federal Theatre* (New York: Duell, Sloan & Pierce, 1940).

FICTION OF THE 1930S: MODERNISM FOR THE MASSES

A Time of Transition. The 1930s were a time of great ferment in American letters. In a period of social crisis American writers, including Theodore Dreiser and Erskine Caldwell, debated how best to create social change through literature, and critics such as Edmund Wilson and Philip Rahv argued about where on the political Left they should position themselves. Literary journalists, including Martha Gellhorn and Josephine Herbst, documented the suffering of the American people. Not all writers, of course, produced what became known as proletarian fiction. Tough-guy writers provided a nihilistic view of a country gone awry, while modernists provided intimate portraits of the American self.

Between 1932 and 1942 Laura Ingalls Wilder (1867–1957) published a steady stream of books recording her girlhood memories of frontier life, beginning with the passage of the Homestead Act of 1862, which enabled settlers to obtain "free land in exchange for their labor." Editors at Harper and Brothers hoped that her first book, *Little House in the Big Woods* (1932), would be the "miracle book that no depression could stop," and their hopes were not disappointed: it was chosen as a Junior Literary Guild selection, and sales were brisk. This first success was followed by a stream of others: *Farmer Boy* (1933), *Little House on the Prairie* (1935), *On the Banks of Plum Creek* (1937), *By the Shores of Silver Lake* (1939), *The Long Winter* (1940), *Little Town on the Prairie* (1941), and *These Happy Golden Years* (1943) became critically acclaimed best-sellers. Five of her books became Newbery Honor books; a branch library in Detroit was named after her, as was the children's section of the public library in Pomona, California. Wilder's books were welcomed by readers hungry for regional literature, a taste that paralleled the Regionalist movements in painting and music. Her tales of surviving blizzards, grasshopper plagues, encounters with hostile Indian tribes, illness, and debt struck a resonant chord in Depression America — and the optimistic conclusion of each volume gave hope to a battered nation.

Sources: Janet Spaeth, *Laura Ingalls Wilder* (Boston: Twayne, 1987);

Donald Zochert, *Laura: The Life of Laura Ingalls Wilder* (Chicago: Regnery, 1976).

Travelogues. Throughout the 1930s a range of prominent writers took to the road in search of America. The works they produced, including Sherwood Anderson's *Puzzled America* (1935), Nathan Asch's *The Road: In Search of America* (1937), Edmund Wilson's *The American Jitters* (1932), James Rorty's *Where Life Is Better: An Unsentimental American Journey* (1936), Dreiser's *Tragic America* (1931), Louis Adamic's *My America* (1938), and John Dos Passos's *In All Countries* (1934), which included accounts of his travels both in and out of the United States, were hallmarks of the decade's travel literature. These trips were, among other things, research that writers did as part of a much larger project: not only to understand America but to be able to, in their fiction, create an image of America that would enable readers to see themselves as participants in the making of history, rather than as spectators at some historical pageant. The new task of the writer, then, would be to effect a full and accurate representation of America as itself, of the "unexceptional American."

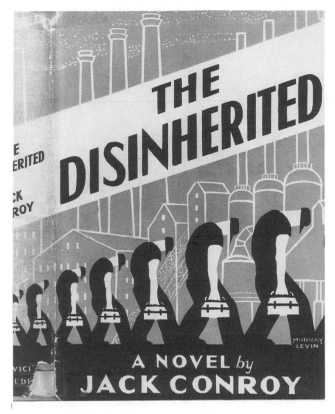

Dust jacket for Jack Conroy's 1933 proletarian novel

Strangers in Their Own Land. These writers were spurred to take their cross-country journeys by their recognition that something had gone terribly wrong and that they needed to understand what it was. Worse, perhaps, was the feeling that their old intellectual habits had become irrelevant and that the old kind of fiction simply was not adequate to the times. What is clear from many of the accounts is the extent to which these writers, even as they struggled to describe as well as survive it, felt baffled by America and uncertain about their place in it. Theirs was to be a mission both personal and political, both experiential and literary, as writers wrestled with trying to discover the forms that would best enable them to depict and analyze the country that seemed in many ways foreign to them. In their travelogues, as well as in much of the radical fiction and drama of the decade, writers were coming to grips with the necessity for new forms and techniques. They used the skills of the muckrakers, offering statistical accuracy in order to stir outrage. They employed the lessons of the modernists while experimenting with the subject, that was, America. Finally, as those who had labored on tabloids and in the advertising industry understood all too well, to succeed, radical writers had to compete with the styles and techniques of mass culture. Sometimes moved, often shocked, and occasionally bored by what they saw, these writers were rediscovering America for themselves and for their readers. Whereas in the 1920s many of these writers had traveled to Europe for inspiration, cheap living, and the intellectual and emotional support of their peers, now

they had come home, and they wanted to know what home was.

The New Literature. The land that socially conscious fiction writers of the 1930s described included inhabitants that had hitherto escaped noncaricatured fictional representation. The homeless were one such group, and Edward Dahlberg in *Bottom Dogs* (1930), Jack Conroy in *The Disinherited* (1933), and Nelson Algren in *Somebody in Boots* (1935) offered a view of life "on the bum." The struggles of workers for justice were dramatized by journalist Mary Heaton Vorse in her novel *Strike!* (1930), Robert Cantwell in *The Land of Plenty* (1934), and by Clara Weatherwax in the award-winning, now largely forgotten *Marching! Marching!* (1935). Henry Roth dramatized the immigrant experience in his modernist novel *Call It Sleep* (1935), and Richard Wright's *Uncle Tom's Children* (1938) offered a view of southern black life. Tess Slesinger in *The Unpossessed* (1934) wrote about the difficulties women radicals faced, a theme shared by Herbst in her trilogy of novels, including *Pity Is Not Enough* (1933), *The Executioner Waits* (1934), and *Rope of Gold* (1939). Herbst was one of several Depression writers who turned to the trilogy form, first used by naturalists, including Dreiser and Frank Norris at the turn of the century. Like their predecessors these radical writers of the 1930s, with their focus on history and in the depiction of broader social problems, wanted a form that would require readers themselves to adopt a historical perspective (among other reasons, by requiring them to remember what had happened in the trilogy's previous volumes). Dos Passos, in his *U.S.A.* trilogy, comprising *The 42nd Parallel* (1930), *1919* (1932), and *The Big Money* (1936), combined modernist techniques such as stream-of-consciousness, montages of newspaper headlines, and capsule biographies of prominent Americans to offer readers a sweeping vision — and an indictment — of American life in the first decades of the century. And James T. Farrell, in his *Studs Lonigan* trilogy (*Young Lonigan*, 1932; *The Young Manhood of Studs Lonigan*, 1934, and *Judgment Day*, 1935), gave readers a vision of an apolitical young worker unable to come to terms with a world in which he no longer has a place.

Things Fall Apart. Not all radical writers produced radical fiction — Dashiell Hammett, who was active in radical movements and later went to prison for his beliefs, specialized in hard-boiled detective fiction, notably *The Maltese Falcon* (1930). Although not all of the decade's fiction was explicitly radical, much of it centered on documenting the American experience — and its failures. Just as Dos Passos, Farrell, and other radical writers were disturbed by the deleterious effects on the populace of mass culture, so Nathanael West savagely portrayed Hollywood in his 1939 novel *The Day of the Locust*. Wallace Stegner depicted the brutalizing effects of poverty on a migrant family in *The Big Rock Candy Mountain* (1938), a year before John Steinbeck blended radicalism and Christian redemption in *The Grapes of Wrath* (1939). Zora

Dashiell Hammett in New York, 1934

Neale Hurston's relatively apolitical narrative about the founders of the country's first all-black town, *Their Eyes Were Watching God* (1937), may not have been radical but was, however, an example of the inclusive, Americanist approach of the decade's burgeoning American Studies movement. Similarly, William Faulkner's modernist novels, including *Light In August* (1932) and *Absalom, Absalom!* (1936), which focused on a tiny region of Mississippi, were marked by an Americanist concern for the deep history of a place. Of course, not all writers shared this concern for depicting America: Ernest Hemingway continued his production of terse, modernist works with *Winner Take Nothing* (1933), *Green Hills of Africa* (1935), and *To Have and Have Not* (1937). Nobel Prize-winner Pearl Buck's *The Good Earth* (1931) took readers far away to China.

The Agrarian Movement and Southern Writing. While many American writers turned to the left, a movement sprung up in the South that was to provide a nostalgic counterbalance. When, in 1930, twelve southern writers produced a manifesto, *I'll Take My Stand*, they staked out a new territory for themselves: that of the idealized agrarian past. Among these writers were four poets who had contributed to the short-lived (1922–1925) Vanderbilt University–based literary magazine *The Fugitive*: Robert Penn Warren, Donald Davidson, Allen Tate, and John Crowe Ransom. Based on the premise that modern urban life was profoundly destructive of culture, the contributors, as they wrote in their introduc-

tory "Statement of Principles," tend to support a southern way of life against what may be called the American or prevailing way; and all agreed that the best terms in which to represent the distinction are contained in the phrase "Agrarian *versus* Industrial." However, the agrarians avoided discussion of social injustice in their manifesto, which contained no mention of the sharecropper system and little of slavery. Caroline Gordon (*Alex Maury, Sportsman,* 1934) was among the writers who followed the path of the Agrarians (Tate was her husband) in blending modernist techniques with a concern for the South's history. Not all southern writers were equally nostalgic, however; Caldwell, whose *Tobacco Road* (1932) was a best-seller, offered a grotesque portrait of sharecropper life: the book opens with a twelve-year-old daughter of a tenant farmer attempting to prostitute herself for a turnip. Wright, in *Uncle Tom's Children,* offered a searing vision of life in the racist South.

Tough-Guy Writers. During the 1930s the genre of the tough-guy novel, or hard-boiled novel, flourished. Writers such as James M. Cain (*The Postman Always Rings Twice,* 1934; *Double Indemnity,* 1936; *Serenade,* 1937), Hammett (*The Maltese Falcon,* 1930; *The Glass Key,* 1931), Raymond Chandler (*The Big Sleep,* 1939), and Horace McCoy (*They Shoot Horses, Don't They?,* 1935) wrote fiction, often in the first person, about protagonists who were usually, though not always, detectives, moving through a harsh, violent world where poverty and lawlessness were rampant. These were novels of action, in which characters spoke with their fists and with their pistols as much as with their words. In the hard-boiled detective novel, the wealthy people who hire the dick often turn out to be as corrupt as the denizens of the underworld through which he normally moves. These popular works offered a vision of Depression America unalloyed by hope: in many ways the hard-boiled novel was the underbelly of the proletarian novel. Indeed, Hammett, a former Pinkerton detective himself, was a committed radical, though his novels are apolitical.

The Great Age of American Criticism. In the 1930s it was still possible for the freelance intellectual to flourish free of attachment to the university system. At the decade's beginning the literary debate swirled around "Proletcult," a movement whose American form was spearheaded by novelist and editor Mike Gold, who suggested politically committed writers employ "Proletarian Realism." This new form of literature would focus on working-class characters, would have social themes, would emphasize political activism rather than internal exploration, and would express the hope offered by the prospect of revolution. Although many writers employed this style of naturalism or realism, others found it unpalatable: many leftist writers employed modernist techniques in the service of socially focused fiction and poetry. Among the critics who entered the fierce debate over the shape of the time's literature were such figures as Malcolm Cowley and Wilson, writing in the pages of the

On 6 May 1926, on being offered the Pulitzer Prize for fiction for his novel *Arrowsmith,* Sinclair Lewis wrote a public letter to the prize committee that concluded: "I invite other writers to consider the fact that by accepting the prize and approval of these vague institutions, we are admitting their authority, publicly confirming them as the final judges of literary excellence, and I inquire whether any prize is worth that subservience." Three years later he concluded one institution was worthy of his attention, and thus he became the first American writer to win the Nobel Prize for Literature, which had a cash award of some $48,000 attached. "Naturally I felt that some day I would get this recognition," Lewis told reporters, "but I didn't know when. I should be just as glad if Eugene O'Neill had received it."

Six years later he did. In 1936 O'Neill became the second American winner of the Nobel Prize for Literature. His award was $40,000. He was a much more gracious winner than Lewis. Unlike the novelist, O'Neill did not use his acceptance speech as an opportunity to hector his critics. Indeed, his speech was short and gracious, expressing his "profound gratitude" to the Swedish Academy. It was delivered by a reader in Stockholm, as O'Neill was severely ill when the award ceremony took place. Appendicitis, complicated by kidney and prostate conditions, kept him hospitalized for a month. His award was presented in a five-minute ceremony at Merritt Hospital in San Francisco by the Swedish consul and witnessed only by O'Neill's physician and a nurse. There was a consensus throughout the English-speaking world that O'Neill was a most deserving recipient.

Not so, with the winner of the 1938 Nobel Prize, forty-six-year-old Pearl Buck, the second youngest recipient in history. (Rudyard Kipling was forty-two when he won.) Though she was awarded a Pulitzer for her 1931 novel about China, *The Good Earth,* she was not regarded as a writer of the first rank by critics in America, and the Swedes' high opinion of her work baffled contemporary observers and even Buck herself. When her secretary informed her she had won the Nobel, she replied, "I think it's reporters' talk, and I shan't believe it until you have called Sweden long distance and inquired." There was a public expression of outrage when the award was announced. Henry Seidel Canby wrote a particularly harsh editorial in the Saturday Review of Literature criticizing the Swedish Academy's choice. Sinclair Lewis, who had some experience in dealing with critics, offered Buck collegial support: "You must write many novels," he told her. "And let people have their little say! They have nothing else to say, Damn them!"

Sources: Arthur and Barbara Gelb, *O'Neill* (New York: Harper, 1962);

Theodore F. Harris, *Pearl S. Buck: A Biography* (New York: Day, 1969);

Mark Shorer, *Sinclair Lewis: An American Life* (New York: McGraw-Hill, 1961).

New Republic, as well as Rahv and William Phillips, writing in the rival *Partisan Review:* most of these writers were politically radical, but the gulf between a Socialist and a Communist was broad indeed.

Sources:
Sherwood Anderson, *Puzzled America* (New York, Scribners, 1935);

Malcolm Bradbury, *The Modern American Novel,* revised edition (New York: Viking, 1992);

Malcolm Cowley, *The Dream of the Golden Mountain* (New York: Viking, 1964);

Joseph Freeman, *An American Testament* (New York: Farrar, Straus & Giroux, 1973);

David Madden, ed., *Tough Guy Writers of the Thirties* (Carbondale: Southern Illinois University Press, 1968);

Richard H. Pells, *Radical Visions & American Dreams: Culture and Social Thought in the Depression Years* (Middletown, Conn.: Wesleyan University Press, 1973);

Joan Shelley Rubin, *Constance Rourke and American Culture* (Chapel Hill: University of North Carolina Press, 1980).

THE FUNNY PAGES AND BEYOND

Beyond Kids. The 1930s ushered in a significant development in comic art: the rise of the adventure strip. From the family strips of the 1920s, which focused on kids and domestic experience, comic strips moved toward the lurid and the action-packed.

Tarzan. "Me Tarzan, you Jane" may have been Tarzan's most lasting contribution to the American vernacular, but it was only one of many. The shaggy, inarticulate hero of Edgar Rice Burroughs's 1914 adventure novel *Tarzan of the Apes* was an orphaned English lord who, following the death of his parents, was raised by the she-ape Kala in the jungles of Africa. Harold Foster's strip, launched as a daily in 1929, was instantly successful: its focus on danger within an exotic locale, its Darwinian leitmotivs, and its thematic preoccupation with eugenics so appealed to readers that by 1931 the strip began appearing in Sunday color supplements.

Leftist political groups of the 1930s held that it was an artist's role in society to record the plight of the proletariat —the working class—which clearly suffered terribly during the Great Depression. The militancy of workers' groups was regarded by leftists as proof of the Marxist theory of class struggle and the emergence of the working class as the dominant element in society. The more naive the worker, the better he or she illustrated the theory. Thus, when coal miners went on strike in eastern Kentucky, one of the most depressed areas of the nation even in flush times, literary leftists rallied to the strikers' support.

John Dos Passos was a vocal supporter of the Kentucky miners. He was chairman of the National Committee to Aid Striking Miners Fighting Starvation and had written a public letter appealing for financial aid. When Theodore Dreiser, chairman of the National Committee for the Defense of Political Prisoners (NCDPP) called for volunteers to go to Kentucky to investigate, Dos Passos answered the call, along with screenwriters Lester Cohen and Samuel Ornitz; Bruce Crawford, Melvin P. Levy; and Dos Passos's Provincetown neighbors Charles and Adelaide Walker. In November 1931 the group left for a two-week visit to Harlan County, Kentucky, where they held public hearings that were recorded by stenographers.

Appalachians are traditionally suspicious of outsiders and hostile to strangers who do not respect the mountain code of minding one's own business. They greeted the committee with attitudes ranging from bemusement to contempt. The strikers, sensing that maybe they could use the committee to voice their complaints, told stories and sang songs in protest meetings at local churches. The mine owners and local police acted to rid themselves of the pesky intruders.

Dreiser, anticipating the drabness of life in Harlan County, brought an attractive female companion, whom he referred to as his secretary. One night when they retired late to his hotel room, the sheriff placed toothpicks against the door, which were found undisturbed the next morning. That was evidence enough in the locals' view to justify charging Dreiser with fornication, a misdemeanor. Judiciously, he left the area the next day to avoid facing charges. The local authorities did not stop with Dreiser, however. Nine days after the committee left Harlan County, charges of criminal syndicalism were filed against Dreiser and the NCDPP, though Harlan County insiders assured Dreiser's attorney that if the committee did not attempt to return to the area the charges would be dropped. Dreiser was happy to accede, but Earl Browder, head of the Communist Central Committee felt that the charges offered an opportunity for a high-profile trial that could be useful as a propaganda tool. Since Dreiser was too busy to go, Browder asked Dos Passos to go back to Kentucky and act as scapegoat. Dos Passos declined the honor and filed the experience in his memory bank to draw upon six years later when he wrote his *Adventures of a Young Man* (1939), an indictment of the manipulative tactics of the Communist Party.

Dos Passos did, however, prepare a report of the NCDPP investigation. *Harlan Miners Speak* (1932), which he called "a volume for the record," consists of transcripts of testimony with continuity and commentary provided by NCDPP members with his guidance. The volume was published without notice in Harlan County, where, by winter 1932, the miners were back at work and there was no sign of an active union.

Sources: *Harlan Miners Speak* (New York: Harcourt Brace, 1932);

Townsend Ludington, *John Dos Passos: A Twentieth-Century Odyssey* (New York: Dutton, 1980).

Moreover, by the end of the 1930s Burroughs had produced twenty-one popular Tarzan novels. In addition, Tarzan was the hero of a daily fifteen-minute radio serial and of sixteen movies, many of them starring former Olympic star Johnny Weismuller.

Prince Valiant. Like Tarzan, Prince Valiant was an adventure hero whose life was far removed from the grim realities of Depression America. And like the Tarzan strip, the prince and his environs were drawn by Harold Foster, whose careful, draftsmanlike work reflected the tradition of the book illustrator rather than that of an artist in the comics tradition. Val, the Arthurian prince, occupied a medieval world whose details were accurately limned by Foster — from the impeccably drawn Camelot, home of good King Arthur, down to the disemboweled bodies littering the battlefields where Prince Valiant spent so much time.

Science Fiction. When readers were not escaping into the world of England, circa A.D. 500, or to distant jungles with Tarzan, they were frequently traveling to far-off galaxies in the company of one of the 1930s science fiction stars. The first of these was Buck Rogers, created

When Will Rogers died in an air crash in Alaska with aviator Wiley Post during the summer of 1935, America lost a man whose homespun humor, cowboy skills, and jest-folks philosophy made him a top box-office draw in the 1930s. The advent of talking pictures provided him with a forum in which to excel as he had not in the silents, and his vehicles, pictures such as *A Connecticut Yankee* (1931), *State Fair* (1933), and *Judge Priest* (1934), were box-office smashes. Rogers's popularity extended far beyond his screen talents: he served as mayor of Beverly Hills; declined the governorship of his home state, Oklahoma; and contributed mightily to the election of Franklin Delano Roosevelt in 1932. Rogers had a great gift for summing up the mood of the country: as he said of Roosevelt in the early days, "The whole country is with him. Just so he does something. If he burned down the Capitol, we would cheer and say, 'Well, at least we got a fire started anyway.' "

Sources: Frederick Lewis Allen, *Since Yesterday* (New York: Harper, 1939);

Ephraim Katz, *The Film Encyclopedia* (New York: Harper Perennial, 1994);

Robert S. McElvaine, *The Great Depression* (New York: Times Books, 1984).

by John Dilles and drawn by Richard Calkins. *Buck Rogers,* launched in 1929 and set in the year 2430, was essentially a strip about pioneer life, set in outer space and replete with gee-whiz gadgetry such as the Super Radiating Protonoformer and the Electrocosmic Spectrometer. The equipment proved as great a hit on Earth as in intergalactica: a line of 20,200 formed outside Macy's the morning after the New York department store advertised a toy version of a Disintegrator Gun.

Flash Gordon. Buck Rogers was not alone in his futuristic adventures; the Yale-educated Flash Gordon made his first appearance on the comic pages in 1934, when creator Alex Raymond engineered the near collision of Earth with the planet Mongo and the subsequent abduction of Gordon and the lovely Dale Arden by an insane rocket-dwelling scientist. Flash's life on the planet Mongo was, needless to say, eventful, and the success of the strip — marked by its witty narrative and slick drawing — led to a series of Flash Gordon movies and Big Little Books — ten-cent, four-hundred-page cubes of text and illustrations.

Dick Tracy: The First Shoot-'Em-Down Strip. In a decade when gangster movies enjoyed unprecedented popularity, and when the bad guys, though they may in the end have died, at least did so in a blaze of glory, uttering unforgettable lines on their way out, Dick Tracy provided a cartoon counterbalance — and, in some sense, a counterpart — to the tide of blood washing over American screens. In 1931 Dick Tracy, just minutes after he announced his engagement, was traumatized by witnessing his fiancée's father gunned down in cold blood by gangsters and joined the police force as a plainclothes detective. From this beginning artist Chester Gould launched a strip in which his square-jawed hero pursued and shot scores of gangsters in the funny pages: the cops-and-robbers format and the sheer level of violence was unprecedented in the world of comics. Tracy proved too powerful a force to be confined to the comics page, however: Quaker Oats soon launched a radio serial linked to a sales gimmick: American children could, by sending in an escalating number of cereal boxtops, join the ranks of Dick Tracy's Secret Service Patrol. Moves up the career ladder in this patrol were marked by badges, and members could also distinguish themselves by wearing club buttons and even official Dick Tracy watches.

Superheroes. The superhero strip was a development of the 1930s. Audiences, beaten down by the exigencies of depression life, responded well to strong men with extraordinary powers. The first of these strips, *The Phantom,* drawn by Lee Falk, appeared in 1936. The Phantom ruled from the skull throne in a deep African forest; it was not until 1939 that an American superhero was born. Who could be better assimilated than Superman, the 1938 refugee from the planet Krypton, who arrived on American shores in order to make the country safe for democracy?

Sources:
Stephen Becker, *Comic Art in America* (New York: Simon & Schuster, 1959);

Wolfgang Fuchs and Reinhold Reitberger, *Comics: Anatomy of a Mass Medium* (Boston: Little, Brown, 1970);

Erling B. Holtsmark, *Edgar Rice Burroughs* (Boston: Twayne, 1986);

Ted Sennett, *This Fabulous Century: The Thirties* (New York: Time-Life Books, 1969).

MOVIES

Hollywood in the 1930s. Movie critics are nearly unanimous in declaring the Depression era to be the most important in the history of film. Technical advances, the seemingly limitless amount of available money, and a pool of talent fed by writers and actors from New York, as well as directors and technicians from overseas, all contributed to make the 1930s the golden era in Hollywood cinema. In 1932 the improvement of three-color Technicolor from the two-color process invented in 1926 enabled studios to create "A pictures" that looked markedly different from the B movies churned out in quantity and helped to stratify the production system, though black-and-white movies were still common throughout the 1930s. Many of the decade's most talented writers, including such noted fiction writers as William Faulkner, Samuel Ornitz, Dalton Trumbo, Dor-

James Cagney, left, in *Public Enemy*, 1931

othy Parker, and Dashiell Hammett, and playwrights Lillian Hellman and Clifford Odets, headed west. As the decade wore on, many of the brightest stars from Europe sought in Hollywood a refuge from fascism. All of these factors, combined with the desperate desire to escape a life that seemed at times insurmountably difficult, drew eighty-five million Americans a week to movie theaters, there to be swept away by glamorous musicals, screwball comedies, and fantastic tales of adventure.

The Studio System. The continued growth and stability of the film industry in a time of economic uncertainty made it attractive to banks and established corporations. Studios ran their own chains of movie theaters, in addition to producing and distributing films. Each studio was guided by production executives such as Jack Warner at Warner Bros. or Darryl Zanuck at 20th Century–Fox, men who worked with an annual budget dictated by the New York office to create a year's worth of entertainment. These executives were micromanagers: they not only coordinated plant operations and conducted contract negotiations, but they also developed stories and scripts, screened dailies, and supervised editing. Moreover, each studio employed a stable of stars, directors, producers, set designers, and technicians, which insured that their products would have a distinctive stamp. For example, during the 1930s Warner Bros. became known for its socially conscious films, including *Heroes For Sale* (1932), *Wild Boys of the Road* (1933), *I Am a Fugitive From a Chain Gang* (1932), and the antilynching films *They Won't Forget* (1937) and *Fury* (1936). Paramount was known for its stylish, witty, elegant movies and its beautiful sets and costumes. Cecil B. DeMille directed such lush, sensual films as his 1934 *Cleopatra* for this studio; Ernst Lubitsch contributed such signature pieces as *Design for Living* (1933) and the Marlene Dietrich vehicle *Angel* (1937). Rouben Mamoulian contributed such works as his 1932 version of *Doctor Jekyll and Mr. Hyde*. If Paramount aimed for a sophisticated audience,

Metro-Goldwyn-Mayer (M-G-M), the richest and most productive of the studios, was known for targeting its films at middle-American audiences. Among M-G-M's successful productions were the Andy Hardy movies, starring Mickey Rooney, and the William Powell–Myrna Loy Thin Man series of six movies, which included *The Thin Man* (1934), *After the Thin Man* (1936), and *Another Thin Man* (1939). Universal was famous for horror, with such productions as James Whale's 1931 *Frankenstein,* starring Boris Karloff, and *The Invisible Man* (1933) with Claude Rains. Tod Browning's *Dracula* (1931) was an example of the terror the Universal artists could evoke.

Molls, Gunslingers, and T-Men. What can account for the incredible popularity of gangster movies during the Depression? In the early 1930s several factors combined to create an atmosphere in which audiences across America flocked to theaters to see the dozens of new gangland pictures. First of all, Prohibition enabled gangsters like Chicago's Al Capone to reap enormous profits by supplying the American public with the alcoholic beverages legally denied them — a service many Americans appreciated. Second, citizens who had become unemployed, or who had lost their property through bank foreclosures, often found themselves admiring the exploits of those 1930s crooks — Pretty Boy Floyd, John Dillinger, and Bonnie and Clyde among them — who fought the system. Although the introduction of the Production Code in 1934 forced studios to pay lip service at least to the notion that crime does not pay, gangsters continued to die in blazes of glory throughout the 1930s. Warner Bros. was the king of the crime flick, with such productions as *Doorway to Hell* (1930) with Lew Ayres, *Little Caesar* (1930) with Edward G. Robinson and Douglas Fairbanks Jr., *Public Enemy* (1931) with James Cagney and Jean Harlow, *The Finger Points* (1931) with Richard Barthelmess and Fay Wray, *G-Men* (1935) with James Cagney and Ann Dvorak, and *Petrified Forest* (1936) with Leslie Howard and Bette Davis; M-G-M produced a series of films based on their hit *Dead End* (1937), featuring Joel McCrea and Sylvia Sidney, including *Angels With Dirty Faces* (1938), starring Humphrey Bogart and Cagney. Paramount produced *City Streets* (1931) with Gary Cooper and Sidney; M-G-M's *The Last Gangster* (1937) with Robinson and James Stewart gave audiences Robinson at his snarling best. United Artists weighed in with such offerings as *You Only Live Once* (1937) with Henry Fonda and Sidney.

Lavish Musicals. Top Broadway dance director Busby Berkeley, lured by Samuel Goldwyn to Hollywood in 1930, provided Depression audiences with some of the most memorably overblown dance numbers in the history of the movies. Berkeley's dance numbers, seen in such films as *Gold Diggers of 1933* (1933), *Stars Over Broadway* (1934), and *Varsity Show* (1937), as well as the movies he directed himself, such as *Gold Diggers of 1935* (1935) and *Stage Struck* (1936), were sensuous extravaganzas, in which dozens of dancers moved in rhythmic patterns —

Scene from Busby Berkeley's *Gold Diggers of 1933*

snowflakes, expanding stars, and so forth. These numbers were filmed as inventively as they were choreographed — using diagonal angles, rhythmic cutting, and what has become known as the "Berkeley top shot" — from directly above the action. In contrast, Fred Astaire and Ginger Rogers, paired in 1933, created ten films together, all of them notable for their gracefully elegant dance numbers. *Flying Down to Rio* (1933), *Top Hat* (1935), *Swing Time* (1936), and *Shall We Dance* (1937) were among the most memorable of these grand productions.

The B Movie. Of course, not all Hollywood movies were star-studded extravaganzas. One feature of the well-stratified studio system was the ability to crank out seemingly endless numbers of B movies, also known as "low-budget" or "cheapie movies." Although some studios released an average of a feature each week, most of these were not top-of-the-line productions. Add in the three hundred or so films made each year by B studios or independents, and it becomes apparent that approximately three-quarters of the films made during the 1930s were B films. B movies, aimed at filling out the double bills that were an established feature of 1930s movie-

going, were produced quickly — often in as little as a week — and utilized actors of dubious box-office appeal. These low-budget movies were rented to exhibitors for correspondingly low fees and thus rarely lost money for studios. Occasionally, a B movie would cross over to A-picture status and score an unexpected success — a case in point would be the 1938 medical drama *A Man to Remember*, which took place at the funeral of a beloved small-town doctor. This, however, was the exception rather than the rule. Some writers and directors seized the chance to make stylistic experiments in a low-pressure, low-stakes venue where there was little to lose. Moreover, B movies could target smaller audiences than A movies.

African American Cinema. "Race movies," as they were known, had their roots in the late 1910s, when black-owned production companies such as the Lincoln Company and the Douglass Film Company created movies whose strong black characters provided a counterbalance to the stereotypes being purveyed by major production companies. The advent of sound film, which few black production companies could afford, and the onset of the Depression changed the way black films were pro-

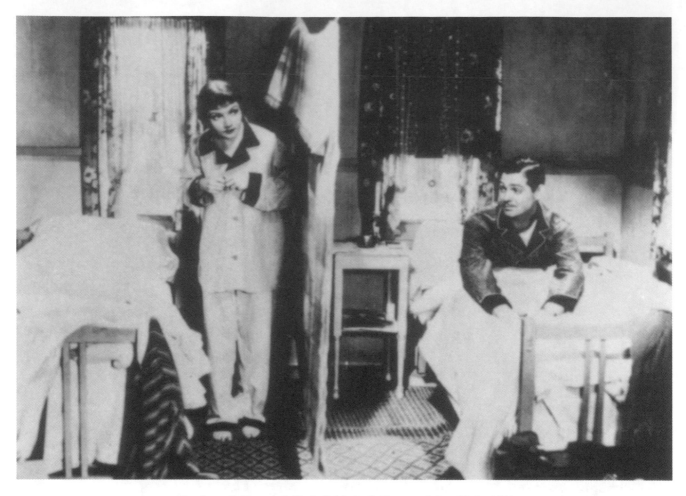

Claudette Colbert and Clark Gable in *It Happened One Night*, 1934

duced: the white director Dudley Murphy, for example, in 1933 directed black actor Paul Robeson in *The Emperor Jones,* based on the Eugene O'Neill play and featuring a prologue by DuBose Heyward, author of *Porgy.* Many "race movies" of the 1930s were Hollywood studio–produced, white-directed shorts in which jazz music and jazz musicians played a prominent role: among the artists who performed in these shorts were the Mills Brothers, Duke Ellington, Ethel Waters, Louis Armstrong, Eubie Blake, and Cab Calloway. Typical of this genre was *Barbershop Blues* (1932), a movie depicting the camaraderie in a black barbershop and featuring the dancing of the Nicholas Brothers to the music of Claude Hopkins's band. New black stars appeared during the Depression, including Bill Robinson, Clarence Muse, Hattie McDaniel, and Louise Beavers. However, most black roles in white movies were still stereotyped portrayals: the most glaring example of this would be the 1939 hit *Gone With the Wind,* with its eye-rolling slaves. Progress, no matter how minor, could be seen in such films as Mae West's *I'm No Angel* (1933), in which mistress and servant were seen to have risen together from poverty, and in which the maid, played by Beavers, was seen to have aspirations for success.

The Screwball Comedy. In such pictures as W. S. Dyke's *The Thin Man* (1934), strong female stars paired off with their male counterparts — in this case, Myrna Loy with William Powell — in relationships that were egalitarian and marked by barbed, witty repartee. With hits such as Frank Capra's *It Happened One Night* (1934), starring Clark Gable and Claudette Colbert, and Howard Hawks's *Twentieth Century* (1934), featuring John Barrymore and Carole Lombard, the cycle was firmly launched: studios would for the next four years produce scores of these comedies. With their roots in slapstick, and coated with an urbane gloss, screwball comedies such as Leo McCarey's 1937 *The Awful Truth,* for which the director won an Oscar, allowed its stars, Irene Dunne and Cary Grant, to escape rigid gender roles as they, playing a divorcing and, ultimately, remarrying couple, teased and tormented one another through a range of hilariously uncomfortable situations.

Sources:

Frederick Lewis Allen, *Since Yesterday* (New York: Harper, 1939);

Tino Balio, *Grand Design: Hollywood as a Modern Business Enterprise 1930–1939,* volume 5 of *History of the American Cinema,* edited by Charles Harpole (New York: Scribners, 1993);

John Baxter, *Hollywood in the Thirties* (London: Tantivy Press, 1968);

Thomas Cripps, *Slow Fade to Black: The Negro in American Film, 1900–1942* (New York: Oxford University Press, 1977);

Ephraim Katz, *The Film Encyclopedia,* revised edition (New York: HarperPerennial, 1994);

John McCarty, *Hollywood Gangland* (New York: St. Martin's Press, 1993);

Thomas Schatz, *The Genius of the System* (New York: Pantheon, 1988).

MUSIC IN THE 1930S

Searching. American music flourished and expanded during the 1930s, driven by a search for authentic American voices and rhythms. From sophisticated symphonic composers, urban recording executives, rural radio-station operators, and the Smithsonian Institution to the Library of Congress, the general trend among music lovers and producers was to seek out voices of the American people and to adapt their songs or record them directly in an effort to capture what was a disappearing authenticity. Radio had arrived full force in the 1920s, and already the folk of rural America were being introduced to a variety of musical styles that they adapted into their traditional sound. But academic and sociological interests were not the only reason for the search for American music. Commercial interests also drove the search. When the 1930s opened, as many as a third of the poorest rural southerners already owned phonographs. The rural blues had already gained popularity on record and was influencing music nationwide. A huge potential market of record buyers and radio listeners existed in regions far from New York and Chicago, the centers of the music publishing and production industries. So while George Gershwin, Aaron Copland, and an entire generation of European-trained composers looked to adapt traditional rural voices into their operas and symphonies, another group, led by Alan and John Lomax, Ralph Peer, David Kapp, Howard Odum, Robert W. Gordon, and John Work, traveled the South and West with recording equipment on board in search of unspoiled native talent. They would find much of it, from the Appalachian Mountains to the Mississippi delta to the Texas heartland, and in bringing the sounds back to rural areas would have a huge impact on commercial music of the following decades.

A Growing Audience. Despite the Depression, American music exploded in its reach and inclusiveness during the 1930s. More people could hear more music than at any previous time. The major reason for this increased exposure was technology. The 1920s had seen a broadening of radio broadcasting which took on added importance during the Depression. Phonograph-record sales had peaked in 1927 at 106 million but within five years had fallen to some 6 million. But radio found new listeners. In 1931 the Metropolitan Opera broadcast a performance for the first time. Hillbilly music gained increasing popularity on Chicago's WLS National Barn Dance and Nashville's WSM Grand Ole Opry programs. The amateur hillbilly shows became increasingly professional and

began sending out touring groups. Hillbilly music found a greater audience from the Mexican border stations, which were two and three times more powerful than allowed by United States law. Funded by incessant advertising, often for disreputable products, the border stations could be heard in all forty-eight states and in Canada and helped the likes of the Carter Family, Jimmie Rodgers, the Callahan Brothers, and cowboy Slim Rinehart reach new audiences. The jukebox became another means of spreading music. In 1933 Prohibition was repealed. As a result, taverns and "juke joints" opened immediately. Within five years more than 250,000 jukeboxes were playing nationwide. Sound became the norm in previously silent motion pictures and became fertile ground for classical composers. But the most concerted broadening of musical education and performance came from the federally sponsored WPA Federal Music Project (FMP). Like other artists, musicians were devastated by the Depression in the early 1930s. Headed by Nikolas Sokoloff, the FMP, founded in 1935, sponsored radio broadcasts and musical-education classes and commissioned work from composers such as George Antheil, William Schuman, and Elliot Carter. The FMP funded an index of American composers from colonial times to the present and sponsored folklorists traveling through the South. Between 1935 and 1939 some seven thousand musicians worked for the FMP in twenty-eight symphonies, ninety small orchestras, sixty-eight brass bands, and thirty-three opera or choral groups. The FMP sponsored African American composers and had a hit with *The Swing Mikado,* Gilbert and Sullivan done to African rhythms in Chicago and New York in 1938 and 1939. Music spread and flourished despite decreased economic activity.

Hillbillies. When the 1930s opened, two distinct hillbilly styles of music had already developed. The traditional style associated with the Southeast and Appalachian Mountains was true folk music and was represented by the legendary Carter Family. A. P. Carter, his wife Sara, and his sister-in-law Maybelle Carter recorded from 1927 to 1941 and influenced all folk music that followed. Maybelle Carter's rhythm guitar on songs such as "Wildwood Flower" ranks among the most influential guitar styles in popular-music history. Traditional songs of the sorrows of rural life such as "Can the Circle Be Unbroken?" made the Carters popular, though they never toured widely. They gained their popularity through recordings and especially via radio boomed out from across the Mexican border. The Carter style of music provided the roots of the bluegrass music that followed later in the decade as traditional music began to diversify into new forms. The Monroe Brothers, the Blue Sky Boys, and the Callahan Brothers were early bluegrass performers who held to traditional mountain music. Roy Acuff and his Smoky Mountain Boys became legendary in the 1930s, singing in the Carter Family tradition. Hits such as "The Great Speckled Bird" made Acuff's name synonymous with the Grand Ole Opry, which he joined in 1938.

The Carter Family: Maybelle, A.P., and Sara

Meanwhile, the other and more popular style of hillbilly music originated with the "Singing Brakeman," Jimmie Rodgers, who from 1927 until his death from tuberculosis in 1933 was the most popular and successful hillbilly entertainer in America. Rodgers is called the "father of country music." He brought a slick professionalism to what had previously been an amateur's calling. His blend of blues music with the traditional hillbilly sounds, and his use of the famous "blue yodel," marked him distinctive. Rodgers influenced contemporaries such as Frank Marvin, Bill Cox, Jimmie Davis, Cliff Carlisle, Wilf Carter, Hank Snow, and Ernest Tubb.

Western Style. The folk and hillbilly music of the 1920s and early 1930s was primarily southeastern in origin. Songs of the South and Appalachia had been discovered and made their way north into cultural centers. The 1930s, however, saw a shift of rural music that would leave its mark in the form of "Western music" that was applied to nearly all country music in the decades that followed. The romantic cowboy image was a growing phenomenon in the 1930s, as the frontier West became the stuff of myth. Inevitably, music reflected that romance. "Singing cowboys" such as Gene Autry, Tex Ritter, Roy Rogers, and the Sons of the Pioneers sang hillbilly music in a Texas-Oklahoma drawl while Hollywood promoted the image of the range and the cowboy. Non-

westerners such as Rogers (Leonard Slye of Ohio) and Snow (of Nova Scotia) began to dress in flashy cowboy outfits based more on myth than reality. Bostonian Billy Hill wrote some of the decade's most popular "western songs" ("The Last Roundup," "The Call of the Canyon"). Other "western styles" took hold as well, supplanting the term *hillbilly*, which became more localized, relating to the music of Appalachia. The fact that "western music" was southern blues and hillbilly music in cowboy dress was of no importance. Texas, booming with oil, became the center of western music. Prohibition was repealed in 1933, and taverns sporting jukeboxes sprang up nationwide. In Texas the traditional values of hillbilly music were inappropriate to the honky-tonk tavern atmosphere. Thus, an edgier, "honky tonk" style developed. Electric guitars appeared in order for bands to be heard above the din of the honky-tonk crowds. Honky-tonk music became contemporary, reflecting social ills, drinking, and loneliness, and did so with a danceable beat. Ultimately, honky tonk, as practiced by such Jimmie Rodgers–inspired performers as Tubb, became the dominant form of country and western music. Meanwhile, a variation called "Western swing," led by Bob Wills and His Texas Playboys, developed late in the decade to become a popular style in the 1940s. As the western style dominated, traditional music evolved into bluegrass or mountain style music of the Monroe Brothers and the Blue Sky Boys.

Bob Wills, left, and his Texas Playboys

Folk. While commercial interests had begun searching rural America for talent in the 1920s, the academics and sociologists took up the search in the 1930s. In 1933 under the direction of John Lomax, the Library of Congress began its own search-and-record program. Lomax, whose son Alan assisted him and continued his work beyond the decade, recorded folk songs of the rural South. In the late 1920s Harvard-sponsored folklorist Robert W. Gordon embarked on a journey with some one thousand recording cylinders that became the anchor of the Archive of American Folk Song. Hillbilly recordings included George Roark, Bascom Lamar Lumsford, Uncle Alec Dunford, and Jilson Setters. Gordon recognized the impact technology was having on the "pure folk songs" and looked specifically for songs of the preradio era. The WPA Federal Writers' Project also sponsored intellectuals in their search for the music of the common folk, resulting in a curious phenomenon. The music of the folk became increasingly popular in the North and especially when associated with labor unions or with the struggle of the poor, as sung by Woody Guthrie. The protest songs that resulted became a subgenre of the folk tradition. In 1933 John and Alan Lomax found one of the most important folk performers of the decade. Huddie "Leadbelly" Ledbetter was discovered in a Louisiana state penitentiary and made his professional debut at the Modern Language Association conference in Philadelphia the following year. Leadbelly's traditional protoblues twelve-

string guitar and vocal style of the field shouter made him an immediate success with the white urban audience of the North. Songs such as "Boll Weevil" and "Goodnight, Irene" exemplified Leadbelly's voice from the past and influenced folk music to follow. By decade's end folk music had obtained political protest connotations in the North, leaving the folk of the South with traditional hillbilly, bluegrass, and blues as its own music.

Protest Songs. The *Depression* defines conditions of the 1930s. Unemployment reached an all-time high. Dust Bowl Oklahomans migrated west looking for work. Labor unions clashed with the forces of capital. The fate of the common workingman became of great interest to the writers and musicians of the northern cultural centers. Inevitably, the music of the decade voiced concerns for social conditions in the form of the protest song. Radical ideas from the North found a home in places such as Harlan County, Kentucky. The hillbilly music of rural areas began to speak to the issues. Aunt Molly Jackson's "Dreadful Memories" spoke of the miners in Kentucky. Slim Smith's "Breadline Blues" and the Martin Brothers' "The North Carolina Textile Strike" spoke directly of contemporary events. Meanwhile, Guthrie wandered around the country performing at union rallies and observing the social conditions of labor and the Okies migrating to California. Guthrie's "Dust Bowl Refugee" and "Ain't Got No Home in This World Anymore" exemplified his brand of social criticism. In 1938 Guthrie moved to New York and took the protest music to the city. He became the archetype "folksinger" and along with Harvard-educated Pete Seeger brought the political connotations to the genre. Ledbetter's "Scottsboro Boys" and "Bourgeois Blues" were popular songs, and Florence Reece penned the union standard "Which Side Are You On?" Songs commemorated every major labor conflict, from the Flint, Michigan, strike of 1935 to the Memorial Day Massacre at Republic Steel in Chicago in May of 1937. The "Ballad of the Chicago Steel Massacre" exemplified the genre with its anticapital narrative:

> On dark Republic's bloody ground
> The Thirtieth day of May
> Oh, brothers, let your voices sound
> For them that died that day. . . .
>
> Men and women of the working class
> And you little children too
> Remember that Memorial Day
> And the men that died for you.

Blues. The blues of the 1930s was the song of the lone bluesmen that had emerged from the American South at the end of the previous decade. The female vocalists such as Bessie Smith and Ma Rainey who had dominated the 1920s gave way to the Delta bluesmen, led by Charlie Patton and his Texas counterparts, as the 1930s opened. Economic conditions were one reason. Due to the Depression and the rise of radio, record sales had plummeted in the late 1920s. The solitary bluesman was the cheapest of all musicians to record, and his records could remain profitable for minimal sales. Another reason was the continued migration of southern blacks to the northern urban centers. The music from home was in demand in urban centers, and the search for new talent continued through the 1930s. Bluesmen such as Patton, Blind Lemon Jefferson, Son House, and Skip James made recordings, but more often they traveled and performed live in the "juke joints" of the South. By decade's end the blues, especially in Chicago, was becoming urbanized and electrified. A variation of the blues was gospel blues — blues guitarists and singers who used music to preach the fire of an evangelist, though more often than not the blues was associated with the difficulties of rural life or sexual relations. The greatest of all the bluesmen was the mysterious Robert Johnson, whose short recording career remains legendary. His "Crossroads Blues," "Preaching Blues," "If I Had Possession Over Judgement Day," and "Hell Hound on My Trail" are blues standards and represent the pinnacle of the Delta blues of Mississippi, though in his own lifetime Johnson sold few records. Other blues developments included barrelhouse piano, which evolved into the boogie-woogie craze of the 1940s. Memphis Slim, Roosevelt Sykes, and Little Brother Montgomery were urban pianists who popularized the barrelhouse style. Blues infused nearly all forms of music in the decade. Gospel would develop from blues origins; jazz remained heavily blues-influenced; and country and

Robert Johnson

honky-tonk music adapted blues to traditional hillbilly music.

Swing. The Jazz Age ended with the stock-market crash of 1929. Thus, when the 1930s opened, jazz was declining in popularity as a whole even while the next stage of its development was proceeding. In terms of a wider public, the tame, quiet, so-called "sweet jazz" exemplified by Guy Lombardo dominated, while the "hot jazz" of Harlem and Kansas City remained a localized phenomenon. Early swing bands, such as the Casa Loma Band, influenced by the black bands of the late 1920s, gradually caught on, leading to the explosion of swing as a phenomenon in 1935 with the popularity of Benny Goodman. Though it was sold as a "new jazz" to the public, swing, which was characterized by members of a large band of ten to twelve playing hot jazz while remaining a cohesive unit, was really ten years old. Fletcher Henderson and Don Redmon provided the musical arrangement in the 1920s, and Henderson had sold his arrangements to Goodman. Swing attempted to apply a field-holler spontaneity to the precision of a large band, and by 1935 the black bands of Chick Webb, Earl Hines, Duke Ellington, Cab Calloway, and Bennie Moten had already succeeded. Goodman brought the big-band sound to the rest of America and provided the country with a music that would dominate the popular scene for ten years and through World War II. Other bands led by Tommy Dorsey, Jimmy Dorsey, Artie Shaw, Bob Crosby, and especially Glenn Miller dominated the era. While swing was king in the late 1930s, Count Basie was

Benny Goodman, 1938

already taking his band in new directions. Drummer Jo Jones and tenor sax player Lester Young began the earliest forays into what would develop as bop in the 1940s. Basie developed a role for the jazz piano in swing arrangements while his band as a unit redefined big band music with its brass and reeds tossing phrases at one another. Jazz singers flourished during the swing era. Teenage Ella Fitzgerald sang with Webb after 1935 and became a bandleader when Webb died in 1939. Red Norvo employed Mildred Bailey, his wife, and Goodman had Helen Ward. Billie Holiday had begun singing as well, though the dominance of the vocalists was still a few years away.

Gospel. Modern gospel music was born in the 1930s. The Depression had hit urban blacks particularly hard, and their churches became community help centers as well as places of worship. Gospel's origins came from an unlikely source. Thomas (not Tommy) Dorsey, who as "Georgia Tom" in the 1920s had composed songs for Ma Rainey and had coauthored one of the decade's most notoriously risque hit songs ("It's Tight Like That") with Tampa Red, began peddling his gospel compositions after 1927 in Chicago. Singing preachers such as Rev.

J. M. Gates, Rev. Moses Doolittle, Rev. H. R. Tomlin, Rev. W. M. Mosely, and evangelist-bluesman Blind Willy Johnson had been a staple of blues music in the late 1920s. Dorsey, however, brought the music into the church. He sold his first gospel compositions at the National Baptist Convention in Chicago in 1930. In 1931 he created the first gospel chorus at the Ebenezer Baptist Church, while also forming the Chicago Gospel Choral Union. The following year, with the organizing help of singer Sallie Martin, Dorsey founded the National Convention of Gospel Choirs and Choruses to promote the music nationwide. In the same year he created the Dorsey House of Music, dedicated solely to publishing and selling black gospel music. Martin was the first of many Dorsey protégés who would become well-known gospel vocalists. Others included Willie Mae Ford Smith, Roberta Martin, Myrtle Scott, the Ward Singers, and Edna Gallman Cooke. In 1932 Chicago's Greater Salem Baptist Church Choir debuted the first superstar of gospel. Mahalia Jackson was a robust, bluesy singer in the field shouter tradition. She recorded "God's Gonna Separate the Wheat from the Tares" in 1937 but did not record again until the late 1940s when gospel entered its golden age. Dorsey was also a prolific composer, writing such

Thomas Dorsey and Mahalia Jackson in his Chicago studio, 1939

standards as "Precious Lord," "Take My Hand," and "There'll Be Peace in the Valley." Similar developments were occurring in Memphis under the guidance of Rev. W. Herbert Brewster, composer of "Move on Up a Little Higher." His East Trigg Choir had an even stronger blues influence than Dorsey's choirs and is said to have even influenced young Elvis Presley in the late 1940s. Memphis had its own star singer in Queen Candace Anderson. Eventually two gospel styles developed, the all-male "gospel quartets" singing a cappella in harmony and the robed, all-female choruses singing with piano and clapping their hands for rhythm. By 1936 Dorsey could charge admission, and gospel, begun as mere inspirational music, achieved professional status. In 1938 Sister Rosetta Tharpe sang gospel in the secular environment of Calloway's show at the Cotton Club in Harlem. Tharpe also became the first major gospel vocalist to record with a major label.

Opera. The stock-market crash of 1929 hit opera companies in America particularly hard. New York's Metropolitan Opera Company saw an almost immediate 30 percent decline in attendance after the prosperous 1920s. Chicago's great opera company, an equal to the Met in previous decades, declared bankruptcy in January 1932 and would not reopen for twenty years. Companies in San Francisco, Boston, and Philadelphia were already in decline when the decade opened. By 1932 the Met, in crisis, became the nonprofit Metropolitan Opera Association. Its season was reduced to sixteen weeks. A radio appeal for funds saved the company from financial ruin, and in 1935 the Committee for Saving the Met was formed. But as commercial companies teetered on the edge of ruin, the music flourished. The Met began broadcasting on 25 December 1931, allowing opera to reach more ears than ever before, redefining its audience. Europeans in exile began arriving to influence American music. The Federal Music Project of the WPA was keep-

THE METROPOLITAN OPERA BEGINS ITS SATURDAY BROADCASTS

On Christmas Day 1931 the Metropolitan Opera in New York broadcast a full live opera for the first time in its history. The Saturday broadcast from the Met was a resounding hit and would quickly become a permanent part of American musical culture. The Met had considered broadcasts before the historic day. In 1909 a microphone had been placed on the Met stage for a few numbers from *Tosca* sung by Enrico Caruso and Emmy Destinn. The few amateur radio pioneers involved had concluded that "insurmountable obstacles would keep opera off of the radio." Twenty-two years later, with the Met surrounded by rumors of financial ruin brought on by the Depression, the NBC broadcast of Engelbert Humperdinck's *Hansel and Gretel* reached millions of listeners from coast to coast in the United States and was picked up by stations in Japan and around the Orient. Composer Deems Taylor served as a commentator for the broadcast, which began at 2:00 P.M. in New York. Within minutes of the start, *The New York Times* reported, hundreds of messages from all over the country had come in with congratulations. On stage the opera went on as usual. No microphones were visible to the audience due to the new parabolic microphone that could be swiveled in order to maximize the sound quality. The broadcast was such an immediate hit that the Met announced within days that the Saturday broadcast would become part of its regular programming, with Taylor continuing as commentator. Opera's audience expanded overnight as the power of radio continued to redefine the musical audience.

Sources: "Metropolitan Christmas Opera to Go on Air; World-wide Audience to Listen to Broadcast," *New York Times*, 16 December 1931, p. 1;

"Metropolitan Broadcasts First Full Opera; Hailed as a Success as Millions Listen In," *New York Times*, 26 December 1931, p. 1.

ing singers and musicians alive while spreading musical forms through educational and performance programs. Most important, however, American composers began to write American opera. The decade's search for native music included classical conductors who tried to deflect criticism that all American classical music was derivative. The Met rarely performed American opera and yet consistently attempted to display the emerging American talent. Joseph Deems Taylor's *Peter Ibbetson* premiered in 1931. In 1933 Louis Gruenberg's *The Emperor Jones*, based on a Eugene O'Neill play, debuted and broke the color line at the Met. Howard Hanson's *Merry Mount* (1934) was yet another attempt at an American idiom, though it was considered to have failed. Only two operas

Sportin' Life (John Bubbles), Porgy (Todd Duncan), and Bess (Anne Brown) in tryouts for the first stage production of *Porgy and Bess,* Boston, 1935

truly stand out as successes, though contemporary audiences had mixed reactions to both. Virgil Thomson's experimental *Four Saints in Three Acts* (libretto by Gertrude Stein) debuted with an all-black cast in Hartford in 1934 before moving to New York for six weeks and to Chicago in the fall. Gershwin's *Porgy and Bess* premiered in Boston in 1935 before moving to New York. Gershwin fused blues, jazz, and southern folk music to create the most American opera of the decade, though it opened to mixed critical response. Marc Blitzstein's *The Cradle Will Rock* was not only American, but political opera. The WPA withdrew funding of the controversial prounion piece, but the show, in a now-famous act of defiance, rented a theater and performed the opera anyway, with singers standing in the audience while Blitzstein himself played the piano onstage.

Chicago. Although Chicago jazz had peaked in the 1920s and the city's opera company shut down in January of 1932, Chicago remained a music center for the United States during the 1930s. The National Barn Dance, broadcast weekly on Chicago's WLS, was the most important radio show in the country for hillbilly music. Chicago, not Nashville, was still the center of the hillbilly music industry. Besides the broadcasts, the National Barn Dance was performing the show live and sending

out touring groups to promote the show and spread the sound of hillbilly music. Gospel was born in Chicago and remained largely a Chicago phenomenon through the decade while spreading east and to the South. Most important, however, was the city's blues culture. The Delta blues of Mississippi had migrated north to Chicago along with the masses of southern blacks during previous decades. Robert Johnson's blues classic "Sweet Home Chicago" is an example of just how entrenched the blues was becoming in Chicago, and Chicago in the blues. Blues became synonymous with the city, especially a new urban style of blues that developed in the city and would become popular in following decades. The electric guitar entered the blues genre, which began to take on the hard edge identified with the city late in the decade. Of course this brand of blues, known as rhythm and blues, would eventually become the source of rock 'n' roll in the 1950s, when white culture caught on to and adapted the rhythm and blues sound. By decade's end the musical center of America had shifted decidedly to New York and toward Nashville, leaving Chicago with a reputation for appreciation of jazz, opera, and hillbilly music but with the blues still all its own.

Classical. American classical music of the 1930s had its foundation in Paris of the 1920s. Nearly every major

By the late 1930s the influence of black Americans on all American music was evident and much discussed. The swing era was in full force. Gospel was spreading. The major blues recordings were approaching twenty years old, and a blues-inspired brand of hillbilly music had taken hold after the fashion of the "blue yodel" of Jimmie Rodgers. But the music was not pure, according to John Hammond. In order to present the true music of black Americans, Hammond organized a concert at Carnegie Hall in December 1938 to "show both the general public and the serious musician just what it [Negro music] is." Hammond, while acknowledging the prodigious talents of Marian Anderson and Count Basie, among others, wanted to showcase the true folk music of the Carolinas, Georgia, Texas, Arkansas, Mississippi, and Missouri. He and others combed the South for music untouched by contemporary popular tastes. In a *New York Times* article a week before the concert, Hammond described in detail the group Mitchell's Christian Singers as an example of what to expect at his forthcoming concert. The a cappella group from North Carolina was utterly unknown. They were untrained and unaware of the popular music of the day. Other performers at the groundbreaking concert were Big Bill Broomzy, an Arkansas blues man, Bessie Smith's niece Ruby Smith, James P. Johnson, and Count Basie himself. Robert Johnson had been scheduled to play but had been poisoned earlier in August. Hammond announced Johnson's death before the concert and played recordings of "Walkin' Blues" and "Preachin' Blues" for the audience.

Sources: Peter Guralnick, *Searching for Robert Johnson* (New York: Dutton, 1989);

John Hammond, "From Spirituals to Swing," *New York Times*, 16 December 1938.

colleges. He scored his first opera, *An Outdoor Overture*, for young orchestras in 1938. His ballet *Billy the Kid* appeared in the same year. *Music for Radio* was composed for CBS in 1937. He wrote a book, *What to Listen for in Music*, in 1938 to popularize classical music and continued to influence music in America for decades to come. Other composers who matured in the 1930s included Harris (*First Symphony*, 1933), Douglas Moore, William Grant Still, Samuel Barber (*Adagio for Strings*, 1936), Piston, Roger Sessions, Thomson, Hanson, and Randall Thompson. Gershwin, already established as America's premier composer, had a productive decade prior to his sudden death in 1937. His *Second Rhapsody* appeared in 1932; his *Of Thee I Sing* won a Pulitzer Prize in 1935; and *Porgy and Bess*, the most famous American opera of the decade, opened in 1935. Meanwhile, as Americans explored their native music, Europeans, because they were Jewish or because their work was considered decadent by fascist forces, began arriving to live out the war in exile. Among those who came were the pioneering modernists: Arnold Schoenberg, Paul Hindemith, Kurt Weill, Béla Bartók, Boulanger, Darius Milhaud, Bohuslav Martino, Arturo Toscanini, Arthur Rubinstein, and Igor Stravinsky. They had a huge impact on American music and musicians in the decades during and after World War II.

Experiments. The experimentation that marked the 1920s declined but carried over into the 1930s as some composers continued to push the definitions of traditional classical music. Taking their inspiration from Schoenberg's experiments, some American composers tried and succeeded to varying degrees with atonal and machine music. Henry Cowell, founder of the quarterly *New Music*, wrote experimental works such as *Synchrony* (1930), *Two Appositions* (1931), and *Four Continuations* (1934) for strings. George Antheil attempted an abstract music inspired by the paintings of Pablo Picasso. His jazz opera *Transatlantic* was performed in Frankfurt in 1930 but found no home in America, though his opera *Helen Retires* was performed at The Juilliard School of Music in 1934 and his *Third Symphony* (1934) found listeners in America. Atonal and fiercely independent composer Carl Ruggles continued into the 1930s with *Sun-Treader* (1933) and *Evocations* (1937). French-born Edgard Varèse was among the most radical experimenters of the decade, and though he completed little work he remained influential. *Density 21.5* (1935) was one of his few works from the 1930s, when experimentation fell out of popular favor. Thomson's experiments made him controversial. Like Copland, Thomson scored film and drama as well as symphonies (*Second Symphony*, 1931). His all-black cast and all-cellophane set for the opera *Four Saints in Three Acts* remain a highlight of the decade. Thomson was also a critic and writer. Finally, America's most radical experimental composer began his career in the 1930s. John Cage studied under Schoenberg in 1935 but quit shortly after. Cage became interested in percussion, space, and noise. Early works include *Sonata for Clarinet* (1933) and

American composer born around the turn of the century had studied in Paris during the 1920s under the tutelage of Nadia Boulanger. Boulanger predicted an explosion of American music in the late 1920s and 1930s. Her students fulfilled her prophecy. Copland, Virgil Thomson, Walter Piston, Roy Harris, Elliot Carter, Blitzstein, and David Diamond were among Boulanger's students who would distinguish the 1930s as the first outstanding decade for American classical music. Ironically, Boulanger's students often found their successes in the American idioms not yet explored in American music. Copland typified the search for an American style of music, applying traditional folk to classical music. He was also among the first composers to widen his market, composing "functional music" for radio, film, ballet, schools, and

Clark Gable and Vivien Leigh in *Gone With the Wind*, 1939

Quartet for Percussion (1935), though Cage became more widely known in the decades to follow.

Sources:

Patrick Carr, ed., *The Illustrated History of Country Music* (Garden City, N.Y.: Doubleday, 1979);

Francis Davis, *The History of the Blues: The Roots, the Music, the People from Charley Patton to Robert Cray* (New York: Hyperion, 1995);

John Dizikes, *Opera in America: A Cultural History* (New Haven: Yale University Press, 1993);

John Tasker Howard and George Kent Bellows, *A Short History of Music in America* (New York: Crowell, 1957);

Bill C. Malone, *Country Music U.S.A.: A Fifty Year History* (Austin: University of Texas Press, 1968);

Eileen Southern, *The Music of Black Americans: A History* (New York: Norton, 1983);

Marshall W. Stearns, *The Story of Jazz* (New York: Oxford University Press, 1956);

John Warthen Struble, *The History of American Classical Music* (New York: Facts On File, 1995).

1939: HOLLYWOOD'S GOLDEN YEAR

Popular Movies. Although the 1930s were generally a very strong decade for the American film industry, 1939 was an extraordinary year, even by Depression standards. This was a year in which two of the American Film Institute's ten most popular films of all time were released — *Gone With the Wind* and *The Wizard of Oz,* both directed by Victor Fleming — and in which the country was treated to William Wyler's memorable adaptation of *Wuthering Heights,* to Greta Garbo's first comic role (in Ernst Lubitsch's humorous treatment of Soviets in Paris, *Ninotchka*), and to Mickey Rooney and Judy Garland's sentimental showbiz comedy *Babes in Arms.*

Americana, Hollywood Style. As Europe teetered on the brink of war, Hollywood regaled American audiences in 1939 with increasingly idealized visions of American life, including director John Ford's account of early pioneer life, *Drums Along the Mohawk,* his Abraham Lincoln biography, *Young Mr. Lincoln,* and his epic Western (Ford's first since 1926), *Stagecoach.* With a simplicity of vision, Ford's films pitted good against evil. *Drums Along the Mohawk* featured strong, courageous settlers battling filthy, terrifying Indians. *Stagecoach,* starring John Wayne, Claire Trevor, and John Carradine, was set amidst the grandeur of the American West and showed the strength of a disparate group of Americans banding together to overcome difficulties. *Young Mr. Lincoln,* with Henry Fonda in the starring role, was one of many movie biographies, or biopics, popular in the 1930s. Ford's film emphasized Lincoln's ties to family and community and was noteworthy for its warm, idyllic qualities rather than its authenticity. The Frank Capra movie *Mr. Smith Goes to Washington* provided audiences with an even more heartwarming view of American politics, as they watched Jimmy Stewart, the naive but idealistic junior senator, do battle against cynicism and corruption — and win.

Sweeping Epics. The gracious life made possible by slavery was the theme of the incomparably nostalgic *Gone With the Wind*, starring Vivien Leigh, Clark Gable, and Leslie Howard. The most expensive picture (and one of the longest) produced up until that point, *Gone With the Wind* was a much-ballyhooed adaptation of Margaret Mitchell's Pulitzer Prize–winning 1936 novel, which had itself broken all publication records (fifty thousand copies sold in a day, a million in six months, two million in a year). Audiences thrilled to the movie's portrayal of rascally Yankees; chivalric Confederates; chaste southern belles; shiftless, eye-rolling slaves; sweeping panoramas of plantation existence — and, of course, tempestuous love scenes between scheming, spirited Scarlett O'Hara and dashing Rhett Butler, scenes that culminated in a touching, romantic episode of conjugal rape. Film historians acclaim *Gone With the Wind* as a high point in Hollywood filmmaking, as one of the screen's great romantic sagas, and the ten Academy Awards it received provide contemporary confirmation of this judgment.

Gunga Din. *Gone With the Wind* may have been the most famous of epics produced that year, but it was not the only one. George Stevens's *Gunga Din*, based on the Rudyard Kipling poem and starring Cary Grant, Douglas Fairbanks Jr., and Joan Fontaine, offered a rousing view of the derring-do of late-nineteenth-century British troops subduing a native uprising in India.

Shirley Temple's Finest Film. *The Little Princess* could be described as the young actress's swan song. Although Temple would continue to make pictures, she would never recapture the phenomenal popularity that had been hers during the 1930s. A whole industry had been created around her; she was the most popular child actress of all time, and Shirley Temple dresses, coloring books, and dolls sold briskly. (The drink which bore her name, a combination of ginger ale and maraschino cherry juice, also enjoyed popularity among the younger set). Throughout the decade she charmed moviegoers with her plucky appearances in milieus ranging from the world of the racetrack (*Little Miss Marker*, 1934) to a post–Civil War southern household (*The Little Colonel*, 1935) to a hotel for vaudevillians *(Little Miss Broadway*, 1938). In addition, she brought children's classics to life, such as *The Poor Little Rich Girl* (1936), *Heidi* (1937), and *Susannah of the Mounties* (1939). It was in this spirit that she was to inhabit Kate Douglas Wiggin's classic *Rebecca of Sunnybrook Farm* (1938) in a role first played by Mary Pickford in the 1917 movie of the same title. By this point Temple was eleven and teetering on the brink of

puberty, the hormonal tragedy that was to destroy her lisping, baby-faced appeal to audiences.

Sources:

Ephraim Katz, *The Film Encyclopedia*, revised edition (New York: Harper Perennial, 1994);

James Martine, ed., *American Novelists, 1910–1945* (Detroit: Gale, 1981);

Ted Sennett, *Hollywood's Golden Year, 1939* (New York: St. Martin's Press, 1989).

PUBLIC WORKS OF ART PROJECT MURALS

The Federal Art Project. Like its counterparts, the Federal Theatre, Writers, Dance, and Music Projects, the Federal Art Project (FAP) was a part of the Works Progress Administration. Preceded by the Public Works of Art Project in 1933 and 1934, founded in 1935, drastically reduced in 1939, and eliminated entirely in 1943, the FAP was responsible for more than 2,500 murals, 11,000 designs, 108,000 easels, and 17,000 sculptures. Perhaps the most famous of all of these endeavors, however, were the commissioned murals of the FAP.

Public Works of Art Project. In 1933 artist George Biddle, known as the father of federal arts projects, wrote a letter to his old classmate Franklin Delano Roosevelt, suggesting a series of publicly commissioned murals by young American artists — murals that would express American ideals and the social vision of the New Deal. The result, after the usual political battles had been fought and won, was the Public Works of Art Project (PWAP), which, with its successor, the Federal Art Project, was to be responsible for more than twenty-five hundred murals in schools, post offices, federal buildings, and other public spaces throughout the nation. These murals were painted by a range of distinguished and soon-to-be-distinguished artists, including Thomas Hart Benton, Grant Wood, Willem de Kooning, Reginald Marsh, Jackson Pollock, Rockwell Kent, Philip Guston, and Stuart Davis. In Oklahoma Kiowa Indians painted murals at two state colleges depicting subject matter from their religious rituals and festivals. While perhaps chiefly inspired by Diego Rivera and other Mexican muralists active in the 1920s, scholars have also detected the influence of Italian Renaissance styles, French academicians and abstractionists, and Asian decorators in the murals. The PWAP artists painted murals that reflected a wide range of aesthetic styles, including both realistic and nonrepresentational elements.

A New Vision. Perhaps most of the PWAP and FAP painters were, like so many other artists and intellectuals, deeply engaged in creating a new vision of American life. While heroic workers and smiling children certainly occupied their share of space in these murals, so did the poor, the homeless, and a range of historical figures, such as Abraham Lincoln and Frederick Douglass. Many murals were controversial: industrialists in Kellogg, Idaho, condemned Fletcher Martin's design, "Mine Rescue,"

THEATER OF THE 1930S

American Themes. As in the other arts, stylistic innovation, a focus on social issues, and a concern with American themes became hallmarks of Depression drama. Most notable, in some ways, was the degree of interaction between seemingly disparate groups. Radical workers' theaters like the Workers Laboratory Theatre, many of them founded by German refugees from fascism, flourished; the experimental Group Theatre had its splashiest success with a play written to benefit workers' theater, while producing other plays on Broadway; Broadway plays themselves tackled social issues such as the problems faced by tenant farmers — albeit in a typically cheerful manner. Although the first three years of the Depression saw no long-running hits, subsequent years were marked by both Broadway smashes and creative ferment in the smaller theaters.

The Group Theatre. Founded by Harold Clurman, Cheryl Crawford, and Lee Strasberg in 1931, the Group Theatre was an outgrowth of the American Laboratory Theatre of the 1920s, which had based much of its approach on that of the Moscow Art Theatre. The twenty-eight group members lived together as well as worked together. For the ten years of its existence, the group had an outsized influence on American theater, primarily for its promulgation, through Strasberg, of Stanislavskian acting technique, an approach based on the use of emotional memory, and one which, under the name of Method acting, subsequently became the standard training for American actors. Not only was the group responsible for several socially conscious Broadway hits but also featured some of the most notable actors on the American stage (and later, American screen), including Morris Carnovsky, Stella Adler, Luther Adler, John Garfield, Franchot Tone, Elia Kazan, Lee J. Cobb, Karl Malden, Howard Da Silva, and J. Edgar Bromberg. The Group Theatre, which stressed politically aware dramas by writers such as Paul Green, John Howard Lawson, and Irwin Shaw, had several Broadway hits, including Sidney Kingsley's 1933 hospital drama, *Men in White,* and Clifford Odets's haunting drama of family life during the Depression, *Awake and Sing!* (1934). However, it was Odets's *Waiting For Lefty* (1934), a play written in three feverish nights, that sealed the group's reputation. A drama based on a New York City cabdrivers' strike and set at a union meeting, its first performance nearly resulted in a riot when sympathetic audience members, in effect, became part of the play. The spontaneous, and resounding, calls of "Strike! Strike!" that filled the theater at play's end made theater history. As historian Wendy Smith writes, *Waiting for Lefty* demonstrated that "theatre at its best could be a living embodiment of communal values and aspirations."

The Mercury Theatre. After John Houseman and Orson Welles had their production for the Federal Theatre Project of Marc Blitzstein's prounion labor opera *The Cradle Will Rock* postponed on the grounds that it was too

George Biddle's mural *Sweatshop* at the Department of Justice Building, Washington, D.C.

while officials of the Mine Workers and Smelt Workers Union praised it: the industrialists prevailed, and Martin substituted a design depicting the arrival of a local prospector, for whom the town was named. In Watango, Oklahoma, Cheyenne Indians pitched a tepee on the post-office lawn until Edith Mahier changed the Indian ponies on her mural, which Chief Red Bird complained looked like "oversized swans." However, on the whole the murals received, and continue to receive, their share of acclaim on social and aesthetic grounds, both from critics and from grateful citizens, including the postmaster of Pleasant Hill, Missouri, who wrote: "In behalf of many smaller cities, wholly without objects of art, as ours was, may I beseech you and the Treasury to give them some art, more of it, whenever you find it possible to do so. How can a finished citizen be made in an artless town?"

Sources:

Richard D. McKinzie, *The New Deal for Artists* (Princeton: Princeton University Press, 1973);

Barbara Melosh, *Engendering Culture: Manhood and Womanhood in New Deal Public Art and Theater* (Washington: Smithsonian Institution Press, 1991).

ARTS 71

Cast singing "It's Not Cricket to Picket" in the International Ladies Garment Workers Union show, *Pins and Needles*

controversial, they defied the order and opened the play under the auspices of the Mercury Theatre, a company formed for this purpose. Although the Mercury Theatre only lasted from 1937 to 1940, it was known for its flamboyant, stylistically innovative plays, most notably a very popular and highly controversial production of *Julius Caesar*, performed in modern costume, textually cut and rearranged, and directed in such a way as to stress the parallels with Benito Mussolini and Adolf Hitler's growing strength. Other productions included Shaw's *Heartbreak House*, a disastrous version of *Danton's Death*, and its final production, Richard Wright and Paul Green's *Native Son*.

Broadway. While revenues continued to drop throughout the 1930s, eroded by the competition from movies and radio, Broadway audiences continued to support the comedies of Kaufman and Hart, whose *You Can't Take It With You* (1936) ran for 832 performances and became a successful Hollywood film, and whose wacky 1939 show, *The Man Who Came to Dinner*, was almost as successful. While apolitical musicals like Ole Olsen and Chic Johnson's almost surrealistic revue *Hellzapoppin'* (1938) and the gentle Howard Lindsay and Russel Course drama *Life With Father* (1939) ran for eight years, Depression themes also proved powerful for audiences.

Tobacco Road (1933), a ribald comedy based on Erskine Caldwell's novel about Georgia sharecroppers, became a runaway hit despite being banned in Boston and Chicago for obscenity: it ran for almost thirty-two hundred performances on Broadway. Most surprising of all was the eleven-hundred-performance run of *Pins and Needles* (1937), a comic revue put on by the International Ladies Garment Workers Union. It was the only Broadway show whose cast members had to take leaves from their factory jobs in order to perform. Other Broadway successes included Eugene O'Neill's psychological drama *Mourning Becomes Electra* (1931) and George Gershwin, DuBose Heyward, and Ira Gershwin's *Porgy and Bess* (1935), hailed as the first musically effective American opera to use a native setting successfully.

Sources:

Charles Alexander, *Here the Country Lies* (Bloomington: Indiana University Press, 1980);

Oscar G. Brockett and Robert Findlay, *Century of Innovation: A History of European and American Drama Since the Late Nineteenth Century* (Needham, N.Y.: Simon & Schuster, 1991);

Harold Clurman, *The Fervent Years: The Story of the Group Theatre and the Thirties.* (New York: Harcourt Brace Jovanovich, 1975);

Wendy Smith, *Real Life: The Group Theatre and America, 1931–1940* (New York: Knopf, 1990).

The Spanish Civil War was a cause célèbre among literary liberals, who saw Francisco Franco's attack against the Third Republican Government in Spain in 1936 as a fascist assault against socialist ideals, with international implications. The German and Italian governments supported Franco with arms and supplies, and the Soviet Union backed the Republican government. John Dos Passos, a Communist fellow traveler who had lived in Spain and had close friends there, felt compelled to tell the world about the conflict in Spain. When his efforts to create a news service to report the war from the perspective of the ordinary Spaniard failed, he conceived the idea of a documentary movie that would explain the effect of the war on Spanish peasants and marshall support for the Republican cause.

Late in 1936 a group called Contemporary Historians was formed to develop the idea for a documentary, which would be called *The Spanish Earth*. Margaret De Silver, wife of Trotskyite journalist Carlo Tresca, put up the seed money. Archibald MacLeish, Lillian Hellman, and Ernest Hemingway were among the other members of the group; they received financial support from Donald Ogden Stewart, Gerald Murphy, and Hellman's friends Dorothy Parker, Dashiell Hammett, Ralph Ingersoll, and Herman Shumlin. Contemporary Historians hired Communists Joris Ivens to direct and John Ferno (Fernhout) to film the documentary, with Ernest Hemingway as the scriptwriter, assisted by Dos Passos.

Once in Spain, early in 1937, Hemingway and Dos Passos were soon at odds. Hemingway was serving as a war correspondent for the North American News Alliance and was actively courting journalist Martha Gellhorn, who became his third wife in 1939. At the Hotel Florida in Madrid, where foreign correspondents stayed, he established himself as the dominant figure. When Dos Passos arrived, Hemingway berated him for not bringing canned food and went on to express his contempt for Dos Passos's unmilitary bearing. Dos Passos soon distanced himself from *The Spanish Earth*, and by summer, when the documentary was released, he and Hemingway were bitter enemies.

Dos Passos's closest Spanish friend was Jose Robles, whom he had met in 1916-1917 when he studied architecture in Spain. Robles taught Spanish at Johns Hopkins University in Baltimore, and he was Dos Passos's Spanish translator. When the war broke out, Robles was vacationing in Spain and decided to join the Ministry of War as the interpreter for the Russian General Goriev, one of the military advisers to the Republicans. Just before Dos Passos arrived, Robles disappeared, and Dos Passos felt it his duty as a friend to find out what had happened. After frustrating days of inquiry, Hemingway gracelessly told Dos Passos that Robles had been executed and apparently suggested that it was with good cause, for talking too freely. Dos Passos took the incident as proof of the repressive tyranny of the Communists. He left Spain in disgust at the behavior of his former friend and at the willingness of the American sympathizers to embrace Communist ideals while failing to see their harmful effect on individuals. He wrote an essay, "Villages are the Heart of Spain" (*Esquire*, February 1938) expressing that notion, and in his next novel, *Adventures of a Young Man* (1939), he portrayed a young idealist victimized by Communist exploitation. Leftist reviewers were shocked by his denunciation of his former political beliefs, and they publicly criticized him and his works as no longer being relevant to political struggle.

Hemingway stayed in Spain throughout the spring of 1937 and returned to the United States a hero. He and Ivens were invited to The White House to show *The Spanish Earth*, which he narrated from his script. The documentary was shown at fundraisers on both coasts. At the politically charged Second American Writers' Congress in June 1937, before an audience of dedicated leftwing writers, Hemingway expressed his solidarity with them—disingenuously, most observers believe now. In 1940 Hemingway published what many critics regard as his last great novel, *For Whom the Bell Tolls*, set during the Spanish Civil War.

Source: Townsend Ludington, *John Dos Passos: A Twentieth Century Odyssey* (New York: Dutton, 1980).

THREE LITERARY SUICIDES

Vachel Lindsay. Vachel Lindsay was fifty-two years old in 1931 when depression overtook him. He had been a practicing populist poet for some thirty years. He published his own work, distributed it freely, and delighted in reading his works publicly. Yet after he married in 1925 and had two children, the schedule of readings he had to maintain to support his family weakened his health and threatened his already fragile mental state. Late in November 1931 Lindsay traveled from his home in Springfield, Illinois, on a lecture tour that included stops in Cleveland and Washington. Neither session went well. He offended his audience, and people walked out. Lindsay complained to his friend Sara Teasdale that audiences only wanted to hear his old poems and did not care for his new work. When he returned to Springfield, he was tired, embarrassed, and sick. He brought seventy-six dollars home from his tour and faced four thousand dollars in debts. Upon his return he began to exhibit manic-depressive behavior so erratic that his wife was advised by a doctor to leave her husband for her own safety. On the evening of 5 December he tarried downstairs at bedtime, and his wife retired alone. Soon afterward, she heard a crash and rushed downstairs to investigate. She encountered her husband, frantic, asking for water. "I took Lysol," he told her. He died soon thereafter. "They tried to get me; I got them first," were his last words.

Hart Crane. Hart Crane was the most promising and the most eccentric of the modernist American poets of the 1920s. He was an impulsive, alcoholic, homosexual genius, who in his long poem *The Bridge* (1930) sought to unite contemporary movements — including modernism, symbolism, and postimpressionism — with the American romanticism of the mid to late nineteenth century. In 1932 Crane was at his most unpredictable. He had received a Guggenheim Fellowship in March 1931 to study European culture, but he used the money instead to go to Mexico, where he engaged in a stormy heterosexual relationship with Peggy Baird Cowley, former wife of influential *New Republic* editor Malcolm Cowley. A mama's boy, Crane was emotionally distraught over a disagreement with his mother about income from a trust fund that had partially supported him since 1928. His father, who had died in 1930, had underwritten some loans that diverted the resources of the estate at a critical time, and Hart Crane was left with an income of only $125 per month, which he felt insufficient to support him in the style of debauchery to which he had become accustomed. He attempted suicide by drinking iodine, risking imprisonment in Mexico for breaking the antisuicide law, and made himself a nuisance to local authorities by drunkenly filing a missing-person report on Peggy Cow-ley, who arrived home late one afternoon. Crane's friends, realizing they had to get him out of the country before he ended up in jail, arranged for him to borrow money for passage from Vera Cruz to New York late in April. His behavior was violent and erratic onboard the ship. He seems to have had an affair with one of the sailors, and he had to be forcibly restrained one night and confined to his quarters. On the evening of 27 April 1932, 275 miles north of Havana on the way to New York, he said goodbye to Peggy Cowley, walked purposefully to the rail of the ship, threw off his overcoat, and jumped. Attempts were made immediately to save him, but, after resurfacing only briefly, his body disappeared without a trace.

Sara Teasdale. Sara Teasdale was a friend of Vachel Lindsay's; he was in love with her and even proposed marriage. She was among the most popular American lyric poets of the 1920s, and her work was praised for its expression of a woman's view of love. Teasdale's life began to sour in 1928, when she left Ernest Filsinger, her husband of twelve years, and began a close companionship with a college student named Margaret Conklin, whom she described as the daughter she had always wanted. Teasdale all but quit writing. She took Lindsay's suicide in 1931 hard and sought to divert her attentions from morbidity by agreeing to edit the love poems of Christina Rossetti. Her research took her to England, where she contracted pneumonia. The physical dimension of her illness was matched by a severe depression. She returned home in the fall of 1932, seemingly to die. As her illness progressed the capillaries in her hands began to collapse, and she was afflicted with progressive paralysis. Early on the morning of 30 January 1933, fearing she was about to have a stroke, Teasdale took a handful of sleeping pills and climbed into a warm bath. Her nurse found her there dead, the water still warm.

Sources:

Margaret Haley Carpenter, *Sara Teasdale: A Biography* (New York: Schulte, 1960);

Edgar Lee Masters, *Vachel Lindsay: A Poet in America* (New York: Scribners, 1935);

John Unterecker, *Voyager: A Life of Hart Crane* (New York: Farrar, Straus & Giroux, 1969).

HEADLINE MAKERS

THOMAS HART BENTON

1889-1975

PAINTER

A Vision of America. The decade's best-known practitioner of Regionalist painting, Thomas Hart Benton's work was aimed, he said, at an audience which "was never subjected to the aesthetic virus." Benton, born in Neosho, Missouri, was the son of a populist congressman, Maecenas E. Benton. On the campaign trail with his father he grew comfortable in Washington salons as well as revival meetings. From a youthful career as a reporter and illustrator for a paper in Joplin, Missouri, he attended the Chicago Art Institute. He moved on to art school in Paris (1908–1911), where he found himself unimpressed by the contemporary artists he met — Diego Rivera, George Grosz, Wyndham Lewis. Between 1918 and 1924 Benton abandoned modernism in favor of what he termed Americanism — a depiction of what he saw as the American character: hardworking, nonintellectual people who sometimes fell prey to circumstance. However, his satiric paintings of American life continued to be influenced by the strong forms and sometimes random use of space characteristic of modernism. His "American Historical Epic," of which he completed eighteen of a planned seventy-five mural studies between 1921 and 1926, was representative of this transformation and led to the paintings which made him famous in the 1930s. His father's death from throat cancer in 1924 marked the beginnings of what were to be Benton's lifelong wanderings around the United States, journeys that provided him with his artistic inspiration. By 1929 he was exhibiting drawings which he grouped into four sets: Holy Roller Camp Meeting, Lumber Camp, King Cotton, and Coal Mines. These were all groups whose representation became emblematic of New Deal art. Although Benton lived in New York City for the first half of the 1930s, becoming known among colleagues for his gifts at self-promotion as well as his artistic talent, in 1935 he returned to Missouri to execute a mural in the state capitol — but not before circulating a farewell letter to New York in which he condemned the city as being overrun by Communists and homosexuals.

Regionalism. The title of the movement with which Benton, Grant Wood, and John Steuart Curry were most closely associated was taken, according to Benton, from the Agrarians — a group of southern writers including Robert Penn Warren, Allen Tate, and John Crowe Ransom — who in "turning from the over-mechanized, over-commercialized, over-cultivated life of our metropolitan centers, were seeking the *sense* of American life in its sectional or regional cultures." However, there were major differences between the two: while the Agrarians eschewed city life, Benton painted factories as well as farms. He did not confine himself to a vision of a single region; rather, he was "after a picture of America in its entirety . . . I ranged north and south and from New York to Hollywood and back and forth in legend and history."

WPA Muralist. Along with Edward Laning, Reginald Marsh, Henry Varnum Poor, Boardman Robinson, and Maurice Sterne, Benton was instrumental in developing the Public Works of Art Project. His own mural contributions to public buildings across the country were often controversial: his 1936 Missouri State Capitol mural presented aspects of the state's history and legend that many citizens would rather had gone acknowledged. Mark Twain's Huck Finn and Jim; Frankie and Johnny, the doomed lovers celebrated in American folk song; and the outlaw Jesse James gazed down at visitors and aroused protests. In response to a museum director's criticism of his murals, Benton asserted, "If it were left to me, I wouldn't have any museums . . . Who looks at paintings in a museum? I'd rather sell mine to saloons, bawdy houses, Kiwanis and Rotary clubs, Chambers of Commerce, even women's clubs. People go to saloons, but never to museums."

Popularity. Although criticized by modernists for what they saw as his clichéd style and by radicals for an insufficient focus on themes of repression, poverty, and injustice, Benton was held in great public esteem and was perhaps the decade's most celebrated painter. He was on the cover of *Time* magazine in 1934 and was lauded in *Life* in 1937. In paintings such as "America Today — Changing West I" (1931), a representation of farms and factories; "I Got a Gal on Sourwood Mountain" (1938), its title derived from an Appalachian folk song; and in his 1939 lithograph "Planting," which depicted poor black farmers, Benton offered a mass audience a vision of American life that affirmed the worth of local expression and which was, for the most part, one of dignity even during times of struggle. Although his critical reputation has waxed and waned over time, his popularity continued unabated until his death, as evidenced by a *60 Minutes* profile, several *Life* magazine pieces, and spreads in *National Geographic* and *Sports Illustrated*.

Sources:

Thomas Hart Benton, *An American in Art* (Lawrence: University Press of Kansas, 1969);

Richard D. McKinzie, *The New Deal for Artists* (Princeton: Princeton University Press, 1973);

Linda Weintraub, *Thomas Hart Benton: Chronicler of America's Folk Heritage* (Annandale-on-Hudson: Edith C. Blum Art Institute, Bard College, 1985).

JOAN CRAWFORD

1904-1977

ACTRESS

An Adaptable Star. One of the leading ladies of Depression Hollywood, Crawford was known for her ability to play just about any role, inhabiting romantic comedies (W. S. Van Dyke's *Forsaking All Others* [1934]; Edward H. Griffith and George Cukor's *No More Ladies* [1935]), gangster films (Harry Beaumont's *Dance Fools Dance* [1931]), historical dramas (Clarence Brown's *The Gorgeous Hussy* [1936]), farces (Van Dyke's *Love on the Run* [1936]), vicious social comedies (Cukor's hit *The Women*), Depression melodramas (Brown's *Possessed* [1931]; Howard Hawks's *Today We Live* [1933]), romantic dramas (Beaumont's *Laughing Sinners* [1931]; Brown's *Chained* [1934]), and even ice-skating pictures (*Ice Follies of 1939*, directed by Reinhold Schunzel). She costarred with Greta Garbo and John Barrymore in Edmund Goulding's 1932 *Grand Hotel*, played opposite Norma Shearer and Rosalind Russell in *The Women*, and had on-screen romances with Clark Gable and with Franchot Tone, to whom she was also married. In short Joan Crawford was the consummate professional, an all-purpose Depression

star. Although her vehicles varied, Crawford tended to play independent women whose choices (or lack thereof) forced them to grapple with issues of survival in the modern world, working girls from the tough part of town clawing their way to the top.

Coming up the Hard Way. Joan Crawford's early beginnings prepared her for a life of hard work. She worked as a laundress, shop clerk, and waitress before winning her first glimmerings of attention in a local Charleston dance contest. Stints as a chorus girl in Detroit and on Broadway gave her the exposure she needed to be spotted by an M-G-M talent agent. Her name by this point had changed from being Lucille Fay Le Seur (her birth name and her waitress name) to Billie Cassin (her stepfather's name and her chorus girl name) to her studio-chosen name, Joan Crawford. Although Crawford was by no means the incarnation of Hollywood glamour or beauty, nor even a great actress, she was above all adaptable, moving from a 1920s flapper image in *The Taxi Dancer* (1926, directed by Harry Millard) to that of an ambitious working girl in the 1930s. Crawford changed hairstyles and colors with a dizzying rapidity as she moved up through the Hollywood ranks, becoming a top star by the late 1920s. She seemed to acquire and shed star husbands at the same fast pace. Her marriage to Douglas Fairbanks Jr. lasted from 1929 to 1933 and was followed by nuptials with Franchot Tone (1935–1939). While her marriage to Philip Terry (1942–1946) also ended in divorce, her final marriage in 1956, to Pepsi-Cola board chairman Alfred Steele, left her a widow in 1959. Her acting career continued in the early war years with such pictures as *A Woman's Face* (1941), directed by Cukor, but her popularity began to decline as she grew older. No matter how changeable she might seem from role to role, she refused to move from the glamour roles to more-maternal assignments. M-G-M's attempt to cast her in screwball comedies was largely unsuccessful as well. After 1937 she was no longer on the list of top moneymaking stars, and in 1944 she was written off by M-G-M.

The Comeback Kid. A survivor in life as on the screen, however, Crawford triumphed in her first Warner Bros. picture, the steamy 1945 domestic melodrama/noir *Mildred Pierce*, based on the James Cain novel and directed by Michael Curtiz. Not only did the picture score several million dollars at the box office, it also resulted in a Best Actress Oscar for Crawford — her first in a twenty-year career as a star. She was nominated for two more Oscars in the course of her career — the first time for *Possessed* (1947) and the second time for *Sudden Fear* (1952). Not only did Crawford succeed in the 1950s, in a string of star vehicles that ran the gamut from Western (*Johnny Guitar* [1934]) to melodrama (*Queen Bee* [1935]), but she had another surprise comeback in 1962, when Robert Aldrich directed her and Bette Davis in the chilling *Whatever Happened to Baby Jane?* She capitalized on her success in a string of other horror movies throughout the 1960s, including *Strait-Jacket* (1964, directed by

William Castle) and *I Saw What You Did* (1965, directed by Castle). Although Crawford wrote two volumes of memoirs, *A Portrait of Joan* (1962) and *My Way of Life* (1971), they have faded from the public eye. The Crawford portrait which survives, however, is her adopted daughter Christina Crawford's *Mommie Dearest*, published in 1978, the year after Joan Crawford's death. The book is notable for the horrific picture it paints of its subject, in Christina's version a parent crazed and vicious enough to be the real-life version of the psychopathic characters Crawford played so well on screen. *Mommie Dearest* was made into a 1981 movie, which flopped, starring Faye Dunaway as Joan Crawford and directed by Frank Perry.

Sources:

Tino Balio, *Grand Design: Hollywood as a Modern Business Enterprise 1930–1939*, volume 5 of *History of the American Cinema,* edited by Charles Harpole (New York: Scribners, 1993);

Ephraim Katz, *The Film Encyclopedia*, revised edition (New York: Harper Perennial, 1994);

Thomas Schatz, *The Genius of the System* (New York: Pantheon, 1988).

WILLIAM FAULKNER

1897-1962

WRITER

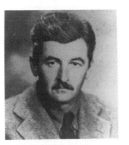

The New Regionalism. William Faulkner, considered by many to be the greatest modern American writer, mined the nineteenth-century history of the imaginary Yoknapatawpha County in his native Mississippi to create a literature that was a fusion of the American tradition of regionalism and modernism. Focusing on a few families to whom he returned in story after story, novel after novel, Faulkner examined the social structure in the Deep South. However, his fiction was anything but the local color of the earlier Regionalists. Rather, Faulkner used the modernist techniques of Eliot and Joyce to create a literature that was dazzlingly complex in form and often violent and tragic in content.

Beginnings. William Falkner, as he was born, was raised in the university town of Oxford, Mississippi, where he grew up as a dreamy, introverted child. After dropping out of high school halfway through his last year, he spent years drifting from a job bookkeeping in his grandfather's bank to joining the Canadian Royal Air Force, where he added the *u* to his name and where, enlisting too late for the war, he never completed his flight training. This fact did not keep him from returning to Oxford with exciting tales of his military adventures, though. His narrative endeavors soon took a different shape when, upon the advice of a friend at the University of Mississippi, he sent a story to the *New Republic*. The

story's publication encouraged him, and he enrolled at the university as a special student for the year 1919–1920. Though his formal education ended that year, it was a productive period for him, during which he wrote a slender volume of poems, as well as a one-act play, *Marionettes*. His wanderings took him to New York, where he worked in a bookstore for a few months, and back to Mississippi, where he wrote for the campus literary magazine and worked, in desultory fashion, as the postmaster of the campus post office, a job from which he was fired in 1924 for failing to deliver the mail. At writer Sherwood Anderson's suggestion Faulkner sent his first novel, the bitter post–World War I narrative *Soldier's Pay*, to Boni and Liveright, where it was accepted and published in 1926. His second novel, a study of an artist's development titled *Mosquitoes*, appeared in 1927. By his third novel, *Sartoris* (1929), Faulkner was beginning to embark on the exploration of the tangled web of southern history and family that was to mark his writing career. However, it was not until he published *The Sound and the Fury* (1929) that Faulkner fully explored the nature both of human consciousness and of history in a prose that was dense, provocative, and destined to stand as one of the monuments of American literature.

The Sound and the Fury. A novel in four parts, *The Sound and the Fury* tells the story of the Compson family and its declining fortunes through different voices, including that of Benjy, the retarded younger brother, and Quentin, the oldest brother, who has suffered a nervous breakdown and who ultimately commits suicide. Like the southern Agrarians, Faulkner charts the rise of commercialism in the South and the corresponding decline of the traditional white upper-middle-class family. In *The Sound and the Fury*, as in the novels to follow, the history of the Compsons and of their region is shown to be violent, sexualized, and marked by insanity and premature death.

A Flourishing Career. Faulkner proved to be as prolific as he was innovative. His next novel, though, was *Sanctuary*, which he had intended as a moneymaker to support him and his new wife, Estelle Oldham Franklin. It was deemed by his editor to be so sensational as to be unpublishable without substantial cuts. *As I Lay Dying* (1930), his next published novel, was as experimental as *The Sound and the Fury*. Narrated by fifteen different voices, the novel tells the story of a single day. Though it was praised by the critics, it did not sell. By this point Faulkner was supporting himself by selling stories to magazines, notably the *Saturday Evening Post*. Although critics were not nearly as impressed by *Sanctuary*, which finally appeared in 1931, as by his earlier work, this study of pure human evil sold extremely well, outraged southern reviewers, and was considered so scandalous that in Oxford's drugstore it was sold in a brown paper wrapper. However, even the extremely well-reviewed novel *Light in August*, which came out the following year, was not enough to support the Faulkners, and when Hollywood called, Faulkner responded.

Hollywood. Faulkner spent most of 1932 in Hollywood, writing screenplays under contract to M-G-M. His first real success came with the Joan Crawford and Franchot Tone vehicle *Today We Live* (1933), which he wrote for director Howard Hawks. Other screenplays included the 1936 war film *The Road to Glory,* which he wrote with Joel Sayre and which was also directed by Hawks, this time for 20th Century–Fox. Faulkner's screenwriting career continued into the 1950s with pictures such as *To Have and Have Not* (1945), the film version of the Ernest Hemingway novel, which he wrote with Jules Furthman, and *The Big Sleep* (1946), the film version of the Raymond Chandler detective novel, which he wrote with Furthman and Leigh Brackett. Although his paychecks may have come from Hollywood, Faulkner's main effort went into his fiction, thirteen volumes of which he published during the 1930s. These works included *Pylon* (1935) and *Absalom, Absalom!* (1936), considered by many critics to be his greatest work, in which he continues to plumb the depths of the southern family.

Nobel Laurels. Faulkner wrote much less during the 1940s and 1950s, and what he wrote was less well received than had been his work during the 1930s. However, critics have recently begun to reevaluate in a more positive light such works as *Go Down, Moses* (1942) and *Intruder in the Dust* (1948), both of which treat black life in the South. The publication of *The Portable Faulkner* in 1946 helped to revive his reputation, and his 1950 Nobel Prize for literature sealed it. In 1955 he was awarded the National Book Award and the Pulitzer Prize for his otherwise ill-received World War II novel, *A Fable.*

Source:
Joseph Blotner, *Faulkner: A Biography* (NY: Random House, 1974).

ELLA FITZGERALD

1920-

JAZZ SINGER

Discovered. Ella Fitzgerald was not quite fifteen years old when she made her professional singing debut at a Yale University party in March 1935. She had been discovered the previous year at the Harlem Opera House, where she won an amateur talent contest for singing a Connie Boswell song. Heartened by the success, Fitzgerald entered more contests, eventually winning a week's performance with Tony Bradshaw's band in February 1935. Bardu Ali, then an announcer with Chick Webb's band, heard her singing for Bradshaw and later brought her to Webb for an impromptu audition, which led to her being hired for the Yale gig a month later. She had made a large leap quickly. Born in Norfolk, Virginia, and raised in Yonkers, New York, by her mother, Ella Fitzgerald made an immediate impact on jazz singing in her time, redefined the role of the jazz singer, and eventually broadened the scope of her music beyond jazz to popular singing.

Early Career. Shortly after Ella's professional debut, her mother was killed in an automobile accident. New York labor laws prevented the fifteen-year-old Fitzgerald from performing without a guardian's consent. The result was that bandleader Chick Webb and his wife legally adopted Fitzgerald and brought her into their home. Webb became a parent, guardian, and teacher to Fitzgerald, developing her singing style and bringing her out slowly to the crowds at the Savoy, Harlem's hottest and most crowded club. The swing era was in full glory when Fitzgerald began recording with Webb in 1936. Songs such as "Sing Me a Swing Song and Let Me Dance," "I'll Chase Your Blues Away," and "If You Can't Sing It, You'll Have to Swing It" (later called "Mr. Paganini") popularized Fitzgerald. In 1937 a *Down Beat* readers' poll confirmed her as the top female vocalist. Fitzgerald, along with Billie Holiday, was among the first female singers to become an integral part of the big band. Webb began to feature Fitzgerald more, arranging songs around her to capitalize on her popularity. She even began to compose and arrange, scoring a huge hit with "A-Tisket, A-Tasket" in 1938. She was eighteen years old.

Bandleader. The success of "A-Tisket, A-Tasket" got the Chick Webb band booked in previously white-only venues such as the Park Central Hotel, where Fitzgerald continued to win fans. But in 1939 the thirty-year-old Webb died of pneumonia. Due to her popularity, Fitzgerald became the band's leader, though primarily in name only. She was among the youngest bandleaders and one of the few women nationwide leading an all-male band. She also continued to write songs, scoring hits with "Just One of Those Nights" and "Serenade to a Sleeping Beauty." Swing was beginning its decline, and Fitzgerald began to branch out. She recorded a single hit ("All I Need Is You") with the Four Keys in 1940 and appeared in Abbott and Costello's movie *Ride 'Em Cowboy* in 1942. But her music suffered in popularity. In the 1941 poll in *Down Beat* she fell to fourth among vocalists. She married dockworker Benny Kornegay in 1941 and had the marriage annulled within two years. By 1942 the Chick Webb band had broken up. The first stage of Fitzgerald's career had come to a halt.

New Directions. In the mid 1940s Fitzgerald moved in new directions that not only revived her stagnant career but also had a great impact on jazz music. She had helped popularize jazz singing in the late 1930s and redefined it in the 1940s. First she began branching out. In 1946 she recorded with Louis Jordan a calypso song "Stone Cold Dead in the Market" and scored a hit. More important, she began singing with Dizzy Gillespie, one of the seminal figures in bop music. In the spirit of bop's emphasis on individual improvisation, Fitzgerald began scat singing, using her voice as an instrument, singing the syncopated improvisations similar to those usually played on saxophone or trumpet. Songs such as "Lady Be Good" and "How High the Moon" popularized bop and made Fitzgerald a favorite in New York at jazz clubs. She married again in 1948 (to bass player Ray Brown) and in the same year made the acquaintance of promoter Norman Granz, the man who led Fitzgerald's career through the 1980s. Granz promoted a touring band called "Jazz at the Philharmonic." The group toured some twenty weeks a year for more than a decade. Granz was not only a promoter and founder of Verve, a recording label, he was also a social activist. "Jazz at the Philharmonic" shows, wherever it toured, resisted segregation at hotels and restaurants. The band, which included Herb Ellis, Gillespie, and Brown, toured worldwide. By 1953 Fitzgerald was again the number one jazz vocalist in the *Down Beat* polls. In 1955 Granz, by then Ella's manager, negotiated her out of her binding deal with Decca records and began recording her on his Verve label.

Songbooks. In 1955 Fitzgerald, always looking for new directions for her singing, agreed with Granz's idea to broaden her career even further. She moved away from the world of jazz with a series of Songbook albums, each focusing on one popular stage composer of previous decades. The first Songbook, a collection of thirty-two Cole Porter songs, sold more than one hundred thousand copies and broadened Fitzgerald's audience even further. She continued with albums of Rodgers and Hart, Irving Berlin, Jerome Kern, Harold Arlen, Johnny Mercer, Duke Ellington, and George and Ira Gershwin. She also recorded three albums with Louis Armstrong, including Gershwin's *Porgy and Bess*. By doing the Songbooks she not only broadened her own audience but also brought much great American music back to life. The Berlin and Ellington Songbooks each won Grammy Awards. Some jazz critics were upset with Fitzgerald's departure from pure jazz for popular music, but the audience response was overwhelming. Fitzgerald had again redefined herself through popular singing.

Legend. Her career slowed after 1960, though she remained a popular touring entertainer. In the 1980s Fitzgerald was still performing thirty-six weeks a year while the honors rolled in. In 1974 the University of Maryland dedicated the Ella Fitzgerald School of Performing Arts. She received honorary degrees from Princeton, Harvard, Dartmouth, Boston University, UCLA, and Washington University, among others. In 1986 Ella Fitzgerald was named doctor of music at Yale University, where fifty-one years before she had begun what would become among the most prominent vocalist careers in American music history.

Sources:

Stuart Nicholson, *Ella Fitzgerald: A Biography of the First Lady of Jazz* (New York: Scribners, 1994);

Carolyn Wyman, *Ella Fitzgerald: Jazz Singer Supreme* (New York: Franklin Watts, 1993).

BENNY GOODMAN

1909-1986

JAZZ MUSICIAN

What Was Swing? Dubbed "The King of Swing," Goodman introduced a jazz style that relied on written arrangements performed by big bands. Swing, a simpler and less improvisational form of jazz than that of the 1920s, one based on the structure of popular songs, was functional dance music. Swing enabled the individual voice to contribute to the collective whole: as historian David W. Stowe notes, swing was another expression of trends that prevailed in American culture throughout the Depression: "both the regionalist paintings of Thomas Hart Benton and swing embodied the ideals of progressive reform and a populist producerist ideology through symbols that embodied the uniquely American values of energy and democracy." The Duke Ellington hit "It Don't Mean a Thing If It Ain't Got That Swing" appeared in 1932: the nation was well on its way to being swing crazy. It was Benny Goodman's 1935 recording triumph, "The Music Goes 'Round and 'Round," that propelled the craze. Although Goodman had had a lukewarm response from audiences when he started his band in 1934, his 1935 radio broadcasts from the Palomar Ballroom in Los Angeles brought him his first real success — and sparked audience interest in his soon-to-be-hit song. Over one hundred thousand copies of sheet music for "The Music Goes 'Round and 'Round" were sold; the song was the most popular on the air; a necktie, a sofa, and a cigarette holder were named after it. Swing gained momentum through 1936 and 1937, and in January 1938 Benny Goodman and His Swing Orchestra played a memorable concert at Carnegie Hall, normally reserved for classical performances. The reception was wildly enthusiastic. As for Goodman himself, his sponsored radio shows included the "Let's Dance" program for National Biscuit Company, the "Camel Caravan," and the "Victor Borge Show." Fans rioted at his shows: during the latter half of the 1930s Goodman achieved first a national, and then an international, reputation. During the 1930s Goodman produced hundreds of records.

Who Was Goodman? Goodman struggled out of a difficult childhood. His father died in a taxicab accident when he was young, leaving him to support his widowed mother and eleven siblings. He served his apprenticeship, at age eleven, in a local theater pit band, then in a five-piece orchestra on a Lake Michigan steamer, then, in the early 1920s, with Jules Herbuveaux, who had a well-known Chicago-area band. Goodman spent the 1920s moving from one coast to the other: first Los Angeles, where in 1925 he joined Ben Pollack and his orchestra at the Venice Ballroom, leaving for short stints with Benny Krueger and Isham Jones. He finally left Pollack for good in 1929 to play with Red Nichols until 1931, after which he spent the next three years doing freelance work. Goodman was twenty-five when, in 1934, he formed his own orchestra in New York, using a library of arrangements written by Fletcher Henderson.

Breaking the Barriers. Benny Goodman is significant, however, for reasons that have to do with more than his sheer popularity. As a clarinetist Goodman's style was unmistakably his own — his use of the high register, of grace notes, variations in dynamics, and, above all, the unprecedented smoothness and control of his tone, all combined to give him his trademark sound — one which he used to highlight the clarinet as an instrument for a front man. Benny Goodman was the first white band leader to break the color bar, first in 1935 by hiring pianist Teddy Wilson and subsequently by including vibraphonist Lionel Hampton, guitarist Charlie Christian, and trumpeter Cootie Williams in his orchestras; pianist Count Basie made frequent guest appearances as well. Nor was his significance confined to his big band sound. In 1935 Goodman formed the first of his smaller combos, featuring such musicians as Lionel Hampton, drummer Gene Krupa, and Wilson, which created a second innovative new sound of the period, one which can be heard on the 1939 RCA recording *Trio-Quartet-Quintet*. By the time of his Columbia recordings in 1939, Goodman's combos, which were called sextets regardless of whether they included six, seven, or even eight musicians, had moved away from the structured arrangements of his big band sound and into freewheeling combo jam sessions. Jazz historians point to electric guitarist Christian's influential style of playing on these disks, especially on the Columbia Jazz Masterpieces recording, *The Benny Goodman Sextet 1939 — 41 Featuring Charlie Christian.*

After the 1930s. The swing craze lasted until the end of the 1930s, and the hiatus Goodman took in 1940, during which he disbanded his orchestra, marked a turning point in his career. Goodman had never had a reputation as an easy man to work with, and by the early 1940s he had replaced many of the players in his orchestra. By the end of the decade he was incorporating bebop into his work, but his popularity was on the wane. Struggles with his record company, MCA, led Goodman to disband his orchestra once again in 1944. Though he returned in 1945, his appearances toward the end of the decade were sporadic. The 1955 release of *The Benny Goodman Story,* which made up in sentimentality what it lacked in accuracy, gave Goodman a new lease on life. He traveled widely throughout the end of the 1950s and the 1960s and made one of his last, triumphant appearances at Carnegie Hall in 1978.

Sources:

Leslie Halliwell, *Halliwell's Film Guide* (New York: HarperCollins, 1991);

Barry Dean Kernfield, *The Blackwell Guide to Recorded Jazz* (Oxford, U.K., & Cambridge, Mass.: Blackwell, 1991);

David W. Stowe, *Swing Changes* (Cambridge, Mass.: Harvard University Press, 1994);

Leo Walker, *The Wonderful Era of the Great Dance Bands* (Garden City, N.Y.: Doubleday, 1972).

WOODY GUTHRIE

1912-1967

FOLK SINGER

The Voice of the Forgotten American. Described by folksinger Pete Seeger as "a national folk poet," Woody Guthrie crisscrossed America throughout the Depression years — walking, hitchhiking, and riding the rails along with the hoboes and migrant laborers during the 1930s. Between 1936 and 1954, when he was hospitalized for Huntington's chorea, of which he would die, he wrote more than one thousand songs chronicling the experience of the common American. Among his best-known songs are "Roll On, Columbia," "This Train Is Bound For Glory," "Hard Traveling," "Union Maid," and "Dust Bowl Refugee."

Early Years. Like so many of the westward migrants during the Depression, Guthrie was an "Okie" — an Oklahoman who found himself forced out of the life he knew by the coming of the Dust Bowl. The soil erosion and resulting dust storms that drove so many Oklahomans from their farms were, however, not the first tragedy to scar Guthrie. When she was fourteen, his sister burned to death; the depressions that plagued his mother — diagnosed, in retrospect, as Huntington's chorea — eventuated in her death in a mental institution when Guthrie was a teenager. His father, unable to compete with the sharp operators who followed the oil boom into the state, experienced a series of devastating business declines. By 1936 his father had closed his real estate office and was living on skid row in Oklahoma City, where he was to die. When Guthrie sang that "I've been doing some hard travelling," he meant it.

An American Repertoire. His first band, the Corncob Trio, which he founded in Pampa, Texas, in the early 1930s, played traditional songs for local barn dances — for audiences whose appetite for country music was being whetted by the recent recording success of the first country music stars, the Carter Family and Jimmie Rodgers. By 1935 Guthrie had already produced his first slim, typewritten volume of original songs; soon he would be documenting the Depression experience in songs such as "Talking Dust Bowl," "I Ain't Got No Home," and his most famous song, "This Land Is Your Land." He shared these ballads with the dispirited men he met in boxcars and flophouses on his endless travels throughout Depression America. By 1937 he had begun his first regularly scheduled Los Angeles radio show, which he did in collaboration with partner Lefty Lou (Maxine Crissman). The fan mail soon began pouring in. His collaborators were amazed by how quickly he could develop songs; it often took just minutes for a sketchy idea to be transformed into an enduring song.

Radical Visions. Guthrie's first real brush with radicalism came from his discussions in hobo jungles with old Wobblies, or members of the Industrial Workers of the World, the militant union which had had its greatest strength before the First World War. The social injustice he saw in California — including the ill treatment of migrant laborers by growers that was to spur John Steinbeck to write *The Grapes of Wrath* — proved a galvanizing force for Guthrie. By 1939 he had become, at his request, a columnist for the Communist Party newspaper, the *People's World,* publishing a weekly humor column called "Woody Sez." His songs reflected a radical version of American identity: in "The Ballad of Pretty Boy Floyd" he glorified the life of the outlaw; in "Pastures of Plenty" he deplored the injustice suffered by farmworkers; in "Do-Re-Mi" he decried the brutality of the Los Angeles police force.

New York Days. In 1940 actor Will Geer invited Guthrie to move to New York, where he befriended such folk-singing luminaries as Pete Seeger, Cisco Houston, and Huddie Ledbetter, better known as Leadbelly. Impressed by Guthrie's performance at a New York benefit, Library of Congress folk-music archivist Alan Lomax began promoting Guthrie's career, interviewing him for a three-record Library of Congress set and arranging for the recording of a Victor Records twelve-record series of his "Dust Bowl Ballads." However, Guthrie's career as a CBS radio star — the next step on a possible road to fame and mainstream acceptance — was short-lived: Guthrie soon headed west again, embarrassed by what he saw as his own sellout.

Lasting Influence. Guthrie's publications, in addition to his many recordings, include his 1943 autobiography, *Bound For Glory, American Folksong* (1947), and a 1965 collection of his prose and poetry, *Born to Win.* Most of all, though, it was his music that inspired later artists such as Joan Baez; Bob Dylan; Odetta; Peter, Paul and Mary; Tom Paxton; and Judy Collins — and, of course, his son, singer Arlo Guthrie. Even as Huntington's chorea, a disease with debilitating physical and mental symptoms, ate away at Guthrie, he remained active into the 1950s, playing with the Almanac Singers (a group that included Pete Seeger, Lee Hays, Millard Lampell, and others). His son, Arlo, has become a renowned folksinger in his own right.

Sources:
Woody Guthrie, *Bound for Glory* (New York: Dutton, 1943);

Joe Klein, *Woody Guthrie: A Life* (New York: Knopf, 1980);

Donald Worster, *Dust Bowl: The Southern Plains in the 1930s* (New York: Oxford University Press, 1979).

DOROTHEA LANGE

1895-1965

PHOTOGRAPHER

Early Years. Born in Hoboken, New Jersey, as Dorothea Margeretta Nutzhorn, Lange early took her mother's maiden name. Disabled by the childhood polio that left her with a lifelong limp, Lange discovered her photographic vocation as she was finishing high school. She apprenticed herself to a series of Manhattan portrait photographers before moving to San Francisco in 1918 to embark on a career doing romantic photographic portraits. During the 1920s she made several long trips with her first husband, painter Maynard Dixon, to the Southwest to photograph.

A Change Wrought by Hardship. Dorothea Lange describes her transformative moment as occurring in 1932 when, from the studio where she sustained her portraiture business, she gazed out into the alley below and witnessed daily scenes of misery and poverty. "The discrepancy between what I was working on in my printing frames and what was going on in the street was more than I could assimilate. I knew that if my interest in people was valid, I would not only be doing what was going on in those printing frames," she wrote. Her first photograph in the documentary style that she was to hone to a fine art was titled "White Angel Breadline" (1932). She continued to photograph scenes of men on state relief, of street demonstrations, of the San Francisco waterfront strike of 1934, and had her first exhibit by Willard Van Dyke of Group f/46, who had a gallery in Oakland. The same year, in collaboration with Paul Taylor, a professor of labor economics and the field director of California's Federal Emergency Relief Agency (FERA) Rural Rehabilitation Division, who was to become her second husband, Lange made a study of the difficulties faced by the Dust Bowl migrants in California. Her photographs, while not referred to in the text, powerfully documented the misery of the workers. These efforts eventuated in her well-received book *American Exodus* (1939).

Farm Service Administration. Lange and Taylor's reports for FERA soon caught the attention of Roy Stryker, an economist for the Federal Resettlement Agency (FRA), and of the documentary filmmaker Pare Lorentz. Impressed, Lorentz invited Lange to shoot stills for a project on the creation of the Dust Bowl, *The Plow That Broke the Plains* (1936). For his part, Stryker asked Lange to join his newly formed Farm Service Administration photographic division. By the end of 1935 Ben Shahn, Arthur Rothstein, Carl Mydans, and Walker Evans had joined the staff, which, during the project's seven-year life, also included John Collier Jr., Russell Lee, John Vachon, Theodor Jung, Paul Carter, Jack Delano, and Marion Post Wolcott. Their task was to document not only the activities of the FRA, but American rural life in general. Lange's "Migrant Mother," a portrait of a dispossessed mother surrounded by her children, became the most widely reproduced of all FSA photos. Lange's photographs are notable for their respect for the integrity of the subject, their refusal to overly sentimentalize the poor, and their emotional complexity. Lange photographed California's Dust Bowl refugees, tenant farmers in the Mississippi delta, former slaves in Alabama, and Texas cotton pickers.

The 1940s and Beyond. Although she was let go by the FSA in 1939 as the project began to close, Lange was granted a prestigious Guggenheim Fellowship in 1941, which enabled her to create a series of photographs documenting life among three contrasting cooperative religious communities: the Mormons in Utah, the Amana Society in Iowa, and the Hutterites in South Dakota. Her deep concern about the internment of Japanese Americans during World War II led her to document their lives in detention camps, work that eventuated in a 1972 book and traveling exhibit called *Executive Order 9066.* From this project Lange went on to work for the Office of War Information, creating photo stories about minority groups on the West Coast. Health problems interrupted her career in 1947; the work she did after this period was slightly less focused on specific social issues. She remained active until her death in 1965.

Sources:

Milton Meltzer, *Dorothea Lange: A Photographer's Life* (New York: Farrar, Straus & Giroux, 1978);

Beaumont Newhall, *The History of Photography* (Boston: Little, Brown, 1982);

William Stott, *Documentary Expression and Thirties America* (Chicago: University of Chicago Press, 1973).

RUTH MCKENNEY

1911-1972

WRITER

Significance. Ruth McKenney is one of the best examples of the ways in which 1930s writers combined radical politics, an appreciation of their audience's need for entertainment, and a desire to document the harsh realities of Depression life. Moving between writing scripts for radio, stage, and screen; light short stories in *The New Yorker;* essays for the Communist weekly *New Masses;* and

journalism for the *World-Telegram* in New York, McKenney seems to embody a certain cultural ethos of the period.

Autobiography. Ruth McKenney is best known today as the author of *My Sister Eileen,* the best-selling account of her family life during her childhood. This 1938 autobiography was a collection of McKenney's *New Yorker* pieces; a second collection appeared two years later under the title *The McKenneys Carry On.* Both volumes were critically acclaimed: *My Sister Eileen* went through more than a dozen printings and became first a Broadway play then a 1942 Hollywood film directed by Alexander Hall and starring Rosalind Russell and Brian Aherne. In 1955 Richard Quine directed a musical version with Betty Garrett, Janet Leigh, and Jack Lemmon; the Broadway version was titled *Wonderful Town.* The book's chapter headings give a fair idea of its general flavor: *Hun-gah* is subheaded "Eileen learns to play the piano and I take elocution lessons"; while *A Loud Sneer for Our Feathered Friends* is further explained as "We go to a girls' camp and don't think much of it, also about birds"; and *The Gladsome Washing Machine Season* is subheaded "Father feels like King Lear, with good reason."

Covering the Bases. This text would hardly identify McKenney as a radical writer of the time, but McKenney wrote other books: in 1939 and 1940 her works included a campaign pamphlet for the Communist Party presidential and vice presidential candidates titled *Browder and Ford for Peace, Jobs and Socialism* and *Industrial Valley,* a documentary account of the successful 1932–1936 rubber strike in Akron, Ohio. Thus, McKenney moved from popular autobiography to documentary labor history to radical pamphleteering. One week she might find herself in Hollywood working on the script of *My Sister Eileen;* the next filing her regular theater review column in *New Masses,* of which she became an editor (1938–1944). In fact, she moved in high Communist circles, spending her vacations with Communist leader Earl Browder and his family. Moreover, sister Eileen was married to modernist novelist Nathanael West, author of *The Day of the Locust.*

Proletarian Documentary. McKenney's early experience as a reporter on the *New York Post* served her well in her work on *Industrial Valley.* Using only two fictitious names in her collective biography of the strikers, McKenney traces the strike's progress using excerpts from newspaper headlines, vital statistics, and editorial comments on national and local affairs. *Industrial Valley* not only exemplifies radical documentary of the period but serves perhaps as its avatar.

Reception. *Industrial Valley* was well received both by radical and mainstream critics and acclaimed by radical literary critic Malcolm Cowley, writing in the *New Republic,* as perhaps the best American example of proletarian literature. The carefully researched *Industrial Valley* stands not just as exemplar for its genre, but as explanation for the genre's importance. Unlike Nathan Asch,

James Rorty, Sherwood Anderson, and others who documented their journeys through America, McKenney keeps herself entirely out of the story. Thus, she avoids the naked methodology of those works, the discussions of how best to represent American culture, to tell the American story. What McKenney does, instead, is to contrast the official truths of Akron, Ohio, as expressed by newspapers and Chamber of Commerce releases, with the unofficial, yet very real, suffering of the population there, as documented by the numbers of people applying for relief, the numbers freezing to death, the number of suicides. Through these often surreal juxtapositions, McKenney forces readers to consider the distance between these two accounts.

Later Career. After the 1930s McKenney continued writing light autobiography, fiction, and travel books. *The Loud Red Patrick,* her 1947 book about her grandfather, was also made into a Broadway show. Her film scripts, cowritten with husband Richard Branstein, included both versions of *My Sister Eileen* (1942, 1955), *San Diego, I Love You* (1944), *The Trouble With Women* (1947), and *Song of Surrender* (1949). She died in 1972 at age sixty.

Sources:

Malcolm Cowley, Review in *New Republic,* 98 (22 February 1939): 77;

M. L. Elting, Review in *Commonweal,* 28 (15 July 1938): 332;

Ruth McKenney, *Industrial Valley* (New York: Harcourt, Brace, 1939);

McKenney, *The McKenneys Carry On* (New York: Harcourt, Brace, 1940);

McKenney, *My Sister Eileen* (New York: Harcourt, Brace, 1938);

Obituary for Ruth McKenney, *Variety* (2 August 1972);

Review [unsigned], *Books* (24 July 1938): 2.

CARL SANDBURG

1878-1967

POET

Origins. Born on a corn-husk mattress in a three-room shack and raised in the prairie town of Galeburg, Illinois, Carl Sandberg, who early changed his name to the more American-sounding Charles Sandburg, was the restless son of semiliterate Swedish immigrants. Sandburg's name change was an early, visible sign of his desire to establish an American identity for himself and to explore the nature of Americanness: in fact, these lifelong preoccupations prepared him to become one of the foremost poetic voices of the 1930s, the decade with which he is most closely associated. Sandburg was only eighteen when wanderlust propelled him out of his rural town and toward Chicago in 1896 and then across the country as part of the stream of hoboes and tramps whose continent-wide odyssey in search of employment prefig-

ured that of the railroad-hopping hoboes of the Depression. Sandburg's quest left him with the indelible images he would later use in his poetry taste for adventure. During his twenties Sandburg was a college student, a soldier, a traveling salesman, a journalist for several Milwaukee and Chicago papers, and an apprentice poet, who recorded his observations and his first attempts at verse in a series of journals. He published his first book of poetry, *In Reckless Ecstasy,* in 1904. He became active in Socialist politics, campaigning for Socialist Party presidential candidate Eugene Debs in 1908, working as the secretary for the Socialist mayor of Milwaukee from 1910 to 1912, and writing Socialist pamphlets. When in 1907 Sandburg met Lillian Steichen, the sister of photographer Edward Steichen, his life changed dramatically. After a brief, primarily epistolary correspondence, the two married: she persuaded him to take back his given name and to try to integrate his American self and his immigrant Swedish self.

Growing Reputation. The publication of a group of Sandburg's poems in Harriet Monroe's magazine *Poetry* in 1914 signaled the emergence of a major American talent. The expectations of critics were met, if not exceeded, by the two books which followed, *Chicago Poems* in 1916 and *Cornhuskers* in 1918. In 1921 Sherwood Anderson declared Sandburg to be "of all the poets in America . . . my poet," and the following year Malcolm Cowley acclaimed him: "Sandburg writes American like a foreign language, like a language freshly acquired in which each word has a new and fascinating meaning." Cowley's praise echoed throughout the following decades, as writers struggled to reconcile the emphasis on language of the Imagist and modernist techniques with the American identity that was theirs. Sandburg, it seemed to many, was the poet best equipped for this sometimes daunting task. His accessible language, his populist concerns, and his graceful tone made him a favorite of audiences, though his reputation among critics had its ups and downs. As Newton Arvin wrote in *The New Republic* in 1936, "Of tenderness, of human feeling, of generous and robust sentiment, there is notoriously a great deal: of strong, sharp and ardent emotion, of the specific passion and intensity of poetry, there is singularly little." However, Sandburg's simplicity and optimism struck a chord for readers beaten down by the Depression, readers who found their experiences affirmed by the voice of the poet whose 1936 volume *The People, Yes* was a popular success. As Henry Steele Commager wrote, "Sandburg is the poet of the plain people, of farmers and steel workers and coal miners, of the housewife and the stenographer, and the streetwalker, too; of children at play and at work; of hoboes and bums; of soldiers — the privates, not the officers — of Negroes as of whites, of immigrants as of natives — of *The People, Yes.*"

Biography. Even as Sandburg was building his reputation with such volumes as *Smoke and Steel* (1920) and *Good Morning, America* (1928), he was becoming known for his monumental biography of Abraham Lincoln, the first two volumes of which appeared in 1926 under the title *Abraham Lincoln: The Prairie Years* and the final four volumes of which were published in 1939 as *Abraham Lincoln: The War Years*. The biography as a whole, which may have been occasionally inaccurate in detail but which was carefully researched and vividly written, was awarded the Pulitzer Prize for history in 1940. Sandburg wrote other biographies, including *Steichen the Photographer* (1929) and *Mary Lincoln: Wife and Widow* (1932), as well as an autobiography, *Always the Young Strangers* (1953).

Continuing Success. As time passed, Sandburg's reputation flourished. His thousand-page novel *Remembrance Rock* appeared in 1948: he collected a brace of honorary degrees from universities and a handful of prizes, including the Swedish Order of the North Star in 1938, a Pulitzer Prize for poetry (1951), and a Presidential Medal of Freedom in 1964. In 1962 he was designated poet laureate of Illinois. Together, these prizes recognized his ethnic roots, his regionalism, and above all his distinctively American voice — fitting tributes for a man who favored, as he wrote, "simple poems published long ago which continue to have an appeal for simple people."

Sources:

Harold Bloom, ed., *Twentieth-century American Literature* (New York: Chelsea House, 1987);

Dorothy Nyren Curley, Maurice Kramer, and Elaine Fialka Kramer, eds., *Modern American Literature : A Library of Literary Criticism* (New York: Frederick Ungar, 1969);

Penelope Niven, *Carl Sandburg: A Biography* (New York: Scribners, 1991).

MAE WEST

1892-1980

ENTERTAINER

Buxom Blonde. More than any other mainstream entertainer, Mae West — with her blonde hair, heavy-lidded eyes, and voluptuous figure — epitomized the liberating force of sexuality — a sexuality that managed to express itself despite the heavy hand of Production Code censors. However, though West is remembered as the heavy-breathing mistress of the double entendre, she is not always recognized for the artistic control she maintained over a career that began when she was five or for acting in stock theater.

Beginnings. By the time she was fifteen West was already starting to rewrite the vaudeville and Broadway revue material in which she appeared. A few years spent in burlesque, where she was billed as "The Baby Vamp," no doubt gave her material for her first play, *Sex*, which she wrote, produced, and directed on Broadway in 1926.

The ten-day jail sentence she received for her conviction on obscenity charges did little to dampen her writing fervor. The very next year she wrote and directed a drama about homosexuals titled *Drag*, which became a hit in Paterson, New Jersey. Heeding warnings, West chose to keep it off the Broadway stage. Here, as later, she managed to address risqué topics in a manner almost, but never quite, obscene. By this time West was piquing the interest of Hollywood producers; her next play, *Diamond Lil* (1928), was not only a Broadway hit but succeeded on the road. After writing two more plays, she accepted a Paramount offer to bring her ribald brand of entertainment to the screen.

Cracking the Code. The introduction of the Production Code on 1 July 1934 cast a pall over Hollywood. The self-regulatory code of ethics created by the Motion Picture Producers and Distributors in 1930 clearly set out guidelines for what could and could not be seen on screen. Gone were pictures that enlisted the sympathies of the audience to the side of crime or wrongdoing, depictions of illegal drug traffic, miscegenation, and comic or villainous portrayals of ministers. Most problematic for West, though, were the regulations concerning representations of sexuality. The code stipulated that "The sanctity of the institution of marriage and the home shall be upheld. Pictures shall not infer that low forms of sex relationships are the accepted or common thing"; "excessive and lustful kissing, lustful embracing, suggestive postures and gestures" were banned, as was "indecent or undue exposure." Seduction and rape, the code said, were "never the proper subject for comedy." Given that West had built a career on sex comedies, what was she to do?

Come Up and See Me Some Time. Triumph was the answer: by 1935 West was the highest-paid woman in the United States. She used her formidable verbal powers (as well as her great skill at physical comedy) to circumnavigate the rocky shoals of censorship. When she asked a handsome costar "Is that a pistol in your pocket, or are you just happy to see me?" or told her maid to "peel me a grape," audiences were vastly entertained — and there was nothing definably obscene about the performance. West was an early avatar of camp: she encouraged moviegoers to laugh a little at her performance, which was both sexy and so exaggerated that it served as a parody of seduction. Throughout the 1930s, West appeared opposite costars including Cary Grant and W. C. Fields in a steady stream of hits: *Night After Night* (1932); *She Done Him Wrong* (1933), the basis for her play *Diamond Lil*; *I'm No Angel* (1933), for which she also penned the story and screenplay; *Belle of the Nineties* (1934), also story and screenplay; *Klondike Annie* (1936), also costory and co-screenwriting credits; *Go West Young Man* (1936), also screenplay; *Every Day's a Holiday* (1938), also story and screenplay; and *My Little Chickadee* (1940), also co-screenwriting credit.

Later Career. Although West may have been down after the failure of her 1943 production *The Heat's On,* she was not out. Her series of comebacks included her 1954 nightclub act in which the sixty-two-year-old West appeared surrounded by a group of muscle-bound hunks, the publication of her 1959 autobiography *Goodness Had Nothing to Do with It,* and her successful appearance in the unsuccessful 1970 film *Myra Breckenridge,* for which she wrote her own dialogue. Her final screen appearance was in *Sextette* (1978), when she was eighty-five.

Source:
Ephraim Katz, *The Film Encyclopedia,* revised edition (New York: HarperPerennial, 1994).

PEOPLE IN THE NEWS

In November–December 1938 poet **Stephen Vincent Benét,** novelist **Willa Cather,** novelist-playwright **Thornton Wilder,** and novelist **Ellen Glasgow** were elected to fill vacancies in the fifty-member American Academy of Arts and Letters.

In January 1930 novelist **Louis Bromfield** went to Hollywood to write screenplay for the new sound motion pictures, telling reporters: "There is intelligence and talent gathering in Hollywood as it never gathered there before. . . . I am fed up with Europe. It gives me a stomach-ache."

In December 1938 the Limited Editions Club presented a gold medal to literary critic **Van Wyck Brooks,** proclaiming his 1937 Pulitzer Prize–winning book *The Flowering of New England* "the most likely to become a classic" of all the books published in the last three years.

In March 1937 director **George Cukor** said the actress he selected to play Scarlett O'Hara in the movie version of Margaret Mitchell's *Gone With the Wind* "must be possessed of the devil and charged with electricity. What I want is a really young and attractive girl, but she must be stupid, cruel and ruthless."

In December 1938 professor-musician-novelist **John Erskine** gave a lecture on "The Rise of Jazz and Swing" before an audience of one thousand at Town Hall in Manhattan. Also on the program were **Benny Goodman** and his band, who played to illustrate some of Erskine's points. According to Erskine, who had taught English at Columbia University and had recently retired from the presidency of The Juilliard School of Music, "Bach plus swing equals vitality."

When movie actor **Douglas Fairbanks Jr.** arrived in Manila in March 1931 en route to Cambodia to hunt big game, all business along the waterfront came to a halt as eight thousand people flocked to the pier to see him.

In January 1931 a reporter for *The American Jewish World* in New York City went to visit the mother of **Michael Gold** (Irwin Granich), editor of the leftist magazine *The New Masses* and author of *Jews Without Money* (1930), a novel Mrs. Granich had apparently not read. The reporter read her some passages that were clearly intended as homage to her dedication and hard work to improve the unsavory living conditions to which poverty had condemned her family, including a description of the fictional mother's "endless frantic war with the bedbugs." Mrs. Granich was enraged: "Wot, my son writes about bedbogs in my house? . . . I got to hev a son writes about bedbogs!"

In April 1931 **Gladys Adelina Lewis** sued playwright **Eugene O'Neill** for $2.5 million, charging that the motif of "selective parenting" in his *Strange Interlude* was plagiarized from her privately printed book *The Temple of Pallas-Athene* (1924), about a temple in Paris where perfect young men were — in the words of the judge hearing the case — "kept at stud as professional fathers." O'Neill had no difficulty convincing the judge that he had never heard of Lewis or her book until he had read in a newspaper that she was suing him.

Speaking at a luncheon in Springfield, Massachusetts, in April 1930 novelist **Sinclair Lewis** said, "A writer will work two or three years on a book, make $40 out of it, and then plunge quickly into two or three more years' work on another book. This kind of pluck reminds me of the chap who asked a lawyer for his daughter's hand. 'You work,' said the lawyer, 'for Blank & Co. What are your prospects for promotion?' 'The very best in the whole office,' said the young man. 'My job is the lowest one they've got.' " In reporting Lewis's remarks *Time* magazine pointed out that in a recent alimony dispute with his former wife, Grace Hegger Lewis, the novelist had claimed that he made less than ten thousand dollars while Mrs. Lewis contended that he had made one hundred thousand dollars in 1929, the year before he won the Nobel Prize.

In January 1930 New York publisher **Horace Liveright** agreed to destroy the plates and remaining copies of *Josephine, The Great Lover* (1929) after the Society for the Suppression of Vice declared it obscene. Liveright explained that the English translation of Pierre Nezelof's book about Empress Josephine, wife of Napoleon I, had not sold well enough to justify the expense of fighting its suppression.

In May 1936 poet **Edwin Markham** celebrated his eighty-fourth birthday at a party given by the English Department at Princeton University. The poet told his hosts, "When you finish a good poem, you must be able to say 'ah,' as though you were hit in the solar plexus."

In December 1930 California socialite **Elsa Maxwell** asked guests invited to her annual Manhattan costume ball to come dressed as their "opposites." Maxwell dressed as Herbert Hoover. Dancer **Adele Astaire** came as a devil. Actress **Ina Claire** dressed as Episcopal bishop William Thomas Manning. Banker Mortimer Schiff was playwright Oscar Wilde for the evening, while composer **Cole Porter** came as an old-time football player.

In February 1930 thirteen-year-old **Yehudi Menuhin** gave a violin recital in New York before a large audience that included Arturo Toscanini, conductor of the New York Philharmonic-Symphony Orchestra. After the recital Toscanini kissed Menuhin and promised to invite him to play a concerto with the orchestra.

In July 1939 movie actress **Pola Negri** sued the Paris weekly *Pour Vous* for one million francs because it reported that she was seeking a job as a Nazi propagandist. A French court awarded her ten thousand francs (then worth about $265).

Returning from a visit to France in late 1933, novelist **Charles Gilman Norris** commented on the effect the Depression was having on tourism in that country: "I am tickled to death to see that France is at last getting it in the neck. Paris has for many years been fattening on Americans visiting there.... History will show that when France is in power there is always trouble."

After fan dancer **Sally Rand** appeared in the 1937 Saint Patrick's Day parade in Cleveland, riding next to a float honoring the Virgin Mary, Bishop Joseph Schrembs of that city declared, "I am deeply humiliated and ashamed. . . . Her inclusion does not represent the mind of the great Irish people."

In January 1930 Irene O'Connor Rockwell divorced artist **Norman Rockwell** in Reno, Nevada, on the grounds of mental cruelty and neglect.

In July 1939, with his novel *The Grapes of Wrath* on the best-seller list, **John Steinbeck** went into seclusion to avoid autograph seekers and invitations to various literary clubs and luncheons: "I'm no public speaker, and I don't want to be," he told the press.

In December 1938 Simon and Schuster withdrew from sale *I Can Get It for You Wholesale* and *What's in It for Me?*, novels by **Jerome Weidman**. According to *Time* magazine (26 December 1938), the books were withdrawn because "their principal character, Harry Bogen, a smart-guy Jew, is enough to arouse anti-Semitic sentiments in a rabbi." At the same time, the publishers withdrew *Miniature Photography* by **Richard Simon,** one of the partners in the firm, because it praised some German-made cameras.

In August 1934, following the centennial of the birth of artist **James Abbott McNeill Whistler,** British reporters talked to Mortimer Menpes, one of Whistler's last surviving friends and students. According to Menpes, "The curious thing about Whistler was that he was simply no good at the technical side of his job. Even his best-known picture, *The Artist's Mother,* is fading rapidly." Menpes also remembered a story Whistler liked to tell about his days as a cadet at West Point: "he plucked and painted an eagle as a cock and entered it in a cock-fighting contest. Of course the eagle demolished the prize birds."

In January 1930 **Mrs. Harry Payne Whitney** told the press of her plans to open the Whitney Museum of American Art in New York City as the first museum devoted exclusively to works by American artists.

In April 1930 violin dealer George Smith of Los Angeles sued violinist **Efrem Zimbalist,** charging that the well-known musician still owned six thousand dollars of the eight-thousand-dollar purchase price for two violins. Zimbalist's lawyer contended that one of the violins, which Smith had called a 1717 Stradivarius, was spurious.

AWARDS

ACADEMY OF MOTION PICTURE ARTS AND SCIENCES AWARDS (THE OSCARS)

1930

Production: *All Quiet on the Western Front* (Universal)

Actor: George Arliss in *Disraeli*

Actress: Norma Shearer in *The Divorcee*

Direction: Lewis Milestone for *All Quiet on the Western Front*

1931

Production: *Cimarron* (RKO)

Actor: Lionel Barrymore in *A Free Soul*

Actress: Marie Dressler in *Min and Bill*

Direction: Norman Taurog for *Skippy*

1932

Production: *Grand Hotel* (M-G-M)

Actor: Frederic March in *Dr. Jekyll and Mr. Hyde* and Wallace Beery in *The Champ*

Actress: Helen Hayes in *The Sin of Madelon Claudet*

Direction: Frank Borzage for *Bad Girl*

1933

Production: *Cavalcade* (Fox)

Actor: Charles Laughton in *The Private Life of Henry VIII*

Actress: Katharine Hepburn in *Morning Glory*

Direction: Frank Lloyd for *Cavalcade*

1934

Production: *It Happened One Night* (Columbia)

Actor: Clark Gable in *It Happened One Night*

Actress: Claudette Colbert in *It Happened One Night*

Direction: Frank Capra for *It Happened One Night*

1935

Production: *Mutiny on the Bounty* (M-G-M)

Actor: Victor McLaglen in *The Informer*

Actress: Bette Davis in *Dangerous*

Direction: John Ford for *The Informer*

1936

Production: *The Great Ziegfeld* (M-G-M)

Actor: Paul Muni in *The Story of Louis Pasteur*

Actress: Luise Rainer in *The Great Ziegfield*

Supporting Actor: Walter Brennan in *Come and Get It*

Supporting Actress: Gale Sondergaard in *Anthony Adverse*

Direction: Frank Capra for *Mr. Deeds Goes to Town*

1937

Production: *The Life of Emile Zola* (Warner Bros.)

Actor: Spencer Tracy in *Captains Courageous*

Actress: Luise Rainer in *The Good Earth*

Supporting Actor: Joseph Schildkraut in *The Life of Emile Zola*

Supporting Actress: Alice Brady in *In Old Chicago*

Direction: Leo McCarey for *The Awful Truth*

1938

Production: *You Can't Take It With You* (Columbia)

Actor: Spencer Tracy in *Boys' Town*

Actress: Bette Davis in *Jezebel*

Supporting Actor: Walter Brennan in *Kentucky*

Supporting Actress: Fay Bainter in *Jezebel*

Direction: Frank Capra for *You Can't Take It With You*

1939

Production: *Gone With the Wind* (Selznick-M-G-M)

Actor: Robert Donat in *Goodbye, Mr. Chips*

Actress: Vivien Leigh in *Gone With the Wind*

Supporting Actor: Thomas Mitchell in *Stagecoach*

Supporting Actress: Hattie McDaniel in *Gone With the Wind*

Direction: Victor Fleming for *Gone With the Wind*

NOBEL PRIZES IN LITERATURE

1930

Sinclair Lewis

1936

Eugene O'Neill

1938

Pearl Buck

PULITZER PRIZES IN LETTERS

1930

Novel: *Laughing Boy*, by Oliver La Farge

Drama: *The Green Pastures*, by Marc Connelly

History: *The War of Independence*, by Claude H. Van Tyne

Biography or Autobiography: *The Raven*, by Marquis James

Poetry: *Selected Poems*, by Conrad Aiken

1931

Novel: *Years of Grace*, by Margaret Ayer Barnes

Drama: *Alison's House*, by Susan Glaspell

History: *The Coming of the War: 1914*, by Bernadotte E. Schmitt

Biography or Autobiography: *Charles W. Eliot*, by Henry James

Poetry: *Collected Poems*, by Robert Frost

1932

Novel: *The Good Earth*, by Pearl S. Buck

Drama: *Of Thee I Sing*, by George S. Kaufman, Morrie Ryskind, and Ira Gershwin

History: *My Experiences in the World War*, by John J. Pershing

Biography or Autobiography: *Theodore Roosevelt*, by Henry F. Pringle

Poetry: *The Flowering Stone*, by George Dillon

1933

Novel: *The Store*, by T. S. Stribling

Drama: *Both Your Houses*, by Maxwell Anderson

History: *The Significance of Sections in American History*, by Frederick J. Turner

Biography or Autobiography: *Grover Cleveland*, by Allan Nevins

Poetry: *Conquistador*, by Archibald MacLeish

1934

Novel: *Lamb in His Bosom*, by Caroline Miller

Drama: *Men in White*, by Sidney Kingsley

History: *The People's Choice*, by Herbert Agar

Biography or Autobiography: *John Hay*, by Tyler Dennett

Poetry: *Collected Verse*, by Robert Hillyer

1935

Novel: *Now in November*, by Josephine Winslow Johnson

Drama: *The Old Maid*, by Zoë Akins

History: *The Colonial Period of American History*, by Charles McLean Andrews

Biography or Autobiography: *R. E. Lee*, by Douglas S. Freeman

Poetry: *Bright Ambush*, by Audrey Wurdemann

1936

Novel: *Honey in the Horn*, by Harold L. Davis

Drama: *Idiot's Delight*, by Robert E. Sherwood

History: *The Constitutional History of the United States*, by Andrew C. McLaughlin

Biography or Autobiography: *The Thought and Character of William James*, by Ralph Barton Perry

Poetry: *Strange Holiness*, by Robert P. Tristram Coffin

1937

Novel: *Gone With the Wind*, by Margaret Mitchell

Drama: *You Can't Take It With You*, by Moss Hart and George S. Kaufman

History: *The Flowering of New England*, by Van Wyck Brooks

Biography or Autobiography: *Hamilton Fish*, by Allan Nevins

Poetry: *A Further Range*, by Robert Frost

1938

Novel: *The Late George Apley*, by John Phillips Marquand

Drama: *Our Town*, by Thornton Wilder

History: *The Road to Reunion, 1865–1900*, by Paul Hernan Buck

Biography or Autobiography: *Pedlar's Progress*, by Odell Shephard; *Andrew Jackson*, 2 volumes, by Marquis James

Poetry: *Cold Morning Sky*, by Marya Zaturenska

1939

Novel: *The Yearling*, by Marjorie Kinnan Rawlings

Drama: *Abe Lincoln in Illinois*, by Robert E. Sherwood

History: *A History of American Magazines*, by Frank Luther Mott

Biography or Autobiography: *Benjamin Franklin*, by Carl Van Doren

Poetry: *Selected Poems*, by John Gould Fletcher

DEATHS

Renée Adorée, 35, film actor (*The Big Parade*, 1925, *Call of the Flesh*, 1930), 5 October 1933.

Roscoe Conkling "Fatty" Arbuckle, 46, film actor (*His Wife's Mother, A Reckless Romance*) accused of causing starlet Virginia Rappe's death in 1921, 29 June 1933.

Mary Austin, 65, author of books on Native Americans, including *Lands of the Sun* (1927) and *One Smoke Stories* (1934), 13 August 1934.

Heywood Broun, 51, writer, journalist, cofounder of Newspaper Guild, 18 December 1939.

Lon Chaney, 47, actor, star of *The Phantom of the Opera* (1925) and *The Hunchback of Notre Dame* (1923), 26 August 1930.

Charles Waddell Chesnutt, 74, novelist (*The Conjure Woman*, 1899), 15 November 1932.

Herbert Croly, 61, author, publisher of the *New Republic*, 17 May 1930.

Marie Dressler, 64, film actor, won 1931 Academy Award for *Min and Bill*, 28 July 1934.

Finley P. Dunne, 68, journalist and humorist, wrote humorous essays in the character of "Mr. Dooley," 24 April 1936.

Harrison Fisher, 58, illustrator of magazine covers, created "Fisher Girl," 19 January 1934.

Pauline Frederick, 53, silent-screen star (*Bella Donna, Madame X*), 19 August 1938.

Mary E. Wilkins Freeman, 77, author of books on rural New England (*Pembroke*, 1894), 13 March 1930.

George Gershwin, 39, composer (*Rhapsody in Blue*, 1924, *Porgy and Bess*, 1935), won first Pulitzer Prize for a musical, *Of Thee I Sing*, in 1931, 11 July 1937.

William James Glackens, 68, impressionist, member of realist school The Eight, later known as the Ashcan School, 22 May 1938.

Alma Gluck, 54, New York Metropolitan Opera soprano (1909–1912) whose recording of "Carry Me Back to Old Virginny" sold two million copies, 27 October 1938.

Zane Grey, 64, writer of Western novels, most notably *Riders of the Purple Sage* (1912), 23 October 1939.

Mary Louise Cecelia "Texas" Guinan, 51, producer, known as "The Queen of the Speakeasies," 5 November 1933.

Frank Harris, 75, author of biography and erotica (*My Life and Loves*), 26 August 1931.

Childe Hassam, 75, impressionist painter, etcher, 25 August 1935.

De Wolfe Hopper (William De Wolfe), 77, actor known for recitation of "Casey at the Bat," 23 September 1935.

Sidney Howard, 48, playwright, screenwriter, won 1939 Oscar for screenplay of *Gone With the Wind* and 1924 Pulitzer Prize for *They Knew What They Wanted*, 23 August 1939.

Edgar Watson Howe, 84, author of early realist novel *Story of a Country Town*, 3 October 1937.

Kin Hubbard (Frank McKinney), 62, creator of cartoon character Abe Martin, 26 December 1930.

James Weldon Johnson, 67, writer (*The Book of American Negro Poetry*, 1902), diplomat, secretary of NAACP, 1916–1930, 26 June 1938.

Ring(gold) Lardner, 48, sportswriter, short-story writer (*You Know Me Al*, 1915), playwright with George S. Kaufman of 1929 hit *June Moon*, 25 September 1933.

Vachel Lindsay, 52, poet (*The Cargo*, 1914, *Johnny Appleseed*, 1928), 5 December 1931.

Horace B. Liveright, 46, publisher, 24 September 1933.

Harriet Monroe, 76, poet and critic, founder of *Poetry* magazine, which publicized work of Ezra Pound, T. S. Eliot and Robert Frost, 26 September 1936.

Paul Elmer More, 72, editor of the *Nation* (1909–1914), leading voice of New Humanism, 9 March 1937.

William Morrow, 58, book publisher, 11 November 1931.

F. A. Parsons, 64, president of New York School of Fine and Applied Arts, 26 May 1930.

Tyrone Power, 62, Broadway matinee idol, 30 December 1931.

Will Rogers, 56, humorist, 15 August 1935.

Ole Edvart Rolvaag, 55, novelist (*Giants in the Earth,* 1927, *Peder Victorious,* 1929), 5 November 1931.

Arthur H. Scribner, 73, book publisher, 3 July 1932.

Charles Scribner, 76, book publisher, 19 April 1930.

John Philip Sousa, 77, bandmaster, composer of 140 marches, including *Stars and Stripes Forever,* 6 March 1932.

Lincoln Steffens, 70, muckraking journalist and editor, exposed municipal corruption in *The Shame of the Cities* (1904), 9 August 1936.

Lorado Taft, 76, sculptor (*Solitude of the Soul*), 30 October 1936.

Sara Teasdale, 50, poet, won 1918 Pulitzer Prize for *Love Songs,* 29 January 1933.

Fay Templeton, 73, actor, vaudevillian whose appearances included *Fiddle-Dee-Dee,* 3 October 1939.

Edith Wharton, 76, novelist and short-story writer (*Ethan Fromme,* 1911), won 1920 Pulitzer Prize for *The Age of Innocence,* 11 August 1937.

Owen Wister, 78, novelist best known for *The Virginian* (1902), 21 July 1938.

Herbert Witherspoon, 61, first basso, New York Metropolitan Opera (1908–1916), director of Met, 1935, 10 May 1935.

Thomas Wolfe, 38, novelist (*Look Homeward, Angel,* 1929; *You Can't Go Home Again,* 1940), 15 September 1938.

Florenz Ziegfeld, 65, producer of long-running musical revue the *Ziegfeld Follies,* 22 July 1932.

Sources:

Beverly Baer and Neil E. Walker, eds. *Almanac of Famous People* (Detroit: Gale Research, 1994);

Miriam Allen De Ford and Joan Jackson, *Who Was When?* (New York: Wilson, 1976).

PUBLICATIONS

Louis Adamic, *My America* (New York: Harper, 1938);

Sherwood Anderson, *Puzzled America* (New York: Scribners, 1935);

Nathan Asch, *The Road: In Search of America* (New York: Norton, 1937);

Cab Calloway, *Hepster's Dictionary* (New York: C. Calloway, 1936);

Malcolm Cowley, *Exile's Return* (New York: Viking, 1934);

Edward Dahlberg, *Bottom Dogs* (New York: Simon & Schuster, 1930);

John Dewey, *Art As Experience* (New York: Minton Balch, 1934);

Waldo Frank, *In the American Jungle* (New York: Farrar & Rhinehart, 1937);

Henry Hart, ed., *American Writers Congress* (New York: International Publishers, 1935);

Granville Hicks, *The Great Tradition* (New York: Macmillan, 1935);

Ruth McKenney, *Industrial Valley* (New York: Harcourt, Brace, 1939);

James Rorty, *Where Life is Better: An Unsentimental American Journey* (New York: Reynal & Hitchcock, 1936);

Gilbert Seldes, *Mainland* (New York: Scribners, 1936);

Gertrude Stein, *Lectures in America* (New York: Random House, 1935);

Margaret Thorp, *America at the Movies* (New Haven: Yale University Press, 1939);

Edmund Wilson, *The American Jitters* (New York: Scribners, 1932).

BUSINESS AND THE ECONOMY

by VICTOR BONDI and ROBERT BATCHELOR

CONTENTS

Sidebars and tables are listed in italics.

1930

- Dry ice is first introduced for commercial purposes.

- Continental Baking introduces the world's first commercial sliced bread loaf, Wonder Bread.

- McGraw-Electric of Elgin, Illinois, introduces the first automatic toaster.

6 Mar. General Foods introduces Birds Eye Frosted Foods to stores in Springfield, Massachusetts. Frozen vegetables, fruits, and meats soon become a staple of grocery stores, despite high retail prices.

17 June Despite a petition signed by 1,028 economists, President Herbert Hoover signs the Smoot-Hawley Tariff — the highest in American history — into law. Other countries will retaliate by raising tariffs against the United States.

3 Oct. In Rusk County, eastern Texas, wildcatter Columbus M. Joiner, 71, brings in a gusher that opens a tremendous new oil field that will produce 3.6 billion barrels of oil.

11 Dec. New York's Bank of the United States, with sixty branches and four hundred thousand depositors, goes out of business.

20 Dec. Congress passes a $116 million public works bill and allocates $45 million for drought relief.

1931

- Lucky Strike outsells Camel cigarettes for the first time. The two brands will spend the next twenty years alternating the lead in cigarette sales.

- The United States produces a record wheat crop, driving prices down and precipitating further financial crisis in the farm belt.

4 May Continuing labor strife between the United Mine Workers and mine operators in Harlan County, Kentucky, leads to a gunfight that ends with three guards and one miner dead and many wounded.

20 June President Hoover proposes a one-year moratorium on war debt and reparations.

4 Aug. Gov. William H. "Alfalfa Bill" Murray of Oklahoma declares martial law and sends troops into the oil fields of the state to shut down production in order to elevate disastrously low prices for crude.

16 Aug. Gov. Ross Sterling of Texas proclaims a state of insurrection and, like Governor Murray, sends troops into oil fields.

1932

22 Jan. Congress authorizes the Hoover administration's request to found the Reconstruction Finance Corporation (RFC) to help ailing businesses.

7 Mar. Police fire into a crowd of demonstrators outside the Ford Motor plant in Dearborn, Michigan, killing four and wounding more than one hundred.

23 Mar. Congress passes the Norris–La Guardia Act, prohibiting the use of injunctions against strikes and contracts that prohibit workers from joining labor unions.

7 July The Dow Jones Industrial Average reaches an all-time low of 41.22.

21 July Congress approves the Emergency Relief and Reconstruction Act, making $2 billion available to the states for relief and public works projects.

22 July   Congress passes a Home Loan Act, establishing twelve federal home loan banks to lend money to mortgage institutions.

9 Aug.   The Iowa Farmers' Union begins a thirty-day strike to drive up farm prices. The strike is accompanied by a high level of violence.

15 Dec.   Six nations, including France and Belgium, default on war debt payments to the United States.

1933

6 Mar.   In response to continuing runs on banks, President Franklin D. Roosevelt declares a national bank holiday. Congress grants Roosevelt sweeping powers to regulate banking the next day; by the following week most American banks have resumed operations.

19 Apr.   The Roosevelt administration abandons the gold standard for American currency in international transactions.

12 May   Congress passes the Federal Emergency Relief Act, disbursing $500 million to states for economic assistance, and the Agricultural Adjustment Act, creating the Agricultural Adjustment Administration to help stablize farm prices.

18 May   Congress authorizes the Tennessee Valley Authority to operate a power plant at Muscle Shoals, Alabama.

13 June   Congress establishes the Home Owners Loan Corporation to provide emergency loans for homeowners.

16 June   President Roosevelt signs the Glass-Steagall Act, providing for government regulation of the banking industry. Congress approves the National Industrial Recovery Act, establishing economic codes for various industries, and the Farm Credit Act, consolidating rural credit agencies.

5 Aug.   The Roosevelt administration establishes the National Labor Board to oversee labor's right to bargain collectively.

9 Nov.   The Civil Works Administration, under former social worker Harry Hopkins, begins efforts to provide emergency jobs for four million unemployed Americans.

11–13 Nov.   A huge dust storm sweeps the drought-stricken Midwest, depositing Dakota soil as far east as Albany, New York.

1934

31 Jan.   Congress passes the Farm Mortgage Refinancing Act to help farmers in danger of having the mortgages on their farms foreclosed.

5 Feb.   Congress appropriates $950 million for the continuation of civil works program as part of the Civil Works Emergency Relief Act.

12 Feb.   The Export-Import Bank of Washington is established, with funding from the Reconstruction Finance Corporation to finance trade.

13 Apr.   Congress passes the Johnson Debt Default Act, prohibiting additional American loans to any country currently in default of debt payments to the United States.

May   Dust storms strip the plains states of three hundred million tons of topsoil, blown as far as the Atlantic Ocean.

9 May President Roosevelt signs the Costigan-Jones Act into law, establishing U.S. sugar import quotas.

22 May Pitched battles surrounding a teamster strike in Minneapolis result in two deaths. Violence throughout the summer will result in more fatalities.

6 June Congress establishes the Securities and Exchange Commission (SEC) to oversee financial and securities speculation. The first head of the commission is Wall Street speculator Joseph Patrick Kennedy Sr.

12 June The Reciprocal Trade Agreement Amendment to the Smoot-Hawley Tariff is passed by Congress, reducing tariffs by up to 50 percent for importers willing to grant the United States reciprocal tariff concessions.

19 June Congress creates the National Labor Relations Board (NLRB) to replace the National Labor Board.

21 June President Roosevelt signs the Dill-Crozier Act into law, establishing a National Railroad Adjustment Board to guarantee rail workers the right to organize.

28 June Congress passes the Taylor Grazing Act to control grazing and soil erosion in the West. The act effectively ends homesteading under the provisions of the Homestead Act of 1862. It also passes the Frazier-Lemke Farm Bankruptcy Act, postponing some foreclosures for five years.

16 July San Francisco is paralyzed by a general strike led by the International Longshoremen's Association, headed by Harry Bridges.

1935

16 Feb. Congress passes the Connally Hot Oil Act, regulating the production of crude oil and providing penalties for excess oil production.

8 Apr. Congress passes the Emergency Relief Appropriation Act, authorizing the disbursal of $5 billion in work relief.

30 Apr. An executive order creates the Resettlement Administration to move farmers from exhausted lands to good lands.

6 May President Roosevelt creates the Works Progress Administration (WPA), headed by Harry Hopkins.

11 May By executive order, Roosevelt establishes the Rural Electrification Administration to increase the electrification of American farms.

27 May In *Louisville Joint Stock Land Bank* v. *Radford*, the Supreme Court rules the Frazier-Lemke Farm Bankruptcy Act of 1934 unconstitutional.

26 June The Roosevelt administration creates the National Youth Administration to provide jobs for young people.

27 June In *Railway Retirement Board* v. *Alton Railway Co.*, the Supreme Court rules the Railway Pension Act of 1934 unconstitutional, a precedent that threatens other New Deal legislation.

5 July Congress passes the Wagner Act, affirming the right of unions to collective bargaining.

9 Aug. Congress places interstate bus and truck lines under the control of the Interstate Commerce Commission.

14 Aug.   President Roosevelt signs the Social Security Act into law, creating a nationwide system of old-age pensions and unemployment benefits.

23 Aug.   President Roosevelt signs the Banking Act into law, increasing the banking oversight power of the Federal Reserve System.

30 Aug.   Congress passes the Revenue Act, taxing inheritances and gifts heavily.

16 Sept.   On Wall Street Morgan Stanley investment firm begins operations. Because the Glass-Stegall Banking Act forbade the type of combined commercial/investment banking formerly practiced by the J. P. Morgan Company, Morgan has created Morgan Stanley to handle investments, while the parent company continues commercial banking.

9 Nov.   Dissidents within the American Federation of Labor (AFL), separate from the organization to form the Committee for Industrial Organization (later called the Congress of Industrial Organizations, or CIO). United Mine Workers president John L. Lewis is the first chairman.

1936

- Douglas Aircraft introduces the DC-3, a two-engine, twenty-one passenger workhorse of a plane that will revolutionize air travel. By 1938 it will have sold $28.4 million worth of the aircraft.

- American Airlines introduces day-long, transcontinental service from Newark, New Jersey, to Glendale, California.

6 Jan.   In *United States* v. *Butler* the Supreme Court rules that the Agricultural Adjustment Act of 1933 is unconstitutional.

14 Feb.   United Rubber Workers of America refuse to leave the Goodyear Tire and Rubber Plant No. 2 after being laid off, inaugurating the sit-down strike.

17 Feb.   The Supreme Court ruling in *Ashwander* v. *Tennessee Valley Authority* upholds the constitutionality of the Tennessee Valley Authority.

12 May   The first Super Chief locomotive leaves Chicago; the luxury liner will reduce Chicago to Los Angeles service to just under forty hours.

18 May   The Supreme Court rules the 1935 Bituminous Coal Conservation Act is unconstitutional.

1 June   In *Morehead* v. *New York ex. rel. Tipaldo* the Supreme Court rules a New York minimum wage law unconstitutional.

20 June   Congress passes the Robinson-Patman Act, supplementing the Clayton Anti-Trust Act of 1914 by forbidding price discrimination in advertising.

29 June   Congress passes the Merchant Marine Act, subsidizing the American carrying fleet.

30 Oct.   Striking maritime workers paralyze American shipping in a job action that begins on the West Coast but soon spreads to every port. The strike will last three months.

31 Dec.   Workers at the General Motors Chevrolet body plant in Flint, Michigan, stage a sit-down strike.

1937

- There are 4,740 work stoppages, working strikes, and lockouts in factories nationwide.

11 Feb. General Motors ends the sit-down strike in Flint, Michigan, by recognizing the United Automobile Workers (UAW) as the sole bargaining agent for its employees.

2 Mar. United States Steel averts a strike by permitting the unionization of its workers.

29 Mar. In *West Coast Hotel* v. *Parrish* the Supreme Court reverses itself and upholds the minimum wage for women.

24 May The Supreme Court upholds the constitutionality of the Social Security Act.

30 May Following labor disputes, Chicago police attack a union picnic of Republic Steel workers, killing ten and injuring eighty-four in the Memorial Day Massacre.

1938

- General Motors and Standard Oil organize Pacific Coast Lines, designed to lobby western cities to convert their streetcars to buses.

- Saltwater injection wells are used for the first time in the oil industry.

27 May Congress reduces the corporation profits tax.

15 June Congress passes the Fair Labor Standards Act, revolutionizing the American workplace. Working hours are limited to forty-four hours per week, after which workers must be paid overtime. A minimum wage is established at 25 cents per hour. The new law affects 12.5 million American workers.

21 June Congress passes the Emergency Relief Appropriations Act to continue government assistance to the unemployed.

23 June Congress creates the Civil Aeronautics Authority (CAA) to oversee the American aviation industry.

27 June The U.S. Food, Drug and Cosmetic Act is signed by President Roosevelt, updating the 1906 Pure Food and Drug Act and providing consumers greater protection.

18 Nov. John L. Lewis is elected president of the Congress of Industrial Organizations.

1939

- The Department of Agriculture introduces food stamps.

- Pall Mall brand cigarettes introduce the first "king-size cigarettes."

- General Electric introduces fluorescent lighting.

- Howard Hughes buys control of Transcontinental and Western Airlines (TWA).

- The Hewlett-Packard electronic instrument firm is founded.

28 June Pan-American inaugurates the first commercial transatlantic passenger air service, a flight that takes 26.5 hours.

OVERVIEW

Transformation. Business and the economy in the 1930s were in a state of upheaval. The Great Depression was an international economic calamity so overwhelming that many around the world considered it an omen of divine disapproval. Old economic solutions failed to resolve it; the normal patterns of capitalism and the business cycle seemed broken. But for all the upheaval and catastrophe, the 1930s were a transitional time in business and economic history, not a break with history. Along with the two world wars, the Depression signaled a difficult shift in the form and practice of industrial capitalism. Nineteenth-century capitalism was militantly nationalistic, focused on seizing exclusive markets and on industrial manufacturing, wedded to an individualistic view of economic psychology that resulted in glaring disparities of wealth. Twentieth-century capitalism was multinational, focused on reciprocal trade and consumer production, and dominated by organic models of economic behavior that rationalized judicious distributions of wealth. So entrenched were the theories and practices of nineteenth-century capitalism that it took two wars and an economic collapse to change them. But they did change.

Stagnation. Even without the stock-market crash of 1929, the 1930s would have been difficult. Many older industries had seemingly reached the limits of their production. Domestic railway construction had long since peaked; in 1931, 755,000 fewer cars were made than were scrapped, replaced, or stored by owners; oil production glutted the market; agricultural prices collapsed because of overproduction. Stagnationism, an influential school of economic thought, took note of these factors, as well as the closing of the frontier and a decline in the birth rate, and argued that capitalism had reached its "mature" phase and was finished growing. They argued that low prices, high unemployment, and oversupply — a stagnant economy — were permanent structural features of the mature economy. In retrospect, stagnation was not the type of permanent structural problem its proponents believed it to be. Older industries — rail, steel, textiles — had displayed limited growth and were stagnating; mass-based consumer industries seemed to promise to be the engine of future economic growth. Unfortunately, these new productive sectors of the economy — armaments,

consumer products, appliances, medical care, and recreation — were in the 1930s only becoming established. The irony of the 1930s was that the consumer economy of the postwar period was being born, but most people were too poor to notice. The gap between the establishment of these newer industries and the collapse of older industries led to a temporarily stagnant economy that made life miserable for millions.

Emerging Consumerism. Many of the unusual economic features of the 1930s evidenced the transition from a manufacturing to a consumer economy. The decline of rail transportation and downturn in the auto market led to cutbacks in iron and steel; yet, simultaneously, the manufacturing of flat-rolled steel and tin plate increased vastly at the end of the decade, as these metal products were used in the manufacture of processed foods, especially canned goods. The processed foods industry was spurred in many ways by the Great Depression. Lower food prices and an increasing number of women working outside the home shifted many American eating habits to canned and processed foods, which were easier and quicker to serve. Retailers responded by revolutionizing the grocery business, turning to canned food and the newly introduced frozen foods to save space and operating expenses. The first true supermarket was opened in 1930; by 1939 nearly five thousand existed around the country. The government revamped the Pure Food and Drug Act of 1906 to meet increased consumer concerns regarding the purity of processed food; sanitary concerns led to a boom in glass products for packaging. Similarly, the chemical and oil industries turned from manufacturing concerns to consumer products. Plunging oil prices forced oil companies to develop innovative methods of refining and forced them to follow the advent of the oil burner and the airplane by developing home and aviation fuels. To cut costs and meet the needs of new markets, chemical manufacturers turned to developing products for consumer use, such as rayon and nylon, or for consumer industries such as motion pictures and electronics. Rather than lower prices, the automobile industry met the slump in the Depression by becoming more responsive to consumer needs, improving the performance and safety of automobiles, inaugurating streamlined auto designs to attract consumer attention, and developing consumer-friendly financing and automobile trade-ins.

Construction. The construction industry shows the changed nature of the economy in the 1930s most clearly. The 1930s were one of the most prosperous periods for construction in history. Many of the structures that have become icons of the American landscape were built in the period: the Empire State Building, the Chrysler Building, Rockefeller Center, the Golden Gate Bridge, Boulder (Hoover) Dam, Coit Tower in San Francisco, the Lincoln Tunnel in New York, the George Washington Bridge, La Guardia Airport, the Supreme Court building, and the Fort Peck Dam in Montana. The building boom of the decade, however, can be divided into two parts: those projects constructed before 1935, usually with private capital (and usually begun before the onset of the Depression), and those built after 1935, usually constructed by the government for the purposes of infrastructure development and unemployment relief. Construction before 1935 was operated according to an older, orthodox economic philosophy that saw productive ventures as the responsibility of private capitalists. As magnificent as were the buildings developers erected, almost all of them were economic failures: office space in the Empire State Building and Rockefeller Center, for example, was largely unoccupied in the midst of depression. On the other hand, the New Deal construction projects, built with mixed funding, were far more successful in accomplishing their goals of alleviating unemployment, flood control, and rural electrification. Projects such as Fort Peck Dam represented a new economic philosophy to fit new economic realities: government intervention in the market to promote growth and aid the private sector. By using government funds to electrify rural areas, the New Deal was making possible the use of electrical appliances by a vast segment of the population (nearly 20 percent of Americans) who had heretofore been unable to use them. To the New Dealers such government spending was a way of bridging the gap between a manufacturing-based and a consumer-based economy and was the surest way of overcoming the stagnation of the 1930s.

The Crash. The stock-market crash of 1929 complicated the temporary stagnation of the economy. Capital liquidity and investor confidence might have spurred the growth of new industries. After the crash, however, capital and confidence were in short supply. Both were undermined by poor economic practices and fiscal mismanagement in the 1920s. Large World War I debts combined with high tariffs made it impossible for Europe to trade its way out of debt with the United States and led to severe imbalances in international payments. Federal Reserve mismanagement of the gold supply and easy credit fueled speculation and undermined bank solvency. Unregulated stock practices and securities fraud drove stock prices far higher than the real worth of American corporations. Production increases in industry were not matched by higher wages, undermining consumer demand. The crash of 1929 reflected investor recognition of the economy's troubled condition. But their panicked sell-off only made matters worse, drying up sources of capital for industrial modernization and forcing bank closings. Thus, at the very moment when American industry was shifting its base, the business cycle began a downturn that made restructuring of the economy particularly difficult.

Philosophy. The painful transition from an industrial to a consumer economy in the 1930s was accompanied by an equally painful shift in the economic philosophy of American business. Investor confidence remained low throughout the decade because many businessmen, wedded to the economic axioms of the 1920s, had little faith in the new economic philosophies that were developed by the end of the 1930s. These older economic axioms, enshrined in what President Herbert Hoover called the "American System," assumed a degree of automatism to the marketplace that simply did not exist. Partisans of the American System waited for the automatic mechanism of the marketplace to restore prosperity after the crash. When it did not, investor confidence plummeted still further. But the new economic philosophy of President Franklin Roosevelt's New Deal also failed to reassure investors. Devaluation of the dollar, reciprocal trade arrangements, government oversight of finance, welfare-state protection for workers, deficit spending, and countercyclical works projects were far too radical for many investors. The very notion of economic planning was alien to businessmen who insisted the marketplace functioned automatically. Thus, just as there was a structural gap in the economy in the 1930s, there was a gap in business philosophy and investor psychology that reinforced the economic impasse of the decade.

Industrial Warfare. Nothing reflects the structural and philosophical impasse of the 1930s better than the debate over the role of labor in the economy. The United States has historically had some of the most severe industrial warfare in the West. Economic orthodoxy denied the right of labor to organize, collectively bargain, or strike. Industrialists consistently articulated the idea that labor was secondary to capital in the productive process; labor was cheap and replaceable; wages were necessarily low, in order to discipline the workforce. The American System tempered this philosophy somewhat, as management assumed a new paternalism toward labor. But the productive gains of labor during the 1920s were not reflected in rising wages, and with the stock-market crash the facade of paternalism dissolved. Treasury Secretary Andrew Mellon almost immediately urged that management liquidate labor. By 1933 more than a quarter of the labor force was unemployed, and much of the remainder was employed part-time. When labor attempted to respond to these conditions by striking or demonstrating, they were often attacked. Hired thugs, paid informants, police — even the National Guard — were used to suppress union activity. Ford's River Rouge plant had a staff of nine thousand paid informants to monitor the workers and planted microphones and patrolled bathrooms to prevent union organizing. The Pittsburgh Coal Company placed machine guns at its coal pits. "You cannot run the mines without them," explained Pittsburgh head Richard B. Mellon. Violence against labor assumed an often ferocious cast: police and Ford guards killed four protesters and wounded more than one hundred in a march on Ford's River Rouge plant in 1932; during the Allegheny coal strike of 1934, mine owners spent $17,000 on munitions and bombed strikers' homes; sheriff's deputies killed six union organizers in Honea Path, South Carolina, during a textile strike that same year; in Minneapolis a teamster strike throughout the summer of 1934 led to battles between workers and police that killed several; during the San Francisco general strike of 1934, the militia was called in and gunned down striking longshoremen; police raided and shot ten workers and wounded eighty-four at a Memorial Day protest near Chicago in 1937; eighteen workers were killed at a 1937 strike against Republic Steel in Cleveland. Beatings of union organizers were innumerable; the Pinkerton National Detective Agency, the leading provider of industrial police forces, made $1.7 million between 1933 and 1936.

Wagner Act. Violence against labor reflected the beliefs of many industrialists that wage and safety demands by labor were illegitimate and communistic. When the New Deal took up the cause of labor with the passage of Title 7(a) of the National Industrial Recovery Act and the 1935 Wagner Act, both of which protected the right to bargain collectively, many in the business community were incensed. At the heart of orthodox economic theory was a belief in what Herbert Hoover termed "rugged individualism," a notion derived from social Darwinian philosophy that maintained that only a few "fit" individuals were capable of economic success and prosperity. By backing the workers, many businessmen felt the New Deal was supporting individuals who had failed in the competition of life; high wages for such people, many felt, would be squandered and wasted. To many businessmen, the New Deal was taking from the most capable and giving to the least deserving. Critics such as Herbert Hoover believed government support for labor would undermine civilization itself, and no act of the New Deal was more bitterly opposed by business conservatives than its support of labor.

A New Philosophy. Not all businessmen were opposed to labor organizing. Ultimately, the vanguard of a new economic philosophy came from the ranks of those businesses that would lead the economy toward consumer production. Many businessmen in mass-consumption-oriented industries (such as retailers like Filenes and Macy's), urban real estate developers, new consumer banks and investment houses (such as Lehman Brothers, the Bank of America, and Goldman, Sachs), and the motion picture, insurance, furniture, and appliance industries supported high wages as a means to increase demand. They often gave political support to the New Deal and sometimes cooperated with the new Congress of Industrial Organizations (CIO). By 1937 a new coalition of New Deal politicians, CIO organizers, and consumer industrialists were developing a new economic philosophy, one based on government regulation of finance and securities, countercyclical deficit spending, progressive taxation, free international trade, labor organization, and high wages. It would become the basis of prosperity after World War II, insuring a quality of life from 1945 to 1972 unparalleled in American history.

TOPICS IN THE NEWS

THE AUTOMOBILE INDUSTRY IN THE 1930S

Economic Leader. In the 1920s the automobile industry overtook steel as the most important sector of the American economy. Approximately 10 percent of the annual income of Americans was taken up purchasing cars and trucks and in buying gas, oil, parts, repairs, and other auto-related items. The automobile industry, led by the "Big Three" companies of General Motors, Ford, and Chrysler, fueled the upswing in the economy in the last half of the 1920s. The increasing importance of the business, however, meant that if car and truck sales slipped the entire American economy would suffer. People soon discovered just how closely the auto industry was linked to the general healthiness of the economy following the stock-market crash in October 1929.

Effects of the Depression. The automobile industry in 1929 set a record by selling more than 5 million vehicles. The next year, even after cutting prices in the wake of the market crash, sales dropped by 2 million. By 1932 the number of vehicles sold plummeted to a paltry 1.33 million, a drop of 4 million from the 1929 record. The Depression affected the entire economy and had a major impact on the car manufacturing areas in the Midwest. Unemployment in Detroit and Flint, Michigan, hit 13 percent in 1930, when the national average was only 6.6 percent. Later, in 1932, half the male population of Detroit was unemployed. Ford employed 120,000 in March 1929, but by August 1931 that number fell to 37,000. After 1932 car sales slowly crept back to mid-1920s levels but slid again in response to the break in the nation's recovery that occurred in 1937 and 1938.

Demise of Independents. The Depression was too much for many of the independent carmakers, including Pierce-Arrow, Peerless, Stutz, Marmon, Du Pont, Durant, Duesenberg, Auburn, Hupmobile, and Kissel. The smaller automakers had sold one-quarter of the cars on the road in 1925, but that number dropped to just over 10 percent by 1933. Some of these companies were able to switch to other products to survive; however, the majority were forced to fold. Most of the smaller companies manufactured high-priced luxury cars, and those were the hardest hit by the collapsing economy. Packard was the

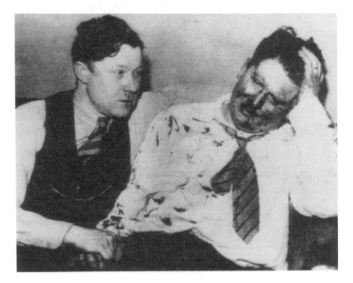

UAW organizers Walter Reuther and Richard Frankensteen after being beaten by policemen hired by Ford during a demonstration at the River Rouge Ford plant on 26 May 1937

only luxury car company to survive outside the Big Three, and it reluctantly introduced a scaled-down version called the "Junior" Packard in an attempt to increase sales. The demise of the luxury car companies had a tremendous impact on automobile parts suppliers and the custom-body companies who made the specially designed bodies for the independent automakers. By the end of the 1930s nearly all of these firms were gone.

Shake-Up at the Top. The fall of the independent companies translated into a larger share of the market for the Big Three. During the Depression their share increased to 90 percent, up from the 75 percent they held in the late 1920s. A restructuring also took place among the Big Three. Ford had reigned supreme at the end of the

1920s with its Model A. However, GM and Chrysler quickly put technological advances to use and began building more-stylish and cheaper automobiles. In 1931 Chrysler's low-priced Plymouth and an improved Chevrolet from GM knocked Ford out of the lead. In the new decade GM's market share increased to over 43 percent, compared to Ford's 28 percent. Just a year later, in 1932, Chrysler closed in on second, selling over 17 percent to Ford's 24 percent. Henry Ford was directly responsible for his company's demise. His outdated management style and autocratic practices contributed to Ford's fall into third place in 1933, a position it held into the 1950s. Henry Ford simply could not compete with the dynamic, and sometimes brilliant, leadership of GM's Alfred P. Sloan Jr., and Walter P. Chrysler.

Unionization and Intervention. Poor economic conditions were not the only thing the Big Three leaders had to contend with in the 1930s. The onset of the Depression led many workers to believe that unionization was the only way they could protect themselves from the companies and have some job security. The Roosevelt administration favored unions and introduced legislation to facilitate unionization. Congress passed the National Labor Relations Act (NLRA) in 1935, which guaranteed the rights of labor and outlawed the heavy-handed measures the companies used to break up unions. The fledgling Committee for Industrial Organizations (CIO) and its offspring the United Automobile Workers (UAW) used the NLRA legislation to organize workers.

Violence. Both the unions and the Big Three prepared for battle in the mid 1930s. GM spent close to $1 million from January 1934 to July 1936 for private detectives and guards to patrol its plants. The Ford Service Department, headed by Harry Bennett, may have been the most violent and corrupt. The Service Department was virtually a gang of thugs and spies with the sole purpose of intimidating Ford workers at the massive River Rouge plant. Bennett and Ford despised unions and used every means at their disposal to keep activists away from River Rouge. On 26 May 1937 UAW leaders Dick Frankensteen and Walter Reuther attempted to hand out flyers at the overpass leading to the main gate but were intercepted and trapped by a group of servicemen. The two union leaders were beaten unmercifully, along with women, reporters, and photographers who were also on hand. The highly publicized event came to be known as the "Battle of the Overpass," although Reuther and Frankensteen and the women involved hardly put up a battle against Bennett's men. The incident only solidified the view of River Rouge as a "gigantic concentration camp founded on fear and physical assault."

Union Success. The UAW used the new tactic of the sit-down strike to close down many plants, in effect. Workers would take physical possession of a plant by remaining inside the building and not letting strikebreakers in, thus stopping all work. By early 1937 the UAW forced GM to accept it as the bargaining agent for its

workers. Chrysler followed suit in April 1937. Ford continued to hold out and used its servicemen to stop unionization. Not until a spontaneous walkout of Ford workers on 1 April 1941 closed the River Rouge plant did Ford capitulate. The UAW won an overwhelming victory in elections at the Ford plant, and Henry Ford signed a formal contract in June that gave his workers more-generous terms than the other major automakers. The victory by the UAW gave workers a larger stake in the automobile business. As World War II approached, the American autoworker made significant strides forward, being helped along the way by the UAW.

Legacy. The automobile industry survived many upheavals in the 1930s. It remained, despite the foundering economy, the dominant industry in the United States. The Big Three expanded as the independent companies were forced out of business. The industry also weathered a changing of the guard as Ford fell from first to third place and GM took its place in the forefront. Most significantly, the automakers eventually accepted industrial democracy in the plants. The wave of unionization, supported by the Roosevelt administration, swept the country and could have been even more violent if the leaders of the auto companies did not realize that they were fighting a losing battle. Taken together, the events of the 1930s solidified the strength of the automobile industry and set the tone for the mobilization effort in World War II and the booming years of the 1950s.

Sources:

Anthony J. Badger, *The New Deal: The Depression Years, 1933-1940* (New York: Noonday Press, 1989);

Irving Bernstein, *Turbulent Years: A History of the American Worker, 1933-1941* (Boston: Houghton Mifflin, 1970);

Allan Nevins and Frank E. Hill, *Ford: Decline and Rebirth, 1933–1962* (New York: Scribners, 1963).

THE CIO AND THE TRIUMPH OF UNIONIZATION

Growth. The 1930s witnessed an incredible growth in union membership. Many factors came together at a crucial time to allow the phenomenal growth, including governmental support for unions and dynamic leadership within the labor movement. The most central issue was the creation of the Committee for Industrial Organizations (CIO), later renamed the Congress of Industrial Organizations, in 1935. Because of the success of the CIO nearly all the major industries in the United States were organized by the end of the decade.

Split. The American Federation of Labor (AFL) failed to meet the needs of the unorganized workers in the mass-production industries in the early 1930s. The fundamental problem was that the AFL did not want to let unskilled workers into the organization, which was dominated by craft unions. The stubbornness of the AFL led United Mine Workers (UMW) leader John L. Lewis to split from the AFL and found the CIO. Lewis created

Banner depicting CIO president John L. Lewis, held by marchers in the Labor Day parade, Toledo, Ohio, 1938

the CIO with the explicit purpose of organizing the mass-productions industries.

Lewis's Gamble. Leading the break from the AFL was a personal gamble for Lewis. He had moved up the ranks within the labor movement and now risked his position on a fledgling organization. The success of the CIO in organizing, however, made him one of the most recognized and powerful men in America. Lewis was wholly committed to advancing the interests of the nonskilled workers through collective bargaining. Lewis was also something of a maverick because he made sure that the CIO ignored the lines of color, sex, and nationality in its efforts. Women, immigrants, and blacks were persuaded to join the new organization.

Government Support. The CIO benefited from the support of the federal government toward unionism. Management could no longer assume that the government would help them in the fight against labor. The Wagner Act of 1935 gave workers the legal right to unionize and protected them from unfair employer tactics, such as firing, espionage, violence, and the use of strikebreakers. The Wagner Act became the keystone of labor's legal protection. Government intervention on the

side of labor played a major role in helping the CIO rise to prominence.

Lewis and Roosevelt. Lewis also involved the CIO in politics. He campaigned heavily for President Roosevelt in 1936, convinced that FDR's reelection was imperative for labor. Lewis spoke at numerous campaign rallies and reached countless workers over the radio airwaves urging them to vote for Roosevelt. After Roosevelt's landslide victory Lewis said, "We must capitalize on the election, the CIO was out fighting for Roosevelt, and every steel town showed a smashing victory for him." The CIO now had the impetus to begin a massive organizing campaign because it had, in Lewis's words, "a President who would hold the light for us."

The Sit-Down Strike. The mass-production workers were eager to join the CIO and were bursting with militancy. An example of their rising enthusiasm was the spontaneous phenomenon of the sit-down strike. The sit-down strike allowed a small minority of workers to take control of an entire plant by occupying the work site and not leaving the premises. In 1936 and 1937 a wave of sit-down strikes involving almost half a million workers occurred across the nation. Sit-down strikes, or the threat of such strikes, led to resounding victories for the CIO against automobile giants General Motors and Chrysler, rubber corporations Goodrich and Firestone, and steel leader United States Steel. The sit-down strike became a major weapon in the CIO's fight to organize workers and gain collective-bargaining agreements.

Radicals. Lewis realized that he needed shrewd, intelligent, and experienced organizers to build the CIO successfully. Many of the best organizers were socialists and communists, veterans of many labor wars. Lewis did not hesitate to use the radicals. This was an opportunistic move, however, not one of support for the revolutionary cause. Lewis did not fear that the communists would take over his organization. He needed good men, and the radicals were often the most dedicated and effective organizers. Communists soon became prominent members of the CIO at both the national and local levels.

Depression. The Depression also helped the CIO organize the nonskilled workers. In times of economic downturns companies were less willing to fight unionization. The CIO was then able to exploit the company's need to maintain production. Antiunion tactics were also costly and cut deeply into a company's profits. During periods of industrial growth the corporations did not want to lose their competitive edge to smaller firms; therefore, they could not risk the plants shutting down. This thinking influenced the U.S. Steel Company to recognize the Steel Workers Organizing Committee (SWOC) unexpectedly and without a real battle in 1937. Under these circumstances, the CIO benefitted regardless of the economy's minor fluctuations.

Setbacks. Lewis did experience some defeat in late 1937 and 1938. The CIO suffered setbacks when the economy took a massive downturn and layoffs and rising inventories curbed the militancy found earlier in the year. Lewis estimated that 8 million to 10 million workers had joined the CIO, but this number was vastly exaggerated. Furthermore, the AFL responded to the challenge by increasing its own organizing and challenging the CIO in many industries.

Success. The CIO made remarkable strides in 1937. Lewis's young organization actually outnumbered the AFL, 3.7 million members to 3.4 million. The unionization effort had effectively succeeded in gaining collective bargaining agreements in the nation's two most antiunion industries, auto and steel. The organization also paved the way for unionization in other industries. The CIO gave millions of workers an opportunity to join a union. Lewis's gamble in forming the CIO paid off, and the organization improved the working conditions for the nation's blue-collar workers. The CIO stands as Lewis's most important contribution to American life.

Sources:

Irving Bernstein, *Turbulent Years: A History of the American Worker, 1933–1941* (Boston: Houghton Mifflin, 1970);

David Brophy, *Workers in Industrial America: Essays on the Twentieth Century Struggle* (New York: Oxford University Press, 1980);

Robert H. Zieger, *John L. Lewis: Labor Leader* (Boston: Twayne, 1988).

"Champagne" Fred Bell, whose fortune during the 1920s was estimated at nearly a million dollars, selling apples on a San Francisco street corner in 1931, having lost his money in the stock-market crash

THE CRASH AND THE GREAT DEPRESSION

The Crash. On 24 and 29 October 1929 prices on the New York Stock Exchange collapsed. The losses among 880 issues were estimated at between $8 billion and $9 billion. The "Great Crash" of 1929 ended a period of tremendous prosperity and inaugurated the Great Depression, but the crash and the Depression were not unprecedented. Since the Civil War, the American economy had suffered periods of depression every eight to twelve years. The last major depression, from 1893 to 1897, had been a period of enormous suffering and widespread political unrest; the economy had been through a smaller depression as recently as 1920–1921. Such depressions had been devastating, but often their impact varied by region, with the worst effects being localized. In the 1930s, however, the United States was financially unified as never before. Harvests in California affected markets in New York. Newspapers, magazines, radio, and cinema linked the nation from coast to coast. The dust bowl in Oklahoma was reported in Florida; hurricanes in Florida were reported in Oklahoma. A national media reinforced the perception that the Great Depression was unprecedented in its intensity and depth. Furthermore, after the prosperity and boosterism of the 1920s, the Depression seemed to many an unexpected and incredible calamity. Capitalism itself appeared to fail.

The Downward Spiral. Although the Great Crash was sudden, the Great Depression descended slowly, spiraling down to deeper and deeper depths of misery. Because of its gradual character, business and political leaders continually expected that the Depression, like those previous, would end, and that the economy would rebound. Repeatedly they discussed the Depression as part of the normal business cycle, advised the public to wait it out, and predicted the return of prosperity. In December 1929 the president of the National Association of Manufacturers, John Edgerton, remarked, "I can observe little on the horizon today to give us undue or great concern." "I am convinced we have passed the worst," announced President Herbert Hoover in May 1930. In January 1931 James Farrell, president of United States Steel, maintained, "The peak of the Depression passed thirty days ago." To the public — and to many businessmen — such pronouncements rang increasingly hollow. The economy only grew worse. Shares of General Motors stock, worth $212 per share in 1928, fell to $8 by 1931; Goldman, Sachs stock traded at 104 during the heyday of prosperity, and at 1 3/4 in 1932. Seventy-four billion dollars in investments were wiped out in the two years following the crash. Banks failed by the score, with 2,294 closing in 1931 alone, taking with them years of personal savings at a time when few businesses offered pensions to their workers. Nine million dollars in savings were wiped out by 1932. That same year twenty thousand businesses went bankrupt. By 1933 nearly a quarter of the labor force was unemployed. Manufacturing was at half the level it had been in 1929; foreign trade reduced by two-thirds. Wages fell nearly below the level of survival: in Pennsylvania sawmill workers received five cents an hour and general contract workers seven and a half cents an hour. Even baseball star Babe Ruth took a $10,000 pay cut. No depression, it seemed, had been as bad as the Great Depression. By 1932 rosy predictions of the return of prosperity became rare. Many businessmen conceded to a Senate committee that the Great Depression was not part of a normal cycle of boom and bust, and that they were helpless to change the situation. Myron C. Taylor of United States Steel told the senators, "I have no remedy in mind." Jackson Reynolds of the First National Bank echoed his sentiments, adding "I do not believe anyone else has."

Weaknesses and Wages. Although historians continue to debate the causes of the Great Depression, most agree that several economic problems combined to make the Great Depression especially severe. First, although the 1920s were a period of prosperity for many, several sectors of the economy were weak, especially agriculture and the coal and textile industries. These weak sectors acted as a drag on the rest of the economy. The relatively impoverished condition of American farmers, who averaged 40 percent of urban laborers' income, meant that they could not afford to buy the consumer products — refrigerators, phonographs, and radios — that fueled the

boom of the 1920s. Indeed, less than 10 percent of American farms were electrified. Similarly, the average wages of the majority of workers were too low. In the mining industry, for example, although output per man rose 43 percent between 1920 and 1929, yearly earnings fell from $1,700 to $1,481. Although wages in other industries rose generally in the same period 11 percent, corporate profits rose 62 percent. By 1929 fifteen thousand families in the United States with incomes above $100,000 per year received as much income as 5 million to 6 million families of poorly paid workers; that same year the top 5 percent of income earners in America held 33.5 percent of the nation's total wealth. Such differential distribution of wealth had several consequences. It meant that the majority of Americans, like the farmers, could not afford to buy the consumer goods of the period, leading to large-scale overproduction. This was not immediately apparent, as the market was driven to artificial highs, supported by wealthy investors. The high stock prices resulted in easy credit so that consumers purchased goods they could not really afford; banks and security firms, moreover, lent speculators as much as half of the cost of stocks, rocketing share prices far above the real worth of companies. The 1929 crash was a function of this overvaluation. In 1926, for example, production of automobiles began to exceed the ability of consumers to purchase them, but easy credit and stock speculation combined to obscure this fact until 1929. After that investors realized the real worth of their stock and began a disastrous sell-off.

Mismanagement and Trade. The crash itself reflected widespread mismanagement of the economy. The Federal Reserve system failed to stem the rise of easy credit by raising the discount rate it charged to member banks. Banking and finance were virtually unregulated, and this led to unsound practices, such as pyramiding industries (utility magnate Samuel Insull held sixty-five chairmanships, eighty-five directorships, and seven presidencies of major corporations), banks lending money for security purchases, and fraudulent investment schemes. Mismanagement was also evident in the American response to problems of world trade. World War I had badly disrupted world trading patterns. European nations, stunned by their strategic vulnerability during the war, responded by raising trade barriers after the conflict, seeking economic self-sufficiency and wrecking traditional channels of trade. The United States did much the same, passing the highest tariff in modern American history in 1922. The tariff was disastrous in the context of the postwar international debt structure. After the war the United States emerged as the leading creditor in the world, the holder of substantial debt owed to it by its wartime allies. Britain owed the United States $4.2 billion; France, $3.4 billion; Italy, $1.6 billion; Belgium, $379 million; and Russia, $192 million. America's European allies had requested debt forgiveness after the war, arguing that full repayment of the debt would retard economic recovery. But American officials refused to forgive the debt, resulting in the Allies demanding war reparations from Germany, radically destabilizing the German economy, and, as predicted, retarding the general European recovery. Moreover, American trade dominance in Latin America, which the United States had seized during World War I, severely restricted a traditional market for European exports. And American trade barriers to European products meant that the Europeans could not trade their way out of debt with the United States. Accordingly, during the 1920s the United States was forced to make more loans — this time to Germany, so the Germans could pay reparations to the French, so the French could then repay their war debt to the Americans, at an interest rate double the original debt. Such a concentration of obligation in the United States naturally had an effect on Wall Street. As confidence in high return rates for American corporations and banks increased, more and more Europeans invested in American corporations and on the stock exchange, driving prices higher and increasing speculation. Gold, the medium of international transfers, concentrated in the United States, further exacerbating problems in international trade. The upshot was an international financial trade situation in the 1920s that defied economic common sense: the United States was deeply engaged in a pattern of international debt while refusing to open its markets to the type of trade necessary to repay those debts. Consequently the Europeans eventually defaulted on their obligations. In 1931 President Hoover placed a one-year moratorium on the repayment of war debts; in 1932 interallied debt and war reparations were repudiated altogether.

STAGNATIONISM AND TECHNOCRACY

Stagnationism and technocracy were two of the more popular schools of economic thought during the 1930s. Stagnationists such as economist Alvin Hansen of the University of Minnesota argued that the Depression was the result of capitalism reaching a full, mature stage. Stagnationists pointed to the closing of the frontier and a declining birth rate in the industrial world and argued that capitalism was done with, as Hansen put it, "the great era of growth and expansion." All the industries that could be built were built; all the rail that could be laid was laid; all the autos sold that could be sold. Mass unemployment was permanent, a consequence of mechanization. Along with the technocrats, the stagnationists believed that absent a sweeping technological innovation, capitalism had reached the limits of its growth and would now stagnate.

The technocrats were similar to the stagnationists in believing that capitalism had entered a "mature" phase; they were, however, less pessimistic about its future prospects. The technocrats believed a technological revolution was just around the corner and would spark a return of prosperity. The technocrats formally organized economists, engineers, and architects into a group called the Continental Committee on Technocracy. In 1933, under the supervision of Columbia University professor Walter Rautenstrauch, they produced what they termed the "Energy Survey of North America." The survey deployed some three thousand charts to prove that the Depression was a consequence of the mechanization of industry. After turn-of-the-century economist Thorstein Veblen, they advocated production for use, not profit; the replacement of politicians with engineers; the abolition of money (to be replaced by units of value they called ergs); the reduction of the workday to four hours; and lowering the retirement age to forty-five. Supposedly, such policies would promote efficiency and prosperity; how they were to be effected was unclear.

Both stagnationism and technocracy were something of intellectual fads, fading as the decade pressed on. Nonetheless, both movements contributed to the developing Keynesian philosophy of mainstream economists. Hansen himself eventually joined the Roosevelt administration and used modified stagnationist principles to press for countercyclical spending as a way of moving capitalism from its "mature" stage to its "advanced" stage.

Source: John A. Garraty, *The Great Depression* (New York: Harcourt Brace Jovanovich, 1986).

Solutions? Because so many business leaders perceived the Depression as part of a natural business cycle, they offered traditional solutions to the problem — solutions that only made the Depression worse. Particularly disastrous was the passage in 1930 of the Smoot-Hawley Tariff, the highest levy in American history. An attempt to shore up the failing agricultural sector, the tariff led to retaliation from Europe and Latin America, further clogging world trade and destabilizing balance of payments. Business leaders, including Bernard Baruch, recommended balancing budgets and belt-tightening, which only furthered the deflationary spiral. A 1930 tax cut failed to stimulate the private sector, while it undermined federal revenues. A 1931 tax increase to balance the federal budget hit the private sector hard. Voluntary business associations continued to be threatened by antitrust laws and were, in any event, insufficient to stem the corrosion of an increasingly brutal market: competitive pressures in the oil industry nearly destroyed the business. President Hoover actually increased antitrust prosecutions in the hope that competition would alleviate the Depression, an error in judgment that moved many businessmen to oppose his election in 1932. He furthermore refused to approve large-scale agricultural subsidies, instead exhorting farmers to curtail their production voluntarily, an impossible request given the market during the Depression. His intention to remain tied to the gold standard as the basis of international trade led to gold exports and made money expensive, offsetting deflationary gains, especially after Britain went off the gold standard in September 1931. International trade arrangements, massive federal expenditures, agricultural subsidies, and the cartelizing of industry were called for; but many businessmen resisted such innovations, wedded as they were to an older economic philosophy. President Hoover was flexible enough to begin to introduce such programs in late 1931, but he did so reluctantly, afraid of undermining the individual work ethic and the operations of the marketplace. His philosophical objections made little sense to millions suffering physical deprivation. In 1932 Hoover was voted out of office, making way for Franklin Roosevelt and his New Dealers, who would attack the Depression with a series of more distinctly innovative economic programs.

Sources:

Robert Heilbroner and Aaron Singer, *The Economic Transformation of America* (New York: Harcourt Brace Jovanovich, 1977);

William Keylor, *The Twentieth-Century World: An International History* (New York: Oxford University Press, 1984);

Joan Hoff Wilson, *Herbert Hoover: Forgotten Progressive* (Boston: Little, Brown, 1975).

THE FARM CRISIS

Demographic Shift. In 1920 the census showed that for the first time in history more Americans lived in urban centers than on farms. The Great Depression, however, sparked an exodus of farmers to the city, irre-

Wisconsin farmers, early 1930s, dumping milk in an attempt to drive up milk prices

versibly transforming the United States from an agricultural to an industrial society. On the farm the Depression was an unalloyed catastrophe made worse by drought. It drove millions to the city. Hundreds of thousands of midwesterners made the trek to California in search of agricultural work, ultimately ending up in the defense factories of World War II. The farm crisis was thus at the center of an enormous demographic shift in American life, one that permanently reshaped the character of the nation.

Falling Prices. The farm crisis did not begin with the Great Crash of 1929. Throughout the 1920s agriculture in America was subject to severe economic stress. During World War I prosperity had been the norm as farmers in America and other areas of the world expanded acreage to fill markets formerly supplied by European farmers. When the war ended and the Europeans returned to cultivation, a worldwide collapse in agricultural prices resulted. The collapse continued and was made worse by lack of international cooperation during the 1920s. Bumper crops in Canadian wheat at the end of the decade depressed world prices. The Soviet Union, determined to gain capital for industrial development through the sale of wheat, dumped grain on world markets, depressing prices and depressing their own ability to earn capital, to which they responded by exporting more wheat — even as their own citizenry began to starve for lack of staples. Australian politicians responded to the onset of depression by undertaking a "Grow More Wheat" campaign that made a bad situation worse. American farmers did much the same. Aided by easy credit during the 1920s, farmers increased acreage and made yields more efficient via increased mechanization

The appearance of Jack Morgan, head of the Morgan financial group, before the Senate Banking Committee became something of a public carnival. The spectacle of the nation's most powerful banker being grilled by bulldog New York prosecutor Ferdinand Pecora inspired a media frenzy. Senators had to request photographers to stop snapping flashbulbs and quit shuffling chairs so they could see and hear the witnesses. "We are having a circus," stammered Virginia senator Carter Glass, "and the only things lacking now are peanuts and colored lemonade."

The next day the circus literally arrived at the Senate. A Ringling Brothers press agent, Charles Leef, had overheard Glass's comment and brought to Capitol Hill a thirty-two-year-old midget named Lya Graf. As the hearing began, Leef took a seat beside Morgan and plopped the twenty-seven-inch-tall Graf on his lap. To the horror of Morgan's partners, Morgan struck up a conversation with the woman, thinking she was a child. Newspapermen from around the country snapped photos of the event, and the pictures became some of the most famous of the decade. Morgan was appalled by the incident, but Graf's shame was greater. Seeking to escape the endless jokes, she quit the circus and returned to her native Germany in 1935. The move was fatal. Prosecuted by the Nazis for her Jewish background, Graf died at Auschwitz during World War II.

Source: Ron Chernow, *The House of Morgan: An American Banking Dynasty and the Rise of Modern Finance* (New York: Simon & Schuster, 1990).

and the use of fertilizers. Both actions made the decline in prices worse and increased the debt burden of American farmers. By 1930 the mortgages on American farms amounted to $9.2 billion, up from $3.2 billion in 1910, and millions of farmers were tenants.

Foreclosures. The economic pressures on agriculture increased following the stock-market crash of 1929. Struggling banks began foreclosing on farms, and farmers attempted to meet their bills in the only way they knew how: by increasing acreage and yields, further driving down prices. By 1932 farm prices were only 40 percent of their already low 1929 levels. Wheat earned only 25 cents a bushel (down from $2.94 in 1920); oats brought 10 cents a bushel; sugar got 3 cents per pound; and cotton and wool garnered 5 cents a pound (down from 37 cents in 1920). By 1933 prices had sunk to 63 percent of their 1929 level. Fundamentally it became impossible for indebted farmers to earn enough to keep their farms. Farmers had to grow nine bushels of wheat to pay for a pair of shoes; in 1909, two bushels would have sufficed. The Smoot-Hawley Tariff of 1930 was supposed to offer farmers some protection, but agricultural surpluses were so huge that its impact was barely felt, and foreign retaliation dried up exports. President Hoover's Federal Farm Board was a similar failure. It purchased selected crops from farm cooperatives in order to drive up prices. The program had negligible results, losing approximately $345 million without achieving price stablization. The Hoover administration finally suggested that farmers voluntarily refrain from growing crops and thus drive up prices. Following the administration's advice, in some midwestern states farmers did declare "strikes" and curtailed production. Nothing protected such farmers from banks, under severe pressure themselves, from calling in loans and foreclosing on farms, and thus attempts at voluntary production limits failed. Although Hoover did loan some $64 million to farmers through his business-oriented Reconstruction Finance Corporation, it was not enough to prevent massive foreclosures. Farmers turned militant in their attempts to stop foreclosures, threatening to kill bank officers and police. Sedition and revolt were in the air. "Unless something is done for the American farmer," Farm Bureau Federation president Edward A. O'Neal told the Senate in January 1933, "we will have revolution in the countryside within less than twelve months."

Agricultural Adjustment Act. The Agricultural Adjustment Act of 1933 was an attempt to coerce reductions of agricultural products, thus driving up prices. Participation in the program was voluntary, but economic reality virtually dictated participation. The Roosevelt administration established the Agricultural Adjustment Administration (AAA) to oversee the reduction of crops and other goods. The AAA paid farmers to leave acreage unplowed and to raise fewer animals. The government also guaranteed participating farmers a minimum price for the goods they did raise, a price secured by taxing food processors and distributors. Finally, the Roosevelt administration established the Farm Credit Administration to protect farmers against creditors, offering generous loans to forestall foreclosure. Because the 1933 growing season had already begun by the time the AAA commenced operations, however, the government was forced to pay farmers to destroy their crops. Ten million acres of planted cotton were plowed under; 6 million baby pigs and 200,000 pregnant sows were destroyed. The spectacle of destroying food at a time when millions went hungry was to many almost surreal. Equally difficult was adjusting farmer's attitudes to the new subsidies. Raised to believe it was sinful to let productive ground lay fallow, many of them found it difficult to adjust to AAA directives. Nonetheless, AAA policy worked. By 1936, with 30 million acres out of cultivation, prices had recovered and farm income had doubled. The AAA had thus set a precedent for farm price supports that continues into the present.

An Oklahoma farm after a dust storm, mid 1930s

Unions. AAA policy did not work exactly as planned. Although the AAA had specifically set up rules to protect tenant farmers and sharecroppers, in the Democratic South it was difficult to enforce these rules, and as large agricultural owners took land out of cultivation, they often threw out the tenant farmers who worked the land. So frequent were the evictions that tenant farmers organized the Southern Tenant Farmers Union in 1934 and became increasingly militant about opposing farmland owners. Tensions between the two groups were often heightened by racial tensions, as many sharecroppers were blacks. Night riders and Klansmen enforced evictions, but the tenants resisted intimidation. Eastern Arkansas, the sugar-beet fields of Colorado, lettuce farms in Arizona, and the orange groves of California were the scenes of armed battles between tenant farmers, sharecroppers, migrant workers, and landowners. Such battles were documented in plays such as Erskine Caldwell's *Tobacco Road*, movies such as Pare Lorentz's *The Plow that Broke the Plains* (1937) and *The River* (1937), and John Steinbeck's novel *The Grapes of Wrath* (1939).

Dust Bowls. Compounding the misery of the Depression, a long drought in the middle of the 1930s brought hardship to millions. Farmers throughout the Midwest literally watched the fruits of their work dry up and blow

away. The farmlands became nicknamed "dust bowls" because of the winds busy drawing the topsoil away. The dust storms caused by the drought were so great that soil was deposited as far east as New York and the Atlantic Ocean. As calamitous as the drought was, however, it combined with the AAA to reduce drastically the number of farmers and farm acreage in the United States, thus driving up prices and facilitating recovery.

Farm Security Administration. Aware of the hardships imposed by AAA policies and the drought visited on farm families, in 1935 the government established an agency that would ultimately be called the Farm Security Administration (FSA). The FSA provided poor farmers with financial relief, health advice, and agricultural information. If it discovered farmers were cultivating substandard land, the FSA resettled them to new, more fertile land and taught them how to farm it scientifically. Of particular importance was instruction in contour plowing, which reduced soil erosion. Entire resettled communities, such as Arthurdale, West Virginia, were established to prove that government assistance and community interest could produce energetic, productive agriculture. The program succeeded, but at such a high price that its economic value was questionable. Ultimately Congress balked at financing so expensive a project and ordered a reduction in FSA programs in 1938. Six years later the project was killed altogether.

Cancellation and Continuance. In 1936 the entire AAA program was eliminated by the Supreme Court, which ruled in *United States* v. *Butler* that Congress had no constitutional right to regulate agriculture, and invalidated the taxes raised to pay for the AAA. Conservatives were heartened by the decision, but their joy was short-lived. The AAA was successful and popular enough that Congress re-created it in a form more acceptable to the Supreme Court in 1936 with the passage of the Soil Conservation and Domestic Allotment Act. To the original AAA programs of price supports, agricultural education, and debt relief were added a system of warehouses, which held agricultural products until a good price for them existed in the marketplace — an idea that had been prominent in the farm belt since the 1880s. Thus, by 1936 the farm crisis was fundamentally over, with the number of American farmers sharply reduced (less than a quarter of the population in 1939), prices for their goods substantially raised, and the model of farm/government cooperation firmly built — a model from which subsequent governments would construct their own farm support policies.

Sources:

Stuart Bruchey, *Enterprise: The Dynamic Economy of a Free People* (Cambridge, Mass.: Harvard University Press, 1990);

Robert Heilbroner and Aaron Singer, *The Economic Transformation of America* (New York: Harcourt Brace Jovanovich, 1977);

Charles P. Kindleberger, *The World in Depression, 1929–1939* (Berkeley: University of California Press, 1986);

Cabell Phillips, *From the Crash to the Blitz, 1929–1939* (New York: Macmillan, 1969).

HARLAN COUNTY AND COAL

"Bloody" Harlan County. The battle between coal miners and operators in Harlan County, Kentucky, in the 1930s lasted the entire decade and became extremely bloody and violent. The struggle ripped through the nation's conscience, drawing more national attention than any other labor conflict in the period. Ultimately, after many long years of strife, the federal government intervened to successfully open the county to unionism. The story of the Harlan Country strike, however, is one of defiance: of the operators forcefully resisting the trend toward unionism sweeping the nation and of the workers no longer willing to accept a coal company controlling their destiny.

Background. Harlan County sits just north of the Cumberland Gap near the intersection of Kentucky, Virginia, and Tennessee. Located in a narrow valley between the Black and Pine Mountains, the area remained uniquely isolated from the outside world. No railroad or highway was introduced until 1910, and the first automobile did not enter the county until 1928. Harlan County retained its seclusion, although the arrival of the railroad spurred the development of the area's coal industry. Coal soon became Harlan County's main industry, and just prior to the Great Depression the county had risen to become one of Kentucky's wealthiest.

Rise of Coal. Three main factors contributed to the rise of the coal industry in Harlan County. First, the high-quality coal in the region sold quickly. Second, the cost of shipping the coal was relatively inexpensive. Third, and perhaps most important, the absence of unions allowed the Harlan County mine operators to exploit the miners for maximum benefit. Several large corporations moved into the area because of these factors. Instead of buying coal from an outside company, corporate giants such as Detroit-Edison, U.S. Steel, and Ford opened mines in Harlan County. The companies were then able to produce the needed coal directly, thus reducing costs and meeting supply demands.

Company Rule. Harlan County's seclusion and lack of well-paying manufacturing jobs worked against its residents. The coal mines became the major source of income for area families. People could not afford to become union activists because the operators had too much power over them. The coal companies virtually controlled every aspect of their workers' lives. Coal miners lived in company-owned houses, shopped in company-owned stores, and even worshiped in company-built churches. Workers who tried to start unions faced the full wrath of the operators and were discharged, evicted, and blacklisted. Most workers were deterred from unionism when faced with the option of having a job without a union or organizing and never working in Harlan County again.

Antiunionism. Coal operators and miners both contributed to the antiunion spirit in Harlan County. The coal companies viewed unionism as a northern conspiracy to destroy the southern coal industry. They believed that the northern coal operators used the federal government and the United Mine Workers (UMW) to force the southern companies into having standardized wages and hours. Higher wages and periodical strikes, imposed by the UMW, would cause southern companies to lose contracts to northern competitors. Operators used the "North versus South" imagery continually to keep the miners from organizing. The 1920s also saw Harlan miners prospering. The thinking of the typical miner helped foster antiunionism. Many were first-generation industrial workers and found the activity and fast pace of the coal camp more exciting than the isolated mountain cabin left behind. Trading impoverished hillside farming for mining greatly increased one's wealth. Until the Great Depression, Harlan County miners profited from the rich coal mines in the region and from lack of unionism.

Misery and Depression. Deteriorating work conditions, low wages, and wholesale unemployment, all resulting from the Great Depression, opened the eyes of the coal miners to unionism. The workers began to see that the hardships following from the Depression were beyond the control of themselves or the paternalistic coal companies. When low wages, irregular employment, and unemployment brought poverty, hunger, and disease to Harlan County, coal workers finally realized that they needed help. As a result of falling wages and severe unemployment, 231 children died of malnutrition in Harlan County from 1929 to 1931. If not for a child-feeding program launched in the fall of 1931 the number would have been much higher. One mine owner sadly remarked, "The miners' families are still able to eat and keep warm, but I don't pretend that they are living as they ought to live." Other miners felt despair because they were unable to feed their families. The coal companies aggravated the harsh conditions faced by the miners by imposing a 10 percent wage reduction on them in early 1931. Harlan miners decided to unite against the operators and felt that they "might just as well die fighting as die of starvation." The resulting battle began a ten-year struggle for unionization.

Fighting Authoritarianism. The battle for unionization in the 1930s was an attempt to improve working conditions and a revolt against the arbitrary economic, political, and social power of the operators. The local mine owners increased their influence over the lives of workers by virtually owning every sheriff, politician, and judge in Harlan County. Every law enforcement agent would then fight against any attempt at unionizing. Sheriff John Henry Blair reported that during the strikes of 1931–1932, "I did all in my power to aid the coal operators." The operators felt that they acted as benevolent patriarchs caring for the workers. As long as miners adhered to the company's moral code that prohibited prostitution, theft, drunkenness, and unionism, they provided a reasonable amount of social security. Unionism gave miners their only chance to fight the authoritarian control of the operators. Two-thirds of the county's labor force mined coal, and the companies employed or controlled most lawyers, ministers, teachers, and law-enforcement officials; thus, the struggle became one of "us" versus "them." Harlan County's violent heritage ensured that the battle for unionism would be bloody. During the 1920s Harlan's homicide rate was the highest in the United States.

Intimidation. The United Mine Workers used the 1931 wage reduction as a springboard for organizing in Harlan County. The operators fought back, however, and used spies to ferret out union sympathizers. Hundreds of men were fired and then evicted for wanting to join the UMW. Most of the displaced workers moved to Evarts, one of the three noncompany towns in Harlan County, and it soon became a center of union agitation. William B. Jones, the secretary of the local union, emerged as the leader of the organizing movement. Hungry strikers, fired by the operators, began raiding company-owned stores to feed their families. Miners were also suffering at the hands of mine guards and deputies who were employed by the operators to intimidate the workers. Rumors circulated alleging that company guards abused

miners' wives and children and openly displayed firearms to cower any opposition.

The Battle of Evarts. Tension escalated between miners and guards, and by March 1931 gunfire became commonplace. Both sides were armed and willing to use their weapons in any dispute. Ambushes, snipers, explosions, and robberies rocked Harlan County, and a *Knoxville News-Sentinel* headline warned, "Flare-Up in Harlan Area Is Expected." Sheriff Blair, responding to a reporter's questions regarding the use of guns, said, "Hell, yes, I've issued orders to shoot to kill." The fight between miners and deputies came to a climax on 4 May when the "Battle of Evarts" broke out. A group of ten mining officials were ambushed by seventy-five union sympathizers, who exchanged gunfire for more than half an hour, resulting in several deaths and a state of chaos in Harlan County. For two days there was no law and order in the region. Public schools closed, and many families fled the area. Gov. Flem Sampson called in the National Guard to restore order to the county. The Battle of Evarts was produced by hunger, the abuses of the private deputies, the operators' unrelenting opposition to unions, and the spontaneous nature of the strike. The battle, however, galvanized the resolve of the operators, and the military occupation undermined the strikers' resolve. UMW officials realized the use of National Guard troops would effectively end the strike without the miners' grievances being remedied. Sheriff Blair and his cronies continued to harass union sympathizers and, in fact, rounded up and jailed all the major union leaders on trumped-up charges relating to the Battle of Evarts. Many union miners who were not permanently blacklisted were forced to return to work. Those who refused to relinquish their union ties were left either to starve or flee Harlan County.

Government Intervention. The historic passage of the National Industrial Recovery Act in 1933 and the Wagner Act of 1935 placed the authority of the federal government behind the efforts to unionize. The notable exception to the movement remained Harlan County. Harlan posed a serious threat because as long as it held out against collective bargaining its competitors in Virginia, Tennessee, eastern Kentucky, and Alabama threatened to terminate their union contracts. Thus, the UMW had to keep up its organizing efforts in Harlan so its entire southern region would not evaporate. At the time of the Wagner Act, however, the miners had made no real strides toward organizing. Eventually, concerted pressure by the Roosevelt administration and the UMW combined in 1937 and 1938 to open Harlan to unionism. New Deal legislation resulted in the abolition of the private deputy system and gave union organizers the freedom to enter the county. Violence in labor disputes gradually gave way to mediation and negotiation. The New Deal did not transfer power from the operator to the worker in the 1930s, but it did create a new balance of power that greatly benefited the miner.

Final Battle. The turbulent decade closed just as it had opened, with a strike. It began as part of the UMW's national strike to obtain a union shop. In Harlan a fifteen-week strike ensued that pitted the operators' association against the county's nine thousand union miners, supported by the federal government, the UMW, and the nation's public and editorial opinion. When the strike began on 3 April 1939, every county mine closed in Harlan County for the first time in history. Union officials, realizing that a return to the violence of the 1931 strike would destroy their cause, urged members not to resort to violence, even after union zealots forcibly baptized nine nonunion miners "in the name of the father, the son, and John L. Lewis." By the strike's seventh week all national operators had signed a union-shop contract except Harlan's. The governor intervened and sent the National Guard to reopen the mines. Remarkably, the union miners showed great restraint, and little violence occurred until a 12 July picket of five mines. National Guardsmen opened fire on unarmed miners in picket lines, and two men were killed and three others seriously wounded. The event was dubbed the "Battle of Stanfill," and the violence was blamed on the Harlan operators who refused to conform to the interests of national coal companies.

Balance of Power. Intervention on the part of the Roosevelt administration and Secretary of Labor Frances Perkins resulted in a settlement being reached on 19 July, the strike's 109th day. The key issue was union security, which Harlan officials conceded. Operators recognized the UMW as sole bargaining agent for all employees, and strikers were immediately rehired. The agreement covered forty-eight hundred workers at twenty-four mines. The 1939 agreement, aided by the wartime coal boom, ended the ten-year struggle in Harlan County and brought a new balance of power in the county.

Success. Without government intervention, Harlan probably could not have been organized. A decade of violence produced several deaths and countless injuries. Unionism, however, brought significant economic and social gains to miners. "Bloody" Harlan County lived through the decade of strife and emerged a better place for miners and their families.

Source:
John W. Hevener, *Which Side Are You On? The Harlan County Coal Miners, 1931–1939* (Urbana: University of Illinois Press, 1978).

A HOLIDAY FOR THE BANKS

The Banker and His Image. Before the Depression, banks and bankers held an interesting place in the American imagination. On one hand, bankers had been among the most esteemed figures in the United States, especially during the boom of the 1920s. For many, bankers were synonymous with sobriety, thrift, and hardheaded realism. Banking was the institution that could lead right-thinking young men to wealth and a place among the

Nearly $3 million worth of scrip issued by the city of Detroit in 1933

elite. On the other hand, the populist tradition in America had long viewed banking as a sophisticated form of loan-sharking. To such people, investment was akin to gambling; interest similar to usury. Enough people remained suspicious of banks that hundreds of thousands kept their savings in tins beneath their mattresses or buried in backyards rather than deposited in banks. J. P. Morgan and Company, in New York, represented both images. To partisans it was responsible and powerful; to antagonists it was a secret government, a cabal defrauding the public of its wealth. During the Depression the suspicions of Morgan's antagonists moved to the fore, banking fell into disrepute, and by the time of Roosevelt's inauguration in 1933 the entire financial structure of the United States was in danger of collapse.

Bank Runs. Nothing symbolized the lack of public confidence in banking during the Depression more than the bank runs. Bank runs were spurred by fears that banks would go bankrupt, taking the savings of depositors with them. The mere hint of a bank closing often was enough to send depositors scrambling to withdraw their money, and banks, which did not keep enough cash on hand to cover all of their deposits, often then collapsed. Bank runs also reflected unsound banking practices. During the 1920s many banks had not acted in a responsible and hardheaded fashion. Some had lent money for dubious investments; others extended dangerously large credit to financial speculators. When the stock market crashed, many banks saw their assets evaporate; creditors liquidated what remained; depositors were left with nothing. Because few companies in the 1920s provided pensions for workers, many used the banks as a place to deposit a lifetime's worth of earnings in anticipation of retirement.

When the banks went under, many of these people, old and unable to work, lost everything. More than fourteen hundred banks collapsed in 1932, taking with them $725 million in deposits. The public scrutinized the remaining banks; at the first sign of trouble, a run on the banks was on, and the banks usually ended up closing, many permanently.

Panic. By the time of Franklin Roosevelt's inauguration in March 1933, banking in the United States was in serious jeopardy. In Detroit the banks were so badly over-extended that Michigan governor William A. Comstock closed all the banks temporarily to give the bankers time to set their affairs in order. The "bank holiday" caught the public by surprise and left everyone with the problem of how to extend the money in their pockets for the duration of the eight-day holiday. They were not alone. In the week that followed, a dozen other states followed Michigan's lead and closed the banks. Rather than reassure people, the bank holidays only increased the panic of the public. Bank runs and closings continued to sweep the country. In the week prior to Roosevelt's inauguration, a quarter of a billion dollars in gold vanished from the nation's vaults. The Department of the Treasury estimated that the nation's banks had a mere $7.37 billion in cash reserves against some $40.5 billion of liabilities in deposits. Treasury experts feared that the nation's banks were coming to a point where they might not survive another business day. Experts urged a nationwide bank holiday and sweeping measures to shore up the banks. President Hoover refused to act, believing that the bank problem was a function of Roosevelt's failure to back his own "sound money" policies. Roosevelt, however, had his own plans.

The Bank Holiday. Roosevelt begged off the inaugural's evening celebrations, meeting with top aides and members of Hoover's Treasury Department throughout the night of Saturday, 4 March, and all the next day. By the dawn of the next business day, Monday, 6 March, Roosevelt had ordered a nationwide bank holiday (violations were punishable by a fine of $10,000 or ten years' imprisonment); soon afterward he embargoed all shipments of gold or silver, called Congress into an emergency session to pass sweeping bank legislation, and ordered leading bankers to Washington to help him deal with the crisis. Rather than provoke public hysteria, as some feared, Roosevelt's actions bolstered public confidence in the banking system. The nation rallied to extend the necessary credit to weather the nine-day holiday. Grocers sold goods on promises, cities paid workers in scrip, movie houses reverted to the barter system. On 9 March Congress passed, virtually unseen, Roosevelt's banking legislation, including a law that made gold hoarding illegal. The next day, reserve banks throughout the United States were filled with people returning their stash of gold. By Saturday night $300 million in gold had been returned, and the Treasury added $750 million in new currency to the nation's vaults. Sunday evening Roo-

sevelt held his first "fireside chat" radio address, designed to bolster the public's confidence in the banks. It worked. When selected banks opened Monday, 13 March, deposits exceeded withdrawals. By the end of the week 75 percent of the banks in the United States were back in business, and the crisis was averted. By the end of the month $1.25 billion in deposits had been made to banks. Two thousand insolvent banks were liquidated or consolidated to more-sound banks. Bank failures fell to less than fifty per year for the remainder of the decade. "Capitalism," New Dealer Raymond Moley later wrote, "was saved in eight days."

Banksters. While the Roosevelt administration was busy resuscitating public confidence in the banks, Congress was punishing bankers for old violations of the public trust. In 1933 and 1934 sensational hearings were held that detailed larceny and fraud on the part of many bankers and other members of the business community, resulting in the introduction of the term *bankster* to the vocabulary. The Senate Banking and Currency Committee, led by New York jurist Ferdinand Pecora, revealed that the brokerage house of Lee, Higginson, and Company had defrauded the public of $100 million; that National City Bank head Charles E. Mitchell, with a salary of $1.2 million, paid no income tax and had issued $25 million in Peruvian bonds he knew to be worthless; that former secretary of the treasury Andrew Mellon and banker J. P. Morgan had also managed to avoid taxes; that twenty Morgan partners had paid no taxes in 1931 and 1932. The public was introduced to such Wall Street tactics as selling short, pooling agreements, influence peddling, insider trading, and the wash sale, techniques by which traders artificially inflated the worth of their stock or gained financial advantage over others. National City Bank, for example, took bad loans, repackaged them as bonds, and sold them to unwary investors. Although such actions were technically legal, many viewed such bankers as unethical and immoral, and the public reputation of bankers and financial businessmen fell to a new low. "You see, there is a lot of things these old boys have done that are within the law," quipped Will Rogers, "but it's so near the edge you couldn't slip a razor blade between their acts and a prosecution."

New Rules. The Pecora investigations did much to invalidate the political clout of big business and opened the way politically for sweeping changes in the nation's financial structure. Against the objections of many orthodox bankers, Congress established the Federal Deposit Insurance Corporation (FDIC) to insure small depositors against the loss of their savings if a bank went under. The government promised to cover deposits up to twenty-five hundred dollars (later raised to five thousand dollars), an act that did much to bolster confidence in banks. The government also required bankers to separate commercial and investment banking and, in order to monitor investments, created the Securities and Exchange Commission (SEC). The SEC, along with the passage of the Public Utility Holding Company Act, prohibited the types of investor fraud that had been endemic in the 1920s, requiring full disclosure of the financial status of certain investments. The J. P. Morgan Company, once the nation's most powerful financial firm, was forced by banking reform to choose between commercial or investment banking; it chose commercial banking. Other established firms, such as Kuhn, Loeb; Goldman, Sachs; and Lehman Brothers, opted for investing. Each choice meant an end to the undivided influence such firms had over the economy and politics. Congressional acts passed in 1935, which concentrated the power of the Federal Reserve in Washington, D.C., also brought the bankers to heel and forced them to submit to political supervision. A shift in public esteem was complete: where once the banker had been the model of public trust and personal rectitude, now the federal authority assumed this role. Roosevelt, naturally enough, expressed the shift in a message to Congress in 1933, in which he reflected on the mix of responsiblity and ambition that had once been the credo of the banker: "What we seek is a return to a clearer understanding of the ancient truth that those who manage banks, corporations and other agencies handling or using other people's money are trustees acting for others."

Sources:

Ron Chernow, *The House of Morgan: An American Banking Dynasty and the Rise of Modern Finance* (New York: Simon & Schuster, 1990);

Cabell Phillips, *From the Crash to the Blitz: 1929–1939* (New York: Macmillan, 1969).

"HOOVERED"

In retrospect President Herbert Hoover's attempts to deal with the Depression were relatively innovative and well intended. Some of his ideas, for instance the Reconstruction Finance Corporation, continued to become part of Roosevelt's New Deal program. Hoover was also personally moved by the suffering of people during the Depression. But Hoover's political style was fixed to an older age, one that saw personal expressions of sympathy as irresponsible. "No president," he told an adviser, "must ever admit he has been wrong." By 1932 Hoover's apparent indifference to the plight of the common man and his unwillingness to develop sweeping programs to deal with the emergency made him the target of bitter mockery by the public. They developed a lexicon of "Hooverisms" that convey something of the misery of the period:

* Hoovervilles: shantytowns of scrap metal and cardboard that sprung up in every major city during the Depression.

* Hoovercarts: automobiles drawn by horses or mules because their owners could not afford gasoline.

* Hooverflags: empty pants pockets turned inside out.

Source: Joan Hoff Wilson, *Herbert Hoover: Forgotten Progressive* (Boston: Little, Brown, 1975).

THE NEW DEAL AND ITS CRITICS

An Evolutionary Force. The New Deal was one of the most powerful economic forces of the twentieth century, incubating economic philosophies and techniques of financial management that dominated American business life from 1945 to 1980. It expressed a shift from infrastructure manufacturing to consumer production; it ushered in large-scale federal oversight of the economy; it forced the development of bureaucratic procedures in business administration; it revolutionized public finance; it pioneered a mixed economy; it erected the welfare state. A combination of businessmen, economists, politicians, and labor leaders managed these transformations, synthesizing often-disparate approaches to the economy. They were often opposed by other businessmen and politicians far more unified in their economic outlook. For all their criticism, however, they could not derail the New Deal. It represented an evolutionary step in modern capitalism that avoided the political dangers attending contemporary alternatives, such as fascist corporatism and Soviet collectivism.

The System of '96. The New Deal's immediate predecessor as a national economic philosophy — and the

President and Mrs. Roosevelt with A. E. Morgan, director of the Tennessee Valley Authority

source of most of the objections to the New Deal — was what businessmen and politicians called "the system of '96." Originally articulated during the presidential election of 1896 by Republican Party leader Mark Hanna, the system of '96 was derived from the philosophy of a nineteenth-century British thinker, Herbert Spencer. Spencer's "social Darwinism" argued that life is an incessant struggle for survival, pitting individuals against each other. The economy reflects this struggle, with wealth and power going to those individuals born "fit" — cunning, disciplined, intelligent enough to prevail in the fight. Such fit individuals were rare, but society progressed by recognizing them and orienting the bulk of resources toward them, as they were best capable of enlightened use of such resources. Partisans of the system of '96 sometimes argued for a laissez-faire economy — a French term meaning an economy that regulated its own conduct, without interference from government and politicians. What the system of '96 meant by laissez-faire, however, was not divorcing government and economy but using government to advance the fortunes of those the economy had selected as fit. The businessmen of the time enjoyed generous tax benefits, high protective tariffs, and grants of land and natural resources. By 1900, 1 percent of the nation's population controlled 88 percent of the nation's wealth. Adherents of the system of '96 felt this was to the good: in Mark Hanna's famous formulation, businessmen and the wealthy would exploit natural resources, and the benefits of their skill would "trickle down" to the less capable. Society would advance by rewarding those most fit: responsible businessmen who had proved themselves in the competition of life.

Progressives. Businessmen were opposed in 1896 by economists and politicians who would later come to be known as progressives. Progressives laid much of the foundation of the New Deal. They attacked both the philosophy and the practice of the system of '96. Sociologist Lester Frank Ward and economist Richard T. Ely repudiated social Darwinism, noting that it was human cooperation — not competition — that allowed civilization to raise itself above the law of the jungle. Economist Thorstein Veblen rejected the notion that businessmen advanced social progress. To him, the opposite was true. Those who advanced society were inventors and engineers who developed new technologies and exploited new resources for the benefit of all. Businessmen and middlemen interposed themselves between the engineer and the public, exploiting invention for personal gain. The only talent businessmen evidence, to Veblen, is the ability to exploit the genius of engineers and inventors, to hoard resources for themselves. Veblen argued that inevitably capitalism became monopolistic. (In his day the Standard Oil Company controlled nearly all the nation's oil production and distribution.) Once a businessman held a monopoly on a particular resource, he would raise its price, violating the law of the market and making expensive and exclusive what in the hands of the engineer was a cheap, usable commodity. The solution to this problem was to abolish the power of the businessman and have engineers and scientists develop natural resources directly for the public good. Another critic of monopoly and the system of '96 was jurist Louis Brandeis. His 1914 book *Other People's Money — And How The Bankers Use It* also attacked businessmen Brandeis felt were hoarding resources that belonged to the public.

Alfred E. Smith addressing the American Liberty League dinner at the Mayflower Hotel, Washington, D.C., on 25 January 1936

Brandeis argued that government should act to break up monopolies and keep business small and localized — where it could be more responsive to public needs. He also favored using the political power of big government to counterbalance the economic power of big business.

The American System. Progressives like Brandeis were successful in breaking up the largest monopolies, such as Standard Oil, and in developing the beginnings of government regulation of business, via legislation such as the Pure Food and Drug Act (1906), the Clayton Antitrust Act (1914), and the establishment of the Federal Reserve banking system (1913). World War I, however, returned the economy to the system of '96. Government put itself at the service of big business: federal funds underwrote factory modernization, created a merchant marine that was turned over to private hands after the war, insured American investment abroad, and suspended antitrust laws for American firms operating overseas. The system of '96 became what Secretary of Commerce Herbert Hoover called "the American System" — a businessman's government that would unleash the power of capitalism for the benefit of all. It fell 24 October 1929. Hoover and partisans of the American System believed it would right itself; they balanced their budgets and waited for market forces to return prosperity. But the market was locked in a disastrous deflationary spiral. Eventually political necessity dictated that Hoover act. When he did, it was in keeping with the philosophy of the American System: he advised business leaders in the hope they would act on his advice. Less than a month after the stock-market crash, he met with leading businessmen including Henry Ford, Pierre du Pont, and Julius Rosenwald to convince them, for humanitarian reasons, to maintain their workforce. He held similar conferences throughout the Depression, seeking voluntary compliance with his economic recovery program. The conferences failed, despite the efforts of businessmen such as Ford to comply. Workers were laid off; factories shut down; strikes erupted. Hoover tried more-assertive actions: incremental increases to public works projects; the creation of a Federal Farm Board to try to raise agricultural prices; the construction of a Home Loan banking system to cover home mortgages. The Reconstruction Finance Corporation, his most original innovation, made government loans to responsible businessmen and insisted that outlays be recoupable. Direct relief to the general public was out of the question, although Hoover did increase loans to state governments for relief. Hoover felt the public would only squander the money, that it would lead to a breakdown in the "sense of responsiblity of individual generosity," just as he felt public works expenditures would dry up capital for investment — axiomatic positions for the economically orthodox. Hoover, more or less, hewed to the straight and narrow; recovery, however, did not come.

The Brain Trust. Roosevelt proved far more flexible than Hoover in his philosophical approaches to the economic emergency. Roosevelt assembled a team of economists, scholars, and businessmen to help him sift through the various approaches to resolving the Depression. The nucleus of this so-called Brain Trust were three Columbia University professors: Raymond Moley, a progressive who believed in government regulation of business; Rexford Guy Tugwell, an economist and expert on agriculture; and Adolf A. Berle, a thirty-eight-year-old corporate lawyer (and registered Republican). Supplementing the work of these three was input from other figures soon to take places in the New Deal bureaucracy: former cavalry officer and businessman Hugh Johnson, agricultural businessman Henry Wallace, industrialist William H. Woodin, Chicago lawyer Harold L. Ickes, social worker Frances Perkins, Arizona politician Lewis Douglas, social worker Harry Hopkins, and corporation lawyer Jerome Frank.

Planning. The New Deal also relied on support from leading investment firms, commercial banks, and industries that in many cases would contribute to the leadership of the Democratic Party for the next forty years: Dillion, Read; Brown Brothers Harriman; Goldman, Sachs; Lehman Brothers; the Bank of America; First National Bank of Chicago; Chase National Bank; Standard Oil of New Jersey; General Electric; IBM; Filene's; Mead Paper; Reynolds Tobacco; American Tobacco; and Coca-Cola. What these banks and companies had in common with the Brain Trust was the belief that capitalism had evolved from its entrepreneurial and manufacturing base to a bureaucratic and consumerist mode. They felt the marketplace needed to be regulated and planned; that international trade should be on a tariff-free basis; that the wages of workers should be sufficient to drive nascent consumer industries. Often these businessmen were from ethnic backgrounds, and in the WASP-dominated market of the 1920s they were consistently slighted — especially on Wall Street. The New Deal was their vehicle of revenge and ascendancy; they succeeded, for example, in using it to split up the Anglophile, Republican powerhouse bank of J. P. Morgan and Company. But they were also aware of the damage an unregulated, uncontrolled market could wreak on business — the Rockefeller interests, for example, suffered from ruthless price competition and an oil glut during the decade — and pressed for price supports and the creation of business cartels. Uncontrolled overproduction had shattered investor confidence in 1929, and unregulated market pressure continued to freeze the movement of capital. The unregulated market of the 1920s led businessmen to seize gains in production for capital, rather than labor, and that seizure ultimately led to overproduction. The Brain Trust and the businesses that supported the Democratic Party felt the time had come for a planned, organized economy.

Reform. Perhaps the greatest innovation of the New Deal was to compartmentalize the problems of the Depression and deal with them on a case-by-case basis, rather than trying to resolve them through use of one sweeping philosophy, as had Hoover. Often this led to programs that contradicted one another, and often it made it difficult to define the New Deal's aims and purposes. Roosevelt sometimes seemed at sea, deploying several different economic programs because he was unable to choose among them. Consistently, however, he tried to reform corporate capitalism without abandoning it wholesale, as had Soviet Russia, or without shifting it into an authoritarian mode, as had Nazi Germany. This was no easy task, as partisans of the American System saw any deviation from their fundamental philosophy as fraught with error; for them, anything less than economic orthodoxy was revolutionary. "There are some principles that cannot be compromised," Herbert Hoover told the 1936 Republican National Convention. "Either we shall have a society based on ordered liberty and the initiative of the individual, or we shall have a planned society that means dictation [sic] no matter what you call it or who does it. There is no halfway ground." Such critics alternated between accusing the New Deal of being communistic and accusing it of being fascistic. The New Deal was vulnerable to attacks from the orthodox precisely because it lacked such ideological consistency. On the whole, however, its ad hoc programs effectively met the needs of the emergency, and by the end of the decade the New Deal had coalesced into a more coherent program.

Cartels and Regulation. To correct what they saw as a lack of economic regulation and federal oversight, from 1933 to 1935 the New Dealers inaugurated a series of reforms of the banking and financial industries. The reforms were designed to systematize investing and banking, prevent fraud, and assure investor confidence. The New Dealers hoped these reforms would spark an investment rally, and there was a small rally, but financial regulation was not enough to reassure the market. Competition was far too fierce; returns on investment far too slim. Accordingly, the government developed the National Recovery Administration (NRA), an agency built upon the model of industrial planning pioneered during World War I. The NRA represented in many ways a break with the Brandeis style of progressivism. It permitted business, in essence, to divide markets and form large productive cartels, thwarting competition, ending surpluses, and assuring returns on investments. To prevent the types of monopolistic abuses that had troubled Brandeis and Veblen, the NRA had the power to establish prices, allocate resources, and set wages. After seemingly endless haggling with the industries, the NRA established more than five hundred codes of business conduct.

Problems. Other New Deal agencies, such as the Tennessee Valley Authority (TVA) and the Rural Electrification Administration (REA) helped the NRA by establishing government-run industries to set codes and to gauge whether the productive costs reported by business were accurate or not. The TVA and REA were thus fundamentally programs that might have been envisioned by Veblen: one where engineers determined the fairest and most efficient cost for a resource and civil servants forced businessmen to hew to this standard. The TVA and REA, however, were concerned primarily with the production of electricity; for most industries, the government had no guide to the fair cost of manufacturing (and hence fair price to consumers) save that provided by industry itself. There were other problems. Small businessmen complained they were being "coded out" of competition. Many repudiated the program and announced a return to "free enterprise." Price increases granted for hardship cases in one industry were then demanded by other industries. The codes discouraged the entry of newer and more-aggressive firms into the marketplace. The codes raised prices and reduced the broader money supply. Provisions for enforcing the code were lax, and many NRA administrators refused to use them, believing they would not survive a court challenge. They were right. On 27 May 1935 the Supreme Court found the NRA unconstitutional, arguing that Roosevelt had exceeded his authority in establishing the codes. For the most part everyone, including Roosevelt, was glad to see the NRA go. It had established important precedents: a forty-hour workweek, a minimum wage, the abolition of child labor, and the beginnings of a systematized textile and oil industry. But it had not sparked a significant recovery.

Wages. The most important provision of the NRA was its codes regarding wages and rules concerning labor.

Believing that a primary cause of the Depression was the low wages of workers, the New Dealers sought to raise wages, limit hours, and improve working conditions. The New Dealers believed that high wages would be used to purchase consumer goods, sparking increased production by industry, and setting the economy on the road to recovery. It was, in a sense, the exact opposite of the "trickle-down" philosophy of the system of '96 — a kind of "trickle-up" theory. As Roosevelt explained it when he signed the National Industrial Recovery Act (the congressional measure that brought the NRA into being):

> The law I have just signed was passed to put people back to work — to let them buy more of the products of farms and factories and start our business going at a living rate again.
>
> In my inaugural I laid down the simple proposition that nobody is going to starve in this country. It seems to me to be equally plain that no business which depends for existence on paying less than a living wage to its workers has any right to continue in this country. . . .
>
> Throughout industry, the change from starvation wages and starvation employment to living wages and sustained employment can, in large part, be made by an industrial covenant to which all employers shall subscribe. It is greatly to their interest to do this because decent living standards widely spread among our 125 million people eventually means the opening up to industry of the richest market the world has ever seen. . . .
>
> I am fully aware that wage increases will eventually raise costs. But I ask that management give first consideration to the improvement of operating figures and to the greatly increased sales to be expected from the rising purchasing power of the public. This is sound economics and good business. The aim of this whole effort is to restore our rich domestic market by raising its vast consuming capacity.

Collective Bargaining. The New Dealers tried to raise wages through Title 7(a) of the National Industrial Recovery Act. Title 7(a) gave labor unions the legal right to bargain collectively, and the Roosevelt administration usually backed labor in its disputes with management. When the NRA was struck down by the Supreme Court, Congress passed the Wagner Act, which continued the right to bargain collectively, authorized the Fair Labor Standards Act, which continued the forty-hour workweek and prohibited child labor, and established the National Labor Relations Board to mediate industrial disputes. When labor unions added the clout of the sit-down strike to government assistance, they secured for themselves living wages and purchasing power.

Other Measures. The Roosevelt administration buttressed increased wages by more equitably distributing wealth in America. Welfare-state programs such as Social Security and unemployment compensation were, in effect, transfers in wealth from employers to employees, although programs such as these were not nearly as radical in the United States as they were in Europe, and many of the benefits of such transfers were offset by indirect taxes. Devaluation of the dollar in 1934 and reform of the Federal Reserve System increased the money supply and eased credit. Finally, the New Dealers shifted the tax burden to the wealthiest Americans, increasing the purchasing power of average citizens. While Roosevelt opponents, such as Louisiana politician Huey Long, suggested a confiscatory 100 percent tax on millionaires, Roosevelt settled for steep inheritance and luxury taxes. The Revenue Acts of 1937 clamped down on tax loopholes for businesses and levied a new tax on undistributed corporate profits. Afraid of war profiteering during World War II, the Roosevelt administration restructured the tax code in 1942 to provide for a 91 percent tax on the highest incomes — a progressive system that, although modified, remained in place until 1964. The increased power of labor unions, welfare programs, and progressive taxation combined to increase vastly the spending power of average Americans, but the effects of such policies would not really be apparent until after World War II.

Deficit Financing. The most radical economic feature of the New Deal took the longest to arrive. In 1929 the federal government operated with a budget surplus of $734 million. By 1932 the government operated with a deficit of $2.7 billion, due to increased outlays and a nearly 50 percent decline in tax receipts. During the 1932 election Roosevelt had promised to balance the budget after the election, a position he shared with his opponent. It was a bipartisan article of economic faith that governments, like households and businesses, had to operate in the black. Originally the New Deal was committed to this end. In May 1933, for example, the Roosevelt administration disbursed $500 million in unemployment relief — precisely the amount the government had saved by cutting federal salaries and reducing payments to veterans with the passage of the Economy Act. In 1936 Congress had to override a Roosevelt veto to pass a veterans' bonus. Like Hoover before him, FDR feared it would badly destabilize the federal budget. Consistently the New Dealers distinguished between "general" outlays — those federal expenditures that predated the Depression — and "emergency" outlays that would be eliminated with recovery. In 1932 very few economists believed that persistent government deficits would lead to anything but calamity. Nearly all economists felt that if government borrowed the savings of the public for its operations, banks and businesses would be "crowded out" — unable to draw on public savings for industrial improvements and expansion. The New Dealers believed that if they kept the deficit down, restructured American finance, and cartelized industry, banks and private loaners would feel confident enough in the economy that they would resume investments. Yet the Roosevelt administration was so economically heterodox, and the international situation so unstable, that large-scale investment failed to take place.

Public Works. The New Dealers thus took the next logical step: they themselves borrowed money from the public to invest in direct relief, public works, and infrastructure development. The New Dealers hoped that projects such as the Public Works Administration, the Works Progress Administration, the Civil Works Administration, the Tennessee Valley Authority, the Civilian Conservation Corps, and the National Youth Administration would hire enough of the unemployed to build bridges, schools, and highways that it would "prime the pump" of broad consumer spending, leading to increased demand for consumer products and setting manufacturing on the road to recovery. Once the economy had recovered, tax revenues from prosperity would enable the government to repay its debts. Such was the New Deal theory behind deficit spending. By 1936 Roosevelt was spending $4.8 billion, an unprecedented sum during a time when total gross national product was about $100 billion. Yet, on the face of it, the expenditures did prime the pump of private sector recovery. Consumer spending grew from $46 billion in 1933 to $67 billion in 1937. Business investment rose from a low of $0.9 billion in 1932 to $11 billion in 1937. Gross national product returned to the levels it held in 1929; unemployment was reduced to 7.7 million. Thus, in 1937, the New Dealers attempted to balance the budget, cutting back its work programs. The action sent the whole economy south, and Roosevelt scrambled to resume deficit spending. The Depression was back.

Selling Capitalism. The New Deal's critics seized on the recession of 1937–1938 with glee, and in 1938 the New Deal was defeated at the polls, the end of a long period of political ostracism for partisans of the American System. Hoover's relative inactivity during the early Depression had discredited much of the prestige that businessmen and orthodox economic thinkers had in the mind of the public. The 1934 Pecora and Nye committee investigations of big business focused public blame for the Depression on orthodox economic thinkers and Republican businesses, such as J. P. Morgan and Company. These businessmen responded by mounting an unprecedented media campaign designed to rehabilitate the system of '96 and defeat the New Deal. By the middle of the decade such businessmen were preoccupied with rebuilding favorable public opinion toward their own version of capitalism. The National Association of Manufacturers (NAM) was determined to use the most modern advertising techniques to sell the idea that capitalism was good "just as continuously as the people are told that Ivory Soap floats or that children cry for Castoria." The NAM posted forty-five thousand billboards with messages such as "What Is Good For Industry Is Good For You" and distributed free, procapitalist radio advertisements. On the other hand, the American Bankers Association seriously threatened a "boycott" if the federal government refused to balance its budget.

The Liberty League. In 1934 the New Deal's economic opponents, including Morgan; R. R. M. Carpenter, vice president of Du Pont; Alfred Sloan and William Knudsen of General Motors; J. Howard Pew of Sun Oil;

and Sewell Avery of Montgomery Ward combined to form and finance the American Liberty League. Its one-hundred-man executive committee comprised seventy presidents or directors of leading corporations or investment firms. Many of Roosevelt's political enemies in the Democratic Party, including John J. Raskob, Jouett Shouse, and Al Smith, also joined. The Liberty League was one of the New Deal's most vitriolic opponents, challenging each economic innovation from the standpoint of the orthodox. To the Liberty League, the NRA smacked of Italian corporatism, and they predicted the New Deal would turn fascistic. They argued equally adamantly that the public works programs and Social Security were communistic. Most important, however, they objected to deficit financing, labor unions, and the redistribution of wealth. Each objection was based on the philosophical core of orthodoxy: redistribution of wealth put money in the hands of people incapable of using it properly; labor unions coddled workers and increased laziness; deficit financing borrowed extravagantly for economic programs whose returns were limited.

Defeat. Critics feared at times that the New Deal was the authoritarian mechanism whereby the American voters traded their freedom for economic security. The presidential election of 1936 did nothing to diminish their fears. The Liberty Leaguers backed the Republican candidate, Gov. Alfred Landon of Kansas, in part because he expressed their sentiments to the American people. The Liberty League sent the public more than five million pamphlets and leaflets explaining their position. The public sent Landon and the Liberty League packing, in the worst political defeat in modern American history. Only after the New Deal stumbled in 1937 and Southern Democrats, concerned with Roosevelt's support for black civil rights, made common cause with Republicans would there be a political rehabilitation for conservatives. Even then, the public — and the business community — never embraced economic orthodoxy. By 1938 many Liberty Leaguers and partisans of economic orthodoxy, who were, for the most part, economic nationalists in favor of high tariffs and an almost mercantilist attitude toward trade, embraced isolationism and opposed American entry into the World War II. What political influence they recovered disappeared with Pearl Harbor. The system of '96 was dead.

Keynesian Economics. World War II and the Cold War validated many New Deal economic theories, at least from the perspective of the majority of the nation's business leaders and politicians. Deficit spending received a theoretical boost with the publication of British economist John Maynard Keynes's *General Theory of Employment, Interest, and Money* (1936). Keynes's argument was that deficit spending could be used to temper the effects of the business cycle. Countercyclical spending could indeed prevent catastrophic depression — but the spending had to be great enough to make a difference. The New Deal's tens of billions, it turned out, were too little; World War II's $240 billion was what was required to spark the private sector economic recovery. High wages due to powerful labor unions and a progressive income tax sustained that recovery. Businessmen not only prospered within the regulative supervision of the government, but they extended its mechanisms to international trade at the Bretton Woods conference in 1944 and through the Marshall Plan and tariff agreements after that. After 1945 politicians from both parties and economists of almost every persuasion unified around a consumer economy and multinational Keynesian economics. The economic transition years were behind; the great age of American prosperity ahead.

Sources:

Michael A. Bernstein, "Why the Great Depression was Great: Toward a New Understanding of the Interwar Economic Crisis in the United States," and Thomas Ferguson, "Industrial Conflict and the Coming of the New Deal: The Triumph of Multinational Liberalism in America," both in *The Rise and Fall of the New Deal Order, 1930–1980,* edited by Steve Fraser and Gary Gerstle (Princeton, N. J.: Princeton University Press, 1989);

Stuart Bruchey, *Enterprise: The Dynamic Economy of a Free People* (Cambridge: Harvard University Press, 1990);

Robert Heilbroner and Aaron Singer, *The Economic Transformation of America* (New York: Harcourt Brace Jovanovich, 1977);

Iwan W. Morgan, *Deficit Government: Taxing and Spending in Modern America* (Chicago: Ivan R. Dee, 1995);

Cabell Phillips, *From the Crash to the Blitz, 1929–1939* (New York: Macmillan, 1969);

Carole Shammas, "A New Look at Long-Term Trends in Wealth Inequality in the United States," *American Historical Review,* 98 (April 1993);

Joan Hoff Wilson, *Herbert Hoover: Forgotten Progressive* (Boston: Little, Brown, 1975).

THE OIL BOOM

Restructuring. The oil industry exemplifies the problems plaguing most industries and businesses in the 1930s. The forces of an unregulated, laissez-faire market glutted the nation with oil, driving prices down to a point where the structure of the oil industry was in peril. In contrast to the laissez-faire ideology, oilmen pressured states and the federal government for regulation and control. It was a decade of tremendous oil strikes, plunging profits and panic, restructuring and regulation: in many ways the decade that created the modern oil industry.

Boom. The oil industry struggled to control the effects of several tremendous strikes during the decade. In 1930 wildcatters struck oil in east Texas, opening a reservoir that proved to be 140,000 acres large — the largest strike in the United States at that time. In 1932 wildcatter Robert Samuel Kerr struck oil within the Oklahoma City city limits; his find would eventually earn over $2 million. On 31 May 1932 Standard Oil of California struck oil in Bahrain; by 1936 production equaled 20,000 barrels per day. In 1938 an equally important reservoir was struck in Kuwait and Saudi Arabia. In 1935 Shell Oil hit oil in Kern County, California; the introduction of a new process for cracking oil into gasoline that same year promised to bring this oil to market cheaply.

Eight thousand people gathered in an east Texas oil field waiting to see if drillers would strike oil, October 1930. Five billion barrels were eventually pumped from this field.

Effects. The consequence of the oil strikes of the decade was to collapse prices for oil. Wildcatters and independent oilmen moved into the new oil fields and pulled the crude from the ground as fast as they could, saturating the market. In 1926 oil had sold in Texas for $1.85 a barrel; by 1930 the price was a dollar a barrel; by 1931 oil was between two and six cents a barrel — almost eighty cents lower than the cost of production. The situation would have been an unmitigated disaster were it not for decreased demand because of the Depression, but the Depression also supplied a steady stream of desperate wildcatters and novice oilmen seeking to strike it rich. Established businessmen and oil companies feared "competitive suicide" for the entire industry. By 1931 they were seeking various ways to reduce oil supplies and drive up prices: "A dollar a barrel" became the rallying cry and goal for many oilmen.

Control. The oil industry tried several approaches to controlling oil supplies and prices. Large oil companies such as Standard Oil of New Jersey and Royal Dutch/Shell began informal meetings to divide overseas markets and set prices, a tactic impossible within the United States because of antitrust laws. Abroad the oil companies went so far as to specify the amount of advertising each company could do in protected markets, but such agreements were always unsteady and were often violated. In America oil companies attempted to control supplies via government regulation. They succeeded in

HITTING THE GUSHER

In 1930 oil wildcatter Columbus "Dad" Joiner, 70, was just about the only driller in the hills of east Texas, an area most experts considered empty of oil. A geologist from Texaco, confident the site was dry, told Joiner "I'll drink every barrel of oil you get out of that hole." He is lucky Joiner did not hold him to his words. In September 1930 one of Joiner's wells tested positive for oil. Word circulated quickly, and a shantytown grew up around Joiner's claim, filled with other wildcatters hoping Joiner would hit oil. On 3 October 1930 he did. As the gurgling and trembling of the pressurized oil grew louder, the oil foreman told an assembled crowd "Put out the fires! Put out your cigarettes! Quick!" As the gusher poured forth, the celebrations of the crowd grew reckless. One man pulled a pistol and starting firing into the sky. Three men quickly wrestled him to the ground. One spark could ignite the natural gas escaping from the well with the oil, killing everyone instantly.

Source: Daniel Yergin, *The Prize: The Epic Quest for Oil, Money and Power* (New York: Simon & Schuster, 1992).

getting Congress to pass a high duty on imported oil, thus protecting the domestic market. In Texas the state legislature stretched the authority of the state railroad commission in an attempt to shut down oil production, but illegal production and sale of oil continued. Federal control was necessary. The Roosevelt administration, committed to economic planning, was glad to comply with oil industry requests to stanch the flow of cheap oil. On 14 July 1933 Roosevelt signed an executive order empowering federal agents to police the oil fields. Prices began to rise. But the Supreme Court's 1935 decision invalidating the Roosevelt administration's National Industrial Recovery Act undercut the federal regulatory effort. Nonetheless, the oil industry and the Roosevelt administration pressed on with their regulatory efforts, passing the Connally Hot Oil Act through Congress in 1935 and restoring the police powers of the administration. Thereafter, via the Connally Act and the Bureau of Mines, the government succeeded in bringing some discipline to the unsteady oil market. For the remainder of the decade, the price for crude varied between $1.00 and $1.18 per barrel. Most important, however, government regulation of the market became a permanent feature of the oil business — one created and promoted by the oil industry itself.

Source:
Daniel Yergin, *The Prize: The Epic Quest for Oil, Money and Power* (New York: Simon & Schuster, 1992).

THE SIT-DOWN STRIKE IN THE 1930S

Background. The New Deal climate of the 1930s gave industrial workers an unprecedented chance to improve their conditions by organizing into unions. Led by powerful labor leader John L. Lewis, the Committee for Industrial Organizations (CIO) was created in 1935 to give the nation's thirty million nonskilled workers a chance to unionize. A major new weapon in organizing workers and fighting for better conditions was the sit-down strike. Prior to the sit-down strike, unions could only overcome the fears and suspicions of workers by mounting a successful strike. Strikes, however, often erupted in violence and were rarely successful unless a majority of the workers supported the effort.

Passive Resistance. Sit-down strikes enabled a small number of workers to stop the production of an entire company by taking physical possession of the plant and its machines. By occupying a single strategic area of a plant, strikers could encourage others to join the strike and shut down the plant until the employer agreed to deal with the union. Sit-down strikes brought production to a total and immediate halt and eliminated the use of scab workers to break the strike. A benefit of the wave of sit-down strikes in the 1930s was that there were no casualties and little property damage as compared to normal strikes. The sit-down strike was a form of passive resistance that moved away from the violence surrounding strikes.

Origins. The first sit-down strike in the United States occurred at the Hormel Packing Company in Austin, Minnesota, in 1933. Over the next two years the phenomenon spread to auto plants in Cleveland and Detroit and to the Goodyear factory in Akron. By 1936 union leaders were relying on it in many industries. According to the Bureau of Labor Statistics, there were 48 sit-downs in 1936, involving 88,000 workers. In 1937 alone the number increased to 477 sit-downs involving 400,000 workers, and in 1938 there were 52 such strikes with 30,000 workers participating.

Impact. The sit-down had its most dramatic effect on the automobile industry. In 1936 the United Automobile Workers of America (UAW) demanded recognition from the major automobile companies according to the provisions of the Wagner Act, but the large corporations were not willing to make concessions. The UAW decided to take on General Motors in Flint, Michigan, a town dominated by GM where the UAW local had only 122 members in early 1936. The sit-down strike began in the Fisher Body plant of GM on 31 December 1936 and lasted forty-four days. Like a brush fire, the strike spread to Detroit, Cleveland, Toledo, and other industrial cities. Soon GM production stood at a standstill, with 112,000 of 150,000 plants idle.

Counterattack. GM called the sit-down an unlawful invasion of property rights and wanted the strikers ejected by force. Homer S. Martin, president of the

Sit-down strikers at an automobile body plant in 1937

UAW, countered, stating, "what more sacred property right is there in the world today than the right of a man to his job?" The CIO was, at first, skeptical of the strike but soon supported the UAW with all its resources. GM demanded that the Michigan state militia be used to break the strike. Gov. Frank Murphy of Michigan, however, was sympathetic to the strikers and feared the bloodshed that would occur if he called in the troops.

Response. GM received a court order setting 3 February as the deadline for the workers to evacuate the plants or risk a penalty of imprisonment and fines. In response to the deadline, the workers cabled Governor Murphy explaining that "unarmed as we are, the introduction of the militia, sheriffs, or police with murderous weapons will mean a blood bath of unarmed workers. We have decided to stay in the plant." The 3 February deadline passed and Murphy refused to unleash the militia on the striking workers. President Roosevelt intervened and requested the continuation of negotiations between the union and GM, so for another week the strikers held the plant until an agreement was reached on 11 February 1937. As a result of the sit-down, GM recognized the UAW as the bargaining agent for the workers, and this opened the way for a collective bargaining agreement.

William S. Knudsen, the antiunion GM executive, hailed the new agreement and said, "Let us have peace and make cars."

Success. The Flint sit-down strike was a major success. It led to many grievances being reconciled. The enthusiasm about Flint led to many autoworkers forming new unions faster than the UAW could send them organizers. The sit-down strike even outgrew the labor leaders and the unions; workers realized that they could strike at will. The UAW could not stop the spontaneous strikes that began to break out nationwide. An important consequence of this movement was that auto union membership increased from 35,000 in 1935 to 375,000 in 1937.

Effects. Because of the increased power of the CIO, many major corporations began to rethink their positions regarding unionism. United States Steel, perhaps the most antiunion large corporation, settled with Lewis without a strike soon after the Flint campaign. Another automotive leader, Chrysler, also settled with the CIO after a short, peaceful, and effective sit-down strike. Over the next two years Firestone, Goodrich, RCA, and General Electric all made collective bargaining agreements and recognized their unions.

Resentment. Although the sit-down strike was a successful tool in organizing unions, it was also a short-lived phenomenon. As the strikes increased across the country, popular resentment grew. Conservative newspapers condemned the strikes, and few supported the workers. After much spirited debate the Senate declared the strikes illegal and a form of trespassing. Gallup polls indicated that an overwhelming majority of people opposed the sit-down strike and that new laws needed to be enacted to curb the power of the unions.

Sources:

Irving Bernstein, *Turbulent Years: A History of the American Worker, 1933–1941* (Boston: Houghton Mifflin, 1970);

Foster Rhea Dulles, *Labor in America: A History* (New York: Crowell, 1949).

STRIKES AGAINST BIG BUSINESS IN THE 1930S

Reasons to Strike. Throughout the 1930s blue-collar workers united against the harsh conditions imposed by the corporate giants and walked off their jobs. The common man, spurred on by increasingly powerful unions, believed that bringing production to a halt in the factories or on the docks was the only way he could effectively fight for a better working environment. Furthermore, workers struck even though they faced unemployment or blacklisting and risked injury at the hands of pro-company police officers and strikebreakers. Workers had much to lose by striking, and many paid the price with their lives or by spilling blood for the cause. However, in an overall sense, workers made tremendous gains by organizing and putting their newfound power to the test. Unions, with the assistance of the federal government, consistently won collective bargaining agreements with the giant corporations, which improved the standard of living for the workers.

Strikes and the Depression. The Great Depression had a life-altering effect on the American worker. The economic crash forced companies to lay off millions, and by 1933 one-fourth to one-third of the labor force was out of work. The massive unemployment and general deterioration of working conditions led to labor unrest and a renewed interest in unionization. Strikes inevitably became labor's most useful weapon against the corporations. In 1934 alone a million and a half workers in different industries went on strike. Soon, major companies were completely disabled by the strikes. Unions used the advent of the sit-down strike to win major victories in the automobile, rubber, and steel industries. In a three-year span from 1936 to 1939 American workers employed the sit-down strike 577 times.

The San Francisco General Strike. The San Francisco longshoremen's strike of 1934 is an example of the tremendous power that unions gained by striking in the 1930s. Beginning on 9 May 1934, the strike by the International Longshoremen's Association (ILA) Local 38-79 developed into a citywide general strike and soon closed ports up and down the Pacific Coast. Harry Bridges, a lean, Australian longshoreman with an irascible, intense nature, led the ILA. By the end of May the strike grew into a stoppage involving almost all maritime workers. After much violence and a failed attempt at mediation by the Roosevelt administration, labor sentiment for a general strike reached a peak. On 16 July sixty-three unions voted to walk off in support of the longshoremen. For several days over 130,000 workers in San Francisco engaged in a general strike, closing down much of the city. Secretary of Labor Frances Perkins stepped into the fray and was able to mediate a settlement. The seventy-nine-day strike ended on 27 July. The strike was a victory for Bridges and the ILA: the longshoremen were awarded wage increases and a thirty-hour workweek.

Violence. Violence was commonplace during strikes. Companies hired men from the lowest rungs of society to break strikes and patrol the factories. Spies and moles among the workers informed company officials of union activity. Often, the local and state authorities sided with the employers and used their superior manpower and weaponry to coerce strikers. In the San Francisco strike police, strikebreakers, and workers viciously battled with baseball bats, bricks, and tear gas on 3 July, and the violence culminated on 5 July, or "Bloody Thursday." The 5 July battle lasted the entire day and was so ferocious that many bystanders and innocent citizens were injured. In the end the poorly armed workers could not withstand the power of the police, and by nightfall two workers were dead and sixty-seven others were seriously injured. The governor of California, Frank E. Merriam, sent in the National Guard to restore order in the city. The two victims, Howard Sperry and Nick Bordoise, became martyrs for labor's cause, and their funeral drew more than ten thousand workers.

The Little Steel Strike of 1937. Later in the decade came another important, but violent, strike. The Little Steel strike of 1937 was unique because the employers were actually able to fend off the organizing forces led by the newly formed Committee for Industrial Organizations (CIO) and its offspring, the Steel Workers Organizing Committee (SWOC). The "Little Steel" companies — Republic Steel, Youngstown Sheet and Tube, Inland Steel, and Bethlehem Steel — were antiunion and refused to accept the SWOC as a bargaining agent for its workers. Organizers believed that the steel industry was a vital proving ground for unionization; therefore, the defeat tested the resolve of the union movement. Ultimately, however, the companies succumbed to the pressure of unionization and were forced to recognize the SWOC.

Bracing for Conflict. Labor officials began their unionization drive against Republic Steel in May 1937. The Little Steel companies were led by Republic Steel's antilabor president Tom M. Girdler. The SWOC organized workers and held rallies to recruit new members. Republic responded through intimidation and by spying

The first computer was built in the late 1930s at the Iowa State University by Dr. John V. Atanasoff and a graduate student, Clifford Berry; it was called the Atanasoff-Berry Computer, the ABC. Their calculating device consisted of two rotating drums that had capacitors mounted in them, and it was driven by an electrical circuit that made use of vacuum tube switches. Data was input on punch cards, and calculations were printed out on cards that were marked in distinctive patterns by sparks emitted by the capacitors. Answers were interpreted from the burn patterns on the cards. The ABC cost about one thousand dollars, but there were few takers. The machine could only be programmed to do one task, and it was best suited for small problems more easily solved by conventional means. The primary importance of the ABC was in the theory of its operation. Dr. Atanasoff was denied credit for his role in the development of the computer until the Honeywell corporation used his invention to challenge the patent of the ENIAC, developed by Drs. John W. Mauchly and J. Presper Eckert during World War II. In 1990 Dr. Atanasoff was presented with the National Medal of Technology by President George Bush for his role in the development of the computer.

on local union leaders. The Little Steel companies braced themselves for battle by increasing their stores of guns, tear gas, and billy clubs. They also added new plant guards to their already large security forces. SWOC locals called for a strike, and seventy-five thousand workers walked off the job on 26 May. In steel towns from Illinois to Ohio SWOC members set up picket lines. The first days of the strike were peaceful.

The Memorial Day Massacre. In Chicago a Republic Steel mill continued to operate with the help of a thousand nonstrikers, even after the general strike began. Chicago police and company guards fought with striking workers constantly. The police forbade union supporters to march and accused them of being members of the Communist Party. Chicago SWOC leaders called for a rally on Memorial Day to protest the way the police dealt with union picketers. When strikers and sympathizers began to march on the plant a force of over three hundred police and company guards intercepted them. After a brief standoff, a bottle or rock was thrown at the police, who responded by opening fire into the crowd. A melee ensued, and many SWOC supporters were attacked and

beaten by police as they were running away or had fallen down. Ten marchers were killed, seven shot in the back and the other three in the side. Eyewitnesses and a movie film taken at the scene proved that the police acted brutally and fired for no reason. Over eighty other marchers were injured in the battle, dubbed the "Memorial Day Massacre," along with twenty-two police officers, though none of the police was injured critically or by gunshot.

Intervention and Failure to Settle. The Memorial Day Massacre elicited a public outcry in favor of the strikers, but the Little Steel companies stood firm. The steel companies refused to negotiate with the SWOC or recognize the union's legitimacy. The strike continued, along with much more violence, even after the Chicago incident. The steel companies began using propaganda and local antiunion committees to turn the public's sentiment away from the strikers. Officials from the Roosevelt administration soon began efforts to settle the strike. The president set up a Federal Steel Mediation Board in 1937 to investigate and search for a way to end the impasse; however, the group did not have any real power to enforce its recommendations. Eventually, President Roosevelt himself turned his back on the strikers, fearing that further support would hurt his chances in the 1940 election. At a press conference in late June, Roosevelt condemned both sides, wishing "a plague on both your houses."

Unionization Defeated for the Moment. The CIO and SWOC were defeated by the Little Steel companies in one of the bloodiest and violent strikes in the 1930s. The victory was only temporary, however, because the National Labor Relations Board ordered the companies to recognize the union four years later. By that time the CIO had organized six hundred thousand steelworkers, and the entire industry was covered under union contacts. The defeat did not ruin the SWOC or the CIO, and the union was able to win collective bargaining agreements and reinstatement of union members fired during the strike.

Conclusion. The Little Steel strike and the San Francisco longshoremen's strike were both brutally violent and typify the relations between big business and the worker in the 1930s. Both strikes pitted aggressive union leaders against powerful company officials and featured intervention by the Roosevelt administration. Ultimately, after much bloodshed and violence, the strikes were successful in that the worker greatly benefited from union representation.

Sources:

Irving Bernstein, *Turbulent Years: A History of the American Worker, 1933–1941* (Boston: Houghton, Mifflin, 1970);

Charles P. Larrowe, *Harry Bridges: The Rise and Fall of Radical Labor in the United States* (New York: Hill, 1972).

HEADLINE MAKERS

DAVID DUBINSKY

1892-1982

Leadership. In the early months of 1933 the International Ladies Garment Workers Union (ILGWU) stood virtually in ruins. Internal factionalism had ripped the union apart. By the end of the year, however, the ILGWU had become one of the most powerful unions in the United States. The man responsible for the dramatic turnaround was a short, squat, feisty leader named David Dubinsky. Dubinsky personally carried the union to the forefront. His deep commitment to industrial democracy and unionism placed Dubinsky among the great leaders of the 1930s.

Background. Dubinsky may have the most interesting background of any union leader from the period. He was born David Dobnievski in Brest Litovsk, Russian Poland, on 22 February 1892. His family moved to Lodz, Poland, the industrial center of the country, where his father owned a small bakery. Dubinsky went to work in his family's bakery at age eleven, and by fifteen he had advanced to master baker. He joined a local bakers' union and became deeply involved in unionism and underground rebellion. Dubinsky quickly became a leader of the union and led a strike against the city's Jewish bakeries, including his father's. He was arrested as a labor agitator and sent to jail. His father bribed the jailer to get his fifteen-year-old released, and Dubinsky spent the next three months hiding in Brest Litovsk. In 1908 a spy betrayed the young man, and he was arrested as a second offender and sentenced to Chelyabinsk, Siberia. Dubinsky spent the next eighteen months in prison. In 1910, on his way to exile, he bribed a guard by giving him his winter clothing and escaped from the train taking him to Siberia. Dubinsky made his way back to Lodz but had to remain in hiding. His brother, Jacob, sent him a ticket for New York City since he could have no future in Lodz. In the fall Dubinsky was smuggled over the German border and sailed from Antwerp, Belgium, on 1 January 1911. Dubinsky was just nineteen years old when he entered the New York harbor.

Craftsman and Leader. Dubinsky arrived in the United States in 1911, and within two weeks he took out citizenship papers, joined the Socialist Party, and enrolled in night school. He became a citizen in 1911 and set out to learn the cloak-cutting trade and joined Local 10 of the ILGWU. Soon Dubinsky became a master of the cloak-cutting craft and one of the best in New York City. His strong interest in unionism and the Socialist Party propelled him to union leadership in Local 10. The branch chapter became like a home for Dubinsky. He was named to Local 10's executive board in 1918 and by 1922 had become the chapter's president and general manager. In that same year he also began his rise in the national organization, being named a vice president and a member of the ILGWU executive board. Dubinsky was elected secretary-treasurer in 1929, and his meteoric rise was capped by being elected president in 1932 on condition that he also remain secretary-treasurer.

Character. Dubinsky was a master at getting along with people. Often called an accommodator and pragmatist, he was able to chart a middle course between feuding labor leaders William Green and John L. Lewis. He was also a man of extremes, sometimes rigidly dieting to lose twenty-five pounds in one month and then falling prey to fits of self-indulgence when he would eat marinated herring and goose pastrami washed down with ample quantities of scotch and rum. Dubinsky, like many other prominent labor leaders, was deeply committed to political and industrial democracy. He was against all forms of discrimination and, although he opposed communism, he allowed some former Communists into the ILGWU. Dubinsky set himself apart from other labor leaders by insisting on a modest salary, and he guarded his union's treasury like a hawk. He was content within the confines of the ILGWU and not as willing to gamble on national unionism as was Lewis or Sidney Hillman.

Reorganizing the ILGWU. The membership of the ILGWU fell from 105,000 in 1920 to 40,000 in 1933. The organization was heavily in debt, and its internal paper, *Justice,* ceased publication. When Dubinsky took over in 1932 he used the initiative of the New Deal to take the offensive in reviving the union. He called for a strike against the nonunion Philadelphia dress industry in May 1933 and was successful, raising the spirits of the entire organization. After the passage of the National Industrial Recovery Act (NIRA), which he helped formalize as a labor adviser to the National Recovery Administration (NRA), Dubinsky called for volunteers to help reorganize the ILGWU. He received a huge response, and hundreds of thousands of circulars were printed; even *Justice* resumed publication. Dubinsky opened organizational drives simultaneously in sixty cities.

Successful Strikes. Dubinsky used the help of the federal government to standardize working conditions nationally through the NRA code. The Roosevelt administration's prolabor stance helped the ILGWU organize and rebuild its membership. Dubinsky called for a general dress strike, and sixty thousand workers walked out in New York City. The employers soon folded under the pressure of union solidarity. After the impressive victory in New York, Dubinsky faced little resistance from other factory owners. Underwear workers struck for three weeks in September 1933 until their wages were increased. Corset and brassiere makers and neckwear and scarf workers also staged brief and successful strikes under Dubinsky's leadership.

Improved Conditions. At the ILGWU convention in May 1934 Dubinsky announced that membership had reached two hundred thousand, making it the third largest union in the American Federation of Labor (AFL). Eighty new locals had been chartered all across the nation and in Canada. Wages, hours, and conditions improved dramatically in all industries. Dubinsky profited from his hard work by being named a vice president of the AFL and a member of its executive council in 1935. Dubinsky, however, agreed with Lewis that the AFL needed to include nonskilled workers. Lewis called on him for help in founding the Committee for Industrial Organizations (CIO). Sensing that his union followed his lead in favoring industrial unionism, Dubinsky pledged five thousand dollars to help form the CIO, even though he was opposed to dual unionism.

Attempted Neutrality. Dubinsky believed that a moderate course could be maintained between the AFL and the CIO. He was a close personal friend of AFL leader William Green and CIO leader Lewis, but the rivalry between the two men made it impossible for Dubinsky to stay neutral. The desire to accommodate both sides in the rupture directly reflects Dubinsky's character. He wanted to commit simultaneously to industrial unionism and to labor unity. Dubinsky wanted to move in a direction that he believed was necessary and still hold on to old ties that had helped his union reach its powerful position.

Independence. Dubinsky and the ILGWU participated actively in CIO ventures. The union contributed $345,000 to organizing efforts in steel and textiles. Dubinsky, however, still tried to bring peace between the AFL and CIO, a fruitless effort, especially after the AFL expelled all ILGWU locals from the organization. Although Dubinsky's efforts at mediating a settlement failed, he supported Lewis and the CIO until Lewis decided to change the committee into a permanent national organization. The ILGWU was isolated between the two groups and remained that way for a year and a half. Independence might have destroyed many unions, but Dubinsky had built the ILGWU to such great strength that it could survive on its own and bide its time until it was feasible to rejoin one of the groups.

Legacy. In early 1940 Dubinsky initiated talks with Green about the ILGWU returning to the AFL. Green wanted the organization back because of the group's largesse and because bringing the ILGWU back within the AFL would be a victory in the war with the CIO. The AFL voted to let the ILGWU back into the group, and the motion passed 640 to 12. By 1945 Dubinsky regained his vice presidency and his position of the executive council. Over the next twenty years Dubinsky remained an active leader, retiring from the presidency of the ILGWU in 1966. In that span he participated in politics and labor concerns and served on various public and private boards and agencies. For the rest of his long, illustrious life Dubinsky sustained his commitment to improving the lives of America's working class.

Source:
Irving Bernstein, *Turbulent Years: A History of the American Worker, 1933–1941* (Boston: Houghton Mifflin, 1970).

ARMAND HAMMER

1898-1990

INTERNATIONAL ENTREPRENEUR

Giant. Armand Hammer was a millionaire for seven of his nine decades, and a most unusual one at that. Physician, pharmacist, mine operator, grain merchant, tractor manufacturer, pencil maker, trader of fine arts and furs, distiller, cattle rancher, oil tycoon — Hammer did many things in his life, all of them with a remarkably deft capacity for negotiation, all of them with unflagging energy, all of them to enormous profit. He was an opportunist, in every dimension, both negative and positive, of that term. He had the capacity to see profits where others saw only loss; he prided himself on doing the impossible; he created a wide network of associates from which to angle every possible gain. He was also ruthless, perhaps unprincipled, constantly fending off lawsuits and indictments. His friends included some of the most important figures of the twentieth century: V. I. Lenin, Eleanor Roosevelt, King

Farouk of Egypt, King Faisal of Saudi Arabia, Prince Charles of England, Nikita Khrushchev, Jonas Salk, Leonid Brezhnev, Jimmy Carter, Deng Xiaoping, Margaret Thatcher, Mikhail Gorbachev. He moved among the circle of giants, and was one of them: the century's most intriguing entrepreneur.

Son of Immigrants. Hammer's parents were Russian Jews who immigrated to New York to avoid the pogroms. His father, Julius, was a physician and pharmaceutical manufacturer active in the Socialist Labor Party and, later, in the Communist Party. Armand was born in New York in 1898. Family lore holds that Julius named his son for the symbol of the Socialist Labor Party, the arm-and-hammer. Following in his father's footsteps, Hammer entered Columbia Medical School in 1915. By the time Armand graduated, Julius Hammer had made millions. His critics found Julius a shady figure, a capitalist active in left-wing causes, a pharmacist whose best-selling concoction was a tincture of ginger that, during Prohibition, had the advantage of being 85 percent alcohol. The government monitored him closely because of his radical activities, a practice they would extend to his son. Julius Hammer was also headed to prison, found guilty of performing an illegal abortion that resulted in the death of the patient. Thus, at the age of twenty-two, Armand Hammer prepared to take over his father's pharmaceutical business.

Soviet Capitalist. Armand Hammer also shared his father's interest in radical causes. In 1921, his medical degree in hand, Hammer traveled to the Soviet Union to help treat victims of starvation and typhus, which was sweeping Russia. He also investigated business opportunities there. Little was available in pharmaceuticals, but Hammer was sufficiently quick to concoct a scheme whereby the Soviets traded mining and fur concessions for badly needed American grain. Surmounting the hurdles to trade imposed by Soviet and American bureaucrats, Hammer became the first American concessionaire in Russia and the first American businessman to establish a bank account in Moscow. So astonishing were Hammer's activities that he became the confidant of Lenin and was granted the sole right to represent American businesses in Russia. Despite Henry Ford's militant anticommunism and even more militant anti-Semitism, Hammer negotiated a deal to import Ford tractors to Russia, and later to build them within Russia. He became a formidable trader in Russian furs. In 1926, with no prior experience, Hammer began manufacturing pencils in the Soviet Union. Hiring German experts, he quickly earned a fortune, eventually exporting pencils to England, Persia, and China.

Trader. Although Hammer left Russia in 1930, he continued to use his Soviet connections to his benefit. In Paris he opened a bank specializing in Soviet bonds. He became the foremost exporter of Russian art treasures, selling them through high-profile galleries and mass-marketing retailers such as Gimbels and Lord and Tay-

lor. For the remainder of his life he would be known as one of the world's foremost art collectors and dealers. Anticipating the end of Prohibition in 1933, Hammer bought a barrel manufacturer. Most barrel manufacturers had gone out of business during Prohibition, so Hammer had the market virtually to himself. The Soviets sold him high-quality white oak for barrel manufacturing at below market cost, and once again Hammer made a fortune. In 1941 he went into the distilling business in earnest, developing innovative refining techniques for vodka, which, naturally enough, he had first learned in Russia. By the end of the 1940s Hammer was one of the nation's leading distillers.

Oil Magnate. Hammer dabbled in several businesses during the 1950s, including cattle ranching and radio. In 1956 he became involved in Occidental Petroleum Corporation, a small Los Angeles–based oil company. Hammer invested in the company thinking it was a tax write-off, but with the usual Hammer luck Occidental began striking new wells throughout California. Hammer took the helm and transformed the company, diversifying its interests into other natural resource production, such as mining and fertilizer. As he had with the Soviet Union in the 1920s, Hammer offered developing nations badly needed goods in trade for access to their raw materials. As he had with pencil manufacturing, Hammer raided other petroleum companies for talent. It was savvy business. By 1966 Occidental had annual sales of almost $700 million. By the 1970s Occidental would have lucrative contracts with Libya, Saudi Arabia, Venezuela, and Singapore. In 1972 Hammer resurrected the deal he had made with Lenin, this time trading the Soviets fertilizer for $20 billion in nickel and other raw materials deliverable over twenty years. Critics and admirers alike called it "the deal of the century."

Teflon Tycoon. The esteem with which Soviet officials held Hammer made him an uncredited American ambassador to Russia and extremely valuable during the 1970s and 1980s. He tried unsuccessfully to resolve Soviet/American tensions over the 1979 invasion of Afghanistan. He marshaled humanitarian assistance to Russia after the Chernobyl disaster. He acted as a mediator negotiating the status of Russian Jews for Israel. He was a lifelong champion of international peace, nominated for the Nobel Peace Prize in 1984. His diplomatic activities provided Hammer with the political support necessary to survive four court challenges to Occidental by the Securities and Exchange Commission. He earned a reputation as a "teflon tycoon," to whom charges of improprieties did not stick, though in 1976 he pleaded guilty to illegal contributions to Richard Nixon's 1972 presidential campaign and was sentenced to a year's probation and a three-thousand-dollar fine. While he continued to enjoy the confidences of the powerful and dismissed the conviction as no more troubling than a speeding ticket, Hammer spent much of the 1980s trying to remove the blot on his good name. On 14 August 1989 his efforts paid off, with a presidential pardon from George Bush. Hammer died absolved on 10 December 1990.

Source:

Steve Weinberg, *Armand Hammer: The Untold Story* (Boston: Little, Brown, 1989).

HOWARD HUGHES

1905-1975

ADVENTURER, AVIATOR, CELEBRITY

Legend. Howard Hughes led a remarkable and bizarre life. There is as much legend to his life as there is reality, which leads to his larger-than-life image. From Hughes's compulsive worries about germs to his links to Richard Nixon and the Watergate scandal, he has been idolized, trivialized, and despised all at one point or another. Obviously there is going to be much mystique surrounding a man who purportedly was seeing Ginger Rogers and Cary Grant while living with Katharine Hepburn and dating Bette Davis. In the 1930s, however, Hughes truly was an American hero and an innovator in the aviation field. In this decade Hughes's internal demons did not prevent him from achieving many remarkable feats.

Background. Hughes was born in Humble, Texas, on 24 September 1905. His father was the outlaw oil wildcatter Howard Robard Hughes and his mother was a neurotic heiress, Allene Gano. The elder Hughes built up a large fortune by making oil drill bits and founding the Hughes Tool Company. Hughes's parents were extremely overprotective and knew how to manipulate the boy. Hughes spent his childhood being shuffled from one private school to another. He often engaged in strenuous physical activity as a boy and excelled in mathematics, physics, and golf. Tragedy struck Hughes early when both his parents died at an early age, his mother while in surgery and his father of a heart attack. Thus, at age eighteen, Hughes inherited a million dollars and his father's empire. To prove that he was old enough to run his father's business, Hughes married Houston socialite Ella Rice in 1924. They had a terrible marriage due to his infidelities and the fact that he beat her.

Motion Pictures. In the early 1920s Hughes entered the world of motion pictures through his uncle, Rupert Hughes, the famous author and movie producer. Hughes, in his compulsive manner, learned every aspect of the motion picture business, including operating cameras, lighting, and editing. The public was generally receptive to Hughes's movies, although since he was an outsider the big movie companies such as M-G-M and Paramount hated him, also due in part to his anti-Semitism. The movie *Hell's Angels* made Hughes the most famous movie producer in the United States. It was a colossal picture about aerial death and dogfighting in World War I. After years of fighting censors over the sexual nature of his films and dealing with the large motion picture companies, Hughes abandoned filmmaking in 1932.

Empire. One of Hughes's greatest moves was to hire a young accountant named Noah Dietrich to run the Hughes Tool Company. Dietrich turned Hughes's $1 million inheritance into a $75 million empire between 1925 and 1930. Dietrich's success with the company allowed Hughes to indulge in other pursuits, including aviation and attempting to break the world land-speed record.

H-1 Racer. Hughes became interested in aviation while filming *Hell's Angels*. Often, when his hired stunt pilots would refuse to risk death for the movie, Hughes would take a plane up himself and do the maneuver. In the early 1930s Hughes hired two men, Richard Palmer and Glenn Odekirk, who helped him realize his dream of breaking the air-speed record. The men began in 1934 to build a plane that would be the fastest in the world and possibly interest the army. By 10 August 1935 the new plane, known as the Hughes 1-B racer, or the H-1, was completed. The plane was completely aerodynamic, and each screw on the plane's surface was tightened so that the slot was exactly in line with the airstream. It was a dream plane, and Hughes decided to go for the record immediately.

Setting Records. Hughes tried for the record on 13 August 1935, ominously a Friday the thirteenth, as Amelia Earhart officially flew cover to make sure he did not break the rules. Hughes set the record by flying 352.388 miles per hour, crushing the old record set by France's Caudron racer. Hughes's next goal was to fly the H-1 nonstop across America. He had Palmer and Odekirk redesign the plane and add new fuel tanks, navigational equipment, and oxygen. On 19 January 1937 Hughes left for New York. He left at 2:14 A.M. and traveled eastward using oxygen and riding the airstream at incredible speeds. The plane touched down in Newark seven hours and twenty-eight minutes later. On the flight Hughes averaged 327.1 miles per hour, and his record stood until 1946. Hughes won the Harmon International Trophy for best aviator of the year in 1937 from President Roosevelt at the White House and decided to attempt an around-the-world record.

America's Idol. Hughes left for Paris from New York on 10 July 1938. He made it to Paris in half the time it had taken Charles Lindbergh. He landed in Moscow the next morning and prepared for the treacherous flight over Siberia. With his wings iced over and running out of fuel, Hughes made it to Alaska in one piece. He flew on to New York, completing his trip in which he flew 14,716 miles in three days, nineteen hours, and eight minutes. Immense crowds greeted Hughes in New York City as he led a ticker-tape parade, and he instantly became an

American hero of a type that others could only portray on film.

Legacy. After the world flight Hughes was worth approximately $60 million. He worried, however, that Hughes Aircraft was being outpaced by every other aircraft company. In 1938 he took interest in TWA and began buying stock, eventually acquiring 78 percent of the company. His flight around the world paved the way for the infant commercial airlines, and TWA became one of the first of this kind. Hughes's interest in aircraft design also set the standard for many others to follow. Engineers borrowed from his thinking to improve many planes.

Downfall. Hughes had a lifelong passion for movies, planes, and beautiful women. He fulfilled his nihilistic pleasures and later in life became a pitiful drug addict and recluse. At the time of his death, Hughes's estate was valued at over $650 million. In the 1980s, however, the empire was destroyed as GM bought Hughes Aircraft and Hughes Tool Company was sold. One cannot view Hughes without seeing his seedier side, but in the 1930s he was a pioneer and an American hero. Few would have believed that Howard Hughes was destined for such a tragic life.

Sources:

Timothy Foote, "A Silver Speedster from the 1930s Evokes the Golden Age of Flight, a Pair of World-Class Speed Records and the Early Triumphs of Howard Hughes' Ultimately Tragic Life" *Smithsonian*, 25 (February 1995);

Charles Higham, *Howard Hughes: The Secret Life* (New York: Putnam, 1993).

HAROLDSON LAFAYETTE HUNT JR.

1889-1974

OIL TYCOON

The Richest Man in America. By 1942 H. L. Hunt was the richest man in the United States, earning roughly a million dollars per week for the oil produced by his east Texas wells. Professional gambler, bigamist, wildcatter, right-wing activist, and health-food fanatic, Hunt took chances, won big, and reveled in his accomplishments. From the 1930s, when he first surfaced as a known national figure, to the end of his life, he embellished his own history with exaggerated stories of his adventures. He was a self-made man who created his own reputation.

Background. Son of a southern farmer and Confederate veteran who moved north during Reconstruction, Hunt was born near Vandalia, Illinois, on 17 February 1889. His father was somewhat prosperous, accounting for his success by embracing a militant social Darwinian philosophy that asserted his genetic superiority to the common man. He passed this ethos on to his son, who articulated it many times during his life. The youngest of eight children, Hunt was doted upon as a boy, evidencing a remarkable talent for mental arithmetic, an independent streak, and a taste for adventure. At age sixteen he struck out on his own, heading west to make his fortune. He took jobs as a dishwasher, a beet topper, a sheepherder, a mule-team driver, a semipro baseball player, a crop picker, a concrete pourer, and a lumberjack. His skill for mental figuring made him an exceptional cardplayer, and eventually he made a living as a professional gambler.

Gambling. In 1911, tiring of life as an itinerant gambler, Hunt made his way to Lake Village, Arkansas, intending to raise cotton. His initial ventures wiped out by floods, he returned to gambling, eventually opening a gambling parlor in the boomtown of El Dorado, about seventy miles west of Lake Village. El Dorado was an oil town, filled with wildcatters, roughnecks, speculators, and prostitutes — perfect for gamblers. Naturally enough, Hunt began dabbling in oil drilling. It was a gamble. Hunt knew next to nothing about geology and had to lease his drilling equipment. He nonetheless proved lucky, striking oil, and then watching the wells go dry, quietly absorbing the nuances of the oil business. By the end of the 1920s he also developed a pattern of oil speculation, where he waited until wildcatters struck oil and then raced to the oil fields to secure leasing rights. He also developed two families, one in El Dorado and one in Shreveport, Louisiana, each oblivious to the presence of the other. He was as successful in bigamy as he was in oil.

East Texas. The basis of Hunt's fortune was laid by a colorful oil wildcatter, Columbus "Dad" Joiner. In 1930 Joiner had been drilling in the oil fields of east Texas for over three years. He had struck nothing, and oil company geologists doubted the area had any oil. They were wrong: in September Joiner struck oil. Soon word of the strike made it into Arkansas. Hunt raced to Joiner's claim, bought up surrounding leases, and offered to purchase Joiner's wells. The wildcatter resisted at first. But Joiner had oversold investor claims to the oil field in order to finance his drilling. As they pressed their claims against him in court, Joiner feared he would lose everything. Wells drilled by others to the east and south of his find proved dry; leading geologists continued to insist the strike was an anomaly. Hunt offered Joiner $30,000 in cash and $1.3 million in future oil royalties. On 26 November Joiner sold Hunt his claim. It was a remarkable coup for Hunt. Personally broke, Hunt had to rustle up the funding for the wells from third parties. There was no guarantee Hunt would be able to placate the investors Joiner had defrauded, although most ultimately settled for a buyout of $250. Hunt had a hunch the oil field was located to the north and west of Joiner's strike, but at the time of the deal only one test well confirmed his guess. Hunt's gambling instincts proved sharp: the east Texas field was indeed north and west of Joiner's well, forty miles long from tip to tip, measuring more than 140,000 acres. It was the largest oil strike ever in the United States, producing more than four billion barrels of crude. Hunt was the single largest independent owner of wells in the field. That made him one of the richest men in the United States.

Prorationing. Hunt's fortune was by no means assured. He was the richest single owner of oil in the field, but he was not the only owner in the field. It was the Depression: thousands flocked to the site hoping to strike it rich. Their wells tapped the same reservoir as did Hunt's; overproduction was bleeding the field dry and driving the prices terribly low. By the spring of 1931 oil was selling for two cents a barrel on the spot market. The boom was turning to bust. Hunt joined forces with the major oil companies to ask the government to shut down oil production and proration it — that is, limit the number of barrels that could be taken out of the ground. Their lobbying efforts were successful. On 16 August 1931 the governor of Texas sent in twelve hundred National Guard troops and shut down the oil field. When he opened it again in September, production was prorationed to 225 barrels of oil per well per day. The prorationing began to drive the smaller drillers out of business. Smuggling became an enormous problem. Vigilantes attacked pipelines and tank trucks. Wells were set on fire. By 1933 the federal government was forced to send agents to east Texas and began a nationwide clampdown of the oil market, driving the price back up to one dollar per barrel. In 1935 Congress passed the Connally Hot Oil Act, making prorationing a national policy and providing penalties for excess production. Hunt's share of the east Texas market was secure. He could now turn to other interests.

Expansion. Ever the gambler, Hunt used his east Texas profits to drill for oil elsewhere, especially Louisiana. He extended his interests to oil refining and trade. He used his fortune to invest in a depressed real estate market. By 1938 he struck deals with the Germans and Japanese for oil equipment and crude, deals that naturally floundered with the outbreak of World War II. The war nonetheless presented Hunt with a steady, high price for crude. He prospered, expanding his operations throughout the South. He opened gas stations to add to his refineries, pipe manufacturing, and drilling. He bought a cattle ranch in Wyoming that, as luck would have it, had oil. He was able to indulge his passion for gambling. He hired a statistician from the Massachusetts Institute of Technology to help him lay bets on horse races around the country. He added a new mistress and child to his collection of families, building them a house located a two-minute drive away from his first, legal family. He now was the patriarch of three separate families. He also began dabbling in politics.

Right-Winger. Despite the fact that Hunt's fortune had been secured by government intervention into the oil market, Hunt's childhood education in the absolutes of social Darwinian philosophy disposed him to conservative politics. In fact, Hunt became one of the most reactionary political figures in the United States. In 1951 he founded and financed Facts Forum, a propaganda agency for the far Right that disseminated pamphlets (*Hitler was a Liberal, Traitors in the Pulpit*) and radio programs attacking communism, liberalism, the United Nations, the State Department, Judaism, and the Catholic Church. Facts Forum and its board (which included Hunt; Norman Vincent Peale; Sears, Roebuck chairman Robert E. Wood; and actor John Wayne) promoted Christianity, Sen. Joseph McCarthy, and Gen. Douglas MacArthur. Hunt wrote off the expenses of running Facts Forum as a donation to charity.

Later Life. The remainder of Hunt's life was filled with notable eccentricities, rather than capital or political adventures. Facts Forum fell into public disrepute with the waning of McCarthyism. Day-to-day operations of the Hunt business were increasingly dominated by his sons. Hunt turned his own attentions to the production of idiosyncratic, utopian novels. He altered a few old habits, giving up gambling and tempering his philandering. He became a partisan of health foods and launched his own company to produce them, an indulgence that cost him millions. He attacked John F. Kennedy in the 1960 presidential election, sponsoring the publication of pamphlets arguing that the election of a Catholic would be disastrous. His status as one of Kennedy's most vocal critics immersed him and his family in the allegations and suspicions that followed Kennedy's assassination. Hunt died in 1974, but in death he turned out to be as impressive a presence as he was in life. His will was bitterly contested by his three families and tied up Texas courts throughout the 1970s.

Sources:

Harry Hurt III, *Texas Rich: The Hunt Dynasty from the Early Oil Days through the Silver Crash* (New York: Norton, 1981);

Jerome Tuccille, *Kingdom: The Story of the Hunt Family of Texas* (Ottawa, Ill.: Jameson Books, 1984).

SAMUEL INSULL

1859-1938

ELECTRICITY MAGNATE

Symbol. In the 1930s Samuel Insull was the symbol of the unprincipled, greedy businessman. His gigantic electricity-generating empire, a series of more than seventy shaky firms piled one on top of the other, had collapsed during the Depression, losing a million investors $2 billion to $3 billion. Indicted for fraud, Insull fled to Europe, from where he was extradited to stand trial. The sensational proceedings occupied the public for months. The writer John Dos Passos described him as "a stiffly arrogant redfaced man with a closecropped mustache," who was "the deposed monarch of superpower." During the 1932 presidential campaign Franklin Roosevelt attacked him repeatedly, denouncing industrialists like "the Insulls, whose hand is against every man's." By most accounts of the day he was shameless and ruthless. But he was also Thomas Edison's personal secretary, a poor boy made good, a business genius, and the builder of the greatest public utilities industry in the United States.

Horatio Alger. Insull was able to weather the investigations and trials of the 1930s with a certain degree of public support because his background was, in many ways, a classic Horatio Alger story of a poor boy rising to wealth. Born and reared in England, Insull was one of eight children. His father was a temperance crusader of modest means. Young Insull briefly attended private school in Oxford with some of England's most privileged children. Teased and slighted by his upper-class schoolmates, Insull embarked on a lifelong drive to earn respectability and wealth. In 1874 the Insull family moved to London, and Insull took work as an office boy. He quickly proved to be diligent and precise in his work habits, learning shorthand after hours and establishing a good reputation as a clerk. In 1879 he began work with the London branch of Thomas Edison's company. He was so successful at his job that in 1881 he immigrated to America to become Edison's personal secretary. He became an American citizen in 1896.

Utilities. Insull arrived just as Edison was about to introduce commercial electric lighting. Insull became Edison's financial manager, finding the money necessary to build the nation's first electricity-generating plants and electric lines. Insull managed to hunt up investors such as Henry Villard and J. P. Morgan to finance the projects. In 1889 he was one of the original directors of the Edison General Electric Company, organizing its manufacturing base and corporate and sales operations. A takeover of General Electric by eastern financiers such as Morgan left Insull powerless and bitter. In 1892 he relocated west, out of the circle of eastern financiers, becoming the president of the Chicago Edison Company. He went on to make Chicago Edison a model of the industry.

Monopolist. The early days of the electricity-generating industry were dominated by several problems Insull deftly resolved. One was competition from the gas industry, which at the turn of the century produced light as cheaply and effectively as did electricity. Another problem concerned the virtues of decentralized versus centralized power generation. Initially bankers and investors would only fund decentralized power generators, building by building, localizing power use. Centralized power required enormous sums of capital up front, and the returns were not certain: central plants, for example, continued operating during the day when usage was low, wasting electricity, whereas power plants located in individual buildings could tailor their electricity generation to specific uses. These factors combined to lead most observers to guess that electricity would be a luxury item, of limited use in the future. Insull's vision was far grander. He was among the first to postulate the idea of generating electricity for mass use (in fact coining the term *mass production*). First, however, he had to resolve the problems plaguing the electricity industry. He recruited bright engineering talent to help refine the production of electricity, introducing the world's first steam turbines to his plants in 1902. Second, he revolutionized utilities financing, introducing open-end mortgages and high-yield bonds to gain investor support. Third, he proved centralized generation profitable by powering electric railways, industry, and an ever-expanding base of consumers. His objective was to supply consumers at the lowest possible price, expanding electric service to millions of homes and broadening the base of his returns. In order to do this, of course, Chicago Edison had to be the exclusive electricity generator for the Chicago area. He made Edison a powerful monopoly, gobbling up competitors, especially during the economic depression of 1893 to 1897. By 1905 annual electricity production for Chicago Edison doubled for the seventh time in thirteen years; by 1907 the company was sixty times larger than it was when Insull took the helm. Chicago Edison was the nation's leading electricity-generating company.

Success. Insull's success in Chicago laid the foundation for his national ambitions. In 1912 he formed the Middle West Utilities Company, a holding company designed to facilitate electrification of the Midwest. It began acquiring local generating companies and electric traction systems, expanding their operations to wider groups of consumers. World War I advanced Insull's efforts. He was head of the Illinois Council of National Defense, a state agency formed to coordinate propaganda and regulate the economy. The federal Council of National Defense spent $2 million to improve electrification of vital industries, moneys naturally benefiting Insull and other utilities magnates in the long run. During the war Chicago Edison (now named Commonwealth Edison) increased its sales fivefold. Insull's participation in the war effort also transformed his business in two other ways. First, his experience as a war propagandist familiarized him with modern advertising techniques, and after the war he formed the Illinois Public Utility Information Committee and other public relations firms to promote the public reputation of the utilities industries. Second, his experience on war-bond drives convinced him to restructure public investment in his utilities. Insull began selling cheap corporate bonds to his electricity customers. By 1930 more than one million people had invested in the Insull companies.

Power. Insull's innovative financial and operational strategies made the 1920s the heyday of his success. Three Insull companies — Commonwealth Edison; Peoples Gas, Light and Coke; and Public Service of

Northern Illinois — each earned more than $175 million annually. Middle West and several hundred subsidiaries were worth $1.2 billion. All totaled, Insull companies were worth nearly $3 billion, had more than one million stockholders, served four million customers, and produced as much electricity and gas as any entire nation on earth other than the United States. Insull's personal fortune was $150 million in 1929. His prestige and power in the United States were matched only by other industrialists of the caliber of Henry Ford or J. P. Morgan. Yet he was about to suffer a devastating series of attacks that would make him one of the most vilified individuals in the nation.

Crash. For Insull several different problems combined with the stock-market crash of 1929 to destroy his fortune and fame. The first was a series of scandals in the utilities business that badly tarnished the reputation of power generation. In 1927 and 1928 congressional committees revealed widespread influence peddling by utilities companies in the Pennsylvania and Illinois elections of 1926. Public sympathy for the utilities business was further undermined by disputes over the proposed Boulder Dam and the federally owned Muscle Shoals plant in Alabama. Politicians hostile to the utilities began speaking of a "power trust," rhetoric bound to impact a monopolist such as Insull. What really destroyed Insull, however, was an attempt to protect Commonwealth Edison from a stock buyout by Cyrus S. Eaton, a Cleveland financial raider. To protect his shares Insull formed the Insull Utility Investments Company and Corporation Securities Company of Chicago, pyramiding his utilities holdings and investment holdings. He refinanced Middle West Utilities, splitting its stock, eliminating its debt, and placing future dividends on a stock, rather than a cash, basis. These moves protected Insull's control of his stock but did not help with shares Eaton had already purchased, as the stock boom of 1929 continually raised the value of Eaton's shares of Commonwealth Edison. Following the crash, with prices declining, Insull bought out Eaton, borrowing money from a variety of sources, including his former enemies in New York. Confident that the Depression would turn out to be brief, Insull was sure he could repay the debt. He was, of course, wrong. As prices in Insull securities continued to fall, the New York bankers turned bearish, driving the stock to lower levels and eliminating their worth as loan collateral. Insull Utility Investments and Corporation Securities were bankrupt; New York took control of Commonwealth, Middle West, and Insull's remaining holdings; Insull resigned from the chairmanships of more than seventy of his companies that were defeated. He had lost everything.

Scapegoat. What happened next was sensational and occupied the press for months. In defeat Insull became a public scapegoat for the impersonal economic forces that had brought on the Depression. He was a ready candidate for the task, as the public stockholders of Insull's companies — ordinary people such as farmers, teamsters, and schoolteachers — had lost their investments when Insull lost his companies. His financial maneuverings of 1930 and 1931 were complex, multifaceted, amoral, and quite possibly illegal; the taint of scandals of the 1920s burdened Insull. John Swanson, state's attorney for Cook County in Chicago, maximized the political potential of this burden during the elections of 1932: on 4 October he secured from a grand jury indictments against Insull for embezzlement, larceny, and mail fraud.

Trial. Getting Insull to face trial was more difficult. After the loss of his power empire, Insull had gone to Europe to rest and recuperate. In 1933 the government moved to force his return for the criminal indictments, chasing him from Paris to Italy to Greece. Greece had no extradition treaties with the United States, but political pressure from the Roosevelt administration prevailed: Insull was returned to the United States in May 1934. On 2 October 1934, at age seventy-four, Insull went on trial in Chicago. The gist of the fifty-page, twenty-five-count indictment was that Insull had engaged in a "simple conspiracy to swindle, cheat and defraud the public." The affair was hardly simple, and the details of Insull's finances bored the jury. But Insull's testimony was riveting, and it was wired to papers around the country. Rather than focus on the details of the indictment, Insull's attorney deftly led the old man to recount his rise from poverty to wealth. In the end the trial was about contrasting stereotypes: Insull the unscrupulous magnate versus Insull the poor boy made good. Horatio Alger won out. Insull was acquitted of all charges. He spent the remainder of his life in exile, retired on the pensions from his former companies. He died in Paris on 16 July 1938.

Source:

Forrest McDonald, *Insull* (Chicago: University of Chicago Press, 1962).

HOWARD JOHNSON

1885-1977

FOUNDER OF NATIONAL RESTAURANT CHAIN

Humble Beginnings. Howard Johnson entered the food-service business in 1924 in Wollaston, Massachusetts, when he bought a debt-ridden soda fountain that also sold newspapers, cigars, and candy. He decided to focus on ice cream and invested $300 in the recipe of an elderly German immigrant whose ice cream had a reputation for high quality. The essence of the recipe was its near-doubling of the butterfat content commonly found in commercial ice cream and its use of natural rather than artificial flavors. By 1928 the gross income from the ice cream sold at the store and on nearby beaches amounted to $240,000.

Opening His First Restaurant. Encouraged by his success, Johnson decided to expand into restaurants. He opened his first restaurant in Quincy, Massachusetts, in 1928 and did a booming business until the stock-market crash in 1929. His restaurant closed. However, Johnson's ice cream business continued to flourish throughout the Depression. He soon had more than a dozen stands in the Boston area that specialized in hot dogs and ice cream. He continued to expand the variety of ice cream flavors he offered, arriving eventually at twenty-eight, a figure that became a trademark for Howard Johnson establishments.

Expansion. In 1929 a family friend, Reginald Sprague, approached Johnson with the idea of opening an ice cream stand on a piece of property he owned on a main highway in southern Massachusetts. Johnson suggested they open a quality restaurant, which they did in 1930. Johnson soon became known as the "host of the highways." He was one of the first to combine a lunch counter, a fast-food takeout, an ice cream stand, and a sit-down restaurant under one roof. His white clapboard buildings trimmed in orange and sea blue became his trademark. Johnson's concern with building a family trade made him scrupulous about cleanliness and hospitality. Waitresses were hired for their courtesy, and all the restaurants were equipped with high chairs. Meals were made available in special children's portions and prices.

Hitting the Big Time. Howard Johnson establishments flourished throughout the 1930s. With the expansion of automobile travel he offered the touring public what they wanted at a reasonable price. By 1940 Johnson had about 135 restaurants in New England, Florida, and Virginia and had become a millionaire.

Weathering the War. America's involvement in World War II dealt a severe blow to Johnson's roadside restaurants. Home-front gas rationing forced 90 percent of his restaurants to close. He survived by acquiring contracts to supply food for workers in large industrial plants and for universities training student officers. He also contracted with the government for the manufacture of candy and marmalade for the armed forces. After the war his business bounced back. In the 1950s he expanded his chains nationally and started to add motor lodges. In 1956 the gross income of the Howard Johnson Company was $175,530,695. In 1959 he passed his business on to his son, Howard B. Johnson.

Source:
Chester H. Liebs, *Main Street to Miracle Mile: American Roadside Architecture* (Boston: Little, Brown, 1985).

JOHN L. LEWIS
1880-1969
LABOR LEADER

Image. John L. Lewis dominated the labor movement in the 1930s. To the millions of blue-collar workers whose lives he improved, Lewis was a saint. His enemies, however, viewed the labor leader as an egomaniac and demagogue. Lewis's enigmatic nature baffled his peers and fueled a mythical, larger-than-life image. Although he had an intense desire for power and wealth, Lewis championed industrial democracy and unionism. He embodied the spirit of the workingmen and workingwomen of the 1930s and devoted his life to helping the industrial worker.

Background. Lewis was born in Cleveland, Iowa, in 1880. His father held a variety of jobs, including coal miner, and moved his family often. One relocation in particular, to the state capital Des Moines, had a major impact on Lewis's life. While his father worked as a police officer, young John was able to complete three and a half years of high school. The basic education he received served as a foundation for his jump into labor politics. Lewis developed a strong ambition after several years of wandering throughout the West and Midwest and many stints working in the mines. He wanted to rise above his coal-mining roots. A move by the entire Lewis clan, including new wife Myrta, to Illinois triggered a meteoric rise by John in the local United Mine Workers (UMW) chapter, capped by Lewis's election as president in 1909.

UMW. John L. Lewis spent the next decade climbing the ladder of the UMW and American Federation of Labor (AFL). He ascended to the presidency of the UMW in 1920 and soon gained unchallenged control of the organization. In Lewis's first ten years as president of the UMW he dealt with plummeting wages, employment, and membership, but his personal power increased. He weathered each storm, and with the election of President Franklin D. Roosevelt and the coming of the New Deal in 1933, Lewis was in a position to have a major impact on the national scene.

Power. Lewis reached the height of his power in the years from 1933 to 1937. Roosevelt's economic advisers and the UMW leader held similar ideas concerning national economic policy. In fact, Lewis and his economic consultant, W. Jett Lauck, were most responsible for Title 7(a) of the National Industrial Recovery Act (NIRA), which endorsed the right for workers to organize. The NIRA put the power and authority of the federal government behind organized labor. As a result, coal miners flocked to join the UMW. Soon the UMW was recognized across the nation in the mines that produced 90 percent of the country's coal. In the mind of the coal worker, Lewis stood alongside the president, and joining the union was a way to participate in the country's recovery. The folklore of the miners pictured Lewis "having beer and sauerkraut with President Roosevelt every night."

Political Ties. In the 1930s Lewis and the UMW became America's largest and most powerful labor union. Lewis used his greatest asset, intervention by the federal government, to improve wage standards and working conditions for his constituents. The demagogic Louisiana senator, Huey Long, gave Lewis his highest praise, calling him "the Huey Long of labor." From 1933 to 1937 the president and the labor leader pursued similar goals. Both realized the connection between New Deal politics and the successful organizing of blue-collar workers. President Roosevelt needed the support of the millions of union men in his reelection bid, and Lewis needed the help of the federal government to fight the corporate giants. National politics, not a philosophical dispute between skilled and unskilled workers, led to a growing split in the AFL and the rise of the Committee for Industrial Organizations (CIO), later to be renamed the Congress of Industrial Organizations.

Breaking Away. Lewis realized that the New Deal gave labor an unprecedented opportunity for the AFL to organize mass-production workers. Lewis, however, had to fight the conservative leadership of the AFL, which was opposed to including the unskilled workers. In 1934 and 1935 Lewis used the power and resources of the UMW to lead the struggle within the AFL. At the 1935 AFL convention Lewis blasted its leaders for what he characterized as "twenty-five years of unbroken failure." William Hutcheson, the leader of the carpenters union, called Lewis a "big bastard" after Lewis announced that the thirty million nonskilled workers should be accepted into the AFL ranks. Lewis jumped over a row of chairs and hit Hutcheson square in the jaw with an uppercut. People scrambled to separate the two, and Hutcheson emerged bloodied. A few minutes later, Lewis relit his cigar and casually strolled back to the podium. The right jab to Hutcheson's jaw may be characterized as "the punch heard 'round the world" because it led to Lewis's most outstanding and lasting contribution to American life, the creation of the CIO.

Founding the CIO. From 1935 to 1937 Lewis presided over the CIO and fought to bring collective bargaining to the auto, steel, rubber, electric, and other manufacturing industries. He poured vast sums of money into Roosevelt's 1936 reelection campaign and personally led the labor movement into the national political arena. He spoke at large campaign rallies and used the radio to address millions more. One admiring journalist called him "the Babe Ruth of the labor movement." By the end of 1937 the CIO had 3.7 million members, compared to the 3.4 million AFL members.

Prestige. The personal leadership of Lewis, the support of the Roosevelt administration, and the advent of the sit-down strike led to several resounding agreements from many large companies, including General Motors and the United States Steel Corporation. Lewis became the most recognized public figure in the United States after Roosevelt, and his image appeared in magazines, newspapers, and even movie theaters.

Downfall. Lewis's victories, however, were short-lived. The CIO was defeated by the "Little Steel" companies, and the nation was beset by an economic downturn in 1937–1938. Coupled with Roosevelt's increasing devotion to international affairs, which further separated the two men, Lewis never fully recovered. The labor leader's reaction was to declare war on the Roosevelt administration, a fight he was destined to lose. Lewis even tied his presidency of the CIO to the presidential election of 1940 and publicly supported Republican candidate Wendell L. Willkie. Lewis urged workers to vote for Willkie and said that if Roosevelt won he would resign as president of the CIO. When Roosevelt won reelection, Lewis was true to his word and stepped down.

Legacy. John L. Lewis was the driving force behind the labor movement in the 1930s. He did not want to overturn the existing economic system — he wanted to improve the lives of working-class citizens. His legacy is that he was able to achieve this goal. In many ways Lewis embodied the American dream. With little formal education or training he was able to become a successful and powerful leader whose actions directly benefited the lives of millions of people.

Sources:
Melvyn Dubofsky and Warren Van Tine, "John L. Lewis and the Triumph of Mass-Production Unionism," in *Labor Leaders in America,* edited by Dubofsky and Van Tine (Urbana: University of Illinois Press, 1987), pp. 185–206;

Robert H. Zieger, *John L. Lewis: Labor Leader* (Boston: Twayne, 1988).

ROSE PESOTTA

1896-1965

LABOR LEADER

Women in the Depression. The Great Depression had a tremendous impact on workers in the United States. While all suffered from the devastating loss of jobs and economic deterioration, women especially were adversely affected. By 1933 almost two million women were unemployed. Married women were discriminated against more than married or single men and single women. Wages for women plummeted, and some women did not even make five dollars for a week's work. Workplace conditions worsened as the Depression increased. In the garment industry, where many women were employed, work standards deteriorated and the sweatshops were revived.

Outsider. Franklin D. Roosevelt took immediate steps to rectify the economic problems facing the country after he was elected president. The prolabor stance taken by the administration helped unions gain tremendous power in the 1930s. One of the most powerful was the International Ladies Garment Workers Union (ILGWU), led by David Dubinsky, aided by a young anarchist named Rose Pesotta, who was often sent to the fiercest antiunion factories to organize workers. As the only paid woman organizer in a male-dominated union, Pesotta had to fight to get her voice heard within the union. Her anarchism and commitment to women made her an outsider and were issues that she had to deal with throughout her career.

Militant. Pesotta was one of the militant female labor organizers working for the ILGWU, a group that included Fannia Cohn, Pauline Newman, and Rose Schneiderman. Each of these early female leaders faced difficult decisions regarding working within the union because of the discrimination they saw in the union hierarchy and in the shops. These women, however, realized that without a union the conditions would be much worse. Pesotta chose to work within the ILGWU and challenged the positions taken by the male leaders. Questioning the authority of the men in the union led Pesotta to be labeled as a troublemaker. Although the women mentioned were able to achieve positions of power, women were still largely absent from union leadership. It was socially unacceptable for women to aspire to these positions.

Vice President. Pesotta used early successes in unionizing on the West Coast, particularly in Los Angeles and San Francisco, as a catapult into the upper echelons of ILGWU leadership. Pesotta was nominated and elected a vice president of the union in 1934, even though she did not agree to be a candidate. She could not logically justify a position on the executive board with her anarchist background. Pesotta seemed to enjoy the honor for her accomplishments and remained a vice president for the next ten years. Dubinsky, like Pesotta, was fiercely anticommunist and an advocate of social reform; thus, he took her under his wing.

Success. Pesotta found success almost everywhere she went, and after the ILGWU pledged itself to the fledgling Committee for Industrial Organizations (CIO) the union began to lend her out to other organizing drives. Pesotta was the only "woman organizer" helping at the United Auto Workers strike in Flint, Michigan, and at the Akron rubber workers strike in the late 1930s. It was Pesotta's job to raise the morale of the strikers by working with the wives, daughters, and sisters. She often spoke at meetings of the strikers and led them in union songs. She also filmed the strikes with her movie camera, and the workers were eager to pose for her, thus increasing her familiarity with the strikers. Pesotta played an important role in the Flint sit-down strike. She was involved in the negotiations and diligently supported the strikers. During this strike thugs attacked and beat her, causing a lifelong hearing impairment. When the strike was finally settled, Pesotta was one of the CIO and UAW leaders who led the workers out.

Difficulty. Pesotta was an anarchist in philosophy but a pragmatist in action. She made the choice to be practical based on her experiences as a union organizer. She came under fire from fellow anarchists for being too willing to compromise and for her position as a bureaucrat. Pesotta also increasingly ran into difficulties with Dubinsky. She criticized him for ruling the ILGWU as a dictatorship and for the sexism she so plainly saw within the union. Publicly she was loyal to Dubinsky, but privately she began to view him as a sellout and lost all respect for him. Their differences grew so great that Dubinsky sent Pesotta to Los Angeles in 1940, a form of banishment to which she vigorously objected.

Return to the Factory. After a difficult time organizing in Los Angeles, marked by internal fighting with local male ILGWU leaders, Pesotta surprised everyone by returning to the sewing machine at a dress factory in New York City. In fact, Pesotta had been devastated by her experiences in Los Angeles. She was not allowed to manage the locals she had organized on the West Coast and felt abandoned by Dubinsky and the other members of the executive board. For the next few years Pesotta searched for purpose in her life after the many years of organizing. Sometimes she lost jobs in the dress industry because of her previous years of agitation.

Legacy. Pesotta was marginalized and isolated from the ILGWU because she was an outspoken woman trying to make changes in a male-dominated hierarchy. Her anarchism further threatened those in power. In many cases women had subservient and powerless roles in the 1930s. Pesotta dared to step out of the role society gave her. She is one of the few women who made it past the bastions of male power in the 1930s and tried to instill her own brand of feminism into the labor movement.

Source:
Elaine Leeder, *The Gentle General: Rose Pesotta, Anarchist and Labor Organizer* (Albany: State University of New York Press, 1933).

PEOPLE IN THE NEWS

In 1937 and 1938 New York patent-law student **Chester Floyd Carlson** developed the xerography process, revolutionizing the process of duplicating business documents. His patent to the process netted him a fortune.

In May 1930 **Ellen Church** became the first airline stewardess. United Airlines hired her and seven other women, all aged twenty-five; single; shorter than five feet, four inches; and lighter than 115 pounds. The airline argued that such women would help allay passenger fears of flying.

Michael S. Cullen, 46, opened the first true supermarket in Jamaica, Long Island, New York, in August 1930. Established in an abandoned garage, the market met with virtually instant success.

In 1932 San Antonio candy maker **C. Elmer Doolin** introduced mass-produced corn chips, Fritos, to the public. Doolin got the recipe from local Mexican café owner Gustave Olgin and produced the chips using a modified potato ricer to cut the tortilla dough.

In 1934 Federal Bureau of the Budget director **Lewis Douglas** resigned in protest of mounting government deficits.

On 4 June 1937 a supermarket in Oklahoma City introduced a supermarket shopping cart, designed by grocer **Sylvan N. Goldman**. The carts were a combination of wicker basket and folding chair and revolutionized American grocery shopping.

In 1930 the first **Howard Johnson** restaurant opened at Wollaston, Massachusetts, on Cape Cod, serving ice cream, frankfurters and fried clams; the next year Johnson began franchising the restaurant, including its menu, famous for its twenty-eight flavors of ice cream.

On 3 October 1930 oil wildcatter **Columbus "Dad" Joiner** struck oil in east Texas, tapping the largest oil reservoir discovered to that point. Joiner soon sold his claim to businessman H. L. Hunt for $1.33 million and then plowed the money back into more wildcatting. When he died at the end of the 1940s, Joiner was nearly pennyless.

In 1930 Russian American economist **Simon Kuznets**, 29, began to formulate models culminating in the creation of an index of national wealth, the gross national product (GNP).

Shipbuilder **David Keith Ludwig** pioneered new techniques for efficient shipbuilding, including side-launching newly built ships and techinques of ship welding. In 1935 he founded National Bulk Carrier.

Freon 12 (dichlorodifluoromethane), a refrigerant gas developed by **Thomas Midgley** of Ethyl Corporation and **C. F. Kettering** of GM, was produced for the first time for use in refrigerators in 1931.

In 1930 **Col. Jacob Schick** introduced the Schick Dry Shaver, an electric razor selling for twenty-five dollars each. By 1937 he had sold nearly 1.85 million razors.

Because of uncontrolled oil production that was driving prices to disastrously low levels, Texas governor **Ross Sterling** declared the oil fields of east Texas in a "state of insurrection" on 17 August 1931. The declaration allowed Sterling to send National Guardsmen and the Texas Rangers into the oil fields to shut down overproducers, but because of smuggling, the effort to raise prices failed.

In September 1931 General Electric president **Gerard Swope** proposed the "Swope Plan" for economic recovery: the creation of trade associations led by representatives of labor and management to coordinate production in industry. "Production and consumption should be coordinated," Swope told the National Electrical Manufacturers Association, "preferably by the joint participation and joint administration of management and employees." Many of Swope's proposals became part of the New Deal's National Recovery Administration.

In November 1933 Secretary of the Treasury **William Woodin** resigned due to illness. He was replaced by **Hans Morganthau Jr.**

DEATHS

Warren Bechtel, 60, railroad builder and construction magnate, helped build the San Francisco–Oakland Bay Bridge and Boulder Dam, 28 August 1933.

Hernand Behn, 53, capitalist, founder of International Telephone and Telegraph Corporation, 7 October 1933.

Robert Somers Brookings, 71, Saint Louis woodenware merchant and philanthropist, generous contributor to Washington University, founder of the Brookings Institution, 15 November 1932.

James A. Campbell, 79, steel manufacturer, president of Youngstown Sheet and Tube Company, third largest in the United States, 20 September 1933.

Howard Earle Coffin, 64, automobile engineer and industrialist, organized the Hudson Motor Car Company, chairman of the Aircraft Board during World War I, 21 November 1937.

William Sloane Coffin, 54, New York furniture maker and real estate magnate, 16 December 1933.

Gilbert Colgate, 74, president of Colgate-Palmolive-Peet Company, grandson of the founder of Colgate Soap Manufacturing, 5 January 1933.

William Ellis Corey, 68, steel manufacturer, former president of U.S. Steel, 11 May 1934.

Robert Dollar, 87, West Coast shipping magnate and lumberman, president of the Dollar steamship company, 16 May 1932.

Alfred I. du Pont, 70, former vice president and general manager of the Du Pont Company, chief stockholder, Florida real estate developer, 29 April 1935.

George Eastman, 77, photographer and philanthropist, inventor of many processes for photography, founder and chairman of Eastman Kodak, 14 March 1932.

Edward A. Filene, 77, Boston retailer and philanthropist, 26 September 1937.

Harvey S. Firestone, 69, rubber manufacturer, founder of Firestone Tire and Rubber, 7 February 1938.

King Camp Gillette, 77, industrialist, inventor of the safety razor, president of the Gillette Safety Razor Company, 10 September 1932.

William Charles Gotshall, 60, electrical railway engineer, developer of high-speed electric traction, 20 August 1935.

Carl Raymond Gray, 71, railroad executive, president of the Union Pacific Railroad (1920–1937), 9 May 1939.

Murry Guggenheim, 81, mining industrialist and philanthropist, 15 November 1939.

Charles Hayden, 66, Boston financier and philanthropist, 8 January 1937.

Morris Hillquit, 63, labor organizer and leader of the Socialist Party of the United States, 7 October 1933.

Samuel Insull, 78, public utilities magnate, fled the United States under indictment for fraud, extradited and found innocent in 1934, 16 July 1938.

Ralph Burkett Ives, 60, insurance executive, president and chairman of the Aetna Fire Insurance Company, 2 January 1934.

Mary Harris "Mother" Jones, 100, fiery orator and legendary labor organizer for the United Mine Workers, 30 November 1930.

Otto Hermann Kahn, 63, railroad financier and banker, senior partner in Kuhn, Loeb and Company, classical music philanthropist, 29 March 1934.

Ivy Ledbetter Lee, 57, public relations expert, founder of Ivy Lee and Associates in 1916, public relations firm for some of the largest industrial interests in the United States, 9 November 1934.

Adolph Lewisohn, 89, mining financier and philanthropist, 17 August 1938.

James Loeb, 65, banker and philanthropist, member of the New York banking firm Kuhn, Loeb and Company, publisher of the Loeb Classical Library, supporter of classical music and literature, 27 May 1933.

Franklin MacVeagh, 96, grocer, banker, and secretary of the treasury (1908–1913), 6 July 1934.

Stephen Tyng Mather, 52, manufacturer and advertiser, developed the famous "Twenty-Mule Team" slogan for the Pacific Coast Borax Company, first director of the National Park Service (1917–1929), 22 January 1930.

Cyrus Hall McCormick, 77, inventor of the reaping machine, founder of International Harvester Corporation, 2 June 1936.

Andrew W. Mellon, 82, financier, founder of the Aluminum Company of America, secretary of the treasury (1921–1932), art philanthropist, 26 August 1937.

Richard Beatty Mellon, 74, financier, president of Mellon National Bank, director of numerous industrial interests, 1 December 1933.

Charles Wyman Morse, 77, speculator and shipping magnate; his illegal banking practices resulted in a fifteen-year jail sentence in 1908; pardoned by President William H. Taft in 1912, after which he returned to the shipping business; indicted again in 1922 on charges of fraud, 12 January 1933.

William Cooper Proctor, 71, president and chairman of Proctor and Gamble Company, son of the founder, 2 May 1934.

John D. Rockefeller, 97, America's first billionaire, founder of Standard Oil, 23 May 1937.

Julius Rosenwald, 69, wholesaler and philanthropist, head of Sears, Roebuck and Company, in 1917 founded the Rosenwald Fund to assist black education, 6 January 1932.

Jacob Schick, 59, manufacturer of electric razors, July 1937.

Charles M. Schwab, 77, industrialist, president of the U.S. Steel Corporation (1901–1903), head of Bethlehem Steel for thirty-five years, 18 September 1939.

Edwin R. A. Seligman, 78, economist, founder of the American Economic Association, tax expert whose advice was sought for many pieces of federal and state legislation, 18 July 1939.

Harry C. Stutz, 53, automobile manufacturer, formed the Ideal Motor Car Company (1911–1919), 26 June 1930.

William Boyce Thompson, 60, mining industrialist and financier, headed the American Red Cross mission to Russia in 1917, 27 June 1930.

Frederick William Vanderbilt, 82, railroad director, grandson of Cornelius Vanderbilt, noted for his skill as a yachtsman, 2 June 1939.

Frank A. Vanderlip, 72, banker, assistant secretary of the treasury during the Spanish-American War, 29 June 1937.

Charles R. Walgreen, 66, merchant and retailer, founder of Walgreen Drug Stores, 11 December 1939.

Graham Wallas, 74, British economist whose work was influential in the United States, especially his 1914 book *The Great Society*, 10 August 1932.

Felix Warburg, 66, banker, partner in Kuhn, Loeb and Company, heavy contributor to Jewish philanthropies, 20 October 1937.

Henry Parker Willis, 62, economist, helped create the Federal Reserve System, 18 July 1937.

PUBLICATIONS

Thurman Arnold, *The Folklore of Capitalism* (New Haven: Yale University Press, 1937);

Benjamin Graham, *Security Analysis* (New York: Whittlesey House, 1934);

Armand Hammer, *The Quest of the Romanoff Treasure* (New York: Payson, 1932);

Alvin Hansen, *Economic Stabilization in an Unbalanced World* (New York: Harcourt, Brace, 1932);

H. V. Hodson, *Economics of a Changing World* (London: Faber & Faber, 1933);

Herbert Hoover, *The Challenge to Liberty* (New York: Scribners, 1934);

Arthur Kallet and F. J. Schlink, *100,000,000 Guinea Pigs* (New York: Vanguard, 1932);

John Maynard Keynes, *The General Theory of Employment, Interest and Money* (New York: Harcourt, Brace & World, 1935);

H. R. Knickerbocker, *The Red Trade Menace* (New York: Dodd, Mead, 1931);

J. K. Lasser, *Your Income Tax* (New York: Simon & Schuster, 1936–), published annually;

Lewis Mumford, *Technics and Civilization* (New York: Harcourt, Brace, 1934);

Ferdinand Pecora, *Wall Street under Oath, the Story of Our Modern Money Changers* (New York: Simon & Schuster, 1939);

F. J. Schlink, *Eat, Drink and Be Wary* (New York: Grosset & Dunlap, 1935);

George Soule, *The Coming American Revolution* (New York: Macmillan, 1934).

EDUCATION

by VICTOR BONDI

CONTENTS

Sidebars and tables are listed in italics.

1930

- Festivities at colleges and in communities around the United States celebrate the Virgil Bimillennium, the two-thousandth anniversary of the birth of the Roman poet.

3 Feb. Some 1.5 million schoolchildren listen to the first educational radio broadcast, transmitted on CBS by the American School of the Air.

1931

- Congress authorizes the National Survey of School Finance to take stock of the condition of schools in the United States.

Jan. The William H. Spencer High School is dedicated in Columbus, Georgia. A model of the industrial-school movement, Spencer High is an all-black school designed to prepare students for industrial jobs rather than college.

Dec. President Herbert Hoover's National Advisory Committee on Education issues its report on American schools, finding them in generally good condition.

1932

- Bennington College in Bennington, Vermont, holds its first classes.

- African Americans in the Philadelphia area found the Educational Equality League to seek desegregation of the public schools, the hiring of black teachers, and the appointment of a black to the school board.

18 Feb. Columbia University professor George S. Counts delivers a speech to a teachers' convention in Baltimore on the topic "Dare Progressive Education Be Progressive?" — launching the social-reconstructionist movement in education.

1933

- The Institute for Advanced Study, a graduate institute that confers no degrees, opens at Princeton University. Educator Abraham Flexner is its first director.

1 Mar. In an address before a school supervisors' convention in Minneapolis, John Dewey casts the U.S. Chamber of Commerce as an enemy of public education for having recently proposed radical cuts in American education as a Depression-era austerity measure.

17 Apr. The first Civilian Conservation Corps (CCC) camp opens. Although the CCC is a New Deal agency directed toward forestry and environmental work, it will also conduct broad educational programs for thousands from impoverished backgrounds.

24 Apr. Five thousand Chicago schoolteachers march on city hall, demanding back pay after having been paid for ten months in scrip.

21 July Twenty-five thousand teachers and supporters fill Chicago Stadium, protesting budget cuts and firings by the Chicago school board.

14 Dec. Ten children are killed and thirty injured when a school bus is struck by a freight train in Crescent City, Florida.

1934

- The Progressive Education Association begins an eight-year study that it hopes will convince colleges to modernize their curricula.

- Indebtedness of school districts in the United States rises to $137 million, up from $93 million in 1930.

1935

-
- Textbook purchases by public schools have fallen by one-third since 1930.
- The average public-schoolteacher's annual salary has dropped 13.6 percent, from $1,420 to $1,227, since 1930.
- Berwyn, Pennsylvania, desegregates its schools after boycotts of segregated schools by the Educational Equality League of Philadelphia.
- A study shows that 98 percent of school superintendents were born in the United States and that 90 percent are from Anglo-Saxon backgrounds.

1 Apr. Nearly twenty thousand schools, mostly in rural areas, have closed for lack of financing.

- Following pressure from the Daughters of the American Revolution, the American Legion, and other groups concerned about political subversion, nineteen states pass laws requiring teachers to swear loyalty oaths.

18 Jan. Brookwood Labor College in New York celebrates its fifteenth anniversary with a commemoration involving more than five hundred graduates and trade unionists.

13 Feb. The Arkansas House of Representatives authorizes an investigation of alleged communist activities at Commonwealth College, a labor college in Mena, Arkansas.

10 June The Tennessee House of Representatives reaffirms the verdict of the 1925 Scopes "monkey trial" by passing a statute prohibiting the teaching of evolution.

26 June The Roosevelt administration establishes the National Youth Administration (NYA) as part of the Works Progress Administration (WPA). The NYA will provide work and education for persons sixteen to twenty-five years of age.

1936

- In *Murray* v. *Maryland* the U.S. Supreme Court orders the University of Maryland Law School either to admit an African American student, Donald Murray, or to create a segregated law school for him alone. Murray is admitted to the law school.

1937

- Queens College is founded in Flushing, New York.
- King William's School in Annapolis, Maryland, becomes St. John's College, under the leadership of Stringfellow Barr and Scott Buchanan.
- Western Auto Supply magnate George Pepperdine funds Pepperdine College, a new school in Los Angeles.

9 Feb. Senators Pat Harrison of Mississippi and Hugo Black of Alabama introduce a bill providing $100 million in federal aid to schools. The bill will be defeated.

28 May President Roosevelt signs a bill repealing the infamous "red rider" to a Washington, D.C., appropriation bill. The rider had required teachers in the nation's capital to sign a loyalty oath.

15 Aug.   Commonwealth College in Mena, Arkansas, formally affiliates itself with the Southern Tenant Farmers Union.

21 Nov.   Brookwood Labor College closes, the victim of the Depression and internal political divisions.

1938

- Congress passes the George-Deen Act, appropriating $14.5 million for vocational education.

6 Feb.   In a published report the Carnegie Foundation for the Advancement of Teaching condemns unfair competitive practices by colleges searching for tuition-paying students.

12 Dec.   In *Missouri ex. rel. Gaines* v. *Canada* the U.S. Supreme Court orders the state of Missouri to provide equal educational accommodations for African American law students.

1939

- George S. Counts begins a campaign to rid the American Federation of Teachers of Communist Party influence.

- Only 4 percent of the professors at large state universities are women, but they hold 23.5 percent of the instructorships.

OVERVIEW

Ideals and Realities. Long before the 1930s the public school was a symbol of American democracy. In many ways it represented the promise of America: a place where hard work and achievement were rewarded, where brilliance was mined from the ore of raw talent — a necessary starting point on the road to success. Pedagogues from Thomas Jefferson to John Dewey argued that the future of the school and the future of democracy were one, that the school was the only nonauthoritarian institution capable of instilling the self-discipline necessary for a self-governing nation. The distance between the American ideal of school and the reality of American schools in the 1930s, however, was striking. Lip service for education was freely available, but financial support for schools and good salaries for teachers went begging. A financially pressed public prioritized its limited resources, and the schools lost out. Early in the decade a blue-ribbon panel of the National Economic League issued a list of "Paramount Problems of the United States"; in 1930 the condition of education was fourteenth among their concerns; in 1931 it was twenty-fourth and in 1932 thirty-second. During the Depression most Americans decided they could not afford their love affair with the school.

The Bottom Line. The goals and ideals of education in the 1930s were in sharp conflict with the economic bottom line, as businessmen repeatedly pointed out. In the 1910s and 1920s American business had been one of the foremost champions of public education, especially of the high school, which was busy training at taxpayer expense the stenographers, secretaries, and clerks of the future. In the 1920s businessmen had generously loaned money for new school buildings and reaped handsome profits as building contractors and school provisioners. During the Depression, however, businessmen had a change of heart. Schools needed tax dollars to survive; businesses needed tax breaks to pay their debts. C. Weston Bailey, president of the National Board of Fire Underwriters, spoke for many when he complained of "exorbitant taxes and bureaucracy" in education and demanded a "prompt stopping of this riot of waste." Businessmen's groups such as the U.S. Chamber of Commerce, the National Committee for Economy in Government, and the National Economic League argued that Americans could no longer afford universal public education. The most extreme among them wanted the schools closed, while the moderates argued that the schools should restrict their instruction to trade skills and job training. They also wanted their school loans paid back, and they wanted school boards to maintain their lucrative provisioning contracts. In Chicago businessmen had their way: the school board fired fourteen hundred teachers, cut the salaries and increased the teaching loads of the remainder, and repaid their building debts to businessmen — even as they retained provisioning contracts, and businessmen received federal bailouts. Georgia and Alabama closed schools, leaving thousands of children without access to formal education. Iowa lowered teachers' salaries 30 percent, to forty dollars a month. By 1933 there were two hundred thousand unemployed teachers; 2.2 million children were out of school; and two thousand rural schools in twenty-four states failed to open. Whatever transcendent values the school had in the American imagination, they were not sufficient to protect education from the Depression.

Meritocracy. Businessmen were the foremost advocates of school retrenchment during the 1930s, not only because they were pressured by the Depression, but also because they embraced a particular outlook regarding the role of schools in American society, one shared by many educators. Businessmen and some educators argued that the role of the school was to select the gifted few from the dull mass, to sort out a capable elite from the incapable many. Given this presumption, education could be ruthlessly slashed: the gifted, the able, those struggling to achieve, would claw their way to success regardless, and the rest would take their place as the underlings of industrial society. In theory anyone, from any class or race, was capable of succeeding in this meritocratic model of education. In practice, however, there were enormous class and racially based barriers to educational success.

Class Barriers. Success in education meant graduation from college. Graduation from college meant access to high-wage jobs and wealth. But college was not open to many. Admission requirements retained from the nineteenth century often stressed a knowledge of archaic languages, such as Latin or Greek, or mastery of subjects such as algebra, not taught in all public schools. The children of wealthy businessmen, trained in private, expensive college-preparatory academies, were well prepared for college-admission tests. Children attending public high schools often were not. Businessmen argued that financing academic training in the high schools was a waste of money: children from working-class, immigrant backgrounds were born for manual labor, and their high-school education should be in metalworking, not Latin. That a child educated in metalworking would be unable to pass an examination in Latin was obvious. Less obvious was the fact that in this manner gifted children from impoverished backgrounds would be prevented from competing with less-talented children from wealthy backgrounds.

Racial Barriers. The manner in which education served to reinforce the economic status quo was illustrated perfectly in the education of African Americans. American education was racially segregated in the 1930s precisely because of the white presumption that blacks were inherently incapable of learning at an advanced level. Segregating white schoolchildren from black schoolchildren meant that white pupils presumably would not be "held back" in the classroom by less-capable black pupils. Black schools, especially in the South, were thus underfunded and rudimentary. There were a mere handful of black high schools throughout the South. Two hundred thirty southern counties did not have a single high school for black students in 1932 — even though every one of these counties possessed a high school for whites. In sixteen states there was not a single state-supported black institution that offered graduate or professional programs. Northern white philanthropists, sometimes explicitly acknowledging that their goal was to prevent "competition between the races," often insisted that their charity be used to build black "industrial schools," training African Americans for manual labor. Only African Americans and some white progressive educators dissented from the mainstream assumption that tax money spent on black education was a waste of money. Black communities throughout the country built schools for themselves and hired instructors for the most difficult subjects. Black academics such as W. E. B. Du Bois, Horace Mann Bond, and E. Franklin Frazier attacked intelligence testing and educational discrimination that validated the status quo. They were combating years of neglect and racism. In 1930, 15 percent of rural adult African Americans had no formal schooling, and 48 percent had never gone beyond the fifth grade. White school boards paid white teachers an average annual salary of $833; black teachers, who had larger teaching loads, were paid only $510. Ironically, the Depression improved the situation of black education in many ways. In northern schools, school boards began to abolish segregated education as a way of saving money; in the South educators fearful of the possible consequences of unschooled, unemployed youths succeeded in getting school districts to build high schools for blacks — if for no other reason than to keep them off the streets. Thanks to such programs and to literacy campaigns mounted by New Deal agencies such as the National Youth Administration (NYA), by 1940 five hundred thousand illiterate blacks had been taught to read and write. The number of African Americans attending high school doubled; the number of high-school graduates tripled; and the percentage of blacks attending school became equal to that of whites.

Progressive Education. Segregation, of course, validated its own racial premises: substandard education was given to blacks because they were presumed to be incapable of intellectual achievement; substandard education then kept blacks from achieving academic success. Progressive educators sought to break this vicious circle of educational failure by changing the criteria for educational success for both poor blacks and poor whites. Progressives argued that colleges should restructure their curricula and admissions requirements to reflect the modern, scientific, multicultural character of American society. They argued that requirements tied to the older collegiate traditions of "gentlemanly education," such as Latin and the classics, ought to be deemphasized in favor of the sciences. In 1934 the Progressive Education Association began a large, expensive experiment, an eight-year study designed to convince colleges to modernize their curricula, which they did after World War II. Progressives also advocated restructuring primary- and secondary-school courses of study, in general favoring a broader evaluation of scholastic performance than strict academic excellence. Often progressives disagreed about how this broadening of education was to take place, but in general they sought an expansion of education to everyone, a leveling of differences in the quality of education provided, and the creation of real opportunities for impoverished students.

Conflict. Expansion, however, was a hard sell during the Depression, especially given business emphasis on retrenchment. During the first half of the decade progressive educators were thwarted at every turn by conservatives and businessmen. Capital outlays for education actually shrank to levels of twenty years earlier. Teachers turned militant, organizing, affiliating with trade unions, and taking their case to the people. They also became politically active, joining the New Deal and left-wing crusades to equalize political and economic power in America. The leading educational philosophy of the decade was a variant of progressivism known as social reconstructionism, which advocated political action for American teachers. After 1935, and something of a return to prosperity, progressives increasingly got their way in the nation's schools, often by enlisting the public in school-funding drives and publicizing the function of the school in a democratic society. In 1936 big business was crushed at the polls, and the public equally rejected business demands for retrenchment in education. In defeat, however, conservatives raised the level of invective directed against the schools, accusing progressives of socialist and communist indoctrination and precipitating a "red scare" whose full effects were not felt until after World War II. Nonetheless, American schools were back on the track set for them by progressive educators, the path on which progressive education gradually improved the character of American democracy, widening opportunity for all and imparting fundamental instruction in civic obligation and self-government.

TOPICS IN THE NEWS

THE DEPRESSION AND EDUCATION

Retrenchment and Reform. The Great Depression profoundly transformed every American institution. In education it eroded significant educational advances begun during the 1920s. Schools were closed; teachers' salaries were cut; school programs were eliminated. Yet in an important sense the Depression precipitated the modernization of American schools. The political trade-off for reduced financing of schools was increased autonomy for school administrators and teachers. Facing budget cuts, teachers organized into militant unions that in many cases successfully represented their interests. Economic consolidation led to standardization of curriculum, textbooks, and testing. The financing of school districts, which had been variable in the 1920s, was reformed and made efficient by the Depression. While the Depression had disastrous consequences for American schools, especially in the early 1930s, it was also instrumental in making education more modern, consistent, and professional.

Boom and Decline. During the boom years of the 1920s, new schools had been built, junior-high schools had been developed, and new programs, such as vocational education, had been expanded. Teachers' salaries were rising. More and more children were attending schools. In Detroit, Michigan, the student population doubled, increasing from 122,690 in 1920 to 250,994 in 1930. So prosperous were American schools that the effect of the Depression failed to impact education significantly until 1932. Enrollments and salaries continued to grow. During the 1931–1932 school year the salaries of school superintendents increased from $4,000 to $4,200. In 1932, however, capital outlays for schools began a precipitous drop, and schools began to decline. In Detroit total school revenues fell from $17.8 million in the 1930–1931 school year to $12.8 million in the 1932–1933 school year. Many school districts were burdened with enormous debts from school expansion in the 1920s, and

Chicago teachers protesting cuts in education spending, 1934

the indebtedness of school districts increased from $93 million in 1930 to $137 million in 1934. Business leaders demanded repayment of these debts; bankers and tax leagues demanded cuts in educational programs and teachers' salaries. Some went further and demanded the closing of entire school districts. By 1934 the number of teachers, supervisors, and principals in education had fallen to the level of 1927; the cost per child enrolled declined to the level of 1922; the average salaries of teachers, principals, and supervisors dropped to the level of 1921; and the total capital outlay for schools was back to the level of 1913. Twenty years of educational advances disappeared, seemingly overnight.

INCOME AND THE TEACHERS

One sign of the increased militancy of teachers during the Depression was their willingness to attack the wealthy. The educational journal *Social Frontier*, for example, published the following list of annual incomes in 1934:

William Randolph Hearst, $500,000, Newspapers

Mae West, $339,166, Movies

B. D. Miller, $337,479, Dime stores

C. W. Guttzeit, $323,250, Electricity

Charles M. Schwab, $250,000, Steel

Bing Crosby, $192,948, Crooner

George Hill, $187,126, Tobacco

R. B. Bohn, $140,860, Aluminum

F. B. Davis, $125,219, Rubber

Arthur C. Dorrance, $112,500, Soups

At the time the average annual salary of an American teacher was slightly more than $1,200; a college instructor was paid slightly more than $1,500.

Source: William Edward Eaton, *The American Federation of Teachers, 1916–1961: A History of the Movement* (Carbondale: Southern Illinois University Press, 1975).

Hard Times. As hard times arrived, people outside education naturally enough wanted to save money by trimming education down to its sparest functions. Many schools were closed. Georgia shut down 1,318 schools, leaving 170,790 children without instruction. During the 1932–1933 school year 81 percent of white children in rural Alabama had no schools. Other districts reduced their hours of operation. In Dayton, Ohio, schools were open only three days a week. By the score, schools cut recently introduced programs such as art, music, manual arts, home economics, physical education, and health. Vocational education, the foremost educational innovation of the 1920s, was virtually eliminated. In New York State, 97 of 110 school districts with populations higher than five thousand had no vocational education. Textbook purchases between 1930 and 1934 fell by a third nationwide. One fifth-grade class in Waukegan, Illinois, was forced to share a single textbook, from which the teacher read aloud. Many schools increased the teacher/student ratio of their classes as an economy measure. In 1934 the average high school had 24.9 students for every teacher, and many schools had classes of 40 students or more. Enrollment in high schools also increased, as students who might have taken jobs if they were available stayed in school for want of work. Between 1930 to 1940 the number of public-high-school students increased from 4.4 million to 6.5 million, straining the resources of financially strapped schools. Some educators

suggested that high-school graduation be made compulsory, as a way of keeping young people out of the labor market. Other educators suggested lowering academic standards because so many new students were poorly prepared for classes — an idea that would find full expression in the "life adjustment curriculum" of the 1940s. Schools also increased the practice of "social promotion" — passing students on to higher grades whether they met academic standards or not.

Salaries. The biggest financial cuts for school budgets came in teacher salaries. School districts expected teachers to accept lowered salaries and increased workloads, and for the most part teachers did, rationalizing that any job was better than no job at all. From 1929–1930 to 1933–1934 teachers' salaries dropped 13.6 percent on average, from $1,420 to $1,227 annually. In Philadelphia the school board "volunteered" a 10 percent wage cut on the part of teachers; Denver teachers were forced to take a 20 percent cut in the same fashion. In New York substitute teachers were hired to replace regular teachers as a technique for cutting wages. The drop in pay was somewhat offset by declining prices for most goods, but teachers' salaries had already been lowest among the professions, and teachers lived in constant fear that they would lose their jobs and end up, like so many others, on the street. The fear was even more acute among married women teachers, often dismissed from their posts because of the argument that what few jobs there were should go to men.

Modernization. The political trade-off for reduced salaries was increased teacher control of schools. Tenure and certification laws were enacted along with salary cuts, making teachers more secure in their jobs. Enrollment in associations such as the American Federation of Teachers (AFT) and the National Education Association (NEA) increased. School surveys were repeatedly undertaken in the hopes of making school more financially and pedagogically effective. The pressure of the Depression resulted in the consolidation of many school districts and school facilities, centralizing and rationalizing control of education — goals education reformers had long sought. Businesses that supplied local school districts with textbooks, furniture, and physical plants standardized their products and homogenized the educational market.

State Financing. The most important change necessitated by the Great Depression was an increase in educational financing from the states. The decline in property values and general prosperity often dried up sources of school funding at the local level. Increasingly states assumed the responsibility of paying for schools, standardizing both financial practices and curriculum. Many states began providing "foundation grants" — a "floor" of guaranteed funding for every district in a state, rich or poor. Localities remained free to spend more or less on their own schools; state funding was designed to ensure that a minimal amount of instruction was financed. Between 1930 and 1940 state support for schools doubled,

THRIFT AND SCHOOLCHILDREN

Some of the economic casualties of the Depression were American schoolchildren. Since 1920 the Savings Bank Division of the American Bankers Association, with the support of the National Education Association, had been promoting thrift campaigns and savings projects in the public schools. The program was touted as an opportunity for schoolchildren to learn finance and personal discipline. By 1930 nearly 4.5 million children in fourteen thousand schools were participating, with deposits totaling more than $29 million. As banks around the country closed, however, the schoolchildren, as well as adults, lost their savings. Teachers sometimes compensated the children for their losses. In 1935 Saint Louis school superintendent Henry J. Gerling gave twenty-five thousand dollars of his own money to cover the losses of schoolchildren. Nothing could compensate, however, for the loss of the bankers' intended lesson about the rewards of frugality.

Source: Edward A. Krug, *The Shaping of the American High School, Volume 2, 1920–1941* (Madison: University of Wisconsin Press, 1972).

covering more than 30 percent of all educational expenses. In 1930 only seven states covered local school costs to that degree; by 1934 eighteen states had assumed this level of support.

Federal Funding. Despite the increase in state funding, the inequality in funding of school districts remained a severe problem that was related to the relative wealth or poverty of the individual states. South Carolina, one of the poorest states in the nation, for example, could not raise the funds necessary to finance schools on the level of a wealthy state such as Delaware. In 1935 the federal government commissioned a study of inequalities in education among the states. Under the leadership of educator Paul Mort, the National Survey of School Finance recommended that the national government provide foundation grants to the states, as the states had to their local school districts. Mort proposed an expenditure of $15 per pupil per year to help schools raise their level of instruction. Similarly, in 1936 Mississippi senator Patrick Harrison proposed a federal grant of $100 million to the states, but the bill was defeated. In 1938 the Roosevelt administration created an education advisory committee, led by Floyd Reeves of the University of Chicago, to make further recommendations concerning educational equality. The commission recommended sweeping changes in educational financing, with the bulk of funding coming from Washington. The recommendation was killed in Congress. Many lawmakers believed increased control of education from Washington would violate the long tradition of local control of schools. Southerners

feared the federal government would desegregate the schools, and budget balancers on Capitol Hill and at the White House were afraid the program would plunge the government into receivership. Although the Great Depression did not lead to federal assistance to schools, it did precipitate increased state funding for education and begin the process of replacing old, localized education with modern, national, integrated schools, a process that would be further advanced by World War II.

Sources:
William Edward Eaton, *The American Federation of Teachers, 1916–1961: A History of the Movement* (Carbondale: Southern Illinois University Press, 1975);

David Tyack, Robert Lowe, and Elisabeth Hansot, *Public Schools in Hard Times: The Great Depression and Recent Years* (Cambridge, Mass.: Harvard University Press, 1984).

EDUCATION FOR AFRICAN AMERICANS

Segregation. American education in the 1930s was racially segregated. With few exceptions living patterns and customs led to segregated schools nationwide; in many places, especially in the South, segregation was the law. As African Americans were often the poorest members of communities, their neighborhood schools suffered from their inability to raise funds for teacher salaries and maintenance. African Americans were also unrepresented on most school boards and hence were unable to push for better funding for their schools. The average expenditure per pupil per year was eighty dollars; for African American students the average was fifteen. Nationally, more than 25 percent of all students were black, but they received only 12 percent of all education revenues and only 3 percent of funds budgeted for school transportation. Many white Americans — including many professional educators — embraced an ideology of Anglo-Saxon racial superiority and believed African Americans could not be educated above rudimentary levels. When sociologists Robert and Helen Lynd asked high-school students in Muncie, Indiana, if the white race was "the best race on earth," 66 percent of boys and 75 percent of girls agreed. Georgia education officials argued that whites were "a thousand years" ahead of blacks in evolution and that African Americans were "a constant menace to the health of the community, a constant threat to its peace and security, and a constant cause of and excuse for the retarded progress of the other race." Such officials believed they were acting in a "progressive" fashion by denying blacks education. Racism, poverty, and neglect thus combined to reduce black education to an inadequate, basic level. As President Herbert Hoover's commission on education put it in 1931, black students were "by far the most heavily disadvantaged group of children in the entire field of education."

Self-Help. What education there was for African Americans was usually the result of concerted programs of self-help. Because white southern school boards routinely denied black taxpayers the funds necessary to con-

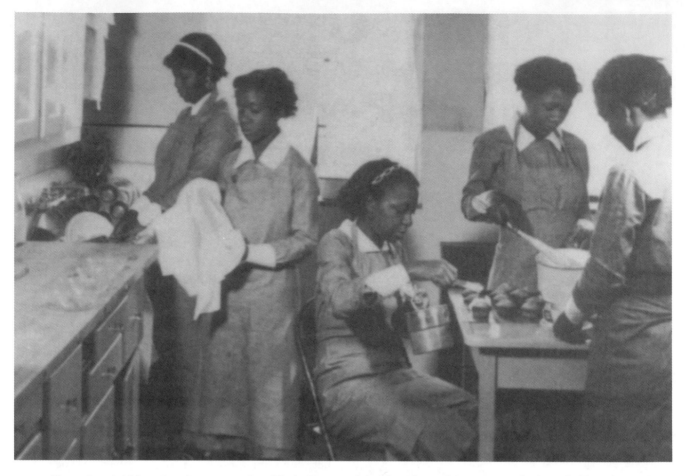

Unemployed African American women in a Works Progress Administration training program for household workers

struct black schools, in the 1910s and 1920s blacks pooled their limited resources and embarked on programs of school construction. Sharecroppers who had been born slaves donated their meager life savings so their grandchildren could have an education. Even people without children mortgaged their homes and lands to fund the schools. Black communities farmed communal lands and used the profits to finance local schools. People who lived in shanties without glass windows or running water banded together to construct one-, two-, and three-room schoolhouses. Those who had no money donated time and labor. Black lumberjacks cut down trees and hewed the pine necessary to build the schools. Women donated food and cooked meals for the laborers. African Americans were often assisted by funds from white philanthropists such as Sears, Roebuck head Julius Rosenwald or from sympathetic white neighbors, but outside funding rarely amounted to more than 12 percent of financing. Nonetheless, in the 1920s and early 1930s African Americans continued to build schools. By 1932 the self-help movement had erected 3,464 schools in 880 southern counties.

Limits. Despite the school-building program blacks in the South had either no schools or inadequate schools. The school-building program of the 1920s served only a fourth of all black students. Most of the schools built,

moreover, were elementary schools; high-school education for blacks remained virtually nonexistent. Nearly half of all black students were in the first two grades of elementary school. Only 19 percent of blacks aged fourteen to seventeen were enrolled in high school, compared to 55 percent of all white students. In some states, such as Mississippi, nearly nine times as many white students attended high school as did black students — despite the fact that black teenagers constituted the majority of the secondary-school-age population in that state. In 230 southern counties African Americans were 12.5 percent or more of the total population; yet there were no high schools. In 195 other counties, there were elementary schools but no high schools. The few black high schools that existed were located in southern cities. There were almost no black high schools in the countryside, although nearly all rural whites had high schools.

Industrial Education. Southern school boards refused to build black high schools because most whites believed blacks were racially incapable of advanced learning. This belief was shared by northern white philanthropists who in the beginning of the decade funded a program of black industrial education that was to take the place of high school. Industrial education was designed to prepare African Americans for low-wage positions in the industrial workplace. Industrial high schools taught carpentry, auto

In 1930 Howard University asked W. E. B. Du Bois, perhaps the most prominent black intellectual in the United States, to deliver its commencement address. Decades earlier, Du Bois had argued that the bulk of the black community's resources should be directed toward the maintenance and cultivation of its brightest and most creative individuals — a "talented tenth" of the African American population that would lead other black people out of racial oppression. Colleges such as Howard University were important parts of this process. Yet by 1930 Du Bois had become profoundly disappointed in the talented tenth. To him, black college students simply imitated their white counterparts, becoming more concerned with the collegiate fads of the Roaring Twenties than with their obligations to the community. His commencement address castigated Howard students for their lack of social consciousness:

> Our college man today is, on the average, a man untouched by real culture. He deliberately surrenders to selfish and even silly ideals, swarming into semiprofessional athletics and Greek letter societies, and affecting to despise scholarship and the hard grind of study and research. The greatest meetings of the Negro college year like those of the white college year have become vulgar exhibitions of liquor, extravagance, and fur coats. We have in our colleges a growing mass of stupidity and indifference.

Source: James D. Anderson, *The Education of Blacks in the South, 1860–1935* (Chapel Hill: University of North Carolina Press, 1988).

mechanics, bricklaying, sewing, laundry working, cooking, and metalworking but almost never literature, mathematics, or history. When New Orleans planned an industrial high school in 1930, the school had no classrooms assigned for traditional academic subjects. The *Times Picayune* explained that industrial education alone would "render the Negro youth more efficient in their chosen tasks and lead them into settled and stable occupations." As the Depression worsened and increasing numbers of blacks migrated from the rural South to southern cities, school boards in those cities began supporting the industrial-school program as a way of keeping unemployed black youths off the street. African Americans, however, pointed out that the Depression had also virtually eliminated jobs for blacks in industry. Vigilantes and white pressure groups such as the Federation of Women's Clubs, the Ku Klux Klan, the Blue Shirts, and the White Knights forced blacks out of jobs that had traditionally been theirs and gave them to white workers. The Jacob Drug Company in Atlanta, for example, fired all its 230 black messengers and replaced them with whites at higher wages. African Americans therefore wanted the industrial schools to include traditional college preparatory curricula. Instead, southern school boards simply stopped building industrial schools. By the end of the decade the absence of black high schools remained striking.

Depression. The Great Depression also ended the self-help program of building elementary schools in most southern communities. Black income, never high to begin with, declined precipitously. In 1934 in some sharecropping areas of the South the monthly per-capita income fell to $1.75. Malnutrition became a serious problem, and less was spent on schools. White school boards were more reluctant than ever to fund black schools. Nonetheless, donations of labor continued to maintain some black schools. In 1933 it was estimated that the total value of labor that rural blacks in Louisiana donated to their schools equaled $2,947.33. Yet books, supplies, and transportation could rarely be donated. Teacher salaries could not be raised. Some black schools in North Carolina could not pay for heating fuel or electricity. A 1934 letter one North Carolina teacher wrote to a white philanthropist expressed the sense of desperation plaguing black educators during the Depression:

> Mr. Embree, I know already that you have almost exhausted your funds on Negro Education and other good causes but we have just got to ask you for a little. Please if you can give us just a little money on our project here in this very humble community of good people. If you can't give us but a little that little will go a long way on our project. Please let me hear from you. If you don't have much money to give us you do have great advice that will go a long way in pointing the way out for us. We do thank you for anything that you have to give us whether it be money, advice or encouragement.

Improvement. Such appeals often went nowhere during the Depression. Black schools remained underfunded and unmaintained. Inadequate education, moreover, was compounded by racial injustice: those African Americans who built and maintained their own schools continued to be taxed by the white school boards who denied black schools funding. Yet the prospects for black education during the Depression were not universally grim. Black colleges prospered during the decade, beneficiaries of donations by northern white philanthropists who weathered the Depression without difficulty. New Deal agencies, especially the National Youth Administration, provided African Americans with instruction in academic subjects, industrial arts, and domestic services. Most important, in northern cities African Americans used the budget cutbacks of the Depression as an occasion to desegregate schools.

An End to Segregation. In cities such as Philadelphia, black educators argued that school systems could conserve scarce financial resources by consolidating the separate black and white school systems. African American citizens developed a variety of techniques to challenge segregation in education. In 1932 African Americans created the Educational Equality League of Philadelphia.

THE PLIGHT OF THE BLACK ACADEMIC

After the Civil War the University of South Carolina hired a black, Harvard-trained teacher named Richard Greener. He left the school in 1873. Between that date and 1940, not a single African American academic was hired as a full-time faculty member at any important white university in the United States. In the 1930s there was a significant number of outstanding black scholars, including educators W. E. B. Du Bois and Horace Mann Bond; political scientist Ernest E. Just; sociologists E. Franklin Frazier, Charles Johnson, and Ira Reid; historians Rayford Logan, Carter G. Woodson, and John Hope Franklin; economist Robert C. Weaver; critic and art historian Alain Locke; poets Sterling Brown and Countee Cullen; and chemist Percy Julian. Although many had been educated at the finest American universities, including Harvard and Chicago, black scholars were offered professorships only at black schools — extremely frustrating given the dismal job prospects during the Depression, when black colleges and universities had even more financial woes than white schools.

Some black universities even refused to hire black professors. Lincoln College, an all-black institution in Pennsylvania, did not hire a black teacher until 1932. Black scholars were often ostracized by their white peers and suffered the everyday indignities in housing and transportation that plagued all African Americans, regardless of education, in the Jim Crow South. The color bar to hiring black faculty at white institutions was broken in 1940, when Allison Davis was hired as a professor of education at the University of Chicago. Before that, by necessity, black scholars formed a tight-knit community whose segregation from the white world ironically, in the words of John Hope Franklin, "made an institution of the field of Negro studies."

Source: Roger Williams, *The Bonds: An American Family* (New York: Atheneum, 1972).

---

forced action from judges and governmental officials. In 1934 the school board in the Philadelphia suburb of Berwyn desegregated its schools. In May 1935 a black surgeon, Dr. John P. Turner, was appointed to the Philadelphia Board of Public Education. By 1938 black teachers were instructing in both black and white schools. Owning to segregated living patterns, segregated schools continued to exist in Philadelphia, but institutional barriers to integrated classes had fallen, and the combination of social, economic, and political pressure proved effective in ending segregation.

The NAACP Plan. Taking stock of the success in Philadelphia, the NAACP began in the mid 1930s to plan legal challenges to segregated education throughout the United States. Under the leadership of a Howard University law professor, Charles Houston, the NAACP began filing suits to end segregation in education. Aware that a direct challenge to the legal foundation of segregation, the 1896 Supreme Court decision *Plessy* v. *Ferguson,* was likely to fail, the NAACP planned a series of challenges to the lack of advanced education or the poor quality of black education, rather than segregation itself. They hoped a court decision demanding that white school boards provide truly equal education to blacks would be so costly for white school districts that they would desegregate the schools voluntarily. An example of the NAACP approach was *Murray* v. *Maryland* (1936), wherein the NAACP helped a black graduate of Amherst College, Donald Murray, file suit to compel his admission to the University of Maryland Law School. When the Court ordered Maryland either to admit Murray or to build a separate law school for blacks, Maryland desegregated its law school. The NAACP successfully repeated the procedure in *Missouri ex. rel. Gaines* v. *Canada* (1938), desegregating the University of Missouri Law School. In the 1940s similar decisions, especially *McLaurin* v. *Oklahoma* (1949), heartened civil rights lawyers. Yet the South resisted, often going to absurd and expensive lengths to keep white and black schoolchildren separated. It seemed a lost cause. In 1954 the NAACP mounted a direct legal challenge to the doctrine of segregation and won a judgment in *Brown* v. *Board of Education* that enshrined a civil rights principle as law: "separate education is inherently unequal."

Sources:

James D. Anderson, *The Education of Blacks in the South, 1860–1935* (Chapel Hill: University of North Carolina Press, 1988);

Vincent P. Franklin, *The Education of Black Philadelphia: The Social and Educational History of a Minority Community, 1900–1950* (Philadelphia: University of Pennsylvania Press, 1979);

Harvard Sitkoff, *A New Deal For Blacks: The Emergence of Civil Rights as a National Issue, Volume 1: The Depression Decade* (New York: Oxford University Press, 1978).

THE EIGHT-YEAR STUDY AND OTHER SCHOOL SURVEYS

Studies and Tracking. The practice of long-term empirical study of curriculum and education, begun in the

---

The league had three main objectives: desegregation of schools, the hiring of black teachers, and the appointment of an African American to the Philadelphia school board. By 1940 they had substantially accomplished all three goals. Lawsuits supported by the National Association for the Advancement of Colored People (NAACP) challenged segregation in the courts. Political activism by the league resulted in the election of white politicians sympathetic to desegregation. Boycotts of segregated education by parents mobilized community opinion and

A BLACK SCHOOL IN EAST TEXAS

Throughout the South black schools were particularly hard hit by the Depression. Underfunded by white school boards in prosperous times, black schools had their budgets virtually eliminated when hard times came. In his *Special Problems of Negro Education* (1939) the noted African American scholar Doxey A. Wilkerson included this description of a black school in east Texas:

> The building was a crude box shack built by the Negroes out of old slabs and scrap lumber. Windows and doors were badly broken. The floor was in such condition that one had to walk carefully to keep from going through cracks and weak boards. Daylight was easily visible through walls, floors, and roof. The building was used for both church and school. Its only equipment consisted of a few rough hewn seats, an old stove brought from a junk pile, a crude homemade pulpit, a very small table, and a large water barrel. . . . Fifty-two children were enrolled. All these crowded into a single small room with benches for but half that number. The teacher and pupils had tacked newspapers on the walls to keep the wind out. Rain poured through the roof, and school was dismissed when it rained. No supplies, except a broom, were furnished the school by the district during the year.

Source: David Tyack, Robert Lowe, and Elisabeth Hansot, *Public Schools in Hard Times: The Great Depression and Recent Years* (Cambridge, Mass.: Harvard University Press, 1984).

1920s, was expanded in the 1930s. Educators framed many new "surveys" to determine the success or failure of curricular innovation and new teaching techniques. These surveys were closely tied to controversies over educational philosophy and the political power and economic strength of certain communities. Their results were accordingly mixed and undermined by charges of partisanship. Despite their inconclusive nature, such surveys thrived in the 1930s.

The Eight-Year Study. The most prominent curricular survey of the decade was the Eight-Year Study. The Commission on the Relation of School and College of the Progressive Education Association ran the study from 1933 to 1941 to evaluate the success of progressive education in placing students in traditional colleges and how well those individuals competed with students from schools with more-conservative curricula. At the time, most colleges had admission standards similar to those of the 1880s, when college curricula were geared toward a privately educated elite. Progressive educators had turned the public schools away from rote memorization, instruction in arcane subjects, and a college-preparatory curriculum that emphasized Latin and Greek. Such students nonetheless had to pass entrance exams filled with academic drills such as translating Latin — and then they had to compete in college with students familiar with such conservative pedagogy. In theory, because progressive education inspired the student to critical thought and

imagination, progressive students should have done better in college than students whose analytic skills and expressiveness were stifled by memorization and authoritarian instruction. By demonstrating the efficiency of progressive education, moreover, progressives hoped to convince conservatives to abandon traditionalism. The Eight-Year Study was begun to see if the theory held up.

Method. Some of the leading progressive educators in the United States oversaw the study: among them were Jesse H. Newlon, Harold Rugg, and Goodwin Watson of the Columbia Teachers College; Superintendent Willard Beatty of the Bronxville, New York, schools; and Wilford M. Aikin of the John Burroughs School in Saint Louis. The study was funded by an unprecedentedly generous endowment of nearly $1.9 million from the Carnegie Foundation and the General Education Board of the Rockefeller Foundation. The study was to track students from selected progressive high schools through their college careers. Thirty-six hundred students from twenty-seven secondary schools participated in the experiment. Nearly three hundred colleges agreed to waive their entrance requirements for graduates of these schools. Because progressive educators argued that their curriculum was more democratic and effective with the ranks of new students filling American high schools, the study was supposed to document the upwardly mobile path of many students from deprived backgrounds. In fact, however, most of the leading progressive schools were located in affluent communities or neighborhoods, such as New Trier Township High School in Winnetka, Illinois; often they were not public institutions but private academies such as the Burroughs School in Saint Louis.

Results. Given the economic and social advantages of such affluent students, it was difficult evaluating whether their educational success was the result of progressive curriculum or their privileged circumstances. Nonetheless, in 1941 evaluators proclaimed progressive education a success, noting that students from progressive schools did as well as students from nonprogressive schools in their college courses. The study also noted that students from the six schools judged most progressive did the best of any group in college. Conservatives were less impressed, arguing that colleges reduced their requirements for the newest crop of poorly educated progressive students. Radicals questioned the worth of the study to students who were not going on to college. The study was constructed carefully enough, however, that it became a model for many regional imitators, including similar surveys in California and Michigan.

Other Studies. Other educational studies during the decade focused on specific academic disciplines. The National Council of Teachers of English revised its curriculum in the 1930s in response to the large number of new students entering high school. Following the progressive educators, they added to traditional subject matter applied English in telephone conversations, business, and other practical settings. In 1940 they published the results of this new "experience curriculum," judging it to be "a model of curriculum construction." Conservatives were less enthusiastic. The writer and critic Wilson Follett condemned the new curriculum. "Pupils," he explained, "who cannot be trusted to give a plural subject a plural verb are now coached in the tricks of dramatic construction, the aesthetics of literary criticism, the canons of the short story, and the composition of free verse, all in the name of 'self-expression.' " Similar curricular innovations and surveys conducted in Pennsylvania, Massachusetts, Virginia, Denver, Los Angeles, and Chicago all ended with contested results. Many surveys followed the development of innovative plans they were designed to validate; when outsiders suggested other evaluative measures, survey administrators often responded that the criteria for evaluation were inappropriate. Thus, the school surveys of the 1930s often simply affirmed programs they were designed to affirm, thrilling supporters but failing to convince critics. In the 1940s controversies in educational philosophy continued to rage — with the surveys barely altering the substance of the debate.

Sources:

Lawrence A. Cremin, *The Transformation of The School: Progressivism in American Education, 1876–1957* (New York: Knopf, 1961);

Edward A. Krug, *The Shaping of the American High School, Volume 2, 1920–1941* (Madison: University of Wisconsin Press, 1972).

FOLK SCHOOLS, LABOR COLLEGES, AND OTHER EXPERIMENTS

Experiments. The 1930s were notable as a decade of remarkable experiments in education, especially at the collegiate level. The Depression challenged many educators' traditional assumptions about teaching as surely as it challenged most Americans' economic and political assumptions. Conservative university curriculum and the role of the college in shaping the economic elite were rethought, in part because of the presence of alternative institutions such as the labor college and the folk school. During the 1930s almost every major American city had a labor college. These schools instituted several educational advances that became common in subsequent decades and challenged mainstream educators to rethink their instructional approaches.

The Folk Schools. The folk schools were derived from nineteenth-century experiments in education pioneered in Denmark. Folk schools broke with the teacher-centered classroom and its emphasis on memorization and recitation. Instead, the folk school stressed interpersonal relations. Teachers and students lived together, and their common labor sustained the operation and financing of the school. Offering courses in labor organizing and political reform, folk schools hoped to become a base for more-sweeping social transformation. They were active in local strikes and health and housing reform. They were often integrated and championed civil rights. They were central in the collection of folk music and pioneered methods of oral history. The best known of the folk

Members of the University in Exile at the New School for Social Research: (seated) Emil Lederer, Alvin Johnson, Frieda Wunderlich, and Karl Brandt; (standing) Hans Speier, Max Wertheimer, Arthur Feiler, Eduard Heimann, Gerhard Colm, and E. von Hornbostel

schools was the Highlander Folk School in Monteagle, Tennessee. Founded in 1932 by a Tennessean named Myles Horton, the school initially relied on support from established educational liberals such as Reinhold Niebuhr and George S. Counts. The school quickly became a center for labor activists and educational experiments. In 1937 Highlander became an official Congress of Industrial Organizations (CIO) educational training center, and it was instrumental in the union's southern organizing drives. In the 1940s and 1950s Highlander established many "citizenship schools" that mounted African American voter-registration drives. Even in the 1930s it trained civil rights leaders in the methods of nonviolent protest, and its role increased in importance during the civil rights campaigns of the 1950s and 1960s. Highlander also became a magnet for attack from conservative groups such as the American Legion, who viewed its civil rights and organizing activities as communistic and subjected it to repeated attacks throughout its history. Other folk schools included the John C. Campbell Folk School in Brasstown, North Carolina, the Pocono Peoples College in Henryville, Pennsylvania, and the American Peoples School in Gladden, Missouri.

The Labor Colleges. The labor colleges were an outgrowth of the noncommunist left-wing labor movement, particularly the socialist Industrial Workers of the World (IWW), and they were often supported financially by trade unions such as the International Ladies Garment Workers Union (ILGWU). Brookwood Labor College in Katonah, New York (founded 1921), Work People's College in Duluth, Minnesota (founded 1903), and Commonwealth College in Mena, Arkansas (founded 1925), were among such schools. Using innovative curricula and

ACADEMIC ANTI-SEMITISM

Although rarely an overt policy, anti-Semitism in higher education was still common in the 1930s. Academically gifted Jewish students were routinely denied admission to many universities, especially those in the Ivy League. Many schools maintained geographic quotas, admitting a set number of students from each region of the nation. Since most Jewish students lived in the Northeast, geographic quotas had the effect of preventing the enrollment of gifted Jewish students while admitting less talented non-Jews from other parts of the country.

Jews were also routinely denied faculty appointments because of their cultural origins, especially in departments of religion, English, and German. In his 1987 memoir Jewish philosophy professor Sidney Hook explained the practice:

> The departments of English were almost everywhere the most intractable and usually the last to come around. It was taken for granted by those who administered the department . . . that the purity of the English language and the effectiveness of instruction in its language and literature required that courses in the subject be taught only by teachers of Anglo-Saxon stock. No one attempted to defend or justify the practice, but it was nonetheless in many institutions until the Second World War.

Many such practices changed radically in the 1930s, as Jewish academics found refuge from the Nazis in the United States and genteel, formerly anti-Semitic scholars abandoned their own prejudices as extremist. A symbolic watershed was crossed in 1938, when Columbia University granted tenure to Lionel Trilling, a Jewish American literary scholar who had earned his undergraduate and graduate degrees at Columbia. The Columbia English department had been a bastion of Anglo-Saxon gentility in multicultural New York for decades. In 1936, when Trilling was a graduate student and part-time instructor at Columbia, his colleagues in the English department attempted to have him dismissed. Although the reasons for keeping Trilling on remain obscure (Hook reports that Trilling threatened to create a scandal), Trilling's dissertation clearly helped to demonstrate a non-Anglo-Saxon's ability to deal with English literature: he wrote on Matthew Arnold, the nineteenth-century British literary scholar whose work did much to enshrine Anglo-Saxon letters.

Sources: Sidney Hook, *Out of Step: An Unquiet Life in the Twentieth Century* (New York: Carroll & Graf, 1987);

Mark Krupnick, *Lionel Trilling and the Fate of Cultural Criticism* (Evanston, Ill.: Northwestern University Press, 1986).

teaching methods, they trained labor organizers, journalists, and lawyers and provided extension-school and non-traditional instruction to adult industrial workers and farmers, as well as literacy courses to laborers who could not read or write. Commonwealth College abolished as "claptrap" collegiate institutions such as fraternities and sororities, varsity sports, and compulsory religious services. At Brookwood the curriculum was heavily geared toward instruction in labor history and economics; the course on advanced economics taught a variety of unorthodox approaches to the discipline, including those of Karl Marx and Thorstein Veblen. Brookwood especially valued instruction that advanced class consciousness and sought to combat the individualistic mores of normal American education. One educator said that the school's goal was to "teach them to get along with people, because you have to live in a community and if you can't live in a community, you can't get along with people, you can't create a union." Administrators, faculty, and students donated labor and time to provide maintenance and services at the institutions. Students at the labor colleges were encouraged to do field work recruiting new workers for the unions and helping to organize strikes. The schools published labor pamphlets and organizing songbooks and distributed them to unions. Most notably, the labor colleges pioneered a variety of activist theater with socialist themes (known as agitprop) that became popular in the 1930s. Commonwealth students wrote and performed prounion plays such as *What Price Coal?* for miners and other workers. Work People's College took its agitprop show on the road to working-class Finnish communities in northern Minnesota and upper Michigan. Brookwood students staged *The Miners — A Drama of the Non-Union Coal Fields of West Virginia*, *The People*, and the musical *The Tailor Shop*, which featured these lyrics:

> Union I swear by you.
> You've made my dreams come true.
> Since I began first to sew,
> You made things better I know.
> I didn't join right away,
> I waited till I was swayed
> I don't know any way I can ever repay —
> Union I swear by you!

Attacks. Agitprop, union organizing, and socialist education were controversial activities, and conservatives repeatedly attacked the labor colleges. Following tenant-farmer organizing and civil rights activities in eastern Arkansas, Commonwealth College was investigated by the state legislature in 1935. Conservatives sought to abolish the school, but they were blocked by nationally known liberals and others, who endorsed the college and raised money for its defense, including Jane Addams, Alexander Meiklejohn, Albert Einstein, H. L. Mencken, Scott Nearing, and George S. Counts. Support from liberals such as John Dewey, Stuart Chase, and Sinclair

Lewis also helped protect Brookwood from political attacks and, more important, from financial insolvency during the Depression. Liberals could not protect the schools from the corrosive effects of competition between different labor unions and political groups. Debates over whether the colleges should affiliate themselves with the American Federation of Labor (AFL) or other groups such as the Conference for Progressive Labor Action (CPLA), the CIO, or the Communist Party split campus unity. Faculty and administrators were divided by labor factions and disputes. Commonwealth experienced rifts in 1932 and 1938, when the school refused to affiliate with the Communist Party, and Brookwood suffered a schism in 1933, when longtime administrator A. J. Muste left because the school refused to affiliate with the CPLA.

Demise. Political divisions, attacks from conservatives, and the financial strain of the Depression combined to destroy the labor colleges. Brookwood closed in 1937, its financial resources exhausted. Conservatives mounted an effective attack against Commonwealth College, weakened by left-wing factional disputes, and succeeded in destroying the school in 1940. Work People's College fell victim to ethnic assimilation as its Finnish-immigrant base joined the mainstream. Classes were suspended in 1941, although summer school continued and the college existed as a financial entity until 1963. Nonetheless, the schools made important contributions to the labor movement. Their students became organizers and leaders of the CIO. Walter Reuther and his brothers, organizers of the United Auto Workers' groundbreaking 1936 sit-down strike against General Motors, were Brookwood alumni, and Brookwood theater skits entertained the strikers during the action. Other labor-college graduates went on to positions in mainstream colleges, making important contributions in various history and sociology departments.

The New School. The New School for Social Research in New York City was similar to the folk schools and the labor colleges in that it emphasized social reform and academic freedom. Less directly tied to the labor movement, it distinguished itself as a more traditional research institution. Founded in 1917 by liberal academics angered over the censorship and intellectual conformity imposed on American universities during World War I, the New School became notable for its combination of experimental pedagogy and high academic standards and for its embrace of adult education and modern art. In 1933 the New School added a self-governing research institute known as the University in Exile, which became an American refuge for intellectuals and academics who had fled Nazism in Europe. New School head Alvin Johnson brought an extraordinary array of talent to New York: economists Gerhard Colm, Karl Brandt, Emil Lederer, and Eduard Heimann; sociologists Hans Speier, Albert Salomon, and Karl Mayer; political scientists Arnold Brecht and Frieda Wunderlich; psychologist Max Wertheimer; and many other scholars. These academics continued the research they had begun in Europe and made a significant impact on many disciplines in America, especially political science. Having lost most of their possessions, their way of life, and many times members of their families, they were sadly qualified to evaluate Nazism and fascism for Americans.

Bennington. Many of the educational experiments of the 1930s were less given to the political radicalism of the folk schools or the labor colleges than to sheer iconoclasm. One of the most innovative schools was Bennington College in Bennington, Vermont. The college began in 1923 when Dr. Vincent Ravi-Booth, minister of the First Congregational Church in Bennington, Vermont, drew the local community and national educators together to study the shortage of quality higher education for women. By 1928, drawing upon a variety of economic resources, including the financial support of the town, Bennington College had been chartered to provide creative, progressive instruction to women. When classes began in 1932, the school did not disappoint. Bennington distinguished itself with innovative programs in the arts and humanities, a liberal admissions policy, and practical interaction between the college and the community. Bennington was especially known for its emphasis on student individuality and willingness to embrace the avant-garde. Innovative artists such as dancer-choreographer Martha Graham taught there, and the college quickly developed a reputation for sending the children of well-heeled families back to their homes filled with radical ideals.

Black Mountain. Another alternative school was Black Mountain College, founded in 1933. The school was established by classical scholar and professional gadfly John Andrew Rice following his dismissal from Rollins College in Winter Park, Florida, over a dispute concerning salary cuts and curriculum innovations. With a group of other dissident Rollins professors, Rice rented a group of buildings owned by the Blue Ridge Assembly of the Protestant Church near Black Mountain, North Carolina, and gained funding from a wealthy New England philanthropist. Like the folk schools, Black Mountain emphasized the college as community and encouraged strong interpersonal relations between teachers and students. It stressed pedagogical experimentation and refused to set fixed regulations or parameters for graduation. Black Mountain established a reputation as a center for avant-garde art in the United States. In its twenty-three year existence, Black Mountain enjoyed the participation of some of the finest creative individuals of the twentieth century: artists Josef Albers, Willem de Kooning, Franz Kline, and Robert Rauschenberg; composer John Cage; dancer-choreographer Merce Cunningham; architect Buckminster Fuller; poets Charles Olson, Robert Creeley, and Robert Duncan; and social critic Paul Goodman. The school was able to begin building its own campus in 1941, but enrollments dropped in the 1950s, and it closed in 1956.

Other Schools. Small colleges were also known for a variety of curricular experiments during the 1930s. Rollins College in Winter Park, Florida, offered students a startling range of curricular choice and instructional freedom. Antioch College in Yellow Springs, Ohio, offered a distinctive blend of liberal-arts education and vocational instruction, alternating between classroom instruction and work internships. Reed College in Portland, Oregon, had already established a reputation for academic seriousness and excellence by the 1930s. Reed was highly selective in its admissions of students, abolished fraternities and sororities, allowed unprecedented participation of the faculty in university administration, imposed rigorous examinations on its students, and refused to field competitive athletic teams. Under President Frank Aydelotte, Swarthmore College near Philadelphia went from a local institution noted for its football program to a national institution respected for its honors program. The Swarthmore honors program set high academic standards that were much imitated by other universities in the 1940s. Such was the value of small experimental colleges such as Swarthmore, Black Mountain, Highlander, and Brookwood, generally: despite the Depression, they pioneered curricular and administrative innovations that larger, more mainstream universities adopted in coming decades.

Sources:

Richard J. Altenbaugh, *Education for Struggle: The American Labor Colleges of the 1920s and 1930s* (Philadelphia: Temple University Press, 1990);

Burton R. Clark, *The Distinctive College: Antioch, Reed & Swarthmore* (Chicago: Aldine, 1970);

Martin Duberman, *Black Mountain: An Exploration in Community* (New York: Dutton, 1972);

Myles Horton, with Judith Kohl and Herbert Kohl, *The Long Haul* (New York: Doubleday, 1990);

Peter M. Rutkoff and William B. Scott, *New School: A History of the New School for Social Research* (New York: Free Press, 1986).

LOYALTY OATHS, RED-BAITING, AND ACADEMIC FREEDOM

Academic Freedom. During the 1930s financial pressures and political factionalism combined to imperil the principle of academic freedom, by which teachers are free to instruct without the imposition of political or ideological agendas. Conservatives in groups such as the American Legion and the Daughters of the American Revolution (DAR) repeatedly attacked the schools as bastions of communist propaganda and sought to have school boards restrict the curricula of public schools and require teachers to sign loyalty oaths. After the Democratic landslide in the elections of 1936, conservatives, smarting from wholesale repudiation at the polls, turned their attention to the schools, attempting to turn them into bastions of conservative philosophy. Although historians normally date the onset of "red-baiting," or "witch-hunting" for

CHARLES A. BEARD ON WILLIAM RANDOLPH HEARST

During the 1930s newspaper publisher William Randolph Hearst was among the most powerful and influential anticommunists in the United States. Anticommunism sold newspapers. Hearst's *New York American* frequently asked questions such as "What will deter this disloyal [Communist] 'party' from making EVERY SCHOOLHOUSE IN THE COUNTRY a center of revolutionary Communist propaganda?" Hearst was flamboyant and indiscriminate in charging communist subversion, and teachers were a favorite target. Hearst newspaper reporters would pose as radical students to get interviews with supposedly left-wing teachers and then quote these teachers out of context. When these reporters in disguise tried such tactics at the Teachers College of Columbia University, canny educators such as George S. Counts thwarted Hearst by having verbatim transcripts made of their interviews with the "students." The methods of Hearst's reporters were deplored by many educators and journalists. When the eminent historian Charles A. Beard denounced Hearst before a convention of the National Education Association in 1935, these words earned him a standing ovation:

> I have never found one single person who for talents and character commands the respect of the American people, who has not agreed with me that William Randolph Hearst has pandered to depraved tastes and has been an enemy of every thing that is best in the American tradition. . . . There is not a cesspool of vice and crime which Hearst has not raked and exploited for money-making purposes. No person with intellectual honesty or moral integrity will touch him with a ten foot pole for any purpose or to gain any end.

The *New York American* report on the convention did not mention Beard's address; instead it fabricated a speech by Willard Givens, secretary of the NEA, wherein Givens supposedly praised Hearst as a benefactor of education. Although Givens publicly denied ever having given such an address, the Hearst press did not report his denial.

Sources: Lawrence J. Dennis, *George S. Counts and Charles A. Beard: Collaborators for Change* (Albany: State University of New York Press, 1989);

Richard Hofstadter, *The Progressive Historians: Turner, Beard, Parrington* (Chicago: University of Chicago Press, 1968);

Robert W. Iversen, *The Communists & The Schools* (New York: Harcourt, Brace, 1959).

communists, after World War II, for teachers red-baiting began in the 1930s.

Red-Baiting. Immediately following the Bolshevik Revolution of 1917, conservatives suspected communists were attempting to take control of the schools so that they could subvert the minds of children. Often such charges were brought by conservatives distraught over the new progressive curriculum and seeking to tar it with the brush of communism. In 1928, for example, the DAR accused the progressive National Education Association (NEA) of being "sympathetic with communist ideals" and denounced it in a pamphlet. The frequency of such charges increased during the Depression, especially after teachers organized to oppose sweeping cutbacks in educational financing and other teachers adopted educational philosophies such as social reconstructionism that were sympathetic to left-wing causes.

Loyalty Oaths. The foremost technique for enforcing political conformity was the loyalty oath. In the 1920s some states required their teachers to swear not to teach ideas or doctrines "subversive" to the status quo. The definition of *subversive* was highly subjective and varied from state to state, encompassing anything from Marxism to civil rights to sexual liberation. The consequence of failing to swear such an oath, however, was clear to everyone: dismissal, a prospect truly intimidating during the Depression. By 1936 twenty-one states were making teachers take loyalty oaths; fourteen of those states had instituted the requirement since the onset of the Depression. Increasingly states also required children to say the pledge of allegiance before the school day began, a practice that would be declared unconstitutional in the 1940s. In the mid 1930s a last-minute rider attached to a congressional appropriation bill for Washington, D.C., required teachers to sign a statement that they were not teaching communism. Educators protested this "red rider" loyalty oath, pointing out that a true subversive would sign anything to achieve his goal; Congress was asking for a conformist gesture of obedience to authority from law-abiding teachers — one that violated the principle of academic freedom and the constitutional right to free political expression in the nation's capital. Pressure from teachers succeeded in rescinding the rider in 1937.

Firings and Dismissals. Throughout the decade there were other challenges to academic freedom. In 1934 six teachers in Toledo, Ohio, were threatened with dismissal for supposedly using radical textbooks, including one by New Deal official Rexford Tugwell. In North Carolina principal James M. Shields was fired for publishing *Just Plain Larnin'* (1934), a novel critical of the tobacco companies. The New York City Board of Examiners began an intrusive screening process to expose subversive teachers. In 1935 Rensselaer Polytechnic Institute in Troy, New York, dismissed English professor Granville Hicks, a noted critic and a communist sympathizer; City College of New York refused to reappoint writer Morris Schappes to the faculty because he had led unionizing activities on campus. At Rollins College in Florida eight faculty members were dismissed in a dispute between the administration and the faculty over a 30 percent pay cut and innovative curriculum.

Attack. Conservatives rarely discriminated in their attacks on the schools, lumping progressives, liberals, socialists, and communists into one subversive group. For some, red-baiting was a business. The Hearst press specialized in boosting newspaper sales by making sweeping and unsubstantiated charges about subversive plots in the schools. "Red Radicalism," William Randolph Hearst hinted ominously, "has planted a soapbox on every campus in America." Cost-conscious school boards routinely dismissed teacher protests against salary cuts as communist inspired. Two teachers in Westchester County, New York, were fired as agitators after protesting a pay cut. Between 1930 and 1936 twenty-five teachers were dismissed and fifty-nine resigned because of budget cuts and protests at the University of Pittsburgh. In Wisconsin Rapids, Wisconsin, thirteen instructors were dismissed on the excuse of their supposed radicalism. Other red-baiters were anticommunist zealots, none more so than Elizabeth Dilling, whose 1934 book, *The Red Network*, sketched out a fantastic communist conspiracy supposedly reaching from the common schoolteacher to the president. Similarly, New York State Economic Council president Merwin K. Hart denounced the popular textbooks of historian Harold Rugg, used in forty-two hundred school systems, as "promoting unrest, of fomenting class struggle, of proposing unworkable government planning, of retailing inaccurate views of the Constitution." Charles Walgreen, the drugstore-chain owner, was sufficiently influential to get the Illinois state legislature to investigate communism at the University of Chicago in 1935. The legislative committee concluded, "Nothing in the teachings or schedule of the school can be held to be subversive of our institutions." *National Republic*, "A Magazine of Fundamental Americanism," advised teachers in 1937 to "Be Loyal to America or Leave It!" Other groups instrumental in pushing for loyalty oaths and dismissals of radicals were the American Legion, the Anglo-Saxon Federation, the Junior American Vigilante Intelligence Federation, and the American Defense Society. In the 1940s such groups stepped up their attacks on American education, and — via investigative agencies such as the House Un-American Activities Committee (HUAC) and the New York State Rapp-Coudert Committee — they successfully purged the schools of presumed radical influences — and of many good teachers.

Orthodoxy. In the 1930s academic freedom was also assailed by Communists on the Left. For the most part teachers' unions and professional groups cooperated with or tolerated Communist functionaries throughout the decade. Often Communists were among the most dedicated teachers and were on the cutting edge of educational reform. The Communist-influenced Local #5 of the AFT in New York, for example, led the nation in providing quality education to black students. While flexible in its pedagogy, the Communist Party nonetheless required rigid adherence to orthodox Soviet politics and sought control of many teachers' unions. Before 1935 Commu-

Members of the Chicago Teachers' Union protesting late paychecks and payment of their salaries in scrip, 1933

nists believed that non-Communist leftists were "social fascists," implicitly giving aid and comfort to reactionaries. In 1934, for example, philosophy professor Sidney Hook, an early left-wing anti-Communist, was simultaneously denounced as a "red" by the Hearst *New York American* and as a "counterrevolutionary reptile" by the Communists. After 1935 Communists abandoned such rhetoric in favor of cooperation with non-Communist leftists, but repeated efforts by Communists to seize control of teachers' unions led many educators to view the Communists with suspicion. Factionalism was so pronounced among the members of the New York Local #5 of the AFT that the non-Communist members of the union left to form the New York Teachers Guild, leaving Local #5 in Communist control. When the Communist Party supported the signing of the Hitler-Stalin Pact in 1939, most non-Communist leftists and liberals broke all ties to the Communists. Disputes with Communists throughout the 1930s increased the stress on teachers and their unions. As Local #5 representative Abraham Lefkowitz put it after a Communist takeover bid in 1933, "Between the bankers and the Communists, we're having a hell of a time."

Sources:

Robert W. Iversen, *The Communists & The Schools* (New York: Harcourt, Brace, 1959);

Marjorie Murphy, *Blackboard Unions: The AFT and the NEA, 1900–1980* (Ithaca, N.Y.: Cornell University Press, 1990);

James M. Wallace, *Liberal Journalism and American Education, 1914–1941* (New Brunswick, N.J.: Rutgers University Press, 1991).

MANAGEMENT AND LABOR IN EDUCATION

Conflict. American education reflected the labor struggles that so dominated industrial relations in the 1930s. While management and labor battled over wages and working conditions in the steel and automobile industry, school administrators and teachers' unions did much the same. Like industrial workers, teachers were concerned with low wages, the lack of pension plans, and control of the workplace. The two leading education organizations, the American Federation of Teachers (AFT, begun 1916) and the National Education Association (NEA, begun 1857) struggled to change these conditions by advocating the "professionalization" of the workplace — by which they meant greater teacher control of schools and increased salaries. Opposing them were school administrators and school boards who had their own definition of professional education — one in which schools were run like businesses and teachers were treated like employees. The conflicts between these groups defined the character of American education in the 1930s.

Tension. Prior to the 1930s most school districts were run on the model of the corporation, with the school board acting as a board of trustees; the school administrators and principals acting as the chief executive officers; and teachers functioning as employees. In the 1920s local school boards composed mostly of wealthy or powerful citizens generally cooperated with school administrators in running schools. Such businesspeople donated funds, advocated raising taxes, and initiated bond drives to help schools. Their cooperation with school administrators was instrumental in improving education in the 1920s. The Depression, however, heightened tensions among these groups. Cost-conscious school boards cut budgets and pressured administrators to cut programs and lower teacher salaries; teachers responded by organizing for higher wages and demanding greater shares in school administration; administrators sought greater autonomy from school boards without any loss in funding. Individualistic leaders such as business analyst Roger Babson blamed educators for the Depression, arguing that they had failed to instill in their students "the desire to struggle and the willingness to sacrifice." Many administrators and teachers came to view such people, often well-represented on school boards, as hostile to education — especially when cost-conscious businessmen began cutting programs and funding. Some educators feared a full-scale elimination of public education. Dean Henry Lester Smith of the School of Education at Indiana University warned that "enemies" of free schools were seeking to destroy them under "the guise of economic necessity," while Chicago educator Helen Hefferan warned against foes "powerful, united, and sinister."

Chicago. Tensions between businessmen and educators in Chicago exemplified national controversies. The local school board was dominated by wealthy businessmen whose priorities during the Depression were lower taxes and repayment of a large school debt, incurred to finance a construction boom in the 1920s. Fred W. Sargent, president of the Chicago and Northwestern Railroad and chairman of the business-sponsored Citizens' Committee on Public Expenditures, demanded a 33 percent cut in educational expenditures. Wealthy Chicagoans organized a tax strike that succeeded in halving city tax collections, forcing reductions in school expenditures. Bankers and businessmen also succeeded in getting the school board to suspend wage payments to teachers, withholding $20 million, or $1,400 per teacher, by 1932. From 1930 to 1934 only nine salary checks were disbursed on time; sometimes wage payments were as late as nine months. The school boards increased the teaching load to six classes per day, with each teacher instructing more than 150 students daily (only 10 percent of Illinois teachers outside Chicago had comparable workloads). The school board also agreed to divert funding from school maintenance to repayment of debt. As a stopgap measure, the school board paid teachers in scrip; large Chicago banks then turned around and refused to honor that scrip. Teachers began to cash in their life savings and insurance policies; unable to pay the mortgage on their homes, many faced foreclosure. According to *The Nation* magazine, the crisis was so severe that teachers went hungry, with some fainting at their desks and others panhandling after school hours.

Response. Especially after the 1932 revelations of financial fraud and misconduct on the part of electricity magnate Samuel Insull and other Chicago businessmen,

teachers turned militant. Responding to the situation in April 1933, a Chicago high-school gym teacher, John M. Fewkes, led twenty thousand teachers, parents, and students on a march against city hall. When that demonstration accomplished nothing, Fewkes sent five thousand teachers into the banks that refused to honor teachers' scrip, where they splashed ink on the walls, jammed tellers' windows, and overturned desks. A follow-up demonstration resulted in pitched battles between male teachers and police. City National Bank chairman Charles C. Dawes, the recipient of a large federal loan, responded to these events by denouncing teachers. "To hell with troublemakers," he said, and the leading newspapers in the city, including the *Chicago Tribune,* agreed. The school board responded by voting on 12 July 1933 to fire fourteen hundred teachers, cut the number of kindergartens in half, abolish the junior-high-school system and special education, stop buying textbooks, and require each elementary-school principal to supervise two schools — while at the same time continuing payments to coal contractors and other well-connected businesses. Despite further protest efforts, including mass petitions calling for a revision of the board decision, the July firings ultimately stood. Due to entrenched business interests and a formidable political machine, it would take thirteen years to pressure the government of Chicago to reform public education. Charles H. Judd, dean of the School of Education at the University of Chicago, observed, "I am filled with resentment when I hear the criticisms of those who say that the American schools are failures. These are the smug exploiters who have been driving communities to the brink of ruin by their greed and self-seeking."

The Florida League for Better Schools. Other efforts to protect schools from budget cuts were more successful than those in Chicago. Although the situation in Detroit was similar to that in Chicago, with a group of businessmen led by banker Ralph Stone pressuring the school board to cut back programs, Detroit mayor Frank Murphy and school superintendent Frank Cody successfully resisted such pressures. While paring some programs, Cody mounted a publicity campaign to get public support for the schools, and teachers and trade unions organized as an effective voting bloc, electing a school board willing to defy businessmen. In Kellogg, Idaho, teachers joined miners to throw businessmen out of important county offices. When Florida legislators cut education while simultaneously increasing spending on highway programs that benefited wealthy contractors, the state education association, led by school administrator Henry Filer, formed the Florida League for Better Schools. The league succeeded in passing a gasoline tax to benefit schools, and it got state legislators to guarantee teacher salaries. The league was stridently denounced by businessmen's groups and the Florida press, but it gained popular support by asserting that it was fighting for "the greatest of all American institutions."

The California Teachers Association. In 1933 educators in California organized to oppose Gov. James Rolph Jr. and the California Taxpayers Association, a consortium of utility companies seeking lower taxes. The California Teachers Association (CTA) combated proposals to cut per-pupil expenditures from thirty to twenty-four dollars per year, to repeal tenure for teachers, and to eliminate kindergarten and adult education. To the *Los Angeles Examiner* such proposals were advanced "by pinchpenny politicians who want to save on education, not for the avowed purpose of balancing state budgets, but to have more money to squander on their friends and supporters." Teachers agreed and rallied local communities to defend their schools. The CTA and public supporters succeeded in getting state funding of thirty dollars per year for each elementary-school child (sixty dollars per high-school student) and an increase in teacher wages.

"Wreckers." In 1932 the United States Chamber of Commerce (an organization of businessmen) proposed a program of sweeping educational cuts, including the elimination of kindergartens and evening classes, the shortening of the school day, and the imposition of tuition at high schools. The NEA responded by establishing the Joint Commission on the Emergency in Education to combat their efforts. The *Idaho Journal of Education* viewed the Chamber of Commerce actions as a "smoke screen," part of a program to eliminate public schools entirely. A 1933 *National Education Association Journal* article denounced "the Wall Street Power Trust oligarchy." Prominent educators, such as Glenn Frank, president of the University of Wisconsin, denounced such businessmen as "wreckers," intent on continuing the "ventures in irresponsibility that landed the nation in economic disaster." Angered by such rhetoric and alarmed at educational movements that advocated increased political action on the part of teachers, many businessmen argued that educators were communistic, busy indoctrinating children in radical ideologies. The cordial relationship between educators and businessmen that had so dominated the 1920s fell into ruin.

Conservatism. Despite such rhetoric, most school administrators remained fairly conservative. A 1934 study found that the 850 local school superintendents in the United States were 98 percent native born and 90 percent Anglo-Saxon in background. Almost all were from rural, Protestant backgrounds, overwhelmingly Republican, and members of local business organizations, such as the Chamber of Commerce. Eighty percent agreed with the idea that pledging allegiance to the flag should be mandatory, and 84 percent agreed that teachers should omit from the classroom "any facts likely to arouse in the minds of the students questions or doubts concerning the justice of our social order." As the economy slowly rebounded from the Depression, school superintendents and administrators mended fences with local business elites, restoring much of the cooperation between the two

groups that had been found in the 1920s. Glenn Frank, in fact, became so friendly with businessmen in the Republican Party that many suggested him as their presidential candidate in 1936 and 1940.

Generosity. While school administrators returned to conservatism, teachers became more militant. Many educators became radicalized by their everyday experience with students, who were miserable for want of good food, clothing, or shelter. In 1932 the New York Health Department reported that 20.5 percent of schoolchildren were suffering from malnutrition. The American Friends Service Committee found similar conditions among 10 percent of students in Illinois, West Virginia, Kentucky, and Pennsylvania. Teachers responded with compassion. In Detroit schoolteachers collected shoes for thousands of barefoot pupils and contributed thirty thousand dollars to a general relief fund; in New York, rather than let their students go hungry, teachers paid for children's lunches from their own meager salaries, feeding more than eleven thousand children; in San Jose, teachers gave 5 percent of their salaries to provide clothing, blankets, medicine, and food. Teachers at Libbey High School in Toledo, Ohio, began a program of student work relief, paid for out of their own pockets.

Unions. Most teachers' organizations originally kept their distance from the organized-labor movement and stayed aloof from affiliated political causes, such as women's suffrage. Teachers usually thought of themselves as professionals, not employees, and were reluctant to unionize. The Depression, however, changed this stance. Memberships in teachers' unions skyrocketed. AFT membership quadrupled, and the group added thirty-three college locals to its complement of public-school guilds. Teachers' unions became more militant and politically active. Unemployed teachers formed their own organization, the Unemployed Teachers Association (UTA), to secure back pay and other benefits from school boards. The Chicago AFT agitated for progressive political causes such as the graduated income tax, unemployment insurance, the planning of public works, and a shorter workweek. In 1934, led by Raymond Lowry, the Toledo AFT searched the city tax records and broadcast over local radio stations the information that, while poorer families had paid their taxes, the wealthiest citizens owed $13.5 million in back taxes. Communist-influenced AFT Local #5 in New York was probably the most radical in the country, its ranks growing as it took stands against any retrenchment by the New York school board. Members of Local #5 agitated against fascism in Europe and supported CIO strikes. It also organized the Harlem Committee for Better Schools, a coalition of parents, teachers, churches, and community groups that successfully petitioned for the construction of two new schools in Harlem in 1938, and it successfully urged the state legislature to grant substitute teachers tenure rights, while limiting their numbers.

Compromise and Conservatism. The militant spirit of the teachers' unions was not applauded by all educators. School administrators, mending fences with the business community, were alarmed at the radicalism of groups such as Local #5. Older teachers objected to the stridency of young radicals. While younger teachers pressed for higher wages and more jobs, older teachers sought pensions, tenure, and professional standards. Communist teachers, among the most militant, alienated many moderates. In 1939, in the midst of the AFT national convention in Buffalo, the Hitler-Stalin Pact was announced, and Communist delegates immediately moved from militant opposition to fascism to an isolationist, pacifist position. Such an ideological shift was too much for most non-Communist educators at the convention. They replaced AFT president Jerome Davis, a Communist sympathizer, with George Counts, an anti-Communist progressive. The election symbolized a shift to the Right that would continue in the 1940s, bringing the radicalism of the unions to heel. Most unions abandoned their broader agendas of social reform and settled for pensions, higher wages, and smaller classes. Constant attacks by conservatives, generational splits, the inability of American Communists to maintain autonomy from Moscow, and an improving economy brought an end to class conflict between management and labor in education. Just as the United Auto Workers abandoned its demand for "industrial democracy" and a say in the management of the auto industry after the General Motors strike of 1945–1946, after 1945 teachers' unions abandoned their demands for control of the profession and settled for better working conditions and higher wages.

Sources:

Edward A. Krug, *The Shaping of the American High School, Volume 2, 1920–1941* (Madison: University of Wisconsin Press, 1972);

Majorie Murphy, *Blackboard Unions: The AFT and the NEA, 1900–1980* (Ithaca, N.Y.: Cornell University Press, 1990);

David Tyack, Robert Lowe, and Elisabeth Hansot, *Public Schools in Hard Times: The Great Depression and Recent Years* (Cambridge, Mass.: Harvard University Press, 1984);

Julia Wrigley, *Class Politics and Public Schools: Chicago, 1900–1950* (New Brunswick, N.J.: Rutgers University Press, 1982).

THE NEW DEAL IN EDUCATION

Adversaries. Although Franklin Roosevelt's New Deal significantly altered practices in business and politics, it did little to change the traditions of American education. For the most part the New Deal left control of schools to localities and failed to deliver federal assistance to schools. Roosevelt cut the budget and staff of the U.S. Office of Education until it was smaller by the end of the decade than it had been at the beginning. Tensions between New Dealers and educators were so high that Roosevelt snubbed the NEA convention of 1934, which had convened in Washington specifically to consider the relationship between the New Deal and education. When it came to education, the New Deal and teachers' groups were adversaries, not allies.

Politics. New Dealers kept their distance from educational reform because the issue was so politically charged. Schools were powerful political symbols to many Americans, representing both progress and independence. Conservatives already accused the New Dealers of attempting to centralize power in Washington; New Deal administration of local schools would only give credence to the accusation. Educational reform furthermore threatened the emerging New Deal political coalition of labor, liberals, southerners, and blacks. Federal financial assistance to public schools, for example, might create tensions between big labor, dominated by Catholics who would seek financial assistance for parochial schools, and liberals opposed to parochial education. Southerners feared federal intervention in their schools would undermine their practice of segregated education. An activist educational policy thus had the potential to disrupt already-tense relationships between antagonistic groups whose political support was vital to the New Deal.

Temperament. New Dealers also kept their distance from educational reform because of a disagreement in temperament between them and professional educators. Before the Depression professional educators tended to be middle-class conservatives, closely allied with local business elites. They often saw their task as one of "elevating" the children of minorities and ethnic groups into the realm of middle-class values, which in the 1920s meant imparting a rural, Protestant, teetotaling — in many ways culturally Republican — ethos. The New Dealers had a different educational sensibility, one given less to moral instruction than to vocational education. Professional educators talked about values; New Dealers talked about skills. Professional educators focused on instruction for the academically gifted; New Dealers focused on education for the masses. Many professional educators considered blacks and other minority groups incapable of education beyond a certain level; New Dealers targeted minorities for instruction, teaching 1.3 million illiterate adults, half of them black, to read. Many professional educators held rigidly to the notion that education took place only in the classroom; New Dealers sought to educate through experience and entertainment, exposing millions to educational theater, films, radio programs, and art exhibits. The cultural tensions between the two groups were exemplified in Roosevelt's tense relationship with his own commissioner of education, John Studebaker. Repeatedly Roosevelt snubbed Studebaker and placed the educational programs that the New Deal did develop in the hands of trusted New Dealers such as Harry Hopkins. Roosevelt's memoranda to Studebaker were sarcastic and derogatory; Studebaker replied in kind, denigrating Roosevelt's pet projects, such as the Civilian Conservation Corps (CCC). Although seemingly natural allies in the cause of educational reform, New Dealers and professional educators were at odds throughout the decade.

Members of the Civilian Conservation Corps learning about automobile mechanics in Washington, D.C.

Assistance. The Roosevelt administration did channel federal assistance to schools through various New Deal agencies. When rural schools began to close for want of funding, Harry Hopkins's Federal Emergency Relief Administration (FERA) paid $14 million in teachers' salaries to keep the schools open, ultimately helping more than four thousand schools and 150,000 pupils. Moreover, when state governments, such as that of Arkansas, threatened school funding, the New Dealers threatened to remove federal assistance for nonschool projects, forcing the states to support their schools. The federal government also funded schools by paying their debts through the Reconstruction Finance Corporation (RFC). Between 1933 and 1939 the federal government subsidized 70 percent of all school construction, and the Works Progress Administration (WPA) painted and restored tens of thousands of schools. Ever sensitive to the dangerous politics of school reform, however, the Roosevelt administration repeatedly refused to finance education directly or engage in sweeping national reform.

New Deal Education. The bulk of Roosevelt's education programs were administered through New Deal agencies such as the Tennessee Valley Authority (TVA),

the WPA, the CCC, or the National Youth Administration (NYA). While the primary goals of the TVA were controlling flooding, generating electricity, and promoting local industry, it also provided an educational program that taught TVA workers skilled trades such as carpentry, electrical work, and auto repair and trained them in engineering, domestic work, and agriculture. The WPA set up the Emergency Education Program to provide nursery schools for poor children and child-care classes for their parents, ultimately serving more than two hundred thousand children. The WPA also ran adult-education classes, which it claimed taught one million people to read and write. The WPA provided health services to millions, built school furniture, and paid for extra teachers in various school districts. Its most successful program was a school-lunch project that distributed a total of 1.25 billion hot lunches to needy children. The CCC and NYA were primarily concerned with keeping unemployed men and teenagers engaged in productive pursuits and away from radical political recruitment. The CCC hired unmarried men ages eighteen to twenty-five to do forestry work and environmental improvement; the NYA paid teenagers to remain in school and provided service jobs to occupy their free time. Both organizations employed people of high-school or college age, and both organizations ran their own educational programs, competing with high schools and colleges — and engendering further animosity between New Dealers and professional educators.

CCC. Run like the military, the CCC was locally supervised by army personnel with help from the Forest Service and National Park Service. During its nine-year life, the CCC built 1,468 camps and enrolled almost 2.5 million young men, nearly all from deprived, rural backgrounds. Although the day work of the CCC occupied these men with planting trees, building campgrounds, and fighting fires, night hours were often spent in educational instruction, as nearly two-thirds of the corps were high-school dropouts. Attendance at classes was voluntary, and teachers struggled to keep the corpsmen motivated. Many classes taught remedial instruction to men who had only rudimentary schooling, while others continued traditional academic instruction. Some corpsmen attended classes in nearby colleges. About a third of all instruction was vocational, instructing the corpsmen in typewriter use, drafting, surveying, construction, agricultural science, and radio and auto repair. One army captain taught a course called "Decisive Battles of the World," and, like this class, many courses were simply interesting ways to pass the time. By the end of the decade, however, educational instruction in the CCC had become mandatory and more professional. Many camps had libraries, classrooms, and facilities for showing educational films. Class attendance rates ran close to 90 percent. More than eight thousand illiterates were taught to read and write; nearly five thousand men received eighth-grade certificates; one thousand graduated from high school; ninety-six earned college degrees. The CCC classroom was an educational success.

NYA. Equally successful were the educational efforts of the National Youth Administration. Led by social worker and lay minister Aubrey Williams, the NYA approached educating young people from a more radical perspective than the CCC. The NYA was also dealing with impoverished people (95 percent were from families on relief), most of whom had not gone beyond the eighth grade. For Williams it was important that the NYA give these people "a decent break" and educate them about the "palpably unfair distribution of wealth" in the United States. Williams was committed to using the NYA to help women and blacks, and he created a Division of Negro Affairs, which ultimately assisted some three hundred thousand African American youths. Although given a slim budget, the NYA provided cash supplements to approximately 6–10 percent of all high-school students, as well as approximately 12 percent of all college students. With NYA help, about two hundred African Americans received Ph.D.'s during the decade — some 155 more than received doctorates in the period prior to the 1930s. In return for the cash, NYA participants worked as teachers' assistants and school groundskeepers or in school cafeterias, laboratories, and workshops. For unemployed dropouts the NYA offered jobs draining swamps, restocking fish hatcheries, working as teachers' and nurses' assistants, and building roads and community centers. Nearly 2.6 million young people participated in the program. Many were housed in NYA "resident centers," where they were taught agricultural science, machine and auto repair, welding, sewing, and painting, as well as remedial courses in grammar and reading. In 1940 Williams reported that a survey of sixty-two thousand NYA students in 666 colleges showed that NYA students ranked higher in scholarship than their fellow students. Like the CCC, the NYA was a low-cost educational success, becoming a blueprint for the social programs of the 1960s — which would be inaugurated by a president who was one of the Texas state directors of the NYA, Lyndon B. Johnson.

Reaction. Implicitly, the success of New Deal educational programs stood as a rebuke to traditional education, proof that vast groups heretofore assumed to be uneducable could learn. Politically, the programs were tremendously popular, a thorn in the side of conservatives and a challenge to the elitism of traditional educators. The New Dealers intended that children, heretofore barred by poverty from getting good educations, would compete educationally with their wealthy neighbors. New Dealers went out of their way to make this point clear. A 1938 educational-commission advisory to Roosevelt condemned the use of schools as "a force to create class . . . race, and sectional distinctions," and Harry Hopkins, director of the WPA, put it thus: "this business of getting an education and going to law school and medical school and dental school and going to college is not to be confined to the people who have an economic status at home that permits them to do it." Such egalitarianism provoked conservatives, who joined with professional educators to abolish New Deal programs. By the beginning of World War II every New Deal youth program was in jeopardy; by the end of the war all had been eliminated. Yet the precedents set by the New Deal, especially its success in educating the most poverty-stricken segments of the population, became a model for reform programs begun in the 1960s.

Source:
David Tyack, Robert Lowe, and Elisabeth Hansot, *Public Schools in Hard Times: The Great Depression and Recent Years* (Cambridge, Mass.: Harvard University Press, 1984).

PROGRESSIVE EDUCATION AND SOCIAL RECONSTRUCTIONISM

Prominent Philosophy. In the 1930s many intellectuals shifted from political liberalism toward more-radical alternatives. Before the Depression the dominant educational philosophy in the United States was the liberalism of progressive education; in the 1930s many prominent progressive educators turned toward a more radical philosophy known as social reconstructionism. Social reconstructionism urged teachers to take an active role in advocating social reform. Some social reconstructionists urged teachers to participate in socialist and communist labor organizing. Other social reconstructionists urged teachers to instruct their students in the follies of capitalism. Almost all social reconstructionists believed that the school was the one institution in American life capable of rapid, yet nonviolent, change. While social reconstructionism was widely publicized in the 1930s, it was never a broad movement among educators, and it had almost no real impact on schools. Its prominence during a politically charged decade, however, affected the debate between conservative and progressive educators about the curriculum of American schools.

Progressive Education. Progressive education appeared in the United States at the turn of the century. Closely associated with the instrumental philosophy of John Dewey, progressive education sought to transform curriculum from rote memorization to active student participation and to integrate abstract subjects into everyday life. At Dewey's well-known laboratory school at the University of Chicago, children building a small-scale log cabin would learn not only basic geometry but also the history of homesteading and western expansion. In the high schools Dewey favored a curriculum that integrated student talents and practical tasks and was an early partisan of vocational education. Such "learning-by-doing" and "child-centered curriculum" were radical innovations at a time when basic reading was taught via Bible recitation and the typical high-school curriculum was dominated by Latin and Greek. In two important books, *School and Society* (1899) and *Democracy and Education* (1916), Dewey had furthermore argued that the greater participation of the child in learning prepared students for scientific thinking and democratic activity. To Dewey progress, democracy, and the future of the school were closely intertwined. During the Depression, when progress stalled and democracy seemed imperiled, Dewey's disciples naturally turned toward the schools as a means to get America back on track.

The New Frontier. Social reconstructionism began with an address titled "Dare Progressive Education Be Progressive?" by Columbia University educator George S. Counts. Speaking to the 1932 convention of the Progressive Education Association, Counts bemoaned the lack of success progressive education had in changing educational curriculum in the 1920s — in many ways a stock complaint of the progressives. He went on, however, to argue that the opponents of progressivism were the same people whose laissez-faire economics, hierarchical social ethic, and conservative political outlook were responsible for the Depression. Counts suggested these individuals be replaced by progressive educators as the leaders of American society and that progressive educators turn the classroom into a forum for political education and social consciousness-raising. The idea was instantly attractive to

many educators. By the next year social reconstructionism was a formal educational movement, centered on a group of intellectuals at the Teachers College of Columbia University. The group included Counts, John Dewey (who had moved from Chicago to Columbia in 1905), William H. Kilpatrick, Harold Rugg, Jesse Newlon, John L. Childs, R. Bruce Raup, and Thomas H. Briggs. These men saw themselves as breaking new intellectual ground and insisted they were pioneering a "new frontier" of social responsibility and democracy. In 1934 they founded a journal, *Social Frontier,* to use as a platform for their philosophy.

Goals. Although a complex movement, social reconstructionism held to four broad ideas: it attacked laissez-faire economics and called for centralized economic planning; it called for a nationalized, centralized educational system; it sought to professionalize and organize American teachers; and it wanted to break the power that local elites (especially businessmen) often held over education. Almost all reconstructionists wanted to replace the individualistic thrust of American education with a more community-oriented curriculum. Although nearly all reconstructionists disavowed Marxism, what many hoped to teach was an Americanized version of "class consciousness." A group of reconstructionist historians argued that "the age of individualism and laissez-faire in economy and government is closing," and that "a new age of collectivism is emerging." A revolution in American education seemed about to begin.

Essentialism. Educational conservatives had long been opposed to progressive education; they were even more opposed to social reconstructionism. Generally insisting that education be directed to the few academically talented and that curriculum be oriented toward the status quo and tradition — which often meant the training of "gentlemen" — the conservatives saw nothing less than barbarism in social reconstructionism, the coddling of the least gifted, a mass philosophy of education akin to communism. Educators such as William S. Learned of the Carnegie Foundation; Abraham Flexner, director of the Princeton Institute of Advanced Study; and University of Chicago president Robert Hutchins urged teachers to choose a philosophy they often called "essentialism," rather than social reconstructionism. Essentialists sometimes advocated a "classical" curriculum for high schools and colleges (based on the "essentials" of Western humanism), and they sometimes advocated sharply hierarchical educational placement. Not all essentialists were political conservatives, and not all of them completely rejected progressive innovations in curriculum. They objected to the tendency of some educators to pass their students on to advanced levels without imparting techniques of critical analysis and mental discipline. One of the most prominent essentialists, William C. Bagley, argued that Latin should be retained as the principal high-school subject precisely because mastering the dead language required great mental discipline, which could be applied in many different fields. Bagley and other essentialists argued that the school electives, practical subject matter, and child-centered curriculum advocated by progressives distracted from the disciplinary goal of the school. To essentialists, social reconstructionism, with its politicization of the classroom, only compounded the mistakes of progressivism.

Opposition. Many progressive educators were also opposed to social reconstructionism. Many were "administrative progressives," who believed schools should be run like businesses. They took offense at the social reconstructionist attack on business. Educators such as David Snedden, Franklin Bobbitt, William Wirt, and Werrett Wallace Charters viewed the Depression as a natural fluctuation in the business cycle. They believed schools should use the Depression as an occasion for increased efficiency and derided the reconstructionists as "romantics" and "utopians." Burton P. Fowler of Tower Hill School in Wilmington, Delaware, warned educators against "short cuts to social efficiency." The superintendent of schools in Allentown, Pennsylvania, wrote that the reconstructionist challenge to local elites was doomed to failure. "Those of us who have not taken leave of our senses," he wrote, "know that the schools and schoolmasters are not generally going to be permitted *to take the lead* in changing the social order, nor in conducting experiments likely to lead to a radical redefinition of the aims of that order."

Division. The opponents of social reconstructionism often found sympathy for their criticisms from social reconstructionists themselves. John Dewey repeatedly condemned reconstructionists who took an overly romantic view of child-centered education. To Dewey children's innate curiosity and willingness to learn was unfocused and chaotic; it needed guidance and direction from teachers. According to Dewey, the educator who made a dogma of educational freedom and waited for the children to, in essence, teach themselves "misconceives the conditions of independent thinking." Dewey and many other reconstructionists were also opposed to the use of political indoctrination in the classroom. Some reconstructionists, including Counts, Thomas H. Briggs, and Charles C. Peters of Pennsylvania State College had maintained that all instruction was a form of indoctrination and that reconstructionists should simply make overt and political a practice that had always been implicit in education. "Why should not high school students have emotionalized attitudes and ideals for a better social order, a better and more just economic order, an improved political order?" asked Oklahoma City principal Lloyd N. Morrisett. Dewey's response trusted that the clear presentation of history and politics would allow children to frame democratic alternatives for the future. Indoctrination discounted the capacity of children to recognize truth and work toward democratic reform, he said. "If the method of intelligence has worked in our own case," he asked, "how can we assume that the method will not work with our students, and that it will not with them generate ardor and practical energy?"

Passing. By the end of the decade the vogue for social reconstructionism was passing. Improvements in the domestic economy and the threat of war from abroad combined to moderate political opinion toward the center. Disagreement over the issue of indoctrination became more charged, fragmenting the reconstructionists. Increasingly, educators of every political persuasion were concerned with new controversies over the control of unemployed youth, and interest shifted from politics to pedagogy. Vocational education was given a boost by its usefulness in defense industries. The philosophical prominence of social reconstructionism, although it changed little in the academic or political landscape, filled conservatives outside education with the fear the schools were being used as a base for subversion — a fear that would return to feed the McCarthyite hysteria after World War II.

Sources:
Edward A. Krug, *The Shaping of the American High School, Volume 2, 1920–1941* (Madison: University of Wisconsin Press, 1972);

Robert Westbrook, *John Dewey and American Democracy* (Ithaca, N.Y.: Cornell University Press, 1991).

RURAL SCHOOLS

Overpopulated and Underfunded. During the 1930s about one-half of all children went to school in rural areas, where the proportion of children to adults was higher than in the cities. In 1930 rural school districts had, on average, 686 children per 1,000 white women; cities had only 384 children per 1,000 white women. There were 799 children per 1,000 black women in rural districts, compared to 360 per 1,000 black women in urban centers. Such ratios meant that rural areas had proportionately fewer adults to educate children than did cities. They also had fewer resources. The states with the highest birth rates — Texas, Louisiana, Virginia, Tennessee, Georgia, Kentucky, North Carolina, South Carolina, Alabama, Mississippi, and Arkansas — also had the highest levels of poverty in the nation and the lowest expenditures on education. Rural schools on average spent about half what urban schools spent per pupil. In 1930 Arkansas spent $33.56 per pupil per year, while New York spent $137.55 and the nation as a whole spent $76.70.

Depression. Of all the schools affected by the Great Depression, already-underfunded rural schools suffered the worst. As farmers went broke and land values plummeted, property taxes fell. Unable to raise funds to continue operation, rural school districts cut teacher salaries, stopped buying supplies, or simply ceased operations. Iowa cut teachers' salaries by 30 percent to a mere $40 per month. By 1934 almost three hundred thousand rural teachers earned less than the National Recovery Administration (NRA) minimum wage of $650 per year. Many rural school districts revived the old practice of "boarding round" teachers — offering them bed and board rather than wages. Arkansas reduced the school year to less than sixty days for three hundred schools. By 1 April 1934 nearly twenty thousand American schools had closed, affecting more than one million students. Ten states reduced the school year to less than three months; twenty-one others cut the school year to less than six months.

Improvement. Yet hard times during the Depression also meant improvement for rural schools. Large school districts were consolidated and made cost effective. Educational reformers forced state governments to bear a larger share of the costs of maintaining rural schools. Declining rural populations meant available resources were shared by fewer students. For rural migrants, however, a move from the homestead to agriculturally productive regions such as California or Florida often ended their formal education. Migrant agricultural workers remained unschooled or poorly schooled well into the 1970s.

HEADLINE MAKERS

CHARLES A. BEARD

1874-1948

HISTORIAN, EDUCATOR

Historian. Along with frontier historian Frederick Jackson Turner, Charles A. Beard was in many ways responsible for creating the modern discipline of American history. His *An Economic Interpretation of the Constitution* (1913) put the study of the past on a modern, economically based foundation and established an interpretative tradition in history that continues to this day. Beard was also an important and controversial educator in the 1930s, author of the most commonly used history textbooks of the day, an activist who challenged political orthodoxy, and a leading proponent of change.

Background. Beard grew up on a prosperous Indiana farm, immersed in the political and ethical certainties of midwestern Republicanism. At Spiceland Academy, a Quaker school not far from his home, he absorbed something of the Friends' vigorous nonconformity. In the midst of his undergraduate career at DePauw University, he spent the summer of 1896 in Chicago, a center of the populist radicalism of the time. There he witnessed the reform efforts of social worker Jane Addams at Hull House. He graduated in 1898 and traveled in Europe for the next four years. In England he was drawn into the circle of the Fabian socialists, who were attempting to build a Labour Party and industrial democracy in Britain. Beard was greatly impressed by John Ruskin's *Unto This Last* (1862), a collection of essays critical of classical economics. He studied at Oxford until 1902, received his Ph.D. from Columbia University in 1904, and then joined the Morningside Heights faculty of that school as a professor of political science.

Maverick. Beard's *An Economic Interpretation of the Constitution* was in many ways the historical equivalent of the muckraking journalism of the progressive era. It submitted to withering inspection the economic motives and self-interest of the Founding Fathers in framing the Constitution. In contrast to the heroic and laudatory understanding of the framers that dominated most American histories, Beard argued that their foremost intention was to protect their property and that the Constitution was in many ways an antidemocratic document. Such an interpretation was shocking to many, but it fit perfectly Beard's maverick dissent from intellectual orthodoxy. Further proof of his independent spirit came in 1917. Although Beard supported American entry into World War I, he opposed efforts to silence antiwar protesters. When three Columbia instructors, J. McKeen Cattell, Henry Wadsworth Longfellow Dana, and Leon Fraser were fired for opposing conscription, Beard resigned from the university, bringing an end to his career as a practicing academic.

Educator. Beard's resignation from Columbia made him a national symbol of academic freedom, and in the 1920s and 1930s his public reputation and educational activities increased. He served as president of both the American Historical Association and the American Political Science Association. In 1919 — along with John Dewey, Alvin Johnson, and James Harvey Robinson — he founded the New School for Social Research in New York. In 1922 and 1923 he advised the city of Tokyo in its rebuilding efforts following a devastating earthquake, and after that appointment he traveled through Asia and Europe. He continued to produce well-received scholarly works and several history textbooks, including *The Rise of American Civilization* (1927), that were standard issue in colleges and high schools of the period.

Social Studies Commission. In 1929 Beard joined the American Historical Association Commission on the Social Studies in the Schools. The commission was organized to set goals for social-studies curricula in the high schools and to reassess college admission requirements in history. Members of the commission were some of the leading American educators — including George S. Counts, Frank Ballou, A. C. Krey, Guy Stanton Ford, Edmund E. Day, Charles Merriam, and Jesse Newlon — but Beard quickly became the dominant intellectual force, responsible for drafting the majority of the commission publications. He reevaluated the objectives of social studies curricula, attacking pedagogy that "assumes a fixed order of society into which each child is to be fitted by a dogmatic system of indoctrination" and urging teachers to use social studies to prepare children for a changing world. Along with Counts, Beard argued that American civilization was progressing from an agricultural and provincial state to an industrial, cosmopolitan democracy. To Beard the successful transition from one to the other depended on centralized economic planning and a willingness for students to work within a new collectivized order. To attain such goals, Beard argued that high-school curricula should be transformed and guided by this agenda.

Critics. Critics of the commission's work seized on Beard's decidedly non-Marxist use of the term *collective* and attacked the commission as communistic, especially following the 1934 publication of the commission's *Conclusions and Recommendations*. In the politically charged Depression, even some commission members found Beard's goals objectionable. Merriam and Day refused to sign *Conclusions and Recommendations*. Political attacks were mounted against commission members. Commission secretary Ballou, superintendent of the schools in Washington, D.C., was ordered to appear before a congressional committee and subjected to relentless grilling by anticommunist Representative Thomas L. Blanton of Texas. The Hearst newspapers made an anticommunist sensation of the commission's work. The most damning complaint against the *Conclusions and Recommendations,* however, was that they were sweeping and vague, of little use to teachers in the classroom. Yet as a statement of educational objectives *Conclusions and Recommendations* remains an important document of a decade when teachers were becoming increasingly politically active.

Isolationist. Beard's later political activities diminished his reputation among educators and progressives. By 1934 Beard began to argue that American imperialism abroad inevitably defeated economic planning at home. He became one of the leading American isolationists, and — after 1937 — a shrill critic of Franklin Roosevelt's foreign policy. Even after the fall of France in 1940, Beard consistently downplayed the dangers of Nazi tyranny and argued against American intervention in World War II. His last two works, *American Foreign Policy in the Making, 1932–1940* (1946) and *President Roosevelt and the Coming of the War, 1941* (1948), demonized Roosevelt and argued that he had conspired to plunge America into the war. Subsequent historians have validated some of Beard's interpretation, but his repeated underestimation of Japanese and German aggression makes these books one-sided and polemical. His stance cost him many friends and affiliations, and toward the end of his life he became increasingly conspiracy-minded and somewhat paranoid. The optimism that characterized his educational works of the 1930s vanished. Nonetheless, during the Depression Beard stood with Counts and Dewey as leading examples of the American teacher as political and social reformer.

Beard's work in education continues to inspire many modern educators.

Sources:

Richard Hofstadter, *The Progressive Historians: Turner, Beard, Parrington* (Chicago: University of Chicago Press, 1968);

Ellen Nore, *Charles A. Beard: An Intellectual Biography* (Carbondale: Southern Illinois University Press, 1983).

MARY MCLEOD BETHUNE

1875-1955

EDUCATOR AND CIVIL RIGHTS REFORMER

Dominant Figure. In the 1930s Mary McLeod Bethune was perhaps the most influential African American woman in the United States. A somewhat domineering woman with an unshakable religious faith, the charismatic Bethune was sometimes considered a female Booker T. Washington. Like him she had the capacity to reassure whites even as she pressed for greater civil and social equality for blacks. In the segregated, Depression-era South, she managed to promote the fortunes of Bethune-Cookman College, which she had founded. By the end of the decade she was the most influential African American administrator in the New Deal, the director of Negro affairs for the National Youth Administration. Her achievements are proof of what diligence and vision can accomplish in education, even under the most trying circumstances.

Background. One of seventeen children of parents freed from slavery after the Civil War, Bethune was born on a farm near Mayesville, South Carolina. Her family recognized early her aptitude for scholarship and singing. She excelled at the mission school she attended as a child. In 1888 she was sent to Scotia Seminary (later Barber-Scotia College), a Presbyterian school for black girls in Concord, North Carolina. The interracial faculty at that school emphasized religion and industrial education. Bethune, who did well at English composition and music, graduated in 1894 and entered the Bible Institute for Home and Foreign Missions (later called the Moody Bible Institute) that same year. Her intention to become a missionary to Africa was thwarted when the Presbyterian Mission Board refused her application on the grounds of race. Instead she taught at Haines Normal and Industrial Institute in Augusta, Georgia, and then at the Kindell Institute in Sumter, South Carolina. There she met her husband, Albertus Bethune, a menswear salesman. They were married in 1898 and had one son. In 1899 the family moved to Palatka, Florida, where Mary Bethune opened a Presbyterian mission; they separated soon after she moved to Daytona Beach five years later to open a school there. Albertus Bethune died in 1918.

Educator. In 1904 Bethune opened the Daytona Normal and Industrial Institute, a girls' school patterned on Scotia Seminary. Possessing canny business skills, she quickly secured funding from influential whites and expanded the school to meet the needs of the local black community. In 1907 she established the Tomoka Mission, a sort of school extension, in the local turpentine camps. The school built a hospital in 1911 and brought black and white visitors and celebrities to the school. Like Tuskegee Institute, the school had its own farm that both supplied the school with food and provided agricultural training. By 1923 the school had a twenty-five-member faculty and a student body of three hundred girls. In that year Bethune merged the school with the Cookman Institute of Jacksonville, making it coeducational. In 1929 a postsecondary division, known as Bethune-Cookman College, was added. Despite the Depression, Bethune continued to have success in soliciting funding for the school. By 1943 the school had become a fully accredited four-year institution and one of the leading teacher-training institutes in the South.

Activist. Deeply religious and believing in the equal worth of all individuals regardless of race, Bethune championed African American equality, even when it put her at risk. In the 1920s she led a successful black-women's voter-registration drive, despite threats from the Ku Klux Klan. She also opposed the Klan in local elections. During World War I she was instrumental in integrating the Red Cross. Bethune's articulateness and emphasis on black pride, on developing "Self-Control, Self-Respect, Self-Reliance and Race Pride," gave her national prominence, and in 1924 she became president of the National Association of Colored Women (NACW). In 1935 she created the National Council of Negro Women (NCNW), which was more activist than the NACW, and served as its president until 1949. Her participation in other national associations was extensive; she was a leader of the National Association of Teachers in Colored Schools, the Commission on Interracial Cooperation, the Southern Conference for Human Welfare, the National Urban League, and the Association for the Study of Negro Life and History. In 1935 she was awarded the Joel E. Spingarn gold medal for service by the National Association for the Advancement of Colored People (NAACP).

New Dealer. A confidant and associate of Eleanor Roosevelt, Bethune has been credited by many with advancing the first lady's stand on civil rights. In 1935 Bethune was appointed to the National Advisory Committee of the National Youth Administration (NYA), a New Deal agency responsible for helping young people stay in school or find work. By 1939 Bethune had become director of Negro affairs for the NYA. Bethune was instrumental in getting the NYA to extend its benefits to African Americans, and she was instrumental in the hir-

ing of many blacks for government positions at both federal and state levels. Under her leadership more than 150,000 African American teenagers went to high school; 60,000 went on to college. She was also instrumental in organizing and focusing the efforts of the Federal Council on Negro Affairs, the so-called "black cabinet" that pressured the Roosevelt administration to improve civil rights. She praised President Roosevelt's 1941 executive order desegregating defense industries and the government, and she promoted the war effort among African Americans. During the war she was also an assistant to Oveta Culp Hobby, commander of the Women's Auxiliary Corps of the U.S. Army, pressing for African American participation in the corps.

Later Career. Bethune left administrative service in 1944, returning to Daytona Beach. Appointed by the Truman administration as a consultant, she attended the San Francisco conference that framed the charter for the United Nations in 1945. In demand as a speaker, she continued to promote African American education before various groups around the country. In the 1940s her civil rights activities led her to be investigated by both the FBI and the House Un-American Activities Committee, but she continued her work undeterred. In 1949 she was invited to participate in the celebration of Haitian independence. In 1952 she traveled to Liberia as a U.S. representative at the inauguration of the new Liberian president. She died of a heart attack in 1955.

Source:

Rackham Holt, *Mary McLeod Bethune: A Biography* (Garden City, N.Y.: Doubleday, 1964).

HORACE MANN BOND

1904-1972

EDUCATOR, COLLEGE PRESIDENT

Black Educator. An imposing figure in a family that produced several important scholars and civil rights leaders, Horace Mann Bond had a career that exemplifies the dilemma of the black educator in the segregated South during the 1930s and 1940s: despising segregation and silently struggling to abolish it, while still helping to improve education for African Americans within its confines. Sociologist, college president, and philanthropic agent, Horace Mann Bond resolved this dilemma with intelligence and diplomacy. His work, and that of other educators like him, set into motion the historic forces that found expression in the civil rights movement of the 1950s and 1960s.

Background. Grandson of slaves, Bond was the child of an extraordinary couple. His mother was a schoolteacher, his father a minister. Both excelled in the network of religious and educational institutions established in the South after the Civil War. Bond was an academic prodigy, graduating from high school at the age of fourteen. He attended Lincoln University, a black college in southeastern Pennsylvania. Lincoln placed a premium on W. E. B. Du Bois's notion that racial improvement in the United States would be accomplished by a "talented tenth" of African Americans. Bond quickly proved himself to be such a leader, graduating with honors in 1923. While taking graduate courses at Pennsylvania State College, Bond earned grades higher than those of his white classmates and returned to Lincoln in 1923 as an instructor. Bond then suffered the only setback to his success: he was dismissed from the college for tolerating a gambling ring in a dormitory he was supervising.

Difficulties. Despite his embarrassment at Lincoln, Bond had a reputation as a fine scholar, and he spent much of the next fifteen years alternating between various jobs as an administrator of African American schools and graduate work in sociology at the University of Chicago, from which he received his doctorate in 1936. Bond's administrative work at Langston University in Langston, Oklahoma, and at Alabama State Normal School in Montgomery taught him valuable lessons in the difficulties of education in the segregated South. To keep the white state legislature funding Langston, for example, Langston faculty had to "fool" visiting legislators into thinking the school taught only domestic sciences and "honest labor and toil," giving visiting legislators sumptuous meals of fried chicken and mounting theatrical displays of teachers picking peas. After the whites left, satisfied that the blacks of Oklahoma were receiving education sufficient for their "place," Langston got back to teaching. Throughout the 1930s Bond was engaged in a similarly difficult and often frustrating relationship with the Rosenwald Fund, a white philanthropy that donated large sums toward black education. The Rosenwald funding was instrumental in Bond's pursuit of his doctorate, as well as in securing Bond's major academic appointments to Fisk University in 1928 and to Dillard University in New Orleans in 1935. Nonetheless, the Rosenwald Fund, enamored of Booker T. Washington's notion that African American improvement was best pursued through industrial and agricultural labor, was often conservative and rarely challenged the segregated status quo in the South. That perspective privately annoyed Bond; during the Depression, however, no responsible educator could antagonize a steady source of funding. Believing in black academic excellence, Bond confronted white resistance to equality as a scholar, attacking one of the cornerstones of segregation: the belief that intelligence testing had "proved" the intellectual inferiority of African Americans.

Intelligence Testing. The U.S. Army had begun intelligence testing during World War I. In the 1920s various academics, such as Carl Brigham of Princeton, used the army data and other studies to argue that intelligence testing demonstrated the innate racial inferiority of African Americans. At Chicago, however, Bond had studied sociology in a department that had pioneered research in the impact of environment and society on individual personality. He had also supervised the creation of a statistical survey on the socioeconomic and educational condition of African Americans for the Tennessee Valley Authority. In a series of important articles, in a book titled *The Education of the Negro in the American Social Order* (1934), and in his dissertation, published as *Negro Education in Alabama: A Study in Cotton and Steel* (1939), Bond assailed intelligence testing for its cultural bias and ignorance of environmental factors in education. White academics argued that "bright" blacks moved North; Bond conducted empirical studies at Lincoln demonstrating no significant difference in innate intelligence between northern and southern African Americans. Many asserted that the decline of black schools was owing to African American indifference; Bond demonstrated that it resulted from poor financing by white-dominated school boards. Bond showed that exceptional black students were usually the products of exceptionally well-financed and well-administered black schools, rather than any genetic characteristic. Bond tied the poor educational performance of African Americans to their political disenfranchisement and economic exploitation. He revealed that in many counties where the majority or near majority of the population was African American, white school boards kept taxes low and financed good schools for white children by directing the bulk of black tax payments to white schools — even as black schools remained substandard. Black taxpayers, in other words, were financing education for their white neighbors. "The School," he wrote in his 1934 book, "has been the product and interpreter of the existing [economic] system, sustaining and being sustained by the social complex." With Du Bois he also inaugurated a revisionist history of southern Reconstruction, which — in contrast to the dominant "Dunning" school of southern history in his time — did not applaud the activities of the Ku Klux Klan in "redeeming" the South after the Civil War.

Administrator. Bond's scholarly work, although fairly radical for the time, was tempered by articles and speeches in which he lauded the work of "Southern white gentlemen" and racial moderates. He also did not recommend the abolition of the segregated school system but instead advocated financing it on a truly equal basis. Such gestures were necessary for the continued functioning of any southern educator committed to improving black education in the Jim Crow South. After 1939 Bond was foremost among such educators. That year he accepted the presidency of Fort Valley State College in Fort Valley, Georgia, a position he held until 1945, when he assumed the presidency of his alma mater, Lincoln. The first black president in the history of Lincoln, Bond held the office until 1957. He used his position to pursue several concerns: pan-Africanism and the development of African studies in American universities (following a trip to Africa in 1949), desegregation in Pennsylvania schools, assistance to the NAACP legal team that argued the *Brown* v. *Board of Education* (1954) suit before the U.S. Supreme Court, and the physical expansion of Lincoln and the improvement of its courses. He increased the number of black faculty members at Lincoln and brought to campus its first Jewish professor. He aroused opposition to his presidency by his activism and in 1957 resigned his office owing to the increased combativeness of the board of trustees. He then became dean of the School of Education at Atlanta University, remaining there until his retirement in 1971. During that time he renewed his criticisms of intelligence testing and standardized achievement tests following a flurry of new activity in those fields in the early 1960s, but increasingly his energy was focused on helping the civil rights activities and political career of his son, Julian Bond. Horace Mann Bond died in December 1972.

Sources:

Wayne J. Urban, *Black Scholar: Horace Mann Bond, 1904–1972* (Athens: University of Georgia Press, 1992);

Roger M. Williams, *The Bonds: An American Family* (New York: Atheneum, 1972).

GEORGE S. COUNTS

1889-1974

EDUCATIONAL ACTIVIST

Lightning Rod. In 1932, with a single address to the Progressive Education Association (PEA), George Counts became the most discussed educator in the United States. His speech — "Dare Progressive Education Be Progressive?" — articulated the anxieties and ambitions of professional educators during the Depression. Calling American teachers to arms, he demanded that they put their talents to work not only as educators but as economic reformers and political activists. Insisting that only education could advance the cause of social reform without revolution, Counts challenged educators to take an increased role in leadership and government and to impart to their students a sense of progressive politics. Denounced by conservatives, he was the foremost advocate of the new educational philosophy of social reconstructionism, a lightning rod for the tensions of the times, the champion of the teacher as social reformer.

Background. Counts was born on 9 December 1889 near Baldwin, Kansas. As a youth, he hoped to become a trapper and evidenced a marked taste for adventure. As the frontier was closed, he gave up his youthful ambition, attending Baker University in Baldwin and majoring in classics. Following college, he taught science in high school, eventually becoming a teaching principal. In 1913 he won a scholarship to study sociology at the University of Chicago, where the faculty included some of the foremost sociologists and educators in America. Counts studied with Albion Small, Frederick Starr, Charles Hubbard Judd, and Charles E. Merriam. All emphasized the social and economic context of education, the way in which the schools reflected their settings. Counts received the first doctorate in the sociology of education granted by the University of Chicago and immediately began serving on a series of faculties: Delaware College, Harris Teachers College in Saint Louis, the University of Washington, Yale University, and the University of Chicago. In 1927 he took a position at the Teachers College of Columbia University, and by the time of his PEA address he was one of the best-known educators in America.

International Education. Counts's reputation as an educator rested on his expertise in international education. In 1925 he had participated in a survey of schools in the Philippines. In 1927 he learned Russian and went to the Soviet Union, becoming among the first Americans to travel to the new Communist state. In 1929 he repeated the journey, driving a Model A Ford from Vienna, Austria, through six thousand miles of western Russia. Counts was impressed by what he saw in the Soviet Union, especially during his 1929 trip. The planned economic system was revolutionizing Russia, transforming an agrarian society into an industrial power. During this period, before the Stalinist purges that began in the mid 1930s, the utopian promise of the Soviet Union seemed great, and the Russian schools were apparently busy creating a democratic, industrial polity from a formerly subordinated peasantry. The contrast between the energy and organization of Russian society and the disorganization of the United States was striking. On his return to America Counts wrote *The Soviet Challenge to America* (1931), a book that established him as the leading American expert in Russian education. In 1929 Counts delivered the Inglis Lectures in Education at Harvard University and joined the American Historical Association Commission on the Social Studies in the Schools, a group reformulating curricula in history and civics. During his service on the commission, Counts developed his philosophy of the educator as social reformer, naturally enough since the mandate to the commission was to consider the relationship between social-studies curricula and society. By 1932 he was the point man for educators seeking broad social change through the schools. In 1934 he helped to launch and edit *Social Frontier*, a lively journal designed to advance "the raising of American life from the level of the profit system, individualism and vested class interests to the plane of social motivation, collectivism and classlessness.... It will place human rights above property rights." *Social Frontier* was one of the leading intellectual journals of the decade, continuing publication until 1943.

Critic. In the 1930s there was an enormous amount of tension between professional educators who argued that education was best pursued by "uplifting" children to the standards of a white, Anglo-Saxon, Protestant, middle-class culture and those who sought to build new, culturally plural standards for educational achievement. The dispute often took the form of debates over standbys of an older educational tradition, such as instruction in Latin, but it also focused on the sort of instruction in politics and economics pursued in the schools. Middle-class educators insisted, even during the Depression, that schools should teach the merits of an unregulated, laissez-faire economy and conservative, Anglo-Saxon political leadership. Counts condemned such an approach, insisting that "it constitutes an attempt to educate the youth for life in a world that does not exist. Teachers cannot evade the responsibility of participating actively in the task of reconstituting the democratic tradition and of thus working positively toward a new society. . . . They owe nothing to the present economic system except to improve it; they owe nothing to any privileged class except to strip it of its privileges."

Anticommunist. Such rhetoric drew considerable fire from conservatives, and Counts was the target of many professional anticommunists, who charged him and the social reconstructionists with subversion. Counts, however, was no communist. In 1936 he made a third tour of the Soviet Union, in time to witness Stalin's purges firsthand. His friend Albert Petrovich Pinkevich, a Russian educator, was sent to a forced-labor camp. When Counts was elected president of the American Federation of Teachers (AFT) in 1939, he began a campaign to purge the union of Communist Party influence, expelling the Communist-led New York Local #5 and other Communist-influenced locals in 1941. In the 1940s and early 1950s he wrote several books concerned with maintaining civil liberties and academic freedom while at the same time opposing communism and the Soviet Union.

Later Career. Counts's activism continued in the 1950s and 1960s. He served on the AFT Commission on Post-War Reconstruction. He traveled to Japan to participate in the reconstruction of the Japanese educational system. With others he helped to found the Liberal Party of New York, unsuccessfully running for the Senate on its ticket in 1952. Against his wishes he was forcibly retired from Columbia in 1955. Tireless, he lectured in Brazil in 1957, joined the faculty of the University of Pittsburgh in 1959, went to teach at Michigan State University in 1960, and in 1961 was appointed to the faculty at Southern Illinois University in Carbondale, where he remained for a decade. He died on 10 November 1974.

Sources:

Lawrence A. Cremin, *The Transformation of the School: Progressivism in American Education, 1876–1957* (New York: Knopf, 1961);

Lawrence J. Dennis, *George S. Counts and Charles A. Beard: Collaborators for Change* (Albany: State University of New York Press, 1989).

GLENN FRANK

1887-1940

UNIVERSITY PRESIDENT, POLITICIAN

A Varied Life. Evangelical preacher, philanthropist, journalist, college president, politician: Glenn Frank had many careers during his short life, and he excelled at each. A colorful, affable, and intelligent man, Frank was one of the leading college presidents and educational reformers in the United States during the 1930s. A moderate conservative who called himself a liberal, Frank proposed modest programs for educational reform at a time of radical alternatives. He successfully held to the center and then became one of the most articulate conservative critics of the New Deal, becoming for a time a figure who was proposed by many for the presidency of the United States.

Background. Frank was born in Queen City, Missouri, on 1 October 1887, and he grew up in nearby Green Top, a small agricultural community where almost everyone was white, Anglo-Saxon, and Protestant. Frank was the youngest — by fifteen years — of four boys. His father was a country schoolteacher, his mother a zealous Methodist, who instilled piety in her son. When Frank was twelve he became a boy evangelist, riding a circuit and giving as many as six sermons a day. In 1903 he was officially ordained a Methodist minister. In 1909 he came to the attention of the famous evangelist Billy Sunday, who hired him to assist in a summer crusade. That fall, however, Frank entered Northwestern University in Evanston, Illinois. Despite a campus atmosphere that was more morally relaxed than his evangelical background, Frank fit in well, becoming a popular fraternity member and editing the *Northwestern Magazine*. He was an outstanding orator, winning several prizes and earning money for college by summer stints on the lecture circuit. His talent was such that the university administration hired him as its alumni fund-raiser following his graduation in 1912. It would not be the last time his skill as a speaker advanced his fortunes.

Among the Elite. In the three years Frank worked for Northwestern, he doubled the endowment fund, recruited many students, and traveled frequently. He developed a national reputation for oratory and made contacts with some of the most influential businessmen in the

United States. In 1915 he became a private secretary for one of them, Edward A. Filene, a Boston retailer and philanthropist. Relocating to Boston was an important step for Frank. In the East he amassed more business contacts, continued to refine his oratory, and took his first steps into politics, helping Filene administer pet projects such as the League to Enforce Peace, an antiwar association. In 1918 he wrote his first book, in collaboration with Lothrop Stoddard, a Harvard Ph.D. *The Stakes of the War* urged Americans to take an active role in the efforts to settle the peace following World War I. The book sold well, and Frank became much in demand as a speaker on political issues. His reputation as a speaker helped Frank to attain the editorship of the prestigious *Century* magazine, a position that gave him access to the political and cultural elite of the United States, and Frank made himself known to them. By 1925 he was a fixture of the American cultural establishment, and his appointment to the presidency of the University of Wisconsin that year was widely applauded.

President. At that time the University of Wisconsin was the premier public university in the United States. In the previous two decades Wisconsin had set national standards for sociological and economic research and provided academic expertise to progressive Wisconsin political reformers, such as Robert La Follette. By 1925, however, the close ties between the university and Wisconsin politics had made the university administration a minefield of special interests and factions. Frank's skills with politics and public speaking made him the ideal candidate for the post of president, which he assumed at the age of thirty-seven. Controversy nonetheless followed him to the office. To learn about the local politics and interest groups, Frank made the mistake of hiring a private detective firm to investigate the faculty, an act which immediately embittered many. As president Frank brought educational reformer Alexander Meiklejohn to the university to establish an experimental college dedicated to revolutionizing curriculum, another act which alienated him from the established faculty. Frank's own program for educational reform included the production of educational movies and the establishment of research laboratories for business and industry. Many found these ideas shallow and academically soft. The Depression forced cutbacks at the school, including the cancellation of the experimental college. Necessary salary cuts angered the faculty, and Frank's demands for continued funding from state legislators hurt his standing with them. In 1932 a scandal involving the moral code at the university was poorly handled by Frank, and the number of his critics increased. In 1935 several faculty firings by the Board of Regents undermined Frank's authority. After professional anticommunists claimed the university was a seedbed of sedition, it was investigated by a legislative committee, which found no subversion. Nonetheless, the ire of local vigilantes was aroused. On 13 May 1935 right-wing students attacked a small meeting of the League for Industrial Democracy, a socialist campus group. Frank denounced the attacking students and threatened them with expulsion, a position that was applauded. While Frank's mild attempts at educational reform had contributed to the accusations of communism, he was far too conservative for Progressive governor Philip F. La Follette. Following his landslide election victory in 1936, La Follette fired Frank.

Politician. In many ways Frank's political ambitions were responsible for his removal. Since the late 1920s he had cultivated powerful friends within the Republican Party, including Calvin Coolidge and Herbert Hoover. Following the election of Franklin D. Roosevelt, Frank became one of the important spokesmen for the business wing of the Republican Party, writing a book, *America's Hour of Decision* (1934), that helped unite business conservatives in their opposition to the New Deal. After 1934 he also turned his oratorical skills toward attacking the New Deal, condemning it as creating the "weapons of power to be captured by some yet-to-arise dictatorial government which will mean the end of all our fathers fought to establish in the American scheme of government." Many thought Frank would become the Republican candidate for president in 1936, but Frank refused to run. After he was fired from Wisconsin, he bought an obscure magazine, *Rural Progress,* and used it as a vehicle to attack Roosevelt. As the 1940 election approached, Frank joined the Republican National Committee, helping to draft the 1940 platform. He also ran for the Republican nomination as a U.S. Senate candidate from Wisconsin, hoping to unseat Robert La Follette Jr., the governor's brother. These ambitions were dashed when Frank died in an automobile accident while campaigning. His death on 15 September 1940 brought to an end an extraordinary career.

Source:

Lawrence H. Larsen, *The President Wore Spats: A Biography of Glenn Frank* (Madison: State Historical Society of Wisconsin, 1965).

CATHERINE BRIEGER STERN

1894-1973

MATHEMATICIAN, EDUCATOR

Elementary Education Leader. An acknowledged leader in the education of kindergarten children, Catherine Brieger Stern immigrated to the United States from Germany in 1938. Stern's innovations in the teaching of elementary mathematics and reading anticipated many of the curricular innovations of the 1960s and 1970s, and her work had a lasting impact on elementary schools.

Background. Born Käthe Brieger, Stern was the only daughter of a medical and academic family in Breslau, Germany. Much influenced by her mother, Hedwig, Stern was educated by a private tutor and at the Mädchen Gymnasium in Breslau. Following in the footsteps of her father, she took a degree in physics at the University of Breslau, where she was awarded a Ph.D. in physics and mathematics in 1918. She met her husband, Rudolf Stern, through a shared interest in literature and the theater; they were married in 1919 and had two children, Toni, a daughter, and Fritz, a son.

Expertise and Exile. Raising her children led Stern to an interest in preschool education, and she studied the Montessori method of teaching. In 1924 she opened Breslau's first Montessori kindergarten, which she later expanded to include the primary grades. Renouncing drills and routinization, Stern developed new materials for teaching reading and mathematics. She published two important works in the field of kindergarten and elementary education, *Methodik der täglichen Kinderhauspraxis* (1932; translated as *Methods of Daily Kindergarten Practice*) and *Wille, Phantasie and Werkgestaltung* (1933; translated as *Will, Fantasy and Work Development*). Far too innovative for the Nazis, Stern was also persecuted for her Jewish background. In 1938 she and her husband immigrated to New York, where she took the name Catherine Stern. She became an American citizen in 1944.

Innovations. In the United States Stern continued the innovations in education she had begun in Germany. Rather than force children to memorize mathematics, she sought to teach them the fundamental relationships of arithmetic. She developed a challenging series of numbered block games to help children make mathematical abstractions concrete. She had children analyze and reassemble words and speech in order to teach reading skills more effectively. After 1940 she began an association with gestalt psychologist Max Wertheimer at the New School for Social Research, fusing her search for more-active methods of pedagogy with his school of psychology. She wrote several influential textbooks, including *Children Discover Arithmetic: An Introduction to Structural Arithmetic* (1949). From 1944 to 1951 she conducted the experimental Castle School in Manhattan with her daughter and Margaret J. Bassett, and she continued to pioneer new methods of instruction, which she and her daughter detailed in books such as *Experimenting with Numbers: Structural Arithmetic for Kindergarten* (1950), *The Early Years of Childhood: Education Through Insight* (1955), and *Children Discover Reading* (1965). In the early 1960s she was a consultant to the School Mathematics Study Group, proponents of the new math program. Even after her death in 1973, Stern's teaching materials continued to be used widely in Europe, Israel, and North America.

Source:
Richard D. Troxel, Entry on Stern, in *Notable American Women: The Modern Period, A Biographical Dictionary*, edited by Barbara Sicherman and Carol Hurd Green, with Ilene Katrov and Harriette Walker (Cambridge, Mass., & London: Harvard University Press, 1980), pp. 659–660.

LOYD S. TIREMAN

1896-1959

PIONEER IN BILINGUAL EDUCATION

Pioneer. During the 1930s Loyd S. Tireman conducted some of the first bilingual education experiments in the United States. At the San José Demonstration and Experimental School in Bernalillo County, New Mexico, and later at the Nambé Community School in Nambé, New Mexico, he developed new methods of teaching reading, bicultural education, and community relations. For thirty-two years he was among the leading American educators who organized bilingual educational programs in the face of much prejudice and opposition.

Background. Tireman was born in Orchard, Iowa, in 1896. The farming community in which he was raised emphasized quality education and tied the schools closely to the local community. For Iowans of that time good schools produced good citizens, and community interest in education was high. Tireman benefited from this attention, graduating from Fayette High School in 1913 and continuing his education at Upper Iowa State University. He graduated in 1917, in time to enlist for service in World War I, after which he returned to Iowa, married, and assumed a position as school superintendent in Hanlontown, the first of several superintendencies he held. In 1924 he earned an M.A. in education from the University of Iowa at Iowa City and continued there until he was granted a Ph.D. in 1927. That year he left Iowa for a position on the faculty of the University of New Mexico at Albuquerque. New Mexico would remain his adopted and beloved home for the rest of his life.

The San José School. School surveys conducted during the late 1920s indicated frequent problems with reading in New Mexican schools. Especially troubling was the disparity between English-speaking and Spanish-speaking children. In the first three grades the two groups scored equally on reading exams, but after that the lack of English reading reinforcement at home for Spanish-speaking children led Hispanic children to score poorly on tests. In 1930 Tireman secured funding (no small task during the Depression) and the cooperation of the Albuquerque public schools to open an experimental school in San José, a Spanish-speaking district near the city. The San José school quickly became a model for those interested in teaching Hispanic students. Tireman constructed a curriculum familiar to a predominantly Hispanic student body from rural backgrounds. Innovative drills in reading skills, the use of peer tutoring, and the use of community resources in the classroom successfully increased student interest in the program. After he witnessed similar programs in Mexico, Tireman began classes in health and hygiene and hired a school nurse to monitor the condition of the students. Tireman also inaugurated a preschool reading program, vastly increasing student performance in the regular grades. In 1932 the

San José school hired a Spanish instructor and made Spanish education an elective for higher grades — one of the first bilingual educational efforts in the nation. The results were encouraging, with students making advances in both Spanish and English courses. Programs developed at San José were quickly instituted at other New Mexico schools.

Problems. Tireman's greatest problem with the San José school was not with the students, but with other educators. During the 1930s the majority of educators believed that African Americans, Hispanic Americans, and Native Americans were racially inferior to whites and incapable of anything but the most rudimentary learning. To such educators, developing curricular programs especially for Spanish American and Native American students was a waste of time and money. These educators argued that the function of the school was to assimilate nonwhite cultures to a standard set by whites, and Tireman's attempts to provide special programs for Spanish speakers was viewed as corrupting educational standards. On the other hand local Hispanic politicians feuding with white authorities and the local police viewed the San José school as a form of white cultural colonization and often opposed Tireman. To meet the objections of these two groups of critics, Tireman became something of a politician and began a teacher-training program at San José designed to recruit new instructors to his cause. The strain of such varied efforts was telling on Tireman personally. By 1938, with funding running out, he wrapped up his participation with the school and moved on to a new project, a new experimental school in Nambé, a village in northern New Mexico.

The Nambé Community School. Nambé was a primarily Spanish-speaking agricultural town with a strong tradition of communal action. It had suffered badly during the Depression, but Cyrus McCormick Jr., the heir to the International Harvester fortune, had moved near Nambé in the early 1930s and decided to fund a school based on the example set by San José. Tireman headed the new school. As in San José, he immediately abandoned the standard curriculum designed for white, eastern students and built a curriculum accessible to the experience of Hispanic, western children. Community problems determined the curriculum at the school; the school in turn acted as a center for improving the health and well-being of the community. With help from several New Deal agencies, the Nambé school also taught the adults of the community scientific farming techniques. As they had at San José, teachers at Nambé took their students on "walks" through the community, using the town and its problems as the basis for instruction. Public health, animal husbandry, and agricultural science joined mathematics and reading as standard parts of the curriculum. Again, however, the Nambé school encountered the same criticisms raised against San José — from professional educators who believed that Spanish-based and community-based curriculum was soft and undemanding and from Spanish-speaking parents who often objected to ideas introduced by teachers from a white, urban culture. World War II redirected much of the community and educational support for the experiment toward the war effort, and in 1942 the school closed.

Later Career. Tireman continued as an educational reformer throughout World War II and the postwar period, traveling to South America and around the United States advising governments on educational reform. The Office of Inter-American Affairs sent him to Bolivia after the war to help reorganize that nation's schools. In 1950 Tireman curtailed many of his public activities because he was suffering from heart disease and leukemia. He died on 25 October 1959.

Source:
David L. Bachelor, *Educational Reform in New Mexico: Tireman, San José, and Nambé* (Albuquerque: University of New Mexico Press, 1991).

PEOPLE IN THE NEWS

In 1933, responding to widespread criticisms that American education was out of step with the times, the U.S. Office of Education asked progressive historian **Charles Beard** to supply high-school libraries with a book list designed to "acquaint teachers and pupils with facts, known and unknown, about this new world we are entering."

In 1930 the New Orleans school board hired sociologist **Mabel Byrd** to investigate black labor conditions in New Orleans and to recommend an appropriate system of African American education. Byrd concluded that African Americans should be given a high-school curriculum designed to improve their low-wage work skills but not their intellectual competence, so as to prevent "increasing competition between the races."

Chemist **James B. Conant** succeeded A. Lawrence Lowell as president of Harvard University in 1933.

On 9 May 1933 the director of the Civilian Conservation Corps (CCC), **Robert Fechner,** approved a U.S. War Department directive that began educational instruction at CCC camps.

On 30 June 1934, in an address to the National Education Association, **Gustave A. Feingold,** principal of Bulkeley High School in Hartford, Connecticut, condemned educators who sought to reduce academic requirements for the soaring enrollments of American schools. "The spreading of the idea that 50 percent of the high school enrollment is unqualified for the traditional high school studies is nothing less than a libel against the youth of the nation," he said.

In 1939 the American Association of University Women published a study on sexual discrimination in college; **Willystine Goodsell** found that only 4 percent of the professorships at large state universities were held by women (as opposed to 23.5 percent of the instructorships) and that 79 percent of women attending college felt discriminated against because of their sex and marital status.

In late 1933 a report issued by New York State Commissioner of Education **Frank P. Graves** called for sweeping revisions to the standard curriculum, in keeping with the needs of a multiethnic, heterogeneous student body.

In July 1939 Howard University psychologist **Martin D. Jenkins** published the results of a comprehensive survey of intelligence testing, attributing, "either in the whole or in part," the difference in intelligence-test scores between blacks and whites to "the environmental factor."

Clarence S. Marsh, dean of the evening session of the University of Buffalo, was appointed educational director of the Civilian Conservation Corps on 29 December 1933.

On 26 September 1936 President Franklin D. Roosevelt appointed **Floyd W. Reeves** chairman of the Advisory Committee on Education, which investigated vocational education and recommended greater federal participation in education. After reviewing the committee's report in 1938, Congress refused to appropriate funds for this purpose.

Writing in the March–April 1937 issue of the *American Teacher,* **Charles H. Thompson** called for a "New Deal" in education for American blacks and estimated that to bring the physical plant of black common schools up to the standards of white common schools would require an outlay of $242 million.

In 1930 educator **Ben D. Wood** founded the Cooperative Test Service, an educational testing organization attempting primarily to standardize admissions tests for colleges.

In 1934 educator **George Zook** resigned as the Roosevelt administration's first commissioner of the U.S. Office of Education, citing insufficient administration financing for education and insufficient commitment to black equality in education.

DEATHS

Felix Adler, 81, educator and social reformer, founder of the Ethical Culture Society, professor of ethics at Columbia University, 24 April 1933.

John Howard Appleton, 86, professor of chemistry at Brown University, author of many popular works on chemistry, 18 February 1930.

Irving Babbitt, 67, influential critic and Harvard University professor of modern languages, founder of the New Humanist movement in American letters, whose best-known work was *Rousseau and Romanticism* (1919), 15 July 1933.

William Henry Black, 75, theologian and educator, president of Missouri Valley College (1890–1925), 23 June 1930.

Frank David Boynton, 61, superintendent of the Ithaca, New York, public schools and president of the New York State teachers' association, 17 June 1930.

Elmer E. Brown, 73, educator, commissioner of education under Presidents Theodore Roosevelt and William Howard Taft, chancellor of New York University (1911–1933), 3 November 1934.

James Joseph Carlin, 58, Jesuit theologian and educator, president of Holy Cross College (1918–1925), 1 October 1930.

John Bates Clark, 91, political economist at Columbia University, president of the American Economic Association (1893–1895), 21 March 1938.

William Stearns Davis, 53, author and historian, professor of history at the University of Minnesota, 15 February 1930.

Alfred Lewis Pinneo Dennis, 56, author and historian, chairman of the history department at Clark University, 14 November 1930.

Melvil Dewey, 80, inventor of the Dewey decimal classification system for libraries, 26 December 1931.

Robert Fechner, 63, labor leader, director of the Civilian Conservation Corps, which provided many educational programs, 31 December 1939.

Frank Johnson Goodnow, 80, educator and legal scholar, president of Johns Hopkins University (1914–1929), 15 November 1939.

Edwin Greenlaw, 57, noted philologist, professor of English literature at Johns Hopkins University, 10 September 1931.

John Grier Hibben, 72, logician and president of Princeton University (1912–1932), 16 May 1933.

Edward Washburn Hopkins, 74, philologist, former president of the American Oriental Society, 16 July 1932.

William Edwards Huntington, 86, theologian and former president of Boston University, 6 December 1930.

Harry Burns Hutchins, 92, lawyer and historian, president of the University of Michigan (1910–1920), 25 January 1930.

Allen Johnson, 60, Yale University history professor, 18 January 1931.

David Starr Jordan, 80, educator and naturalist, first president and chancellor of Stanford University (1890–1916), peace activist and president of the World's Peace Congress in 1915, 19 September 1931.

Charles Knapp, 67, philologist and classical scholar at Barnard College, 17 September 1936.

John Holladay Latane, 62, diplomatic historian, dean at Johns Hopkins University, 1919–1924, 1 January 1932.

James Laurence Laughlin, 83, political economist at the University of Chicago, helped establish the federal reserve system, 28 November 1933.

Emil Lederer, 57, German economist and educator, forced to leave Germany by the Nazis, found many fellow exiles positions at the New School for Social Research in New York City, 29 May 1939.

Anne Mansfield Sullivan Macy, 70, teacher at the Perkins Institution for the Blind in Massachusetts and lifelong companion of Helen Keller, 20 October 1936.

Charles Carroll Marden, 64, professor of the Spanish language at Princeton University, 11 May 1932.

George Herbert Mead, 58, educator and pragmatic philosopher, chairman of the philosophy department at the University of Chicago, 25 April 1931.

Paul Elmer More, 72, essayist and literary scholar, professor at Princeton University, founder with Irving Babbitt of the New Humanist movement, 9 March 1937.

George Daniel Olds, 77, mathematician, president of Amherst College (1924–1927), 11 May 1931.

Frederick L. Ransome, 66, geologist and educator, member of the faculty at the University of Arizona and the California Institute of Technology, 6 October 1935.

James Harvey Robinson, 73, historian, professor of history at Columbia University, founder of the New School for Social Research, 16 February 1936.

Ole Edvart Rölvaag, 55, head of the Department of Norwegian Language and Literature at St. Olaf College in Northfield, Minnesota, author of the novel *Giants in the Earth* (1927), 5 November 1931.

Julius Sachs, 94, New York educator, professor at the Teachers College at Columbia University, 2 February 1934.

Nora Smith, 74, kindergarten educator and reformer, author of children's books, 1 February 1934.

William Edward Story, 69, educator and chairman of the mathematics department at Clark University (1889–1921), 10 April 1930.

James A. Tufts, 73, educator, professor of English at Phillips Exeter Academy (1878–1928), editor of textbooks, 21 November 1938.

Frederick Jackson Turner, 70, historian, influential founder of the school of historical interpretation that located the motive behind American history in the effects of the frontier, 14 March 1932.

William A. Wirt, 64, educational conservative, superintendent of the Gary, Indiana, schools, 11 March 1938.

George Edward Woodberry, 74, author, critic, and educator, influential professor of literature at Columbia University, author of studies of nineteenth-century American literary figures, 2 January 1930.

John Wesley Young, 52, Dartmouth College mathematician, 17 February 1932.

PUBLICATIONS

American Association of School Administrators, *Schools in Small Communities* (Washington, D.C.: American Association of School Administrators, National Education Association, 1939);

American Association of School Administrators, *Youth Education Today: Sixteenth Yearbook* (Washington, D.C.: American Association of School Administrators, National Education Association, 1938);

American Historical Association, Commission on the Social Studies in the Schools, *Conclusions and Recommendations of the Commission* (New York & Chicago: Scribners, 1934);

American Youth Commission, American Council on Education, *What the High Schools Ought to Teach: The Report of a Special Committee on the Secondary School Curriculum, Ben G. Graham, Chairman* (Washington, D.C.: American Council on Education, 1940);

Byron K. Armstrong, "Factors in the Formulation of Collegiate Programs for Negroes," dissertation, University of Michigan, 1939;

Charles A. Beard, *A Charter for the Social Sciences in the Schools* (New York: Scribners, 1932);

Beard, *The Nature of the Social Sciences in Relation to Objectives of Instruction* (New York: Scribners, 1934);

Howard Bell, *Youth Tell Their Story* (Washington, D.C.: American Council on Education, 1938);

Boyd H. Bode, *Progressive Education at the Crossroads* (N.p.: Newson, 1938);

Horace Mann Bond, *The Education of the Negro in the American Social Order* (New York: Prentice-Hall, 1934);

Bond, *Negro Education in Alabama: A Study in Cotton and Steel* (Washington, D.C.: Associated Publishers, 1939);

Thomas Monroe Campbell, *The Movable School Goes to the Negro Farmer* (Tuskegee, Ala.: Tuskegee Institute Press, 1936);

George Counts, *Dare the School Build a New Social Order?* (New York: John Day, 1932);

Counts, *The Schools Can Teach Democracy* (New York: John Day, 1939);

Counts, *The Social Foundations of Education* (New York: Scribners, 1934);

Counts, *The Soviet Challenge to America* (New York: John Day, 1931);

Merle Curti, *The Social Ideas of American Educators* (New York: Scribners, 1935);

Charles W. Dabney, *Universal Education in the South*, 2 volumes (Chapel Hill: University of North Carolina Press, 1936);

Kingsley Davis, *Youth in the Depression* (Chicago: University of Chicago Press, 1935);

Maxine Davis, *The Lost Generation* (New York: Macmillan, 1936);

John Dewey, *Experience and Education* (New York: Macmillan, 1938);

Harl Douglass, *Secondary Education for Youth in Modern America* (Washington, D.C.: American Council on Education, 1937);

Ella Enslow, with Alvin Harlow, *Schoolhouse in the Foothills* (New York: Simon & Schuster, 1935);

Abraham Flexner, *I Remember* (New York: Simon & Schuster, 1940);

Flexner, *Universities: American, English, German* (New York: Oxford University Press, 1930);

Dwight Oliver Holmes, *The Evolution of the Negro College* (New York: Teachers College, Columbia University, 1934);

Robert Maynard Hutchins, *The Higher Learning in America* (New Haven: Yale University Press / London: Oxford University Press, 1936);

Lance G. E. Jones, *The Jeanes Teacher in the United States, 1908–1933: An Account of Twenty-five Years' Experience in the Supervision of Negro Rural Schools* (Chapel Hill: University of North Carolina Press, 1937);

William H. Kilpatrick, ed., *The Educational Frontier* (New York: Century, 1933);

Howard Langford, *Education and the Social Conflict* (New York: Macmillan, 1936);

Joseph Lash and James Wechsler, *War Our Heritage* (New York: International Publishers, 1936);

William S. Learned, *The Student and His Knowledge: A Report to the Carnegie Foundation on the Results of the High School and College Examinations of 1928, 1930, and 1932* (New York: Carnegie Foundation for the Advancement of Teaching, 1938);

Betty and Ernest Lindley, *A New Deal for Youth: The Story of the National Youth Administration* (New York: Viking, 1938);

Fred McCuiston, *The South's Negro Teaching Force* (Nashville, Tenn.: Julius Rosenwald Fund, 1931);

Theophilus E. McKinney, ed., *Higher Education among Negroes: Addresses Delivered in Celebration of the Twenty-fifth Anniversary of the Presidency of Dr. Henry Lawrence McCrorey of Johnson C. Smith University* (Charlotte, N.C.: Johnson C. Smith University, 1932);

Bruce L. Melvin, *Youth — Millions Too Many?* (New York: Association Press, 1940);

Thomas Minehan, *Boy and Girl Tramps of America* (New York: Farrar & Rinehart, 1934);

Charles A. Prosser, *Secondary Education and Life* (Cambridge, Mass.: Harvard University Press, 1939);

Homer P. Rainey, with Arthur Brandon, M. M. Chambers, and others, *How Fare American Youth?*, Report to the American Youth Commission of the American Council on Education (New York & London: Appleton-Century, 1937);

Edward E. Redcay, *County Training Schools and Public Secondary Education for Negroes in the South* (Washington, D.C.: John F. Slater Fund, 1935);

John L. Tildsley, *The Mounting Waste of the American Secondary School* (Cambridge, Mass.: Harvard University Press, 1936);

Goodwin Watson, *How Good Are Our Colleges?* (New York: Public Affairs Committee, 1939);

James Wechsler, *Revolt on the Campus* (New York: Covici, Friede, 1935);

M. R. Werner, *Julius Rosenwald: The Life of a Practical Humanitarian* (New York: Harper, 1939);

Doxey A. Wilkerson, *Special Problems of Negro Education* (Washington, D.C.: U.S. Government Printing Office, 1939);

Arthur D. Wright, *The Negro Rural School Fund, Inc., 1907–1933* (Washington, D.C.: Negro Rural School Fund, 1933);

Caroline Zachry, *Emotion and Conduct in Adolescence* (New York: Appleton-Century, 1940);

Journal of Negro Education (1932–   );

Social Frontier, Journal of the Progressive Education Association (1934–June 1939); retitled *Frontiers of Democracy* (October 1939–December 1943).

FASHION

by JANE GERHARD

CONTENTS

Sidebars and tables are listed in italics

1930

- Architect Raymond Hood completes the Daily News Building in New York City. With its lively cubist pattern of red and black bricks, it is one of the foremost examples of art deco architecture.

- Developer Hugh Prather plans and builds Highland Park Shopping Village in Dallas, Texas, the first unified commercial development where stores surround a parking lot rather than facing the street.

- In response to the stock-market crash, independent automakers Willy-Overland and Hudson produce one-third fewer cars than in 1929.

- Auto factories cut wages, shorten the workweek, institute periodic shutdowns, and fire thousands in an effort to cut costs.

- Ford's forty-horsepower Model A is hugely popular, and 1.15 million cars are sold.

- Reflecting a new interest in simple, ordinary fabrics, French designers Jean Patou and Gabrielle Chanel show elegant evening clothes made of cotton and cotton variants such as organdy.

1931

- The Chrysler Building opens in New York City. Designed by William Van Alen, it is a testimony to art deco with its crown of zigzag triangular windows.

- Architect Raymond Hood completes the sixty-story McGraw-Hill Building in New York City.

- The world's longest suspension span, the George Washington Bridge, is completed across the Hudson River, connecting New York and New Jersey.

- The American West continues to be the fastest-growing automobile market in the United States, with Los Angeles topping the list of cities with the highest number of cars each business day.

3 Mar. As the international depression deepens, the fashion world reels. *The New York Times* reports that French dress imports have dropped more than 40 percent since 1926.

30 Apr. The Empire State Building in New York City opens to the public.

1932

- Hailed as the most advanced skyscraper of its time, the Philadelphia Savings Fund Society Building, designed by architects George Howe and William Lescaze, is completed.

- Eliel Saarinen is appointed president of the Cranbrook Academy of Art in Bloomfield Hills, Michigan.

- The Museum of Modern Art's International Exhibition of Modern Architecture, assembled by Henry-Russell Hitchcock and Philip Johnson, introduces modern architecture to America. Hitchcock and Johnson publish a monograph from the show, *The International Style,* the same year.

- Construction begins on Rockefeller Center, a proposed complex of modern high-rises in New York City.

- Congress appropriates more than $13 million to improve automobile access to the national parks, specifically targeting access roads and roads within the parks in an effort to stimulate tourism.

- To cut costs and boost efficiency, General Motors drops the Viking and the Marquette, companion cars to the Oldsmobile and Buick.

- Despite the popularity of the new Plymouth, the Chrysler Corporation's profits drop $11 million from the previous year.

- The Ford Motor Company has its worst year on record, with production falling from a 1929 peak of 1.5 million cars to a low of 232,000. The company cuts its workforce from 170,502 in 1929 to 46,282 as the Depression worsens.

- First Lady Eleanor Roosevelt wears a Sally Milgron original to President Franklin D. Roosevelt's inaugural ball.

Spring   Lord and Taylor begins window displays that identify American designers by name as a way to promote homegrown talent.

31 Mar.   Ford introduces the V-8 convertible, notable for its powerful new engine.

Aug.   As more and more roadside eateries, gas stations, and campgrounds spring up to meet the needs of American travelers, *Ladies' Home Journal* proposes an architectural contest to improve what it calls the "hideous American roadside spectacle."

Oct.   General Motors sells a total of 5,810 cars for the fiscal year, a figure that all its dealers combined reached each week in 1929.

1933

- The Century of Progress Exposition, celebrating technology and modernity, opens at the Chicago World's Fair.

- Palm Beach and Miami Beach in Florida become boomtowns, as most Americans no longer travel abroad. Resort wear becomes fashionable, as do suntans.

- The term *supermarket* is introduced by Albers Super Markets of Cincinnati, Ohio, marking the long decline of mom-and-pop speciality stores and the rise of discount shopping.

- The federal government imposes a new gasoline tax to finance its road-construction projects across the country. Gas-station attendants claim it is the most popular tax they have ever seen.

11 Jan.   *Business Week* announces that the 1933 Automobile Show features more radical changes in car design than seen since "the horseless carriage became a motor car." Lower, longer, and more unified, the new designs mark the beginning of a modern look for cars.

7 Mar.   An autoworkers' union stages a march of the unemployed at the Ford River Rouge Plant in Dearborn, Michigan, to protest layoffs and deteriorating work conditions.

6 June   Richard M. Hollingshead Jr. opens the first drive-in movie theater in Camden, New Jersey.

1934

- The RCA Building, part of the three-block Rockefeller Center complex in downtown New York, is completed.
- The Ford Motor Company loses $120 million between 1931 and 1934.
- Much to the dismay of Detroit, Americans maintain their passion for automobiles by purchasing used cars, buying 171 used cars for every 100 new ones.

Apr. German chancellor Adolf Hitler announces that Germany should triple its number of cars in order to reach the "motorized glory" of the United States.

1935

- The United States Supreme Court building, designed by Cass Gilbert of New York, is completed.
- Howard Johnson opens his first roadside restaurant in Boston, Massachusetts.
- Detroit introduces the "passing beam" headlight, intended to redirect the headlight away from the oncoming driver's eyes.
- As automakers make bigger and better cars without pricing them higher, automobile executives start moving toward increased automation and mechanization as a way to hold down prices by cutting back on human labor.
- Fighting a valiant battle against the Big Three, independent car manufacturers record a year of good sales. Packard announces that sales are up 120 percent from 1934 levels; Auburn increases by 63 percent; and Nash increases by 61 percent.
- Designer Valentina features oriental details in her designs, including mandarin jackets and pointed coolie hats.
- Katharine Hepburn wears designer Muriel King's clothes in the movie *Sylvia Scarlett.*

Apr. Frank Lloyd Wright's designs for decentralizing urban America, Broadacre City, are exhibited in New York's Rockefeller Center to forty thousand viewers.

5 July The National Labor Relations Act ensures the rights of workers to organize and bargain with employers for "fair labor practices," spurring the growth of unions and strikes in the auto industry.

1936

- Architect John Russell Pope wins approval for his designs of the Jefferson Memorial and the National Art Gallery.
- Architect Frank Lloyd Wright captures the new spirit of Streamline Moderne architecture in his Johnson Wax Company Administration Building in Racine, Wisconsin; it is completed in 1939. Its curved bands of brick walls and glass-tube glazing give the building the aerodynamic look of a Buick or an airplane.
- The San Francisco Bay Bridge is completed.
- General Motors reports that its annual profits are only $10 million short of its peak profits in 1929, proving to Detroit at least that the economy has turned a corner toward improvement.

1937

- The automotive industry uniformly adopts steel tops and all-steel bodies that are longer and wider than on previous models, adding about one hundred pounds to the weight of 1937 models.

- Trailer manufacturing becomes the fastest-growing U.S. industry, as many Americans hit the road and tour the country.

- Red is popular with women, with matching rouge, lipstick, and nail enamel in such variations as "bright red," "gay red," "poppy," and "geranium."

- Run-proof mascara is invented.

Oct. Despite an improving economy, the 1936 Cadillac Series 60 is priced at $1,645, $700 less than Cadillac's lowest-priced 1935 model.

- A poll taken by *Architectural Record* finds that the Colonial Style is still the most popular home in America, constituting 85 percent of homes costing less than ten thousand dollars.

- The Lincoln Tunnel under the Hudson River opens, connecting New York and New Jersey.

- German architect Walter Gropius is appointed head of the Harvard University School of Architecture.

- The Golden Gate Bridge near San Francisco is completed.

- *Business Week* announces that the luxury car is making a comeback, with the new Lincoln Zephyr, Cadillac LaSalle, and Chrysler Custom Imperial all selling at impressive rates.

- Independent automaker Nash's "Young Man's model" offers its drivers a bed-conversion option in its sedans.

- Americans who can afford to vacation do so by car, pushing the number of auto travelers from 45 million in 1929 to 52 million.

- Packard announces it expects to make and sell 130,000 cars in 1937.

- Solid-disk steel wheels replace steel-spoke wheels and secure the dominance of chrome-plated hubcaps on American cars.

- Muriel King designs dresses for Katharine Hepburn and Ginger Rogers for the movie *Stage Door*, introducing her designs to women across the country.

1938

- General Motors leads the American auto industry, claiming 43 percent of all passenger cars sold in the United States, with Chrysler second at 25 percent and Ford third with 22 percent.

- Designer Claire McCardell's "monastic dress" becomes her first commercial success, with its monklike cut that can be worn full, swinging from the shoulders, or belted.

- Du Pont announces it has devised "whole new schools of fabrics," including rayon, synthetic silk, and an early version of nylon.

- As the Depression drags on, Macy's advertising states the obvious and proudly declares, "It's smart to be Thrifty."

1939

- Milliner Lilly Dache opens her design house on East Fifty-sixth Street in New York City and upholsters a room in gold for her brunette customers and one in silver for her blond ones.

Jan.   *Architectural Record* devotes an entire edition to Frank Lloyd Wright's Usonia house designs, his utopian solution to the American housing shortage.

3 July   President Franklin D. Roosevelt formally dedicates the Gettysburg Memorial by lighting the eternal light, a flame intended to represent the nation's strength and unity.

30 July   Auto manufacturer Henry Ford is presented with Germany's highest honor given to foreigners, the Grand Cross of the Supreme Order of the German Eagle, for making motorcars available to the masses.

- The Museum of Modern Art in New York shows the work of the Bauhaus.

- Eliel Saarinen designs the Crow Island School in Winnetka, Illinois, which is completed the following year.

- Heralded by some as a safety improvement, some American cars begin to feature gearshifts connected to the steering wheel instead of the floor of the car.

- Valentina designs Katharine Hepburn's costumes for Philip Barry's play *The Philadelphia Story*.

Feb.   The Golden Gate World's Fair in San Francisco opens. This mile-long fair, erected on a man-made island, cost more than $40 million to construct.

OVERVIEW

Endings and Beginnings. The 1930s were fundamentally and irrevocably shaped by the stock-market crash on 29 October 1929. As the decade began, Americans still had not recognized the full extent of the economic disaster. Auto magnate Henry Ford was still playing by the old rules when he tried to bolster the economy by lowering prices on his popular Model A and raising his employees' daily pay by one dollar. But even Ford could not prop up the sagging market: by 1933 the country was mired in the worst depression in its history. Wall Street bulls such as Ford and William Durant, both heavy hitters in automobiles, the nation's proudest industry, conceded defeat and started their painful readjustment to the new game of austerity, cutbacks, and shutdowns.

Adjusting to Austerity. In the realm of fashion and design — clothing, architecture, interior design, and automobiles — the new reigning philosophy was "use it up, wear it out, make it do, or do without." French fashions were suddenly too expensive for middle-class customers. Classic clothes that could be worn for many seasons became popular. American designers found a new niche for themselves, as Paris originals became too expensive for all but the richest consumers. Automobile owners patched their old cars with spare parts, nursing them along until better times returned. A lucrative used-car market also developed. As Detroit struggled to find a response to sagging sales, companies such as General Motors and Chrysler trimmed their offerings, focusing their energies and resources on fewer cars. New looks in furniture and interior design appeared at the Century of Progress Exhibition at Chicago's World Fair in 1933, but these modern home adornments did not become available for the average consumer until after World War II.

Streamline Moderne. Despite such a glum beginning, the decade nonetheless witnessed a significant transformation in design. The excesses of art deco and Victorianism, with their busy patterns and elaborate adornments, were replaced by a new style of efficiency and function that took inspiration from the machine. Streamline Moderne, as it was called, communicated its alliance with the future and the values of technological progress. The aerodynamic shapes of airplanes, trains, and cars influenced the new look. By the middle of the decade the elegant curves, rounded corners, and long and lean shapes of Streamline Moderne could be found on toasters, fountain pens, tableware, radio cases, and furniture.

The Bauhaus. In architecture technology and the machine inspired a new generation of practitioners. In 1937 Walter Gropius, founder of the Bauhaus school of architecture in Germany, immigrated to the United States, where he introduced functionalist architecture to his Harvard University students. Committed to revitalizing design, he encouraged his students to collaborate, to learn by doing, and to embrace the social possibilities of technology. His teaching techniques and his philosophy of design helped to translate modern technology into dwellings that supported human communities.

Organic Architecture. American-born architect Frank Lloyd Wright also explored the human aspects of technology in his designs. His view of design was modeled after nature and the environment. Each structure had an organic life of its own uniquely attuned to its locality. He married his appreciation of organic structures with the modern fascination with machines. His Johnson Wax Company Administration Building (1936–1939) in Racine, Wisconsin, perfectly captured the design advances of the decade. Its interior looked like a forest, with its towering curved pillars that supported circular disks. A large, spiraling, rounded tower was his experiment with the look he would perfect in the Guggenheim Museum in 1959. Taliesin West (begun 1939), his winter residence and school in Scottsdale, Arizona, and Fallingwater in Bear Run, Pennsylvania (1936), were testimonies to the possibility that technology and nature could dwell peaceably together.

A New Look for Cars. In 1933 Detroit also took a giant leap into the future by reinventing the look of the car. The look Ford had pioneered in the Model T and Model A, with their high-perched chassis, square engines, and exterior trunks, disappeared. Passengers now sat lower in the car, between the front and rear axis. Chassis and bodies were now welded together. Trunks, bumpers, and engines were molded into a unified whole. Longer and lower, these new cars had more horsepower and offered their passengers smoother rides. Rounded corners, steel roofs, and shiny new colors marked them as distinctive and, most important, modern.

American Fashion. In response to the Depression, dress designers adopted the values of simplicity and efficiency. Paris remained the world's fashion capital, but French fashions were too expensive for most Americans, so American clothes manufacturers copied Parisian originals for the average woman at a price she could afford. A new generation of young designers, including Claire McCardell, Elizabeth Hawes, Charles James, and Muriel King, translated French fashion for a range of consumer pocketbooks, from French-influenced originals for those who could afford them to modestly priced copies for the average shopper. By offering American women fashions with flair, style, and sensible prices, American designers in the 1930s laid the groundwork for what in the 1940s would become a distinctive American style.

Hollywood. While New York City imitated Paris, it also felt competition from the other great influence on American style, Hollywood. Americans loved the movies almost as much as they loved their cars. In the 1930s hundreds of thousands Americans went to the movies, where they reveled in the new looks of their favorite stars. Bette Davis, Katharine Hepburn, Joan Crawford, Marlene Dietrich, and Greta Garbo set the nation's fashion trends. Hollywood's premier costumer, Adrian, introduced a new classicism to his designs. His sober, beautifully draped, floor-length dinner dresses and elaborate afternoon or cocktail dresses relied on expert cutting, simple yet rich fabrics, and elegant brooches, silk scarves, or unusual collars for their grace. King dressed stars in wide satin pajamas, while Lilly Dache designed unusual hats.

Daily Wear. Men's fashions emphasized the chest. Jackets had wide, short lapels, slightly tailored waists, and high pockets. Pants were wide and high-waisted. Variety was added to the three-piece suit of jacket, vest, and pants by wearing V-necked or vest sweaters instead of a vest. In the 1930s men had a new option for evening wear. Long dinner jackets and cummerbunds were not always required. A shorter black dinner jacket worn with a crisp white shirt and a simple black bow tie was considered high fashion, thanks to the example of Britain's Prince of Wales. Women's daytime fashions bore little resemblance to the dominant flapper look of the 1920s. Dresses had waistlines and bustlines and fell farther below the knee. The most popular dress of the 1930s was the simple print dress, with its loose half-sleeves, belted waist, and blousy top. Most women no longer were able or encouraged to change their look with each passing season. Instead, they accessorized their standard look with costume jewelry, dramatic hats, long or short gloves, and stylish handbags.

Roadside Americana. As the Depression wore on, Americans took to the roads by the thousands. Many relocated in an effort to find better luck in California. Others hit the road to camp and tour the country. The government levied new gasoline taxes to finance major road construction in an effort to keep up with traveler demand and to stimulate the economy. Campgrounds and motor courts sprung up from Cape Cod, Massachusetts, to Miami Beach, Florida, to the Grand Canyon in Arizona. With so many tourists on the road, America witnessed the birth of a uniquely homegrown style of architecture: roadside Americana. Familiar roadside institutions such as Howard Johnson's and Big Boy restaurants had their starts in the 1930s. Stranger manifestations also sprouted up in such forms as giant ducks, milk pails, and tepees selling gasoline, hot dogs, ice cream, or just a place to pull over and sleep. Many critics and civic clubs bemoaned such roadside clutter, but there was no stopping the synergy between Americans' love of driving and their restless search for adventure. Roadside Americana was here to stay.

Getting By. Americans nursed their optimism that better times were coming by making do as best they could under adverse conditions. As the decade ended, rumors of war in Europe and Asia took up more headline space than President Franklin D. Roosevelt's New Deal, and Americans soberly prepared for what many viewed as the country's inevitable entrance into the hostilities. Few would guess the impact the war would have on the country, pulling it out of its long economic crisis and making the United States the leading political and economic force in the world. Yet in the late 1930s Americans continued to focus on getting by, making do, or doing without. Many enjoyed their cars, their movies, and their new roads as they waited for better times.

TOPICS IN THE NEWS

AMERICAN AUTOMOBILES

The Automobile and the American Dream. In the 1930s cars were the nation's symbol of leisure, convenience, and security. Middle-class and farming families were understandably reluctant to give up driving even in the worst years of the Depression. As the country reeled from the effects of the stock-market crash, the auto industry seemed resistant to the Depression. Sociologists Robert and Helen Lynd noted in 1932 that the Depression had not changed the public's commitment to automobiles. Car ownership, the Lynds concluded, was synonymous for many Americans with self-respect and the American dream.

Of Bulls and Cars. The American automobile industry embodied the weaknesses of the national economy in the late 1920s. Throughout the heyday of the 1920s the industry saturated the market with cars by coming out with new models each year and encouraging buyers to purchase new models rather than maintaining existing ones. Consumers traded in their now "old" cars for rebates and agreed to pay for new cars over a three-year period. The line between so-called old and new cars was established through design and styling. While such emphasis on styling brought important innovations to car design, this selling strategy based on planned obsolescence also left automakers such as Ford, Chrysler, and General Motors (GM) short of cash, as they invested capital in producing new styles. In addition, manufacturers and dealers had lots full of well-running used cars.

Sloanism. Alfred P. Sloan of GM weathered the Depression by intensifying and refining what he called "constant upgrading of product," another name for planned obsolescence. By producing a car "for every purse and purpose," his strategy called for blanketing the market with a car at the top of every price range and encouraging consumers to trade up — for instance, from a midprice Chevrolet to a Cadillac via a Pontiac, Oldsmobile, or Buick. Sloanism, as it was soon called, propelled GM to new dominance of the automobile industry, beating Ford in sales throughout the decade. Sloan's emphasis on styling and trade-ins perfectly matched the public's appetite for new styling and more-exciting automobiles.

Advertisement for the 1934 DeSoto

Styling. Sloan's emphasis on upgrading and style pushed GM to the forefront of design innovation. With the company's emphasis on planned obsolescence, GM designers were encouraged to rethink the fundamentals of auto design. Under the supervision of chief designer Harley J. Earl, GM's Styling Section set into motion the institutionalization of auto design by professional designers rather than leaving it to engineers or salesmen. After World War II, Ford and Chrysler also adopted styling departments, many of whose employees were trained by Earl at GM.

CROSSLEY'S LITTLE CAR

Powel Crossley, a British inventor of inexpensive radios and refrigerators, spent much of the Depression tinkering with lightweight automobiles. In 1938 he proudly displayed his small, sleek, rakish convertible sedan with tiny wheels, wide doors, and neatly streamlined hood and front end. Its eighty-inch wheelbase, forty-inch tread, and two-cylinder engine gave the car an upper speed of fifty miles per hour, and it ran efficiently at fifty miles per gallon. Selling for $325, the Crossley undersold the only other midget on the automotive market, the American Bantam. Crossley dealers rolled their small cars onto sales floors among radios and refrigerators. The target audience: the man who could not afford a new higher-priced car or the family who needed a second car for shopping, commuting, and taking the children to school.

Source: "Little Fellow," *Time*, 33 (8 May 1939): 56.

Streamlining. The biggest innovation in car design was aerodynamic styling, or streamlining. Auto manufacturers modeled their new cars on the design principles of airplanes and high-speed trains. Technically, aerodynamic streamlining reduced the car's drag and resulted in better fuel economy and speed; it also diminished wind noise and made the ride smoother. Structurally, streamlining transformed distinct component frameworks into one larger framework, which resulted in a unified, welded body that merged the once-separate chassis and body. Visually, streamlining integrated the car's visible features into a more unified and flowing whole, in contrast to the odd mix of shapes and angles of earlier automobiles such as the Model T.

A New Look for Cars. The styling department at GM broke new design ground with its program to eliminate projections and to make cars appear lower and longer. The 1932 Cadillac was the first car to eliminate the separate, boxlike trunk that sat above the rear axle in earlier models. In incorporating the trunk into the body of the car, the 1932 Cadillac and the low-priced 1933 Chevrolet offered consumers a new, aesthetically pleasing automobile. In the 1933 Chevrolet the radiator was hidden behind the grille; the gas tank was covered; and fenders blended more smoothly into the body of the car. The 1938 Cadillac 60 Special was the first American car to eliminate the running board, a change that allowed the car's body to be widened enough to hold six passengers. By the end of the 1930s American auto manufacturers had taken decisive steps away from the early appearance of the Model T. With their unified structure and their lower and wider passenger compartments, American cars assumed the look they would keep well into the 1950s.

NATION OF NOMADS

No one knows exactly who devised the automobile trailer, but everyone who participated in the mass movement onto the highways in the early 1920s remembered the ugly, ungainly, lopsided wooden boxes. Not only did trailers look, as one commentator put it, "like outhouses on wheels," they were relatively rare. Then overnight, it seemed, the public bought trailers. All over the United States improved, streamlined, metallic trailers rolled onto the highways. *Time* reported in its 15 June 1936 issue that trailer manufacturing had become the fastest-growing industry in the United States. Reporting that between three hundred and two thousand companies manufactured trailers, *Time* explained that producers were working overtime to meet the burgeoning demand. "Since 1933 demand for trailers has at least trebled every year. . . . Last week Covered Wagon Co. of Mt. Clemens, Michigan, the largest manufacturer in the business, doubled the size of its paint shop to keep pace with a production schedule up 600% over last year."

From fourteen to thirty feet long, the typical trailer was a streamlined lozenge of light metal with curtained windows, chromium fittings, and a simple swivel joint at the bow, where it joined with the automobile. Inside, it was like the cabin of a small cruiser. Many came with such amenities as stoves, iceboxes, chemical toilets, and breakfast nooks. They featured running water, insulation, electric light, and heat. Costs ranged from four hundred to twelve hundred dollars. No longer an ugly wooden box, the trailer became a conspicuous symbol of a new automobile-powered nation of nomads.

Source: "Nation of Nomads?," *Time*, 27 (15 June 1936): 53–55.

"Drop Frame." Ford's 1932 V-8 model also contributed to the look of automobiles. Its "drop-frame" construction brought the passenger compartment down from its high perch up on the axles to its now-familiar position between the front and rear axles. This lowered the car's height and its center of gravity. The engine was moved over the front axles, and the hood was expanded outward. Like the Model T and Model A, it had a favorable power-to-weight ratio, and its sixty-five-horsepower capacity gave it significant strength.

Ford's V-8. Ford's new V-8 appeared to rave reviews. Testimonials arrived in Dearborn, Michigan, Ford's home, from unexpected sources. "You have a wonderful car. It's a treat to drive one. . . . I can make any other car take a Ford's dust," wrote John Dillinger, who at the time was considered by the Federal Bureau of Investigation to be Public Enemy Number One. Likewise, notorious bank robber Clyde Barrow wrote, "I have drove Ford's exclusively when I could get away with one. For sustained speed and freedom from trouble, the Ford has got every other car skinned." Barrow concluded by conceding that "even if my business hasn't been strictly legal it don't hurt anything to tell you what a fine car you got in the V-8." He and Bonnie Parker took pictures of each other posing with their pride and joy, a 1932 V-8 they had stolen in Texas.

The Airflow. The most revolutionary car of the 1930s was the 1934 Chrysler and DeSoto Airflow models. While not particularly popular with the public, the Airflow represented the cutting edge of engineering and aesthetic auto production. The Airflow was the first car to feature a unified chassis and body, which gave the car a roomier interior and gave it a sturdiness on the road that earlier models lacked. The car's aerodynamic shape included an art deco grille, an integrated trunk, and rounded headlights mounted over the front fenders. At the Chicago Century of Progress Exhibition an Airflow sedan was displayed next to the new Union Pacific M-1000 Streamliner train to suggest the similarity in design concepts. However, the Airflow was out of step with the buying public, which found it unattractive. Fewer than eleven thousand units were sold before production was shut down in 1937. Despite the failure of the Airflow, Chrysler integrated the technical advances learned from the Airflow into its line of midpriced sedans.

The Birth of the Big Three. Although car sales plummeted, they never completely evaporated. Big companies such as Ford and GM responded to the economic crisis by cutting prices and limiting trade-ins but nonetheless continued to produce new cars with new features and designs. Smaller companies folded. Such conditions consolidated the automobile industry, driving out small independent producers and strengthening the hold of larger companies on the market. The Depression in essence created conditions for the modern "Big Three" to emerge and dominate the international automotive industry.

Thinning the Market. Car sales hit their lowest levels in 1932. By 1933 the market for cars slowly began to recover, and the Big Three began to turn small profits. However, this upturn came too late for many of the independent automakers. By the mid 1930s some of the most celebrated American marques had succumbed. Jordan, Kissel, Ruxton, Mood, Dobel, Gardner, Stearns, and the American division of Rolls-Royce went under in 1932, while Peerless, Marmon, Du Pont, and American Austin were in their death throes. Durant Motors failed in 1936, and Pierce-Arrow in 1938. The last Auburn was built in 1936, the last Cord and Duesenberg in 1937.

Page from the 1936 Sears, Roebuck catalogue advertising simple print dresses

The Little Five. Not all the independents succumbed. Charles Nash managed to keep his company solvent despite low sales. In 1932 he produced fewer than eighteen thousand cars and turned a profit of one million dollars, six times that of GM. Hudson, under the guidance of Roy Chapin, introduced the low-priced Terraplane and emerged in good health from the Depression. By 1937 the Packard sold more than twice its 1928 figures. Thanks to brilliant leadership, Willy-Overland and Studebaker also rode out the Depression intact and poised to compete in the post–World War II market.

Sources:

James J. Flink, *The Automobile Age* (Cambridge, Mass., & London: MIT Press, 1988);

Stephen W. Sears, *The Automobile in America* (New York: American Heritage Publishing, 1977).

AMERICAN FASHIONS

No More Flappers. The Depression of the 1930s left little in the United States unchanged. As with other sectors of the economy, the crisis profoundly shaped what Americans wore, what they bought, and what they desired. Overnight, the high-spirited look of the flapper evaporated; the long, lean, tubular chemise, the signature look of the fashionable woman, disappeared. In its place a mature elegance emerged. Ageless, classless, and reus-

Page from the 1934 Sears, Roebuck catalogue advertising men's suits

and donned glamorous dresses that the public ogled through *Life* and the *Saturday Evening Post*. Debutantes frequently modeled clothes at department stores and charity events.

The Simple Print Dress. For the rest of the country, the dominant look for women's everyday wear was the simple print dress made from synthetic material. Most strikingly different from the 1920s silhouette was the print dress's waistline and longer hemline. Belted just above the hips, the dress fell five inches below the knee and flared slightly. The top bloused loosely, with only a few pleats to accommodate the return of the bustline. Collars were rounded, shoulders unstructured, and sleeves midlength. The dresses appeared as a complete unit, with their small floral prints unbroken by visible seams or large patterns. Women's shoes returned to being practical, with lower heels, sturdy straps or ties, and pointed toes. Women tended to wear their hair longer, with more waves, and they often parted it on the side. Hats had smaller crowns and upturned brims and were often worn tilted forward over one eye. Most women no longer painted their faces as dramatically as in the 1920s, preferring a more natural look. By the end of the decade the look became more stylized, with broader shoulders coming to dominate women's wear. Padded shoulders dramatically contrasted with narrowing waistlines and straighter skirt lines that fell just below the knee.

The Look for Men. Men's suits continued to emphasize the chest. Jackets were high-waisted and had higher pockets and buttons and short, wide lapels. The double-breasted reefer jacket, with its two rows of buttons, wide front, and trim flanks, was enormously popular. Trousers were of medium width, cut long in the leg with turned-up hems. Pleats and a top waistband continued from the 1920s. For business and formal wear, a black jacket with striped trousers and a dark, long suit remained popular. The modern two-piece suit was introduced in the 1930s, with the traditional vest replaced by a V-necked sweater or sweater vest. Men's shoes had low heels and remained heavy as a balance to the wide pants. Many men also donned finger waves in their hair, which they wore shorter than in previous decades. As with women's fashions, menswear was increasingly stylized by the end of the decade. Shoulders were padded and squared, lapels widened, and suits narrowed. Many men abandoned parting their hair, preferring a brushed-back look. Hat brims widened and lowered.

The Star and the Prince. Men's clothes reached a new elegance in the 1930s. Clark Gable, whose career as a movie star lent him unprecedented authority in the world of fashion, set new looks for men. His double-breasted suits became widely popularized. American men's fashions came not only from Hollywood but from England, specifically from the Prince of Wales. The prince was innovative, and trendsetters followed his every fashion move. Among his novelties were double-breasted dinner jackets, midnight blue for evening, the larger Windsor

able looks that were flexible, reasonably priced, and easy to accessorize reflected the style of the 1930s and the new sobriety of the nation's collective mood.

Café Society. Yet while most of the country suffered the effects of the stock-market crash, many of the nation's wealthiest families continued to make money throughout the decade. High society went on unabated by Hoovervilles, food lines, and strikes. Families such as Chicago's Marshall Fields, Boston's Kennedys, and New York's Vanderbilts threw lavish parties, covered their women with jewelry, and bought fancy Paris originals. Many women in such families competed with Hollywood stars in setting fashion trends.

Debutantes. December debutante balls, in which families "introduced" their sixteen- and seventeen-year-old daughters to society, were among the decade's most striking fashion events. Such parties cost anywhere between $10,000 and $100,000. Families outspent each other in their attempts to make their daughter's or niece's ball the season's best. Champagne rivers, ballrooms full of fresh flowers, elegant tables, liquors, desserts, and eye-catching stage sets made these events monuments to conspicuous consumption. Debs, as they were called, attended dances nearly every night from late November to early January

knot in a necktie, and the wider-set flat collar to accommodate it. The backless waistcoat that joined at the back of the collar and at waist level with a strap and button became popular in 1934. These were worn with dinner jackets, starched white shirts, and black ties. Other popular looks were "teddy bear" coats, oversized and unstructured fleece jackets with wide shoulders, loose-fitting trench coats, and in 1936 waist-length gold jackets in suede or proofed gabardine. By 1938 men's suits were straighter, with well-padded square shoulders and wider lapels. Pants came in a different shade than jackets and narrowed in the leg, with zippers replacing buttons in the fly.

A New Generation of Designers. With the collapse of the international economy, American fashion designers found themselves in an unusual position. Paris had long been the center of Western fashion, particularly in the 1920s, when many Americans were rich and shopping was a national pastime. But as savings disappeared businesses went bankrupt and cash grew increasingly scarce, and most Americans were no longer in a position to buy expensive French originals. American designers, who labored in relative obscurity throughout the 1910s and 1920s, found an opportunity to cater to the needs of Americans in a new way. American women wanted inexpensive, well-made, fashionable clothes, and a new generation of designers gave them just that. Elizabeth Hawes, Charles James, Valentina, Nettie Rosenstein, Muriel King, Claire McCardell, and Hattie Carnegie soon became significant names. They set the look of American fashion until the end of World War II.

Home-Grown Talents. Although American fashion was known for its sporty, relaxed style, there was great variety among this generation of designers, as each addressed a market composed of a wide range of tastes, pocketbooks, climates, and types. There were sophisticated designers, such as Germaine Monteil and Mollie Parnis, who specialized in evening clothes ranging in price from $79 to $195. Wholesale houses known for sportswear, such as William Bloom and Helen Cookman, designed suits, vest blouses, and jumpers that worked on their own and together and used knits and tweeds. Designers Tina Leser and McCardell reinvented women's sportswear by discarding the model set by men's sports clothing.

Buy American. The most well-known American designer of the 1930s was Hawes, whose appreciation of the power of the press catapulted her into prominence. In 1932 she took a collection of twenty-five dresses and held a fashion show in Paris on the Fourth of July to prove that Americans could produce lovely, stylish clothes. Later that year, at the lowest point of the Depression, she rallied spirits by designing for tony Lord and Taylor a ready-made checkered dress and dark coat combination for $10.75, one-tenth of the cost of her custom pieces.

Trendsetting Designers. King was also a prominent 1930s designer. Lord and Taylor show-cased her designs in their 1932 promotion of American fashion. While she ran a booming business in expensive custom-designed wear, King's ready-made dresses sold for $25 at Lord and Taylor. She fashioned everything from bathing suits and skating clothes to evening gowns, and her designs were worn by Hollywood stars such as Katharine Hepburn and Ginger Rogers. Clare Potter was known for her painterly use of colors and her beautifully cut pants, shorts, pajamas, and other sportswear. The designs of Nettie Rosenstein, known for their elegant lines, were also popular. Rosenstein relied on an unusual set of principles: she worked by draping fabric on the figure, and her ready-made dresses were made by a single sewer from start to finish. Her prices ranged from $89.50 to $794 for evening wear.

New Vogue for Simplicity. A fundamental rule of fashion is that the cost of manufacturing a dress affects its appearance. Because the effects of the Depression were so far-reaching, cost became a consideration in dress design on all levels, from material to cut and decoration. Given the strict limits in which designers and couturiers worked, designers creatively used materials that had previously been overlooked or dismissed. Gone were the expensive excesses of the 1920s party dress, with its beaded and embroidered dresses and fragile silk jerseys, chiffons, and velvets. The Depression triggered a return to simple, ordinary fabrics. Evening wear now came in cotton varieties such as organdy, piqué, and lace. Corduroy, bouclé knit, and wool, once exclusively daytime materials, appeared as elegant night wear.

Innovations. Fit became a concern, as designers tried to accommodate a range of figures and sizes in mass-

Paramount Pictures costume department, 1930

produced clothing. The zipper, introduced in the late 1920s, became widespread in the 1930s. It was cheaper to install in a dress than hand-sewn hooks and eyes or snaps. Charles James, among other American designers, started incorporating the zipper as a design element. A newly invented elastic substance, Lastex, found a new niche in sportswear such as ski pants and bathing suits. The belt, long scorned in high fashion, returned as an integral feature of dress design. Hawes made the belt an important part of the dress while letting it accommodate women's diverse figures. Belt buckles were adorned as accessories, sometimes lending the dress an art deco feel. The 1930s were also the first decade in which different-length dresses were worn at different times of the day. Evening events called for long dresses, while midcalf lengths prevailed in the day.

Accessories. Accessories became an increasingly important aspect of fashion, as most women no longer traded dresses in with each fashion season. Hats, pocketbooks, shoes, gloves, and jewelry now helped change the look of a relatively simple suit or dress from one wearing to the next. Hats came in all sizes and shapes, from the fedora to the turban. Pocketbooks were longer and shaped like envelopes, with large jeweled clasps and an occasional shoulder strap. Longer gloves became popular. Costume jewelry also became fashionable. The American costume-jewelry industry was centered in Rhode Island, and Miriam Haskell, the best-known name in costume jewelry, gained recognition for her unusual mix of baroque designs in bright colors and interesting shapes.

Hollywood. The United States not only had its own fashion industry in the 1930s, it had Hollywood, whose golden age began in the 1930s. Thousands more women

BOOTLEG FASHIONS

Twice a year, in February and August, the great Parisian couturiers held grand openings to show their new collections. About fifty designers displayed approximately five thousand designs at each semiannual exhibit. Guests at these closely guarded affairs included socially prominent Europeans, fashion writers, manufacturers, and buyers. Most important for American fashion was the attendance of big American department-store representatives. As *Newsweek* reported, buyers bought hundreds of gowns at the August 1936 show, each averaging in price from three hundred to five hundred dollars. Instead of selling these dresses, American fashion manufacturers took advantage of an export loophole to make bootleg versions of Parisian originals. Export law held that if the dresses were returned to France within six months, the store paid no significant import duty. Meanwhile, the store made as many duplicates from the original as desired within the six-month limit. These copies were advertised as coming from Chanel, Vionnet, or whoever designed the original. Under this system American stores often sold exact copies of a five-hundred-dollar Paris creation for less than one hundred dollars. Before the six months were up the shopworn original was usually sent back to France and sold to a backstreet dress establishment for whatever it would bring — sometimes as little as ten dollars in American currency.

Source: "Fashion: Paris Couturiers Hold Open House, Decree Coronation Elegance for Winter of 1936–7," *Newsweek*, 8 (15 August 1936): 32–34.

went to the movies than followed high-fashion developments, and for many one of the most pleasurable aspects of going to the movies was seeing what the stars wore. Hollywood, however, broke away from the slavish trends of the fashion industry and instead came up with its own blend of classicism. Adrian was the preeminent Hollywood costume designer and dressed the decade's most notable stars — including Greta Garbo, Joan Crawford, and Marlene Dietrich — with his simple yet elegant clothes. Dresses that were successful on film were those that not only flattered the actress but also had a timeless quality. Clothes had to look good in black-and-white or in the early attempts at color photography. Hollywood tended toward simple designs covered with furs, hand-sewn sequins, and bugles that shone for the camera. Printed fabrics were rare, and emphasis was placed on a few memorable details: a low-back décolletage seen when the actress turned away from the camera, white or glittering jewels, and striking accessories. Stores soon learned

CINEMA FASHIONS

Few people did more to increase the influence of Hollywood on American fashion than Bernard Waldman, president and founder of the Modern Merchandising Bureau in New York, which functioned as a clearinghouse for styles shown in the movies. The bureau provided retail shops with models of hats and dresses worn by the stars of current films. The business was much more complicated than it appeared at first glance. First the bureau had to study stills of coming attractions and figure out what was going to be popular. Then it arranged with the manufacturers to have the dresses made before the release of the picture. Finally it had to supply retail shops with advertising that mentioned the movie from which the model was taken and the theater at which it was playing. Waldman received a 5 percent commission on all sales, and the studios traded cash payments for the free publicity the clothes brought them. Macy's in New York was Waldman's first customer. Fashion commentators rejected the arrangement, deeming it vulgar, but the public embraced it wholeheartedly. Soon critics agreed that the movies taught many American women how to dress.

Source: "Cinema Fashions," *Fortune*, 15 (January 1937): 38–39.

---

to watch Hollywood for specific items to copy, and a debate arose over whether Hollywood or New York was America's fashion center.

Hollywood Costuming. As Hollywood took greater notice of its fashion influence, studios responded by expanding their costuming departments. The construction of glamorous dresses seen on the screen was backbreaking work requiring long hours from the dozens of mostly immigrant women who cut, stitched, and beaded dresses. Designers such as Adrian sent sketches to the costuming department, where the cutters and fitters made the pattern. A trial garment was quickly made up in cotton for approval by the designer and the star. Then the fitter would model the cotton pattern on the star, take the garment apart, and cut the finished costume from the proper fabric. The beaders had the hardest job of all. M-G-M employed at least twenty expert Mexican American women beaders. Long gowns took up to three months to bead. Beaders worked twelve hours a day six days a week stooped over their fabrics. Other minorities found work with such specialized skills: Armenian workers crocheted, Middle Eastern workers wrapped turbans, and Japanese and Chinese women embroidered. In the costume shops English was often a second language.

Long Hours, Little Glamour. In the 1930s studio costume departments were crowded with workers day and night, as costumers rushed to complete clothes for a movie in production. Grueling shooting schedules often required costumers to stay all night working. In big feature films copies of dresses were necessary. In the 1939 classic *Gone with the Wind* the dress Vivien Leigh wore as Atlanta burned was in fact twenty-seven versions of the dress in various stages of deterioration. While the hours were long and the pay low, costume workers in the 1930s were glad for the work. Hollywood studios cranked out feature films at a fierce pace, and each one required the labor of many hands to give it the fashion sensibility it needed.

Sources:

Caroline Rennolds Milbank, *New York Fashion: The Evolution of American Style* (New York: Abrams, 1989);

Elizabeth Nielsen, "Handmaidens of the Glamour Culture: Costumers in the Hollywood Studio System," in *Fabrications: Costume and the Female Body*, edited by Jane Gaines and Charlotte Herzog (New York: Routledge, 1990), pp. 160–180;

Anne V. Tyrrell, *Changing Trends in Fashion: Patterns of the Twentieth Century, 1900–1970* (London: Batsford, 1986).

ARCHITECTURE

Art Deco. The 1930s opened with some of the most dramatic applications of art deco to modern skyscrapers. The art deco style originated in Europe and became widely popular in the United States in the 1920s. Characterized by its geometric patterns, surface ornamentation, and rich materials, art deco styling could be found in entrance portals and elevator lobbies, where the display of fancy metalwork, colored marbles, and contrasting wood veneers could be fully seen and appreciated. Architects William Van Alen, along with John and Donald Parkinson, among others, took art deco to new heights — literally. Van Alen's crown for the Chrysler Building in New York (1928–1930) terminated in a needlelike spire that rose from diminishing semicircles, with each circle set with a zigzag of triangular windows. Recognizing that it was the top of the skyscraper that gave it a distinctive identity, Van Alen broke new ground.

Functionalism and Constructivism. The influence of art deco on American architecture declined by the early 1930s and was replaced by a new conception of beauty and design inspired by the machine and technology. Constructivism in architecture originated in Moscow just after World War I with the work of two brothers, Naum Gabo and Antoine Pevsner. Drawing from Cubism in painting and sculpture, constructivism emphasized spatial relationships and viewed geometric forms as essential structures. They stripped their designs of ornamentation and simplified their buildings to emphasize their structure and form. All traditional accessories of a building, such as ornament and style, were discarded to make the structure and form stand out. The aesthetic effect of a building, then, depended on the formal relations of mass and space resulting from the most efficient construction. Constructivism was part of the broader movement of functionalism, which claimed that any object that was

The top of the Chrysler building, designed by William Van Alen and completed in 1930

enced modern architecture. He believed that architects should be artists as well as engineers. The distinction between artist and craftsman, he believed, no longer applied to the modern age. Gropius contended that architects should be trained as artists and should work in a wide variety of materials to gain an appreciation of their qualities. He also believed architects should study theories of form and design. By joining arts and handicrafts with applied engineering, architects could reinvent architectural form for the modern technological age.

Buildings for a Mass Society. Fascinated with the utopian implications of the machine, Gropius sought to promote social unity through functionalist designs. He dreamed of inventing a socialist architecture in which simple utilitarian structures could be cheaply mass-produced. He and his students experimented in producing inexpensive buildings of quality, simple in design and utilitarian in form, for people of all classes. With the threat of war growing, Gropius left Germany and immigrated to Chicago in 1937. He eventually settled in Boston, where he headed the Harvard University School of Architecture. From Harvard his Bauhaus philosophy and training directly shaped American architecture.

Frank Lloyd Wright. American architect Frank Lloyd Wright was also fascinated by the idea of building affordable houses for the masses. Yet he approached the problem from an entirely different point of view than did Gropius and other Bauhaus architects. Wright's guiding principle, "out of the ground, into the light," was organic and drew predominantly from nature for its inspiration. According to Wright, architects must design buildings and homes to fit both their natural environments and the needs of their occupants. Buildings, he believed, must be as individual as their owners.

Broadacre City. With the Depression undercutting much of his business, Wright turned his attention in the 1930s to urban decentralization, a problem he felt plagued American cities. Disillusioned with urban sprawl, he drew up plans for Broadacre City, a model suburb of planned construction and uniform design. The buildings of Broadacre were to be geometric, deceptively simple, and low to the ground, with Wright's signature overhanging roofs. They would mold to the shape of the land on which they sat or to their environments, whether marked by a river, lake, or hillside. The plans of Broadacre reflected Wright's vision of a democratic society in harmony with nature. Gas stations would be community centers; parks and sports fields would abut government offices and businesses. Houses would come in all sizes, but, reflecting Wright's populism, every family would own its own.

"Usonia." Wright's house designs constitute some of his most significant architectural work. Beginning in 1936 he applied the term *Usonia* to a series of small houses that many viewed as realizing the impossible: distinctive architecture at a modest price. Usonia encapsu-

efficiently made for its purpose was both aesthetically pleasing and utilitarian. In functionalism beauty followed form and efficiency. The efficient machine was cited as the standard of excellence.

The Bauhaus. Another group of architects took different inspiration from technology and the machine. Walter Gropius, the German founder of the Bauhaus design school, developed a new philosophy that radically influ-

On May Day 1931 New York City celebrated the opening of what was called the eighth wonder of the world, the 1,248-foot-high Empire State Building at the corner of Fifth Avenue and Thirty-fourth Street, the tallest building in the world. Former governor Alfred E. Smith, president of the Empire State Building Corporation, presided. Guests of honor included Gov. Franklin Delano Roosevelt, Mayor Jimmy Walker, and architect R. H. Shreve of Shreve Lamb and Harmon, who had designed the structure. Shreve reminded the audience that the Empire State Building weighed 600 million pounds, but due to its placement on 220 columns it had the impact on the earth beneath it of only a forty-five-foot-high pile of rock. Col. Paul Starrett, president of Starrett Brothers and Eken, who had built the Empire State Building, praised the citizens of New York, who had been willing "to convert dollars to structures and keep the procession of structures moving." President Herbert Hoover in Washington threw the switch that symbolically lit the building, and then more than two thousand invited guests traveled to the 102nd-floor observatory.

Opening as it did in the depths of the Great Depression, the Empire State Building was a testimony to "the vast energy that threw [it] upward and that is certain to reassert itself," as *The New York Times* observed. The reassertion was anxiously awaited by the Empire State Building Corporation, who had rented only just over a quarter of the two million feet of office space available at the time of the opening; full occupancy was not attained until the late 1940s. The $40,948,900 building (including land where the Waldorf-Astoria Hotel had formerly stood) was constructed of ten million bricks, 2.5 million feet of electric wire, fifty miles of radiator pipe, and 3,500 miles of telephone and telegraph cable. It had sixty-seven elevators traveling in seven miles of elevator shaft and consumed some 35 million kilowatt-hours of electricity annually. Throughout the years the building was modified as needs required, and in 1995, a television tower having added 222 feet to its height, it remained the fifth tallest building in the world.

Source: Theodore James Jr., *The Empire State Building* (New York: Harper & Row, 1975).

lated the values of Broadacre. Its best-known example was the Herbert Jacobs House in Madison, Wisconsin (1937). Anticipating prefabrication, Wright simplified the construction by standardizing the whole plan on a modular two-by-four-foot grid. The living and dining rooms opened to the kitchen, giving the interior of the house a new spaciousness and a sense of community. The bedrooms, on the other hand, were closed and smaller, opening off a narrow hallway. The total cost of the house, including Wright's fee, was less than six thousand dollars. The Jacobs House became a prototype for a series of houses Wright built in the 1930s. The significance of the Jacobs House was not only that in it Wright realized all his technical innovations but also that these innovations were quietly integrated into a plan and lifestyle that matched the changed social habits of the late 1930s. The values of informality, simplicity, and community were amply manifest in the Jacobs House.

Fallingwater. Fallingwater (1936), another of Wright's houses, is one of the most famous houses of the twentieth century. His concept of organic architecture guided the design. Poised over a rocky stream in Bear Run, Pennsylvania, the house incorporated both modern and "natural" aspects of contemporary life. The rocks that form the waterfall also structure the house. Wide cement porches lean over the falls, tracing the movement of the water in horizontal planes as modern as any building in the 1930s. Vertical slabs rise and cross the horizontal porches and tower among the trees around the falls. The incorporation of glass as a wall structure sent light deep into the interior. Many critics still view Fallingwater as one of the freshest monuments of modern architecture.

The Johnson Wax Building. Another masterpiece in modern architecture was Wright's designs for the Johnson Wax Company Administration Building in Racine, Wisconsin (1936–1939), an eclectic blend of organic form with modern materials. The curved bands of brick walls and glass-tube windows gave the building the look of a modern steel train. Inside, the open central hall was punctuated with fifty-four white concrete supports, reinforced with metal mesh, that elegantly tapered downward to a slim nine-inch-diameter base. The large concrete disks on top of the supports formed the roof, with the spaces between the disks filled with tubular opaque glass. He called it "as inspiring a place to work as any cathedral was in which to worship." To maintain its conceptual integrity Wright designed everything, down to the chairs and desks that carpeted the grand hallway. By 1938 Wright's international reputation had attracted many students who wanted to learn under him. He responded by establishing an architectural fellowship where students could apprentice with him. Taliesin West in Scottsdale, Arizona, became the home of several of his disciples and his winter home.

A New Home for the Met. Rockefeller Center in Manhattan was planned as the first skyscraper city, and it stands as a major architectural achievement. The concept was born in the late 1920s when the directors of the Metropolitan Opera decided they needed to a new home. MET supporters, investment banker Otto Kahn chief among them, developed the concept of a arts center that included a complex of retail shops on the site of their new theater. They identified the area bounded by Forty-Eighth and Fifty-First Streets and Fifth and Sixth Avenues as the location for the center and enlisted the financial support of John D. Rockefeller, one of the wealthiest men in the nation. Rockefeller began buying property in the area, including a large tract from Columbia University, and planning construction. Then came the stock market crash. The Metropolitan Opera Company decided the costs were too great for them and they withdrew, leaving Rockefeller with promising plans for an arts complex, a lot of property in what was then a run-down part of the city, and the need the capitalize on his investment.

Rockefeller's Center. Rockefeller's decision to proceed with the project delighted city officials, who welcomed the jobs and the business activity in the darkest days of the Depression. He decided to build a small city, consisting of living space, office space, restaurants, commercial shops, and theaters. Due to a zoning regulation that tied the height of new buildings to the amount of free ground space on the property, architects were able to design skyscrapers as part of the center, arranged around a large mall. The original Rockefeller Center, built between 1932 and 1940, included thirteen buildings. The seventy-story RCA Building, the British Empire Building, the International Building, the Associated Press Building, and Radio City Music Hall are among the most impressive of the original structures. In the view of many, the public areas of Rockefeller Center are the most enlightened aspect of the design. Public gardens in the large plaza and display areas for art, including murals and sculptures, demonstrate the concept of Rockefeller Center as a people's complex that departs from strict utilitarianism.

Government Funding. In an unprecedented attempt to revive the economy President Franklin D. Roosevelt worked for the passage of several acts that poured money from the treasury into various public works. For architects, the bill that had the most direct effect was the formation in 1932 of the Public Works Administration (PWA), led by Secretary of the Interior Harold Ickes. The PWA authorized $3.3 billion for the construction of roads, public buildings, and other projects. By the end of the decade the PWA had spent more than $4.2 billion building roads, schools, post offices, bridges, courthouses, and other public buildings around the country.

WPA. Government-sponsored architecture revived a neoclassical vernacular in the United States. Deemed the most suitable for institutional buildings and monuments, the classical designs of government-funded construction visually enhanced the Enlightenment values of democracy. The Works Progress Administration (WPA) supported the creation of several buildings, bridges, and monuments across the country, including the Philadelphia Court House (1934), the United States Naval Hospital (1935), the San Francisco–Oakland Bay Bridge (1934), the New York Triborough Bridge system (1936), the Cincinnati Railway Terminal (1933), the North Dakota state capitol (1934), and in Washington, D.C., the U.S. Supreme Court Building (1935), the Jefferson Memorial (1937), and the National Gallery of Art (1937). Many of the buildings were decorated by federally commissioned works of art through a separate fund set aside for this purpose.

Sources:

Barbara Melosh, *Engendering Culture: Manhood and Womanhood in New Deal Public Art and Theater* (Washington, D.C., & London: Smithsonian Institution Press, 1991);

Marcus Whiffen and Frederick Koeper, *American Architecture 1607–1976* (Cambridge, Mass.: MIT Press, 1981).

ROADSIDE ARCHITECTURE

Goodbye Europe, Hello America. Many cash-poor Americans hit the road in the 1930s with a vengeance and by doing so transformed the landscape. Tourist courts, with shanty cafés and gas pumps, sprang up on highways all over the country, hoping to tempt drivers to buy ice cream, sodas, and trinkets. Since the mid 1920s the American public's celebration of the automobile had included road trips. As the Depression and oil strikes lowered gasoline prices, America's appetite for travel seemed endless. For many, road travel seemed the quickest way to escape the grinding misery of economic hard times. Some Americans traveled by car to relocate in California in hope of finding work, while others simply drove as recreation. As the federal government expanded the nation's public parks, camping mushroomed. The tourist court, a clustering of amenities including washrooms, single-room cabins, and restaurants, sprouted up to serve nomadic Americans.

National Parks. Throughout the Depression both federal and state governments levied gasoline taxes to finance massive road construction projects, which greatly improved tourism. Some travelers opted to visit newly opened national parks in the 1930s, such as Williamsburg, Virginia; the Great Smoky Mountains National Park in Tennessee and North Carolina; Nags Head in North Carolina; and the National Shore Line on Cape Cod, Massachusetts. Beginning in the 1920s Congress passed a series of funding packages intended to improve the quality of roads leading to and within national parks. As access by train and car improved, the number of tourists increased. A range of housing options emerged to meet the growing need. Visitors could choose to stay at a high-priced lodge, stay in a small cabin, or camp out.

Roadside camp in Henderson, North Carolina. Camp space was thirty cents a night, and cabins rented for $1.25 to $2.50 a night.

Cabin Camps and Motor Courts. Small motels, or cabin camps, as they came to be called, were predominantly mom-and-pop operations, cheaply constructed and run with family help. They remained the major roadside lodging for noncampers until the end of World War II. The cabins offered easy access from the highway, free parking, no clerks or tipping, informality, and privacy. Motor courts were first built in California, Florida, and Texas. These establishments combined the advantages of the cabin camp with sturdier constructions and hotel-type conveniences such as indoor plumbing and private bathrooms.

From the Bizarre to the Regional. To catch the eye of travelers, enterprising entrepreneurs starting in the late 1920s built a strange assortment of attractions. Giant dogs, frogs, and ducks sprang up along the nation's roadsides. The giant dog where a traveler could buy a frankfurter, a huge dairy pail hawking ice cream, and an oversized toad that advertised the Toad Inn became part of the American landscape. The best known of these attractions was the Big Duck in Riverhead, Long Island, built in 1931. Designed for the Long Island duck magnate Martin Maurer, it measured twenty by thirty by fifteen feet and was wildly successful at catching travelers' eyes. The largest concentration of these fanciful structures was in the Los Angeles area. Historical or regional motifs also became popular. Dad Lee's in Carlin, Nevada, a cabin camp, combined the shanties of the gold-rush era with Native American tepees. New England stops drew on colonial imagery, and in Arizona travelers could eat in adobe structures evocative of Mexico. Chinese pagodas, Dutch windmills, and other such structures appeared from Maine to Wisconsin.

Howard Johnson. Amid the clutter of large frogs and colonial nostalgia, roadside restaurant chains took hold. In 1935 businessman Howard Johnson opened the first of what would become a chain of roadside eateries throughout Massachusetts. The popularity of his establishments spread as word of his extrarich ice cream got out. Johnson made his cones distinctive by offering a range of flavors and by using a scoop that formed a rim of extra ice cream at the bottom, suggesting to customers that they were getting an exceptionally large serving. Johnson's restaurants also offered what was then an unusual combination: he offered a full-meal dining room, a quick-bite counter, and a fast-food menu under one roof. In 1935 he began franchising his restaurants; by 1940, 125 Howard Johnson restaurants, a third of them company owned, were in business from Maine to Florida and grossing $14 million a year. Johnson secured the popularity of his orange-roofed establishments by building the largest roadside restaurant in the world on Queens Boulevard in New York City in 1939 to serve visitors to the New York World's Fair.

Sources:

James J. Flink, *The Automobile Age* (Cambridge, Mass., & London: MIT Press, 1988);

Chester H. Liebs, *Main Street to Miracle Mile: American Roadside Architecture* (Boston: Little, Brown, 1985).

STREAMLINE

Streamline Moderne. American design underwent an enormous transformation in the 1930s. Inspired by technology and a fascination with the machine, Streamline Moderne was a rigorously modern aesthetic that emphasized speed and efficiency. Shedding the eclecticism of Victorianism and its ornate designs, historicism, and

The Burlington Zephyr

cluttered aesthetic, Streamline Moderne marked a radicalization of design.

Modernism in Motion. The most popular and influential source of the new aesthetic was the Zephyr high-speed train. First designed by engineer Edward G. Budd, the stainless steel, lightweight 1932 Zephyr translated the aerodynamic principles of modern airplanes to ground transportation. The Zephyr's smooth curves, rounded corners, and powerful diesel engines replaced the older square steel and wooden trains. This generation of high-speed trains, which also included the Super Chief and the M-10001, reached speeds of 120 miles per hour while using a fraction of the fuel consumed by earlier trains. With their speed and efficiency, trains such as the Zephyr embodied the future and futuristic longings for wealth and a society freed from scarcity.

From Trains to Cars. Budd first applied his stainless-steel designs to automobiles and throughout the 1920s worked for Nash Motors. His steel-bodied cars were unique in an industry that preferred wood. By the 1930s the use of stainless steel in automobiles was widespread. The ease with which steel could be shaped helped transform the look of modern cars. With their curved fenders, rounded hoods, and long, sleek shapes, the newest generation of cars in the 1930s adopted the look Budd made popular with the Zephyr.

Architecture. Streamline Moderne architecture also utilized the symbolism of speed and efficiency popularized by fast motorcars, airplanes, and trains. Many architects incorporated mechanically perfect curves at the corners of buildings, cylindrical helix stairs, circular windows, and spherical knobs into their buildings. The Philadelphia Savings Fund Society building was one of the first and most exciting examples of Streamline Moderne architecture. Designed by George Howe in 1932, it was one of the first skyscrapers to use ribbon windows that folded around the corners of the building. This skyscraper solved a chronic problem of tall buildings: how to make the towering surface planes pleasing to the eye. Taking inspiration from the machine, Howe's answer was minimalist. The giant building's ornamentation was sculptural and formal: by means of sharp, thin detailing, the masonry veneer of polished granite, limestone, and smooth brick appeared as a continuous skin. Together with the curving bands of windows, this gave it the appearance of texture and motion.

Popularizing the New Look. The Streamline Moderne style appeared not only in high-rises in New York and Chicago but in gas stations and restaurants. Corporations hired industrial designers and architects to prepare prototypes for their roadside outlets, and the idiom trickled down to mom-and-pop outfits. Do-it-yourself magazines and trade journals offered handymen advice on streamlining their buildings. By the late 1930s everything from hot-dog stands to motor courts sported smooth surfaces and rounded corners.

Sources:

Chester H. Liebs, *Main Street to Miracle Mile: American Roadside Architecture* (Boston: Little, Brown, 1985);

Marcus Whiffen and Frederick Koeper, *American Architecture 1607–1976* (Cambridge, Mass.: MIT Press, 1981).

VARIATIONS IN HOME DESIGN

Interior Design. As the United States slipped deeper into hard times in the 1930s, manufacturers turned to industrial designers in hopes of stimulating plummeting sales. Manufacturers challenged industrial designers to develop a visual idiom capable of communicating such positive thoughts as "up-to-date," "technologically advanced," and "modern" for their products and thus attract an uncertain buying public. Leading industrial designers, including Henry Dreyfuss, Norman Bel Geddes, and Walter Dorwin Teague, set about reinventing a range of household gadgets from irons to blenders. They were influenced by the rounded corners and streamlining of modern airplanes, trains, and automobiles. Radio cabinets, furniture, pens, toasters, and silverware appeared in shiny metals with curves, etchings, and the appearance of technological advancement.

The Tubular Chair. Several important modern architects experimented with furniture design in the 1930s. In 1925 Hungarian architect Marcel Breuer, a student of Walter Gropius and the Bauhaus, designed his first tubular chair, whose simple lines gained popularity in the 1930s. Composed of two leather squares framed by parallel steel tubes, the chair was shaped like the numeral *5* without the horizontal top. Ludwig Mies van der Rohe's 1930 Barcelona chair and Alvar Aalto's 1934 lounge chair followed Breuer's innovation. Trimmed of all ornament and embellishment, the tubular chair expressed the streamline aesthetic of modernism.

Functionalism. The Century of Progress Exhibition of 1933–1934 introduced functionalism to the American public in its "House of the Future" show. There the public saw the machinelike contours of new tables, chairs, dishes, and household items. Throughout the exhibition and particularly in the "House of the Future," the future was conceived of as technologically advanced by its rejection of Victorian excesses. Ornamentation was discarded for streamlined simplicity. Gone were overstuffed chairs and sofas cluttered with pillows and finely handcrafted details. Modern sofas were narrower, with slim cushions and armrests, and were unadorned by complicated patterns or pillows. Chairs were noted for the prominence of the frames. Solid wood frames with one- or two-toned colored cushions were popular. Rooms were planned to enhance their function as living spaces rather than being museum-like parlors from which to conduct business. Bookshelves were incorporated into the walls, and carpets

The Butler House, 1937, a residence in Des Moines, Iowa, designed by Kraetsch and Kraetsch

were of single, subdued colors. Functionalism in furniture design remained out of the reach of all but the most affluent consumers until the late 1940s, when the designs were adapted for mass production.

American Homes. The Colonial Revival style home remained the most popular house in the United States during the 1930s. These homes typically included an accentuated front door with a decorative crown supported by slender columns to form an entry porch. The symmetrical facade generally included first-floor double windows with double-hung sashes and second-floor single windows. A revival of the Dutch Colonial style was particularly popular in the 1930s. The distinguishing features of these homes were the roofs, which sharply sloped upward to a triangular peak. Many of these homes had front porches composed of a steep overhanging roof and narrow columns. These homes were typically found on the eastern seaboard.

Varieties. A revival of the Tudor Style was also popular in the 1930s. These homes had steeply pitched roofs, with side gables and a facade marked by prominent cross gables. In imitation of British country homes, Tudor homes had tall, narrow windows that typically clustered in groups with multipane glazing. The facades also relied on brick or stone, with stucco or wood exteriors. In western states the Spanish Eclectic style was popular. These homes had low-pitched, red-tiled roofs with little or no eaves overhanging, stucco exteriors, and arches popular in Spanish architecture over the door or windows. A variation on the Spanish Eclectic was the Monterey home, a two-story home with a low-pitched gabled roof, balconies, and mission-style windows. This style blended Spanish adobe construction with pitched-roof English shapes brought to California from New England and fused Spanish Eclectic and Colonial Revival details.

Throughout the 1930s these homes tended to favor Spanish detailing.

High Style. Art deco and modernist aesthetics made themselves felt in home designs during the 1930s. Modernist houses had smooth wall surfaces generally of stucco, flat roofs, asymmetrical facades, and often horizontal grooves or lines. Many incorporated the modern emphasis on curves and continuous round corners. Typically these homes had small windows. International Style homes also had flat roofs and smooth, unornamented walls but none of the detailing of art deco buildings. In many International Style houses walls were not used for structural support but were instead more like curtains hung over a structural steel skeleton. Freeing exterior walls from structural demand permitted greater variation in the exteriors, such as long ribbons of windows, some of which wrapped around the building's corners, and large floor-to-ceiling plate-glass windows. These homes were rare and avant-garde, mostly clustered in fashionable suburbs in the northeastern states and in California.

Sources:

Virginia and Lee McAlester, *A Field Guide to American Houses* (New York: Knopf, 1992);

Meyric R. Rogers, *American Interior Design: The Traditions and Development of Domestic Design from Colonial Times to the Present* (New York: Norton, 1947).

HEADLINE MAKERS

HATTIE CARNEGIE

1889-1956

DRESS DESIGNER

From Hats to Dresses. Hattie Carnegie, born Henrietta Kanengeiser in Vienna in 1889, was one of the premier dress designers of the 1930s. Not only did she make her mark through her elegant designs, she also trained a generation of fashion designers that shaped American style for decades. Carnegie started her career as a milliner. Her father, an artist and designer, introduced her to the world of fashion and design, and by age fifteen she had found work trimming hats. Five years later she opened a shop on East Tenth Street in New York called Carnegie — Ladies Hatter. The shop was successful, and within a few years she moved to the tony Upper West Side, where she took up dress design. However, she never learned to sew. A friend explained that "Hattie couldn't sew a fine seam, but she had a feeling about clothes and a personality to convey her ideas to the people who were to work them out." She changed the name of her business in 1914 to Hattie Carnegie, Inc., and by the 1920s was the toast of the fashion world from her new location in the Upper East Side.

"Simple, Beautiful Clothes." Carnegie's belief in simplicity fit perfectly with the streamlining of 1930s design. She believed that "simple, beautiful clothes . . . enhance the charm of the woman who wears them. If you have a dress that is too often admired, be suspicious of it." The dress, she insisted, must fit and not overpower the woman who wears it. She was unabashedly devoted to Paris fashion and made regular buying trips throughout the 1920s and 1930s. Yet while she was a self-declared Francophile, she adapted French style to American tastes by offering a blend of style and comfort that suited many fashion-conscious Americans who still wanted their clothes to have a French flair.

Designing for the Middle Class. Carnegie's expensive original designer clothes were out of reach for many Americans, but this did not limit her influence on American design. Hers were among some of the most widely copied designs by popularly priced designers. As the decade wore on, Carnegie added a modestly priced, ready-to-wear line of clothing that proved to be the most lucrative of her enterprises. She made her modestly priced clothes more available to the average consumer by permitting some department stores to carry the new line, breaking from her usual practice of selling her clothes at her own shop. This practice secured her influence over both haute couture and popular wear.

Training a New Generation. Throughout the 1930s Carnegie's booming business attracted several young designers who trained under her. Norman Norell, Claire McCardell, Paula Trigère, Pauline De Rothschild, and Jean Louis, among others, spent years working under her tutelage. As her business grew, so did her interests. She added accessories, perfumes, chiffon handkerchiefs, silk hose, and cosmetics. By the 1940s Carnegie was well established as one of America's top designers.

Sources:
L. H., "Profiles: Luxury, Inc.," *New Yorker*, 10 (31 March 1934): 23–27;

Caroline Rennolds Milbank, *New York Fashion: The Evolution of American Style* (New York: Abrams, 1989).

LILLY DACHE

1913-1990

MILLINER

The Well-Designed Hat. "A hat that is well designed never goes out of fashion," claimed Lilly Dache. "I wear some of mine three and four years." Dache was the best-known milliner of the 1930s. By 1940 she had produced around nine thousand hats, which sold for twenty-five dollars at forty-seven department stores across the country. In the 1930s she was best-known for her half-hat, a hat with a narrow brim and crown that sat on the back of the head. The millinery industry embraced the half-hat as its best weapon against what it called the insanity of "the hatless craze." Dache was also attributed with starting the popularity of the turban in the 1930s.

Bicycle Cap as Inspiration. From age ten Dache displayed a flair for original hats. When her mother ordered her a traveling suit composed of a black-and-white checkered skirt and bright red jacket, Dache promptly stopped at a bicycle store and bought herself a red cap to go with her new outfit. She never completed her purchase, as the store owner sought confirmation from her mother. Yet the experience left its mark on the young Dache: no collection she designed was ever without the visored cap for travel.

Early Life. Born in Beiles, France, Dache started sewing doll clothes at a young age from expensive fabric scraps from her mother's wardrobe. She hated school and was truant so often that when she was fourteen her parents refused to spend any more

money on books that she did not read. As a teenager she apprenticed with an aunt who was a milliner in Bordeaux. In the 1920s Dache immigrated to the United States with fifteen dollars in her pocket and was promptly hired as a salesgirl in a New York millinery.

Starting Her Own Shop. Within a few years Dache had saved enough money to open her own shop and began producing forty to fifty hats a day. She soon had a devoted following and in the early 1930s moved into a complete building. During the decade she made hats for such stars as Marlene Dietrich, Carmen Miranda, Carole Lombard, Joan Crawford, and Sonja Henie. Her hat sales triggered lines outside her building that at times led to disagreements with the police.

Sculptural Hats. Dache's hats had unusual designs and utilized a range of fabrics previously unseen in the millinery industry. Usually they were asymmetrical; crowns and brims were often tilted to one side, and some hats were trimmed with veils designed to hang down on one side of the head, turn under the chin, and be pinned with a brooch to the hat on the other side. During World War II, when materials were in short supply, she made hats from mop yarn and gold epaulets from uniforms. In the summer she made hats from dress buttons, topstitching the brims to give them the proper shape. In the 1940s she expanded her business into perfumes called Drifting and Dashing and added dresses and accessories to her millinery designs.

Sources:
Caroline Rennolds Milbank, *New York Fashion: The Evolution of American Style* (New York: Abrams, 1989);

"1940 Design Prizes Awarded to Four," *New York Times*, 30 April 1941, p. 15.

WALTER GROPIUS

1883-1969

ARCHITECT

Founder of the Bauhaus. Walter Gropius's philosophy, his functionalist designs, and his renowned teaching abilities profoundly influenced the modern movement in Western architecture. As chairman of the Department of Architecture in the Graduate School of Design at Harvard University, he headed the top architecture school in the United States from 1938 to 1952. Under his direction Harvard architecture students began learning by doing, a technique he applied at the Bauhaus, the German school of architecture and design he had established in the early 1900s. While at Bauhaus, Gropius made a name for himself in architecture, furniture design, industrial design, and city planning. Other examples of his work include residences, housing developments, prefabricated houses, theaters, academic buildings, and factories constructed in the United States, Germany, and England.

Early Life. Walter Adolf Gropius was born on 18 May 1883 in Berlin, Germany, to a family long associated with architecture and painting. Having intended from an early age to become an architect, Gropius volunteered to work in the firm of Solf and Wichards at the Technische Hochschule in Munich. After serving in the military and later traveling through Europe, Gropius established his own practice in 1910. He designed factories and residences noted for their clean, functional lines, their austerity, and for the unusual materials he used, such as cement and steel.

Fascination with the Machine. After World War I Gropius became the director of the Grand Ducal Saxon school of arts and crafts in Weimar, Germany, which he later reorganized into the Staatliches Bauhaus. "The foundation and development of the Bauhaus," he wrote in *The New Architecture and the Bauhaus* (1935), "aimed at the introduction of a new educational method in art and a new artistic conception that derived development of all artistic form from the vital functions of life and from modern technical means of construction." Gropius was one of the first architects to take inspiration from modern technology and felt strongly that designers must explore the design elements the machine made possible. "The object of the Bauhaus," he wrote, "was not to propagate any 'style,' system or dogma, but simply to exert a revitalizing influence on design." He brought in leading names in painting, typography, furniture, ceramics, weaving, stage design, and other applied arts.

Emigrating from Fascism. In 1928 Gropius resigned the directorship of the Bauhaus to go into private practice in Berlin, where he designed important institutional structures. As chairman of the design committee of the Adler automobile company (1929–1933) he also designed automobile bodies. Dismayed at Adolf Hitler's Germany, Gropius left for London in 1934. In 1937 he and Marcel Breuer moved to the United States to complete a three-year project in Massachusetts. Over the next two years the two designed their own houses in Lincoln, Massachusetts; the Hagerty House in Cohasset, Massachusetts; the Abele House in Framingham, Massachusetts; and the Frank House in Pittsburgh. They also did projects for the Pennsylvania state exhibition at the New York World's Fair in 1939 and for Black Mountain College in North Carolina and Wheaton College in Massachusetts.

Harvard. In 1937 Gropius was named senior professor of architecture at Harvard University, and in 1938 the chair of the department where he trained a generation of architects. In 1941 the federal government commissioned him to design a 250-unit defense-housing project, Aluminum City, in New Kensington, Pennsylvania. Gropius and Breuer provided the units at a cost of $3,280 each. Many critics believe Gropius's most significant American building was the Harvard Graduate Center (1950) in Cambridge, Massachusetts. Designed by the Architects' Collaborative — a firm in which Gropius was one of eight partners, some of whom were his former students — the Graduate Center was a testimony to modern architecture. In July 1952 Gropius retired from his position at Harvard.

Sources:

Dorothy Adlow, "Walter Gropius: An Architect Who Has Blazed a Way," *Christian Science Monitor*, 21 January 1952, p. 9;

"Retrospect in Boston," *Time*, 59 (21 January 1952): 58.

ELIZABETH HAWES

1903-1971

DESIGNER AND CRITIC

Selling Dresses and Opinions. Throughout the 1930s Elizabeth Hawes built a reputation in dress design and fashion commentary. Her best-known book, *Fashion Is Spinach* (1938), debunked the endless search for newness driving the fashion industry. Style is functional, she claimed in her best-seller. But fashion, that "deformed thief," was based purely on the whims of designers and manufacturers, she claimed. Her battle cry throughout the 1930s was that a good dress could last for more than one season.

Early Life. Hawes began making clothes as a child in Ridgewood, New Jersey. By age nine she sewed her own clothes, and at twelve she made clothes for her mother's friends' children. She wanted to go to art school, but her mother insisted she attend Vassar College. During summer break of her sophomore year she attended Parson's School of Fine and Applied Arts in New York. The next summer, in 1924, she went to work as an unpaid apprentice at Bergdorf Goodman, convinced that art school would not teach her what she needed to know.

Living in Paris. After graduating in 1925, Hawes was determined to go to work in Paris to learn the fashion business firsthand. She found a job at a Paris copy house that followed famous French designers. In 1928 she quit to make sketches for American buyers and manufacturers in Paris. This work consisted of accompanying buyers to the important fashion openings and sketching those dresses they wanted to copy but did not wish to buy. Combining writing with drawing, she also worked as the Paris correspondent for *The New Yorker* and an American fashion syndicate.

Opening Her Own Shop. In 1928 Hawes returned to New York, determined to design and make clothes for American women that suited the lives they led. This goal was still radical in the late 1920s, as most Americans copied French design and viewed American designs as purely for leisure and sportswear. On her twenty-fifth birthday she opened her first shop with a debutante,

Rosemary Harden. They opened to much fanfare but had difficulty turning a profit. In 1929 Hawes became the sole owner. She struggled to keep her shop alive through the Depression. Ever imaginative, she organized a publicity stunt by showing her American designs in Paris in 1931. It was the first time the world's fashion center had been invaded from overseas, and the stunt won Hawes considerable attention.

Designs for Average Women. Before the Depression Hawes had designed clothes for well-to-do women. In 1933 she hired herself out to a dress manufacturer to design ready-made clothes. Her moderately priced designs appeared in a storm of advertisements and promotion pieces, and she startled the retail trade with her unusual color combinations and designs. Though making a great deal of money, Hawes severed her connections with the manufacturer in 1934 when she discovered that dresses bearing her name were being made from inferior fabrics. Yet the money she earned in ready-made clothing financed the return of her own business, Hawes, Inc. In 1939, one year after the success of *Fashion Is Spinach,* she published *Men Can Take It,* an indignant attack on the uncomfortable clothing men wore. She advocated functional clothing without stiff collars, heavy belts, and stiffly buttoned coats.

Writing. In 1940 Hawes retired from fashion designing, returning only to create a uniform for Red Cross volunteers in 1942. She turned her attention to writing, penning a column for an afternoon-evening newspaper called *PA* and writing more books. To gain insight into the plight of women machine operators, she took a night job at an airplane plant during the war and wrote an exposé called *Why Women Cry; or, Wenches with Wrenches* (1943). In 1948 she reentered the fashion world, opening a shop on fashionable Madison Avenue. When she closed the shop in 1949 it marked the end of her professional involvement with fashion. Up to her death in 1971 she designed for herself and for her friends, specializing in hand-knitted separates.

Source:
Caroline Rennolds Milbank, *New York Fashion: The Evolution of American Style* (New York: Abrams, 1989).

CHARLES JAMES

1906-1978

DRESS DESIGNER

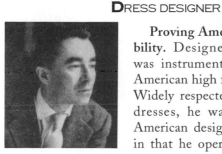

Proving American Style Sensibility. Designer Charles James was instrumental in introducing American high fashion to Europe. Widely respected for his original dresses, he was unique among American designers in the 1930s in that he operated on the Paris pattern, creating clothes for private clients and then selling the original models to leading stores throughout the United States. In 1952 he entered the wholesale business, making his designs available to the general public through mass production. In 1955 he opened his own retail stores.

Early Life. Charles Wilson Brega James was born in England in 1906. Finding school dull, he refused to attend the college his father had chosen for him. Instead, he went to work with a family friend who taught him the basics of business. In 1927 James moved to the United States and opened a dress shop in New York. He presented his first collection in London in 1928 and opened European branches in London and Paris.

Life in Europe. James's business took off in the 1930s. He began producing designs, including linens, accessories, and sportswear, for American buyers such as Best and Company, Marshall Field, Taylor Importing Company, and Casino Frocks. He divided his time between London and Paris while regularly sending dresses to the United States. In 1936 he became the toast of Paris with his first show there. Paul Poiret, one of the great Parisian couturiers, declared to James that "I pass you my crown. Wear it well." James stayed in Europe until 1939, when the war interfered with his work there.

Unusual Textures and Colors. James worked within his own vision of the silhouette. His asymmetrical draped clothes were made in lustrous, weighty fabrics such as heavy faille, slipper satin, and velvet and combined fabrics of different textures in the same dress. One of his best-known designs was the complicated culotte, which had one trouser leg and one skirtlike leg folded over to the other side. He also experimented with colors in his evening clothes, combining apricot and eggplant, shell pink and ginger, and orange and rose.

Back to America. Upon his return to the United States in 1939, James set out to promote native American designers. Besides gaining respect from Wall Street financiers who backed his work, he was also recognized by fashion mogul Elizabeth Arden, who in 1944 hired him to design, staff, and decorate her fashion floor. Both James and Arden were known for their fiery tempers, and the two severed their relationship shortly after he showed his first collection under the Arden label.

Winning a Coty. James reopened his New York stores in 1945 and began selling original dresses to Lord and Taylor, Neiman-Marcus, Bergdorf Goodman, and other stores. In 1947 he showed his designs in Paris to rave reviews. Virginia Pope, the *New York Times* fashion editor who covered the show, praised him as offering the most sensational designs of the show. In 1950 he was awarded the American Fashion Critics Award (Coty) for his "great mystery of color and artistry of draping." Throughout the 1950s and 1960s he continued selling his original designs to major department stores.

Sources:
Caroline Rennolds Milbank, *New York Fashion: The Evolution of American Style* (New York: Abrams, 1989);

Amy Porter, "Young Man of Fashion," *Collier's*, 120 (20 September 1947): 100–101, 104.

MURIEL KING

1900-1977

FASHION DESIGNER

Classic Designs. Muriel King preached the importance of designing dresses that looked good the first, second, and third season well before the Depression of the 1930s. Good design, she believed, never went out of fashion. Her philosophy of classic fashion served her well in the 1930s, as consumers who could do so stopped replacing their wardrobes each season and looked for clothes that would look good for years.

Fashion Drawing. As a girl King dreamed of being an artist. After studying art at the University of Washington she went to New York to study fashion at the New York School of Fine and Applied Arts. While in school she freelanced as a fashion artist for *Women's Wear Daily, Vogue,* and various New York department stores, which she continued to do throughout the 1920s. Friends encouraged her to design her own clothes, and in 1932 she began. She was proclaimed the creator of fashions that revealed "the artist's impatience with monotony," and her designs were introduced by Lord and Taylor, a New York department store. Each of the originals accompanying her debut was priced at $125, with copies ranging from $29.50 to $49.50.

Striking Out Alone. A few months after her debut King opened her first salon. Taking a risk by opening a new venture in the depths of the Depression, she reassured herself by thinking that the salon could serve as a home to her family if the business did not succeed. Her worries never materialized. In fact, she soon expanded her salon from one to three floors. In 1935 King went to Hollywood to design costumes for Katharine Hepburn for the film *Sylvia Scarlett.* She was amused by the experience: "I flew out and back to California twice, and worked very hard when I was there," she said, "and what designs do you think finally appeared in that picture? A cotton dress, a clown suit, and a raincoat!" In 1937 she did the costumes for Hepburn and Ginger Rogers in *Stage Door.*

King's Creative Techniques. King described her designing process as "backwards." She first sketched the dress in color. When the outline and drape of the garment were complete, she chose the fabric. Contemporaries agreed that if she knew more about cutting and sewing she might be restrained by technical difficulties from trying for certain effects. Her defiance of traditional rules gave her clothes the freshness for which she was famous.

Designs for the People. Throughout the 1940s King continued to design for Hollywood, and in 1940 she abruptly closed her high-priced salon, claiming it was too elitist. She began working on a series of dress-design patterns for a women's magazine, offering quality patterns to women who could not afford her originals. In 1943 she designed Flying Fortress Fashions for women workers in the aircraft industry, which workers and critics adored.

Source:
Women's Wear Daily, 14 September 1932, 28 September 1937, and 13 January 1942.

VALENTINA

1904-1989

FASHION DESIGNER

An Architect of Dress. A leading member of haute couture, Valentina considered herself an architect of dress. Claiming inspiration from Grecian architecture, she used fabrics to accentuate their textures, shadows, and highlights in order to create the desired architectural effect. "Color," she once explained, "should never be obvious, static, or flat" but rather should move and flow. Commentators agreed that she achieved dramatic effects in her gowns without, as one put it, "resorting to extreme cuts."

Early Life. She was born Valentina Sanina in Kiev, Ukraine, in 1904 to a wealthy family. Her education at the school of dramatic arts in Kiev was interrupted by the Russian Revolution in 1917, in which her mother and brother were killed. At fifteen she fled alone to the Crimean peninsula, carrying only the family's jewels. Two years later she married and immigrated to Athens, where the couple struggled to survive. In 1923 she moved to New York City, where she began designing clothes.

Establishing a Name. After a series of efforts in different fashion salons, the husband-and-wife team opened Valentina Gowns, Inc., in 1928 and soon began to make a profit. Valentina's dresses were complicated and difficult to reproduce. She believed that each dress should be individual and suited perfectly to one person. She regularly traveled to Paris to study the new fashions. She would then bring her designs back to New York, where she would fashion originals for her high-paying customers.

Costuming and the Theater. In the 1930s Valentina began designing costumes for the stage, which she had loved since her days in Kiev, and Hollywood. In 1933 she designed costumes for Judith Anderson for the play *Coming of Age*, which established her as a costume designer. By 1936, when she did Lynn Fontanne's clothes for the role of a White Russian pseudocountess in the play *Idiot's Delight*, the designer was well known enough for columnists to recognize her work. Valentina also did stage costumes for Helen Hayes, Mary Martin, and Vera Zorina as well as Clifton Webb's dressing gowns and pajamas for the play *The Man Who Came to Dinner*. Her Hollywood following included Norma Shearer, Rosalind Russell, and Greta Garbo.

The Art of Fashion. Valentina combined her belief in the individuality of every woman with her passion for the stage. "On-stage or off," she wrote, "it is essential to know a woman's physical and psychological equipment as well as . . . she knows it herself, in order to create a dress that will have meaning in relation to her as a woman. . . . Every dress should identify a personal style through the elements of personality which it accentuates. Otherwise, it cannot be called a piece of art." She was particularly known for using hoods, large fur hats, dolman sleeves, pleated skirts and blouses, and scarf handkerchiefs.

Source:
"*Life* Calls on Valentina," *Life,* 16 (31 January 1944): 98–101.

FRANK LLOYD WRIGHT

1867-1959

ARCHITECT

America's Premier Architect. One of the world's most famous architects, Frank Lloyd Wright had a profound and enduring effect on Western architecture. His professional career spanned seventy years, starting with a revival of past styles and continuing through the beginnings of modern architecture, a movement in which he played a major role. Throughout his career he maintained a strong reverence for life and nature. His architecture was always far ahead of the work of other architects. He was a creative innovator and experimented throughout his long career with structure, using great steel and concrete cantilevers and poured concrete. He was one of the first architects to see the design capability of concrete blocks, designing buildings of custom-cast blocks with patterns. He also introduced open planning in buildings, letting spaces flow into each other rather than enclosing them with walls. He was interested in machines and was an early advocate of factory-manufactured products in his buildings.

Early Life. Frank Lloyd Wright was born in Richland Center, Wisconsin, on 8 June 1867. His father deserted the family when Wright was sixteen. His mother was a strong-willed woman who had decided that her son should become an architect. Starting when he was seven, his mother tutored him in the art of building designs by playing with blocks and paper, a technique originated by Friedrich Froebel. Using a basic set of blocks and other simple materials, Wright drew plans for buildings and constructed them, furniture and all. At eighteen he went to Chicago to work in the offices of Louis H. Sullivan. As a designer and draftsman in the firm of Adler and Sullivan, Wright worked on some of their finest buildings, such as the Wainwright Building (1891) in Saint Louis. Most important, he absorbed much of the philosophy, design principles, and engineering knowledge of the two partners. He left the firm in 1893 to set up his own practice.

The Prairie Style. During his early career Wright worked from a studio in downtown Chicago. He designed houses, gradually developing what he called his Prairie Style, which adopted the horizontal lines of the Great Plains. He also built the Larkin Building (1904) in Buffalo and the Robie House (1907) in Chicago. Throughout these years he developed his mature philosophy of an organic architecture, an architecture that grew like living organisms by adaptation to specific environments, sites, uses, and materials.

Wright's Mature Period. The second, or mature, period of Wright's career began when, in 1911, he built his home and studio, Taliesin, in Spring Green, Wisconsin. It burned twice and was rebuilt each time. Notable buildings from this period include Midway Gardens (1914), a great indoor and outdoor amusement center in Chicago; the Imperial Hotel (1922) in Tokyo, which survived the great earthquake of 1923; and the Millard House (1923) in Pasadena, California.

Usonian. Faced with fewer commissions in the 1930s, Wright started a new series of houses he called *Usonia*, a term for the United States used by Samuel Butler in his 1872 novel, *Erewhon*. Usonia was Wright's utopian vision of an American democracy in which life was led closer to nature, where architecture supported community, and where every family had a beautiful home. With these houses, many of which were in California, Wright pioneered the custom-designed concrete block, a material no other architect used toward such aesthetic ends. At the end of the decade he produced some of his finest buildings. He designed what many view as a residential masterpiece, the Kaufmann House (1936), called Fallingwater because it was built over a waterfall in Bear Run, Pennsylvania. In 1939 he completed the Johnson Wax Company Administration building in Racine, Wisconsin. In 1940 he started the designs for Florida Southern University at Lakeland, which was completed in 1952. He also began work on his own winter house and school, Taliesin West, in Scottsdale, Arizona, in 1939, on which he worked until his death in 1959. In 1949, when he was eighty years old, he was awarded the Gold Medal of the American Institute of Architects.

Sources:
Henry-Russell Hitchcock, *In the Nature of Materials, 1887–1941: The Buildings of Frank Lloyd Wright* (New York: Duell, Sloan & Pearce, 1942);

Robert C. Twombly, *Frank Lloyd Wright: His Life and His Architecture* (New York: Wiley, 1979).

PEOPLE IN THE NEWS

New York department store Bonwit Teller hired Spanish painter **Salvador Dalí** to design a group of its store windows, marking the influence of Surrealism on American fashion.

Lewis Gannett, conservationist, was one of the earliest critics of the automobile's impact on national parks, complaining in 1937 that "the floor of Yosemite is an amusement park, as crowded a city as New York's Central Park. . . . Nothing in America is less wild than . . . Yosemite Valley."

Noting the growing dependence on the car in Los Angeles, critic **Douglas Haskell** commented in *Architectural Record* in 1937 that "Los Angeles is a city built on the automobile as Boston was built on the sailing ship. It appears to the casual view as a series of parking lots interspersed with buildings."

In 1934 entrepreneur **Richard M. Hollingshead Jr.,** with help from **Willis Warren Smith,** formed Park-In Theaters, a chain of drive-in movie houses. Business proved so good that they franchised Park-In Theaters for one thousand dollars each plus 5 percent of gross earnings.

At the 1931 Conference on Home Building, President **Herbert Hoover** explained the significance of home ownership to the American dream. The aspiration to own a home, he said, "penetrates the heart of our national well being. . . . There can be no fear for a democracy or for self-government or for liberty and freedom from home owners no matter how humble they may be."

Federal Bureau of Investigation chief **J. Edgar Hoover** complained in 1939 that the popular tourist camps located on the outskirts of towns and cities across the country not only were stopovers used by tourists but were becoming "camouflaged brothels."

New York store Bonwit Teller, with offices in Paris and London, appointed **Hortense Oldlum** president of the company in 1937, making her the first woman to head a major American department store.

In 1932 **Dorothy Shaver,** vice president of Lord and Taylor, explained that while she appreciated French designers, "American designers are best equipped by tradition, background and feeling to understand the needs and demands of American women's clothes."

Trailer manufacturer **George Sherman,** founder and president of the Covered Wagon Company, displayed his first streamlined, modern trailer at the 1930 Detroit Automobile Show and began to fill orders at a rapid pace as Americans' passion for travel took the auto industry by storm.

Ever optimistic about the utopian implications of technology, architect **Frank Lloyd Wright** predicted in 1932 the existence of a "great architectural highway with . . . roadside markets, super-service stations, fine schools and playgrounds, small, integrated, intensive farming units . . . and fine homes winding up the beautiful natural features of the landscape."

DEATHS

Clement C. Cassell, 70, architect of Roosevelt Park, a colony for the elderly in Millville, New Jersey, sponsored by the Works Progress Administration, 1 November 1939.

F. Bunham Chapman, 53, beaux arts architect, 29 April 1935.

Frank Davis Chase, 60, industrial architect, designer of plants for the *Saint Louis Star-Times*, the *Oklahoman*, and the *Milwaukee Journal*, 21 July 1937.

Arthur Dillon, 66, architect of Atlanta's Masonic Temple and All Saints Episcopal Church, 7 January 1938.

Frederick Dinkelberg, 74, architect of the Hayworth Building in Chicago, 18 February 1935.

Isaac E. Ditmars, 84, architect of many Catholic churches and institutions, 26 February 1934.

William J. East, 71, architect for more than 150 ecclesiastical buildings, 3 May 1936.

Vincent J. Eck, 45, architect for the Roman Catholic Diocese of Trenton, New Jersey, 23 May 1938.

George W. Eckles, 65, architect of many schools, colleges, hotels, and churches, 5 March 1932.

Gilbert Gass, 75, architect well-known for his beaux arts buildings such as the U.S. Custom House (1907) and the Woolworth Building (1913), both in New York City, 19 May 1934.

Earl Hallenbeck, 58, head of the Department of Architecture at Syracuse University, 1 June 1934.

Raymond Mathewson Hood, 53, architect of the Chicago Tribune Building (1925), the Daily News Building (1929) in New York, and the McGraw-Hill Building (1930) in New York's Rockefeller Center, 15 August 1934.

Franklin H. Hutchins, 63, Boston architect who specialized in banks, 14 February 1934.

William B. Ittner, 72, a nationally noted figure in the field of school design, 2 March 1936.

Louis E. Jackson, 54, Boston architect who worked with Harry Vaughan in designing the Washington Cathedral, 10 October 1932.

George W. Jacoby, 56, architect who designed an addition to the New York Stock Exchange in 1922, 21 February 1937.

Irving John, 66, a pioneer in the modern movement in architecture, 7 October 1936.

James H. Johnson, 74, New York architect who built the United Office Building in Niagara Falls, New York, as well as several bridges and support buildings for the region, 5 April 1939.

Charles Z. Klauder, 66, a specialist in collegiate architecture, building on campuses such as Princeton University, Pennsylvania State College, and the University of Pittsburgh, 30 October 1938.

John Russell Pope, 63, beaux arts architect famous for his memorials, 27 August 1937.

Louis Comfort Tiffany, 85, designer of Art Nouveau stained glass, 18 January 1937.

PUBLICATIONS

Naum Gabo and others, eds., *Circle: Survey of Constructive Art* (London: Faber & Faber, 1937);

Walter Gropius, *The Bauhaus: 1919–1928* (New York: Museum of Modern Art, 1938);

Gropius, *The New Architecture and the Bauhaus*, translated by P. Morton Shand (New York: Museum of Modern Art, 1935);

Elizabeth Hawes, *Fashion Is Spinach* (New York: Random House, 1938);

Hawes, *Men Can Take It* (New York: Random House, 1939);

Henry-Russell Hitchcock and Philip Johnson, *The International Style* (New York: Museum of Modern Art, 1932);

Jonathan R. Leonard, *The Tragedy of Henry Ford* (New York: Putnam, 1932);

Robert S. Lynd and Helen M. Lynd, *Middletown in Transition: A Study in Cultural Conflicts* (New York: Harcourt, Brace, 1937);

Frank Lloyd Wright, *An Autobiography*, 5 volumes (New York: Longmans, Green, 1932–1943);

Wright, *An Organic Architecture: The Architecture of Democracy* (London: Lund Humphries, 1939);

Wright and Baker Brownell, *Architecture and Modern Life* (New York: Harper, 1938);

Architectural Record, periodical;

Women's Wear Daily, periodical.

GOVERNMENT AND POLITICS

by JOHN LOUIS RECCHIUTI

CONTENTS

Sidebars and tables are listed in italics.

1930

Jan. Unemployment reaches four million.

10 Feb. In Chicago more than one hundred people are arrested for distributing whiskey. Bootlegging has increased as opposition grows to Prohibition, instituted in 1919 by the Eighteenth Amendment to the Constitution.

17 June President Herbert Hoover signs into law the Smoot-Hawley Tariff Act, setting tariffs on imported goods at the highest rates in American history.

3 July President Hoover signs into law an act establishing the Veterans Administration.

21 July The Senate confirms the London Naval Treaty, in which the United States, Great Britain, and Japan agree to limitations on the size of their navies. The treaty supplements the Washington Naval Treaty of 1922, which also includes limitation agreements.

4 Nov. In the congressional elections the Democratic Party gains a majority in the House of Representatives. In the Senate the Democrats gain eight seats, leaving the Republicans in the majority by 48–47. The remaining seat is held by a member of the Farmer-Labor Party.

11 Dec. One of the largest banks in the country, the Bank of the United States in New York, closes. Its more than four hundred thousand depositors lose most of their savings.

20 Dec. At President Hoover's request Congress passes legislation appropriating $116 million for public-works projects.

1931

7 Jan. President Hoover's committee on unemployment reports that almost five million Americans are without work.

19 Jan. The Wickersham Committee, appointed by President Hoover, says Prohibition is not working and calls for revisions in the Eighteenth Amendment and federal laws that support its enforcement.

27 Feb. Congress overrides President Hoover's veto of the Veterans' Bonus Act, which will lend veterans of World War I 50 percent of a bonus they were promised in 1924.

3 Mar. President Hoover signs a bill making "The Star-Spangled Banner" the national anthem.

20 June President Hoover proposes a moratorium on the payment of debts incurred during World War I. French delays in agreeing to Hoover's proposal cause a further deepening of the worldwide economic crisis.

July In Iowa and Kansas farmers stage strikes and demonstrations as prices for their crops continue to tumble.

Sept.–Oct. Hoarding of gold increases as the economic depression worsens; banks are failing in great numbers (522 close during October alone), and their depositors, uninsured by the government, lose most of their savings.

1932

7 Jan.   Secretary of State Henry L. Stimson announces, "The United States cannot admit the legality nor does it intend to recognize" the puppet government Japan has installed in Manchuria after a successful invasion of that northern province of China. His assertion that the United States will not accept any Japanese action that endangers the sovereignty of China or the Open Door trade policy, by which the Western powers maintain equal trading rights in Asia, becomes known as the Stimson Doctrine.

2 Feb.   On the recommendation of President Hoover, Congress establishes the Reconstruction Finance Corporation, giving it wide-ranging power to extend credit to private banks and businesses. In half a year it authorizes more than a billion dollars in loans to banks, insurance companies, and farmers' credit corporations.

27 Feb.   Congress passes the Glass-Steagall Credit Expansion Act, making $750 million of the government gold reserve available for industrial and business needs.

23 Mar.   Congress passes the Norris–La Guardia Act, which is then signed by President Hoover; the legislation is hailed by labor for its restrictions on federal injunctions against strikers.

29 May   Calling themselves the "Bonus Army," a thousand veterans of World War I arrive in Washington, D.C., hoping to persuade Congress to pay them all the bonus money promised them in 1924. Within weeks about twenty thousand of them are camped out in shanty towns around the city.

21 July   Congress passes the Emergency Relief and Reconstruction Act, increasing to $3 billion the amount of money the Reconstruction Finance Corporation can loan to states and businesses.

22 July   Congress passes the Federal Home Loan Bank Act, making $125 million available to financial institutions in an effort to reduce foreclosures and encourage new housing starts.

28 July   The remnant of the Bonus Army is routed from its camp at the Anacostia Flats in Washington, D.C., by U.S. Army troops under the command of Gen. Douglas MacArthur.

1 Sept.   Mayor James "Jimmy" Walker of New York resigns while under investigation for corruption.

31 Oct.   President Hoover warns that "the grass will grow in streets of a hundred cities" if the Democratic presidential candidate, Gov. Franklin D. Roosevelt of New York, wins the election.

8 Nov.   Franklin D. Roosevelt is elected president of the United States, winning 472 votes in the Electoral College to Hoover's 59. Democrats gain 90 seats in the House of Representatives and 13 in the Senate.

1933

- Congress passes the Farm Credit Act to help farmers refinance the mortgages on their farms rather than lose them to foreclosure.

- Congress passes the Emergency Railroad Transportation Act to allow the financial reorganization of the nation's railroads.

- Congress passes the National Industrial Recovery Act (NIRA), which establishes the Public Works Administration (PWA) and the National Recovery Administration (NRA). This act is the last major piece of legislation passed during President Roosevelt's first one hundred days in office.

- Congress passes the Agricultural Adjustment Act (AAA), designed to raise sagging prices of farm products by restricting production.

- Approximately 25 percent of working-age Americans are unemployed.

4 Feb.   Louisiana declares a one-day bank "holiday" in an effort to stem the tide of depositors withdrawing their savings.

6 Feb.   The Twentieth Amendment to the U.S. Constitution, the "lame duck" amendment, is ratified. It moves the date of the presidential inauguration from 4 March to 20 January and sets the beginning of terms for senators and congressmen as 3 January, which is also established as the first day of the new session.

14 Feb.   The governor of Michigan declares an eight-day bank holiday. Twenty-one other states quickly follow suit.

15 Feb.   In Miami, Florida, Italian immigrant Joseph Zangara fires six shots at President-elect Roosevelt. Though he misses Roosevelt, others in the party are wounded, and Mayor Anton J. Cermak of Chicago dies a few days later.

25 Feb.   The USS *Ranger,* the first U.S. aircraft carrier, is christened at Newport News, Virginia.

4 Mar.   Franklin D. Roosevelt is inaugurated as president of the United States.

5 Mar.   President Roosevelt declares a four-day national banking holiday and calls for a special session of Congress to open on 9 March.

9 Mar.   Congress convenes to deal with the banking crisis, beginning the "First Hundred Days" of the "First New Deal." The special session runs until 16 June and passes many bills designed to improve the economy and ease the suffering of the poor and unemployed.

The Emergency Banking Relief Act is introduced, passed by both houses of Congress, and signed by the president.

12 Mar.   President Roosevelt's first "Fireside Chat" is broadcast over the radio.

15 Mar.   The National Association for the Advancement of Colored People (NAACP) unsuccessfully sues the University of North Carolina on behalf of Thomas Hocutt. The suit serves as an opening salvo in the NAACP's drive against segregation in American education.

20 Mar.   Congress passes the Economy Act, reducing government salaries and veterans' benefits and reorganizing some government agencies in the face of price deflation brought on by the Depression.

22 Mar.   Congress legalizes alcoholic beverages with 3.2 percent or less alcohol content by weight, signaling the beginning of the end for Prohibition.

31 Mar.   Congress passes the Reforestation Relief Act, which establishes the Civilian Conservation Corps (CCC) to provide work for unemployed young men. By 1941 it will have employed more than two million.

19 Apr.   The United States officially abandons the gold standard.

12 May   Congress approves the Federal Emergency Relief Act, creating the Federal Emergency Relief Administration (FERA) to spend $500 million in grants to the states.

18 May   Congress establishes the Tennessee Valley Authority (TVA) to control flooding and provide electricity to the region.

27 May	Congress passes the Truth-in-Securities Act, designed to keep investors informed about the stocks and bonds in which they invest.
12 June–27 July	At the London Economic Conference, European nations and the United States are unable to develop a plan for international cooperation in ending the wide fluctuation of exchange rates and reducing trade barriers.
13 June	Congress passes the Home Owners' Refinancing Act, which creates the Home Owners' Loan Corporation (HOLC) to help people avoid foreclosure by refinancing their home mortgages.
16 June	Congress passes the Glass-Steagall Banking Act, which forbids banks to sell stocks and bonds and creates the Federal Deposit Insurance Corporation (FDIC) to insure deposits against bank failure; initially, the FDIC insures only deposits under $5,000.
5 Aug.	The National Labor Board, authorized under the NIRA, is established by President Roosevelt.
20 Oct.	The American Federation of Labor (AFL) begins a boycott of German-made goods in response to the rising Nazi antiunion sentiment in Germany.
7 Nov.	Fiorello La Guardia is elected mayor of New York on a Fusion ticket.
8 Nov.	Congress authorizes the Civil Works Administration (CWA) to give work to the unemployed.
16 Nov.	The United States formally recognizes the Soviet Union, sixteen years after the Bolshevik Revolution of 1917.
5 Dec.	The Twenty-first Amendment to the Constitution is adopted, repealing the Eighteenth Amendment.

1934

- Arthur L. Mitchell of Chicago becomes the first African American elected to Congress as a Democrat.
- Congress passes the National Housing Act, which establishes the Federal Housing Administration (FHA).

30 Jan.	Congress passes the Gold Reserve Act of 1934, giving the government greater control over the value of the dollar.
31 Jan.	Congress passes the Farm Mortgage Refinancing Act.
2 Feb.	The Export-Import Bank of Washington, D.C., is created through funding from the Reconstruction Finance Corporation to promote international trade.
15 Feb.	Congress passes the Civil Works Emergency Relief Act, authorizing an additional $950 million to be spent on civil-works projects.
23 Feb.	Congress passes the Crop Loan Act, which gives farmers loans for planting and harvesting their crops.
27 Mar.	The federal government authorizes the building of a thousand airplanes and a hundred warships within five years.
12 Apr.	The Senate authorizes the Nye Committee to look into profiteering by U.S. businesses during World War I.

28 Apr.   In an effort to revive the building industry Congress passes the Home Owners' Loan Act to help people buy new houses or refinance their current homes.

6 June   Congress passes the Securities Exchange Act, which creates the Securities and Exchange Commission (SEC) to regulate stock exchanges.

12 June   Congress passes the Trade Agreements Act, authorizing the president to cut tariffs for nations that grant the United States "most-favored-nation" trading status.

19 June   Congress creates the Federal Communications Commission (FCC) to oversee the telephone, telegraph, and radio industries.

28 June   Congress passes the Frazier-Lemke Farm Bankruptcy Act, creating a five-year moratorium on farm-mortgage foreclosures. On the same day it also passes the Taylor Grazing Act to prevent further wind erosion of the western plains by setting up a program to control grazing.

16 July   In solidarity with striking longshoremen, a general strike begins in San Francisco.

6 Aug.   The United States withdraws its troops from Haiti, where they have been since 1915, when President Woodrow Wilson sent in U.S. Marines to impose martial law after a coup toppled the government of Guillaume Sam.

6 Nov.   Gaining nine seats in both the Senate and House, Democrats increase their strength in Congress.

29 Dec.   The Japanese denounce the Washington Naval Treaty of 1922.

1935

4 Jan.   The "Second New Deal" begins as President Roosevelt outlines a program for social reform that will benefit laborers and small farmers.

8 Apr.   The Works Progress Administration (WPA) is created under the auspices of the Emergency Relief Appropriation Act; the WPA will employ more than eight million people in building parks, airports, and highways.

27 Apr.   Congress passes the Soil Conservation Act, which establishes the Soil Conservation Service.

11 May   By executive order President Roosevelt establishes the Rural Electrification Administration.

27 May   The NIRA is declared unconstitutional by the U.S. Supreme Court.

26 June   The National Youth Administration is established under the WPA to provide jobs for Americans aged sixteen to twenty-five.

5 July   Congress passes the National Labor Relations Act, which strengthens the National Labor Relations Board (NLRB) and restores the right of workers to form unions, which was part of the NIRA.

14 Aug.   Congress passes the Social Security Act.

26 Aug.   Congress authorizes the Public Utilities Act.

31 Aug.   Congress passes the Neutrality Act of 1935, which outlaws shipment of arms to countries at war.

| 8 Sept. | Sen. Huey Long of Louisiana, founder of the "Share-Our-Wealth" Societies, is assassinated. |
| 30 Dec. | The United Auto Workers (UAW) begins a wildcat sit-down strike in Flint, Michigan. |

1936

Jan.	First Lady Eleanor Roosevelt begins publishing a syndicated column called *My Day*.
6 Jan.	The U.S. Supreme Court declares the AAA unconstitutional.
29 Feb.	Congress passes the Neutrality Act of 1936, which extends and augments the Neutrality Act of 1935.
June	Mary McLeod Bethune is appointed head of the Division of Negro Affairs in the National Youth Administration.
3 Nov.	Franklin D. Roosevelt is elected to a second term as president in a landslide victory over Republican Alfred M. Landon of Kansas. There will be only 89 Republicans in the new House of Representatives and only 16 in the Senate.
8 Dec.	The NAACP files *Gibbs* v. *Board of Education;* the Supreme Court decision in the case establishes the precedent of paying black schoolteachers the same salaries as white schoolteachers.

1937

6 Jan.	The U.S. Congress outlaws supplying weapons to either side in the Spanish Civil War.
20 Jan.	President Roosevelt begins his second term, declaring, "I see one-third of a nation ill-housed, ill-clad, ill-nourished."
5 Feb.	President Roosevelt requests that Congress pass legislation to increase the number of justices on the U.S. Supreme Court to as many as fifteen. His proposal is decried as "court packing" by many.
1 Mar.	Congress passes the Supreme Court Retirement Act, which provides for justices to retire at seventy with full pay if they wish.
	U.S. Steel recognizes the United Steelworkers as the collective bargaining agent for its employees.
29 Mar.	The U.S. Supreme Court upholds the principle of a minimum wage for women.
12 Apr.	The U.S. Supreme Court upholds the constitutionality of the National Labor Relations Act.
1 May	Congress passes a third Neutrality Act, introducing the "cash-and-carry" policy, which allows warring nations to buy weapons (but not ammunition) if they pay for them in cash and carry them away on their own ships.
24 May	The U.S. Supreme Court validates the Social Security Act.
22 July	Congress establishes the Farm Security Administration (FSA), which offers low-interest loans to sharecroppers and farm laborers.

2 Sept.   President Roosevelt signs the National Housing Act, creating the U.S. Housing Authority.

5 Oct.   President Roosevelt urges an international "quarantine" of aggressor nations in an effort to preserve peace.

12 Dec.   Japanese planes bomb and sink the U.S. gunboat *Panay* on the Yangtze River in China; two American sailors are killed. Two days later Japan formally apologizes for the incident, but relations between the Japan and the United States are further strained.

1938

- The stock market, after recovering somewhat in previous years, falls by fifty points between August 1937 and March 1938.

3 Jan.   President Roosevelt's State of the Union message focuses on the need to strengthen the nation's defenses.

11 Jan.   Prime Minister Neville Chamberlain of Great Britain rejects President Roosevelt's proposal for a world conference on arms reduction.

28 Jan.   President Roosevelt proposes major military spending in an effort to shore up the nation's defenses.

16 Feb.   President Roosevelt signs the second Agricultural Administration Act, replacing the first AAA, which had been declared unconstitutional in 1936.

17 May   Congress authorizes a ten-year program to build up the U.S. Navy.

26 May   The House Un-American Activities Committee (HUAC) is established.

27 May   Congress reduces corporate taxes in an effort to stimulate the economy.

25 June   Congress passes the Fair Labor Standards Act, establishing federal standards for the length of the workweek (forty-four hours) and a minimum wage (initially forty cents an hour). It also prohibits the employment of children under sixteen at many sorts of labor.

4 July   President Roosevelt declares that the South is "the nation's No. 1 economic problem" in a message to the National Emergency Council.

27 Sept.   President Roosevelt appeals to Hitler for a peaceful solution to the crisis in the Sudetenland.

29 Sept.   The Munich Pact, signed by Hitler and Prime Minister Chamberlain of Great Britain, cedes the Sudetenland to Germany.

8 Nov.   Republicans register their first congressional gains since the beginning of the Depression by gaining seven seats in the Senate and eighty in the House of Representatives; despite their loses, Democrats retain commanding majorities in both houses of Congress.

14 Nov.   The United States recalls its ambassador from Germany in protest over the treatment of German Jews; the German ambassador is recalled to his country four days later.

1939

4 Jan.   In his State of the Union message President Roosevelt stresses the dire international situation.

5 Jan.	The president's budget calls for more than a billion dollars for national defense.
27 Feb.	The U.S. Supreme Court rules wildcat strikes (strikes in violation of a contract) to be illegal.
1 Apr.	The United States recognizes the government of Gen. Francisco Franco in Spain.
3 Apr.	Congress passes the Administrative Reorganization Act of 1939, aimed at increasing government efficiency.
14 Apr.	President Roosevelt appeals to Adolf Hitler of Germany and Benito Mussolini of Italy to ensure European peace, and he calls for a world disarmament conference.
16 May	The U.S. Department of Agriculture introduces food stamps, which needy people can redeem for surplus agricultural goods.
1 July	The Federal Works Agency (FWA) is established to consolidate several New Deal programs and allow for staff reductions.
2 Aug.	Congress passes the Hatch Act, which prohibits federal employees from participating in political campaigns.
	Albert Einstein writes President Roosevelt a letter about the possibility of building an atomic bomb.
1 Sept.	Germany invades Poland; the Second World War begins.
3 Sept.	Responding to the German invasion of Poland on 1 September, Great Britain and France declare war on Germany. On the same day thirty Americans are killed when Germany sinks a British passenger ship; President Roosevelt restates U.S. neutrality.
4 Sept.	Secretary of State Cordell Hull asks Americans to keep their travel to Europe to a minimum.
5 Sept.	President Roosevelt officially declares U.S. neutrality and bans the export of weapons to warring nations.
8 Sept.	President Roosevelt declares a limited state of emergency, giving him the ability to act quickly if needed.
11 Oct.	The NAACP Legal Defense and Education Fund is organized and pledges an all-out fight against discrimination.
18 Oct.	The president declares U.S. territorial waters off-limits to the submarines of the warring nations.
20 Oct.	The U.S. government recognizes the Polish government in exile.
4 Nov.	A fourth Neutrality Act repeals all but the "cash and carry" clauses of the previous restrictions on supplying belligerents with arms.
30 Nov.	The United States declares its support for Finland as that nation is invaded by the Soviet Union.

OVERVIEW

The Depression Decade. In the United States the greatest legacy of the years 1930–1939 was the creation of the modern bureaucratic welfare state, which arose in response to the worst economic collapse in national history. Unlike other economic crises, the Great Depression was not short-lived. It persisted throughout the 1930s, affecting all aspects of society. The critical political controversy of the decade focused on how government ought to be used to bring the Depression to an end. Every political quarter proposed solutions. In the desperate times of severe economic crisis patience often grew thin, and debates became strident. The major political contest took place between Republicans and Democrats. Together these parties consistently drew about 97 percent of ballots cast, and the debate over how to end the Depression was generally carried out on ideological terrain defined by individuals and groups within them. Yet other groups — with a broad spectrum of alternative political visions — also influenced the debate and sometimes policy. On the political Left were small numbers of socialists, communists, and anarcho-syndicalists; and on what is sometimes called the "far Right" there were tiny groups of American fascists and Nazi sympathizers. The severity of the Depression and the immediacy of the need to bring the nation back to prosperity galvanized politics in the 1930s. Still, the problems of the United States in the Great Depression must be kept in perspective. For all of the hardships, most Americans continued to work; and in contrast to other countries suffering from the international economic depression, the United States remained among the wealthiest nations in the world.

President Hoover's Problem. Republican Herbert Hoover was president when the stock market crashed on 29 October 1929. This crash on Wall Street in New York was part of a series of events — a sort of chain reaction — in which unemployment, credit contraction, deflation, depressed agricultural prices, and international problems all played parts. With the economy spiraling downward, the pressing question became what, if anything, government should do. President Hoover's first response to the onset of the Depression was to allow traditional market forces to make correctives with a minimum of government intervention. In this view the overheated economy would self-adjust if given time. As Andrew Mellon, Hoo-

ver's secretary of the treasury, declared, it was necessary to "purge the rottenness out of the system" by allowing the downturn to run its expected course. Hoover himself asserted that "Economic depression cannot be cured by legislative action or executive pronouncements. Economic wounds must be healed by the action of the cells of the economic body — the producers and consumers themselves." While seeking to convey a spirit of optimism, Hoover also met with business leaders and asked them to keep their workers' wages at current levels, even if working hours had to be cut back. This measure, it was hoped, would keep prices up and give workers purchasing power, but it did not work. Unemployment rose precipitously, and the economy staggered. By early 1932, with the November elections less than a year away, Hoover changed course away from his initial "laissez-faire" approach and initiated the greatest peacetime government expenditure program in the nation's history to that time. The Reconstruction Finance Corporation (RFC) made more than one billion dollars of federal money available in "loans for income producing . . . enterprises which will increase employment." When the hoped-for recovery did not materialize, Hoover was routed by Democrat Franklin D. Roosevelt in the 1932 presidential election.

The New Deal. Using the democratic measuring stick of popular votes, there can be no doubt that Franklin D. Roosevelt, the Democrats, and the New Deal dominated the 1930s. Roosevelt's take-charge, action-oriented, pragmatic brand of politics was welcomed by most Americans who had watched as the number of shanty towns — called "Hoovervilles" by many — grew larger. Alongside poverty, strikes by industrial workers increased and were sometimes violent and bloody. Voices from the political Left and Right captured people's attention in ways that they had not done in pre-Depression years. In response Roosevelt's political program promised a reshuffling of the cards of American government, economy, and society in a "New Deal" for the American people. The New Deal set out to bring relief, recovery, and reform, and in the process the federal government was vastly expanded. Roosevelt accomplished his sweeping legislative reforms (and his election to four terms as president) by building the New Deal coalition, which was to endure for more than two decades after his death. Drawing together elements from urban ethnic groups, labor, women, African Americans, and middle-class liberals, Roosevelt used, for the first time in American history, the power of government to sustain a series of bureaucratic institutions to administer such new programs as unemployment insurance, public housing, and social security. The New Deal created the modern welfare state.

The First New Deal. When Franklin D. Roosevelt took office on 4 March 1933, unemployment was at 25 percent nationwide. In Toledo, Ohio, three-quarters of those looking for work could find none. There was no federal welfare system, no federal unemployment insurance, no public housing. When people did not find work, they turned of necessity to charitable organizations that were usually run by churches and synagogues. The enormity of the Depression overwhelmed these traditional means of aid to the needy, and it became clear to the president that government-run relief efforts were required. Within exactly one hundred days of taking office, Roosevelt introduced fifteen major legislative bills to Congress. All were passed. In the next two years Roosevelt embarked on a vast array of relief and reform programs in an effort to place the U. S. economy on its feet. To bring the economy back from the brink, the initial stages of the New Deal allowed limited collusion among businessmen in setting prices and standards within an industry. To increase employment, and with it consumer spending, the New Deal used deficit spending, pouring billions of dollars into relief and jobs programs. It dealt with the banking and securities-market crises through reform legislation and bolstered farmers' beleaguered economic position with price supports.

The Second New Deal. In 1935 Roosevelt made a decided move to the political Left in what historians have labeled "the Second New Deal." Less than two years into his first term, the economy began to falter. Though the federal government had pumped billions into works proj-

ects and relief, the much-vaunted recovery had not taken shape. Roosevelt was pilloried from both the Right and Left by popular figures such as Sen. Huey Long of Louisiana, Father Charles Coughlin, the "radio priest" of Detroit, and Dr. Francis Townsend of California. In response Roosevelt orchestrated the beginning of the modern welfare state. A significant part of this "new Roosevelt" was his anticorporate tone. His "Soak the Rich" progressive tax (which proposed taxes as heavy as 75 percent on the wealthiest Americans) and his efforts to rein in the power of utility trusts marked a break with the relief policies of the previous two years. The keystone of this Second New Deal phase of Roosevelt's reform efforts, however, was the Social Security Act of 1935.

Isolationism. The United States did not enter World War II in September 1939, when England and France declared war on a belligerent Germany. During most of the 1930s Americans were deeply isolationist. One poll revealed that 64 percent of Americans supported isolationist policies as late as 1937. Nevertheless, after the Hitler-Stalin Pact of August 1939 and the German invasion of less than a month later, the isolationist mood in the United States waned. By the end of the decade, with war raging across Europe and relations between the United States and Japan becoming increasingly tense, the United States had begun to prepare for war.

The Depression Ends in War. Though the economy had somewhat recovered by the end of the 1930s, many problems remained. Unemployment, an important economic indicator, remained extremely high. In 1939, 9.5 million Americans (17 percent of the labor force) were out of work. Not until the United States entered World War II in 1941 did the Great Depression finally come to an end. It ended not so much because of the actions of presidents or political parties but because of the military expenditures of World War II.

TOPICS IN THE NEWS

AMERICA AND THE CRISIS OF THE DEPRESSION

Hoover's "Rugged Individualism." Herbert Hoover was elected president in the economically flush times of the late 1920s. During the 1920s the gross national product of the United States rose an astonishing 25 percent. Millions of Americans purchased refrigerators, washing machines, radios, and cars for the first time. In this economic boom many Americans attributed the nation's success to the ideology of "business Republicanism." They believed that the nation would flourish in proportion to the support that large and small businesses received from government. They supported policies that made mills, mines, banks, factories, and farms more profitable: a protective tariff, right-to-work (that is, antiunion) laws, the gold standard, and a government that purposively restrained itself from intervention in capitalist markets. From 1921 onward, during nearly a decade of dynamic and expansive growth, Americans elected business Republican presidents. Their view was summarized by Republican president Calvin Coolidge in 1924: "The chief business of America is business." Herbert Hoover, coined the term *rugged individualism* during his 1928 presidential campaign: "We were challenged with a peace-time choice between the American system of rugged individualism and a European philosophy of diametrically opposed doctrines — doctrines of paternalism and state socialism," he said in a campaign speech and added that America had chosen well, opting for the path to prosperity. During this campaign Hoover capitalized on the successes of the Republican Party in the 1920s and on the apparent health of the economy, and he won. One indication of the American spirit of optimism in 1928 was Hoover's assertion that "We in America today are nearer to the final triumph over poverty than ever before in the history of any land. The poorhouse is vanishing from among us. . . . We shall soon with the help of God be in sight of the day when poverty will be banished from this nation." At the 1928 Republican National Convention this sentiment was greeted by wide acclaim. A little more than a year later, the mood of the nation was dramatically different.

The Crash. Only seven months after Hoover's in-auguration as president, he faced an enormous economic crisis. On Tuesday, 29 October 1929, the stock market crashed. Stock prices plummeted. On 3 September General Electric stock had traded at $396 a share; by 13 November it was trading at $168. Stock prices for General Motors, Woolworth, and Westinghouse declined by one-half. Similar stories were repeated across the stock index. Tens of thousands of investors who had purchased stocks on margins went bankrupt. (It was estimated that at the time of the crash about one million Americans had purchased some stocks on margin bids.) Others suffered severe economic losses, and the ramifications of the ensuing economic downturn were enormous. Between 1929 and 1933 the real gross domestic product — a measure of how the economy is faring — fell by 30 percent. In human terms this decline meant unemployment, homelessness, and heartache for millions. People who had been gainfully employed only weeks before spent sleepless nights wondering how they would pay mortgages or buy food for their children. Managers, office clerks, and laborers turned to selling apples on the streets; many scrounged through garbage cans in alleys behind restaurants in hopes of finding food. In New York a forty-eight-year-old man died after carrying a bag of coal, given to him by city workers, up a flight of stairs. According to *The New York Times,* witnesses attributed his death partly to "the bitter disappointment of a long day's fruitless attempt to prevent himself and his family being put out on the street." By 1933 an astonishing 25 percent of the labor force — thirteen million people — were unemployed. Personal income fell, on average, by 25 percent in these same years. Without jobs people could not pay debts, and thousands were evicted from their farms, houses, or apartments. One man wrote the president in imperfect English, "If I wont get any help . . . I will take my life away." Another wrote the chief executive, "I am badly in need of your help. . . . The doctor came [and] said that they [the children] was not getting enough to eat."

Encouraging Words, Traditional Practice. In early 1930 President Hoover offered words of encouragement and optimism, proclaiming on one occasion (against all the evidence) that the "fundamental business of the country is on a sound and prosperous basis." Otherwise, he

A Seattle "Hooverville," one of many shantytowns set up by homeless people in or near major cities in the United States during the 1930s

kept the government out of the way of the hoped-for self-adjustments in the capitalist markets. Eight months after the stock-market crash, however, the president and Congress made what is now considered to have been a major blunder. Congress enacted the Smoot-Hawley Tariff, which the president signed into law on 17 June 1930. Promoted by the Republican Party, the new law raised tariffs (taxes on goods coming into United States from foreign countries) to 49 percent on agricultural raw materials and 34 percent on many manufactured goods — the highest levels in American history. The tariff proved to be a disaster. Within two years America's major trading partners retaliated by putting up high tariff barriers of their own. As a result, the already bad international economic situation worsened. By spring 1931 international financial woes, exacerbated by the Smoot-Hawley Tariff, reached a crisis level. Soon it was clear that the Depression was worldwide. There would be no quick recovery.

Hoover's Political Downfall. At the time, however, people could not know how long and how severe the

Depression would be. The nation had experienced many economic crises in the past, and the mechanisms of the capitalist marketplace had generally restored prosperity without much government intervention. President Hoover's lack of action during the opening months of the crisis should not be viewed as uncaring. It was a calculated effort to allow the economy to bounce back on its own. In 1929 economic experts generally agreed that government intervention would only serve to slow the recovery. Nevertheless, the president's inaction was interpreted by many as a failure of office. The political ideology of business Republicanism that had suited the three previous presidents became an albatross around Hoover's neck.

The "Bonus Army." Amid the precipitous decline in the national economy, President Hoover faced another public-relations nightmare. Americans who had served in World War I, which President Woodrow Wilson had labeled "the war to end all wars," had been promised bonuses to be paid by the federal government in 1945 —

as a kind of retirement supplement for risking their lives defending democracy. With the onslaught of the Great Depression, many veterans called for early payment of their bonuses. In February 1931 Congress agreed to lend them half their bonus money but would not pay them their full bonuses outright, in part because the available money in the U.S. Treasury was shrinking in the economic downturn. Beginning in May 1932, some twenty thousand veterans started arriving in Washington and setting up "Bonus Army" encampments around the city, insisting that they would stay until Congress met their demands. In mid July police tried to drive some of these veterans from some empty federal buildings they had occupied. In the confusion that ensued, police shot and killed two protesters. Many in the "Bonus Army" still refused to leave the nation's capital. President Hoover ordered the U.S. Army to come to the aid of police. On 28 July, armed with machine guns, tear gas, and bayonets, active-duty military men under the command of Gen. Douglas MacArthur chased the Bonus Army down Pennsylvania Avenue and burned their encampment to the ground. In the melee a baby was killed and more than one hundred protesters were injured. Newspaper accounts associated the president with this debacle in Washington and increased adverse public opinion of him.

Hoover Changes Course. By mid 1931 Hoover understood that his earlier economic policies were not working. He reversed his earlier course and embraced a policy of federal economic activism. He also understood that economic recovery in the United States would be predicated upon improvements in the international financial picture. To address these problems he urged that major adjustments be made in international finance. In June he suggested a suspension of international debts. On the domestic front he promoted, and Congress enacted, increased funding for home-loan banks. In early 1932 Hoover also championed the enactment of the Glass-Steagall Credit Expansion Act and the creation of the Reconstruction Finance Corporation (RFC). The RFC was the largest federal loan program up to that time. With a budget of $1.5 billion it made money available for states to develop relief programs and public works. It also provided federal loans to corporations and banks. Yet because of Hoover's ideological views, the federal government gave no direct assistance to the unemployed and hungry, and in the apportioning of funds, the Hoover administration was cautious. Only a fifth of the budgeted funds were actually spent, and those were generally given out as loans or to projects that raised revenue (and so could return the borrowed money to the federal treasury). The economy worsened.

Sources:

Frederick Lewis Allen, *Only Yesterday: An Informal History of the Nineteen-Twenties* (New York: Harper, 1931);

William J. Barber, *From New Era to New Deal: Herbert Hoover, the Economists, and American Economic Policy, 1921–1933* (Cambridge & New York: Cambridge University Press, 1985);

Set up in anticipation of veterans' bonus checks, this bank at a Bonus Army encampment in Washington, D.C., closed after Congress failed to pass the Bonus Bill.

Otis L. Graham Jr., *An Encore for Reform: The Old Progressives and the New Deal* (New York: Oxford University Press, 1967);

Joan Hoff-Wilson, *Herbert Hoover, Forgotten Progressive* (Boston: Little, Brown, 1975);

Elliot Rosen, *Hoover, Roosevelt, and the Brains Trust: From Depression to New Deal* (New York: Columbia University Press, 1977).

DEMOCRACY AND THE NEW DEAL

Progressivism Resurgent. In the 1932 presidential election Hoover was easily defeated by the Democratic governor of New York, Franklin D. Roosevelt. Roosevelt's political program called for a vastly expanded role for the federal government. Under this "New Deal" a broad array of modern liberal reforms — from government regulation of industries to social security for the elderly, young, and handicapped — were implemented. The ideas of these and other like-minded reforms was not wholly new to the American political landscape. The New Deal was the politics of progressivism resurgent. From 1900 until 1917 political progressivism had galvanized American politics. Progressivism had its heyday in 1912, when, under the banner of Franklin Roosevelt's distant cousin Theodore Roosevelt, the Progressive Party had placed second in the presidential election — behind Woodrow Wilson and the Democrats but ahead of incumbent president William Howard Taft and the Republicans. The Progressive Party platform had called for "a system of social insurance" to be used "against the hazards of sickness, irregular employment and old age." It had also called for "a strong National regulation of inter-

In 1932 most African Americans who were able to vote cast their ballots for Republicans, as they had since the Civil War. Blacks voted for the Republican Party because, as the party of Abraham Lincoln, it had freed them from slavery and supported them during the Reconstruction period. By 1936, however, more than 90 percent were voting the Democratic ticket. President Roosevelt and the New Deal had won their allegiance. (About the same percentage of African Americans vote Democratic in the 1990s.)

Though Roosevelt's support of civil rights for African Americans was weak and halting, they appreciated what he had done. Roosevelt appointed African Americans to important positions within his administration, and one group of African American men and women — led by Mary McLeod Bethune, William Hastie, and Robert Weaver — became known as the "Black Cabinet." The African American community also benefited from the New Deal relief programs and from the Social Security Act. One historian has estimated that about one-third of blacks received governmental assistance. For a group that was used to being "the bottom rail" in society, such support was welcomed, even if clearly inadequate.

Roosevelt had to be cautious, however, in helping blacks because he also needed the votes of the white racists in the South and elsewhere in the nation. Catering to the white vote, Roosevelt did not support a federal antilynching law aimed at stopping the murders of blacks by racist whites. The Roosevelt administration's federal farm policies offered almost no assistance to poor sharecroppers (black and white alike), many of whom were evicted from the land they worked by its owners. Furthermore, the Works Progress Administration and other New Deal programs almost invariably gave blacks the lowest-paying jobs. It is a telling measure of the intensity of racism in the 1930s that despite all these problems African Americans rushed to support the Democrats.

Source: David E. Kyvig, ed., *FDR's America* (Saint Charles, Mo.: Forum Press, 1976).

Raymond Moley and President-elect Franklin D. Roosevelt working on Roosevelt's first inaugural address in the library at Hyde Park

Roosevelt's policies brought to completion the political project his cousin had begun a quarter century before.

"The Brain Trust." Intellectuals have contributed mightily to the creation of the national political agenda throughout the twentieth century, but their power was nowhere more impressive than during the New Deal. In the months prior to the 1932 election, Roosevelt repeatedly consulted three Columbia University professors: Raymond Moley, Rexford G. Tugwell, and Adolf Berle. Roosevelt came to rely on their proposals for solving the nation's economic and social ills. Taking note of Roosevelt's frequent meetings with these three men, a reporter for *The New York Times* labeled the professors the "brains trust" (later, "brain trust"). The leading member of the group was Raymond Moley, a professor of government and public law at Columbia. Moley had assisted Roosevelt as early as 1928 in preparing political speeches, and he had served on several of Governor Roosevelt's commissions in New York State. It was Moley who incorporated the phrase *New Deal* into Roosevelt's acceptance speech at the 1932 Democratic National Convention and earlier collaborated with Roosevelt on the April 1932 radio speech asserting that the government must think in terms of "the forgotten man at the bottom of the economic totem pole" — sounding a theme that reverberated throughout the campaign. Moley also deserves much credit for steering Roosevelt toward increasing the role of the federal government in the economy and a lion's share of the credit for promoting massive government deficit spending in "an emergency budget." Moley's emergency-

State corporations," for the prohibition of child labor, for progressive taxation, and for greater protection for unions. These and many other goals of the progressives were instantiated in the legislative framework of the New Deal. Indeed, it would not be unfair to say that Franklin

Franklin Delano Roosevelt was a member of one of the wealthiest families in the nation, one that could trace its American heritage back to a Dutch farmer who settled in New Netherlands in 1644, not long before it was ceded to the British and became New York. Aristocratic, handsome, and well educated, he might have been a snob, but he was not. His charismatic charm and reassuring, patrician fatherliness made him remarkably popular with the American people throughout his presidency. One measure of the people's affection for Roosevelt was the large number of portraits of him that ordinary Americans hung on the walls of their homes. Another was the enormous amount of mail he received.

On average about five thousand Americans in all walks of life wrote to President Roosevelt each day. In the week after his first inauguration alone, almost half a million Americans wrote to their president. The volume of mail he received dwarfed that which even the most popular presidents had received before him. In previous administrations one person had generally been employed to open and sort the president's mail. Fifty people were needed to sort Roosevelt's, and First Lady Eleanor Roosevelt received a large amount of mail as well.

Among the most moving letters to the president were the simple, sometimes inarticulate letters from poor and working-class Americans who were reaching out for understanding, consolation, or help. One such letter, dated 10 April 1934, came from a man with five children in Middletown, New York:

> Mr. President:
>
> I am badly in need of your help. I have a home but I have a mortgage and they have hand me notice that they are goint to close said mortgage because I am not able to pay. . . . Now, Mr. President, we are in a land of plenty but I see that good many of us are starving. I am a world war veteran. Mr. President try to Help me in this thing if you can. I do not ask this for me but for my children. Thank you.

In another letter — written on 24 October 1934 from Columbus, Georgia — an unemployed cotton-mill worker outlined the economic hardships he and his family were undergoing and asked, "wont you try to help us wont you appeal, 'for us all,' to the real estate people and the factories." Its author concluded, simply, "I've always thought of F.D.R. as my personal friend."

Still another letter — written in spring 1936 from Oliver Spring, Tennessee, and signed simply "J.B." — said, "All of the working men are for you. For you sure have been good to the Poor and help us out, and we sure do aprishate your kindness."

Source: Robert S. McElvaine, *Down and Out in the Depression: Letters from the "Forgotten Man"* (Chapel Hill: University of North Carolina Press, 1983).

spending plan, which included direct federal payments to destitute Americans, came to fruition in the Federal Emergency Relief Administration and other New Deal agencies. An economist, Tugwell headed the planning of the Roosevelt administration's farm policy and served for a time in the U.S. Department of Agriculture. His radical call for the nation to forsake capitalism for an economy planned by the government never took root. Adolf A. Berle Jr., a law professor at Columbia, regarded Tugwell's notions of a planned economy as untenable, though he did sympathize with the need to regulate business by governmental action. Berle was a major architect in the expansion of the Reconstruction Finance Corporation and in the development of federal farm and home owners' mortgage programs. In fact, the brain trust shaped much of the legislation that President Roosevelt sent to Congress during his first hundred days in office. By late 1933 Roosevelt had many new advisers, and thereafter the labels *brain trust* or *brains trust* began to be applied to all presidential advisers.

The First Hundred Days. By spring 1933 the country had been immersed in a terrible Depression for more than three years. Calm assurance had been widely replaced by anxiety, uncertainty, and despair. Roosevelt's charismatic personality helped change the mood of the nation almost overnight. With his election in November 1932, the country became hopeful. In his first inaugural address, on 4 March 1933, Roosevelt declared: "the only thing we have to fear is fear itself," and he proclaimed to the American people that he was asking Congress for "broad Executive power to wage a war against the emergency." In this speech, and in the frequent "fireside chats" he broadcast to the nation over the radio, the new president's strong, reassuring voice exuded confidence and heartened millions. His steady and encouraging words meant as much to some as the policies he promoted.

Experimentalism. Roosevelt always remained the consummate practical politician, first and foremost a pragmatist. His call for "bold, persistent experimentation" captures the core of this approach. In 1933 he sent the Agricultural Adjustment Act to Congress with the words "I tell you frankly, that it is a new and untrod path. But I tell you with equal frankness that an unprecedented con-

A BOWL FULL OF DUST

Caroline Henderson lived on a farming homestead in Oklahoma in the 1930s with her husband and children. The dust storms of the 1930s struck terror into the hearts of many who had worked so hard to cultivate the semiarid earth. In 1935 she wrote:

There are days when for hours at a time we cannot see the windmill fifty feet from the kitchen door. There are days when for briefer periods one cannot distinguish the windows from the solid wall because of the solid blackness of the raging storm. Only in some Inferno-like dream could anyone visualize the terrifying lurid red light overspreading the sky when portions of Texas "are on the air."

Source: T. H. Watkins, *The Great Depression* (Boston: Little, Brown. 1993).

dition calls for the trial of new means to rescue agriculture." The president's "take-charge" approach was nowhere more evident than on Capitol Hill. During its first hundred days the Roosevelt administration proposed fifteen major legislative reforms, and all were enacted.

An Alphabet Soup of Agencies. During the 1930s many economists argued that one of the ailing nation's primary needs was an infusion of money into the economy to check the downward spiral of unemployment. The Roosevelt administration responded with such a wide array of agencies, administrations, and acts — most of which were referred to by acronyms formed from the initial letters in their names — that some glibly referred to them as an "Alphabet Soup of Acts and Agencies."

Sources:
Paul K. Conkin, *F.D.R. and the Origin of the Welfare State* (New York: Crowell, 1967); republished as *The New Deal* (New York: Crowell, 1969);

Steve Fraser and Gary Gerstle, eds., *The Rise and Fall of the New Deal Order, 1930–1980* (Princeton, N.J.: Princeton University Press, 1989);

Raymond Moley, *The First New Deal* (New York, Harcourt, Brace & World, 1966);

Rexford G. Tugwell, *The Brains Trust* (New York: Viking, 1968).

THE FARM CRISIS

Farm Problems before the Crash. Economic depression had struck American farmers earlier than any other element in American society. Indeed, by the early 1920s American farmers were already enduring a severe economic crisis. During World War I the American economy, including farming, had gone into an all-out sprint of productivity. When the war ended, however, the European markets in which American food had been sold were closed off by tariff restrictions. Newly and traditionally cultivated lands in the United States continued to be

farmed with ever-more-efficient machinery and higher-yielding fertilizers. The result was a vast surplus of agricultural goods and livestock. In the competitive domestic marketplace the purchasing power of Americans could consume only so much cotton, corn, wheat, beef, and pork. As farmers competed to undersell their competitors, who were often their neighbors, prices fell through the floor.

The Onset of the Depression. As the Depression of the 1930s gripped the nation, the farmers' plight worsened. In 1920 wheat sold for $2.94 a bushel in Chicago. In 1929 it commanded only $1.00, and by 1932 it sold for a scant $.30. The price of cotton, a staple crop across much of the South, fell from $.37 a pound in 1920 to an unprofitable $.065 by 1932. During the same period prime beef fell from $14.95 per hundredweight to $5.78. In 1920 U.S. farming had generated $16 billion in sales, but by 1932 this figure had fallen by $10 billion. During the 1920s Congress passed the McNary-Haugen Bill, designed to dump surplus crops in foreign countries and raise prices in the domestic market. President Calvin Coolidge twice vetoed the bill. In 1929 President Hoover allowed the creation of the Federal Farm Board (FFB). The FFB bought up cotton and wheat surpluses in that year, but because it did nothing to halt the farmers' annual race to bring more and more crops and livestock to market, the FFB failed to alter the problem of "overproductivity."

Agricultural Unrest. Exhausted and frustrated, farmers sometimes joined together to protest their plight. In Wisconsin in 1932 angry dairymen hijacked milk trucks and spilled the milk onto the ground. Across the nation farmers with shotguns in hand stopped the sales of friends' farms or forced auctioneers of foreclosed farms to sell them back to their original owners at nominal prices. In summer 1932 farmers in Iowa joined together in the Farmers' Holiday Association, trying to raise prices through a farmers' strike that they hoped would spread across the nation. When violence between striking and nonstriking farmers broke out in western Iowa, however, Milo Reno, the colorful leader of the association, ended the strike.

The AAA: Federal Aid for Troubled Farmers. Many New Deal laws were passed in the effort to address the needs of the American farmer. In the early days of Roosevelt's first administration, Secretary of Agriculture Henry A. Wallace worked with presidential adviser Rexford G. Tugwell and M. L. Wilson of Montana State College to develop and promote the Agricultural Adjustment Act. Signed into law in early May 1933, the act created the Agricultural Adjustment Administration (AAA), whose major task was to coordinate an acreage-reduction plan. By reducing the amount of food going to market, the federal government hoped to drive farm-commodity prices upward. Farmers who complied were paid by the federal government for leaving a portion of their farmland idle. By the time the AAA was estab-

Secretary of Agriculture Henry A. Wallace (right) discussing plans to limit hog production under the Agricultural Adjustment
Act of 1933

lished, farmers had already begun their growing season. If price controls were to be effective in 1932, some crops would have to be plowed under and some livestock killed. Tens of thousands of acres of cotton plants were plowed under and left to rot, while more than six million pigs were slaughtered and their carcasses burned or buried. Many Americans, however, looked on these actions with shocked disbelief. They could not understand how the government could be complicit in destroying food or reducing its production in a nation where many were going to bed hungry.

The Dust Bowl. In some states during the 1930s overproduction was not the problem. Prolonged misuse of grasslands in parts of Kansas, Colorado, New Mexico, Texas, and Oklahoma led to one of the greatest environmental disasters in American history. For years farmers had torn off the grassy mantle of the Great Plains by overgrazing and overfarming. By late 1933 — after a year and a half of drought — hundreds of square miles of parched topsoil were churned up by violent winds and swirled upward, creating huge dust storms. Fine dust filled the air and blackened the skies for miles. Scientists

calculated that the worst of the dust storms carried 300 million tons of topsoil. By 1935, it was estimated, nine million acres of the Great Plains had been eroded. With crops destroyed and livestock dying, farmers of the Dust Bowl headed westward to California seeking prosperity. The Taylor Grazing Act of June 1934, which set up a program to limit grazing and thus prevent further wind erosion, could not help those who had already lost everything, nor could the Soil Conservation Service, established in 1935. In four short years more than three hundred thousand poor and disheartened farm families migrated to California. On the road from Oklahoma to California a seemingly endless stream of old, overladen cars filled with gaunt, sallow-faced families made their way west. The new arrivals in California needed work. In desperation entire families turned to low-paying jobs picking crops and lived in one-room shacks. "When they need us they call us migrants," said one forlorn farmer. "When we've picked their crops we're bums and we've got to get out."

The Success of the AAA. Yet the AAA did help farmers. By early 1936 their net income had risen by more than $3 billion, while the government had spent $1.5 billion on the program. In 1936 the Supreme Court declared the AAA unconstitutional, but to meet the Court's objections Congress rewrote the act as the Soil Conservation and Domestic Allotment Act. Farmers continued to receive payments from the government for not producing various crops and livestock. Through agencies such as these, as well as federal projects that brought electricity to the countryside and federal programs to resettle those laboring on poor soil, the government greatly improved life for American farmers.

The Farm Credit Administration. Along with the regulation of Wall Street and the banks, President Roosevelt and Congress also created programs to offer farmers and home owners respite from foreclosures on the mortgages to their homes and farms and simultaneously put unemployed building-industry workers back on the job. Through the Farm Credit Administration (FCA), established in 1932 and expanded under the Roosevelt administration in 1933 — as well as in the Home Owners Loan Corporation (HOLC), created in 1933, and the Federal Housing Administration (FHA), set up in 1934 — they were successful in stemming the flood of foreclosures that began in the early 1930s. The U.S. Housing Authority, created in 1937, made half a billion dollars in government loans available for public housing for the poor, augmenting earlier New Deal legislation in support of the middle class.

Sources:

William E. Leuchtenburg, *Franklin D. Roosevelt and the New Deal, 1932–1940* (New York: Harper & Row, 1963);

Leuchtenburg, *New Deal and Global War* (New York: Time-Life Books, 1964);

Arthur M. Schlesinger Jr., *The Politics of Upheaval*, volume 3 of his *The Age of Roosevelt* (Boston: Houghton Mifflin, 1960).

President Roosevelt signing the Emergency Banking Relief Act, 9 March 1933

THE FINANCIAL AND BANKING CRISIS

The Banking Crisis. In the banking and fiscal crisis of the Great Depression, the heady days of the 1920s were well-nigh forgotten. More than five thousand banks closed in the three years before President Roosevelt took office in March 1933. By then about nine million people had lost their savings and it was clear that some action was necessary. In the "interregnum," Hoover's final days as a "lame-duck" president between Roosevelt's election in November 1932 and his inauguration the following March, state after state declared banking "holidays," briefly closing local banks in efforts to prevent nervous depositors from creating bank failures by rushing to withdraw their savings from banks believed to be financially unstable. The day after his inauguration, President Roosevelt called Congress into special session and announced a four-day nationwide banking holiday. While the banks were closed, the president introduced the Emergency Banking Act, which Congress passed the same day. During this bank closure many people ran short of cash. In an era before credit cards, people without hard currency were unable to purchase groceries or attend public events. Shows at Radio City Music Hall in New York were all but empty. At Madison Square Garden people "paid" admission to boxing matches with spark plugs, jigsaw puzzles, and other items deposited with the attendants at the door. Yet these short-term and relatively minor hardships were offset by the fact that the federal banking holiday worked. In his first radio "fireside chat," broadcast three days after the banks were closed, President Roosevelt reassured the public that the banks had been made safe. The president's personal charm and his penchant for decisive action were apparent in this first New Deal success. Within the month banking deposits had grown by more than a billion dollars.

The Pecora Investigation. In January 1933 the Senate Banking and Currency Committee appointed Ferdinand Pecora as legal counsel for an investigation of banking and securities trading. In 1933 and 1934 Pecora — an Italian immigrant educated at City College of New York and New York Law School — captured headline after headline in his unflagging efforts to reveal corruption in American financial institutions. His investigations uncovered unethical and criminal activities by some of the most revered financial giants. In addition to securities and tax fraud he found a web of complicated holding companies controlled by single interests and stock-market trusts manipulated by major financial players. Pecora's investigation proceeded in two steps. First, he sent more than a hundred investigators and accountants into various banks and other financial institutions. Second, armed with information from these reconnaissance forays, Pecora questioned witness after wealthy witness before the Senate committee, usually before a crowd of about three hundred witnesses. His handling of the first investigation set the tone for more than a year of probing by the Senate committee. Charles E. Mitchell, president of National City Bank of New York, was the first financial magnate called before the committee. During three days of testimony, Mitchell admitted to feigning the sale of $2.8 million in stocks to his wife so that he could declare an income loss for tax purposes. (He received a salary of $1.2 million). He told how he and other high-ranking bank officials lent themselves more than $2 million interest-free to cover losses that they had incurred during the stock-market crash of 1929. At the time of the hearing virtually none of that loan had been repaid. He also testified that hundreds of lower-level bank employees had suffered severely in the crash but that they had received no help from National City Bank. When Mitchell had finished, Sen. Burton Wheeler of Montana said, "If it's right to send Al Capone to the Federal penitentiary for income tax evasion, some of these crooked bank presidents ought to go too." Much of the public agreed with Wheeler, but Mitchell served no prison time.

Banking Regulation: The FDIC. The first reform to derive from the Pecora investigation was the Glass-Steagall Banking Act, sponsored by Sen. Carter Glass of Virginia and Rep. Henry Steagall of Alabama in 1933, amid a rash of bank failures. The law regulated many of the unsound practices that contributed to the Depression, including making it illegal for banks to deal in stocks and bonds. It also created the Federal Deposit Insurance Corporation (FDIC). The FDIC initially guaranteed deposits to a maximum of $5,000. (In the 1990s it guarantees deposits up to $100,000.)

Taming Wall Street: The SEC. The greatest legacy of the Pecora investigation was the creation of the Securities and Exchange Commission (SEC) in 1934. Working with the Federal Reserve Board, the SEC has successfully regulated financial markets and prevented subsequent depressions. When Roosevelt named Joseph P. Kennedy (father of John F. Kennedy, future president of the United States) the first chairman of the SEC, critics said that appointing a man reputed to have made his fortune through some of the practices the SEC was supposed to prevent, was like hiring a fox to guard the henhouse. Yet under Kennedy's leadership the SEC became a model government regulatory agency. In administering the Securities Act of 1933, the SEC protects investors against fraud and malpractice, supervising the New York Stock Exchange and other securities markets where stocks, bonds, and commodities are brokered and requiring that anyone offering securities register with the SEC.

Sources:

Paul K. Conkin, *F.D.R. and the Origin of the Welfare State* (New York: Crowell, 1967); republished as *The New Deal* (New York: Crowell, 1969);

Steve Fraser and Gary Gerstle, eds., *The Rise and Fall of the New Deal Order, 1930–1980* (Princeton: Princeton University Press, 1989);

William E. Leuchtenburg, *Franklin D. Roosevelt and the New Deal, 1932–1940* (New York: Harper & Row, 1963);

Cabell Phillips, *From Crash to the Blitz, 1929–1939* (New York: Macmillan, 1969);

Arthur M. Schlesinger Jr., *The Coming of the New Deal*, volume 2 of his *The Age of Roosevelt* (Boston: Houghton Mifflin, 1958);

Schlesinger, *The Politics of Upheaval*, volume 3 of his *The Age of Roosevelt* (Boston: Houghton Mifflin, 1960).

HELP FOR THE COMMON MAN

The CCC. Founded on 31 March 1933, the Civilian Conservation Corps (CCC) was one of President Roosevelt's first New Deal programs. During its nine-year existence the CCC employed more than 2.5 million young men in temporary camps administered by the U.S. Army. In 1935, at the high point of its activity, the CCC employed half a million men in twenty-five hundred camps nationwide. For about a dollar a day the young members of "Roosevelt's Tree Army" restored historic sites, built park facilities, cleaned reservoirs, fought forest fires, and planted more than two billion trees. The CCC also taught thirty-five thousand illiterate young men to read. Though considered one of the most successful programs created during Roosevelt's first hundred days in office, the CCC was not without its flaws. Women were excluded from its membership rolls; and, though more than two hundred thousand African Americans did serve in the CCC, the discriminatory policies of its director, Robert Fechner, meant that sometimes a young African American man could join only after another quit.

FERA and the CWA. Signed into law in May 1933, the Federal Emergency Relief Administration (FERA) provided cash grants to states for distribution to the unemployed. Under the able administration of Harry Hopkins, FERA distributed nearly $500 million in short order. Recognizing, however, that many Americans wanted to work for the money they received, Hopkins and Roosevelt developed the Civil Works Administration (CWA), which was approved by Congress in November. With a budget of more than a billion dollars, the CWA put more than four million people to work at temporary jobs during its first six months. The CCC, FERA, and CWA signaled the beginning of the federal policy of deficit spending, by which the government can mitigate economic downturns in the short term by infusing capital into the economy.

The PWA. Also established in 1933, and run by Secretary of the Interior Harold Ickes, the Public Works Administration (PWA) had a budget of more than $3

The first Civilian Conservation Corps recruits in New York City lining up outside the Army Building

billion with which to hire unemployed Americans for jobs created by the federal government. Tens of thousands of PWA workers across the country built housing projects, schools, hospitals, power plants, highways, dams, and new buildings on military bases. Instead of wandering as hoboes in search of nonexistent work, the people employed by the PWA were able to retain their pride and put food on the table for their families.

The TVA. On 18 May 1933 President Roosevelt signed the bill establishing the Tennessee Valley Authority (TVA), one of the greatest successes of the New Deal. The TVA was an ambitious project that revitalized a broad region of the rural Southeast. The TVA began by building a series of dams on government-owned land at the point where the Tennessee River descends almost 150 feet in thirty miles. These dams generated electricity and controlled flooding in the valley. Before they were built only 2 percent of the people in the valley had electricity; after their completion nearly 100 percent did. The TVA also provided jobs in government-constructed factories that produced nitrate fertilizers using electricity generated by the dams. Other TVA projects included reforestation and industrial and agricultural revitalization. The government followed up the successes of the TVA by building a series of dams in the Pacific Northwest and with the Rural Electrification Administration (REA) of 1935. Before the REA only 10 percent of farms in the nation had electricity. Fifteen years later, nearly 90 percent had light and power.

A Further Flurry of Government Activity. The Roosevelt administration restructured the Reconstruction Finance Corporation (RFC), which also contributed to improving economic conditions. The "common man" was also helped by economic regulations such as the Securi-

ties Act of 1933, which curtailed the Wall Street malpractice that had contributed to the great crash of 1929. In early 1934 the country seemed to be on the road to recovery. The worst of the Depression was behind. Crowds cheered the president. Within months, however, the economy began to sputter, and by December unemployment had reached the levels of a year before. With the economic downturn and the president's luster a bit tarnished, an air of radicalism — on both the Right and Left — was becoming apparent.

The Second New Deal. In January 1935 President Roosevelt altered his course and began the "Second New Deal." Massive governmental spending in a dozen different agencies had pumped billions of dollars into works projects and relief, but with the economy still in the doldrums the president was coming under increased attacks from both the political Right and Left. Responding to the challenge, Roosevelt turned leftward.

Social Security. Signed into law on 14 August 1935, the Social Security Act (SSA) created a federal old-age insurance system for the first time in American history. The act provided a modest monthly payment for Americans aged sixty-five and older. It also provided for unemployment compensation as well as governmental support for the handicapped and for single mothers with dependent children. The SSA was not initially considered a system of welfare. Intended to function as a forced savings plan, the program required all employed people to contribute a small percentage of their pay into a general Social Security fund for the duration of their working years. In the initial years it would serve as yet another deficit-spending element in the New Deal's arsenal. After that, however, Americans would be able to collect modest Social Security checks from the federal government only after a working life spent contributing to the fund. Yet the SSA did more than simply assure working people an income in old age. Its Aid to Dependent Children provision provided single mothers with a means to make ends meet; and support payments to single mothers, as well as to the handicapped, grew enormously in subsequent years. Initially a minor provision of the SSA, it was renamed Aid to Families with Dependent Children in the 1950s, and in the Great Society programs of the 1960s the program became the backbone of an expanded welfare state.

The WPA. By May 1935 Roosevelt, in council with his brain trust, decided to enter into deficit spending in drastic ways. In its day the Works Progress Administration (WPA), with an initial budget of $5 billion, was the most expensive single governmental program in the history of the United States. Ably administered by Harry Hopkins, the WPA gave millions of unemployed Americans jobs and buoyed the economy with its infusion of cash. From its creation until it was dismantled at the beginning of World War II, WPA projects employed an average of two million workers. Men were set to building or renovating bridges, post offices, roads, and schools;

The NRA parade in New York City, 13 September 1933, one of the many events organized to promote compliance with codes established by the National Recovery Administration

women were generally employed as child-care givers or in sewing or other handicraft projects. The art, theater, and writers' projects of the WPA gave men and women the chance to earn a modest living in pursuit of their creative vocations. (Fading murals in Depression-era high schools and post offices are the legacy of this element of the New Deal.)

The NYA. The National Youth Administration (NYA), begun in June 1935, assisted millions of Americans between the ages of sixteen and twenty-five. Motivated in part by the desire to dispel potential radicalism among young Americans, the NYA gave out 620,000 high-school and college scholarships. It created an additional four million part-time jobs for young Americans in such areas as roadwork and building renovation. By the end of the 1930s the NYA had helped more American young people than the CCC. Unlike the CCC, the NYA created a special Division of Negro Affairs. Under the administration of African American reformer and educator Mary McLeod Bethune, this division helped young black men and women secure scholarships and part-time jobs.

Sources:

Paul K. Conkin, *F.D.R. and the Origin of the Welfare State* (New York: Crowell, 1967); republished as *The New Deal* (New York: Crowell, 1969);

Martha Derthick, *Policymaking for Social Security* (Washington, D.C.: Brookings Institution, 1979);

Preston Hubbard, *Origins of the TVA* (Nashville: Vanderbilt University Press, 1961);

William E. Leuchtenburg, *Franklin D. Roosevelt and the New Deal, 1932–1940* (New York: Harper & Row, 1963);

Betty and Ernest K. Lindley, *A New Deal for Youth: The Story of the National Youth Administration* (New York: Viking, 1938);

Thomas K. McCraw, *TVA and the Power Fight: 1933–1939* (Philadelphia: Lippincott, 1971);

Cabell Phillips, *From Crash to the Blitz, 1929–1939* (New York: Macmillan, 1969);

Edwin Witte, *The Development of the Social Security Act* (Madison: University of Wisconsin Press, 1962).

INDUSTRIAL POLICY

The NIRA. The first New Deal efforts to respond to corporate bankruptcies and the concomitant unemployment came in the form of an omnibus legislative bill. The National Industrial Recovery Act (NIRA) was passed by Congress in mid June 1933. An extremely complex bill, the NIRA was intended to stop the crippling deflation that was ruining American industries. The NIRA suspended antitrust laws and allowed industries to collude in setting prices. The NIRA created the Public Works Administration (PWA), and in its now-famous section 7(a) allowed workers to organize into unions with the assurance that they could not be "coerced, harassed, or intimidated" by their employers. The National Recovery Administration (NRA) was established under the NIRA to set codes for industrial compliance. Under the capable leadership of Hugh S. Johnson, the NRA instituted codes calling for minimum wages, maximum hours, and an end to child labor. Industries that complied with NRA codes were allowed to display a "Blue Eagle." Almost overnight the Blue Eagle and the accompanying slogan "We Do Our Part" were being displayed in factories and stores nationwide. In Philadelphia the owner of a new National Football League franchise even named his team the Eagles. In May 1935, however, the U.S. Supreme Court declared the NIRA unconstitutional. Congress extracted the labor provision of the NIRA, which, passed as the Wagner National Labor Relations Act of 1935, encouraging labor organization in the United States.

THE NIRA AND AN "UNFIT CHICKEN"

The NIRA was a complex, multibillion-dollar federal law that based its authority on the inter-state-commerce clause of the U.S. Constitution. Ironically, this major piece of New Deal legislation was brought down by two poultry wholesalers from Brooklyn, New York. The Schechter brothers operated a chicken slaughterhouse under the provisions of Jewish dietary law. Kosher law, however, conflicted with the Live Poultry Code of the NIRA, and in April 1935 the Schechter brothers were found guilty of eighteen counts of conspiracy to violate the poultry code. In part the government charged that they were selling "an unfit chicken." In May the Schechters appealed their case to the U.S. Supreme Court, giving that body the opportunity to subject the entire NIRA to judicial review. As a result the court not only overturned the Schechter Poultry conviction on the grounds that the company was not engaged in interstate commerce, but it also ruled the entire NIRA unconstitutional. Chief Justice Charles Evans Hughes, delivering the majority opinion, argued that "extraordinary conditions do not create or enlarge constitutional power." Thus, the omnibus NIRA was defeated by "The Sick Chicken Case."

Source: Arthur M. Schlesinger Jr., *The Politics of Upheaval*, volume 3 of his *The Age of Roosevelt* (Boston: Houghton Mifflin, 1960).

The Fair Labor Standards Act. One consequence of a reinvigorated labor movement was the passage in 1938 of the Fair Labor Standards Act. The law established for the first time a minimum wage for working people (initially twenty-five cents an hour) and, beginning in 1940, set the maximum workweek at forty hours.

Sources:

Irving Bernstein, *Turbulent Years: A History of the American Worker, 1933–1941* (Boston: Houghton Mifflin, 1970);

Ellis W. Hawley, *The New Deal and the Problem of Monopoly* (Princeton: Princeton University Press, 1966);

Robert F. Himmelberg, *The Origins of the National Recovery Administration* (New York: Fordham University Press, 1976);

John H. Leek, *Government and Labor in the United States* (New York: Rinehart, 1952);

Michael M. Weinstein, *Recovery and Redistribution under the NIRA* (New York: North-Holland Publishing, 1980).

INDUSTRY AND LABOR

Labor Organization and Unrest. Industrial wage earners became increasingly militant during the 1930s. Both unions and capitalists frequently resorted to violence. Republic Steel was said to have purchased more tear gas than any other institution, and a Senate report noted that 282 companies had spent almost $10 million for ammunition, spies, and replacement workers from 1933 to 1937. Ten thousand garment workers, including many women, went on strike in New York in 1935. The previous year thousands of workers walked out of textile mills from Massachusetts to Georgia (and elsewhere) in the largest strike in the nation's history to that time. That same year, in Minneapolis, four men died as a result of violent struggles between striking truck drivers and deputized businessmen. Minnesota governor Floyd B. Olson, who had been elected on the Farmer-Labor ticket in 1932, sympathized with the strikers, who were actively supported by the Farmers' Holiday Association, a group allied to the Farmer-Labor Party, but he finally declared martial law to end the violence. By the mid 1930s Olson was considered the most radical governor in the nation, claiming openly "You might say I'm radical as hell!"

The San Francisco Longshoremen's Strike. In summer 1934 tensions between San Francisco longshoremen and their employers spilled over into the entire city. The longshoremen had gone on strike in May, refusing to unload any more cargo after their employers failed to recognize the International Longshoremen's Association. Two months later thousands of tons of food, steel, and other goods clogged docks and warehouses. On 4 July San Francisco erupted in traditional celebrations of the nation's independence. The following morning the streets again erupted, this time in labor violence. Determined to open the port, a broad alliance of business leaders got the mayor to order police to clear the docks of picketing strikers. In the daylong battle between police and workers, two strikers were killed, and hundreds on both sides were injured. "Bloody Thursday" galvanized the unions and working people of the city. Workers from many industries joined in a general strike, which began on 16 July. For four days roads were blockaded, and stores were closed as even conservative trades unionists joined in. Government officials from Washington, D.C., to San Francisco were greatly alarmed; but after hurried meetings between civic officials and strikers, tensions subsided, and the strike was called off.

Industrial Labor: Agitate, Educate, Organize. The 1930s were a decade of vigorous organization among American workers. Skilled workers such as carpenters, steampipe fitters, and stonemasons had been organized in the American Federation of Labor (AFL) since the late nineteenth century. As a result of unionization, these skilled workers had better pay, benefits, and working conditions than other workers. Semiskilled and unskilled laborers — those who could be taught their job in a matter of a few minutes or a few days — were often fired by their employers when they attempted to unionize. Yet in the 1930s, buoyed by the government support of unionization in the NIRA and in the Wagner Act, unions grew rapidly.

The United Mine Workers. John L. Lewis, charismatic leader of the United Mine Workers, began to organize the unorganized in the early 1930s. Frustrated at AFL opposition to unionization of the semiskilled and unskilled workers in American factories, mines, and mills, Lewis went to the AFL national convention at Atlantic City, New Jersey, in October 1935 determined to act. Toward the end of a tumultuous meeting, when "Big Bill" Hutcheson, the head of the carpenters' union, cursed him, Lewis marched across the floor and punched the stocky carpenter with such force that he fell to the ground. Soon both men were wrestling on the floor. This fight signaled the immense tensions between unionized skilled workers and nonunionized mass-production factory workers. Three weeks after the fight, Lewis established the Committee for Industrial Organization (CIO), which was expelled from the AFL soon thereafter. In 1938 Lewis and his followers — retaining the same acronym — changed the name of their group to the Congress of Industrial Organizations.

CIO Unionization. By 1936 the CIO was vigorously organizing steelworkers, textile workers, automotive assembly-line workers, and others across the nation amid much violence between management and labor. Bloody battles, started by either side, were not uncommon. In Seattle there was an abortive effort by workers to call a general strike. Perhaps the most innovative forms of worker protest, however, were the sit-down strikes at mid decade. Rather than leaving the plants and marching outside at the gates as in traditional strikes, the "sit-downers" elected to occupy the plants — literally to sit down next to their machinery — until their demands were met. The best known of these sit-down strikes was launched just before Christmas 1936 by the automotive assembly-line workers. Supported by their wives and others on the outside, who organized food and blanket brigades to help them, the workers occupied automotive factories for weeks. In February 1937 General Motors agreed to their demands for recognition of their union and increased wages. Soon sit-down strikes were being waged by women clerks in Woolworth stores and elsewhere across the nation.

Sources:

Irving Bernstein, *Turbulent Years: A History of the American Worker, 1933–1941* (Boston: Houghton Mifflin, 1970);

David Brody, *Workers in Industrial America* (New York: Oxford University Press, 1980);

Bert Cochran, *Labor and Communism: The Conflict That Shaped the Unions* (Princeton: Princeton University Press, 1977);

Melvyn Dubofsky and Warren Van Tine, *John L. Lewis: A Biography* (New York: Times Books, 1977);

Sidney Fine, *Sit-down: The General Motors Strike of 1936–1937* (Ann Arbor: University of Michigan Press, 1969).

NEW DEAL OPPONENTS

Alternatives on the Left and Right. American politics consists of the interplay of individuals, interest groups, and their contending worldviews. The politics of the 1930s were extraordinarily dynamic. As the economy tumbled ever more swiftly downhill in the early 1930s, Americans contemplated the social, economic, and political conditions that had — to a greater or lesser extent —

Strikers during the "Little Steel" dispute of 1937, one result of CIO efforts to unionize steel workers

ruled the United States since its founding. Some individuals began to question the free-market capitalism and constitutional republicanism (representative democracy) that had been foundational tenets of American history. Though the gross domestic product (GDP) of the United States rose from $56 billion in 1933 to $72 billion in 1935, unemployment remained at more than 10 million workers. The optimism of Roosevelt's first hundred days was increasingly replaced by frustration and anger. Voices of protest were heard from the political Right and Left.

Share-Our-Wealth Societies. The greatest challenge to Roosevelt and the New Deal in the mid 1930s proved to be Sen. Huey P. Long of Louisiana, whose "Share-Our-Wealth" clubs, organized in early 1934, spread rapidly across the country. Millions of Americans supported Long's proposals. Calling for redistributing the nation's wealth through heavy taxation of the rich, Long's plan guaranteed every American an annual income of twenty-five hundred dollars (a middle-class income in the 1930s) and a "homestead allowance" of five thousand dollars. Critics considered the plan unworkable, and Roosevelt called Long "one of the two most dangerous men in America." Nevertheless, a poll conducted in mid 1935 found that Long would get 10 percent of the vote if he were to run for president. Soon after Long was assassinated in September 1935, the "Share-Our-Wealth" movement collapsed.

The National Union for Social Justice. Another challenge to the programs and policies of the New Deal came from a "radio priest" in Royal Oak, Michigan. A Catholic priest named Father Charles E. Coughlin, who had been broadcasting his radio show since the mid 1920s, began attacking communism. The popularity of his show grew enormously during the early days of the Depression. In 1934 Coughlin received more mail than

Upton Sinclair during his 1934 campaign for the governorship of California

bers each. A Townsend Plan bill was introduced in Congress, but the Social Security Act of 1935 — developed in part because of the political pressure brought to bear on the administration by Townsend's supporters — dissipated much of the movement's energy.

A Left Alternative: EPIC. Upton Sinclair, well known as the author of *The Jungle* (1906), a fictionalized exposé of conditions in the Chicago meatpacking industry, moved into the national spotlight in 1933 and 1934 with a program he called EPIC (End Poverty in California). EPIC caught fire with many farmers and unemployed workers. Among its principal demands was that uncultivated farmland should be given to unemployed men and women. On this land, Sinclair asserted, cooperative farm colonies, model factories, and workers' villages would be constructed. Claiming that capitalism had "crumbled like a dry-rotted log," Sinclair said it was necessary to replace the production-for-profit system with the quasi-socialistic "production for use" of EPIC. In a close race for the governorship of California in 1934, Sinclair was narrowly defeated by the incumbent, Republican Frank F. Merriam, and thereafter EPIC faded from the headlines.

Communists. The political Left remained small during the 1930s, but it exercised influence on politics in proportions greater than its numbers. After the Spanish Civil War broke out in 1936, more than three thousand American leftists traveled to Spain to fight for the democratically elected republican government against the fascist troops of Gen. Francisco Franco. On the home front Communists and other leftists pointed out that the economic collapse of 1929 occurred in an economy where wealth was not equally distributed. The richest fifth of the American population owned more than half the nation's wealth, while the poorest 40 percent of Americans owned only about 10 percent of the wealth. Communists argued that the unrelenting Depression signaled the end of such an inequitable system, which would be replaced by communism. Communists organized a hunger march on Washington, D.C. (1931), organized black sharecroppers, and worked within unions to foment radical action against the industrial order. In 1932 William Z. Foster, the Communist Party presidential candidate, received a scant 102,785 votes. In 1935 Foster, under direction from Moscow, reversed the Communists' strategy of separatism from other leftist and liberal political groups. Hailing a "Popular Front" of all leftists to fight fascism, Foster declared, "Communism is twentieth-century Americanism." The strategy produced poor results; in 1936 Communist presidential candidate Earl Browder won only 80,869 votes. Throughout the 1930s the Communist Party in the United States kept close contact with and was often controlled by Joseph Stalin and Soviet Communists. In August 1939, after party leaders were ordered by Moscow to support the nonaggression pact signed by Stalin and Adolf Hitler, many party members

any other American, and an estimated 30 million to 45 million Americans listened to his show each week. At first Coughlin supported Roosevelt. During the 1932 election he told his audience that it was "Roosevelt or ruin," and in 1933 he said that "the New Deal is Christ's deal." Yet Coughlin soon turned against Roosevelt. Blaming the Depression on Jews and Communists, he began to espouse what analysts of his broadcasts have called an ideology of fascism. By 1935 Coughlin was calling Roosevelt "anti-God," and he relabeled the New Deal "The Jew Deal." In 1934 Coughlin began the National Union for Social Justice, which had half a million members at its peak, and in 1935 he helped found the Union Party to challenge Roosevelt's bid for reelection.

The Townsend Plan. In 1934 Dr. Francis E. Townsend of California also mounted a challenge to the New Deal, calling for the government to give two hundred dollars a month to all Americans who were sixty years of age or older. Critics of the Townsend Plan noted that more than half of the nation's taxes would go to compensate less than 10 percent of the population. Nonetheless, by January 1935 there were more than three thousand Townsend clubs claiming half a million mem-

resigned in disgust over the Soviets' reversal of their policy toward fascism.

The Socialist Challenge to the New Deal. The Socialist Party of America, led by Norman Thomas, contained within it both reformist and revolutionary elements. During the 1920s the party had often emphasized the need for revolutionary change, but in the 1932 election, with Thomas as their presidential candidate, Socialists offered a largely reformist platform — albeit reforms they hoped would lead toward a restructuring of the nation's polity. In their 1932 platform Socialists called for social insurance for the unemployed and elderly, as well as for national medical insurance, federal relief payments to the unemployed, federal jobs programs, a minimum hourly wage, the right for workers to bargain collectively in unions, a federal program to refinance people's homes and farms, repeal of Prohibition, and arms reduction. When Franklin D. Roosevelt was elected president (on a much more conservative Democratic Party platform), the Socialists were shocked to find that he implemented almost all of their programs. "What cut the ground pretty completely from under us was," Thomas said, "Roosevelt in a word." Yet Thomas and other Socialists believed that Roosevelt had implemented reforms to save capitalism rather than to cultivate socialism. In 1936 the Socialist Party called for further relief spending, a thirty-hour workweek, and more aid for farmers. Whereas Thomas had received 881,951 votes in the presidential election of 1932, he received only 187,720 votes in 1936. Factional fights between Old Guard Socialists and the revolutionary left wing of the party further weakened the organization in the late 1930s. By 1938 party membership was down to seven thousand (from a high of around twenty-one thousand in 1934). While they could claim success in seeing the implementation of many of the reforms they had proposed, Socialists were disheartened by the lack of growth in their movement.

The Silver Shirts. Extremist right-wing hate groups also formed in the United States during the 1930s, though their memberships remained relatively small. The fascist movements flourishing in Germany and Italy gave rise to imitative organizations in the United States. The Silver Shirts was founded by journalist William Pelley in 1933. Pelley claimed that in 1928 he had been dead for seven minutes and had gone to heaven, where he was instructed to form a fascist organization to support Hitler in the United States. The anti-Semitic Pelley and his followers harangued the president and New Deal supporters for being, among other things, agents of communism. Pelley was arrested for fraud in 1934, and in 1942 he was convicted on charges of sedition and sent to prison for eight years. The Silver Shirts disappeared soon thereafter.

The German-American Bund. Organized in 1932 as part of the international Friends of the New Germany, the German-American Bund sought to educate Germans living in the United States about the Nazi ideology then

A German-American Bund Rally at Madison Square Garden in New York City, 20 February 1939

gaining favor in the fatherland. Fritz Kuhn was the American leader of the Bund. From 1936 to 1939 many Americans were horrified by the racist and anti-Semitic views of the Bund, which at its peak may have had as many as twenty-five thousand members. In 1939 Kuhn was convicted of embezzling Bund funds; his imprisonment, along with rising anti-Nazi sentiment in the United States, led to the demise of the organization.

The American Liberty League. The American Liberty League (ALL) was the greatest voice of political conservatism during the second half of the 1930s. During its six-year existence the ALL gained support from some of the wealthiest businessmen and professionals in the United States. Among them were Irénée du Pont of the Du Pont company; Nathan Miller, head of U.S. Steel; Edward F. Hutton of General Foods; and John Jacob Rascob, former director of General Motors and onetime head of the Democratic Party. Among other disillusioned Democrats active in the ALL were two former Democratic presidential candidates: John W. Davis, who lost to Calvin Coolidge in 1924, and Alfred E. Smith, who lost to Hoover in 1928. The ALL offered cogent conservative criticism of the New Deal. Its stated purpose was "to defend and uphold the Constitution . . . [and] to teach the duty of government to protect individual and group initiatives. . . ." Claiming that the New Deal threatened the constitutional system of checks and balances by concentrating power in the chief executive, the ALL also opposed the New Deal's monetary policy, its deficit spending, its progressive taxation of businesses, and its efforts to enlarge government in general. Though the ALL suffered from its popular image as a club for millionaires and did not gain wide popular support, its membership reached almost 125,000 at its height, prior to the election in 1936. The league foundered after Roosevelt's decisive electoral victory that year. Alf Landon, Roosevelt's Republican opponent in that election, said that an endorsement from the ALL was "the kiss of death."

Martin Dies and HUAC. Though best known for its activities in the 1950s, the House Un-American Activities Committee (HUAC) had its start in the late 1930s, when it served as an irritant to Roosevelt. Founded on 26 May 1938 and chaired by Martin Dies of Texas, the HUAC was created to investigate fascist organizations such as the German-American Bund and the Silver Shirts, but it rapidly expanded its efforts to include investigations of socialist, communist, and liberal organizations. The committee played an instrumental role in closing the Federal Writers' Project in 1938 and the Federal Theatre Project the following year. Its attacks against New Deal supporter Frank Murphy, governor of Michigan, for his sympathies with sit-down strikers played a crucial role in Murphy's defeat when he ran for reelection in 1938.

Sources:

David Bell, *Marxian Socialism in the United States* (Princeton: Princeton University Press, 1967);

David H. Bennett, *Demagogues in the Depression* (New Brunswick, N.J.: Rutgers University Press, 1969);

Alan Brinkley, *Voices of Protest: Huey Long, Father Coughlin, and the Great Depression* (New York: Knopf, 1982);

James MacGregor Burns, *Roosevelt: The Lion and the Fox* (New York: Harcourt, Brace & World, 1956);

August Raymond Ogden, *The Dies Committee* (Washington: D.C.: Catholic University of America Press, 1945);

Arthur M. Schlesinger Jr., *The Politics of Upheaval*, volume 3 of his *The Age of Roosevelt* (Boston: Houghton Mifflin, 1960);

David Shannon, *The Socialist Party in America* (New York: Macmillan, 1955).

THE NEW DEAL STALLS

Court Packing. Reassured by his landslide reelection in 1936, Roosevelt overextended his political power in the following year. Believing that his popularity was a mandate to drive forward with his reformist policies, he overreached his grasp and suffered politically for doing so. The greatest blunder Roosevelt made after 1936 was in trying to pack the U.S. Supreme Court with additional justices. Since *Marbury* v. *Madison* established the principle of judicial review in 1803, the Supreme Court's job has been to decide on the constitutionality of laws. By declaring a law to be unconstitutional, it checks and balances the powers of the legislative and executive branches. Its methods of interpretation are open to question, however, and by the mid 1930s Roosevelt had be-

come increasingly irritated as the highest court in the nation ruled against one New Deal act after another. By 1936 the Supreme Court had found both the AAA and NRA unconstitutional, and many New Deal supporters believed that the court would soon strike down other reformist legislation. Furious with the conservatism of the Supreme Court and buoyed by the 1936 election results, Roosevelt made plans to change the court's composition. In February 1937, hiding behind the pretense that he wanted to free aging justices from a mountainous backlog of cases, Roosevelt made proposals that would have increased the number of Supreme Court justices from nine to as many as fifteen, with the addition of new justices more ideologically attuned to the New Deal than the old. Yet in spring 1937 public opinion, so supportive of its chief executive only months before, increasingly turned against him. At a time when the cult of personality had led such figures as Mussolini, Hitler, and Stalin to dictatorial power in Europe, many Americans found chilling the prospect of the American president's thwarting the Constitution, and they believed the court-packing plan would unreasonably enhance the president's power in a way that the Founding Fathers had never intended. Dixiecrats, Southern Democrats who had been vexed by Roosevelt's dismissal of the two-thirds rule at the Democratic convention, as well as by his increasing drift to the Left, sounded strident calls of disapproval during his court-packing efforts. Chastised by politicians and the press, Roosevelt nevertheless continued to promote his plan. The tension broke in March 1937 when two Supreme Court justices — Chief Justice Charles Evans Hughes and Associate Justice Owen Roberts — abandoned their conservative stances and began voting with the more liberal justices. To the surprise of many, the court quickly proceeded to find the Wagner National Labor Relations Act, the Social Security Act, and other New Deal legislation constitutional. In July the president abandoned his court-packing plan.

The Roosevelt Recession. In summer 1937, basking in what appeared to be the success of the New Deal, Roosevelt moved to cut government expenditures and raise interest rates, hoping to slow inflation and begin to withdraw the heavy hand of the government from the economy. Within weeks, however, the economy was in a tailspin, and by autumn 1937 the economy was back in the doldrums. Suddenly, four million workers were out of work, and economic indicators foretold a worsening future. The Roosevelt administration returned to its policy of massive government spending, and the Federal Reserve loosened its monetary policy. In spring 1938 Roosevelt called for an additional $5 billion in public expenditures. By late 1938, however, the New Deal was drawing to a close. Foreign policy was increasingly occupying the concerns of a nation not yet recovered from the traumas of economic depression.

An Unsuccessful "Purge" of the Democratic Ranks. Dixiecrats — conservative Southern Democrats in Congress — had long disrupted Roosevelt's reform legislation. In 1938, convinced that his landslide victory in 1936 proved the American people were behind him, Roosevelt set out to "purge" the party ranks of those Democrats he considered the most noxious. His efforts met with little success and contributed to the collapse of the New Deal majority in Congress. For the remaining two years of his second term as president, Roosevelt and the New Deal were on the defensive. In fact, many historians argue that the New Deal came to an end with the congressional elections of 1938.

Sources:

James MacGregor Burns, *Roosevelt: The Lion and the Fox* (New York: Harcourt, Brace, 1956);

Paul K. Conkin, *F.D.R. and the Origin of the Welfare State* (New York: Crowell, 1967); republished as *The New Deal* (New York: Crowell, 1969);

William E. Leuchtenburg, *Franklin D. Roosevelt and the New Deal, 1932–1940* (New York: Harper & Row, 1963);

Cabell Phillips, *From Crash to the Blitz, 1929–1939* (New York: Macmillan, 1969);

Arthur M. Schlesinger Jr., *The Politics of Upheaval*, volume 3 of his *The Age of Roosevelt* (Boston: Houghton Mifflin, 1960);

Dixon Wecter, *The Age of the Great Depression, 1929–1941* (New York: Macmillan, 1948).

POLITICS: THE 1930 ELECTIONS

Congressional Election Issues. The stock-market crash of October 1929 set the tone for the congressional elections of 1930. With more than five million people unemployed, fear and uncertainty gripped large portions of the electorate. Democrats campaigned primarily on the issue of the economy, accusing the Republican president and the Republican-controlled Congress of failing to deal with the yearlong economic downturn. Prohibition was a secondary, but important, issue in the states. Alignment for or against Prohibition was nonpartisan, some Democrats and some Republicans falling on either side of the issue. *The New York Times* estimated that prior to the 1930 elections 344 members of the House of Representatives supported Prohibition, but after the elections only 298 congressmen-elect supported it.

Democratic Gains. The elections resulted in a severe setback for the Republican Party, which barely maintained its majorities in both houses of Congress. Republican Senate seats fell from 56 to 48, and the number of Republicans in the House of Representatives dropped from 267 to 214. In the Senate, when the 47 Democrats and the 1 Farmer-Laborite voted together, it was necessary for Vice President Charles Curtis to cast the tie-breaking vote. When President Hoover was elected in 1928 it had looked as though he would be working with a friendly Congress, but only two years later the Republican majority was beginning to evaporate.

Sources:

Kristi Andersen, *The Creation of a Democratic Majority, 1928–1936* (Chicago: University of Chicago Press, 1979);

Samuel Lubell, *The Future of American Politics*, third edition, revised (New York: Harper & Row, 1965);

Senate	71st Congress	72nd Congress	Net Gain/Loss
Democrats	39	47	+8
Republicans	56	48	-8
Other	1	1	0

House	71st Congress	72nd Congress	Net Gain/Loss
Democrats	167	220	+53
Republicans	267	214	-53
Other	1	1	0

Governors	1928	1930	Net Gain/Loss
Democrats	18	25	+7
Republicans	30	21	-9
Other	0	2	+2

Elliot Rosen, *Hoover, Roosevelt, and the Brains Trust: From Depression to New Deal* (New York: Columbia University Press, 1977).

POLITICS: THE 1932 REPUBLICAN NOMINATION RACE

An Unpopular President. By the time the Republican National Convention opened in Chicago on 14 June 1932, the U.S. economy was near collapse. Almost one in four Americans was out of work, and many who still had jobs were suffering the hardships created by reduced hours and lower pay. Because of President Herbert Hoover's unpopularity, brief efforts were made to draft an alternative Republican candidate. Progressive senators Hiram Johnson of California and William E. Borah of Idaho were mentioned, but both declined to be considered. There was also a short-lived effort to place Calvin Coolidge's name into nomination, but the former president refused to begin an insurgent movement within his own party. Only Joseph France, a conservative former senator from Maryland, challenged Hoover. Though France won a few inconsequential primaries, he was never a serious contender, and in the end Hoover won renomination easily. In a colorful moment at the Republican National Convention, France was dragged from the convention hall by police as he tried to ascend the podium to give an unscheduled speech. The alleged reason for his detainment was his failure to produce proper credentials. Convention organizers seemed to be trying to avoid any hint of dissent from the party's renomination of the president.

The Republican Platform. The Republican National Convention was filled with an air of despair. In light of the Depression, defeat in November seemed almost certain. The delegates focused attention away from the troubled economy with a major debate on the prohibition of alcoholic beverages, which had been instituted in 1919 with the Eighteenth Amendment to the U.S. Constitution. After much debate, the delegates voted for a vaguely worded resolution to "allow states to deal with the problem [of prohibition] as their citizens may determine." The 1932 elections were the last in which Prohibition was an issue, because in December 1933 the Twenty-first Amendment to the U. S. Constitution repealed the Eighteenth Amendment. The Republican Party platform called for rugged individualism, asserting that "The people themselves, by their own courage, their own patient and resolute effort . . . can and will work out the cure" to the Depression. Convention speakers L. J. Dickinson of Iowa and Joseph L. Smith of California tried to rouse the delegates' enthusiasm by recounting Republican Party successes of the 1920s, but to little avail. Charles Curtis of Kansas was unenthusiastically nominated for vice president after the favored candidate, Gen. Charles G. Dawes, who had been Coolidge's vice president, refused to be drafted for the job. Hoover, who controlled the convention from the outset, easily won renomination on the first ballot.

POLITICS: THE 1932 DEMOCRATIC NOMINATION RACE

Roosevelt the Frontrunner. Gov. Franklin D. Roosevelt of New York was the frontrunner for the Democratic nomination for president, but with victory for the Democrats almost a certainty, stakes were high, and an internecine primary battle broke out in the Democratic ranks. Challenging Roosevelt were a series of "favorite son" candidates, including Gov. George White of Ohio, Gov. William "Alfalfa Bill" Murray of Oklahoma (with his "Bread, Butter, Bacon, and Beans" campaign), Sen. James H. Lewis of Illinois, Speaker of the House John Nance Garner of Texas, and former senator James A. Reed of Missouri. Of these challengers Garner, promoted by newspaper publisher William Randolph Hearst, had the most convention delegates lined up behind him. Roosevelt faced his greatest challenge, however, from the party's 1928 presidential nominee, Alfred E. "Al" Smith of New York. Smith, supported by party conservatives, had almost two hundred delegate votes when the Democrats opened their convention in Chicago on 27 June. Because the Democratic Party had a rule requiring a candidate to have two-thirds of the delegate vote to win the nomination, Roosevelt, though he held a majority of delegate votes (with 682 votes cast for him early on the morning of 1 July), was 89 votes short of the nomination after three ballots. At this point Garner had 101 delegate votes. To break the impasse Roosevelt's campaign headquarters intimated to Garner — who had the support of the delegates from California and Texas — that the vice-presidential spot on the ticket would be his if he supported Roosevelt. On the fourth ballot Garner released his delegates to vote for Roosevelt. Califor-

nia and Texas moved into the Roosevelt camp, and Roosevelt received 945 votes to become the Democrats' nominee for the presidency. Smith and other conservatives, motivated by what historian Frank Freidel has called a "fierce hatred of Roosevelt," refused to make the nomination unanimous. Elated by his success, Roosevelt broke with tradition — which called for a candidate to wait at home to be informed of his nomination — and flew to Chicago from Albany, New York, to accept the nomination. In his rousing speech to party delegates Roosevelt said,

> On the farms, in the large metropolitan areas, in the smaller cities and in the villages, millions of our citizens cherish the hope that their old standards of living and of thought have not gone forever. Those millions cannot and shall not hope in vain.

> I pledge you, I pledge myself, to a new deal for the American people. Let us all here assembled constitute ourselves prophets of a new order of competence and of courage. This is more than a political campaign; it is a call to arms. Give me your help, not to win votes alone, but to win in this crusade to restore America to its own people.

Democratic Platform. Roosevelt ran on a party platform that offered a mix of conservative and progressive solutions to the economic woes of the day. Condemning "the disastrous policies" of the Republican administration, the platform lambasted President Hoover for failing to balance the federal budget and promised to do so if the Republican candidate were elected. On the progressive side, the Democrats promised a series of federal work programs and relief payments to the needy. Roosevelt hinted at aid for farmers and railroads, as well as at the introduction of industrial planning and governmental regulation of banks and public utilities.

Senate	72nd Congress	73rd Congress	Net Gain/Loss
Democrats	47	60	+13
Republicans	48	35	-13
Other	1	1	0

House	72nd Congress	73rd Congress	Net Gain/Loss
Democrats	220	310	+90
Republicans	214	117	-97
Other	1	5	+4

Governors	1930	1932	Net Gain/Loss
Democrats	25	38	+13
Republicans	21	8	-13
Other	2	2	0

A bumper plate promoting the 1932 Democratic candidates for president and vice president and their stand against Prohibition

POLITICS: THE 1932 ELECTIONS

Roosevelt Wins Big. On election day Roosevelt carried forty-two states. He received a total of 22,809,638 votes (57.4 percent of the popular vote) to Hoover's 15,758,901 (39.7 percent) and won 472 electoral votes to only 59 for Hoover. The Democrats also trounced the Republicans in congressional races. Democrats won 310 seats in the House while Republicans won only 117. The Democrats took control of the Senate, where they outnumbered the Republicans 60–35. The small Farmer-Labor Party captured 5 House seats and 1 Senate seat. The Republicans had been handed the worst electoral defeat in their history, as the Democrats won an impressive mandate from the American people.

Sources:
Frank Freidel, "Election of 1932," in *History of American Presidential Elections 1789–1968*, edited by Arthur M. Schlesinger Jr., volume 3 (New York: Chelsea House/McGraw-Hill, 1971), pp. 2707–2805;

William E. Leuchtenburg, *Franklin D. Roosevelt and the New Deal, 1932–1940* (New York: Harper & Row, 1963).

POLITICS: THE 1934 ELECTIONS

Democrats Increase Their Majority. As off-year elections go, 1934 was a splendid year for the Democrats. The general trend in American history is that the party that wins the presidency loses ground in the following congressional election. Not so in 1934. The majority of voters were impressed with the flurry of activity in Washington during the opening years of the Roosevelt administration. Recalling the failures of the Republicans, voters bucked historical trends and increased the already sizable Democratic majorities in both houses of Congress. Dem-

ocrats ran on their legislative successes and on the popularity of the president, promising future successes if returned to office.

Republicans Attack the New Deal. Conversely, Republican National Chairman Henry P. Fletcher of Pennsylvania engaged his party in an all-out attack on the New Deal. His "Declaration of Policy" warned voters of "domination of an all-powerful central government." If the New Deal policies of the Democrats were continued, he wrote, there would be "limitless inflation." He charged

Senate	73rd Congress	74th Congress	Net Gain/Loss
Democrats	60	69	+9
Republicans	35	25	-10
Other	1	2	+1

House	73rd Congress	74th Congress	Net Gain/Loss
Democrats	310	319	+9
Republicans	117	103	-14
Other	5	10	+5

Governors	1932	1934	Net Gain/Loss
Democrats	38	38	0
Republicans	8	8	0
Other	2	2	0

that Democrats were "seeking covertly to alter the framework of American institutions" and buying votes through the various New Deal programs, then giving millions of Americans work, relief, or farm subsidies. Not all Republican congressional candidates embraced the "Declaration of Policy" — indeed, in many locales it was all but ignored. In Wisconsin Sen. Robert La Follette Jr., a supporter of much that Roosevelt was seeking to accomplish, abandoned the Republican Party to run successfully for reelection to the Senate on the Progressive Party ticket; and the reconstituted Progressive Party also captured seven seats in the House that year. In September 1934 the *Saturday Evening Post* published a series of articles in which former president Hoover attacked the New Deal. For all such efforts Republicans were able to garner only 103 seats in the House against 319 for the Democrats (and 10 for the Farmer-Labor Party). The Democrats increased their number of Senate seats to 69. The 1934 elections were the first — and to date the only — off-year elections in which a first-term president's party gained seats in both houses of Congress. The voting so affirmed the New Deal policies that journalist William Allen White said of Roosevelt, "He has been all but crowned by the people."

Sources:

Kristi Andersen, *The Creation of a Democratic Majority, 1928–1936* (Chicago: University of Chicago Press, 1979);

William E. Leuchtenburg, *Franklin D. Roosevelt and the New Deal, 1932–1940* (New York: Harper & Row, 1963).

POLITICS: THE 1936 REPUBLICAN NOMINATION RACE

Drawing Ideological Battle Lines. The presidential election of 1936 was one of the most ideologically charged in American history. The policy differences between Democrats and Republicans expressed in that year would continue in the same general outline for the rest of the twentieth century. Traditionally the party of states' rights, the Democratic Party became the party of the federally constructed welfare state. Conversely, Republicans abandoned their defense of federal power, a position they had held since the Civil War and Reconstruction, and embraced local and states' rights.

The Republican Candidate Search. The impressive gains of the Democrats in the 1932 and 1934 elections made it difficult for the Republicans to find a viable candidate. Frank Lowden, a former governor of Illinois, was promoted by those who wished to see a moderately liberal probusiness candidate. Lowden, a contestant for the Republican presidential nomination in 1920, was in his seventies and declined to run. Sen. Arthur Vandenberg of Michigan, with aspirations focused on the 1940 presidential election, also refused. Sen. William E. Borah of Idaho was a possibility early on, but he was opposed by party conservatives, and his chances dwindled. Frank Knox, publisher of the *Chicago Daily News,* was also a contender for the nomination, but it was the middle-of-

the-road governor of Kansas, Alfred M. "Alf" Landon, who quickly became the front-runner. As the only Republican governor elected in the Democratic landslide of 1934, Landon, poised and with a proven track record, could, it was hoped, draw votes. At the Republican National Convention, which began on 9 June in Cleveland, Landon was nominated on the first ballot. Knox became the Republican vice-presidential candidate after Vandenberg declined Landon's request. Knox, one of Theodore Roosevelt's Rough Riders in the Spanish-American War in 1898 and a colonel during World War I, used his editorial skills to mount a vigorous attack on the policies of the New Deal, accusing Roosevelt of leading the country down the path toward communism. Landon, a longtime progressive, sought to mitigate the influence of the party's conservative wing, but his success was uneven. Displeased with some aspects of the party platform, Landon sent a message to the convention that emphasized his support for legislation to regulate the hours and wages of women and children and his belief in the need for an expanded civil service. Though divided between conservative and progressive factions, the Republican Party mounted a vigorous campaign against Roosevelt. The Republicans berated the Democrats for fiscal irresponsibility, abandoning the gold standard, and establishing a social-security system that would, they argued, lower workers' purchasing power by its increased tax demands. Nevertheless, Landon seemed at times to be promising to outspend the Democrats on federal support for farmers and aid to the unemployed. To promote their candidates, Republicans hired a New York advertising agency, spending $14,198,203 on the campaign, while the Democrats spent $9,228,407. In the month before the election a *Literary Digest* poll — which had never been wrong — predicted a victory for Republicans and gave them hope that their strategy had worked.

POLITICS: THE 1936 DEMOCRATIC NOMINATION RACE

Democratic National Convention. President Franklin Delano Roosevelt was unopposed for the Democratic presidential nomination. The platform, adopted after the Democratic National Convention opened in Philadelphia on 22 June, echoed the Declaration of Independence, stating:

> *We hold this truth to be self-evident* — that government in a modern civilization has certain inescapable obligations to its citizens, among which are:
> (1) Protection of the family and the home;
> (2) Establishment of a democracy of opportunity for all the people;
> (3) Aid to those overtaken by disaster.

The president and platform also roundly criticized big business and finance capital.

"Rendezvous with Destiny." The president arrived at

Republican presidential candidate Alfred M. Landon (center) campaigning in La Salle, Colorado, 1936

the Democratic National Convention to accept his renomination on 27 June and delivered one of his most frequently quoted speeches, attacking "economic royalists" who were seeking to impose a "new industrial dictatorship." The crowd of one hundred thousand people cheered uproariously as the president said,

> Governments can err, Presidents do make mistakes, but the immortal Dante tells us that divine justice weighs the sins of the cold-blooded and the sins of the warm-hearted in different scales.

> Better the occasional faults of a Government that lives in a spirit of charity than the consistent omissions of a Government frozen in the ice of its own indifference.

> There is a mysterious cycle in human events. To some generations much is given. Of other generations much is expected. This generation of Americans has a rendez-vous with destiny.

At the convention Roosevelt was able to dismantle the traditional two-thirds rule. One effect of this rule change was to weaken the Southern Democrats' power in the party because it took away the ability of a minority faction to exercise what amounted to a veto of a candidate favored by a majority of the delegates.

Attack on Big Business. Roosevelt's "Second New

Deal," which had begun in 1935, had rhetorically declared something of a war on large and powerful corporations. As part of their strategy, Democrats spent much time and energy attacking the conservative American Liberty League and the ideology of business Republicanism. Roosevelt asserted that his New Deal policies had saved capitalism though public-works programs, regulatory reforms, and the Social Security Act. This attack had enhanced the president's standing with the New Deal coalition of voters.

Democratic Coalition Building. Under the able leadership of James A. Farley, the Democrats put together the famous New Deal coalition, a broad spectrum of supporters that included labor, farmers, the unemployed, Southerners, many urban voters, Catholics, Jews, and, for the first time in the nation's history, an overwhelming majority of the African American vote. The New Deal coalition centered its efforts in the cities, courted city machine bosses, and developed a friendly relationship with American Catholics. Whereas Republican presidents during the 1920s had named only eight Catholics to federal judgeships, Roosevelt had appointed fifty-one during his first term of office. Catholic priests praised the president and his programs from their pulpits.

POLITICS: THE 1936 ELECTIONS

Democrats at the Height of Their Power. In the elec-

Senate	74th Congress	75th Congress	Net Gain/Loss
Democrats	69	76	+7
Republicans	25	16	-9
Other	2	4	+2

House	74th Congress	75th Congress	Net Gain/Loss
Democrats	319	331	+12
Republicans	103	89	-14
Other	10	13	+3

Governors	1934	1936	Net Gain/Loss
Democrats	38	39	+1
Republicans	8	6	-2
Other	2	3	+1

tions of 1936 the Democratic Party reached the zenith of its power in the twentieth century. The terms of the 1936 presidential debate would resonate in elections for the remainder of the twentieth century. There was no doubt in 1936 where most Americans stood. The Democratic Party surpassed even its own stratospheric election results of two years before.

A Flawed Poll. During the election campaign the Democrats were given a brief scare. Public-opinion polling was then in its infancy, and a flawed poll conducted by the *Literary Digest* in October 1936 incorrectly predicted a landslide victory for Roosevelt's Republican opponent, Alf Landon of Kansas. As it turned out, the poll sample had been skewed because the poll takers had relied on *Literary Digest* subscription lists and on phone books to compile their polling sample. In the mid 1930s a relatively small number of Americans — generally the wealthier and more conservative ones who voted Republican — owned telephones. The *Literary Digest* predicted that 55 percent of the vote would go to Landon. They were wrong. Election day 1936 was the day of greatest electoral triumph for the Democrats in the party's history. The president received 27,752,869 votes (60.8 percent of the popular vote) to Landon's 16,674,665 (36.5 percent), while Union Party candidate William Lemke received 882,479 votes. In the electoral college Landon, who won in only Maine and Vermont, got only 8 votes; Roosevelt received 523. After the president's landslide victory his supporters gleefully revised the old saying "As Maine goes, so goes the nation" to "As Maine goes, so goes Vermont."

Congressional Elections. In Congress the results were equally one-sided. In the new House of Representatives there would be 331 Democrats and only 89 Republicans (with 13 other seats going to Farmer-Laborites, Progres-

sives, and Socialists). The numbers in the Senate were equally astounding: 76 Democrats and only 16 Republicans (with 4 Farmer-Laborites).

Sources:
Kristi Andersen, *The Creation of a Democratic Majority, 1928–1936* (Chicago: University of Chicago Press, 1979);

Harold F. Gosnell, *Champion Campaigner: Franklin Roosevelt* (New York: Macmillan, 1952);

William E. Leuchtenburg, "Election of 1936," in *History of American Presidential Elections 1789–1968*, edited by Arthur M. Schlesinger Jr., volume 3 (New York: Chelsea House/McGraw-Hill, 1971), pp. 2809–2913;

Samuel Lubell, *The Future of American Politics*, third edition, revised (New York: Harper & Row, 1965).

POLITICS: THE 1938 ELECTIONS

Republican Advance. The congressional elections of 1938 were a major setback for the Democrats. After five years of New Deal policies the Depression had not ended. In late 1937 a severe recession had begun, and by fall 1938 the country had not yet recovered. Increasing numbers of Americans were becoming disenchanted with the New Deal policies. Roosevelt made matters worse for his party in two ways. First, his court-packing scheme struck many Americans as an inappropriate use of executive power. Second, flushed with the gigantic vote of confidence he had received in the 1936 election, Roosevelt believed that by politicking in various states he could help to elect congressmen who would support his agenda and convince voters to withhold support from congressmen he wanted out of office. He miscalculated. In his effort to "purge" the Democratic Party of its most conservative members he began the 1938 campaign season with a train tour through various parts of the country. In New York he opposed Congressman John J. O'Connor; in Georgia he appealed to voters to oust Sen. Walter George; in South Carolina he blasted Sen. Ellison "Cotton Ed" Smith; in Maryland he called for the defeat of Sen. Millard Tydings; and in Iowa he spoke out against Sen. Guy Gillett. He failed. All but O'Connor won reelection.

Republicans Attack the New Deal. In the elections of 1938 Republicans were able to capitalize on the 1937–1938 recession and on the dissension in the Democratic ranks. Their biggest gains came in the Midwest, where they made substantial headway in Illinois, Indiana, Iowa, Michigan, Minnesota, Nebraska, Ohio, and Wisconsin. They fared well in Pennsylvania and New Jersey as well. In California Townsendite Sheridan Downey was elected to the Senate on a platform calling for "Thirty-Dollars-Every-Thursday" as a pension system for the elderly; the plan was subsequently defeated in Congress. While the Democrats maintained their majorities in both houses of Congress, the Grand Old Party (GOP) added 75 seats in the House and 7 in the Senate. The Associated Press calculated that overall the Democrats had received 49 percent of the ballots cast, and the Republicans 47.8 percent — with 3.2 percent going to various other par-

Senate	75th Congress	76th Congress	Net Gain/Loss
Democrats	76	69	-7
Republicans	16	23	+7
Other	4	4	0

House	75th Congress	76th Congress	Net Gain/Loss
Democrats	331	261	-70
Republicans	89	164	+75
Other	13	4	-9

Governors	1936	1938	Net Gain/Loss
Democrats	39	30	-9
Republicans	6	18	+12
Other	3	0	-3

ties. The election of 1938 pumped new life into the Republican Party.

Sources:
James MacGregor Burns, *Roosevelt: The Lion and the Fox* (New York: Harcourt, Brace, 1956);

Samuel Lubell, *The Future of American Politics,* third edition, revised (New York: Harper & Row, 1965);

James T. Patterson, *Congressional Conservatism and the New Deal* (Lexington: Published for the Organization of American Historians by University of Kentucky Press, 1967).

TOWARD WAR: U.S. FOREIGN POLICY AND ISOLATIONISM

American Foreign Policy in the 1930s. In the opening years of what would be a decade of worldwide depression, President Herbert Hoover made a series of proposals to quiet rising international tensions. In 1930 his administration extended the naval-limitations agreements of the early 1920s. In 1931 he proposed a moratorium on international debt, while refusing to cancel those lingering World War I debts owed to the United States by the European powers. Further, Hoover pressed for an international agreement on arms limitation, but the World Disarmament Conference, held in Switzerland in 1932, failed to achieve its goals. International economic and military pressures intensified. Fueled by the global depression, Fascism in Italy, Nazism in Germany, State Socialism in the Soviet Union, and militarism in Japan were ascendant.

Roosevelt and Foreign Policy in the 1930s. Roosevelt's initial foreign policy was mixed. His administration took an isolationist stance at the World Economic Conference in June 1933, when it refused to cooperate in the effort to stabilize world currencies. In 1934, however, he took an internationalist stance in the U.S.-negotiated Reciprocal Trade Agreements on tariff reductions. His vacillating policies reflected his political priorities: at the beginning of his administration domestic issues were more important than foreign policy.

The "Good Neighbor Policy." In December 1933 Secretary of State Cordell Hull committed the United States to a new policy toward Central and South America. Signing an international accord that declared, "No state has the right to intervene in the internal or external affairs of another," Hull initiated an agenda that was to characterize Roosevelt's presidency. This "Good Neighbor Policy" put an end to the repeated U.S. military interventions in Latin America. Critics of the policy have argued, however, that it was a smokescreen for redoubled economic intervention and exploitation of the region by the United States.

Isolationism. Isolationists held the view that America ought not get involved in European wars and in other "entangling alliances." They believed that it was not the role of the United States to be policeman to the world or to make over other nations in its own image. Isolationism was not restricted to one end of the political spectrum. Conservatives, liberals, and radicals might be isolationist. Indeed, in the early and mid 1930s most Americans were isolationist.

Roosevelt and the Isolationists. In his first term Roosevelt worked closely with isolationist progressives such as Senators Robert La Follette Jr. of Wisconsin, Hiram Johnson of California, George Norris of Nebraska, and Burton K. Wheeler of Montana. Other influential isolationists in the Senate included William E. Borah of Idaho, Gerald P. Nye of North Dakota, Henrik Shipstead of Minnesota, and Arthur Vandenberg of Michigan. During his second term Roosevelt gradually broke with the isolationists as international tensions rose. In October 1937 Roosevelt's famous quarantine speech — which called for international cooperation in bringing unspecified economic and diplomatic pressure to bear on aggressor nations — irritated the isolationists. Beginning in 1937 they increasingly, and sometimes angrily, turned against the president. After France fell to Germany in 1940, however, isolationists were forced to rethink their position.

The Nye Investigating Committee and Neutrality Acts. In 1934–1936 the discoveries of a Senate investigating committee headed by Senator Nye helped to fuel the nation's mood of isolationism. Exposing war profiteering by banks and corporations during World War I, the Nye committee investigation led many to conclude that the interests of American banks and corporations had driven the United States into a war the nation should have avoided. Many isolationists believed that the Atlantic and Pacific Oceans afforded the United States sufficient protection from foreign aggression. The Senate's refusal to allow the United States to join the World Court in 1935 was another

In July 1936 Gen. Francisco Franco, commander of the Spanish troops in North Africa, led an uprising against the democratically elected government of the Spanish Republic. This Popular Front coalition of antifascists, socialists, and communists was widely supported by liberals and leftists both in Spain and worldwide. Franco was backed by the conservative elements of Spanish society, including most of the hierarchy of the Catholic Church. He was also aided by Fascist Italy and Nazi Germany, both of which quickly sent troops and weapons. A few months later the Soviet Union entered the conflict on the side of the Republic but provided less military aid than Italy and Germany were giving Franco.

Great Britain then began a campaign to keep the rest of the major powers out of the civil war in Spain. Despite a mutual-aid agreement between France and Spain, Foreign Secretary Anthony Eden of Great Britain persuaded the French Popular Front government of Léon Blum to declare its neutrality. Wanting to offend neither British allies nor isolationists, Catholics, and anticommunists at home, President Roosevelt had no difficulty in invoking the Neutrality Act of 1936, and by the following January Congress had specifically outlawed supplying weapons to either side in the conflict. Although this embargo applied to both sides, it was far more damaging to the ill-equipped troops of the Spanish Republic, especially in the face of the modern, mechanized German army that was turning Spain into a testing ground for new tanks and aircraft. The only nations willing to sell weapons openly to the Republic were Mexico and the Soviet Union, and many shipments were impounded in neutral France before they could reach Spain. (The U.S. merchant marine smuggled arms and supplies to both sides.)

Some Americans sided with Franco. Large corporations helped Franco by providing items such as trucks and fuel, which were not covered under the embargo. Many other Americans, particularly liberals and leftists, deplored their government's refusal to help the Republic and pointed with alarm to the spread of fascism in Europe. Some twenty-eight hundred Americans defied a U.S. State Department ban on travel to Spain, and — along with about thirty-five thousand volunteers from other countries, including Great Britain, Canada, Ireland, and France — they fought for the Spanish Republic in the International Brigades set up by the Soviet Union under the aegis of Comintern (the Communist International movement). The Americans were organized in the Abraham Lincoln Battalion, the George Washington Battalion, and the John Brown Battery. (The first of these units, often incorrectly called the Abraham Lincoln Brigade, is the best known, and American veterans of the Spanish Civil War were often called Lincolns.) More than a hundred other Americans helped the Republican cause as medical personnel and ambulance drivers. Americans fought bravely for the Republican cause, and more than seven hundred had died by the time Franco's troops took Madrid in March 1939.

Back in the United States prominent Americans such as Albert Einstein, Dorothy Parker, Paul Robeson, Helen Keller, A. Philip Randolph, and Gypsy Rose Lee lobbied the federal government to end the arms embargo and raised money to buy medical supplies for the Republican troops. Well-known American writers also went to Spain and covered the war for newspapers and magazines back home. Novelists Ernest Hemingway and John Dos Passos and playwright Lillian Hellman were part of a group that went to Spain to produce *The Spanish Earth* (1937), a documentary movie presenting a pro-Republican view of the war.

While many combatants and noncombatants were Communists or Communist sympathizers, others were simply antifascists with a fervent belief in democratic principles. Once in Spain, some pro-Republicans — notably Dos Passos — discovered the Kremlin was deeply entrenched in policy making. Communist factions of the coalition government were becoming more concerned with weeding out the anarchists and Trotskyites within their own ranks than with fighting Franco. While remaining antifascist, some Americans came home from Spain equally fearful of International Communism — and their fears were confirmed by the Hitler-Stalin Pact of August 1939.

Sources: Ronald Fraser, *Blood of Spain: An Oral History of the Spanish Civil War* (New York: Pantheon, 1979);

Peter Wyden, *The Passionate War: A Narrative History of the Spanish Civil War, 1936–1939* (New York: Simon & Schuster, 1983).

indication of the isolationist mood pervading the country. Fearful of being pulled into a war from which it would suffer but not benefit, Congress passed three acts that declared American neutrality. In the event that a

Sen. Gerald P. Nye, Assistant Secretary of State R. Walton Moore, and Sen. Key Pittman, chairman of the Senate Foreign Relations Committee, during the campaign for passage of the Neutrality Act of 1936

war broke out between other countries, the Neutrality Acts of 1935 and 1936 made it clear that the United States would not supply either side with weapons or ammunition. The Neutrality Act of 1937 moved the nation further in the direction of isolation and asserted a "cash-and-carry" policy by which warring countries could purchase weapons but not ammunition in cash only and that those supplies could be shipped from American ports only in the bottoms of the belligerents. When the Spanish Civil War broke out in 1936, the United States remained on the sidelines. When tensions rose in Asia as a result of Japan's expansionist foreign policy, Roosevelt's quarantine speech, in which he called for expansionist nations to be contained, was ill received. When, on 12 December 1937, Japanese airplanes sank the *Panay*, a U.S. gunboat navigating the Yangtze River in China, Americans were ready to forgive the incident after a formal Japanese apology.

The Open Door in China, War with Japan. In 1899 and 1900 Secretary of State John Hay had unilaterally asserted the "Open Door policy" to Asia. It was, he declared, the right of all countries to equal trading opportunities in China. Two decades later, in 1922, the Open Door was made international law in the Nine Power Treaty. In 1931, after Japan occupied the region of China known as Manchuria in direct defiance of the Open Door Policy, tensions ran high between Washington and Tokyo. President Hoover's secretary of state, Henry L. Stimson, viewed the Japanese invasion and takeover of Manchuria as a challenge to U.S. foreign policy in the East. The Stimson Doctrine of January 1932 called for the United States to refuse recognition of the Japanese puppet government in Manchuria. After Roosevelt became president his secretary of state, Cordell Hull, sent occasional notes of protest to Japan, but the severity of

such criticism was mitigated by the fact that Japan was an important trading partner with the United States. In 1937, when war erupted between Japan and China, Roosevelt was inhibited by broad national sentiments of isolationism and acted cautiously, hoping that Japan would agree to withdraw its troops. By 1939 Roosevelt recognized the need for firmer action. He canceled the 1911 U.S. trade agreement with Japan, and when the Japanese signed the Tripartite Pact with Germany and Italy in September 1940, President Roosevelt initiated a partial embargo against Tokyo. Thus, it was that the Japanese challenge to the Open Door Policy became a major cause of the disagreement between the United States and Japan that exploded with the bombing of Pearl Harbor on 7 December 1941.

Drifting toward War. As the 1930s drew to a close, the United States stood by as Hitler began his expansionist push eastward. Congress and the president reasserted American neutrality as Hitler moved troops into the Rhineland in 1936, marched on Austria in March 1938, and seized the Sudetenland from Czechoslovakia the following September. Hitler violated the Munich Accord, invaded Czechoslovakia in March 1939, and signed a nonaggression pact with Stalin later that year. As German soldiers invaded Poland, the United States remained on the sidelines. As World War II began, Roosevelt declared, "This nation will remain a neutral nation," but he called for a revision of the Neutrality Acts to allow the United States to sell England and its Allies weapons and ammunition. Skeptically, Congress allowed them to purchase the arms on a cash-and-carry basis.

War Ends the Depression. Ironically, European orders for war goods sparked a phenomenal economic boom that brought the United States out of the Depression for good. So long as America stayed out of the war, it seemed, both peace and prosperity were possible. Members of the Roosevelt administration, however, leaned toward American intervention in the European conflict. Economists within the administration warned that German success in Europe and Japanese victory in Asia would irrevocably close huge markets for American goods. Unless the United States intervened in these conflicts, they argued, America's economic future would be worse than the Great Depression. Such arguments, in concert with war atrocities on the part of Germany and Japan, convinced Roosevelt and his administration that the United States must set isolationism aside and take an active hand in the European and Asian wars. Ever the political leader, Roosevelt devoted himself to convincing his countrymen to enter the greatest military conflagration in world history. While the 1930s ended with the disappearance of the Great Depression, peace, too, was fading away.

Sources:

Wayne S. Cole, *Roosevelt and the Isolationists, 1932–1945* (Lincoln: University of Nebraska Press, 1983);

Robert A. Divine, *The Illusion of Neutrality* (Chicago: University of Chicago Press, 1962);

Manfred Jonas, *Isolationism in America, 1935–1941* (Ithaca, N.Y.: Cornell University Press, 1966);

William R. Keylor, *The Twentieth-Century World: An International History*, second edition, revised (New York: Oxford University Press, 1992).

HEADLINE MAKERS

HERBERT HOOVER

1874-1964

PRESIDENT OF THE UNITED STATES (1929-1933)

Depression-Era President. The thirty-first president of the United States, Herbert Hoover was chief executive at the beginning of the worst economic depression in American history. His was a serious, incorruptible, and independent intellect. He lacked the personal charm and charisma of other politicians, but there was probably little that any sitting president could have done to win the popularity contest at the polls in 1932, and he lost the election to Democrat Franklin D. Roosevelt.

Background. Born in Iowa on 10 August 1874, Herbert Clark Hoover was orphaned as a child. A Quaker known from his childhood as "Bert" to his friends, he began a career as a mining engineer soon after graduating from Stanford University in 1895. Within twenty years he had used his engineering knowledge and business acumen to make a fortune as an independent mining consultant.

Public Service. In 1914 Hoover administered the American Relief Committee, which assisted more than one hundred thousand Americans trapped in Europe at the outbreak of World War I. During the war he was praised for his efficiency as head of the Commission for Relief in Belgium, as U.S. Food Administrator, and as chairman of the Interallied Food Council. After the war he directed the American Relief Administration. All told, Hoover was responsible for distributing more than $5 billion worth of food, clothing, and supplies during and after the war, and he was deservedly acclaimed worldwide as a great humanitarian. From 1918 into the early 1920s Europeans sent him tens of thousands of cards, letters, and drawings to express their gratitude for

their "Hoover lunches." In Finland to "hoover" came to mean to act in a kindly and helpful manner. In the United States to "hooverize" came to mean to ration one's food and supplies, because while he was U.S. Food Administrator in 1917–1918, Hoover importuned the nation to conserve voluntarily resources and comply with meatless and wheatless days. Franklin D. Roosevelt said of Hoover in 1920, "He is certainly a wonder and I wish we could make him President of the United States. There could not be a better one." In 1919 Hoover founded the Hoover Institution on War, Revolution, and Peace at Stanford University. As secretary of commerce in the Harding and Coolidge administrations (1921–1929), Hoover was widely celebrated for his leadership. In 1928 he defeated Democrat Al Smith for the presidency.

The Great Depression. Inaugurated on 4 March 1929, Hoover had been president only seven months when the stock market crashed. Ironically, at the start of his campaign he had declared that Americans were approaching "the final triumph over poverty," and he praised Americans' "rugged individualism" as a solution to the nation's economic problems. When it became clear that the Depression could not be ended without government intervention, Hoover reversed his stand and initiated a series of innovative federal programs in an attempt to counteract the economic downturn. But the economy continued to worsen, and he was handily defeated by Roosevelt in the presidential election of 1932. During Hoover's 1932 campaign one of his critics, Walter Lippmann, observed: "Mr. Hoover has long since abandoned his old faith in rugged individualism. His platform is a document of indefatigable paternalism. Its spirit is that of the Great White Father providing help for all his people. Every conceivable interest which has votes is offered protection, or subsidies, or access of some kind to the Treasury."

Out of Office. After his defeat Hoover kept silent on public policy for two years. In late 1934 he began his attack on the New Deal with *The Challenge to Liberty*, a book in which he articulated his ideological views. He remained active in the Republican Party, quietly and unsuccessfully seeking his party's presidential nomination in 1936 and 1940. As an elder statesman he headed government commissions under Presidents Harry S Truman and Dwight D. Eisenhower. After years of service to the nation, Herbert Hoover died on 29 October 1964.

Sources:
David Burner, *Herbert Hoover: The Public Life* (New York: Knopf, 1978);

Joan Hoff-Wilson, *Herbert Hoover, Forgotten Progressive* (Boston: Little, Brown, 1975).

CORDELL HULL

1871-1955

SECRETARY OF STATE (1933-1944)

A Popular Democrat. Cordell Hull was the longest-serving secretary of state in American history. For much of that time he was one of the most popular Democrats in the nation, and until President Franklin D. Roosevelt announced his intention to seek an unprecedented third term, Hull was considered the frontrunner for the Democratic presidential nomination in 1940.

Background. Born in Tennessee, Hull graduated from Cumberland University Law School in 1891 and was elected to the Tennessee legislature two years later. After serving in the Spanish-American War and working as a lawyer, he was appointed a Tennessee circuit court judge in 1903. In 1907 he was elected to the U.S. House of Representatives, where as a progressive Democrat he was instrumental in sponsoring several important tax laws, including the Federal Income Tax Act of 1913. During the 1920s he actively promoted reciprocal trade agreements as a means to enhance U.S. foreign trade. In 1930 he was elected to the U.S. Senate, where he served until he became Roosevelt's secretary of state in March 1933. Under Hull's leadership the State Department successfully negotiated reciprocal trade agreements with Britain, France, and many Latin American countries. Hull spearheaded the administration's "Good Neighbor Policy" with Central and South America.

World War II. As tensions increased in Europe in the years prior to World War II, Roosevelt increasingly held the reins of American foreign policy, and Hull, ever loyal to the president, was to some degree pushed aside. To a large extent Hull was in charge of the unsuccessful negotiations with the Japanese until the month before Pearl Harbor was attacked. Roosevelt directed much of European foreign policy himself, relying on Undersecretary of State Sumner Welles, sometimes to Hull's great vexation. (Instead of sending Hull as special emissary to Europe in 1940, Roosevelt sent Welles, who was a personal friend.)

Roosevelt reportedly told W. Averell Harriman that he did not take Hull to his conferences with Churchill and Stalin because Hull was "difficult to handle. . . . [and] would be a nuisance." In private conversations Hull sometimes expressed his frustration with the president's "treatment of the [State] Department and encroachment in foreign affairs." During the war Hull reportedly told Treasury Secretary Henry Morgenthau Jr., "The President runs foreign affairs. I don't know what's going on. . . . Since Pearl Harbor he does not let me help in connection with foreign affairs." In public, however, Hull supported Roosevelt with vigor.

Creating the United Nations. Hull succeeded in ousting Welles from the State Department in 1943 and thereafter enjoyed more involvement in and control over U.S. foreign policy and negotiations. In October 1943 Hull met with Anthony Eden of Great Britain and V. M. Molotov of the Soviet Union in Moscow to lay the groundwork for the creation of the United Nations. Addressing a joint session of Congress on his return from Moscow, Hull declared that in the postwar world "there will no longer be need for spheres of influence. . . ." In this judgment — as well as in his assessment of Stalin as "a remarkable personality, one of the great statesmen and leaders of his age" — Hull missed the mark. Hull contributed further to establishing the groundwork for the United Nations, playing prominent roles at the Dumbarton Oaks Conference (August–October 1944), where proposals for the charter were drawn up, and at the founding conference in San Francisco (April–June 1945). In 1945 he was awarded the Nobel Peace Prize for his efforts.

Retirement. Having resigned as secretary of state in December 1944, Hull spent the early years of his retirement writing his memoirs. After a lengthy illness, he died in 1955.

Sources:
Robert Dallek, *Franklin D. Roosevelt and American Foreign Policy 1932–1945* (New York: Oxford University Press, 1979);

Cordell Hull, *The Memoirs of Cordell Hull*, 2 volumes (New York: Macmillan, 1948);

Julius W. Pratt, *Cordell Hull, 1933–44* (New York: Cooper Square, 1964).

FIORELLO LA GUARDIA

1882-1947

MAYOR OF NEW YORK (1934-1945)

A Popular Politician. Fiorello La Guardia was a leading progressive in New York politics from the 1920s until his death in 1947. During the 1930s his flamboyant political style and his hardworking nature made him one of the most popular political figures in the United States.

Background. La Guardia was born in New York City to an Italian father and Jewish mother. Because his father was in the U.S. Army, La Guardia spent much of his youth living on army posts in Arizona, South Dakota, and other western states. La Guardia also spent time with his mother's family in Trieste, then part of Austria. From 1901 to 1906 La Guardia, who knew six European languages in addition to English, worked at American consulates in Hungary and Austria. He entered New York University Law School in 1906, and while he was a student there he worked part-time as an interpreter on Ellis Island and with labor and immigrant groups on the Lower East Side of Manhattan. After graduating in 1910 he began practicing law in New York City. While serving as deputy attorney general of New York (1915–1917), he fought vigorously against the corruption of Tammany Hall, the Democratic political machine that controlled city politics. He was elected to the U.S. House of Representatives in 1916, but in 1917 he stepped down from his congressional seat to serve as a pilot in World War I. After the war he was president of the New York City Board of Aldermen (1920–1921) before he was reelected to Congress in 1922. In Congress he fought for labor reforms, including the Norris–La Guardia Act of 1932, which restricted the use of federal court injunctions against striking workers.

Mayor of New York. Having run for mayor of New York in 1929 and lost, La Guardia ran again in autumn 1933 on a Fusion ticket and was elected. Often called "The Little Flower" (a translation of his first name as well as a reference to his diminutive stature), La Guardia was well known for his charm and charisma. He read the comics to children over the radio during a newspaper-delivery strike; riding in the sidecar of a motorcycle, he went to burning buildings and once helped rescue a fireman from under a fallen beam; he also distributed presents to the sick during the holiday season. For three consecutive terms of office his leadership of New York was bipartisan and honest. The Roosevelt administration worked closely with La Guardia and helped the city develop parks, schools, highways, and an airport (subsequently named after La Guardia). A vigorous supporter of Roosevelt in the 1936 election, he hoped to be rewarded by being appointed Roosevelt's secretary of war during World War II, but it was not to be. In 1945 he chose not to seek a fourth term as mayor, and in 1946 he served as director of the United Nations Relief and Rehabilitation Administration. His autobiography was posthumously published in 1948.

Sources:

Thomas Kessner, *Fiorello H. La Guardia and the Making of Modern New York* (New York: McGraw-Hill, 1989);

Fiorello La Guardia, *The Making of an Insurgent: An Autobiography, 1882–1919*, edited by Morris R. Werner (Philadelphia: Lippincott, 1948).

ALFRED M. "ALF" LANDON

1887-1987

GOVERNOR OF KANSAS (1933-1937)

REPUBLICAN PRESIDENTIAL CANDIDATE (1936)

Republican Candidate. A middle-of-the-road Republican, Alf Landon took on a popular president in an election that gave the American people their first chance to express their opinion of the major expansion of the federal government that had taken place in the last four years. Unlike many fellow Republicans, Landon supported some New Deal programs and offered his own solutions for the nation's economic woes, but the voters in the 1936 presidential election overwhelmingly preferred President Franklin D. Roosevelt and his "Alphabet Soup of Acts and Agencies" and handed him a landslide victory over Landon.

Background. Born in Pennsylvania, Alfred Mossman Landon grew up in Marietta, Ohio. In 1904 his family moved to Independence, Kansas, and for the next four years Landon studied law at the University of Kansas. Though admitted to the bar in 1908, Landon chose to enter the business world. After a brief time as a banker he worked as an oil driller and in other commercial endeavors. Following his father into the Progressive wing of the Republican Party, Landon became county chairman for the short-lived Progressive Party in 1914 and secretary to Kansas governor Henry J. Allen in 1922. In 1924, at a time when the racist Ku Klux Klan was a force in Kansas politics, Landon worked closely with newspaperman William Allen White in White's anti-Klan campaign for the governorship. By 1928 Landon had become chairman of the Republican state committee, and he managed Clyde Reed's gubernatorial campaign that year.

Governor of Kansas. In 1932 Landon successfully ran for governor of Kansas on the Republican Party ticket. His success at a time when Republican candidates were generally being savaged at the polls catapulted him to the forefront of Republican Party politics. Declaring that people "cannot get something for nothing," Landon cut taxes, reorganized the state administration, reformed state finances, and sponsored legislation to regulate banks and utilities. Landon also sponsored legislation to make farm foreclosures more difficult and for a time halted foreclosures altogether. He worked closely with the Democratic-controlled federal government, securing $300 million from Washington for projects in his state and helping to write the oil code for the National

Recovery Administration. He also supported Roosevelt's conservation efforts, the attempts of the Agricultural Adjustment Administration to raise farm prices, and governmental programs to assist the unemployed. In 1934 Landon won reelection to the governorship of Kansas. He was the only Republican governor elected in that year.

Presidential Candidate. Landon won the Republican presidential nomination in 1936. He and his running mate, Frank Knox of Chicago, actively challenged the policies of the New Deal. Declaring, "We must drive the spenders out," Landon attacked the Democrats for deficit spending, for unsound monetary policy, and for their failure to solve the problem of unemployment. He attacked Franklin Roosevelt for exceeding the bounds of his constitutional authority by usurping the legislative power of Congress. Overall, Landon sought to take a moderate position. He proposed to aid farmers and promised to treat organized labor and the poor fairly. As president, he asserted, he would seek legislation to regulate big business and expand world trade. He emphasized the need for a balanced budget and more efficient administration of the federal government, as well as denouncing racism. Many other Republicans urged a more conservative approach. Leading members of the American Liberty League, as well as the Republican National Committee chairman, made scathing attacks against the New Deal, and the election of 1936 became one of the most ideologically charged elections in American history. Landon was trounced. Roosevelt's New Deal coalition of workers, minorities, the poor, urban machines, Southerners, and factions of capitalists and commercial bankers — along with the stinging memory of Hoover's failed policies — posed an unconquerable opponent for Landon. He received only 16,674,665 votes to Roosevelt's 27,752,869 and carried only two states, with 8 electoral votes against Roosevelt's 523 electoral votes.

Later Career. In 1938 Roosevelt appointed Landon vice chairman of the Inter-American Conference in Peru. During World War II Landon roused Republican opponents to support some of Roosevelt's policies. After the war Landon attended to his business interests. Although he was respected as a party elder he had little influence.

Sources:

Donald R. McCoy, *Landon of Kansas* (Lincoln: University of Nebraska Press, 1966);

Frederick Palmer, *This Man Landon: The Record and Career of Governor Alfred M. Landon of Kansas,* revised and enlarged edition (New York: Dodd, Mead, 1936);

William Allen White, *What It's All About: Being a Reporter's Story of the Early Campaign of 1936* (New York: Macmillan, 1936).

HUEY P. LONG

1893-1935

GOVERNOR OF LOUISIANA (1928-1931)

U.S. SENATOR (1932-1935)

"The Kingfish." During the first two years of Franklin D. Roosevelt's presidency, Sen. Huey P. Long, nicknamed "The Kingfish," was a demagogic opponent of the New Deal, offering his own popular solution for poverty and unemployment.

Background. Huey Pierce Long Jr. was born and grew up on his family's farm in northern Louisiana. He attended the University of Oklahoma School of Law for a semester and passed the Louisiana bar examination in 1915 after further study at the Tulane University Law School. In 1918 Long was elected to the state railroad commission, which became the public-service commission in 1921. Long became its chairman in 1924, the year in which he narrowly lost his first bid for the governorship. He ran again in 1928, campaigning with a banner that read "EVERY MAN A KING, BUT NO ONE WEARS A CROWN" and won. He achieved nearly absolute power as governor and was often called the "dictator of Louisiana." Once, when an opponent tried to show him that he was violating the state constitution, Long brushed the document aside and said, "I'm the Constitution around here now." While he built roads, bridges, and government buildings and improved the state's schools, there was an undercurrent of corruption in his methods. In 1929 he was impeached, but not convicted, on charges of bribery and misconduct. Though elected to the U.S. Senate in 1930, the ever-colorful Long refused to take the office until 1932. If he had gone to Washington in 1930, he would have been succeeded by the lieutenant governor, who was a political opponent. By waiting until his term as governor expired in 1932, he was able to engineer the election of a hand-picked successor. Long continued to control the state from Washington.

Senator Long. By 1934, with Roosevelt's New Deal policies having only partial success in improving the economy, a spirit of radicalism was catching fire in parts of the nation. Frustrated and disillusioned by the severity and length of the Depression, some Americans enthusiastically embraced Long's agenda for redistributing the nation's wealth. His Share-Our-Wealth Society offered a plan to divide the nation's wealth equally among all Americans, guaranteeing everyone a middle-class income of twenty-five hundred dollars and a five-thousand-dollar "homestead allowance." By the end of 1934 millions of supporters were singing the society song, which included the lines "Ev'ry man a king, ev'ry man a king, / . . . / There's enough for all people to share."

Assassination. Long traveled with a contingent of bodyguards, but they were unable to protect him on 8 September 1935, when Dr. Carl Weiss assassinated the forty-two-year-old demagogue in the Louisiana State Capitol building. In response Long's bodyguards riddled Weiss's body with sixty-one bullets. The story of Long's rise and fall is the basis for Robert Penn Warren's Pulitzer Prize–winning novel *All the King's Men* (1946).

Sources:
Alan Brinkley, *Voices of Protest: Huey Long, Father Coughlin, and the Great Depression* (New York: Knopf, 1982);

T. Harry Williams, *Huey Long* (New York: Knopf, 1969).

FRANCES PERKINS

1882-1965

SECRETARY OF LABOR (1933-1945)

First Woman Cabinet Member. Frances Perkins was the first American woman appointed to a cabinet post. As secretary of labor under Franklin D. Roosevelt, she was a leading force in New Deal labor policy.

Background. Born in Boston, Frances Perkins was a vigorous advocate for social justice. After graduating from Mount Holyoke College in 1902, she became a teacher. In 1904, when she took a job at a school in Lake Forest, Illinois, she began volunteer work in Chicago settlement houses, learning firsthand the problems of the poor. In 1907 she moved to Philadelphia, where she became general secretary of the Research and Protective Association. After moving to New York in 1909 and earning an A.M. in economics and sociology at Columbia University in 1910, she became secretary of the New York Consumers' League (1910–1912). She worked to address the problems of working conditions and lobbied the state legislature for industrial reform. While she was secretary of the Committee on Safety of the City of New York (1912–1915), she exposed the horrors of sweatshops.

New York State Appointments. In 1918 Gov. Alfred E. Smith appointed Perkins to the New York State Industrial Commission, where she headed the Bureau of Mediation and Arbitration and worked to settle strikes. She lost that post when Smith was defeated in the 1920 gubernatorial election, but when Smith was elected governor again in 1922, she regained her job on the renamed New York State Industrial Board and took over the handling of workmen's compensation cases. Smith made her head of the board in 1926, and in 1928 he named her state industrial commissioner. When Franklin D. Roosevelt became governor in 1929 he reappointed Perkins, who became a trusted adviser. She worked tirelessly for the eight-hour day, stricter factory-safety laws, and protective labor laws for women and children. When the Depression hit, she encouraged Roosevelt to implement state unemployment insurance as well as relief payments to the poor.

Madame Secretary. After Roosevelt was elected president in 1932, he named Perkins to his cabinet. As U.S. secretary of labor, Perkins enlarged the department's Bureau of Women and Children and put its Mediation and Conciliation Service on firm footing. She played a commanding role in developing the Civilian Conservation Corps, the National Industrial Recovery Act, and the Fair Labor Standards Act. As chair of the president's Committee on Economic Security, Perkins contributed substantially to crafting the Social Security Act of 1935. During World War II Perkins used her power as secretary of labor to resist conservatives' efforts to undo the labor legislation of the 1930s. After Roosevelt's death in 1945, she resigned her cabinet post, and from that year until her death in 1965 she served on the Civil Service Commission.

Sources:
George Martin, *Madam Secretary: Frances Perkins* (Boston: Houghton Mifflin, 1976);

Frances Perkins, *The Roosevelt I Knew* (New York: Viking, 1946).

ELEANOR ROOSEVELT

1884-1962

FIRST LADY OF THE UNITED STATES (1933-1945)

Political Influence. Though not an elected or appointed governmental official, Eleanor Roosevelt, wife of President Franklin D. Roosevelt, was a towering figure in the politics of her day. In her travels, lectures, and writing, she promoted a liberal political agenda. Her discussions with her husband and her reports to him on what she had seen and heard on her travels were important in determining Roosevelt's political strategies. James Farley, an important adviser and campaign manager to Roosevelt, called her "the most practical woman I've ever met in politics."

Background. A distant cousin of Franklin D. Roosevelt, Anna Eleanor Roosevelt was born into a patrician family whose history stretched back to the colonial era, but her early life was not an easy one. Both of her parents died when she was a young girl. In 1899 she was sent to London, England, to study at a private boarding school for three years. As she was later to recount, she received intellectual and emotional support from the headmistress at the school. In 1905 she and Franklin Roosevelt married. Soon her life was filled with the demands of five children and a politician husband. During World War I her involvement in organizing a soldiers' canteen and her activities for the Red Cross led to a concern for social welfare that would shape her life's work.

Humanitarian, Feminist, Civil Rights Activist. Eleanor Roosevelt spoke out, both privately and publicly, on a variety of issues. Though she opposed the Equal Rights Amendment during the 1930s (believing that women needed special protection at work), she was, nevertheless, a powerful force for women's rights. Many historians credit President Roosevelt's appointment of the first woman cabinet member — Secretary of Labor Frances Perkins — to his wife's influence. The first lady worked for children's rights, showed compassion for working people and the unemployed, and promoted civil rights. "I always looked at everything from the point of view of what I *ought* to do, rarely from what I wanted to do," she once commented. Beginning in January 1936 she wrote a syndicated newspaper column, *My Day*, in which she put a human face on many of the pressing political issues of the day.

Civil Rights for African Americans. Supporting civil rights for African Americans, Eleanor Roosevelt championed a federal antilynching law and successfully pressed for the appointment of African American activist Mary McLeod Bethune to the National Youth Administration. In 1939, after the Daughters of the American Revolution (DAR) refused to let African American vocalist Marian Anderson rent their Constitution Hall for a concert, the first lady personally invited Anderson to perform at the Lincoln Memorial, where she attracted a crowd of seventy-five thousand people. Eleanor Roosevelt resigned her membership in the DAR over the incident. During World War II she directed her efforts toward helping wounded veterans and Jewish refugees from Hitler's Germany. When she died at age seventy-eight, she was mourned by many as "First Lady of the World."

Source:

Joan Hoff-Wilson and Marjorie Lightman, eds., *Without Precedent: The Life and Career of Eleanor Roosevelt* (Bloomington: Indiana University Press, 1984).

FRANKLIN DELANO ROOSEVELT

1882-1945

PRESIDENT OF THE UNITED STATES (1933-1945)

Influential Politician. One of the most influential politicians in the history of the United States, Franklin Delano Roosevelt (often referred to by his initials, FDR) was elected to an unprecedented four terms as president. His administrations created the modern bureaucratic welfare state. He set the political tone for the 1930s in his acceptance speech at the 1932 Democratic National Convention. Breaking with the tradition of accepting the nomination in a formal ceremony after the end of the convention, Roosevelt had flown to Chicago to address the delegates in person.

On 2 July 1932 he declared, "You have nominated me and I know it, and I am here to thank you for the honor. Let it . . . be symbolic that in so doing I broke tradition. Let it be from now on the task of our Party to break foolish traditions." Toward the end of his stirring address he spoke the phrase that was to symbolize his presidency: "I pledge you, I pledge myself, to a new deal for the American people." This "New Deal" was to reshape life for "the forgotten man at the bottom of the economic pyramid" and for other Americans as well. In bold, experimental measures Roosevelt would do nothing less than reconstruct the face of the federal government. Leading the nation through times of economic depression and world war, the thirty-second president was to become one of the most beloved politicians of the twentieth century.

Background. Born into a patrician family in New York, Roosevelt, who grew up on the family estate at Hyde Park, New York, was an only child and pampered by his parents. A fifth cousin of Theodore Roosevelt, twenty-sixth president of the United States, Franklin attended the exclusive Groton School in Massachusetts before entering Harvard University in 1900. After graduating from Harvard in 1904, he entered law school at Columbia University, and the following year he married Anna Eleanor Roosevelt, his fifth cousin once removed. Unlike Theodore Roosevelt, who was a Republican, Franklin Roosevelt threw in his lot with the Democratic Party. His political career was launched in 1910, when he was elected to the New York State Senate. After campaigning for Woodrow Wilson in 1912, he was rewarded by being named assistant secretary of the navy (1913–1920). After running unsuccessfully for the vice presidency on the Democratic ticket with James M. Cox of Ohio in 1920, Roosevelt had to overcome the greatest challenge of his personal life. In 1921 he was stricken with polio, and until the end of his life he would never again walk unassisted. Most often restricted to a wheelchair, he was able to stand only for brief periods with the help of aides and steel leg braces. After a period of convalescence Roosevelt returned to politics and was elected governor of New York State in 1928. He developed a reputation as an honest reform-minded politician and was elected to a second term in 1930.

President of the United States. At his inauguration as president on 4 March 1933, Roosevelt lifted the spirits of millions of Americans by declaring that, though the economy was in collapse, "the only thing we have to fear is fear itself." An accomplished politician, he immediately called an emergency session of Congress and presented to it fifteen major proposals for economic relief and reform. At the end of his first hundred days in office a cooperative Democratic Congress had passed them all. Through a vast array of initiatives he instituted cooperation among capital, labor, and government, as well as government planning and a program of federal deficit spending that many historians credit with saving an economy teetering on the brink of complete ruin. Two years into his first term Roosevelt moved to the left with a series of reforms, including a "soak-the-rich" tax scheme and the establishment of federal Social Security. Some members of the upper-class circles in which he had traveled as a young man labeled him a "class traitor."

Second Term. Beloved by many farmers, laborers, and unemployed Americans, Roosevelt was reelected in 1936 with a landslide victory over Republican Alfred M. Landon. In 1937, confident in his popularity with the American people, he made what was probably his most serious political mistake, causing an uproar with his plan to "pack" the U.S. Supreme Court with justices sympathetic to his New Deal agenda. By 1939 his attention was focused increasingly on the coming war, and by the early 1940s "Dr. Win-the-War" had, as he said, replaced "Dr. New Deal." He toiled indefatigably during World War II, and as his health grew frail he traveled abroad several times to meet with Winston Churchill and Joseph Stalin to coordinate military strategy and plan the postwar peace. Franklin D. Roosevelt died of a cerebral hemorrhage on 12 April 1945 at Warm Springs, Georgia.

Source:
Arthur M. Schlesinger Jr., *The Age of Roosevelt,* 3 volumes (Boston: Houghton Mifflin, 1957–1960).

ROBERT F. WAGNER

1877-1953

U.S. SENATOR (1926-1949)

A Voice for the Common Man. Robert Wagner, Democratic senator from New York, was one of the major architects of the modern American welfare state. A voice in the Senate for working people, the poor, and minorities, Wagner was a political activist who picked his political fights with care and often won. Wagner often relied on social scientists to conceive the initiatives he sponsored.

Background. Born in Germany, Wagner immigrated to New York City with his family at the age of eight. He attended City College of New York, earned a law degree, and then worked his way up the political ladder by forging an urban-progressive coalition. As a New York State assemblyman (1904–1909) and a New York State senator (1910–1918) he became a vocal advocate of laws to protect working people. Elected a justice on the New York State Supreme Court in 1918, he continued to champion the rights of labor.

A New Deal Senator. Wagner's concern for the well-being of working people continued after he was elected to the U.S. Senate in 1926. In 1931 he sponsored a $2 billion public-works program, which President Herbert Hoover signed into law as the Emergency Relief and Reconstruction Act of 1932. After Franklin D. Roosevelt was elected president in 1932, Wagner became the Senate's leading advocate of New Deal legislation. In 1933 he sponsored the Federal Emergency Relief Act, worked vigorously for the inclusion of public-works provisions in the National Industrial Recovery Act (NIRA), and was the primary advocate of its provisions supporting the rights of labor to organize and bargain collectively. That same year he became the first head of the National Labor Board. When the NIRA was declared unconstitutional in 1935, it was Wagner who sponsored the bill that salvaged its labor provisions as the National Labor Relations Act (often called the Wagner Act in his honor). In that same year Wagner introduced the Social Security Act on the Senate floor. At a time when African Americans were often the victims of brutal racist hate crimes, Wagner sponsored an unsuccessful effort to make lynching a federal crime. Always an advocate for the poor, he sponsored public-housing projects with the Wagner-Steagall Housing Act of 1937. In the late 1930s and early 1940s he was an advocate of health-care grants, national unemployment benefits, and government-sponsored health insurance. Resigning from the Senate in 1949 because of ill health, Robert Wagner died in 1953. His son, Robert F. Wagner Jr., was also involved in politics, most notably as mayor of New York City from 1954 until 1965.

Source:
J. Joseph Huthmacher, *Senator Robert F. Wagner and the Rise of Urban Liberalism* (New York: Atheneum, 1968).

PEOPLE IN THE NEWS

On 10 December 1931 **Jane Addams** and **Nicholas Murray Butler** were jointly awarded the Nobel Peace Prize. Addams, a social worker, was the founder of Hull House in Chicago and the first president of the Women's International League for Peace and Freedom. Butler was president of Columbia University and a strong supporter of the Kellogg-Briand Pact of 1928.

In December 1935 the National Council of Negro Women (NCNW) was organized, with **Mary McLeod Bethune** as the first president. Bethune was a leading member of President Franklin D. Roosevelt's "Black Cabinet," a group of African American leaders who lobbied for political reforms.

In April 1935 **William E. Borah,** a senator from Idaho, successfully demanded that funding for the Emergency Relief Appropriation Act and other New Deal relief efforts not be used to build munitions or warships. A persistent opponent of President Roosevelt's foreign policy and the leader of isolationists in the Senate, Borah was a progressive Republican who supported many New Deal programs, including the Tennessee Valley Authority, the Securities and Exchange Commission, National Labor Relations Act (Wagner Act), and Social Security.

In a special election on 12 January 1932 **Hattie Caraway** of Arkansas became the first woman elected to the U.S. Senate, when voters chose her to fill out the remaining year of her late husband's term. Having first filled the seat by appointment of the Arkansas governor after her husband's death in 1931, Caraway was elected to a full term in the Senate in November 1932 and continued to serve there through 1945.

On 10 July 1932 the Farmer-Labor Party nominated **Jacob S. Coxey** as its presidential candidate. He received just more than seven thousand votes in the November election.

In 1932 Mayor **James Michael Curley** of Boston, one of the most prominent urban Democratic political bosses in the 1930s, overcame his initial opposition to Roosevelt's reformist tendencies and supported him for the presidency.

In March 1933 President Franklin D. Roosevelt ap-

pointed **James A. Farley** postmaster general of the United States. Considered one of the most astute and successful campaign managers in U.S. history. As chairman of the Democratic National Committee, Farley orchestrated Roosevelt's 1932 and 1936 presidential election victories.

On 28 May 1932 the Communist Party USA nominated **William Z. Foster** of New York as its presidential candidate and James W. Ford, an African American, as Foster's running mate. The ticket garnered slightly more than one hundred thousand votes in the election.

In early July 1932 powerful urban political boss **Frank Hague** agreed to support the Roosevelt ticket. Mayor of Jersey City from 1917 to 1947, Hague once boasted to a constituent, "I am the law." Roosevelt relied on the political machines in several states as a crucial part of his New Deal coalition. As a reward for Hague's early support, Roosevelt subsequently channeled New Deal aid to New Jersey through Hague's machine.

On 19 May 1933 President Roosevelt appointed **Harry L. Hopkins** administrator of the Federal Emergency Relief Administration (FERA). One of the president's most valued advisers, Hopkins also headed the Works Progress Administration (1935–1938) and other New Deal programs before becoming secretary of commerce (1938–1940) in Roosevelt's cabinet.

On 9 November 1932 President-elect Roosevelt appointed **Louis Howe** his chief secretary. Howe — who once quipped, "It's no trick to make a President. Give me a man who stays reasonably sober, shaves and wears a clean shirt every day" — was among Roosevelt's closest political advisers.

In February 1933 President-elect Roosevelt announced that **Harold Ickes** would be his secretary of the interior. While holding that post until 1946, "Honest Harold" also headed the Public Works Administration and the National Resources Planning Board. A staunch civil rights advocate, Ickes integrated the cafeteria at the Department of the Interior, and, along with Eleanor Roosevelt, he persistently supported civil rights causes.

Hugh S. Johnson stepped down as the head of the National Recovery Administration (NRA) on 15 October 1934. Johnson, who designed the NRA industrial codes, as well as its "blue eagle" symbol, later attacked Roosevelt and the New Deal as socialistic.

On 27 November 1930 **Frank B. Kellogg** was awarded the Nobel Peace Prize for negotiating the Kellogg-Briand Pact of 1928, which outlawed war.

Herbert Lehman, a close friend of Franklin D. Roosevelt, was elected to the first of his four terms as governor of New York State on 8 November 1932. The president referred to Lehman as "my good right arm." As governor Lehman implemented a "Little New Deal" for New York State. Later, as a U.S. senator (1949–1957) Lehman was one of the last of the New Dealers in Congress.

In January 1937 Gov. **Frank Murphy** of Michigan, an ardent liberal and an early supporter of President Roosevelt and the New Deal, came under attack for his support of the sit-down strike by automotive workers in Flint, Michigan. Murphy had previously served the Roosevelt administration as governor general of the Philippines (1935–1936). Roosevelt made him attorney general of the United States in 1938 and appointed him associate justice of the U.S. Supreme Court in 1940.

In December 1937 Sen. **Gerald P. Nye,** a progressive Republican and leading isolationist from North Dakota, claimed that Roosevelt had promoted the Japanese bombing of the U.S. gunboat *Panay* on the Yangtze River in China.

On 13 April 1933 **Ruth B. Owen** became the first female foreign minister from the United States when President Roosevelt appointed her minister to Denmark.

On 1 July 1932 political boss **Thomas Pendergast** of Kansas City, Missouri, agreed to support Roosevelt's candidacy at the Democratic National Convention. As president Roosevelt enhanced Pendergast's hold on the Missouri political machine by dispensing federal patronage to Missouri through him.

In September 1935 **Gerald L. K. Smith,** a protofascist, took over leadership of the Share-Our-Wealth Society after the assassination of Sen. Huey Long. Smith subsequently helped to found the Union Party in 1936, formed the Committee of One Million, and organized the America First Party. In 1944 he ran as the America First Party's presidential candidate.

During the Socialist Party of America convention on 22–24 May 1932, **Norman Thomas** was nominated to run for president on the Socialist Party ticket. Thomas, who ran in every presidential election from 1928 through 1948, got his highest vote, 881,951, in 1932; he received only 187,720 votes in 1936.

Secretary of Agriculture **Henry A. Wallace,** who once said he aspired "to make the world safe for corn breeders," led the Roosevelt administration in developing the Agricultural Adjustment Act, passed on 12 May 1933. Wallace served as vice president during Roosevelt's third term (1941–1945).

In April 1933 Roosevelt appointed his close friend and adviser **Sumner Welles** ambassador to Cuba. As assistant secretary and undersecretary of state (1933–1943) Welles helped to shape U.S. policy toward Latin America and is credited with coining the phrase "Good Neighbor Policy."

DEATHS

Grace Abbott, 61, social worker, head of the U.S. Children's Bureau (1921–1934), active in shaping New Deal policies, 19 June 1939.

Jane Addams, 74, social worker, the first president of the Women's International League for Peace and Freedom, winner of the 1931 Nobel Peace Prize, 21 May 1935.

Newton D. Baker, 66, secretary of war (1916–1921) under President Woodrow Wilson, 25 December 1937.

Albert Sidney Burleson, 74, U.S. congressman from Texas (1899–1913), postmaster general (1913–1921) under President Wilson, 24 November 1937.

Pierce Butler, 83, associate justice of the U.S. Supreme Court (1923–1939), one of the four conservative justices who opposed the New Deal, 16 November 1939.

Joseph Wellington Byrns, 66, U.S. congressman from Tennessee (1909–1936), majority leader of the House of Representatives (1932–1935), and speaker of the House of Representatives (1935–1936), 4 June 1936.

Benjamin N. Cardozo, 68, associate justice of the U.S. Supreme Court (1932–1938), 9 July 1938.

William Patrick Connery Jr., 48, U.S. congressman from Massachusetts (1923–1937), supporter of Roosevelt's New Deal as chair of the House Labor Committee, 15 June 1937.

Royal S. Copeland, 69, medical doctor in Michigan (1889–1908); mayor of Ann Arbor, Michigan (1901–1903); dean of the New York Flower Hospital and Medical College (1908–1918); U.S. senator from New York (1923–1938); a Democratic critic of the New Deal, 17 June 1938.

Edward Prentice Costigan, 64, U.S. senator from Colorado (1931–1937), a leading progressive, 17 January 1939.

John Joseph Coughlin, 78, political ward boss in Chicago for more than fifty years, 8 November 1938.

James Joseph Couzens Jr., 64, U.S. senator from Michigan (1922–1936) who became known as the "New Deal Republican" during the 1930s, 22 October 1936.

Herbert Croly, 61, political writer whose progressive views influenced Franklin D. Roosevelt, 17 May 1930.

Charles Curtis, 76, U.S. congressman (1893–1906) and senator (1907–1913, 1915–1929) from Kansas, vice president (1929–1933) under President Herbert Hoover, 8 February 1936.

Bronson M. Cutting, 46, U.S. senator from New Mexico (1927–1935), a Republican who supported the New Deal, died in a plane crash, 6 May 1935.

George Henry Dern, 63, governor of Utah (1924–1933), secretary of war (1933–1936) under President Franklin D. Roosevelt, 27 August 1936.

Joseph M. Dixon, 67, U.S. congressman (1903–1907) and senator (1907–1913) from Montana, governor of Montana (1921–1925), first assistant secretary of the interior (1929–1933), a manager of Theodore Roosevelt's 1912 presidential campaign, 22 May 1934.

Simeon Davison Fess, 75, conservative U.S. congressman (1913–1923) and senator (1923–1935) from Ohio, Republican whip (1929–1933), Republican National Committee chairman (1930–1932), 23 December 1936.

Duncan Upshaw Fletcher, 77, U.S. senator from Florida (1909–1936), a moderate Democrat active on the Senate Banking and Currency Committee, 17 June 1936.

Charlotte Perkins Gilman, 75, feminist, socialist, and a founding member of the Woman's Peace Party (1915), 17 August 1935.

Louis McHenry Howe, 65, secretary to President Franklin D. Roosevelt, 18 April 1936.

William Lorimer, 72, U.S. congressman (1895–1901, 1903–1909) and senator (1909–1912), a Republican expelled from the Senate in 1912 for employing "corrupt methods and practices" in his Senate campaign, 3 September 1933.

Floyd B. Olson, 44, Farmer-Labor Party governor of Minnesota (1930–1936), 22 August 1936.

Milo Reno, 70, a leader of the Farmers' Holiday Association, 5 May 1936.

Joseph T. Robinson, 64, U.S. congressman (1903–1913)

and senator (1913–1937) from Arkansas, Democratic leader in the Senate (1923–1937), ran unsuccessfully for vice president on the ticket with Alfred E. Smith (1928), 14 July 1937.

Thomas D. Schall, 57, U.S. congressman (1915–1925) and senator (1925–1935) from Minnesota, a conservative Republican and a vociferous opponent of Roosevelt and the New Deal, blinded by an accident in 1907, died after being struck by a car in Washington, D.C., 22 December 1935.

John Simpson, 62, head of the Oklahoma Farmers' Union (1917–1931), president of the National Farmers' Union in the early 1930s, 15 March 1934.

Hoke Smith, 76, secretary of the interior (1893–1896) under President Grover Cleveland, governor of Georgia (1907–1909, 1911), U.S. senator (1911–1921), leader of the campaign to disenfranchise African Americans in Georgia, 27 November 1931.

Melvin A. Traylor, 55, businessman and informal adviser to the New Deal on financial matters, 14 February 1934.

George F. Warren, 64, expert on farm management and a fiscal adviser to President Franklin D. Roosevelt, 24 May 1938.

PUBLICATIONS

Grace Adams, *Workers on Relief* (New Haven: Yale University Press / London: Oxford University Press, 1939);

Frederick Lewis Allen, *Only Yesterday: An Informal History of the Nineteen-Twenties* (New York: Harper, 1931);

Joseph Alsop, *Men Around the President* (New York: Doubleday, Doran, 1939);

Joseph Alsop and Turner Catledge, *The 168 Days* (Garden City, N.Y.: Doubleday, Doran, 1938);

Charles A. Beard, *America Faces the Future* (Boston: Houghton Mifflin, 1932);

Charles A. Beard and Mary R. Beard, *America in Midpassage*, 2 volumes (New York: Macmillan, 1939);

Adolf A. Berle and Gardiner C. Means, *Modern Corporation and Private Property* (New York: Commerce Clearing House, 1932);

Stuart Chase, *A New Deal* (New York: Macmillan, 1932);

W. E. B. Du Bois, *Black Reconstruction: An Essay Toward a History of the Part Which Black Folk Played in the Attempt to Reconstruct Democracy in America* (New York: Harcourt, Brace, 1935);

James A. Farley, *Behind the Ballots: The Personal History of a Politician* (New York: Harcourt, Brace, 1938);

Herbert Hoover, *American Ideals versus the New Deal: A Series of Ten Addresses upon Pressing National Problems* (New York: Printed by the Scribner Press, 1937);

Hoover, *The Challenge to Liberty* (New York & London: Scribners, 1934);

Hoover, *Shall We Send Our Youth to War* (New York: Coward-McCann, 1939);

Theodore G. Joslin, *Hoover Off the Record* (Garden City, N.Y.: Doubleday, Doran, 1934);

Betty and Ernest K. Lindley, *A New Deal for Youth: The Story of the National Youth Administration* (New York: Viking, 1938);

Ernest K. Lindley, *Half Way with Roosevelt* (New York: Viking, 1936; revised, 1937);

Lindley, *The Roosevelt Revolution, First Phase* (New York: Viking, 1933);

Walter Lippmann, *The New Imperative* (New York: Macmillan, 1935);

Lippmann, *Notes on the Crisis* (New York: John Day, 1931);

Lippmann, *The Supreme Court, Independent or Controlled?* (New York: Harper, 1937);

Leverett Lyon, *The National Recovery Administration* (Washington, D.C.: Brookings Institution, 1935);

H. L. Mencken, *Making a President* (New York: Knopf, 1932);

Mencken, *Treatise on Right and Wrong* (New York: Knopf, 1934);

Raymond Moley, *After Seven Years* (New York: Harper, 1939);

Edwin G. Nourse, *Three Years of the Agricultural Adjustment Administration* (Washington, D.C.: Brookings Institution, 1937);

Frederick Palmer, *This Man Landon: The Record and Career of Governor Alfred M. Landon of Kansas,* revised and enlarged edition (New York: Dodd, Mead, 1936);

Roy V. Peel and Thomas C. Donnelly, *The 1932 Campaign: An Analysis* (New York: Farrar & Rinehart, 1935);

Eleanor Roosevelt, *It's Up to the Women* (New York: Stokes, 1933);

Roosevelt, *This Is My Story* (New York: Harper, 1937);

Roosevelt, *This Troubled World* (New York: H. C. Kinsey, 1938);

Gilbert V. Seldes, *The Years of the Locust (America, 1929–1932)* (Boston: Little, Brown, 1933);

Upton Sinclair, *The EPIC Plan for California* (New York: Farrar & Rinehart, 1934);

Rexford G. Tugwell, *The Battle for Democracy* (New York: Columbia University Press, 1935);

Tugwell, *The Industrial Discipline and the Governmental Arts* (New York: Columbia University Press, 1933);

Henry A. Wallace, *America Must Choose* (New York: Foreign Policy Association, 1934);

Wallace, *New Frontiers* (New York: Reynal & Hitchcock, 1934);

William Allen White, *What It's All About: Being a Reporter's Story of the Early Campaign of 1936* (New York: Macmillan, 1936).

LAW AND JUSTICE

by JACK BENGE

CONTENTS

Sidebars and tables are listed in italics.

1930

3 Feb.	President Herbert Hoover nominates Charles Evans Hughes, a former associate justice of the United States Supreme Court who had resigned his position to run for the presidency in 1916, to become the new chief justice.
13 Feb.	Following a fierce debate in the Senate, the appointment of Charles Evans Hughes as chief justice is confirmed.
13 Mar.	The trial of Edward Doheny, accused of bribing former Secretary of the Interior Albert Fall to obtain leases for the Elk Hills naval oil reserve, begins in Washington, D.C.
21 Apr.	A conflagration breaks out in the Ohio state penitentiary in Columbus that, while designed to hold a maximum of 1,500 prisoners, holds 4,300 on the day of the fire. Of the prisoners, 318 die when efforts to contain the fire fail.
20 May	Senate approves the nomination of Owen J. Roberts to the United States Supreme Court. Two weeks earlier, by a single vote, it had rejected President Hoover's first choice, Judge John J. Parker.
26 May	The Supreme Court issues a decision holding that the purchase of intoxicating liquor is not a violation of the Volstead Act.
3 July	The Veterans Administration is established by an act of Congress.
9 Sept.	The State Department, citing increased and alarming rates of unemployment throughout the nation, prohibits further immigration of foreign laborers.

1931

19 Jan.	The Wickersham Commission, originally formed to study the problem of enforcing Prohibition, delivers its report recommending that Congress consider more effective means of control.
24 Jan.	The Supreme Court defeats an attempt to declare the process in which the Eighteenth Amendment was adopted invalid by reversing a district court's ruling finding Prohibition unconstitutional.
27 Feb.	Congress overrides President Hoover's veto of the Bonus Loan Bill, permitting veterans to cash up to 50 percent of the value of their bonus certificates.
13 Mar.	The Massachusetts state legislature petitions Congress to initiate proceedings for the repeal of the Eighteenth Amendment.
17 Mar.	Mayor James J. "Jimmy" Walker of New York City is charged with malfeasance and neglect of his official duties.
25 Mar.	Nine young black men, later to become known as the "Scottsboro Boys," are arrested in Alabama and charged with raping two white women.
26 July	The Wickersham Commission delivers its final report, recommending major reforms in the federal prison system and greater use of parole.
17 Oct.	Alphonse Capone is sentenced to an unprecedented eleven years in prison for income tax evasion.

1932

- Benjamin N. Cardozo is appointed to the United States Supreme Court.

12 Jan. Associate Justice Oliver Wendell Holmes resigns from the Supreme Court after almost thirty years of service.

15 Jan. Congress passes President Hoover's proposal for the establishment of the Reconstruction Finance Corporation to spur the economy.

1 Mar. The twenty-month-old child of Charles and Anne Morrow Lindbergh is kidnapped from his parents' home in New Jersey.

3 Mar. The Twentieth or "Lame Duck" Amendment is submitted by Congress for ratification by the legislatures of the various states.

7 Mar. Striking employees of the Ford Motor Company organize a demonstration at the company's Dearborn plant in Michigan. Violence erupts and four people are killed.

14 Mar. Benjamin N. Cardozo is appointed to the seat on the Supreme Court vacated by the retiring Justice Holmes.

23 Mar. The Norris-LaGuardia Act, prohibiting the use of court injunctions as a means of maintaining antiunion employment contracts or to inhibit peaceful strikes, is passed.

29 May Large numbers of primarily unemployed veterans begin arriving in the nation's capital to support a bill in Congress that would provide them with the full value of their bonus certificates previously issued in recognition of their service in World War I.

17 June The Senate rejects the bill that veterans of the "Bonus Army" had demanded to be passed, inducing many of the disappointed veterans to leave the nation's capital.

7 Nov. The Supreme Court, in *Powell* v. *Alabama,* rules that the "Scottsboro Boys" were not properly represented at their trial, setting the foundation for a new trial.

1933

6 Feb. The Twentieth Amendment is adopted.

15 Feb. An attempt to assassinate Franklin D. Roosevelt in Miami, Florida, fails, but Anton J. Cermak, mayor of Chicago, riding in the president-elect's car, is killed by the bullets fired by a lone gunman, Giuseppe (called Joseph) Zangara.

20 Feb. Congress votes to submit the Twenty-first Amendment, repealing Prohibition, to the states for ratification.

27 May The Federal Securities Act, establishing, among other things, requirements for the registration of stocks and bonds, is passed by Congress.

16 June President Roosevelt signs into law the National Industrial Recovery Act, which established the Public Works Administration and the National Recovery Administration.

5 Aug. The National Labor Board is created by executive order. Sen. Robert Wagner of New York is appointed its first chairman.

5 Dec. The Twenty-first Amendment is adopted, bringing an end to Prohibition.

1934

5 May   Bonnie Parker and Clyde Barrow, bank robbers believed to be responsible for twelve murders and sought by authorities in three states, are killed by a posse of lawmen outside Rustin, Louisiana.

18 May   The Lindbergh Law, making the death penalty available for offenses involving cross-state kidnappings, is passed by Congress.

6 June   The Securities and Exchange Act, which establishes the Securities and Exchange Commission to regulate stock and bond transactions, is signed into law.

19 June   Responding to increased pressure from labor groups, Congress passes a joint resolution favoring the replacement of the National Labor Board with a prolabor National Labor Relations Board.

28 June   Congress passes the Federal Farm Bankruptcy Act (the Frazier-Lemke Act), which places a moratorium on the foreclosure of farm mortgages.

16 July   In support of the striking members of the International Longshoremen's Association of San Francisco, unions in that city call for a "general strike" which, in violation of a court-issued injunction, is widely observed.

22 July   John Dillinger, "Public Enemy No. 1," is shot and killed outside a Chicago movie theater by agents of the FBI and local police.

6 Nov.   Nebraska, by means of an amendment of its state constitution, adopts a unicameral legislature.

27 Nov.   George "Baby Face" Nelson, a bank robber responsible for the deaths of three FBI agents, is mortally wounded in a gun battle with law enforcement officers near Barrington, Illinois.

3 Dec.   The right of land-grant colleges to require military training of students is upheld by the United States Supreme Court in *Hamilton* v. *Regents of the University of California.*

1935

16 Jan.   Arizona Clark Barker, also called "Kate" or "Ma," and her son Fred are killed in a gun battle with a small army of police and FBI agents.

29 Jan.   Membership of the United States in the World Court is rejected by the Senate, which refuses to do anything which could be seen as compromising the nation's sovereignty.

19 Mar.   Rumors and accusations of police brutality in the case of a sixteen-year-old black youth caught shoplifting in a department store touch off a riot in Harlem resulting in the deaths of three persons and damages in excess of $200 million.

27 May   The National Industrial Recovery Act of 1933, cornerstone of the New Deal program, is declared unconstitutional by the Supreme Court in the case of *Schechter Poultry Corp.* v. *United States.*

5 July   The National Labor Relations Board is created to protect the rights of workingmen to join labor unions, to vote for their own collective bargaining units, and to seek redress from the unfair labor practices of an employer.

29 July Thomas E. Dewey is appointed as a special prosecutor in New York to lead a drive against crime and corruption, a crusade that quickly brings him national attention.

8 Sept. Sen. Huey Long of Louisiana is shot during a visit to the state capital and dies two days later.

23 Oct. Mobster Dutch Schultz, who is rumored to have been planning the murder of "gangbuster" Thomas Dewey, is killed by his fellow gangsters while dining in a Newark, New Jersey, tavern.

1936

6 Jan. The Agricultural Adjustment Act of 1933 is declared unconstitutional by the Supreme Court in *United States* v. *Butler*.

3 Apr. Bruno Hauptmann, the convicted kidnapper of Charles Lindbergh Jr., is electrocuted.

5 May Bank robbers Alvin "Creepy" Karpis and Fred Hunter are arrested in New Orleans by J. Edgar Hoover and a small force of FBI agents.

30 June The Walsh-Healey Public Contracts Act, requiring firms with government contracts to observe specific minimum-wage rates, an eight-hour day, and a forty-hour week and expressly prohibiting the use of child labor, is passed.

30 Nov. The Circuit Court of Appeals upholds a ruling allowing a doctor to distribute prophylactic devices.

30 Dec. The United Auto Workers begin a strike against the General Motors Fisher Body plant in Flint, Michigan, employing a new tactic, the sit-down strike, in disregard of a state court's ruling that they are in violation of the law.

1937

• Associate Justice Willis Van Devanter of the United States Supreme Court retires.

1 Mar. Congress passes the Supreme Court Retirement Act, permitting justices to retire at the age of seventy with full pay.

26 Mar. William H. Hastie, the first black federal judge, is sworn in.

29 Mar. The United States Supreme Court, in a complete reversal of the position it had taken in an earlier case, upholds a Washington State law establishing a minimum wage for women (*West Coast Hotel* v. *Parrish*).

12 Aug. Sen. Hugo Black of Alabama is nominated by President Roosevelt to replace retiring Supreme Court justice Van Devanter and wins Senate confirmation the following week.

26 Aug. Accepting the defeat of his original proposal to increase the number of justices in the Supreme Court, President Roosevelt signs into law a compromise bill that principally affects lower federal courts.

1938

• Supreme Court Associate Justice George Sutherland retires, Associate Justice Benjamin Cardozo dies, and Stanley F. Reed is nominated and confirmed as an associate justice.

10 Jan.   The Ludlow proposal is defeated by a majority in the House of Representatives who vote to return the resolution to the Judiciary Committee. The measure called for amending the Constitution to provide that, except in cases of invasion, the nation could engage in war only when a majority of the people so voted in a national referendum.

12 Apr.   New York becomes the first state to pass a law requiring a medical test as a prerequisite to the issuance of a marriage license.

26 May   The House of Representatives establishes a committee to investigate the potentially "un-American" activities of suspect groups such as communists, fascists, Nazis, and others. Representative Martin Dies of Texas is selected to be the committee's first chairman.

25 June   President Roosevelt signs the Fair Labor Standards Act into law, establishing a minimum wage of forty cents an hour and a maximum workweek of forty hours for businesses engaged in interstate commerce.

7 Oct.   Comedians George Burns and Jack Benny are arrested and charged in New York City with smuggling gems into the country.

1939

• Justice Pierce Butler dies. The appointments of Felix Frankfurter and William O. Douglas as associate justices are confirmed.

7 Jan.   Tom Mooney, widely believed to have been wrongly convicted of the 1916 Preparedness Day bombing in San Francisco, is given a full pardon and released from prison.

13 Feb.   Justice Louis Brandeis retires from the Supreme Court at the age of eighty-two.

18 Feb.   The University of Wisconsin refuses to accept a donation that, by the stipulation of the donor, can only be used to benefit white students.

27 Feb.   In its decision in the case of *NLRB* v. *Fansteel Metallurgical Corp.*, the United States Supreme Court rules that sit-down strikes are in violation of the Constitution.

2 Mar.   A young man and woman, found together in a lover's lane outside of Atlanta, Georgia, are whipped to death for violating the "Moral Kode" of the Ku Klux Klan.

3 Apr.   The Administrative Reorganization Act is signed into law despite expression of deep misgivings in Congress that passage of the act would provide the president with dictatorial powers. The bill consolidated and coordinated many federal agencies including a number created during the New Deal.

2 Aug.   The Hatch Act, which limits the political activity of federal government employees and officeholders, is enacted and becomes law.

OVERVIEW

The Birth of a New Era. The 1930s represented one of the most significant periods of reform legislation in the history of the United States. During this decade, there occurred developments in the law that contributed significantly to the emergence of the modern American state. The expansion of the role and the power of government and its involvement to an unprecedented degree in the daily life of the ordinary citizen were made possible by equally astounding shifts in social values and general perceptions regarding the purpose and function of government. These changes were the result of conditions that had emerged in the previous decade, when the end of an era of prosperity had brought ruin to many and an economic depression far more disastrous than any other in memory. Over sometimes strong opposition, and reflecting the prejudices of its day, the national government gradually and fundamentally altered its relationship with the people and the states.

Prohibition and Social Control. By 1932 public support for the prohibition of the manufacture and sale of alcoholic beverages had dropped to a point where the Democratic Party could, with little fear of alienating the voters, include repeal of the Eighteenth Amendment (prohibiting the sale, manufacture, or transportation of intoxicating beverages) in its platform. Inconsistency in the law's application, doubt as to its enforceability, disgust with the little respect shown for the law itself, and changes in public attitude all combined to make the first-ever repeal of a constitutional amendment possible. The Depression may have raised more serious concerns for Americans to ponder, but many were also dismayed by the federal government's inability or unwillingness to assume a more aggressive role in pursuing Prohibition's objectives and in bearing the cost of its enforcement.

Crime. In the early part of the decade there was a resurgence in banditry, capturing the public imagination and attracting enough attention in the media and films of the day to become a diversion in these hard times. Opinion in regard to the outlaw was initially ambivalent, reflecting a highly romanticized view of his origins and serving as an outlet for the hostility many felt toward the financial institutions and other symbols of the establishment. That soon changed as more and more people were swept up by enthusiasm for the New Deal and its emphasis upon cooperation and interdependence. The outlaw came to be seen as a brutal and murderous predator, his pursuer, now better armed and more mobile, as the public's protector. Even the advantage the outlaw once had in being able to move from one jurisdiction to another faded in the face of a newly revitalized and now-armed FBI. The federal kidnapping statute known as the Lindbergh Law and others like it increased the responsibilities of the various federal enforcement agencies and provided them with the authority to act as more effective crime fighters. That did not, however, translate into action against organized crime, which, following a murderous period of reorganization in the early 1930s, became more pervasive in its influence and far less publicized.

Bigger Government. The growth of government was spurred on by an increasing recognition that reliance upon self-regulating agreements and cooperative ventures was not producing results. The Roosevelt administration's commitment to an aggressive expansion of federal power and to governmental regulation of the economy would inevitably raise new constitutional questions. Such policies tended to alter relations between levels of government while affecting the nation's citizenry and its economic activity in ways long viewed as beyond the government's ability or authority.

The Great Crisis. President Roosevelt's attempt to protect his legislative program and to ensure promised changes precipitated the greatest constitutional and political crisis of the decade. Rulings by the lower courts, particularly, placed much of the New Deal's future in serious jeopardy. Like the Supreme Court itself, the federal judiciary resisted the creation of a large bureaucracy and limited the power of Congress and the president. The president's court-packing scheme, by which he hoped to liberalize the Supreme Court, did not receive sufficient support in either the Congress or the electorate. The need for a radical restructuring of the courts, and particularly the Supreme Court, suddenly disappeared when the Supreme Court, adopting a new interpretation of the government's role and power in the economic affairs of the nation, issued a series of decisions favorable to the New Deal program. The crisis had passed.

The Supreme Court in Transition. The year 1937 was a major turning point in the history of the Supreme Court. Two years before, it had rebuffed efforts to resuscitate a severely depressed economy by limiting the government's power to act under the Commerce Clause of the Constitution (*Schechter Poultry Corp.* v. *U.S.*) and, again, the following year, by restricting its power to tax for purposes other than for raising revenue (*U.S.* v. *Butler*). In each instance the Court's majority had acted on the basis of a legal doctrine that, despite its long history, had already shown signs of strain. For many years beforehand the courts had focused judicial review almost entirely upon questions relating to the kind and source of power the government was permitted to exercise to the exclusion of any consideration of the purposes or the results of the government's use of such power. This highly mechanistic view of the operation of law did not go without challenge in the 1930s. In 1934 the Court, by a narrow majority, upheld the state of New York's au-thority to regulate the price of milk, explaining that the states were free to adopt whatever economic policies they felt could promote the common welfare and, in doing so, did not act in a manner that was either arbitrary or discriminatory (*Nebbia* v. *New York*). In 1937 the Court began to distance itself from its previous restrictive views and to adopt a new test by which to measure the constitutionality of the enactments and regulatory powers of government. Henceforth, a law would be valid if there was any rational basis to determine that it would accomplish permissible objectives. Having resolved that issue, the Court was moving steadily toward taking on a far more active role in scrutinizing laws affecting individual rights. In 1938 by means of a simple footnote in a decision it rendered in the case of *U.S.* v. *Carolene Products Co.*, the Supreme Court alerted all concerned of its intention to enter a new phase in its history — one that would result in the expansion of civil rights after World War II.

TOPICS IN THE NEWS

THE ANTILYNCHING BILL

The New Deal and Civil Rights. The New Deal marked the beginning of a shift in the federal government's recognition of civil rights as an emerging national problem, but it was not until 1940 that this concern was actually translated into action. Even then the government's role was seen as having more to do with combating discriminatory employment and housing practices than with the promotion of equality and basic civil rights. Discrimination against persons of color remained deeply rooted in American life in the 1930s and was generally acceptable to a majority of the population. There were limits, however, to prejudice and discrimination in the law. In 1931 the Supreme Court in the case of *Aldridge* v. *United States* protected the right of a defendant in a criminal trial to question prospective jurors regarding their racial views. In 1932 the Court in *Nixon* v. *Condon* struck down a law in Texas allowing political parties to establish race-based qualifications for voters in primaries. In that manner many black voters were excluded from exercising their right to vote. Nonetheless, progress in civil rights was undramatic, was still forthcoming, and set the stage for an era of far greater consequence. The campaign for a federal antilynching law, though failing to achieve its objective, would contribute significantly to that advance.

The First Wagner-Costigan Antilynching Bill. Previous attempts to introduce antilynching legislation at the federal level had met with no success. In 1902 Rep. George White of North Carolina, the most recent black man to have been elected to Congress from a southern state, had struggled for the passage of such a bill. In 1921, even with the support he received from the Commission On Interracial Cooperation and the Southern Women for the Prevention of Lynching, Congressman Leonidas Dyer was unable to overcome opposition to a lynch law in the Senate. It fell, finally, to the NAACP to take up the cause, and that it did with a strategy designed to mobilize support through a program of public education.

Introduction and Opposition. In 1934 the NAACP, under the leadership of its national secretary Walter White, launched its campaign to obtain passage of an antilynching bill introduced by Senators Edward P. Costigan of Colorado and Robert Wagner of New York. Like those that preceded it, the Wagner-Costigan bill placed responsibility for its enforcement with local authorities. Sheriffs who failed to take appropriate action to protect prisoners in their custody could be penalized under the

NAACP headquarters in Manhattan in 1934

act. Provision was also made to compensate the families of those who had been victimized by mob action. White believed that the president's support would be critical and was able to secure a promise from President Franklin D. Roosevelt that he would confer with the bill's sponsors and encourage the congressional leadership to move for an early vote. A filibuster was immediately organized to resist the bill's passage in the Senate. Opponents of the legislation continued to protest the bill until pressure to get on with other pending matters became so great as to force an agreement among the bill's sponsors and opponents to postpone any further consideration of it on the Senate floor.

The Killing of Claude Neal. In October 1934 a young white woman was found murdered in the Florida panhandle. Among those who were first suspected was Claude Neal, a black employee of the victim's father. Neal was soon found and arrested by authorities in a neighboring state. Before he could be taken to a place of greater safety, however, a mob arrived, forcibly removed him from the jail, and returned him to Jackson County, Florida. The following day, the mob holding Neal sent out invitations to his lynching. Local newspapers and a radio station, announcing that a "Negro" would be "mutilated and set afire," provided details concerning the place and time of the anticipated event. That afternoon, quite unexpectedly, news of the scheduled lynching was picked up and distributed nationally by the Associated Press. The response of the NAACP and many other concerned people to this news moved Florida governor David Sholtz to offer the Jackson County sheriff the assistance of the state's national guard. The offer was refused. The mob forced Neal to eat his penis, stabbed him with a knife repeatedly in his sides and stomach, and cut off several of his fingers and toes. After suffering such torture for almost two hours, Neal died before the hundreds of people who had gathered in a carnival-like atmosphere could see him lynched. Disappointed and enraged, the crowd — including many families — resumed the mutilation of the body before burning and hanging it from a nearby tree.

The Second Wagner-Costigan Bill: The New Deal Backs Down. Neal's death was widely reported in the national press and provoked a strong reaction. The

Federal legislation introduced in the 1930s defined lynching as the act of a mob, consisting of three or more persons, that punished or killed its victim without the authority of law. Throughout the nation's history, such "extralegal" action had been directed at any number of people who were believed to have threatened a significant common interest or violated a moral or social convention. Mobs formed for a variety of reasons: to seek vengeance, to ensure punishment, or to intimidate; but in all such instances, they drew their power from the weaknesses of their victims and the mob's willingness to resort to violence at the slightest provocation.

By the 1930s lynching had become closely associated with the subject of race relations. As a practice it was largely confined to the southern part of the United States, and even there, more often than not, to more rural and poverty-stricken areas. Historically, the worst period for lynching had followed the Civil War and continued to just after the turn of the century. Lynching as an instrument of terror had proved useful in reestablishing the dominance of whites in the South and in maintaining the social boundaries between black and white people. In the 1880s the average number of black persons reported lynched annually throughout the country numbered 116; the annual average was 71 in the 1890s, 50 in the 1910s, 28 in the 1920s, and 15 for the years between 1930–1935 (the annual average for the years 1933 through 1935 was much greater, however, at 19).

Only six states in the 1930s had statutes in force that specifically prohibited lynchings. Four (Alabama, Kentucky, North Carolina, and South Carolina) were in the South. But even in these states officials rarely took any action against those who joined lynch mobs. Between the years 1900 and 1930, fewer than 1 percent of those arrested for lynching were ever convicted. The lynch mob offered not only anonymity but protection through its numbers. State control over local enforcement agencies was often weak and rarely sufficient to motivate local lawmen, many of whom had been elected to their positions, to defy public sentiment. The fact that lynching often found support within the community was a factor many believed distinguished it from murder.

After 1935 the era of lynchings came quickly to an end. Increasingly, white people came to view such violence against blacks as unconscionable and repulsive. Modern technology in the form of newspapers, radio, and photography, all with a potentially national audience, stripped the mob of its anonymity, gave individual communities unwanted attention, and made state officials more sensitive to the social and economic repercussions of these displays of lawlessness. Transformation of the relations between the races themselves would eventually make lynching a thing of the past.

Source: James R. McGovern, *Anatomy of a Lynching: The Killing of Claude Neal* (Baton Rouge: Louisiana State University Press, 1982).

NAACP moved quickly to mobilize public opinion to pressure the administration and Congress into taking action. Senators Costigan and Wagner reintroduced their bill, and pledges of support were obtained from nine state governors, fifty-eight churchmen, and fifty-four university and college presidents. A memorial art exhibit was assembled and sent out on tour to generate further publicity. The Senate Judiciary Committee recommended passage. Forty-three senators and 123 congressmen declared their support for the bill. Elsewhere, however, progress was not quite as dramatic or as promising.

Political Considerations. Under Walter White the NAACP had pressured the president and his attorney general to make public their support for the bill, but to no avail. Homer Cummings, the attorney general, was stubbornly resistant to any direct federal involvement in the investigation of Neal's death. White had called upon him to pursue Neal's abductors and torturers under the Kidnapping Act, popularly known as the "Lindbergh Law."

Cummings declined to do so, steadfastly holding to an interpretation of the act that required a demand for ransom be made before the provisions of the law could be invoked. The mob had made no such demand with respect to Neal. The affair, therefore, remained a matter of legal concern solely to the state of Florida. Never expressed were the attorney general's fears of what federal intervention could do to the congressional support he required for the passage of a comprehensive federal crime package. The president shared those concerns. Like his attorney general, he was not willing to risk losing what progress he was making in forging a new relationship between the states and the federal government. The results of the congressional elections in 1934 convinced him that the majority of the voters favored increased social and economic reforms. Worried that the coalition he had formed in support of his New Deal program would prove too fragile to survive a confrontation over

Alvin Karpis, left, handcuffed to an FBI agent in May 1936. He was sentenced to life imprisonment for armed robbery.

what seemed a less vital and essentially racial issue, he refused to use his influence on behalf of the bill.

Opposition: Opposed to the bill were several senators, mostly representing the southern states, who were growing increasingly sensitive to the erosion of what they believed were the rights of the individual states to exercise authority expressly reserved to them by the Constitution. Concerns regarding federal encroachment were particularly intense when joined with fears that such legislation would cause an upheaval of the South's racial caste system. South Carolina senator Ellison "Cotton Ed" Smith acted swiftly to organize a filibuster to kill the proposal. Josiah Bailey of North Carolina took the Senate floor to warn his colleagues that "this is a cause worth dying for. It is a battle worth fighting if it takes until Congress begins its next session in January 1936.... We'll speak day and night if necessary." Costigan's response was equally swift but still conciliatory: this was not, he proclaimed, a bill aimed specifically at the South. California governor James Rolph's praise for the deadly work of a mob in his state had been met, the senator said, with a wave of antilynching sentiment. The time for action was obviously at hand. Unmoved, the southerners refused to relinquish their control of the Senate floor. By the end of the filibuster's seventh week, feeling in the

Senate against any further delay in taking up other, pending legislation began to weigh heavily against the bill's sponsors. Unable to bring the debate to an end and anxious to consider a relief bill that could add an additional half million people to the rolls of the Works Progress Administration, those in favor and those opposed to the bill eventually agreed to shelve it indefinitely. Not until 1937, and for the final time, would a more strongly worded antilynching bill be introduced in the Senate. It, too, would meet defeat in the face of an unyielding filibuster.

Sources:
Robert S. McElvaine, *The Great Depression: America, 1929–1941* (New York: Times Books, 1984);

James R. McGovern, *Anatomy of a Lynching: The Killing of Claude Neal* (Baton Rouge: Louisiana State University Press, 1982);

Newsweek (4 May 1935): 10;

Newsweek (21 January 1938): 13–14.

BANDITS AND GANGSTERS

Crime Wave. The 1930s are regarded as an era of widespread lawlessness and violence. The great "midwestern" crime wave lasted but for a brief time during the early part of the decade and captured the imagination of the public like little else could. Between "Baby Face"

Nelson, "Pretty Boy" Floyd, and "Creepy" Karpis on the one hand, and the ruthlessness of urban criminal gangs and the frequent revelations of police and political corruption on the other, the 1930s have earned a reputation for lawlessness that tends to obscure other more significant developments in the history of law and order.

Crime Pays. These same outlaws inspired a new war on crime. In the 1920s Americans had displayed a rather surprising tolerance for criminals, particularly those involved in the bootlegger's trade. In an age when the consumption of alcohol had become a symbol of independence and sophistication, the escapades of the bootlegger, whether acting alone or in a gang, offered an exciting form of entertainment. Even when the gangs engaged in the most violent behavior, the high drama they afforded seemed just enough removed from the lives of ordinary citizens to raise few alarms. That sense of security or confidence began to change after the collapse of the nation's economy in 1929. Wealth and power, the prestige symbols of the Roaring Twenties, gradually came to signify all that had become wrong with society. Lawlessness was now seen as evidence of weakened moral values and failing public order. But in the early 1930s the public appeared to be in no hurry to condemn the holdup men and bandits who flouted authority and got away with it. Public ambivalence toward them was picked up by the motion picture industry, which rushed to take advantage of the gangster mystique.

Crime on the Screen. The outlaw was seen not as a troubled or even vicious man but an outcast, the victim of an injustice against which he was expected to direct his rage. In 1931 the actor James Cagney appeared in the movie *Public Enemy* and, like few other actors, would come to personify this sentiment. As a man who is victimized by some injustice, Cagney wages a violent and single-minded war against his oppressors, dying only when the criminal nature of his conduct becomes all too evident; but he never loses his faith in values, which are similar to those of the audience. This theme retained its popularity throughout the early years of the decade. Hundreds of such movies were produced and distributed to an eager public. Then the world changed again. With the arrival of the New Deal, some sense of order, hope, and even belief that justice would be returned to the "little man" was gradually restored. The outlaw no longer fit comfortably into this new society where cooperation, integrity, and devotion to the public interest were the hallmarks of the day. James Cagney would return, this time as a special agent, in *G-Men,* portraying a courageous, tenacious, and ultimately successful man of the law. The movie crime wave would, as it did in real life, come to a swift and bloody end.

The Outlaw. People were no more inclined to romanticize the brutality and ruthlessness that were characteristic of the outlaws of the day than they were at any other time of their history. When individual bandits captured the public imagination, public sympathy proved less en-

HARRY J. ANSLINGER AND THE BUREAU OF NARCOTICS

If J. Edgar Hoover suffered a blind spot when it came to the influence of organized crime, one federal law enforcer did all he could to stem its growth and power. In 1930 Harry J. Anslinger was appointed commissioner of the Department of Treasury's Bureau of Narcotics. Dissatisfied with his opportunities for advancement in the Department of State, where he had been employed for eight years in consular offices in Europe and South America, Anslinger had requested transfer to the Department of Treasury, where he was assigned to the division of foreign control as a prohibition enforcement agent.

Harry Anslinger's strengths lay in his willingness to experiment with new methods of investigation and to adjust his operations to accommodate better ongoing developments in one of the bureau's lesser-known areas of interest, the international narcotics trade. He was interested in results and gave his agents, some of whom were famous or infamous for their eccentricity and independence, considerable autonomy in the performance of their duties. Unlike his counterpart in the FBI, Anslinger encouraged his men to develop networks of informants, many of whom were paid for their information, and to engage in undercover assignments whenever the potential rewards justified the risk. He was among the first federal enforcement agency heads to employ ethnic Americans as investigators, a policy that provided the bureau with immediate and incalculable benefits.

In the early part of the decade, control over the nation's illicit narcotic traffic was dispersed among many small groups, the most active of whom were in New York. Mobsters such as Lepke Buchalter, "Waxey" Gordon, and Mendy Weiss were among the most prominent and ruthless of the traffickers, and, therefore, the focus of one of the bureau's most intensive investigations. In the mid 1930s an organization that would eventually be identified as the American branch of the Sicilian mafia would begin to assume control of the drug trade, a development that, though not escaping the bureau's notice, had implications that were not fully understood until 1939, when the evidence collected by Anslinger's agents could no longer be ignored.

Source: Steven R. Fox, *Blood and Power: Organized Crime In the Twentieth Century* (New York: Morrow, 1989).

during. Clyde Barrow was, after all, responsible for the deaths of half a dozen lawmen; George "Baby Face" Nelson, another sociopath, was the slayer of three special

John Dillinger, early 1930s

agents of the FBI. The public, even in the darkest days of the Depression, could never accept that kind of violence. But initially and from a distance, these outlaws seemed to possess something neither the urban gangster nor the corrupt cop could — an audacity and resourcefulness many couldn't help but admire. When "Pretty Boy" Floyd rushed into a bank waving his machine gun, he was as apt to take with him (and destroy) as many mortgage notes as bills of currency. Such a populist spirit could neither be completely ignored nor unappreciated.

Dillinger. John Dillinger was a believer in the quick strike — one of his accomplices would stand in a bank doorway counting the seconds off while the rest of the gang would loot for as long as their plan allowed. He used high-powered cars and modern weapons, preplanned escape routes, "safe houses," and information regarding police activity obtained from a network of informants to elude his pursuers. He was very good at staying one step ahead of the law, or, when they were able to catch up, to take another, often dramatic step ahead. His escape from a small army of local and FBI agents who had almost

surrounded the Little Bohemia Lodge near Rhinelander, Wisconsin, not only embarrassed the government but may have convinced Congress to pass ten of the twelve anticrime bills for which the administration had been struggling for approval. Every twist and turn in the months-long chase that followed was reported daily and in great detail by newspapers and radio stations all over the nation.

FBI Manhunts. Within two years of Dillinger's death (at the hands of waiting FBI agents) on 22 July 1934, law enforcement officials had killed "Pretty Boy" Floyd, "Baby Face" Nelson, and "Ma" Barker and her son Fred. One of the last holdouts, Alvin "Creepy" Karpis, was tracked down in New Orleans and arrested, legend has it, by J. Edgar Hoover himself. The FBI's success in these manhunts, much heralded in the movies of the day, would establish it forever as the country's premier law enforcement agency.

The Mobster. The mobster in the 1930s was a new class of criminal. Prohibition had changed the nature of organized crime for all time. Distinctions between criminal and legitimate activities became blurred, affording opportunities for expansion and concealment that exceeded the wildest dreams of the Capones and others among the old bootleggers and racketeers. Prohibition had given the bootlegger an incentive to expand his operations beyond his original areas of control, to establish cooperative arrangements with other gangsters, and, with its repeal, to diversify. An increased level of violence among gangsters introduced in the 1920s continued into the early 1930s. Such warfare, much of it drawn along ethnic lines, had become an acceptable means of determining territorial control, eliminating or subduing competition, and settling differences. But such conflict would inevitably extract an ever-costlier toll, the loss of a gang's political connections, interruption of the flow of income, and almost always the unwelcome interest of the public or the police. The murder of Alfred "Jake" Lingle, a reporter for the *Chicago Tribune,* on 9 June 1930, for example, caused a major uproar and an intensive manhunt for his killer, led to two state investigations, and resulted in the forced resignation or indictment of numerous police officials and the city's police commissioner. Little attention was paid to evidence of the reporter's connections to the Capone organization or to rumors that he had been killed in retaliation for his shift in allegiance to one of the mobster's chief rivals, "Bugs" Moran. Capone had welcomed the public's attention, but because of his notoriety he had to contend with the raids of Eliot Ness and his treasury agents, countless political reformers, and the Internal Revenue Service, which finally succeeded in putting him in prison. The lesson was not lost on the new breed.

The Syndicate. In May 1929 mobsters from practically every region in the United States gathered in Atlantic City, New Jersey, to confer with one another. Among those in attendance were Johnny Torrio, Meyer Lansky,

Clash between bonus marchers and police, 28 July 1932, on Pennsylvania Avenue, Washington, D.C., in which two marchers were killed

"Lucky" Luciano, Alphonse Capone, and Frank Nitti, along with the mob leaders of Cleveland, Detroit, Philadelphia, and other major cities. The conference produced agreements about regional boundaries and the creation of a national commission that would oversee relations among the various groups represented. In this manner, the foundation of a national crime syndicate was laid. Those who would not abide by the agreements were dealt with harshly. In New York several of the older mob chieftains, including Salvatore Maranzano and Joe Masseria, were purged and replaced by, among others, Luciano and Joseph Bonanno. Further evidence of continuing attempts to organize cartels surfaced in Chicago in 1932 with the arrests of New York mobsters Meyer Lansky and "Lucky" Luciano. In 1933 Lansky would conclude negotiations with the Cuban dictator Fulgencio Batista for gambling concessions in that small country. These activities and others generally escaped public attention, and, on those few occasions where they didn't, virtually no one could envision what the implications meant.

Thomas E. Dewey. Efforts to curb the mobsters were infrequent, uncoordinated, and often delegated to prosecutors and teams of investigators working in ignorance of each other's efforts and almost always within their jurisdictional limits. The federal government lacked the means and the inclination to coordinate or to give guidance to these investigations, and local governments usu-

ally were without the resources to be effective against the mobs and lacked the will, given the existence of links between the politicians and the mobsters, to try. Still there were moments of high drama in the 1930s: Thomas E. Dewey's investigation of the rackets in the East caused considerable hardship for the top mobsters, including Dutch Schultz (who was murdered by "Lucky" Luciano's triggermen for his plan to kill Dewey), "Waxey" Gordon, and "Lucky" Luciano, who was sent to prison. Federal probes of political machines in Boston and Kansas City resulted in many more convictions; and Dewey's investigation led to the eventual destruction in the early 1940s of a murder-for-hire organization dubbed "Murder, Inc."

Sources:

Dennis Eisenberg, *Meyer Lansky: Mogul of the Mob* (New York: Paddington Press, 1979);

John Toland, *The Dillinger Days* (New York: Random House, 1963).

CIVIL UNREST AND THE BONUS ARMY

Desperation Sets In. By 1930 life for many Americans had become unbearably grim. The country's economic collapse called for emergency measures and resources beyond the capacity of local and even state governments. Millions of Americans were displaced from homes and jobs — losses of an intensely personal nature. The obvious helplessness of elected officials and the reluctance of national government to consider larger and sometimes more unconventional measures of relief did little to earn

Louis Ludlow had introduced a resolution to amend the constitution to require a national referendum on any declaration of war, except in those instances where the nation was being invaded. Held up by the House Judiciary Committee for almost a year, the resolution was not placed before the full House until two days after a navy gunboat was sunk by Japanese warplanes in China. The resolution received strong support from a coalition of liberal and conservative congressmen who were opposed to any foreign policy beyond a posture recognition of strict neutrality. During the course of the debate that followed, the house speaker was advised by the president that such a resolution would seriously weaken the world's perception of the nation's willingness to act in the defense of its own interests and would cripple the president in the conduct of the country's foreign relations. Even after considering these concerns, the House came within but twenty-one votes of approving the resolution.

Source: William E. Leuchtenburg, *Franklin Roosevelt and the New Deal* (New York: Harper & Row, 1963).

the public's confidence. Disillusioned, desperate for solutions that were not forthcoming, and filled with despair, people banded together to take whatever action seemed justified by conditions they saw as not of their own making. In Arkansas a band of nearly five hundred armed farmers demanded food from a Red Cross administrator. When told that all supplies had been exhausted, the farmers descended upon the town of England and stripped its stores of food. Relief demonstrations broke out spontaneously across the nation. In Iowa councils of defense were organized to forestall farm foreclosures. Dairymen in Sioux City declared a general farm strike and prevented shipments of produce from reaching that city. Encouraged by their success, groups of farmers elsewhere came together to carry out similar strikes. Violence frequently resulted. In Nebraska in 1933 farmers, forcing their way past police barricades, marched on the state capitol to demand passage of a moratorium on the repayment of farm debt. In Crawford County, Iowa, bands of farmers and local authorities engaged in pitched battles that were ended when the governor imposed martial law. None of these demonstrations, however, quite achieved the notoriety or caused the federal government more concern than that of the veterans' "bonus march."

The Bonus March. In 1924 Congress, in a display of patriotic emotion and public gratitude, enacted a bill that awarded veterans for their service in World War I a "bonus" payment redeemable in full in 1945. Many veterans, experiencing financial problems both pressing and unanticipated, were eager to receive an earlier payout, a preference provided for in a bill introduced in 1932 by Congressman Wright Patman. In an effort to convince Congress to pass the bill, veterans began to gather in Washington to express their support. Among the first to arrive were a group of several hundred who, under the leadership of Walter W. Waters, referred to themselves as the Bonus Expeditionary Force. It is estimated that the veterans' numbers may have well exceeded sixteen thousand at the peak of their summer encampment in the nation's capital. While a few of the demonstrators occupied empty Treasury Department buildings along Pennsylvania Avenue, the majority settled on vacant land situated in the Anacostia flats along the Potomac River.

The Bonus Riots. On 17 June 1932 the Patman bill failed to pass the Senate, and Congress adjourned without taking any further action. Several of the demonstrators left the city, but the mood among the five thousand or more who remained was sullen. The government, under increased pressure from local residents to remove the veterans, was also running out of patience, but government officials remained undecided as to what action they should take. Tension increased as the marchers set up picket lines around government buildings, including the White House. On 28 July Treasury Department officials asked the police to evict a group of the bonus marchers who had settled into offices on Pennsylvania Avenue. The squatters resisted eviction, and, in the melee that followed, two of the veterans were killed by police, who claimed to have shot in their own defense. Without conferring with the district's police chief, Pelham Glassford, a former brigadier general sympathetic to the plight of the veterans, the police commissioner asked President Hoover for federal troops. Chief of Staff Gen. Douglas MacArthur was sent to survey the scene and to make an independent assessment of the situation. The general, for reasons which are still unclear, did more than he was asked to do. The cavalry troops MacArthur dispatched to clear the scene drew their sabers and rode into the crowds gathering there. Tear gas was used against demonstrator and onlooker alike. As people fled the area, the cavalrymen, now reinforced with armored vehicles and infantry, moved across the bridge and into the bonus army's encampment, where they met fierce resistance from brick-and-rock-throwing veterans. Initially repulsed, the army returned more determined than ever to overcome any and all resistance. The shelters and possessions of the veterans were burned. Those detained were considered prisoners and roughly treated. For the next two days the demoralized veterans were rounded up, forced into trucks, and transported under guard to areas some distance from the capital, where they were released.

Fallout. This demonstration of raw power touched a sensitive nerve with the public. Though he was cheered in some quarters for taking decisive action against radicalism and rebellion, the president's handling of this crisis revealed him to many as an inept and weak leader.

In May of 1929 President Hoover established the National Commission On Law Observance and Enforcement, later to become known as the Wickersham Commission after its chairman George W. Wickersham. A former attorney general in the Hoover cabinet, Wickersham was joined on the commission by a select group of judges, sociologists, educators, and distinguished lawyers. Their task was a formidable one: to investigate conditions and study all facets of the administration of justice throughout the nation's jails, prisons, courts, and prosecutorial offices, and to report their findings to the president and the public. Eleven subcommittees were formed to facilitate the commission's work and to expedite the collection and analysis of an enormous amount of information.

The best known of the commission's final reports, one of fourteen volumes completed and presented to the president in 1931, concerned Prohibition. It was also the most controversial, drawing much criticism from both those who were supportive and those who were opposed to repeal of the Volstead Act. While the report acknowledged that Prohibition agents had been effective in seizing some 15,703 distilleries, 11,416 stills, and more than 1.14 million gallons of spirits in 1929, the commission noted that in 1927 the consumption of beer alone in the country had exceeded 543 million gallons. Anxious to avoid the debate concerning the enforceability of the act, the commission instead chose to make several recommendations for the improvement of enforcement efforts, among them:

1. the consolidation and codification of some twenty or more "dry" laws to facilitate application and to make enforcement across the country more uniform;

2. transfer of the principal responsibility for enforcement of the Volstead Act from the Department of Treasury to the Department of Justice;

3. the reclassification of many of the prohibition violations to lesser offenses to permit them to be disposed of in the federal magistrate courts, thereby relieving congestion in the federal court system.

Among those who sat on the commission was the dean of the Harvard Law School, Roscoe Pound. A highly regarded administrator and legal educator, his opinions were widely respected. Disagreeing with the majority of the commission, Pound had prepared a statement in which he expressed his view that the Volstead Act had failed miserably as a national policy and should be abandoned. In 1932 and 1933, during the many debates that were to take place in connection with the repeal of the Eighteenth Amendment, his position was often, and with some effect, cited as evidence of the need for change.

Against American veterans President Hoover had sent battalions of armed American soldiers, a decision that he, while never comprehending how unsettling an experience it had been for the nation, would have to take full responsibility. It was the last straw for many a voter. That became a lesson not lost on President Hoover's successor, Franklin D. Roosevelt, who, when confronted in 1935 with another bonus march, did not hesitate to provide the demonstrators with quarters in a nearby army depot and, in a further display of his compassion, with quantities of food and even entertainment.

Sources:

William E. Leuchtenburg, *Franklin Roosevelt and the New Deal* (New York: Harper & Row, 1963);

Page Smith, *Redeeming the Time, A People's History of the 1920s and the New Deal*, volume 8 (New York: Penguin, 1987).

CRIME AND PUNISHMENT

An Antiquated System. The investigation and punishment of crime had always been considered a state or local function. When President Hoover's attorney general reminded the president's critics that the federal government carried no constitutional responsibility for fighting crime, most Americans not only understood but agreed with him. This was a time when agents of the Department of Justice's Bureau of Investigation (the forerunner of the Federal Bureau of Investigation) were authorized neither to carry weapons nor to make arrests. The use of the nation's taxing power to send some of its more notorious gangsters to prison for income tax evasion was a rare demonstration of the federal government's policing power. That power was concentrated primarily in two departments, postal and treasury, and was closely associated with the federal government's responsibility to resist attempts to misuse the mail, to circumvent Prohibition, and to avoid payment of the excise tax. Despite the country's increasing unease with conditions brought on by the Depression, with unemployment and with evidence of increasing disrespect for the law, crime had not been a significant issue in the election of 1932. In effect, while the New Deal had promised to bring reform to practically every aspect of national life, its view of crime, deterrence, and the duties of the federal government were no different from that of the previous administration.

In 1937 Lewis E. Lawes, warden of New York State's Sing Sing prison, became known as a playwright with the production of his first dramatic effort, *Chalked Out*. This renowned champion of the rehabilitative approach to penology and opponent of the death penalty had become famous for his experimental work at Ossining (Sing Sing) prison in the 1920s where, as a disciple of the great reform penologist Thomas Mott Osborne, he instituted many needed changes and eliminated much of the brutality that had characterized the treatment of prisoners in the facility since the turn of the century. These accomplishments had done much to enhance his reputation as an expert on prison management and policy, but his popularity came from his weekly radio program, which brought him more than two hundred fan letters a week, and from his book, *Twenty Thousand Years In Sing Sing* (1932), a best-seller, which would become the subject of a Warner Bros. movie of the same title (1933). A firm believer in providing each prisoner with treatment geared to serve his individual needs and a leading supporter of parole reform, Lawes did not hesitate to use his radio program and his writings to advocate for more active parole supervision and training for convicts, a position that often angered J. Edgar Hoover, director of the FBI. Hoover took every opportunity to criticize the warden and his theories, which he dismissed as inadequate and unrealistic, but Lawes was not one to back down and had come to the defense of the Federal Bureau of Prisons when Hoover had attacked its parole decisions. For years afterward, Hoover would go to great lengths to publicize cases in which convicts paroled from Warden Lawes's prison would commit new crimes after their release.

Sources: Curt Gentry, *J. Edgar Hoover: The Man and His Secrets* (New York: Norton, 1991);

Newsweek (3 April 1937).

Obstacles to Federal Intervention. In 1934 President Roosevelt was forced to include in his State of the Union message some comment respecting law and order. In the year since he had taken office, the nation's attention, when it was not focused upon the torrent of social and economic legislation flowing out of Washington, had become transfixed by news accounts of a violent crime wave rocking the Midwest. Local enforcement agencies, many riddled with corruption, had proven unable to cope with this outbreak of lawlessness, and, increasingly, as they had for relief and jobs, people turned to the federal government for a solution. Crimes of organized banditry and kidnapping were threatening the nation's security, the president said, and that made it a national concern. But translating concern into a plan of action was entirely another matter. The man whom the president had made his attorney general, Homer S. Cummings, a former prosecutor and mayor, shared the New Deal's faith in the benefits from the consolidation of power, but he was sensitive to the states' traditional role in the struggle against crime. The new attorney general was determined to convince Congress that it had to enact a comprehensive law enforcement program, but he could not afford to alienate a public still distrustful of the concept of a centralized police authority. To eliminate resistance to federal intervention, Cummings attempted to develop a new relationship between the states and the federal government through which their respective roles in the war against crime could be more clearly defined. To accomplish this, however, he had to avoid recommending fundamental changes in the law while remaining tied to the constraints imposed under the Constitution, which limited the federal government's enforcement function to its powers to levy taxes and to regulate interstate commerce.

The New Deal's Anticrime Proposals. The twelve-point anticrime package that Cummings crafted and sent to Congress for enactment was cautiously received. No one seriously questioned that local law enforcement agencies seemed to lack the technology and means of coordination needed to deal with this outbreak of lawlessness, but concerns regarding the long-term impact of the changes the attorney general had recommended persisted. To overcome this resistance, Cummings and his department set out to define more clearly those areas of enforcement that were of particular concern to the federal government. The package he presented became one of the most important and least recognized of the New Deal reforms. For the first time in its history the federal government would receive a comprehensive criminal code, outlawing the interstate transportation of stolen property, racketeering in interstate commerce, and flight across state lines to avoid prosecution, and also making it a federal offense to rob banks insured by the Federal Deposit Insurance Corporation. The Lindbergh kidnapping law was to be amended to include stiffer penalties, and special agents of the Bureau of Investigation were to be given the authority to carry weapons, execute warrants, and make arrests. Still, Congress remained hesitant to act, that is, until the occurrence of the "Kansas City Massacre."

The First War on Crime. Frank Nash was a wanted bank robber and prison escapee when he was tracked down in Arkansas. Agents of the Bureau of Investigation, accompanied by police officers, were escorting him back to prison at Leavenworth, Kansas, when three men armed with machine guns approached them outside of the Kansas City train station and opened fire. None of the special agents was armed. The deaths of four of the officers, including one of the agents, enraged the nation. The incident was followed by the news of two spectacular kidnappings for ransom and a jailbreak that involved ten prisoners, four of whom had been the objects of enormous manhunts. Nothing could have done more to convince the public that the police were unable to deal with criminals who resorted to unprovoked violence and knew no physical boundaries in their forays. Congress was finally forced to act, if only in a piecemeal fashion at first. Within a year it had passed ten of the twelve proposals, and the war on crime was well on its way.

Racketeering and the Copeland Committee. Organized crime was not entirely overlooked during the years of the New Deal, but, unlike the midwestern bandits, organized gangsters received virtually no attention from the federal government. The repeal of Prohibition had encouraged them to pursue other rackets — gambling, prostitution, and drug trafficking — but new enterprises, such as labor racketeering, interstate theft, political corruption, and payoffs were developed. The renamed Federal Bureau of Investigation (FBI) considered investigations into such activity too costly, time-consuming, and politically sensitive to justify the effort. Certainly these criminal activities were difficult to investigate and nowhere near as dramatic or newsworthy as chasing and shooting bandits.

Hearst Attacks Racketeers. That is not to say that no effort was made. In 1933 New York senator Royal S. Copeland, a physician, former New York City health commissioner, and chairman of the Commerce Committee, scheduled a series of hearings that resulted in conflicting testimony and revelations so startling as to draw the public's attention immediately. Many of the early witnesses, who included police chiefs and district attorneys, denied the existence of any organized criminal activity in their respective jurisdictions, claims that were disputed by the Hearst press. The appearances of two witnesses in particular threw the proceedings into an uproar: New York criminal attorney Samuel Liebowitz testified at length to the political corruption that he had observed in the New York City police force. Sing Sing Warden Lewis Lawes went a step further, stating his belief that if law enforcement could be made invulnerable to corruption, racketeering would be eliminated and its hold upon unions and the economy destroyed. Lawes called upon the federal government to wage a "national war" on crime by making all major offenses violations of federal law. The Copeland Committee had now gone too far. The senator's ties with the New York political machine, Tammany Hall, were urging caution; Cummings and J. Edgar Hoover, among others, spoke out against a national police force; and President Roosevelt moved quickly to steal the senator's thunder by declaring that the war on crime had already begun. It had, but not against racketeering. That responsibility remained for the states alone until well into the 1950s.

Prisons and Punishment. The 1930s were not a period of great consequence in the history of penology, at least not in terms of advancements in rehabilitation or the development of new methods of punishment. The death penalty was readily available for a variety of offenses ranging from rape to murder and was employed in virtually every state of the union and by the federal government. But there were problems that, left unattended since the late 1920s, had begun to surface in a way that stretched the nation's prison systems to the brink of their capacity. Prohibition had quickly become the single and foremost offense for which people were incarcerated in the decades of the 1920s and 1930s. In April 1930 Attorney General William Mitchell appeared before the Senate Judiciary Committee to beg for extensive revision of the Volstead Act. Rebuking Congress for failing to provide President Hoover with the moneys requested to support an ambitious prison construction program, he advised that Prohibition alone was more responsible for the growth of the prison population in the country than any other offense. In 1929 the federal prison population had increased by 23 percent, the overwhelming majority of the new prisoners having been convicted of prohibition act violations. Prisons resorted to releasing inmates early and in the same numbers that they were absorbing those more recently sentenced. Congress allocated some funds for the expansion of existing facilities and in 1933 authorized the creation of a "super prison" at Alcatraz for the worst-behaved of the federal prisoners.

Reform. The situation was even more critical at the state and local level where penitentiaries and jails were already filled to capacity. In the late 1920s news stories of spectacular crime and gang violence increased interest in longer sentences for convicted offenders and habitual-criminal statutes. Harsher sentences soon caused these institutions to be overwhelmed. Their function as rehabilitation centers, the product of twenty years of reform sentiment and theory, was reduced to containment only. Little was done until conditions in the prisons became so severe as to cause extensive rioting in 1929, the beginning of a nationwide wave of prison riots that lasted through 1932. In New York in 1930 conditions in the state's penitentiaries deteriorated so dramatically that then-governor Franklin D. Roosevelt was forced to ask the state assembly for emergency appropriations with which to finance a program of significant prison construction, temporary work camps for nonviolent felons, an increase in parole officers, and improvements in the training and selection of prison guards. In an impassioned speech, Roosevelt specifically blamed overcrowded conditions with helping to "breed the fierce despair among herded inmates." The New York State prison reform program served as a model for twenty-three other states, which adopted special penalties for recidivists, of mandatory life imprisonment for any person convicted of four or more felonies.

Sources:
G. Russell Girardin, *Dillinger: The Untold Story* (Bloomington: Indiana University Press, 1994);

Jordan A. Schwartz, *The New Dealers: Power Politics In the Age of Roosevelt* (New York: Knopf, 1993);

Time (3 December 1934): 14.

DEVELOPMENTS IN THE LEGAL PROFESSION

The Crowded Profession. Overproduction and reduced consumer demand were concerns not just for the nation's manufacturers and businessmen but for the legal profession as well. Among law practitioners everywhere, overcrowding was a much-discussed topic. Such worries actually translated into far more specific concerns: declining incomes from increased competition and the need to restrict the flow of new lawyers flooding the field. Between 1932 and 1937, nine thousand aspiring lawyers graduated each year from law schools throughout the nation. Many found the traditional road to career success blocked by the absence of available jobs with the more-established law firms. Upheaval in the country's economy had resulted in the reduction or closing of an astonishing number of corporate legal departments. The New Deal and the Roosevelt administration had offered new employment opportunities but principally to those who had more recently completed their legal training and others who were better connected. There were other reasons for diminished workloads: as a result of decreased business activity and depressed earnings, some 70 percent of the work that would normally have been referred to a lawyer was instead being withheld or postponed.

Limiting Lawyers. The idea of limiting access to the practice of law, however uncomfortable the thought might have made many lawyers feel, increasingly found support among two factions in the organized bar. Since the 1920s, law school programs had been plagued by a consistently high failure rate in the first and, to a lesser extent, second years of education. For some the explanation was quite clear; the fault lay with the admission standards employed by the schools. A second faction believed that the problem of too many attorneys was a consequence of there being too many law schools. For this group the problem arose from the differences that existed between the university-affiliated law schools and "proprietary" schools, those that were not associated with any university and offered evening programs and less formal methods of instruction.

The ABA. The establishment in 1878 of a national association of lawyers, the American Bar Association (ABA) came about, in great part, because of the inability of the legal profession to resolve either of these conflicts. The existence of an unregulated system of legal instruction had reached a point where, many lawyers believed, the practice of law itself was threatened. While the ABA grew, both in numbers and in importance as the voice of the profession, its influence with the local bar associations increased accordingly. In the 1930s it chose to use its influence to develop uniform standards for admission to law school and the requirements for both graduation and admission to the bar. Many of these standards, in fact, would come to be fixed by law. The consequences of this policy were swift and quite dramatic. Between 1928 and 1935 enrollment in schools not approved by the ABA fell by more than ten thousand, and the share of students attending approved law schools increased by nearly 17 percent.

Changes in Law School Curricula. The New Deal and the prospect of ready employment in government attracted many practicing attorneys and quite a few law professors, some of whom would return to teaching determined to "modernize" the law school curriculum. Until the late 1920s the study of law emphasized the analysis of established legal principles and the rules and legal customs that governed their interpretation and application. Law was viewed as a closed system, providing answers to all questions in the form of legal precedent. But efforts were under way to develop a new mode of training lawyers: an approach that focused narrowly upon the use of multidisciplinary tools and the collection of data to understand and evaluate legal systems. Among the legal scholars who were first to promote this concept were Jerome Frank of the Yale Law School and Karl Llewellyn of Columbia University. In 1928 the Columbia Law School became one of the first to adopt this new approach, developing and offering classes in landlord and tenant law, trial practice, corporate finance, evidence, legislation, and administrative law. Textbooks were developed that drew from a variety of fields, including psychology, sociology, and history. Such views, however, were not shared by the majority of the faculty at Columbia. The realists, as they were called, were criticized and ultimately departed for other law schools, the most receptive among them being the Yale Law School under Robert Hutchins, who had been appointed dean in 1927 at the age of twenty-eight.

Realism. Robert Hutchins was determined to transform the Yale Law School into one of the nation's foremost centers for empirical legal research. Embracing "realism" wholeheartedly, he helped establish programs that studied court administration, the trial process, and bankruptcy, the last the pet project of the eminent realist, professor and future Supreme Court justice William O. Douglas. Hutchins continued, through both his writing and teaching, to encourage adoption of the realist approach. In 1929 he left Yale to assume the presidency of the University of Chicago and was instrumental in extending the influence of realism throughout the Great Lakes region. In 1934, however, Hutchins, like many other realists, began to lose his enthusiasm for realism. As a mode of instruction, it had never found wide acceptance among the more-traditional educators, had distracted from efforts to train students to acquire lawyering skills, and had received little in the way of meaningful theoretical contributions from the social sciences. By 1939 realism had been abandoned and would find few, if any, adherents until the 1960s.

Police attacking picketers at the front gates of Republic Steel Company, Memorial Day, 1937

Sources:

Newsweek (27 June 1938): 30;

Newsweek (8 August 1938): 18;

Robert Stevens, *Legal Education In America From the 1850's to the 1980's* (Chapel Hill: University of North Carolina Press, 1983).

LABOR AND THE LAW

Labor on the Defensive. The coming of the Depression hurt the unions as much as it did any other organization. Like everyone else, the unions were unprepared at first to deal with the drastic changes these new conditions brought to the workplace. Membership declined as layoffs increased and shops closed. Without an effective plan or vision, organized labor's response to the desperation many workers felt was erratic and often ineffectual. Disputes between management and the workers, however, continued and even worsened as the availability of a cheap pool of labor grew. President Roosevelt's approach to the problems of labor in the early days of the New Deal was that of a conciliator. He believed that through cooperation the interests of both would be inevitably served, and toward that end he attempted to gain the workers' confidence by acknowledging that they were entitled to a voice in industry. No other piece of legislation more reflected this attitude than did Section 7(a) of the National Industrial Recovery Act (NIRA), which gave la-

borers the right to organize and to bargain collectively through unions of their own choosing. There were some in Congress and many more in the unions who believed the president was placing too much faith in the employers' goodwill. They felt that his paternalistic views of the workers' needs and his belief that it was the government's responsibility to administer to those needs were preventing organized labor from getting the recognition and bargaining equality it was due.

Labor Ignored. By 1934, moreover, it was becoming increasingly apparent to the now rapidly growing unions that the intent of Section 7(a) was being subverted. Employers had taken advantage of the provision to establish company unions that they used to factionalize their labor forces. Under the NIRA employers had been given the authority to create and impose industrywide codes controlling not only prices and production but also wages, a power which they frequently abused to protect profits. In practically every industry employers were resisting collective bargaining demands, and doing so successfully. Neither Section 7(a), which lacked any enforcement mechanism, nor the president had been of much help. But Congress was. Later that same year Sen. Robert Wagner introduced a bill to protect the nation's industrial workers by assuring them of the right to organize and by establishing a National Labor Relations Board. The board would be authorized to prohibit unfair practices by employers opposed to the unionization of their employees and to conduct elections to determine whether workers wished to bargain collectively and, if so, whom they desired to represent them for that purpose. Nothing could have conflicted more with the president's approach to the relations between management and labor, and he refused to endorse the bill, thereby delaying its consideration until after Congress had reconvened in 1935.

"Labor's Great Friend." The year 1935 was to be eventful. The results of the midterm and congressional elections held late the previous year clearly showed that the public was prepared to go yet further in implementing reform. Organized labor had been a major contributor to the Democratic Party's election success and expected to wield greater influence with the membership of the new, far more liberal Congress. None of this was lost on the president, who had become increasingly disappointed with the NIRA and the failure of his national labor policy. With some adroit maneuvering on the part of its sponsor and his allies, the Wagner bill was passed in the Senate and sent to the House of Representatives for its consideration. The president, perhaps sensing that any further opposition to the bill would prove futile, reversed his position in time to see and take credit for the passage of the National Labor Relations Act (the Wagner Act) on 5 July.

The Supreme Court Steps In. In quick succession, the Supreme Court delivered a series of decisions that would affect labor no less than it did any other group or aspect of national life. On 7 January 1935 in what became known as the "Hot Oil Cases" (*Panama Refining Company* v. *Ryan*), the Court invalidated the provision in the NIRA that regulated the oil industry, having found the act to be an unconstitutional delegation of legislative power. On 6 May the Supreme Court, by a vote of five to four, found the Railroad Retirement Act — an act similar in structure to the social security bill then under consideration in the Congress — unconstitutional because it was a violation of due process and involved matters beyond the scope of the commerce clause. Then, on 27 May in the "Sick Chicken" case (*Schechter Poultry Corp.* v. *U. S.*), the Court invalidated the NIRA itself. Section 7(a) had been eliminated.

. . . And Labor Steps Out. The National Labor Relations Board, to which the Wagner Act had given birth, began operating on 27 August and was immediately inundated with lawsuits challenging its authority and existence. Spurred on by the Supreme Court's recent opinions in the *Schechter* case, organizations such as the ultraconservative, anti–New Deal American Liberty League sought injunctions to paralyze the board and to prevent it from pursuing its congressional mandate. While the government was struggling to respond to the challenge, labor grew increasingly restless and belligerent. Toward the end of the year the major rubber companies announced an increase in work hours with no corresponding increase in pay. The workers reacted swiftly: they struck the plants and in the process refused to give up possession of the company's factories. To its first important test the newly formed Congress of Industrial Organizations (CIO) responded with both aid and leadership, major factors in bringing about the manufacturers' capitulation.

The Battle for Flint. In 1935 automobile-plant workers in Michigan reached the limit of their patience with conditions in their plants. Both the CIO and the United Auto Workers had been hamstrung by the reluctance of the employers to reach an agreement. At meetings convened by the unions' leadership, a proposal to strike was approved, but it was postponed pending further attempts to negotiate. On 30 December, however, the workers took matters into their own hands and shut down the plants. Two weeks later, police and striking workers who were gathered outside the plant clashed. The police, in what became known as the "battle of the running bulls," were forced to retreat, and the sit-down was expanded to include other manufacturing plants in the Chevrolet division. The auto companies were able to obtain an injunction against the strikers, but there was no attempt to enforce it, a factor that contributed to the strike's settlement sometime thereafter.

The Memorial Day Massacre. Many of the country's largest corporations entered into contracts with CIO member unions, effectively recognizing the unions' authority to bargain on behalf of the companies' workforces. Still, there were others who continued to resist, including Republic Steel. In 1937 the Steel Workers Organizing Committee ordered a work stoppage and posted pickets around many of Republic's mills. At one in south Chicago, the picketing was stopped by the police. A protest was organized and generated a march on the plant's main gate, where waiting police confronted the crowd and, in the melee that followed, killed ten of the demonstrators. Despite the outcry that followed, public reaction to labor's renewed militancy, its use of the sit-down strike to deprive company owners of their property, and its defiance of the law left many Americans with ambivalent feelings respecting labor's methods. When the Supreme Court eventually concluded, in the case of *NLRB* v. *Fansteel Metallurgical Corp.*, that the sit-down strike was an unconstitutional abridgment of the rights of property holders, the decision was met with some relief by many citizens.

The Supreme Court Steps Back . . . a Little. Whatever effect the president's court-packing plan may have had in 1937, the fact that labor benefited from the rather sudden and startling change in the Supreme Court's position regarding a host of concerns to its membership is undisputed. In 1938, in the case of *Lauf* v. *E. G. Shinner & Co.*, the Court sustained the constitutionality of the Norris-LaGuardia Act of 1932, which prohibited federal courts from issuing injunctions against strikers in all but certain rare instances. The year before, in *National Labor Relations Board* v. *Jones & Laughlin Steel Corp.*, the Court had upheld the National Labor Relations Act, laying to rest the fear that the protections it afforded the working man would be driven into oblivion. The decision also meant that the National Labor Relations Board could resume its function, free of the harassment it had suffered since its formation. During that period complaints of unfair labor practices had increased from a few hundred annually to more than nine thousand.

Sources:

Irving Bernstein, *Turbulent Years: A History of the American Worker, 1933–1941* (Boston: Houghton Mifflin, 1970);

Robert S. McElvaine, *The Great Depression: America, 1929–1941* (New York: Times Books, 1984);

Newsweek (13 February 1937): 10–11;

Newsweek (17 April 1937): 7–9.

THE LINDBERGH KIDNAPPING

The Public Hero. America has rarely given its heroes the stature it accorded Charles Lindbergh following the completion of his flight across the Atlantic. The image of a fearless pilot, master of one of the world's newest and most promising technologies, acting alone to risk all in his attempt to set a world record was simply irresistible. The "Lone Eagle" was exalted above all other modern-day heroes as a living example of the nation's greatest values. No greater symbol of all that was uniquely great about America could have been created by or for a public so sorely in need of a hero. Whether he enjoyed it or not, the adulation he inspired would achieve an intensity well beyond anything previously experienced by his contemporaries. Not until recent times would a trial be more widely followed, incite more passion, or do more to unite a people in their desire for retribution, than did the trial of Bruno Hauptmann, the nondescript man who stood accused of kidnapping and killing the hero's son.

The Kidnapping. On 1 March 1932 the country was stunned by the news that the twenty-month-old child of Charles and Anne Lindbergh had been abducted from his home in New Jersey. A search for the child was begun immediately and soon encompassed a five-state area. Kings and presidents sent their condolences, and people prayed for the safe return of the child as hundreds of press representatives from all over the world descended upon the Lindbergh home. Governor Roosevelt of New York offered to place the New York State police at the disposal of New Jersey's state police superintendent H. Norman Schwarszkopf. The police discovered few clues, and, as time passed, the absence of any news concerning the progress of the investigation left people feeling increasingly angry, frustrated, and vengeful. The outrage and disgust that had characterized the public's reaction to the news of the abduction was too real to be dissipated by the passage of time and would remain oddly disturbing to many.

The Arrest. What few not actually connected with the investigation knew was that the kidnapper or kidnappers had established contact with the Lindbergh family

Wood expert Arthur Koehler examining the homemade ladder the kidnapper of the Lindbergh baby used in March 1932 to gain entrance to the Lindbergh home

through an intermediary, the eccentric Dr. John Condon. Arrangement was made for a partial payment, the sum of fifty thousand dollars, to be made in a cemetery in the Bronx. This exchange, which took place in the dead of night, brought the doctor into contact with the kidnapper and gave Lindbergh, who was also present, but at some distance, an opportunity to hear an accented voice, if only for a few seconds, call out to Condon. In May, approximately one month after the first of the ransom notes was delivered and a portion of the ransom paid, the body of the Lindbergh child was discovered a short distance from his parents' home. No further demands for the payment of ransom were ever received. Despite the false leads reported to the police, Chief Schwarszkopf's grudging acceptance of the federal investigative assistance, and continuing public interest, there were no further developments in the case until almost two years later. In September 1934 several gold certificates bearing serial numbers that identified them as part of the ransom paid in the case began to surface in New York. One of the bills was traced to a gas station attendant, who provided a description of the man who had used it to purchase gasoline for his car. The trail the police followed finally led them to Bruno Hauptmann.

The Suspect. Hauptmann, a carpenter by trade, had illegally entered the United States from Germany in 1924. Soon after, he married Anna Schoeffer and settled in New York City where he found work as a carpenter. Over the next few years the couple developed a small circle of friends, purchased a car, and managed, through their combined labor, to save approximately ten thousand dollars. In 1932 the couple moved into an apartment in the Bronx where Hauptmann, in his spare time, constructed a garage on the adjoining lot. That same year, while Anna was in Germany visiting family, Hauptmann and an acquaintance, Isidor Fisch, pooled their resources to set themselves up in a business. Hauptmann's first venture into a business of his own would eventually fail, taking with it a goodly portion of the couple's savings. Unbeknownst to Hauptmann, Fisch was also involved in a fencing operation, purchasing "hot," or stolen, currency at a discount, and would remain so involved until 1933 when he returned to Germany. Fisch died there the following year. Hauptmann testified that in August 1934 he had discovered among the possessions Fisch had stored in Hauptmann's home a small box containing more than eleven thousand dollars in cash. Sometime thereafter, having heard nothing more from Fisch, he had decided to use some of the money to cover his own expenses.

The Trial. Hauptmann's trial began on 2 January 1935. Never before in the nation's history had the press been so vigorous or single-minded in its pursuit of a story — every event, however remotely connected and irregardless of its significance, if any, was given a full measure of attention by a press corps supremely confident of the insatiability of the public's interest. Often distorted, rarely accurate, fully self-serving, the news reporting did little more than reinforce a nearly universally held opinion that the discovery of the ransom money in Hauptmann's possession was conclusive and overwhelming proof of his guilt.

The Evidence. The evidence against Hauptmann raised as many questions as it did inferences of guilt: Dr. Condon described his meeting with the kidnapper in convincing detail despite the fact that he was terribly nearsighted and, though unbeknownst to the jury, had been inconsistent in the statements he had offered the investigators over the length of the investigation; Lindbergh saw no one but did hear a voice say "Hey, Doc," a voice he connected with that of the defendant some three years after the fact; the ladder used by the kidnapper to gain access to the Lindbergh's house was a ramshackle affair, suggesting it had been assembled by someone unfamiliar with the carpenter's trade. Hauptmann's defense team suffered its moments of failure: no effort was made to exploit the disagreements that arose among handwriting experts respecting the authorship of the ransom notes. Documentary evidence showing that Hauptmann was at his place of employment around the time of the kidnapping was ignored and eventually misplaced. Hearsay evidence was permitted; other evidence was intentionally suppressed. It all made little difference. At the conclusion of the trial the jury acted quickly to condemn the defendant. Those errors that were identified after the trial were eventually found to be insignificant. In an atmosphere in which Hauptmann's guilt was so completely evident in the eyes of so many as to be beyond question, his request for a new trial was barely given consideration. Hauptmann maintained his innocence until he was executed on 3 April 1936.

Source:
Ludovic Kennedy, *The Airman and the Carpenter* (New York: Viking, 1985).

THE NEW FEDERALISM AND ERIE RAILROAD V. TOMPKINS

Common Law and Diversity Jurisdiction. The Constitution distinguishes between the powers of the states and those of the federal government. The states are empowered to make all laws affecting matters of concern to their citizens. The laws enacted by the federal government, on the other hand, are limited to those areas designated by the Constitution. Under our constitutional form of government, the making of laws is a function of the legislature. The courts are expected to interpret and enforce the laws passed. To accomplish this task, however, the courts found it necessary to develop rules, which they standardized, in the interest of maintaining uniformity. These rules, sometimes referred to as common law, differ from state to state. Laws passed by the states or the federal government are called statutory law. The Court's rules had gradually taken on the force of law, some even being adopted by the legislatures of the different states and passed as statutes. In 1789 Congress had passed the Judiciary Act, which required federal courts to use state law when hearing diversity jurisdiction cases, that is, cases involving citizens of different states, but questions soon arose as to what Congress meant by "law." Did it include common law, or was it limited to the statutory law enacted by the different state legislatures only? In 1842, in the case of *Swift* v. *Tyson*, Supreme Court justice Joseph Story, writing for the majority of the justices, interpreted the word "laws" to mean statutes only. The rules of court made doctrine by the state courts thus became excluded by definition. The federal courts were expected and even encouraged to continue developing their own common law. If, for example, a particular state prohibited its citizens from recovering damages for some types of injury, the federal court could apply its own common law in a way that could produce an entirely different result, and that, in fact, is what happened.

Mr. Tompkins Goes to Court. Late one night in July 1934, near Exeter, Pennsylvania, an iron molder by the name of Harry Tompkins was walking alongside a railroad track on his way home. A door on a refrigerator car of a passing train unexpectedly flew open, striking Tompkins and knocking him to the ground. As a result of this accident, Tompkins lost an arm. The lawyer retained by Tompkins to represent him in a suit for damages knew that just getting to court posed a major problem. Pennsylvania law classified anyone walking on a railroad right-of-way as a trespasser who was, therefore, denied the right to recover for injuries that might have resulted from his trespass on the railroad's property. The operator of the train, the Erie Railroad, however, had been incorporated in the state of New York, where the courts had ruled differently, respecting the train operator's duty of care toward people like Tompkins. Since a citizen of one state may sue a corporate "citizen" of another in federal court, Tompkins's lawyer proceeded to file his lawsuit in New York. When the case was finally heard in the federal district court in New York, the railroad's attorney's objection to the federal court's use of New York instead of Pennsylvania common law was overruled. Tompkins won his suit and was awarded thirty thousand dollars.

The Erie Rule. The Erie Railroad appealed and again lost, the federal circuit court of appeals applying the precedent established in *Swift* v. *Tyson*. Not satisfied, the railroad took the case to the Supreme Court. Given ninety-six years of precedent, no one could have anticipated what happened next. The Supreme Court rejected the reasoning of *Swift* and, in doing so, broke with a tradition that had permitted federal courts to impose their own law upon the states under the constitutional protection afforded by the *Swift* decision. The decision came to be considered one of the most momentous of all those issued by the Court during the New Deal era. From that point on, federal courts were required, in cases where there was diversity jurisdiction, to apply state law, whether that passed by the legislature or that developed by the state courts. Federal common law would be restricted to areas of purely federal concern.

Sources:
Gerald T. Dunne, *Hugo Black and the Judicial Revolution* (New York: Simon & Schuster, 1977);

Newsweek (16 May 1938).

PRESIDENT ROOSEVELT'S COURT-PACKING PLAN

The President Looks for a Solution. By the end of 1936 some of the most important legislation passed in connection with the New Deal had been invalidated by the Supreme Court. Both the National Recovery Act and the administrative machinery created by the Agriculture Adjustment Act had been rendered useless, the problems they were intended to correct as yet unresolved. Other New Deal landmark legislation, including the National Labor Relations Act, had yet to be subjected to the Court's scrutiny. Convinced the Supreme Court was not likely to alter its fundamentally conservative interpretation of the Constitution nor be moved by the economic crisis the nation faced, President Roosevelt introduced a plan he believed would protect the portion of his New Deal program still intact. That plan was presented in the guise of court reform. It would ultimately bring more harm than good to the president's legislative program and stir up a debate that would harden the president's oppo-

---

"FEDERAL JUDICIARY FACTS"

Public reaction to the president's plan revamping the judiciary was initially difficult to gauge. Most elected officials interviewed by the press were surprised by President Roosevelt's announcement and initially guarded in their reaction. Many of the periodicals noted that, on one or two occasions, such plans had been considered and discarded by presidents in the past and that such a reorganization of the high court was not constitutionally prohibited. Most were quick to focus on the president's chief complaint — the fact that so many of the judges were old. The result of surveys like the one below appeared in many newspapers. It was not until sometime later that the full implications of the proposal and the possible motives of the president for making it became the chief topics of discussion.

"Total of life tenure federal judgeships: 237

Age distribution of present incumbents: 10 percent 40-49 years

    33 percent 50–59 years

    45 percent 60–69 years

    5 percent 70–74 years

    5.5 percent 75–79 years

    1.5 percent 80 and over

Vacancies filled to date by President Roosevelt:

    Supreme Court, none;

    lower courts, 91.

Vacancies filled by President Hoover:

    Supreme Court, 3;

    lower courts, 95."

Source: *Newsweek* (13 February 1937): 7.

---

nents and reduce the strength of his popular support until the outbreak of World War II.

"Black Monday." It had been the president's hope that the Supreme Court justices would allow him some discretion in producing the various plans for social and economic reorganization that had become collectively known as the New Deal. Some of the earlier enactments that had emerged from Congress and been signed into law had been rushed through the process under emergency conditions. But the Court's majority was immune

The United States Supreme Court, 1937: (first row, left to right) Justices George Sutherland, James Clark McReynolds, Chief Justice Charles Evans Hughes, Justices Louis D. Brandeis, and Pierce Butler; (back row) Justices Benjamin N. Cardozo, Harlan Fiske Stone, Owen J. Roberts, and Hugo L. Black

to such pressure. Beginning in early 1935 it issued a series of decisions that eliminated much of the New Deal's early legislative program and placed other portions of it in legal limbo. Among its more consequential decisions were the "gold clause cases" (*Perry* v. *U.S.*, *Nortz* v. *U. S.*, and *Norman* v. *Baltimore & Ohio Railroad*) in February, in which the Court, while upholding a congressional resolution voiding clauses in private contracts requiring payment in gold, questioned whether the government actually had the power to annul its own contractual obligations; the 6 May holding in *Railroad Retirement Board* v. *Alton Railroad*, in which a law requiring employers to contribute to plans was found to be beyond the power granted Congress to regulate interstate commerce; and, finally, the decisions on 27 May, a day the press named "Black Monday," when the Court voided a federal moratorium on the repayment of farm mortgages (*Louisville Bank* v. *Radford*), limited the president's power to fire a high-level federal appointee (in this case, a Republican), prevented the president from removing the commissioners of independent regulatory bodies without the consent of Congress (*Humphrey's Executor* v. *U.S.*), and gutted the keystone of the early New Deal, the National Industrial Recovery Act (*Schechter Poultry Corp.* v. *U. S.*). The "Sick Chicken case," as it became known, was adopted as the symbol of the Court's conservatism. The Schechter brothers purchased their poultry from sources outside the

state of New York where they did business and sold their products locally. The Schechters were also guilty of selling substandard and poor-quality processed chickens to their customers, a practice that, along with their payment of substandard wages, violated the codes established by the poultry industry under the NIRA. The Supreme Court concluded that such codes affect interstate commerce, a power delegated under the Constitution solely to Congress; and that the Schechters were not engaged in interstate commerce (and that the chickens came to "a permanent rest within the state") and thus not subject to the law anyway.

The Judicial Reorganization Bill. On 5 February 1937 the president presented his proposals to Congress. He recommended expanding the federal judiciary to include, up to a maximum of fifty, one new judge for each sitting judge over the age of seventy. Other aspects of his plan included sending appeals of constitutional questions directly from the district court to the Supreme Court and requiring government attorneys to be present before an injunction could be issued questioning the constitutionality of any act of Congress. The president went to great lengths to explain that in light of the enormous workloads of the federal courts and the aging justices' diminishing capacities, he felt compelled to submit the plan in the interest of preserving efficiency in the courts. If passed, the proposal would allow the president to appoint six new associate justices, tipping the balance in favor of those on the Court who had demonstrated their support for the New Deal's economic and social measures.

The President Stumbles. In presenting and promoting his plan, however, the president committed two major errors. He failed to consult with the members of his party in Congress, and he was trying to obscure the real purpose of his proposals, which was to safeguard New Deal legislation as yet unaffected by the Court's power of review. Many congressional Democrats were taken completely by surprise by the president's plan: some expressed their support of the president, but with serious reservations. Others indicated they needed time to consider the feelings and views of their constituents. Many were opposed. Most who saw through the president's strategy were left feeling uncomfortable with the course the president had chosen over alternatives they felt had not been explored. The president was not prepared for the reaction he received. Having just been reelected by a wide margin of the popular vote, he thought his popularity would carry the day. Congress's response had been mixed and far from satisfactory. The public's reaction had been far from clear, at least at first.

Reaction. Democrats in Congress began to take one of three possible positions. The first, outright opposition to the plan, was exemplified by Senators Wheeler and Glass, both conservatives who viewed the president's proposal as an attack upon the Supreme Court, the country's greatest continuous symbol of orderly and stable government. In an age that had witnessed the rise of totalitarianism and the destruction of democratic institutions elsewhere, such fears were too "frightful" to consider. In that regard the conservatives might not have been alone. The public's response, somewhat slow in coming, moved from confusion to nagging concern. Within months ten state legislatures passed resolutions condemning the plan. Seven others voted in its favor. If the president had hoped to mobilize the American people to pressure Congress into accepting his proposal, he failed miserably. His plan had done nothing more than cause deep division over the place of the Court in the nation's government. The second group of Democratic congressmen, only slightly fewer in number, were unable to decide where they stood. Pressured by both those who backed the president and those who opposed him, they chose to postpone taking a position. Sen. Hiram Johnson of California initially placed himself in this group, but, recognizing that the debate would afford him an opportunity to take a more independent position respecting the administration's economic policies, he, and many others, joined with the conservatives. Even the president's allies, such as Sen. George Norris, questioned why the president had not attempted to make the changes he desired by means of a constitutional amendment.

The President Responds. It soon became apparent that the president would have to promote his plan more actively. He complained to audiences everywhere that the courts had placed the government's ability to act in matters involving the nation's economic and social welfare in jeopardy. The *Schechter* decision, among others issued in May 1935, had been followed by a flood of requests for injunctions in the lower federal courts. In the time since, federal judges had issued more than sixteen hundred restraining orders preventing governmental officials from carrying out much of the New Deal legislation. The president had been disturbed by the Court's rejection of his program, and he could not understand why his plan was not getting more public support. The only practical recourse available to him was, as he saw it, a full reorganization of the judicial system. There was little question that the president considered the Court's conservative justices enemies of his New Deal and its struggle for social justice. In attempting to avoid the appearance of a political solution, however, he had clashed wih an institution that could muster significant emotional and symbolic support in its own defense. Shortly after the plan had been sent to Congress, Senator Wheeler had convinced Chief Justice Charles Evans Hughes to provide him with a letter, which he later made public, answering each of the specific charges the president had leveled at the Court. The chief justice's reply made a shambles of the president's avowed purpose for recommending his reorganization plan.

"A Switch In Time, Saves Nine." The situation was beginning to change for the president, however. Overlooked in all the excitement was the Supreme Court Retirement Act, passed on 1 March 1937, which allowed the justices to retire at age seventy with full pay. In May Justice Willis Van Devanter announced his retirement. More important in defusing the crisis, however, was a series of opinions the Court issued between March and May upholding important New Deal legislation, including the Social Security Act (*Helvering* v. *Davis,* in which Justice Benjamin Cardozo, writing for the majority, ruled that the general welfare clause did not prohibit the government from spending for a particular group as long as the benefit is national in scope) and the Wagner Labor Relations Act (*NLRB* v. *Jones & Laughlin Steel Corp.*). The Court even reversed itself on the constitutionality of minimum wage laws in the case of *West Coast Hotel Co.* v. *Parrish.* Whatever may have prompted the court to change its position, the effect was to eliminate much of the criticism that had been leveled at the Court. The crisis had passed.

The President Gets His Chance. On 2 July the Senate voted to return the president's bill to the Judiciary Committee for further study — which meant indefinitely. On 26 August the president signed into law a much modified measure that made changes in the procedures used by the lower federal courts, but which did not affect the Supreme Court. In the next four years Roosevelt would fill seven vacancies on the Court, thus finally fulfilling his hope for the changes he had risked and lost so much in bringing about.

Sources:

Henry J. Abraham, *Justices and Presidents: A Political History of Appointments To the Supreme Court* (New York: Oxford University Press, 1985);

William E. Leuchtenburg, *Franklin Roosevelt and the New Deal* (New York: Harper & Row, 1963);

Richard L. Pacelle Jr., *The Transformation of the Supreme Court's Agenda* (Boulder, Colo.: Westview Press, 1991);

Newsweek (13 February 1937): 7–9; (20 February 1937): 17–19; (27 February 1937): 10; (13 March 1937): 7–8; (3 April 1937): 10–12; (24 July 1937): 7–9.

PROHIBITION AND THE TWENTY-FIRST AMENDMENT

The Eighteenth Amendment and the Volstead Act. In the years before World War I, the temperance movement had succeeded in convincing the legislatures of twenty-six states to enact laws banning the manufacture and sale of alcoholic beverages. The culmination of a long campaign directed initially against saloons and more recently against the production of alcoholic beverages, the movement's success was dramatically affected by the nation's mobilization for war. The need to conserve grain, the importance of maintaining some semblance of discipline and devotion to a patriotic cause, and the will to win all required a demonstration of the nation's sober determination to protect its interests. Toward the end of 1917, both houses of Congress had approved a resolution to amend the Constitution to prohibit the manufacture, transportation, or sale of alcoholic beverages. By January 1919 three quarters of the states had ratified this proposal, and it became effective on 16 January 1920. The prohibitory language of the Eighteenth Amendment became the law of the land. Meanwhile, the Volstead Act was passed despite President Woodrow Wilson's veto in October 1919 to provide for the enforcement of the amendment.

Efforts to Enforce Prohibition. Support for the amendment remained strong in the years immediately following its ratification. As late as 1928, those calling for its repeal were a minority. Indications were that enforcement of the Volstead Act was having the intended effect, but clearly large numbers of people still wanted to drink. While overall production had been severely restricted, prices had risen accordingly, spawning an era of lawlessness greater than any in recent memory. Enforcement became increasingly difficult and, much to the disgust of Prohibition's adherents, unenthusiastic. Closing the legitimate channels of supply had given thousands the incentive to become bootleggers and operators of clubs that dispensed liquor and became infamous as "speakeasies." Liquor dealers in Canada, the Caribbean, and Europe provided a ready and unimpeded source of alcoholic beverages, and there were many who were prepared to risk arrest to take advantage of the opportunities afforded. Toward the end of the Prohibition era, much of the organized effort to transport, sell, and distribute alcohol had fallen under the control of criminal gangs, many of which reflected a particular ethnic origin and possessed sufficient wealth and political influence to link cities and entire regions within the networks they had created. As the gangster gained in power and prominence, and as the perception of public corruption and general social decay became more acute and widely held, Americans became increasingly dismayed with the efforts of government to enforce the law.

The Crime Business. The discovery off the New Jersey coast of a flexible pipeline used to connect the bootleggers' boats to the bootleggers' fleets of trucks spoke volumes not only about their ingenuity and brazenness but also about the extent to which local and national prohibition agents had become powerless to do anything meaningful about it. In 1921 Mabel Walker Willebrandt was appointed an assistant to the United States attorney general. Assigned the task of overseeing the Justice Department's efforts to enforce the newly passed Volstead Act, she discovered that few of her colleagues took this responsibility seriously. Worse still was the fact that her authority did not extend to local police officers upon whom the brunt of the enforcement burden fell. In New York, where a state prohibition law had been in effect since 1921, sixty-nine hundred arrests had been made during one three-year period, but only twenty convictions had been obtained. Willebrandt's attention soon focused upon the U.S. attorneys in federal districts around the country, many of whom she criticized for their lack of enforcement zeal. Corruption was rampant among the prohibition agents (they would not be included in the civil system until 1927), and Willebrandt gave up in disgust in 1928. In 1930 Attorney General William N. Mitchell appeared before the Senate Judiciary Committee to rebuke Congress for not providing President Hoover with the funds he needed to improve the government's ability to enforce Prohibition. Admitting that efforts to enforce the law were losing their vigor, he called for more prisons and longer prison terms for offenders. Many who doubted the tide could be turned by any measure the government might adopt marveled at the attorney general's persistence. He would have done better, they felt, if he had heeded the advice of his former assistant Willebrandt when she concluded that what federal enforcement required was not more men, money, and ammunition but greater respect for its own purpose and responsibility.

Repeal. What no one could have anticipated was the direction America's postwar society would take in the late 1920s. A new and more exploitive age had arrived, a social order of a more cosmopolitan nature than the nation had ever known. Older forms of social control and the traditional values that had sustained them gave way to an entirely different outlook, the product of increased mobility, wealth, and opportunity. The Depression and the changes it would bring marked the end of an era. Prohibition simply no longer fit the American lifestyle. By 1932 the public's feelings respecting Prohibition had

Repeal campaign car, Wilmington, Delaware, 1932

changed dramatically, a fact that did not escape the attention of the Democratic Party, which included repeal in its election platform. The strength of the Democratic showing in 1932 and the outpouring of public sentiment the election generated in favor of repeal was enough to move Congress to pass a resolution calling for the adoption of the Twenty-first Amendment, repealing the Eighteenth Amendment on 20 February 1933. The Twenty-first Amendment was put to the states for ratification, and on 5 December it was ratified by the required number of states, becoming law.

Source:
J. C. Furnas, *The Life and Times of the Late Demon Rum* (New York: Putnam, 1965).

THE SCOTTSBORO BOYS

The Arrests. On 25 March 1931 a white youth, one of several who had picked a fight with a group of young black men aboard a Memphis-bound freight train, filed a complaint with local authorities in the town of Stevenson, Alabama. The police in neighboring Scottsboro were contacted and asked to stop the train, but it had already passed through. The Jackson County sheriff called a deputy near the next stop, Paint Rock, and had him deputize every available man to stop the train, arrest every black man on it, and return them to Scottsboro. Nine black youths, all transients and ranging in age from thirteen to twenty, were taken at gunpoint from the freight car in which they were found and arrested. Also discovered

aboard were two white female mill workers, Victoria Price, age nineteen, and Ruby Bates, age seventeen. Fearful that they, too, would be arrested, they reported how they had been repeatedly raped by the black men in custody and forced to remain where they had been discovered. The nine, Olen Montgomery, Clarence Norris, Haywood Patterson, Ozie Powell, Willie Roberson, Charles Weems, Andrew Wright, Roy Wright, and Eugene Williams, were jailed, charged with rape, and held for trial in Scottsboro.

The First Trial. The trials of the nine defendants began twelve days later in an atmosphere so charged with racial hatred that their safety could only be assured by the presence of a small force of deputies. Local editors had already concluded that the youths were guilty and should be treated severely, if only for the fact that they had dared to assault a white woman. The defendants were divided into four groups, based on their ages and the strength of the evidence against them. The first to be tried were Weems and Norris. Questions regarding the strength of the evidence against them arose almost immediately. The medical doctors who had examined the women testified that they had found little physical evidence of rape, that they had observed only minor bruises or lacerations on the body of Victoria Price and none on Ruby Bates, and that neither of the victims had displayed any sign of emotional trauma. There were inconsistencies as well in the accounts given by the women. Nonetheless, the all-white juries hearing the testimony were not disposed to

Attorney Samuel Leibowitz with the Scottsboro Boys in the Decatur, Alabama, jail

render any verdict other than guilty. Eight of the nine were sentenced to be executed for their parts in the rape. Wright, age thirteen, was sentenced to life imprisonment.

Public Reaction and Appeal. Shortly after the trials had been concluded, the cases of the young blacks came to the attention of the Communist Party and its affiliate, the International Labor Defense (ILD). With the assistance of such groups as the Anti-Imperialist League and the League of Struggle for Negro Rights, demonstrations were organized to publicize the plight of the young men and to raise funds for appeals of convictions. Taken by surprise by the strong public reaction to the unfairness of the proceedings in Alabama, the National Association for the Advancement of Colored People (NAACP) attempted to assume control of the litigation but was rebuffed by the ILD. In the "Scottsboro Boys" the Communist Party had found a cause through which they hoped to demonstrate the extent to which the American judicial system had been corrupted. They had no intention of relinquishing control over the case. After the convictions of seven of the eight defendants who had received the death penalty had been upheld by the Alabama Supreme Court (which granted Williams a new trial), the United States Supreme Court, in the case of *Powell* v. *Alabama*, determined on 7 November 1932 that

the defense of the Scottsboro Boys had been so seriously compromised by the errors and inadequacies of their lawyer that they had essentially been deprived of their constitutional right to counsel.

Retrial. The new trials of the Scottsboro Boys, this time followed closely by the national media, began in March 1933 in nearby Decatur. Haywood Patterson was the first to be tried. Arrangements had originally been made for Clarence Darrow to defend the young men, but he had not been able to work with the ILD lawyers assigned to the case. Lead counsel for the nine would instead be the renowned criminal defense lawyer from New York Samuel Leibowitz. Conditions surrounding the new trials were virtually identical to those that had characterized the first. Leibowitz was maligned both for being Jewish and for his willingness to defend blacks. His defense strategy was an aggressive one. The testimony of Victoria Price was picked apart and her credibility destroyed. Ruby Bates took the stand and admitted that her and Price's accusations of rape had been fabricated. Other witnesses appeared to refute much of the state's evidence, but the jury remained unmoved. At the conclusion of the trial Patterson was found guilty and sentenced to death.

Another Retrial. In June 1933 the judge who had presided over the retrial, James Edwin Horton, startled everyone by granting the defense's request for a new trial and transferring the case of Eugene Williams to juvenile court. A fair-minded jurist, he had not been impressed with the credibility of much of the testimony that had been offered against Patterson. Moreover, he was troubled by something he had not dared share with anyone at that time. During one of the trial's recesses, one of the medical doctors who had examined the victims had confronted each with his suspicions regarding their claims of rape, suspicions that the women did not deny. The doctor informed the judge that he could not testify to this exchange for fear that he would lose his practice as a result. As a result of his unpopular decision, Judge Horton was relieved of his assignment (and defeated for reelection to his judgeship in 1934), and another jurist was brought in to replace him. That yet another set of juries would again convict the seven defendants tried in Judge Horton's court in a series of trials in winter 1933 came as a surprise to no one.

Another Appeal. In the fall of 1934, unknown to Leibowitz, two ILD attorneys offered Price $1,500 to repudiate her testimony. She informed the police and the attorneys were arrested with the bribe money still in their posession. The ILD was thoroughly discredited, and groups that originally had been held at arm's length became centrally involved in the defense effort. On 1 April 1935, in the case of *Norris* v. *Alabama*, the verdicts of the Scottsboro Boys were reversed on the grounds that Alabama had systematically excluded blacks from jury service, a deprivation of the defendant's right to a fair trial. The reaction in Alabama revealed the depth of feeling that had been aroused by the critical attention the case had focused on the state. Gov. Bibb Graves was moved to caution against any display of resistance to the ruling and instructed the state's courts to begin impaneling blacks as jurors. The newly formed Scottsboro Defense Committee, created in December 1935 and comprising members of the interested groups, assumed control of the case for the next round of trials, in 1936 and 1937, with Leibowitz still acting as chief counsel, though he ceded the questioning of witnesses to a southern attorney.

And Yet Another Trial. Once again Patterson was to be the first to be tried, and once again he was convicted, though his sentence this time was seventy-five years in prison. Clarence Norris was tried next; he was convicted and sentenced to death. The trials of Andrew Wright and Charles Weems followed. The verdict for each was guilty, and they were sentenced to ninety-nine years and seventy-five years, respectively. Ozie Powell, who had assaulted a police officer on his return to prison after Patterson's most recent trial, was tried for assault only. He pleaded guilty and was sentenced to twenty years. The prosecution declined to pursue charges against the other four defendants, and they were released.

The End. Efforts to secure a pardon for those convicted met with stiff local opposition, though Governor Graves commuted Norris's death sentence to life imprisonment. Graves was invited to meet socially with President Roosevelt at Warm Springs, Georgia, though guessing that the president intended to ask him to consider a pardon, the governor declined to meet. In November 1943 the state released Weems, and in January 1947 Andrew Wright and Norris were paroled; though they left the state without permission and were sent back to prison. Charles Weems received his second parole in 1946, the year Ozie Powell was freed. Haywood Patterson escaped in 1948 and settled in Michigan, which refused to extradite him. In June 1950, the last of the Scottsboro Boys in prison, Andrew Wright, was paroled a second time. The case of the Scottsboro Boys remained a matter of general interest for more than the better part of the decade. No other event so clearly demonstrated the extent of racial injustice in the South. Prejudice of the most extreme kind possible had infected the proceedings from the beginning and had been responsible for its many questionable outcomes. The case remains an enduring symbol of "southern justice" that even the passage of time has failed to erase completely.

Sources:
Dan T. Carter, *Scottsboro: A Tragedy of the American South* (Baton Rouge: Louisiana State University Press, 1969);

Newsweek (13 April 1935): 19.

THE SEABURY INVESTIGATION AND MUNICIPAL CORRUPTION

From Small Acorns . . . Aside from the evidence provided by occasional appearances of anticrime crusaders or the statements by legislative committees of investigation, Americans in the 1930s lacked the means to ferret out collusive arrangements among their elected representatives, organized criminals, and corrupt police. They did not have available to them the legal framework with which these forms of criminal conspiracy could be more vigorously prosecuted, nor the enforcement machinery for detecting and investigating this type of criminal activity. Throughout the nation's history, however, it had been proven time and again that even the most corrupt politicians could not withstand the pressure of an aroused and interested public. While attempts to reform government and to right wrongs involving the public trust often achieved no more than limited goals, they did serve the far more important function of reaffirming community values and protecting the public. Such was the case in New York with the Seabury Commission.

Arnold Rothstein. In 1928 the gambler and loan shark Arnold Rothstein was shot dead, presumably for failing to pay his gambling debts. Rothstein had gained national attention in 1919 in connection with the bribing of eight members of the Chicago White Sox baseball team to throw the World Series. Pressured by New York mayor Jimmy Walker to bring the killers to justice, the police arrested two of the gambler's associates. In the absence of any evidence of their involvement in Rothstein's murder, however, the charges were dismissed. Nothing more came of the matter until the following year when Walker found himself running against Fiorello La Guardia, a Republican congressman, for the office of mayor. La Guardia claimed that the police knew who had killed Rothstein but had decided not to pursue the investigation for fear of the scandal that might result if news of the payments the gambler had made to one of the city's judges became known. Walker was reelected and again the matter was dropped.

Judge Crater. On 6 August 1930 New York Supreme Court judge Joseph Crater disappeared amid rumors that he had been accepting bribes and was involved in a series of shady financial manipulations. The scandal that resulted forced New York governor Franklin Delano Roosevelt to ask the appellate division of the state court to conduct an investigation of New York City's magistrate courts. The appellate division, with the governor's blessing, asked Samuel Seabury to conduct the official inquiry.

Judge Seabury. Samuel Seabury was a lawyer who had been elected a city court judge at the age of twenty-eight. He eventually rose to the office of a state supreme (district) court judge before resigning in 1916 to launch an unsuccessful bid for the governorship. A serious man with a courtly demeanor, Seabury was a devoted progressive and a firm believer in the integrity of public office. Following his appointment by the appellate division in 1930, Seabury received two additional commissions: the first, assigned to him by the governor, was to investigate charges of corruption and malfeasance made against the city's district attorney; the second, under the authority granted him by the state legislature in his newly assigned role as counsel for the Hofstadter Joint Legislative Committee, was to undertake an investigation of the city's government. Seabury's probe continued for two years and resulted in disclosures that were widely reported in the press.

Police Corruption. The investigation got off to a rocky start. Rumors and tips were plentiful enough, but hard evidence of wrongdoing, particularly among the members of the police vice squad, was more difficult to come by. Seabury knew that many of the lower court magistrates had been placed in their positions through an elaborate system of graft and payoffs. Judges appointed under the system returned the favor to those responsible for their appointment by dismissing the cases of criminals who in turn paid for the consideration they received. Such schemes involved the police, the courts, bondsmen, lawyers, and members of organized crime. The mobsters paid enormous sums of money for the privilege of engaging in their many criminal activities without fear of police interference. With the help of informants Seabury subpoenaed the records of some two thousand banks and brokerage houses in New York. From the information he was able to obtain, cases against several police officers and others who had been involved with them in the taking of graft were easily made. The prosecutions that followed resulted in numerous convictions, and even more resignations, among officers and police officials, including the sheriff of Manhattan. The commission's work was not without an element of danger; in the course of its investigation, two of the investigation's witnesses were murdered, and another disappeared.

Tammany Hall. Nor did the political machine that had controlled the city's administration for decades escape Seabury's scrutiny. Day after day, witnesses, eventually some twenty-four hundred in number, appeared before the legislative investigating committee for which Seabury served as directing counsel and were subjected to an aggressive and often accusatory examination. The committee learned that the bribery of public officials was so rampant as to be an essential part of doing business in the city — without payoffs one could not obtain basic services or franchises or necessary permits. Special consideration was given to known gamblers, bootleggers, and leaders of organized crime, including the heads of the Luciano-Costello crime empire. As Seabury's investigation continued to expand, his staff discovered evidence of suspicious deposits suggesting a pattern of bribery implicating the mayor of New York himself.

Jimmy Walker. Unable to develop any concrete evidence against the city's district attorney, Seabury turned his attention to the mayor. Jimmy Walker was perhaps one of the most popular mayors in the city's long history. Tammany Hall's choice for mayor in 1925 seemed to personify the carefree and debonair spirit of the city. Mixing easily with politicians, businessmen, gangsters, and his adoring public, the mayor rarely felt pressured by the responsibilities of his office and seemed to be more concerned with maintaining and enjoying an active social life. Walker's humor and quick wit initially distracted the legislators on the investigating committee, but when examination resumed the following day, it was Seabury who asked the questions, leading the mayor through a history of his personal finances and into making some shocking disclosures. Cash, bonds, checks, and dividends — almost three-quarters of a million dollars all told — had poured into an account that Walker shared jointly with an acquaintance. Walker first denied that the money was his but finally admitted to having withdrawn more than half of it for his own use. This proved to be one of two such accounts in which the mayor was a joint account holder. Walker could no more explain why he had been entitled to the moneys he had withdrawn than he could relate how he had earned the twenty-six thousand dollars he had received from the owner of a fleet of city cabs. In 1932 the mayor resigned, and the Seabury investigation was concluded.

Citizen Seabury. Seabury chose not to capitalize on his fame or reputation as an honest reformer, but this did not prevent him from forming a fusion ticket with Fiorello La Guardia as its candidate for mayor (the Democratic machine, Tammany Hall, had been discredited, but New York City remained a Democratic stronghold. A fusion candidate could appeal to both Democrats and Republicans for support). Once La Guardia had been elected, Seabury withdrew from politics and returned to his private practice. He died in 1958.

Source:
Steven R. Fox, *Blood and Power: Organized Crime In the Twentieth Century* (New York: Morrow, 1989).

HEADLINE MAKERS

ARIZONA CLARK "KATE" OR "MA" BARKER

1871-1935

"Ma" and Her "Boys." As a historical figure, "Ma" Barker is something of a puzzle. Never arrested for committing a crime, she was nevertheless suspected of being the leader of a gang J. Edgar Hoover considered one of the most vicious with whom the FBI ever had to contend. The public, feeding on newsprint that detailed the escapades of her "boys" and their friends, perceived her as a mother whose love for her children was so extreme as to have twisted both her conscience and her judgment. To the members of the gang, or so those who survived would later relate, she was no more than a dowdy and simple-minded, middle-aged woman whose use to them was limited to her willingness to hide them from the law and doing what she could to raise bail money or otherwise to secure their release on parole. What, then, was the truth?

Background. In an era famous for its bandits, shoot-outs, and chases, Arizona Clark Barker was a rarity, a female bandit leader. She had been born and raised in Springfield, Missouri, where as a child she had once seen the legendary Jesse James. In 1892, already displaying the dowdiness and plumpness that were to become her hallmark, she married farm laborer George Barker, who, like her, seemed to be resigned to a life of poverty. What is known about her married life is that it was hard, unhappy, and taken up with the raising of her four sons, Herman, Lloyd, Arthur (who was called "Doc"), and Fred. Her loyalty to her children and the fierceness with which she protected them from the consequences of their delinquent behavior became something of a legend itself in the Ozark Hills in which they lived.

Herman Barker. In the 1920s she could no longer shield her sons from the law and the punishment meted out for their increasingly serious offenses. Doc was arrested in Oklahoma for killing a night watchman during a bungled burglary and sentenced to life imprisonment.

In 1927 Herman was stopped by two officers outside of Wichita, Kansas, for questioning in connection with a recent robbery. Pulling his gun, he shot one of the policemen in the head and was shot, in turn, by the other. Badly wounded and fearing capture, Herman killed himself. Ma Barker grieved for weeks afterward.

The Barker Boys. Struggling to find some motive for Ma's criminal activities, the FBI later explained that the death of her eldest child drove her into a vengeance-seeking orgy of violence. She was reputed to have carried out a series of bank robberies and kidnappings unequaled in the annals of modern crime. The truth may well have been quite different, but by then it hardly mattered. After the death of Herman, little more was heard concerning the Barkers until 1932, the year Lloyd was arrested for mail robbery and sentenced to a twenty-five-year term. Fred had been serving a term in prison for the shooting of a town constable who had caught him attempting to steal a car. In 1933, under conditions that suggested his freedom may have been purchased, Fred was released and returned home to Ma in the company of Alvin "Creepy" Karpis. It is likely that Fred was the first of the two Barker brothers to form an alliance with Karpis, who quickly became one of Ma's favorites. This was a time when membership in the gang was in steady flux, and Ma provided shelter to several wanted men, including Frank Nash. There was no evidence to show that she had ever participated in the gang's robberies or that the FBI suspected her of being its leader. That would come later.

Kidnapping. In a move that gave J. Edgar Hoover fits, the state of Oklahoma pardoned Doc, who promptly rejoined the gang and assumed, with Karpis, a leadership role. Shortly after Doc's return, Ma's paramour, Arthur Dunlop, whom the gang suspected of being an informant, was killed. A year later, in 1934, the gang gunned down one of its own members, an act that ultimately led to their destruction. In 1933 George Ziegler, World War I veteran, college graduate, engineer, and a Capone gunman, had joined the gang. Ziegler, who had connections throughout the Great Lakes region, was said to have been the first to suggest the gang try its hand at kidnapping. The gang's first target was the Minneapolis banker Edward Bremer, for whom they received a two-hundred-thousand-dollar ransom. But it would appear that the Barker-Karpis gang had already gained some previous experience in the field, having, with the assistance of a local crime boss, abducted the founder of Minneapolis's largest brewery, William Hamm, just six months before. Following the second kidnapping and ransom payment, Ziegler, who had been responsible for the two kidnappings which had so shocked the nation, revealed the gang's participation to friends. He had to be silenced immediately. He was killed in Cicero, Illinois, on 22 March 1934.

Shootout. While the FBI was looking through Ziegler's personal effects and tracing the leads they provided, Ma was dispatched to see Ziegler's widow, whom she convinced to turn over the money concealed by her late husband. Returning to the gang's hideout, Ma discovered the place in an uproar: the FBI was closing in and the gang would have to scatter. Ma's days of handing payoffs to officials and running other errands in complete anonymity were over. The FBI had decided that she had been the brains behind the gang's activities, and, whether she had earned the reputation or not, she was stuck with it. In January 1935 Doc was apprehended by the special agent in charge of the FBI's Chicago field office, Melvyn Purvis. Eight days after Doc's arrest Fred was located in a rented cottage near Lake Weir, Florida. The house was quickly surrounded, and at the end of a four-hour gun battle both Ma and Fred were found dead, a Thompson submachine gun lying between their bodies. The mystery of Ma's place in the gang was never solved, but the story of her death took a permanent place in the bandit lore of the day.

Hugo Black

1886-1971

Associate Justice of the Supreme Court

The New Deal's Champion. President Roosevelt's choice of Hugo Black to become an associate justice on the Supreme Court did not surprise those who were familiar with Black's political record as a senator from the state of Alabama. The very same month the president had revealed his preference for Black, he had been forced to accept the senate's defeat of his plan to increase the size of the Court. The opportunity presented by Justice Willis Van Devanter's retirement came as a particularly welcome relief to those in the president's party who opposed his "court-packing" plan. The opportunity to place a confirmed New Dealer on the high-court bench offered the hope that future consideration would be more favorable to New Deal legislation. As a supporter of the act creating the Tennessee Valley Authority and a highly visible senatorial advocate of President Roosevelt's Emergency Relief Appropriation Act, Black had been regarded as a man with a firm and personal commitment to the goals of the New Deal and as its most devoted legislative champion. What many had not anticipated was the extent to which his nomination would be so bitterly opposed by people representing such a cross section of political sentiment and affiliations. His nomination was one of the most closely followed in history, at least until more recent times, and no newcomer to the Court was ever more scrutinized than he.

The Senator. Born into poverty in rural Alabama, Black as a child was fascinated by the lawyers he observed at the courthouse. It had come as no surprise to his family when he announced his intention to become a lawyer. Graduating from the University of Alabama Law School at age twenty, he settled in Birmingham and developed a specialty in labor law. Four years later he became a police court judge, serving until he was elected county prosecutor, a position to which he would return after service in the Army during World War I. In private practice Black developed a reputation as a lawyer who would represent aggressively the interests of the workingman against his employer, a reputation that stood him well in his campaign for a congressional seat in 1926. As a senator, Black's devotion to the New Deal was unsurpassed. During President Roosevelt's first term alone, Black voted in favor of each of the twenty-four major pieces of New Deal legislation introduced.

The President's Choice. Relations between the president and Senator Black were not always close. Soon after taking office, Roosevelt decided to postpone taking on the problems of industrial recovery, preferring instead to give encouragement to American industry to take the initiative in pursuing economic recovery. In December 1932 Senator Black, in complete disregard of the consensus of the president's conservative supporters, introduced a bill limiting the number of hours and days workers involved in interstate commerce could be required to work. Endorsed by both the American Legion and organized labor, the bill passed in the Senate and was sent on to the House of Representatives. Finding himself suddenly forced to take action, the president, upset that the proposed law would allow him no flexibility in its application, arranged for the introduction of another bill, soon to become law as the National Industrial Recovery Act, to counteract the far more liberal and aggressive provisions of the Black bill. If the president had been disappointed with the senator then, he would soon regard him as an indispensable ally, a man whose loyalty to the president was unswerving (at the end, only Black and a small minority of senators had remained steadfast in their support of his court-packing bill). In Black the president had found a perfect candidate for the high-court bench: at fifty-one he was much younger than any of the "nine old men," whose age and capacity for work the president had questioned, an unwavering supporter of the New Deal, and a senator and thus assured of swift confirmation, or so he thought.

Confirmation. Hardly had the nomination been announced when it became evident that the president's strategy could not be achieved without a struggle. Some of the senators viewed the appointment as a rebuke for their opposition to the president's proposal for judiciary reorganization; others saw it for what it was, an attempt to ensure the success of future New Deal legislation and a blatant attempt to influence the Court's interpretation of the law. Outside the Congress Black was assailed, on the one hand, for his liberal views, his sympathy for labor, and his support of what many considered the more-intrusive and regulatory facets of the New Deal program. On the opposite end of the political spectrum, questions were raised respecting his southern heritage, his opposition to the proposed antilynching law, his past membership in the Ku Klux Klan, and his lack of judicial experience. In August 1937, after six hours of rancorous debate, Hugo Black was confirmed as a new associate justice of the Supreme Court.

The Great Dissenter. Early reviews of the justice's performance were not all complimentary. Remarks attributed to Justice Harlan Stone and excerpts from a speech delivered by Chief Justice Charles Evans Hughes were interpreted as evidence of the justices' unhappiness with Black's legal craftsmanship and respect for precedent. Rumors abounded that his opinions had been the work of New Deal lawyer and Roosevelt confidant Thomas Corcoran. The truth, as it would become known, was quite a different story. In his first eight months on the bench Black wrote thirteen dissents, one of which would form the basis of the majority opinion in the case of *Erie Railroad* v. *Tompkins*. The new justice was among the first to discard Justice Louis Brandeis's progressivism, which stressed the need to disperse economic power to prevent its concentration and the likelihood of abuse. Brandeis's views had been influential in shaping the early New Deal, but the subsequent failure of many of these programs to achieve their goals had convinced many that such concentration was inevitable, perhaps even beneficial, and that the proper role for government was one of intervention and regulation. Black was a firm believer in the latter approach, a position that would give him, in the face of enormous governmental growth, a special sensitivity to the rights of the individual in such a society. Black's sense of independence was not questioned, but his real contribution became more evident by the end of the decade. Black's appointment was followed in due course by the confirmation of other justices sympathetic to the New Deal's aims. None, however, did more to move the Supreme Court beyond its preoccupation with cases involving regulation of the nation's economy toward the consideration of issues concerning individual freedoms and protections than the former senator from Alabama.

Sources:

Gerald T. Dunne, *Hugo Black and the Judicial Revolution* (New York: Simon & Schuster, 1977);

Newsweek (21 August 1937): 7–9;

Newsweek (30 June 1938): 30.

BENJAMIN V. COHEN

1894-1983

LAWYER, NEW DEAL INSIDER

The New Dealer. Few administrations have ever spawned as much legislation as did that of President Roosevelt, and fewer yet could claim to have had as many of its proposals enacted because of the drafting skills of a single person. Benjamin V. Cohen's fame as the New Deal's most brilliant and tireless legal craftsman and adviser spread well beyond the inner circles of the Roosevelt administration. Originally induced by his mentor, then–Harvard professor Felix Frankfurter, to employ his considerable skills in the service of the New Deal, he found himself prevailed upon to stay, lending his legal talents and analytical mind to many, such as Secretary of the Interior Harold Ickes and Sen. William Borah of Idaho, who found them indispensable. Identified variously as a "brain truster," an enigma, one-half (with his roommate Thomas Corcoran) of the "Gold Dust Twins," the extent of his knowledge regarding the workings of government and his insight of the legislative process were universally respected.

The Lawyer. Born in Muncie, Indiana, Cohen attended the University of Chicago before enrolling in the Harvard Law School, from which he was graduated at the age of twenty-two. Initially employed as a clerk for Circuit Court judge Julian Mack, then for Justice Oliver Wendell Holmes, he later found employment as counsel for the shipping board combating waste and overcharges in the government's World War I contracts for ocean-going transport. Leaving governmental service at the end of the war, he appeared at the Versailles peace conference as a legal adviser to American Zionists pressing for a Jewish homeland in Palestine. Cohen was later to become involved in a lucrative business-law practice in New York, where he developed a reputation as a brilliant draftsman. His sense of public duty, however, motivated him to devote large portions of his time to the preparation of a minimum-wage law for the National Consumers League and to advising Gov. Herbert Lehman, an early Roosevelt supporter, regarding social legislation.

The Insider. A private man, Cohen was perfectly suited for the role of insider and trusted adviser. In April 1933 the administration found itself in some difficulty in framing legislation for the securities industry. Could Professor Frankfurter be of any assistance? He could, and to

Washington he dispatched two of his former students, James Landis, who would later be made the head of the Securities Exchange Commission, and Ben Cohen. Closeting themselves in a hotel for four days, the two produced a revised version of the bill and watched with not a little satisfaction as it was enacted into law. It would be a while before Cohen returned to New York. He was appointed legal counsel for the Public Works Administration, where he prepared the drafts of what would become the Federal Securities Act of 1933, the Securities and Exchange Act of 1934, the Utility Holding Act of 1935 (the constitutionality of which he personally had to defend before the Supreme Court in 1938), and the Fair Labor Standards Act of 1938.

The New Deal Goes into High Gear . . . Again. Like Corcoran's, Cohen's influence and importance grew as the New Deal progressed beyond its initial stage. By 1935, in the face of increased business opposition, the New Deal began to move away from its cooperative or consensus approach of solving the nation's economic problems to one of economic regulation. The "Second New Deal," as this period became known, emphasized the development of regulatory machinery and rules by which the government's control could be extended. That task fell to the administration's legal draftsmen. Cohen's skills became even more in demand as he raced from one crisis to another, revising enactments that had been weakened through the process of judicial review and explaining the intricacies of the administration's proposals to congressional sponsors. Cohen would move on to serve in the Department of State and in other related capacities, including a term as a member of the War Refugee Board, until the 1970s when, in ill health, he was forced to retire.

Sources:
William E. Leuchtenburg, *Franklin Roosevelt and the New Deal* (New York: Harper & Row, 1963);

Arthur M. Schlesinger, *The Politics of Upheaval* (Boston: Houghton Mifflin, 1960);

Newsweek (13 July 1935): 24–25;

Newsweek (21 February 1938): 13–14.

J. EDGAR HOOVER

1895-1972

FBI DIRECTOR

The Director. The FBI established itself in the 1930s as the nation's premier police force and in doing so changed forever the public's view of professional law enforcement. It did more than that, of course. Through its vaunted centralized crime records section, its crime lab, its training academy, and other services, the bureau became an im-

portant resource for police departments across the country, setting standards and providing a model sorely needed in some areas of the nation. That all of this was due in great part to a single man was as much a reflection of the times as it was a measure of Hoover's control over an agency that played the principal role in establishing the federal government's moral leadership in suppressing crime. Hoover was as much criticized for his obsession with the bureau's image and his insatiable appetite for publicity as he was for his claim of invincibility. These traits certainly did not endear him to all, and particularly not to those local police who were often as involved in the bureau's spectacular manhunts as were the special agents themselves. But the special agents served an important function, a fact not lost on the bureau's director, who more than anyone else appreciated the predicament in which the FBI found itself in the early and mid 1930s. In the end Hoover's penchant for manipulative public relations and sense of drama may have been as responsible for winning back and maintaining the people's faith in the New Deal's war on crime as any other development throughout the decade.

The Bureau of Investigation. Hoover was appointed the bureau's assistant director in 1921 largely on the basis of his work as the supervisor of the department's alien registration section and later as the head of the general intelligence division under Attorney General A. Mitchell Palmer. In 1924 when he was elevated to acting director by the subsequent attorney general and future chief justice Harlan Fiske Stone, he had developed a reputation for his devotion to his work and as a stickler for efficiency and order. The bureau's powers, however, would not be substantially expanded until 1934, the year before it became the Federal Bureau of Investigation. Until that time Hoover and his agents had to be content with the collection of data and the pursuit of interstate car thieves. Many of the resources that would be used so effectively in the future to create the bureau's reputation were sharpened during these years: a crime records section and a filing system capable of enormous expansion were established; relations with the press were improved; and the bureau actually developed its own public relations arm. Hoover's recruitment of college-educated men, many with professional skills, was indeed part of his plan to eliminate all those whose positions were owed to political favor and to improve the quality of the bureau's performance. But it was important for another reason far more relevant to the task of creating a respected and powerful agency. In the early 1930s the public's regard for policemen generally bordered on contempt. Sometimes brutal, frequently reactionary in the execution of their duties, and often regarded as corrupt, police of that day and age were viewed as inept and seriously outclassed in their struggle against the bandit and the gangster, whose cunning and fearlessness seemed unmatched. Hoover understood that unless he could distance himself and his agents from such perceptions, he could not give the public reason to distinguish between the lowly flatfoot and the incorruptible federal crime fighter. Neither his agency nor the power of the federal government would be sufficient to convince people of the soundness of the nation's security.

Crime Fighting. Many mistakes were made at first, and for the bureau the possibility of failure was always real and just a step away. The shooting of three innocent bystanders during the attempted capture of John Dillinger at the Little Bohemia Lodge, as well as the horribly excessive violence used to flush a wanted bank robber out of a New York City tenement that left the structure in flames and the FBI's relationship with one of the nation's largest police departments in shambles, raised serious questions regarding the bureau's readiness to assume the duties given it. Quietly, secretly, Hoover recruited men with extensive histories in local law enforcement — two-fisted, hard-nosed lawmen who made up in their skills as manhunters what they lacked in polish and sophistication. (One of the "hired guns," as they became known within the bureau, was Clarence Hurt, a former chief of detectives in Oklahoma City. As a special agent, he was one of two who actually shot Dillinger outside the Biograph Theater in Chicago and was personally responsible for arresting Alvin "Creepy" Karpis.) But Hoover's persistence, luck, and tightfisted control over the soul and body of his agency would eventually win out, and with success would come an independence and power unheard of among governmental entities.

The Director and the President. In 1935 Hoover discovered that he could be indispensable to the administration in other ways, that he had access to information of a political value that could be used to ensure his continued access to the president. As the government grew increasingly anxious respecting the growth of totalitarian regimes abroad and radical movements internally, it undertook to investigate the backgrounds of large numbers of federal job applicants and appointees. Much of that task fell to the FBI and with it the temptation, rarely resisted, to pursue investigations wholly unjustified under federal regulations. In this Hoover was given some encouragement by the president, who also sanctioned, sometimes unwittingly, the use of wiretaps and break-ins to collect information of a sometimes intimate and potentially scandalous nature. Hoover's reports regarding his investigation's findings and his assurances that the secrets learned would remain safe with him gave him and his bureau a power of intimidation and influence unequaled in government. Even as the decade closed and the bureau devoted more and more of its attention to problems of subversion and espionage, Hoover continued to hoard such information, remaining ever-vigilant against those who might threaten his power.

Source:
Curt Gentry, *J. Edgar Hoover: The Man and His Secrets* (New York: Norton, 1991).

CHARLES EVANS HUGHES

1862-1948

CHIEF JUSTICE OF THE SUPREME COURT, 1930-1941

Judicial Statesman. Charles Evans Hughes assumed the responsibilities of the Supreme Court chief justice at the onset of this nation's worst economic crisis. Little did anyone suspect at the time of his appointment that his varied and extensive experience would become so critical a factor in steering the institution of the Supreme Court through one of its most challenging periods. If anything, the public perception of the chief justice was one that evoked an image of an austere, remote, and humorless man who had once pursued the presidency on a platform remembered for its probusiness and antilabor positions. His name remains linked with the public perception of the early New Deal Court as having been blindly conservative and much out of step with the nation's Depression-era needs and priorities. However conservative Hughes's economic views may have been, he, above all others, was responsible for successfully guiding the Court through one of its most difficult crises. Less well understood is his role as a protector of civil liberties.

Lawyer and Politician. Reared as an only child in a family that placed considerable value upon purposeful action and the performance of one's duty, Hughes was something of a prodigy in his youth. His extraordinary memory and drive led him first to Brown University, then to the Columbia School of Law, where his passion for precise thought and thoroughness in preparation brought him the highest honors. In 1884 he joined a New York law firm, becoming a full-fledged partner only three years later. Thereafter, and in short order, he taught law at the Cornell Law School and served as counsel for a legislative committee investigating the illegal practices of the utilities industry in New York City. His success in this role and as the principal legal counsel for yet another legislative committee investigating the life insurance industry catapulted him into the public eye as a Republican reform candidate for the state's gubernatorial office. In 1910 President William Howard Taft, the man he would succeed in 1930 as chief justice, nominated Hughes to become an associate justice of the Supreme Court, a position he would retain until 1916 when he ran for the presidency against Woodrow Wilson. Having lost the election, he returned to private practice, where he specialized in corporate law. In 1921 he became President Harding's secretary of state, a post he held until 1925, when he was appointed to The Hague Tribunal; later, in 1928, he was made a judge on the Permanent Court of International Justice.

The Chief Justice. When Hughes replaced the ailing Taft as chief justice, he was described as possessing a "judicial tendency" toward a conservative philosophy a little "less cheerful than Mr. Taft's." What was overlooked in this assessment was the chief justice's earlier record as a progressive who had twice urged the New York legislature to consider public regulation of business and, as governor, had established regulatory commissions equipped with both investigatory and rate-fixing powers. Aligned against the four conservative justices on the Court were three who fit squarely in the liberal camp. Only Justice Owen Roberts and the chief justice were considered moderates, their voting tendencies too unpredictable for them to be so easily classified. Among the first pieces of Depression-generated legislation to reach the Court in 1934 were two of special concern. The first (*Home Building & Loan Assn.* v. *Blaisdell*) involved a moratorium upon the foreclosure of mortgages in Minnesota, and the second a question concerning the extent to which the state of New York could establish price controls over milk (*Nebbia* v. *New York*). Both laws were upheld, an indication of the chief justice's willingness to grant government, within limits, the authority it required to meet the pressing needs of a Depression-racked constituency. The justice's concerns regarding the constitutional implications of the centralization of government power would not fully surface until later.

The "Sick Chicken" Case. In 1935 the Court found itself at the center of controversy involving the New Deal's ambitious legislative program. In January the Court invalidated, as an improper delegation of congressional authority, a portion of the National Industrial Recovery Act affecting the regulation of the oil industry. A few months later, Justice Roberts joined the conservatives in a five to four decision invalidating the Railroad Retirement Act, the chief justice having aligned himself with the Court's liberals. Clearly Justice Roberts had become the swing vote, more often than not aligning himself with the more conservative members of the Court against the chief justice and Associate Justices Louis Brandeis, Benjamin Cardozo, and Harlan Stone. On 27 May the remainder of the National Industrial Recovery Act was declared unconstitutional in a decision that would temporarily cast a cloud over all other New Deal legislation. That case involved the administration's use of the constitution's commerce clause to extend its regulatory powers, in this case, over the operation of a poultry packer and distributor.

The Crisis. Not quite two years later, in response to the Court's invalidations of other portions of his program, President Roosevelt introduced a plan to increase the number of justices on the Court. The explanation he offered involved his concerns respecting the ages of the justices and the burdens of their respective offices. Chief Justice Hughes, however, proved to be a shrewd, if somewhat restrained, opponent of the proposal. At Sen. Burton K. Wheeler's suggestion, the chief justice composed and released a letter that refuted many of the reasons the president had offered in support of his plan. In an unprecedented step, Hughes, in the company of two other justices, appeared before the Senate Judiciary Committee to explain the Court's position and to emphasize the constitutional significance of its independence. The presence of additional members of the Court, he insisted, would only create delay and foster impression that the Court would be ever thereafter subject to the ebb and flow of politics. Gradually, public and congressional opinion shifted against the president's plan, and, as the Court's cause was taken up by members of the president's own party, it became evident that the proposal would meet with defeat. Two weeks later Justice Roberts joined the chief justice and the more liberal wing of the Court in issuing two opinions, one upholding a minimum-wage law similar to another it had previously rejected only a few years before, and the other in which the Wagner Act was found to be constitutional. Hughes denied that the Court had been pushed to reverse itself: Justice Roberts had acted independently in reconsidering his earlier position, and the chief justice himself, it was noted, had remained consistent with the reasoning of an opinion he had written in connection with a similar case where he had approved of the government's use of its power to control commercial activity, even where it was only loosely associated with interstate commerce. The president's effort to influence the Court's deliberations by expanding its membership had been effectively neutralized.

The Chief Justice's Remaining Terms. In the years remaining, Hughes proved instrumental in the Court's transformation from its role as the protector of property rights to defender of personal liberties. An outspoken critic in the post–World War I hysteria, which had encouraged official action against radical political groups, the chief justice was actively involved in defining those liberties in the context of one's right to free speech and assembly and to be free, under the Fourteenth Amendment, from state interference in the free exercise of the rights specifically protected by the federal constitution. Hughes had long maintained an interest in such issues, having written the Court's majority opinions in *Aldridge* v. *U. S.* (jury panelists can be questioned regarding their racial attitudes), *Stromberg* v. *California* (a free-speech issue involving the display of a red flag as a symbol of opposition to the government, a violation of state law), *Near* v. *Minnesota* (the illegal use of an injunction to suppress critical articles in a newspaper), and *DeJonge* v. *Oregon* (overturning the conviction of a communist organizer as a violation of the defendant's right of assembly). He would, as chief justice, preside over the Court during its change in direction away from principally economic issues toward three decades of involvement in the individual rights of the nation's citizenry.

Sources:

Alpheus Thomas Mason, *The Supreme Court from Taft to Burger* (Baton Rouge: Louisiana State University Press, 1979);

Richard L. Pacelle Jr., *The Transformation of the Supreme Court's Agenda* (Boulder, Colo.: Westview Press, 1991);

Newsweek (13 June 1938): 26;

Time (10 February 1930): 11.

THOMAS J. MOONEY

1882-1942

LABOR RADICAL AND PRISONER

The Bombing. In the early afternoon of 22 July 1916 a powerful bomb exploded among a group of onlookers who had gathered to watch a Preparedness Day parade in San Francisco. Ten people were killed and many more injured by the detonation that echoed through the streets of the downtown district. The bombing was thought to be the work of unknown anarchists opposed to the nation's preparation for war in the face of an armed conflict that had engulfed the nations of Europe.

Suspects. There were no witnesses to the planting of the bomb and virtually no hard evidence that could be used in the identification of the bomber, but the public's outraged insistence on some form of retribution placed considerable pressure upon the authorities. Suspicion soon focused upon five radical labor unionists, among them Warren Billings, a laborite who had been previously convicted of a conspiracy in which a bomb was to have been used, and his good friend Thomas Mooney, an iron molder and labor organizer. Arrests soon followed.

The Trial. From the very beginning of Mooney's trial, there were indications of a frame-up. Testifying against Mooney were two witnesses whose truthfulness and motives for testifying became highly questionable. Evidence of prosecutorial misconduct and the manipulation and distortion of the evidence produced by police investigators began to surface even before the trial ended. In response to the prosecution's accusations, the defense called witnesses who had occupied the building overlooking the site of the explosion and who could testify that Mooney had not been observed in that area. An alibi witness, an amateur photographer, produced photographic evidence that Mooney and his wife were standing one and a half miles away from the site of the explosion only moments before the bomb detonated. Nonetheless, Mooney was convicted, the jury voting for the death penalty. Not until years later did it become known that the principal witness against Mooney had perjured himself and that the foreman of the jury had been a close personal friend of the prosecutor, with whom he had continued to meet during the course of the trial.

The Prisoner. Mooney's conviction was as much a product of the times as it was the result of a concerted effort to skirt the law. Even before the trial had begun, there had been an ominous shift in public opinion away from the liberalism of the progressive era toward a more conservative view of the world. The threat to deeply held notions of democratic ideals seemed very real to most people. The possibility of becoming embroiled in a war had intensified feelings of patriotism while creating greater antagonism toward anything that smacked of a foreign or radical influence. This fear, which would peak in the postwar years, affected judge and jurors alike in Mooney's case, giving them ample reason, they believed, to ignore evidence of misconduct on the part of the police and the prosecutors. The prosecution's theory, which found no support in the evidence, was that Mooney had intended to start a revolution in California, and the jury seemed disposed to believe it.

Reaction. Mooney's case was propelled into a cause célèbre by the verdict and his sentence of death. Labor organizations in the United States and throughout the world sponsored rallies and otherwise protested the outcome of the trial. President Wilson was moved to appoint a commission, chaired by the secretary of labor, to conduct an inquiry into the circumstances surrounding Mooney's conviction. The subsequent report condemned the atmosphere in which the trial had been held and suggested that there had been a concerted effort on the parts of certain commercial interests to ensure that a conviction resulted regardless of whether it was supported by sufficient evidence. Mooney's trial judge, troubled by the report and other disclosures made during the course of the commission's investigation, prevailed upon the state's attorney general to reopen the case. The state supreme court, however, refused to take any action. The law of the state of California at the time made no provision for the introduction of newly acquired evidence after the conclusion of a trial, and the court refused to allow an exception. Finally, at the request of President Wilson, the governor commuted Mooney's sentence to life imprisonment.

The Case That Would Not Die. Mooney's cause was not helped by events that occurred in the ensuing years. His close identification with radical labor and the Socialist Party became reason enough in the public's mind for his incarceration. At the height of the red scare public attitudes in California hardened against him, and the chances of securing his release or a new trial diminished with each affirmation of his conviction on appeal. Numerous appeals were prepared and raised in his behalf and helped to keep the case in the public's eye well into the 1930s. With each appeal, however, interest in the case grew and the public came to feel considerably more sympathetic toward a man whose case seemed to resemble so closely that of France's Dreyfus Affair. In July 1931 Sherwood Anderson wrote, "He should be turned loose. They should quit it. There should be a limit, even to our human cruelty."

Habeas Corpus. California's officialdom was not entirely impervious to mounting criticism of its handling of the matter. In 1933 Gov. James Rolph convened a pardon hearing. The committee that was to deliberate on the matter debated the issues for three months before concluding that Mooney was in fact guilty and not deserving of a pardon. This time interest in the case did not wane. With the assistance of the American Civil Liberties Union, a new team of lawyers was formed to pursue a writ of habeas corpus on a ground never before tried — a violation of due process based upon perjured testimony. The petition was denied at the federal district court level, then brought directly to the attention of the United States Supreme Court by means of an appeal of the lower court's refusal to consider the petition for a writ. In January 1935 the Supreme Court, with Justice Charles Evans Hughes speaking for the majority, reversed the district court's ruling in a momentous decision (*Mooney* v. *Holohan*) but determined that the petition would first have to be pursued in the state courts before it could again be considered in the federal judicial system.

A New Hearing. Mooney's petition for a writ of habeas corpus was, as he expected, denied at both the trial and the intermediate appellate levels, but the California Supreme Court did act on his petition and scheduled what was to become one of the lengthiest habeas corpus hearings in the nation's history. In October 1937 the Court denied the writ in a lengthy opinion in which it detailed the record before it and concluded that in the absence of any proof of fraud, perjury, or suppression of evidence, it lacked any authority to overturn the jury's verdict. In yet another extraordinary move, Mooney obtained permission to appear before the state assembly to plead his case and won from the legislators a resolution supporting a full pardon. That resolution, however, was defeated in the state senate, and Mooney was returned to San Quentin prison. One of the senators who had heard Mooney, however, was Culbert Olson. Olson was convinced of Mooney's innocence. Two years later, after he was elected governor, Olson summoned Mooney to his office and conducted a parole hearing, which resulted in Mooney's exoneration and complete pardon. Warren Billings was also released that same year, but not in time to participate in the demonstrations, including a parade through San Francisco, celebrating Mooney's release. Labor's aging and ailing martyr soon slipped back into obscurity.

Source:
Richard H. Frost, *The Mooney Case* (Stanford: Stanford University Press, 1968).

PEOPLE IN THE NEWS

In 1936 the screen actress **Mary Astor** became involved in a highly sensationalized divorce proceeding filed against her by her husband, Dr. Franklyn Thorpe, after he had discovered in the actress's diary proof of her affair with playwright and critic George S. Kaufman; excerpts were published in the tabloids, embarrassing several of her fellow actors in Hollywood about whose private lives she had written in often crude and intimate detail.

In 1935 film actress **Constance Bennett** was taken to court by an artist whom she had commissioned to paint her portrait and had refused to pay his fee of thirty-five hundred dollars because she was dissatisfied. At trial Bennett complained that the portrait exaggerated the size of her thighs and that the painter had not done enough to make her image appear more flattering. The argument was not enough to win the sympathy of the jury but did convince the starstruck judge to direct the jury to find in the actress's favor.

In 1935 a bawdy play based on **Erskine Caldwell**'s novel *Tobacco Road* (first published in 1932) opened in Chicago and was promptly closed by Mayor Edward Kelly, who revoked the license of the theater; the producers obtained a temporary injunction against the city but lost their case at trial after the mayor and several witnesses testified that the play was obscene by local community standards, a decision later upheld by the United States Circuit Court of Appeals.

America's most notorious mobster, **Alphonse Capone**, was convicted of tax evasion in 1931 and sent to the federal prison on Alcatraz Island to prevent him from communicating with his fellow "racketeers." In 1935 a reporter of the *San Francisco News* learned from a confidential source that Capone was suffering bouts of dementia, behaving like a raging, spitting madman. The prison psychiatrist who was called to examine Capone confirmed that Capone was indeed losing his mind because he was in the late stages of syphilis infection. In reply to a reporter's question as to whether Capone could be feigning, the doctor had replied: "Paresis can't be faked."

On 11 April 1938 former child actor **Jackie Coogan** unsuccessfully sued his mother and stepfather, who was his business manager, in the Los Angeles County Superior Court, claiming that they had withheld more than four million dollars he had earned during his fifteen-year film career. But shortly after Jackie's twenty-first birthday, his stepfather denied him any further claim to the fortune he had accumulated during his performing years. While the trial and the appearance of the actor's wife, the actress Betty Grable, drew much attention and the actor himself much sympathy, Coogan was to lose his suit and never to recover the moneys he had earned during his childhood.

In 1932 **Clarence Darrow** was hired to defend naval Lt. Thomas Massie; Mrs. Granville R. Fortescue, a prominent socialite; and two ordinary seamen charged with the murder of a Hawaiian whom they believed responsible for raping the lieutenant's wife, Mrs. Fortescue's daughter. In a racially charged atmosphere Mrs. Massie originally accused the victim and four of his companions, all native Hawaiians, of assaulting her but later refused to testify at their trial. The evidence against the men was weak, and, after the jury became deadlocked, a mistrial was declared. Rioting and other violence erupted in the streets of Honolulu. Lieutenant Massie and two sailors later kidnapped one of the Hawaiian youths whom Mrs. Massie had identified as one of her assailants in an attempt to force him to confess but killed him instead. The lieutenant, his mother-in-law, and the two sailors were arrested after their car was stopped by police, who had been alerted to the young man's abduction by eyewitnesses. Swayed by Darrow's arguments, the four were found guilty of manslaughter, a verdict regarded by the local population as too lenient and that touched off another round of rioting among enraged Hawaiians. Support for the defendants, however, had steadily grown on the mainland: the Hearst newspapers were referring to the matter as the "honor slaying." The four were brought to the governor's office, where they were detained for one hour before their sentences were commuted with the understanding that they would leave the islands immediately.

In 1934 Chicago grain merchant **Robert A. Gilchrist**, invoking the "Informer Law" of 1863, which permitted ordinary citizens to sue at their expense to recover moneys rightfully owing but unlawfully kept from the government, and entitled "informers" to half of the funds recovered as a reward, filed a complaint for fraud against the Grain Stabilization Corporation in New York's federal district court seeking more than one billion dollars in damages and five million dollars in fines for some twenty-five hundred different violations the corporation committed prior to becoming insolvent. The suit was dismissed in 1935 by Judge John C. Knox with the explanation that Gilchrist did not have legal standing to pursue such an action, casting doubt on the applicability of the statute.

In 1935 Los Angeles attorney Richard Bird learned from a newspaper account that his client **Rush Griffin,** a black man convicted of murder, had been executed the day before. The appeal Bird had filed on Griffin's behalf was unprocessed. The court clerk's office had failed to forward the brief requesting a stay of execution to the state's supreme court. Bird's request eventually was forwarded to its intended destination, where his request for a postponement of Griffin's execution pending the appeal was routinely granted after the fact.

In 1932 **Angelo Herndon,** a black youth and communist organizer, was arrested while handing out leaflets urging people, particularly blacks, to organize. He was charged with and in 1933 convicted of violating a 131-year-old statute prohibiting anyone from inciting "insurrection among slaves and other Negroes" and sentenced to eighteen to twenty years at hard labor on a chain gang. His appeal was rejected by the Georgia Supreme Court. Whitney North Seymour, the nation's former assistant solicitor general, argued the matter before the United States Supreme Court, which rejected the appeal after finding that the central issue in the case — the constitutionality of the Georgia anti-insurrection statute — had not been raised before the courts in Georgia. Associate Justice Roberts postponed execution of the sentence, pending action on Herndon's request for a new hearing. Herndon was freed in 1935 after a Georgia court found the statute too vague and indefinite to be constitutionally sound.

In 1935 **Ben B. Lindsey,** a former Denver, Colorado, juvenile court judge well known as an advocate of special juvenile courts and revision of delinquency laws, as well as for his management of the Denver juvenile and family courts, was reinstated as a member of the Colorado state bar from which he had been suspended in 1927 for endorsing the concept of companionate (trial) marriage. The adverse publicity he received resulted in the loss of his position as a judge and, two years later, his disbarment; he was elected to the bench in California and characterized his reinstatement as a complete vindication.

In 1935 **Eliot Ness** was hired by the reform mayor of Cleveland to investigate the racketeers who had placed a stronghold on the city's commercial activity. Ness introduced a program to reform the police force, attacking bribery and graft in the department and reducing crime by 25 percent. During the next three years a combination of surveillance and undercover work was used against organized criminal gangs and labor racketeers, the conviction of two of the most powerful of whom signified the changing times.

In 1930 the United States Senate refused by a single vote to confirm President Hoover's nomination of Judge **John J. Parker** to the Supreme Court. Criticized for his lack of scholarship and judgment, Parker was said to possess a certain "animus toward Negroes" and a willingness to accept the legitimacy of "yellow dog" contracts (employment made contingent upon a laborer's agreement not to join a union). But the most damaging evidence was found in a letter written by President Hoover's political adviser to the secretary of the interior, suggesting that the North Carolina judge's appointment would strengthen the president's popularity in a state that had given him a significant majority of its votes in the last presidential election.

In 1934 **Melvyn Purvis,** special agent in charge of the Federal Bureau of Investigation's office in Chicago, received word that the nation's most notorious bank robber, John Dillinger, had driven a stolen car across a state line, a violation of federal law, to make good his escape from an Indiana jail. Purvis and the bureau's efforts to locate and apprehend America's "Public Enemy No. 1" were closely followed by both press and public for some four months, a chase filled with all the melodrama of an exciting and violent adventure. On 22 July acting on a tip, Purvis and a squad of agents shot Dillinger as he attempted to resist capture outside a movie theater in Chicago.

In 1936 the Senate impeached **Halsted Ritter,** a United States district judge in Florida and the first sitting judge removed for general misbehavior. The judge had continued to practice law while serving as a federal judge, a practice that left him open to suspicions that his conduct as a judge could be influenced for private gain. The notoriously headstrong judge ignored the Senate's impeachment order and had to be evicted from chambers by the U.S. marshal.

In 1934 "Little" **Gloria Vanderbilt,** granddaughter of the railroad baron Cornelius Vanderbilt, was removed from the custody of her mother, judged neglected because of her mother's self-indulgent lifestyle, and named a ward of the court under the care of her paternal aunt. Income from Gloria's trust fund, set up by her father to provide for her, was redirected to her aunt.

In 1932 **James J. "Jimmy" Walker,** the flamboyant Democratic mayor of New York City, was charged with some fifteen counts of malfeasance and other related offenses by a committee organized in response to an outcry for the reform of the city's municipal government. Gov. Franklin D. Roosevelt arranged for an investigation of the magistrate courts in the borough of Manhattan, which eventually was expanded under the direction of Judge Samuel Seabury to include other public offices, including that of the mayor. No proof of malfeasance or graft-taking on the part of Mayor Walker was found, but the results of the investigation clearly demonstrated that Walker had been neglectful of his duties, at least on one occasion. The mayor resigned from office and left the country, a decision many viewed as an admission of guilt.

DEATHS

Arthur "Doc" Barker, bank and armored-car robber and founding member of the Barker-Karpis gang, killed while attempting to escape the federal penitentiary on Alcatraz Island, 14 June 1939.

Benjamin N. Cardozo, 68, United States Supreme Court associate justice (1932–1938) and acclaimed legal scholar whose belief that law should be molded to fulfill the needs of a society deeply influenced that Court in the later days of the New Deal era, 9 July 1938.

Clarence Darrow, 80, who, as the "attorney for the damned," was one of the nation's most famous criminal lawyers, defending, among others, Nathan Leopold and Richard Loeb, Eugene V. Debs, J. T. Scopes (the "Monkey Trial"), and the McNamara brothers who were accused of bombing the *Los Angeles Times* building, 21 March 1938.

Izzy Einstein, 57, Prohibition agent and master of disguises who was personally responsible during his career for the arrest of some forty-nine hundred persons for violation of the Volstead Act, 28 February 1938.

Charles Arthur "Pretty Boy" Floyd, killed in a gun battle with FBI agents on the outskirts of East Liverpool, Ohio, 22 October 1934.

William A. Glasgow, 64, chief counsel for the United Mine Workers of America and adviser to its president, John L. Lewis; became known as the union's advocate against the use of the injunction to suppress strikes by workers in the nation's coal fields, 24 March 1930.

William J. Hickson, 61, psychopathologist and criminologist, who, as founder and director of the Chicago Municipal Court's pathology laboratory, testified as an expert at the Leopold-Loeb murder trial, 4 October 1935.

William Hitz, associate justice of the District of Columbia Court of Appeals (1916–1931) who presided over the oil-reserve scandal trials called the "Teapot Dome" scandal of oilman Harry F. Sinclair and former secretary of the interior Albert B. Fall, 3 July 1935.

Oliver Wendell Holmes, 93, associate justice of the United States Supreme Court (1902–1932), known as the "Great Dissenter" for the minority opinions he wrote in such cases as *Lochner* v. *New York,* in which he expressed his belief that government should be given wide discretion to address problems concerning the general welfare, 6 March 1935.

William McAdoo, 76, former congressman and assistant secretary of the navy under Woodrow Wilson, who in the latter part of his career in public service assumed the post of New York City's chief magistrate, instituting much-needed reform in that city's judicial system, 16 June 1930.

Jack "Machine Gun" McGurn (real name, James De Mora), 32, one of Alphonse Capone's most feared gunmen, having been implicated in some twenty-eight gangland killings and believed to be a participant in Chicago's "St. Valentine's Day Massacre," killed by unknown assailants, 13 February 1936.

John George Milburn, 78, counsel for the New York Stock Exchange and defender of the nation's largest trusts (Standard Oil and Union Pacific); when President William McKinley was mortally wounded by an assassin's bullet in 1901, he was taken to the Milburn home where he died a week later, 25 August 1930.

Frank "Jelly" Nash, 49, bank robber, killed by gunmen believed to have been sent to free him from the custody of federal and local police officers, in Kansas City, Missouri, 17 June 1933.

Albert Ottinger, 59, former New York attorney general and the Republican Party's candidate for governor who lost by only twenty-five thousand votes to Franklin D. Roosevelt, 24 January 1938.

Francis Raule, 83, former president (1902–1903) of the American Bar Association and that organization's last surviving founder, 10 February 1930.

Edward T. Sanford, 64, associate justice of the United States Supreme Court (1923–1930), 8 March 1930.

Frederick Steiwer, 55, a former United States senator from Oregon (1926–1938) who gained national recognition as President Roosevelt's chief opponent in his attempt to reorganize the Supreme Court and one of the Court's principal congressional defenders, 3 February 1939.

William Howard Taft, 72, the twenty-seventh president of the United States and former chief justice of the Supreme Court (1921–1930), where he presided as a conservative in his judicial thinking and as an advocate of efficiency in the work of the court, 8 March 1930.

William G. Thompson, 70, attorney and chief counsel for Sacco and Vanzetti from shortly after their arrest in 1922 until their execution in 1927, September 1935.

Ansley Wilcox, 74, the Buffalo, New York, lawyer in whose coat and library Theodore Roosevelt took the oath of office to become the president of the United States following the assassination of President McKinley, 12 September 1935.

Giuseppe Zangara, 33, an unemployed millhand and self-proclaimed anarchist who attempted to kill then-president Franklin D. Roosevelt but did succeed, quite unintentionally, in mortally wounding Chicago mayor Anton Cermak on 15 February 1933, in Miami, Florida, by execution, 6 March 1933.

PUBLICATIONS

Dean Alfange, *The Supreme Court and the National Will* (Garden City, N.Y.: Doubleday, Doran, 1937);

Ernest Sutherland Bales, *The Story of the Supreme Court* (Indianapolis: Bobbs-Merrill, 1938);

Harry Best, *Crime and Criminal Law in the United States, Considered Primarily in Their Present-Day Social Aspects* (New York: Macmillan, 1930);

Bibliography of Crime and Criminal Justice, 1932–1937 (New York: Wilson, 1939);

Louis D. Brandeis, *Mr. Justice Brandeis: Essays* (New Haven: Yale University Press, 1932);

James H. Chadbourn, *Lynching and the Law* (Chapel Hill: University of North Carolina Press, 1933);

Homer S. Cummings, *Selected Papers of Homer Cummings, Attorney General of the United States, 1933–1939* (New York: Scribners, 1939);

Mary Dennet, *Who's Obscene* (New York: Vanguard, 1930);

Morris Leopold Ernst: *The Ultimate Power* (Garden City, N.Y.: Doubleday, Doran, 1937);

Felix Frankfurter, *Law and Politics: Occasional Papers, 1913–1938* (New York: Harcourt, Brace, 1939);

Frankfurter, *Mr. Justice Holmes and the Supreme Court* (Cambridge: Harvard University Press, 1938);

Charles Furman, *Mr. Justice Miller and the Supreme Court, 1862–1890* (Cambridge, Mass.: Harvard University Press, 1939);

J. Edgar Hoover, *Persons in Hiding* (Boston: Little, Brown, 1938);

Law: A Century of Progress, 1835–1935: Contributions in Celebration of the 100th Anniversary of the Founding of the School of Law of New York University (New York: New York University Press, 1937);

David Lawrence, *Nine Honest Men* (New York: Appleton-Century, 1936)

Maury Maverick, *In Blood and Ink* (New York: Modern Age, 1939);

Morris Ploscow, *Crime and Criminal Law* (New York: Collier, 1939);

Frederick Seaton Siebert, *The Rights and Privileges of the Press* (New York & London: Appleton-Century, 1934);

Southern Commission on the Study of Lynching, *Lynchings and What They Mean* (Atlanta: The Commission, 1931);

Henry Torrschaefer, *Handbook of American Constitutional Law* (St. Paul, Minn.: West, 1939);

John Barker Waite, Criminal Law in Action (New York: Holston House/Sears, 1934).

LIFESTYLES AND SOCIAL TRENDS

CONTENTS

Sidebars and tables are listed in italics.

1930

- The number of miles of paved roads in the United States has doubled since 1920, reaching 695,000. Gasoline consumption is at 16 billion gallons per year, up from 2.7 billion gallons in 1919.

- With smoking glamorized by the movies, 124 billion cigarettes are produced in the United States, up from less than 9.7 billion in 1910.

- The United States has 6.3 million farms, and a quarter of its population either lives on farms or grew up on farms.

- New Mexico's 46,753-acre Carlsbad Caverns is made a national park by an act of Congress.

- The first Dutch elm disease kills trees in Cleveland and Cincinnati. Introduced to the United States by furniture lumber shipped from Europe, the disease will kill 13 million trees in the next forty years.

- For the first time in history, emigration from the United States exceeds immigration.

6 Mar. General Foods introduces Birdseye Frosted Foods: frozen peas and spinach, three kinds of berries, fish, and various meats. Because the prices of these products are relatively high (thirty-five cents for a package of peas, as opposed to ten to thirteen cents for a pound of dried navy beans) and because they are hidden away in grocers' ice cream freezers, frozen foods are not immediately successful.

7 Mar. Commenting on the stock-market crash of October 1929, President Herbert Hoover tells the American public: "All evidences indicate that the worst effects of the crash upon unemployment will have passed during the next sixty days." Unemployment has grown from 1.5 million to 3.2 million in the five months since the crash.

30 Mar. Nearly one million people take part in "hunger marches" across the country.

May The first airline stewardess, Ellen Church, begins work for United Airlines. Her primary task is to ease passengers' fears of flying. The job requirements are female, single, over twenty-one, no taller than 5 feet 4 inches, under 115 pounds, and friendly personality.

Aug. Flashbulbs, which produce an odorless, smokeless, and noiseless light to use with cameras, are introduced by General Electric seven weeks before they are patented by German inventor Johannes Ostermeir.

7 Aug. President Hoover tells governors from the drought-stricken Midwest to establish local and state committees to handle the problem.

Oct. With unemployment at 4.5 million, President Hoover appoints a Committee for Unemployment Relief.

11 Dec. The Bank of the United States in New York, with sixty branches and 400,000 depositors, collapses. It is one of more than thirteen hundred banks to close in 1930.

20 Dec. Congress responds to President Hoover's request for funding for public works construction by authorizing a $116-million public works loan. It also authorizes $45 million in drought loans for farmers in the Midwest and South.

1931

- To generate income by attracting visitors from other states, Nevada legalizes gambling and institutes a six-week residency period for divorces (far shorter than elsewhere in the nation).

- Sales of glass jars increase dramatically while sales of canned goods decline — indicating that people are saving money by preserving food at home.

- Schick Dry Shaver, Inc., begins marketing the first electric shaver, selling three thousand at twenty-five dollars apiece in 1931 and more than ten thousand in 1932.

- Hundreds of unemployed workers in New England dig clams and sell them door to door for twenty-five cents a peck.

- Social worker Jane Addams wins the Nobel Peace Prize.

Jan. President Hoover insists, "No one is going hungry and no one need go hungry or cold."

The New England Telephone and Telegraph Company lays off all its married women workers.

Feb. A group of 6,024 Americans of Mexican origin leave Los Angeles for Mexico on the Southern Pacific Railroad at a cost of $77,247 to the city of Los Angeles. These *repatriados* are the first of some 400,000 to repatriate voluntarily or be deported forcibly to Mexico under a program initiated by the U.S. Department of Labor.

3 Mar. Congress designates "The Star Spangled Banner" the national anthem.

Nov. Hattie T. Caraway is the first woman to be elected to the U.S. Senate.

1932

- Congress passes Section 213 of the Federal Economy Act, prohibiting more than one family member from working in the federal civil service. Many married women will be thus barred from government employment.

7 Mar. Leaders of the Trade Union Unity League (TUUL) and the Detroit Unemployed Council organize a hunger march from Detroit to the River Rouge Ford Motor Company Plant, in Dearborn, Michigan. Four men are killed when police fire into the crowd. Dozens are arrested.

12 Mar. Six thousand dissidents march in Detroit, while the band plays the Communist anthem, "The Internationale."

June-Aug. Thousands of World War I veterans, calling themselves the Bonus Expeditionary Force (BEF), camp in Washington, D.C., to petition Congress to pass a bill granting early payment of bonuses authorized by the Adjustment Compensation Act of 1924 but not due until 1945. Violence with police on 28 July results in the deaths of two veterans.

Nov. The Iowa Farmers' Union stages a thirty-day strike, urging supporters to "Stay at Home! Buy Nothing! Sell Nothing!" They hope to force the federal government to institute a farm program to stabilize prices and provide mortgage relief.

8 Nov. Franklin D. Roosevelt is elected to his first term as president of the United States with 22,800,000 popular votes to 15,750,000 for Herbert Hoover.

1933

- One survey estimates that illness is 40 percent higher among the jobless.

- The marriage rate is down 40 percent from the 1920s level.

Mar. Frances Perkins becomes the first woman cabinet member when President Roosevelt names her secretary of labor.

5 Mar.	President Roosevelt declares a four-day national bank holiday.
9 Mar.	Congress passes the Emergency Banking Act.
May	First New Deal legislation passes: the Federal Emergency Relief Administration (FERA) is created to give direct relief to the unemployed; the Public Works Administration (PWA) is established, utilizing private contractors for dams and bridges; the Civil Works Administration (CWA) authorizes employment for civic purposes, such as parks, roads, and schools.
27 May	The Century of Progress World's Fair opens on the South Side of Chicago.
16 June	The National Industrial Recovery Act passes, setting up National Recovery Administration, regulating prices and wages.
9 July	National Labor Relations Board meets for first time.
Oct.	*Esquire,* the first magazine for men, begins publication; it features cartoons and drawings of scantily dressed women.
Nov.	Elijah Muhammad (formerly Elijah Poole) succeeds Farad Muhammad (formerly W. D. Fard) as leader of the Nation of Islam.
30 Nov.	Eleanor Roosevelt convenes the White House Conference on the Emergency Needs of Women, "to pay attention that women are employed wherever possible."
5 Dec.	The prohibition of the sale of alcoholic beverages, in effect since 1920, is repealed. Six southern states, as well as Kansas and North Dakota, remain dry.

1934

- Food-shopping patterns shift, as Americans buy more red meats, fruits, green vegetables, and dairy products.
- Coca-Cola sales drop with the repeal of Prohibition.
- In the Plains states 300 million tons of soil blow away in the "black blizzard."
- Huey Long receives more mail than any other person in America this year.

9 May	Some twelve thousand West Coast longshoremen and seamen strike.
28 May	The Dionne quintuplets are the world's first five infants on record to be born during one delivery. They soon become a media sensation.
5 July	Police clash with striking San Francisco waterfront workers, fatally shooting two workers.
3 Sept.	Sixty-five thousand textile workers strike in North Carolina.
8 Sept.	The S.S. *Morro Castle* sinks in the Atlantic; 125 lives are lost.
Oct.	The Federal Farm Bankruptcy Act, the Federal Surplus Relief Corporation, the Commodity Credit Corporation, and the Jones-Connally Farm Relief Act pass, responding to the farm crisis and expanding government's role in farming.

1935

- One out of four households is on relief; 750,000 farms have been foreclosed since 1930.

- Thousands of migrants from Oklahoma, Texas, and Missouri move to the West Coast.

- Bingo begins in movie houses and becomes popular with charities.

- The ten-cent chain letter fad begins. Denver postal employees work at night to sort thousands of letters.

- Twenty million Monopoly sets are sold in one week.

- Funded by John Rockefeller, Jr., the eight-year task of reconstructing colonial Williamsburg, Virginia, is completed.

- The 193,593-acre Shenandoah National Park is established in the Blue Ridge Mountains.

- The first canned beer is introduced, by Krueger Beer of Newton, New Jersey.

- Eastman Kodak introduces Kodachrome for sixteen-millimeter movie cameras.

6 Apr. The Emergency Relief Appropriation Act is signed, establishing the Works Progress Administration to create relief jobs in public works. Start of the "Second New Deal."

10 June In New York former alcoholic Bill Wilson and drinking companion Dr. Robert H. Smith found Alcoholics Anonymous.

5 July Roosevelt signs the National Labor Relations Act, known as the Wagner Act, boosting organized labor.

7 Aug. Roosevelt signs the Social Security Act of 1935, a historic turning point in government responsibility for the welfare of its citizens.

15 Aug. Pilot Wiley Post and humorist Will Rogers are killed when Post's plane crashes near Point Barrow, Alaska.

22 Nov. Pan Am's flying boat, the *China Clipper*, leaves Alameda, California for the Philippines, inaugurating transpacific commercial air and mail service.

3 Dec. The nation's first public-housing project opens on New York's Lower East Side.

5 Dec. The National Council of Negro Women, founded by Mary McLeod Bethune, begins advocating civil rights.

1936

- A U.S. Circuit Court of Appeals judge rules that shipping contraceptives by mail does not violate antiobscenity Comstock Laws.

- Dust storms denude vast farmlands of Kansas, Oklahoma, Colorado, Nebraska, and the Dakotas.

- A Colorado farm survey shows that half of the six thousand farmhouses in one region are abandoned.

- WPA Federal Art Project employs 3,500 artists; the Federal Writers' Project employs 6,500 writers; the Federal Music Project employs 15,000 musicians from thirty different orchestras.

- Six hundred thousand acres are added to state park preserves.

- A *Fortune* magazine poll reports that 67 percent of the respondents favor birth control.

- Herbert LeRoy Hechler runs a flea circus on New York City's Forty-second Street. For thirty cents viewers can watch trained fleas juggle, dance, walk a tightrope, and operate a carousel.

- Seven million women pay more than $2 billion for 35 million hair permanents.

- A sleeper berth from Newark to Los Angeles costs $150; the Fifth Avenue double-decker-bus fare goes up from five cents to ten cents.

- Tampax is introduced on the market.

13 Mar. Floods in central New England kill twenty-nine, and cause $50 million in damage.

3 June John Hope, president of Atlanta University, is honored by the NAACP for his achievements in education and civil rights.

23 Oct. The streamline train *Burlington Zephyr* sets a new time record for train service from Chicago to Denver: 12.5 hours.

8 Dec. Case of *Gibbs* v. *Board of Education* of Montgomery County, Maryland, is filed. The eventual decision sets a precedent for equalizing the salaries of black and white teachers.

11 Dec. Press and public alike thrill to British king Edward VIII's announcement that he is renouncing the throne in order to marry an American divorcée, Wallis Warfield Simpson.

1937

- W. H. Carothers of Du Pont patents nylon.

- Congress establishes the Cape Hatteras National Seashore, the first national seashore.

- The George A. Hormel company introduces the canned meat Spam.

- The Indian Reorganization Act, known as the Indian New Deal, passes, enabling Indian culture to survive, though not thrive, within white society.

- The United Autoworkers Union (UAW) is recognized as sole bargaining unit for workers at General Motors.

- A massive flood of the Ohio River leaves 500,000 homeless.

- As a result of the Tennessee Valley Authority dams, the Tennessee River does not flood.

- A Gallup poll shows that 80 percent of respondents approve of relief through paid work rather than a dole.

- One study reports that people spend an average of 4.5 hours a day listening to the radio.

- Thousands of Americans join the Abraham Lincoln Battalion to fight with the Loyalists against Francisco Franco's fascist forces in the Spanish Civil War. Among the writers who go to Spain are John Dos Passos, Ernest Hemingway, Malcolm Cowley, and Upton Sinclair.

Mar.	U.S. Steel agrees to the terms of a CIO agreement without a strike, a triumph for John Lewis and for unions.
15 Mar.	The first state contraceptive clinic opens in Raleigh, North Carolina.
18 Mar.	A waste-gas pipeline explodes beneath the New London Consolidated School in east Texas, killing 294, most of them schoolchildren.
26 Mar.	William H. Hastie becomes first African American federal judge.
26 May	Walter Reuther, William Frankensteen, and two other UAW organizers are beaten by Ford Motor Company police at a union rally at Ford's River Rouge plant.
June	From September 1936 to 1 June 1937, 484,711 workers participated in sit-down strikes across the country.
2 July	Walter F. White, writer and civil rights leader, is honored by NAACP for his work as the organization's executive secretary, his investigations of lynchings, and his lobbying for a federal antilynching law.
2 July	On a Pacific flight from New Guinea to Howland Island, aviatrix Amelia Earhart disappears.
2 Aug.	President Roosevelt signs the Marijuana Traffic Act, outlawing the sale and possession of the drug.
1 Sept.	Congress creates the U.S. Housing Authority (USHA) to remedy the nation's housing shortage.

1938

•	Congress creates the Olympic National Park in the Pacific Northwest.
Mar.	In a new economic crisis, known as the "Roosevelt Recession," unemployment rises to nearly 20 percent of the labor force.
26 May	Texas Congressman Martin Dies is given congressional approval for his Special Committee to Investigate Un-American Activities, with "Un-American" principally meaning communist.
July	At a conference of twenty-seven European and Latin American countries on the question of Jewish emigration, Roosevelt says that the United States will not raise its immigration quotas to the victims of Hitler's Nazi regime.
19 July	Douglas Grace Corrigan lands in Dublin after a twenty-eight-hour flight from New York. After authorities contend the flight is unauthorized, Corrigan insists he intended to fly to Los Angeles, earning him the moniker "Wrong-Way" Corrigan in the press.
21 Sept.	A hurricane devastates Long Island and southern New England, killing 680, leaving 63,000 homeless, and causing $400 million in damage.
31 Oct.	On his Mercury Theatre on the Air radio show, Orson Welles broadcasts "Invasion from Mars," a dramatization based on H. G. Wells's "The War of the Worlds," and panic-stricken listeners think Martians have landed in New Jersey.
12 Dec.	In the NAACP-supported case *Missouri ex rel Gaines,* the U.S. Supreme Court declared that states must provide equal, even if separate, educational facilities for blacks within their boundaries.

1939

22 Feb. A rally of the pro-Nazi Bund organization at Madison Square Garden in New York is disrupted when Jewish activist Isadore Greenbaum attempts to pummel Bund founder Fritz Kuhn.

9 April Black contralto opera singer Marian Anderson performs to an audience of seventy-five thousand at the Lincoln Memorial. When the Daughters of the American Revolution refused to give permission for Anderson to perform in Constitution Hall, Eleanor Roosevelt resigned from the DAR in protest. Secretary of the Interior Harold Ickes invited Anderson to perform at the Lincoln Memorial in Washington, D.C., an Easter Sunday in an event cosponsored by Mrs. Roosevelt.

July and Aug. With Congress cutting their budgets, New Deal programs are dismantled. 775,000 WPA workers are let go.

23 Nov. By presidential proclamation Thanksgiving Day is celebrated on the fourth Thursday in the month rather than on the last, in order to lengthen the Christmas shopping season.

OVERVIEW

The Great Depression. The period between the stock-market crash of October 1929 and the bombing of Pearl Harbor in December 1941 was dominated by one of the worst economic crises in American history. One observer called the 1930s "years of standstill," when "everybody and everything marked time." The confidence of Americans in progress and prosperity, so marked during the 1920s, suddenly vanished. But hard times were not new, and many Americans had suffered even during the prosperous 1920s, especially workers in textile and mining industries. Unemployment had risen from 1.5 million in 1926 to nearly 2.7 million in 1929. During the 1920s millions of Americans were forced off farms by deflated crop prices, soil depletion, and farm mechanization. Yet the Great Depression of the 1930s hit with unprecedented force. Millions of Americans who had recently joined the middle class because of easy credit, installment buying, and low-cost stocks lost everything. For working-class Americans and the poor, the situation was worse: jobs were nowhere to be found; many sharecroppers were thrown off their farms; malnutrition and despair were constants. Worse still was the condition of the elderly, children, and families. Seniors who lost years of savings in the banking collapse were too old to find work and were forced to rely on hard-pressed families and charity to survive. Education was slashed, and millions of children lost their schools. They too had to work at whatever they could find, contributing their meager earnings to their families. The normal stresses of family life were compounded by unemployment and malnutrition. Many families were forced to "double up," sharing small apartments and homes between two families. Many American families were confronted for the first time with unemployment, uncertainty, and the loss of sustenance. It was a situation alien to a society and economy geared to abundance, unlimited growth, and opportunity.

Economic Crisis. After the stock-market crash the American economy went into a tailspin. National income was cut by one half between 1929 and 1932, and one-fourth of the workforce was unemployed. U.S. Steel cut its full-time payroll from 225,000 in 1929 to zero on 1 April 1933. Agriculture was also hit hard. Farm income went down by 20 percent in 1930 and plunged by 30 percent in 1931. Farm families who could not meet mort-

gage payments saw their homes and farms auctioned off in foreclosure proceedings. Urban families suffered as well. Ninety-five people were reported starved in New York City in 1931, with countless others made seriously ill because of malnutrition. The situation prompted citizens of the Cameroon to collect $3.77 and send it to New York to aid "the starving." The economy plummeted even lower in 1933. In that year unemployment peaked at between 12 million and 15 million workers, and it hovered around 8 million workers for the rest of the decade. Out of work year after year, many grew increasingly demoralized: "There is something about the anniversary of your layoff," lamented an unemployed laborer, "which makes you feel more helpless."

Assistance. President Herbert Hoover's Republican principles of self-reliance limited his response to the Depression. He opposed direct relief to the unemployed, believing it would "destroy character." Hoover instead favored grants to corporations, believing that putting industry back into gear would indirectly help the unemployed. He also favored loans to states and charities, believing they should be responsible for relief — aid that, from his perspective, had to be repaid. Most Americans shared his philosophy. Like Hoover, they believed the Depression was part of a natural business cycle and would cure itself. They believed that government should have a limited role in social and economic affairs. They believed that misfortune could be best handled by charity, repentance, and hard work. Yet the Depression grew worse and spread more widely through society. In the winter of 1931 farmers in eastern Arkansas were near starvation, and Red Cross assistance had failed. Local governments, traditionally responsible for economic relief, like those in Arkansas, were bankrupted by the staggering numbers of people applying for assistance, and turned to state governments, which also lacked the necessary resources.

Exhausted Charities. By 1933 nearly one thousand local governments had defaulted on debt payments. Private charities failed to pick up the slack, with many of them financially overextended or liquidated by their wealthy patrons. By 1932 nearly four hundred private charities had disappeared in New York City, one third the 1929 total. The winter of 1932–1933 was a low point:

by that time private charity and local welfare agencies had exhausted their resources. Desperation became acute. Thousands of food stores in the United States were looted, the reports of which were generally suppressed by the press, afraid of creating widespread panic. Yet panic was building. By 1933 banks around the United States were collapsing as depositors withdrew their savings and hoarded their resources. Farmers in the Midwest destroyed their crops in a desperate attempt to inflate agricultural prices. Industrial laborers and police fought pitched battles at factories. Tenants in major cities conducted rent strikes and forcibly resisted eviction. A host of experts paraded to Capitol Hill to warn that the nation was in danger of revolution. Normally conservative businessmen began to rethink their philosophy of "natural" economics, limited government, and private assistance. Even Hoover inaugurated a program of loans to industry and states. The Depression did more than cause widespread misery. It forced Americans to rethink the fundamental organization of power and wealth in society. Americans developed new concepts of social justice and fairness.

A New President. The election of Franklin D. Roosevelt to the presidency in 1932 reflected the new thinking of many Americans. Roosevelt offered a planned economy, an activist government, and federal assistance to the disadvantaged. Hoover wanted to keep government as much as possible out of the lives of private citizens. Yet the Depression exposed the degree to which wealthy and powerful private citizens used government to their benefit. At the local and state levels, lucrative provisioning contracts and generous bonds to businessmen continued to be paid, even as city councils and school boards canceled public relief programs and closed schools. When local governments defaulted on their debts to the rich in order to keep schools and welfare services open, wealthy citizens organized tax strikes and liquidated private charities. At the federal level congressional investigations in 1933 and 1934 revealed sensational securities fraud, profitable ties between business and government (especially in the airmail business), and the tax loopholes provided for the wealthy. The public was outraged, and Roosevelt took advantage of this anger to reverse the relationship of government to the powerful, placing government at the service of common people.

A New Deal. Roosevelt's New Deal intervened at an unprecedented level in the lives of average Americans. Direct emergency relief, although meager, kept many from starving; public works projects provided temporary jobs for millions; federal insurance protected the life savings of American workers; housing and farm loans protected millions from foreclosure; Social Security provided retirement and unemployment protection; Roosevelt's support for organized labor insured millions of workers of high wages and safer working conditions. Such policies laid the foundation of the welfare state and were overwhelmingly supported by the public. But they did not

cure the Depression, and the New Deal's critics saw them as a harbinger of federal despotism in the private lives of Americans. Many businessmen and politicians of Hoover's stripe were bitterly opposed to such programs. Other businessmen and politicians pointed out that the New Deal was fundamentally conservative and supported the New Deal as a reform necessary to prevent revolution. Most Americans had already adopted the communitarian, interdependent perspective of the New Deal. The Great Depression forced friends, family, and ultimately government to help one another. It made hash of the "rugged individualism" often rhetorically evoked by conservatives and reflected a deeper historical fact: the Great Depression disrupted the norms of American life; the New Deal redefined those norms.

The Family. The Great Depression hit families who had felt insulated from economic crises. Families who based their security on savings accounts and home ownership were suddenly penniless and unable to pay off their mortgages. Some nine million families lost their savings in the Depression, and by 1934 two-fifths of all homeowners in twenty cities had defaulted on their loans. The Depression created two kinds of poor Americans. The traditional poor, whose poverty began before the Depression, included tenant farmers, the elderly, single-parent families, and the disabled. The "new" poor included thousands of formerly middle- and working-class families suddenly impoverished by the loss of jobs, homes, and savings. Unemployment or low-paying part-time work caused financial uncertainty and lower standards of living for many families. The self-esteem of men eroded as they were unable to fulfill their roles as breadwinners for the families. Needy relatives stretched thin the resources of extended families. Marriage and birth rates declined, as many couples decided to wait until they could afford marriage and children. Single people in their late teens and early twenties, as well as young married couples, were forced to live with parents, creating tight quarters, frustration, and tension. Rates of divorce declined, in part because divorce became too expensive, but husbands deserted their wives in record numbers. Undernourished children contracted nutritional-deficiency diseases such as rickets and pellagra. The destructive impact of the Depression on families is undeniable, but it also brought families closer together, forcing family members to rely on each other. As writer Louis Adamic observed, "On the one hand, thousands of families were broken up, some permanently, some temporarily, or were seriously disorganized. On the other hand, thousands of families became more closely integrated than they had been before the Depression."

The Plight of the "New Immigrants." Already economically disadvantaged, immigrants were especially vulnerable to the economic hardships of the Depression. In the 1920s members of the "new immigrant" groups — such as the Poles, Italians, and Jews who came to the United States in the late nineteenth and early twentieth centuries — still depended on local ethnic institutions such as charities, loan associations, and banks for survival. During the Depression these agencies lack sufficient resources to meet the increased demands of the needy in their communities, and they folded quickly in the nationwide banking crisis of the early 1930s. Many ethnic Americans lost not only their savings but also the sense of trust and stability within their communities.

Blacks. Blacks also lost traditional means of support in the 1930s. Already poorly paid and badly treated, thousands of southern tenant farmers and sharecroppers were forced off the land as banks foreclosed on the owners of a third of all cotton fields. Always the first to be fired, blacks were especially discriminated against during the Depression. In one Chicago manufacturing plant African American employment went from a high in the 1920s of 18 percent to 10 percent by 1940. Unemployed white workers were willing to take unpleasant jobs they might previously have disdained, and employers were far more likely to hire even inexperienced whites rather than experienced blacks. As a black meatpacking-house worker complained, "They were hiring young, white boys, sixteen and eighteen years old, raw kids, didn't know a thing," instead of black workers who knew how to do the job. Thus, unemployment rates for blacks in the Depression were far higher than the national average. Roughly 25 percent of the national workforce was unemployed in 1932, but the national unemployment average for blacks stood at 48 percent, and in Pittsburgh 70 percent of blacks were unemployed.

Mexican Americans. When the Depression hit, most Mexican immigrants and Mexican Americans were already living at or below the poverty line, and during the 1930s their underemployment and unemployment increased. At a time when noncitizens were frequently blamed for taking jobs away from American citizens and burdening relief services, Mexican Americans often lost their jobs because federal and local officials mistook them for foreigners. Mexican immigrants were seen as a public burden: their children required special language instruction in public schools, or increased education costs in districts that chose to establish separate "Mexican schools." Mexicans and Mexican Americans were also seen as a public-health problem; they were more likely to contract infectious diseases because they lived in overcrowded housing, and they were alleged to practice poor hygiene. Finally, they were thought to have difficulty assimilating into American society because they were clannish and clung tenaciously to their own culture. As a result of these arguments, the U.S. Department of Labor initiated a program of forced deportation and voluntary repatriation. Between 1929 and 1934 some four hundred thousand Mexican immigrants and U.S. citizens born to Mexican parents were deported or repatriated to Mexico.

Woman as Homemaker. In 1933 Eleanor Roosevelt called on American women to pull the country through the crisis of the Great Depression. In her book *It's Up to the Women* she wrote, "The women know that life must go on and that the needs of life must be met and it is their courage and determination which, time and again, have pulled us through worse crises than the present one." The collective contributions of women were critical during the 1930s. With Americans turning inward and relying on their families for survival, woman's role at the center of the family gained in significance. Overall, the Depression served to reinforce traditional gender roles. During the Depression the vast majority of American women were neither rich nor poor but somewhere in between. Most women were married, and their husbands remained employed, but they probably took pay cuts to keep their jobs. If a middle-class man lost his job, his family typically had enough resources to make do without turning to relief or losing their property. While life was not easy for these women, it was not all bleak either. The ingenious survival strategies of middle-class married women helped their families to make do. They saved money by buying day-old bread, relining coats with old blankets, cutting adult clothing down to children's sizes, and saving anything that might be useful someday (such as string and broken crockery) or could be sold as scrap (such as old rags). As Eleanor Roosevelt commented, women were responsible for "endless little economies" as a hedge against "some catastrophe such as accident or illness which may completely swamp the family budget." Even the middle class lived in fear of poverty, with no social safety net to protect against unforeseen disaster.

Gender Roles. Men's lives were more disrupted by the Depression than women's. As men tried desperately to remain breadwinners for their families, their self-esteem suffered when they lost their jobs. Discouraged after daily searches for hard-to-find jobs, they frequently had time on their hands. Sociologists Robert and Helen Lynd described the difference in gender roles in a 1937 study: "The men, cut adrift from their usual routine, lost much of their sense of time and dawdled helplessly and dully about the streets; while in the homes, the women's world remained largely intact and the round of cooking, housecleaning, and mending became if anything more absorbing."

Resentment. While some unemployed men willingly pitched in with housework, many men found being asked to do "women's chores" a deeper insult to their already fragile masculinity. Male anger and resentment was typical, especially when it was the women who had a job. As the Lynds put it: "Time hung on his hands. In the morning before she left for work his wife told him to make the beds. The children, seeing him in this new role, sometimes laughed at him. I came upon a man who, making the beds one day, was so enraged by his son's laughter that he had nearly killed the child." In general these role reversals were not desired by either men or women, and most couples tried to maintain traditional, patriarchal gender roles through the dislocations of the Depression. Yet simple survival required change. The collapse of the traditional male sphere of business increased the importance of the traditional female sphere of the home. Despite often fierce resistance, the Depression radically altered traditional ideas of male privilege, economic conservatism, and social conformity.

"The People, Yes!" The 1930s has been dubbed the "Red Decade," the decade of the people, when culture embraced the common folk. It was a decade when communists and intellectuals kept happy company. As critic Malcolm Cowley commented, membership in the Communist Party held intellectual status in the 1930s: "There was an enormous prestige at that time for people who belonged to the party. They were listened to as if they had received advice straight from God." Participation and belonging, both intellectually and politically, were central to the culture of the 1930s. Nowhere was there a greater sense of intellectual belonging than in the rich intellectual circle of New York City. In leftist journals such as the *Nation, Partisan Review, New Masses,* and *The New Republic,* and in Greenwich Village coffeehouses, New York intellectuals debated a broad range of topics from wages to Stalin to psychoanalysis, art, aesthetics, and religion.

Escape. Such intellectual engagement coexisted with a contrasting experience in the culture of the 1930s: escape fantasies, which helped people lift, at least temporarily, the burden of the Depression. Hollywood provided images of escape for the masses, via films about high society, ease, and luxury, featuring glamorous film stars. The escape fantasy also manifested itself in an increase in popular participation in sports and games, specifically gambling. Bingo nights, chain-letter schemes, and the Irish sweepstakes attracted tremendous interest, and the board game Monopoly was an enormous success. Each enabled players to "make it" in ways that current economic conditions forbade. Escape fantasies of the 1930s involved taking chances, competing, and, above all, winning.

TOPICS IN THE NEWS

CHILDHOOD AND THE DEPRESSION

Children in Poverty. The Depression brought extreme poverty to families who were already poor or in low-paid jobs. Children went hungry and contracted disease. Malnutrition was reported to be over 90 percent in the coal-mining regions of Illinois, Kentucky, Pennsylvania, Ohio, and West Virginia. Investigators found Kentucky children so hungry they had begun to chew their own hands. One-fifth of the children in New York City were malnourished. A teacher reportedly told a hungry child to go home and eat, and the child replied, "I can't. This is my sister's day to eat." In some communities children could not go to school because schools closed for lack of funds. Poor children contracted pellagra and rickets, diseases that indicated malnourishment. According to a 1937 Children's Bureau report, many children found themselves, "going for days at a time without taking off their clothes to sleep at night, becoming dirty, unkempt, a host to vermin. They may go for days with nothing to eat but coffee, bread and beans."

Children's Contributions. Children who were over age twelve were often enlisted in their families' efforts to cope with the economic loss of the Depression. Children's labor made a vital contribution to home pro-

A Hooverville, circa 1931

duction. Girls helped their mothers cook, clean, and sew; boys assisted their fathers repairing the house or working the farm; both genders ran errands when necessary. Chil-

A FARM MOB

The 1920s and 1930s were a grueling time for American farmers. Tens of thousands lost their farms. Many blamed uncaring bankers for their plight, and by the late 1920s there was increasing resistance to farm foreclosures. Armed farmers sometimes tried to stop auctions of foreclosed farms by threatening local officials. *The New York Times* reported one such incident, which occurred on 4 January 1933 in Lemars, Iowa. Carrying a rope, some eight hundred farmers and townspeople gathered at the entrance to the county courthouse for the auction of a farm belonging to their neighbor John A. Johnson.

The farm was to be sold to satisfy a $33,000 mortgage held by a New York insurance company. Johnson had defaulted after corn, which cost 80 cents a bushel to raise, had dropped to 10 cents a bushel at the market. Johnson's neighbors did not intend to prevent the sale. They just wanted to be sure that it sold for the full amount of the mortgage so that Johnson would not have sell livestock and other possessions to make up the difference.

The only bid was $30,000, offered by Herbert S. Martin, an attorney representing the mortgage holder. When the crowd insisted that he offer the full value of the mortgage, Martin responded that he was not authorized to go higher. The mob seized Martin, the sheriff, and a judge who threatened to telephone for help, as their leaders announced that they would hang Martin from "the highest tree in Lemars."

"Tar and feather him. Ride him on a rail!" others in the crowd cried.

Martin's neck was saved when he agreed to telegraph the insurance company asking permission to increase the bid to the full amount of Johnson's debt. His wire ended: "Rush answer. My neck at risk."

Once the message was sent, Martin, the sheriff, and the judge were released, a bit bruised but otherwise unharmed. A little while later the insurance company sent a message agreeing to pay the full price.

Source: "Lynching Threat Halts Sale of Farm," *New York Times*, 5 January 1933, p. 14.

dren also helped supplement family income by earning money at jobs in the community. Children worked as baby-sitters, store clerks, and newspaper boys. Boys (and some girls) were often sent to work as part of migrant labor forces, harvesting crops and returning with their earnings. Most children made these economic contributions to their families while remaining in school; but many high-school dropouts were caused by the need for teenagers to contribute substantial wages to the family income.

Curtailed Childhoods. Performing economically valuable roles at younger ages had positive effects on children growing up in the Depression. "It was an enormously hard life" recalled one child of the Depression, "but there was also a sense of great satisfaction in being a child with valuable work to do and being able to do it well and function in the world." Children who performed economically valuable roles developed sound work habits, reliability, judgment concerning the use of money, awareness of the needs of others, and social independence. The economic need for children's labor presented these children with a moral challenge that called for their best efforts. For boys, who were employed outside the home more often than girls, paid jobs fostered independence and self-direction. Household tasks for girls, on the other hand, brought them closer to the family and kept them involved in domestic tasks. But these Depression children grew up faster than children who were not economically deprived. Childhood as a time of play and leisure was foreshortened for children whose labor was required by their families, and these children entered the adult world, at least in terms of their attitudes. Those who held jobs, boys especially, preferred the company of adults to children; they also identified with adults and aspired to adult status.

Sources:
Glen Elder, *Children of the Great Depression: Social Change in Life Experience*, (Chicago: University of Chicago Press, 1974);

Steven Mintz and Susan Kellogg, Domestic Revolutions: A Social History of American Family Life (New York: Free Press, 1988).

FARMERS AND THE GREAT DEPRESSION

Disaster. The Depression was one of the most devastating agricultural disasters in American history, and American farmers suffered terribly. In 1934 more than 30 percent of all Americans still lived on farms, and agriculture — even in that drought year — produced $9.5 billion. But a combination of natural disasters and human miscalculations devastated American farming in the 1930s. The decade opened with a series of natural catastrophes: in 1930 hail destroyed wheat crops, and 1932 to 1935 were years of unrelenting drought. This, combined with plummeting agricultural prices, ruined countless farm families. Caroline Henderson, who lived on her family farm in Shelton, Oklahoma, wrote in the summer of 1935: "[Our] daily physical torture, confusion of mind, gradual wearing down of courage, make that long continued hope look like a vanishing dream. . . ."

Despair. Such despair was common among farmers and their families. Rural America had traditionally embraced bedrock values such as hard work, thrift, religion, and self-reliance. Few understood the impersonal force of

Okies setting up camp near a California pea field, mid 1930s

world agricultural markets that continued to drive down agricultural prices: the harder the farmers worked, the cheaper the product, and the less money they made. For traditionalists the Depression created an inverted world where the values they embraced only made things worse. Yet they were reluctant to ask for help, viewing their problems as a consequence of their own incompetence, or as divine punishment for sins. Shame and guilt compounded a bad situation. Some turned to God and interpreted the events of the 1930s as presaging the apocalypse. Some turned to politics and organized farm strikes and vigilante actions against bankers. But most adjusted their individualistic outlook and took what help they could find. The rest moved to the cities, advancing the depopulation of the countryside, a long-term historical trend that by 1960 resulted in fewer farmers than college students in the United States.

Bad Practices. Farmers were partially to blame for the agricultural depression. The lowered agricultural prices and easy credit of the 1920s meant that farmers put more land into production, exploiting millions of acres of farmland, grazing, plowing, planting, and harvesting. Many of these farmers engaged in unsound agricultural practices, such as plowing straight up and down inclines and hills and refusing to allow fields to lay fallow. Topsoil was accordingly exhausted or eroded, and unable to support productive crops. Western grazing land was overgrazed, its stock of hearty grasses depleted. For generations American farmers had simply exhausted the land and then moved on to new farms on the western frontier. In the 1930s the frontier was closed, and the Depression forced farmers to reconsider their agricultural habits.

Government Aid The federal government intervened in the farm crisis, but its help was insufficient. The Soil Erosion Service was established in 1933 to organize farmers into soil conservation districts, but the repair process was slow and farmers could not wait. The Taylor Grazing Act of 1934 was slightly more successful. The Taylor Act established carefully monitored grazing districts that helped to stabilize the depletion of range, although it could not repair longstanding damage. Between 1933 and 1934 the Federal Emergency Relief Administration also spent $85 million to buy out farmers and take land out of production, partially restoring its fertility.

Foreclosure and Dispossession. Between 1930 and 1935 nearly two hundred of every thousand farms in the states of the Midwest, the South, and the Plains succumbed to foreclosure proceedings. When the owners failed, croppers and tenants were also forced off the land. Increasingly, farmers banded together to oppose the bankers and government agents throwing them off their land. Iowa farmers threatened to lynch bank agents who came to repossess farms. Wisconsin farmers hijacked milk trucks and spilled their contents in an effort to raise milk prices and protect their farms. Socialist leader Norman Thomas organized the Southern Tenant Farmers Union in 1934 to protect the interests of Arkansas sharecroppers. The Roosevelt administration inaugurated several programs to help farmers pay their mortgages, such as the Federal Emergency Relief Administration, the Farm Resettlement Administration, and the Farm Security Administration. Their financial supplements, price supports, and debt relief eased the pain of dispossession, but only temporarily. The historical trend was inexorable and unmistakable: the economy had shifted to an industrial base and could no longer sustain millions of American farmers.

Migration. People forced off the land in the South in the mid 1930s had to leave not only their farms but their home states, because there were no jobs. Oklahoma lost more than 440,000 people, and Kansas lost 227,000 in the 1930s. A total of 2.5 million people left the Plains states in the 1930s. Most moved to neighboring states, but some 460,000 people moved to the Pacific Northwest, where they found jobs in lumbering or building the Bonneville and Grand Coulee Dams. More than 300,000 more moved to California.

"Okies" Move to California. Called "Okies," masses of poor white families displaced by farm failure in Oklahoma, Arkansas, and Texas sought opportunities in the Golden State. Some had relatives waiting with homes and even jobs. But most were rural refugees who quickly discovered that California's large-scale agribusiness left no room for a family farm. Learning this, many settled in California's major cities, where they were hardly welcomed. Los Angeles authorities were already busy shipping Mexican Americans back to Mexico, and they balked at the prospect of yet another burden on their charity rolls. In February 1936 Los Angeles police chief James E. Davis sent 125 police to patrol the state's borders at Arizona and Oregon, trying to keep transients out. Davis's gesture was unconstitutional. The city was sued by the American Civil Liberties Union and widely ridiculed.

Okies. Thus, Okies continued to flow into California, many scattering into poor and middle-class white urban neighborhoods, while 110,000 others joined California's population of 200,000 migrant farmworkers. Okies arrived after intense labor activism by California's farmworkers in 1933 and 1934. Thirty-seven strikes involved more than fifty thousand workers producing everything from cotton to walnuts. The strikes achieved as much as a twenty-five-cent increase in the hourly wage and greater union recognition.

Crackdown. But California agribusiness thought the increase excessive and responded in the summer of 1934 with a crackdown against the union. With union leaders in jail on charges of criminal syndicalism, labor agitation subsided. Okies in fact contributed to the union's decline. They were white, Christian fundamentalists, with little union experience or sympathy. Bringing southern racism to California, they were not inclined to mix with Mexican American farmworkers who supported the union, and the Okies were strikebreakers more often than strikers.

Poor Living Conditions. These white migrants soon made up almost half of California's farm labor. Working as families, they traveled up and down the state, from the southern Imperial Valley to the northern Sacramento Valley. They lived in squalid shacks in communities called ditch camps, located on the sides of the road where

Homemaker canning fruit

water ditches ran. Hardly fit for human habitation, ditch camps were filthy and disease-ridden. At one point, two children a day were reported dying in Tulare County; in another county fifty babies died of diarrhea and enteritis in only one picking season. Wages were too low to get these families out of poverty; average income for a white farm-labor family was $1,300 per year, $500 less than the average for all white California families, but $315 higher than the average for nonwhite Californians. These poor migrants gained the contempt of their neighbors, as one woman complained: "These 'share croppers' are not a noble people looking for a home and seeking an education for their children. They are unprincipled degenerates looking for something for nothing."

Source:
James N. Gregory, *American Exodus: The Dust Bowl Migration and Okie Culture in California* (New York: Oxford University Press, 1989).

MAKING DO: FAMILY LIFE IN THE DEPRESSION

Budgeting. In the 1930s more than half of American families earned between $500 and $1,500 per year. In 1935–1936 the median family income was $1,160. An income of $2,000 per year guaranteed a comfortable lifestyle and put a household at the top 10 percent of incomes. On an average annual income of roughly $1,000, most families had between $20 and $25 per week for food, clothing, and shelter. Budgeting and stretching scarce resources was essential. In adapting to economic deprivation families used two strategies: they curtailed expenses and found alternative sources of income. Expenses were curtailed by using family labor to produce goods that used to be store bought, such as food, clothing, and home repairs. This reponsibililty typically fell on

Although population rates declined during the Depression, the movement to provide birth control to families continued during the decade. Margaret Sanger and other birth control advocates not only lobbied to make contraceptives legal for married couples (they were illegal in most states) but championed the cause of national health and child care.

In spirit, birth control advocates had the support of the Roosevelt administration. In the 1920s Eleanor Roosevelt had served on the board of Sanger's American Birth Control League. But Franklin Roosevelt depended heavily on the support of the Catholic Church and southern Democrats and thus refused to acknowledge the movement, fearful of alienating these conservative political supporters. Eleanor Roosevelt in fact resigned from Sanger's league when her husband ran for president in 1932. The New Deal nonetheless funded birth control surreptitiously, paying nurses in the employ of New Deal agencies such as the Farm Security Administration to bring birth control information and contraception to poor farm women and women in migrant labor camps.

More-overt efforts to fund birth control waited until southern governments began to fear the increasing rate of births among blacks. In 1937 North Carolina became the first state to offer contraception as part of its public health service, followed by South Carolina, Virginia, Georgia, Mississippi, Alabama, and Florida. All these states were already burdened with expensive relief payments and supported birth control as a means of keeping down costs. All these states also had high populations of blacks and few Catholics.

Source: Rosalind Rosenberg, *Divided Lives: American Women in the Twentieth Century* (New York: Hill & Wang, 1992).

women, who did most of the household spending. The government gave guidelines for a family budget, recommending setting aside 35 percent of the family income for food, 33 percent for shelter, and 4 percent for taxes. One wit reacted to such budgets by noting, "In order to run a budget, you have to have money . . . I don't feel that I can afford one right now — there are so many other things I need worse."

Prices. Tight budgets demanded that women watch every penny. If a woman shopped carefully, she could feed a family of six on five dollars per week. Low food prices helped: milk cost ten cents a quart; a loaf of bread was seven cents; a pound of butter cost twenty-three cents; and two pounds of hamburger cost twenty-five cents. To stretch their pennies, some women shopped with a friend so that they could split the cost for, say, two pounds of hamburger meat, alternating on who paid the extra penny each week.

Recipes for Frugality. Radio shows broadcast money-saving recipes such as poor man's cake, made without flour, and green tomato mincemeat. Women temporarily stopped buying ready-made goods and began making food and clothing at home. Women did their own canning, pickling, preserving, and baking. Sales of glass jars reached an eleven-year high in 1931, as the demand for store-bought canned and bottled foods declined. In these ways women helped the household economy by expanding their unpaid labor at home. By substituting their own labor for goods and services that were previously purchased, women enabled their families to maintain their former standard of living despite decreased incomes. As the Depression lessened, however, women returned to their roles as consumers of household products — now consuming new products, such as frozen foods, introduced during the decade.

Declines in Marriage and Divorce. The Great Depression affected more than the household economy. It caused many couples to delay marrying and having children; both became too expensive. Divorce also was too expensive, although Nevada reaped a fortune in tax receipts midway through the decade by offering quick, low-cost divorce. Between 1930 and 1935 there were 170,000 fewer divorces than would have occurred if the divorce rates of the 1920s had continued. This did not mean that marriages were happier in the Depression. Rates of desertion rose, as husbands left their families without divorce, and by 1940 there were more than 1.5 million married women living apart from their husbands. Fifteen percent of all households were headed by females that year, as opposed to only 12 percent in 1930. Hard times may have made some couples stick together, but others stayed married because it was easier to qualify for relief if there was a family to support. The divorce rate increased again after 1933, as families finally collapsed under the financial strain; by 1940 divorces would exceed the level of the 1920s.

Unmarried Women. The marriage rate was 10.14 per 1,000 persons in 1929 but dropped to 7.87 per 1,000 in 1932. By 1938 hard times forced an estimated 1.5 million people to postpone marriage. For some couples postponing marriage meant never marrying. Schoolteacher Elsa Ponselle explained: "Do you realize how many people in my generation are not married? It wasn't that we didn't have a chance. I was going with someone when the Depression hit. We probably would have gotten married. He was a commercial artist and had been doing very well . . . Suddenly he was laid off. It hit him like a ton of bricks. And he just disappeared." Ponselle was typical of women in her age group: the number of women who never married is 30 percent higher among those who were aged

THE DIONNE QUINTUPLETS

The focus of enormous public attention, the Dionne quintuplets were five girls born during one delivery to Elzire and Oliva Dionne, a farm couple with six other children in Corbell, Ontario, 28 May 1934. The multiple birth was so rare that Morris Fishbein of the American Medical Association reported that only thirty cases had been reported in the five hundred previous years; in none of those thirty, according to Fishbein, did all five children live longer than fifty minutes. The public was more than intrigued. Progress of the quints was eagerly reported by the press; their eating habits, spirits, and illnesses were scrutinized by the public; gifts of money, food, clothing, and toys poured in to the Dionnes. The government of Canada, viewing them as national treasures, made them wards of the state and built a new home and provided subsidies for them. The king of England gave Oliva Dionne a royal bounty of five pounds for her troubles. The grandfather of the family made a healthy profit on a souvenir stand set up on the farm. Elzire Dionne continued to farm. His daughters continued to garner public attention throughout the 1940s as they grew into healthy adulthood.

Source: Cabell Phillips, *From the Crash to the Blitz, 1929–1939* (New York: Macmillan, 1969).

twenty-five to thirty-five in 1935 as compared to women of the same age group five years earlier.

Long Engagements. More common than broken engagements were prolonged ones that frustrated young people and worried moralists. In a mock trial of "Society," staged by the Council of Social Agencies in 1935, one of the eighteen charges brought against society was "allowing conditions to exist under which young people are unable to marry due to a lack of employment." The mock jury of twelve adults held society guilty on six counts, one of which was negligence in creating the material conditions conducive to marriage.

Frustrated Couples. Some psychologists believed that postponing marriage was detrimental to the mental health of young people. Moralists feared a rise in premarital and extramarital sexual activity, and longer engagements did result in premarital sex. In 1937 the Roper Organization asked a representative sample of the American public if the government should give financial assistance to young couples to help them get married and establish homes. This proposal represented a startling departure from the deeply held view that government should not to intervene in private matters such as mar-

riage, but more than 38 percent answered yes. Women supported the proposal more than men, and older women liked the idea most of all. This response reflected public discomfort with premarital sex; young marriage with financial dependence was preferable to sexual activity before marriage. Overall, prolonged rather than broken engagements typified the 1930s, and the marriage rate rose significantly by 1940.

Falling Birthrates. During the early years of the Depression the birth rate dropped sharply from 21.2 live births per 1,000 in 1930 to 18.4 by 1933. For the first time in U.S. history, the birthrate was below the level needed to replace the population. Couples deliberately put off having children or had fewer children than they wanted. Many explained, "I don't want to bring children into a world that has no use for them." Pregnancy was often viewed as unfortunate rather than joyful. The use of contraceptives increased and forced revisions in legal prohibitions against birth control. Illegal abortions also increased, as did the desertion of infants. As the economy improved, however, the birthrate began to rise.

Family Interdependence. The Depression brought some families closer together, forcing them to pool resources and turn toward one another in what was called "intelligent independence." As a newspaper in Muncie, Indiana, put it, "many a family that has lost its car has found its soul." Everyone pitched in to get by. In those families where wives were not engaged full-time in stretching the household economy, they found part-time work to supplement the family income. Children took part-time jobs running errands, mowing lawns, babysitting, shining shoes, and selling newspapers. Rural families sent their teenage boys and girls out to work as migrant field hands, hoping they would return with their earnings. The 1930 census indicated that one-third of all American families had more than one wage earner, and a quarter had three or more earning income. The multigenerational extended family, long in decline, returned, as many elderly lost their means of financial independence and moved in with their children. Relatives in nearby communities often turned to one another for help. Fifty percent of working wives in Utah, and 40 percent in Cleveland, Ohio, helped support relatives living outside the home. For many, in fact, the Depression helped to renew a sense of family compromised by the materialism of the 1920s. With less money to spend on entertainment outside the home, families gathered around the radio in the evening or played cards, checkers, or the new board game Monopoly. Although such family closeness was an important source of psychological support, for many Americans it was too confining. Families forced to share a common home — a phenomenon known as "doubling up" — sometimes complained about lack of privacy, as did young people, who often chafed under close parental supervision. After World War II, when sound, cheap housing became available, the extended Depression family quickly fragmented, demonstrating that it was an ar-

Black family in Gee's Bend, Alabama, 1937

rangement of necessity as much as an expression of values.

Sources:

Steven Mintz and Susan Kellogg, *Domestic Revolutions: A Social History of American Family Life* (New York: Free Press, 1988);

Rosalind Rosenberg, *Divided Lives: American Women in the Twentieth Century* (New York: Hill & Wang, 1992);

Susan Ware, *Holding Their Own: American Women in the 1930s* (Boston: Twayne, 1982).

A New Deal for Blacks

Blacks and the New Deal. While the Great Depression dealt blacks a severe blow, with the New Deal the federal government addressed the issue of black poverty for the first time. In doing so, the New Deal marked a turning point in American race relations. Blacks needed government intervention, since they suffered severe economic dislocation in the Depression: by the mid 1930s the proportion of blacks on relief doubled that of whites, and in some southern cities 80 percent of the black population needed public assistance.

The Black Family. The Depression severely disrupted lower-class black family life. Rural black poverty was extreme in the late 1920s, but the Depression made it still worse. Payment for picking cotton dropped to a low of sixty cents for a fourteen-hour day. Sharecropping families were given as little as ten dollars a month for a family of six or eight to live on. The Depression also erased the

host of menial "Negro jobs" that had provided employment for blacks, especially in the urban South. Instead, unemployed whites took jobs they formerly disdained: street cleaning, garbage collection, elevator operation, domestic service. Whites organized vigilante groups such as the Black Shirts and the Ku Klux Klan to terrorize blacks and take their jobs. By 1932 half of all blacks living in the urban South could find no work. In the North, where three million blacks lived in the 1930s, conditions were equally bad. The median income of skilled workers declined 48.7 percent. Kelly Miller, a Howard University sociologist, estimated in 1932 that one-third of blacks were unemployed and another third were underemployed, commenting that the African American was "the surplus man, the last to be hired and the first to be fired."

Blacks in the North. Many northern businesses refused to hire blacks; two-thirds of Manhattan's hotels had no African American employees. Black families suffered under the compound stress of unemployment, poverty, and racism. Mortality rates were high among black men. In Chicago two out of five black women were without husbands. In one neighborhood on Chicago's West Side, half of all black households lacked a husband or a father. Nationally, nearly 30 percent of black households were headed by women. High rates of unemployment, the lack of stable jobs, and low wages made it impossible for lower-class black men to function as breadwinners and to survive. Black women were left caring for their children, and they often relied on relatives for help. But the employment prospects for black women were equally dismal. In 1935, 25 percent of all black women workers were on relief, and two-fifths of these were heads of households. Menial occupations that typically employed black women declined; families could no longer afford to hire domestics. Black families turned to their churches and charitable institutions to help sustain them through the Great Depression, but these organizations could do little, and by 1932 most private charities had exhausted their resources. Detroit's charities granted the destitute fifteen cents a day to get by — until they went out of business.

Relief. For the Roosevelt administration and the New Dealers, black poverty was one among many problems. New Deal agencies were reluctant to address black issues independent of overall New Deal programs for fear of alienating Roosevelt's political support among Southern Democrats. The Federal Housing Administration, for example, constructed segregated housing for the poor and refused to make loans to blacks buying homes in white neighborhoods. Roosevelt himself did not publicly associate with black leaders or causes until 1935. Behind the scenes, however, the New Deal quietly began to address the special needs of blacks. In 1933 Roosevelt approved of the appointment of a white civil rights activist, Clark Foreman, and a black academic, Robert Weaver, to assume responsibility for the fair treatment of blacks by his administration. Early programs that provided food, shelter and clothing helped blacks significantly. These included the Federal Emergency Relief Administration (FERA), the National Recovery Administration (NRA), the Works Progress Administration (WPA), the Agricultural Adjustment Administration (AAA) and the National Youth Administration (NYA). Implementing these programs at the local level was no simple matter, since federal officials encountered customs and laws that led to racial discrimination and inequities. Roosevelt attempted to overcome this by issuing an executive order forbidding discrimination in the WPA, but the order was ignored. In Atlanta average monthly relief checks to whites totaled $32.66; to blacks, $19.29. The Tennessee Valley Authority rarely hired blacks to work on its construction projects. Mississippi, with blacks forming more than half the population, permitted only 1.7 percent of its participants in the Civilian Conservation Corps (CCC) to be black. Federal officials, reluctant to antagonize southern support, tolerated such discrimination.

Other Programs. Elsewhere in the nation New Deal programs, notably the CCC and the National Youth Administration (NYA), operated with minimal discrimination. In 1935, the peak year of the CCC, there were more than half a million boys in integrated conservation camps. The NYA, for which Mary McLeod Bethune served as administrator of Negro Affairs, provided young men and women with student relief programs that enabled them to stay in school. In distributing more than $40 million, the NYA provided significant help to black youth. The Public Works Administration (PWA) turned more than one-third of all the housing units it built over to blacks, many times in integrated apartment buildings. Despite the best efforts of the PWA's director, Harold Ickes, the agency remained segregated in the South, but its contributions to black communities in the form of schools, hospitals, and recreational facilities was substantial. The WPA's educational and cultural program gave wholehearted support to the work of blacks. Nearly a quarter of a million blacks were taught to read and write by the WPA. Black music, literature, and art — including that of artists such as Jacob Lawrence and Samuel Brown — were produced by the Federal Art Project in the WPA. The Roosevelt administration, especially via the efforts of First Lady Eleanor Roosevelt, also won other victories for the African American cause, such as securing increased funding for Howard University and Freemen's Hospital in Washington, D.C. The Roosevelt administration placed the first African American on the federal bench and peopled the judiciary with friends sympathic to the cause of racial equality. Eleanor Roosevelt was seemingly tireless in her pursuit of racial equality, securing important posts for blacks within the administration (tripling the number of blacks working for the federal government) and pleading the cause of racial tolerance in speeches, radio broadcasts, and newspaper editorials. By 1935 Roosevelt was being unofficially advised by what the press termed "the black cabinet," a score of African American New Dealers, including Rayford Logan and Ralph Bunche, as well civil rights activists outside the administration, including NAACP head Walter White and union leader A. Philip Randolph. The administration even supported a three-day National Conference on Problems of the Negro and Negro Youth in Washington, D.C., in 1937. Such efforts, symbolic and substantial, impressed blacks, gave them hope, and caused them to switch their political allegiance to the Democratic Party. The attitude of blacks toward the New Deal was summed up by a group of black social workers who visited Hyde Park in 1939: "For the first time Negro men and women have reason to believe that their government does care."

Sources:

Leslie Fishel Jr., "The Negro in the New Deal Era," in *America's Black Past*, edited by Eric Foner (New York: Harper & Row, 1970);

Harvard Sitkoff, *A New Deal for Blacks: The Emergence of Civil Rights as a National Issue, Volume I: The Depression Decade* (New York: Oxford University Press, 1978);

T. H. Watkins, *The Great Depression* (Boston: Little, Brown, 1993).

PROHIBITION ENDS

First Night. At 5:32 P.M. EST on 5 December 1933, the "noble experiment" called Prohibition came to an end when the state of Utah became the thirty-sixth state to ratify the Twenty-first Amendment to the Constitution. The amendment, which had been passing feverishly through state legislatures across the country since 10

Beer parade in Seattle, 1932

April, repealed the Eighteenth Amendment (1919), which had barred sales and consumption of alcohol nationwide for nearly fourteen years. As expected, there was dancing in the streets, but only a little dancing. The police in Los Angeles and New York had put their entire forces on call to combat the anticipated celebrations, but Prohibition passed away more quietly than expected. Both *The New York Times* and the *Los Angeles Times* reported subdued celebration, though patrons of the St. Moritz Hotel in New York did dance their way single file to the lake in Central Park for a symbolic drowning of Old Man Prohibition. Similar effigies were burned, drowned, buried, and shot nationwide.

Call for Restraint. One reason for the subdued party was the late-afternoon ratification. Although liquor was distilled and loaded, ready to be delivered at the crucial hour of repeal, the timing of Utah's vote was too late for many deliveries in the East. Only a few of the larger hotels and clubs in New York were able to procure the now-legal beverages. Essentially, Prohibition was to last another night for many people, though that did not necessarily mean abstinence. The fact that Prohibition had failed and was by 1933 being essentially ignored in many states also dampened the party. Procuring a drink at one of New York's thousands of speakeasies had been commonplace for years. The small detail of its new legality meant very little. It was business as usual that Tuesday night. President Roosevelt requested cooperation in a nationwide address. He called for restraint, asking consumers to buy only from legal dealers. He asked that the saloon atmosphere that had preceded Prohibition not

return to American life. Roosevelt, while running for office the previous year, had asked for repeal of the Eighteenth Amendment. It had come even more quickly than he had imagined.

Prohibition's Demise. That Prohibition would end was a foregone conclusion. The rapidity with which the Eighteenth Amendment was repealed only emphasized the unpopularity of the Volstead Act, the legislation passed subsequent to the Eighteenth Amendment that had provided the enforcement authority to bar the sale and consumption of alcohol. Prohibition ended for several reasons, all of which had appeared within a year or two of its inception in January 1920. Through the 1920s the problems of Prohibition were well known, but political timidity in the face of strong, mostly rural Protestant support kept Prohibition alive. Enforcement of the law was Prohibition's greatest problem. In 1920 Congress appropriated a measly $2.2 million enforcement for the entire nation. That amount tripled in 1921 and by 1926 had reached $10 million. Yet enforcement remained impossible. In 1929 Prohibition commissioner James M. Doran estimated that strict enforcement would require at least $300 million annually. Congress never appropriated more than one-tenth of that figure. The result was that the liquor industry continued to flourish, though now underground. Besides the expenditures for the ineffective enforcement, Prohibition cost the nation millions in unearned revenue. Instead of money flowing to the federal government in the form of taxes on alcohol sold and tariffs on alcohol imported, the money remained in the hands of a new class of criminal, the bootlegger. Men

CONSUMERISM

The consumer movement, long a minor fixture in American economic life, became increasingly important during the 1930s. One catalyst was the Depression, which convinced many consumers that businesses were practicing price gouging and other forms of consumer fraud. Another stimulus was the books of writer Fred J. Schlink, whose 1927 study, *Your Money's Worth*, and 1933 sequel with Arthur Kallet, *100,000,000 Guinea Pigs*, exposed a host of fraudulent practices and merchandiser chicaneries. In the early 1930s the Federal Radio Commission also turned up glaring examples of medical fraud by radio advertisers. Consumer cooperatives were also instrumental in the rise of consumerism. Various groceries, meat markets, pharmacies, gas stations, and medical clinics were run cooperatively, meaning that members of the co-op contributed cash or labor toward the maintenance of the co-op. The co-op in turn cut out middlemen as much as possible and brought goods to the consumer for a cheaper price. The most important factor in the rise of consumerism in the 1930s, however, was the host of new, processed foods being introduced onto the market. Manufacturers such as Birdseye wanted to reassure consumers that their frozen foods and newly canned products were safe for use. Their support was instrumental in getting Congress to revise the Pure Food and Drug Act in 1938 — an act that did much to police the marketplace, to the benefit of both large food processors and consumers.

Source: Cabell Phillips, *From the Crash to the Blitz, 1929–1939* (New York: Macmillan, 1969).

R. H. Macy and Company. Clearly, a business and industrial elite, fearing the economic fallout of Prohibition while citing concern for constitutional freedoms, began to oppose Prohibition and to influence debate about it. By the mid 1920s newspaper polls showed an immense majority of the population interested in either repeal or modification of the Eighteenth Amendment. By 1929 a women's anti-Prohibition group had been founded by Pauline Sabin, wife of Charles Sabin. The Republican Party had been staunchly "dry" earlier in the decade, but at the Women's National Republican Club in 1929, Pauline Sabin shocked her audience by announcing her opposition to Prohibition. Women were a new political force in the 1920s due to the Nineteenth Amendment of 1919, which finally gave them the right to vote. By election time in 1932, more than a million "Sabin women" had joined Sabin's Women's Organization for National Prohibition Reform. The consolidation of the "wet" vote across party lines helped send Franklin Roosevelt to the White House in 1932, though Prohibition was not the major issue of the campaign. After the stock-market crash of 1929 and the Depression that set in, repealing Prohibition became important to stimulate the economy. Upon his inauguration in 1933, Roosevelt called for a change in the Volstead Act to allow beer consumption. Congress enacted changes within nine days, just before the Twenty-first Amendment began its roll toward repeal in Michigan on 10 April. By year's end the noble experiment would be over, a victim of economic and political forces, but also of simple public demand for the freedom to drink.

Sources:

John Kobler, *Ardent Spirits: The Rise and Fall of Prohibition* (New York: Putnam, 1973);

Cabell Phillips, *From the Crash to the Blitz, 1929–1939* (New York: Macmillan, 1969);

Page Smith, *Redeeming the Time: A People's History of the 1920s and the New Deal* (New York: McGraw-Hill, 1987).

such as Chicago's Al Capone and Cincinnati's George Remus made millions of tax-free dollars by producing and distributing alcohol. Prohibition was a boon to organized crime.

Speakeasies. Private speakeasies flourished, providing customers with good, cheap food because alcohol was so expensive and profitable. The federal war to support Prohibition had cost a lot of money and many law officers' lives but all for naught. Prohibition failed for political as well as economic reasons. Increased taxes to account for the lost revenue from alcohol turned some Prohibition supporters into ardent opponents. Most notable was Pierre Samuel du Pont, who was a staunch Prohibitionist until 1926, when he became the leader of the Association Against the Prohibition Amendment (AAPA), a group founded in 1918 by Capt. William H. Stayton. Other members of the AAPA included business leaders Elihu Root, Herbert Pratt of Standard Oil, Charles Sabin of Guaranty Safe Deposit Company, and Percy S. Straus of

THE RED DECADE: SOLIDARITY AND INDIVIDUALISM IN THE 1930s

From Individual to Community. The 1930s were a decade of community and class consciousness unprecedented in American history. A 1937 poll revealed that the majority of impoverished Americans did not "think that today any young man with thrift, ability, and ambition has the opportunity to rise in the world, own his own home, and earn $5,000 a year." The traditional radical individualism of most Americans was abandoned, and people began to conceive of themselves as parts of communities and distinct interest groups. This consciousness was an important component of many of the important political events of the decade, responsible for the repeal of Prohibition, the success of labor organizations and strikes, the passage of the Social Security Act, and the creation of the federal bureaucracy. Most important, however, the collective consciousness Americans developed in the 1930s was instrumental in providing the

The Veterans of Future Wars (deliberately abbreviated VFW, to the annoyance of the Veterans of Foreign Wars) was a campus-based antiwar protest movement of the 1930s. Launched at Princeton University in 1936, it had chapters on more than fifty campuses within a year. Antiwar students drew attention to their pacifist stand by demanding a cash "bonus" similar to the bonus provided by Congress to World War I veterans — for their participation in future wars. Like the Bonus Marchers of 1932, the students reasoned that the thousand-dollar bonus, to be awarded to each future soldier (plus 3 percent interest, compounded annually) would provide them, all consumers, with the spending money necessary to help raise the nation out of Depression. They failed to convince government officials, however, and by the time of World War II this VFW was moribund.

Source: Cabell Phillips, *From the Crash to the Blitz, 1929–1939* (New York: Macmillan, 1969).

social cohesion necessary to carry the United States through World War II. In the 1930s Americans began to conceive of themselves as a "people"; in the 1940s Americans realized themselves as a nation.

Progressives. The new community consciousness of Americans had several sources. One was simply the widespread misery of the Great Depression. Americans were by necessity forced to rely on one another, and that sense of mutual dependence strengthened families, communities, and labor unions. The influence of progressive intellectuals and social reformers such as Jane Addams, Florence Kelly, John Dewey, and Louis Brandeis was also important. At the turn of the century such Americans had challenged the concept of individualism by noting that industrial societies were defined more by productive interdependence than by rugged individualism. By the 1930s only the third of Americans living on farms could make a case for their absolute self-reliance. Everyone else was dependent on others for food, clothing, work, and amusement. Even farmers depended on the labor of urban workers to produce their farm implements and clothes. Social reformers such as Addams and Kelly had long argued that industrial society was as dependent upon its component parts as a family was upon its independent members; expanding on the analogy, they crusaded for a more humane, loving, familylike society, and pushed legislation such as the Social Security Act. Many such progressives became New Dealers, and the New Deal itself did much to develop class and community consciousness, through artistic products such as plays and books commissioned by the Works Progress Administration.

Conservatives. The New Dealers were often opposed by conservatives and businessmen who insisted that individual initiative was the key to American success. Although conservatives such as Hoover and advertiser Albert Lasker recognized that modern society was an interdependent entity, as the Depression proceeded their rhetoric became stridently individualistic. Their invective only served to advance the communal consciousness of the average American, as conservatives often tied their individualism to the economic and political practices of the 1920s, which, after congressional investigations and journalistic exposés, many among the public blamed for the Depression. Individualistic attitudes were also undermined by the sheer force of the Depression. Hardworking farmers, for example, each year witnessed diminished returns from their labor. While millions of Americans were burdened by guilt and shame for their destitute condition, especially early in the 1930s, many finally accepted the explanation of leading economists and New Dealers that their poverty was due to impersonal forces and poor policies, which affected each of them as members of a whole.

Socialists and Communists. Communal consciousness was also stimulated by the activities of socialists and communists throughout the 1930s. Although probably fewer than 100,000 Americans were members of socialist or communist parties in the 1930s, enough prominent intellectuals joined or gave their support to such parties, and enough strikes and demonstrations were led by such groups, to earn the 1930s the title of "the red decade" from some historians. For both socialist and communist groups the goal was not communal consciousness, but class consciousness — a recognition by the poor and the workers in America of their common plight and of their common exploitation by the rich. Socialist and communist political parties often required extraordinary dedication from their members to the cause — in the case of the Communist Party, the near-complete subordination of their individual lives to collective action and party leadership. Socialists and communists sponsored colleges, newspapers, journals of opinion, plays, art exhibits, folk-music concerts, parades, and summer camps to promote class consciousness. Socialists and communists led various labor and farm unions and sought to build class solidarity among these members.

The Popular Front. Although many socialists and communists initally opposed the New Deal, after 1936 Communists pursued the political strategy of the "popular front" and supported the New Deal, liberal reformers, and labor unions dominated by noncommunists. Earlier, Communists and many leftist intellectuals had argued that the New Deal and liberalism would lead to fascism, as they believed had occurred with powerful national governments in Italy and Germany. Leftist intellectuals sympathetic to communism, such as Lewis Mumford, George Soule, and John Burnham, looked at early New Deal programs as the last gasp of liberal reform.

Communist Party Headquarters in Union Square,
Manhattan, 1930

Hart Benton and Stuart Davis sought to give the American spirit expression in art; writers struggled to produce the "great American novel." As in Europe, much of the artistic effort was an attempt to define what was unique to "the people," a catch-all term that signified a distinct communal identity. Who "the people" were was never quite established; but by the time of Pearl Harbor the concept served to focus public attention on what many saw as America's unique mission in world history: to win the war and establish order in the postwar world. Beyond that, the communal consciousness of the 1930s served to advance distinct group identities: union member; Chicagoan; Democrat; African American; Italian American; southerner — identities that would become more sharply and precisely defined in the postwar era.

Sources:

Robert S. McElvaine, ed., *Down and Out in the Great Depression: Letters from the Forgotten Man* (Chapel Hill: University of North Carolina Press, 1983);

Richard H. Pells, *Radical Visions and American Dreams* (New York: Harper & Row, 1973).

Burnham thought the New Deal was moving dangerously close to a dictatorship and that it could not remain neutral much longer in the struggle between fascist reaction and socialist revolution. Burnham believed Roosevelt would come down on the side of fascism. Mumford, in a typical indictment, saw the New Deal as nothing but "aimless experience, sporadic patchwork . . . an uncritical drift along the lines of least resistance, namely the restoration of capitalism." Such critics often advocated violent revolution to overthrow capitalism and were more critical of liberals — whom they believed retarded the development of class consciousness — than they were of conservatives and reactionaries. In Europe, however, such an outlook had helped fascist political parties such as the Nazis to political victory by dividing the Left and the center. The popular-front strategy was designed to prevent this by making common cause with liberals. Thus, from New Dealers, progressives, socialists, and communists, the public at the end of the 1930s were treated to newspapers, magazines, plays, and films stressing the importance of community and union.

Nationalism and War. Nationalism also played a role in forming communal consciousness. The fascist dictatorships of Europe, and the Soviet Union, had mounted massive propaganda campaigns to help their citizens identify themselves as part of a group; so did American intellectuals. Defining what was distinctly "American" was an intellectual and artistic preoccupation throughout the decade. Aaron Copland sought to define a distinctive brand of classical American music; Martha Graham established the uniqueness of American dance; Thomas

WORKING WOMEN IN THE 1930S

Working Women. The Depression did little to alter the role of women in the American workplace. According to the 1930 census almost eleven million women, or 24.3 percent of all women in the country, were gainfully employed. Three out of every ten of these working women were in domestic or personal service. Of professional women three-quarters were schoolteachers or nurses. The 1940 census did not post dramatic changes in the numbers of working women: thirteen million women, or 25.4 percent of all women over the age of fourteen, worked. The greatest numbers of women continued to work in domestic service, with clerical workers just behind. Out of every ten women workers in 1940, three were in clerical or sales work, two were in factories, two in domestic service, one was a professional — a teacher or a nurse — and one was a service worker. Women in the 1930s in fact entered the workforce at a rate twice that of men — primarily because employers were willing to hire them at reduced wages. In unionized industries, however, women fared better. Women constituted 7 percent of all workers in the automobile industry and 25 percent of all workers in the electrical industry. The integrated International Ladies Garment Workers Union had 200,000 members and secured for pressers in Harlem high wages of $45 to $50 per week.

Poor Working Conditions. Such pay was exceptional. For the most part women worked long hours for low wages in the 1930s. More than half of all employed women worked for more than fifty hours a week, and more than one-fifth worked for more than fifty-five hours. According to the Social Security Administration, women's average annual pay in 1937 was $525, compared with $1,027 for men. The Depression caused women's wages to drop even lower, so that many working women

Women demonstrating against the employment of married female workers

could not meet basic expenses. Certain industries such as canning, textiles, candy, and meatpacking gladly hired women at reduced wages. Added to these poor working conditions and low wages, women who worked faced social criticism in the 1930s, since they were believed to be taking jobs away from men. In most cases of the replacement of men by women, however, women were doing work at wages most men would not accept.

Work and the Married Woman. Married women who worked faced particular hostility. A 1936 poll in *Fortune* magazine asked, "Do you believe that married women should have a full time job outside the home?" Only 15 percent of the respondents approved, while 48 percent disapproved, with the remaining 37 percent giving it conditional approval. Common arguments against married women working were that they were taking jobs away from men, that the woman's place was in the home, and that children needed a mother at home full time. Both private companies and the government dismissed large numbers of married women and made it difficult for married women to get high-paying professional or cleri-

cal jobs. Section 213 of the 1932 Federal Economy Act prohibited more than one family member from working for the government, barring many married women from federal employment. Even positions that were traditionally held by women, such as teacher and librarian, were affected. In 1930, 81 percent of teachers had been women; in 1940, 76 percent were women; the percentage of women librarians fell from 91 in 1930 to 86 in 1940. Despite these restrictions, the Depression pushed many married women into the workforce. Married women sought jobs out of economic necessity, when their husbands lost their jobs, or when the husbands' wages were too low to support their families. The percentage of married women who worked rose from 11.7 in 1930 to 15.2 in 1940.

Difficulty Getting Relief Jobs. New Deal legislation provided relief to both male and female workers in need, although women often did not receive their full share of benefits. For example, in 1933 the National Recovery Administration (NRA) designed codes that improved women's wages, shortened their hours, and increased the

THE CHAIN-MAIL FRENZY

In the spring of 1935 the country was caught up in a get-rich-quick scheme that enraged mail carriers and postal officials. The chain-letter craze clogged post offices, burdened letter carriers, and dominated public conversation. The chain letter featured a list of six names. Recipients of a letter were asked to send a dime to the person at the top of the list, scratch that name out, add their own at the bottom, and send the letter on to five friends. Presumably, after five such progressions, the individual's name would reach the top of the list, and they would be deluged with 15,625 dimes — $1,562.50 — no small sum during the Depression. Of course, if anyone broke the chain, the payoff became uncertain, and while the basic premise was preposterous, millions of Americans participated in the scheme. Post offices had to hire extra help to process the flood of mail. Racketeers — dubbed "chainsters" by the press — sent off hundreds of letters with their name heading each list. Banks ran out of dimes. President and Mrs. Roosevelt received hundreds of such letters, as did the president's political opponent, Al Smith. The town of Springfield, Missouri, was virtually shut down for two days as its citizens went into a frenzy over the chain mail, but by summer the craze was over, with mail officials cracking down on the practice and occasionally fining malefactors.

Source: Cabell Phillips, *From the Crash to the Blitz: 1929–1939* (New York: Macmillan, 1969).

number of women employed. But NRA codes did little for the two million women who lost their jobs and sought relief. Nor did most New Deal public works projects provide much assistance for women. The Civil Works Administration (CWA) employed four million people in large-scale construction projects in January 1934. These projects were defined as unsuitable for women, and the CWA employed only 300,000 women. Starting in 1935, the Works Progress Administration (WPA) oversaw federal relief projects. While the WPA launched successful projects for women, notably sewing rooms where women repaired old garments, women had difficulty getting such jobs. Only one member of a household was eligible to qualify for a relief job, and women had to prove themselves economic heads of households. Women with physically able husbands could not qualify, since men were considered heads of households, even if they were unable to find jobs.

Single Women. The 1930s have been called a "golden age for spinsters." In the 1920s and the 1930s some women, especially college-educated women, chose to remain single. These women expected to find spiritual and emotional — perhaps sexual — fulfillment from other women. The decision to remain single was often part of a commitment to a career in social reform, academic life, or a profession. In spite of the discrimination women faced in the tight labor market, the Depression provided opportunities for these young women to become self-reliant. Their experiences of economic independence inhibited their desires to hurry into the dependency of marriage. As one women from Providence, Rhode Island, explained, "It's not that I didn't want to get married, but when you are working and have your own money. . . ." The Depression also created a scarcity of men financially able to marry and led to many broken engagements. Another woman explained that she did not choose to remain single, but her obligations to her family came first: "During all the years I worked, I had a boyfriend, but we both had responsibilities at home. . . . Now they say 'career woman,' but at the time you wouldn't call yourself that. It's just because you felt you had a responsibility at home too." Whether committed to lives with other women, or inspired by their experience of economic independence, more than six million single women supported themselves or contributed to their parents' households in the 1930s.

Feminism. Though some historians have argued that "feminism died" during the Depression, the economic emergency of the 1930s led to substantial political gains for women. The expansion of social welfare services in the New Deal, a field dominated by women, led to the appointment of more women in high government positions than ever before. As feminists, these women used their government posts to work on behalf of other women. New Deal politician Molly Dewson observed, "The change from women's status in government before Roosevelt is unbelievable." Prominent women appointed by Roosevelt included Frances Perkins, secretary of labor; Ellen Sullivan Woodward, head of the Women's and Professional Projects for the Works Progress Administration; Josephine Roche, assistant secretary of the treasury; and Lucille Forster McMillin, civil service commissioner. These and other appointments marked firsts for women: the first cabinet member, the first director of the mint, first woman ambassador, first judge on the Court of Appeals.

Reasons for Gains. Several factors led to these gains for women in the New Deal. First, government organizations and bureaucracies in the area of social welfare were expanding, and women's opportunities are greatest when organizations are in their formative stage. Second, Eleanor Roosevelt, called "the conscience of the country," crusaded for disadvantaged Americans and promoted women's issues as well. She worked to increase the number of women in high government posts. Franklin Roosevelt himself gained experience working with talented women, many of whom he met through Eleanor, and recognized the importance of women to the future of the Democratic Party. Finally, feminist political activist

Molly Dewson, head of the Women's Division of the Democratic National Committee, worked effectively for women in politics. Dewson was a close friend of the Roosevelts, and a dynamic politician. She used her position to increase women's roles in the Democratic Party and to promote major appointments for women under the New Deal.

Source:
Susan Ware, *Holding Their Own: American Women in the 1930s* (Boston: Twayne, 1982).

WORLD'S FAIRS

Pastime. One of the most popular American pastimes of the 1930s was attending fairs. A long-standing tradition, especially in rural areas, fairs took various forms. Many were local events, tied to special holidays; some were county fairs, often celebrating a historical occasion; and many states held fairs, usually annual events. A variety of events took place at these fairs: bartering and trade, especially of agricultural products; cooking competitions; prizes for the fattest hog, the largest tomato, or the longest-jumping frog; exhibitions by schools, community groups, and business; rodeos and other sporting contests; daredevil airplane performances featuring parachutists and wing walkers; and carnival rides of various sorts. Such fairs were an opportunity to express civic pride, social occasions welcomed by isolated rural people, and an opportunity for cheap fun, a rare commodity during the Depression.

Large Scale. While fairs were held all over America, the world's fairs got the majority of the press and public attention. World's fairs took place on a scale that dwarfed even the large state fairs. World's fairs usually cost millions of dollars, and financing was often raised by both private investors and governments. Planning for these events took years, and unlike state fairs, which usually ran a few days, the world's fairs lasted for months. Corporations usually fielded exhibits, and most fairs established a unifying theme. Public response was tremendous. Attendance ran in the millions. The world's fairs usually captured the tenor of the times as did few institutions, and exhibits often contributed something permanent to the broader culture. Several previous fairs had been occasions of national pride, such as the Columbian Exposition of 1893 in Chicago, the Louisiana Purchase Exposition of 1904 in Saint Louis, and the Panama Pacific International Exposition of 1915 in San Francisco. Because the Depression brought civic and national pride to a new low, the world's fairs of the 1930s were especially valued and touted. Many proponents actually believed they might lift the United States out of the Depression.

Chicago. The Century of Progress Exposition in Chicago (1933–1934) is a good example of a world's fair designed to help alleviate the Depression. Although planning for the exhibition began before the Depression, by the time of the fair's opening, 27 May 1933, planners hoped that the tourism generated by the exhibition would

The 250-foot-high Lifesavers Parachute Jump introduced at the 1939 New York World's Fair

spark an economic recovery in Chicago. Although these hopes were not realized, the fair was popular, with 22.5 million tickets sold in 1933 and 16.4 million tickets sold in 1934. Attendees found themselves in a dreamworld of fairyland architecture and futuristic exhibits that contrasted sharply with the unemployment and financial misery of Chicago. The fair's theme of scientific and industrial progress reaffirmed the faith of many in inevitable progress, a faith badly shaken by the Depression. Big businesses used the occasion to repair their tarnished reputation. Visitors viewed operating oil refineries, automobile assembly lines, a radio-controlled tractor and toothpaste tube–packing demonstrations, as though American industry had never been affected by the economic downturn. The Ford Motor Company, suffering from bad publicity due to industrial warfare, built a $5 million, nine-hundred-foot long building with a rotunda displaying a twenty-foot globe of Ford's international operations and featuring an automobile assembly plant as well as re-creations of historic highways. It was the most popular industrial exhibit of the fair, and it did much to rebuild public goodwill for Ford.

Fan Dances and Fanfare. As popular as the industrial exhibits were, the entertainment exhibits in Chicago really drew the crowds. The Sky-Ride, a two-hundred-foot tall transportation system, shuttled visitors around the fair in "rocket cars"; Spoor's Spectaculars featured giant movie screens and 64-mm films; the Odditorium displayed exhibits from Robert Ripley's "Believe It or Not"; and the Midget Village starred sixty midgets in plays and other entertainments. Sally Rand was the greatest headline grabber of the fair, however. Rand was a burlesque dancer who starred in a notorious "fan dance" that featured her nude body, made up to look like an alabaster statue, behind two large, feathery fans. She was arrested twice in 1933 for her risqué dance, and the fair directors announced they would suspend her from the exhibition, but in the 1934 season she was back, this time with a dance that featured a five-foot semitransparent bubble. More-highbrow fare could be found in the Chicago Symphony series conducted on the fairgrounds and in the joint exhibit on American art at the Art Institute of Chicago, near the exhibition site. Visitors also enjoyed exhibits from foreign countries, especially a model Belgian village, artifacts from Mayan ruins, and a reproduced Chinese temple. There were also special celebrations, such as the national boys' marbles championship and the celebration of the end of Prohibition, when the fair directors provided the public with free beer and sandwiches, all in the name of what they termed "Personal Responsibility Day." Although attendance was high for the fair, the receipts from the 1933 season were not enough to cover the financing of the project, and thus the fair directors reopened the exhibition in 1934. They managed to eke out a profit with the additional year, but the Depression bit deeply, and plans to make the exhibition a permanent feature were dropped. In the end the Depression proved greater than the ability of the exhibition to cure it.

San Diego. Alleviating the Depression was also the foremost concern of the directors of the California Pacific International Exposition in San Diego (1935–1936). Like Chicago, San Diego had been the site of an earlier world's fair, had built the new fair on the old fairgrounds, and had featured corporate entertainment and foreign exhibits. The most distinctive feature of the San Diego fair was the replica of the Globe Theater, where abbreviated versions of William Shakespeare's plays were performed; it later evolved into one of the nation's most important regional theaters. As in the case of the Century of Progress Exhibition, San Diego fair directors ran the exhibit for two seasons; they too were disappointed in the ultimate profits and discovered the fair did little to lift the Depression.

San Francisco. The Golden Gate International Exposition, held in San Francisco in 1939 and 1940, was also motivated by the Depression. Taking stock of the boost to employment the construction of the Golden Gate Bridge and the San Francisco–Oakland Bay Bridge had given the San Francisco economy, fair planners sought to build an exhibition that would not only attract tourists, but provide jobs for the unemployed. To generate work, they built Treasure Island, a four-hundred-acre island in the middle of San Francisco Bay. Ferries provided access to the site, as did a road connected to nearby Yerba Buena Island, the focal point of the Bay Bridge. The Golden Gate Exposition was notable for its meandering gardens on Treasure Island, providing fine vistas of San Francisco. It also featured magnificent arches and towers, and architecture reminiscent of the Cambodian ruins of Angkor Wat. The exhibits were dominated by Pacifica, an eighty-foot statue by Ralph Stackpole celebrating peace. Like the exhibits in Chicago and San Diego, corporations were well represented, with General Motors displaying a translucent Pontiac and Westinghouse introducing a robot, "Willie Vocalite." Ferris wheels, a roller coaster, and a diving bell provided amusements. Sally Rand broadened her act to make a complete "Nude Ranch." Although the fair entertained seventeen million visitors, it lost money, closing with a $559,423 deficit. The Pacifica and other exhibits were dismantled, and Treasure Island was turned over to the navy during World War II.

New York. The greatest fair of the decade was the New York World's Fair (1939–1940). Like the fairs in Chicago and San Diego, fair directors planned the exhibition in an attempt to improve the Depression-plagued economy of New York City. Designed to coincide with the 150th anniversary of George Washington's inauguration as the first president of the United States, the fair's theme was nonetheless forward-looking: "The World of Tomorrow." With this theme in mind, fair designers built one of the most distinctive icons of the decade, the futuristic Trylon and Perisphere (a triangular tower 610 feet high and a globe 180 feet in diameter). Inside the Perisphere the fair's focal exhibit was displayed: a city of the future, which the planners called, a "Democracity." From there, visitors could appreciate the plan of the exhibition. The site (a former ash dump in Queens) was divided into nine zones — Amusement, Communications and Business Systems, Community Interests, Food, Government, Medicine and Public Health, Production and Distribution, Science and Education, and Transportation. Each of these zones was colored in progressively darker hues as one moved from the pure-white Trylon and Perisphere. Each zone featured exhibits by major corporations, including RCA, American Telephone and Telegraph, Kodak, Firestone, Heinz, U.S. Steel, Westinghouse, General Electric, National Cash Register, and the three major automakers.

Futurama. In keeping with the theme of the fair, corporation exhibits specialized in displaying innovative products that awed the crowd. RCA introduced the public to television and broadcast a transmission of President Roosevelt, the first television address by a president. General Motors thrilled the public with its Futurama, an exhibit featuring designer Norman Bel Geddes's model of the world of 1960. As visitors sat in an armchair fixed to a conveyor belt, a speaker in the back of his chair described the American future, a place where automated cars race along superhighways, fueled by liquid air; cancer and polio have been eradicated; and nearly everyone is a high-school graduate. General Electric demonstrated artificial lightning and interred a time capsule, featuring photographs, newsreels, books, speeches, and the Lord's Prayer in three hundred languages, fifty feet into the ground, with orders that it be opened in A.D. 6939. The Borden company demonstrated its new automatic cow-milking machine, the Rotolactor. The Eastern Railroad's Presidents' Conference offered visitors the biggest model railroad ever built and a stage show demonstrating the development of the streamline locomotive. Westinghouse allowed visitors to fire an "electron gun," into gas, producing a luminous streak. There were more-pedestrian thrills in the Amusements zone: Midget Auto Race, Aerial Joy Ride, the Parachute Jump, Nature's Mistakes, and Auto Dodgem. Sally Rand's brand of entertainment was represented by Yvette Dare, who trained a macaw named Einstein to remove her bra to the beat of primitive tom-toms. The most popular attraction was Billy Rose's Aquacade, a water show spectacular featuring "Aqua-femmes" splashing about to waltz music. The fair also featured exhibits by individual states and exhibits by fifty-eight nations, the most spectacular of which was that offered by the Soviet Union, which was removed for the 1940 season due to World War II.

Optimism. Financially, the New York World's Fair was a failure. Despite an incredible publicity blitz, featuring radio advertisements, newsreels, and print and newspaper ads, the fair posted only 25.8 million paid attendees in its first season — not enough to offset the $67 million cost of the fair. A second season in 1940 did little to help: ultimately the fair lost $18.7 million. As with the other world's fairs of the decade, the New York World's Fair proved to be a victim, and not a cure, of the Depression. Yet, the fair's striking iconography — especially the Trylon and Perisphere — captured the imagination of the public and set the image of the future for the future. The hopes and aspirations of the 1930s were encapsulated in the fair as surely as they were packed into General Electric's time capsule. The optimism toward progress and the future would not survive the Second World War and its barbarities. Neither would the World's Fair. During the war the Trylon and Perisphere were dismantled, and the steel within them was sold for scrap.

Sources:

John E. Findling and Kimberly D. Pelle, eds., *Historical Dictionary of World's Fairs and Expositions, 1851–1988* (Greenwood, Conn.: Greenwood Press, 1990);

David H. Gelernter, *1939: The Lost World of The Fair* (New York: Free Press, 1995);

Peter Kuznick, "Losing the World of Tomorrow: The Battle over the Presentation of Science at the 1939 New York World's Fair," *American Quarterly*, 46 (September 1994): 341–373.

YOUTH, DATING, AND SEX

Doing Without. The Depression hit youth aged sixteen to twenty terribly hard. Maxine Davis described the despair she saw when she traveled the country in 1936, talking to young people: "The depression years have left us with a generation robbed of time and opportunity just as the Great War left the world its heritage of a lost generation." More than 200,000 youth left home in the 1930s and took to the road, seeking better opportunities. For the rest, coming of age in the Depression meant doing without, lowering expectations, making do. A special issue of *Life* magazine in 1938 devoted to "The Youth Problem," explained, "by and large, U.S. youths today are a sober lot."

Idle Youth. While families depended on the economic contributions of their children, pervasive unemployment made getting jobs hardest for young people. With prospects for employment so bleak, many youth responded by staying in school: in 1930 less than half the youths between fourteen and eighteen attended high school; in 1940 three-quarters of this age group were in high school. Numbers of young people completing high school rose markedly during the Depression. Those who did not continue to college typically faced complete idleness until they reached their early twenties and found a first job.

Job Hunting. In 1935 young people of both sexes sought work in massive numbers; it typically took several years to find a job. Six months after graduating from high school, over one in four males in New York State in 1936 was still unemployed, and one in seven was employed only part-time or seasonally. Although it qualified them for better jobs, the job market was so poor that graduating from high school did not improve the likelihood that these young men would find any employment. The prospects were even bleaker for young women. Thus, young people remained dependent on their families longer in the 1930s than they had been in the 1920s.

College Youth. Fewer youths could afford to attend college in the 1930s than in the 1920s. Many young people only attended "the college of hard knocks" during the Depression. "Almost everyone knew someone who couldn't go to college," wrote Caroline Bird. Most students able to attend college in the 1930s were on strict budgets, took part-time jobs, or had families willing to sacrifice for their education. Students had to economize, and few could afford to join Greek societies. These costs and sacrifices made students intensely serious and devoted to learning.

Campus Radicals. The hard times of the Depression spurred radical political debates that extended onto the ever-serious college campuses. Campus political radicalism in the 1930s extended from on campus causes to worldwide revolutionary theory. College radicals took on the elitism of Greek societies, opposed military recruitment and training on campus, and supported union organizing. Student councils and newspapers endorsed the Oxford oath, which originated in England, and pledged its takers to oppose their government in future war. Anti-war strikes initiated by radical campus groups became annual events in the 1930s. Nowhere were left-wing politics more hotly debated than at the City College of New York. City College enrolled children of immigrants who entered college with sophisticated political educations that began well before high school; many of their parents were socialist and communist activists. Writer Irving Howe remembered the impassioned political debates in the college lunchroom. His corner was Alcove 1, where the anti-Stalinist, Trotskyist Left hung out, next to Stalinist Alcove 2, where many of the four hundred members of the Young Communist League argued. They debated day and night, arguing the issues that divided the Left: the New Deal, the Stalinist purges, the war in Spain. "I can remember getting into an argument at ten in the morning," recalled Howe, "going off to some classes, and then returning at two in the afternoon to find the argument still going on, but with an entirely fresh cast of characters." College rebels also popped up in remote, elite schools as well as on urban, multicultural campuses, where it was most expected. Writer Richard Rovere remembered that he entered Bard College an unquestioning conservative in 1934, but he "became a radical almost overnight . . . I am sure that the fact that the Vassar girls I knew . . . were members of the Young Communist League had a lot to do with my speedy conversion."

Dating. When they were not debating revolutionary politics, studying, or working a job, college students and other youths in the 1930s found time to socialize. While tight budgets forced young people to cut down on entertainment and clothing, dating rituals continued the patterns developed in the 1920s. Indeed, in the context of the bleak job market and overall deprivation facing youth in the 1930s, dating provided an important outlet for

THE SHIRLEY TEMPLE CRAZE

In households around America during the 1930s, mothers scraped together what funds they could to take their daughters to the hairdresser's and have them put fifty-six curls in their daughters' hair in imitation of the child-star phenomenon of the decade, Shirley Temple. Temple was only five when she appeared in her first starring role, *Stand Up and Cheer* (1934). With her perky demeanor, apple cheeks, and curly hair, she quickly became an audience favorite, the top box-office draw in Hollywood from 1935 to 1938, with most of her movies grossing more than five million dollars each. But Temple was much more than a movie star; she was a national icon. Her face adorned buttons, books, soap boxes, ribbons. Six million Shirley Temple-endorsed dolls were sold per year, for prices ranging from three to thirty dollars each. "Moppet contests," featuring girls who looked like Temple, were held throughout the United States. What the craze meant depended on the interpreter; perhaps Temple symbolized an optimism and innocence Americans were loath to part with during the Depression. Clearly, the public had a seemingly endless appetite for Temple and her movies — films that writer Leo Gurko characterized as, "small miracles of inoffensive sentimentality."

Source: Leo Gurko, *The Angry Decade* (New York: Dodd, Mead, 1947).

youthful desires. Thwarted in their ambitions for jobs and independence, dating provided youth with an avenue to social prestige that helped compensate for cut-off economic opportunities.

Dating and Rating. A 1937 study of dating by sociologist Willard Waller described the competitive system of American dating as the "campus rating complex." In his detailed study of students at Penn State, the "dating and rating" system was based on clearly defined standards of popularity. According to these middle-class standards, even in the Depression years, to be popular men needed to possess material symbols of power and wealth, such as the right clothes, a car, or money. A woman's status was based on her reputation. Women had to "be seen" with the right men, in just the right place, and play "hard to get" by turning down last-minute dates. In this way a young woman cultivated the image of being special, popular — a woman in demand. College women would then "rate" men and other women based upon their conformity to the dating standard. Sorority women at the University of Michigan in 1936 assigned certain men the title BMOC (Big Man on Campus) according to their "dating value." Even to be considered a BMOC, men had to have dated several women. Then they were rated: "A — smooth;

B — OK; C — pass in a crowd; D — semigoon; or E — spook." The sorority women copied the rating list and distributed it around campus. According to the school newspaper, the lists were used "quite extensively" by women to check the ratings of blind dates. An article in *Woman's Home Companion* explained modern dating to its readers: "If you have dates aplenty you are asked everywhere. Dates are the hallmark of personality and popularity. No matter how pretty you may be, how smart your clothes — or your tongue — if you have no dates your rating is low . . . The modern girl cultivates not one single suitor, but dates, lots of them . . . . Her aim is not a too obvious romance but general popularity."

Popularity. This rating system for popularity spread from college campuses to youth culture at large. High-school students of the late 1930s imitated the dating and rating system. *Senior Scholastic,* a national magazine for high-school students, began running an advice column in 1936. The column took for granted that teenage girls wanted to be popular and advised them how to do it. Keeping oneself available for a variety of dates was crucial. Gay Head, the column's pseudonymous author, advised girls never to brush off a boy in a rude way, since "he may come in handy on an off-night." A *Ladies' Home Journal* advice column for "sub-debs" (female teenagers) suggested that refusing blind dates was "public proof" of a slow social life and unpopularity. Even imperfect "blind dates help keep you in circulation. They're good press agents. They even add to your collection." The more dates a girl had, the higher she rated; the higher a girl was rated, the more dates she would have. Ideally a girl was to become so popular that she could turn down requests from boys because she already had a date for the evening. In contrast to dating rituals after World War II, the object of the dating and rating system was not to "go steady," but to cultivate a wide circle of potential male suitors. The more suitors one had, the greater one would attract suitors of a high caliber, with one's hand in marriage presumably going to the best of them.

Petting. The dating and rating system implicitly suggested sexual promiscuity as a means to increase one's popularity, and by the 1930s sexual foreplay, "necking and petting," were expected elements in romantic relationships between adolescents. As *Parents* magazine explained in 1931, when a girl pets, "she is acting according to the code of her own adolescent world, she feels behind her the approval of her own age group, and she is serenely sure that she is all right." Polls, which measure attitudes and not actual behavior, told youth in 1938 that 88 percent of American women "believed most youth petted." A 1939 poll reported that "41.7 percent of high school girls dated boys who expected a good-night kiss."

Going Too Far. Parents were less enthusiastic about adolescent petting, fearing it would lead to sexual intercourse and pregnancy. Much of the advice literature to youth included strong proscriptions against necking, petting, and intercourse. Colleges enacted strict in loco pa-

rentis (in the place of parents) rules in an attempt to control the sexual activity of youth. Access to female dormitories was strictly controlled, and most women students were subject to curfews and punishments for sexual transgressions. Parents of high-school youth set curfews for dates and, to limit privacy, required group and double dating and restricted access to the family car. But young lovers found privacy. In 1937 *Pulse,* the University of Chicago's student magazine, listed nine "tried and true" necking places on campus, but recommended cars "whenever possible," for complete privacy.

Sex. Necking and petting in seclusion led naturally to premarital intercourse. A 1938 study of 1,364 college students, *Youth and Sex,* by Dorothy Bromley and Florence Britten, reported that one-half of the male students and one-quarter of the female students had premarital sex. A 1938 survey of 777 middle-class families found that among those born between 1890 and 1900, 74 percent remained virgins until marriage, but among those of the generation born after 1910, only 31.7 percent remained virgins. Clearly, a change in sexual morality was occurring. Premarital sexual partners were typically fiancés, although this was more true of women than of men. Contraceptives became more widely available in the 1930s, and among the college students surveyed in *Youth and Sex* condoms were the most frequently used form of contraception. Four percent of the women in Bromley and Britten's sample said that they had homosexual experience. Another study, *New Girls for Old* (1930), by psychologists Phyllis Blanchard and Carolyn Manasses, reported that one-third of females had crushes on girls and 20 percent continued to prefer girls to boys. Blanchard and Manasses predicted that the number of women seeking intimate companionship with other women would increase as the number of professional women choosing not to marry increased: "The new freedom of woman and her ability to achieve economic independence should favor the homosexual types in making life adjustments." Data on male homosexuality was more difficult to find, but Alfred Kinsey's 1948 study of male sexuality reported that one-third of men had experienced a homosexual encounter.

The Depression and Youth Culture. Clearly, the dating and rating system and the increase in premarital sex expressed the fact that American youth, forced to adopt adult economic roles during the Depression, were also adopting adult morality. The dating and rating system developed by young people was, in fact, derived from the limited economic prospects of young adults: lacking the means to compete economically, young people began to compete sexually. In subsequent decades, however, many young people would view both the dating and rating system and the Depression as exceptional: the Depression as an aberration from the norm of prosperity; the dating and rating system as an aberration from the norm of going steady. Both the economic and sexual independence of young people during the decade, however, were instrumental in the development of a more distinctive youth culture after World War II.

Sources:
Beth L. Baily, *From Front Porch to Back Seat: Courtship in Twentieth-Century America* (Baltimore: Johns Hopkins University Press, 1988);

Susan Ware, *Holding Their Own: American Women in the 1930s* (Boston: Twayne, 1982).

HEADLINE MAKERS

ELLA REEVE "MOTHER" BLOOR

1862-1951

R**ADICAL, LABOR ORGANIZER, JOURNALIST, SUFFRAGIST**

Radical Activist. A radical activist, Ella Bloor had little patience with ideological debate. Her single goal was "to make life happier for the world's unfortunates." Reeve grew up on Staten Island, New York. She attended public schools, briefly went to the Ivy Hall Seminary, and then was taught by her mother at home. When Reeve was seventeen, her mother died in childbirth, and Ella was responsible for caring for her nine younger siblings.

Early Political Interests and First Marriage. Reeve's father leaned toward political and religious conservatism, so that when she became interested in social and political reform as a teenager, she turned to her great uncle, Dan Ware, who was an abolitionist, Unitarian, and freethinker. Ware had a strong influence on her intellectual growth. When she was nineteen, Reeve married Dan Ware's son, Lucien Ware, an aspiring lawyer. She gave birth to six children over eleven years. During those years Ella Ware was introduced to the woman's suffrage movement and became active in the Women's Christian Temperance Union and the Ethical Culture Society of Philadephia. She also became interested in the labor movement and organized the Philadelphia streetcar workers in the early 1890s. Her political activism caused tension in her marriage, and the couple separated and were divorced in 1896.

Second Divorce and Radical Exploration. After her divorce Reeve was active and independent, exploring possible occupations. She took courses at the University of Pennsylvania and wrote two children's books. She and her children then moved to the utopian community of Arden, Delaware, which was established by socialists. In 1897 she married socialist Louis Cohen, and the couple had two children but were separated in 1902 and later divorced.

Political Activism. Reeve then became a political activist. She was always committed to improving the status of women but devoted her energies to left-wing politics and the labor movement. Ella Cohen met Eugene Debs in 1895, and he convinced her of the necessity of socialism. She joined the Socialist Labor Party in 1901. In 1905 she moved to Connecticut and became the state organizer for the party.

Investigating Meatpacking Industry. In 1906 her friend, writer Upton Sinclair, urged Ella Cohen to investigate conditions in the Chicago meatpacking industry. Sinclair wanted her to gather evidence for a government investigation documenting the charges he made against the industry in *The Jungle.* Richard Bloor, a fellow socialist and young pottery worker, went along to protect her. Sinclair feared it would be scandalous to have an unmarried team of investigators and convinced Ella Cohen to publish the reports under the name Ella Bloor. Although the couple quickly split up, she continued to use the name Ella Bloor for the rest of her life.

Socialism. Bloor spent the next twelve years organizing for the Socialist Party and for the United Cloth Hat and Cap Makers Union. Her work on behalf of coal miners won her an honorary membership in the United Mine Workers of America. Bloor opposed World War I as imperialist and was arrested for antiwar activities. Disillusioned by the support of many Socialist Party leaders for the war, in 1919 Bloor helped form the Communist Party. Bloor worked devotedly for the party for the rest of her life.

Communist Party Activism. In 1925, at the age of sixty-three, Ella Bloor hitchhiked from New York to San Francisco on a cross-country tour for the *Daily Worker*. She held meetings in cities along the way, recruiting party members and selling subscriptions. In the 1920s she was active in the unsuccessful defense of Nicola Sacco and Bartolomeo Vanzetti. She also continued her labor organizing work, traveling to the coal mines to support strikers.

The 1930s. When the Depression hit, Mother Bloor, as she was then called, went to Washington to join the hunger marches of the unemployed. By the 1930s, when she was in her seventies, Mother Bloor was a sought-after speaker for the Communist Party and traveled extensively. While traveling to North Dakota to rally support for the United Farmers' League, she met Andrew Omholt, a farmer and Communist Party candidate for Congress in North Dakota who soon became her third husband. She continued her party campaigning and labor organizing through the 1930s. In 1937 she made her second visit to the Soviet Union as an honored guest at the celebration of twentieth anniversary of the October Revolution. Her final campaign was during World War II, when she spoke at public rallies and on the radio on the theme "Win the War Against Fascism." In her life-long fight for the "world's unfortunates," Mother Bloor suffered more than thirty arrests, countless threats of violence, and frequent harassment by police.

Source:
Thomas L. Edwards and Richard C. Edwards, Entry on Bloor, in *Notable American Women: The Modern Period,* edited by Barbara Sicherman, Carol Hurd Green, Ilene Kantrov, and Harriette Walker (Cambridge, Mass.: Harvard University Press, 1980), pp. 85–87.

MARY WILLIAMS DEWSON

1874-1962

SOCIAL WORKER, SUFFRAGIST, DEMOCRATIC
PARTY LEADER

Childhood and Education. Mary Dewson, known as Molly, grew up in Quincy, Massachusetts, the youngest of six children. Because of her father's poor health, her mother became the backbone of her family. Dewson acquired her father's interest in history and government and would always remember her mother's happiness in being a wife and mother. She was also influenced by her neighbor Elizabeth Cabot Putnam's idealism and commitment to prison reform. Dewson was educated at Dana Hall School in Wellesley and at Wellesley College. There she studied economics, history, and sociology and related these subjects to emerging industrial problems. As president of the senior class at Wellesley, Dewson demonstrated her leadership and organizational talents and the class predicted she would become president of the United States.

Domestic Reform. After graduating from Wellesley in 1897, she became secretary of the Domestic Reform Committee of the Women's Educational and Industrial Union, Boston's most influential women's social and reform club. Dewson was charged with finding out ways to professionalize housework, in order to provide working women with alternatives to factory work, and to free middle-class women to pursue work outside the home. Dewson conducted statistical studies of the home, reorganized the union's domestic employment office, and taught at a school of housekeeping organization by the leader of the home economics movement, Ellen Richards. From this experience Dewson viewed the reform of consumption and housework as keys to the improvement of society.

Probation Reform and Minimum Wages. In 1900 Dewson became superintendent of the Parole Department of the Massachusetts State Industrial School for Girls. There she studied causes of female delinquency and methods of rehabilitation. Dewson applied social casework methods to penal reform, establishing close contact between the social worker, the ward, and the family. In 1912, after publishing several articles on probation, Dewson became involved in the minimum-wage movement and was appointed to study the wages of women and children in Massachusetts. Her report became the basis of the minimum wage act of 1912, the first of its kind in industrial America.

Domesticity. Dewson's report also led to several job offers, which she declined because of her grief over her mother's death. She had lived with her mother in the family's home in Quincy, and in 1913 she and an old friend, Mary G. Porter, settled down to run a dairy farm near Worcester. Dewson and Porter lived together for the rest of her life.

Suffrage Movement and World War I Service. Drawn again into active political life, in 1915 Dewson turned to the woman's suffrage movement and became a leader in the Massachusetts Suffrage Association. Like many social workers, Dewson traveled to Europe during World War I, serving as chief of the American Red Cross's Bureau of Refugees in France's Mediterranean Zone.

National Consumers' League. After the war Florence Kelley of the National Consumers' League appointed Dewson her chief assistant in the league's drive for state minimum-wage laws for women and children. Dewson's contribution was to compile data used in briefs by league attorney Felix Frankfurter, in his court defense of the California and District of Columbia minimum-wage laws. When the courts ruled against the laws, Dewson concluded that a national minimum-wage crusade was hopeless and resigned. Dewson became president of the New York Consumers' League from 1924 to 1931 and played a central role in the passage of a 1930 New York law limiting women's workweeks to forty-eight hours.

Democratic Party. Dewson then became involved in New York Democratic Party politics. At Eleanor Roosevelt's request Dewson organized Democratic women in Alfred E. Smith's 1928 presidential campaign and did the same for Franklin D. Roosevelt's 1930 New York gubernatorial campaign and his presidential campaign of 1932.

Influence in Roosevelt Administration. Eleanor Roosevelt brought Dewson into national politics by getting her a position in the Women's Division of the Democratic National Committee. Dewson set out to create a nationwide network of party workers similar to the core that sustained the reform of the Democratic Party in New York. Dewson's first step was to secure government jobs for women party workers. She won important jobs for key party women at both the state and national levels. Her influence helped secure the appointment of Frances Perkins as secretary of labor, the first woman cabinet member. Working through the help of Eleanor Roosevelt, Dewson arranged for high-level appointments of women throughout the administration of New Deal programs. Dewson believed that women should be promoted in politics because their special sensitivity to human welfare was needed in public life.

Reporter Plan. In 1934 Dewson instituted the Reporter Plan, a national program to train women campaign workers to understand and explain the New Deal. The goal of the plan was to make the Democratic Party more attractive to issue-oriented citizens of both sexes and ensure its victory in the polls. Dewson persuaded President Roosevelt to allocate Democratic National Committee funds for headquarters for the Women's Division between election years. In 1935 the Women's Division started holding regional conferences to train women in carrying out the Reporter Plan, and by the eve of the 1936 election the Women's Division was better prepared than any other group of the party.

Record of Accomplishments. Heart problems caused Dewson to give up direction of the Women's Division after the election of 1936, but she remained responsible for the appointment of its directors until 1941. In the 1930s Dewson's leadership was responsible for bringing large numbers of women into Democratic Party politics. The number of women campaign workers increased from 73,000 in 1936 to 109,000 in 1940. She was also a member of the President's Committee on Economic Security, responsible for shaping the Social Security Act of 1935. Roosevelt then appointed her as a member of the Social Security Board, a role in which her political finesse helped establish effective state-federal working relationships in the administration of old-age assistance and unemployment insurance.

Retirement. Ill health forced Dewson to resign from the Social Security Board in 1938 and kept her in semi-retirement for the rest of her life. In her retirement she

and Mary Porter moved to a home in Castine, Maine. Dewson still kept a hand in politics, serving as elder stateswoman to the Women's Division of the Democratic National Committee and as vice president of Maine's Democratic Advisory Committee in 1954. She died in 1962.

Source:
Paul C. Taylor, Entry on Dewson, in *Notable American Women: The Modern Period*, edited by Barbara Sicherman, Carol Hurd Green, Ilene Kantrov, and Harriette Walker (Cambridge Mass.: Harvard University Press, 1980), pp. 188–192.

W. E. B. DU BOIS

1868-1963

SOCIOLOGIST, CIVIL RIGHTS LEADER

Education. William Edward Burghardt Du Bois grew up in rural Tennessee, where the terrible social and economic conditions in which blacks lived inspired him to devote himself to improving the status of blacks. He believed that higher education was the best means to overcome racial oppression. W. E. B. Du Bois received his bachelor's degree from Fisk University and a second bachelor's in philosophy and a Ph.D in history and social sciences from Harvard University. Du Bois wrote his doctoral dissertation on the suppression of the African slave trade. He also received a fellowship to study at the University of Berlin, where he wrote another thesis on agricultural economics in the American South. In 1895 he became the first black to receive a Ph.D. from Harvard University.

Ambitions. On the night before his twenty-fifth birthday Du Bois described himself in his journal as "either a genius or a fool" and declared his ambition to "make a name in science, to make a name in literature and thus to raise my race. Or perhaps to raise a visible empire in Africa thro' England, France, or Germany." In 1894 Du Bois embarked on his academic career. His first academic post was as professor of classics at Wilberforce University in Ohio. His doctoral thesis, *The Suppression of the African Slave-Trade to the United States of America, 1638-1870*, was published as part of a Harvard series of historical works.

Social Change Through Knowledge. In 1896 Du Bois was appointed assistant professor of sociology at the University of Pennsylvania. He was asked by the university to conduct a sociological study of the black population of Philadelphia, which was published in 1899 as *The Philadelphia Negro*, the first sociological analysis of a black urban community. At this point in his career Du Bois believed deeply that social science would provide

America's white leaders with the "knowledge necessary to eliminate racism and solve the race problem."

Agitation and Protest. In 1897 Du Bois moved to Atlanta University, where he remained until 1934, as professor and chairman of the departments of History and Economics, and then Department of Sociology. He continued his research on the urban black community and published his influential *The Souls of Black Folks* in 1903, which examined both the damaging effects of racism and the strengths of the black community. Du Bois described black identity in the United States in these terms: "One ever feels his two-ness, — an American, a Negro; two souls, two thoughts, two unreconciled strivings; two warring ideals in one dark body, whose dogged strength alone keeps it from being torn asunder." Du Bois wrote prolifically throughout the first decade of the century, but his publications were ignored. Du Bois reconsidered his strategy and concluded that agitation and protest, not knowledge, were necessary to bring social change.

Rift with Booker T. Washington. In turning to direct activism Du Bois continued to believe in access to higher education for blacks as a means to full political rights. In this he differed from the moderate stance of black leader Booker T. Washington, who supported vocational education for blacks and their gradual assumption of full citizenship and accommodated to white leaders. Though the two leaders tried to resolve their differences, they were unable, and in 1905 Du Bois set out on his own.

The Niagra Movement. On 11 July 1905 Du Bois organized a meeting of leaders committed to his goal of immediate full economic and political rights for blacks. This split the black movement into Du Bois's "Niagra Movement," and Washington's "Tuskegee Machine," which advocated elementary and industrial education for blacks. Leaders of the Niagra Movement called for a complete rejection of racism and insistence on fundamental human equality. The radical Niagra movement lacked the political and financial support enjoyed by Washington, and though Du Bois built momentum for his movement over the next several years, the movement fragmented and disbanded in 1910. Some historians attribute the demise of the Niagra movement to the nation's "virulent racism."

A Founder of the NAACP. Learning from the failure of the Niagra Movement, Du Bois decided that an interracial organization representing beliefs different from the Tuskegee group was necessary to end racism. Thus, in 1910 he became a founder of the National Association for the Advancement of Colored People, an interracial organization whose goal was to end discrimination. Du Bois became director of publications and research for the NAACP and edited its journal, *Crisis,* for twenty-five years. Internal conflicts at the NAACP, such as Du Bois's advocacy of segregation as a means to advance blacks in education and the economy, led to Du Bois's

resignation from the editorship of *Crisis* in 1934. He returned to Atlanta University as chair of the Department of Sociology.

Arrogant and Autonomous. Du Bois often changed positions, asserting his independent response to the changing racial climate. These shifts, along with what has been described as his arrogant personality, created continual conflict between Du Bois and other black leaders. He embraced the Pan-African Movement in the 1920s, but his belief in self-government for oppressed black people living in colonial regimes led to clashes with the views of nationalist leader Marcus Garvey. Du Bois exposed corruption and poor management in Garvey's Black Shipping Line, which led to Garvey's arrest. In his later years Du Bois joined the Communist Party and distanced himself from the mainstream of the U.S. civil rights movement. In the 1950s he traveled to the Soviet Union and Africa and moved to Ghana, West Africa, just before his death. When Du Bois died in 1963, *Crisis* described him as "the prime inspirer, philosopher and father of the Negro protest movement."

Source:
Francis L. Broderick, *W. E. B. Dubois: Negro Leader in a Time of Crisis* (Stanford: Stanford University Press, 1959).

A. PHILIP RANDOLPH

1889-1979

LABOR AND CIVIL RIGHTS LEADER

Early Years. A leading labor organizer and civil rights leader, A. Philip Randolph's nonviolent activism against American racism improved the position of blacks in the twentieth century. Randolph believed that improving the economic position of blacks was essential to achieving justice for them within American society. Randolph grew up near Jacksonville, Florida, reading Karl Marx's *The Communist Manifesto* while still in high school. His father, an itinerant minister, wanted him to enter the clergy, but his early sense of social injustice against blacks led him toward a career in political activism. He attended City College of New York, working as a porter, a waiter, and an elevator operator to support himself.

At City College. While at City College Randolph met Chandler Owen, a law student at Columbia University who shared his socialist vision, and the two started a small employment agency for untrained blacks arriving in New York from the South. Randolph and Owen also founded a radical magazine, *The Messenger,* to address social injustice against blacks. During World War I Randolph and Owen used the paper as a forum to protest U.S. involvement in the war and to urge blacks around the country to arm themselves against white violence.

Randolph was arrested for opposing black support for World War I. The U.S. attorney at the time called Randolph "the most dangerous Negro in America."

Organizing Pullman's Union. Randolph's brief imprisonment did not stop his organizing on behalf of black unions and civil rights. It took until 1925, after Randolph and Owen parted, for Randolph to be asked to unionize the Pullman Railroad Company's sleeping-car porters after the porters heard his brilliant demands for racial justice. Pullman, the largest employer of blacks in the country at the time, had resisted the attempts of its porters to organize since 1909, firing porters who rallied their coworkers for wage increases and improved working conditions. This was a challenge for Randolph, since blacks tended to assume that unions were only for whites, and since many blacks believed that porters enjoyed good working conditions. Randolph prevailed in his persistent, dignified negotiations with prosegregation Pullman executives, who went so far as to offer Randolph a ten-thousand-dollar bribe, which he refused. In 1925 the Pullman Company sanctioned the Brotherhood of Sleeping Car Porters, the first black union in the country, and granted a $2 million wage increase.

St. Philip of Pullman Porters. This increase was a triumph for black workers and for Randolph's leadership, and he became known as "St. Philip of Pullman Porters." Randolph rose through the ranks of organized labor, establishing the Negro American Labor Council and becoming the first black vice president of the American Federation of Labor and Congress of Industrial Organization (AFL-CIO), the largest federation of unions in the country. Under Randolph's leadership the union's membership and bargaining power increased. Randolph persistently argued that full equality for blacks rested on equality of economic opportunity. Randolph pursued his vision of economic egalitarianism through building coalitions with whites, a strategy that angered more-militant and separatist blacks. As Randolph explained in this 1969 quote from *Ebony* magazine, "The idea of separatism is harkening to the past and it is undesirable even if it could be realized, because the progess of mankind has been based upon contact and association, upon social, intellectual and cultural contact."

1941 March on Washington. Randolph viewed U.S. mobilization for World War II as an opportunity to push for an end to racial discrimination. Randolph warned President Roosevelt that if discrimination in the military and all federal hiring did not end, he and fifty thousand blacks would march on Washington, D.C. Randolph carried out his threat. On 25 July 1941, less than a week before the scheduled demonstration, Roosevelt issued Executive Order 8802, banning discrimination in the defense industry. While Executive Order 8802 led to the establishment of the Fair Employment Practices Committee, Roosevelt failed to provide an effective means of enforcing it, and blacks were often forced to take low-paying, menial jobs. But an important barrier to racial equality had been breached, and the civil rights movement was surging ahead.

Forced Desegregation of the Military. Frustrated with the continued segregation of the military, in 1948 Randolph informed a congressional committee that he would advise black and white youth to boycott the military unless it was integrated. Now challenging President Harry Truman, Randolph stated he would oppose a "Jim Crow Army until he rotted in jail." Though Truman was as reluctant as Roosevelt to give in to Randolph, since Truman was in the midst of a reelection campaign, he issued to Executive Order 9981, forcing desegregation of the military.

Last Years. Randolph was among the prominent black leaders at the 28 August 1963 March on Washington, where Martin Luther King Jr. gave his impassioned "I Have a Dream" speech. Randolph viewed that march as more than for civil rights, as a "challenge to the conscience of the country." Randolph worked on behalf of civil rights until his death in 1979.

Source:
Jervis Anderson, *A. Philip Randolph: A Biographical Portrait* (Berkeley: University of California Press, 1986).

PEOPLE IN THE NEWS

In 1930 **Jessie Daniel Ames**, a white suffragist from Texas, formed the Association of Southern Women for the Prevention of Lynching (ASWPL), dedicated to challenging the southern, male pretense that lynching was a chivalrous act designed to protect white female purity.

Father Charles E. Coughlin began to give weekly radio sermons from Detroit in 1922. By 1930 his sermons were broadcast over seventeen networks in the East and Midwest. In 1934 the "radio priest" founded the Union for Social Justice, which served as a platform for his growing bigotry, anticommunism, and anti-Semitism.

In 1935 Parker Brothers of Salem, Massachusetts, released Monopoly, a board game adapted by unemployed engineer **Charles B. Darrow** from the turn-of-the-century Landlord's Game, originally designed to exemplify the economic theories of single-tax advocate Henry George. Darrow's patent to the game made him a millionaire.

Dorothy Day founded the Catholic Worker Movement with French poet and philosopher Peter Maurin in 1932. Through the movement Day attempted to reconcile radical politics with the teachings of the Catholic Church and was devoted to improving conditions of the poor.

The Peace Mission movement, founded by **Father Devine** (George Baker), had a membership of nearly two million in the mid 1930s. He preached peace on earth, an end to racism, and food for the hungry to his predominantly black followers. All were welcome to share in his enjoyment of food.

Elizabeth Gurley Flynn, longtime labor activist, joined the Communist Party in 1936 and became one of the leading public speakers for communism in the country.

William H. Hastie was confirmed as the first African American federal judge in 1937. He served for two years on the District Court of the Virgin Islands and was appointed assistant solicitor in the Department of the Interior early in the New Deal.

Lorena Hickok was part of a circle of women journalists who were Eleanor Roosevelt's closest friends. A star Associated Press (AP) reporter in the late 1920s and early 1930s, she resigned from the AP in 1933 because she was unable to write objectively about Eleanor Roosevelt.

Lawyer **Charles H. Houston** led the NAACP Legal Defense and Educational Fund's effort to fight discrimination sanctioned by law, starting in 1939.

John L. Lewis, president of the United Mine Workers, dominated the labor movement from 1935 until World War II, organizing textile, steel, and automobile workers.

Writer and civil rights leader **Walter F. White** was honored in 1937 by the NAACP for his work as its executive secretary, for his advocacy of a federal antilynching law, and his investigations of lynchings. Antilynching measures came before Congress in 1935 and 1940 but died in the Senate.

Ellen Sullivan Woodward was head of the Women's and Professional Projects for the Works Progress Administration, which was responsible for women's relief programs.

DEATHS

Grace Abbott, 60, social worker, director of the Federal Children's Bureau from 1921 until 1934, 19 June 1939.

Jane Addams, 74, social reformer, settlement founder, peace worker; founded the Hull House settlement in Chicago in 1889, which housed clubs, classes, a day nursery, a dispensary, and served as a cooperative boardinghouse for working girls, 21 May 1935.

Alexander Berkman, 65, anarchist and associate of Emma Goldman, shot Carnegie Steel head Henry Frick during the Homestead strike of 1892; was deported from the United States in 1919, 28 June 1936.

Marion Butler, 75 educator and lawyer; led fight for state university at Greensboro, North Carolina; led fight for appropriation to save state university at Chapel Hill; led fight to improve public schools, favored cooperative marketing of cotton and tobacco, 3 June 1938.

Louise Bryant, 40?, wife of radical leader John Reed, journalist for the Hearst papers following his death; briefly married to United States envoy to the Soviet Union William Bullitt, 6 January 1936.

Hugh Frayne, 65 labor organizer, prison reformer, began work at age nine as breaker boy in a coal mine in Pennsylvania; learned sheet metal trade and served as general vice president of the Sheet Metal Workers Union from 1901 to 1904 and as general organizer of American Federation of Labor, in charge of New York offices from 1901 to 1910; a member of the National Commission on Prisons and Prison Labor and received a gold medal from the NCPPL for prison reform; spoke on labor, social and civil problems and was an authority on trade-union law, 13 July 1934.

James Norris Gamble, 96, of Proctor and Gamble, manufacturer of soap, candles, and oils, 1862–1890; vice president of Proctor and Gamble from 1890 until his death, 1932.

Charlotte Perkins Gilman, 75, feminist and author of the groundbreaking *Women and Economics* (1898), and *The Yellow Wallpaper* (1899), 17 August 1935.

Kate Gleason, 68, business promoter and community developer, lauched several low-cost, standardized residential construction projects, 9 January 1933.

Anna Gordon, 77, temperance reformer; organized children's work for the Women's Christian Temperance Union; served as vice president from 1898 to 1914 and president of the WCTU from 1914 to 1925, 15 June 1931.

Florence Kelley, 73, social reformer, secretary of the National Consumers' League from 1899 until 1932; a tireless advocate of child-labor laws and laws protecting women in the workplace, 17 February 1932.

Samuel Edgar Nicholson, 71, prominent Quaker and prohibitionist, 17 April 1934.

John Ringling, 70, circus owner and entrepreneur, 2 December 1936.

Lucy Slowe, 52, educator, college dean, taught at Columbia University; appointed dean of women at Howard University in 1922; helped establish National Council of Negro Women in 1935, 21 October 1937.

Cora Frances Stoddard, 63, temperance worker, author of many books on alcohol, 13 May 1936.

Rose Pastor Stokes, 53, poet and radical, nearly imprisoned for sedition after World War I, 20 June 1933.

Martha Van Rensselaer, 68, home economist, organized an extension course at Cornell University for the wives of farmers in 1900, which culminated in the establishment of the New York State College of Home Economics at Cornell University in 1925, with her as the first codirector, 26 May 1932.

PUBLICATIONS

Louis Adamic, *My America, 1928–1938* (New York & London: Harper, 1938);

Herbert Agar and Allen Tate, eds., *Who Owns America? A New Declaration of Independence* (Boston & New York: Houghton Mifflin, 1936);

Robert C. Angell, *The Family Encounters the Depression* (New York: Scribners, 1936);

Mary Beard, *A Changing Political Economy as It Affects Women* (Washington, D.C.: American Association of University Women, 1934);

Ruth Shonle Cavan and Katherine Howland Ranck, *The Family and the Depression* (Chicago: University of Chicago Press, 1938);

Maxine Davis, *The Lost Generation: A Portrait of American Youth Today* (New York: Macmillan, 1936);

John Dewey, *Freedom and Culture* (New York: Putnam, 1939);

Margaret Jarman Hagood, *Mothers of the South: Portraiture of the White Tenant Farm Women* (Chapel Hill: University of North Carolina Press, 1935);

Karen Horney, *The Neurotic Personality of Our Time* (New York & London: Norton, 1937);

Grace Hutchins, *Women Who Work* (New York: International Publishers, 1934);

Robert M. Hutchins, *The Higher Learning in America* (New Haven: Yale University Press / London: Oxford University Press, 1936);

Charles S. Johnson, *Shadow of the Plantation* (Chicago: University of Chicago Press, 1934);

Robert S. Lynd and Helen Merrell Lynd, *Middletown in Transition: A Study in Cultural Conflicts* (New York: Harcourt, Brace, 1937);

Elton Mayo, *The Human Problems of an Industrial Civilization* (New York: Macmillan, 1933);

Lewis Mumford, *The Culture of Cities* (New York: Harcourt, Brace, 1938);

Mumford, *Technics and Civilization* (New York: Harcourt, Brace, 1934);

Lorine Pruette, ed., *Women Workers Through the Depression: A Study of White Collar Employment Made by the American Woman's Association* (New York: Macmillan, 1934);

Eleanor Roosevelt, *It's Up to the Women* (New York: Stokes, 1933);

Roosevelt, *This is My Story* (New York: Harper, 1937);

Constance Rourke, *American Humor: A Study of the National Character* (New York: Harcourt, Brace, 1931);

Samuel A. Stouffer and Paul Lazarsfeld, with the assistance of A. J. Jaffe, *Research Memorandum on the Family in the Depression* (New York: Social Science Research Council, 1937);

Bertha Thompson, *Sister of the Road: The Autobiography of Box-Car Bertha,* as told to Dr. Ben L. Reitman (New York: Gold Label, 1937).

CHAPTER NINE

MEDIA

by VICTOR BONDI, DARREN HARRIS-FAIN, and JAMES W. HIPP

CONTENTS

Sidebars and tables are listed in italics.

1930

- *The Smart Set* magazine ceases publication.

- The first issues of *Astounding Science-Fiction* are published.

13 Jan. The *Mickey Mouse* daily comic strip, drawn by Floyd Gottfredson until 1975, makes its debut. A Sunday page is added on 10 January 1932.

20 Jan. WXYZ in Detroit airs the first episode of the radio drama *The Lone Ranger*.

Feb. The first issue of Henry Luce's *Fortune* magazine is published.

Apr. Ham Fisher's comic strip *Joe Palooka* makes its debut, reflecting a contemporary interest in boxing and in adventure comics.

30 July *Death Valley Days* debuts on the NBC-blue Network. The series moves to CBS in 1941 and continues until 1945.

8 Sept. Chic Young's *Blondie* first appears in newspapers.

29 Sept. Lowell Thomas begins a nightly radio news program. NBC carries the program until 1946, when it moves to CBS, which carries it until 1974.

1931

- The first issues of *Apparel Arts* (later *Gentleman's Quarterly,* or *GQ*) are published.

6 Apr. The NBC-blue Network introduces *Little Orphan Annie,* a radio adaptation of Harold Gray's popular comic strip.

1 June In *Near* v. *Minnesota* the U.S. Supreme Court rules that a 1925 Minnesota law banning publication of a "malicious, scandalous and defamatory newspaper, magazine or other periodical" is unconstitutional.

12 Oct. Chester Gould's *Dick Tracy* begins appearing regularly in newspapers.

1932

- German photographer Erich Solomon takes an illegal picture of the U.S. Supreme Court in session.

- Walt Disney receives a special Academy Award for his creation of Mickey Mouse, who first appeared in 1928.

19 Mar. Carl Anderson's *Henry* begins in the *Saturday Evening Post.*

2 May The radio comedy *The Jack Benny Show* premieres on NBC. The program featuring the violinist-comedian will run for twenty-three years on radio and for ten more years on CBS television.

22 May The first national gathering of the Communist-sponsored John Reed Clubs convenes in Chicago. The clubs were organized to promote the dissemination of Communist propaganda in music, film, and magazines.

Sept. *Family Circle,* the first magazine marketed exclusively through grocery stores, begins publication; by 1939 it will have a circulation of 1.44 million.

23 Oct. The radio program *The Fred Allen Show* premieres on CBS and will be on the air until 1949.

7 Nov. The radio adventure drama *Buck Rogers in the Twenty-Fifth Century* premieres on CBS. The program will air until 1947.

4 Dec. *New York Daily Mirror* columnist Walter Winchell starts broadcasting his enormously popular radio program, which begins, "Good evening, Mr. and Mrs. America and all the ships at sea."

1933

- *Reader's Digest,* which has reprinted previously published articles since its formation in 1922, publishes its first original signed articles.
- *U.S. News & World Report* is founded.
- Dorothy Day's magazine *Catholic Worker* is first published.
- Ernie Bushmiller introduces Nancy to his *Fritzi Ritz* Sunday comic; she and her friend Sluggo become so popular that the strip is renamed *Nancy* in 1938.
- Milton Caniff's *Dickie Dare* first appears in the comics.

17 Feb. British-American journalist Thomas John Cardel Martyn publishes the first issue of *News-Week* magazine, a newsweekly designed to compete with Henry Luce's *Time.*

17 Feb. Blondie Boopadoop and Dagwood Bumstead marry in *Blondie.*

Mar. The first issue of *Doc Savage* magazine is published.

12 Mar. President Franklin D. Roosevelt delivers the first of his radio addresses known as "fireside chats."

1 June The bankrupt *Washington Post* is bought by California chemical millionaire Eugene Meyer, who will ultimately turn over the paper to his daughter, Katharine Graham.

31 July KBBM of Chicago airs the first episode of the enormously popular radio adventure program *Jack Armstrong, the All-American Boy.*

7 Aug. V. T. Hamlin's comic strip *Alley Oop* makes its debut in daily newspapers. It first appears in Sunday newspapers on 9 September 1934.

Oct. *Esquire,* at first a men's fashion magazine, begins publication. The first issue features a story by Ernest Hemingway, and the magazine quickly establishes a reputation for publishing exceptional writing.

Dec. The American Newspaper Guild is founded.

1934

- The Wagner-Hatfield bill, proposing that 25 percent of radio channels be reserved for educational purposes, is defeated.
- WLW in Cincinnati begins broadcasting at 500,000 watts, becoming one of the most influential radio stations in the Midwest.
- Alex Raymond and Don Moore's *Flash Gordon* first appears in newspapers.
- Whitman Publishing offers an unauthorized book about L. Frank Baum's Oz, *The Laughing Dragon of Oz,* in a Big Little Book.

Jan. The comic strip *Secret Agent X-9,* written by Dashiell Hammett and drawn by Alex Raymond, first appears in newspapers. Both leave it in other hands in 1935.

15 Apr. Dagwood and Blondie have a baby, Alexander.

9 June Donald Duck makes his screen debut with a small part in "The Wise Little Hen," one of Disney's *Silly Symphonies*. On 11 August he is a featured character in a Mickey Mouse cartoon, "The Orphans' Benefit."

10 June Congress authorizes the creation of the Federal Communications Commission (FCC) to oversee the nation's mass-communications industry.

16 June FM (frequency modulation) radio is tested for the first time.

13 Aug. Al Capp's *Li'l Abner* debuts in eight newspapers. By 1939 it has been picked up by four hundred.

Sept. The Mutual Broadcasting Network is created.

Oct. The soap-opera strip *Apple Mary* first appears in newspapers. It is later renamed *Mary Worth*.

8 Oct. In a decision widely condemned by engineers and scientists, the U.S. Supreme Court rules that the patent rights to the superregeneration circuit, an essential component of radios, belong to Lee De Forest rather than its inventor, Edwin Howard Armstrong.

1935

- The verdict in the Lindbergh baby kidnapping trial is broadcast over radio.

- The American Institute of Public Opinion is established by George H. Gallup to measure reader response to newspaper features. The following year it accurately predicts the results of the presidential election.

23 Feb. Marjorie "Marge" Lyman Henderson creates Little Lulu for the *Saturday Evening Post*.

16 Apr. NBC-blue Network airs the first episode of the radio comedy-drama *Fibber McGee and Molly*. The program will run until 1952.

13 May Attacked throughout the early 1930s for its many laxative commercials, CBS announces that it will ban ads for laxatives and other products for which the "good taste" of ads could be questioned.

Nov. FM pioneer Edwin Howard Armstrong demonstrates his invention for the press.

1936

- The Republican Party produces a radio "dramatization," *Liberty at the Crossroads,* as part of the 1936 presidential campaign.

- RCA begins television field tests.

- Moses L. Annenberg purchases the *Philadelphia Inquirer* for a reported $15 million.

- *Consumer Reports* is first published.

- In a poll relying on Republican-heavy telephone and automobile owners, *Literary Digest* inaccurately predicts the defeat of Franklin D. Roosevelt in the presidential election. The magazine folds in 1937.

Nov. A harsh critic of the Roosevelt administration, Father Charles Coughlin, the "radio priest," temporarily leaves the air as promised following Roosevelt's landslide reelection.

The Clock, the first masked crime fighter to appear in comic books, simultaneously makes his debut in *Funny Pages* and *Funny Picture Stories*. In December he also appears in *Detective Picture Stories*.

23 Nov. The first issue of Henry Luce's *Life* is published.

1937

- Martyn's *News-Week* becomes *Newsweek* and becomes a far more effective competitor to *Time*.
- *Des Moines Register* publisher Gardner Cowles launches *Look,* a pictorial bi-weekly, to compete with Henry Luce's *Life*.
- A&P begins publication of *Woman's Day* magazine.
- *Popular Photography* begins publication.
- NBC hires Arturo Toscanini to conduct its new NBC Symphony.
- The American Bar Association adopts Canon 35, barring microphones and photographers from courtrooms.

25 Jan. NBC airs the first episode of its soap opera *The Guiding Light*. It will run as a radio program until 1956, after which it will become a television program.

Mar. *Detective Comics,* which becomes the longest-running comic book in existence, first appears on newsstands.

4 Mar. CBS broadcasts its *Columbia Workshop* production of Archibald MacLeish's radio verse play *The Fall of the City*. Its cast includes Burgess Meredith and Orson Welles.

9 May NBC debuts *The Charlie McCarthy Show,* featuring ventriloquist Edgar Bergen with his dummy Charlie McCarthy. The program will air on NBC until 1948 and then on CBS until 1954.

6 June Walter Piston's piano concertino is broadcast by CBS from New York.

21 Dec. Disney's *Snow White,* the first feature-length animated motion picture, is released.

1938

- CBS purchases Columbia Records.
- Bugs Bunny makes his screen debut.

13 Mar. Edward R. Murrow and William L. Shirer describe the German annexation of Austria from Vienna for American radio audiences.

June *Action Comics* #1 introduces Jerry Siegel and Joe Shuster's Superman.

Sept. Jerry Iger and Will Eisner's Fiction House introduces Sheena, Queen of the Jungle, in the first issue of *Jumbo Comics*.

30 Oct. Orson Welles's Mercury Theatre on the Air performs a radio adaptation of H. G. Wells's 1898 novel *The War of the Worlds*. The program is so realistic it causes panic in many areas.

1939

- FM radio receivers go on sale for the first time.

- The National Association of Broadcasters adopts a code that promotes objectivity in news broadcasts.

- The FCC ends WLW's superpower broadcasts at 500,000 watts; the Cincinnati station scales back to 50,000 watts.

- *Philadelphia Inquirer* publisher Moses L. Annenberg is indicted on charges of income-tax evasion. He ends up paying some $9.5 million in taxes, penalties, and future interest and is sentenced to the federal prison in Lewisburg, Pennsylvania.

- Pocket Books, the first modern American paperback company, is founded.

30 Apr. NBC televises the opening of the New York World's Fair.

May Bob Kane and Bill Finger's Batman is introduced in *Detective Comics* #27.

Summer The first issue of *Superman Comics* appears.

Aug. The Blue Beetle makes his comic-book debut in *Mystery Men Comics* #1.

6 Aug. *The Dinah Shore Show* premieres on NBC radio.

14 Oct. Broadcast Music Incorporated (BMI) is founded to provide musicians an alternative licensing agent to the American Society of Composers, Authors, and Publishers (ASCAP).

Nov. *Marvel Comics* make their debut with stories featuring the Human Torch and the Sub-Mariner.

OVERVIEW

The Rise of Mass Media. The 1930s made a lasting impact on American mass media. Despite the Depression several of the mass media in the United States underwent considerable growth during the 1930s. Even though their numbers decreased, newspapers maintained their readership. In 1920 the United States had 2,042 daily newspapers with a total circulation of 27,791,000. By 1930 there were a thousand fewer dailies, but their circulation had risen to 39,589,000. In 1939 the number of papers had dropped to 1,888, but those papers had 39,671,000 subscribers. The enormous growth of radio in the 1920s continued during the 1930s. In 1930 there were radios in 29 million households, less than half the households in the United States. Ten years later 80 percent of American households (35 million) had radios. The 1930s were a heyday for magazines. In 1935 there were 6,546 in the United States — half monthlies and one-quarter weeklies. Pulp fiction, comic books, and the new animated cartoons with synchronized sound were also popular. In the 1930s newspapers and radio were radically restructured, both in their operational foundation and in their content. Federal regulations governing mass media were established and remained in place, with little alteration, until the 1980s. Journalistic ethics and business protocols developed in the 1930s continued to govern mass media in the postwar era. The decade gave American mass media a distinct character.

Entertainment. In many ways the American mass media as we know it is a product of the Depression. Mass media provided the Depression-era public with projections of their thwarted ambitions and expressions of their deep frustrations. Mass media was foremost entertainment, even in radio and newspapers, which were well suited for communication of news or other vital information. Like other businesses in the Depression, the mass media were forced to scale down and pay close attention to what the public wanted. Some newspapermen continued to fulfill their journalistic responsibilities to inform and educate the public. Others, such as William Randolph Hearst, understood that sensationalism — not detailed news presentation and analysis — sold papers. Hearst survived the Depression, but many of his idealistic competitors did not. Like other big businessmen, Hearst, David Sarnoff of RCA, Henry Luce of *Time,* William

Paley of CBS, and other magnates of the communications field saw the Depression as an opportunity to expand their holdings, driving competitors out of business. The economics of the Depression and the psychological impact of the downturn on the public thus combined to strip the educational and informational potential from the mass media and turn them almost exclusively toward entertainment. In the early part of the decade the NBC-red network broadcast no news programming; educational radio was virtually nonexistent; pulp fiction presented lurid sex and violence; and newspapers focused on sensational events, simplistic presentation of news, and comic strips. All were well-loved by the public; all were highly profitable; all provided a temporary escape from the misery of the period. Mass media in the early 1930s thus pandered to the lowest — and sometimes the worst — common denominator of the American public.

Critics. Many enlightened observers realized that the mass media were not reaching their full potential. Many European conservatives viewed American mass media with contempt, as an expression of democratic politics in culture. To them the mass media created a mass human — unserious, superstitious, disrespectful of tradition and authority. Their fears were echoed by many in the United States who despised the comedy on radio, the thrill of pulp fiction, or the glossy fantasy of the mass magazine. Other critics took a different, but equally condemning, perspective, arguing that the mass media were a modern form of "bread and circuses" — a means whereby the rich and powerful who owned them kept the public entertained and thus politically immobilized. The philosopher John Dewey addressed this problem repeatedly during the decade but never with more precision than in *The Public and Its Problems* (1927). "The smoothest road to control of political conduct is by control of opinion," he wrote. "As long as interests of pecuniary profit are powerful, and a public has not located and identified itself, those who have this interest will have an unresisted motive for tampering with the springs of political action in all that affects them." To Dewey and others the aspirations of democracy were thwarted by big business and its ownership of the media.

A New Culture. Yet the mass media also had the

capacity to present culture and politics in a new, innovative fashion. While the mass media in the 1930s were diversionary and entertaining, quite often that entertainment was implicitly political. Comedy, the most popular genre on radio during the decade, often got its laughs with the plot line of a poor person disrupting the social occasions of the rich, a technique the Marx Brothers perfected in the movies. As the decade wore on, comic strips became more and more overtly political. To some extent they always had been political: *Blondie* always mocked middle-class mores; *Little Orphan Annie* always supported the economic status quo; *Li'l Abner* always exaggerated the most ridiculous features of American culture. Pulp fiction and comic books were much the same. The crime fighter was certainly a political figure at a time when many were equating the gangster and banker. Batman, Superman, and the Green Hornet suggested the wealthy and the gifted should turn their resources to improving the community. In the 1920s pulp fiction had begun pioneering two types of literature that became representative of Depression-era America: the hard-boiled detective story and the science-fiction tale. Both offered implicit and explicit commentary on contemporary society. Through the cheap and accessible medium of pulp fiction, talented writers such as Raymond Chandler, Robert A. Heinlein, and H. P. Lovecraft offered sobering studies of amorality, self-deception, and social breakdown. Although not "classic" literature, such fiction nonetheless addressed many of the same preoccupations of so-called high-minded novelists. By the middle of the 1930s many were recognizing the emergence of a new, vibrant mass culture in the pulp fiction, radio, and magazines of the decade.

Recognition and Transformation. Some of this recognition came from those who had once asserted traditional "high" culture against the culture of the mass media. Many writers of the 1930s had been searching for a "proletarian" literary form that would appeal to the masses and inspire progressive political action. In the sensationalism and amusements of the mass media many discovered new techniques of expression. John Dos Passos literally transcribed pieces of newspaper items and radio stories in his masterpiece, *U.S.A.* With the economic downturn many literary figures looked to the pulps and the movie industry for income. William Faulkner and F. Scott Fitzgerald were among the many novelists who had stints in Hollywood, with Faulkner adapting Chandler's *The Big Sleep* for the silver screen. The Federal Artists Project of the Works Progress Administration (WPA) was instrumental in facilitating the fusion of high and mass culture that characterized the late 1930s. Many writers, such as Richard Wright, were supported by the WPA; more important, WPA support for the theater sustained men like John Houseman, Burgess Meredith, and Orson Welles, who took radio drama to new heights of sophistication in the late 1930s. By the outbreak of World War II the mass media had become *the* distinctive form of American culture: exciting, pluralist, somewhat optimistic, and liberal.

The New Deal. In contrast to Dewey's fears, moreover, the mass-media audience had become politicized. Conservatives, rather than dull the sensibilities of Americans through entertainment, had done their best to use the media to maintain the status quo in the early 1930s. Led by *The Chicago Tribune*, American newspapers were quite nearly unified in their opposition to the New Deal policies of President Roosevelt, and the papers continued to criticize him throughout the decade. In the early years of the Roosevelt administration, radio was also opposed to the New Deal. Programs such as *The Crusaders, Ford Sunday Evening Hour,* and *Forum of Liberty* hammered Roosevelt. Their editorial efforts bore little fruit, primarily because they worked against the implicit politics of mass-media entertainment — which was paying the bills. The sensationalism and superficiality of the newspapers, for example, played to Roosevelt's political strengths, especially in the election of 1932, when his energetic and colorful campaign appearances contrasted starkly with Herbert Hoover's uncharismatic and dry recitation of his economic philosophy. Radio comedy was peopled with ethnic groups heretofore underrepresented in mainstream culture. These groups recognized themselves in the broadcasts of the time, which portrayed economic and cultural situations markedly different from that of the Anglo-Saxon businessmen who supported Hoover in 1932 and Landon in 1936. Roosevelt built an enormous political base among these various ethnic groups, using the new medium of radio to expert advantage to address Americans in his "fireside chats." Unlike his opponents, he did not talk down to Americans. They could envision Roosevelt in their own living rooms. Roosevelt's radio talks transmitted his personal concern for the average American. He set aside older, individualistic notions of government and economy to help the common man; the mass media of the 1930s set aside older standards of cultural correctness to entertain America. One innovation reinforced the other. Ironically, in their desire to make a profit in mass-media entertainment, the owners of those media undercut their own political agenda.

Media Planning. Because conservative owners of the mass media continued to think of politics, entertainment, and culture as distinct entities, they consistently underestimated the power of their products. New Deal politicians did not, and during the 1930s they set out to regulate the mass media in ways that reflected their understanding of how the mass media influenced American politics. Part of their agenda derived from their efforts to plan the broader American economy. The Federal Communications Commission (FCC), created in 1934, attempted to bring order to an anarchical situation in the electromagnetic spectrum. Because radio must transmit on a particular bandwidth, stations around the country were interfering with each other's signals. The FCC sought to resolve this problem by assigning specific bandwidths with specific levels of transmission to specific regions. The Roosevelt administration and its allies in Congress were also concerned with limiting the impact of any one media owner on public opinion. The Depression had forced the buyout and consolidation of many radio stations and newspapers. The FCC sought to limit the number of media outlets an individual could own in a single market, and it forced large companies such as RCA to divest themselves of many of their media holdings. To New Deal politicians the airwaves were a public trust; they sought to plan and administer that trust to public — as well as private — profit.

The News Drama. By the middle of the 1930s the greedy and unprincipled businessman had become a staple of radio and the pulps, as well as of Roosevelt's rhetoric. Programs such as Norman Corwin's *Pursuit of Happiness* characterized the United States to Americans as a nation of tolerant, fair-minded people, liberal in their politics and human sympathies. Americans also began to view events abroad as a form of drama — and brought their expectations from radio and pulp drama to these world events. In 1934 and 1935 advertisers realized they could make money by sponsoring news broadcasts, something they had not heretofore believed. Sponsored news began to fill the airwaves, bringing the dramatic events of Europe and Asia home to Americans, who interpreted them much as they did drama — making villains of Benito Mussolini, Adolf Hitler, and Tojo Hideki, and heroes of the people they attacked, the Ethiopians, the Jews, and the Chinese. Aware of the influence they had on public opinion, American newscasters debated over how much they should editorialize in broadcasts, with William S. Paley of CBS leading the way by arguing that news broadcasts should be as dispassionate as possible. Yet the public was already interpreting news, no matter

how dry, from the standpoint of entertainment. It was natural enough that they would get the two confused: the news drama of war averted in the September 1938 Munich Crisis was soon followed by the panic inspired by Orson Welles's dramatization *War of the Worlds,* which employed a news-broadcast format. When real war came on 1 September 1939, the radio transmission of the event on CBS was of course followed by an announcement:

> We should like to express our appreciation again at this time to the makers of Oxydol, sponsors of *The Goldbergs;* the makers of Ivory Soap, sponsors of *Life Can Be Beautiful;* the makers of Chipso, sponsors of *The Road of Life;* the makers of Crisco, sponsors of *This Day is Ours.* . . .

An American Culture. To the sensibility of the proponent of high culture, such commercialism diminished the significance of the event. Most Americans, however, accepted it as normal. In the new mass media advertising and entertainment were a given. The question debated then and now was the extent to which advertising and entertainment distracted from the need for media to inform and enlighten. The synthesis that developed in the 1930s suggested that media could advertise and inform, entertain and enlighten, equally well. The synthesis itself was in many ways unprecedented, breaking with cultural values established in the West in the preceding two hundred years. At the time it was unique to the United States; in Depression-era Europe the new mass media was used for state indoctrination, and it made sharp distinctions between high and low culture. Owned by private individuals and regulated by the government in the public interest, the American mass media proved extremely receptive to the public need for both entertainment and enlightenment and set a precedent that would serve Americans well for the next forty years.

TOPICS IN THE NEWS

ANIMATED CARTOONS

The Golden Age of the Movies. Many businesses suffered severe losses during the Depression. The movies were not among them; in fact, they were so popular and so successful that many historians consider the 1930s to be their golden age. Full-length motion pictures were most popular, but short animated films were also audience favorites.

Adding Sound to Cartoons. Animated cartoons had existed since the 1910s, and during the 1920s successful silent-cartoon characters included Otto Messmer's Felix the Cat, Max and Dave Fleischer's KoKo the Clown, and Walt Disney's Oswald the Rabbit. In 1928 Disney and Ub Iwerks created a new character, Mickey Mouse, and featured him in *Steamboat Willie,* the first animated cartoon with synchronized sound. As with regular movies, sound rapidly displaced the silent film.

New Characters and Trends. As major animation studios, Disney and the Fleischer Brothers were soon joined by Warner Bros. in the 1930s, a decade that witnessed the introduction of several new characters and trends. One of the first new animated characters of the decade was Betty Boop, created by Grim Natwick for the Fleischers. Based on singer Helen Kane, who in the late 1920s included the phrase "boop-boop-a-doop" in the popular song "I Wanna Be Loved By You," Betty Boop repeatedly found herself in comic predicaments. The character was immediately successful and was highly merchandised. Another popular Fleischer character, introduced in 1933 opposite Betty Boop, was Popeye the Sailor. The character had made his comic-strip debut four years earlier in E. C. Segar's *Thimble Theatre.* The ambitious Walt Disney began the decade with his remarkable "Silly Symphonies" and ended it with the first feature-length cartoon, *Snow White* (1937). Disney also began work on its next animated features, *Pinocchio* (1940) and *Fantasia* (1940). In between Disney continued to produce popular Mickey Mouse cartoons as well as other shorts such as "The Three Little Pigs" (1933) — whose song, "Who's Afraid of the Big Bad Wolf?," was a Depression favorite. In 1932 Disney won a special Academy Award for his Mickey Mouse cartoons, one of which introduced the immediately popular Donald Duck that year.

Warner Bros. Other studios fought to share in the successes of animated cartoons, including Terrytoons and Walter Lantz. Warner Bros., which entered the field relatively late, in 1930, toward the end of the decade began to assume dominance in the short animated cartoon. Porky Pig first appeared in 1935, followed two years later by Daffy Duck and three years later by Warner Bros.' most famous character, Bugs Bunny. On such popular characters the studio proceeded to build a cartoon empire, owing much of its success to the innovative talents of animators and directors such as Tex Avery, Bob Clampitt, Friz Freleng, and Chuck Jones.

Sources:

Leslie Cabarga, *The Fleischer Story* (New York: Nostalgia Press, 1976);

John Grant, *Encyclopedia of Walt Disney's Animated Characters,* revised edition (New York: Hyperion, 1993);

Norman M. Klein, *Seven Minutes: The Life and Death of the American Animated Cartoon* (London & New York: Verso, 1993);

Leonard Maltin, *Of Mice and Magic: A History of American Animated Cartoons,* revised edition (New York: New American Library, 1987);

Steve Schneider, *That's All Folks! The Art of Warner Bros. Animation* (New York: Holt, 1988).

COMIC STRIPS AND THE BIRTH OF THE COMIC BOOK

Beginnings. The first comic strip, Richard Outcault's *The Yellow Kid,* appeared in the *New York World* in 1895. In the next twenty-five years comic strips became one of the most popular forms of entertainment in the United States thanks to the talents of such writer-artists as Out-

Front cover for the first comic book featuring Superman

cault, who also created *Buster Brown;* Rudolph Dirks with his *The Katzenjammer Kids;* Winsor McCay, particularly with his *Little Nemo in Slumberland;* Bud Fisher with his *Mutt and Jeff,* the first daily comic strip; George Herriman, the genius behind the surreal *Krazy Kat;* George McManus with his *Bringing Up Father;* and many others. Most comic strips in the first decades of the form relied on humor, earning them the names *comics* and *funnies,* and often on fantasy as well. In addition, several adventure strips, including Roy Crane's *Wash Tubbs* and Richard Calkins and Philip Nowlan's *Buck Rogers,* began to appear in the 1920s. These trends, along with more-realistic depictions of American life, would prevail in comic strips throughout the 1930s, the decade that also witnessed the birth of a near relative, the comic book.

New Faces on the Funny Pages. While many older strips continued to prosper into the 1930s, many of the most popular were introduced during the decade. Chic Young's *Blondie* first appeared in 1930. Beginning as a lighthearted satire of young people in the Jazz Age, it soon evolved into a popular comic examination of American work and family life. An established strip, Billy DeBeck's *Barney Google* (introduced in 1919), underwent a striking transformation: in 1934 the eponymous character inherited a cabin in the hill country of North Carolina and met an equally diminutive character named Snuffy Smith, who then began to steal the show. By the end of the 1930s the strip was named *Barney Google and Snuffy Smith*. After DeBeck's death in 1942 his assistant, Fred Lasswell, took over, and Barney Google was eventually supplanted by Snuffy Smith and his kin and neighbors. Also set in the South, but more sharply satirical than *Barney Google*, was Al Capp's *Li'l Abner*, introduced in 1934, with the denizens of Dogpatch making fun of contemporary social issues. Other strips combined humor and fantasy with adventure, among them V. T. Hamlin's *Alley Oop*, which first appeared in 1933. At first set in a prehistoric land called Moo, the strip began to vary its potential for humor and action when Hamlin introduced a time machine that allowed the strip's caveman protagonist and his friends to travel to a wide range of times and places.

Action and Adventure. Some strips of the 1930s seemed to defy the "funnies" label by adhering to action and adventure rather than humor. One example was Milton Caniff's *Dickie Dare*, introduced in 1933. The strip featured a twelve-year-old boy who first imagines himself as part of classic adventure tales, such as those with Robin Hood and Robinson Crusoe, then takes part in real adventures with his globe-trotting writer friend Dan Flynn. At the end of 1934 Caniff left the strip, which continued until 1957 under other hands, to create *Terry and the Pirates*, another adventure strip. The most beautifully drawn adventure strip of the decade, Alex Raymond and Don Moore's *Flash Gordon*, first appeared in 1934. Other noteworthy adventure strips introduced during the decade include Frank V. Martinek's *Don Winslow of the Navy* (1934), Lee Falk and Phil Davis's *Mandrake the Magician* (1934), Falk and Ray Moore's *The Phantom* (1936), and Hal Foster's *Prince Valiant* (1937).

Reflections of Hard Times. Not every comic strip during the 1930s provided such escapism. The 1930s was a decade of depression and high crime rates, and several strips reflected the reality that the newspapers in which they appeared described daily. The best-known strip of this kind was Chester Gould's *Dick Tracy*, which started appearing regularly on 12 October 1931. Combining cartoonish art with realistic violence, the strip was instantly popular, its hero taking his place with other popular detectives of the 1930s. In an era obsessed with gangsters, Dick Tracy fought gangsters of every conceivable shape and aspect. While the strip had elements of humor and warmth, the urban setting in which Tracy worked was filled with darkness and crime, a clear reflection of contemporary concerns and moods. Similarly, one of the most popular strips of the decade, Harold Gray's *Little Orphan Annie* (introduced in 1924), dealt with the hard times of the decade through Annie's unbending optimism and pluck and Gray's increasingly blatant critiques of the New Deal.

The Creation of the Comic Book. Reprint collections of comic strips were popular before the 1930s. In 1933 a

---

BIG LITTLE BOOKS

The first comic book, a collection of comic strips called *Funnies on Parade*, appeared in 1933, but it was not the first time comic strips had been collected. Books of collected strips had been published for decades, and one year earlier a form of collected comic strips first appeared and enjoyed immediate and substantial success: Whitman's Big Little Books.

Big Little Books were small, thick "novels" alternating a page of text with a captioned illustration. First sold in discount stores for ten cents apiece, the books were extremely popular with children of various ages, who could read them at whatever level they were comfortable. Most of the first Big Little Books adapted stories and characters from comic strips; the first three titles, for instance, featured Dick Tracy, Mickey Mouse, and Little Orphan Annie. Other sources came from movies and radio shows. From 1932 to 1938 Whitman Publishing sold 250 separate titles, by some estimates selling one million books a month at their most successful. The number of titles offered would more than double by 1950, when Whitman stopped creating the books. They have since revived the format at various times.

Source: Ron Goulart, ed., *The Encyclopedia of American Comics* (New York & Oxford: Facts On File, 1990).

---

new type of collection, *Funnies on Parade*, reprinted strips in color in a 7 1/2" x 10" magazine with a slick paper cover and inadvertently created a new medium, the comic book. Its ten thousand copies, given away with Proctor and Gamble products, were extremely popular with the public, and the following year its publisher created another reprint comic, *Famous Funnies*, to be sold for ten cents; it became the first monthly comic book. Its thirty-five thousand copies sold quickly, and it was rapidly imitated. In 1935, starting with *New Fun Comics* (later *More Fun*), National Periodical Publications (later DC Comics) began seeking original stories to publish, and comic books quickly assumed an independent identity. They were especially popular during the next decade, which many historians label the golden age of the comic book.

The Age of the Superhero. It is unlikely that comic books would have become as popular as they did, however, without the advent of a new concept in their pages, the costumed crime fighter. The idea of mystery men who took the law into their own hands was not entirely new, having originated during the early 1930s in popular pulp magazines such as *The Spider* and *The Shadow*. With the introduction of Superman in the first issue of *Action Comics* (June 1938) the comic book had a creature all its own — the *superhero.* Though other kinds of comic books — featuring funny animals, romance, war, science fiction, Westerns, teenagers, and so on — would appear and succeed, it was superheroes such as Superman and Batman (introduced in *Detective Comics* #27 in 1939) that ensured the continued prosperity of the form into the next decade and beyond.

Up, Up, and Away! Superman was created by two nineteen-year-olds from Cleveland, Jerry Siegel and Joe Shuster. An amalgam of pulp-magazine science fiction and comic-book fantasy, the Man of Steel was the first superhero. For a long time he was also the most popular — even with competition from a plethora of costumed crime fighters introduced in the late 1930s and early 1940s. Next in popularity was Batman, created by Bob Kane and Bill Finger, who were influenced from even more directions: pulp-magazine figures such as the Shadow and Doc Savage; radio crime fighters such as the Green Hornet and the Lone Ranger; Zorro and gangsters from the movies; and comic-strip characters such as the Phantom. Superheroes quickly fell into two camps: either they were like Superman in exhibiting unusual abilities, soon labeled *superpowers,* or they were "normal" men (and occasionally women) who fought crime, like their archetype Batman, using a combination of physical strength and skill, intelligence, and fancy equipment. Thus, the comic-book pages were filled with such colorful characters as the Atom, Batman, Blackhawk, Blue Beetle, Captain America, Captain Marvel, Daredevil, Doll Man, the Flash, Green Arrow, Green Lantern, Hawkman, the Human Torch, the Phantom Lady, Plastic Man, the Sandman, the Sub-Mariner, Superman, Wonder Woman, and many, many others. These characters shared certain traits that struck a chord with young readers: they had exciting abilities and adventures, and they almost always had a secret identity — a winning combination for children and adolescents who often felt overpowered by the world and believed that no one understood them. In addition, many of these superheroes had youthful sidekicks — Batman had Robin; the Human Torch had Toro; Captain America had Bucky — with whom youthful readers could identify.

Sources:

Mike Denton, *The Comic Book in America: An Illustrated History,* revised edition (Dallas: Taylor, 1993);

Ron Goulart, ed., *The Encyclopedia of American Comics* (New York & Oxford: Facts On File, 1990);

Richard Marschall, *America's Great Comic-Strip Artists* (New York: Abbeville, 1989).

COMMUNICATIONS ACT OF 1934

The Radio Act of 1927. The regulation of the burgeoning broadcasting industry began with the Radio Act of 1927, which for a few years brought order to chaos. But the 1927 act treated radio broadcasting differently from telephone and telegraph communications and set up a confusing range of federal agencies with control over different aspects of the industry. During the first few years of the Radio Act of 1927 it became clear that, while the legislation had done a good job with the radio portion of the industry — especially with the formation of the Federal Radio Commission — it had failed by not including the telephone and telegraph industries within its scope.

Government Regulation. By 1929 many of the ideas later incorporated into the 1934 act had been discussed and agreed upon by members of Congress but not passed into law. During the first several years of the Great Depression, Congress was more concerned with the economic collapse than with regulatory tinkering. With the election of Franklin D. Roosevelt in 1932 and a new activist attitude toward government regulation, the Communications Act of 1934 took its place among the other regulatory milestones of the New Deal — the Securities Act of 1933, the Securities Exchange Act of 1934, the National Labor Relations Act of 1935, and the Civil Aeronautics Act of 1938. Like many of these acts, the Communications Act of 1934 was the product of ideas, laws, and negotiations that existed before the Depression.

Utilities and Regulation. In a message asking Congress to pass the bill regulating communications, President Roosevelt defined communications vendors as specific utilities and pointed out the singular lack of regulation concerning communications: "I have long felt that for the sake of clarity and effectiveness, the relationship of the Federal government to certain services known as utilities should be divided into three fields: Transportation, power, and communications. The problems of transportation are vested in the Interstate Commerce Commisssion, and the problems of power . . . in the Federal Power Commission. In the field of communications, however, there is today no single Government agency charged with broad authority." As the bill was already written, it was quickly passed as the Communications Act of 1934.

Federal Communications Commission. The centerpiece of the legislation was the reformulation of the old Federal Radio Commission as the Federal Communications Commission (FCC), with little new structure but with new responsibilities to oversee the telecommunications industry as well as broadcasting. According to the act, the role of the FCC was "to make available, as far as possible, to all the people of the United States a rapid, efficient, Nation-wide, and world-wide wire and radio communications service with adequate facilities at reasonable charges." The act was not intended to make the industry competitive, nor to make the prices charged a function of market mechanisms. The subjects of the six major chapters of the act show the scope and intentions of the legislation:

1. Setting up of the FCC.

2. Common carriers, being the telephone and telegraph companies.

3. Broadcast licensing, general powers of the FCC, requirement that candidates for public office be treated equally and that sponsors be identified.

4. The right to appeal FCC decisions.

5. Enforcement procedures.

6. War emergency powers of the president.

Public Interest. The clause that defined the powers of the FCC in relation to the content and structure of the broadcasting industry included the idea of the "public interest" as the measure of whether something should be allowed to be broadcast or someone should be given a broadcasting license. Such a vague and ultimately undefinable term as "public interest" gave almost unlimited power to the FCC. But the FCC exercised those powers in a limited way, controlling advertiser fraud over the airwaves and insuring community standards of decency. The full scope of that power was not made explicit until 1975, when a federal appeals court stated that "since the public cannot through a million stifled yawns convey that their . . . fare is not in their interest, the Congress has made the FCC the guardian of that public interest." Despite that power, and the fear of critics that the FCC would seek to impose a partisan political agenda on local radio broadcasts, the FCC left local stations free to express virtually any opinion.

Lasting Influence. The Communications Act of 1934 set up a structure that lasted through the rise of television and the telecommunications giants of the late twentieth century. Its broadcast standards, licensing procedures, and tariff policies withstood almost fifty years without radical change. As with so many of the New Deal–era legislative juggernauts, the Communications Act of 1934 is only in the 1990s facing a fundamental rewrite.

Sources:

Sydney W. Head and Christopher H. Sterling, *Broadcasting in America: A Survey of Television, Radio, and New Technologies,* fourth edition (Boston: Houghton Mifflin, 1982);

Max D. Paglin, ed., *A Legislative History of the Communications Act of 1934* (New York: Oxford University Press, 1989).

ESQUIRE MAGAZINE

Born in the Depression. *Esquire: The Quarterly for Men* made its debut on 15 October 1933, near the trough of the Great Depression. The idea of a new men's fashion magazine for the public came from C. F. Peters, a Scandinavian fashion artist, who told three men associated with the trade paper *Apparel Arts* that a magazine that could be sold or given away to clothing customers would be successful. The three men — David A. Smart, William H. Weintraub, and Arnold Gingrich — worked for nearly a year before coming up with a design for the new magazine, which would combine fashion illustrations and advice with cultural writing.

Quick Growth. The 5,000 copies of the first quarterly issue reserved for newsstand sales sold out within five

David A. Smart, publisher (sitting), and Arnold Gingrich, editor of *Esquire*

hours. The *Esquire* staff scrambled to recall 95,000 of the 100,000 copies presold to menswear stores so they could be shipped to newsstands. The success of the magazine was so great and such a shock that Smart, Weintraub, and Gingrich quickly retooled *Esquire* into a monthly, which began publication with the issue dated January 1934. That issue sold more than 60,000 copies. By the end of 1934, sales had reached more than 135,000. With Smart as publisher and Gingrich as editor, sales of *Esquire* rose to more than 700,000 copies in 1938.

Targeting the Middle Class. Gingrich marketed the magazine as a guidebook to leisure for middle-class men, a risky idea for a country in the midst of the Great Depression. In addition to its fashion, food, and leisure advice, *Esquire* also featured drawings of scantily clad women, which became used as pinups during the 1940s. Full-page cartoons were also a fixture of the magazine. Yet *Esquire* was best known for its ability to attract some of the best American fiction writers as contributors. The first issue featured work by Dashiell Hammett, Ring Lardner, John Dos Passos, Ernest Hemingway, and others. To get Hemingway's contribution for this issue Gingrich reportedly kept after Hemingway so persistently that the author agreed to contribute a story if

Gingrich could shoot more beer cans than he could. Gingrich did, later saying, "I guess he was drunker than I was." Hemingway not only became a regular contributor but introduced Gingrich to other prominent writers of the time, including Dos Passos and Lardner. *Esquire* soon built a reputation for publishing the best writers of the period, among them William Faulkner, F. Scott Fitzgerald, and Sinclair Lewis.

A Bellwether. The importance of *Esquire*, besides its literary pedigree, was its influence on the development of future magazines. Shown by the success of *Esquire* that a male magazine market existed, other publishers brought out offerings such as *Sports Illustrated* and *Playboy* after World War II. While successful to a degree even into the 1990s, *Esquire* never regained the singularity it held in the 1930s.

Source:
Arnold Gingrich, *Nothing But People: The Early Days at Esquire, A Personal History, 1928–1958* (New York: Crown, 1973).

THE GOLDEN AGE OF RADIO

The Broadcast Center. The 1930s were truly the golden age of radio. Radio had been a nationwide phenomenon during the 1920s, broadcasting jazz; it was a fixture of the 1940s, connecting the home front to the war; but during the Depression era of the 1930s radio was something more than an entertainment or communications medium. It was a source of solace, of relief from everyday troubles; a means of escaping hardship, if only for a few minutes. It also embodied the political tensions of the decade. President Franklin D. Roosevelt reassured the nation by radio during his "fireside chats"; H. V. Kaltenborn's broadcasts from Munich in 1938 focused the nation's anxieties on Europe. During the 1930s radio was at the center of American culture.

The Depression. The Depression affected the radio business much as it did other industries. Large radio manufacturers and broadcasters were hurt slightly; small radio manufacturers and broadcasters were driven out of business. Small radio stations, when they did not fold, weathered the Depression by occasionally trading air time to advertisers in return for room and board for their personnel. Wealthy entrepreneurs unaffected by the Depression increasingly bought up local radio stations, forming chains of broadcast sites and radio networks. If anything the Depression was good for the radio business. Advertisers, hunting for maximum exposure for the minimum price, increasingly chose radio over newspapers. Even in the worst years of the Depression the major networks continued to post profits: in 1932 the National Broadcasting Corporation (NBC) made just more than $1 million; the Columbia Broadcasting System (CBS), $1.6 million.

The Popular Imagination. Radio was profitable because it was popular: the *Amos 'n' Andy* program was such a fad that during its broadcast time, between 7:00 and

7:15 P.M. each evening, telephone use in the country dropped 50 percent and movie theaters interrupted showings to pipe in the program. Enough Americans were listening to radio by 1930 that the first analysis of the listening audience, organized by Archibald Crossley of the Association of National Advertisers, began attempting to rate the popularity of various programs. Social workers reported that some destitute families would give up their iceboxes or furniture before they would part with their radios. In 1933, 3.6 million radio sets were sold, in the depths of the Depression. By 1939 about 80 percent of Americans owned radios. Audiences loved radio because it provided them with an excitement often missing

Freeman Gosden and Charles Correll — Amos 'n' Andy

in their lives: romance, adventure, wealth, and ease. But audiences also loved radio because it invited them to participate in its scripted fantasies. Radio conveyed its message by sound; listeners had to provide the visualizations. Broadcast dramas used various sound effects to evoke slammed doors, automobiles, and telephones, but listeners pictured the majority of the script in their imaginations, filling in the features of the hero or heroine as they pleased. Few in the audience knew that the Lone Ranger's faithful horse, Silver, was actually a couple of coconut shells on a soundboard; even had they known it, fewer still would have imagined Silver as anything but a gallant steed.

From Vaudeville to Radio. Radio borrowed much of its broadcast format from other entertainment media. Sports, of course, were a fixture of radio — sometimes even in the absence of actual games. The future president Ronald Reagan, a sports announcer at WHO in Des Moines, Iowa, during much of the Depression, called play-by-play for the Chicago Cubs in a studio three hundred miles from the actual game. Linked to the baseball

field by telegraph relay, Reagan was fed the raw data from the game and invented the remainder of the action — which was in turn reimagined by his audience. Baseball, boxing, and college football were favorites of broadcasters. Radio also borrowed much of its entertainment talent from vaudeville, a type of stage variety show that was in decline. Radio comedies, like vaudeville, were usually performed before live audiences, and audience reactions were considered part of the program — so much so that microphones were hung over the crowd. Vaudevillians such as Eddie Cantor, Ed Wynn, Jack Pearl, Fred Allen, George Burns and Gracie Allen, Jack Benny, Fanny Brice, and Edgar Bergen were stars of radio, and the variety show, usually featuring the name of its advertising sponsor in the title (for example, *Texaco Five-Star Theater, Kraft Music Hall, Maxwell House Showboat*), made the transition to a nonvisual medium by emphasizing singers and comics.

Amos 'n' Andy. The most popular radio show of the decade was also borrowed from an older entertainment tradition. Minstrelsy was an old vaudeville genre in which white entertainers painted their faces black and sang "Negro" songs or poked fun at African Americans. Although minstrelsy was often offensive to blacks, white audiences loved it. Two white vaudevillians, Freeman Gosden and Charles Correll, brought this genre to radio, with amazing results. Audiences could not get enough of the escapades of the stereotypically "black-sounding" protagonists — who usually ran into trouble trying to rise above their social "place." Even President Roosevelt listened to *Amos 'n' Andy.*

Comedy. Led by *Amos 'n' Andy,* comedy ruled the airwaves during the 1930s. Inevitably the most popular programs offered some levity during hard times. One of the most popular performers was Fred Allen, an intelligent actor whose program featured characters such as the voluble Senator Claghorn and the opinionated Mrs. Nussbaum. Jack Benny, another radio wit, repeatedly offered gags about his penny-pinching and his ability as a violin player. One episode featured Benny being robbed. The thief demanded, "Your money or your life!" After a pregnant silence Benny responded with, "I'm thinking it over." Ratings soared when Allen and Benny met on the air in March 1937, culminating years of good-natured feuding over their acts. The show concluded with an off-air "fistfight" between the two, after which they returned to the studio to deliver the punch line: when Benny's wife, Mary, asked Benny how he got a black eye, he responded by fibbing, "I was writing a letter," to which Allen quipped, "And I dotted his eye." Other popular comedy acts and shows included George Burns and Gracie Allen as a straight-man husband and a scatterbrained wife; *Easy Aces,* on which writer Goodman Ace and his wife, Jane, entertained with puns, non sequiturs, and malapropisms; *Fibber McGee and Molly,* a situation comedy about an accident-prone couple; and Edgar Bergen and Charlie McCarthy, a ventriloquist act whose suggestive banter with guests such as Mae West and Dorothy Lamour brought many complaints to the Federal Communications Commission.

Music. Music, of course, was also a staple of radio, brought from the stage and concert hall to the studio. Live symphonic orchestra performances were common, with CBS sponsoring broadcasts by the New York Philharmonic and NBC building an orchestra around Italian maestro Arturo Toscanini. But the most popular music on radio came from vaudeville and the dance hall, with singers such as Rudy Vallee, Kate Smith, Bing Crosby, Ella Fitzgerald, and Dinah Shore leading the pack of audience favorites. Established swing and jazz stars often performed on the radio, especially Louis Armstrong, Cab Calloway, Benny Goodman, Tommy Dorsey, Paul Whiteman, Artie Shaw, and Duke Ellington. Such broadcasts were almost always live, as few records were licensed for radio broadcast — a reflection of a long-standing royalty dispute broadcasters had with the American Federation of Musicians and American Society of

Gracie Allen and George Burns

Composers, Authors and Publishers. The dispute dragged on throughout the decade.

Soap Operas. A more original staple of radio was the soap opera, so named because they were usually sponsored by household-products advertisers, such as soap makers. The soap operas were serial melodramas aimed toward a daytime, female audience. They served up heady doses of middle-class family crisis and tepid romance to enthusiastic millions. Typical of the plot dilemmas of soaps was that of *Just Plain Bill,* where Bill, the midwestern protagonist, fears that his daughter, raised in eastern finishing schools, will be "too good for me." *Our Gal Sunday* continued for years, probing the basic question "Can a girl from a little mining town in the West find happiness as the wife of a wealthy and titled Englishman?" *Big Sister* concerned the travails of a heroine in love with a man whose wife was insane. One of the most interesting of the soap operas was *The Goldbergs,* the story of an urban Jewish family. Millions of upwardly mobile families of every ethnic background responded to the Goldbergs' pursuit of the American dream. Regular listeners wrote letters addressed to soap opera characters, offering them advice with their problems. The first soap opera was *The Romance of Helen Trent,* about a widow. It made its debut in 1933 and was still on the air in 1960. Others included *Myrt and Marge, Ma Perkins, Life Can Be Beautiful,* and *Against the Storm.*

Amateur Hours, Game Shows, and Advice. Programming staples of radio were the amateur hour and the game show. *Major Bowes' Amateur Hour* was the most popular of these programs, highlighted by a deep brass gong tolling the end of a performance from the less-than-gifted. Others included *Professor Quiz, Information Please,* and *True and False.* The advice and instructional program was drawn in many instances from newspapers. The program hosted by Mary Margaret McBride's "Martha Deane" character and other similar shows proved popular, especially with women. McBride conducted interviews with famous and ordinary people and dispensed advice in ad-libs. Other programs, such as *Betty Crocker*, passed along recipes or home-decorating tips.

Drama. Radio also developed its own version of the drama, featuring narrators, actors speaking lines, and sound effects. In the early 1930s the most popular of these dramas were crime and suspense stories, sometimes drawn from the pulp fiction or the comic books of the day. They included *The Shadow, Charlie Chan, Eno Crime Clues,* and *Sherlock Holmes.* Other dramas — such as *Death Valley Days, Roses and Drums, Soconyland Sketches,* and *Moonshine and Honeysuckle* — were oriented toward adventure. Some dramas were specifically designed for preadolescent and adolescent males and usually featured some variant of the superhero. *Tom Mix, Tarzan, The Lone Ranger, The Green Hornet, Superman, Buck Rogers in the Year 2430,* and *Jack Armstrong, the All-American Boy* were among these shows. In 1937 both CBS and NBC began broadcasting Shakespeare plays. The horror drama *Lights Out* was also popular and challenged sound-effects technicians to produce sounds such as the squishing of blood and guts (a bathroom plunger in warm spaghetti) and the crunching of bones (Lifesavers broken between the teeth, very close to the microphone).

Norman Corwin. One of the most original dramatists on radio in the 1930s was a young writer, Norman Corwin, who integrated word and sound in an innovative fashion. In 1938 Corwin began to produce "word orchestrations" — programs in which sound effects reinforced the narration. In his production of the Old Mother Hubbard nursery rhyme, for example, the rattling of cups and china is heard as she goes to her cupboard. Similar orchestrations were put to other nursery rhymes and to poetry by Edgar Lee Masters, Carl Sandburg, and Stephen Vincent Benét — often with the assistance of the poets themselves. On Christmas Day 1938 Corwin presented *The Plot to Overthrow Christmas,* a half-hour verse play that became an audience favorite. In 1939 his orchestrations began commenting on political events. *They Fly Through the Air* was critical of fascism. *Pursuit of Happiness,* which made Corwin famous, focused on Americana, featured an orchestra, and starred Burgess Meredith as the master of ceremonies. A variety show with a liberal, nationalist bent, *Pursuit of Happiness* introduced comedian Danny Kaye and balladeer Woody Guthrie, among other folksingers. It also premiered the rousing "Ballad for Americans," sung by African American baritone Paul Robeson, which culminated in a recitation of the Declaration of Independence. In the period just before World War II it thrilled millions. Corwin went on to be one of the most effective radio propagandists of the war. His broadcast on V-E day, "On a Note of Triumph," remained unforgettable to listeners.

Fusions. Another interesting use of radio was *The*

March of Time, a dramatization of the day's news with fictional dialogue. Produced by *Time* magazine, *The March of Time* featured actors such as Welles and Ray Collins portraying public figures such as Roosevelt, Benito Mussolini, and Huey Long. Audiences were less impressed by the dramatizations than the rich baritone of narrator Westbrook van Voorhis, whose announcement that "Time . . . marches on!" became endlessly parodied in later years as "the voice of doom." Also fusing news and drama, fiction and reality, were the "insider" and "gossip" programs of figures such as Walter Winchell and Louella Parsons. Winchell's breathless broadcasts promised the listener the inside story on world events, calamities, and celebrity marriages and divorces. Parsons's broadcasts on *Hollywood Hotel,* along with other programs such as *Forty-five Minutes in Hollywood,* included both gossip and publicity items supplied by Hollywood studios.

News. In the early 1930s news and other information broadcasting were rarely welcomed by radio-station owners. NBC-red, one of the major networks, carried no news programming. NBC-blue had only one news program, as did CBS, although it occasionally carried news commentary during unprofitable hours. Viewing radio essentially as an entertainment and commercial medium, broadcasters were reluctant to enter into news broadcasting. In 1934 they struck a deal with newspaper publishers to limit the number of news broadcasts and delay news releases. The deal failed, but not until advertisers came forward to sponsor news programming — often demanding veto rights over controversial news stories. Nonetheless, some journalists who emerged on radio during the decade set high standards for reporting. Hans von (H. V.) Kaltenborn was a Milwaukeean who had earned a reputation as an insightful commentator on contemporary events for the *Brooklyn Daily Eagle*. His clipped, energetic discussions of world events translated easily to radio. He became famous for his broadcasts from Europe, where he interviewed world leaders such as Mussolini and Adolf Hitler. His broadcasts from Spain during the civil war did much to rally American opinion against fascism. Edward R. Murrow, a young reporter with a rich voice, managed to broadcast from Vienna during the Anschluss and went on to make gripping reports from London during the Blitz. Like Kaltenborn, Murrow was an employee of CBS, which built a large news staff during the latter part of the decade, including reporters such as William L. Shirer, Edgar Ansel Mowrer, Pierre Huss, Frank Gervasi, and Robert Trout. The entire news team participated in the most dramatic news broadcasts of the decade: reports of the Munich Crisis. From 12 to 29 September 1938 American listeners waited by their radios for the CBS broadcasts from Europe, which repeatedly interrupted regular programming with a breathless "Flash!" As Europe was mobilizing for war, Kaltenborn and the others reported on the distribution of gas masks in Prague, Hitler's fiery threats from Berlin, the paralysis of the French cabinet in Paris. Each day war drew closer. Then, at the last minute, British prime minister Neville Chamberlain flew to Germany to meet Hitler and averted war — albeit temporarily. Kaltenborn was there, translating French and German, interpreting events for the American public. The Munich crisis made him the nation's leading broadcast journalist.

Education. Educational programming was virtually nonexistent on radio during the early 1930s. During the 1920s educators around the nation urged the government to nationalize the airwaves and provide instructional, informational, and educational programming, as did the British Broadcasting Corporation. But teachers were completely outmaneuvered by commercial broadcasters. By the 1930s there were only two full-time educational radio stations in the United States — and they, like other part-time, college-based radio stations, broadcast from noncommercial bandwidths and were limited to low-power transmissions. Large commercial broadcasters did transmit educational and public-service programs such as *American School of the Air*, *America's Town Meeting of the Air*, *NBC University of the Air*, *Cavalcade of America*, and *University of Chicago Round Table*, but they did so primarily to deflect criticism of their commercial broadcasts. In 1934 educators and politicians mounted an attack on the overcommercialization of radio with the introduction of the Wagner-Hatfield bill in the Senate. The bill proposed turning over one-fourth of all radio allocations to "educational, religious, agricultural, labor, cooperative and similar non-profit-making associations." The bill

CRASH OF THE HINDENBURG

The crash of the German dirigible *Hindenburg* on 6 May 1937 in Lakehurst, New Jersey, was one of the most spectacular disasters ever captured on film. A total of thirty-six people were killed in the terrible explosions and fire that lit up the evening sky in New Jersey. The coverage of the crash by newsreel and radio brought home the awesome immediacy of the media in delivering information. The images of destruction and death contained in the reports of the crash of the *Hindenburg* were a vision of a coming world that would be more subject to the emotional response of human beings to the suffering of others.

The radio report by Herb Morrison for WLS, Chicago, has become well known for its stark emotionalism, a response not in the later tradition of unemotional reporting.

Here it comes, ladies and gentlemen, and what a sight it is, a thrilling one, a marvelous sight. . . . The sun is striking the windows of the observation deck on the westward side and sparkling like glittering jewels on the background of black velvet. . . . Oh, oh, oh . . . !

It's burst into flames. . . . Get out of the way, please, oh my, this is terrible, oh my, get out of the way, please! It is burning, bursting into flames and is falling. . . . Oh! This is one of the worst. . . . Oh! It's a terrible sight. . . . Oh! . . . and all the humanity.

Morrison's emotional response — he sobbed through most of the broadcast — was seen as a human response to tragedy. It has later been held up as an example of emotion intruding on objective reporting.

Source: Michael Macdonald Mooney, *The Hindenburg* (New York: Dodd, Mead, 1972).

floundered because of a provision allowing nonprofit stations to sell commercial airtime to meet their bills, but an important precedent was set. For the remainder of the 1930s the Federal Communications Commission would review the licenses of broadcasters to ensure that they transmitted educational and public-service programs — which they did, primarily during noncommercial hours such as Sunday morning, when few people were listening.

End of an Era. By 1939 American radio had reached the height of its creativity and power. News broadcasts were providing a degree of insight and immediacy unprecedented in history. The variety and scale of entertainment programming was tremendous. The profits for advertisers and broadcasters from radio were staggering.

Although television technology had been present throughout the 1930s, with competing systems developed by RCA scientist Vladimir K. Zworykin and inventor Philo Farnsworth, the public was for the most part unaware of television, except as a convention in science fiction. Experimental on-air broadcasts of television were conducted during the decade, but the real public debut of television took place 30 April 1939 at the New York World's Fair. The fair's theme was "The World of Tomorrow," and television was just one of the marvels, along with nylon stockings and a cigarette-smoking robot named Elektro. To great public acclaim and much publicity, RCA chairman David Sarnoff opened the fair by addressing the public through television, as did President Franklin D. Roosevelt, who became the first president to appear on television. Sarnoff also took advantage of the fair to display RCA's first television receivers, bulky models with five- and nine-inch cathode ray tubes, ranging in price from $199.50 to $600. Regular broadcasts from NBC's studio 3H in Manhattan, featuring plays, bits of opera, comedians, and singers, kept the screens lit. The public was awed, and those who could afford it immediately placed orders for television receivers. They would have to wait. World War II soon intervened, placing television's development on hold. After the war, however, consumer savings fueled a boom in purchases — making the 1950s the first real decade of television.

Source: Erik Barnouw, *The Golden Web: A History of Broadcasting in the United States, Volume II, 1933 to 1953* (New York: Oxford University Press, 1968).

Yet radio was nearing the end of its days as the foremost communications medium in American culture. Royalty disagreements between musicians and broadcasters were about to be resolved, leading radio to recorded music and spelling the end of live broadcasts of orchestras. The federal government was about to order the end of radio-station chains on the grounds that they violated antitrust laws. World War II led to closer government scrutiny of radio, and its focus shifted to news. Most important, at the 1939 New York World's Fair, the public was introduced to a new electromagnetic technology few had seen before: television. Although World War II would delay the deployment of this new technology, it spelled the end of radio. By 1949 many of the stars of radio had gone to television, and the networks focused their resources on the new medium. The golden age of radio was over.

Sources:
Erik Barnouw, *The Golden Web: A History of Broadcasting in the United*
States: Volume II, 1933 to 1953 (New York: Oxford University Press, 1968);

Barnouw, *A Tower in Babel: A History of Broadcasting in the United States: Volume I, to 1933* (New York: Oxford University Press, 1966);

Cabell Phillips, *From the Crash to the Blitz, 1929–1939* (New York: Macmillan, 1969).

THE MARTIAN INVASION

The Mercury Theatre on the Air. On 30 October 1938, a Sunday evening, the United States was invaded by Martian hordes — or so hundreds of thousands of people believed. Howard Koch's radio adaptation of H. G. Wells's 1898 novel *The War of the Worlds* was performed on CBS radio by the Mercury Theatre on the Air, directed by twenty-four-year-old Orson Welles. CBS took great pains to ensure that the broadcast seem fictional, including changing real names of institutions to made-up names in the script and announcing at the beginning that the program was an adaptation of *The War of the Worlds*. Nonetheless, the clever narrative strategy of Koch and Welles and the verisimilitude of the production caused listeners who did not hear the opening of the show to panic when they heard that Martians had landed in New Jersey and were spreading across the country.

The Dangers of Verisimilitude. Welles and Koch so successfully imitated other types of radio broadcasting — weather reports, dance music, news bulletins — that much of the audience was convinced that they were actually hearing a series of news reports, regardless of their patently fantastic nature. Listeners purportedly heard reporters from Grover's Mill, New Jersey, Washington, D.C., and elsewhere describe Martian spacecraft and weaponry; some reports were cut off in the middle, leaving audiences to suspect the worst. Concerned listeners called police stations and newspaper offices; others jumped in their cars to flee what they believed was imminent death at the hands of technologically superior Martian invaders. In New York sailors on shore leave were requested to return to their ships. Many listeners in one Washington town panicked when the broadcast happened to coincide with a power failure.

Many associated with the project thought it would be a failure because listeners would not accept its fantastic content. Yet the broadcast so successfully convinced so many people of its truth that CBS had to promise not to air any more fictionalized news events. Many commentators believed that the astonishing reaction of the public expressed hidden concerns about the prospect of another world war, to which contemporary events in Europe and Asia were then inexorably leading.

Sources:
Erik Barnouw, *The Golden Web: A History of Broadcasting in the United States, Volume II, 1933 to 1953* (New York: Oxford University Press, 1968);

Hadley Cantril with Hazel Gaudet and Herta Herzog, *The Invasion from Mars: A Study in the Psychology of Panic* (Princeton: Princeton University Press, 1940).

Man in Grover's Mill, New Jersey, prepared for a Martian invasion after Orson Welles's broadcast of *The War of the Worlds* on the Mercury Theatre on the Air, 30 October 1938

NEW MAGAZINES

Boom Times. While the 1930s were a difficult decade for many businesses, magazine publishing flourished during the period. From the pulp magazines to the more respectable "slicks," magazines of widely varying content found a ready market among Americans who wanted either to read about, or, more usually, to distract themselves from, the troubles of the times. General magazines founded before the 1930s, such as the *Saturday Evening Post* and *Reader's Digest,* did well, as did Henry Luce's newsweekly *Time.* Several narrow-interest magazines also succeeded. Though the Depression would hardly seem an ideal time to launch a new business venture, many magazines that have lasted until the end of the twentieth century got their starts in the 1930s.

Success Stories. Luce's business magazine *Fortune,* for instance, made its debut in 1930 and quickly offered some of the best contemporary treatments of the Depression. Its generous use of photographs and stylish design influenced Luce's later creation, *Life,* and many other magazines as well. *Family Circle,* introduced in 1932, was one of the first women's magazines to be distributed exclusively through grocery stores. The marketing strategy worked. Like its similarly distributed competitor *Woman's Day,* introduced in 1937, it offered a combina-

tion of food and entertainment ideas, housekeeping and fashion tips, fiction, and other features.

Magazine Fiction. One of the most noteworthy new magazines of the 1930s was *Story,* introduced in 1931 by Whit Burnett and Martha Foley. During the 1930s it was commonly regarded as the best place to find good contemporary short fiction. Other significant literary periodicals introduced during the decade include the *American Spectator* (1932) — with a founding editorial board of Ernest Boyd, James Branch Cabell, Theodore Dreiser, George Jean Nathan, and Eugene O'Neill — and the *Kenyon Review* (1939), initially edited by John Crowe Ransom, who made the magazine a vehicle for advocating the New Criticism.

Newsmagazines. At the beginning of the 1930s *Time* reigned as the only noteworthy weekly newsmagazine. It remained in this position throughout the decade, but its isolation ended with the introduction of two more newsweeklies in 1933, *U.S. News & World Report* and *News-Week. News-Week* became *Newsweek* in 1937, and — thanks to the financial and marketing expertise brought to the magazine by real estate titan Vincent Astor, railroad heir W. Averell Harriman, McGraw-Hill president Malcolm Muir, and new editor Raymond Moley, a member of Roosevelt's original "brain trust" — it would mount a serious challenge to the dominance of *Time* in the 1940s.

Picture Magazines. In 1936 Luce, always an innovator, introduced *Life*, a general-interest magazine with extensive photographs. The following year Gardner Cowles created a similar magazine, *Look*, as competition. Like *Fortune*, Luce's new magazine featured the work of talented photographers such as Margaret Bourke-White. Both magazines influenced others in ushering in a new era of photojournalism, a term coined in 1938 to describe the telling of a story primarily through photographs. *Life* in particular excelled at this, offering readers stark images of the Depression as well as colorful common-interest stories. Both *Life* and *Look* prospered for decades and were imitated until the market for general-interest magazines began to shrink. *Look* folded in 1971, with *Life* following the next year. *Life* resumed publication in 1978.

Sources:

Amy Janello and Brennon Jones, *The American Magazine* (New York: Abrams, 1991);

Frank Luther Mott, *A History of American Magazines*, 5 volumes (Cambridge, Mass.: Harvard University Press, 1938–1968).

PULP MAGAZINES

A Popular Medium. Inexpensive magazines publishing fiction that appealed to a popular audience dated back to the end of the nineteenth century. The pulp magazines — so named for the thick, inexpensive pulpwood paper on which they were printed — got their start early in the twentieth century. The pulps flourished in the 1930s, along with radio shows and motion pictures, as a reasonably priced form of escapist entertainment. Hundreds of these magazines appeared between the 1920s and the 1950s, when they disappeared because of competition from paperbacks and television. At their peak pulps were purchased by millions of readers.

Violence. The pulps were more adventuresome than radio or movies, which catered to family audiences. The world of the pulps was generally a violent place, whether the stories dealt with cowboys and Indians, crime fighters and gangsters, spacemen and bug-eyed monsters, or warriors such as Robert E. Howard's Conan the Barbarian in *Weird Tales*. Crime was on the minds of many Americans during the 1930s, and the pulps offered plenty of brave, capable men who could fight it successfully. Colorful heroes abounded, including *The Shadow* (introduced in 1931) and *Doc Savage* and *The Spider* (both introduced in 1933). More down-to-earth were the hard-boiled private eyes who appeared in such magazines as *Black Mask* and *Dime Detective*, including Dashiell Hammett's Sam Spade.

Reputations. While the pulps were extremely popular, they were often dismissed as a lowbrow form of entertainment by those who did not read them. Such a perception was natural: the pulps generally featured bright,

Front cover of the fiftieth-anniversary issue of the pulp magazine *Argosy*, 30 July 1932

often lurid covers, usually showing men with weapons and scantily clad women cowering in fear. In addition to using the cheapest paper possible, the magazines crammed stories onto pages, using small type and double columns. They catered to the oddest advertisers imaginable, and they published thousands of poorly written stories. But their detractors also missed out on the early work of several writers who went on to make names for themselves, including Hammett, Robert A. Heinlein, and H. P. Lovecraft. While many editors simply bought material to fill their pages, others — such as Joseph T. Shaw at *Black Mask* and John W. Campbell Jr. at *Astounding Science-Fiction* — took their tasks seriously and made their magazines highly sought-after collectibles for later aficionados.

Categories and Top Magazines. Frank Munsey's *Argosy* and *All-Story*, both launched around the turn of the century, were among the first popular-fiction magazines to be printed on pulp paper. Like many of the first pulps, they offered a variety of story types. *Argosy* continued to do so into the 1930s, after most other magazines had specialized. One of the first specializations was the genre of horror and fantasy. Street and Smith's unsuccessful *The Thrill Book* made its debut in 1919, followed four

Books published with paper covers had appeared before the 1930s. For instance, in 1929 Charles Boni launched Boni Paper Books, which offered paperbound books first through a mail-order club and then, as Bonibooks, through bookstores. The books were beautifully designed, but the series ended in 1932 because of the Depression. The first books published with stiff covers in perfect-bound format in a size close to that of modern paperbacks did not appear until later in the 1930s. The first were Penguin Books, begun in England in 1935. The first American paperback publisher was Pocket Books, started by Robert de Graff in 1939 with Pearl Buck's novel *The Good Earth*. De Graff followed with such titles as James Hilton's *Lost Horizon*, Thorne Smith's *Topper*, and Samuel Butler's *The Way of All Flesh*. Designed to appeal to readers with limited budgets — they sold for twenty-five cents — who desired easily portable books, paperbacks were quickly successful, and Pocket soon had plenty of competition. By the 1940s the popularity of the format was assured.

Sources: Thomas L. Bonn, *Under Cover: An Illustrated History of American Mass Market Paperbacks* (New York: Penguin, 1982);

Piet Schreuders, *Paperbacks, U.S.A.: A Graphic History, 1939–1959*, translated by Josh Pachter (San Diego: Blue Dolphin, 1981).

years later by *Weird Tales*, one of the most striking and respected pulps of the 1920s and 1930s thanks to the contributions of writers such as Howard, Lovecraft, Clark Ashton Smith, Robert Bloch, and many others who made names for themselves in horror, fantasy, and science fiction. Hugo Gernsback's *Amazing Stories* was the first pulp devoted to science fiction, but in the 1930s more writers sought to be published in *Astounding Science-Fiction*, founded in 1930. Under the editorship of Harry Bates and F. Orlin Tremaine, the magazine attracted such popular writers as Murray Leinster, Jack Williamson, E. E. "Doc" Smith, Campbell, and others. When Campbell took over the reins in 1937 the magazine, and science fiction in general, entered a golden age. Previous editors of the magazine had stressed good story-telling, in contrast to Gernsback's fascination with technology; Campbell not only sought well-told stories but stories, as he put it, that could be read as realistic stories set centuries in the future. Writers such as Heinlein, Isaac Asimov, Theodore Sturgeon, and A. E. Van Vogt gave him what he wanted and changed the face of American science fiction in the process. Founded in 1939, *Unknown* was Campbell's noteworthy but largely unsuccessful attempt to challenge *Weird Tales*. As influential in detective fiction as Campbell was in science fiction, "Cap" Shaw took over the six-year-old *Black Mask* in

1926 and nurtured the creation of a whole new style, hard-boiled detective fiction, during his ten years as editor. He was aided by the work of such talented writers as Hammett, Raymond Chandler, and several others who made *Black Mask* the classiest pulp on the market. Its rival *Dime Detective* also published several noteworthy writers and stories. In addition, pulp magazines devoted to such genres as general adventure, the Western, sports fiction, romance and sexier "spicy" stories, and prototypes of the comic-book superhero were also popular during the decade.

The Beginning of the End. The 1930s were the last prosperous decade for the pulps. Media that proved to be serious competitors in the 1940s — paperbacks, comic books, television — had their beginnings in the 1930s, and the paper shortages caused by World War II drove many pulp magazines out of business. By the 1950s the heyday of the pulps had passed.

Sources:
Tony Goodstone, ed., *The Pulps: Fifty Years of American Popular Culture* (New York: Chelsea House, 1970);

Ron Goulart, *Cheap Thrills: An Informal History of the Pulp Magazines* (New Rochelle, N.Y.: Arlington House, 1972);

Lee Server, *Danger Is My Business: An Illustrated History of the Fabulous Pulp Magazines* (San Francisco: Chronicle, 1993).

RADICAL JOURNALS

Heyday. The 1930s were the heyday of the radical journal. Magazines and newspapers of political opinion, cultural criticism, science, and literature, the radical journal was an important forum for expression during the decade. Although radical journals never had substantial readership, their influence on American intellectual and political life was great. Published primarily in New York City, journals such as *Partisan Review, The New Masses*, and *Modern Monthly* shaped opinion far from Manhattan, even influencing political opinion abroad. The journals also provided many writers outlets for work that might otherwise have gone unpublished during the Depression, and they gave writers and critics who would become well known in subsequent decades their first experience in political journalism. Most radical journals were exceptionally critical of capitalism, and almost all advocated some type of reform. But they also analyzed, criticized, and introduced new art and literature. Especially in New York, the radical journals of the 1930s were at the center of a vibrant literary culture.

From Masses to New Masses. Most radical journals of the 1930s followed the stylistic precedent set by the groundbreaking journal *The Masses* (1911–1918). A combination of socialist advocacy, muckraking journalism, poetry, and art, *The Masses* featured illustrations by well-known artists such as George Bellows and John Sloan and established the reputations of important American writers such as John Reed, Max Eastman, and Floyd Dell. The combination of cultural criticism, Greenwich Village bohemianism, and socialist advocacy in *The Masses* was imitated by other journals such as *Smart Set, The Seven Arts, The Dial,* and *The Liberator* (the successor to *The Masses*). Few of these magazines survived World War I. Like *The Masses,* many succumbed to government censorship, which became particularly fierce during the red scares of 1919–1920. The 1920s were also profoundly unreceptive to radical combinations of art, literature, and politics. Still some radical journals soldiered on. In 1926 the remains of *The Liberator* and *The Masses* staff launched a new journal, *The New Masses.* Like *The Masses,* it featured art and politics and was important in rallying support for radical causes, such as the protest against the executions of anarchists Nicola Sacco and Bartolomeo Vanzetti, widely believed to be innocent of the murders of which they had been convicted. With the Depression *The New Masses* became an important shaper of public opinion, its denunciations of capitalism keyed to the sentiments of the time. It was also one of the best sources for information on labor activism, civil rights, and artistic innovation. It spawned a host of imitators.

Party Lines. The radical journals were some of the best places for American readers to find discussions of cutting-edge artistic and philosophical developments such as suprematism, Futurism, Dadaism, Nietzscheanism, and psychoanalysis. As advocates of political reform or revolution, they were also inevitably caught up in the polarized politics of the 1930s. By 1930 *The New Masses* was firmly affiliated with, and subordinated to, the Communist Party of the United States. Under the leadership of an acerbic intellectual named Mike Gold, it faithfully interpreted the day's events from the perspective of the party leadership, itself parroting the party "line" on events dictated by Moscow. When Joseph Stalin exiled Leon Trotsky from Russia, *The New Masses* condemned Trotsky — even though he had been the darling of leftist intellectuals during the 1920s. When Moscow quit lumping liberals and fascists together in 1935, *The New Masses* also quit the practice; when Stalin signed a nonaggression pact with Hitler in 1939, *The New Masses* warmed toward the fascists. Many intellectuals were less galled by such ideological shifts than by the tendency of *The New Masses* to condemn art, literature, or journalism that was not sufficiently "proletarian." The Depression caused many middle-class intellectuals — including Theodore Dreiser, Waldo Frank, Sherwood Anderson, Edmund Wilson, Granville Hicks, Malcolm Cowley, Lionel Trilling, and John Dos Passos — to endorse communism and socialism as a means of resolving the nation's problems. Some such writers journeyed to Harlan County, Kentucky, early in the decade to report on a bloody miners' strike. Fifty-two of them, including Anderson, Wilson, Cowley, Frank, Dos Passos, Lincoln Steffens, Erskine Caldwell, Countee Cullen, and Langston Hughes, endorsed William Z. Foster, the Communist Party presidential candidate in 1932. Their efforts meant little to Gold and *The New Masses,* who continually castigated such intellectuals for their ideological and artistic deviations from Commu-

Front cover of the communist magazine *The New Masses*

nist orthodoxy. Gold was searching for a journalism that would appeal to the "working stiffs" in America and pressured writers to work in a "realistic" idiom appropriate for factory workers. Eventually, he began to favor the writings of factory workers over those of the intellectuals. *The New Masses* and the Communist Party sponsored the John Reed Clubs writers' workshops for aspiring workers. Toeing the party line became too difficult for talented and idiosyncratic middle-class writers. American intellectuals had to "take Communism away from the Communists," asserted Wilson, and they sought a more heterodox forum for their opinions. In V. F. Calverton's *The Modern Quarterly* they found such an organ.

The Modern Quarterly. *The Modern Quarterly* (later *The Modern Monthly*) was the almost single-handed production of a Baltimore autodidact, George Goetz, who took the pen name V. F. Calverton. Begun in 1923, the journal reflected Calverton's sweeping interest in just about everything imaginable, from communism to fascism to psychoanalysis, civil rights, anthropology, sex, art history, and literary criticism. The journal was eclectic, exciting, iconoclastic. In its pages leading intellectuals and superb writers debated Stalinism, fascism, the New Deal, romantic poetry, and American history. Unlike *The New Masses,* Calverton boasted that he at one time or another printed something by "almost every left-wing liberal and radical who had artistic aspirations." In 1934 Wilson joined Calverton as an editor of *The Modern Quarterly,* and it became an important journal for anti-

Stalinist and anti-Communist leftists, including Max Eastman and Sidney Hook. When Calverton died in 1940 he took with him one of the most interesting publications of the decade.

Popular Front. Tensions between middle-class intellectuals and Communists diminished greatly after Moscow announced the policy of the Popular Front in 1935. No longer did Gold and *The New Masses* suggest that the intellectuals were too middle class; now middle class and working class were to unite to combat fascism. Many of the country's leading middle-class, liberal journals of opinion, including *The Nation* and *The New Republic*, now became repositories for many of the same types of political and cultural analysis appearing the *The New Masses* and *The Modern Quarterly*. Under the editorial leadership of Malcolm Cowley, *The New Republic* featured the same sort of social criticism found in *The New Masses*. The association was too much for many intellectuals who had broken with Gold and the Communists, Popular Front or not. Many protested when Cowley followed Gold and Moscow in representing Stalin's purge trials as legitimate judicial procedures rather than kangaroo courts and in supporting a Soviet Union that had become murderous and authoritarian under Stalin. Cowley argued with his liberal friends until 1939, when he joined them in condemning the Hitler-Stalin Pact. *The New Masses*, naturally enough, approved of the treaty; but liberal journals such as *The New Republic* used the occasion to depart from the Left and rejoin the center.

Partisan Review. Another radical journal, *Partisan Review*, broke with the Communists before the Hitler-Stalin Pact. Originally a product of the John Reed Clubs, *Partisan Review* made its debut in 1933. It featured the usual combination of art and politics, but its editors, Philip Rahv and William Phillips, quickly chafed at the restrictions imposed on their journal by Communist orthodoxy. The two were far more interested in literature than in politics, and they admired the innovations of the literary modernists before World War I. Although they originally tried to develop a Marxist/modernist aesthetic in their magazine, they abandoned the project in 1936 and quit the Communist Party. In 1937 they resurrected *Partisan Review* as an independent Marxist quarterly. Thereafter, the magazine enjoyed remarkable growth, becoming notable by the 1950s as a publisher of Delmore Schwartz, Dwight Macdonald, Robert Penn Warren, Stephen Spender, Mary McCarthy, Clement Greenburg, Irving Howe, James Dickey, Norman Mailer, Amos Oz, and many other writers. From the late 1930s to the early 1950s, *Partisan Review* was the foremost journal of literature, criticism, and politics in the United States.

Writers on the Right. Left-wing writers were not the only intellectuals publishing journals in the 1930s. Conservative journals of opinion, criticism, and the arts also existed, although they tended toward aesthetic issues far more than politics. H. L. Mencken distinguished himself as America's foremost iconoclast in the pages of *American Mercury*. The *National Republic* called itself "A Magazine of Fundamental Americanism" and advocated military preparedness, high protective tariffs, and fundamentalist Christianity. *American Review*, edited by Seward Collins, embraced almost any antimodern philosophy of the age, from Allen Tate's southern Agrarianism to Irving Babbitt's New Humanism to Benito Mussolini's Fascism.

Other Journals. The richness of radical journalism in the 1930s is not only evident in quality journals, such as *Partisan Review*, but in the many lesser journals that circulated throughout the decade. *Menorah Journal* began in 1915 as a magazine designed to promote a nonsectarian and humanist spirit in the university. By the 1930s it was one of the leading journals of political and cultural opinion and gave some of the best writers of the time, including Lionel Trilling, Elliot Cohen, Herbert Solow, and Clifton Fadiman, their start. Catholic intellectuals published four periodicals: *America, Commonweal, Catholic World*, and the more radical *Catholic Worker*. Protestants sponsored *Christian Century*. Many ethnic and political newspapers published literature, criticism, and art, including *Labor Age, The Daily Worker, The Communist, Challenge of Youth, Negro Worker, Harlem Liberator, Southern Worker*, the NAACP periodical *The Crisis*, the African American *Chicago Defender*, the *Jewish Daily Forward*, the Italian American *Il Mondo*, and Carlo Tresca's Italian-language *Il Martello*. American partisans of Leon Trotsky's version of communism published *The Militant* and *The New International*; members of the Socialist Labor Party published *The Weekly People*; and the Socialist Party published *Appeal* and *American Socialist Quarterly*. There were also many other journals, including *Americana, The New Tide, Prolit Folio, Rebel Poet, Symposium, Anvil, Miscellany, Labor Action, New Militant, Left Front, International, Midland, New Challenge*, and the superb socialist theoretical journal *Marxist Quarterly*. All such journals and the talented writers who worked for them made the 1930s one of the most exceptional decades for critical and political publishing in American history.

Source:
Daniel Aaron, *Writers on the Left* (New York: Harcourt, Brace & World, 1961).

THE RISE OF THE AMERICAN NEWSPAPER GUILD

A White-Collar Union. A union of newspaper reporters and editors, the American Newspaper Guild (ANG) was founded in 1933 as a result of the Depression; by 1936 it had affiliated with the American Federation of Labor. One of the nation's first white-collar unions in the United States, it protected the job security of members and agitated for higher wages and better working conditions. The rise of the guild was highly controversial and was accompanied by conservative charges that the ANG was a communist agency seeking to take over the nation's press. The growth of the union was nonetheless striking, and by the end of the decade the ANG had become a permanent feature of the news business.

Romance and Reality. Although newspaper work was often romanticized during the 1930s, with movies and novels portraying the reporter's life as adventurous and exciting, the reality was far less glamorous. Most newspaper reporters were poorly paid, with small-town and suburban reporters earning as little as six dollars per week or one dollar per day. Working hours were long, ten to twelve hours per day, six days a week. Reporters were regularly told to "stick with" a story even if it meant working fifteen-hour days or longer. So poor was the pay and so long were the hours that many newspapers discouraged their reporters from marrying, aware that such a schedule could not be followed if reporters had family commitments. Walter Howey, the managing editor of the *Chicago Tribune*, threatened to cut salaries or fire reporters if they married. Firings were simple for management. Reporters rarely had job security or severance pay and were often informed of pay cuts on payday. As a result of these conditions, graft was a constant of newspaper life in the 1930s. Reporters routinely took bribes and kickbacks for stories favorable to wealthy and powerful figures. Sportswriters were especially venal, taking shares of sporting events for their coverage. The boxer Gene Tunney, for example, paid 5 percent of his purse to sportswriters early in his career. Although some newspaper columnists and reporters earned high salaries (newspaper publishers were often fabulously wealthy), for the majority of those in the newspaper business work was long; pay was low; the temptation of corruption was great; and the rewards were few.

Depression. The Depression made a bad situation worse. Newspaper revenue from advertising dried up, falling almost 40 percent from 1929 to 1933. Radio increasingly seized the attention of advertisers — as well as their business. By 1933 radio was absorbing almost half the advertising revenues in the United States. Newspapers around the country ceased operations or merged with one another. By 1933 more than 87 percent of the cities with populations less than one thousand had only one newspaper. In most large cities only one morning and one evening newspaper remained financially viable. The newspaper crunch meant that few reporters could choose between employers. And most newspapers, seeking to reduce operating expenses, balanced their budgets by firing reporters and editors, lowering the wages of the remainder, and increasing the workload. The Bureau of Labor Statistics reported that among thirty-one dailies the number of editorial workers dropped from 1,506 in April 1930 to 1,248 in April 1933. In San Francisco reporters took a 10 percent pay cut from the city's three newspapers; the wages of reporters in Cleveland were cut by 30 and 40 percent. Henry Justin Smith of the *Chicago Daily News* argued that such policies would improve newspaper reporting, leading to "survival of the fittest," but few reporters saw it that way. Job insecurity was

constant. Most reporters feared being dismissed with barely a week's pay, a frightening prospect during the Depression.

Organization. Unlike the typesetters, teamsters, and other blue-collar workers in the newspaper industry, reporters were not unionized. Cutting the salaries of typesetters would lead to strikes and undermine production, but dismissing reporters had few repercussions for publishers. Reporters naturally concluded that they could improve their job prospects by organizing. There had been efforts to unionize writers and editors prior to the 1930s. A branch of the International Typographical Union tried to organize reporters in the 1890s. Boston newspapermen organized in 1919. Editorial workers in Scranton, Pennsylvania, unionized in 1907. With the exception of the Scranton union, almost all these efforts failed. Most reporters and editors thought of themselves as professionals, white-collar workers, individualists. "DITCH DIGGERS HAVE UNIONS WE DONT," telegraphed two Chicago newsmen responding to an invitation to join the ANG. Such attitudes were common as the ANG organized, but conditions during the Depression forced a shift in perspective and gave the ANG an intellectual cohesiveness its predecessors lacked.

The NRA. The ANG began, essentially, as a professional association. Opposition to it by newspaper publishers turned it toward the trade-union movement. The central issue between the ANG and publishers concerned the relationship of reporters and editors to the industrial codes established by President Franklin D. Roosevelt's National Recovery Administration (NRA). The NRA divided markets and granted industries immunity from antitrust laws in exchange for their adherence to industrial codes that mandated a fair price for goods and services and higher wages and improved working conditions for workers. Hoping the NRA would organize the newspaper business and grant them job security and higher wages, reporters and editors began the ANG as a series of independent regional associations designed to bring their case before the government body establishing industrial codes. On 15 December 1933 the ANG established itself as a national body, with noted columnist Heywood Broun its president and foremost spokesman. Broun and the ANG tried to get the NRA administrators to establish several provisions for reporters and editors in its industrial codes for newspapers: a five-day, forty-hour workweek; overtime compensation; restoration of pay cuts; vacations; a minimum wage; and advance notice for dismissals.

Opposition. Unfortunately for the ANG, the American Newspaper Publishers Association (ANPA) had their own representatives and sought to block the creation of any NRA code that fundamentally altered their business practices. The ANPA was particularly troubled by NRA codes eliminating child labor (hence newsboys), by provisions for unionization and limiting working hours per week, and by governmental licensing of industries (which was believed to interfere with freedom of the press). Ultimately, the ANPA prevailed on the government to create an industrial code for newspapers that maintained publisher control of the business. While the NRA codes did mandate suggestions forwarded by the ANG, loopholes and temporary exceptions to the code undermined their utility in changing the work conditions of reporters and editors. Publishers also began dismissing ANG leaders from their jobs. Many ANG members agitated for the type of job action typical of trade unions: the strike.

Strikes and Affiliation. The first ANG strikes were against New York papers in the summer and fall of 1934. Strikers at the *Long Island Daily Press,* the *Jewish Daily Bulletin,* and the *Staten Island Advance* generally were well paid and well treated. What they struck for was the right to associate with the ANG. Often organized labor lent their support; during the Staten Island strike, the projectionists' union lent the strikers a sound truck. These short strikes accomplished little in the newspaper room, but the better relations between the ANG and the trade unions were a harbinger of things to come. On 17 November the editorial staff of the *Newark Ledger* walked out, angered over lack of job security and low pay. It was the first strike at a major, mass-circulation newspaper. Despite charges of communist subversion and a court injunction, the strike ended in victory for the guild on 28 March 1935. That victory, combined with the 1935 Supreme Court ruling eliminating the NRA, led the guild in a more radical direction. In October 1935 it successfully won a strike against the *New Amsterdam News,* a black-owned New York newspaper opposed to guild organizing. In February 1936 the Scripps-Howard chain of newspapers negotiated new contracts with regional representatives of the ANG. In that same month members of the Milwaukee ANG struck the Hearst newspaper, the *News.* Hearst put up a tremendous fight, refusing to meet with Broun and representatives of the ANG. Strikers were fired. Injunctions against picket lines were secured. Strikers, including Broun, were arrested during labor rallies. Strikers responded by calling every number in the Milwaukee phone book and canvasing the city, door to door, in an effort to get subscribers to boycott the paper. ANG members at Hearst's paper in Seattle mounted a sympathy strike. Most important, however, was the ANG's decision in June to affiliate with the AFL, thus gaining enormous political clout with which to force a resolution. On 2 September 1936 the strike ended, fundamentally in victory for the guild. The next year the ANG switched its affiliation to the Congress of Industrial Organizations (CIO), extending its membership throughout the newspaper business. Far from being the professional association its original members intended, the ANG had become a part of the trade union movement and a permanent feature of the publishing industry.

Sources:

John Diggins, *Up From Communism: Conservative Odysseys in American Intellectual History* (New York: Harper & Row, 1975);

Daniel J. Leab, *A Union of Individuals: The Formation of the American Newspaper Guild, 1933–1936* (New York: Columbia University Press, 1970);

Richard Pells, *Radical Visions and American Dreams: Culture and Social Thought in the Depression Years* (Middletown, Conn.: Wesleyan University Press, 1973);

Alan Wald, *The New York Intellectuals: The Rise and Decline of the Anti-Stalinist Left From the 1930s to the 1980s* (Chapel Hill: University of North Carolina Press, 1987).

HEADLINE MAKERS

MOSES ANNENBERG

1875-1942

NEWSPAPER PUBLISHER AND RACING-NEWS ENTREPRENEUR

Immigrant Beginnings. The son of Prussian Jewish immigrants, Moses Annenberg rose from poverty to become a powerful newspaper publisher and racing-news entrepreneur. In 1900, after a meager education and jobs as a junkman, a Western Union messenger, a livery stable boy, and a bartender, Annenberg became a subscription solicitor for the *Chicago Evening American* newspaper, recently purchased by William Randolph Hearst. In 1904 Hearst started a morning newspaper, the *Examiner*, and appointed Annenberg circulation manager to establish a place for the paper in the highly competitive morning market. It was Annenberg's job to obtain prime sales locations on street corners. The competition quickly erupted into gang warfare, and Annenberg, along with his brother Max, were deeply involved in the violence. His involvement colored Annenberg's reputation throughout his life.

Wisconsin and Success. In 1907 Annenberg moved to Milwaukee, Wisconsin, and started an agency to distribute all the Chicago newspapers. The agency was successful, and he started similar businesses in twenty other cities. He also earned a large amount of money with a promotion idea devised by his wife. With the newspapers he distributed coupons offering teaspoons decorated with state seals. Annenberg invested the money in Milwaukee real estate.

Publishing with Hearst. In 1917 Annenberg became the publisher of Arthur Brisbane's *Wisconsin News* and

quickly tripled its circulation to eighty thousand. Brisbane then sold his interest in the paper to Hearst. After a year Hearst moved Annenberg to New York, where he became circulation manager for all Hearst's New York papers and magazines. In 1924 Hearst named him president and publisher of the newest Hearst paper, the *New York Mirror*.

Horse-Racing Papers. In 1922 Annenberg had bought the *Daily Racing Form*, which printed information about horse racing. In 1926 he resigned his position with Hearst to concentrate on serving the horse-race business. He bought many other racing papers, and in 1927 he became involved in racing wire services, which supplied quick information to subscribers, mostly bookmakers. He bought interests in competing businesses in the wire-service industry and used his positions to drive out his partners. After 1930 Annenberg had a virtual monopoly in the wire-service business, transmitting information from twenty-nine tracks to fifteen thousand betting establishments around the country.

Prospering through Depression. In 1930 Annenberg's net worth was estimated at more than $8 million. By 1938 that figure had increased to almost $20 million. He did not forget his roots in the newspaper business. In 1934 he founded the *Miami Tribune*, which he sold in 1937. In 1936 Annenberg bought the respected 107-year-old *Philadelphia Inquirer*. By adding more comic strips and a weekend magazine with photographs he was able to increase circulation by 23 percent during the week and by 55 percent on Sundays.

Trouble with the Government. In 1939 U.S. attorney general Frank Murphy announced that a grand jury was looking into Annenberg's tax returns from 1932 to 1936. Annenberg was indicted for filing false returns for those years and for evading more than $3 million in taxes. The government also began investigating his track-information monopoly. Annenberg immediately sold his wire-service business, and in 1940 he pleaded guilty to one year of evading taxes. He also agreed to pay nearly $10 million to settle any and all claims dating back to 1923. In return for the dropping of other charges against him and his son Walter, he was sentenced to three years in prison.

Death. In June 1942, after serving two years of his sentence, Annenberg was released from prison. A month later he died of a brain tumor. Even after all his legal expenses, Annenberg's property was valued at $8 million when it was reorganized after his death into Triangle Publications, under the direction of Walter Annenberg. Walter Annenberg later became the publisher of *TV Guide* and a United States ambassador.

Source:
John E. Cooney, *The Annenbergs* (New York: Simon & Schuster, 1982).

EDWIN HOWARD ARMSTRONG

1890-1954

INVENTOR OF FM RADIO

Last Great Inventor. Edwin Howard Armstrong ranks with Alexander Graham Bell and Thomas Edison as one of the greatest of American inventors. Like them, he was a gifted and original thinker, as responsible for modern radio as Edison was for the electric light or Bell for the telephone. Like them, Armstrong worked obsessively and held himself to high moral standards. Unlike them, Armstrong was born in a century when science was rapidly moving from the inventor's shed to the corporate laboratory. In a sense Armstrong was the last of the great nineteenth-century inventors, an individualistic genius who fit poorly into the modern technocracy. While Bell and Edison reaped the rewards of their skills in wealth and prestige and built modern corporations on their inventions, Armstrong spent his life defending his inventions from corporations and had his wealth and prestige stripped from him. By 1954, despondent, bankrupt, his life and marriage shattered by four decades of lawsuits, he killed himself. It was a tragic end for one of the most gifted engineers of the twentieth century.

Background. Edwin Howard Armstrong was born in 1890 to a prosperous New York family. His mother was a teacher, and his father was an executive for Oxford University Press. Armstrong grew up immersed in middle-class Presbyterian values, eagerly absorbing tales of thrift, persistence, and honesty associated with successful inventors such as Edison and Guglielmo Marconi. By high school he was consumed with the new "wireless" (radio) craze, building his own receivers and antennas and communicating in Morse code with stations as far away as Key West. He attended the School of Mines, Engineer-ing and Chemistry at Columbia University, where he learned about the latest innovations in electricity and physics. By the time he was graduated in June 1913 he had earned distinction as a highly unorthodox, inquisitive, and original student. He had already built two inventions that would transform radio technology: a feedback circuit that increased the receptive power of radio receivers, and a feedback circuit that transmitted continuous radio waves. These two inventions made modern radio possible. He followed them with the superheterodyne, a device capable of tuning in and deciphering radio signals transmitted at a very high frequency. Built while Armstrong served in the U.S. Army Signal Corps during World War I, the superheterodyne remains the tuning mechanism used in radio and television today. By the early 1920s the patent rights for the superheterodyne and a superregeneration circuit had made Armstrong wealthy, and he was among the most acclaimed inventors in the United States. By the 1930s his title to his inventions had been stripped from him.

Patents. Armstrong filed for a patent on his feedback receiver on 19 October 1913; on 18 December of that year he filed for a patent on the circuit capable of generating continuous radio waves. But he was too late. His circuit worked in a device invented by Lee De Forest, the audion. De Forest filed his own patent for a similar amplification circuit in 1915. Although De Forest did not file for his patent until after Armstrong had filed for his, on the face of it De Forest had a strong claim to have built the refinement to his own invention, which he claimed to have done in 1912. For the next nineteen years Armstrong and De Forest filed infringement suit after infringement suit against one another. The suits demonstrated the strength of Armstrong's claim, and he won several judgments against De Forest. But the regeneration circuit became essential in commercial radio, and large corporations, such as Radio Corporation of America (RCA) and American Telephone and Telegraph (AT&T), had vested interests in the outcome of the case, royalties to be gained by their ownership of De Forest's patent. Despite the previous rulings against De Forest, RCA and AT&T appealed the case to the U.S. Supreme Court, and AT&T hired a former associate justice of the Supreme Court, Charles Evans Hughes, to argue for de Forest. Armstrong lost the case and his legal right to royalties from his invention. Similarly, AT&T used a dispute with a former associate of Armstrong's, Lucian Levy, to file a case against Armstrong's patent rights to the superheterodyne. In 1928 the courts awarded the patent to AT&T. Armstrong, however, was undeterred. In 1933 he filed a case on somewhat different grounds to regain his patent to the regeneration circuit and once again won decisions against De Forest in the lower courts. In the Supreme Court, however, Armstrong was again defeated in a decision whose embrace of flawed science was condemned by many engineers and scientists. In 1934 the professional body of the Institute of Radio

Engineers affirmed that, whatever the judgment of the Supreme Court, Armstrong was the inventor of the regeneration circuit.

FM. Chastened by his experience in the courts, Armstrong returned to his laboratory for his next technological breakthrough, FM (frequency modulation) radio. FM radio solved one of the most vexing problems in early radio, the presence of static in the transmission. Caused by electrical interference, thunderstorms, car engines, and sunspots, static frequently interrupted radio broadcasts. Armstrong solved the problem by inventing a technology that most engineers and scientists considered impossible in theory and unworkable in practice. Rather than modulating the amplitude (height) of the carrier wave, Armstrong varied the frequency (length) of the carrier wave. FM required that Armstrong construct a completely new technology of broadcasting, and it worked. FM transmissions were free of static and, moreover, carried a wider range of sound, giving birth to the first high-fidelity transmissions. Once again, Armstrong had revolutionized radio.

Stalled. Armstrong's revolutionary technology, however, was too radical for the times. Despite conclusive tests demonstrating the efficacy of FM, skeptics denied what their own ears heard. Mathematical models had indicated that FM could not work, and therefore they remained convinced that it did not work. Commercial radio, moreover, was becoming slightly less lucrative. The Depression cut into advertising revenues, and technological improvements in AM transmission drove down the profitability of radio receivers. FM technology would entail huge start-up costs and compete with existing AM systems, further eroding profits. Large corporations such as RCA were banking on a new broadcast technology, television, and were scarcely interested in FM, which they considered merely a refinement in AM broadcasting. Armstrong, unfortunately, was contractually bound to offer the new technology to RCA. RCA did not want the new system, but they did not want their competitors to get it either, and they did everything they could to prevent the introduction of FM. Because RCA would not allow him to use their transmitters, Armstrong applied for an experimental broadcast license to begin FM transmissions. Then RCA imposed on friends at the Federal Communications Commission (FCC) to deny Armstrong a license. With virtually no merit, RCA contested Armstrong's FM patents with the U.S. Patent Office and then imitated his circuits in slightly modified form, arguing that their technology was original and unique. Simultaneously, RCA engineers testified in FCC hearings and in the newspapers that FM technology was unworkable.

World War II. World War II disproved the claims of FM detractors. The new technology proved vital to battlefront communications, becoming standard issue in walkie-talkies, tanks, and jeeps. Armstrong himself modified the technology for use in radar, creating early-warning radar and other applications that remain classified in the 1990s. In 1946 he successfully bounced an FM-modified radar signal off the moon, inaugurating modern earth-to-space communications. As a patriotic gesture, Armstrong waived all rights to patent royalties on his products for the duration of the war, an act that cost him millions. RCA was not nearly so generous, receiving cost-plus contracts for goods based on Armstrong's inventions and an annual royalty of $4 million.

Last Battle. The efficacy of FM during the war moved RCA to redouble its efforts to squelch it after the war. In 1945, with prodding from RCA, the FCC moved FM transmissions from the very high frequency bandwidths of the electromagnetic spectrum to the untested ultra high frequency range. The decision immediately made fifty FM broadcasting stations and a half million FM radios obsolete. When the FCC followed this decision with one reducing the wattage of FM transmitters, FM seemed nearly dead. But Armstrong fought on. He modified FM technology for the new transmission bands and continued to challenge RCA in court. Ultimately, in the 1970s, Armstrong's efforts resulted in FM becoming the dominant radio medium around the world. In the 1950s, however, Armstrong was racing against time and money. RCA's efforts to marginalize FM effectively limited Armstrong's royalties and income; patents on some of his technologies were due to expire in 1950, after which his abilities to pay court costs would be further compromised. RCA stalled, tying Armstrong up in court, bleeding his financial resources. Still Armstrong was able to produce technical innovations. In 1953 he and his associate John Bose developed FM multiplexing, the sending of different signals on a single carrier wave, which made stereo broadcasting possible. It was his last invention. By 1954 Armstrong was bankrupt, and his thirty-year marriage had collapsed. On Sunday, 31 January 1954, Armstrong jumped from a thirteenth-floor apartment in New York City. Less than a month later, David Sarnoff, chairman of RCA, announced to stockholders that RCA's profits had reached an all-time high of $850 million.

Source:
Tom Lewis, *Empire of the Air: The Men Who Made Radio* (New York: HarperCollins, 1991).

AL CAPP

1909-1979

COMIC-STRIP CREATOR

Famous Comic-Strip Artist. At age twenty-five Al Capp created the comic strip *Li'l Abner*, which he wrote and drew until he ended it forty-four years later. During his career Capp was one of the best-known comic-strip creators in the United States, and he courted the media attention that came his way. John Steinbeck hailed him as "the best satirist since Laurence Sterne," adding, "He has taken our customs, our dreams, our habits of thought, our social structure, our economics, examined them gently like amusing bugs. Then he has pulled a nose a little longer, made outstanding ears a little more outstanding, described it in dreadful folk poetry and returned it to us in a hilarious picture of our ridiculous selves."

Early Life and Career. Born Alfred Gerald Caplin in New Haven, Connecticut, he grew up experiencing hunger and want, which he made humorous in the hillbilly setting of *Li'l Abner*. At age nine he lost his left leg after being run over by an ice truck; as a result he read voraciously and took an interest in art at an early age. In his mid teens he hitchhiked through the South, visiting Memphis and the Ozarks, where he gained impressions of backwoods life that would later fuel his career. He studied art at several schools before dropping out to join the Associated Press in 1932. Working in New York, he drew a daily strip called *Mister Gilfeather* with little success. He left the Associated Press a few months later and shortly thereafter met Ham Fisher, the creator of the successful comic strip *Joe Palooka*. Fisher hired the young artist to help him with an overdue strip and then hired him as an assistant. Though Capp later referred to Fisher as a leper and "a veritable goldmine of swinishness," he learned a great deal about the comic-strip business under Fisher. He did some writing for *Joe Palooka* as well as some of the artistic chores. In particular, he began experimenting with southern characters and began creating sample strips of his own.

Success. After King Features hesitated about accepting *Li'l Abner,* United Features took up the strip, which made its first appearance on 13 August 1934. Capp, as he began to call himself, got less money but more artistic freedom with United. The money soon failed to matter, as *Li'l Abner* steadily grew in popularity — helped by a contemporary fascination with images of backwoods America. Hailed as a skilled satirist, Capp became a wealthy man. Set in the fictional hillbilly community of Dogpatch, *Li'l Abner* presented a broad cast of characters, including the dense but good-hearted Abner Yokum, his Mammy and Pappy, and the beautiful Daisy Mae, who longs to marry the virile but clueless Abner. Through his characters and setting Capp was able to satirize humanity's worst characteristics while keeping humor and occasionally sentiment close at hand. At the height of its popularity in the 1940s, the strip appeared in nine hundred newspapers across the country, and its characters appeared in comic books and movies and even on Broadway. In the late 1930s it also introduced a concept that was practiced in many high schools and colleges during the 1940s and 1950s, the Sadie Hawkins Day, an annual event in which single women would pursue single men.

Publicity. With the success of *Li'l Abner* Capp was almost as much in the public eye as his creations. He appeared in magazines and was interviewed on radio and television, and he increasingly turned over much of the work on *Li'l Abner* to assistants. The strip was always his, though, and in the 1960s his growing conservatism and his satires of liberal causes and figures lost him many young readers. The strip was dropped from several papers in the 1970s before he decided to drop the strip itself.

Sources:

Arthur Asa Berger, *Li'l Abner: A Study in American Satire* (New York: Twayne, 1970);

Ron Goulart, ed., *The Encyclopedia of American Comics* (New York & Oxford: Facts On File, 1990);

Richard Marschall, *America's Great Comic-Strip Artists* (New York: Abbeville, 1989).

PHILO T. FARNSWORTH

1906-1971

TELEVISION PIONEER

The Importance of Technology. The real pioneers of television were not entertainers or financiers; they were scientists. One of the most important was Philo Farnsworth, who when only a teenager designed the basic system needed to transfer moving pictures over the air waves.

High-School Prodigy. Farnsworth was fifteen years old, and a high-school student, when he read of the research being carried out in the Soviet Union by Boris Rosing on transmitting moving images by electricity. He quickly designed a schematic drawing of the required system. Farnsworth entered Brigham Young University the next year and remained for two years until the death of his father. A San Francisco banker named William H. Crocker built a laboratory for Farnsworth so that he could continue his research into the practical development of his television system.

Patents and Corporations. Farnsworth developed his laboratory into the Farnsworth Radio and Television Corporation, which later became the Capehart Farnsworth Electronics Company. In 1927 he transmitted his television picture. In 1928 he received his first patent, covering a complete electronic television film.

Competition. By working essentially on his own without major corporate backing, Farnsworth was at a great disadvantage. His main competition was the Radio Corporation of America (RCA), whose effort was headed by David Sarnoff and the scientific genius of Vladimir Zworykin. Zworykin had been a graduate student of Boris Rosing in Russia and was working on a television based on a system different from Farnsworth's.

Public Demonstration and Legal Troubles. During the 1930s Farnsworth's research costs were borne by the Philco Corporation, whose resources were less than

RCA's. Farnsworth gave a public demonstration of his television system at the Franklin Institute in Philadelphia for ten days in 1935. Despite the public success much of the 1930s was taken up with patent litigation. Unable to match the financial might of RCA, Farnsworth finally settled with RCA on a cross-patent agreement in which Farnsworth shared in the profits from the development of RCA's system. In 1949 Farnsworth's company was bought by International Telephone and Telegraph (ITT), which kept Farnsworth as the head of its research unit. During his career Farnsworth held more than 135 patents in television and other fields.

The Place of Research. Farnsworth was a throwback to American entrepreneurs such as Henry Ford who developed their technology into large manufacturing businesses. By the 1930s American business had changed, and corporate finances were able to overwhelm individual American genius. Still, American television would not have developed in the 1930s and 1940s without the vision of Farnsworth.

Sources:

Michael Emery and Edwin Emery, *The Press and America: An Interpretive History of the Mass Media* (Englewood Cliffs, N. J.: Prentice Hall, 1992);

George Everson, *The Story of Television: The Life of Philo T. Farnsworth* (New York: Norton, 1949).

CHESTER GOULD

1900-1985

COMIC-STRIP CREATOR

A Unique Comic Strip. Introduced on 12 October 1931, *Dick Tracy* quickly became one of the most popular comic strips of the 1930s and beyond. Its creator, Chester Gould, tapped into a contemporary fascination with crime and gangsters through the popular medium of the comic pages to invent one of the most durable characters in American culture. While other comic-strip creators dealt with crime or detectives, none did so with the visual flair for the urban violence and grotesque villains.

Inspiration. Gould was born in Pawnee, Oklahoma, in 1900. His father published a weekly newspaper, and although Gould studied business administration in Chicago, where he moved in 1921, he went from college to a job drawing for newspapers. An avid fan of comic strips in his youth, he drew his own strips during the 1920s while working for newspaper art departments. In creating *Fillum Fables* he became one of several cartoonists at the time who offered comic treatments of popular movies, including detective stories. That influence — combined with his youthful admiration for Sir Arthur Conan Doyle's Sherlock Holmes and his experience with gang-

sters in contemporary Chicago — led Gould to create Dick Tracy, "a comic strip character who would always get the best of the assorted hoodlums and gangsters." Tracy was tough yet honest, a cartoon tribute to contemporary heroes such as Eliot Ness. He also packed a gun and was the first comic-strip character in the newspapers to use one. He got plenty of chances to use it: the hoodlums and gangsters kept coming, and by the end of the decade the villains started becoming as horrid in their appearances as in their crimes. The grimness of the strip was relieved by Tracy's love interest, Tess Trueheart, and his young friend Junior.

Popularity. The stories, characters, and distinctive visual style of *Dick Tracy* won it a large audience. It also spread to other media, including Big Little Books and movie serials in the late 1930s and early 1940s. It was parodied in "Fearless Fosdick," Al Capp's strip-within-a-strip in his *Li'l Abner*. Gould accepted the parody as free advertisement. *Dick Tracy* remained popular into the 1960s, when it became too eccentric for many readers' tastes; Gould increasingly was perceived as out of touch, worrying that government was tying the hands of law enforcement and giving more power to criminals. He retired in 1977 and left *Dick Tracy* to other hands, where it has continued, even after Gould's death in 1985.

Sources:

Ron Goulart, ed., *The Encyclopedia of American Comics* (New York & Oxford: Facts On File, 1990);

Jay Maeder, *Dick Tracy: The Official Biography* (New York: Plume, 1990);

Richard Marschall, *America's Great Comic-Strip Artists* (New York: Abbeville, 1989).

JOSEPH T. SHAW

1874-1952

EDITOR OF BLACK MASK, 1926-1936

Influential Editor. Joseph T. Shaw made *Black Mask* one of the most respected pulp magazines of the 1920s and 1930s. By publishing the early work of such noteworthy writers as Raymond Chandler, Dashiell Hammett, and Erle Stanley Gardner, the magazine helped to define a whole style, commonly known as hard-boiled detective fiction.

Early Career. Born in 1874 in Gorham, Maine, Shaw edited the campus newspaper at Bowdoin College in Brunswick, Maine. Graduating in 1895, he was briefly employed at the *New York Globe* and worked for a wool company. He served in World War I, earning the rank of captain and the nickname "Cap." He was also a champion fencer, and when he later lived in New York he was licensed to carry a sword cane. Shaw remained in Europe for five years after the war, distributing food for the American Relief Administration. When he returned to the United States, he did some freelance editing and writing for popular magazines such as *Field and Stream* and the *Saturday Evening Post*. From the editor of *Field and Stream* he learned in 1926 that *Black Mask* needed a new editor; he got the job.

Black Mask. Founded in 1920 by H. L. Mencken and George Jean Nathan, both of whom distanced themselves from the magazine, *Black Mask* was a successful monthly pulp periodical specializing in detective fiction, mysteries, and adventure stories. Though Shaw knew nothing about the magazine when he applied for the position, he threw himself into making it the best of its kind and increasing circulation. Dashiell Hammett was among the most popular writers for *Black Mask* before Shaw took over the editorship of the magazine. Hammett had stopped submitting stories when he could not get a pay increase for his work. Shaw convinced Hammett to return to the magazine and then sought other writers of a similar caliber. Before long there was talk of a "*Black Mask* School" of detective fiction featuring tough, street-wise protagonists in grittily realistic urban American settings, a stark contrast to the genteel British detective tradition. The *Black Mask* approach proved popular: circulation soared, reaching a high of 103,000.

Tireless Advocate. He set his magazine above other pulps of the time, referring to it instead as a "rough-paper book." While most pulp writers were treated as hacks and expected to crank out stories rapidly for the many magazines that were published in the 1920s and 1930s, Shaw treated his writers like craftsmen. *Black Mask* was one of the best-paying pulps of the period and one of the most difficult in which to publish. Shaw promoted the writers whose stories he accepted both in the editorials and in his efforts to secure book contracts for some of them; he also helped to get some of their works adapted for the movies. Hammett flourished in this environment, serializing his first three novels in *Black Mask*. He dedicated his first novel, *Red Harvest* (1929), to Shaw. After Hammett stopped writing for the magazine in 1930, writers such as Raymond Chandler, George Harmon Coxe, Paul Cain, Norbert Davis, W. T. Ballard, and Horace McCry helped to ensure the continuing popularity of *Black Mask*.

The End of an Era. The Depression cut into *Black Mask* sales, and during a salary dispute with its publishers Shaw was relieved of his duties in 1936, sparking an exodus of several of his faithful writers from the magazine. *Black Mask* continued until 1951. By this time Shaw had become a literary agent, a job he held for ten years until his death in 1952.

Sources:

Ron Goulart, *The Dime Detectives* (New York: Mysterious Press, 1988);

Goulart, *The Hardboiled Dicks* (New York: Pocket Books, 1967);

William F. Nolan, ed., *The Black Mask Boys* (New York: Morrow, 1985);

Lee Server, *Danger Is My Business: An Illustrated History of the Fabulous Pulp Magazines* (San Francisco: Chronicle, 1993).

LOWELL THOMAS

1892-1981

NEWS COMMENTATOR

On the Radio. Lowell Thomas made his debute as a newsreader and commentator in September 1930 and continued daily broadcasts until 14 May 1976. Before he became a radio personality, Thomas was already famous as an author, traveler, and lecturer, best-known for *With Lawrence in Arabia* (1924), the story of his time with T. E. Lawrence during World War I. Thomas's radio job was the result of CBS Radio president William S. Paley's attempt to convince the *Literary Digest* to sponsor a news broadcast on CBS instead of the news show it had on NBC. Once Thomas made a trial broadcast, *Literary Digest* publisher R. J. Cuddihy immediately fired his present reader, Floyd Gibbons, and hired Thomas. For six months Thomas's fifteen-minute nightly broadcasts were heard on NBC in the East and on CBS in the West. After that Thomas was heard only on NBC until 1947.

An American Voice. Thomas had an American voice, without a trace of a foreign or patrician accent. His commentary was balanced politically though always pro-American. His first broadcast included commentary on Benito Mussolini and a little-known German named Adolf Hitler: "There are now two Mussolinis in the world. . . . Adolf Hitler has written a book in which this belligerent gentleman states that the cardinal policy of his powerful German party is the conquest of Russia. That's a tall assignment, Adolf. You just go ask Napoleon." His informed, yet folksy, opinions quickly gained Thomas a nightly audience of between ten million and fifteen million listeners.

Newsreel Voice. 20th Century–Fox hired the popular broadcaster for their Movietone newsreels, and through his experience in radio and film, he became an important figure in the development of television broadcasting. In 1939 Thomas broadcast the first televised news program for NBC. During his world travels he did radio and newsreel reports on the coronation of King George VI in 1937 and on the increasing world tensions in Europe during the late 1930s.

A News Fixture. Thomas was one of the news commentators who made radio such an important part of the way Americans received information. His tag line, "So long until tomorrow," was a reassuring promise in a world that seemed increasingly strange and dangerous. Thomas and other radio commentators such as H. V. Kaltenborn laid the foundation of public trust for radio and television figures such as Edward R. Murrow.

Source:
Michael Emery and Edwin Emery, *The Press and America: An Interpretive History of Mass Media* (Englewood Cliffs, N.J.: Prentice Hall, 1992).

WALTER WINCHELL

1897-1972

JOURNALIST, RADIO COMMENTATOR

Controversial Columnist. Walter Winchell was the most famous, most popular, and most controversial "gossip" columnist in twentieth-century American journalism. He made a career of printing scoops about celebrities and making "informed" predictions (many of which did not come true). In the 1930s he also began to make partisan political pronouncements.

Background. Winchell was born in 1897 and left school in 1910 to work as a vaudeville performer. After years of minimal success he enlisted in the U.S. Navy in 1917 and worked in New York City as a receptionist for Adm. Marbury Johnston at the New York Customs House. In 1919 he returned to vaudeville and started a newsletter that featured light vaudeville news and punnish quips such as "You tell'em Quija, I'm bored." In 1922 the *Vaudeville News,* a paper run by a vaudeville circuit, hired Winchell at the salary of twenty-five dollars a week.

Journalism. In 1924 Winchell became a dramatic critic and Broadway columnist for the *New York Evening Graphic.* He worked for the *Evening Graphic* until 1929, his salary rising from one hundred dollars a week in the beginning to three hundred dollars a week before he left for William Randolph Hearst's *New York Daily Mirror.* The publishers of the *Graphic* credited Winchell with attracting 75,000 of its overall 350,000 subscribers.

A National Audience. The move to the Hearst newspaper gave Winchell a tremendous increase in salary. He was signed to the King Syndicate, which distributed features to more than 170 newspapers. His initial contract with King paid him $25,000 annually. Winchell used his national platform to improve the quality of his gossip. In the early 1930s he also started a weekly radio program, broadcast on Sunday night and sponsored by the Jergens Lotion Company. By the late 1930s he was earning in excess of $130,000 per year. Winchell's popularity was in no small measure due to his skill at language — he was a constant spouter of flashy phrases. Some of his linguistic creations include *Joosh* for Jewish, *pash* for Passion, *shafts* for legs, *Wildeman* for homosexual, and *the Hardened Artery* for Broadway.

Political Commentary. The national audience and his newfound prominence with political figures (he was staunchly pro-Roosevelt and a friend of FBI director J. Edgar Hoover) led him to begin take an interest in national and international affairs. Very early he denounced Adolf Hitler and the National Socialists. On 2 September 1939, just before the beginning of World War II, Winchell sent a cable to British prime minister Neville Chamberlain suggesting that the wording of the expected declaration of war be worded as a declaration of war against Hitler personally and not against Germany in general. When Chamberlain issued a statement worded in that way, Winchell wrote a column seeming to take credit for the distinction between Hitler and the German people.

A Popular and Trusted Reporter. The self-importance shown in the episode was typical of Winchell and a key to his success and his controversy. His audience of seven million readers and twenty million listeners considered him someone who would let them know what was *really* going on. During the Depression he was the voice and words of New York City, the entertainment center of the United States. Winchell's slangy language and his secret information made him a great entertainer in the guise of a reporter. In that sense he was a man ahead of his time.

Sources:
Michael Emery and Edwin Emery, *The Press and America: An Interpretive History of the Mass Media* (Englewood Cliffs, N.J.: Prentice Hall, 1992);
St. Clair McKelway, *Gossip: The Life and Times of Walter Winchell* (New York: Viking, 1940).

VLADIMIR ZWORYKIN

1889-1982

TELEVISION PIONEER

The Importance of Technology. Along with Philo Farnsworth, Vladimir Zworykin developed the technology that made television possible. Because of the success of his technology and the company who produced it, Zworykin is known as the father of television.

A Russian Beginning. Zworykin was born near Moscow in 1889, graduating from the equivalent of high school in 1906. He received his electrical engineering degree in 1912 from the Saint Petersburg Institute of Technology, where he remained to study under Boris Rosing, one of the early scientists who developed the idea of television. Later in 1912 he traveled to France, where he studied physics until the outbreak of World War I. After the war, during which he was a signal officer working on radio, Zworykin escaped the Russian Revolution by immigrating to the United States. He eventually found work at the Westinghouse unit of the Radio Corporation of America (RCA).

Early Television. Because of his background with Rosing, Zworykin worked at developing television. In 1923 he filed his first patent application, for a transmitting tube called the iconoscope. He displayed his invention to Westinghouse management in 1924, but they informed him that while his "demonstration had been extremely interesting," it would be better if he spent his "time on something 'a little more useful.'" Instead he continued to develop television. Later in 1924 Zworykin filed a patent on the kinescope, the first television picture tube. It was publicly demonstrated in November 1929.

The Cost of Development. That same year David Sarnoff, the head of RCA, moved Zworykin from Westinghouse to RCA. Zworykin filed his patent for color television that year, and Sarnoff asked him how much it would cost to perfect his invention. Zworykin said

$100,000. During the 1930s and 1940s RCA would spend more than $50 million on its development.

The Eye of the Public. Zworykin developed other uses for his technology during the 1930s, thinking that by 1937 the basic issues concerning television had been resolved. He was instrumental in developing early versions of night-vision glasses and radio-controlled missiles, both inventions that aided efforts in World War II. He also developed the idea of the electron microscope. RCA marketed the first television sets in 1939 — $199.50 for a three-inch screen and $600 for a twelve-inch model. The scale of Zworykin's achievements reached the headlines, and he was widely hailed as the father of television. His book *Television*, which he wrote with coworkers at RCA, was published in 1940.

Source:
Michael Emery and Edwin Emery, *The Press and America: An Interpretive History of the Mass Media* (Englewood Cliffs, N.J.: Prentice Hall, 1992).

PEOPLE IN THE NEWS

In April 1930 **Frank R. Birdsall,** editor and publisher of the *Yazoo City Sentinel* in Mississippi, was shot and killed by Mayor **John T. Stricklin** because Birdsall had published damaging reports about Stricklin just before the local mayoral election in February.

In February 1937 **Walter J. Black** introduced *Book Digest* magazine, which published condensed versions of nonfiction best-sellers; he developed the idea after noticing the immense popularity of *Reader's Digest* condensed books.

In 1938 **O'Brien Boldt,** editor of the *Daily Dartmouth*, developed a plan to send **Adolf Hitler** a Christmas present of four test tubes containing samples of Jewish, Negro, Mongolian, and "Aryan" blood contributed by undergraduates and to challenge Hitler to tell the difference. The plan fell through when no "pure Aryan" blood could be found.

In July 1939 colorful, well-known *New York World-Telegram* columnist **Heywood Broun** advertised for a job because his contract expired in December and would not be renewed. With thirty-one years' newspaper experience, he ended up at the *New York Post*, working for one-quarter of his previous salary.

American Fiction Guild President **Arthur J. Burks** gave encouragement to pulp writers hurt by the Depression when he announced in early January 1933 that Dell Publishing Company's three pulp magazines were accepting new material and that Clayton Magazines were again paying authors on acceptance of their stories.

Seward Collins, editor of the *American Review*, revealed in November 1936 that he and **Dorothea Brande,** his associate editor, had married secretly in Manhattan.

In October 1938, addressing the Eighth National Eucharistic Congress in New Orleans, Louisiana, **Joseph Vincent Connolly,** general manager of all Hearst newspapers, condemned the "diabolical paganism behind Nazi and Communist persecutions" and said, "the time to fight in America is NOW."

In August 1939 **Eddie Cramer,** a reporter for the *Wilmington* (North Carolina) *Star-News*, telephoned his city editor to report on an automobile accident in which he had been injured. A few minutes later Cramer died.

Cyrus Hermann Kotzschmar Curtis's *New York Evening Post* confused and amused readers in March 1933

when it accidentally ran an advertisement for **Charles** and **Mary Beard**'s *The Rise of American Civilization* upside down.

In January 1930 *The New York Times* ran a full-page testimonial to its reliable reporting from **Charles Gates Dawes**, vice president under **Calvin Coolidge**. According to Dawes, "The *Times* stands like a beacon light in what is at times pretty foggy weather."

In May 1932 **Rudolph Dirks**, creator of the comic strip *The Captain and the Kids* (originally called *The Katzenjammer Kids*), was replaced as cartoonist for the strip by a young understudy, **Bernard Dibble**, after United Features Syndicate acquired the syndicate contracts of the *New York World*.

In April 1936 **Dorothy Dix** (Elizabeth Meriwether Gilmer), the popular author of the internationally syndicated weekly women's column "Sunday Salad," was honored at several parties by her friends and colleagues at the *New Orleans Times Picayune*, the first paper to first run her column, for her four decades of hardheaded domestic advice giving and commonsense writing.

In Kentucky **Jack Durham**, city editor of the *Danville Advocate* and local correspondent for the Associated Press, and **Wesley Carty**, reporter for the *Louisville Courier-Journal*, were fined and jailed in August 1934 after they refused, citing professional ethics, to tell a judge who was responsible for the hanging in effigy of a state representative.

In August 1939 **James Lawrence Fly** was appointed chairman of the Federal Communications Commission by President **Franklin D. Roosevelt** after the resignation of controversial **Frank Ramsay McNinch**, who Roosevelt had appointed two years earlier to "clean house."

In November 1938 **Stanton Griffis**, executive committee chairman at Paramount Pictures, announced that the company would soon begin telecasting from a highly effective, far-reaching transmitter in Montclair, New Jersey. The transmitter was developed at **Allen B. DuMont**'s laboratories.

In March 1933 chemist **Charles Holmes Herty** produced the first significant run of newspaper made from southern pine trees at his plant in Savannah, Georgia. Paper made from the pines is cheaper, stronger, and lighter in weight than paper from spruce pulpwood.

Harrison Holliway, manager of Los Angeles radio stations KFI and KECA, challenged social taboos in December 1938 by broadcasting the medical program *Why Not Have A Baby?* During the program an anonymous obstetrician gave plain-spoken answers to questions about prenatal care, paternal and maternal hygiene, sterility, and danger of miscarriage.

In October 1935 *Kansas City Star* editors replaced *Moon Mullins* comic strips that featured a snake charmer with one of her reptiles coiled around her neck with *Moon Mullins* strips from 1927 and 1929 because publisher **George Baker Longan** had a snake phobia.

In 1936 cartoonist **Reuben Lucius**'s *"Rube" Goldberg* comic strip gained national popularity after he added a new character: Lala Palooza, a fat, rich, and stupid female clown.

In January 1937 **Charles Fulton Oursler**, editor in chief of *Liberty* magazine, filed a libel suit against **Mary McFadden**, divorced wife of *Liberty* publisher **Bernarr "Body Love" McFadden**, because she had accused Oursler and her former husband of conspiring to kidnap **Charles Lindbergh**'s child as part of a plan to increase magazine sales.

In April 1932, during a presentation of a melodrama from radio station WAE in Hammond, Indiana, sound expert **Roland G. Palmer** fired a pistol when the script called for a gunshot — and accidentally shot off two of his fingers.

In March 1933 publisher **Joseph Medill Patterson** promised in his *New York Daily News* that "whatever [President **Franklin D. Roosevelt**] does or doesn't do, we're going to be for him. We're going to withhold hostile criticism for one year at least."

After his life was threatened by fascists in London, New York publisher **George Palmer Putnam** returned to the United States in early 1930 with the manuscript for an antifascist book by Francesco Nitti, nephew of former Italian prime minister Francesco Saverio Nitti.

In a March 1931 editorial *New York Herald Tribune* publishers **Mr. and Mrs. Ogden Reid** condemned New York tabloids and daily newspapers, including the Hearst daily *New York Journal*, for printing sensational and damning speculations about the murdered vice-investigation witness **Vivian Gordon**. The woman's sixteen-year-old daughter had read the papers and then committed suicide.

In March 1937 First Lady **Eleanor Roosevelt** announced at a gathering of writers, editors, and critics that *Ladies' Home Journal* would publish the first installment of her autobiography, *This Is My Story*.

David Sarnoff, a Russian immigrant who worked his way up from the duties of messenger boy, was elected president of Radio Corporation of America (RCA) in January 1930. He succeeded **James Guthrie Harbord**, who became board chairman, and **Owen D. Young**, who became head of a new executive committee.

When **William C. Shepherd**, managing editor of the *Denver Post* since 1912, was elected to succeed the late **Frederick G. Bonfils** as president, editor, and publisher in February 1933, the newspaper claimed that it would "continue to be THE PAPER WITH A HEART AND SOUL."

In September 1934 cartoonist **Otto Soglow** dressed as his

Little King and made a cross-country tour to celebrate the debut of his well-known *New Yorker* comic strip in *Puck,* a weekly funny paper published throughout the United States in Hearst newspapers.

In October 1935 Scripps-Howard executive editor **John Sorrells** forced *Indianapolis Times* editor **Talcott Powell** to resign after Powell's accusing several county officials of corruption led him into personal battles with local politicians.

In March 1937 *New York Times* photographer **George Strock** helped catch the *New York Examiner* in reprinting *Times* photographs without permission. He snapped an angled shot of Los Angeles district attorney **Buron Fitts** on a hospital stretcher with cigarette in hand and had the art editor blot out the cigarette; the *Examiner* printed the same photograph, also without the cigarette. The next day *The New York Times* published the retouched photograph alongside the original under the headline, "HERE IS A STUDY IN PICTORIAL JOURNALISM PRACTICE 'FOR PEOPLE WHO THINK.' "

Claiming homesickness for California aggravated by the high cost of living in Manhattan, **Edgar Marshall Swasey** resigned in June 1932 as publisher of the *New York Evening Journal,* the largest Hearst newspaper, to resume his former work as western advertising representative for the Hearst *American Weekly.*

In April 1931 *New York Herald Tribune* editor **Stanley Walker** publicly apologized for using the word *Negress,* a word considered inappropriate by leading African American newspapers. In the future, when race must be designated, Walker said only the word *Negro* should be used, unless the reference involves crime; then the description *colored* would be used.

Former *Stars and Stripes* cartoonist **Abian Anders "Wally" Wallgren**'s comic strip *Hoosegow Herman,* based on his misadventures while he was a U.S. Marine private during World War I, began national syndication in October 1938.

In July 1934 **William, Edward,** and **Henry Woodyard** became owners of the largest weekly newspaper chain in the United States when they acquired eight weeklies on the North Shore of Long Island, New York, and linked them with their fifteen county-seat weeklies in West Virginia.

In late February 1933 well-known wrestler **Stanislaus Zbyszko** won a libel suit against the *New York American,* which had printed his picture next to one of a gorilla — with the caption "Stanislaus Zbyszko, the Wrestler, Not Fundamentally Different from the Gorilla in Physique" — as an illustration for an article on evolution.

AWARDS

PULITZER PRIZES FOR JOURNALISM

1930

Meritorious Public Service: No award

Reporting: Russell D. Owen, *The New York Times*

Correspondence: Leland Stowe, *New York Herald Tribune*

Editorials: No award

Editorial Cartoons: Charles R. Macauley, *Brooklyn Eagle*

1931

Meritorious Public Service: *Atlanta Constitution*

Reporting: A. B. MacDonald, *Kansas City Star*

Correspondence: H. R. Knickerbocker, *Philadelphia Public Ledger* and *New York Evening Post*

Editorials: Charles S. Ryckman, *Fremont* (Nebr.) *Tribune*

Editorial Cartoons: Edmund Duffy, *Baltimore Sun*

1932

Meritorious Public Service: *Indianapolis News*

Reporting: W. C. Richards, D. D. Martin, J. S. Pooler, F. D. Webb, and J. N. W. Sloan, *Detroit Free Press*

Correspondence: Walter Duranty, *The New York Times,* and Charles G. Ross, *Saint Louis Post-Dispatch*

Editorials: No award

Editorial Cartoons: John T. McCutcheon, *Chicago Tribune*

1933

Meritorious Public Service: *New York World-Telegram*

Reporting: Francis A. Jamieson, Associated Press

Correspondence: Edgar Ansel Mowrer, *Chicago Daily News*

Editorials: *Kansas City Star*

Editorial Cartoons: H. M. Talburt, *Washington Daily News*

1934

Meritorious Public Service: *Medford* (Oreg.) *Mail Tribune*

Reporting: Royce Brier, *San Francisco Chronicle*

Correspondence: Frederick T. Birchall, *The New York Times*

Editorials: E. P. Chase, *Atlantic* (Iowa) *News-Telegraph*

Editorial Cartoons: Edmund Duffy, *Baltimore Sun*

1935

Meritorious Public Service: *Sacramento Bee*

Reporting: William H. Taylor, *New York Herald Tribune*

Correspondence: Arthur Krock, *The New York Times*

Editorials: No award

Editorial Cartoons: Ross A. Lewis, *Milwaukee Journal*

1936

Meritorious Public Service: *Cedar Rapids* (Iowa) *Gazette*

Reporting: Lauren D. Lyman, *The New York Times*

Correspondence: Wilfred C. Barber, *Chicago Tribune*

Editorials: Felix Morley, *Washington Post*, and George B. Parker, Scripps Howard Newspapers

Editorial Cartoons: No award

1937

Meritorious Service Award: *Saint Louis Post-Dispatch*

Reporting: John J. O'Neill, *New York Herald Tribune;* William L. Laurence, *The New York Times;* Howard W. Blakeslee, Associated Press; Gobind Behari Lal, Universal Service; and David Dietz, Scripps-Howard Newspapers

Correspondence: Anne O'Hare McCormick, *The New York Times*

Editorials: John W. Owens, *Baltimore Sun*

Editorial Cartoons: C. D. Batchelor, *New York Daily News*

1938

Meritorious Public Service: *Bismarck* (N.Dak.) *Tribune*

Reporting: Raymond Sprigle, *Pittsburgh Post-Gazette*

Correspondence: Arthur Krock, *The New York Times*

Editorials: William Wesley Waymack, *Des Moines Register & Tribune*

Editorial Cartoons: Vaughn Shoemaker, *Chicago Daily News*

Special Citation: *Edmonton* (Alberta) *Journal*

1939

Meritorious Public Service: *Miami News*

Reporting: Thomas L. Stokes, Scripps-Howard Newspapers

Correspondence: Louis P. Lochner, Associated Press

Editorials: Ronald G. Callvert, *The Oregonian*

Editorial Cartoons: Charles G. Werner, *Oklahoma City Daily Oklahoman*

DEATHS

Ernest Hamlin Abbott, 61, editor of the religious magazine *Outlook,* 8 August 1931.

John Alden, 73, editor and poet, 4 March 1934.

Paul Y. Anderson, 45, journalist; his articles on the Teapot Dome and Elk Hills oil leases resulted in the reopening of a Senate investigation and won him the 1928 Pulitzer Prize for reportorial work, 6 December 1938.

Benjamin Harris Anthony, 69, became president of E. Anthony and Sons, publishers of the *New Bedford Evening Post* and the *New Bedford Morning Mercury* after the death of his father in 1906; also served as second vice president of the Associated Press and as president of the New England Daily Newspaper Alliance, 16 October 1932.

Daniel Reed Anthony Jr., 60, congressman and editor of the *Leavenworth* (Michigan) *Times,* 4 August 1931.

Elbert H. Baker, 79, director of the Associated Press after 1916, director (1907–1924) and president (1912–1914) of the American Newspaper Publishers Association, 26 September 1933.

Hugh Bancroft, 54, lawyer and publisher; president of the Boston News Bureau Co. and of Dow, Jones and Co., publishers of the *Wall Street Journal,* 17 October 1933.

Charles Eugene Banks, 80, editor and author, 29 April 1932.

Col. James Barnes, 69, author, magazine and newspaper editor, 30 April 1936.

David Sheldon Barry, 75, newspaperman and sergeant at arms for the U.S. Senate, a post from which he was dismissed because he had written an article concerning members of the Senate for *The New Outlook,* 10 February 1936.

John Foster Bass, 65, war correspondent for the *Chicago Daily News,* 16 April 1931.

Winifred Black (Annie Laurie), 65, reporter for the *San Francisco Examiner,* 25 May 1936.

Frank Le Roy Blanchard, 77, editor and advertising manager, 30 May 1936.

John Theodore Boifeuillet, 74, journalist and politician, 30 May 1934.

Peyton Boswell, 57, art critic for several New York newspapers, 18 December 1935.

Clarence Winthrop Bowen, 83, historian and publisher of *The Independent* (New York), a religious journal, 2 November 1935.

Edward E. Brodie, 63, diplomat; editor and publisher of the *Oregon City Morning Enterprise* (1908–1935), 27 June 1939.

Louise Bryant, 40?, a reporter for the Hearst newspapers; obtained the first newspaper interview granted by Premier Benito Mussolini, 6 January 1936.

Elisabeth Luther Cary, 69, editor of *The New York Times* art department (1908–1936), 13 July 1936.

Herman Casler, 42, inventor of the Biograph, forerunner of the modern motion-picture projector, 20 July 1939.

Joseph Edgar Chamberlin, 83, newspaper editor, 6 July 1935.

Henry Kellet Chambers, 67, editor for the Hearst newspapers in San Francisco; edited the column "The Sun's Rays" for the *New York Sun,* 5 September 1935.

Selah Merrill Clarke, 79, night city editor of the *New York Sun* (1881–1912), 26 July 1931.

John Sanford Cohen, 65, held several positions with the *Atlanta Journal,* including reporter, Washington correspondent, managing editor, and in 1917 editor and president of the Atlanta Journal Company, 13 May 1935.

Abram Coralnik, 54, associate editor of *The Day,* a New York Yiddish-language daily newspaper, 17 July 1937.

Erwin Craighead, 79, served successively as city editor, managing editor, vice president, and editor emeritus of the *Mobile Register,* 3 February 1932.

Walter Hill Crockett, 61, editor of several Vermont newspapers, 8 December 1931.

George Dale, 69?, publisher of the *Muncie* (Indiana) *Post-Democrat,* a weekly newspaper known for its editorial attacks on the Ku Klux Klan, 27 March 1936.

George Herbert Daley, 68, sports editor of the *New York Tribune* (1900–1906), *World* (1916–1931), and *Herald Tribune* (1931–1938), 8 February 1938.

George Aaron Dame, 66, advertising expert and drama critic, 3 February 1934.

Harry Grant Dart, 69?, cartoonist; originated *The Joy Family* in the *New York Tribune* and *Mr. Home, Sweet Home* in the *World*, 15 November 1938.

Oscar King Davis, 66, publicist and correspondent, served as vice president of the Pan-American Postal Congress and as secretary of the National Foreign Trade Council, 3 June 1932.

Holman Francis Day, 69, editor and author, 19 February 1935.

Stoddard Dewey, 80, correspondent for several publications, including the *New York Tribune* and the *New York Evening Post*, 30 July 1933.

Grace Gebbie Drayton, 58, comic-strip illustrator; known for originating the idea of the Campbell Soup Kids, 31 January 1936.

Wells Drury, 80, newspaperman and author, 4 May 1932.

James O. G. Duffy, 69, held several editorial positions at the *Philadelphia Press*, 9 January 1933.

John Robertson Dunlap, 80, editor and publisher of engineering magazines, 5 June 1937.

Harry Stillwell Edwards, 83, author and editor of the *Macon* (Georgia) *Telegraph* (1881–1887), 22 October 1938.

Martin Egan, 66, journalist and publicist, 7 December 1938.

George Buchanan Fife, 69, journalist; managing editor of *Harper's Weekly* (1906–1911), literary editor of *The New York Times* (1911), and with the *New York Evening World* (1912–1917; 1920–1931), 12 March 1939.

Fabian Franklin, 85, newspaper editor and author, 9 January 1939.

Clinton Wallace Gilbert, 61, worked as reporter and as editor for several New York newspapers, 17 May 1933.

Joseph Benson Gilder, 75, journalist, cofounder of *The Critic* (1881), which later became *Putnam's Magazine*, 9 December 1936.

Franklin Potts Glass, 75, publisher and editor, president of the Southern Newspaper Publishers' Association (1910–1911) and of the American Newspaper Publishers' Association (1918–1920), 10 January 1934.

William Elliot Gonzales, 71, editor of *The State* in Columbia, South Carolina, 20 October 1937.

Ruf Gonzalez, 46?, typographical expert; designer of the "Ruf Bold" type for display cards and various prize-winning types; on the staff of the *New York Herald Tribune* after 1924, 6 June 1938.

William Griffith, 60, editor and author, 17 May 1936.

John Gruelle, 57, cartoonist and writer; originator of the comic strip *Brutus*, which won the *New York Herald* competition in 1910, 9 January 1938.

Herbert Foster Gunnison, 74, occupied several positions at the *Brooklyn Eagle*, ending with the presidency; founder of the American Newspaper Publishers Association; vice president of the Associated Press in 1921 and 1922; president of the New York City Publishers Association in 1925, 25 November 1932.

Alfred Holman, 72, reporter and editor, 14 December 1930.

Robert E. Howard, 30, pulp-magazine writer who created Conan the Barbarian in *Weird Tales*, 11 June 1936.

Edgar Watson Howe, 84, editor, publisher, and author, 3 October 1937.

Louis McHenry Howe, 65, staff member of the *New York Herald* (1888–1915); secretary to the assistant secretary of the navy, Franklin D. Roosevelt, 18 April 1936.

Thomas Sambola Jones, 73, editor of *The Louisiana Educator* and of *The State Journal* of Louisiana, 15 May 1933.

Charles William Kahles, creator of the comic strip *Hairbreadth Harry*, 1931.

Edward Windsor Kemble, 72, illustrator for the *Daily Graphic, Century, Life, Collier's, Harper's Weekly,* and other magazines, 19 September 1933.

James Kerney, 60, publisher of the *Trenton* (N. J.) *Times* and of the *New Jersey State Gazette*, 8 April 1934.

Frederick A. King, 74, literary editor of *The Literary Digest* (1909–1933), 31 October 1939.

Stoddard King, 43, editorial writer and conductor of a column titled "Facetious Fragments" for the *Spokane Spokesman-Review*, 13 June 1933.

Karl Kingsley Kitchen, 50, newspaper columnist, 21 June 1935.

Adolph Klauber, 54, Sunday editor (1904–1906) and drama critic (1906–1918) of *The New York Times*, 7 December 1933.

Amy Leslie, 78, drama critic for the *Chicago Daily News* (1890–1930), 3 July 1939.

Walter William Liggett, 49, editor and newspaper publisher, assassinated on 9 December 1935.

Ray Long, 57, newspaper and magazine editor, 9 July 1935.

Robertus Love, 63, editor of the *Daily Press* of Asbury Park, N.J. (1892–1895), and of the General Press Bureau of the Saint Louis Exposition (1903–1904), 7 May 1930.

H. P. Lovecraft, 46, popular writer of weird fiction for pulp magazines such as *Weird Tales,* 15 March 1937.

Frederick Rollins Lowe, 75, editor and engineer, 22 January 1936.

Charles Raymond Macauley, 63, political cartoonist whose work appeared in such publications as the *New York Morning World* and *Life* magazine, 24 November 1934.

Frank Pitts MacLennan, 78, president of the Associated Press (1910–1911) and a director of the organization after 1919, 18 November 1933.

Walt Mason, 77, columnist with the *Emporia* (Kans.) *Gazette* since 1907, 22 June 1939.

Thomas Lansing Masson, 67, literary editor of *Life* magazine (1893–1922); associate editor of the *Saturday Evening Post* (1922–1930), 18 June 1934.

Clark McAdams, 61, editor and columnist for the *Saint Louis Post-Dispatch,* 29 November 1935.

Nelson McAllister Lloyd, 60, on the staff of the *New York Evening Sun* for seventeen years, 1 February 1933.

Winsor McCay, pioneering cartoonist (*Little Nemo in Slumberland, Dreams of a Rarebit Fiend, Gertie the Dinosaur*), 1934.

Valentine Stuart McClatchy, 80, publisher and owner with his brother of the *Sacramento Bee,* 15 May 1938.

William O'Connell McGeehan, 74, reporter, editor, and columnist for several New York newspapers, including the *Tribune* and the *Herald,* 29 November 1933.

William L. McLean, 79, publisher of the Philadelphia *Bulletin;* director of the Associated Press (1896–1924) and of the American Newspaper Publishers Association (1899–1905), 30 July 1931.

Edwin Doak Mead, 87, author; editor of the *New England Magazine,* 17 August 1937.

Charles Henry Meltzer, 83, dramatist and critic, 14 January 1936.

Henry Harrison Metcalf, 90, editor, publisher, and member of the Michigan bar, 5 February 1932.

Michael Monahan, 68, newspaperman and founder of the magazine *Papyrus,* which was later renamed the *Phoenix,* 22 November 1933.

Frederick Cook Morehouse, 64, editor of religious magazines, 25 June 1932.

Frederick Craig Mortimer, 78, held many positions at *The New York Times;* created the *Topics of the Times* column for that paper, 27 January 1936.

Edward J. Neil, 37, Associated Press correspondent, 2 January 1938.

James Banks Nevin, 58, editor in chief of the *Atlanta Georgian* (1910–1931), 18 November 1931.

Clarence Herbert New, 70, author, editor, and foreign correspondent, 8 January 1933.

Lucius W. Nieman, 77, publisher of the *Milwaukee Journal,* which was awarded the Pulitzer Prize for "the most disinterested and meritorious service rendered by an American newspaper in 1918," 1 October 1935.

Moissaye J. Olgin, 61, founder and editor in chief of *The Morning Freiheit,* a Yiddish Communist daily, 22 November 1939.

William Belmont Parker, 63, magazine editor and author, 6 October 1934.

Charles Melville Pepper, 70, correspondent for the *Chicago Tribune* (1886–1895) and the *New York Herald* (1896–1897), 4 November 1930.

Charles Phillips, 53, newspaper editor, poet, and playwright, 29 December 1933.

Thomas E. Powers, 68, political cartoonist; associated with the Hearst newspapers (1896–1937), 14 August 1939.

Frank Presbrey, 81, publisher and advertising expert, 10 October 1936.

George Bronson Rea, 67, correspondent and diplomat, 21 November 1936.

Harrison Robertson, 83, editor in chief of the *Louisville Courier-Journal* after 1929, 11 November 1939.

Jason Rogers, 63, publisher and author; helped form the American Newspaper Publishers Association, 26 April 1932.

George Henry Sandison, 84, editor, 31 October 1934.

Charles Frederick Scott, 78, U.S. representative and publisher of the *Iola* (Kans.) *Register* (1887–1938), 18 September 1938.

Robert Paine Scripps, 42, newspaper publisher; became editorial director in 1927 of the Scripps-McRae newspapers under his father, later uniting with Roy Howard to form the Scripps-Howard chain of twenty-four newspapers, 3 March 1938.

Wallace McIlvaine Scudder, 77, founder, publisher, and editor of the *Newark News,* 24 February 1931.

Elzie Crisler Segar, 43, cartoonist; originator of the *Thimble Theatre,* a comic strip that included characters such as Popeye the Sailor, J. Wellington Wimpy, Alice the Goon, Eugene the Jeep, Olive Oyl, and Castor Oyl, 13 October 1938.

Don Carlos Seitz, 73, held positions at several New York newspapers, including correspondent, business manager, city editor, managing editor, assistant publisher, and advertising manager, 4 December 1935.

William Gunn Shepherd, 55, correspondent for the

Newspaper Enterprise Association and for the United Press Association, 4 November 1933.

Chesla C. Sherlock, 42, editor of *Better Homes and Gardens* (1922–1927), *Ladies' Home Journal* (1929–1933), and *St. Nicholas Magazine* (1935–1937), 30 June 1938.

Sime Silverman, 61, reporter for the *New York Morning Telegraph* and founder of *Variety,* a theatrical newspaper, 21 September 1933.

Edward Alfred Simmons, 56, president of Simmons Boardman Publishing Company, publisher of trade journals, 30 September 1931.

George H. Simmons, 67, editor, and founder of *Hygeia Health Magazine* (1923), 1 September 1937.

Samuel White Small, 80, editorial staff member of the *Atlanta Constitution* (1875–1931); also helped found the *Oklahoma City Oklahoman* in 1889, 21 November 1931.

Frances Stanton Smith, 60, music editor for the *Buffalo Express* and the *Buffalo Courier;* editor of the women's page of the *Buffalo Enquirer,* 30 June 1931.

Ormond Gerald Smith, 72, founder of several pulp magazines, 17 April 1933.

Seymour Wemyss Smith, 35, newspaper editor and author, noted for his contention that John Hanson and not George Washington was the first president of the United States, 4 January 1932.

Sydney Smith, 58, cartoonist responsible for *The Gumps,* a comic strip which achieved nationwide fame, 20 October 1935.

John Randolph Spears, 85, author; journalist with the *Buffalo Sun* and the *New York Sun,* 25 January 1936.

Rufus Steele, 58, held editorial positions with several California newspapers, 25 December 1935.

Pleasant A. Stovall, 77, part owner of the *Savannah Press;* editor of the *Savannah Evening Press,* 14 May 1935.

Walter Ansel Strong, 47, served successively as audit clerk, auditor, business manager, and publisher of the *Chicago Daily News,* 10 May 1931.

John Adams Thayer, 75, printer, typesetter, and publisher, 21 February 1936.

Gabriel Thorne, 85, president of the Newark Call Printing and Publishing Company from 1899, 13 July 1935.

Eugene Thwig, 70, editor and publisher of *The Circle* and of *Success Magazine,* 29 May 1936.

Gilbert Milligan Tucker, 84, editor in chief of the *Country Gentleman* (1897–1911), a farm magazine, 13 January 1932.

Samuel E. Vail, 74, editor and manager of *The Wood County Sentinel* of Bowling Green, Ohio, for twenty years, 29 November 1937.

Lapsley Greene Walker, 84, editor of the *Chattanooga Times* (1903–1932), 12 July 1939.

William Henry Walker, 66, cartoonist; credited with first using lithograph crayon for cartooning, 18 January 1938.

Walter Wellman, 75, founder of the *Cincinnati Evening Post* (1879); Washington correspondent for the *Chicago Herald* and the *Chicago Times-Herald,* 31 January 1934.

Peter Wiernik, 70, editor of Jewish newspapers, 12 February 1936.

Louis B. Wiley, 65, staff member of *The New York Times* beginning in 1896, played an outstanding part in building the newspaper up to its present standard, 20 March 1935.

John Elbert Wilkie, 74, journalist, detective, and traction executive; worked for Chicago newspapers the *Times* and the *Tribune;* was appointed chief of the United States Secret Service in 1898, 13 December 1934.

Alfred Brockenbrough Williams, 74, editor of several Virginia newspapers, including the Richmond-based *News, News-Leader,* and *Evening Journal;* and the *Morning Times* and *Evening World News* of Roanoke, 11 March 1930.

Eugene Zimmerman, 72, political and comic cartoonist for both *Puck* and *Judge* magazines, 26 March 1935.

PUBLICATIONS

Waldo Abbot, *Handbook of Broadcasting: How to Broadcast Effectively* (New York & London: McGraw-Hill, 1937);

John E. Allen, *Newspaper Makeup* (New York & London: Harper, 1936);

Gleason L. Archer, *Big Business and Radio* (New York: American Historical Co., 1939);

Eric Barnouw, *Handbook of Radio Writing: An Outline of Techniques and Markets in Radio Writing in the United States* (Boston: Little, Brown, 1939);

Silas Bent, *Newspaper Crusaders: A Neglected Story* (New York & London: Whittlesey House, McGraw-Hill, 1939);

Simon Michael Bessie, *Jazz Journalism: The Story of the Tabloid Newspapers* (New York: Dutton, 1938);

Karl A. Bickel, *New Empires: The Newspaper and the Radio* (Philadelphia: Lippincott, 1930);

F. Fraser Bond, *Breaking Into Print: Modern Newspaper Technique for Writers* (New York & London: McGraw-Hill, 1933);

Herbert Brucker, *The Changing American Newspaper* (New York: Columbia University Press, 1937);

Ben H. Darrow, *Radio: The Assistant Teacher* (Columbus, Ohio: R. G. Adams, 1932);

Charles Kellogg Field, *The Story of Cheerio, By Himself* (Garden City, N.Y.: Garden City Publishing, 1937);

John J. Floherty, *Your Daily Paper* (Philadelphia & London: Lippincott, 1938);

S. E. Frost Jr., *Is American Radio Democratic?* (Chicago: University of Chicago Press, 1937);

Robert E. Garst and Theodore Menline Bernstein, *Headlines and Deadlines: A Manual for Copyeditors* (New York: Columbia University Press, 1933);

Laurence Greene, *America Goes to Press: The News of Yesterday* (Indianapolis: Bobbs-Merrill, 1936);

Harold L. Ickes, *America's House of Lords: An Inquiry Into the Freedom of the Press* (New York: Harcourt, Brace, 1939);

Hans von Kaltenborn, *I Broadcast the Crisis* (New York: Random House, 1938);

George L. Knapp, *The Boy's Book of Journalism* (New York: Dodd, Mead, 1932);

Ruth Adams Knight, *Stand By for the Ladies! The Distaff Side of Radio* (New York: Coward-McCann, 1939);

Sherman Paxton Lawton, *Radio Speech* (Boston: Expression, 1932);

Peter Morell, *Poisons, Potions, and Profits: The Antidote to Radio Advertising* (New York: Knight Publishers, 1937);

William Murrell, *A History of American Graphic Humor*, 2 volumes (New York: Whitney Museum of Art/Macmillan, 1933, 1938);

Robert M. Neal, *Editing the Small City Daily* (New York: Prentice-Hall, 1939);

Arthur W. Page, Harold D. Arnold, and others, *Modern Communication* (Boston & New York: Houghton Mifflin, 1932);

Philip W. Porter and Norval Neil Luxon, *The Reporter and the News* (New York & London: Appleton-Century, 1935);

Richard Reid, *The Morality of the Newspaper* (Notre Dame, Ind.: Notre Dame University Press, 1938);

George Eaton Simpson, *The Negro in the Philadelphia Press* (Philadelphia: University of Pennsylvania Press, 1936);

A. Walter Socolow, *The Law of Radio Broadcasting* (New York: Baker, Voorhis, 1939);

Lowell Thomas, *Magic Dials: The Story of Radio and Television* (New York: Polygraphic Company of America, 1939);

Laura Vitray, John Mills Jr., and Roscoe Ellard, *Pictorial Journalism* (New York & London: McGraw-Hill, 1939);

James Whipple, *How to Write for Radio* (New York & London: Whittlesey House, McGraw-Hill, 1938);

Annual Report of the Federal Communications Commission to the Congress of the United States, periodical;

Wireless World, periodical.

MEDICINE AND HEALTH

by JOAN D. LAXSON

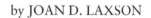

CONTENTS

Sidebars and tables are listed in italics.

1930

- Karl Landsteiner wins the Nobel Prize for medicine or physiology for discovery of the blood groups.

- Duke University Hospital and Medical School open.

- The National Institute of Health is created.

- Anesthesia is advanced with the increased use of Avertin, originally developed in Germany.

- Tincture of merthiolate gains widespread popularity for painting cuts and scratches after adding a little alcohol to make it sting and vegetable dye to make it show on the skin.

- A tiny virus that causes the common cold is discovered.

- The culturing of the rickettsia bacterium promises a means of immunizing humans against typhus.

- Harvard Medical School scientists find a lack of vitamin B in the diet causes a paralysis in animals similar to that of humans suffering from pernicious anemia.

- Cornell University scientists discover that injected adrenaline increases blood pressure and is valuable in treating traumatic shock, bronchial asthma, hives, and hay fever.

- Johns Hopkins University scientists develop a new method for diagnosing brain tumors by injecting air into the brain under local anesthesia, then using X rays.

- Spleen X rays are accomplished by injecting emulsions of iodized nutrient oils into the bloodstream.

- *The Human Mind* by Menninger Clinic psychiatrist Karl Menninger popularizes psychiatry as a legitimate source of help for the mentally ill.

28 Jan. Prohibition reaches its tenth anniversary as the Metropolitan Life Insurance Company reports that deaths from alcoholism are soaring.

Apr. Isolation of the hormone cortin from the cortex of the suprarenal glands proves useful in the treatment of Addison's disease.

24 May A *Reader's Digest* poll shows the majority of Americans favor repeal of Prohibition laws.

30 May The first International Congress of Mental Hygiene is held in Washington, D.C.

6 June Frozen food arrives on the market.

27 June Diathermy — an electrical method of elevating body temperature — is used to treat patients with paresis, a disease of the central nervous system caused by syphilis.

Sept. The *American Journal of the Diseases of Childhood* reports that a balanced diet rich in vitamin D is a powerful preventive agent against caries (cavities) in the teeth of children but that the local use of antiseptic mouthwashes is of little value.

25 Oct.   An artificial respirator treats acute respiratory failure of infantile paralysis, newborn asphyxia, and other diseases.

Dec.   Hungry people protest in New York City as unemployment climbs.

1931

- A severe polio epidemic centers public interest on the disease.

- The poliomyelitis virus is cultured and the disease reproduced in monkeys.

- Alka-Seltzer gains acceptance for treating headaches, hangovers, and upset stomachs.

- Death rates from childbirth are greater in the United States than in any other of the twenty nations with available statistics; doctors attribute this to the isolation of pregnant women from medical care.

- Ernest Goodpasture adopts the technique of inoculation on the chorioallantoic membrane of a chick for use in virology.

- Wolferth and Wood introduce chest lead for routine use in suspected myocardial infarction.

- The electron microscope is developed.

- Metropolitan Life Insurance Company statistics show the mortality rate from acute appendicitis continues to increase.

- New York obstetricians report the drug pernocton makes childbirth nearly painless without the possible harm to the baby from other drugs.

Jan.   Rheumatoid arthritis is identified as a streptococcal infection.

3 Jan.   Five hundred Arkansas farmers storm a small town demanding food.

The Journal of the American Medical Association reports early diagnosis of pregnancy by injecting small quantities of a woman's urine into a castrated female mouse; if estrus is induced in the mouse (that is, if the mouse goes into heat), the woman is shown to be pregnant.

20 Mar.   U. S. Federal Council of Churches approves the use of limited birth control.

23 Aug.   Ford Motor Company orders employees to grow vegetables or give up their jobs.

3 Sept.   Chemists find a growth hormone in the pituitary gland.

17 Oct.   The National Advisory Council on Radio in Education begins a series of fifteen-minute radio talks called *Psychology Today*.

31 Dec.   Dr. Frederick Eberson of the University of California Medical School announces that he has succeeded in culturing the poliomyelitis virus and has reproduced the disease by inoculation into monkeys; he hopes that his discovery might make possible the preparation of a vaccine for the disease.

1932

- Riboflavin is discovered.

- Harvey Williams Cushing describes the syndrome that bears his name.

- Goldblatt produces experimental hypertension by renal-artery stenosis.

- The Chicago Institute for Psychoanalysis is established.

- The Benzedrine Inhaler is introduced as a nasal decongestant with amphetamine as its active ingredient.

- Scientists at Northwestern University School of Medicine demonstrate that extract of the gastric mucous membrane of swine, served in ice cream, malted milk, or fruit juices, is an effective cure for stomach ulcers.

- A new immunization serum is developed for the treatment of yellow fever.

- The formerly invisible poliomyelitis virus is isolated, grown in test tubes, and observed.

- The United States Public Health Service begins the Tuskegee Syphilis Study on African Americans in Alabama that seeks to determine the impact of syphilis if left untreated.

4 Apr.   Vitamin C is identified and isolated.

Sept.   In sixty-two cities 944,609 meals are provided for homeless and transient persons as compared to 472,688 meals in September 1931.

23 Dec.   The needy receive 185 tons of food in a Christmas welfare gesture.

1933

- T. H. Morgan wins the Nobel Prize for medicine or physiology for his studies of genetics.

- Hamilton designs the manometer for measurement of intravascular pressure.

- Scientists present a new method for treating certain forms of chronic heart disease; the metabolic rate is lowered by removing the normal thyroid gland, thus decreasing the body's demand on the heart.

- Sodium pentothal, an intravenous barbiturate, is used to anesthetize a patient before surgery.

- The Blue Cross insurance program for hospital costs is created.

- The U.S. Children's Bureau estimates that about one-half of all preschoolers and schoolchildren show the effects of Depression-related poor nutrition, inadequate housing, and lack of medical care.

22 Mar.   President Franklin D. Roosevelt signs a bill legalizing the sale of beer and wine.

5 Apr.   The first successful surgery to remove an entire cancerous lung is performed.

Aug.   An amoebic dysentery epidemic in Chicago calls attention to the disease as not being limited to tropical areas, as had been thought.

7 Aug.–
10 Sept.   An encephalitis epidemic in Saint Louis claims more than 115 deaths.

4 Nov.   Scientists report success in treating obesity by using the drug alpha-dinitrophenol to increase the patient's metabolism but caution against the drug's potential fatal toxicity.

	11 Dec.	A newly developed technique for the transplantation of human tissue is reported to transplant portions of the thyroid and parathyroid glands from one patient to another.
	21 Dec.	The first dried human blood serum is prepared.

1934

- George Hoyt Whipple, George Minot, and William P. Murphy win the Nobel Prize for medicine or physiology for liver therapy against anemia.
- Mayo Clinic scientists isolate the suprarenal cortical hormone in crystalline form.
- The Rockefeller Institute for Medical Research makes a vaccine for psittacosis (parrot fever).
- Evipan, a new German anesthetic, is first tried in the United States in a George Washington University Medical School postgraduate clinic.
- Liver extract cures agranulocytosis, a blood disease that was 100 percent fatal.

1935

- Edward Calvin Kendall and Tadeus Reichstein isolate cortisone.
- The first hospital for drug addicts is founded at Lexington, Kentucky.
- Riboflavin (vitamin B_2) is synthesized.
- Polio vaccine trials inoculate three thousand children — several contract polio and one dies, leading to public suspicion about human vaccination.
- Yale scientists observe that primates who have had a bilateral prefrontal lobotomy are calm, even when presented with difficult problems.
- Congress enacts the Social Security Act, which includes funds to the states for setting up public health programs.
- Stomach ulcers are attributed to pure gastric juices.

	May	The Board of Education of New York City reports 18 percent of the city's pupils lack proper food.
	10 June	Alcoholics Anonymous is founded in New York City.
	20 June	Dr. Alexis Carrel, surgeon and biologist, with the assistance of aviator Charles A. Lindbergh, announces the perfection of the first mechanical "heart," a pumping device that can keep different types of tissues and organs alive outside the body.
	June/July	Epidemics of polio occur throughout the country.

1936

- Long and Bliss introduce sulfa drugs in the United States.
- The alkaloid ergonovine is used effectively in obstetrics to treat postpartum uterine bleeding.

- Dilantin (diphenylhydantoin) comes on the market as the first successful anticonvulsive treatment for epilepsy since phenobarbital and is also used to treat abnormal heartbeats.

- The Federal Children's Bureau notes a downward trend in infant mortality but calls attention to an "alarmingly high" maternal mortality rate of fifty-nine per ten thousand live births in 1934.

- Schizophrenic patients are treated with insulin doses to create hypoglycemic shock.

- Thiamine (vitamin B_1) is synthesized.

- Poliovirus is grown in human brain cells at the Rockefeller Institute.

14 May   Missouri doctors criticize the use of drugs for painless childbirth.

14 Aug.   The Social Security Act calls for setting aside funds for grants-in-aid to states for maternal and child-health services, especially in poor and rural areas.

30 Nov.   Birth control under medical direction is recognized as legal by the United States Circuit Court of Appeals for the Second Circuit.

1937

- Angiocardiography is introduced.

- Ochsner and DeBakey describe lung cancer in cigarette smokers.

- Zinc protamine insulin — the most important advance in the treatment of diabetes since Sir Frederick Grant Banting's discovery of insulin in 1922 — is introduced.

- The National Cancer Institute is established.

- A new vaccine prevents yellow fever.

- A new closed-plaster method for treating compound fractures reduces infections.

- Children die after treatment with an elixir of the antibacterial drug sulfanilamide containing the solvent diethylene glycol.

- Nicotinic acid treats pellagra, a dietary deficiency disease.

- Karen Horney's *The Neurotic Personality of Our Time* attacks Freudian anti-feminism.

- Sulfanilamide (para-amino-benzene-sulfonamide) is used experimentally to treat streptococcus infections.

- The Stanford-Binet intelligence test is revised.

15 Mar.   The first modern blood bank is established at the Cook County Hospital in Chicago.

1 Apr.   Forty-two states approve plans for crippled children under the Social Security Act.

June   The American Medical Association approves birth control as an essential part of medical practice and education.

23 June   Yale University professors announce the isolation of the pituitary hormone.

1938

Aug. A Federal Children's Bureau study announces the mortality rate of African American infants for the years 1933 to 1935 is 86 per 1,000 live births as compared to 53 per 1,000 for white infants.

30-31 Aug. The first meetings of the American Association of Applied Psychologists are held.

23 Sept. The National Foundation for Infantile Paralysis is founded in Warm Springs, Georgia.

- Pellagra is proven to be a deficiency disease and is treated with niacin.

- Congress enacts the Venereal Disease Control Act, which provides federal funds for the prevention, treatment, and control of venereal disease.

- Increasing the prothrombin content of the blood by administering vitamin K derived from putrefied fish meal, bile, and bile salts treats hemorrhage in jaundiced patients.

- Coccidioidomycosis, or "valley fever," common in California, is discovered to result from inhalation of dust containing the fungus coccidioides, which produces an infection of the upper respiratory tract.

- Sodium diphenyl hydantoinate is used to treat epilepsy.

24 Feb. The first commercial product using the synthetic fabric nylon — toothbrushes with nylon bristles — goes on sale in New Jersey.

12 Apr. New York becomes the first state to require medical tests for marriage license applicants.

20 Apr. Birth-control movement pioneer Margaret Sanger declares birth control is finally legal in the United States, except for Connecticut, Mississippi, and Massachusetts.

27 June After more than 107 people die from a popular antibiotic, Congress enacts the Food, Drug, and Cosmetic Act, which bans potentially dangerous drugs.

1939

- Edward Doisy isolates vitamin K from alfalfa and determines its structure.

- René Dubos introduces tyrothricin (gramicidin), which leads the Australian scientist Howard Walter Florcy to the revival of penicillin.

- The Rh factor in human blood is discovered.

- Tyrocidine and gramicidine are isolated from swamp soil; effective against a broad spectrum of gram-positive bacteria, they are too toxic for human use.

- Sherman Anti-Trust Act proceedings are brought against the American Medical Association, the Medical Society of the Washington, D.C., and other medical societies and hospitals.

- State public-health agencies receive federal payments totaling $3,724,362 under the Social Security Act Amendments of 1939.

- The U.S. Census Bureau reports the lowest maternal and infant mortality rates on record for the United States in 1938.

- Patent ductus arteriosus (a vascular anomaly that causes regurgitation of blood into the pulmonary circulation) is surgically corrected.

- The synthetic hormone diethylstilbestrol treats menopause symptoms in women.

- Addison's disease is treated with the synthetic crystalline hormone desoxycorticosterone acetate.

- The New York City Department of Health reports success in curing early syphilitic infections with massive doses of neoarsphenamine, a chemotherapeutic agent.

- The Blue Shield insurance plan is created to pay for physicians' charges.

23 Jan. President Roosevelt proposes a national health program.

28 Feb. The Wagner Health Bill proposal is introduced in the Senate, but no action is taken by year's end.

26 Apr. The first session of the White House Conference on Children in a Democracy is held in Washington.

1 May President Roosevelt proclaims this day as Child Health Day.

OVERVIEW

The Biggest Health Concern. In the 1930s the biggest health concern of America was how to pay for medical needs. The national income was less than half of what it had been in 1929, and in several states as many as 40 percent of the people were on relief. Many Americans could not pay their medical bills, and visits to physicians and hospitals decreased. Before the Depression, physicians charged a fee-for-service on a sliding scale and collected their bills as best they could. They also saw some patients on a charity basis and passed the expenses along to those who could pay. Loss of medical services and reduced ability to pay meant lower incomes for physicians, too. While doctors as a group fared better than many other professions during the Depression, in many cases they also saw their incomes halved. Hospitals were in similar trouble. Beds went empty as patients could no longer afford a two-week hospitalization, which was the average in 1933. Bills were unpaid, and charitable contributions to hospital fund-raising efforts fell.

The Health of the Nation. In the first three years of the 1930s the leading causes of death were 1) heart disease, 2) cancer, 3) pneumonia, and 4) infectious and parasitic diseases, including influenza, tuberculosis, and syphilis. Large increases in the mortality rate occurred from cancer and other malignant tumors and diseases of the circulatory system and heart. Motor-vehicle deaths dropped in 1933 from earlier years, and, despite the Depression accidental deaths from hunger and thirst totaled less than one per one hundred thousand of the total population. Perhaps reflecting the Depression, the birth rate in 1933 was the lowest since the establishment of the federal birth registration area in 1915. Many of America's old health nemeses, such as diphtheria and typhoid, were firmly controlled by public health and medical measures, but vaccines and cures for such diseases as polio and tuberculosis were still in the future. Acute diseases were being replaced with an increase in chronic diseases such as heart disease, hardening of the arteries, rheumatism, or mental diseases. Syphilis raged in as much as 10 percent of the population, and maternal mortality — the highest known in the part of the industrialized world that kept statistics — was a major cause for concern. Both the federal government and the medical profession gave their okays to birth control by 1938, but there were still a few states that were holdouts.

Polio. Polio troubled the nation. Large outbreaks occurred in the northeastern part of the United States in 1931, Philadelphia in 1932, Los Angeles in 1934, and South Carolina and Buffalo, New York, in 1939. At the beginning of the decade, little was known about the cause and transmission of the disease. Treatments using serum derived from animals that had survived the disease was finally recognized as ineffective after two decades of hopeful efforts. Experiments in 1931 marked a revival of virologic studies on patients in attempts to isolate the poliovirus in human victims and duplicate the disease in experimental animals. Until 1938 with the advent of the amended Food, Drug and Cosmetic Act, vaccines did not have to undergo the lengthy process of being approved and licensed by the U.S. Public Health Service. The individuals who prepared and promoted the vaccines were the only ones responsible for the safety of their product. Premature vaccine trials on humans in 1935 led to a rate of vaccine-associated poliomyelitis cases that may have been as high as one per one thousand. These trials set research into the subject of human immunization against the disease back by a decade. Unknown to many Americans, their president, Franklin D. Roosevelt, was a crippled poliomyelitis victim. He provided his leadership to help create one of America's greatest medical research fund-raisers, the National Foundation for Infantile Paralysis's March of Dimes campaign, in 1938. Out of this program came funds for many polio victims and funds for the research that supported the ultimate discovery of the miraculous polio vaccines in the 1950s.

Scientific Research. American research moved into high gear by the 1930s, and several Americans won or shared Nobel Prizes for their work in medicine or physiology. Karl Landsteiner won America's second Nobel Prize in medicine for his identification of the blood groups; Thomas Hunt Morgan for his research in genetics; and George R. Minot, William P. Murphy, and G. H. Whipple for their work on pernicious anemia. As polio and various forms of encephalitis began to strike more often, American researchers began to pave the way for the treatments to come. In 1931 Austrian scientists discovered two strains of poliovirus, leading the way for Drs. Albert B. Sabin and Peter K. Olitsky of the Rockefeller Institute in 1936 to grow poliovirus in human brain cells.

Scientific Medicine. Medicine had both its feet firmly planted in the modern scientific era. The modern age of chemotherapeutic treatments loomed on the horizon with the introduction of the sulfa drugs from Germany in 1936, and new advances in anesthesia promised better means of conquering surgical pain. Improvements in blood transfusion techniques and the opening of the first blood bank in 1937 made more complicated surgical procedures feasible. Newer and faster forms of X-ray equipment aided physicians in identifying tuberculosis in an earlier stage when better treatment might be more effective. Hormones, vitamins, and insulin were a part of daily use and saved many citizens from the ravages of deficiency diseases. Americans were confronted with a bewildering variety of modern machines and techniques for diagnosis and treatment. Still, every day one out of twenty people was too sick to go to school or work, and every American averaged ten days of such incapacity a year.

The Intellectual Diaspora. The increasing unrest in Europe in the 1930s had a great impact on both American medicine and psychiatry as many scientists fled the Nazis and came to the United States. American psychiatry in particular was heavily influenced by this intellectual diaspora, which brought many Freudian psychiatrists and psychologists from Austria and Germany. Many of these settled in urban areas, and their practices influenced the field of psychoanalysis for decades to come.

Health and the New Deal. President Roosevelt's New Deal was the first attempt to elevate the social welfare programs that had previously been confined to the states to a national level. Under the terms of the New Deal, Washington was to become the guardian of the weak and unfortunate and the source of security for all Americans. Almost every New Deal agency, temporary or permanent, made some contribution to health. As early as June 1933, the Federal Emergency Relief Administration authorized the use of its funds for medical care, nursing, and emergency dental work. The Resettlement Administration of 1935 and the Farm Security Administration (FSA) of 1937 provided for cooperative medical prepayment plans among the poor farmers they were assisting. These plans covered a quarter of the population of North Dakota and South Dakota. In 1935 Titles V and VI of the Social Security Act authorized the use of federal funds for crippled children, maternal and child care, and the promotion of state and local public health agencies. The Food, Drug, and Cosmetic Act of 1938 was one of the last of the New Deal enactments and gave Americans new protection from medical quackery or adulterated and dangerous drugs.

Health Insurance. Congress debated national health insurance but did not enact it. A National Health Conference convened in July 1938, emphasized the need for a national health program, and a bill incorporating the report's recommendations was introduced in 1939. Although it passed by the Senate, the Wagner bill died in the House. The 1930s did see a major breakthrough in private voluntary health insurance in the emergence of the Blue Cross–Blue Shield plans. The American Hospital Association created the Blue Cross plan for hospital costs in 1933 that led to the Blue Shield (medical and surgical) program in 1939. The American Medical Association (AMA) was dubious of these plans at first but gave in when faced with what they perceived as the more radical alternatives of national health insurance proposals. Instead of a single health insurance system for the entire nation, America would have a system of private insurance for those who could afford it and public welfare services for the poor.

Professional Medicine's Response. The medical profession felt threatened by the increased government involvement in health care. Even though many European nations had already moved to some form of a nationalized health care system by 1930, the United States was slow to respond. Medicine in the United States was traditionally practiced on an individualized, fee-for-service pattern. Such group practices that did exist were seen by many physicians as forms of corporate or "socialized" medicine that could erode their traditional professional autonomy. In 1931 there were 156,440 physicians in the 48 states ranging from a low of 131 in Nevada to a high of 21,008 in New York. Doctors were becoming clustered in the cities and rarer in the remote rural areas of the country. According to the 1930 U.S. Census there were 122,775,046 Americans, which meant that for every 10,000 citizens, there were 12.74 physicians available to them. In 1934, 28 percent of medical schools had never graduated a woman; in 1939, 19 percent were still restricting their enrollment to men. In 1934, 43 percent of hospitals in the country had never employed a woman physician. The initial response of the AMA in 1934 to the increased federal involvement was to limit enrollments to medical school. Fewer physicians would mean a greater demand for their services and would insure that their salaries would remain high. The AMA in particular responded to proposals for a national health insurance with major publicity campaigns. There were also a great number of new medical specialty boards that came into existence in the 1930s. These boards were created not only to oversee the quantity and quality of new specialists but to stem the tide of what the medical profession saw as a potential for increased external controls.

The Age of Reform. Medical practice and financing in the 1930s was in need of reform. Because of the Depression, many Americans had to go without health care and many others could not pay for even part of their medical bills. By 1932 tax funds met 14 percent of the national medical bill, mostly for care in government hospitals. But voluntary hospitals were going under. People came to hospitals more for outpatient care; and the decreased use of inpatient beds forced a financial crisis. It seemed likely that the government would have to intervene in health services and many of Roosevelt's New Deal enactments did make some contributions to the nation's health. Three of every four citizens polled in the mid and late 1930s approved of government help in paying for their medical care. The inability of many Americans to afford the medical care they needed led to changes in health insurance and changes in the government's role in pro-

viding funds for health care and medical costs. The great increase in the role of hospitals, clinics, and laboratories created the need for reform within the organization of medicine, which led to the growth of the medical specialty boards. Had the private fee-for-service medical system worked as effectively as its AMA advocates insisted, it is likely that the hodgepodge of government and private agencies involved in the delivery of medical care would not have come into existence. The questions of medical reform were not solved in the 1930s and would affect issues of medicine in the United States for decades to come.

TOPICS IN THE NEWS

BIRTH CONTROL

Margaret Sanger, Birth Control Pioneer. Margaret Sanger, the great pioneer of the birth control movement in the United States, declared in a 1938 article in the *New Republic*, "At last birth control is legal in the United States." As a nurse in New York City slums, Sanger was appalled at deaths from self-induced abortions. One of every four maternal deaths was due to abortion. In 1916 she opened a birth control clinic in Brooklyn and was arrested for creating a public nuisance. But by 1938 she could proclaim that federal law finally recognized the right to provide contraceptive information and service under medical direction. This right was legal under state laws in all but three states, Connecticut, Mississippi, and Massachusetts.

Legal and Medical Sanctions for Birth Control. Prior to 1930 the Comstock laws of 1873 — Section 211 of the United States Penal Code — outlawed the dissemination of birth control information even by a physician and forbade any information about the subject from being sent through the mails or other carriers. Other sections criminalized the possession of any contraceptive article with fines from one thousand dollars to five thousand dollars, or imprisonment for five years, or both. Even married couples were forbidden by law from buying condoms and other contraception, especially through the mail. In 1930, after yet another trial of a physician who had prescribed contraceptive devices, the National Committee on Federal Legislation for Birth Control endorsed the lifting of federal restrictions. The National Committee consisted of nearly a thousand organizations with

about twenty million members; and they filed 325,000 individual endorsements with Congress. On 30 November 1936 the United States Circuit Court of Appeals for the Second Circuit decided that federal obscenity laws did not apply to the legitimate activities of physicians and that physicians could prescribe contraceptives in the interests of the health and general well-being of their patients. Its objective won, the National Committee disbanded. A few months later, in June 1937, the AMA approved birth control as an essential part of medical practice and education and urged that physicians be informed of their legal rights in relation to the use of contraceptives.

The Last Holdouts. But in 1938 Connecticut, Mississippi, and Massachusetts continued to hold out. In Connecticut the use of contraceptives was forbidden even though there were seven birth control clinics in operation in the state. Mississippi made no exceptions in its laws, which banned even verbal information. In Massachusetts eight birth control clinics operated for many years without legal problems even though the state laws made no exceptions in forbidding birth control. In the summer of 1937 three Massachusetts clinics were raided, and doctors, nurses, social workers, and officials were arrested, convicted, and fined. The cases were appealed to the higher courts, and all clinics in the state were closed. Even with this situation, Sanger persisted in her belief that these outmoded statutes in these three states would be reinterpreted and these states would "now catch up with public sentiment, judicial interpretation and the demand for contraceptive services by clarifying and mod-

Sen. Henry D. Hatfield of West Virginia with Margaret Sanger prior to her testimony before a U.S. Senate Judiciary Subcommittee.

ernizing their laws." In 1938 when she published her article in the *New Republic,* there were only 350 birth control centers in the country. But Margaret Sanger, the pioneering woman who coined the term *birth control* and created the Planned Parenthood Federation, did not give up. Her decades-long struggles with the law had finally won doctors the right to dispense birth control information to their patients.

Source:
Margaret Sanger, "The Status of Birth Control: 1938," *New Republic* (20 April 1938): 324–326.

THE BLUES — BLUE CROSS AND BLUE SHIELD

Hospitals and the Financial Crunch. One of the effects of the Depression was to increase public interest in prepayment for medical care. Until the 1930s hospitals primarily depended on endowment income, charitable gifts, and patients' fees to function. But with the advent of the Depression, these sources dried up. The high rate of unemployment forced hospitals to provide more free hospital care than they had done in the past, and their finances were in crisis. In just one year after the 1929 stock market crash, average hospital receipts per person fell from $236.12 to $59.26. In 1931 only 62 percent of the beds in voluntary hospitals were occupied on an average day, compared to 89 percent in government hospitals where costs were covered. The financial insecurity of the nation's voluntary hospitals encouraged them to turn to insurance for a solution and led to the organization of the Blue Cross plans. Americans were already familiar with policies offered by certain commercial insurance companies that offered part payment for medical expenses, especially those in hospitals. Labor unions, industries, lodges, and fraternal orders also offered similar prepayment plans, but the number of persons covered by these programs was small and declined during the Depression years.

The Emergence of Blue Cross and Blue Shield. In 1933 the American Hospital Association approved hospital insurance for the costs of hospital care. Subscribers paid a monthly fee, and the hospitals agreed to provide them full care in semiprivate accommodations for three weeks at a prearranged daily rate to be paid by Blue Cross. The American Hospital Association adopted some guiding principles. The plans were to be nonprofit and were only to cover hospital charges. This way they did not interfere with private practitioners. They were also to provide a choice of physician and hospital, which ruled out any single-hospital plan. Physicians' and surgeons' fees were not covered. In 1939 Blue Shield plans were organized to take care of the doctors' bills, but unlike the Blue Cross plans, Blue Shield did not cover the entire bill. Blue Shield began as the California Physicians Service, which originally offered coverage for home and office visits as well as doctors' services in the hospital. That same year, the medical society in Michigan also organized a prepayment plan, and in the following years, similar plans were started in other states.

Voluntary Health Insurance. The medical profession committed itself to private health insurance by endorsing hospital insurance and in actively developing proposals for medical service plans such as Blue Shield. The label of "voluntary" health insurance was attached to the "Blues" and to other insurance companies' health plans. Voluntary health insurance differed from other proposals for a publicly organized national system. It joined private fee-for-service practice as a desirable feature of the health system from the medical profession's point of view and supported the image of medical professionals as independent entrepreneurs. Thus, these nationally organized, privately operated, nonprofit Blue Cross and Blue Shield plans shored up the physicians' and voluntary hospitals' independence and helped to steer the country away from national health insurance proposals.

Sources:
James Bordley and A. McGehee Harvey, *Two Centuries of American Medicine, 1776–1976* (Philadelphia: W. B. Saunders, 1976), p. 120;

Paul Starr, *The Social Transformation of American Medicine* (New York: Basic Books, 1982), pp. 295–310;

Rosemary Stevens, *American Medicine and the Public Interest* (New Haven: Yale University Press, 1971), pp. 270–271.

THE COST OF BEING SICK

Caught in the Middle. In 1930 a major concern for Americans was whether or not they could afford to be sick. The wealthy could pay for their own medical expenses, and the decade of the 1920s had seen a continuation of the development of charitable organizations that helped to support the very poor. But families of moderate means were caught in the middle. A number of trends in medicine contributed to the mounting costs of medical care, including the increased use of hospitalization for patients, medical specialization, the "sliding scale," and charity work of physicians.

Costs and Trends in Medicine. By the fourth decade of the century medicine entered an age of hospitalization. Hospitals originated as charitable institutions for the poor, with a few private rooms added for the wealthy. As health care and technology improved, medical care focused more on hospital treatment and hospitals increased in number and complexity. As this change occurred, the proportion of medical school graduates settling in large cities near large hospitals increased. With the increase in doctors and medical complexity, many general practitioners began to specialize, partly to compete and partly to solve the problem of keeping up to date in the enormous field of medicine that lay outside their particular speciality. Costs were also driven up for average Americans by their doctors' practice of the sliding scale, or "what the traffic will bear," for charging for medical care. Most doctors set apart a portion of their time for charity work and the costs were also passed along in higher rates to their paying clients. Citizens of 1930 saw a rough justice in "charging the rich man's gout for the poor man's physic" but complained about "charging the man of moderate means a compulsory poor tax, which he cannot pay."

Solutions. Suggestions to solve these problems included prepaid sickness insurance, more middle-priced hospitals for patients of moderate means, group practices, and preventive medicine, including earlier trips to physicians before an incipient health problem grew more costly. Many critics noted how well Americans were provided with death insurance but commented on the need for "sickness" insurance for all Americans to avoid doctors passing on the costs of those who could not pay to those who received the bills. In 1930 the public called for more group practices as an antidote for the burdensome costs of increasing specialization and a "practical answer to the dreaded demand for state medicine. . . . a more socialized — . . . [not] socialistic or Bolshevistic! — medical practice . . ." Americans thought costs should be reduced if they could be, or at least more equally distributed. In previous decades they would not have issued such open challenges to the medical profession, but by

HOSPITAL COSTS AND MEDICAL EXPENSES

In 1930 in a moderately priced hospital such as the new Baker Memorial Pavilion of the Massachusetts General Hospital, a bed in a nine-bed ward cost $4 a day; in a four-bed room, $4.50 a day; in a two-bed room, $5.50 a day; and in a single room, $6.50 a day. These rates did not include private nursing or private medical and surgical care.

By mid decade medical expenses for the average family amounted to $56 dollars a year. Individuals averaged $18. Families with an income of less than $500 a year paid an average of $16 a year for their health care, while wealthier families making more than $20,000 paid an average of $899 a year for their medical expenses. Measles cost $4.81 to treat; chicken pox, $1.82; and whooping cough, $6.27. A fractured limb meant an expense of $18.07, and a tonsillectomy cost $47.37. Childbirth costs averaged $98.74. Chronic diseases meant a lifetime outlay of $25.56 to treat neuralgia, $30.52 for rheumatism, and $63.24 for diabetes. Cancer treatments averaged $341.51 over an individual's lifetime, and heart trouble cost $49.56.

The average American counted on averaging between one and two disabling illnesses every year. Most common were respiratory or digestive diseases, and each time they incapacitated, on average, for eight days. The individual paid an average of $5.91 for treatment of each minor respiratory disease and $6.89 for a common digestive disturbance. A more serious case of pneumonia, which could be fatal, would cost $58.72 to treat.

Sources: Frederick L. Collins, "The High Cost of Being Sick," *Ladies' Home Journal* (October 1930): 16–17+;

"The Medical Problem," *Fortune* (November 1938): 154;

Statistical Abstract of the United States, 1940 (Washington, D.C.: United States Government Printing Office, 1941): 318–319.

1930 they cried, "It is we who must see that this question [of cost] is settled and settled right!"

Source:
Frederick L. Collins, "The High Cost of Being Sick," *Ladies Home Journal* (October 1930): 16–17+.

THE DAWN OF THE SULFA DRUGS

The "Sulfa" Drugs. Infectious diseases had no truly effective agents for treatment available until the 1930s, when sulfonamides were developed as the first systemic drugs effectively used to fight the major killers of the twentieth century. The first of the sulfa drugs, Prontosil, was discovered by the German physician and chemist

Gerhard Domagk. In 1932 he noticed that Prontosil, a red azo dye used in the laboratories of the dye industry, cured streptococcal infections in his laboratory mice. Domagk was awarded the 1939 Nobel Prize for medicine or physiology for his research, but the Nazis forced him to decline it. Workers at the Pasteur Institute (Paris) found that the active component of the dye was sulfanilamide, and the dawn of the modern era of antibacterial chemotherapy truly began.

American Contributors. American scientists Perrin H. Long and Eleanor A. Bliss brought Prontosil to the United States and used it in clinical applications at the Johns Hopkins Hospital beginning in 1936. Their invitro experiments and experimentation on mice led them to conclude, "the careful clinical use of para-amino-benzene-sulfonamide and its derivatives in the treatment of human beings ill with infections due to beta-hemolytic streptococci is warranted." Another major contributor to the modern age of chemotherapy was E. Kennerly Marshall Jr., a professor of pharmacology at Johns Hopkins, who created a process for determining the amount of sulfanilamide in the blood of patients receiving it. Clinical experience proved the drug was effective in streptococcus and other bacterial organisms such as meningococcus and gonococcus.

The Beginning of the Revolution. The sulfonamides soon offered a more hopeful outlook for sufferers of gonorrhea and streptococci infections, but there were certain drawbacks. The drugs often created serious side effects such as kidney failure. Other patients showed such allergic reactions as rashes and fever. Strains of bacteria, especially gonococci, developed a resistance to the sulfonamides, and the drugs had a relatively narrow range of activity since many infectious diseases were not affected by their action. The greatest development of the sulfa drugs came in the decade of the 1940s when the needs of the war promoted their research and development. They later came to be overshadowed by the development of newer antibiotics such as penicillin and tetracycline. But the 1930s marked the real beginning of the revolution of the management of many important infectious diseases, and the sulfonamides continue to be widely used today.

Sources:

James Bordley and A. McGehee Harvey, *Two Centuries of American Medicine, 1776–1976* (Philadelphia: W. B. Saunders, 1976), pp. 447–448;

Theodore L. Sourkes, *Nobel Prize Winners in Medicine and Physiology. 1901–1965* (London: Abelard-Schuman, 1966), pp. 214–215, 219.

THE FOOD, DRUG, AND COSMETIC ACT OF 1938

A Terrible Mistake. The press widely praised sulfanilamide as a miracle medicine. But in 1937 a terrible mistake was made. The chief chemist at a small pharmaceutical plant in Bristol, Tennessee, trying to create a liquid dosage form, found that the solvent diethylene glycol would dissolve sulfanilamide. With the solvent he created a liquid form of sulfanilamide called an elixir of sulfanilamide. The chemist tested the elixir for appearance, fragrance, and flavor but neglected to consult the scientific literature or make animal tests to determine the effect on the body. Nearly two thousand pints of the liquid were made, but not one named the solvent on the label. Its presence in the elixir was toxic. The Food and Drug Administration (FDA; created in 1906 with the passage of the Pure Food and Drug Act) began hearing a rumor that deaths were occurring from some sulfa compound. By the time the investigation was over, the "elixir," according to FDA calculations, had killed some 107 people, many of them children who suffered long and painful deaths. A victim's mother wrote to President Franklin Roosevelt, telling how her little girl of six had died in agony and begging the president to support legislation to prevent other families from suffering similar tragedies. She included a picture of her daughter with the letter. The chemist who created the elixir committed suicide, and the doctor who owned the company paid a fine of $26,100, the highest ever levied under the 1906 law. An outraged public begged Congress to amend the earlier law to insure such mistakes would never again occur.

Federal Regulations. The Pure Food and Drug Act marked the beginning of federal drug regulation, but it had several loopholes. It did not require the disclosure of all contents, except for narcotics; and it did not regulate the bold claims of drug makers except in cases that were "false and fraudulent." State and federal drug officials and the AMA continued the struggle to expose quackery and to strengthen the drug laws. Although some progress was made, it took the national drug scandal over "Elixir Sulfanilamide" to bring about a major revision of the act.

A Last Measure from the New Deal. On 27 June 1938 President Roosevelt added his signature to the Food, Drug, and Cosmetic Act. It was one of the last major domestic measures to come from the New Deal. Any false and misleading statement in labels was now banned, and the government no longer needed to prove fraudulent intent in lawsuits. Labeling required warnings when medication might be hazardous. Now the names of all active ingredients were required on the label for over-the-counter remedies; and quantity and proportion had to be given for a list of potent drugs and habit-forming narcotics and hypnotic substances. New drugs could not be marketed until their manufacturers persuaded FDA officials that the drugs were safe. With their new law as a weapon, the FDA launched a full-scale campaign to make self-medication and cosmetic products safe. Its first seizure under the new law was an aniline eyelash "beautifier" that blinded the women who used it.

Sources:
"Two New Treatments and Two New Dangers," *Scientific Monthly* (January 1938): 63;

Paul Starr, *The Social Transformation of American Medicine* (New York: Basic Books, 1982), p. 131;

James Harvey Young, *The Medical Messiahs* (Princeton, N.J.: Princeton University Press, 1967), pp. 184–188.

THE "GOOD SLEEP" — A NEW ERA IN SURGERY

News Flashes. In 1933 Americans could ponder such news flashes from the world of "astonishing, modern surgery" as:

•A patient in a New York hospital who read a newspaper throughout his painless operation.
•A seventy-year-old surgeon who performed a major abdominal operation upon himself.
•A Long Island patient who carried on a conversation with the surgeon during a forty-five-minute operation on his brain.

Anesthesia and Medical Progress. One of the most significant American contributions to the history of medical progress was the introduction of surgical anesthesia. In 1844 Horace Wells, a dentist from Hartford, Connecticut, began to use nitrous oxide ("laughing gas") during dental extractions. Two years later another dentist, William T. G. Morton of Boston, who had experimented with ether for pulling teeth, administered it for a surgical operation performed by John C. Warren at the Massachusetts General Hospital. Chloroform was introduced in Europe in 1848, but it was never very popular in the United States. The danger was that even a little too much in the bloodstream might paralyze the heart.

Ether. By the early 1930s ether was still the main anesthesia of choice, but it had its own problems. It caused stomach upsets, and because it was an intoxicant the human system developed a tolerance for it, just as with alcohol. During the second of the four stages of

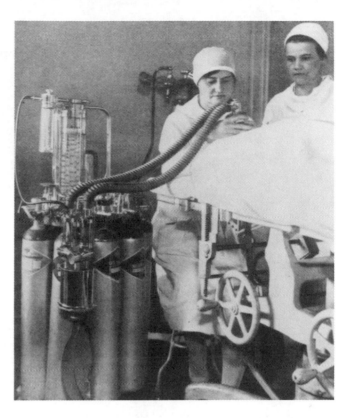

Hospital staff using the latest equipment to administer anesthetic to a patient before surgery

administration of ether, the patient could become excitable and need physical restraint. It was also highly explosive, and the sparks from an X-ray machine could touch off a blast. Extensive precautions had to be taken. Most surgical anesthesia techniques used nitrous oxide and oxygen until the patient lost consciousness. Then ether was administered by breathing through a cone, finishing off with nitrous oxide again to reduce post-operative vomiting. Nitrous oxide was the safest anesthetic; chloroform the most dangerous but the most efficient; ether the best for all-around work. Electric anesthetic machines and batteries of cylinders filled with different vapors under high pressure were part of the equipment of the surgery room. Watching the dials, the expert in charge controlled the strength and flow of the anesthetic by means of levers. Besides keeping the patient unconscious by replacing the ether lost in breathing, he watched the type of tissue through which the surgeon was cutting, since some tissues were more sensitive and would require an extra amount of anesthetic to prevent pain and shock. The patient's color had to be carefully watched to determine the need for more or less oxygen. Jaundiced persons and dark-skinned African Americans were difficult subjects for the doctor in charge of the anesthetic.

New Developments. New developments in anesthesia in the early 1930s created dramatic changes in surgery. Neocaine, a French drug, was used in spinal anesthesia. Injected into the lower spine, it deadened the abdomen and lower extremities, allowing the patient to remain

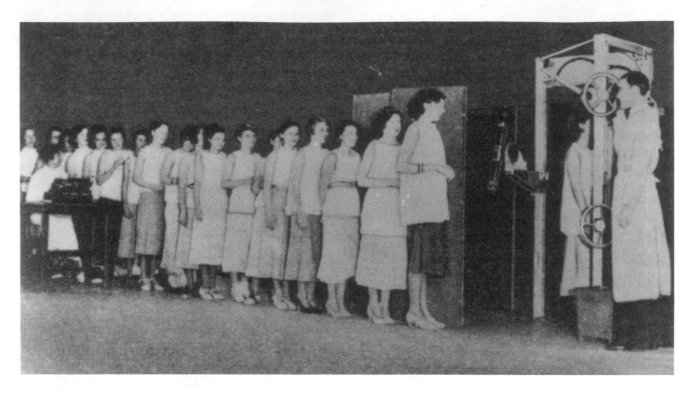

Students in line for lung X rays used to detect tuberculosis, which were administered at the rate of four per minute

fully conscious and to retain full use of his arms. It eliminated nausea after the operation, and there was no excitement stage, as there was with ether. Avertin, introduced from Germany in 1930, was given rectally and used for short operations, since its effects lasted only about an hour. Pernocton, taken by mouth or injected into the veins, put the patient into a deep sleep that lasted for several hours. It was used in childbirth with less harmful effects to the baby than other drugs. Local anesthetics such as novocaine (one-seventh as dangerous as cocaine), eucaine, and benzyl alcohol were also used frequently in major operations in place of ether. Novocaine was the drug used by the surgeon who operated upon himself. Sitting on the operating table, propped up by pillows, he swabbed the right side of his abdomen with iodine and alcohol and then injected novocaine from a small hypodermic syringe along the line he intended to cut. He was out of the hospital following the operation in far less time than usual. He pointed out his experiment proved that when the patient's system was not burdened with a general anesthetic, recovery was quicker. The newest local anesthetic in 1933 was diothane, developed by two Cincinnati, Ohio, chemists. It deadened pain longer than either novocaine or cocaine, had no habit-forming properties, and was considered valuable because it kept the patient comfortable longer after surgery.

Conquering Pain. By 1933 eighty-seven years had passed since Morton demonstrated the powers of ether fumes. World War I stimulated the use of anesthesia, and with later developments of local anesthesia and spinal anesthesia the trained physician anesthetist came into his

own. The nurse anesthetist was also well established, and many of the medical anesthesiologists of the 1930s were introduced to anesthesia during their internship by nurse anesthetists. Month by month, surgeons reported new feats to Americans, adding fresh chapters to the age-old story of conquering pain.

Sources:

James Bordley and A. McGehee Harvey, *Two Centuries of American Medicine, 1776–1976* (Philadelphia: W. B. Saunders, 1976), p. 79;

F. Damrau, "Safe Pain Killing Drugs Bring New Era in Surgery," *Popular Science* (February 1933): 32–34.

"THE GREAT WHITE PLAGUE" — TUBERCULOSIS BEFORE THE AGE OF ANTIBIOTICS

A Chronic Infectious Disease. Pulmonary tuberculosis — also known as consumption, phthisis, or the "great white plague" — was still an insidious, chronic presence in the 1930s. The disease is caused by a tubercle bacillus, or germ, contained in the sputum coughed up by patients with tuberculosis of the lungs, and it is spread from sick to well individuals by close personal contact. After the discovery of the bacillus in 1882, doctors and the public hoped that a means could be found to kill it within the body or to immunize the individual from its threats, but this did not exist in the 1930s. In 1930 the tuberculosis mortality rate was seventy per one hundred thousand population per year. It took more lives than any other contagious disease. In 1936 the U.S. Bureau of the Census estimated that one out of every twenty-one deaths was due to tuberculosis. Its greatest toll was in young

MALPRACTICE PROTECTION

When, in 1935, doctors found themselves increasingly the targets of malpractice litigation, they received advice from a fellow doctor in *Clinical Medicine & Surgery*:

•Never under any circumstances promise a cure or use language which might be interpreted as such a promise.

•Be careful of diagnoses and when there is doubt don't "affix a label."

•When calling a consultant, select one who knows more than you do.

•In surgical cases, in unfamiliar surroundings, see that a careful count of all sponges is kept all the time, and be sure that the count is verified before closing the incision.

•If an operation is to be performed, have the patient, or his guardian, give consent in writing, or verbal consent in the presence of a witness.

•Collect your fees when they are due. It is a well-recognized fact that many malpractice suits are started because physicians try to force payment from delinquent patients.

•Do not become nervous. If things have gone wrong, do not inform the patient, his family or friends that an error has been committed. It is not necessary to misrepresent the condition, but it is easy to evade direct replies until you can determine the end results.

•Terminate your relations tactfully with patients who seem contentious or litigious.

Source: "Malpractice Protection," *Time* (18 November 1935): 54.

---

people between the ages of fifteen to forty-five, and it affected proportionately more women than men.

Treatment. Although deaths from tuberculosis were still high, mortality rates had declined from the two hundred tuberculosis deaths per one hundred thousand population per year in 1900. Several factors contributed to this steady decline, including the public concern raised by individuals and organizations such as the National Tuberculosis Association. By 1930 scientists better understood how the disease was spread; earlier diagnosis by means of X-ray machines and tuberculin tests prevented the more serious forms of the disease; the testing and elimination of tubercular cows and the pasteurization of milk eliminated the infection in children from cows' milk; and more-widespread institutional care in private

sanatoriums and state and municipal TB hospitals provided both quarantine and better medical supervision. Treatment still consisted primarily of rest, a well-balanced diet rich in vitamins and minerals, an "abundance of fresh air and moderate amounts of sunlight," or even surgery to collapse the diseased lung for treatment or to remove the diseased part of the lung.

Christmas Seals. In most European countries the government funded health and welfare programs to combat tuberculosis, but in the United States both the federal and the state governments were slow to become involved. Consequently, lay associations such as the American Red Cross and the National Tuberculosis Association funded most of the tuberculosis programs. The best-known fund-raiser was the brightly colored little stamps called Christmas seals, which cost only a penny. The bright red double-barred cross that was the insignia of antituberculosis work throughout the world identified them, and they were used as decorations on mail and packages.

A New X-Ray Machine. With fears of a spread of tuberculosis from the poverty of the Depression, one of the few advances against the disease made in the 1930s was the movement for X-raying schoolchildren. The use of X rays in the diagnosis of TB was nothing new in itself, but the novelty in 1933 lay in a new weapon — a machine capable of taking X rays of the lung at the rate of four X rays a minute. The high speed and precision of the new machines made it possible to examine large numbers of schoolchildren in a very short time. They lined up near the machine, and one by one they stepped up and were "shot" at the rate of 150 or more an hour. The new, portable equipment lowered the price of X-ray diagnosis and improved treatment possibilities. The X-ray exam could spot early lesions in the lungs. In its earliest stages, before the victim was even aware of its presence, tuberculosis cure was comparatively easy and sure. In the later stages it was much more difficult. Public health officials hoped that with periodic X-ray exams of all children and adolescents, cases could be found and treated, eventually wiping out tuberculosis. By 1938 the tuberculosis death rate had been reduced to 56 per 100,000 population per year. Yet the greatest twentieth-century innovation in the treatment of tuberculosis, Selman Waksman's chemotherapeutic agent streptomycin, was a decade away.

Sources:

James Bordley and A. McGehee Harvey, *Two Centuries of American Medicine, 1776–1976* (Philadelphia: W. B. Saunders, 1976): 202–213;

Herman N. Bundesen, "Tuberculosis," *Ladies' Home Journal* (April 1939): 82+;

"The Dragnet for Tuberculosis," *Scientific American* (June 1938): 354;

"A Rapid-Fire Weapon to Fight Tuberculosis," *Scientific American* (November 1933): 215;

Sheila M. Rothman, *Living in the Shadow of Death* (New York: Basic Books, 1994);

A. Schaeffer Jr., "Tuberculosis and the Depression," *Journal of Home Economics* (December 1932): 1076–1078.

President Roosevelt signing the Social Security Act, 14 August 1935. From left: Edwin E. White, Robert L. Doughton, Alben W. Barkley, Robert F. Wagner, unidentified man, Frances Perkins, Byron Patton Harrison, and Davis J. Lewis.

HEALTH AND THE NEW DEAL

Social Reform. Franklin Delano Roosevelt's inaugural speech on 4 March 1933 set the tone for the early months of what would come to be called the New Deal. The Depression affected the priorities of social reform in the United States. The consequences of the sudden, enormous unemployment after 1929 fell first on local governments, which, as they always had, retained primary responsibility for relief of the poor. But relief payments were pitiful, and private agencies also could not cope with the massive unemployment and suffering. By 1932 even President Hoover had to admit that Americans needed federal help. During earlier eras in U.S. history, health insurance was the top item after workmen's compensation. European countries typically developed health insurance from a system of insurance against industrial accidents. Old-age pensions were next, and unemployment insurance came last. But in America, with millions out of work, unemployment insurance became the leading priority. Roosevelt told the American people that "fear it-

self" was the chief danger and proposed programs to ease the economic hardships suffered by millions with relief measures that would put jobless people to work and lead to economic recovery. Through New Deal programs, the federal government came to play such an unprecedented part in people's daily lives that its critics decried it as "socialism."

Contributions to the Nation's Health. Even though it appeared that national health insurance would have to wait, almost every New Deal agency, temporary or permanent, made some contribution to the nation's health. As early as June 1933 the Federal Emergency Relief Administration used some of its funds for medical care, nursing, and emergency dental work, and Civilian Conservation Corps workers received medical care as part of their benefits. The Civil Works Administration promoted rural sanitation and helped control malaria; and both the Works Progress Administration and the Public Works Administration built hospitals, sewer plants, and other public health projects.

The Frontier Nursing Service nurse provided medical services including handing swaddled newborn babies — "least-uns" — to their mothers after riding to their mountain cabins on horseback. Rural eastern Kentucky in 1937 had seven hundred square miles of mountainous land with no railroad, only twenty-four miles of gravel road, and one hospital with eighteen beds. Frontier nurses rode horses, mules, or flat boats to assist in childbirth, give inoculations against communicable diseases, and wage a vigorous campaign against the diseases of rural poverty — trachoma and hookworm.

Patients paid according to their means — the mother of the new "least-un" who rarely had thirty dollars a year might pay only a dime. A bill of five dollars was likely to be paid in goods — three shoats, a rifle, two split-bottom chairs, or a load of hay.

Source: "Frontier Nurse," *Literary Digest* (28 August 1937): 12.

The Social Security Act of 1935. The Social Security Act had far-reaching consequences for American life. Even though other nations had adopted systems of health insurance for their citizens and social security for the unemployed, the handicapped, and the aged, the United States had left such social problems to the individual to solve. The Social Security Act established a system of unemployment insurance, set up a pension scheme for retired people over sixty-five and their survivors, and provided federal funds to the states to aid them in caring for the blind and for destitute children. It extended the government's role in public health by providing states funds on a matching basis for maternal and infant care, rehabilitation of crippled children, and general public health work.

Significance for Health. While the Social Security bill itself included only one minor reference to health insurance, it was of special significance, since it established a permanent machinery for distributing federal funds for health purposes and recognized special needs in allocating these funds. Appropriations for health under the Social Security Administration grew rapidly in the late 1930s. A National Health Survey in 1935–1936 confirmed that the lowest economic groups were at the greatest risk for sickness and disability, while receiving the least medical care. The survey aroused public awareness of health problems, and in 1939 the Wagner bill was introduced into Congress to establish a national health program. But President Roosevelt's preoccupation with the fascist aggression, the opposition of organized medicine including the AMA, and other factors prevented its passage.

Sources:

John Duffy, *The Healers: The Rise of the Medical Establishment* (New York: McGraw-Hill, 1976), p. 317;

Michael B. Katz, *In the Shadow of the Poorhouse. A Social History of Welfare in America* (New York: Basic Books, 1986);

Paul Starr, *The Social Transformation of American Medicine* (New York: Basic Books, 1982), pp. 266–270.

THE MARCH OF DIMES AND THE NATIONAL FOUNDATION FOR INFANTILE PARALYSIS

President Roosevelt and Polio. Of all the major ills that still plagued Americans in the 1930s, polio became a community rallying point and an urgent subject for medical research. Polio was an enemy that struck the nation's young in a vicious manner, often paralyzing or crippling victims for life, if it was not fatal. The nation's first citizen was its foremost victim. In 1938 not all Americans knew that their president, Franklin Delano Roosevelt, was a paraplegic, a crippled victim of poliomyelitis. Roosevelt disguised his paralysis with strong steel braces on his paralyzed legs when he had to stand and often appeared seated in open-topped automobiles where the crowds could not see his disability. He was only photographed in a wheelchair once during his entire political career. But the story of his apparent "victory" over the disease was common knowledge. He made frequent therapy visits to Warm Springs, Georgia, to the Warm Springs Foundation, which ran a treatment center for polio victims. In 1934 the foundation needed financial support, and the decision was made to ask the public for contributions. President Roosevelt lent his name to the fund-raising campaign, which was based on a series of annual balls held in various cities on Roosevelt's birthday, 30 January.

The National Foundation for Infantile Paralysis and the March of Dimes. In January 1938 President Roosevelt provided his leadership to expand the Warm Springs Foundation into a national organization — the National Foundation for Infantile Paralysis. A dynamic lawyer named Basil O'Connor, who had once practiced law in New York City with Roosevelt, took command. The new foundation's stated purpose was "To lead, direct, and unify the fight against every aspect of the killing and crippling infection of poliomyelitis." The plan was to collect small contributions from a large number of people, and its fund-raising campaign became famous as the "March of Dimes." The campaign soon captured the imagination of the country. At halftime at basketball games in small towns a big canvas was spread on the court to receive the change that the spectators showered down. The Disney Studios created a cartoon for the foundation featuring Mickey Mouse, Donald Duck, and friends marching off to fight polio:

Heigh-ho, heigh-ho
We'll lick ol' polio,
With dimes and quarters

President Roosevelt with patients at the National Foundation for Infantile Paralysis in Warm Springs, Georgia, mid 1930s

And our doll-aaars —
Ho, heigh-ho!

Research as a Popular Cause. Roosevelt believed that poliomyelitis could be conquered with a program of scientific education and research and the organization of the National Foundation for Infantile Paralysis. Ordinary people came to see research as a popular cause, and the March of Dimes annually raised more money than any other health campaign. The millions of people who gave money every year to the March of Dimes did so because they wanted to care for polio patients and to wipe out the disease that had so injured them. The scientists — microbiologists, biochemists, or the newly emerging specialists in virology and immunology — desired to solve the mystery of poliomyelitis and to understand the nature of viruses and the way they spread. Out of this program came the research that supported the ultimate creation of the miraculous Salk and Sabin polio vaccines in the 1950s.

Sources:
James Bordley and A. McGehee Harvey, *Two Centuries of American Medicine, 1776–1976* (Philadelphia: W. B. Saunders, 1976), pp. 647–648;

Geoffrey Marks and William K. Beatty, *The Story of Medicine in America* (New York: Scribners, 1973), p. 281;

Edward Shorter, *The Health Century* (New York: Doubleday, 1987), p. 64;

Jane S. Smith, *Patenting the Sun. Polio and the Salk Vaccine* (New York: Morrow, 1990).

MATERNAL MORTALITY — WHY MOTHERS DIED

A Cause for Concern. A major health concern of the decade was the high rate of mothers who died giving birth. In 1936 the Federal Children's Bureau called attention to an "alarmingly high" maternal mortality rate of 59 mothers per 10,000 live births in 1934, the highest among the industrialized nations. More women in the reproductive period of life from ages fifteen to twenty-four died from diseases and complications of pregnancy and childbirth than from any other cause except tuberculosis. The specific reasons recorded on death certificates for these 12,859 deaths included septicemia or puerperal fever, a contagious infection responsible for about 40 percent of the deaths. Twenty-three percent of maternal mortalities were due to albuminuria with eclampsia, a condition of protein in the urine which can lead to coma and convulsions. "Other causes," a blanket group of emergencies, abnormalities, operative procedures, etc., accounted for about 37 percent of the mothers' deaths.

To make a preventive vaccine for a virus, you have to catch it first. But the common-cold virus was invisible under the best microscope and so tiny it slithered right through the finest-grained porcelain filter. In 1935 Dr. Alphonse Raymond Dochez, a professor of medicine at the College of Physicians and Surgeons at Columbia University, announced he had isolated the cold virus. First he took throat washings from victims, then he filtered out bacteria and left the virus floating in the sterile water.

Next Dochez had to find at what temperature the viruses thrive and in what medium they thrived. On a chicken embryo diet they multiplied rapidly. Thus, for the first time in medical history, Dochez cultivated the virus outside the body. Making a preventive vaccine was the next step. Dochez worked on it, and so, to this day, have many others!

Source: "MEDICINE: N.Y. Doctor Finally Discovered Common-Cold Bug," *Newsweek* (9 November 1935): 42.

Poverty and Rural Isolation. Although unlisted on death certificates, poverty and rural isolation from prenatal and obstetrical care were major causes of maternal deaths. Prenatal care meant visits to the doctor, and visits to the doctor, when there was one available, cost money. The comparison of maternal mortality rates for white and African American women was an additional cause for concern. The mortality rate for African American women for 1934 was 93 per 10,000 live births as compared with 54 for white women. In the early part of the decade home births were still traditional. In Europe trained midwives were often more highly skilled in obstetrics than physicians, but the midwife profession was not as well developed in the United States. By 1930, 80 percent of the forty-seven thousand midwives in the United States were practicing in the rural South where maternal mortality rates ran as high as 114 deaths per 10,000 live births in some states.

Cultural and Medical Attitudes toward Pregnancy. Poorly trained midwives were not the only cause of the high mortality rates. The philosophy of the medical world of the day was that childbirth was a "physiological function" and nothing to worry about. General practitioners attended about two-thirds of the births, and a surprising number of physicians knew very little about it. Although obstetrics and pediatrics grew as medical specialties during the 1920s, obstetrics was still given short shrift in medical schools. At the end of 1929 the Council of Medical Education of the American Medical Association reported that of 1,491 interns in approved teaching hospitals, 334 graduated without having delivered any babies and 235 had not even observed deliveries. By 1931 there were only about 8,000 obstetrical specialists in the country, the majority of them in the Northeast.

The Childbirth Profession. The medical profession regarded the midwives who still existed in the early 1930s as only a temporary expedient until all patients could be delivered by physicians, and midwifery laws gradually legislated them out of existence. The concerns over the high rates of maternal mortality encouraged higher standards of medical obstetrics and gynecology as well as the elimination of the untrained general practitioner-surgeon. Ironically, the emphasis on obstetrics as a specialty contributed to some of the deaths from "other causes," as obstetricians became enthusiastic — sometimes overenthusiastic — surgeons. By 1930 caesarean section was a fashionable method of childbirth, both because of improvements in technology and safety compared with an earlier generation and because of the increasing number of patients who sought obstetrical services in hospitals. Between 20 to 25 percent of hospital deliveries in New York and Philadelphia in the early 1930s involved operative procedures, especially for private patients. Any physician could legally perform surgical obstetrics, and there was a high correlation between maternal mortality and operative interventions.

Board Certified. Except in ophthalmology and otology, where the specialty boards were long established, hospitals had no guidelines to evaluate the abilities of their staffs. In 1930 the American Board of Obstetrics and Gynecology was established to detach the two specialties from general surgery and to make sure that no part-time specialists would be certified. Candidates were required to limit their practice to obstetrics and gynecology. The board defined specialist boundaries, and the general practitioner was rejected from board certification. The overt function of certification was to establish recommended patterns of training, and, since the boards were professional organizations, to decide on acceptable modes of practice and behavior, thus reducing maternal mortality rates. But the GPs continued to resist any attempt to give the specialists exclusive privileges over obstetrical work and continued, with relatively little training, to deliver babies.

Sources:
Mary Sumner Boyd, "Why Mothers Die," *Nation* (18 March 1931): 293–295;

Paul Starr, *The Social Transformation of American Medicine* (New York: Basic Books, 1982), pp. 223–224;

Rosemary Stevens, *American Medicine and the Public Interest* (New Haven: Yale University Press, 1971), pp. 99–100, 180, 200–204;

Frank H. Vizetely, ed., *The New International Year Book for the Year 1936* (New York: Funk & Wagnalls, 1937), p. 154.

THE NATION'S HEALTH

The Science and Status of Medicine. By the late 1930s medicine was well established as a science. The

Hospitals decreased in number from 6,719 in 1930 to 6,437 in 1933 to 6,166 by 1938. In 1933 the country had a variety of hospitals offering different types of services:

Hospitals by type of service:

General 4,237

Nervous and mental 621

Tuberculosis 497

Maternity 134

Industrial 118

Convalescent 130

Isolation 71

Children's 58

Eye, Ear, Nose, and Throat 56

Orthopedic 69

Hospital departments of institutions 343

The rate of patient occupancy in general hospitals was 59.9 percent. The average length of stay in a general hospital was 14 days in 1933, which decreased to 12.6 days by 1937. One American in fourteen became a hospital patient in 1933. Only one-third of all births were in hospitals in that same year.

Sources: *The World Almanac and Book of Facts, 1935* (New York: New York World-Telegram, 1935): 278;

The World Almanac and Book of Facts, 1940 (New York: New York World-Telegram, 1940): 326, 519.

modern age of chemotherapy had arrived with the sulfa drugs, and the age of antibiotics was to come in the next decade. Hormones, insulin, and vitamins were used in daily life. Blood transfusion was one of the most common hospital procedures, together with a bewildering variety of diagnostic and therapeutic procedures, including X-ray procedures, electrocardiographs, and basal metabolism techniques. In the first thirty years of the century public health measures had alleviated much human misery. Diseases such as typhoid fever, dysentery, and diphtheria were rapidly disappearing. Other diseases, previously unknown, were taking their place: allergies, diabetes, arthritis, and diseases of the peripheral blood vessels. There were still epidemics and some diseases, which, as one doctor put it, "many a research man would literally give

his right arm if he could just find a clue as to how [it got] around." Infantile paralysis, or polio, was still a mystery disease, and so were spinal meningitis and sleeping sickness. German measles and the common cold were acknowledged threats, and tuberculosis, or the "white plague," still was mainly being treated by sunshine, fresh air, and rest.

A Report on the Nation's Health. In 1938 Surgeon General Thomas Parran published a report on the nation's health and revealed to his countrymen that every day one out of twenty people was too sick to go to school or work, and each citizen on average suffered ten days of incapacity during the average year. Forty-two percent of those who were sick every day suffered from chronic diseases such as heart disease, hardening of the arteries, rheumatism, or mental diseases. Sixty-five thousand people in a national population of 130 million were totally deaf; 75,000 were "deaf and dumb"; 200,000 lacked a hand, arm, foot, or leg; 300,000 had permanent spinal injuries; 500,000 were blind; and a million more were permanent cripples. The average life expectancy for a white male born during the decade was 60.6 years; for a white female, 64.6 years. Nonwhite males had a life expectancy of only 49.4 years; and nonwhite females, 52.1 years.

Health and Socioeconomic Status. Socioeconomic status had a clear impact on an American's health. Parran's report indicated that two persons on the Relief income level (less than a thousand dollars yearly income for the entire family) were disabled for one week or longer for every one person better off economically. Only one in 250 family heads in the income group of more than $2,000 yearly could not seek work because of chronic disability. In Relief families one in every twenty family heads was disabled. Relief and low-income families were sick longer as well as more often than wealthier families, although they called doctors less often. But the poor, especially in big cities, got to stay in hospitals longer than their better-off neighbors. Parran concluded: "It is apparent that inadequate diet, poor housing, the hazards of occupation and the instability of the labor market definitely create immediate health problems." He had cause for concern as he ceremonially broke ground for a new group of U.S. Public Health Service research buildings near Washington to aid in improving the nation's health.

Sources:
G. H. Estabrooks, "They Shall Not Pass . . ." *Scientific American* (December 1937): 340–342;

E. Eastman Irvine, Ed., *World Almanac and Book of Facts for 1943* (New York: New York World-Telegram, 1943), p. 470;

"Sickness Survey," *Time* (31 January 1938): 22+;

Rosemary Stevens, *American Medicine and the Public Interest* (New Haven: Yale University Press, 1971), pp. 179–180.

THE NEW DEAL, HEALTH INSURANCE, AND THE AMA

Physicians' Autonomy versus the Great Depression. The traditional forms of medical practice in the United States evolved during the nineteenth and early twentieth centuries. Individual doctors cared for the sick and regulated their fees according to their patients' ability to pay. There were few group practices and fewer prepaid medical plans. This individualized fee-for-service system did not always provide economic security for the physician since it also rested on his ability to charge and to collect his fees. But it did mean that physicians had full control over their profession, with no other organization able to dictate their income and conditions of practice. This was a powerful tradition for the medical profession and one that they feared losing. American health insurance had been a political issue ever since World War I, after nearly all the major European countries had adopted programs. In the United States, what prepaid health insurance or third-party payments that existed came mainly from labor unions, and even these came from the local rather than the national organizations. There was some commercial health insurance, but it was little developed. Blue Cross and Blue Shield originated during the 1930s to provide some relief, but the Great Depression brought about calls for the greater reforms, as private physicians and private charities could no longer afford to meet the demand for free services. The public agitated for state-sponsored national health care. The powerful medical lobby fought "compulsory socialized medicine" as "another insidious step towards the breakdown of democracy."

The American Medical Association. The medical profession was organized through the American Medical Association (AMA), founded in 1846. By the 1930s the AMA was a very powerful political organization that controlled medical schools and medical education and defined the nature of medical practice in the United States. It fought third-party-payment insurance schemes for decades because it saw most insurance schemes and other potential external controls as forms of governmental paternalism, or "creeping socialism." Dr. Morris Fishbein, the editor of the AMA's publications and its primary spokesman in the 1930s, warned that any form of group health insurance or governmental aid in medical care "breaks down that initiative and ambition which are the marks of a young country going ahead," and the young doctor who steps into such a job, "begins a mechanized routine type of service that is harmful not only to his patients but to his own character and advancement."

Increases in Government Assistance Programs. Because of the economic crisis of the Depression, federal and state funds began increasingly to pay for medical services. The Resettlement Administration and Farm Security Administration subsidized cooperative medical prepayment plans among the poor farmers it assisted, and local medical societies agreed to accept limits on the fees they would receive. These new developments disturbed the AMA. They feared increasing government control of their profession, yet the Depression posed a severe test to the status quo. Physicians themselves were in economic difficulty. The initial response of the AMA to the national health crisis emphasized restricting the supply of doctors. In 1934 the AMA warned medical schools against admitting too many students, and enrollments declined. The prices physicians charged thus remained high, but limiting the number of doctors only exaggerated the lack of affordable health services for the public. By the late 1930s a new push for health insurance developed within the Roosevelt administration, although the president was tentative in its full backing.

A Profession or a Trade? As public interest in national health insurance programs became widespread, the AMA launched a counterattack. In response to the increasing evidence that a high percentage of Americans received little or no medical care, the AMA conducted its own survey and declared that the only citizens receiving inferior care were those under the jurisdiction of governmental agencies. The AMA rallied political support by accusing national health plans of destroying the medical profession, reducing doctors to mere laborers. ". . . Medicine . . . is practiced as an art and as a science, without any reference to hours of work or any fixed formula for its administration. These are the characteristics of the profession and the question which we must answer for ourselves and for the people is simply the question as to whether medicine shall remain a profession or become a trade," challenged Fishbein.

A Counterattack against National Health Insurance. Not all members of the AMA agreed with Fishbein. As political pressure began to build in support of a national health bill in the late 1930s, the AMA modified its earlier opposition to voluntary health insurance. Recognizing that voluntary programs were the lesser evil compared to compulsory ones, the AMA stopped opposing all insurance programs in general. Instead, it defined "acceptable" voluntary programs and insisted that there be no direct intervention in the doctor's business by any insurance company. Although the AMA's official viewpoint about health insurance was not unanimous, urban specialists controlled the organization and acted as its spokespersons as they fought to control their interests. In February 1939 Sen. Robert Wagner of New York introduced a national health insurance plan, which the AMA fought. But the bill died out as the United States became increasingly involved in the declining fortunes of the New Deal and then World War II. The American Medical Association was highly organized and very prepared to challenge any attempts to interfere with physicians' professional autonomy in the 1930s.

Sources:

Current Biography 1940 (New York: H. W. Wilson, 1940), pp. 297–299;

John Duffy, *The Healers: The Rise of the Medical Establishment* (New York: McGraw-Hill, 1976), pp. 304–305;

"Nationalized Doctors?" *Time* (21 June 1937): 26+;

Paul Starr, *The Social Transformation of American Medicine* (New York: Basic Books, 1982), pp. 235–279;

Rosemary Stevens, *American Medicine and the Public Interest* (New Haven: Yale University Press, 1971).

PSYCHOANALYSIS IN AMERICA AND THE IMPACT OF THE EUROPEAN INTELLECTUAL MIGRATION

The Nazis Ban Psychoanalysis. In October 1933 Nazi Germany labeled psychoanalysis a "Jewish science" and banned it from the Congress of Psychology in Leipzig. The Nazis burned psychoanalytic literature, and practicing psychoanalysts, mostly from Berlin, first joined Sigmund Freud for a brief stint in Vienna or left directly for the United States to save their lives and their practices. Their contributions made a profound impact on American psychology and contributed to the growth of a more influential psychiatric profession in the United States.

The Psychoanalytic Diaspora. Freud is honored as the genius of psychoanalysis, but not all American academicians or medical psychiatrists were ready to accept his ideas wholeheartedly. In the first third of the century there was a great deal of ambivalence to his ideas in the United States. Other schools of thought, such as behaviorism and experimental psychology, were more popular. The European psychoanalysts were accustomed to the lukewarm embrace of psychoanalysis. Analysts were to a large extent outsiders in their own countries and subject to the hostile climate of opinion that surrounded Freud's European psychoanalytic movement. But they brought certain strengths to the United States. They already knew their American colleagues from the international congresses of the psychoanalytic movement, and as practitioners of a middle- and upper-class urban profession, they were financially well situated. They settled in New York, Boston, Chicago, Philadelphia, Detroit, Los Angeles, and San Francisco and were soon busy in private practice, as professors, and as supervisors of a new generation of American psychiatrists.

The Popular Success of Psychoanalysis. The Great Depression was a time of much soul-searching for the American middle class, and these European psychoanalysts arrived at a time when there was a need to explain an event and the feelings it provoked in a new way. Popularized versions of Freudian theory reassured many that there were reasons for failure beyond their control — perhaps something from early childhood. The tremendous success of psychoanalysis in the popular culture forced academics to take a closer look. Beginning in 1936, a series of seminars was organized at Yale University with the aim of "achieving a synthesis of conditioning theory [behaviorism] and psychoanalysis." These seminars brought psychoanalysis to the center of attention at the Yale Institute of Human Relations. They were an important step for the history of Freud's influence on American psychology because they made many of his psychoanalytic concepts familiar-sounding and talked-about by psychologists.

American versus European Psychology. Much of American psychology emphasized measurement and scientific classifications; European psychoanalysis focused on imagery and dreams. Immigrants such as Ernst Kris and René Spitz, Else Frenkel-Brunswik, and Käthe Wolf adapted American methodologies and fused empirical research to psychoanalysis. Other Europeans combined different psychological schools with American practices. Gestalt psychology, with its emphasis on empirical research, was a good methodological fit and was carried into the United States by Wolfgang Köhler, Kurt Koffka, Max Wertheimer, and Alfred Lewin. Although Adler's individualist psychology did not interest academic psychologists, it was recognized and used by clinical workers to treat patients. It is not possible to separate completely the influence of the European intellectual migration of the 1930s from the natural evolutionary course of American psychiatry in understanding the convergence of psychoanalysis and general psychology. The fields of psychology that were the most affected by the Freudian diaspora included: abnormal, personality, developmental, industrial and social, and psychotherapy. But the fact remains that America has become a world center of psychoanalysis, while, in Europe, Freud is honored as a genius of a past epoch and psychoanalysis is mostly ignored.

Sources:

Marie Jahoda, "The Migration of Psychoanalysis: Its Impact on American Psychology," in *The Intellectual Migration. Europe and America, 1930–1960,* edited by Donald Fleming and Bernard Bailyn (Cambridge: Harvard University Press, 1969): 420–445;

David Shakow and David Rapaport, *The Influence of Freud on American Psychology* (Cleveland: Meridian Books, 1964), pp. 135–142, 194.

SEX, DISEASE, AND THE NEW DEAL

The Conquest of Infectious Disease. The most important health change during the century was the successful conquest of many infectious diseases through both public health measures and scientific medical advances. Diphtheria, typhoid, and dysentery no longer threatened Americans with terrible epidemics, yet venereal diseases remained uncontrolled. Modern antibiotic treatments for them were not available in the 1930s; but control was also defeated by a conspiracy of silence that prevailed in the country over issues of sexual morality. During World War I, newspapers and magazines dramatically publicized the problem, but in the years after the war the antivenereal campaign began to fail. If all conditions due to syphilis had been reported as such, it was believed that syphilis would have been found to be the leading cause of death in the United States. It was responsible for 10

Connecticut public service announcement promoting prenatal blood tests for venereal disease

percent of all insanity, 18 percent of all diseases of the heart and blood vessels, and many of the stillbirths and deaths of babies in the first weeks of life. In 1935 the disease attacked and disabled more than half a million people. There was more of it than measles, twice as much as tuberculosis, a hundred times as much as polio. The spirochete organism that causes syphilis was identified in 1905, and the following year August Wassermann and his colleagues developed a diagnostic test for the disease. In 1910 Paul Ehrlich discovered salvarson ("606") for use against syphilis, but his "magic bullet" was only partially effective, and until the advent of the sulfa drugs there was no important successor.

The Surgeon General's Campaign. During the years of the New Deal, Thomas Parran, the surgeon general under President Roosevelt, committed the country to the eradication of venereal disease by dramatically publicizing these infections. By the time Parran, a member of the Public Health Service since World War I, mounted his attack, publicizing it first in the *Survey Graphic* and then in the *Reader's Digest,* the Great Depression had eroded funds for venereal-disease control. According to the moral precepts of such groups as the American Social Hygiene Association, the disruption in traditional family roles created by the Depression generated higher rates of venereal disease. Syphilis and gonorrhea were seen as the consequences of the Depression's social instability rather

Nowhere was the campaign against syphilis pursued with more vigor than in Chicago. On 13 August 1937 a syphilis parade marched from the Loop to City Hall carrying banners proclaiming, "Friday the thirteenth is an unlucky day for syphilis." Even the Federal Theatre Project joined in with the production of Arnold Sundgaard's "living newspaper," *Spirochete*. This "fictionalized-documentary" reviewed the history of medical treatment for the disease, attacked the conspiracy of silence, and urged on the Wassermann campaign of testing and treatment. During intermission, theatergoers were invited to be tested in the lobby. *Spirochete* later opened in Boston, Seattle, and Philadelphia.

Source: Allan M. Brandt, *No Magic Bullet. A Social History of Venereal Disease in the United States Since 1880* (New York: Oxford University Press, 1985), p. 152.

than as infectious diseases. Without question, the economic crisis did lead to a greater prevalence of the infections because fewer people could afford the expensive treatments. In the early 1930s the cost of treatment using injections of arsenic compounds alternated with injections of bismuth to reduce the chance of toxic reaction averaged between $305 to $380 but could cost as much as $1,000. Typically more than one member of a family needed treatment. Because of the expense and the stigma surrounding venereal diseases, many victims turned to quacks and patent medicines. Parran attacked the traditional argument that VD victims got what they deserved and calculated the larger social costs of the diseases. Millions were spent in treating syphilis, and the costs went even higher as the complications of the untreated disease developed. Parran also calculated the costs of the venereal diseases to American industry and estimated a loss of more than $100 million annually. Since the disease could be diagnosed and treated, Parran believed it could join the ranks of other controlled communicable diseases and set out to publicize it.

The Mask of Secrecy. His article, "The Next Great Plague To Go," tore away the mask of secrecy. In 1937 Parran published a book about his campaign against syphilis, *Shadow on the Land*, which became a best-seller. He defined venereal disease as the most pressing of all public health problems and called for a "New Deal" for its victims. His campaign made dramatic strides against venereal diseases, and he committed the federal government to its resolution. By 1938 he had the following results to show:

•New laws, requiring both applicants for a marriage license to show medical certificates that they were free from syphilis, had gone into effect in several states.

• Billboard posters all over the country, showing a happy couple playing with their healthy baby and urging: "Safeguard Baby's Right to Be Born Healthy. Every expectant mother should go early to a physician for an examination and blood tests."

•The organization of an American Academy of Dermatology and Syphilology.

•Postgraduate courses on venereal-disease control for health officers and private practitioners in many institutions of medicine and public health.

•A survey by the American Institute of Public Opinion establishing that the majority of American residents interviewed were in favor of federal clinics for the treatment of venereal disease.

VD and New Deal Reform. Parran's program represented the most positive elements of Roosevelt's New Deal reform. Parran rejected the traditional emphasis on morality and ethics and defined the disease as a combatible infectious disease. He attempted to force the government to accept certain basic responsibilities for the care of venereal-disease victims and to commit federal funds to its eradication, as he had seen done in several European countries. Unfortunately, the tide of public opinion about sexually transmitted diseases undermined his goals. Public fears about the danger of venereal disease meant it ultimately would not join the ranks of diseases that the techniques of medicine and public health could effectively control. His attempts to redefine venereal disease as curable met with only partial success, and his goal of a nation freed from the burden of sexually transmitted diseases was never reached. The old triad of fear, stigma, and taboo formed an alliance that would stretch much further into the twentieth century.

Sources:
Allan M. Brandt, *No Magic Bullet. A Social History of Venereal Disease in the United States Since 1880* (New York: Oxford University Press, 1985);

"Safeguard Baby," *Time* (14 February 1938): 47–48.

SPECIALIZATION VERSUS GENERAL PRACTICE

Planning and the Structure of the Medical Profession. During the 1920s the growing complexity of medicine led to a bewildering range of new information for a physician to assimilate. Hospitals and clinics grew in number, and medical costs ranged upward to pay for them. Resources, both in medicine and for the public, were maldistributed, with physicians forced to make compromises in the treatment of patients between what was medically desirable and what the patient could afford to pay. All these issues affected the way medicine was organized and the quality and distribution of the service offered. Such problems were brought to a head by the social turbulence of the early 1930s. One of the most important issues facing medicine concerned the organization of the profession. The Depression cut doctors' profits, raised hospital costs, and strained medical services. As they did in other industries, New Dealers advocated economic planning, the imposition of codes and practices, and general federal regulation of the health profession. But health professionals mobilized to oppose federal regulation, national health insurance, and governmental oversight of their profession. In the process the health industry became more specialized, more professionalized, and more able to protect itself from outside regulation.

Life, Death, and Medicine. Unlike other industries, of course, medicine was not simply a for-profit enterprise. Medicine was a science, with developing methods and procedures; a profession, with common social assumptions and guild practices; and a public service, whose life-and-death character made for volatile politics. It was also the province of increasingly wealthy and powerful members of American society. Physicians insisted on protecting their ability to negotiate their division of labor instead of having it hierarchically imposed upon them by a corporate structure. As a group doctors fared better than other Americans during the Depression, but there were differences within the medical hierarchy. A 1930 survey in Wisconsin showed an income range from less than one thousand dollars to more than twenty thousand dollars. Surgeons and other specialists were at the top of the scale, and general practitioners ranged toward the bottom. GPs had the most difficult time collecting bills; full-time specialists the least. Relationships between general practitioners and specialists, already strained by questions of prestige and status, became more stressful. The technological advantages of a hospital affiliation became linked to economic advantages. Professional interests and ideals also influenced the increasingly complex division of labor between general practitioners and the specialty occupations that emerged with the growth of modern hospitals, clinics, and laboratories.

The General Practitioner versus the Specialist. By 1930 nonphysician specialists were under the doctors' authority, but general practitioners resisted any efforts to give specialists exclusive privileges over some kinds of medical work. There was no way to prevent GPs from practicing as specialists. In England there was a two-tiered system where patients had to be referred to specialists through their general practitioners, and only specialists could consult in the hospitals. In the United States patients could go directly to specialists. Specialists were concentrated in the major cities and towns, GPs in the more-rural areas. There was no clear solution to questions of bringing quality medical services equally to all citizens, but professional organizations began to form rapidly within the medical profession. The AMA had already emerged as the powerful political spokesman for the physician, and in response both to the continuing development of specialist fields and to the economic problems of the Depression, medical specialties became formalized.

The Specialty Boards and the "System" of Medical Care. Many specialty boards developed during the 1930s, including the American Boards of Obstetrics and Gynecology, Internal Medicine, Surgery, Pediatrics, and others. These boards professionally regulated physicians admitted to the specialty and defined and controlled the quality of practice. Three years of training after internship were required. Candidates for a specialty board were looked at for moral and ethical standing, and they had to be members of the AMA. The boards also were a response to what seemed the inevitable alternative of specialist licensing by the states. But the question "Who should control specialization?" was only partially answered by the end of the decade. Once approved, a specialty board was not subject to any common, outside control. No one had primary responsibility — the AMA, the licensing boards, the National Board, the hospitals, or any other group. There had been little involvement of the public or their elected representatives during the evolution of the new structures. Physicians had still preserved their traditional autonomy and professional sovereignty and protected their practices from governmental oversight. There was still no consideration of specialty certification in terms of the overall organization and delivery of medical care for the country. The American system of medicine remained a "non-system."

Sources:

Paul Starr, *The Social Transformation of American Medicine* (New York: Basic Books, 1982), pp. 220–225;

Rosemary Stevens, *American Medicine and the Public Interest* (New Haven: Yale University Press, 1971), pp. 75–266.

HEADLINE MAKERS

ALEXIS CARREL

1873-1944

AMERICA'S FIRST NOBEL PRIZE WINNER
IN MEDICINE—
SCIENTIST AND ECCENTRIC PHILOSOPHER

The Threads of Life. Alexis Carrel was born in Lyons, France, on 28 June 1873. He became a physician in Lyons, began his experimental work in surgery in 1902, and then immigrated to the United States in 1904. When the Rockefeller Institute for Medical Research opened its doors in New York in 1906, it included Carrel among its outstanding investigators. In 1912 the Nobel Prize Committee awarded him the first Nobel Prize in medicine given to an American in recognition of his work on the suturing together of blood vessels and the transplantation of blood vessels and organs. The development of this technique laid the foundation for vascular surgery, heart surgery, and transplantation of organs.

Eccentric Philosopher. In the 1930s Carrel became one of the first medical scientists in America to attract widespread public attention. In 1935, late in his career as a laboratory scientist, he wrote a nonmedical book, *Man, the Unknown,* which became a best-seller. In this work he presented his social views and his ideas for an institute that would study "man as a whole" and develop "leaders" for the state. His book became popular because he voiced the public concern of the time that science was not doing enough for humanity and that the rapid development of technology might be detrimental to mankind. To widen the popular appeal of his work, he included several topics, such as sex, which in those days was not often discussed in popular writing. He also proposed that dangerous criminals and the criminally insane should be "humanely and economically disposed of in small euthanasic institutions supplied with proper gases … Modern society should not hesitate to organize itself with reference to the

normal individual. Philosophical systems and sentimental prejudices must give way before such a necessity." Liberal minds were disturbed that a book such as this became a best-seller in the year Mussolini attacked Ethiopia and Hitler enacted the Nuremberg Laws. They were also troubled by the effect Carrel might have upon his most famous associate, America's greatest hero, aviator Charles A. Lindbergh.

Charles A. Lindbergh and Alexis Carrel. With Lindbergh, Carrel made the headlines again in 1935, when they announced the development of a mechanical "heart," in which the heart, kidney, and other internal organs of an animal could be kept alive for study in glass chambers supplied by circulation of artificial blood. Carrel's medical work provided him with a long-standing interest in the preservation of tissues and organs for surgical use and transplantation, but he was unable to succeed in perfecting a system to allow an organ to survive outside of the body. Lindbergh's involvement in this biological problem came when his sister-in-law's heart was damaged by rheumatic fever. Physicians told him that heart repair was impossible because the heart could not be stopped long enough for surgeons to work on it. Lindbergh saw this as an engineering problem; he undertook to develop a pump that could take over the heart's functions during surgery, and he pressed his physiological questions upon his family doctors. One of them offered to introduce him to a man he knew, a medical researcher who was working on the problem of a heart pump. On 28 November 1930 Lindbergh met Carrel. There was an immediate rapport between the tall, lean aviator and the short, stocky, pink-faced scientist, and together they set to work, announcing the success of their collaboration in 1935. The relationship between them was particularly intense in the middle and late 1930s. When Lindbergh exiled himself to England in 1936, the two men were drawn even closer together, visiting with each other on Carrel's island off the coast of Brittany. Many of the philosophical concepts Lindbergh held in later life, such as his later writings on the wisdom of nature and natural selection, can be traced to his association with Carrel.

Philosopher and Mystic. When Carrel had to retire from the Rockefeller Institute because of his age in 1939, he had become more of a philosopher and mystic than a productive scientist. Carrel was the first Rockefeller scientist to be forced to retire under the institute's new mandatory retirement policy. His entire Division of Experimental Surgery was closed, and his staff disbanded, when he reached the age of sixty-five. It is possible that the division's dissolution may have been directed at Lindbergh rather than at Carrel. The administration of the Rockefeller Institute did not wish to be associated with political stands, and by this time Lindbergh had begun to be controversial on the scene of national politics. When World War II broke out, Carrel returned to France and joined a special mission for the French Ministry of Public Health. He ended his days there in 1944 amid the confusion of World War II and its aftermath.

Sources:

Kenneth S. Davis, *The Hero, Charles A. Lindbergh and the American Dream* (New York: Doubleday, 1959);

Theodore I. Malinin, *Surgery and Life. The Extraordinary Career of Alexis Carrel* (New York: Harcourt Brace Jovanovich, 1979);

Walter S. Ross, *The Last Hero: Charles A. Lindbergh* (New York: Harper & Row, 1964).

MORRIS FISHBEIN

1889-1976

AMERICAN MEDICAL ASSOCIATION SPOKESMAN

 **A "Socialized Medicine" Opponent.** One of the strongest opponents of "socialized medicine" in any form was Dr. Morris Fishbein, editor of the *Journal of the American Medical Association* and of *Hygeia.* When the Group Health Association (GHA) of Washington formed a medical cooperative in November 1937, Fishbein led the battle to oppose them. For years the American Medical Association and most of its state and county medical societies were guided by the principle that a corporation could not practice medicine, and Fishbein was its primary spokesman. The idea behind a medical cooperative such as the GHA was to give patients financial relief with prepaid health insurance "premiums" and to improve the incomes of physicians by paying them fixed salaries from these premiums. In less than a year this medical corporation had nearly twenty-five hundred members. The Medical Society of Washington, D.C. (a branch of the AMA), threatened the doctors who worked for the group plan with loss of membership in the AMA and in August 1938 expelled one. It also applied pressure upon Washington hospitals to exclude GHA doctors. Most American physicians were very attached to their traditional patterns of professional autonomy and saw any form of "socialized medicine" as outside intervention that could in-

terfere with their long-standing individual fee-for-service practices. The AMA was the primary opponent of any form of imposed change to the medical profession.

A Federal Indictment. In response to these actions, the United States Department of Justice indicted the AMA, the local medical society, and twenty-one physicians under the Sherman Antitrust Act on charges of restraining trade. Fishbein, speaking for the AMA, pledged a legal effort to "establish the ultimate right of organized medicine to use its discipline to oppose types of contract practice damaging to the health of the public." In August 1939 the indictment was dismissed on the ground that the term "trade" did not include the medical profession. In March 1940 the Circuit Court of Appeals reversed the decision and said that the AMA's interference with doctors who worked for the GHA was a violation of the Sherman Antitrust Act.

Influential Spokesman. Fishbein was the most effective spokesman the medical profession ever had, in spite of the fact that he had had little personal contact with patients and never practiced medicine on his own. Born in Saint Louis, Missouri, in 1889, he received his M.D. from Rush Medical College in 1912. He then spent one year as a fellow in pathology at Rush and then had one year's service in the Durand Hospital of the McCormick Institute for Infectious Diseases. In 1913 he was proposed for the post of assistant to the editor of the *Journal of the American Medical Association,* and, when the editor retired in 1924, Fishbein became editor of the journal and of *Hygeia.* As editor, according to a 1938 issue of *Fortune,* he "has been a promoter. He has promoted the AMA from a mild academic body into a powerful trade association." A popular public speaker, he amused AMA delegates in 1931 by beginning a speech, "Unaccustomed as I am to public speaking . . ." Fishbein received much support for his views among AMA members, but he also aroused significant opposition. An opponent even went so far as to refer to him as a "medical Mussolini." To many people his view seemed out-of-date in light of the various health insurance programs in existence, the New Deal programs the government had instituted, and the widespread practice of socialized medicine in many of the European countries. Still, he remained the most prolific and articulate of the leaders of the AMA. His arguments against any form of group health insurance or governmental aid in medical care were a major influence on the medical profession and American public alike.

Sources:

"The A.M.A. Voice," *Fortune* (November 1938): 152+;

Morris A. Bealle, *Medical Mussolini* (Washington, D.C.: Columbia Publishing, 1938);

Current Biography 1940 (New York: H. W. Wilson, 1940): 297–299;

Fishbein, *Morris Fishbein, M.D. An Autobiography* (New York: Doubleday, 1969);

Paul Starr, *The Social Transformation of American Medicine* (New York: Basic Books, 1982), p. 305.

KAREN HORNEY

1885-1952

PSYCHOANALYST

From Germany to the United States. On 22 September 1932 a German psychoanalyst who was to influence American psychotherapy and personality theory greatly arrived in the United States. Dr. Karen Horney accepted a job offer from her former student, Hungarian analyst Franz Alexander, as assistant director of his newly established Psychoanalytic Institute in Chicago. Horney received her M.D. degree at the University of Freiburg in 1913 and underwent psychoanalytic training with Karl Abraham, a friend and close associate of Sigmund Freud. She enjoyed her life in the Weimar Republic in the 1920s, but the 1929 Wall Street crash with its resulting economic hardship and the growth of Nazism encouraged her to accept Alexander's offer. Horney worked briefly at the Chicago institute and then moved to New York City, where she joined the New York Psychoanalytic Institute. The New School for Social Research had set up a University of Exile for German academics threatened by Hitler's 1933 rise to power, and Horney was invited to teach there. Her lectures became popular, and although her appealing lecture style was interrupted by endless smoking, students hung onto her every word. Her first book, *The Neurotic Personality of Our Time* (1937), attracted attention, too.

Karen Horney versus Sigmund Freud. Her lectures and book critiqued Freud's male-biased view of feminine psychology. Where Freud felt that neurosis came from social repression of instinct, Horney argued it came instead from the parents' attitudes in socializing the child. If a child was not dealt with warmly by its parents, it might express its frustration through anger. If parents met that anger with more intimidation, the child was likely to suppress its feelings of rage. Horney taught that neurosis was motivated by these "basic anxieties" rather than having its genesis in childhood sexuality. She was more optimistic than Freud, who believed that some degree of neurosis was inevitable given the conflict between instinct and conscience and between the individual and society. Horney argued that people were always capable of growth and change and were capable of fending for themselves and meeting their needs on their own.

Conflicts with Psychoanalysts. Horney was soundly criticized for abandoning Freud's theory of infantile sexuality even though she agreed with him that neurosis did not stem from anything internal to the child but came from external abuse of the child by its caregivers. In 1939 she published her second book, *New Ways in Psychoanalysis,* where she further broke from Freudian orthodoxy and suggested major revisions in psychoanalytic therapy,

which was rejected by analysts at the time. Ironically, many later adopted her suggestions, particularly her insistence that it was just as important in therapy to deal with the real-life, present-day problems as it was to reconstruct childhood emotional states and fantasies.

Future Acclaim. Her critiques of Freud and the popularity of both her writing and her teaching alienated her fellow teachers in the New York Psychoanalytic Institute, and by late 1939 the stage was set for her future break with the institute. After her break she helped to found the Association for the Advancement of Psychoanalysis and the American Institute for Psychoanalysis. In later decades Horney's work received increased attention, especially from feminists and psychoanalysts interested in self-esteem.

Sources:

Bernard J. Paris, *Karen Horney: A Psychoanalyst's Search for Self-Understanding* (New Haven: Yale University Press, 1994);

Susan Quinn, *A Mind of Her Own. The Life of Karen Horney* (New York: Summit Books, 1987);

Jack L. Rubins, *Karen Horney: Gentle Rebel of Psychoanalysis* (New York: Dial, 1978);

Janet Sayers, *Mothers of Psychoanalysis* (New York: Norton, 1991).

KARL LANDSTEINER

1868-1943

THE FATHER OF IMMUNOLOGY

America's Second Winner of the Nobel Prize for Medicine. Karl Landsteiner devoted years of his life to classifying the different types of human blood. A "modest, reticent man with a drooping moustache," Landsteiner became the United States' second winner of the Nobel Prize for medicine in 1930. The Austrian-born physician received his doctor of medicine degree from the University of Vienna in 1891 and was a pathologist at the university from 1909–1919. Poor working conditions forced him to leave Vienna in 1919, but facilities in The Hague were no better. He accepted an offer from the Rockefeller Institute in New York City and went to the United States in 1922, becoming an American citizen in 1929. His 1909 classification of the four main types of human blood (A, B, AB, and O) made possible the safe transfusion of blood from one person to another, although several years passed before the knowledge was put to practical use.

Man and the Apes. Landsteiner had a wide range of research interests. He was also known for his studies of poliomyelitis and was the first to infect monkeys with the poliovirus, which gave bacteriologists a means of studying the disease in animals and for experimenting in attempts at human immunization. He dealt with therapeutic blood transfusions, serological specificity, paroxysmal nemoglobinuria, and syphilis. In 1925 Landsteiner and Dr. C. P. Miller of the Rockefeller Institute published a series of articles on "Serologic Studies on the Blood of Primates," which showed that there was a far closer biochemical relationship between man and apes than between man and monkeys.

The Rh Factor. In 1939 Landsteiner and his co-workers Alexander Wiener and Philip Levine discovered a new factor in human blood. Named the Rh, or rhesus, factor after the rhesus macaque laboratory monkey, this new knowledge led to the prevention of permanent brain damage and death in newborns whose Rh incompatibility with their Rh negative mothers led to jaundice at birth. The Rh factor was also critically important in blood transfusions. If Rh positive blood is transfused into Rh negative patients, Rh antibodies are formed, and further transfusions could lead to severe hemolytic reactions and death. This modest, self-critical, rather timid man of science whose work saved thousands of lives was known for his wide reading. He was also an excellent pianist.

Sources:

Charles Coulston Gillispie, *Dictionary of Scientific Biography*, volume VII (New York: Scribners, 1973), pp. 622–625;

"Nobel Prize in Medicine for America," *Literary Digest* (22 November 1930): 33.

KARL MENNINGER

1893-1990

POPULARIZER AND PUBLICIZER OF PSYCHIATRY

The Human Mind. In 1930 the American psychiatrist Karl Menninger published his best-seller, *The Human Mind,* a book that gave the psychopathology of everyday life and the workings of the mind a new meaning to many Americans. The psychiatrist in *The Human Mind* took the reader into his practice and let him see how the world looked when viewed through a psychiatrist's eyes. Menninger openly discussed the everyday problems of mental illness, and, in doing so, the reading population of the country developed new insights into both mental illness and the psychiatric specialty. Menninger's name appeared widely in newspapers and magazines as he also published articles and reached the public in the *Nation*, the *New Republic*, and the *Ladies' Home Journal.* In many minds Menninger's name and psychiatry became indivisible. Psychiatry had found a spokesman, and the Menninger family became the family psychiatrists of America.

A Medical Dynasty. Menninger was born in Topeka, Kansas, on 22 July 1893 to a medical dynasty. His father was Dr. Charles Frederick Menninger, a prominent physician from Topeka who found himself impressed with the Mayo Clinic's pioneer work in group practice in Minnesota. When he returned to Topeka after visiting the Mayo Clinic, arriving just in time for breakfast with his family, Charles Menninger bowed his head for the morning prayer. At last he raised his head, looked at each of his three sons in turn, and said, "I have been to the Mayos and I have seen a great thing. You boys are going to be doctors and we are going to have a clinic like that right here in Topeka." Two of his sons, Karl and William, became physicians, and both shaped the future of American psychiatry. Dr. Karl, as he was to become known, completed his medical training at Harvard Medical School in 1917. After his internship in Kansas City, he worked with Professor Ernest Southard in the Boston Psychopathic Hospital and taught in the Harvard Medical School. In 1920 he returned to Topeka to join his father in practice. The two conceived the idea of giving Topeka a group of physicians who could complement each other's work and agreed to dedicate their future to psychiatric practice. They were joined by two other physicians, and the first patients were admitted to the Menninger Clinic in 1925. The clinic was to become one of the greatest psychiatric clinics in the world.

Dr. Karl's Psychiatry. Dr. Karl carried the message of psychiatry to the public with a missionary's enthusiasm but tempered his writing with a scientist's caution. In the same year that *The Human Mind* was published, he completed his psychoanalytic training under Dr. Franz Alexander and received the first certificate of the Chicago Institute for Psychoanalysis. He published several additional books with his 1938 book, *Man Against Himself,* also reaching both a popular and scientific audience. The Menningers leaned toward the Freudian concept of personality structure but rejected Freud's therapeutic recommendations. Menninger was not convinced that months on the couch could bring about cure or improvement and developed more effective short-term therapies. One of the clinic's most important innovations was the creation of a milieu therapy program. Both activities and attitudes were prescribed because of their specific therapeutic value for the individual patient. Every member of the hospital staff considered what attitude to display to the patient, whether it was "loving and tender care" or "firm but friendly encouragement." The shortage of psychiatrists in America made the Menninger Clinic a major teaching hospital and training center for doctors interested in psychiatry. The clinic got the approval of the AMA to train psychiatric nurses in 1931 and physicians in 1933. In 1938 they established the Topeka Institute of Psychoanalysis. Because of the work and dedication of the three Menninger physicians and the message of psychiatry from Dr. Karl, physicians flocked to Topeka to be trained. By mid century, the directors of some of America's greatest psychiatric clinics were the men who were in Topeka during the 1930s and 1940s.

Source:

Walker Winslow, *The Menninger Story* (Garden City, N.Y.: Doubleday, 1956).

Thomas Parran

1892-1968

THE NATION'S FAMILY DOCTOR AND CRUSADER
AGAINST THE LAST GREAT PLAGUE

A Censored Broadcast. In November 1934 the Columbia Broadcasting Company scheduled a radio address by New York State Health Commissioner Thomas Parran Jr. on future goals for public health. But he never delivered his talk. Listeners who tuned in heard piano melodies instead. Moments before he was scheduled to go on the air, CBS told him that he could not mention syphilis and gonorrhea by name. In response, Parran refused to go on and complained in a press release that his speech should have been considered more acceptable than "the veiled obscenity permitted by Columbia in the vaudeville acts of some of their commercial programs." During Roosevelt's New Deal, Parran, as the surgeon general of the United States, committed the nation to the eradication of venereal disease by dramatically bringing these infections to the center of public consciousness. Barred from the radio in 1934, he found his picture on the cover of *Time* in 1936, as he embarked on a major campaign to take the prudery out of the war against social diseases and eradicate syphilis from the country.

United States Surgeon General. Parran entered the health service of the United States in 1917 when he was twenty-five years old and two years out of Georgetown University School of Medicine. During the influenza epidemic of 1918, he was in charge of an improvised hospital barracks for government men working to build a dam. Ten thousand of them were sick with influenza. Parran frantically wired for supplies but received no answer to his pleas for sheets, bandages, and medicine. On a trip to the railroad yard to see if anything had arrived, he found a trainload of army supplies headed for a camp. He weighed his options of court-martial versus having lifesaving materials for his men and stole the supplies. Instead of being court-martialed, he was promoted. By 1925 he was chief of the Public Health Service's Division of Venereal Diseases. He stayed there until 1930, when he was made commissioner of the New York State Department of Health. In 1936 President Roosevelt appointed him surgeon general at a salary of $9,800 a year, and he began his historic public campaign with a lengthy article called "Stamp Out Syphilis," which appeared first in *Survey Graphic* and then in *Reader's Digest*.

Parran's Program. Parran led the fight to see venereal disease as a social problem worthy of governmental intervention, rather than a problem of moral turpitude. His campaign fit into the larger picture of New Deal reform as he battled to show the social and economic costs of not dealing with the problem by dismissing it as a failure of individual responsibility. Although his redefinition of venereal disease as a curable illness met with success, Parran's goal of freeing the nation from the burden of venereal diseases was never reached. In spite of his efforts, these diseases remained for most Americans moral problems, symptoms of social decay and sexual evil.

Sources:

Allan M. Brandt, *No Magic Bullet. A Social History of Venereal Disease in the United States Since 1880* (New York: Oxford University Press, 1985), p. 122;

Current Biography 1940 (New York: H. W. Wilson, 1940), pp. 629–631;

"Great Pox," *Time* (20 October 1936): 60–64.

Francis Everett Townsend

1867-1960

THE "STEPFATHER" OF THE SOCIAL SECURITY ACT
OF 1935

A Generous Man with a Tender Heart. According to the story promoted by his loyal followers, one morning Francis Everett Townsend, an elderly retired assistant medical officer in Long Beach, California, was startled to see three old women rummaging for food in some garbage cans outside his window. He let forth a shocked bellow that brought his wife, who cautioned him that he should not shout because the neighbors would hear. "I want all the neighbors to hear me!" he defiantly shouted. "I want God Almighty to hear me! I'm going to shout till the whole country hears!" And thus Townsend became identified as the champion of old people, credited by many with the creation of state-supported pensions — social security.

Old-Age Benefits. Although a form of national health insurance had been one of the top concerns during the Progressive Era, the Depression sidetracked it in favor of other priorities. With millions out of work, unemployment insurance became the leading priority. Old-age benefits were a second and often unaddressed issue. A generous man with a tender heart, Townsend was outraged by the lack of public concern for the elderly victims of the Depression. In 1933 he suggested that all retirees over the age of sixty should receive two hundred dollars a month (in scrip) on the condition that they retire and "spend the money as they get it." The plan, popularly known as "$60 at 60," thus would help elderly citizens and stimulate consumer spending, at that time extremely low. The funds were to come from a national sales tax.

The "Townsend Plan." The kindly doctor told audiences all over the country that his "Townsend Plan" would provide security for the nation's elderly and would reinvigorate the economy by creating jobs for young men and women. The following year Townsend established Old Age Revolving Pensions, a loose organization of local clubs that within two years numbered seven thousand — with a total membership of about 1.5 million. Although his unlikely scheme would have turned over half the national income to 8 percent of the population, its following of older people led many of their congressmen to pledge themselves to work for its enactment and the Townsend Plan was incorporated into a bill introduced in Congress in early 1935.

The Social Security Act versus the Townsend Plan. When critics, including President Roosevelt, attacked the measure as unworkable, the *Townsend Weekly*, the doctor's editorial voice, responded with an angry attack on the administration. Townsend joined the opposition and made plans to link his movement to that of Roosevelt's most serious political rival, New Deal Sen. Huey P. Long of Louisiana. To steal the stage from Townsend, Roosevelt supported the Social Security Act of 1935. Many congressmen breathed a sigh of relief and saw support of the Social Security Act as a way to escape from their improbable commitment to the Townsend Plan. The Social Security Act's pensions were tiny compared with Townsend's call for two hundred dollars a month, but for the first time the United States government assumed responsibility for the welfare of people who were disabled or too old to work.

A Step Along the Way to Medicare and Medicaid. In the summer of 1936 Townsend emerged as a principal backer of the third-party candidacy of Rep. William Lemke for president. Allied with him were the Reverend Charles E. Coughlin, the Detroit radio priest, and the Reverend Gerald L. K. Smith, the national organizer for Sen. Huey P. Long's Share Our Wealth Society. Townsend's excursion into national politics alienated a substantial part of his following and led to lawsuits and disputes. But the plan still continued in popularity for several decades after the 1930s with claims of at least five million members in 1953. Townsend traveled extensively and appeared at different Townsend clubs throughout the country, discussed his plan with various political leaders including Presidents Truman and Eisenhower, and addressed rallies of elderly people. His greatest triumph, he said, was the "actual proving" of his contention that there must be no power that shuts off the circulation of money. While the Social Security Act itself included only one minor reference to health insurance, it did extend the government's role in public health and was a major step along the way toward the Medicare and Medicaid amendments to the Social Security Act in 1965.

Sources:

Abraham Holtzman, *The Townsend Movement, A Political Study* (New York: Bookman Associates, 1963);

Obituary, *New York Times,* 2 September 1960, p. 1;

Paul Starr, *The Social Transformation of American Medicine* (New York: Basic Books, 1982), pp. 266–267.

PEOPLE IN THE NEWS

In 1937 **Dr. L. B. Alford,** Saint Louis, stated that brain operations indicated that a small section of the left side of the posterior brain in right-handed persons controlled the functioning of the mind.

Dr. C. W. Alvarez of the Mayo Clinic found disease of the gallbladder to be the most frequent cause of indigestion or abdominal distress in 1930.

Drs. Charles Armstrong and **W. T. Harrison,** National Institute of Health, reported in 1935, that a solution of alum used as a spray enabled 74 percent of the animals so treated to survive infantile paralysis. In 1936 the doctors announced their nasal spray of picric acid-sodium alum offered hope of a successful preventive for infantile paralysis; the drugs used in the spray could be purchased at any pharmacy

Working independently in 1937, **Dr. Charles Armstrong,** National Institute of Health, and **Drs. E. W. Schultz** and **L. P. Gebhardt,** Stanford University, found that inoculation with a zinc sulphate or with picric acid and alum solution successfully immunized monkeys against infantile paralysis.

Autopsy reports studied by **Drs. D. L. Augustine** and **W. W. Spink,** Harvard University, revealed in 1936 that 20 percent of the individuals had suffered from trichinosis, the disease caused by worm-infested pork.

On 8 August 1930 **O. T. Avery** and **René Dubos** announced that an enzyme, isolated from New Jersey cranberry bog soil, was effective in treating pneumonia in mice.

Dr. L. W. Aycock of Harvard Medical School announced in 1930 that infantile paralysis was due to the destruction of muscle-controlling nerve cells in the spinal cord.

In 1934 Dr. L. W. Aycock of the Harvard University Infantile Paralysis Commission stated that studies suggested susceptibility to polio might be inherited.

In 1930 Dr. W. S. Baer of Johns Hopkins Medical School introduced the use of maggots into infected bone cavities of osteomyelitis sufferers to remove the dead tissue and products of infection with no harm done to the patient.

Subjecting pituitary and adrenal glands to X rays was found an effective treatment for diabetes in animals, according to Drs. B. O. Barnes, W. L. Culpepper, and J. H. Hutton, Chicago, in 1935.

In 1931 Dr. Walter Bauer and associates at the Massachusetts General Hospital discovered that the intense pain of lead colic, gallstone colic, and urethral colic was relieved by slow injections of calcium chloride into the veins.

In 1938 Dr. H. C. Bazett, University of Pennsylvania, stated that all individuals had 30 percent more blood in spring than in fall and winter.

In 1937 George Beadle and Edward Tatum developed the one gene-one enzyme theory that stated that all chemical reactions in the cell are controlled by enzymes and that each enzyme is controlled by a single gene; the two won the 1958 Nobel Prize for medicine or physiology for their work.

Dr. Alfred Blalock of Vanderbilt University Medical School studied surgical shock in 1931 and recommended the replacement of fluid loss stemming from surgery as a valuable treatment.

Dr. Sidney Bliss of Tulane University reported evidence in 1931 that lack of iron in the diet was the cause of pellagra.

Dr. Emil Bogen, Olive View, California, asserted in 1934 that cancer of the breast in women was the penalty for not nursing their children.

Drs. Paul Boyle and David Weisberger, Harvard University, reported in 1937 that a deficiency of vitamin C, the cause of scurvy, might also be the cause of pyorrhea.

Professors Jean Broadhurst, Columbia University, and Gladys Cameron, New York University, reported in 1938 that their researches indicated scarlet fever was caused by a nasal virus rather than a streptococcus.

In 1934 Drs. Maurice Brodie and A. R. Elvidge, working under Dr. W. H. Park, New York City Department of Health, produced a serum for infantile paralysis that was apparently successful on a test group of children. Their findings confirmed Dr. Simon Flexner's theory that the olfactory nerve might be the gateway by which the virus penetrated the nervous system.

In 1935 Dr. Maurice Brodie, New York Health Department, working under the direction of Dr. W. H. Park, announced that animals had been successfully immunized against sleeping sickness.

In 1931 Dr. J. Bronfenbrenner and associates at Washington University developed a process for changing the chemical nature of the proteins in protective or curative serums.

In 1932 Dr. Reginald Burbank reported the development of a vaccine for chronic rheumatism.

Dr. C. G. Burn, Yale University, reported the isolation of a disease-producing bacterium from patients dying of meningo-encephalitis in 1935.

In 1931 Dr. Walter B. Cannon of the Harvard Medical school discovered a new hormone, sympathin, which is similar to adrenalin; in 1933 Cannon announced two forms of the hormone sympathin.

Dr. Robert Chambers, New York University, stated in 1937 that injection of grain cornstarch caused almost complete disappearance of cancerous growths in 45 percent of the experimental mice.

Patients with slowly knitting broken bones might be helped by the administration of hydrochloric acid, according to Drs. W. W. Cornell and Alice R. Bernheim, New York City, in 1936.

Dr. G. W. Crile reported in 1931 successfully treating diabetes, goiters, and stomach ulcers by severing the nerve connection between the brain and the adrenal glands.

Studies on deafness made by Dr. S. J. Crowe of the Johns Hopkins Medical School in 1931, showed that certain forms might be due to alteration in the rigidity of certain small bones in the inner ear and that pressure on a membrane in the inner ear might increase hearing.

The study of brain electrograms in 1936 by Drs. Hallowell Davis and Pauline A. Davis, Harvard Medical school, revealed that identical twins have identical patterns of brain activity.

In 1935 Dr. D. B. Dill, Harvard University, made experiments which led him to advise athletes to eat starches and sugars during the twenty-four hours before an athletic event.

In 1937 studies of water moccasin snake serum were made by Dr. R. L. Ditmars, assisted by Dr. C. R. Schroeder, New York Zoological Park, which confirmed the hypothesis that the drug was helpful in the treatment of epilepsy.

Colds and influenza were probably caused by filterable viruses, according to Dr. A. R. Dochez, Rockefeller Institute, in 1936.

In 1939 vitamin K was isolated and synthesized by **Edward Adelbert Doisy**; the biochemist won the 1943 Nobel Prize for his work.

In 1936 **Drs. L. R. Dragstedt, John van Prohaska,** and **H. P. Harms,** University of Chicago, reported that the new hormone lipocaic, obtained from the pancreas, might prove effective as a supplement to insulin in the treatment of diabetes.

Dr. George Draper pointed out in 1931 that until the exact mode of polio transmission was known, questions of isolation and quarantine presented great difficulties.

On 25 October 1930 **Dr. Philip Drinker** of Harvard Medical School reported successful treatment of acute respiratory failure in polio cases with the use of an artificial respirator.

René Jules Dubos, at the Rockefeller Institute for Medical Research, isolated tyrocidine and gramicidine from swamp soil in 1939; effective against a broad spectrum of gram-positive bacteria, they were too toxic for human use.

In 1934 **Dr. J. G. Dusser de Barenne,** Yale University, described a method of destroying any number of consecutive layers of nerve cells in the cerebral cortex of the brain; the discovery was expected to aid in the study of which particular areas controlled various bodily activities.

In 1931 **Dr. R. E. Dyer** and associates at the United States Public Health Service, demonstrated that fleas, long suspected of transmitting typhus, were indeed the disease vectors.

Dr. H. L. Eder, Santa Barbara clinic, found in 1935 that the administration of iron would help lessen or prevent sunburn of persons who were abnormally sensitive to the sun.

Drs. C. A. Elsberg, Irwin Levy, and **E. D. Brewer,** Neurological Institute, New York, reported success in locating brain tumors in more than one hundred patients by testing their sensitivity to odors of coffee and the chemical citral in 1936.

In 1933 **Drs. Conrad A. Elvehjem** and **W. S. Sherman,** University of Wisconsin, announced that the role of copper in the treatment of pernicious anemia was to transform iron into hemoglobin.

Dr. Conrad A. Elvehjem and associates in the agricultural chemistry department of the University of Wisconsin discovered nicotinic acid as a cure for pellagra in 1937.

In 1936 an extract from the placenta was found to be helpful in treating patients with hemophilia, according to **Drs. R. C. Ely** and **C. F. McKhann,** Boston; the same extract also stopped bleeding after mastoid and adenoid operations.

On 15 March 1937 **Bernard Fantus** developed the first modern blood bank at the Cook County Hospital in Chicago.

In 1931 **Dr. S. M. Feinberg** announced the relief of asthma symptoms by raising patients' body temperatures through the passage of electrical currents through their bodies.

Dr. N. S. Ferry, Detroit, reported the successful use of a spinal meningitis antitoxin in 1935.

In 1936 **Drs. Isidore Finkelman** and **Daniel Haffron,** Elgin, Illinois, reported that their studies indicated that schizophrenia was the result of a disturbance of the hypothalamus in the forebrain.

Drs. Earl W. Flosdorf and **Stuard Mudd** of the University of Pennsylvania prepared the first dried human blood serum on 21 December 1933.

Drs. Earl W. Flosdorf and **L. A. Chambers,** University of Pennsylvania, advanced the theory in 1934 that high-pitched sound, which kills bacteria, may aid in producing immunity to disease; such sounds were found to catalyze chemical changes in egg albumen.

Dr. Walter Freeman, Washington, D.C., demonstrated a way of taking pictures of the living brain in 1934.

In 1935 Yale scientists **John Farquhar Fulton** and **Carlyle F. Jacobsen** observed that primates who had had a bilateral prefrontal lobotomy were calm, even when presented with difficult problems.

In 1933 **Dr. Sidney Garfield** created a prepaid medical plan to provide medical care for five hundred workers building a California aqueduct.

In 1938 **Dr. Sidney Garfield** established a prepaid group health plan for Grand Coulee Dam workers at the request of **Henry J. Kaiser.**

Daily administration of insulin to schizophrenics resulted in the recovery of sanity by 68 percent of the patients, according to **Dr. Bernard Gluck,** Ossining, New York, in 1936.

After treating dementia praecox patients with large doses of insulin in 1937, **Dr. D. S. Griffin,** Central State Hospital, Norman, Oklahoma, reported that eight of twenty-nine patients completely recovered their sanity and the others were improved.

Drs. Arthur Grollman and **W. M. Firor,** Johns Hopkins University, isolated crystals of the hormone of the adrenal gland cortex in 1933.

In 1938 **Dr. Robert E. Gross** surgically repaired a congenital heart defect.

Typhoid carriers might be rendered harmless by the application of X ray to the livers and gallbladders of the affected persons, according to **Dr. Lars Gulbrandsen,** University of Illinois, in 1935.

In 1936 **Dr. O. J. Hagen,** University of Minnesota, reported the identification of a new disease, terminal or regional ileitis, that had in the past probably been confused with cancer and intestinal diseases; the prognosis of ileitis was favorable if early diagnosis and treatment were obtained.

In 1930 **Dr. F. S. Hammett** found that sulfahydril compounds stimulated the rapid growth of tissues, healing stubborn wounds.

In 1938 **Dr. Edith Haynes,** Indiana University School of Medicine, reported that sores kept wet with a water solution of pectin healed rapidly.

Drs. H. E. Himwich and **J. F. Fazikas,** Yale University, found that sugar was a source of energy for the brain in 1935.

Subjecting rabies virus for a short time to ultraviolet rays allowed **Dr. H. L. Hodes** and his associates at the Rockefeller Institute for Medical Research to prepare an effective but nonvirulent type of vaccine in 1938.

The injection of meningococcus serum into the veins rather than into the spinal cord of meningitis patients reduced the death rate to 11.8 percent, according to **Dr. A. L. Hoyne,** Chicago, in 1936.

In 1931 **Dr. W. C. Hueper** developed a leukemia treatment serum from rabbit blood by injecting leukemic white blood cells raised in cultures from patients' blood into the blood of rabbits.

In 1933 **Dr. A. S. Hyman** announced an "artificial pacemaker" that had restored life to 60 percent of the patients whose hearts had stopped through shock, when used within five or ten minutes after the heart stopped beating.

A device to take infrared ray photographs that reveal early stages of heart trouble was made by **Dr. A. S. Hyman** and his associates at Beth David Hospital, New York, in 1935.

In 1932 **Drs. Raphael Isaacs** and **C. C. Sturgis** of the University of Michigan developed a chemically pure liver extract that could be administered intravenously in the treatment of pernicious anemia.

Dr. Benjamin Jablons, New York, reported in 1937, that tubulin, extracted from animal kidneys and used in the treatment of nephritic hypertension, had restored patients from uremic coma.

Dr. H. A. Kelly of Johns Hopkins University reported continued success with electrical surgery in treating cancer in 1930.

In 1937 **Dr. J. F. Kelly,** Creighton University, Omaha, reported that X-ray treatment of gangrene was successful in 100 percent of the cases when used within twenty-four hours of the discovery of the disease; the treatment effectively removed the necessity for amputations in most cases.

Dr. Garnet King, Los Angeles, reported a method of preheating to make ether nonexplosive and pneumonia-free in 1937.

In 1936 **Dr. H. A Kipp,** Pittsburgh, during an operation, measured the variations in bile pressure and found that laughing, coughing, and standing up affected the rate of flow of bile in human beings.

A mathematical formula that diagnosed at birth congenital hip deformities that would produce lameness was described by **Drs. Samuel Kleinberg** and **H. S. Lieberman,** New York City, in 1935; remedial measures were simple if early diagnosis was made.

In 1933 **Drs. W. B. Kouwenhoven** and **D. R. Hooper** of Johns Hopkins University found that the rhythm of a beating heart could be controlled by interrupted direct currents of electricity.

Dr. S. D. Kramer, Brooklyn, announced in 1934 that he had successfully immunized animals against polio and believed that the vaccine could be adopted for human beings.

In 1933 **Dr. I. N. Kugelmass** of New York City reported that giving babies a solution containing gelatin, dextrose, and salt instead of the usual feedings following birth reduced the loss of weight in the newborn to 2 percent or less.

Insertion of a minute glass tube into a single capillary in the bed of a man's nail allowed **Dr. E. M. Landis,** University of Pennsylvania, to measure the passage of fluid through the walls of these blood vessels in 1936; this method was expected to reveal knowledge of diseases of blood vessels and edema.

In 1936 **John H. Lawrence** of the University of California at Berkeley introduced the radiophosphorus treatment of leukemia.

In 1932 **Dr. C. D. Leake** and associates at the University of California announced their discovery of a new anesthetic through the purification of divinyl oxide; it was quicker, lasted longer, and was free from the effects of other anesthesias, such as ether and chloroform.

Dr. W. G. Lennox, Harvard Medical School, reported in 1938 that insulin shock treatments relieved mild forms of epilepsy.

In 1939 **Philip Levine, Rufus Stetson, Alexander Wiener,** and **Karl Landsteiner** discovered the Rh factor in human blood.

In 1931 **Dr. Erlich Lindemann** of the University of Iowa announced that small doses of sodium amytal were effective in getting even the most reserved patient to discuss his or her emotions.

The virus theory of cancer was supported in 1936 by experiments conducted by **Dr. Baldwin Lucke,** University of Pennsylvania, who found that frogs developed kidney cancers when inoculated with cell-free dried extracts made from cancerous frog kidneys.

In 1933 **John Lundy** an anesthesiologist, used an intravenous barbiturate, sodium pentothal, to anesthetize a patient before surgery.

Dr. Madge T. Macklin, reporting in 1936 on cancer in human beings, stated that members of the same family tended to have the same type of cancer, in the same organ, at about the same time of life.

In 1933 **Dr. M. J. Mandelbaum,** New York City, developed a tiny ultraviolet lamp that could be inserted in the bronchial tubes for treatment of tuberculosis.

Dr. David Marine and his associates, of Montefiore Hospital, New York, announced in 1933 that vitamin C offered a means of controlling goiter.

Information on sleep was obtained in 1935 by **Dr. L. W. Max,** New York University, from the electrical currents in the arms and fingers of sleeping deaf-mute persons.

In 1933 **Drs. E. V. McCollum, H. D. Kruse,** and **Elsa Orent,** Johns Hopkins University, found that when an animal got too little magnesium in its diet, it died as a result of the faulty use of the fats by the body.

Drs. Ellice McDonald and **E. F. Schroeder** and their associates at the University of Pennsylvania reported in 1934 that phosphatase, an enzyme in the kidneys, apparently furnished immunity to cancer.

Dr. W. A. McGee announced success in using ether injections to treat whooping cough in 1930.

In 1936 Harvard researchers **H. Houston Merritt** and **Tracy J. Putnam** developed Dilantin (diphenylhydantoin) as the first anticonvulsive treatment for epilepsy since phenobarbitol.

Dr. Richard Miller developed a camera for photographing the interior of the human ear in 1931.

In 1931 **Dr. R. A. Millikan** of the California Institute of Technology announced the development of a million-volt X-ray tube for cancer research.

In 1933 **Dr. Marjorie B. Moore** of the Abbott Laboratories and **Dr. Leon Unger** of Northwestern University announced that the cause of hay fever was the protein rather than the sugary or starchy constituents in pollens.

In 1933 **Thomas Hunt Morgan** was awarded the Nobel Prize in medicine "for his discoveries concerning the function of the chromosome in the transmission of heredity."

Dr. R. S. Morris, University of Cincinnati, reported that several conditions besides pernicious anemia were successfully treated with addisin, a newly discovered blood-forming hormone, in 1933.

In 1934 **Dr. W. P. Murphy,** Boston, discovered that liver extract was a cure for agranulocytosis, a fatal blood disease.

In 1935 **Dr. W. P. Murphy,** in collaboration with **Dr. G. W. Clark,** invented an inexpensive method of injecting liver extract directly into the muscle of pernicious anemia victims.

In 1938 **Basil O'Connor** founded the March of Dimes to finance research into poliomyelitis (also known as infantile paralysis or polio).

Dr. E. L. Opie and **Dr. Jules Freund,** Cornell University, reported in 1938 the discovery of a new vaccine for tuberculosis made from dead bacteria, which after two years' successful application to animals was to be tried on human beings.

A closed-plaster method for treating compound fractures used principles developed in 1937 by Lincoln, Nebraska, physician **H. Winnett Orr** to save Spanish Civil War fracture victims and reduce the need for amputation.

Dr. E. D. Osborne and **Miss B. S. Hitchcock** effectively treated ringworm infection with sodium hypochlorite in 1931.

Dr. R. L. Osborne, Columbia University, described a new local anesthetic, epicaine, which combined the action of novocaine and epinephrine without the tendency of the former to dilate peripheral blood vessels and of the latter to induce nervousness; the anesthetic was still in the experimental stage in 1937.

High blood pressure was normal for some persons and lowering the pressure was actually dangerous, according to studies made by **Dr. O. H. P. Pepper,** Philadelphia, in 1936.

In 1934 **Dr. G. E. Pfahler,** University of Pennsylvania, expressed the conviction that radioactivity could be used successfully on 75 percent of skin cancers.

Drs. Henry Pinkerton and **G. M. Hass,** Harvard University, investigating the filterable viruses in 1934, found evidence that the inclusion bodies might be compact clusters or colonies of minute organisms.

Dr. Bret Ratner, New York University, stated in 1936 that a fifteen-year study showed hay fever and other allergy diseases were not hereditary.

In 1938 **Dr. E. T. Remmen's** report of the more than three hundred nurses and doctors at the Los Angeles Hospital attacked in 1934 and 1935 by a mysterious disease revealed that the malady was a new one, named polioencephalitis.

In 1931 **Dr. H. B. Richardson** and associates at Cornell University isolated a single tuberculosis germ and studied its entire life cycle.

Heart muscles, when injured in such diseases as coronary thrombosis, formed different patterns on electrocardiograms, according to **Dr. Jane S. Robb** and her associates, Syracuse University, who succeeded in identifying some patterns in 1935.

Dr. E. C. Rosenow, Mayo Clinic, reported in 1937 that a serum to prevent the crippling effect of infantile paralysis was being developed, based on the discovery that the virus causing the disease was a transformed streptococcus germ.

In 1936 tests of a childbirth anesthetic consisting of paraldehyde and benzyl alcohol developed by Drs. G. B. Roth and Howard Kane relieved mothers of pain and made it unnecessary to slap or hold the babies upside down at birth to start them breathing.

Dr. L. G. Rowntree, Philadelphia Institute for Medical Research, reported in 1935 that normal stature evidently depended upon the maintenance of a proper balance between the large thymus glands and the small pineal glands of growing children.

In 1937 Dr. L. G. Rowntree and his associates reported that mice fed wheat germ oil developed cancer; this was the first record of a cancerous growth produced by a vegetable substance.

In 1936 Drs. Albert B. Sabin and Peter K. Olitsky of the Rockefeller Institute grew the poliomyelitis virus in human brain cells.

Drs. Florence R. Sabin and A. L. Joyner, Rockefeller Institute for Medical Research, reported in 1938 progress in the development of a chemical treatment for tuberculosis.

Drs. W. A. Sawyer, S. F Kitchen, and Wray Lloyd of the Rockefeller Foundation announced the development of a new immunizing serum for the treatment of yellow fever in 1932.

In 1934 Dr. Franz C. Schmelkes, Belleville, New Jersey, reported a new germicide, which he called azochloramid, to be more effective than iodine or Dakin's solution.

Using a bacterium filtrate method, Dr. Gregory Schwartzman, Mount Sinai Hospital, New York City, developed a new serum for typhoid fever in 1934.

Dr. Florence Seibert, University of Pennsylvania, produced the first pure tuberculin in 1934.

Drs. Atherton Seidell and M. I. Smith, U.S. Public Health service, succeeded in obtaining crystaline vitamin B_1, preventive of beriberi and other nerve disorders, in 1933.

Dr. Oliver B. Simon, Batavia, Illinois, successfully administered oxygen under the skin in 1934, a method that might eliminate the necessity of oxygen tents.

In 1933 Dr. Margaret C. Smith discovered specialized particles known as inclusion bodies in the tissues of encephalitis victims, which proved the disease was caused by a virus.

In 1938 Dr. Tom D. Spies proved that pellagra was a deficiency disease; he treated it with niacin.

In 1935 Rockefeller Institute biochemist Dr. Wendell Meredith Stanley demonstrated the proteinaceous nature of viruses, proving that they were not submicroscopic organisms as was commonly believed.

In 1936 Dr. Wendell Meredith Stanley reported that his studies with mosaic disease indicated that viruses were chemical rather than animal entities.

In 1933 Drs. W. W. Swingle, J. J. Pfiffner, and their associates at Princeton University announced that the function of the cortex of the adrenal gland was to maintain the blood supply at normal volume.

In 1937 Dr. Max Theiler developed a vaccine for yellow fever.

Dr. Walter Timme of the New York Neurological Institute announced in 1930 that a deficiency of calcium in the blood produces crossness, tiredness, and misbehavior.

In 1932 Dr. M. V. Veldee of the U.S. Public Health Service developed a new scarlet fever treatment by treating the scarlet fever antitoxin with formalin, then keeping it warm for two months; it lost its toxic quality but retained its immunizing effects.

In 1936 Miss Mary E. Warga, University of Pittsburgh, announced that identification of silicon in the lungs of silicosis patients was possible through the use of a spectroscope.

In 1933 Drs. R. M. Waters and E. A. Rovenstine, Wisconsin General Hospital, developed an oxygen tube to supplant tents in oxygen administration.

Drs. L. T. Webster and G. L. Fite, Rockefeller Institute, developed a serum in 1934 that immunized mice from encephalitis, sometimes called sleeping sickness.

Drs. Soma Weiss and R. W. Wilkins, Boston, stated in 1937 that they had discovered a previously unrecognized heart disease induced by malnutrition; vitamin B was said to be specific in treating the condition.

In 1933 Dr. D. B. Wells announced a method of treating extensive burns by a three-hour bath in tannic acid.

The 1930 prize award for *Popular Science Monthly* went to Dr. George H. Whipple of the University of Rochester School of Medicine and Dr. George R. Minot of Harvard Medical School for their work which led to the effective treatment of pernicious anemia by feeding liver to victims; as a result of their work, this formerly fatal disease now had an adequate and specialized treatment.

In 1934 Dr. G. H. Whipple, Rochester, New York, and Drs. G. R. Minot and W. P. Murphy, Boston, shared the Nobel Prize in medicine for "their discoveries on liver therapy in the anemias."

In 1935 Dr. L. R. Whitaker, Memorial Hospital, Boston, devised an "electric knife" that would remove large sections of the intestine and join parts without opening the intestine itself; the method was also applicable to gallbladder and other abdominal operations.

Dr. L. R. Williams of the National Tuberculosis Association reported in 1930 that from half to nine-tenths of the American population carried tuberculosis germs in their bodies and urged the entire population to have annual X-ray exams to help prevent the disease.

In 1936 **Robert R. Williams** synthesized thiamine (vitamin B_1).

Dr. M. M. Wintrobe, Johns Hopkins Hospital, reported in 1938 that powdered yeast proved effective in the treatment for patients with pernicious anemia.

Drs. R. C. Wise and **O. H. Schettler** reported in 1938 that three capsules a day of carotene in oil relieved eye fatigue for industrial workers and that vitamin A was the helpful agent.

In 1933 **Dr. Hans Zinsser** and associates of Harvard University, working under the auspices of the U. S. Public Health Service, developed a vaccine and a serum against typhoid fever.

AWARDS

NOBEL PRIZE WINNERS IN MEDICINE OR PHYSIOLOGY

1930

Karl Landsteiner (Austrian-born American) for the identification of human blood into the major groups A, B, AB, and O.

1931

Otto Warburg (Germany) for his discovery of the nature and mode of action of the respiratory enzyme.

1932

Edgar D. Adrian and **Charles S. Sherrington** (United Kingdom) for their discovery regarding the functions of the neurons.

1933

Thomas Hunt Morgan (United States) for his discovery of the heredity transmission functions of chromosomes.

1934

George R. Minot, William P. Murphy, and **George H. Whipple** (United States) for their work on liver extract therapy to overcome anemia.

1935

Hans Spemann (Germany), embryologist, for discovering the organizer effect in embryonic growth.

1936

Henry H. Dale (United Kingdom) and **Otto Loewi** (Austria) for their discovery of the chemical transmission of nerve impulses.

1937

Albert Szent-Györgyi (Hungarian-born American), biochemist, for his identification and isolation of vitamin C (ascorbic acid).

1938

Corneille Heymans (Belgium) for his discovery of the role played by the sinus and aortic mechanisms in the regulation of respiration.

1939

Gerhard Domagk (Germany) for his discovery of the antibacterial effects of Prontosil, the first sulfa drug.

AMERICAN MEDICAL ASSOCIATION DISTINGUISHED SERVICE AWARD RECIPIENTS

The AMA Distinguished Service Award honors a member of the association for general meritorious service. It was first awarded in 1938.

1938

Rudolph Matas, New Orleans, Louisiana

1939

James B. Herrick, Chicago, Illinois

JOHN PHILLIPS MEMORIAL AWARD

American College of Physicians

1932

Oswald T. Avery, New York, New York

1933

William B. Castle, Brookline, Massachusetts

1934

No award

1935

Leo Loeb, Saint Louis, Missouri

1936

Eugene Markley Landis, Boston, Massachusetts

1937

Richard E. Shope, Princeton, New Jersey

1938

Harry Goldblatt, Cleveland, Ohio

1939

Tom Douglas Spies, Birmingham, Alabama

SEDGWICK MEMORIAL MEDAL

American Public Health Association

1930

Theobald Smith

1931

George W. McCoy

1932

William H. Park

1933

Dr. Milton J. Rosenau

1934

Edwin O. Jordan

1935

Haven Emerson

1936

Frederick F. Russell

1937

No award

1938

Wade H. Frost

1939

Thomas Parran

DEATHS

Herman Morris Adler, 59, psychiatrist and criminologist who perfected a lie detector for use in criminal investigation and whose work dealt primarily with the personality and behavioral difficulties and mental factors in criminology, in Boston, 7 December 1935.

Freeman Allen, 59, anesthesia expert and grandson of Harriet Beecher Stowe, in Boston, 3 May 1930.

Frank Allport, 78, ophthalmologist and otologist who advocated the examination of schoolchildren's eyes and ears and was reportedly the first to cure vernal conjunctivitis, in Nice, France, 3 August 1935.

James Meschter Anders, 82, physician whose particular areas of interest were medical diagnosis, clinical medicine, and the function of transpiration; at the Medico-Chirurgical College in Philadelphia he served as professor of forestry, specializing in the relationship of plant life to health, and chaired the Department of Clinical Medicine at the University of Pennsylvania Graduate School of Medicine; among his writings was *House Plants as Sanitary Agents* (1887), in Blue Hills, Maine, 29 August 1936.

Bailey Kelly Ashford, 61, surgeon who determined that hookworm was responsible for widespread anemia in Puerto Rico and organized a government campaign for the eradication of the hookworm disease with the use of the drug thymol; in World War I he received the Distinguished Service Medal and was made a companion of the British Order of St. Michael and St. George in recognition of his laboratory discoveries and war service, in San Juan, Puerto Rico, 1 November 1934.

Astley Paston Cooper Ashhurst, 56, physician and author of surgical texts; he was the colonel in charge of Base Hospital 34 of the American Expeditionary Force in France during World War I and won a citation for his services; professor of clinical surgery at the University of Pennsylvania School of Medicine, in Philadelphia, 19 September 1932.

William Easterly Ashton, 73, physician, surgeon, and author; he took part in the Saint Mihiel and Meuse-Argonne offensives as regimental surgeon to the 309th Field Artillery of the 78th Division during World War I and received the Distinguished Service Cross in 1918; he was the inventor of several surgical instruments, in Philadelphia, 30 March 1933.

Charles Edwin Atwood, 69, neurologist, editor, and author, in New York City, 19 February 1930.

Frederick Henry Baetjer, 58, roentgenologist; a pioneer in X-ray techniques, he was also a martyr to science when he suffered the loss of all of his fingers and serious injury to an eye; professor of roentgenology at Johns Hopkins University and Hospital, in Baltimore, 17 July 1933.

Clarence Bartlett, 77, physician and author who created the department of nervous diseases at the Hahnemann Medical College and Hospital in Philadelphia in 1883, in Philadelphia, 26 August 1935.

Emanuel DeMarnay Baruch, 65, physician, author, and philanthropist; the writer of many articles on medical subjects, he also produced a play, *Judith and Arropherius*, in London in 1928 and in Darmstadt in 1929, in Valhalla, New York, 1 July 1935.

Edwin Beer, 62, urologist; chief of the urological service of the Mount Sinai Hospital, New York; his method of treating tumors of the bladder by high-frequency current was generally adopted; he received the first gold medal of the International Society of Urology in Brussels in 1927, in New York City, 13 August 1938.

Joseph Augustus Blake, 72, surgeon and professor of surgery at the College of Physicians and Surgeons of Columbia University; during World War I he was head of the American Red Cross Military Hospital and received the Cross of the Legion of Honor; after the war he became chief surgeon of the reconstruction Hospital and the Tarrytown Hospital, in Litchfield, Connecticut, 12 August 1937.

Joseph Colt Bloodgood, 67, surgeon and cancer fighter who instructed surgeons in the best way to diagnose the disease; he received the gold medal of the Radiological Society of North America in 1929 for his work in the study of bone malignancy diagnosis and its treatment by X ray and radium, in Guilford, Maryland, 22 October 1935.

Walter M. Brickner, 54, surgeon, and lieutenant colonel with the Medical Reserve Corps during World War I; he was consultant in neurosurgery for the American Expeditionary Force and editor of the *American Journal of Surgery* from 1905 to 1927, in Atlantic Beach, Long Island, New York, 22 July 1930.

Kate Brousseau, psychologist and director of the psychological service of the Los Angeles Institute of Family Relations; during World War I she served with the French army and was decorated by the French government, 9 July 1938.

Lawrason Brown, 66, physician, author, and tuberculosis expert; he was a founder of the American Sanatorium Association and a pioneer in work on intestinal tuberculosis, in Saranac Lake, New York, 26 December 1937.

Albert Harrison Brundage, 74, toxicologist, professor of toxicology and physiology at Marquette University; during World War I he was with the Volunteer Medical Corps and after 1918 lectured for the American Red Cross; he founded the first open-air classes for the Brooklyn public schools, in Central Islip, Long Island, New York, 12 March 1936.

Carroll Gideon Bull, 46, pathologist; associate of pathology at the Rockefeller Institute, New York City, where in collaboration with Ida W. Pritchett he discovered an effective antitoxin for war gangrene; he specialized in research in bacteriology and sources of the common cold, in Baltimore, 31 May 1931.

Henry Turman Byford, 84, gynecologist and author who extensively researched anemia in women and eczema, in Chicago, Illinois, 5 June 1938.

Augustus Caille, 81, pediatrician and author who invented a perforated trocar for use in abdominal puncture and devised a scratch test to detect people sensitive to the animal serum used in inoculations, in New York City, 10 October 1935.

Henry Ware Cattell, 73, pathologist and author known for his expertise in murder cases; during World War I he had charge of the postmortem records of the American Expeditionary Force, in Washington, D.C., 8 March 1936.

John Roberts Caulk, 56, urologist whose important innovations in surgical practice included ultraviolet-ray treatment of tuberculosis of the bladder, simplified kidney surgery, an operation for the relief of megaloureter, the cautery punch operation for prostatic growths, and the infiltration method of anesthetizing the neck of the bladder, in Saint Louis, 13 October 1938.

Robert A. Chesebrough, 96, inventor of the petroleum product Vaseline, who attributed his longevity to ingesting one spoonful of the product every day of his life, 9 September 1933.

Eugene Christian, 72, dietician who lived on spinach and orange juice, in San Diego, 9 March 1930.

John Woolman Churchman, 60, bacteriologist whose work in experimental bacteriology led to the discovery of the selective bacteriostatic properties of various triphenyl menthane dyes; in 1925 he recommended to the American Chemical Society the use of dyes in the treatment of infectious diseases, in Amityville, New York, 13 July 1937.

L. Pierce Clark, 63, physician, neurologist, and writer; Clark was president of the New York Psychiatric Society, National Association for the Study of Epilepsy, and the American Psychopathological Association; during his later years he became noted for his psychobiographies, including those of Abraham Lincoln, Alexander the Great, and other famous historical characters, in New York City, 3 December 1933.

Robert Calvin Coffey, 64, surgeon who was best known for his contributions to the eradication of cancer; he devised the "hammock operation" in the field of abdominal surgery and was credited with being the first surgeon to remove the head of the pancreas experimentally, implanting the remaining part into the intestine, near Portland, Oregon, 9 November 1933.

Harvey Cushing, 70, neurosurgeon and author who made notable contributions to brain surgery, 7 October 1939.

Condict Walker Cutler, 71, general practitioner, author, physician in chief of the New York dispensary and professor of dermatology at the University of Vermont, in Morristown, New Jersey, 9 July 1930.

John Chalmers Da Costa, 69, surgeon whose demonstrations of surgical practice and addresses to his students received much attention in the medical field and attracted prominent surgeons of the world to see and listen; his *Manual of Modern Surgery,* revised through ten editions from 1895 to 1925, was the authoritative work on the subject, in Philadelphia, 16 May 1933.

Charles Loomis Dana, 83, known as the dean of American neurologists, Dana's prolific interests and research and writing encompassed public health, neurology, psychiatry, physiology, psychology, archaeology, the application of pathology to neuropathology, pathology of paralysis agitans and of combined sclerosis and douloureux, cerebral localization of cutaneous sensations, alcoholism, and alcoholic meningitis, in Harmon-on-Hudson, New York, 12 December 1935.

A. B. Davis, 69, a founder of the American College of Surgeons, in New York City, 13 August 1930.

George Van Ness Dearborn, 69, neuropsychiatrist who was one of the first to explore scientifically the relationship between emotion and blood pressure, in New York City, 12 December 1938.

Frederick Shepard Dennis, 83, surgeon and author who in 1874 was one of the first American converts to Joseph Lister's theory of applying the principles of antiseptics to treating wounds, in New York City, 8 March 1934.

Richard (Smith) Dewey, 87, psychiatrist; during the Franco-Prussian War he was a volunteer assistant surgeon at the field hospital at Pont à Mousson, France; upon his return to the United States in 1872, he served in several facilities for the insane and was chair of mental and nervous diseases at the Chicago Post-Graduate Medical School; in 1896 he was president of the American Medico-Psychological Society (now the American Psychiatric Association), in La Cañada, California, 4 August 1933.

Alvah Hunt Doty, 79, physician and author; chief of the Bureau of Contagious Diseases in New York from 1905 to 1911, through the system of quarantine sanitation that he established, he prevented the spread of contagious diseases brought by immigrants, in Pelham Manor, New York, 27 May 1934.

John Douglas, 63, surgeon and clinical professor of surgery at New York University and Bellevue Medical College, who disproved the theories of his day that cancer was hereditary, in New York City, 5 December 1938.

Charles Edward Dowman, 49, surgeon; in World War I he served at the mobile hospitals in the Saint Mihiel and Argonne offensives; as a neurological surgeon, he became noted especially for his delicate brain operations, in Atlanta, 14 November 1931.

John William Draper, 59, associate in surgery and director of the laboratory of surgical research at the New York University medical school and attending surgeon at the New Jersey State Hospital for the Insane; at the time of his death he was director of the Andrew Todd McClintock Foundation in New York City, in New York, 26 January 1931.

George Peter Dreyer, 64, physician; known for his discovery of the secretory nerves of the suprarenal glands and his work on blood proteins and differential respiration, in La Grange, Illinois, 27 February 1931.

Arthur Baldwin Duel, 65, surgeon and author; with Sir Charles Ballance he originated an operation for facial paralysis; elected a fellow of the American College of Surgeons, he was made a Knight Commander of the Order of the Crown of Rumania in 1927, near Pawling, New York, 11 April 1936.

Charles A. Eastman (Ohiyesa), Native American (Santee Dakota) physician; in 1891 he was a doctor at Pine Ridge Agency at the time of the Ghost Dancers' Battle of Wounded Knee and described the tragedy in his autobiography, *From the Deep Woods to Civilization*; in 1933 he received the first Indian Achievement Medal awarded by the Indian Council Fire of Chicago, in Detroit, 8 January 1939.

Robert Gibson Eccles, 86, Scottish-born pharmacist who served as a chemist with the U.S. Bureau of Indian Affairs and a professor of organic chemistry at the Brooklyn College of Pharmacy; his research concerned antiseptics and sepsis, in Brooklyn, New York, 9 June 1934.

Harry Belleville Eisberg, 45, surgeon who was recognized as an authority on intestinal obstruction and abdominal wounds and injury, in New York City, 10 August 1935.

Maurice Fishberg, 62, Russian-born physician and author and one of the leading authorities on tuberculosis; he attracted attention in the field of physical anthropology with his research on the physical anthropology of the Jews, in New York City, 30 August 1934.

Lawrence F. Flick, 81, physician whose fight against tuberculosis led to the founding of the Benjamin Rush Hospital in Philadelphia, the White Haven Sanitarium, and the Phipps Institute for the Study of Tuberculosis; he cured himself of tuberculosis early in life and later proved the disease was not hereditary, in Philadelphia, 7 July 1938.

Joseph Irwin France, 65, physician and former senator from Maryland who opposed American membership in the League of Nations and advocated recognition of Soviet Russia, in Port Deposit, Maryland, 26 January 1939.

Otto "Tiger" Freer, 74, laryngologist who invented the Freer instruments that were used by surgeons to perform the submucus resection of the septum, in Chicago, 21 April 1932.

Wade Hampton Frost, 58, epidemiologist and dean of the Johns Hopkins School of Hygiene and Public Health; he studied epidemiology, polio, stream pollution, and influenza, in Baltimore, 30 April 1938.

John Samuel Fulton, 72, physician and public health administrator; secretary-general of the sixth International Congress on Tuberculosis in 1908 and of the fifteenth International Congress on Hygiene and Demography in 1912, and director of the State Board of Health of Maryland from 1923 to 1928, in Baltimore, 12 August 1931.

Frederick Parker Gay, 64, pathologist and university professor at the University of California and Columbia University; his research interests included the impact of sulfanilamide in streptococcus infection, typhoid fever, leprosy, and sleeping sickness, in New Hartford, Connecticut, 14 July 1939.

John Harvey Girdner, 77, surgeon who attended President James A. Garfield during his eighty-day struggle for life after he was shot on 2 July 1881; Girdner was said to be the first surgeon to succeed in grafting skin from a dead body onto a living one; he invented the telephonic bullet probe, widely used before the discovery of X rays, and the phymosis forceps, in Islip, Long Island, New York, 27 October 1933.

Lucio and **Simplicimo Godino,** 28, Filipino conjoined twins, joined by a thick muscular coupling at the base of their spine; after Lucio died of lobar pneumonia on 24 November 1936, surgery was performed to separate the dead twin from the live one, followed by a second operation to restore Simplicimo's large intestine, which had protruded into the connecting band; his condition was reported favorable for eleven days before he contracted spinal meningitis and died on 5 December 1936; had he survived, he would have been the only living adult formerly conjoined twin, in New York City.

James Riddle Goffe, 80, surgeon and president of the International Congress of Obstetricians and Gynecologists in 1915; lecturer at the New York Polyclinic Medical School and Hospital and at the Dartmouth Medical School, and attending surgeon at the Polyclinic Hospital and the Woman's Hospital, New York City, in Bronxville, New York, 24 December 1931.

Anna Adams Gordon, 77, temperance worker and president of the National Woman's Christian Temperance Union from 1914 to 1925, in Castile, New York, 15 June 1931.

Amédée Granger, 60, radiologist and professor of radiology; he was the discoverer of Granger's Sign and Granger's Line and in 1926 received the gold medal of the Radiological Society of North America, in New Orleans, 15 December 1939.

William Phillips Graves, 62, surgeon and professor of gynecology at the Harvard Medical School; he was president of the American Gynecological Society in 1931 and the first American to be honored as an honorary fellow of the British College of Obstetricians and Gynecologists, in Boston, 25 January 1933.

Robert Battey Greenough, 65, surgeon who was known throughout the country for his fight against cancer; he served as president of the American Association for Cancer Research and was an early advocate of health insurance but did not favor the socialization of medicine, in Boston, 16 February 1937.

Clyde Graeme Guthrie, 51, physician and associate professor of medicine at Johns Hopkins Medical School; his research dealt with chemical infections of the blood and body secretions and parasites in the liver and intestines; he also studied the matching of blood for transfusion, in Cincinnati, Ohio, 14 December 1931.

Melvin Everett Haggerty, 62, psychologist and authority on educational psychology; after service in World War I he was assigned to the Surgeon General's Office in

charge of the reeducation of disabled soldiers, in Minneapolis, 6 October 1937.

Carl August Hamann, 61, surgeon and educator, professor of applied anatomy and clinical surgery and dean of Western Reserve University Medical School in Cleveland, Ohio, in Cleveland, 12 January 1930.

George Tryon Harding Jr., 55, physician, psychiatrist, and brother to President Warren G. Harding; after serving as a member of the Medical Reserve Corps in World War I, Harding became examining neuropsychiatrist for the U.S. Veterans' Bureau, in Worthington, Ohio, 18 January 1934.

Louis Israel Harris, 56, Austrian-born physician and commissioner of the New York City Board of Health who reorganized the department and initiated many reforms in public health procedure, in New York City, 6 January 1939.

William C. Hassler, physician who served for more than thirty years as public health officer of San Francisco, leading the campaign for the extermination of waterfront rats during the rebuilding of the city after the earthquake and fire of 1906 to reduce the menace of bubonic plague; in 1931 he was elected president of the American Public Health Association, in San Francisco, 2 August 1931.

Clarence Floyd Haviland, 54, clinical professor of psychiatry at Columbia University; in 1914 he made a survey of conditions of the care of the insane in Pennsylvania, in Cairo, Egypt, 1 January 1930.

James Ramsay Hunt, 63, neurologist and Columbia University School of Medicine professor of neurology; he wrote many authoritative articles for medical journals, and many of the diseases that were first described and recognized by him bear his name in medical literature, in Katonah, New York, 22 July 1937.

Byron H. Jackson, 65, roentgenologist who was a pioneer in the use and development of the X ray, in Luzern County, Pennsylvania, 16 May 1939.

Edward Starr Judd, 57, chief of the surgical staff of the Mayo Clinic in Rochester, Minnesota; Judd was acknowledged as an authority on biliary, gastrointestinal, and genitourinary tracts and the thyroid, in Chicago, 30 November 1935.

George Hughes Kirby, 60, psychiatrist and authority on alcohol psychoses, race psychopathology, and manic-depressive psychoses; as a member of the Medical Corps in World War I, he helped organize a unit for the care of soldiers suffering from mental or nervous disorders, in Portsmouth, New Hampshire, 11 August 1935.

Alexander Lambert, 77, physician and medical head of the American Red Cross in France in World War I, president of the American Medical Association in 1919, and former chairman of the New York State

Narcotic Commission, in New York City, 9 May 1939.

Charles Augustus Leale, 90, surgeon; on 14 April 1865, when President Lincoln was shot, Leale was the first physician to reach the president's side and was authorized by Mrs. Lincoln to take charge of the president, remaining continuously by him until he died the next day; he later became a medical practitioner in New York City, in New York City, 13 June 1932.

Joseph Leidy, 66, physician; in 1900 he was appointed official delegate for the U.S. government on the international jury at the Paris Exposition and was decorated by France as an Officer of Public Instruction; after serving in World War I and as instructor and medical director of gas defense with the 30th Division, he returned to the U.S. and became a leading neurologist, in Philadelphia, 6 July 1932.

John Levy, 41, psychiatrist and chief of the Child Guidance Clinic of the Columbia-Presbyterian Medical Center, New York City; author of *The Happy Family*, in Boston, 11 July 1938.

John Alden Lichty, 66, physician and radiologist; while studying in Berlin from 1895 to 1896, he became interested in the future possibilities of the Roentgen rays (X rays) and was an expert exponent of their use, in Rochester, New York, 2 May 1931.

Charles S. Little, 67, psychiatrist under whose direction the Letchworth Village in New York, a mental institution, became a model asylum housing thirty-five hundred patients, in Letchworth Village, New York, 6 June 1936.

Andrew Stewart Lobingier, 76, surgeon, author, and one of the founders of the American College of Surgeons, in Los Angeles, 31 July 1939.

Brig. Gen. Theodore Charles Lyster, 58, army surgeon who served in the Philippines, the American occupation of Veracruz, Mexico, and World War I as chief of aviation and professional services in the surgeon general's service in France during the winter of 1917–1918; on his retirement in 1919, Lyster became a director of yellow fever research at the Rockefeller Foundation in New York City; in 1930 he was commissioned brigadier general by a special act of Congress, in Los Angeles, 6 August 1933.

C. J. MacGuire, 82, surgeon; forty-five years with Saint Vincent's Hospital in New York City, in New York City, 6 May 1930.

Stephen John Maher, 79, physician and authority on tuberculosis who served as chairman of the Connecticut Tuberculosis Commission for twenty-eight years and was the U.S. government representative at several International Tuberculosis Conferences, in New Haven, Connecticut, 6 June 1939.

Emil Mayer, 77, laryngologist; from 1893 to 1904 he was surgeon and chief of clinic in the throat department of the New York Eye and Ear Infirmary, and during 1904 to 1919, attending laryngologist at Mount Sinai Hospital, retiring in 1926; in 1920 he was president of the American Academy of Ophthalmology and Otolaryngology and in 1922 of the American Laryngological Association, in New York City, 20 October 1931.

Lewis Linn McArthur, 76, surgeon; a pioneer in the use of antiseptic surgery, he was noted for his research on opsonin, tuberculosis, and the thyroid gland; his World War I service led to his decoration as a chevalier of the Order of Leopold of Belgium, in Chicago, 5 November 1934.

Alfred Watterson McCann, 52, food expert and author who was director of the Alfred W. McCann Laboratories in New York City and was associated for many years with Dr. Harvey Wiley in his crusade for pure food, in New York City, 19 January 1931.

Stewart LeRoy McCurdy, 72, surgeon and author; from 1896 he was professor of anatomy and oral surgery in the dental department of the University of Pittsburgh and was also assistant professor of surgery in the medical department of the university, surgeon for the Pennsylvania Railroad, and orthopedic surgeon at the Columbia Hospital, Pittsburgh, in Pittsburgh, 8 September 1931.

John Rich McDill, 74, soldier and surgeon whose service in the Spanish-American War led to his organization of the Woman's Hospital in Manila and his work in other Philippine hospitals; his World War I service resulted in his appointment as consultant in reconstructive surgery in the Surgeon General's Office and his work as chief medical officer on the Federal Board for Rehabilitation of Disabled Soldiers; he was also a founder and fellow of the American College of Surgeons, in Cornwall-on-Hudson, New York, 14 September 1934.

Earl Baldwin McKinley, 43, bacteriologist and expert on tropical diseases and immunology; dean of the medical school of George Washington University; lost when the *Hawaii Clipper* disappeared on a Guam-Manila flight, 29 July 1938.

Frank Ebenezer Miller, 73, laryngologist, author, and a tenor singer who made a special study of the singer's voice; he invented a system of "finger surgery" used in the treatment of deafness and an electrical system used to produce musical tones, in Copake, New York, 15 April 1932.

Roger Sylvester Morris, 56, physician and author who developed, with his associates, a method of treatment for pernicious anemia using intramuscular injections of gastric juice; his other research pertained to normal and subnormal basal metabolic rate and to the treatment of bacterial hypersensitivity in the intestinal tract, in Cincinnati, Ohio, 2 March 1934.

Charles Norris, 77, physician and chief medical examiner for New York City; Dr. Norris's research on sudden death led him to become an authority on wood alcohol, tetra ethyl lead, and carbon monoxide poisoning, in New York City, 11 September 1935.

William Perry Northrup, 84, pediatrician and author who was one of the first practicing pediatricians in New York City and who introduced the first open-air hospital ward for the treatment of pneumonia, in New York City, 20 November 1935.

G. L. Noyes, 57, dean, University of Missouri Medical School, Columbia, Missouri, 4 February 1930.

James Thomas Orbison, 72, psychiatrist who testified in several sensational murder trials, including those of Thomas Massie and William Edward Hickman, in Sawtelle, California, 26 March 1938.

Payn Bigelow Parsons, 59, bacteriologist; in 1905 he was appointed bacteriologist for the New York subway air investigation and in 1907 was a member of the Pollution Commission and the Metropolitan Sewerage Commission, directing the laboratories from 1909 to 1913; also chief bacteriologist for the New York laboratory of the U.S. Bureau of Chemistry; after 1925 he was bacteriologist for the New York State Conservation Commission, in New York City, 19 September 1931.

Edward Lasell Partridge, 76, general practitioner and obstetrician and a pioneer in the movement to develop the Highlands of the Hudson River as a state reservation, in New York City, 2 May 1930.

J. D. Patterson, 82, former president of the American Dental Association, in Kansas City, Missouri, 12 January 1930.

Roger Griswold Perkins, 61, bacteriologist and professor; a member of the American Red Cross Commission to Romania in 1917–1918, he was medical associate to scientific attachés at the American Embassy in Paris in 1918, and director of the sanitation division of the Red Cross Commission to the Balkan States in 1919, in Providence, Rhode Island, 28 March 1936.

Lewis Stephen Pilcher, 89, surgeon and editor who served as a hospital steward with the federal army during the Civil War; he was a founder and editor for fifty years of the *Annals of Surgery;* upon the fiftieth jubilee of his medical school graduation in 1916, he was awarded a special medal by the American Surgical Association, in Upper Montclair, New Jersey, 24 December 1934.

Charles Winfield Pilgrim, 78, psychiatrist; a former president of the American Psychiatric Association, Pilgrim spent his career trying to raise the standard of medicine and nursing care of the insane and was a pioneer in the establishment of outpatient departments of state hospitals with their accompanying social service and mental clinics, in Central Valley, New York, 3 May 1934.

John Osborne Polak, 61, gynecologist and author whose works included *Students' Manual of Obstetrics* (1914) and *Students' Manual of Gynecology* (1915), in Brooklyn, New York, 29 June 1931.

Charles Allen Porter, 64, surgeon in chief at the Massachusetts General Hospital; he was associated with the Harvard Medical School as John Homans professor of surgery and was also a past president of the New England Surgical Society, in Boston, 3 July 1931.

Otto Rank, 55, Austrian-born psychologist; an associate of Sigmund Freud for twenty years, he left Freud in 1925 to develop his own technique, which emphasized the importance of the conscious, in New York City, 31 October 1939.

Mortimer Williams Raynor, 56, psychiatrist and neurologist who served as consulting psychiatrist and neurologist at various hospitals throughout New York State and whose interests lay in the parole system, social work, and medical service in state hospitals and prisons, in White Plains, New York, 5 October 1935.

Henry Cottrell Rowland, 59, adventure-story author and physician who fought in the Spanish-American War and was assistant surgeon with the U.S. forces during the Philippine Insurrection of 1900; after the entry of the United States into World War I, he became a special agent in France of the Intelligence Department of the U.S. Navy, in Washington, D.C., 5 June 1933.

Lena Kellogg Sadler (Mrs. William Samuel), 64, gynecologist and associate director of the Chicago Institute for Research and Diagnosis and coauthor of several books with her husband, in Chicago, 8 August 1939.

Thomas Edward Satterthwaite, 91, physician and author; while studying in Vienna after receiving his M.D. from Columbia University, the Franco-Prussian War broke out and Satterthwaite received a commission as assistant surgeon in the Prussian army; on his return to the United States, he worked as a microscopist and pathologist at various New York City hospitals and founded and cofounded the Babies' Hospital and Post-Graduate Medical School, New York City, 19 September 1934.

David Henry Shelling, 40, pediatrician who developed medicine for softening and reshaping the bones without an operation in cases of rickets and studied lead poisoning, the parathyroid, and other bone diseases, in Brooklyn, New York, 17 May 1938.

William I. Sirovich, 57, physician and Democratic congressman from New York City, in New York City, 17 December 1939.

Arthur Donaldson Smith, 74, physician, author, and explorer who received the Callum gold medal of the American Geographical Society for his explorations under the auspices of the British Museum, in Philadelphia, 19 February 1939.

Charles Morton Smith, 70, dermatologist with the Harvard Medical School and Massachusetts General Hospital, he was noted for syphilis research, in Boston, 8 January 1938.

George Rinaldo Southwick, 70, gynecologist, and professor of gynecology at Boston University School of Medicine; president of surgery and gynecology of the American Institute of Homeopathy, in Boston, 7 January 1931.

Daniel Atkinson King Steele, 79, surgeon; in 1882 he was one of the founders of the College of Physicians and Surgeons of Chicago and also acted as president from 1894 to 1913 when the college was presented to the University of Illinois as its permanent medical department; during World War I he was chief surgeon at the U.S. Army General Hospital No. 9, Lakewood, New Jersey, in Sarasota, Florida, 19 July 1931.

Louis William Stern, 66, German-born psychologist who was a pioneer in the field of mental testing and who developed the personalistic approach to psychology, in Durham, North Carolina, 27 March 1938.

George David Stewart, 70, surgeon, professor and visiting and consulting surgeon to several New York institutions; he was a founder of the American College of surgeons. Stewart gained notoriety in 1927 when, at a banquet at the American College of Surgeons, he maintained that alcohol was a valuable remedy that medical men should be allowed to prescribe regardless of the Eighteenth Amendment, in New York City, 9 March 1933.

Edgar James Swift, 72, psychologist, author, and educator; from 1920 to 1924 he was a special lecturer on applied psychiatry at the Post-Graduate School of the U.S. Naval Academy and the Naval War College, in Hollis, Maine, 30 August 1932.

Rudolf Bolling Teusler, 58, physician who went to Japan in 1900 as medical missionary for the Protestant Episcopal Church; he received many decorations from the Russians, Czechoslovaks, and Japanese for his service as commissioner of the American Red Cross to Siberia during 1918 to 1921; in June 1933 Teusler saw his dream of a great medical center for the Far East materialize when a 275-bed hospital was dedicated in Tokyo, in Tokyo, Japan, 10 August 1934.

Walter Nelson Thayer, 60, physician, prison doctor, and Commissioner of Correction for the State of New York from 1930; he was a believer in the parole system and a writer of monographs and articles on crime problems, in Napanoch, New York, 6 January 1936.

Benjamin A. Thomas, 51, surgeon and educator, professor and vice dean of urology in the University of Pennsylvania Medical School, 29 May 1930.

Thomas Wingate Todd, 53, anatomist noted for his studies of the growth of the skeleton, the size of the brain, and the action of the stomach, in Cleveland, Ohio, 28 December 1938.

Leonard Thompson Troland, 43, scientist, psychologist, author, and inventor; assistant professor of psychology at Harvard; coinventor of the color process for motion pictures and vice president of the Technicolor Motion Picture Corporation; during World War I he helped develop a submarine listening device, in a mountain-climbing accident on Mount Wilson, California, 27 May 1932.

Fenton Benedict Turck, 75, surgeon who was admitted to practice in New York State without examination by the Board of Regents because of his notable record in Philadelphia, Chicago, and at the University of Rome in Italy; he invented the gyromele and other medical instruments, in New York City, 16 November 1932.

Charles R. Walgreen, 66, merchant, founder, and president of the Walgreen Company, retail drugs, in Chicago, 11 December 1939.

Theodore Weisenburg, 58, neurologist whose research involved cerebellar localization, aphasia, and polio; he was among the first neurologists to use motion pictures in studying the expressions and actions of people with nervous disorders, in Philadelphia, 3 August 1934.

William Henry Welch, 84, pathologist whose work gave Johns Hopkins Medical School its preeminent position in the field of pathology; dean of the medical school, and director of its school of hygiene and public health; Johns Hopkins named its new medical library for him in 1928 and perpetuated his memory through John Sargent's portrait of "The Four Doctors" which depicts Welch, Sir William Osler, Dr. William S. Halsted, and Dr. Howard A. Kelly and hangs in the great hall of the Welch Medical Library, in Baltimore, 30 April 1934.

Reynold Webb Wilcox, 75, physician and author; among the organizations of which he was president were the American Therapeutic Society, the American Association of Medical Jurisprudence, the American Congress on Internal Medicine, and the American College of Physicians, in Princeton, New Jersey, 6 June 1931.

Frankwood Earle Williams, 54, psychiatrist and author; as director of the National Committee for Mental Hygiene, he planned the program for the first international congress on mental hygiene held in Washington in 1930, died at sea, 24 September 1936.

Herbert Upham Williams, 72, pathologist and professor at the University of Buffalo Medical School; he was noted for his research on diseases of ancient times, in Buffalo, New York, 8 December 1938.

Linsly Rudd Williams, 58, physician and tuberculosis expert who served as deputy commissioner of health for the state of New York until 1917 when at the request of the U.S. Army Medical Reserve Corps he investigated sanitary conditions in France and England; after the armistice he remained in France to direct the tuberculosis work conducted with the support of the Rockefeller Foundation; after his return to the United States he continued to be important in the field of public health, in New York City, 8 January 1934.

John Whitridge Williams, 65, physician; dean of the Johns Hopkins Medical School and president of the American Gynecological Society, the American Association for the Study and Prevention of Infant Mortality, and the Medical and Chirurgical Faculty of Maryland, in Baltimore, 21 October 1931.

Mrs. Josephine Woodbury, a pioneer Christian Scientist, in France, 3 March 1930.

John Henry Wyckoff, 55, physician and educator who was in charge of the cardiac clinic at Bellevue Hospital in New York and aided in the establishment of the Department of Cardiography and the Department of Forensic Medicine at the Bellevue Hospital Medical College, in New York City, 1 June 1937.

PUBLICATIONS

American Academy of Political and Social Science, *The Medical Profession and the Public: Currents and Counter-Currents* (Philadelphia: American Academy of Political and Social Science, 1934);

American Medical Association, Bureau of Medical Economics, *Economics and the Ethics of Medicine* (Chicago: American Medical Association, 1935);

L. F. Barker, *Live Long and Be Happy; How to Prolong Your Life and Enjoy It* (New York: Appleton-Century, 1936);

Bertram M. Bernheim, *Medicine at the Crossroads* (New York: Morrow, 1939);

Esther Lucile Brown, *Physicians and Medical Care* (New York: Russell Sage Foundation, 1937);

P. Brown, *American Martyrs to Science through Roentgen Rays* (Springfield, Ill.: Charles C. Thomas, 1936);

Alexis Carrel, *Man, the Unknown* (New York: Harper, 1935);

Carrel and Charles A. Lindbergh, *The Culture of Organs* (New York: Paul B. Hoeber, 1938);

Elizabeth M. Chesser, *Vitality; a Book on the Health of Women and Children* (New York: Oxford University Press, 1935);

Logan Clendening, *Behind the Doctor: The Romance of Medicine* (New York: Knopf, 1933);

Committee on the Costs of Medical Care, *Medical Care for the American People* (Chicago: University of Chicago Press, 1932);

Royal S. Copeland, *Home Medical Book* (Philadelphia: Winston, 1934);

J. L. Corish, ed., *Health Knowledge* (New York: Medical Book Distributors, 1936);

Nelson A. Crawford and Karl A. Menninger, *The Healthy-Minded Child* (New York: Coward-McCann, 1930);

Margaret W. Curti, *Child Psychology* (New York: Longmans, 1930);

George Gordon Dawson, *Healing: Pagan and Christian* (New York: Macmillan, 1936);

Albert Deutsch, *The Mentally Ill in America* (New York: Doubleday, Doran, 1938);

David Dietz, *Medical Magic* (Toronto: McClelland, 1938);

Paul A. Dodd, *Economic Aspects of Medical Services* (Washington, D.C.: Graphic Arts Press, 1939);

George Draper, *Infantile Paralysis* (New York: Appleton-Century, 1935);

Anne Ellis, *Sunshine Preferred: The Philosophy of an Ordinary Woman* (Boston: Houghton Mifflin, 1934);

Morris Fishbein, *Do You Want to Become a Doctor?* (Toronto: McClelland, 1939);

Fishbein, *Fads and Quackery in Healing* (New York: Covici, 1932);

Fishbein, *Frontiers of Medicine* (Toronto: McClelland, 1933);

Fishbein, *Syphilis; the Next Great Plague to Go* (Philadelphia: McKay, 1937);

Fishbein, ed., *The Modern Home Medical Adviser, Your Health and How to Preserve It* (Garden City: Doubleday, 1935);

I. S. Falk, *Security Against Sickness* (Garden City: Doubleday, Doran, 1936);

Falk, C. Rufus Rorem, and Martha D. Ring, *The Cost of Medical Care* (Chicago: University of Chicago Press, 1933);

Iago Galdston, ed., *Medicine and Mankind* (New York: Appleton-Century, 1936);

Arthur T. Gersild, *Child Psychology* (New York: Prentice-Hall, 1933);

Howard W. Haggard, *Doctor in History* (New Haven: Yale University Press, 1934);

Haggard, *The Lame, the Halt, and the Blind; the Vital Role of Medicine in the History of Civilization* (Toronto: McClelland, 1935);

T. S. Harding, *Fads, Frauds, and Physicians: Diagnosis and Treatment of the Doctors' Dilemma* (New York: Dial Press, 1930);

A. E. Hertzler, *The Horse and Buggy Doctor* (New York: Harper, 1938);

Karen Danielson Horney, *The Neurotic Personality of Our Time* (New York: Norton, 1937);

P. P. Jacobs, *Christmas Seals Around the World* (New York: New York Tuberculosis and Health Association, 1937);

Joseph Jastrow, *Piloting Your Life; The Psychologist as Helmsman* (New York: Greenberg, 1930);

Journal of Social Psychology, first published February 1930;

W. N. and L. A. Kellogg, *The Ape and the Child* (New York: Whittlesey House, 1933);

L. M. Klinefelter, *Medical Occupations Available to Boys When They Grow Up* (New York: Dutton, 1938);

L. M. Klinefelter, *Medical Occupations for Girls; Women in White* (New York: Dutton, 1939);

Roger I. Lee, Lewis Webster Jones, and Barbara Jones, *The Fundamentals of Good Medical Care* (Chicago: University of Chicago Press, 1933);

Morris Lichtenstein, *Cures for Minds in Distress* (New York: Jewish Science Publishing, 1936);

Ralph H. Major, *Doctor Explains* (New York: Knopf, 1931);

L. C. Marsh, A. G. Fleming, and C. F. Blacker, *Health and Unemployment; Some Studies of Their Relationship* (New York: Oxford University Press, 1938);

Franklin H. Martin, *Fifty Years of Medicine and Surgery: An Autobiographical Sketch* (Chicago: Surgical Publishing, 1934);

L. B. Mendel, et al., *The Vitamins*. A symposium of eleven articles that appeared in the *Journal of the American Medical Association* between April and August, 1932. Reprinted in a special edition by Mead Johnson, Evansville, Ind., 1932;

Karl Menninger, *The Human Mind* (New York: Knopf, 1930);

Menninger, *Man Against Himself* (New York: Harcourt Brace, 1938);

Harry A. Millis, *Sickness and Insurance* (Chicago: University of Chicago Press, 1937);

The Modern Psychologist, first published in 1933;

Robert T. Morris, *Fifty Years a Surgeon* (New York: Dutton, 1935);

Wendell Muncie, *Psychobiology and Psychiatry* (Saint Louis: Mosby, 1939);

Marian S. Newcomer, *Bewildered Patient* (New York: Hale, 1936);

Edna E. Nicholson, *A Study of Tuberculosis Mortality among Young Women* (New York: National Tuberculosis Association, 1932);

Francis B. Packard, *History of Medicine in the United States*, 2 volumes (New York: Paul B. Hoeber, 1931);

Rachel Palmer and Sarah Greenberg, *Facts and Frauds in Women's Hygiene* (New York: Vanguard, 1936);

Thomas Parran, *Shadow on the Land: Syphilis* (New York: Reynal and Hitchcock, 1937);

E. Podolsky, *Medicine Marches On* (New York: Harper, 1934);

Psychoanalytic Quarterly, first published April 1932;

Louis S. Reed, *Midwives, Chiropodists, and Optometrists: Their Place in Medical Care*. Committee on the Costs of Medical Care Publications, no. 15 (Chicago: University of Chicago Press, 1932);

David Riesman, *Medicine in Modern Society* (Princeton: Princeton University Press, 1939);

Victor Robinson, *The Story of Medicine* (New York: Boni, 1931);

James Rorty, *American Medicine Mobilizes* (New York: Norton, 1939);

Henry E. Sigerist, *American Medicine* (New York: Norton, 1934);

Sigerist, *Man and Medicine* (New York: Norton, 1932);

Frederic A. Washburn, *The Massachusetts General Hospital: Its Development, 1900–1935* (Boston: Houghton Mifflin, 1939);

Leslie Dixon Weatherhead, *Psychology in Service of the Soul* (New York: Macmillan, 1930);

Herman G. Weiskotten, Alphonse M. Schwitalla, William D. Cutter, and Hamilton H. Anderson, *Medical Education in the United States, 1934–1939*. Commission on Medical Education. (Chicago: American Medical Association, 1940);

Lucy Wilder, *The Mayo Clinic* (Springfield, Ill.: Charles C. Thomas, 1936);

George D. Wolf, *The Physician's Business* (Philadelphia: Lippincott, 1938);

Walter B. Wolfe, *How to Be Happy Though Human* (New York: Farrar & Rinehart, 1931);

R. S. Woodworth, *Contemporary Schools of Psychology* (New York: Ronald, 1931);

Hans Zinsser, *Rats, Lice, and History* (Boston: Little, Brown, 1935).

RELIGION

by JOHN SCOTT WILSON

CONTENTS

Sidebars and tables are listed in italics.

1930

- Marc Connelly's *The Green Pastures,* a retelling of biblical stories by southern blacks, opens. The play, based on Roark Bradford's sketches *Ol' Man Adam an' His Chillun* (1928), wins the Pulitzer Prize for drama.

- Charles Fuller, perhaps the most popular evangelist to appear on the scene between Billy Sunday and Billy Graham, begins his long-lived radio program *The Radio Revival Hour,* later called *The Old Fashioned Revival Hour.* In 1937 he moves to the Mutual Broadcasting Network, where he developed one of the largest audiences ever for religious programs.

- W. D. Fard begins preaching in Detroit's African American community that blacks are members of a Muslim "lost-found tribe of Shabazz" and that separation from whites, self-knowledge, and self-help will restore them to their proper place in the world. He founds a Temple of Islam, a University of Islam, and the Fruit of Islam (a self-defense organization) before his mysterious disappearance in 1934. His follower, Elijah Muhammad, continues the development of the Nation of Islam.

2 Oct. Prof. Walter A. Maier presents the first broadcast of *The Lutheran Hour* on the CBS radio network. In 1935 the program is moved to the Mutual Broadcasting Network for an extended career.

31 Dec. Pope Pius XI issues the encyclical *Casti conubii,* in which he prohibits Catholics from using artificial birth control under penalty of grave sin, claiming that it is against the laws of God and nature. The rhythm method, in which couples refrain from intercourse during ovulation, is permitted.

1931

- Edgar J. Goodspeed works with J. M. Powis Smith to complete a translation of the Old and New Testaments into the current American vernacular. This "American Bible" begins a series of such translations in the following decades.

- The American Lutheran Church is organized from a merger of the Lutheran Synod of Buffalo, the Evangelical Lutheran Synod of Iowa, and the Evangelical Lutheran Joint Synod of Ohio.

- Best-selling advertiser Bruce Barton publishes his biblical study *He Upset the World.*

- The General Council of Congregational and Christian Churches is formed by the union of the National Council of Congregational Churches and the General Convention of Christian Churches.

- The International Bible Students Association changes its name to Jehovah's Witnesses. In 1939 the organization is incorporated as the Watch Tower Bible and Tract Society of Pennsylvania.

20 Mar. The use of contraceptives as birth control is defended before the Federal Council of Churches.

1932

- Lloyd C. Douglas publishes his religious best-seller *Forgive Us Our Trespasses.*

- Xavier University in New Orleans is dedicated. Founded in 1915 by the Sisters of the Blessed Sacrament for Indians and Colored People, Xavier is the first Roman Catholic university in the United States created specifically for African American students.

- Rev. John Ralph Voris organizes Save the Children, a charity designed to relieve the plight of poor children in the southern Appalachian mountains.

1 May   The *Catholic Worker*, founded by Dorothy Day, distributes its first issue, charging one cent a copy. Within three years more than 150,000 copies per issue are printed, and the Catholic Worker movement spreads across the nation's cities.

1933

- Herbert W. Armstrong starts the World Wide Church of God after a series of revival meetings in Eugene, Oregon.

- Rev. Norman Vincent Peale, recently named pastor of the Marble Collegiate Church (Reform) in New York City, begins his radio broadcast for the Federal Council of Churches of Christ, *The Art of Living*. The Saturday program becomes one of the most successful religious programs of the decade.

- Bob Jones moves his Bob Jones College to Cleveland, Tennessee. The college, founded in 1926, offers a fundamentalist view of Christianity and education.

- Congress modifies the Volstead Act, which established Prohibition, to allow the sale of beer and wine with a 3.2 percent alcohol content. The Twenty-first Amendment, repealing the Prohibition amendment, is adopted, ending an experiment in social control passed largely with the support of Protestant churches.

- "The Humanist Manifesto I" appears in the May–June issue of *The New Humanist.*

- Theologian Paul Tillich — whose first book, *The Religious Situation* (1925), was translated by Richard Niebuhr in 1932 — arrives in the United States as a refugee from Nazi Germany after being dismissed from the University of Frankfurt. He is hired as a visiting professor at Union Theological Seminary in New York when the faculty at that institution pools 5 percent of their salaries for his pay. His position later becomes permanent.

1934

- Professor Mordecai M. Kaplan publishes his influential book *Judaism as a Civilization,* which insists that Judaism is not only a religion but an entire way of life.

- Rev. George W. Truett of Dallas is elected president of the Baptist World Alliance at its meeting in Berlin.

- The Evangelical and Reform Church is organized from the union of the Reformed Church in the United States and the Evangelical Synod of North America.

- The National Council of Methodist Youth is formed in response to a growing demand by young people for an organization concerned with their interests. Eventually, the organization moves to the Left on the political issues of the day, effectively opposing capitalism.

- U.S. ambassador to Mexico Josephus Daniels praises the rural school program of former president Plutarco Elías Calles. Followers of Calles still control Mexico and continue his anticlerical policies, limiting the power and activities of the Roman Catholic Church. American Catholics, already concerned with the administration's failure to protest or block the Mexican government's activities, are enraged and bitterly protest Ambassador Daniels. The nation's bishops issue an unusual letter of protest, warning that even innocent remarks "give color to the boast of supporters of tyrannical policies, that the influence of our American government is favorable to such policies."

10 Jan. Rev. Billy Sunday begins a two-week revival in New York City, his first series of services in that city since his great meetings in 1917.

10 June Bill Wilson (as Bill W.) and Robert E. Smith hold the first meeting of Alcoholics Anonymous (AA) in a New York hotel room. AA expands through word of mouth and with support from churches and synagogues. Bill W.'s name is revealed after his death in 1971.

1935

- Herbert W. Armstrong of the World Wide Church of God begins his radio ministry, *The World Tomorrow*.

- Rev. Martin Luther King Sr. leads a march of several thousand African Americans from his Ebenezer Baptist Church to Atlanta's city hall to protest the denial of black voting rights.

1936

- Rev. Ralph W. Sockman of Christ Church, Methodist, in New York City begins his twenty-five-year radio program *The National Radio Pulpit*.

- The Union Party, organized by the forces of Sen. Huey Long, Francis Townsend, and Father Charles E. Coughlin, nominates William Lemke for the presidency. Long, the logical nominee, had been assassinated the previous year. His following supposedly is led by Rev. Gerald L. K. Smith, who later establishes a career as an anti-Semite.

- Eugenio Cardinal Pacelli, papal secretary of state, visits the United States, the first man holding that office to do so. In 1939 he is elected Pope, taking the name Pius XII.

1937

- The Central Conference of American Rabbis, meeting in Columbus, Ohio, adopts the Columbus Platform, which reflects a growing interest in reviving traditional Jewish religious practices. The platform supports the Saturday, rather than the Sunday, Sabbath and historic Jewish festivals and holy days and replaces "confirmation" with the bar mitzvah. The platform also encourages the use of Hebrew and cantorial music and the optional use of prayer shawls and yarmulkes. The platform commits Reform Jews to Zionism, saying, "We affirm the obligation of all Jewry to aid in [Palestine's] upbuilding as a Jewish homeland by endeavoring to make it not only a haven of refuge for the oppressed but also a center of Jewish cultural and spiritual thought."

1938

- Louis Finkelstein of the Jewish Theological Seminary of America invites prominent Christians, such as Henry P. Van Dusen and Henry Sloane Coffin of Union Theological Seminary, the prominent Protestant pastor Harry Emerson Fosdick, and John Courtney Murray, S.J., to help him organize the Institute for Religious and Social Studies. This ecumenical group begins a process of dialogue across religious lines that continues throughout the twentieth century.

1939

- Martin Wersing and John C. Cort found the Association of Catholic Trade Unionists, an organization that fights both communism and racketeering in labor unions.

- President Franklin D. Roosevelt moves Thanksgiving from the last Thursday to the fourth Thursday in November to extend the Christmas shopping season.

10 May The Northern and Southern Methodist Churches unite after 105 years of separation; they had split in 1844 over slavery. They are joined in the union by the Methodist Protestant Church, which had become separate in 1830. The new denomination, the Methodist Church, becomes the largest Protestant church in the United States, with more than seven million members.

25 Dec. President Franklin D. Roosevelt appoints Myron C. Taylor, an Episcopalian, as his personal representative to the Vatican, arousing a chorus of opposition from Protestants who oppose direct ties between the United States government and a religious institution.

OVERVIEW

Tests and Trials. For many, the 1930s were a squalid decade, introduced by financial collapse that threatened the foundations of the nation and ended by the threat of involvement in wars in both Europe and Asia. The streets were filled with ragged men, women, and children through most of these years. The American economic and political systems teetered on the verge of collapse, and even when they were righted and the nation moved on, there were many on both the Right and the Left who insisted that the changes that had occurred were a mistake that would lead to disaster. For many, religion fueled their emotions and supported their arguments, as when in 1932 the General Assembly of the Northern Presbyterian Church resolved that "there is nothing more obvious than that the present economic order is now on probation and its continued existence and justification must be found not in the wealth produced or the power gained, but in its contribution to social service and social justice."

Comfort and Conviction. For others, religion offered the solace of continuity and a sense of contact with something transcending the problems of this world, and many rejected mixing politics and religion — except where alcohol was concerned, perhaps. This did not stop some from supporting economic and political tradition, however. In 1938, for instance, the Southern Baptist Convention resolved, "There ought to be no room for radical Socialism and for atheistic Communism in the United States of America." Many premillennialists not only rejected politics but optimistically saw the catastrophes of the decade as signs of the imminent return of Christ that would usher in a thousand years of his reign on earth.

Hard Times. The stock-market crash of 1929 was not a simple financial panic, as had happened in the past. This was not a replay of the hard times the nation had faced nearly forty years earlier. This time the economic downturn failed to bottom out, until it was stimulated by the spending programs of the New Deal, and even the government was unable to provide work for all who needed it. Many people began to assume that massive unemployment was permanent.

Declining Attendance. The economic collapse had a direct effect on religious groups. Regular attendance at religious services dropped, perhaps because the recently poor were embarrassed by their new status. Only a third of the population reported attending services once a week. Also, membership failed to increase in step with the population. The admittedly flawed Religious Census of 1936 showed membership, however counted, increased by only 1,231,000 in the previous decade. The denominations showing the largest increase were the conservative churches, including the Pentecostals.

Declining Contributions. Clearly reflecting the impact of the Depression was the drop in contributions to religious organizations. Total contributions to churches declined 36 percent between 1926 and 1936. Denominations with large rural and poor memberships dropped most seriously. The Southern Baptist Convention, then still located primarily in the largely rural South, saw a 54 percent drop in contributions between 1926 and 1936. The Methodist Episcopal Church, South, in the same region and also with many rural congregations, saw contributions for missionary efforts drop from a high of $1,618,000 in 1927 to a low of $438,000 in 1932.

Declining Construction. More spectacular was a decline in church building during the decade. In the 1920s about 10 percent of the budgets of large denominations went to building. During the 1930s that part of the budget dropped to 2.5 percent, and some of that reflected commitments made in previous years. When the Lynds returned to Muncie, Indiana, to continue their study of Middletown, they saw that the major Protestant congregations were conducting services in large, new structures begun in the prosperous days of the 1920s, but repaying those building costs drove those churches' budgets into the red. One congregation was unable to finish its building and held its services in its new basement.

Religion and Politics. Religion often became involved in the intense politics of the 1930s, and people were divided in their support of President Franklin D. Roosevelt and his New Deal. Jews and Roman Catholics tended to vote Democratic, while Protestants, with the exception of African Americans and southern whites, tended to stay with the Republicans. One 1936 study reported that 70 percent of Protestant ministers opposed the New Deal.

International Issues. Religious communities also took sides on international issues. The Roman Catholic

Church gave solid support to the fascist rebels in the Spanish Civil War, and a few prominent Catholic figures such as Father Charles E. Coughlin, "the Radio Priest," not only fomented anti-Semitism but supported the emerging fascist powers in Europe. Catholic opposition to communism seemed to explain support for any group that called itself anticommunist, even if, as in the case of the Nazis, they were anti-Christian. Many Protestants, less directly involved in choosing sides in the European struggles, repented their support for World War I and moved to a pacifism on the eve of World War II, contributing to the isolationism of the decade. Pacifists were generally liberal in their domestic views and believed war should be avoided at all costs.

Political Concerns. As domestic and foreign politics became pressing, the churches and their leaders struggled for answers. Conservatives such as evangelist Billy Sunday reminded people that religion did not promise its rewards in this world but that its consolations would come in the next. The Roman Catholic Church reassured its parishioners that the church, its offices, and their faith were eternal and assured the faithful of a reward in heaven. Yet Sunday did concern himself with things of this world, as he spoke as vigorously for Prohibition in 1932 as he had in 1917, and the Catholic Church worried about the threat of communism, the property of the church in Mexico and Spain, and the injustices of the economic system. Theological radicals such as Harry F. Ward and his colleague and opponent Reinhold Niebuhr moved directly into politics, insisting that the message of Jesus did apply to this life and demanded that people take responsibility for improving this world through politics.

Protestant Dominance. For most Americans religion was a part of their inheritance, a community culture that not only gave meaning to their lives but also told them who they were. Most white Protestants continued to assume that they were the most authentic Americans and continued to exercise their cultural dominance. Leaders worried both about their churches' tendencies toward extensive accommodation with the world and about an equally irrelevant rejection of the world and its concerns. Another issue that worried Protestants was the growing strength of the Catholic community. The 1928 election of the Republican candidate, Herbert Hoover, over Alfred E. Smith, the first Roman Catholic to run for the presidency, reassured Protestants that they still controlled the nation, but the bitterness of the election tainted relations between the two largest Christian communities, and the growing population of Catholics suggested that they would be even more powerful in the future. The repeal of Prohibition was evidence of the need for old-line Protestantism to fight to retain its cultural authority.

Mainline Protestantism. During the 1930s mainline Protestants still seemed to be the voice of authentic Protestantism. The six leading Protestant denominations — Baptist, Methodist, Lutheran, Presbyterian, Episcopa-lian, and Christian Church (Disciples of Christ) — enrolled the vast majority of the people within Protestantism. Perhaps the event that best symbolized this dominance came in 1939 when the three main branches of Methodism finally merged, after decades of discussion, to create the largest and most evenly distributed Protestant denomination in terms of both geography and class.

Challenges to the Mainline Churches. This dominance, however, obscured significant changes taking place within the Protestant community. While the mainline churches dominated the culture, the radio airwaves reflected the fact that the fastest-growing Protestant groups were the small, conservative denominations then labeled as fundamentalist and the even-less-observed groups labeled as Pentecostal.

Fundamentalism. The fundamentalists sullenly withdrew into political quiescence with the repeal of Prohibition in 1933. Most were premillennialist in their theology, believing that the world would continue to deteriorate until Christ's return. The interpretation of such signs led evangelist Charles Fuller to take advantage of the weakness of the Mutual Broadcasting Network and buy time to broadcast his *Old Fashioned Revival Hour* in 1937, in contrast to the earlier practice of stations giving religious broadcasters free airtime. His repetition of the tenets and experiences of traditional religion would make him one of the most popular evangelists of the century.

Pentecostals. Another Protestant contingent, then dismissed by the mainline leaders as Holy Rollers, were those groups, black and white, swept up in the Pentecostal revival that began at the turn of the century. In the 1930s the Pentecostals were still on the margins socially, culturally, and religiously. But like the Joad family in John Steinbeck's novel *The Grapes of Wrath* (1939), they were moving out of their southern center into the rest of the nation and growing rapidly everywhere. Within a few decades their members would rise economically and socially, and in time they would change the face of American Christianity.

African American Believers. A third group of Protestants, which also was ignored by the general religious community, were African Americans. Here too Baptist and Methodist groups — such as the National Baptist Convention of America; the National Baptist Convention of the United States; the African Methodist Episcopal Church; the African Methodist Episcopal Church, Zion; and the Colored Methodist Episcopal Church — predominated. General newspapers reported on exotic African American religious figures such as Father Devine and Daddy Grace, but the African American community was deeply embedded in Christianity, which offered them solace in this world and hope for the next.

Roman Catholicism. The Catholic community, emerging from its status as an immigrant church, continued to feel the prejudice it encountered in the 1928 election and eagerly counted Catholic appointments to the

Roosevelt administration as evidence of their arrival into the center of American life. In spite of Catholic defensiveness, they were moving to the center of the culture, as would be recognized after World War II. Evidence of this move was available in the 1930s. In 1936 the papal secretary of state, Eugenio Pacelli, later Pope Pius XII, toured the United States, reflecting the Vatican's increased awareness of the American church's position in world Catholicism as well as the importance of the United States in world affairs. At the end of the decade President Roosevelt appointed Myron C. Taylor, an Episcopal layman, as his personal envoy to the Vatican. This appointment aroused bitter opposition in Protestant circles, but since Taylor served as a personal envoy and at his own expense the protests were in vain. The question of a regular ambassador would wait another decade.

Catholics in the Movies. Further evidence of Catholic acceptance in the larger culture was seen in the representation of Catholics, especially religious Catholics, in Hollywood. The positive treatment of priests and nuns in the movies of the 1930s partly reflected the industry's awareness of Catholic power in the Legion of Decency, whose members pledged they would not attend movies with unacceptable ratings. At the end of the decade Hollywood released a series of movies, such as *You Only Live Once* (1937), *Boys Town* (1938), and *Angels with Dirty Faces* (1938), in which priests were shown positively to a nation whose population was largely non-Catholic. While the Catholic community still seemed to view the world defensively, its size, wealth, and leadership made it one of the major religious forces in the decade.

The Jewish Community. The third major religious community in the interwar period was the Jews. They too were sharply divided. One of the most obvious divisions was among the Reform, Conservative, and Orthodox communities, but those divisions were also split along other lines, such as between the conservative, assimilated German Jews who tended to blend into the larger culture and the rising, culturally distinct east European Jews. Another fissure that split the Jewish community was Zionism. How much support should American Jews give to aiding their coreligionists' settlement in Palestine, the old land of Israel? With its commitment to Zionism, the Columbus Platform that the Reform Jews adopted in 1937 marked a significant change of attitude in an important sector of the American Jewish community.

Response to European Persecution. Finally, the Jewish community was split on how to respond to the persecution of their fellow Jews, first in Germany and then in the rest of eastern Europe. Highly visible Jewish leaders such as Rabbi Stephen S. Wise sought to combine two concerns by seeking security for Jewish refugees in Palestine or in the United States. Others, more cautious and concerned with rising anti-Semitism in the United States, tried to avoid such dramatic positions that would alienate significant groups of Christians. The divisions in the community hindered massive fund-raising and left the Jewish community without a unified response. Even then, few people of any faith could imagine the coming efforts of the Nazis to destroy the Jewish people as a whole.

The End of the Decade. Desperate as the decade seemed when it opened, it closed on a more dismal note with a war that would dwarf World War I in cost of men and money and shatter the illusion of humanity as essentially good. The war would raise even-more-troubling questions about the role of God in allowing evil to flourish on such a scale.

TOPICS IN THE NEWS

AMERICAN RELIGIOUS COMMUNITIES AND NAZI GERMANY

The German Church under Attack. When Adolf Hitler came to power in Germany in January 1933, most Americans were more concerned about the collapsing domestic economy than what he might do with or to the German people because of their ethnic backgrounds or religious views. But the vigorously antireligious Nazi movement made it clear that German religious communities would face challenges to their beliefs and actions. In 1933 Paul Tillich, already recognized as one of the most distinguished German theologians, was dismissed from his position at the University of Frankfurt. He was invited to teach at Union Theological Seminary in New York, eventually becoming an American citizen and continuing his contributions to theology. Dietrich Bonhoeffer, another distinguished German theologian, had studied at the Union Theological Seminary in 1930–1931. His friends in the United States also invited him to accept a visiting professorship in 1939, and he traveled to New York intending to remain. But after two weeks he decided to return to Germany to work with and guide his fellow Germans in the anti-Nazi German Confessing Church. He was imprisoned and killed before the war was over. Catholics also found the antireligious actions of the Hitler government offensive but found some comfort in its anticommunism. The Left developed a deep suspicion of the relations between the Vatican and the fascist governments of Europe, including Nazi Germany.

The Response to Anti-Semitism. The Nazi government's arrest, imprisonment, and harassment of German Jews was of great concern to the religious. Nazi anti-Semitism attracted the attention not only of Jews but of Protestants and Catholics. Initially, Christians primarily expressed concern for German Christians who happened to have some sort of Jewish ancestry, but they gradually extended their concerns to all German Jews.

Speaking Out against the Nazis. In March 1933 Rabbi Stephen S. Wise of the Free Synagogue in New York, founder of the Zionist American Jewish Congress, organized a meeting in Madison Square Garden to protest the new German government's persecution of Jews.

A RESPONSE TO THE OUTBREAK OF WORLD WAR II

When World War II broke out in Europe in 1939, most Americans believed in staying out of the conflict, not knowing that the United States would be pulled into it two years later. Many in religious communities especially clung to the pacifism fostered after the end of World War I. For instance, the Rev. Dr. George A. Buttrick, president of the Federal Council of Churches, said in 1939, "We [Americans] must be neutral from high and sacrificial motives — not for physical safety, not in an attempt to maintain an impossible isolation from world problems, assuredly not for commercial gain, but rather because we know war is futile and because we are eager through reconciliation to build a kindlier world." Ironically, American involvement in the war in the early 1940s would prove the decisive factor in its end.

Source: "Peace and Neutrality Sought by American Churches," *Christian Century*, 56 (20 September 1939): 1124.

An estimated fifty thousand people, more than the arena could hold, showed up to hear former New York governor Alfred E. Smith, current New York senator Robert Wagner, Bishop William Manning of the Episcopal Church, and Methodist bishop Francis McConnell join Rabbi Wise in condemning Nazi atrocities.

Different Responses. Many leading Jews, however, opposed the rally. They feared attracting attention to themselves, desiring to avoid the rising anti-Semitism in the United States. These Jews, many of whom had emigrated from Germany in the nineteenth century and had now assimilated to the United States, sought to blend into the larger community and block old charges that they were more concerned with their coreligionists in Germany than with their fellow Americans. For some time Jews in the United States as well as in Germany and other central European nations saw the outrages of the decade as simply another example of their centuries-old mistreatment, which could be endured and even overcome. Few had any notion that the long-range Nazi goal was the eradication of the Jewish people. At the time the concept of genocide was incomprehensible. Throughout the decade the American Jewish community was divided and unclear on how to respond to the worsening situation in Europe.

No United Front. While religious figures and publications noted the intensifying persecution of German Jews, there seemed no American solutions for their plight. In the isolationist, antiwar climate of the decade, few Americans wanted to involve themselves in the internal affairs of Germany, even after the promulgation in 1935 of the Nuremberg Laws that excluded Jews from German citizenship and protection under the law. While some Christians, such as Dorothy Day's Catholic Workers, joined Jews and leftists in protests outside German facilities and boycotted German products, they also did not know of effective ways of alleviating the worsening plight of German Jews.

Inaction. The issue was not simply a lack of knowledge about German barbarism. The liberal Protestant journal *The Christian Century* called attention to the plight of German Jews by publishing the report of James McDonald, the League of Nations High Commissioner for Refugees from Germany, when he resigned in frustration in 1935 and spelled out his condemnation of Nazi actions. But even those who saw the moral evil of the antireligious and racist policies of the Hitler government could think of no effective way to change those policies. Dreadful as the regime was, no one knew how to interfere with Germany's internal affairs short of war, which was unacceptable to many.

Attempts at Aid. If nothing could be done in Germany, what could be done for those who sought to flee or were forced from that country? In spite of the example of Protestants such as Tillich and Bonhoeffer, refugees generally meant Jews. There were some attempts, led by Wise and other prominent Jewish leaders, to raise funds to aid Jewish refugees. Most of this money was administered by the Joint Distribution Committee, but until the end of the decade the Joint, as it was called, focused on helping the poverty-stricken Jews of Poland and eastern Europe rather than the more prosperous Jews of Germany.

Seeking Refuge. The major problem concerning the refugees was finding them a haven. Some Jews sought to merge Zionist interests with their plight by trying to gain a refuge for them in Palestine, but the British government first tried to limit immigration and then blocked access to the territory to avoid enraging its Arab population. Others, including some Christians, tried to ease the admission of Jewish refugees to the United States by encouraging them to fill the German immigration quota. (The Immigration Act of 1924 not only limited the number of immigrants admitted to the United States each year but also restricted their country of origin to keep out "undesirables," emigrants from southern and eastern Europe). The German quota was only filled for the first time during the decade in 1938.

Resistance to Refugees. Most Americans, even those sympathetic to the people fleeing Germany, saw the plight of German-Jewish refugees as a less important problem than domestic unemployment and wanted no refugees looking for the few jobs that existed. Increased immigration was opposed by labor unions and others who called attention to the estimated eleven million unemployed as late as 1938. This attitude was callously exploited by nativists and anti-Semites, who used any excuse to keep Jews, even children, from sanctuary in America. Among the most outspoken and effective of these were Father Charles E. Coughlin and his Christian Front; Rev. Gerald B. Winrod's Defenders of the Christian Faith, a fundamentalist Protestant group; and Gerald L. K. Smith, who organized a variety of anti-Semitic groups at the end of the decade.

The Evian Conference. The refugee problem became greater and more daunting with the German annexation of Austria in 1938, which brought even more Jews into the Nazi maelstrom. Other nations in central Europe also began to take actions against their Jewish populations. In response to the growing desperation of the situation, President Franklin D. Roosevelt helped organize a conference on refugees to meet at Evian, France, in the fall of that year. The rising tide of intolerance around the world, not just in Europe and the United States, caused the conference to center on the general question of refugees, rather than only the plight of the Jews. The Evian Conference was futile. No nation was willing to accept the hundreds of thousands of people who were being forced from their homes, and diplomats spent their time charging each other's country with failing to take responsibility for the problem.

Kristallnacht. In November 1938, in response to the assassination in Paris of a German diplomat by a Jewish youth desperate over the plight of his refugee parents, the Nazi regime in Germany instituted a nationwide pogrom, *Kristallnacht,* the Night of Broken Glass. Synagogues were burned, and Jewish cemeteries were desecrated. Jewish businesses were looted and destroyed, and Jews were attacked in an orgy of violence. American Jews were joined in their horror and outrage by other religious leaders and groups. The Federal Council of Churches of Christ, the large interdenominational Protestant organization, was prominent in its condemnation of German actions, pointing out that while the pogrom was clearly organized by the government, the German people had enthusiastically participated as well. The Episcopal journal *The Churchman* engaged in a series of reports and editorials on the situation in Germany. *The Christian Century,* the leading liberal Protestant publication, reported on Germany also, but few were as critical as Dorothy Day's *Catholic Worker.*

Not to Decide . . . Condemning Germany was one thing; deciding what to do was another. Inaction was an action itself, as seen in the ill-fated voyage of the S.S. *Saint Louis,* which sailed for Havana in 1939 with more than nine hundred Jews fleeing Europe among its passengers. They hoped the tourist visas to Cuba they had secured would give them enough time in that country to find a haven in the United States or some other country in the Western Hemisphere. The Cuban government, however, refused to honor the visas, and the ship was forced to leave harbor. It delayed off the coast of Florida for several days, hoping some sort of arrangement could be made with the American government. When no permission to enter the United States was granted, the *Saint Louis* sailed back to Europe. While various western European countries finally agreed to accept the refugees, only those admitted to Britain escaped the camps of the Holocaust.

Political Responses. Religious leaders often joined the political opponents of Nazism in condemning anti-Semitism. Left-wing groups, particularly front organizations of the Communist Party, were able to draw upon a sense of religious anger as the party opposed Nazism. The American League for Peace and Freedom, the reorganized League Against War and Fascism, offered a place for religious leaders such as Harry F. Ward of Union Theological Seminary. At its peak, just before the Soviet-German nonaggression pact in 1939, the American League for Peace and Freedom claimed an inflated membership of six million, many of them affiliated with churches and religious groups. When war erupted in September that year, the league collapsed.

The Problem of War. World War II created an enormous problem for religious people. The clear Nazi aggression of the past seven years had culminated in outright war, and most religious people condemned the aggressor. Few, with the exception of Coughlin, offered support for the Axis powers, but just as few were eager for the United States to enter the war. People could now only wait, watch, and pray.

Sources:

Yehuda Bauer, *American Jewry and the Holocaust: The American Joint Distribution Committee, 1939–1945* (Detroit: Wayne State University Press, 1981);

Robert W. Ross, *So It Was True: The American Protestant Press and the Nazi Persecution of the Jews* (Minneapolis: University of Minnesota Press, 1980);

"Tragedy Afloat: Ships Roam American Waters Seeking Jewish Refugee Haven," *Newsweek,* 13 (12 June 1939): 21–22;

Stephen S. Wise, *As I See It* (New York: Jewish Opinion Publishing, 1944).

CHURCH UNIONS AND REUNIONS

A Decade of Mergers. The 1930s saw a series of unions among Protestant groups, usually bringing together people of different ethnic backgrounds who shared a religious tradition. In 1931 members of the Lutheran Synod of Buffalo joined the Evangelical Lutheran Synod

---

A RELIGIOUS RESPONSE TO THE DEPRESSION

At a 1932 meeting the New York East Conference of the Methodist Episcopal Church unanimously adopted a report that held that toleration of poverty is sinful and that "all the evils of our present form of capitalism can be traced back to the motive of acquisitiveness." The report further contended that the "principal means of production and distribution which are now privately owned, controlled and operated, mainly for the benefit of a relatively small portion of our population, must be brought under some form of social ownership and management. Private ownership, with its emphasis upon private profits, has failed to keep industry functioning, and we have the sad spectacle of thousands of our magnificent factories and millions of our workers standing idle."

Source: "Eastern Methodists Go Socialist," *Christian Century,* 49 (13 April 1932): 467.

---

of Iowa and the Evangelical Lutheran Joint Synod of Ohio to form the American Lutheran Church; in 1934 two groups from the Calvinist tradition joined to create the Evangelical and Reform Church out of the Reformed Church in the United States and the Evangelical Synod of North America; and in 1931 two theologically liberal and congregationally organized denominations, the National Council of Congregational Churches and the General Convention of Christian Churches, joined to form the General Council of Congregational and Christian Churches.

The Methodists Merge. The most impressive and important merger of the decade took place in 1939, when three branches of American Methodism finally reunited after more than a century of separation. In 1830 the Methodist Episcopal Church split over questions of organization, and a small splinter group, the Methodist Protestant Church, emerged. In 1844 a more serious split occurred, this time over slavery, which resulted in the creation of the Methodist Episcopal Church, South. The sectional division proved the most bitter and intensified during and after the Civil War, when the two separate churches fought over the same territories and properties. The sectional division became permanent and took on new intensity as Southern Methodists saw their northern brothers and sisters fall prey to the forces of modernism. As recently as 1922 the Southern Methodists had refused to join their northern counterparts, largely because of regional chauvinism but also from a fear of liberalism in the northern church.

Merger at a Price. But the ecumenical force that proved so powerful in the middle of the century was too strong to be denied. The various issues that separated Methodists came to be seen as less important than the issues that united them. The Depression challenged the fund-raising and church-building of both groups; unification promised to lessen the economic strain. When the final issue, the place of the three hundred thousand black Methodists in the reunited church, was resolved, union was finally possible. The compromise, as often happened in American life, came at the expense of African Americans. The reunited church was divided into five jurisdictional conferences based on geography. A sixth, the General Conference, included black congregations wherever they might be. In spite of some protests by black Methodists, the compromise satisfied the custom of segregation and resolved racist concerns in all parts of the nation. In July 1939, at a Uniting Conference in Kansas City, the Methodist Church was formed — the largest Protestant denomination at the time and the one that covered the nation most thoroughly in geography, class, culture, and race. The new denomination had around seven million members.

Sources:

Jerald C. Brauer, *Protestantism in America: A Narrative History* (Philadelphia: Westminster, 1953);

Roger Finke and Rodney Strunk, *The Churching of America, 1779–1990: Winners and Losers in Our Religious Economy* (New Brunswick, N.J.: Rutgers University Press, 1992);

Martin E. Marty, *Pilgrims in Their Own Land: Five Hundred Years of Religion in America* (Boston: Little, Brown, 1984).

"THE HUMANIST MANIFESTO"

Publication. The May–June 1934 issue of the *New Humanist* contained what was called "The Humanist Manifesto," a statement that sought to offer an alternative for people unwilling to rely on religion for an explanation of life and its meanings. The signers of the manifesto included distinguished figures such as Harry Elmer Barnes, Robert Morss Lovett, Charles Francis Potter, Llewellyn Jones, and, most important, philosopher John Dewey.

Science over Supernaturalism. "The Humanist Manifesto" sought to focus attention on the evidence science gave about nature and life in order to encourage people to reject supernaturalism. It included such points as the need to recognize that the universe was "self-existing," not created, and that humanity was a part of nature and had evolved as part of a continuing process. The manifesto rejected the old question of the duality of mind (or soul) and body by incorporating the mind and its functions as a part of the body. Religion, it insisted, was a product of human development and changed according to historical changes. In its fifth point the manifesto insisted that "the nature of the universe depicted by modern science makes unacceptable any supernatural or cosmic guarantees of human values. . . . Religion must formulate its hopes and plans in light of the scientific spirit and method." Having eliminated God and soul, the manifesto continued by seeking to eliminate the perception that life had eternal meaning by insisting that the religious person

John Dewey in his early seventies

should consider "the complete realization of human personality to be the end of man's life and [seek] its development in the here and now." The statement concluded by opposing the current system of capitalism.

Response. "The Humanist Manifesto" attracted little attention at the time, although it gave new material for conservatives and reactionaries who disliked Dewey and his ideas. In the charged political climate of the 1930s it was easy for them to link his acknowledged secularism and socialist views with his efforts to reform education and to see "progressive education," as it was called, as advancing liberal, if not socialist or even communist, ideas. Criticism of the ideas espoused in "The Humanist Manifesto" has continued to resurface on a regular basis — most recently in the 1980s, when religious conservatives warned of the dangers in schools and in society of secular humanism.

Source:

Paul Kurtz, ed., *Humanist Manifestos I and II* (Buffalo: Prometheus, 1973).

THE MOVIES AND THE CHURCHES

Guardians of Morality. From the days of the early nickelodeon, conservatives and protectors of morals had been concerned about motion pictures and their impact on their viewers, particularly the young. In the first decade of the twentieth century, Chicago, New York, and later other cities established local censorship boards to review films to ensure that their content did not corrupt the morals of the young. A variety of censoring boards with a variety of views came into being, but none was able to impose a national standard on the movie industry.

The Hays Office. This situation threatened to change when a series of scandals, including rape, murder, drug use, and general sexual misconduct, swept through Hollywood in the early 1920s. In the face of demands for some sort of government regulation, in 1922 the industry created the Motion Picture Producers and Distributors of America (MPPDA), later the Motion Picture Association of America (MPAA), and hired Postmaster General Will Hays to serve as its head in an effort to block attempts to establish a national censorship agency. It was assumed that this Presbyterian elder and member of the Warren Harding administration was familiar enough with sin to be able to know it when he saw it on the screen. The Hays Office, as it was called, established and published a code for the industry in an attempt to avoid offending the general public and so managed to blunt the demand for government censorship.

Back to Sex and Violence. But by the 1930s concern over the impact of films on morals returned, as Hollywood, feeling the pinch of the Depression and responding to the new potential of talking films, produced a series of films that treated violent and sexual themes with an unusual directness. There were gangster films with criminal protagonists reveling in excess in the first reels and receiving their just desserts only at the end. Also, movies such as *The Story of Temple Drake* (1933), based on William Faulkner's novel *Sanctuary* (1931), dealt with rape and prostitution in a sensational manner. Mae West, who had long recognized the effectiveness of notoriety in advancing her stage career, became a symbol of this development when she moved to Hollywood and made a series of comedies filled with double entendres and frankly sexual situations. Rising concern about the content and effect of movies was widened when in 1933 Henry James Forman published *Our Movie Made Children,* based on a twelve-volume study of movies and their audiences sponsored by the Payne Fund. Forman's study indicted movies for weakening traditional moral standards and thus contributing to the problem of unruly youths of the decade. Something, he said, should be done.

The Breen Office. While Protestant groups, churches, and publications protested declining moral standards, they were too fragmented to mount an effective attack on what they perceived as Hollywood's moral vacuum. The Roman Catholic Church, however, devised means of raising the moral standards of the movie industry, partly through the influence of Joseph I. Breen, an assistant to Hays, who became head of the MPPDA's Production Code Administration in 1934. Breen was finally able to impose the regulations agreed upon in the Production

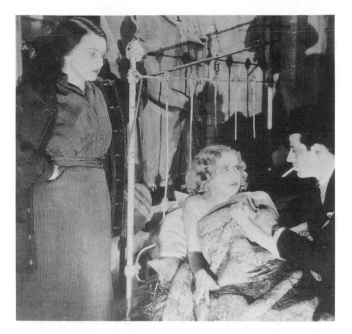

Florence Eldridge, Miriam Hopkins, and Jack La Rue in *The Story of Temple Drake* (1933), adapted from William Faulkner's novel *Sanctuary*

Code, which had been adopted but generally ignored four years earlier. Now the Breen Office, as it was called, saw to it that the regulations were enforced.

The Code. The Production Code demanded cautious treatment of a variety of topics, including crime, sex, vulgarity, obscenity, profanity, dances, and repellent subjects such as brutality, apparent cruelty to children or animals, and the sale of women. Evil was always to be presented in a negative light and good in a positive light. Crime and sin were always to come to a bad end before the close. The code banned outright the depiction of white slavery, the use of drugs or the drug traffic, sexual "perversion," sexual relations between blacks and whites, and nudity. Religion and its ministers were always to be shown in a positive light.

The Legion of Decency. The Breen Office was able to impose its standards in large part because of the power of a new organization, the Legion of Decency, created in 1934 by the American Catholic bishops. Members of the legion, mostly Catholic, pledged "to remain away from all motion pictures, except those which do not offend decency and Christian morality." Through this threatened boycott the legion was able to deny to a significant section of the moviegoing public those films it deemed objectionable. The legion worked out a four-part category system for films as a guide for its estimated six million members. A-I was "Morally Unobjectionable for General Patronage"; A-II was "Morally Unobjectionable for Adults"; B films were "Morally Objectionable in Part for All"; and C movies were "Disapproved" for all members of the legion. Children who belonged to the legion could attend A-II movies if their parents or guardians permitted. Joining the Legion of Decency became a regular part of Catholic behavior for nearly thirty years, offering an effective weapon to the power of the Breen Office in Hollywood.

Effects of Breen and the Legion. With the Breen Office reviewing content in Hollywood and the Legion of Decency certifying the morality of films actually brought into distribution, cries for censorship quickly died. The film industry monitored itself and adhered with little expressed grumbling to the Production Code standards. Consequently, the Legion of Decency found little to condemn. From February 1936 to November 1937, for instance, it reviewed 1,271 titles. Of these, 1,160 were rated A-I or A-II, and only thirteen were rated C — all of them European or independent productions. The restrictions were so effective that in 1939 there was general concern whether Rhett Butler could end his marriage with Scarlett O'Hara in *Gone with the Wind* with the widely known dialogue from Margaret Mitchell's 1936 novel. In response to her question about what would become of her if he left, Butler responds, "Frankly . . . I don't give a damn." To the relief of many and the consternation of a few, the Breen Office permitted Clark Gable as Butler to say the startling phrase. Some things were too sacred for meddling.

Sources:
Andrew Bergman, *We're in the Money: Depression America and Its Films* (New York: New York University Press, 1971);

James M. Skinner, *The Cross and the Cinema: The Legion of Decency and the National Catholic Office for Motion Pictures, 1933–1970* (Westport, Conn.: Praeger, 1993).

PACIFISM

"Never Again." In the early years after the Great War of 1914–1918, a sense of revulsion swept over the Western world as the cost of that war in men and money was reckoned. Americans in particular felt they had been pulled into a conflict of little direct importance and of little positive consequence. A strong mood of "never again, never again war" developed. War itself was the enemy, since it resolved little and destroyed much. This antiwar mood intensified in the first half of the decade, when domestic issues dominated the American consciousness and when conflicts raged in Asia, Africa, and Europe in the second. The antiwar mood in the United States was not just an opposition to wars that did not affect American interests but to war itself. Pacifism became a deeply held conviction, particularly in religious circles.

Catholic Attitudes toward War. The Roman Catholic Church was lightly affected by this pacifist mood. The church had long ago worked out a concept of just wars, wars that in Catholic theology did not violate Christian ethics, that limited the impact of pacifism within its ranks. In addition, the immigrant backgrounds of many in the American Catholic community, with their ties to family members and friends in their countries of origin, gave the American church an interest in accepting the wars of the 1930s. However, Dorothy Day, who did not abandon her left-wing pacifism when she converted to Catholicism, spoke vigorously and openly against war during the decade. Her Catholic Worker movement insisted that Christians, especially Catholics, live their religious values, and one of the greatest of these was to oppose killing. For her there was no just war, only war.

Protestant Pacifism. Pacifism ran most deeply in the Protestant community, although even there it was shallower than it sometimes appeared. Several antiwar activists came from the Protestant clergy. The clergy, regretting the excessive enthusiasm with which they supported the American effort in World War I, seemed convinced they would not allow themselves to be used in the same way again. Many of these ministers, particularly the younger ones, admired and respected the example of Norman Thomas, who as a Presbyterian minister refused to support World War I and moved from that antiwar position into the Socialist Party as the organization that would most effectively prevent wars in the future.

The Fellowship of Reconciliation and The World Tomorrow. Thomas was one of the founders and the first editor of the pacifist magazine *The World Tomorrow,* the voice of the antiwar Fellowship of Reconciliation (FOR). In the 1930s the journal was edited by Kirby Page, a minister in the Christian Church (Disciples of Christ). While FOR had a modest membership on the left wing of Protestantism and *The World Tomorrow* had a modest circulation, their existence reflected an important view in the early part of the 1930s. In 1934 *The World Tomorrow* conducted a mail poll of thirteen thousand Protestant clerics. Of the respondents 85 percent said they would not support the United States if another war were declared.

Conflict. FOR and *The World Tomorrow* both suffered as men and women wrestled with the issue of violence for political aims. Could and should force be used to make a better world? Theologian Reinhold Niebuhr answered yes in his influential book *Moral Man and Immoral Society* (1932), in which he suggested a major weakness of liberalism was its inability to understand the nature of power and the unwillingness of those who have it to give it up voluntarily. Force could be used to bring justice to an unjust world. Protestants in groups such as FOR and the Socialist Party split over the question of force in 1934 and over the issue of whether violence could be used to advance the cause of the working class. When the Socialist Party adopted a platform that supported force in a revolutionary situation, social democrats charged that this position was just communism in another guise and left the party. FOR split effectively over the same issue the same year, and both organizations drifted into impotence. *The World Tomorrow* ceased publication with the reorganization of FOR when J. B. Matthews, later a paid witness before anticommunist congressional committees, tried to urge FOR to accept revolutionary violence by workers.

Communism. While some Protestants worked with pacifist and socialist antiwar organizations, others drifted into the Communist Party as a way of expressing their revulsion with war. The party was particularly effective in setting up organizations that attracted people who supported issues currently advanced by the party. After 1935 many of these were "front" groups — organizations often financially supported by the Communist Party but headed by liberals, socialists, or those sympathetic to Communist causes. One of the largest was the League Against War and Fascism, headed by Harry F. Ward, a prominent Methodist minister and professor at Union Theological Seminary. This antiwar group gave Ward an opportunity to advance his beliefs in the ethics of Jesus and join with large groups of people in the United States and abroad who would work to block the coming of another war. The league became the largest front for the Communist Party. The league was able to expand its influence and take along with it fellow travelers such as Ward when it was reorganized to support collective security — that is, to support armed conflict against the aggressive fascist powers — as the League for Peace and Freedom in 1938. Real pacifists left, but they were replaced by others who had no objection to working with Communists against the increasing threat of Germany, Italy, and Japan.

Other Approaches to Pacifism. Realists such as Niebuhr refused to follow the various leads of the Communist Party, but others like him insisted that a great weakness of modernist Protestants was their refusal to understand power, at first in the class struggle and then, as the decade wore on, in the aggression that characterized the last half of the decade. Niebuhr's influence was great, but many prominent Protestants remained committed to the ideals of pacifism. Some worked with the concepts of passive resistance being developed by Mohandas K. Gandhi, and others committed themselves to an attempt to understand the pacifist message of Jesus. Leaders such as Harry Emerson Fosdick, John Haynes Holmes, and Bishop Francis McConnell continued to insist, even after war erupted in China and Europe, that if Christianity were to have real meaning and a real connection with Jesus' words, then his followers must be willing to turn the other cheek when attacked and strive to find alternatives to violence before being attacked. They believed reason and moral suasion could make a difference in human affairs.

Sources:
Devere Allen, *The Fight for Peace* (New York: Macmillan, 1930);

Manfred Jonas, *Isolationism in America, 1935–1941* (Ithaca, N.Y.: Cornell University Press, 1966);

John K. Nelson, *Peace Prophets: American Pacifist Thought, 1919–1945* (Chapel Hill: University of North Carolina Press, 1967).

PROHIBITION

Prohibition and the Churches. Even as the Depression that followed the stock-market crash of 1929 deep-

ON AN AMENDMENT TO REPEAL PROHIBITION

In a 1933 article called "This *Is* Armageddon," the liberal *Christian Century* spoke out against the widespread call to repeal Prohibition. "It is perfectly true," the article said, "that no law can be enforced or ought to be enforced in a democracy unless it is supported by the sober and deliberate judgement of a majority of the people. Especially this is true of a law that touches so intimately the habits and behavior, the civil rights and moral welfare of all the people. But it does not follow that a majority vote may not sometimes be got for a law the people do not really want." It continued, "It has been claimed that the enactment of prohibition was the results of high pressure political salesmanship which made people vote for what they did not really want. . . . The question of the hour is whether high pressure political salesmanship is going to be the chief force in determining the ratification of the repealing amendment. For years the press of almost the whole country has been shipping the public into a furor on the subject of the evils of prohibition. It was easier to do this because the evils of the old regime are hidden by the dust of years. Now the star salesmen of repeal make great promises of revived private industry and increased public revenue. Such alluring but deceptive promises confuse the main issue." The article concluded with the claim that "we shall fight to the limit of our power" against repeal, but such fervor was not enough to stop the end of Prohibition.

Source: "This *Is* Armageddon," *Christian Century*, 50 (1 March 1933): 279–281.

ened to unprecedented lows, Americans were preoccupied with the Eighteenth Amendment to the Constitution, which prohibited the manufacture, sale, and transportation of alcoholic beverages. That amendment, which had been ratified in 1919, was the result of long, dedicated effort by reformers, many of them active in Protestant evangelical groups. The Women's Christian Temperance Union reflected the links between the effort to dry up America and the Protestant churches. The Anti-Saloon League, with strong ties to the Methodist Church, called itself the Protestant church in action.

Taking Sides. National Prohibition was controversial from the beginning, with soldiers returning from World War I protesting that they had been kept from voting on the issue by failure of the states to provide adequate machinery for absentee voting. Within a short period the "wets," critics of the amendment and the Volstead Act, its enabling legislation, raised challenges about this con-

The White Ribbon Special, a chartered train from Chicago to Houston, site of the 1930 WCTU National Convention

stitutional effort to legislate morality and behavior. The "dry" forces found dubious allies, including corrupt politicians and bootleggers who profited from the traffic in homemade and imported liquor. Perhaps a more shady ally was the revived Ku Klux Klan, which supported small-town Protestant values in the face of changes brought about by industrialization, urbanization, and modernization. In addition to fighting bootleggers and rumrunners, however, the Klan also targeted blacks, Jews, and Roman Catholics and served as a leading nativist force in the nation during the first half of the 1920s.

Prohibition and Politics. Prohibition quickly moved back into politics. While the Republican Party, with its large Protestant support, remained in the dry camp, the Democratic Party, with its combination of dry Protestant southerners and wet urban Roman Catholics, split sharply over the issue. In 1924 the Democrats met in New York City, a center of illicit liquor, and split over the question of the Ku Klux Klan; they suffered a humiliating defeat in that year's presidential election.

A Divisive Issue. In 1928 the question of Prohibition was even more divisive, and the wet forces intensified their organizational efforts. Herbert Hoover, the Republican nominee, called Prohibition "an experiment noble in purpose" and promised a review of the government's support for it. The Democrats nominated a wet, Alfred E. Smith, the Roman Catholic governor of New York. The Republicans, favored by a decade of peace and prosperity, seemed invincible that year, but alcohol and religion both became election issues with the Smith nomination. The Anti-Saloon League, now dominated by Bishop James A. Cannon Jr., head of the Temperance and Social Service Commission of the Methodist Episcopal Church, South, helped split the upper South from the Democratic lower South for the first time in the twentieth century. The link between liquor and the Roman Catholic Church was too strong for traditional white southern Protestants to maintain their old loyalty to the party of their fathers. The upper south voted for Prohibition and against Roman Catholicism in the 1928 election.

Enforcing Prohibition. The question of Prohibition would not go away. In 1929 President Herbert Hoover appointed a commission to review the enforcement and effectiveness of prohibition. The Wickersham Commission split sharply over the effectiveness of Prohibition but nevertheless gave general support for the idea, and President Hoover provided more money for enforcing the Volstead Act. Few proponents or opponents doubted that Prohibition was here to stay.

Bishop James A. Cannon, his second wife, Helen, and codefendant Mrs. Ada L. Burroughs leaving court after their acquittal on charges of failing to account for funds donated to his Anti-Saloon League, 27 April 1934

Challenges to Prohibition. The wet forces were strengthened by the creation in 1929 of the Women's Organization for Prohibition Reform, which challenged the assumption that all women supported prohibition. Perhaps equally telling was the defection from absolute Prohibition by drys such as the Rev. Dr. Clarence True Wilson of the Northern Methodist Church, who announced that he would not oppose light wines and beer as a way to control bootlegging as long as saloons were banned. In 1932 Rev. Charles Stezle of the Presbyterian Church, a longtime dry proponent, came out for repeal, arguing that Prohibition did not work and was worse than the alternative.

Problems with Prohibition. Prohibition collapsed because of the economic issues of the Depression of the 1930s, but other factors played a part. In the early years of the decade Bishop Cannon became embroiled in a series of scandals, ranging from the revelation that he had been gambling on the stock market to his sudden marriage to his secretary shortly after his wife's death to charges that he had misspent campaign money in the election of 1928. While he escaped conviction for his activities, he helped discredit both Prohibition and evangelical Protestantism

in the eyes of many. When Billy Sunday returned to Detroit for a revival in 1932, he was no longer able to whip up the enthusiastic support for Prohibition that he had in his last revival there. The issue no longer attracted deep interest with the general public.

Repeal. Even so, when the political parties met in their presidential conventions in 1932 and capitalism in the United States seemed on its last legs, the key issue for both parties, as the famous journalist H. L. Mencken reported, was their stand on liquor. The Democrats, despite reservations from dry southern delegates, nominated Franklin D. Roosevelt and pledged to overturn the Eighteenth Amendment. When Herbert Hoover accepted his party's nomination, he too joined the chorus for repeal. Effectively, the "noble experiment," as President Hoover's remark was usually misquoted, was over. As soon as the election results were in, plans to repeal the Eighteenth Amendment were put into action. When the Congress met in special session in March 1933 to enact the first hundred days of New Deal legislation, one of its first acts was to revise the Volstead Act to allow the manufacture and sale of beer. The beer parades of 1933 echoed the funerals for John Barleycorn that signaled the ratification of the Prohibition amendment fourteen years earlier. The repeal amendment swept through state ratification, and in December 1933 the Twenty-first Amendment was declared ratified. Once again the states were able to decide the alcohol question for themselves.

Last Efforts. While they had lost the conflict, many Protestants and their organizations were unwilling to give up the struggle. They turned again to local communities to try to limit alcohol sales and consumption. In many states they formed umbrella groups, with names such as Christian Action or Christian Social Response, to coordinate their efforts, sometimes to great effect. Will Rogers, the cowboy humorist, remarked of his native Oklahoma that the people there would vote dry as long as they were sober enough to stagger to the polls. But the national war over alcohol was over for now.

Sources:

"Baptists and Methodists Fight Repeal," *Literary Digest,* 115 (10 June 1933): 15;

Sean Dennis Cashman, *Prohibition: The Lie of the Land* (New York: Free Press, 1981);

Larry Engelmann, *Intemperance: The Lost War Against Liquor* (New York: Free Press, 1979);

David E. Kyvig, *Repealing National Prohibition* (Chicago: University of Chicago Press, 1979).

RELIGIOUS RESPONSE TO THE SPANISH CIVIL WAR

Contention. In July 1936 military officers, led by Gen. Francisco Franco, declared war against the government of the Republic of Spain and launched a four-year civil war between his rebels and the loyalists supporting the republic. The Spanish Republic was created in 1931 after King Alphonso XIII left the country and initially had fairly wide support. But monarchists were soon joined by opponents of the republic's policies, which affected large landowners, the wealthy, and the institutions of the Roman Catholic Church. The military also became disaffected, and many troops followed Franco into revolt. The Spanish Civil War, which lasted until Franco's Flangist

forces won in 1939, was a foretaste of the approaching world war.

Divided Opinions in the United States. As the war dragged on, American religious communities were sharply divided in their attitudes toward the competing armies and their actions. The rebels were vigorously supported by most American Catholics and Catholic clerics, who had been horrified by the republic's confiscation of church land and popular violence directed against Catholic officials. They were also concerned by the growing role Communists played in Republican forces. Protestants and Jews tended to support the loyalists, pointing out that the republic was the legitimate government of Spain and recognized as such by the United States. The political Left charged that Franco's Nationalists were a part of the growing fascist threat to peace and democracy in Europe. A 1938 Gallup public-opinion poll revealed that 58 percent of American Catholics were pro-Nationalist, while 83 percent of Protestants were pro-loyalist. The only significant Catholic publication to express reservations about the Nationalists was Dorothy Day's *Catholic Worker*, which was both pacifist and antifascist. In 1938 there was an internal revolt in the staff of *Commonweal*, an independent Catholic journal. The opponents of the previous pro-Nationalist editors gained power and established a neutral editorial position with regard to the war. There was a rapid 25 percent drop in circulation.

Tensions between Catholics and Protestants. Their opposing stands regarding the civil war led to increased tensions between American Protestants and Catholics. In the summer of 1937 the Spanish Catholic hierarchy published an open letter condemning the loyalist forces and the Republican government for their alleged abuses of priests and nuns and of church property. A week later, to the outrage of Catholics, 150 prominent Protestant clergymen took out an advertisement to attack their position. Catholic-Protestant relations dropped further as, a week later, 175 Catholic clerics responded, asking if these Protestants actually approved the persecution of Christians.

Deepening Distrust. The conflict between the two religious communities deepened as Protestants charged that Catholics had sabotaged an attempt to bring a group of Basque orphans to the United States and that they were responsible for blocking attempts to allow the loyalists to buy arms in the United States. As Communists seemed to gain tighter control over the loyalists and turned against their rivals in the republic, Catholics seemed to bind themselves even closer to the approaching triumph of Franco's Nationalists. For Protestants this was further evidence of the antidemocratic tendency of Roman Catholicism. The strident anti-Semitic charges and antidemocratic statements of Father Charles E. Coughlin and the support he gained in Catholic communities in the northeastern states only confirmed Protestant suspicions. Catholic support for Franco's antidemocratic forces in Spain led many to doubt Catholic support for democracy in the United States.

Sources:

George Q. Flynn, *American Catholics and the Roosevelt Presidency, 1932–1936* (Lexington: University Press of Kentucky, 1968);

Flynn, *Roosevelt and Romanism: Catholics and American Diplomacy, 1937–1945* (Westport, Conn.: Greenwood Press, 1976);

Allen Guttman, *The Wound in the Heart: Americans and the Spanish Civil War* (New York: Free Press, 1962);

John F. Thorning, "Why the Press Failed on Spain," *Catholic World*, 146 (December 1937): 289–291.

HEADLINE MAKERS

FRANK N. D. BUCHMAN

1878-1961

MINISTER

Founder of the Oxford Group Movement. A Pennsylvania-born Lutheran minister, Frank N. D. Buchman founded the Oxford Group Movement in 1921 in an effort to organize a "God-guided campaign to prevent war by moral and spiritual awakenings." In the following two decades he and his followers sought to change people through the use of home meetings where people came together to explore religious issues and make contact with God. The Oxford Group, as it came to be called, believed that those who experienced a conversion, the Change, would surrender their lives to God's control and that gradually the world would come under divine direction.

Controversy. The Oxford Movement aroused much controversy as it attracted increased public attention in the 1930s. The house parties, the informal format Buchman used to spread his movement, were held in large homes and expensive hotels in the United States and Europe and so gave the appearance that the movement was snobbishly directed toward the upper classes. Buchman, however, justified this target, insisting that if the world's leaders were brought under "God-control" through the Change, their nations would move under God-control, and so political problems, including war, could be resolved. A controversial aspect of his God-control was his insistence that his followers use a quiet time, preferably early in the morning, during which they would open themselves to God's direction. They would keep paper and a pen handy to write down the instructions that came into their heads in order to carry out the divine will. Critics wondered just what fleeting thoughts might be confused with this divine revelation.

Criticism. Another issue that was raised about the house parties was the assertion that participants were encouraged to confess their misbehavior to the other par-

ticipants, especially their sexual activities. Critics found it easy to smirk at the titillation these revelations might give their listeners or even the power they might give over those who confessed. The Left found the upper-class ambience and focus on the trivial by the Oxford Movement repellent.

Troubling Statements. Buchman, like many religious leaders of the decade, was adamantly opposed to communism and the Soviet Union. In 1936 he gave an interview in which he was alleged to have said, "[T]hank Heaven for a man like Hitler who built a first line of defense against the Anti-Christ of Communism. . . . Think what it would mean to the world if Hitler surrendered to God. . . . Through such a man God could control a nation overnight and solve every last bewildering problem." This statement seemed to fit into his pattern of pandering to the powerful and supporting not only the status quo but also fascism. The fact that he and his entourage did not directly raise funds for themselves and their cause but depended on God's bounty, which always seemed to be provided by people from the upper classes, solidified liberal and radical criticism of him and his movement. He and his followers were subjected to close examination by the press and some governments as the decade wore on.

Moral Re-Armament. Buchman changed with the times. In 1938 in London he said, "The crisis [of war or peace] is fundamentally a moral one. The nations must re-arm morally. Moral recovery is the forerunner of economic recovery. . . . We need a power strong enough to change human nature and build bridges between man, faction and faction. . . . God alone can change human nature." Around this time he and his followers began to call the movement Moral Re-Armament (MRA). Despite a shift in focus to exclusively social questions, the MRA remained suspect in many circles and lost members and influence in the war years. Only when the Cold War began would it once more become vital, as it focused its energies in building networks of Christians from Europe and the United States to the emerging new nations of the world.

Sources:

Charles Samuel Braden, *These Also Believe: A Study of Modern American Cults and Minority Religious Movements* (New York: Macmillan, 1950);

Tom Driberg, *The Mystery of Moral Re-Armament: A Study of Frank Buchman and His Movement* (New York: Knopf, 1965).

Bishop James Cannon Jr.

1864-1944

RELIGIOUS LEADER AND PROHIBITION SUPPORTER

Behind Prohibition. James Cannon Jr. was elected a bishop of the Methodist Episcopal Church, South, in 1918. The election reflected an esteem for his work in the denomination as president of Blackstone School, a women's college in Virginia. It also reflected enthusiasm for his efforts as editor of the Richmond *Virginian,* which served as a voice for the Virginia Anti-Saloon League, an organization he also led, and his work as chair of the Southern Methodist Board of Temperance and Social Service. Cannon served as the major voice of the Prohibition movement in the South. His work culminated with the 1919 ratification of the Eighteenth Amendment to the Constitution, which prohibited the manufacture and sale of alcoholic beverages in the United States.

Politics. In the 1920s Cannon became the effective head of the national Anti-Saloon League. He attracted national attention in the presidential campaign of 1928 when he led a split in the southern ranks of the Democratic Party over the nomination of Alfred E. Smith. Smith not only was a product of Tammany Hall, the notorious political machine in New York City, but he was also a wet, having stopped the enforcement of the Eighteenth Amendment in New York. Smith was also Roman Catholic. For all these reasons, the Smith candidacy encountered resistance in the deeply Protestant and mostly dry South, resistance that Cannon organized and used to help defeat Smith. His efforts, backed in part by money from the Republican National Committee, led many Democrats to vote Republican with a clear conscience, and Herbert Hoover broke the South for the Republican Party for the first time in the century, winning the electoral votes of five states in the upper South.

Stock-Market Scandal. After the 1928 election H. L. Mencken called Cannon "the most powerful ecclesiastic ever heard of in America." Newspapers and reporters attended his actions, which in the long run proved his undoing. He first encountered national scandal in 1929 when it was revealed that he had been speculating on the stock market with a notorious Wall Street bucket shop that had recently gone into bankruptcy. In eight months between 1927 and 1928 they had bought stocks for him worth $477,000 and sold them for $486,000, all on his investment of $2,500. Not only had Cannon been gambling, but he had been one of the largest customers of a company whose leaders were indicted for using the mail to defraud. The bishop was not brought to trial by his denomination, but his reputation was seriously damaged.

Marriage Scandal. More damage occurred in 1930, when it was announced that Cannon had quickly remarried after the death of his first wife. Initially, his new wife was identified as his secretary, who had traveled with him on several trips abroad. But after the marriage, stories began to circulate about his meeting her in a New York hotel under an assumed name and then supporting her in a New York apartment as his wife's health declined. He was with his secretary in New York when he learned of his first wife's approaching death. He returned to his future wife immediately after the funeral of his first. Once again charges were brought before the Southern Methodist Church, this time for immorality. Once again he was able to block the attacks when twelve bishops investigated the charges and countercharges and concluded that there was no evidence to warrant bringing Cannon before a church trial.

Campaign Scandal. In the meantime questions had been raised about election money directed to Cannon in 1928 and its use. A sum of $48,300 (equal to more than half a million dollars in 1990s currency) was not accounted for. The bishop successfully refused to testify before a Senate committee investigating lobbying but was brought before the Senate Committee on Campaign Expenditures. That committee charged that in December 1931 Cannon had failed to comply with election laws by his failure to account for $71,451.62 in contributions to block Smith's election. He was finally brought to trial in federal court in 1934 on charges that he had conspired with his secretary to defraud the government. The government's case fell apart when the secretary testified that she had no knowledge of the money that had been given to Cannon. The conspiracy failed to be proved, and both defendants were declared not guilty.

Hurting the Cause. The variety of scandals that enveloped the bishop, even though he surmounted each, helped to discredit the cause he had served so valiantly. One prominent anti-Prohibition activist insisted that Cannon was the person most responsible for repeal. Although his reputation was in ruins by the middle of the 1930s, he still had supporters in dry circles in the South and in the Southern Methodist Church. That support was not sufficient to have him elected presiding bishop, the highest office of his denomination, even though his seniority justified that elevation. Nor did it keep his fellow bishops from placing him on the retirement list shortly after his successful defense in federal court in 1934. He had become a liability for his cause.

Later Life. Cannon lived his later years in quiet retirement in Richmond. His income was limited; he had spent money not only in trials defending himself but also in suing others for defamation of his character. By the time of his death in 1944, biographer Virginius Dabney says, "he seemed almost a ghost out of the past."

Sources:

James Cannon, *Bishop Cannon's Own Story: Life as I Have Lived It,* edited by Richard L. Watson (Durham, N.C.: Duke University Press, 1955);

Virginius Dabney, *Dry Messiah: The Life of Bishop Cannon* (New York: Knopf, 1949).

FATHER CHARLES E. COUGHLIN

1891-1979

PRIEST AND RADIO FIGURE

Early Career. Father Charles E. Coughlin was born in Hamilton, Ontario, to an American father and Canadian mother, which raised questions about his constitutional eligibility when his more zealous followers urged him to run for president in the 1930s. In 1926 the bishop of Detroit appointed the newly ordained priest to the new parish of the Little Flower, named in honor of the recently consecrated Saint Thérèse of Lisieux, in suburban Royal Oak, Michigan. In an effort to attract people, Father Coughlin began a series of Sunday-evening broadcasts of his sermons on a Detroit radio station in a program called the *Radio League of the Little Flower.*

From Religion to Politics. Father Coughlin's engaging voice, speaking skills, and message attracted a large audience, and his parish grew quickly. In the early days of his radio ministry he focused on religious and moral issues, but after the stock-market crash of 1929 he began to speak about current topics and their moral implications. His audience continued to grow. In 1930 he entered a contract with the Columbia Broadcasting System radio network, linked to sixteen stations in the Northeast, and his talks became increasingly political. When questions were raised about a radio priest in politics, CBS dropped his contract, and he established an independent network of stations to carry his broadcast.

Success. Throughout his radio career, Father Coughlin's primary audience consisted of Roman Catholics living in eastern industrial cities, but he also attracted a significant audience of Protestants in the Midwest who appreciated his views on political subjects, if not his church. By 1932 his office was receiving as many as eighty thousand letters a week, and he had created a thriving parish and built a large, new sanctuary with a modern radio office for his broadcasts.

Coughlin and Roosevelt. The radio priest became sharply critical of President Herbert Hoover's inability or unwillingness to deal with the Depression and in the 1932 election endorsed Franklin D. Roosevelt's candidacy with the slogan "Roosevelt or Ruin." Father Coughlin always believed he was responsible for Roosevelt's 1932 victory and initially assumed he would be an important adviser to the new president. He endorsed the early programs of the New Deal, and Roosevelt did consult Father Coughlin from time to time. But the president followed little of the priest's advice, especially concerning ways to inflate the currency. Father Coughlin was convinced, as were many others, that cheaper money would ease the ongoing financial crisis and in 1933 supported the idea of shifting the nation from the gold to a silver standard within a year's time. He would later propose another inflationary measure, that of replacing the Federal Reserve System with a federally owned central bank that would issue paper currency in response to consumer demand. Roosevelt was not interested in the silver standard, and Father Coughlin was embarrassed when the administration published a list of people who owned large amounts of silver. The treasurer of the Shrine of the Little Flower was one of the largest silver holders in the nation. Since it was obvious that she had not plunged into the silver market on her own, it appeared that the radio priest was playing the futures market in silver.

Divergent Views. Father Coughlin then began to criticize specific New Deal programs and even the president himself from time to time but did not yet break with Roosevelt. In November 1934, however, he organized the National Union for Social Justice, with himself as head, as a way to assemble his millions of followers into an effective force for change. The organization grew quickly. He claimed to have millions of members, although more-careful estimates suggest that about a million people belonged to the National Union for Social Justice at its peak. He took credit for blocking attempts to have the United States join the World Court in 1935, although in the isolationist atmosphere of the mid 1930s many opposed entangling the United States in the organization and only a few were committed enthusiasts for the court. By mid decade he was periodically indulging in anti-Semitic remarks on his radio program. His anti-Semitism increased over the course of the decade. While there were others who were more strident in their charges against Jews, none had his audience.

Against Roosevelt. In 1936 Father Coughlin finally launched a full assault on Roosevelt, charging the New Deal had brought the nation "Roosevelt and Ruin." The president, according to him, was leading the nation in the direction of communism. He then began to work with other popular political movements of the time, including Francis E. Townsend's Old Age Revolving Pension program and the remnants of Huey Long's Share Our Wealth program. After some negotiation, they agreed to support William Lemke, a congressman from North Dakota, in a presidential run under the banner of the Union Party.

Defeat. Despite the apparent strengths of the coalition that supported the Union Party — Father Coughlin's National Union for Social Justice in the Northeast, Share Our Wealth in the South, and Lemke in the West — none of these leaders was able to bring the mass of his followers with him. Father Coughlin's direct attack on Roosevelt caused a serious split in his movement, as many admirers and beneficiaries of Roosevelt and the New Deal stayed with the president and the Democratic Party. Lemke received fewer than a million votes in 1936 and received no electoral votes; Roosevelt was overwhelmingly reelected.

Fascism and Anti-Semitism. Father Coughlin had promised to leave the radio if the Lemke campaign failed; for a short time he kept his word, but by 1937 he was back on the airwaves. Now his speeches and his newspaper, *Social Justice*, reflected his increasingly bitter anti-Semitism and his fascistic positions on current issues. By the end of 1937 he was attacking the nature of democracy itself, and in the next year he organized the Christian Front Against Communism to bring discipline and "God's will" to America. Bullyboys associated with the Christian Front attacked Jews in cities such as New York and Boston. In 1938 *Social Justice* published the blatantly anti-Semitic *Protocols of the Elders of Zion,* a document forged earlier by the czarist government of Russia to discredit Jews by charging that they planned to gain control of the world. Father Coughlin championed Adolf Hitler when war began in Europe in 1939. Only in 1942 was he finally silenced by government pressure on his church. He continued to work at the Shrine of the Little Flower until his retirement in 1966.

Sources:

David H. Bennett, *Demagogues in the Depression: American Radicals and the Union Party, 1933–1936* (New Brunswick, N.J.: Rutgers University Press, 1969);

Alan Brinkley, *Voices of Protest: Huey Long, Father Coughlin and the Great Depression* (New York: Knopf, 1982).

DOROTHY DAY

1897-1980

CHRISTIAN MAGAZINE PUBLISHER AND SOCIAL WORKER

Conversion. After spending her young adulthood in nonreligious, left-wing circles in New York City, Dorothy Day was received into the Roman Catholic Church in 1927, shortly after the baptism of her illegitimate daughter. Although the American Catholic Church tended to adopt conservative political and religious views in the first half of the twentieth century, Day continued her work for peace and religious meaning while criticizing capitalism. In 1932 she met Peter Maurin, a French immigrant, who introduced her to his ideas about Christians taking personal responsibility for living a Christian life and thus creating a Christian world.

Catholic Worker. After being persuaded by Maurin's ideas, Day took responsibility for publicizing them and putting them into action. In 1933 she began publishing the *Catholic Worker,* a name that became associated with the movement she and Maurin started. He presented his thoughts in the *Catholic Worker,* which competed with the Communist *Daily Worker,* and Day wrote a regular column for the newspaper called "Day by Day" that expressed her thoughts and views as they developed.

Christian Charity. Insisting that Christians assume responsibility for the needs of their fellow human beings, the Catholic Worker movement opened hospices that provided shelter for the ever-growing needy in the early days of the Depression. "Every house should have a Christ's room. It is no use turning people away to an agency, to the city or the state or the Catholic Charities. It is you yourself who must perform the works of mercy."

The Movement. Day's *Catholic Worker* launched a movement. More Catholic Worker houses were opened, as were Workers' schools and farms. She not only put out the *Catholic Worker* but also traveled extensively to bring news of the movement to others. While Maurin sought to avoid the whole issue of labor unions — for him they were a part of an unchristian system — Day endorsed the widespread union activity of the 1930s, and Catholic Workers walked picket lines in the heady days of union organization.

Conflict. Day's old radical reputation haunted her, especially when she and the *Catholic Worker* took stands opposing church involvement in the Spanish Civil War, in which Francisco Franco was widely supported by American Catholics. There were also periodic clashes between Catholic Workers and followers of Father Charles Coughlin's anti-Semitic Christian Front organization in the northeastern cities where both were active.

Pacifism. While Day's charisma and her efforts to create a Catholic radical stand on social and moral issues attracted a devoted group of followers, she encountered deep opposition both in and out of the movement when she took a firm pacifistic stand at the outbreak of World War II. For her and Maurin, war was wrong and the Roman Catholic Church was misguided in refusing to oppose military conflicts. She and her movement would encounter new resistance as the United States drifted into the conflict.

Sources:

Dorothy Day, *From Union Square to Rome* (Silver Spring, Md.: Preservation of the Faith Press, 1938);

William D. Miller, *The Long Loneliness* (New York: Harper, 1952);

Mel Piehl, *Breaking Bread: The Catholic Worker and the Origins of Catholic Radicalism in America* (Philadelphia: Temple University Press, 1982).

FATHER DEVINE

1877?-1965

RELIGIOUS LEADER

God or Man? One of the most colorful religious personalities of the decade, Father Devine challenged religious convention, distributed food to the needy, and conducted healing services. Although his followers often confused Devine with God, few outside his church did. His charity and preaching of interracial tolerance nonetheless won him many admirers and made him the most well known of Harlem's many preachers.

Gaining a Following. In the dark years of the early Depression, increasing numbers of people took advantage of Father Devine's charity. The crowds swelled around his Sayville, New York, home, and the number of his followers expanded. In 1931 protests from his neighbors led to charges that, because of the crowds and traffic problems, he was disturbing the peace. While the community insisted they were concerned with the large crowds Father Devine attracted, his followers believed part of the opposition came from the fact that whites, especially white women, attended his services and joined his group. He was convicted of disturbing the peace and given the maximum sentence, one year in prison. Two days later the presiding judge died, and Father Devine was alleged to have remarked, "I hated to do it." The remark became legendary among followers certain that Devine was God incarnate. His following grew, and he became a public figure.

Plenty in the Midst of Want. One reason for the growth of Devine's Peace Mission Movement, as it was eventually called, was the open hospitality people were given in the "heavens" (as he termed his homes and churches) that he created during the Depression years. He purchased hotels in which his followers were given food and shelter for modest sums. In 1934 he claimed seventy-two "Kingdoms, Extensions, and Connections," names for his various units. By 1939 they had increased to 152, mostly centered around New York.

Becoming a Public Figure. Father Devine and his followers were adamantly opposed to the racism that pervaded American society in the 1930s. It was this multiracial aspect of his followers as much as the generosity of his "heavens" that attracted attention during the decade. This multiracial quality was almost as important as the claims he was God in attracting press attention as he took on the qualities of a celebrity during the decade.

Sources:

Kenneth E. Burnham, *God Comes to America: Father Devine and the Peace Mission Movement* (Philadelphia: Imperial Press, 1982);

Robert Weisbrot, *Father Devine and the Struggle for Racial Equality* (Urbana: University of Illinois Press, 1983).

HARRY EMERSON FOSDICK

1878-1969

MINISTER AND PROFESSOR

Prominent Protestant. Harry Emerson Fosdick was one of the major voices of liberal Protestantism in the middle of the twentieth century. As pastor of the spectacular, nondenominational Riverside Church in New York City and as the leading Protestant speaker on radio, he helped to define the personality and meaning of mainline Protestantism for thirty years.

Early Recognition. Fosdick was born in upstate New York and entered the Baptist ministry after graduating from Union Theological Seminary in New York. His talents and abilities were quickly recognized. He became professor of practical theology at Union in 1911 and taught there until he retired in 1946. In 1918, even though he was a Baptist, he was called to the pulpit of the First Presbyterian Church in New York City. In 1922 he attracted national notoriety when he preached a sermon called "Shall the Fundamentalists Win?," which entered him in the battle between modernists and fundamentalists that splintered many Protestant denominations in the 1920s. The furor over the sermon led to efforts to move him from a Presbyterian pulpit. While his congregation supported Fosdick, he decided to accept an offer to pastor the Park Avenue Baptist Church. That congregation then decided to move to a new sanctuary to be built on Riverside Heights near Union and Columbia University. The Riverside Church, which was generously supported by John D. Rockefeller Jr., was dedicated in 1930.

Riverside. The Riverside Church was one of the largest churches in the nation, with more than two thousand members and a staff of seventy. The structure contained facilities for its varied urban ministry as well as a radio studio for the production of Fosdick's radio sermons. With the support of a professional staff and its extensive facilities, the congregation played an active role in the affairs of the neighborhood and city.

Radio Preacher. Fosdick engaged in a vigorous ministry during the decade. One of his most effective ways of influencing people was through his nationally broadcast program, *The National Vesper Hour*. It was estimated that he reached more people than any other preacher in his nineteen years of broadcasts over NBC's Red Network. Some suggested that a reason for the decline in church attendance in the 1930s was because people stayed home from their local congregations to hear Fosdick.

Critic of Modernism. Though Fosdick entered the battle against fundamentalism in 1922, he also challenged the supremacy of modernism in a widely discussed 1935 sermon, "Shall the Church Go Beyond Modernism?" While he still insisted that modernism had played an essential role in the development of current Christianity, he asserted that religion must go beyond it. This meant advancing beyond a modernist emphasis on intellectualism, which seemed to attempt to adjust Christianity to the world. "Our modern world cries out ... for souls maladjusted to it, not most of all for accommodators and adjusters but for intellectual and ethical challengers." People must realize, he said, that "*Sin is real ... and it leads men and nations to damnation....*" Modernism, he claimed, had watered down the essential truth of religion, the reality of God. Finally, he said, modernism had lost its ethical standards and its ability to attack the problems people face. "What Christ does to modern culture is to challenge it."

Away from Liberalism. Fosdick's sermon reflected the growing influence in Protestant theological circles of the new theology being introduced by Karl Barth, Paul Tillich, and Americans such as Reinhold Niebuhr and his brother, H. Richard. But equally important in challenging the accommodating qualities of American Protestantism were the questions raised by the Depression and by war and the threat of war. What did the spreading totalitarian regimes of Adolf Hitler's Germany, Benito Mussolini's Italy, and Joseph Stalin's Soviet Union say about humanity and the historical moment? For Fosdick, the dictator invalidated many liberal and modernist assumptions about humanity's essential good nature.

A Spiritual Leader. In his many sermons and books Fosdick offered guidance to the American people through the events and issues of the day. No other preacher of his time seemed to speak so directly to the time and his audience.

Sources:

Harry Emerson Fosdick, *The Living of These Days: An Autobiography* (New York: Harper, 1956);

Robert M. Miller, *Harry Emerson Fosdick: Preacher, Pastor, Prophet* (New York: Oxford University Press, 1976).

JOHN HAYNES HOLMES

1879-1964

MINISTER

Pacifist. John Haynes Holmes was a leading political and religious liberal in the first half of the twentieth century. He was ordained in the American Unitarian Association in 1904 and in 1907 moved to the Church of the Messiah in New York City, where he remained until he retired in 1949. He was deeply disturbed by World War I and helped organize the American branch of the pacifist organization the Fellowship of Reconciliation. He was a leader in the American Union Against Militarism, an umbrella organization that opposed American involvement in World War I. The controversy over his pacifist views caused him and his church to leave the Unitarian Association, and the name of the congregation was changed to the Community Church. Following the lead of Holmes, the Community Church remained one of the most active liberal groups in the nation.

Civil Liberties. After the United States entered the war in 1917, Holmes helped to create an organization to protect the rights of pacifists to resist conscription into the military. After the war the Civil Liberties Bureau became the American Civil Liberties Bureau, later the American Civil Liberties Union (ACLU). Holmes remained active with the ACLU and its efforts to protect the constitutional rights of free speech throughout his life.

Social Critic. Holmes believed that the horrors of the Great War came in part from the deep flaws of capitalism and its connection with imperialism. He was sharply critical of the two leading American political parties and sought to create an alternative political alliance that would bring together the nation's progressive forces to create true reform. He was not a Marxist and had reservations about aspects of socialism, but his antiwar beliefs committed him to supporting the Socialist Party, which opposed most conflicts. He was a close associate of Norman Thomas, a former Presbyterian minister, and supported Thomas in his various campaigns on the Socialist ticket in the 1920s, including Thomas's first campaign for the presidency on the Socialist Party ticket in 1928. Thomas was soundly beaten, and in 1929 Holmes joined other liberals in organizing the League for Independent Political Action. But the league failed to create a new political coalition, and again in 1932 and afterward Holmes supported Thomas's campaign efforts.

Antiwar Efforts. In the 1930s Holmes worked actively to stop war, a commitment that led to his being named honorary chair of the War Resisters' League; he also became an ally of the Keep America Out of War Committee. While he opposed war as barbaric and useless, he had no illusions about totalitarian states, either of the Left or the Right. When war finally came after the 1939 German-Soviet nonaggression pact and the American Communist Party shifted its position to oppose the collective security policies it had favored up to the outbreak of war, Holmes joined others on the board of directors of the ACLU to force those close to the Communist position from the board of directors. Holmes replaced Harry F. Ward as chair of the ACLU as the threat of war and its challenges to civil liberties moved closer to the United States.

Sources:

John Haynes Holmes, *Rethinking Religion* (New York: Macmillan, 1938);

Holmes, *A Sensible Man's Guide to Religion* (New York: Harper, 1932).

FATHER JOHN A. RYAN

1869-1945

PRIEST AND PROFESSOR

Vocation. Father John A. Ryan was born in Minnesota to an Irish immigrant family. While attending a Christian Brothers school he decided to become a priest, and during his training he was deeply influenced by the publication of Pope Leo XIII's encyclical *Rerum novarum*, which spoke for social justice and condemned both the excesses of capitalism and the dangers of socialism. He was also impressed by the ideas of Archbishop John Ireland of Saint Paul, who sought to acculturate the Roman Catholic Church to the United States without compromising any of its essential qualities.

Reforming Capitalism. Ryan was ordained in 1898 and earned a Ph.D. at Catholic University in Washington, D.C. His dissertation, published as *The Living Wage* (1906), presented his belief that capitalism should be reformed to accord with Christian concepts of brotherhood and community. In 1915 he returned to Catholic University for a lifelong teaching career. When the National Catholic Warfare Conference proved successful in coordinating Catholic efforts during World War I, American bishops decided to create a permanent organization to direct Catholic charities. Ryan became head of the Social Action Department of the new National Catholic Welfare Conference and quickly moved into the public eye.

Outspoken Catholic. While Father Ryan attracted attention for his progressive stands on social issues, his public support for traditional Catholic views on the relations between church and state triggered much concern and criticism in Protestant circles, although he insisted that he believed in religious liberty. When he became an active supporter of the presidential candidacy of Alfred E. Smith in 1928, his views on the state and Catholicism confirmed the fears of anti-Catholic Protestants.

Against Capitalist Excess. Ryan's course, already set by *Rerum novarum*, was further influenced by Pope Pius XI's *Quadragesimo anno* in 1931, which again condemned laissez-faire capitalism and repeated the need for economic systems to reflect the values of Christianity: "Free competition has destroyed itself: economic dictatorship has supplanted the free market; unbridled ambition for power has likewise succeeded greed for gain; all economic life has become tragically hard, inexorable, and cruel."

Pope Pius XI called for a new partnership between labor and capital to replace the present system without adopting the excesses of Marxism. Ryan found this sufficient basis for his support of the New Deal programs of President Franklin D. Roosevelt. Now a monsignor, he became the most visible Catholic cleric defending the president, repeating that the reform programs of the New Deal were as conservative as the ideals of the Pope.

Countering Coughlin. In the election year of 1936 Father Ryan agreed to give a radio response to the anti-Roosevelt, anti–New Deal tirades of Father Charles E. Coughlin. In his speech, "Roosevelt Safeguards America," Ryan dismissed the radio priest's charges that the New Deal was communistic or that the administration was filled with Communists. Instead, Ryan insisted, the New Deal programs were actually checking the growth of communism. Those who charged to the contrary were breaking the Eighth Commandment, against bearing false witness. Father Ryan then attacked Coughlin's economic ideas, insisting that they did not conform to papal encyclicals on economics and social justice. Father Ryan later concluded that the speech was "one of the most effective and beneficial acts that I have ever performed in the interest of my religion and my country."

Catholics and Roosevelt. It is impossible to estimate how many voters Father Ryan persuaded in 1936, but Roosevelt attracted a vast majority of Catholic votes to the Democratic column. A crucial part of the Democratic Party for the next thirty years would be composed of urban Catholic voters who joined Roosevelt's New Deal coalition. Father Ryan was instrumental in building that coalition. He retired from Catholic University in 1939 and died in 1945.

Sources:

Francis L. Broderick, *The Right Reverend New Dealer: John A. Ryan* (New York: Macmillan, 1963);

John A. Ryan, *Social Doctrine in Action: A Personal History* (New York: Harper, 1941).

GERALD L. K. SMITH

1889-1976

MINISTER AND POLITICIAN

Early Ministry. Gerald L. K. Smith was born in Wisconsin and ordained when he was eighteen in the denomination that modestly called itself the Christian Church. After successfully serving a series of churches in Indiana, he moved to Shreveport, Louisiana, in 1928 to give his ailing wife a better climate. There he led the largest church of his denomination in that state. Smith quickly recognized the usefulness of radio and developed a large local following with the broadcasting of his sermons, which focused on reform topics.

From Preaching to Politics. In the early days of the Depression Smith began to attack the actions of important business leaders of Shreveport, including members of his own congregation. These people joined others in his church who charged that he was neglecting some of his pastoral responsibilities. The dissension in his church and his personal ambitions made Smith responsive to a chance to join Huey Long's organization. By 1934 Long was ready to challenge both the New Deal and President Franklin D. Roosevelt. That year he established Share Our Wealth, which proposed a massive redistribution of individual fortunes and massive taxation of high incomes. Smith left his congregation in Shreveport to become the national organizer for Share Our Wealth and rapidly expanded the movement across the South and into the border states. Smith was a dynamic speaker, as his congregations well knew before he moved into politics. H. L. Mencken described him as "the gutsiest and goriest, loudest and lustiest, the deadliest and damndest orator ever heard on this or any other earth . . . , the champion boob-bumper of all epochs."

After Long. Smith seemed to have Long's confidence, but he did not have time to ingratiate himself with the politicians in the Long machine before the senator was assassinated in September 1935. Smith attempted to seize the leadership of the Long movement and gave the dramatic funeral address to more than a hundred thousand mourners at the new capitol building at Baton Rouge. But he then chose the weaker side of the splitting Long movement in Louisiana and was forced out of Long's organization. When Smith failed to find the crucial national mailing lists of Share Our Wealth he found himself with the shell of a movement and no real power.

The Union Party. Nevertheless, Smith attempted to parlay the assets he had and, claiming to speak for Share Our Wealth, aligned himself with Francis E. Townsend and his Old Age and Revolving Insurance Plan in early 1936. Smith then joined these two movements with Social Justice, the movement of radio priest Father Charles E. Coughlin, to support the presidential campaign of William Lemke's Union Party. Norman Thomas, the leader of the Socialist Party, called the Union Party "fascistic" and characterized Smith as having a "great and sinister influence" in the Union Party.

Fringe Politics. These ambitions came to nothing when Lemke's campaign failed to gain any electoral votes and disappeared. Share Our Wealth was never able to regain the membership of the Long days and disappeared into irrelevance. Smith cast about for a new way to remain in the political spotlight. He worked with a group he called the Committee of One Million for a couple of years, using the organization to preach for what he called Americanism, which he opposed to communism. He also

consistently expressed anti-Semitic views that had become central to his thinking. He appeared in the last years of the decade at various sites of union activity, which he opposed. He was particularly opposed to the efforts of the Congress of Industrial Organizations (CIO), which he charged was infiltrated by Jews and their communist allies. He continued what became a lifelong career of fringe politics and gained a reputation as the nation's leading anti-Semite. Almost all his efforts attempted to use Christianity to justify his attacks on Jews and communists, usually linking the two groups together. Never again, however, did he have the spotlight he obtained for a few short months with Share Our Wealth.

Source:
Alan Brinkley, *Voices of Protest: Huey Long, Father Coughlin, and the Great Depression* (New York: Knopf, 1982).

HARRY F. WARD

1873-1966

MINISTER, ACTIVIST, AND PROFESSOR

Varied Career. Harry F. Ward was probably the best-known fellow traveler of the Communist Party among American Protestant clergy in the 1930s. He was born in England in 1873 and came to the United States in 1881. He was ordained in the Methodist Episcopal Church, the northern branch of the Methodist denomination, and quickly became active in reform movements in the early part of the century. He was one of the principal authors of "The Social Creed of the Churches," the most widely circulated expression of the Social Gospel, which attempted to articulate the social ethics of Christianity. In 1907 he organized the Methodist Federation for Social Action (later the Methodist Federation for Social Service). After teaching at Boston University, he joined the faculty of Union Theological Seminary in New York City, where he taught social ethics until his retirement in 1941.

Activism. There is no evidence that Ward ever joined the Communist Party, but he was a prominent supporter of organizations associated with the party during the 1930s. He criticized the actions of the both the American Communists and the Soviet Union from time to time but had little difficulty in following the general shifts in Communist positions through the turbulent decade of the 1930s. He served as president of the American League Against War and Fascism when it criticized American rearmament and the foreign policies of the Western democracies, and he remained president when the league was reorganized in 1938 as the American League for Peace and Freedom, which supported the rearming of the democracies and their united front with the Soviet Union against the growing threat of Nazi Germany.

Criticism. Ward's actions attracted widespread criticism and seemed to offer support for conservative charges that communists had infiltrated the Protestant clergy. In 1952, in the anticommunist climate of the Cold War, the Methodist Church severed its connections with the Federation for Social Service, but Ward remained a target of the red-baiting forces of that period.

Source:

Ralph Lord Roy, *Communism and the Churches* (New York: Harcourt, Brace, 1960).

STEPHEN SAMUEL WISE

1874-1949

RABBI

Productive Career. Stephen S. Wise came to the United States as a child when his father, also a rabbi, accepted a congregation in New York City. He graduated from the City College of New York and took a Ph.D. at Columbia University. He served a series of congregations, including one in Portland, Oregon. He returned to New York and in 1907 founded the Free Synagogue of New York, where he spent the rest of his career as a leading rabbi in Reform Judaism and a leading reformer in New York politics. He founded the Jewish Institute of Religion, now a part of the Hebrew Union College.

Zionism. Wise was one of the first Reform rabbis to champion the cause of Zionism, the return of Jews to Palestine. He helped found the Federation of American Zionists in 1897 and served as its first secretary. He also helped organize its successor, the Zionist Organization of America.

Against Nazism. When Adolf Hitler came to power in Germany in 1933, Wise attempted to encourage and organize opposition to the Nazis' anti-Semitic actions. In March 1933 he organized a mass meeting in Madison Square Garden that attracted an estimated twenty-two thousand people inside the building and another thirty thousand outside. The meeting was addressed by Wise and former governor of New York Al Smith, Sen. Robert Wagner, and Bishops William Manning of the Episcopal Church and Francis McConnell of the Methodist Episcopal Church. Wise helped organize a boycott of German products and worked in vain to stop American participation in the Olympic Games, which were held in Berlin in 1936.

Jewish Immigration. As Nazi persecution of German Jews intensified, Rabbi Wise attempted to ease immigration to the United States over vigorous opposition. This opposition came in part from concern about bringing new workers into the country when unemployment remained high, but many opponents simply did not want to allow the immigration of Jews. Jewish emigration from Germany increased during the decade, rising from 1,372 in 1933 to 5,800 in 1937.

Seeking a Jewish Refuge. As it became clear that the Western democracies would not offer a refuge for the victims of Nazi persecution, Rabbi Wise intensified his Zionist efforts. In response to Jews who feared that Zionism stoked domestic anti-Semitism by suggesting that Jews were divided in their national loyalties, Rabbi Wise responded, "I have been an American all my life, but I have been a Jew for four thousand years."

Sources:

Carl H. Voss, *Rabbi and Minister: The Friendship of Stephen S. Wise and John Haynes Holmes* (New York: Prometheus, 1980);

Stephen S. Wise, *The Challenging Years* (New York: Putnam, 1949).

PEOPLE IN THE NEWS

In 1934 **Evangeline Booth** — a daughter of Gen. William Booth, founder of the Salvation Army, and its head in the United States since 1904 — was elected general of the International Salvation Army and moved to Britain for five years. She retired in 1939 and returned to her home in the United States.

Marie Joseph Butler, founder of Marymount School (later Marymount College) in Tarrytown, New York, founded new Marymount Colleges in Rome (1930) and Santa Barbara, California (1938).

Mother Frances Xavier Cabrini, who became an American citizen in 1909 and died in 1917, was beatified in

1937, the first American to achieve that status. In 1946 she was canonized as the first American saint, and she was named Patroness of Immigrants in 1950.

Warren Akin Candler, who helped to develop Emory University of Atlanta into a distinguished institution, bitterly opposed the union of the northern and southern branches of Methodism. He helped to block a merger in 1922 but failed to stop the great Methodist merger of 1939. He refused to follow his denomination into the new organization and remained in the old Southern Methodist Church.

Distinguished church historian **Shirley Jackson Case** served as dean of the Divinity School of the University of Chicago from 1933 to 1935, developing it into one of the most distinguished divinity schools in the nation. In the 1930s he also published *Jesus Through the Centuries* and *The Social Triumph of the Ancient Church.*

In the 1930s **Rufus Matthews Jones,** the leading Quaker of the period, and the American Friends Service Committee — which he helped found in 1917, initially to use Quaker conscientious objectors in noncombat service during World War I — helped to alleviate the plight of Jews in Germany, including helping refugees. In 1937 he became chairman of the second World Conference of Friends.

George William Cardinal Mundelein, appointed archbishop of Chicago in 1915 and named cardinal in 1924, took on the cause of naming Mother Cabrini to the sainthood and saw her beatified in 1937. He

worked effectively with members of the Roosevelt administration and was the first cardinal to have dinner at the White House.

After retiring as senior minister of the Marble Collegiate Church in New York City, **Daniel Alfred Poling** purchased the *Christian Herald* and became its editor, turning it toward an increasingly conservative focus.

During the Depression years **Adam Clayton Powell Sr.,** pastor of the Abyssinian Baptist Church, one of the most distinguished African American churches in New York City and one of the largest congregations in the nation, raised large sums of money for the relief of the homeless and the unemployed.

Abba Hillel Silver helped move Reform Jews into the Zionist camp as expressed in the Columbus Platform of 1937. He served as chair of the United Palestine Appeal in 1938 and then as chair of the United Jewish Appeal.

In 1932 **Francis Edward Spellman,** the first American attached to the Secretariat of State of the Vatican, was named auxiliary bishop of Boston and was the first American to be consecrated bishop in Rome. In 1936 he guided papal secretary of state Eugenio Cardinal Pacelli on his historic tour of the United States. In 1939 Pacelli, as the newly elected Pope Pius XII, appointed Spellman to the archbishopric of New York City. Spellman was then named vicar to the American armed forces. He quickly became the most powerful Roman Catholic clergyman of his time.

DEATHS

Jane Addams, 75, founder of Hull House and active in antiwar groups, the second American to win the Nobel Peace Prize, 22 May 1935.

Felix Adler, 82, founder of the Ethical Culture Society in 1876, 24 April 1933.

Guy Warren Ballard, 51, cofounder with his wife of the I Am Religious Activity, 29 December 1939.

Annie Besant, 85, a convert to theosophy who attracted many followers in the United States, from 1907 head of the World Theosophical Association, 20 September 1933.

William Montgomery Brown, 82, Episcopal bishop of Arkansas until his retirement in 1922, deposed by his

church in 1925 because of his communist views, 31 October 1937.

Samuel Parks Cadman, 72, leading Protestant liberal who conducted a series of radio broadcasts over the National Broadcasting Corporation beginning in 1928, elected moderator of the national Council of the Congregational and Christian Churches in 1934, 12 July 1936.

Leopold Cohn, 75, founder of the American Board of Missions to Jews, 19 December 1937.

James Martin Gray, 84, president of the Moody Bible Institute, 1925–1935, 21 September 1935.

Patrick Joseph Hayes, 71, former archbishop of New York, 4 September 1938.

Charles Edward Jefferson, 77, pastor of the Broadway Tabernacle Church, the "Skyscraper Church," 12 September 1937.

Harvey Spencer Lewis, 55, founder of the Ancient and Mystical Order of the Rosae Crucis in 1915, 2 August 1939.

J. Gresham Machen, 55, Old School theologian and professor at Princeton Theological Seminary until 1929, when he left to found the Westminster Theological Seminary to teach his conservative views, helped to organize the Orthodox Presbyterian Church after being expelled from the Presbyterian Church of the United States of America (Northern) in 1936, 1 January 1937.

Helen Barrett Montgomery, 73, president (elected in 1921) of the Northern Baptist Convention, became the first woman to head a major denomination, 19 October 1934.

Charles Parkhurst, 91, pastor of the Madison Avenue Presbyterian Church who stunned the city with charges that prostitution was openly practiced in New York with the obvious tolerance of the police, 8 September 1933.

Richard G. Spurling Jr., 76, one of the founders of the Church of God in Cleveland, Tennessee, one of the leading Pentecostal denominations of the early part of the century, 24 May 1935.

PUBLICATIONS

Devere Allen, *The Fight for Peace* (New York: Macmillan, 1930);

Joseph B. Code, *Spanish War and Lying Propaganda* (New York: Paulist Press, 1938);

Dorothy Day, *From Union Square to Rome* (Silver Spring, Md.: Preservation of the Faith Press, 1938);

George Sherwood Eddy, *The Challenge of Europe* (New York: Farrar & Rinehart, 1933);

Eddy, *The Challenge of Russia* (New York: Farrar & Rinehart, 1931);

Eddy, *Revolutionary Christianity* (Chicago: Willett, Clark, 1939);

Harry Emerson Fosdick, *As I See Religion* (New York: Harper, 1932);

Fosdick, *A Guide to Understanding the Bible: The Development of Ideas within the Old and New Testament* (New York: Harper, 1938);

Fosdick, *The Secret of Victorious Living: Sermons on Christianity Today* (New York: Harper, 1934);

John Haynes Holmes, *Rethinking Religion* (New York: Macmillan, 1938);

Holmes, *A Sensible Man's Guide to Religion* (New York: Harper, 1932);

Mordecai M. Kaplan, *Judaism as a Civilization* (New York: Macmillan, 1934);

Kaplan, *Judaism in Transition* (New York: Covici–Friede, 1936);

Robert S. Lynd and Helen Merrell Lynd, *Middletown in Transition: A Study in Cultural Conflict* (New York: Harcourt, Brace, 1937);

H. Richard Niebuhr, *The Kingdom of God in America* (Chicago: Willett, Clark, 1937);

Reinhold Niebuhr, *Beyond Tragedy: Essays on the Christian Interpretation of History* (New York: Scribners, 1937);

Niebuhr, *Moral Man and Immoral Society: A Study in Ethics and Politics* (New York: Scribners, 1932);

Kirby Page, *Individualism and Socialism: An Ethical Survey of Economic and Political Forces* (New York: Farrar & Rinehart, 1933);

Page, *20,870 Clergymen on War and Economic Justice* (Long Island, N.Y.: Kirby Page, 1934);

Harry F. Ward, *Which Way America?* (New York: Macmillan, 1931);

America, periodical;

Christian Century, periodical;

Christian Herald, periodical;

Commonweal, periodical;

World Tomorrow, periodical.

SCIENCE AND TECHNOLOGY

by GUILLAUME DESYON

CONTENTS

Sidebars and tables are listed in italics.

1930

- Cadillac offers V-16 and V-12 models for sale, while Studebaker introduces the freewheel transmission.

- Louis Bamberger and his sister, Mrs. Felix Fuld, the widow of his late partner, found the Princeton Institute for Advanced Study.

- Transcontinental and West Airlines establish the first transcontinental New York–Los Angeles air link.

- In Boston the first institute for training psychoanalysts in the United States opens.

- Vannevar Bush succeeds in building the first analog computer, which he calls a differential analyzer. An analog computer uses mechanical or electrical devices to represent numbers being manipulated.

- Chemist Thomas Midgley Jr. develops the manufacturing process for Freon, a gas used in refrigerators and air conditioners.

- Sliced bread is introduced at American markets.

- Chemist W. L. Semon of B. F. Goodrich invents polyvinyl chloride (PVC), used in electrical insulation and pipes.

- Andrew Ellicott Douglass, an anthropologist, develops the science of dendrochronology when, while working at a Native American site, he uses tree rings observed in artifacts to determine the age of the site.

- Harlow Shapley calculates the Milky Way galaxy to be 250,000 light years in diameter.

25 Jan. A new amendment to the Air Commerce Regulations sets five hundred feet as a minimum altitude at which aircraft may fly except during landing and takeoff.

18 Feb. Clyde William Tombaugh confirms the existence of Pluto, the ninth and last planet in Earth's solar system, which had been calculated by Percival Lowell in 1906.

10 Mar. Eleanor Smith establishes a women's flight altitude record of 27,418 feet.

4 Apr. The American Interplanetary Society (later the American Rocket Society) is founded for the "promotion of interest in and experimentation toward interplanetary expeditions and travels."

22 Apr. W. A. Mudge at International Nickel produces the first age-hardening wrought-nickel alloy, K-monel.

1931

- Pontiac offers its V-6 and V-8 models. Oldsmobile introduces a downdraft carburetor and synchromesh transmission.

- Harold Urey, a professor at Columbia University, discovers heavy water, thus named because it contains deuterium, a rare hydrogen isotope that has an extra neutron.

2 Jan. Ernest O. Lawrence invents the cyclotron, the first operational particle accelerator, thus inaugurating the modern era of high-energy physics.

4 Mar. Congress appropriates more than $100 million for military, naval, and commercial aviation for the coming year.

1932

11 Apr.   The Empire State Building, begun in 1930, is completed in New York City. The tallest building in the world for forty years, it represents a marvel of engineering and architectural science.

27 May   The first full-scale wind tunnel for testing airplanes is dedicated at the Langley Memorial Aeronautical Laboratory in Hampton, Virginia.

24 Oct.   The George Washington Bridge, built under the direction of O. H. Ammann, chief engineer of the New York Port Authority, is dedicated. The new crossing is thirty-five hundred feet long between the two suspension towers.

28 Dec.   The George Westinghouse Bridge on the Philadelphia-Pittsburgh pike, begun in May 1930, is completed at a cost of $1.6 million. It has the longest central concrete arch in the United States at the time.

- The Ford V-8 supplants the Model A. The Pierce-Arrow company introduces hydraulic valve lifters in its new models, while Buick, Lasalle, and Cadillac all offer vacuum-operated clutches.

- Carl David Anderson discovers the positron, a positively charged particle and the first identified antiparticle, when examining cosmic-ray tracks, thus confirming physicist P. A. M. Dirac's hypothesis of its existence.

- RCA gives the first demonstration of television with a cathode-ray screen.

25 Aug.   Amelia Earhart, who recently received the Gold Medal of the National Geographic Society and the Distinguished Flying Cross from Congress, completes the first nonstop transcontinental flight, from Los Angeles to Newark, New Jersey, in nineteen hours, five minutes. The following year she breaks her time by almost two hours.

21 Sept.   Robert A. Millikan, head of the California Institute of Technology, completes a series of important measurement tests on the intensity of cosmic rays at various altitudes.

1 Dec.   The first teletypewriter weather map service is introduced by the U.S. Department of Commerce.

1933

- The use of the accelerator pedal to start the car is generalized in the United States. Independent wheel suspension is also introduced.

- Biochemist Roger J. Williams isolates pantothenic acid, a substance useful in fighting beriberi.

- The determination of the speed of light, begun by Albert Michelson, is completed. It is estimated to travel at 300,000 kilometers per second, or 186,000 miles per second.

- The Du Pont Company acquires the Remington Arms Company to secure a market for its smokeless powder, to be used by hunters.

- Albert Einstein immigrates to the United States and becomes professor emeritus at the Institute for Advanced Study at Princeton University.

- William J. Eckert, an astronomy assistant at Columbia University who had been the first to use an electric Munroe calculator in a science class, asked and obtained from IBM a series of computing machines that formed the basis for the Astronomical Computing Bureau.

4 Apr.   The navy dirigible *Akron* crashes at sea, killing seventy-three.

1934

- Both Chrysler and De Soto introduce streamlined Airflow models that include automatic transmission overdrives. Knee-action (front wheel independent suspension) is introduced in the United States.

- The Communications Act of 1934 creates the Federal Communications Commission, which replaces the Interstate Commerce Commission as the agency overseeing phone service.

- Lincoln Ellsworth and Baard Holth attempt to fly from the Antarctic Peninsula to the Ross Sea, but their efforts are hampered by poor weather. A short flight along the east coast of Trinity Peninsula is nevertheless carried out in 1935.

- Charles William Beebe and Otis Barton set a depth record by diving in a tethered bathysphere to a depth of 1,001 meters.

- American biochemist J. P. Lent discovers an anticoagulant now known as coumarin.

29 Nov.   The American Polar Society is founded in New York.

1935

- George Horace Gallup founds the American Institute of Public Opinion. Using statistical methods to poll small yet representative sections of the American population, he predicts electoral returns the following year more closely than any other statistical group.

- The beer can is first introduced in the United States.

Nov.   Lincoln Ellsworth, along with Canadian pilot Herbert Hollick-Kenyon and Hartreg Olsen, makes the first transantarctic flight, from Dundee Island to the Bay of Whales.

11 Nov.   In a flight sponsored jointly by the National Geographic Society and the U.S. Army Air Corps, Capt. O. A. Anderson and A. W. Stevens rise to an altitude of 13.71 miles (72,395 feet) aboard the balloon *Explorer II*, thereby exceeding all previous attempts to reach the stratosphere.

1936

- The Reo company ceases producing cars and concentrates on trucks. Its Diamond-T company builds a diesel-powered truck.

1 Mar.   The Hoover Dam, in the Black Canyon on the Colorado River, is completed, thus making Lake Mead the world's largest reservoir.

23 Nov.   The fluorescent lamp is first introduced during the centennial celebration of the U.S. Patent Office.

1937

- Ford offers customers a choice of sixty- or eighty-five-horsepower engines on its models. The steering column gearshifts are reintroduced on some automobiles, while Buick and Oldsmobile now offer automatic transmissions.

- Following the institution of the Social Security Act of 1935, the employment records of some twenty-six million working Americans had to be kept by the federal government. To assist the program, IBM develops the model 077 collator. Such a machine, which uses punched cards, allows the government to implement other national programs in the following years.

6 May   The German airship *Hindenburg* is destroyed by fire upon landing in Lakehurst, New Jersey.

Sept.   Grote Reber completes the first radio telescope in Wheaton, Illinois.

1938

- Chrysler introduces fluid coupling for transmissions.

- Perlon, a synthetic fiber, is developed.

- J. Robert Oppenheimer and George Michael Volkoff predict the existence of pulsars, which is confirmed three decades later.

22 Oct.   American physicist Chester F. Carlson, assisted by German engineer Otto Kornei, succeeds in making the first copy by an electrostatic process called xerography.

1939

- Oldsmobile offers a "hydramatic" drive, an automatic dive that uses hydraulic pressure to shift gears, while automatic overdrive becomes more widely available.

- German engineer Hans von Ohain devises the first practical jet engine. The first flight occurs in August 1939 with a Heinkel 179 test aircraft.

- The first handheld electric slicing knife begins to appear in American kitchens.

15 Feb.   Physicist J. Robert Oppenheimer, with the assistance of George Michael Volkoff, presents his calculations on the nature of black holes, stellar matter collapsing under intense gravitation.

4 Apr.   Following the introduction by Western Union of a cable system that allows transmission of six-by-seven-inch photographs, the first such picture, of a hydroplane, is sent from London to New York and published in American newspapers.

2 Aug.   At the suggestion of fellow physicist Leo Szilard, Albert Einstein writes President Franklin D. Roosevelt to recommend development of an atomic bomb.

14 Sept.   Igor Sikorsky's first helicopter designed for mass production flies for the first time.

31 Oct.   The New York World's Fair ends its first of two seasons, reaching a total attendance of about 25.8 million visitors.

OVERVIEW

Technological Utopians. Although the 1930s saw considerable growth and maturation in science and technology, the outlook they inspired owed much to the legacy of dozens of technological utopians who, from the late nineteenth century until the mid 1930s, published accounts of how technology would help achieve the perfect society. Industrialization and its negative aspects, ranging from smokestacks to cramped living quarters and long workdays, was considered only a stage that would give way to a clean, harmonious world. Whereas religion, ideologies, and revolution always seemed to provide but a part of the answer to life's challenges, technology might be the tool that truly fixed all troubles. Although such an ideal never materialized, the 1930s became the proving ground for many utopian technological predictions, from skyscrapers to airships. It also became the era when such expectations were tempered, despite scientific and mechanical successes.

The Machine as Inspiration and Threat. The worldwide depression that followed the stock-market crash of October 1929 had a surprisingly limited impact on scientific research. In fact, substantial progress was made in atomic physics, and even scientific applications to industrial and business fields continued at an accelerated pace. The belief in the positive impact of technology remained strong in the American consciousness and reflected the daily reports of new technical records and scientific discoveries. Visions of a mechanized world flourished, in which humanity would either be free of routine labor or become a slave of machinery. The Committee on Technocracy, formed in 1932 and led by Howard Scott Loeb, was inspired by Thorstein Veblen's concept of a "Soviet of Technicians" and argued for an increased role of the engineering profession in running the country. It argued, among other things, "All social activity must obey the laws of physics." This adoption of an action-reaction view of the world was best summarized in the technocrats' use of the ancient Chinese symbol of yin-yang, suggesting a dynamic equilibrium. Technocracy came to the fore as a movement and stirred many debates, from church pulpits to university seminars and press editorials. Despite abundant criticism, the technocratic movement led many scientists to view themselves as potential managers of change. Some felt that in order to succeed science required a true socialist transformation, while others believed that the acceptance of the status quo and even open support of government policies in the face of fascist and communist threats was the best way to make a difference.

Fascination. Elsewhere in America, the machine age had been welcomed by such industrialists as Henry Ford, who, although he equated technological and social progress, did not foresee the possibility of utopia. In fact, his plans and designs soon ran afoul of strong workers' unions, which called for better wages and working conditions. Social scientists, in particular Lewis Mumford, also became interested in the promises and dangers of technology. Following a study of the interaction of technology and society, Mumford brought out a pioneering book on the nature and function of cities, *The Culture of Cities* (1938), and proposed various solutions to the problems of urban development and disintegration. Long overlooked in practical terms, this study gained in relevance when the predicted dangers of urbanization came to increased public attention in the 1960s. In a similar fashion, new scientific breakthroughs such as plastics manufacturing were hailed at first as ultimate progress.

The Plastic Age. One industry tagged as the savior of the new age was plastics. Still in its infancy, the manufacture of the new substance seemed to suggest new, better things for a bright future. People in the 1930s could claim to have seen or touched one thing or another made out of plastic and found its resistance to humidity and sturdy pliability unique. Though wide use of plastic did not come until the 1950s, the "miracle" material's outlook seemed bright, as manufacturers scrambled to promise marvelous deeds for the sake of ensured sales. Americans were offered plastic options for a wide range of items, from germ-free unbreakable utensils to car accessories to replacement teeth. What distinguished plastic, as one columnist pointed out in *American Weekly* in 1936, was that it was not created from nature, nor could it be turned back into its components. This praise was also a hidden omen, as consciousness of the problems of pollution and biodegradability was raised several decades later. In the 1930s, however, plastics were the epitome of modern design, and the Bakelite Corporation led the charge to convince manufacturers that plastic was both trendy and practical, as proved by the success of plastic radio casings. The utopian associations of plastic eventually died down as its use expanded and its image suffered; yet for most of the 1930s it seemed that the United States had entered a "plastic age" of sorts, in which everything, including homes, might be mass-produced at cheap prices.

Houses by the Dozen? The housing boom that characterized the United States during the 1920s was driven both by rising standards of living and the new stylistic movement known as modernism — especially Bauhaus, from the school that originated it in Germany. The Swiss architect Le Corbusier summarized modernism's mechanical dimension by suggesting that the house was a "machine for living." Beyond the issue of modern design was that of modern building: how did one respond to the heavy demand for private roofs and walls? The basic solution was, as the slogan went, to "build houses like Fords." Prefabrication of elements was undertaken, and one company, General Houses, was fairly successful in marketing a four-thousand-dollar one-story, flat-roofed house. Unfortunately, building a house was less of an issue than establishing the necessary infrastructure, from building permits to water pipes and phone lines. One solution to such red tape was the appearance of "ready-to-build" units shipped by trucks. Yet for all the original designs proposed by such architects as Frank Lloyd Wright, as well as novel gadgets such as the electric garage door, the mass-housing effort failed, partly for lack of money. Another reason was, as Mumford noted, that a communism of sorts appeared in the manufacturing: there was no taking into account the surroundings or what communities really wished for, not to mention individuals.

Attacking the Machine Through Literature. In 1932 British author Aldous Huxley in his novel *Brave New World* took the opposite step to utopian accounts by proposing a dystopian outlook, a world in which the machine was the instrument of control rather than of help, of oppression rather than freedom. This dystopian outlook — that not all is for the best in the best of machine worlds — stuck in contemporary minds and was echoed later in other works, such as British novelist George Orwell's *Nineteen Eighty-Four* (1949). Echoing them as well as Mumford's analyses, British author John Drinkwater in *This Troubled World* (1933) offered a stern warning about the mechanistic worldview yet suggested there was hope in humanity. Others seemed to suggest that humanity could do little.

Attacking the Machine through Film. In 1936 Charlie Chaplin starred as a factory worker in the movie *Modern Times*. Although as a motion picture it was obviously a reflection of the mechanization of the arts, it actually attacked the process of machinery in no uncertain terms despite its comic content. As his character tries to adapt to the ever-increasing speed of the conveyor belt, he becomes part of the cogs. To rebel is to face physical and mental trouble as well as to lose one's job. Although at times heavily ideological and exaggerated to please audiences, *Modern Times* represented a mechanized attempt at understanding machine technology. As if to symbolize the inexorable march of progress, for the first time in his movies Chaplin's voice was heard, indicating that another page in technical mastery had been turned.

World Fairs. In the 1930s two great American world fairs introduced Americans to marvels of their era, maintaining the dream aspect of science and technology despite the grim realities of industrialization and economic depression. At the Century of Progress exposition in Chicago in 1933–1934 spectators were able to admire a "crystal house" of tomorrow as well as an impromptu visit by the German airship *Graf Zeppelin*. The various shows and exhibits were as much popular entertainment as they were a way to bolster the image of the industries involved in putting the fair together. By 1939, when light shows and grandiose construction might not outdo the real thing in modern New York City, the landscaping of the future and the successes of scientific research were emphasized. It was as if, now that tools such as the airplane, the locomotive, and the skyscraper were common, it were possible to concentrate on the big picture; even the risk of natural catastrophes was mentioned as a solvable problem. There was nothing to worry about, as if one were vacationing in a theme park. The expectation that humanity would succeed and survive was perhaps best summarized by the sealing of a time capsule to be opened in the year 6939, which contains, besides messages from several luminaries, a blueprint for America's future as seen from 1939.

Malaise and New Horizons. Although the 1930s were a period of doubt and skepticism over the Depression and the fears of war, they also became the setting of remarkable successes in the sciences. Such achievements, contrasted with concerns over their use, characterized what is called the second stage of modernism. A side effect of this new stage was the new lease on life given both science and technology in science fiction. Although not utopian in outlook, in much science fiction of the decade humanity might still succeed in overcoming its problems provided it paid more attention to the consequences of what was being viewed as progress. In the 1930s the seeds for a technological consciousness were planted, but it would take the risk of atomic annihilation that appeared in the 1940s to make these seeds flourish.

TOPICS IN THE NEWS

ASTRONOMY

Astronomical Leaps. In astronomy the greatest advance of the 1930s involved the discovery of the planet Pluto, the ninth and last in the solar system. The planet's existence was confirmed, almost by chance, on 18 February 1930 at the Lowell Observatory by Clyde William Tombaugh. Eight years later Seth Barnes Nicholson discovered the tenth and eleventh satellites of Jupiter. Solar research also advanced as astronomers learned, thanks to the advent of long-distance radio, the effects of solar activity on the earth's ionosphere. Such influence often caused static and blackout in communications. In 1932 an international network of solar observatories was created to ensure that the sun's activities could be observed around the clock. That same year the field of planetary physics also progressed when Walter Sydney Adams and Theodore Dunham Jr., both at the Mount Wilson Observatory, identified a thick layer of carbon dioxide as causing the absorption bands in the atmosphere of Venus.

New Answers and Questions about the Universe. In galactic astronomy Karl Jansky, a researcher at Bell Labs, discovered in 1931 a radio disturbance that became stronger every time he pointed a rotating antenna toward the center of the galaxy; unknowingly, he had noticed the radio emissions of the galaxy, a fact with important future consequences. Another fundamental step, this time in the field of stellar energy, was made in 1939 at Cornell University by German-born physicist Hans Bethe. He pointed out that stellar energy was in fact the result of nuclear fusion reactions, which formed a carbon-hydrogen cycle that later carried his name. His discovery made possible new advances in nuclear physics and posited a temperature of 18.5 million degrees Kelvin (approximately 333 million degrees Fahrenheit) at the center of the sun, a figure fairly close to British physicist Arthur Stanley Eddington's earlier prediction of 19 million degrees Kelvin (approximately 342 million degrees Fahrenheit). Bethe's theory also helped explain how stars enter

phases in which they can maintain stationary states thanks to the carbon-hydrogen cycle.

Hubble's Legacy. Meanwhile, astronomer Edwin Powell Hubble proposed a constant to determine the age of the universe that gave a result of only two billion years. This contradicted what was already known about the age of the earth and other celestial objects. Subsequent measurements corrected the discrepancy, and Hubble's research was summarized in his 1936 book *The Realm of the Nebulae*, widely considered a milestone in the history of astronomy. His work opened the possibility of investigation into the nature of star clusters, especially with regard to their dynamics and mass. Similarly, research on stellar evolution brought about theories on the nature of neutron stars, believed to be composed of protons and electrons melted together. The nature of the interaction of subatomic particles, however, remained the chief concern of physics.

Sources:

Arthur Stanley Eddington, *The Expanding Universe* (Cambridge: Cambridge University Press, 1933);

Edwin Hubble, *The Realm of the Nebulae* (New Haven: Yale University Press, 1936).

ATOMS AND MORE: PHYSICS

The Physical World. Physics arguably got one of its great boosts in the 1930s thanks to work in the United States and Europe. However, the flow of scientists fleeing European dictatorships for the United States also contributed substantially to progress in America. Cosmic rays constituted a subject of interest in astrophysics, as Carl David Anderson in 1932 confirmed the existence of the antielectron, or positron, whose existence the British physicist P. A. M. Dirac had predicted. Pursuing research together with Seth Neddermayer, Anderson discovered the existence of another particle in 1937, which he first called a meson; its mass was greater than that of the electron but smaller than that of the proton. This discovery caused several problems in the establishment of experimental conditions in a particle accelerator; since the direction of these particles' energy could not be predicted, detectors might not react with the expected accuracy. Eventually the presumed meson failed to react as predicted by other scientists, and its name was changed to muon because of its differing characteristics.

New Aspects of the Atom. The Berkeley Laboratory in California, under the leadership of Ernest O. Lawrence, attracted many scientists interested in working with the first cyclotron, a particle accelerator invented by Lawrence and built by Niels Edlefsen and the ancestor of the huge circular accelerators of the post–World War II era. In 1932 James Chadwick of England discovered the neutron, which forms the basis of nuclear fission. In 1934 Frédéric Joliot-Curie and Irène Joliot-Curie announced the first case of artificially produced radioactivity. Two years later Hungarian-born American physicist Eugene Paul Wigner established the mathematics that ruled the way in which neutrons were absorbed by an atom's nucleus and how the mathematics varied according to the neutron's energy. Thus, the neutron became the particle of choice in bombarding elements to obtain isotopes. Specialists in the field included Enrico Fermi and Emilio Segrè, both of whom would later work in the United States. In 1938 this line of work gained in importance with the discovery in Germany and Sweden by Otto Hahn, Lise Meitner, and Fritz Strassmann that bombarding a uranium isotope could result in liberating enormous amounts of energy. In New York in 1939 Danish physicist Niels Bohr described this process of fission at a meeting of the American Physical Society.

Working toward the Bomb. By that time scientists working in the United States were especially concerned with drawing the interest of the American government to

Nobel Prize winner Ernest Lawrence with his cyclotron, built in 1937

the potential of atomic science, fearing that other nations might gain an advantage. Fermi, Leo Szilard, and several other physicists took steps first to interest the American military in 1938, then to draw President Franklin D. Roosevelt's attention. Szilard convinced the openly pacifist Albert Einstein to write the president on 2 August 1939 to request that an atomic bomb be built before Nazi Germany could develop one.

Sources:

J. L. Heilbron and Robert W. Seidel, *Lawrence and His Laboratory* (Berkeley: University of California Press, 1989);

Richard Rhodes, *The Making of the Atomic Bomb* (New York: Simon & Schuster, 1986).

CHEMISTRY

New Elements and Substances. In chemistry in the 1930s most of the holes on Dmitry Ivanovich Mendeleyev's periodic table of chemical elements were filled. Emilio Segrè, working from the foundation of demonstrations carried out by Robert Oppenheimer, tracked down the element with atomic number 43, technetium, which turned out to be the simplest element with no isotope. Only the elements for atomic numbers 61, 85, and 87 were missing, with 87 being discovered by French chemist Marguerite Perey in 1939 and named francium for her native country. Work on discovering stable isotopes to various elements also continued. In 1931 Harold Urey was able to isolate an isotope of hydrogen with one proton and one neutron, which was named deuterium. In 1935 physicist Arthur Jeffrey Dempster showed that uranium has one isotope occurring in one out of 140 atoms, uranium 235. This substance would become essential to the manufacture of the first atomic bomb.

Early refrigeration units used ammonia and sulfur dioxide to lower temperature through evaporation. These substances were quite dangerous, however, and a search for a stable and odorless liquid was pursued. American chemist Thomas Midgley had discovered such a liquid in 1921, but it was not until 1930 that he synthesized a substance with these properties. Trademark uses were established, and such products as Freon, deemed completely safe at the time, went on sale and were used in refrigeration units. A 1931 survey by twenty leading refrigerator manufacturers revealed that three million Americans protected their food through the use of electric refrigerators. In 1930 1,002,000 refrigerators were sold. Of these, 770,000 were household refrigerators sold for a total of $223,320,000, or approximately 31 percent of the value of all household electric appliances. Nevertheless, these impressive numbers paled when compared to the number of American homes actually equipped with refrigerators: 14.7 percent, mostly in urban areas already served by electric power plants.

Source: F. D. McHugh, "The Scientific American Digest," *Scientific American,* 144 (May 1931): 350.

Vitamins. Several vitamins and substances were either discovered to exist or were successfully synthesized during the 1930s. Vitamins had been known since the 1900s, but despite their use in nutrition and medicine their molecular structure remained unknown. This changed in 1930 when the Swiss chemist Paul Karrer synthesized vitamin A, which resembles half a molecule of carotene. Two years later American biochemist Charles Glen King claimed that he had discovered vitamin C; however, within weeks biochemist Albert Szent-Györgyi claimed the same result with hexuronic acid. Although the latter was the correct form, the controversy raged on while the two were still alive. In 1933 British chemist Sir Norman Haworth synthesized vitamin C and named it ascorbic acid; he later received the Nobel Prize for his effort. In 1936 Roger J. Williams was able to synthesize vitamin B, found in rice and used to prevent beriberi. In 1939 Edward Adelbert Doisy, working from studies done by Danish scientist Carl Peter Henrik Dam, was able to synthesize vitamin K, a substance essential to blood coagulation, for the first time.

The Nature of Enzymes. American chemists also made great progress in isolating enzymes during the 1930s. The crystallization process, by which a liquid solution is saturated, thus forming crystals, was difficult — its first success dated to 1926 — yet essential in determining the nature of enzymes, because when successful, it allowed a more precise identification of the substance under investigation. In 1930 John Howard Northrop was able to crystallize a digestive enzyme named pepsin, and he showed it to be a protein. His success inspired biochemist Wendell Stanley to use a similar technique to define the structure of viruses. He started work by growing tobacco and infecting it (the tobacco mosaic virus was the first recognized as a virus in the late nineteenth century). He then mashed the leaves and put them through the same procedures as those used to extract enzymes. In 1935 he isolated fine crystals with the same properties as the virus. He thus proved that crystallization was not a life-ending process and that viruses were such a simple life form that they could live in a crystalline state. In the field of hormone research Edward Kendall isolated twenty-eight different cortical hormones and selected the most effective compounds for tests. One of them, isolated as compound E, showed remarkable results in fighting inflammations and became known as cortisone.

Industry and Research. In 1930 about 945 science doctorates were conferred in the United States, including 332 in chemistry and 109 in physics. Ten years later the overall number in doctorates conferred would reach 1,452, with a slight increase in the percentage of chemistry degrees (33.4 percent or 532 degrees) and a decrease in physics degrees (9 percent or 132, down from 11.5 percent). Such numbers reflect the strong influence of chemistry in American science. The predominance of the discipline was further confirmed by the number of prestigious awards going to chemists as well as the naming of such scientists to high academic posts. Furthermore, the trend toward the formation of chemical laboratories in the 1920s continued in the 1930s thanks to the support of the chemical-process industries. Between 1927 and 1938, for example, the number of research workers at Dow Chemical jumped from one hundred to five hundred, while those in the petroleum industry increased from several hundred to more than five thousand in the same period.

Professionalization. As the number of chemists grew, so did specializations. The 1930s witnessed the creation of two new associations, thus further recognizing subspecialties in the field: the American Society of Brewing Chemists was formed in 1934, followed a year later by the American Microchemical Society. A new publication, the *Journal of Organic Chemistry,* was established in 1936, thus becoming the eleventh American chemistry journal since the appearance of the *Journal of the American Chemical Society* in 1876. (Of those, six were founded in the 1920s.) The 1930s, especially the later part of the decade, thus witnessed a jump in the professionalization of the field.

Source:
Arnold Thackray and others, *Chemistry in America 1876–1976* (Hingham, Mass.: Kluwer Academic Publishers, 1985).

THE DECLINE OF THE EUGENICS MOVEMENT

The Origins of Modern Eugenics. The modern idea of eugenics originated in England in 1883 with Sir Francis Galton, a cousin of Charles Darwin who helped found a British society to study eugenics. A sister organization to the British group, the American Eugenics Society, was formed in the United States in 1935. The implicit belief of eugenicists was that races were genetically superior or inferior and that to mix races meant putting "pure racial stocks" at risk. Scientific evidence gathered through the genetic study of plant observation suggests that the contrary result is the case.

Eugenics in the United States. In the early 1930s the concept of selected sterilization, mostly of those in mental institutions, was commonly accepted in twenty-seven states, although several eventually withdrew the legislation authorizing the practice. The idea behind the practice was that to succeed in building a strong nation, social engineering had to extend into controlling the human reproductive cycle. In 1934 *Scientific American* did not hesitate to proclaim that "one-fifth of the population of the United States today is surplus," while noting that the eugenics movement had not yet proved its case for full population control. Such caveats did little to temper the partisans of full-scale eugenics.

The German-American Connection. Until 1933 the American eugenics movement displayed strong power in influencing domestic legislation concerning race and racial purity, and American eugenicists received praise from Europeans, especially German eugenics advocates. By the time the Nazis came to power it was commonly believed that the two leading eugenics movements were in the United States and Germany. Nazi Germany purported to follow the precedents set by American sterilization policies, especially the California sterilization law. Soon, however, Nazi propaganda took the lead in explaining the benefits of sterilization for a "purer race." Furthermore, Nazi policies extended to the whole German nation, while eugenic laws in the United States encountered obstacles at federal, state, and local levels. The secretary of the American Eugenics Society, Leon F. Whitney, reported on a regular basis on the progress of Nazi policy. It seemed to American eugenicists that the German treatment of the Jews, including sterilization, beatings, and arbitrary arrests, was no different from the American treatment of blacks and was therefore acceptable in their eyes. However, as German measures against the Jews became even more radical, including deportation and summary executions, relations between the American and German eugenics movements cooled considerably. Nazi abuses of eugenics in the name of anti-Semitic policy tainted the term and might have contributed to the toning down of American rhetoric in the field. The rise of genetics as an established field of biology also dispelled eugenic myths.

UNITED STATES PLANT PATENT Nº 1

Working on raising trailing roses, Henry F. Rosenberg of New Brunswick, New Jersey, was able to reproduce asexually a new kind, previously unknown in the United States or elsewhere. Under the conditions set forth in Section 4886 of the Revised Statutes of Patents approved by Congress on 23 May 1930, Rosenberg filed an application on 6 August 1930 for a "climbing or trailing rose" that was approved on 18 August 1931. The patent claimed an "everblooming habit" from spring through fall in the New Brunswick region. At the time the value of granting plant patents was deemed recognizable only in cases in which a legal battle over property ensued. No thoughts were given yet to the development of agricultural farming seeds mutated for greater returns.

Source: Orson D. Munn, "United States Plant Patent No. 1," *Scientific American*, 145 (November 1931): 303.

Sources:

Ignatius Cox, "The Folly of Human Sterilization," *Scientific American*, 151 (October 1934): 188–190;

Stefan Kühl, *The Nazi Connection: Eugenics, American Racism, and German National Socialism* (New York: Oxford University Press, 1993);

J. H. Landman, "Race Betterment by Human Sterilization," *Scientific American*, 150 (June 1934): 292–295.

DEVELOPMENTS IN BIOLOGY

Genetics Comes to the Fore. In the 1930s the study of genetics was the focus of both heavy activity and frustration. By then it had become clear that to investigate how genes mutated would require methods beyond those used in most experiments. Genetics as a field was subjected to two main schools of thought. One was German biologist August Weismann's study of germ plasm, which focused on the transmission of dominant and recessive traits. The other was Hugo de Vries's work on mutation, which sought to explain how genetic traits are altered. The studies conducted up to the 1930s led to an important question: how do fixed genes nonetheless produce species mutation? Furthermore, microscopy was not advanced enough to provide more information, since even large genes could not be observed. In Germany and Russia botanists and geneticists took steps to ensure the purity of the genes analyzed so as to ensure maximum certainty of the results obtained, as in the case of studies of the fruit fly. These steps, which included strict selection of specimens analyzed, were essential in adding new information to what was known about genes, but not until the 1950s did a clearer understanding of the role of genes in biology appear. Meanwhile, the slow progress of genetics prompted the development of a movement bent on merging genetics and embryology, arguably the strongest fields of American biology. In the nineteenth century genetics and embryology had been identical disciplines, but in the decades prior to the 1930s researchers rarely combined the two. The pioneering embryologist Thomas Hunt Morgan succeeded in combining the statistic-genetic and the microscopic research methods in hereditary research, an approach he described in his book *Embryology and Genetics* (1934), which emphasized the overlap between the two disciplines and thus the need for collaboration instead of competition. This was difficult for many embryologists, who began to view geneticists as an open threat in both research and teaching. Nevertheless, between 1938 and 1940 several attempts were made at healing the rift between the two fields. The German-Jewish émigré Richard B. Goldschmidt and E. E. Just both issued studies summarizing the issues. Both, however, were ignored, and Just left the United States when it became clear that he would be more easily accepted in Europe as a black scientist than in his native country. Eventually, a truce was reached when British biologist C. H. Waddington demonstrated the clear need for separate programs of research.

Primatology. The study of primates also took off during the 1930s, albeit at a slow speed. A pioneer in the field was Clarence Ray Carpenter, who studied hierarchical dominance and contrasted observations of laboratory specimens with results obtained through field research. In so doing he built on the work of Robert M. Yerkes, who focused on the chimpanzee as a base model of human life, thus suggesting that certain basic behaviors in groups were common to both species. Carpenter was able to observe many primates imported into the United States for use in medical experimentation. His work was further distinguished by his use of social-science techniques and his theoretical complexity. This method, sociometry, was in common use in social psychology in the 1930s and involved diagrams in which each individual of a group was placed in relation to the others, permitting a structural analysis of the group as a whole and clarifying the function of the group according to the activity of each individual. Another method he applied was semiotics, a science of signs, in an attempt to clarify communications within the group studied. The two approaches, as well as physiology, became a common part of primatology in the 1940s.

Sources:

Scott F. Gilbert, "Ernest Everett Just, Richard B. Goldschmidt, and the Attempt to Reconcile Embryology and Genetics," in *The American Development of Biology*, edited by Ronald Rainger, Keith Benson, and Jane Maienschen (Philadelphia: University of Pennsylvania Press, 1988), pp. 311–346;

Donna Haraway, "Signs of Dominance: From a Physiology to a Cybernetics of Primate Society — C. R. Carpenter, 1930–1970," in *Studies in Biology*, volume 6, edited by William Coleman and Camille Limoges (Baltimore: Johns Hopkins University Press, 1983), pp. 129–219;

Ernst Mayr, *The Growth of Biological Thought: Diversity, Evolution, and Inheritance* (Cambridge, Mass.: Harvard University Press, 1982).

EARTH SCIENCES

Looking at Earth. The earth sciences in the 1930s pitted competing theories of continental drift against one another. German scientist Alfred Wegener's theory, proposed in 1912, was supported by geological and paleontological comparisons between South Africa and South America; similarities found on both continents suggested that they might have been joined before being forced apart. Other scientists, such as Hans Cloos, continued to oppose the idea of a continental drift caused by shifting tectonic plates, while others thought the theory helped explain the structures of certain mountain chains as well as other features.

Studies of the Weather. Meteorology in the 1930s was dominated by ideas originating in Norway regarding isobaric observations as more effective, precise, and practical than previous options for the study of weather. The challenge was to adapt them for use in other regions of the globe with varying climatic pressures. The radiosonde — a radio transmitter, usually carried on a weather balloon, used to collect information on weather conditions — was widely in use by the end of the decade and allowed the drawing of isobaric surfaces, regions where similar barometric pressures exist, both in absolute terms and relative to a selected altitude. Such diagrams had existed as early as 1910, but it was not until 1934 that they were introduced on a daily basis by the German scientist Richard Scherhag. In addition, the theory devised around 1930 by T. Bergeron and W. Findeisen in the field of dynamic climatology (the statistical treatment of air masses and fronts) contributed to explaining precipitation.

Redefining Earthquakes. In January 1935 seismologist Charles Richter, working at the California Institute of Technology in Pasadena, devised a new way of determining the intensity of earthquakes. He defined the magnitude of a quake as the logarithm of the height of its seismograph trace in microns (one micron is one one-thousandth of a millimeter). If the trace of an earthquake reached one centimeter (ten millimeters, or ten thousand microns), the magnitude would be four, for ten to the fourth power; at ten centimeters (one hundred thousand microns) it would be five. The basis of the measurement was a seismograph magnifying the ground movement twenty-eight hundred times at a distance of one hundred kilometers (sixty-two miles) from the quake's epicenter. Richter also established conversion charts for the previously used Rossi-Forel and Mercalli scales. He first described his scale in the January 1935 issue of the *Bulletin of the Seismological Society of America*. Later Richter further refined his scale with the help of Beno Gutenberg by devising measuring scales for both surface and body waves. This in turn allowed him to correlate seismic waves with the energy output of a quake, whereby each Richter magnitude corresponds to a thirtyfold increase in energy. The determination of this relationship furthered the understanding of earthquake phenomena, most nota-

Dr. Charles Richter, director of the Carnegie Institution Seismological Laboratory, 25 January 1939

bly what forces are at work within the earth. Although Richter's scale was widely adopted by the scientific community, it did not become widely known to the media and the public until the 1950s.

Sources:
George A. Eiby, *Earthquakes* (New York: Van Nostrand Reinhold, 1980), pp. 78–80;

C. F. Richter, *Elementary Seismology* (San Francisco: Freeman, 1958).

ENGINEERING IN BRIDGE BUILDING

Great Structures. The 1930s witnessed the construction and completion of some of the most famous bridges in the United States. Some incorporated novel experimental approaches, as in the case of the Rogue River Bridge in Gold Beach, Oregon. This structure, comprising seven 230-foot two-rib arch spans, employed precompression techniques developed in France earlier in the century and was completed in 1931. Other projects not only proved to be engineering challenges but captured public attention. Ideas about extending a new

bridge from Manhattan directly into New Jersey over the Hudson River had been proposed since the 1890s but were bogged down in bureaucratic and political issues, ranging from concerns about hindering river traffic to engineering disagreements. Such disagreements still occur despite the successful completion and use of the George Washington Bridge. Thirty-five hundred feet long with a wire-cable suspension system, it was begun in 1927 and completed four years later under the supervision of Othmar H. Ammann, a Swiss-born engineer.

The California Challenge. In San Francisco plans for extending a massive bridge to Oakland had been proposed since the 1850s. Repeatedly these ideas were deemed utopian in view of the huge dimensions of the proposed project. Nevertheless, demands for construction became increasingly pressing. By 1928 about thirty private construction proposals existed, but California decided to build one bridge with public funds following the example of the George Washington Bridge. With the help of President Herbert Hoover, California established the Transbay Bridge (San Francisco/Oakland Bay

Site of the Golden Gate Bridge across the San Francisco Bay in 1935. Construction was begun 5 January 1933, and the bridge was opened on 1 October 1937.

Bridge) Project in September 1929. Following the submission of tentative layouts in the summer of 1930, the California legislature appropriated more funds the following year for further studies. The U.S. War Department, which controlled the mouth of the bay, revised the plans to allow easier water navigation below, and a construction permit was obtained on 19 January 1932. The next challenge was to solve the distance problem. While a suspended bridge was the preferred design, it was unclear where it could actually be suspended over a two-mile length over water. The final decision called for two suspended bridges placed back to back, with an overall length of 8,100 feet (43,500 feet including the approaches), which would make the project the largest suspended bridge in the world. Groundbreaking took place on 9 July 1933. Despite the national economic crisis, financing was solved with the issuing of bonds by the Reconstruction Finance Commission. The final cost of construction was $79.5 million. The bridge opened on 12 November 1936.

The Golden Gate. Plans for building a bridge over the Golden Gate had flourished during World War I, but it was not until the 1920s that projects were seriously developed and permissions granted. The Golden Gate Bridge Company, established in 1928, appointed Joseph Strauss as chief engineer in August 1929. Following multiple ground surveys and test borings, ground was broken on 5

January 1933. Not only did construction face the challenge of strong sea tides that required the construction of a fender-shaped seawall, but the question of whether the tower foundation could withstand an earthquake caused serious concern and still remains an issue. Despite such problems, the Golden Gate Bridge opened on 1 October 1937. The construction stands as a masterpiece of modern American bridge design and engineering.

Sources:

David Nye, *American Technological Sublime* (Cambridge, Mass.: MIT Press, 1994);

Daniel L. Schodek, *Landmarks in American Civil Engineering* (Cambridge, Mass.: MIT Press, 1987).

FROM RAILS TO ROADS: THE PLIGHT OF ROADS AND RAILROADS

The Value of Railroads. When the first American railroad experiments took place near Baltimore in the 1830s, horrified stagecoach drivers clamored for protection, fearing their livelihood was coming to an end in the face of the iron horse. Less than a century later it was the railroads' turn to scream for help. The Depression's impact on transportation was felt most notably in the railroad system, in which the number of carloads dropped from an average 4.5 million in 1929 to approximately 3 million in 1932. Due to a 1922 decree of the Interstate Commerce Commission, railroad operators were not allowed to exceed a profit of 5.75 percent on their invest-

Senator Clarence C. Dill and Rep. Sam Rayburn watching President Franklin D. Roosevelt sign the Railroad Reorganization bill in 16 June 1933

ments, yet even in the best years of the late 1920s they hardly reached that limit. Railroads complained of over-regulation; local, state, and federal taxation rules; and financial ratings lower than those of other transportation industries. Freight-car loading declined in the face of increasing truck competition, especially since trucking companies were not subjected to review by the Interstate Commerce Commission. Lack of taxation of roads and waterways was not the only problem for the nation's rail companies: shipments of oil, which had ensured a substantial income for years, slowly disappeared as pipelines were installed. Even the airplane, although it remained a means of transportation open only to a few well-to-do people, attracted some 327,211 passengers in 1930 and added around 21,000 passengers the following year, eroding the passenger base for the railroads.

Staying Afloat. In response, railroad companies fought to modernize. The Pennsylvania Railroad electrified its lines, while the Baltimore and Ohio introduced air-conditioned dining-car service, extending the "refrig-erated principle" to entire trains later in the decade. Long-distance speed trains, such as the Zephyr streamliner in use on the Minneapolis-Chicago line, were introduced; traveling eighty miles an hour, they would arrive on time even in tough winter weather. At the freight level, pickup and delivery service was instituted for distances where rail remained competitive with trucking. Yet these very pickup services demonstrated the interrelationship between highway and railroad in more-efficient transportation. Rail service remained important and efficient because the roads were in poor condition. In 1930, of the 325,000 miles of state and federal roads, only 226,000 were surfaced, while out of the 2.68 million miles of local roads, only 467,000 were covered. The impetus for surfacing the remainder, as argued by advocates, was commerce. Transportation experts envisioned that the railroads would service certain distances while goods could then be picked up by truck and carried to local destinations. Such reasoning became the foundation of the New Deal's road-building program.

Roosevelt's Roads. During one of his 1932 campaign speeches Franklin D. Roosevelt promised to develop both roads and railroads. The main issue in his view was "the entire absence of national planning." Good, cheap, and efficient transportation was vital to economic recovery, he said. The National Industrial Recovery Act (NIRA) called for federal involvement in putting the unemployed to work on a national road system. "We Do Our Part" became the NIRA motto and adorned many windshields. New parkways were built, based on designs of the 1920s. In the 1930s the Blue Ridge Parkway and the Natchez Trace Parkway, as well as many other roads, were opened to traffic. The NIRA put half a million men back to work building roads. One of the results was the ambitious Pennsylvania Turnpike, completed in 1940. A new kind of attraction, the highway, had appeared in American life.

Sources:

George H. Douglas, *All Aboard! The Railroad in American Life* (New York: Paragon House, 1992);

Stephen B. Goddard, *Getting There: The Epic Struggle Between Road and Rail in the American Century* (New York: Basic Books, 1992).

THE HOOVER DAM

The Value of a Dam. On 17 September 1930 U.S. Secretary of the Interior Ray Lyman Wilbur formally launched construction of the Boulder Dam at a site in the Black Canyon on the Colorado River, some hundred miles upstream from Needles, California, and 440 miles from the entrance of the Colorado River into the Gulf of California. The dam's location affected the water supply of six states: Arizona, California, Nevada, New Mexico, Utah, and Wyoming. Hence each of the concerned states wanted to obtain electricity from the dam project.

Planning. Following a federal government decision in 1922, the Colorado River Compact was created. U.S. Secretary of Commerce Herbert Hoover, also a respected engineer, not only ushered the projected dam through Congress but drafted solutions for an equitable distribution of the electricity produced by the dam. The projected cost of the construction was $165 million, which the federal government agreed to finance as a fifty-year loan. Once completed, the dam and the power plant were to provide between 1.6 and 1.8 million horsepower of electricity. The initial construction, begun in March 1931, consisted of driving four diversion tunnels and two spillways and lining them all with concrete. Construction of the intake towers began on 1 March 1932. The first concrete for the dam face itself, prepared at a special Nevada plant half a mile upstream from the inlet portals, was poured on 5 March 1932.

Distribution. Los Angeles, 266 miles away, applied to receive nearly all of the electricity produced at Boulder, eventually winning about a 65 percent allocation for itself and neighboring regions. The advantages were notable: while one kilowatt-hour of electricity produced at an oil-fired power plant cost four-tenths of a cent, the power

The Hoover Dam under construction, 17 August 1934

coming from the Boulder Dam cost less than half that amount. This allowed Los Angeles consumers to save approximately $1.3 million during the dam's first year of operation.

Achievement. Completion of the dam was a phenomenal feat, both for the designers and for those on the scene, who often worked in temperatures of one hundred degrees Fahrenheit or more. Many died from heat exhaustion, but contrary to popular myth no one was entombed in the concrete of the dam. Enthusiastic pride characterized those who worked on the construction, a reflection of the esteem of the public for technology and for the jobs and industries generated by the dam. In 1935 the dam was officially dedicated, and the first regular supply of electricity to Los Angeles occurred in the fall of 1936. Originally called Boulder Canyon Dam after the initial project name, it was renamed after President Hoover by an act of Congress in 1947. In addition to the stunning engineering feat of the Hoover Dam, it was completed ahead of schedule, and its federal loan was repaid on time.

Source:

J. E. Stevens, *Hoover Dam: An American Adventure* (Norman: University of Oklahoma Press, 1988).

THE RISE OF THE AIRPLANE

Messengers of Modernity. Among the most noticeable improvements in technology during the 1930s, aeronautics exhibited many successes. Apparently simple innovations introduced in the previous decade suddenly
yielded remarkable results, and aviation as a whole increased in importance in the public eye thanks in part to
publicity flights. In 1932, for example, Franklin D. Roosevelt, then governor of New York, chose to fly to Chicago to accept the Democratic presidential nomination,
introducing a new sense of modernity that suggested
progress might solve the economic decay of the nation.
Beyond politics, aviation matters also attracted public
attention, as speed and distance records were regularly
broken, making for front-page news. In 1931, for example, Wiley Post flew around the world in barely nine days,
only to renew the exploit two years later, this time in
eight days. The record would be cut in half in 1938 by a
young millionaire, Howard Hughes, whose business acumen was equaled only by his passion for aviation and who
would play an important role in the development of several airlines in the following decades. The 1930s also saw
the rise of aviatrix Amelia Earhart, who completed the
first female solo transatlantic crossing in 1932 and went
on to establish multiple distance and speed records until
her mysterious disappearance during a Pacific Ocean
flight in 1937. Charles Lindbergh, who had successfully
soloed across the Atlantic in 1927, carried on long-
distance flights in the company of his wife, writer Anne
Morrow Lindbergh, and served as an adviser to Pan
American Airways, which pioneered long-distance links
across the Pacific.

Records. The decade also witnessed the expansion of
specially designed races pitting daredevils against each
other in oddly shaped planes, such as the Gee Bee racer.
Although clearly more of a spectacle than a true technological competition, such races had valuable side effects,
spurring the introduction of retractable landing gear and
of more-powerful and more-reliable engines. The military would enjoy the benefits of such technical tinkering,
even though limited budgets and bureaucratic infighting
prevented a substantial air corps program until 1938.
Thus, during most of the decade the primary beneficiaries of such new technical systems would be civil and
commercial aircraft.

Transport Planes. The machines North American
Airlines bought in the 1930s represented the culmination
of earlier work in streamlining and metal and engine
development, thanks in part to studies undertaken by the
National Advisory Committee on Aeronautics (NACA)
and the aerial laboratory at the California Institute of
Technology funded by the Guggenheim family. Competition among the airlines advanced comfort and efficiency, thus resulting in the building and operation of
such machines as the Boeing 247 but most important in
the creation of the famous DC-3. At the invitation of
TWA, which wanted to compete with United's new

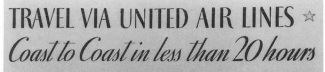

July 1933 advertisement for transcontinental air
passenger service

247s, Donald Douglas assembled a proposal to build the
DC-1 (DC standing for "Douglas Commercial"). The
DC-1, which like the 247 had an all-metal skin, offered
variable-pitch propellers, which allowed better modulation of speed, and NACA-designed wings. Instead
of the 247's ten-passenger capacity, the Douglas machine promised to seat twelve. By the time the prototype
flew on 1 July 1933 the decision had been made not to
build a series of it but rather to upgrade it with new
engines and rename it the DC-2. The new version established itself as one of the fastest passenger airliners. The
Douglas Company decided to consolidate its advance
over Boeing by offering American Airlines a new, larger
aircraft capable of carrying fourteen sleeping berths for
long distances. The Douglas Sleeper Transport (DST),
later known as the DC-3, could also be converted to carry
twenty-one passengers in a "day version." A cargo version, known as the C-47, was later built and provided
great service in air forces around the world. The passenger aircraft were not the only airplanes to mark the 1930s.
The decade also witnessed the creation of large flying
boats such as the Sikorsky S-42, the Martin Clippers, and
the Boeing 314, especially on the Pan Am Pacific routes.
Until the development of long-range pressurized four-
engine airliners in the 1940s, these flying boats would

The *Akron* dirigible being commissioned by Mrs. Herbert Hoover in Akron, Ohio, on 8 August 1931

represent the epitome of luxury in air travel — surpassed only by dirigible airships, whose advantages soon disappeared.

Sources:

Roger Billstein, *Flight in America* (Baltimore: Johns Hopkins University Press, 1985);

F. Robert van der Linden, *The Boeing 247* (Seattle: University of Washington Press, 1991).

SHIPS IN THE CLOUDS: THE GOLDEN AGE OF AIRSHIPS

U.S. Involvement. America's relationship to rigid airships was a troubled one. Aside from Germany and Great Britain, nowhere else was the promotion of dirigible transport such a large-scale affair. Beginning in the 1920s Goodyear built blimps for the U.S. Navy. However, the apparent sturdiness of bigger machines with an internal metal structure to sustain them had become legendary as a result of German airship operations during World War I. Eventually, following the purchase of a German-built machine, the *Los Angeles,* a contract with the Zeppelin Company in Germany cleared the way for the transfer of technological experience that would allow the construction of large rigid airships in the United States. Slow negotiations eventually led to a navy contract for two 6.5-million-cubic-foot airships, numbered ZRS-4 and ZRS-5, valued at $8 million each, signed in October 1928. The dock for the construction of the airships was completed a year later, and the first dirigible girders were laid in March 1930.

Akron and Macon. The main frames of the new dirigibles were large enough to permit crew members to

Indigenous in great quantities only to the United States, helium soon became the nonflammable gas of choice for lighter-than-air craft. In February 1930 the federal government inaugurated a new plant seven miles south of Amarillo, Texas, where a virgin gas field of approximately fifty thousand acres was thought to lie. Not only was the mined gas about 2 percent helium, but the pressure at which it was extracted from the ground required no further compression to carry out the extraction of the helium from the gas mixture. After purifying the natural gas of its relatively high carbon dioxide content (about 0.5 percent), separation of the helium from the other elements (mainly methane, ethane, and nitrogen) was carried out immediately upon cooling the compound to −300 degrees Fahrenheit, at which helium naturally separates itself from the other liquefied gases. Shipment of the helium, whose purity ranged from 40 to 80 percent, to army and navy flying fields was often done by tank trucks capable of holding some 200,000 cubic feet of helium.

Source: Clifford W. Seibel, *Helium, Child of the Sun* (Lawrence: University Press of Kansas, 1968).

Intended to celebrate the centennial of the founding of Chicago, the Century of Progress Exposition was a powerful event at its opening, thanks to its upbeat emphasis on scientific progress in stark contrast to the gloomy Depression atmosphere of the time. Architectural novelty was a trademark of the show, which included a cable-suspended dome inspired by the suspended bridge, as were unique forms of entertainment, including the visit of the *Graf Zeppelin* airship in the fall of 1933. The most popular exhibit of 1934 was the Industrial Hall, in which the latest technological innovations of Ford were displayed. By the time it closed, the exposition had attracted about sixteen million visitors.

Source: Robert W. Ryddell, "The Fan Dance of Science: America's World's Fairs in the Great Depression," *Isis*, 76 (December 1985): 525–542.

---

climb into them, as the navy had insisted that all areas be accessible in flight. The ships were constructed with wire-braced frames and three keels to prevent any risk of a structure breakup in flight, as had happened in 1925 to the navy's first rigid airship, the *Shenandoah*. The most interesting feature of the navy's new dirigibles was the intention to use them as flying aircraft carriers. Using a trapeze system that would allow airplanes with specially designed hooks to be caught in flight, the airships would thus become advanced scouting units. On 8 August 1931 the first machine was christened *Akron* before a crowd of 150,000. In November, following air trials, she made her first flight as a commissioned vessel of the U.S. Navy. Public relations played an important role in the ship's activities, as many within the public and the military remained skeptical of the value of airships as tactical weapons. Nevertheless, impressive long-distance flights — no airplane could ever claim to be able to spend sixty hours aloft during a strategic exercise — increased the reputation of the airship as a marvel machine. By spring 1932 the first "hook-ons" of airplanes were carried out. By then, however, funding for further operations slowed down, with the *Los Angeles* decommissioned as a cost-saving measure, and in July the *Akron* was detached from the fleet and assigned to train the crew of her sister ship, still being built. On the evening of 3 April 1933 the *Akron* took off on a routine training mission but encountered an unexpected storm in which she broke up: only three of the seventy-six crew members survived. The accident shook public confidence in the large-airship program, and opponents within the military saw this as their chance to reduce further funding. However, on 11 March ZRS-5 had been completed and was christened the *Macon*. A virtual copy of her ill-fated sister ship, she first flew three weeks after *Akron*'s crash and was commissioned on 23 June. In October *Macon* flew to her new base in California, leaving Lakehurst Naval Air Station in New Jersey for the last time. From then on the East Coast base would service only blimps and the German airships *Graf Zeppelin* and *Hindenburg* on their Atlantic crossings. American airship activities were scaled down, as training of airship personnel dwindled and Congress refused to appropriate further money for the construction of a machine to replace the *Akron*. Out in California, however, the *Macon* was successfully pressed into operations, patrolling small coastal areas rather than carrying out long-range flights. Nevertheless, she became the aircraft carrier navy planners had envisioned. On 12 February 1935, however, during what was intended as a routine scouting training between San Diego and Long Beach, a sudden gust of wind struck the machine, breaking one of the rear frames and damaging gas cells. Listing to the rear, the ship hit the water and sank within forty-five minutes. All but two of the crew survived. Thus ended the era of the American rigid airship.

Germany Remains. In Germany plans for the construction of a huge passenger airship bigger than the American models proceeded apace. Plans even called for the construction in the United States of civilian machines that would help establish a regular service between Europe and the United States throughout the year; at the time, winter flying was not under consideration. The airship *Graf Zeppelin,* considered a test machine, had already successfully crossed the Atlantic and visited Lakehurst several times. What was needed, however, was a machine able to carry fifty passengers with all the comfort and amenities available. In May 1936 the new ship, christened *Hindenburg,* first reached Lakehurst. A special American Airlines DC-3 service then took the passengers to the airport in Newark, and the apparent routine of the feat was noted in the media. Ten round trips had been made by the time the 1936 flying season came to an end. Each of these scheduled trips was printed in newspapers just like any other steamship, thus showing how the American public was beginning to accept the idea of air transport, including by passenger airships. The 1937 season, however, brought disaster. On arrival after her first North Atlantic crossing of the year, the *Hindenburg* caught fire, probably as a result of a static electricity buildup and because it contained hydrogen instead of helium, and was destroyed. Thirty-six passengers and crew died. Thus ended what has been termed the golden age of rigid airships. The last American airship, the *Los Angeles,* was broken up in 1939, and from then on only blimps were used by the U.S. Navy. The rigid airship thus represented a failed technology, although reasons for its demise were not singly attributable to poor design; political and financial reasons were just as important. While the airship would likely have lost out in due time to the speed and comfort provided by newer airplanes, its existence remains an important chapter in the history of American and world aviation.

Sources:

Harold Dick and Douglas Robinson, *The Golden Age of the Great Passenger Airships* (Washington, D.C.: Smithsonian Institution Press, 1985);

Richard K. Smith, *The Airships Akron and Macon* (Annapolis, Md.: Naval Institute Press, 1965).

SYNTHETIC RUBBER OR NYLON?

The Nature of Rubber. In the past rubber had to be imported from tropical lands where rubber trees grew. The material's strategic value was emphasized in World War I during the blockade of Germany, when shortages complicated the construction of military and civilian vehicles. After the war Du Pont began work on synthesizing artificial rubber. Using chloroprene, a product derived from acetylene, as a primary ingredient, the firm's chemists, in particular F. B. Downing, W. H. Carothers, and Ira Williams, eventually reached a satisfactory rubber substitute by incorporating substances derived from limestone, coal, salt, and water. The new product, christened "duprene" and introduced officially in late 1931, was intended to supplement natural rubber at first but already displayed one significant advantage in its properties, that of resisting the degrading effects of oxygen, kerosene, and gasoline. It also did not require the addition of sulfur to be vulcanized; heat alone was sufficient. Meanwhile, two

Nylon stockings being exhibited at the 1939 World's Fair in New York

other rubber technologists at Du Pont, Oliver M. Hayden and Ernest R. Bridgewater, working on a sample of duprene, concluded that what most differentiated this artificial rubber from previously produced kinds was that it had the same molecular structure as natural rubber. Du Pont also found that chloroprene could be used to make artificial latex, a waterproofer that could be applied to porous materials that usually could not be impregnated with natural latex. Yet when the new product was officially announced, the company was not sure what uses might exist for the product, which was turning out to be quite different from a mere rubber substitute. Not until 1937, after manufacturing problems had been solved, did neoprene — its name changed from the Duprene trademark — first become available commercially.

Looking for a Use for Nylon. Meanwhile, in another Du Pont laboratory a new synthetic material was being processed. Beginning in 1934 a joint effort was undertaken by separate Du Pont labs to develop a material that would be provided as an alternative to silk on the hosiery market. By 1936 determination of the polymer to be used was complete, and both financing and test production were under way. A year later small-scale equipment produced yarns of the new material known as "Fiber 66," which were knitted into hosiery. In the following months these stockings and their silk counterparts appeared indistinguishable. Early tests showed that it could be given

On 30 April 1936 at a joint meeting of the American Physical Society and the Institute of Radio Engineers, both George C. Southworth of the Bell Laboratories and Wilmer L. Barrow of MIT, working independently of each other, announced the invention of a coaxial cable utilizing ultrahigh-frequency radio waves. This cable allowed an increase in the number of phone communications being carried over a single line. The Bell system, which had been tested between New York and Philadelphia, allowed as many as thirty-five voice channels. A coaxial cable was formed of two copper tubes about as thick as a pencil, each carrying messages in one direction. In the middle of each tube a wire was held by pieces of hard rubber so that it would not touch the metal. Eventually, the first commercial link, in the summer of 1941, would provide six hundred channels.

Source: George P. Oslin, *The Story of Telecommunications* (Macon, Ga.: Mercer University Press, 1992).

The idea of making electric typewriters to increase their speed and efficiency was applied experimentally as early as 1900, but repeated experiments failed to convince manufacturers and clients that such complicated contraptions might become part of everyday life. By the 1930s the concept of portable mechanical typewriters was aggressively marketed, and despite the Depression the typewriter industry managed to survive, since its product had become so essential to the business world — even bankruptcy papers required typing. Among the typewriter companies either failing or being taken over, the Northeast Electric Company, which had been attempting to expand the use of electricity in offices, was bought out by International Business Machines (later IBM). The office giant in effect rescued an idea from experimental oblivion, as it started work toward what would later become the standard office business typewriter. It would be another quarter century, however, until the electric machine truly gained a foothold in American businesses.

Source: Bruce Bliven Jr., *The Wonderful Writing Machine* (New York: Random House, 1954).

a variety of shapes or forms yet retain its properties. A pilot plant was then built and started up in the summer of 1938. All that remained was to find a name. Of the 395 suggested by a committee, nuron came closest to the chosen name, and following two changes to avoid close-sounding names, nylon was chosen but not registered. It was left in the public domain, where it soon became a synonym for stockings. As of March 1939 some five thousand pairs of "nylons" had been sold out of the pilot plant, and licensing was soon under way.

Source:
David A. Hounshell and John Kenly Smith Jr., *Science and Corporate Strategy: Du Pont R&D, 1902–1980* (New York: Cambridge University Press, 1988).

TELEVISION

The Struggle to Transmit. The origins of television date back to 1884 with a patent given to Paul Nipkow of Germany for an image-sensitive disk. By 1931, following experimentation in radio laboratories, television was tried out in several "public" experiments. One group involved in attempting to develop the medium was the Jenkins Television Corporation in New York City, which installed a five-thousand-watt television transmitter in the same building as its studios. Collaborating with Jenkins, the General Broadcasting System used station WGBS on Long Island to schedule the synchronized sound equipment needed for the television studios. At the receiver end two units were required, one normal broadcast receiver and one short-wave television screen. Although the two units were separate, the idea was that since both signals were beamed at the same time, they should be

received at the same time, albeit on different frequencies, and thus synchronize automatically. The reconstitution of the image left much to be desired and depended as much on the scanning of the image at the source as it did on atmospheric conditions separating the places of emission and reception. At the receiving end the problem depended on the projection of light onto the screen. Devices ranged from neon-powered "crater lamps" modulated by incoming radio waves to modified shadow boxes or even a complex disk made of some sixty lenses to scan the light. Finally, to see the image, usually limited to one or two characters, one had to be in direct line with the television. Even a ten-foot-wide experimental receiver built by Sanabria suffered from such impediments, meaning that television images did not yet reach a level of quality comparable to that of early movies. Experimental emissions nevertheless continued.

Early Operations. In 1935 RCA, owner of NBC Radio, announced that it would spend $1 million on transmissions out of its New York Radio City base using the Empire State Building as a transmitter. By 1937 experimental programs were well under way, and technical standards had improved thanks in part to a new camera known as the iconoscope. A year later mobile units were available, and NBC conducted interviews with passersby in Rockefeller Plaza. The company went on to prepare a formal broadcast of the inauguration of the

New York World's Fair on 30 September 1939. Thus, President Franklin D. Roosevelt became the first American leader to appear on television as he opened the exhibit. Of course, few saw him on the screen. A television set at the fair was to be had for $200 to $660, depending on the options included, at a time when an average new car cost $1,000, and the amount of programming was limited to ten to fifteen hours a week. Not until transmission and reception standards improved several years later did television truly spread among the American public.

Sources:

A. P. Peck, "Where Is Television?," *Scientific American*, 146 (May 1932): 284–285;

D. E. Repogle, "Television Now on Schedule," *Scientific American*, 145 (July 1931): 33.

WOMEN IN SCIENCE

More Female Scientists. The number of female scientists increased substantially in the 1930s, rising approximately 320 percent beyond what it was in the early 1920s yet remaining low in relation to the number of men who earned degrees in the sciences. A 1938 survey listed a total of 1,726 women scientists, excluding the medical sciences. The largest numbers in 1938 were spread over zoology (281), psychology (277), and botany (256), while the lowest were in engineering (8), anthropology (29), and astronomy (36). The statistics, however, only indicate the number of female scientists who actually got jobs, as opposed to those who had trained in those fields but got by on various grants. How widely a scientific field was taught, in addition, was likely to influence the accessibility of the field to women. Female zoologists graduated from 105 different institutions, while the sixty-three physicists came from some thirty-three schools. Thus, the greater number of some women in one discipline reflected its wider presence in the culture. Many of these women had earned Ph.D's.

Source:

Margaret W. Rossiter, *Women Scientists in America: Struggles and Strategies to 1940* (Baltimore: Johns Hopkins University Press, 1982).

HEADLINE MAKERS

RUTH BENEDICT

1887-1948

ANTHROPOLOGIST

The Role of a Father. When asked about her formative years, Ruth Benedict acknowledged the important role her father had played in her childhood. A homeopathic surgeon whose success was thwarted by illness and who died when she was twenty-one months old, he became in her understanding of his memory a man fascinated with work and research, which she sought to equal. She attended Vassar College and graduated in 1909 after having been exposed to various ideas concerning women's rights, including the rights of women to study and have a profession. In 1914 she married Stanley Rossiter Benedict, a professor of biochemistry. In 1921, after spending eighteen months at the New School, she entered the Ph.D. program at Columbia, where Franz Boas became her mentor. She enjoyed anthropology because of the community of minds she encountered and also for the challenge of creating a space for herself as a woman.

Coming to the Fore. By December 1921 Benedict had presented her first paper at the meeting of the American Anthropological Association. The meticulousness of her investigation of visions in the cultures of the Great Plains Indian tribes impressed the audience, and it was immediately accepted for publication in the association's respected journal. Her chosen byline for it and for her dissertation, finished soon after, was Ruth Fulton Benedict, her maiden and married names combined — a feminist move that raised eyebrows at the time. Despite her early success, throughout the 1920s she jumped from one academic position to another. Thanks to Boas, in June 1931 she became assistant professor of anthropology at Columbia University.

The Importance of Culture. In 1934 Benedict published *Patterns of Culture*, her most popular work of anthropology. Not only did it open new directions in anthropological studies, it also raised new issues and concerns in philosophy and methodology by reintroducing subjectivity, which had previously been rejected in anthropology. The main thrust of her argument was that cultures should be studied as a whole rather than by their specific traits alone. This idea contributed to a split between the "scientific" and "historical" sides of the discipline. Nevertheless, her advocacy of cultural relativism, the idea that unacceptable behavior in one culture might in fact be tolerated or even welcome in another, set the stage for an anthropological focus on culture and the individual. Benedict also worked on issues of racism, striving to dispel racial myths. This also led her to apply some of her conclusions to politics. For example, she suggested in 1943 in her article "Recognition of Cultural Diversities in the Postwar World," published in the *Annals of the American Academy of Political and Social Sciences*, that democracy and its practice might be understood and applied differently in the United States and elsewhere in the world.

Benedict's Legacy. Besides initiating a culture and personality movement within anthropology, Benedict's *Patterns of Culture* is also a major work in twentieth-century American intellectual history; it provided a framework of thought in pre–World War II America in which relative statements replaced absolute ones. Her later books, including *The Chrysanthemum and the Sword: Patterns of Japanese Culture* (1946), carried on this legacy. Although her advocacy that each culture is unique and can be measured and understood only on its own terms caused serious controversy in post–World War II American anthropology, some of its associated ideas of dispelling stereotypes and fighting racism remain respected ideals.

Source:
Judith Schachter Modell, *Ruth Benedict: Patterns of a Life* (Philadelphia: University of Pennsylvania Press, 1983).

FRANZ BOAS

1858-1942

ANTHROPOLOGIST

The Science of Anthropology. Whereas Ruth Benedict offered new directions in anthropology, Franz Boas is probably the figure that made anthropology a scientific endeavor. Born in northern Germany in 1858, he studied at the universities of Heidelberg, Bonn, and Kiel, earning a doctorate in physics with a minor in geography. Following his first study expedition, to the Arctic, he visited the United States in 1884 and two years later emigrated from Germany because he perceived greater freedom in the United States to develop his own path of study. Following a brief stint as assistant editor for the journal *Science,* he taught and researched at Clark University, the University of Chicago, the American Museum of Natural History, and Columbia University. During his career he published about ten thousand pages on northwestern Native American societies. He also published general and specialized scientific books.

The Engaged Scientist. Boas's effort to teach anthropology at the turn of the century met with various difficulties. Such posts were few, and anthropology was rarely considered a science in its own right, alternately treated as part of psychology or natural history. His justification for studying foreign cultures — that closer political and economic relations with such nations as Japan required a better understanding of the culture to be successful — predated such a common-sense approach by half a century in some cases. He also led the mapping and study of North American and Asian aboriginal societies, using data gathered by the Jesup North Pacific Expedition. Such endeavors confirmed the need for on-site investigations, as opposed to the armchair comparative research that had been the preferred method for decades. However, Boas did not go so far as to consider analyzing common societal problems within different societies. This particular field of cultural anthropology, or ethnology, still lacked the tools necessary to understand truly and compare different societies in their cultural contexts and would require the contributions of some of Boas's students, including Benedict, before coming to fruition. Nonetheless, his concerns with human inequality established the bases necessary to further ethnological studies.

Fighting Racism through Science. Throughout his studies Boas was interested in the issues surrounding the classification of human types and the conclusions derived from it, which included claims of racial superiority and inferiority. He attacked the issue by elaborating on specific concepts, thus slowly chipping away at the greater issues. For example, he showed how variations among individuals within one race were greater than those among races; thus, to emphasize "racial" difference was to ignore the basic unity of human form. It followed that the difference between "primitive" and "civilized" ways of life could not be determined based on how and where a people lived and that there was a need to study definitions of "progress" more closely. Thanks perhaps to the open scientific mind he had cultivated and to the work he had done on race, he became an involved citizen, treating questions of nationalism and eugenics. When Adolf Hitler became chancellor of Germany in 1933, Boas tirelessly criticized him and his actions, warning of the dangers of fascist thought. He further combated racism through his work, including *The Mind of Primitive Man,* which, although first published in 1911, underwent a third edition in 1938 and involved issues of practical humanitarian consequences for future public policy.

Boas's Anthropology. Some of Boas's pioneering efforts remained in the vanguard of anthropology well after his death. In particular, his effort at applying anthropological methods to everyday problems signaled a marked difference between the traditional field, limited to museums and university training, and the wider sphere of public pedagogy. While some scholars have referred to a "Boas school" of anthropology to designate his approach to teaching and research, this phrase is likely a misnomer since many of the students he trained, including Benedict, became significant scholars in their own right. What Boas communicated was an open-mindedness necessary to consider the different ways humans can behave, the tools to distinguish behavior from other traits, and a sense of responsibility for what one wrote or said based on the research conducted. His legacy included uncovering the complexities of African culture and dispelling many myths of inferiority that provided the basis for segregation in the United States, as well as advocating as early as 1906 equal levels of education. Such efforts demonstrated the duties of the scientist as an engaged citizen.

Sources:

Franz Boas, *The Shaping of American Anthropology 1883–1911: A Franz Boas Reader,* edited by George W. Stocking Jr. (New York: Basic Books, 1974);

June Helm, ed., *Pioneers of American Anthropology: The Uses of Biography* (Seattle: University of Washington Press, 1966).

RICHARD E. BYRD

1888-1957

EXPLORER

The Fascination with Exploration. Born to an established family, Richard E. Byrd — whose brother, Harry Flood Byrd, was governor of, and later U.S. senator from, Virginia — attended the U.S. Naval Academy in Annapolis, Maryland, and started an officer's career through which he rose to the rank of commander. Although he was forced to retire in 1916 because of a bad leg, he remained active in a variety of land posts, in particular in Pensacola, Florida, where he learned to fly. Throughout he remained fascinated with the various attempts that surrounded polar exploration and soon convinced several industrialists as well as the National Geographic Society to support a flight attempt to the North Pole from the islands of Spitsbergen north of Norway, a preferred departure point for air expeditions. In May 1926 Byrd succeeded in flying to the North Pole. Although his claim to success has been challenged several times, he nevertheless gained heroic status in the American public's mind. The image stuck when he also successfully flew across the Atlantic shortly after Charles Lindbergh. Byrd's interest then shifted to the South Pole, where throughout the 1930s he and his teams would distinguish themselves through many successful firsts.

The Polar Quest. In November 1929 Byrd flew over the South Pole, taking off from his base of "Little America" some seven hundred miles away and thus becoming "the man who flew over both poles." Other flyers had preceded him in the Antarctic, but Byrd was also able to use his machine to place a geological survey party on the Rockefeller Mountains. He also had a photographer on board to record the territory overflown. However, his efforts were unsuitable for cartographic work. It was not until the 1950s that proper coordination for the purpose of map surveying would be achieved. Admiral Byrd returned several times to the Antarctic in the 1930s, supported by funding from the National Geographic Society. Each time new or improved means of carrying out a scientific investigation were provided. A Kellett autogiro, the first vertical-takeoff machine used in a polar region, was employed on the second expedition for atmospheric checks. Ground installations also evolved. The first expedition had established several buildings for geological, meteorological, and physical purposes. The radio lab was just a corner of the administrative building, but on the second expedition a "science hall" went up, intended to investigate twenty branches of the sciences in the region. Improvements in living conditions were also noticeable, as in the case of making orange juice, a source of vitamin C, available on the first Byrd expedition. Several unique flights were successfully undertaken, crisscrossing the Antarctic continent and thus helping establish reference points for use by later surveys. The limits of technological support became clear, however, in 1939 on the third Byrd expedition. Previously he had used several snowmobiles to carry seismic survey equipment too heavy for dog sledges. In this case Thomas Poulter, a physicist who had served on the second expedition, designed a thirty-ton snow cruiser with living quarters, a machine shop, supply storage, and gasoline tanks for both the cruiser and an airplane carried atop the mechanical monster. Tested success-

fully on sand, it failed in the field, sinking in the snow under its own weight.

The End of Exploration. Byrd, along with other flyers and explorers, ironically contributed through his exploratory successes to the termination of grand exploration. As he helped demystify some of the globe's unknown regions, his small teams of intrepid men eventually were replaced with large groups of trained scientists and logistical support groups specializing in specific aspects of the Antarctic region. Public enthusiasm surrounding Antarctic exploration subsided and focused instead on other events. Byrd turned to cultivating his image as a prestigious retired explorer. Nevertheless, the Byrd expeditions represented a unique example of the interrelated growth of science and technology, a necessary step toward the full-scale development of Antarctic science and research.

Sources:

G. E. Fogg, *A History of Antarctic Science* (New York: Cambridge University Press, 1992);

Richard Montague, *Oceans, Poles and Airmen* (New York: Random House, 1971).

AMELIA EARHART

1897-1937?

AVIATRIX

The Road to Flight. Raised in a traditional Kansas family, Amelia Earhart faced difficult times when her parents, although well-to-do, overspent themselves. Her mother was able to recover some money from the estate and enroll Amelia in a school in Pennsylvania, but she never graduated, preferring instead to work as a nurse in a war hospital in Toronto. Meanwhile, she became the subject of a seven-year courtship, which she eventually rejected, fearing that the traditional limits of marriage would prevent her from attaining a meaningful life as an active woman. On Christmas 1920 her father took her to an air show inaugurating the opening of an airfield in Long Beach, California. Fascinated by the show, they went three days later to Rogers Field, where he bought her a ticket for a ride with pilot Frank Hawks. From that point she became obsessed with the idea of flying. She convinced Neta Snook, a female manager at Kinner Airfield, to teach her to fly and paid for her lessons, at a dollar per minute in the air, with Liberty Bonds. Her first successful record was set in October 1922, when she reached an altitude of fourteen thousand feet without wearing an oxygen mask. On 15 May 1923 she became the sixteenth woman to receive the coveted pilot's license of the Fédération Aéronautique Internationale.

Lady Lindy. Earhart was broke by the time she was licensed. Following a sinus illness, she had no choice but to take whatever job she could find, including teaching English. In the fall of 1927 she took more flying lessons to strengthen her experience. Bearing an uncanny resemblance to Charles Lindbergh, who had crossed the Atlantic alone in May 1927, she quickly gained the nickname "Lady Lindy." The identification spread like wildfire once she completed a team transatlantic crossing in 1928, landing in Wales. She loathed such comparisons, however, because she felt she had done nothing that truly compared to Lindbergh's success. That would change in the 1930s.

Chasing the Records. Though she married publisher G. P. Putnam in 1931, Earhart continued her flying career. On 20 May 1932 she became the first woman and only the second person to fly solo across the Atlantic. This event inaugurated a string of speed and distance records throughout the 1930s that would be interrupted abruptly by her disappearance during a transpacific flight attempt in July 1937. Such records included the first solo flight between Hawaii and the mainland in 1935. Some of her ventures, clearly intended to raise money for other records, brought her strong public criticism that male pilots had never faced. As she explained to one of her contemporaries, the pattern was a simple one: "I make a record and then I lecture on it. That's where the money comes from. Until it's time to make another record." She sold the airplanes she used to buy newer, more powerful machines that would take her to her next successes. She also became an active spokesperson for the six hundred female pilots in the United States and headed the aviatrix club the Ninety-Nines. Her flight schedule became increasingly full, as her husband attempted to add various tours and stunts to what was already perceived as excess advertising. Earhart played along, including on her final expedition, although it appeared that a few more months of work would be necessary before a successful world flight could be attempted. This did not happen, however, as her last transmission from her plane came on 5 July 1937 as she was crossing the Pacific.

A Feminist by Action Rather Than Words. Throughout her career Earhart represented the modern woman using technology as a means to liberate herself from social constraints. She viewed aviation as "this modern young giant," something that would give equal opportunity to both men and women. Such a line of thought clearly reflected a utopian view of technology still in vogue in the 1930s. Her need to make a difference through aviation as well as the pressures of public scrutiny are believed to have contributed to her decision to attempt her last long-distance flight ahead of schedule; had she succeeded, such a "stunt" would likely have placated critics into silence. She remains nevertheless a great inspiration to all pilots.

Sources:

Doris L. Rich, *Amelia Earhart: A Biography* (Washington, D.C.: Smithsonian Institution Press, 1989);

Susan Ware, *Still Missing: Amelia Earhart and the Search for Modern Feminism* (New York: Norton, 1993).

THEODORE VON KÁRMÁN

1881-1963

ENGINEER DYNAMICIST

The Road to California. Theodore von Kármán, born to a middle-class Jewish family, grew up in Budapest, Hungary. By the time he was six it was discovered that he had a gift for mathematics, able to calculate multiplications instantly and develop solutions to factor problems. His father, afraid that his son would waste his resources on pointless arithmetic tricks, ordered him to drop any interest in the subject for several years and to concentrate on the parental curriculum, which included history, geography, literature, and the study of six languages. By the time he was allowed to return to his mathematical interest, he had lost the capacity to calculate rapidly, and even when he regained some of it, the skill remained restricted to operations in Hungarian. In the meantime he developed an early interest in dynamics and applied mechanics, but when the time came to enroll in a university program he chose engineering rather than the sciences on the advice of his father. Graduating from Royal Joseph University in Budapest, Kármán then served in the army before undertaking studies at Göttingen, Germany. Then followed various teaching posts and a directorship of the Aeronautical Institute at Aachen. Kármán met Robert Millikan at a scientific conference in 1924 and two years later agreed to visit the California Institute of Technology for a few months. In December 1929, following negotiations, Kármán immigrated with his mother and sister to the United States.

Building the Aeronautics Field. Kármán was given the task of making the Guggenheim Aeronautical Laboratory and wind tunnel there a leader in the field in order to draw aeronautical industries, and therefore financial support, to southern California. One of the early successes of wind-tunnel research under Kármán involved testing models of the Douglas Commercial aircraft models DC-1, DC-2, and DC-3. Less successful because of circumstances beyond his control, Kármán's study of weather turbulence and stresses came too late to help the U.S. Navy's rigid-airship program, despite efforts to establish a research center, with a special wind tunnel, in Akron, Ohio. Of great importance was Kármán's devising of a formula that explained systematically the impact of molecules on hard surfaces. The Kármán law of turbulence, established in 1930, had great consequences for the future design of airships, airplanes, and rockets. In addition to his research, Kármán taught a small group of students enrolled at the California Institute of Technology, usually applying the tutorial method to encourage the free flow of ideas. At formal lectures — he believed that, contrary to common college practice, prestigious professors should teach undergraduate classes rather than just graduate seminars — he would fascinate his students with intricate yet clear solutions to various problems.

Moving On to Rocketry. In the late 1930s Kármán supported a group of California Institute of Technology students interested in rocketry. Attempts at cooperation with pioneer rocket scientist Robert Goddard had failed, so it was his influence that allowed the group to carry on its experiments, which had varying degrees of success. He even had the basement of the California Institute of Technology opened to the young scientists, although he almost regretted it when poisonous fumes escaped through the building. Nevertheless, standing by what became known as the Suicide Club bore fruit. He had made the acquaintance of Hap Arnold, who was to become a leader of the American air effort in World War II. Arnold eventually became interested in the use of rocketry as applied to "jet-assisted takeoff" (JATO) for airplanes, and by 1939 the first tests were under way.

Putting America Ahead. Kármán's work was so influential that, as General Arnold later put it, "it showed the military that a college professor was good for something." The training he provided students at the California Institute of Technology, as well as the information he made available to aeronautical scientists throughout the world, was substantial, and the risks he took with rocket science allowed the United States to start its space program. Not only did the impact of his work continue into the 1960s, but its quality easily justified his receiving the first National Medal of Science in 1963, shortly before his death.

Sources:

Michael H. Gorn, *The Universal Man: Theodore von Kármán's Life in Aeronautics* (Washington, D.C.: Smithsonian Institution Press, 1992);

Theodore von Kármán and Lee Edson, *The Wind and Beyond: Theodore von Kármán, Pioneer in Aviation and Pathfinder in Space* (Boston: Little, Brown, 1967).

DAVID E. LILIENTHAL

1899-1981

NATURAL RESOURCES MANAGER

Rising to the Challenge. Born in Illinois of Czechoslovakian parents, David Lilienthal graduated from Harvard Law School in 1923, where he had studied with Felix Frankfurter, then a professor at the school. Lilienthal went to work in Chicago for a private law firm. His personal interests centered around issues of conservation and development of natural resources. Following his successful handling of a difficult telephone rate case before the U.S. Supreme Court, he was appointed head of the State Utility Commission of Wisconsin in 1931. Two years later, on the advice of Supreme Court Justice Frankfurter, President Franklin D. Roosevelt invited Lilienthal to join the board of the Tennessee Valley Authority (TVA).

The TVA. In April 1933 President Roosevelt asked Congress to create an agency to oversee the use, development, and conservation of the Tennessee River Valley. This proposal included safe navigation, reforestation, industrial and agricultural programs, national defense production management, and the production and distribution of power at Muscle Shoals in northern Alabama, where the river's sudden drop made possible the establishment of a hydroelectric dam. The TVA was to be run by a committee of three men: Arthur Morgan, Harcourt Morgan, and Lilienthal.

The Challenge of Cheap Power. From 1933 to 1938 a battle raged within the triumvirate that administrated TVA. Its first chairman, Arthur Morgan, was most interested in national economic planning through cooperation between government and business. He argued for the selling of electric power at the same rates as those set by private companies, which viewed government involvement as a threat to their business advantage. Lilienthal believed otherwise. He suspected that centralized control of the means of production might be self-defeating. If a monopoly on the price of electricity existed, then the purpose of government involvement to put people to work and make power affordable, thus spreading its use, would be lost. Instead, he argued that public power had to compete directly with private business by selling at lower rates, thus driving prices down and ensuring competitiveness among all groups involved. The disagreement between the two men became so strong that it reached the White House, and Morgan was fired in 1938 and replaced as chair by Harcourt Morgan, an ally of Lilienthal's whose vision of cheap power for everyone thus prevailed. More trouble loomed on the horizon, however. The major private utility in the Tennessee River Valley — the Commonwealth and Southern Corporation, headed by Wendell Willkie — accused Lilienthal of trying to drive it out of business. Although the charges were denied, by 1939 the federal government had purchased a substantial amount of shares in the corporation. Though this move was controversial, it reflected the shift to antitrust competitiveness and government spending that had started with the firing of Arthur Morgan and that helped establish TVA as the biggest producer of power, with nine dams, and as a provider of work in a region of three million people whose average income was less than half the national average.

Lilienthal's Legacy. Lilienthal, who succeeded Harcourt Morgan as head of TVA in 1941, successfully pursued a career as a "power public servant." Although he was given a second nine-year term as TVA chair in 1945, he left his post to become the first head of the Atomic

Energy Commission in 1946 and went into private business in 1950. His optimistic belief in "power for the people," thus associating the benefits of technology with a greater sense of democratic values, made him a popular hero of sorts, even when he was criticized as too aggressive in his beliefs. His work with TVA gave it the necessary foundations to thrive and become the largest producer of electric power in the United States well into the 1980s.

Sources:

William Chandler, *The Myth of TVA: Conservation and Development in the Tennessee Valley, 1933–1983* (Cambridge, Mass.: Ballinger, 1984);

David Lilienthal, *The Journals of David Lilienthal* (New York: Harper & Row, 1964).

ROBERT A. MILLIKAN

1868-1953

PHYSICIST AND ADMINISTRATOR

Self-Starter. Born in 1868 in Morrison, Illinois, to a preacher and a former dean of a Michigan college, Robert A. Millikan spent his childhood in Iowa. Self-taught in physics while at Oberlin College, he graduated in 1893 with a master's degree and enrolled at Columbia University the same year as its sole graduate student in physics. There he studied with Michael Pupin, another self-starter, who had risen from immigrant status to that of respected inventor. Following the completion of his Ph.D. in 1895, Millikan was invited to the University of Chicago to assist Albert Michelson, whom he knew from having taught a course for him the preceding year. Because Michelson disliked lecturing, Millikan assumed heavy teaching loads yet found the time to initiate his own program of research, achieving notice for his studies of electric charges and the photoelectric effect. While at Chicago he wrote several texts that were eventually used by generations of science students. He also became a member of the prestigious National Academy of Sciences and later assumed the research directorship of the National Research Council (NRC), formed in 1916 to mobilize America's talents for defense purposes. He later moved to the California Institute of Technology and received a Nobel Prize in physics in 1923 for his 1916 confirmation of Albert Einstein's 1905 theoretical predictions about quanta. Interestingly, he did not believe in quanta himself until several years later.

Building a New University. In 1919 Millikan moved to California as a visiting professor at the Throop College of Technology in Pasadena. His reputation as an administrator had preceded him, since after the war he successfully built a postdoctoral research program attached to the NRC for young Americans interested in scientific

professions. Later, as chair of the Executive Council of Throop College, he was offered its presidency but declined it, asking instead that the name be changed to the California Institute of Technology, and he maintained an influential role as an administrator and promoter of science. Through his untiring devotion "Caltech" became as famous an abbreviation as MIT, and the quality of American science and scientific education increased substantially. Each year, for example, the California Institute of Technology would host a group of young NRC postdoctoral students so they could enjoy a stimulating place in which to present, compare, and develop their ideas.

The Controversies of Science. While he was busy teaching and administering at the California Institute of Technology, Millikan became embroiled in a debate with physicist A. H. Compton over the nature of cosmic rays. Millikan was convinced that such rays were composed of photons of the same nature as those in X rays and gamma radiation. Compton found "no way of reconciling the data with the [Millikan] hypothesis." Millikan then claimed that the experiments carried out by Carl Anderson confirmed his views, while Compton maintained that the properties of earth's magnetism implied that such cosmic rays were composed of protons. Later experiments confirmed Compton's hypothesis.

Advocating the Sciences in the United States. By the time he retired in 1945 at age seventy-seven, Millikan had built the California Institute of Technology into a world-class institution, attracting a wide variety of scientists to lecture and research there. He never lost sight of the need to justify the uses of science to a skeptical public. To those who viewed it as a threat to religion and jobs, he stressed its positive role in strengthening the United States, thus contributing further to the maturation of the field; America needed science to assert its place in the world, and the sciences required an American setting of individual freedom of opinion to develop fully.

Sources:

L. A. Dubridge and P. S. Epstein, "Robert Andrews Millikan," *National Academy of Sciences Biographical Memoirs*, 33 (1959): 241–282;

Robert A. Millikan, *The Autobiography of Robert A. Millikan* (New York: Prentice-Hall, 1950).

HAROLD C. UREY

1893-1981

CHEMIST

Focus on the Problem. Indiana-born chemist Harold C. Urey first taught high-school classes before entering college at the University of Montana, where he majored in biology. In order to pay for his studies, he worked as a waiter, a construction worker, and eventually as a biology instructor. After graduation he worked as an industrial chemist in Philadelphia during World War I. His dislike of the industrial setting prompted him to pursue a university career. He entered graduate school at the University of California, Berkeley, in 1921, earning his doctorate two years later and then traveling to Denmark to study with physicist Niels Bohr. Of his time in California, Urey recalled both the collegiality and the hardworking atmosphere that permeated the small chemistry department, which inspired him to apply himself fully to the field. His early papers, using quantum theory, concerned the way molecules interact with light.

Working on Isotopes. Moving to Columbia University in 1929, Urey started research on isotopes. The concept was still new — it had been introduced in 1913 — and the periodic table of elements was being actively searched for stable isotopes. Those for oxygen had already been found, but Urey was more interested in the hypothesis that hydrogen had an isotope, an idea that had existed since the concept of isotopes was first developed. It was commonly understood that if there were a hydrogen isotope with heavier nuclei, it would appear only in small quantities. Hypothesizing that evaporation might help isolate the substance, Urey proceeded to evaporate four liters of liquid hydrogen slowly, leaving only one cubic centimeter and analyzing its spectrum. The substance's existence was confirmed by the appearance of faint lines on the chart alongside the normal absorption line of hydrogen. The new substance was called deuterium (meaning "the second one"). Water made with deuterium atoms was called heavy water and included in its properties the fact that it boiled a few degrees higher than normal water. For his success Urey received the Nobel Prize in chemistry in 1934.

Contributions beyond the Nobel Prize. Urey went on to investigate and discover several other isotopes, including carbon 13 and nitrogen 15, thus helping fill the periodic-elements table. His contributions also included practical assistance to colleagues and students; for example, he loaned some of his Nobel money to Isidor Rabi for research that earned Rabi a Nobel Prize, and he later helped one of his graduate students stay in school by covering some of her tuition. Urey also became the first editor of the *Journal of Chemical Physics.* Because his work on deuterium had been instrumental in the development of the atomic bomb, Urey felt a deep sense of responsibility following the bombings of Hiroshima and Nagasaki in 1945. With other scientists he devoted his time to lobbying in favor of controlling nuclear power through international agreements. Later he turned to applying chemistry to determining the age of fossils, and he pioneered the field of cosmochemistry.

The Selfless Scientist. Urey published his last scientific paper at age eighty-four. The stories and events linked to him were many, and many were simple rumors. He expressed himself often, including on the nature of his success; he explained that intelligence, determination,

and the ability to pick up on a problem were the essence of finding a solution. Such drive also made Urey somewhat of a stereotypical scientist, as he forgot faces, names, and even going to lunch whenever he was drawn into a scientific issue that demanded his full attention. His generosity, kindness, and dedication also stood out, making him the epitome of the selfless scientist committed to the greater good.

Sources:

S. K. P. Cohen and others, "Harold Clayton Urey," *Biographical Memoirs of the Royal Society,* 29 (1983): 623–659;

Harold C. Urey, *Some Thermodynamic Properties of Hydrogen and Deuterium* (Stockholm: Norstedt, 1935).

JOHN VON NEUMANN

1903-1957

MATHEMATICIAN, PHYSICIST, COMPUTER PIONEER

Polymath. In an age of increasing specialization within the sciences, John von Neumann seemed to be involved in everything, from mathematics to physics to computers. During the 1930s he was notable for his applications of mathematics to quantum physics and his pioneering work in game theory. He possessed an inquisitive mind and an extraordinary ability to learn about new fields quickly and offer solutions others had not considered.

Prodigy. Born Johann von Neumann in Budapest, Hungary, in 1903, at age twenty he offered a definition of ordinal numbers that was adopted everywhere. He completed a bachelor's degree in chemical engineering at the Zurich Institute in 1925, and the following year, at age twenty-three, a Ph.D. in mathematics at the University of Budapest. His dissertation on set theory was also widely influential. At age twenty-nine he published *Mathematische Grundlagen der Quantenmechanik* (1932; translated as *Mathematical Foundations of Quantum Mechanics,* 1955), an important contribution to quantum physics, then a relatively new area of interest. During the late 1920s and early 1930s he also began to theorize about the new interdisciplinary field of game theory, which deals with strategies for making decisions when interests conflict. In 1944 he and Oskar Morgenstern published a seminal work in the field, *Theory of Games and Economic Behavior.*

Princeton. In 1930 von Neumann was invited to Princeton University as a visiting lecturer, and the following year he became a professor there. In 1933 he joined Princeton's new Institute for Advanced Study, where he remained until his death from cancer in 1957. He became a United States citizen in 1937. Throughout the 1930s he taught, studied, and wrote about mathematics and logic. His work in logic systems led to his becoming one of the pioneers of computer science in the 1940s and 1950s. He was also active in the development of the atomic bomb in the mid 1940s. He was appointed to the Atomic Energy Commission in 1954.

Source:
Steve J. Heims, *John von Neumann and Norbert Wiener: From Mathematics to the Technologies of Life and Death* (Cambridge, Mass.: MIT Press, 1980).

PEOPLE IN THE NEWS

Astronomer **Walter Sydney Adams** had already contributed significantly to the study of white dwarfs when he applied some of his methodology to planets, thus determining in 1932 that the atmosphere of Venus is rich in carbon dioxide.

Naturalist **Charles William Beebe** decided to explore ocean depths by building a heavy steel shell, a bathysphere, that in 1934 helped him reach a record depth of 1,001 meters.

In 1937 botanist **Albert Francis Blakeslee** discovered that the alkaloid colchicine, obtained from the autumn crocus, could cause mutations in plants, an important step in identifying chemical influences in heredity.

In 1934 **P. W. Bridgman,** a Harvard professor of mathematics and physics, received the National Academy of Sciences Comstock Prize for devising and using various apparatuses to apply pressures of up to six hundred thousand pounds per square inch to determine how materials behave under high pressure.

Successful in developing the differential analyzer in the early 1930s, **Vannevar Bush,** a professor of electric power transmission and vice president of MIT, was named president of the Carnegie Institution in Washington, D.C., in 1939.

As president of the National Academy of Sciences, an agency of the federal government, **W. W. Campbell** reported at its 1933 meeting that while the Depression had not affected research, more needed to be done to deal with the unsympathetic stance of the legislature toward science, which might cause further cuts in spending.

Physicist **Arthur Holly Compton,** who had shown that electromagnetic radiation is both wave and particle, started studying the interaction of cosmic rays and earth magnetism in 1930.

Czech-American biochemist **Carl Cori** and his wife, **Gerty Cori,** obtained results in their investigation of the process of glycogen breakdown in the human body in 1936 and 1938.

Walter Elsasser, later known for his work on radar during World War II, suggested in 1939 that the planet's liquid iron core, although not naturally magnetic, was rendered so by the earth's rotation, which creates eddies in the molten core.

Following orders from Massachusetts authorities to stop experimenting with rockets there, pioneer rocket scientist **Robert Goddard** moved to New Mexico in 1930 to carry on his work thanks to the help of philanthropist Daniel Guggenheim. His results included the patenting of a multistage rocket.

While still an undergraduate at Harvard, **Edwin Herbert Land** devised a method of lining up, under plastic, small crystals that could polarize light. The process was given the name Polaroid, and in 1937 Land organized a corporation by the same name.

A 1925 graduate of the California Institute of Technology, chemist **Linus Pauling** used quantum theory to study the bonds formed by carbon atoms. His 1939 book *The Nature of the Chemical Bond and the Structure of Molecules and Crystals* is widely considered one of the most influential scientific works of the century.

A radio engineer by training, **Grote Reber,** after unsuccessfully trying to bounce radio signals off the moon, read of Karl Jansky's work and in 1937 built the first radio telescope in his backyard in Wheaton, Illinois, using a thirty-one-foot-wide reflector. By 1939 he was able to obtain positive results, such as the exact level of radio-wave emission by the galaxy. His results were first published in 1940.

In 1935 biochemist **William Cumming Rose** discovered threonine, an amino acid essential to a balanced diet. Two years later he showed that only ten amino acids out of approximately twenty present in a protein molecule are truly essential to a balanced diet.

Astronomer **Henry Norris Russell** spread interest in astronomy to readers of *Scientific American* through his concise articles throughout the decade.

In 1937 **Glenn Theodore Seaborg**, a recent Ph.D., assisted physicists Jack Livingood and Emilio Segrè in discovering several radioisotopes before making a name for himself the following decade.

In his 1937 master's thesis written at MIT **Claude E. Shannon** described a way of using symbolic logic to improve electrical switching circuits. This paper proved that programming an electronic digital computer would be complicated less by mathematics than by logic.

In 1930 astronomer **Harlow Shapley** determined the diameter of the Milky Way galaxy, estimated to be 250,000 light-years in diameter.

Despite his lack of formal education, self-taught **Lee A. Strong** rose through the ranks of the U.S. Department of Agriculture to become the new chief of the Bureau of Entomology in 1934. His lifework was the prevention of the spread of plant diseases to help farmers avoid losing their crops.

Swiss-born astrophysicist **R. J. Trumpler,** who had been studying the dark regions of space known as dark clouds, determined in 1930 that these areas are regions of absorption rather than of no stars because dark clouds block the light coming from the stars.

Alan Mathison Turing, a British mathematician from Cambridge University, became interested in the logical foundations of mathematics and sought to determine which functions were computable by machine. His solution, published in 1936 while he was on a fellowship at Princeton University, presented the basic principles of the computer.

After graduating from Tufts College at age fifteen and completing his education at Cornell University, **Norbert Wiener,** a professor of mathematics at MIT, was elected in 1934 as one of the approximately five hundred members of the National Academy of Sciences.

Interested in the state of matter and its colors, **Robert Williams Wood** observed in 1933 that alkaline metals experimentally exposed to ultraviolet radiation become transparent.

AWARDS

AWARDS FOR AERONAUTICS

The Guggenheim Award, intended to recognize significant progress in aeronautics, was first bestowed upon Orville Wright for 1929 on 8 April 1930. The Robert J. Collier Trophy had a similar purpose but tended to focus more on engineering achievements.

Guggenheim:

1930

Ludwig Prandtl, for his work on aerodynamics.

1931

Frederick Lancaster, for his work on aerodynamics.

1932

Juan de la Cierva, for his original development of the autogiro.

1933

Jerome C. Hunsacker

1934

No Award.

1935

William Durand, for his achievements in the development of aircraft-propeller theories.

1936

No Award.

1937

Hugo Eckener, for his work in promoting the transport airship.

1938

No Award.

1939

Donald Douglas, for outstanding contributions to the design and construction of transport aircraft.

Collier:

1930

Harold F. Pitcairn and Associates, for their work in the development of the autogiro.

1931

Packard Motor Company, for its development of the diesel engine for airplanes.

1932

Glenn L. Martin, for the development of a two-engined, high-speed, weight-carrying airplane.

1933

Hamilton Standard Company, for the development of a controllable-pitch propeller.

1934

Albert F. Hegenberger, for his successful development of a blind-landing system.

1935

Donald W. Douglas and the personnel of his company, for developing a successful twin-engine transport plane.

1936

Pan American Airways, for the establishment of the transpacific line.

1937

The U.S. Army Air Corps, for construction and successful operation of the XC-35, the first substratospheric airplane with a pressure cabin.

1938

Howard Hughes and his associates, for a round-the-world flight.

1939

The airlines of the United States, for their high record of safety in air travel.

NOBEL PRIZE WINNERS

During the 1930s there were seventeen Nobel Prizes awarded in chemistry and physics. Of those, six were won or shared by Americans. The Nobel Prize is widely considered to be the highest honor bestowed upon scientists and signifies worldwide recognition of their work.

1932: **Irving Langmuir** wins the Nobel Prize for chemistry for his discoveries in, and investigations of, surface chemistry, in particular the interaction of thorium on tungsten and oil films on water.

1934: **Harold C. Urey** wins the Nobel Prize for chemistry for isolating a hydrogen isotope heavier than the common hydrogen atom and called deuterium.

1936: **Carl D. Anderson** of the United States and **Victor Franz Hess** of Austria share the Nobel Prize for physics — Anderson for his discovery of the positron, Hess for his discovery of cosmic radiation.

1937: **Clinton J. Davisson** of the United States and **Sir George Paget Johnson** of England win the Nobel Prize for physics for their respective work on electron diffraction by crystals.

1938: **Enrico Fermi** wins the Nobel Prize for physics for his work with neutrons.

1939: **Ernest O. Lawrence** wins the Nobel Prize for physics for his invention of the cyclotron.

DEATHS

Cleveland Abbe Jr., 62, geographer, 18 April 1934.

John Jacob Abel, 81, respected biochemist, 26 May 1938.

Edward Goodrich Acheson, 75, inventor who studied the properties of carbon, 6 July 1931.

Harold D. Arnold, 49, physicist noted for his invention of the three-electrode high-vacuum thermionic tube, 10 July 1933.

Louis Austin, 64, physicist, 27 June 1932.

James Baldwin, 73, noted psychologist who edited *Psychological Review*, 8 November 1934.

Samuel P. Baldwin, 70, geological explorer who became a pioneer in ornithology and bird-banding, 31 December 1938.

L. A. Bauer, 67, physicist who studied magnetism, 12 April 1932.

Bernard Behrend, 67, construction engineer and inventor, 25 March 1932.

Calvin Bridges, 49, early geneticist who worked on the interpretation of deficiencies in genetic data, 27 December 1938.

Mary Emma Byrd, 84, professor of astronomy who joined the faculty of Smith College, resigning in 1906 to protest the college's acceptance of Rockefeller and Carnegie foundation grants, 30 July 1934.

W. W. Campbell, 76, astronomer, 14 June 1938.

William Campbell, 60, metallurgist who advised the federal government and several city and state commissions, 16 December 1936.

Wallace H. Carothers, 41, chemist who investigated synthetic rubbers and polymers, 29 April 1937.

Louis George Carpenter, 74, consulting engineer who specialized in hydrology and hydrography, 12 September 1935.

Cornelia Clapp, 85, one of six women to earn one of the 150 stars given zoologists in the first edition of *American Men of Science* (1906), a key figure in the development of the Mount Holyoke seminary and college, 31 December 1934.

George Herbert Condict, 62, electrical engineer and inventor who worked on electric cars, 9 April 1934.

Glenn H. Curtiss, 52, aviation pioneer, 23 July 1930.

John V. Davies, 66, civil engineer who designed many important railroad tunnels, 4 October 1939.

Herman S. Davis, 64, astronomer, 23 May 1933.

George Eastman, 77, developer of the Kodak photographic process, 14 March 1932.

Thomas Alva Edison, 83, prolific inventor of the phonograph, the microphone, the incandescent light, and the Kinetoscope, 18 October 1931.

Reginald Fessenden, 65, Canadian-American physicist who worked with George Westinghouse, second to Thomas Edison in the number of patents obtained, 22 July 1932.

J. Walter Fewkes, 79, ethnologist who helped oversee the Harvard Peabody Museum for thirty years, 31 May 1930.

Fanny Gates, 58, physicist who held multiple fellowships to study at physics departments in European universities, taught at Grinell College in Iowa and at the University of Illinois, 24 February 1931.

William Gotshall, 60, pioneer in the electrification of railroads, 20 August 1935.

Daniel Guggenheim, 74, philanthropist who promoted progress in the aeronautics, 28 September 1930.

George Ellery Hale, 69, noted astronomer who had large telescopes built on Mounts Wilson and Palomar, 21 February 1938.

Edwin Herbert Hall, 83, physicist who discovered the "Hall effect" of a magnetic field applied perpendicular to an electric current, 20 November 1938.

Ellen Amanda Hayes, 79, controversial mathematics professor at Wellesley College (1882–1916), denied appointment to professor emeritus upon her retirement because of her socialist and feminist views, 27 October 1930.

Albert Spear Hitchcock, 70, botanical explorer and taxonomist, 16 December 1935.

Charles L. Jackson, 88, early organic chemist and pioneer of chemistry education, 31 October 1935.

Charles Francis Jenkins, pioneer in the development of television, 5 June 1934.

Karl Frederic Kellerman, 53, bacteriologist, 30 August 1934.

Vernon Kellog, 69, zoologist, 8 August 1937.

Arthur Edwin Kennelly, 77, electrical engineer who served two terms as president of the American Society of Electrical Engineers, 18 June 1939.

Christine Ladd-Franklin, 82, mathematician whose dissertation on symbolic logic written at Johns Hopkins University did not earn her the Ph.D. because the school, although it allowed her to study there, did not grant degrees to women, 5 March 1930.

William D. Matthew, 59, paleontologist who served as chief curator of the American Museum of Natural History, 24 September 1930.

Albert Michelson, 78, the first American to win a Nobel Prize for physics, 9 May 1931.

Leroy Moodie, 53, paleontologist whose specialization in anatomy led him to study ancient diseases, 16 February 1934.

Anne Moore, 65, head of the biology department at the State Normal School in San Diego, 25 September 1937.

Charles Munroe, 89, chemist who experimented with smokeless powder, 7 December 1938.

Julius Nieuwland, 58, chemist whose studies of acetylene contributed to the invention of nylon and synthetic rubber, 11 June 1936.

Emmy Noether, 53, renowned German mathematician who immigrated to the United States in August 1933 after the German Nazi Party had removed her from teaching, 14 April 1935.

Mary Paine, 67, mathematician whose work centered on the history and philosophy of mathematics, 19 November 1939.

Martha Austin Phelps, 63, in 1908–1909 one of the first female chemists to work for the National Bureau of Standards, 15 March 1933.

William Henry Pickering, 79, astronomer who discovered Saturn's ninth satellite, 17 January 1938.

Michael Pupin, 76, Yugoslav-American physicist who devised a long-distance, distortion-free wire transmission method, 12 March 1935.

John Shaffner, 72, botanist and pioneer in cytology, 27 January 1939.

Elmer Ambrose Sperry, 69, inventor noted for perfecting the gyroscope, 16 June 1930.

Charles Spiro, 83, inventor who patented the Columbia, Bar-Lock, and Visigraph typewriters, 17 December 1933.

George Owen Squier, 69, leading radio technician, 24 March 1934.

Frederick Starr, 74, anthropologist who worked in Asia and Mexico, 14 August 1933.

Charles Rupert Stockard, 60, biologist and anatomist, 7 April 1939.

Horace E. Stockbridge, 73, agricultural chemist who served as chief chemist for the Japanese government, 30 October 1930.

William Story, 79, editor of the *Mathematical Review*, 10 April 1930.

Joseph Strauss, 68, chief engineer for the Golden Gate Bridge in San Francisco, 16 May 1938.

Charles Strobel, 83, construction engineer who pioneered the use of steel structures in Chicago buildings, 4 April 1936.

Alex Summers, 76, education statistician, 31 January 1933.

George Swain, 74, civil engineer who was the first recipient of the Lamme Engineering Medal in 1928, 1 July 1931.

Edgar James Swift, 72, psychologist, 30 August 1932.

James Edward Talmage, 70, geologist and theologian, 27 July 1933.

Charles Talman, 71, meteorologist with the U.S. Weather Bureau, 24 July 1936.

William Tefft, 50, construction engineer, 24 June 1932.

Carl Thomas, 55, engineer who invented the Thomas electric gas meters, 5 June 1938.

Edward Thompson, 74, archaeologist who discovered the "Hidden City" in Yucatán, Mexico, 11 May 1935.

Elihu Thomson, 83, electrician and inventor, 13 March 1937.

Leonard Troland, 43, research engineer who worked on the Technicolor manufacturing process for film, 27 May 1932.

Milton Updegraff, 77, astronomer, 12 September 1938.

John Waddell, 84, construction engineer who designed bridges in seven countries and twenty-five American cities, 3 March 1938.

Frank Wadsworth, 69?, engineer and inventor of various manufacturing machines, 11 April 1936.

James van Wagenen, 54, civil engineer who also invented radio and automotive devices, 17 May 1935.

Henry Heileman Wait, 62, engineer and inventor of various dynamos and other generator systems, 16 November 1931.

Howard Crosby Warren, 66, psychologist, 4 January 1934.

Henry Stephens Washington, 66, mineralogist who investigated various geological occurrences, 7 January 1934.

Walter Wellman, 75, colorful air pioneer who tried twice to reach the North Pole by dirigible and then attempted a transatlantic crossing by the same means in 1910, 31 January 1934.

Louis Eugene Wettling, 74, railroad statistician, 15 November 1938.

PUBLICATIONS

Arthur Albert, *Fundamental Electronics and Vacuum Tubes* (New York: Macmillan, 1938);

John Stuart Allen and others, *Atoms, Rocks and Galaxies: A Survey in Physical Sciences* (New York: Harper, 1938);

Cyril Andrews, *The Railway Age* (New York: Macmillan, 1938);

George Pierce Baker, *The Formation of the New England Railway Systems* (Cambridge, Mass.: Harvard University Press, 1937);

Ernest Barnes, *Scientific Theory and Religion* (New York: Macmillan, 1933);

Franz Boas, *General Anthropology* (Boston: Heath, 1938);

Boas, *The Mind of Primitive Man*, third edition (New York: Macmillan, 1938);

W. Boyle, *The City That Grew* (Los Angeles: Southland, 1936);

P. W. Bridgman, *The Physics of High Pressure* (London: Bell, 1931);

W. E. Butler, *The Engineer's View of the Promised Land* (New York: Fortuny's, 1939);

Richard E. Byrd, *Alone* (New York: Putnam, 1938);

Byrd, *Discovery* (New York: Putnam, 1935);

Alexis Carrell, *Man, the Unknown* (New York: Harper, 1935);

Walter Chrysler, with Boyden Sparks, *Life of an American Workman* (Philadelphia: Curtiss, 1938);

James Collins, *Test Pilot* (Garden City, N.Y.: Doubleday, Doran, 1935);

Ray Compton and Charles Henry Nettels, *Conquests of Science* (New York: Harcourt, Brace, 1939);

Douglas Corrigan, *That's My Story* (New York: Dutton, 1938);

W. Jefferson Davis, *Air Conquest* (Los Angeles: Parker, Stone & Baird, 1930);

Arthur Stanley Eddington, *The Expanding Universe* (Cambridge: Cambridge University Press, 1933);

Albert Einstein, *The World As I See It*, translated by Alan Harris (New York: Covici, 1934);

Einstein and Leopold Infeld, *The Evolution of Physics: The Growth of Ideas from Early Concepts to Relativity and Quanta* (New York: Simon & Schuster, 1938);

George F. Eliot, *Bombs Bursting in the Air: The Influence of Air Power on International Relations* (New York: Reynal & Hitchcock, 1939);

Federal Trade Commission, *Report on the United States Automobile Industry* (Washington, D.C.: Government Printing Office, 1939);

Enrico Fermi, *Thermodynamics* (New York: Prentice-Hall, 1938);

Henry Ford and Samuel Crowther, *Moving Forward* (Garden City, N.Y.: Doubleday, Doran, 1930);

William Herbert George, *The Scientist in Action: A Scientific Study of His Methods* (New York: Emerson, 1938);

William Stephen Grooch, *Winged Highway* (Boston: Longmans, 1938);

Benjamin Gruenberg, *Science and the Public Mind* (New York: McGraw, 1935);

William Haynes, *Men, Money and Molecules* (Garden City, N.Y.: Doubleday, Doran, 1936);

David Hinshaw, *Look and Listen: Railroad Transportation in the United States* (Garden City, N.Y.: Doubleday, Doran, 1932);

Clarence Lewis Hodge, *The Tennessee Valley Authority: A National Experiment in Regionalism* (Washington, D.C.: American University Press, 1938);

Edwin Hubble, *The Realm of the Nebulae* (New Haven: Yale University Press, 1936);

Herbert Jennings, *Universe and Life* (New Haven: Yale University Press, 1933);

Waldemar Bernhard Kaempfert, *Science Today and To-morrow* (New York: Viking, 1939);

Otto Kuhler and Robert Selph Henry, *Portraits of the Iron Horse* (New York: Rand, MacNally, 1937);

Victor Lefebure, *Scientific Disarmament* (New York: Macmillan, 1931);

Anne Morrow Lindbergh, *Listen! the Wind* (New York: Harcourt, Brace, 1938);

Lindbergh, *North to the Orient* (New York: Harcourt, Brace, 1935);

John Kennedy Maclean and Chelsea Curtis Fraser, *Heroes of the Furthest North and the Furthest South*, revised edition (New York: Crowell, 1938);

W. F. Magie, *A Source Book in Physics* (New York: McGraw-Hill, 1935);

Robert Andrew Millikan, *Science and the New Civilization* (New York: Scribners, 1930);

Thomas Hunt Morgan, *Embryology and Genetics* (New York: Columbia University Press, 1934);

Morgan, *The Scientific Basis of Evolution* (New York: Norton, 1932);

A. Cressy Morrison, *Man in a Chemical World: The Service of Chemical Industry* (New York: Scribners, 1937);

Lewis Mumford, *The Culture of Cities* (New York: Harcourt, Brace, 1938);

Mumford, *Technics and Civilization* (New York: Harcourt, Brace, 1934);

Linus Pauling, *The Nature of the Chemical Bond and the Structure of Molecules and Crystals* (New York: Cornell University Press, 1939);

Pauling and E. B. Wilson, *Introduction to Quantum Mechanics with Applications to Chemistry* (New York: McGraw-Hill, 1935);

George Albert Pettitt, *So Boulder Dam Was Built* (Berkeley, Calif.: Lederer, Street & Zeuss, 1935);

Arthur Pound, *The Turning Wheel: The Story of General Motors Through Twenty-Five Years* (Garden City, N.Y.: Doubleday, Doran, 1934);

William J. Powell, *Black Wings* (Los Angeles: Privately printed, 1934);

Lawrence Redman and Austin van Hoesen Mory, *Romance of Research* (New York: Appleton-Century, 1934);

Donald Richmond, *Dilemma of Modern Physics: Waves or Particles?* (New York: Putnam, 1935);

Alfred Sherwood Romer, *Vertebrate Paleontology* (Chicago: University of Chicago Press, 1933);

Charles E. Rosendahl, *What About the Airship?* (New York: Scribners, 1938);

Bertrand Russell, *The Conquest of Happiness* (Garden City, N.Y.: Garden City Publishing, 1933);

Russell, *Scientific Outlook*, third edition (New York: Norton, 1931);

Robert Rakes Shrock and William Twenhofel, *Invertebrate Paleontology* (New York: McGraw, 1935);

Erwin Schrödinger, *Science and the Human Temperament*, translated by James Murphy and W. H. Johnston (New York: Norton, 1935);

Charles Schuchert, *Outlines of Historical Geology*, third edition (New York: Wiley, 1937);

Cyrus Fisher Tolman, *Ground Water* (New York: McGraw-Hill, 1938);

Herbert A. Toops and S. Edson Haven, *Psychology and the Motorist* (Columbus, Ohio: Adams, 1938);

Frank C. Waldrop and Joseph Borkin, *Television: A Struggle for Power* (New York: Morrow, 1938);

David Woodbury, *The Glass Giant of Palomar* (New York: Dodd, Mead, 1939);

Ernst Zimmer, *The Revolution in Physics* (New York: Harcourt, Brace, 1936);

Current Science, periodical;

Journal of Organic Chemistry, periodical (begun in 1936);

Mechanix Illustrated, periodical;

Polar Times, periodical (begun in 1935);

Popular Mechanics, periodical;

Railroad Magazine, periodical (begun in 1937);

Scientific American, periodical.

SPORTS

by RICHARD ORODENKER

CONTENTS

Sidebars and tables are listed in italics.

1930

- The first James E. Sullivan Memorial Trophy, awarded to the country's top amateur athlete, goes to golfer Bobby Jones. Jim Bausch, Glenn Cunningham, Lawson Little, and Don Budge are other winners during the decade.

18 Mar. Montreal Canadien center Howie Morenz, called the "Babe Ruth of Hockey," scores five goals in one game against the New York Americans.

17 May Gallant Fox, ridden by jockey Earl Sande, wins the Kentucky Derby. The three-year-old will go on to win the Preakness and Belmont Stakes and virtually every major race this year.

31 May Bobby Jones wins the British Amateur, the only title he had never won before, on his way to the grand slam of golf this year.

20 June Jones wins the British Open, shooting 291 for seventy-two holes, ten strokes lower than Walter Hagen's record-breaking score in 1924.

12 July Jones wins the U.S. Open, his fourth Open victory and twelfth golf title.

Sept. Hack Wilson of the Chicago Cubs ends the season with 190 runs batted in, and Bill Terry of the New York Giants hits .401 in the most successful year in baseball for hitters. Attendance climbs to more than 10 million, a figure that will not be reached again until after World War II.

18 Sept. The racing yacht *Enterprise* defeats Sir Thomas Lipton's *Shamrock V* to win the United States' seventy-ninth consecutive America's Cup. It is Lipton's fifth loss to the Americans in thirty-two years of competing.

27 Sept. Jones completes his grand slam victory at the Merion Cricket Club in Ardmore, Pennsylvania. He is the first man to win the amateur and open titles of Great Britain and the United States.

8 Nov. In Knute Rockne's last great game as Notre Dame coach, the Fighting Irish crush the University of Pennsylvania 60–20 in one of college football's most devastating running attacks — 567 yards, including three touchdowns by Marty Brill, a halfback who a few years earlier could not make the Penn regulars.

1931

- Frankie Frisch of the Saint Louis Cardinals becomes the first player to win Most Valuable Player honors, awarded by the Baseball Writers' Association of America.

13 May In the first international Golden Gloves boxing tournament, the United States defeats France, five bouts to three.

12 Nov. Conn Smythe's Maple Leafs Gardens, the Yankee Stadium of hockey, opens in Toronto on the first day of the 1931–1932 season.

21 Nov. Unbeaten in three years, Notre Dame, leading 14–0, loses to Southern California 16–14 in the last fifteen minutes of play.

1932

4–13 Feb. Winter Olympic Games open in Lake Placid, New York, the first time Olympic events have been held in the United States since 1904.

2 June   In Montgomery Lake, Georgia, George W. Perry catches a 22-pound 4-ounce largemouth bass, still an IGFA Freshwater All-Tackle world record.

21 June   Jack Sharkey defeats world champion Max Schmeling through fifteen rounds in what sportswriter Paul Gallico calls "one of the dullest heavyweight fights in the history of the ring."

30 July   After twelve years of planning and nine years of labor, the Summer Olympics open in Los Angeles, California.

31 July   Five Olympic track-and-field records are set in one day by U.S. athletes, including Babe Didrikson's javelin throw of 143 feet, 4 inches and Eddie Tolan's 10.4-second 100-meter run.

6 Aug.   Former University of Kansas football fullback Jim Bausch comes from fifth place to win the pole vault and javelin throw and set new world and Olympic records in the decathlon.

30 Sept.   In the third game of the Yankees-Cubs World Series, Lou Gehrig and thirty-eight-year-old Babe Ruth hit two home runs each. Ruth's second, in the fifth inning, is his famous "called shot."

1933

- The National Football League (NFL) makes the forward pass (previously permitted only five yards behind the line) legal anywhere behind the line of scrimmage.

3 Apr.   In the last game of the Stanley Cup semifinals, the Boston Bruins and the Toronto Maple Leafs play 164 minutes and 45 seconds of scoreless hockey. Into the sixth overtime by 4 minutes and 46 seconds, Toronto's Ken Doraty beats Tiny Thompson, the league's best goalie that year.

6 May   Broker's Tip wins the fifty-ninth Kentucky Derby, and jockeys Donald Meade and Herbert Fisher come to blows after Fisher charges Meade with a foul, which officials disallow.

25 June   Al Simmons of the White Sox tops all major-league players in nationwide voting of baseball fans for participants in the first All-Star Game (the brainchild of sportswriter Arch Ward of the *Chicago Tribune*), to be played in July at Comiskey Park in Chicago.

29 June   Primo Carnera knocks out Jack Sharkey in the sixth round of the heavyweight title bout in Madison Square Garden.

6 July   The American League team, managed by Connie Mack, defeats the National League team, managed by John McGraw, 4–2 in the first All-Star Game, behind the pitching of Lefties Gomez and Grove.

Aug.   Negro League teams begin their annual East-West All-Star Game ritual at Comiskey Park in Chicago. Upwards of fifty thousand fans attend a premier showcase of black baseball talent.

27 Aug.   Helen Jacobs wins her second straight national women's singles tennis championship at Forest Hills when Helen Wills Moody defaults ("because of pain in my back and hip and a complete numbness of my right leg") in the third set.

7 Oct.   The Washington Senators lose the last World Series game they will ever play to the New York Giants, who take the series 4–1.

12 Dec.   Ace Bailey of the Toronto Maple Leafs is nearly killed by an unprovoked blind-side check from Boston's Eddie Shore, who is suspended. Bailey suffers a fractured skull and never plays hockey again.

1934

- Yachting reporter William H. Taylor of the *New York Herald Tribune* becomes the first sportswriter to win a Pulitzer Prize (in reporting) for his coverage of the America's Cup races.

- The Augusta National, a golf course inspired by Bobby Jones, becomes the site of the Masters Tournament, won by Horton Smith.

1 Jan.   In its first-ever appearance in a Rose Bowl, Columbia upsets Stanford 7–0.

14 Feb.   As a benefit for the injured Ace Bailey, the National Hockey League (NHL) holds an All-Star Game: Toronto versus the best players from around the league. Toronto wins 7–0. Two other fund-raising all-star games will be held on 2 November 1937 and 29 October 1939.

8 May   Mack Garner, a veteran jockey, rides Cavalcade to a Kentucky Derby victory at Churchill Downs, Garner's first in a twenty-year career.

14 June   Max Baer becomes heavyweight champion of the world on a TKO of Primo Carnera, who drops to the canvas eleven times during the bout.

30 June   After defeating Bill Bonthron and George Venzke at the Princeton University invitation games two weeks earlier with a world-record 4-minute, 6.7-second mile, Glenn Cunningham loses to Bonthron in the fifth and deciding 1500-meter race at the National Amateur Athletic Union (AAU) championship meet in Milwaukee, Wisconsin. Bonthron sets a new world record: 3 minutes 48.8 seconds.

31 Aug.   A crowd of 79,432 fans packs Soldier Field in Chicago to watch the collegiate all-Americans play the professional champion Chicago Bears to a scoreless tie in the first all-star football game.

20 Sept.   Jim Londos becomes the undisputed heavyweight wrestling champion of the world by pinning Ed "Strangler" Lewis, who had defeated Londos fourteen times before.

9 Oct.   Saint Louis's "Gashouse Gang" wins a bitterly fought World Series against Detroit. In the seventh game a riot almost breaks out after a spiking incident involving Joe Medwick and Marvin Owen. Tiger fans pelt Medwick with pop bottles and fruit, and Commissioner Landis orders Medwick out of the game, which the Cardinals win, 11–0, behind six-hit pitching by Dizzy Dean.

17 Nov.   Playing flawless defense, Yale upsets Princeton 7–0 on a sensational first-quarter touchdown catch by right end Larry Kelley.

1935

1 Jan.   As the era of the forward pass dawns, Alabama, led by the great future NFL receiver Don Hutson, defeats Stanford 29–13 in the Rose Bowl. The Crimson Tide completes ten out of thirteen passes for a total of 210 yards, which one sportswriter terms an "amazing record."

24 May   Cincinnati hosts Philadelphia in the first major-league night game. President Franklin D. Roosevelt illuminates Crosley Field by pressing a button at the White House.

25 May	Ohio State University's Jesse Owens breaks five world records and ties another in one afternoon at the AAU Nationals outdoor track-and-field meet in Ann Arbor, Michigan.
28 May	Barney Ross regains the welterweight title by unanimous decision in a fifteen-round bout with Jimmy McLarnin at the Polo Grounds in New York.
30 May	Amelia Earhart is honorary judge at the Indianapolis 500, won by thirty-one-year-old California fruit merchant Kelly Petillo in record time.
13 June	At the Long Island City Bowl James J. Braddock outscores Max Baer on points to become the heavyweight boxing champion of the world.
6 July	An aging Helen Wills Moody wins her seventh Wimbledon title by defeating Helen Jacobs 6–3, 3–6, 7–5.
14 Aug.	Greyhound, a three-year-old gray gelding, clocks in a record time in two heats, the first, 2 minutes, 2.25 seconds, to win the Hambletonian Stakes at Goshen, New York.
31 Aug.	Glenna Collett (Mrs. Edwin H. Vare Jr.) wins the women's national golf championship for the sixth straight year, at the Interlachen Country Club in Hopkins, Minnesota.
3 Sept.	For the first time a race car driver exceeds 300 mph: Sir Malcolm Campbell, at Bonneville Salt Flats, Utah.
14 Sept.	British Amateur champion Lawson Little Jr. of California wins the U.S. Amateur Open at the Country Club of Cleveland.
7 Oct.	Mickey Cochrane's Detroit Tigers win their first world championship, beating the Cubs four games to two.
2 Nov.	Losing 13–0 going into the fourth quarter, Notre Dame scores three touchdowns in less than fifteen minutes to defeat Ohio State 18–13 at home.

1936

•	The Associated Press poll of writers selects its first National Collegiate Athletic Association (NCAA) football champion: Minnesota.
8 Feb.	The NFL holds its first college player draft (in Philadelphia). Jay Berwanger, University of Chicago halfback and winner of the first Heisman Trophy the year before, is the first pick, but he decides not to turn pro.
24 Mar.	In the first of a best-of-five playoff, respective division champs the Detroit Red Wings and the Montreal Maroons play to 16:30 of the sixth overtime — the longest game in NHL history — before Detroit wins 1–0.
19 June	Max Schmeling knocks out undefeated Joe Louis in the twelfth round of their first fight.
1 Aug.	Ten African American athletes, labeled "American auxiliaries" by Adolf Hitler, participate in the Eleventh Olympiad opening in Nazi Berlin. All but one of the men win gold medals.
2–9 Aug.	Jesse Owens wins four gold medals, in the 100-meter and 200-meter races, the long jump, and the 4 x 400-meter sprint relay.

6 Aug.	In the Olympic 1500-meter race Jack Lovelock of New Zealand defeats his old foe Glenn Cunningham in world-record time.
8 Aug.	Eleanor Holm (Jarrett), backstroke champion, recently dropped from the U.S. swim team for drinking, shooting craps, and violating curfew while on board the ship carrying U.S. athletes to Germany, is barred from further amateur competition for writing daily stories for an American news syndicate.
2 Oct.	In game two of the World Series, the Yankees crush the Giants 18–4 on their way to the first of four consecutive world championships.

1937

- George Preston Marshall moves his Eastern Division champion Boston Redskins to Washington, D.C.

- College basketball eliminates the center jump after every basket; games become faster and more wide open.

22 June	Joe Louis knocks out Jim Braddock in the eighth round at Comiskey Park in Chicago to begin his long reign as heavyweight champion of the world.
20 July	After defeating Baron Gottfried Von Cramm, Wimbledon champion Don Budge is on a pace to lead the United States to its first Davis Cup since 1926.
5 Aug.	The New York Yacht Club again wins the America's Cup as Harold S. Vanderbilt's *Ranger* defeats *Endeavour II* of the Royal Yacht Squadron of Cowes, England.
17 Oct.	For the third straight year Fordham University and Jock Sutherland's Rose Bowl champion University of Pittsburgh Panthers play to a scoreless tie.

1938

- White-water trips in cataract boats down the Colorado River start as a commercial venture.

- The first National Invitational Tournament (NIT) in basketball is held, Temple defeating Colorado 60–36.

1 Jan.	Stanford's Hank Luisetti, master of the running one-handed jump shot, scores fifty points in a game against Duquesne.
25 Mar.	Man O' War scion Battleship wins the 100th Grand National Steeplechase in Aintree, England — the first horse bred and raced in the United States *and* owned by an American to win the event.
12 Apr.	Winners of only fourteen of forty-eight regular season games, the long-shot Chicago Black Hawks defeat the league title winner Toronto Maple Leafs 4–1 to capture their second Stanley Cup.
11–15 June	Cincinnati's Johnny Vandermeer throws back-to-back no-hitters: 3–0 against the Boston Braves and 6–0 against the Brooklyn Dodgers, the latter the first night game in New York.
23 June	Heavyweight champion Joe Louis evens the score by knocking out Max Schmeling in the first round of a title fight at Yankee Stadium.

17 Aug.   In a lightweight match Henry Armstrong defeats Lou Ambers at Madison Square Graden to become the first man to hold three boxing titles at one time. Armstrong won the welterweight title on 31 May and the featherweight championship on 29 October 1937.

24 Sept.   Don Budge becomes the first player to win all four of the major world tennis titles in the same year by beating Gene Mako at Forest Hills 6–3, 6–8, 6–2, 6–1.

1 Nov.   Seabiscuit (grandson of Man O' War) beats War Admiral (son of Man O' War) at Pimlico by three lengths and in record time, returning better than two-to-one odds.

12 Dec.   Professional football comes of age as the Giants win the championship game against the Packers 23–17 before 48,120 people. A short while later the NFL's first Pro Bowl is played in foggy Los Angeles as the champion Giants win 13–10 against the best players from other teams.

1939

- The Montreal Maroons withdraw from the NHL, which ends its old divisional format; six of the seven teams can now qualify for the 1938–1939 Stanley Cup playoffs.

- The NCAA holds its first Final Four championship at Northwestern University in Evanston, Illinois: Oregon versus Oklahoma and Villanova versus Ohio State in the semifinals; Oregon beat Ohio State 46–33 in the final.

- Little League baseball is born in Williamsport, Pennsylvania.

2 May   Lou Gehrig takes himself out of the starting lineup, ending his consecutive game streak at 2,130. The "Iron Man" streak spanned fifteen years, having begun 31 May 1925.

12 May   With war perilously close at hand, the European Golden Glove team defeats the Chicago team, five bouts to three.

11 June   After winning the first match 11–7 on 4 June, the U.S. polo team wins the International Cup series against Great Britain 9–4 at the Meadow Brook Club in Westbury, Long Island. The English have not beaten the Americans since 1914.

8 Oct.   The Yankees take their fourth straight World Series, defeating the Cincinnati Reds in four straight games.

OVERVIEW

The Golden Age Ends. The 1920s were called the golden age of sports. Every sport seemed to be dominated by a single personality. Though several of these athletes were still active in the 1930s, the golden age essentially ended with the retirement of golfer Bobby Jones in 1930. In the new decade, titles and records would be won and shattered many different times by different people, and no one, with the possible exception of Joe Louis in the second half of the decade, came to dominate his or her respective sport. Sports fans today continue to draw comparisons between modern athletes and those of the 1920s and 1930s.

The Depression. The social and economic upheavals of the 1930s took their toll on all sports. In baseball, attendance plummeted and park renovations came to a halt. Ballplayers' salaries dipped (Lou Gehrig, at $36,000–$41,000 a year, was the highest-paid player in the Depression years), holdouts (such as Bill Terry in 1932 and Joe DiMaggio in 1938) were received unfavorably in the press, and even commissioner Judge Kenesaw Mountain Landis took a $10,000 pay cut. Rosters were pared down from twenty-five to twenty-three. Some players, even as Prohibition ended in 1933 and beer flowed once more at ballparks, took their playing (and sobriety) more seriously so as not to risk unemployment. Connie Mack sold nine of his championship Philadelphia Athletics just to keep his ballclub afloat. Several longtime National Football League (NFL) teams withdrew from the league, and others lost money. There was talk of postponing the 1932 Winter Olympic Games for financial reasons. The 11 June 1930 Jack Sharkey–Max Schmeling bout was the first to fail to reach the $1 million mark in gross gate receipts since the golden age. Still, sports furnished a kind of palliative for the hardships many faced on a daily basis. Ironically, out-of-work Americans had more time on their hands, and sports helped fill the long, empty hours. On another positive note, the Works Progress Administration (WPA) saw to the building of many neighborhood sporting facilities during the Depression.

New Promotions. The Depression forced sporting promoters to look for new ways to increase attendance and interest. As a result sports became more and more commercialized, a trend that bothered many sportswriters, who were convinced that sport was becoming a gaudy spectacle for mass entertainment. The 1930s saw the advent of night baseball, particularly in the minor leagues and the Negro League. All-star games in both baseball and football and in black baseball drew record crowds. The House of David religious cult, whose baseball players wore their hair down to their waists, and other teams (including major leaguers) barnstormed across the country. Race tracks introduced the daily double, and in August 1939 Washington Park in Illinois paid a record $10,772 for a single $2 bet (on Joy Bet and Merry Caroline).

Faster Sports. Sports fans demanded greater speed and faster games, as records fell in sports from swimming to powerboat racing. Every year Sir Malcolm Campbell seemed to break a new automobile speed record with his car, *Bluebird*. In football the development of a skinnier ball led to more passing and higher scoring. The elimination of the center jump after each score picked up the tempo of basketball games. Fans grew excited as track stars broke records in the 100-yard dash and closed in on the four-minute mile. The pursuit of adventure and speed got off to an extraordinary start in 1932 when Amelia Earhart flew from New Zealand to Ireland — a world record — to become the first woman to fly solo across the Atlantic. That same year she flew 2,600 miles from Los Angeles to Newark in nineteen hours five minutes to become the first woman to complete a transcontinental flight.

Radio Times. Radio, more than other medium, came of age in the 1930s and brought sports into people's homes and, later, their automobiles. Americans could listen to boxing title fights, Army-Navy football games, and horse racing, among other sporting events. In 1934 NBC broadcast tennis matches from England and France, with John R. Tunis, noted author and sportswriter, doing the commentary. A turning point for radio sports was the 1932 Winter Olympics from Lake Placid, New York. Though sports were essentially "free" on the airwaves, broadcast rights and commercial airtime had to be purchased. Judge Landis sold the rights to the World Series in 1934 for $100,000 (to Ford Motors). For most of the 1930s baseball teams were reluctant to broadcast games out of fear that fans would not come to the parks. Two-city teams agreed not to broadcast any away games, and no New York teams broadcast games until Larry McPhail, the enterprising young general manager of the Brooklyn Dodgers, sold the team's broadcast rights for the extraordinary sum of $70,000 a year. Companies such as Gillette, a razor manufacturer, were willing to pay big money to hawk their products during national and regional broadcasts. The voices and nuances of sportscasters such as Graham McNamee and Bill Stern, whose Colgate Sports Newsreel debuted in September 1939, became widely known and imitated. Former baseball stars, including Cleveland's Jack Graney and Washington's Walter Johnson, paved the way for former player Dizzy Dean and others as announcers in later years. Bobby Jones had a radio program as early as 1931, in which he gave golf tips and lumped professionals and amateurs together as "golfologists."

Hollywood Beckons. Being a professional in sports did not just mean playing in professional competitions; to support themselves athletes had to take on other jobs, sometimes modestly paying ones but not always. Lucrative offers to sports heroes from Hollywood made it difficult for many amateur athletes to resist temptation. Early in 1930 swimmer Johnny Weissmuller took a screen test and became filmland's "Tarzan, King of the Jungle." Olympic swimmer Buster Crabbe, a bronze medal winner in 1928 and a gold medal winner in 1932, starred as Flash Gordon and Buck Rogers in the movies. Bill Tilden signed a contract with M-G-M in 1931 and thus terminated his amateur status as an athlete. Sonja Henie began her successful film career after the 1936 Olympics. Babe Ruth and Knute Rockne also signed Hollywood contracts in 1931, and later in the decade so did Eleanor Holm and Hank Luisetti, who starred with Betty Grable in the 1938 box office bomb *Campus Confessions*. Daredevils ventured into sports as dangerous as bullfighting and speed racing, often in the hope of landing a movie deal. For swimming sensations there was entrepreneur Billy Rose's Aquacade, with Weissmuller and Esther Williams as featured attractions. Williams, who won the AAU 100-meter freestyle in 1939, went on to a successful career in films.

Sports America. In the 1920s Europeans could boast of miler Paavo Nurmi and tennis greats Suzanne Lenglen and Henri Cochet, but American athletes continued to lead in world sports competition throughout the 1930s. One strong reason is that more and more Americans actively participated in sporting activities through longstanding amateur clubs and organizations. Intramurals and gymnasium requirements were becoming important parts of collegiate life. Skiing was the fastest-growing sport in America in the 1930s. Railroads carried ski enthusiasts to New Hampshire's White Mountains and New York's Adirondacks. After the 1932 Winter Olympics in Lake Placid, New York, downhill trails and winter resorts appeared throughout New England and New York and the Rockies and Sierra Nevada out west.

The Emergence of Black Athletes. Desegregation in sports and throughout American life was still many years away, but black athletes in all types of sports finally started to achieve recognition in the 1930s. Colleges plodded toward integration, most notably in track and field and football. Negro League baseball was on many levels the equal of the white majors, and players from both leagues, including Dizzy Dean and Satchel Paige, occasionally barnstormed together. Jesse Owens, Eddie Tolan, and Ralph Metcalfe demonstrated superior abilities in track and field, though white sportswriters were quick to remind readers that these athletes were "colored." Grantland Rice, among others, while praising such athletes, could get by with such offhand remarks as "Negroes generally function best in intense heat." Some writers were more blatantly racist or stereotypical in their reportage; but gradually black athletes were treated with more dignity and respect. Separate but rarely equal organizations, leagues, and even collegiate policies prevailed, and the NFL, which had been sparsely integrated until 1933, remained all-white until 1946. Jim Crow laws still prevailed, but Americans, through the exploits of black athletes, were taking the first step to a growing awareness of the problems of racial injustice and segregation.

Women in Sports. The achievements of Babe Didrikson alone would have been enough to put women prominently on the map of the sporting world in the 1930s. She entered 634 amateur athletic competitions during the 1920s and 1930s and won 632 — the losses were in a basketball game and a disqualification in a high-jump contest in which she appeared to set a world record. But there were also Helen Wills Moody, the undisputed queen of tennis, and Sonja Henie, who transformed figure skating into the popular spectacle it is today. Didrikson and Henie became millionaires from their sporting activities. Women golfers such as Virginia Van Wie garnered amateur crowns and national attention. In 1931 the Amateur Athletic Union (AAU) staged its first gymnastics championships for women, and in 1939 the first bicycling championship for women took place. A woman coxswain led a men's varsity crew to victory; a woman bowled a 300 game for the first time. A female tennis player also wore shorts for the first time at Wimbledon. Verne Beatrice Mitchell became the first woman to sign with a professional baseball team, the Chattanooga Lookouts of the Southern Association. She achieved a measure of immortality on 2 April 1931 when she struck out Babe Ruth and Lou Gehrig in an exhibition game. The decade began with women seeking to achieve equal opportunities and social development. By the end of the decade various sporting organizations were beginning to recognize the competitive needs of women athletes as well.

Burgeoning Technology. Technology continued to boom, and it swept sports along with it. Accuracy and efficiency became more attainable. A motorboat with a pair of 12-cylinder motors and 2,200 horsepower hit a record 101.351 mph in 1931. Two weeks later another boat clocked in at 103.4 mph. A diesel-engine race car completed the Indianapolis 500 without making a pit stop, as its driver boasted it would, though it came in thirteenth place at 86.17 mph. Totalizers came to Hialeah, as did the photo-finish camera in 1936. One year later the AAU introduced underwater photography to determine swim-meet finishes. Baseball parks began using the public-address system, and hockey introduced the four-sided clock so that fans, from any angle, could watch the seconds tick away. By the end of the decade there were twenty-three television stations around the country offering limited programming, including sports. Television was still a decade away from becoming the dominant influence on popular culture and the great link between the American fan and sports, though.

Youth Prevails. Athletes seemed to be a lot younger in the 1930s. The image of a youthful, graceful Bobby Jones of the 1920s lingered in many people's minds. America's image was that of a young, vibrant nation. Babe Didrikson was eighteen at the 1932 Summer Olympics. Sidney Wood, age nineteen, won at Wimbledon. Sportswriter Allison Danzig described 1931 star Ellsworth Vines, barely twenty, as "the youngest-looking player ever to win the national crown [in tennis] though there have been others to come to the throne at a slightly more tender age." In Cleveland seventeen-year-old Stanislawa Walasiewicz ran the 220-yard dash in 26 4/5 seconds and then broke her own record one week later in 26 1/10 seconds. In the 1936 Olympics thirteen-year-old Marjorie Gestring won a gold medal in the springboard diving event. In 1938 twenty-two-year-old Eddie Arcaro rode Lawrin to the first of his record five Kentucky Derbys. At eighteen Joe DiMaggio signed with the San Francisco Seals and hit safely in 61 straight games for a Pacific Coast League record. DiMaggio, along with a youthful Ted Williams, attracted the attention of local and nation-wide sportswriters. Bobby Feller became a major league pitcher at seventeen in 1936 and struck out fifteen in his first major league start. The Iowa farm boy kept getting better. He pitched a no-hitter when he was twenty-one, already a five-year veteran, and won 107 games before his twenty-second birthday.

The Specter of Fascism. The 1936 Olympics had been a showcase for Hitler to tout his theory of Aryan superiority on his German athletes. Despite the strong showing of the United States and its black athletes, Germany still won the most medals. Many sportswriters were impressed. Charles Lindbergh stood by Hitler's side during the ceremonies. Olympic officials brushed anti-Semitism aside by claiming that Jews had never really been Olympic-caliber athletes or that "the customs of other nations are not our business." In the late 1930s fascist countries continued to use sports for propagandistic purposes. The second Joe Louis–Max Schmeling fight turned into a symbol of freedom versus fascism, with Louis, America's first black hero, triumphant.

The Coming War. The possibility of America's becoming involved in the war in Europe, despite Roosevelt's promises of noninvolvement, increased with each passing day. Roosevelt had recalled the U.S. ambassador to Germany in 1938 and a year later asked Congress for half a billion dollars in defense money, while demanding further assurances of nonaggression from Mussolini and Hitler. On 1 September 1939 Germany invaded Poland, and two days later the war began. The Depression, which had inaugurated the decade, was just about over; the U.S. economy, suddenly invigorated by preparations for war, boomed once more as the decade ended on an ominous note. It also ended on a sad one for many: Lou Gehrig, suffering gravely from amyotrophic lateral sclerosis, was honored at Yankee Stadium on 4 July 1939 and gave his now-famous speech in which he said that he still considered himself "the luckiest man on the face of the earth." He died at the age of thirty-seven not two years later, six months before the United States entered the war.

TOPICS IN THE NEWS

AMATEURISM VS. PROFESSIONALISM

Battle over Definitions. Whether sports should be played for physical well-being, competition, recreation, and character building, or primarily for profit and the accumulation of victories has been a long-standing debate in this country since the middle of the nineteenth century. The definition of *amateur* has blurred, depending upon the governing rules of the sport or of the AAU and often upon the athlete in question. Sportswriter Paul Gallico defined an amateur as "a guy who won't take a check." But many amateur athletes could earn money in a variety of other ways, including endorsing products, padding expense accounts, or cashing in the gold and silver prizes they won. Many factors, including the Depression, forced officials to look the other way; but once in a while someone got caught: Finnish runner Paavo Nurmi was barred from the 1932 Olympics because he had made a small profit on his expense account during a trip to Germany. The Missouri Valley football conference questioned Jim Bausch's job selling insurance while he was playing fullback for the University of Kansas. Jesse Owens's amateur status was put in jeopardy because he accepted a patronage job as a page in the Ohio state legislature. The public cared little about these minor infractions and under-the-table dealings, but sportswriters like Gallico and John R. Tunis were often incensed at the hypocrisy of the amateur governing bodies.

Lack of Standards. Amateur sports were often sources of lucrative gate receipts, and amateur athletes usually had to practice the same long hours as professional athletes. After Bobby Jones retired in 1930, there were few pure amateur athletes in America who could compete with — and defeat — professional athletes. Amateurs were often treated like professionals, especially if they failed to live up to contractual obligations. When Jessie Owens backed out of a track-and-field engagement in Sweden, the AAU suspended him. This often forced athletes (such as Monte Irvin in 1937) to play professional sports under an assumed name so as not to jeopardize their amateur collegiate status.

College Football and Amateurism. In the 1930s the NCAA had no restrictions concerning eligibility requirements or compensation of athletes. The 1932 Marx Brothers film *Horse Feathers* lampooned the manner in

Jesse Owens and Tippy Dye, Ohio State Senate pages, 1935

which college football teams cavalierly recruited players, many of whom were not legitimate students. Few schools were willing to take the step Robert Maynard Hutchins did when he abolished the long-established football program at the University of Chicago in 1939. During the first College All-Star Game in 1934, in which the best major-college players challenged the NFL champions, a great defense helped the amateurs blank the NFL Chicago Bears in a scoreless tie. As late as 1950, Army head coach Red Blaik was still convinced that college football was truer sport than professional football.

Source:
Paul Gallico, *Farewell to Sport* (New York: Knopf, 1938).

BASEBALL

Hitters Go Wild. In 1930 the National League batting average was just over .300, with almost 900 home runs. Chicago's diminutive powerhouse Hack Wilson hit 56 homers and 190 RBIs. Bill Terry of the Giants became the last National Leaguer to hit over .400. Even the last-place "Futile" Phillies batted .315 as a team. The American League overall hit less well, but the New York Yankees and Philadelphia Athletics matched the older league in most respects. Some folks insisted that the ball was juiced up. Whatever the reason, fans loved it and came to the ballparks in record numbers. The following year the ball was deadened with a looser covering and higher stitching. As a result, what Ring Lardner (in a 1930 *New Yorker* piece) called "B'rer Rabbit Ball" came to an abrupt end. Averages and run production dropped markedly (run-scoring sacrifice flies were now counted as a time at bat, though, too) and so did attendance. Fans not only missed the great hitting but also began to feel the effects of the Depression. So did the owners, who used the national economic crisis as well as the 1931 drop in batting averages to lower salaries.

Red Ink. From a high of 10.1 million in 1930, attendance dropped to 8.1 million in 1932 and 6.3 million one year later. The American League lost more than $2 million in a three-year period. Major-league salaries were cut overall by a million dollars between 1929 to 1933, and even by 1939 the average major-league salary was $200 below the 1929 figure. Weaker clubs suffered the most, having to sell their best players to financially healthier clubs. Organizations with deep, well-developed farm systems (such as Branch Rickey's Saint Louis Cardinals) could unload their player surplus or begin rotating minor-league talent to the parent club. As the farm system burgeoned in the 1930s, the rich teams got richer — and better. And there was always money to be made by renting out ballparks to Negro League teams. Night games, radio, and a brighter economic outlook for the country starting in 1935 also eased some of the burdens.

Black Ball. Baseball was America's favorite sport, and the major leagues achieved a rare level of stability, with no significant rule changes and only one aborted franchise shift (the Saint Louis Browns). One consequence of that status quo, however, was the gentleman's agreement that kept African Americans from entering the major leagues. Nonetheless, black baseball was more exciting than ever, even though the Depression had virtually wiped out the organized league. While gambling once nearly destroyed Major League Baseball, tavern owner W. A. "Gus" Greenlee used money he made in the numbers racket to organize and support the Pittsburgh Crawfords, the greatest team of the reborn Negro National League in the 1930s. The league consisted mostly of eastern teams, including "Cum" Posey's famed Homestead Grays. In 1936 the Negro American League included teams in cities in the South and the Midwest. The Crawfords could boast of a lineup including baseball im-

mortals Josh Gibson, Satchel Paige, Oscar Charleston, Cool Papa Bell, and Judy Johnson. But the black leagues had no real stability, no reserve clause, and often no formal contracts, so players could — and did — jump from team to team whenever they got a better offer to play.

BASEBALL'S HALL OF FAME

Though the historical evidence was dubious at best, Baseball's Centennial Commission accepted the findings of the Mills Report of 1907 that Abner Doubleday was the founder of baseball in 1839 in Cooperstown, New York. In 1936 the Hall of Fame was founded in that quaint community, and the first inductees were selected by the Baseball Writers Association of America commission and a special veterans' committee. Players inducted in the 1930s were as follows:

1936:
Ty Cobb
Honus Wagner
Babe Ruth
Christy Mathewson
Walter Johnson

1937:
Cy Young
Tris Speaker
Napoleon Lajoie
Morgan G. Bulkeley
Ban Johnson
Connie Mack
John McGraw
George Wright

1938:
Grover Cleveland
Alexander Cartwright
Henry Chadwick

1939:
Cap Anson
Eddie Collins
Charles Comiskey
Candy Cummings
Buck Ewing
Lou Gehrig
Wee Willie Keeler
Charles Radbourn
George Sisler
Albert G. Spalding.

The 1930s were the last great days of semiprofessional, independent, and amateur baseball and in many cases produced some of the wildest baseball west of the Mississippi and in the South. There were various leagues and federations, each of which had its own rules and regulations. Most popular of all were the various tournaments — an outgrowth of the Depression — run on the local, state, and national level. The tournaments were important for a variety of reasons:

1. They were the closest reminders of what the game was like before the era of organized baseball;

2. they became a way for organized baseball to recruit young players, especially for the new minor-league farm teams. Eighteen-year old Bob Feller was playing for a Des Moines semipro club when he was signed by a major-league scout;

3. they helped keep the spirit of amateurism alive;

4. they were, for a while at least, one of the few bastions of integrated baseball. In 1934 Satchel Paige led the House of David team to victory in the prestigious *Denver Post* tournament against his old teammates the Kansas City Monarchs. The next year Paige pitched the semipro Bismarck club (for which he played all season) to a championship in the first national tournament of Hap Dumont's National Baseball Congress in Wichita;

5. they became dependable sources of revenue;

6. they demonstrated the possibilities of spectacle and promotion at ballparks long before the major leagues got into the act;

7. they offered substantial prize money for players during hard times;

8. they provided a diversion for unemployed men and helped them establish business contacts with industrial firms that sponsored teams;

9. they ushered in the era of international baseball, especially in Mexico, Central America, and Japan.

Source: Harold Seymour, *The People's Game* (New York: Oxford, 1990).

The Gashouse Gang. Young and old Cardinals combined to form the most colorful team of the mid 1930s. Managed by Frankie Frisch, the "Gashouse Gang" got its name either from its filthy uniforms or the American League belief that the team was "just a lot of gashouse ball players." Also, the team reminded many old-timers of the down-and-dirty teams of the 1890s, like the old Orioles. Several players (like Pepper Martin) had played for the 1931 championship squad, but young stars like Dizzy Dean and Joe Medwick turned the team into a legend in 1934. The zany Dean won thirty games and saved seven that year, and the Cardinals won the pennant in seven games, defeating a Detroit team featuring Mickey Cochrane, Charlie Gehringer, and Hank Greenberg. Dean and his brother Paul (called "Daffy") won all four games. In game five Dizzy Dean was knocked unconscious. Myth has it that one newspaper headline announced: "X-RAYS OF DEAN'S HEAD SHOW NOTHING."

The Yankees Rule. The Yankees, managed by Joe McCarthy, were again the dominant team in the American League; they would win four consecutive world championships between 1936 and 1939. Babe Ruth was released by the Yankees at the end of the 1934 season and signed with the Boston Braves for 1935. He retired for good in early June. His crowning moment came in the fifth inning of the third game of the 1932 World Series when he allegedly, in the words of sportswriter Joe Williams, "went so far as to call his shot." Whether he actually did or not (and it became doubtful, even to Williams, that he did) remains the stuff of baseball lore. Lou Gehrig stepped into the spotlight through the first half of the decade and became one of the greatest and most beloved players ever to play the game. His famous uniform number 4 (numbers were a Yankee innovation in 1929) reflected his place in the lineup (other teams began issuing player numbers on the backs of uniforms in the 1930s). In 1936 twenty-one-year-old Joe DiMaggio was the full-time centerfielder, already on his way to a phenomenal career. By 1939, with veterans like Lefty Gomez, Bill Dickey, and Joe Cronin, and with the help of an excellent farm system, the team's second dynasty was under way.

Sources:
Robert W. Creamer, *Babe: The Legend Comes to Life* (New York: Simon & Schuster, 1974);

Frederick G. Lieb, *The St. Louis Cardinals* (New York: Putnam, 1944);

John Thorn and Pete Palmer, eds., *Total Baseball*, second edition (New York: Warner, 1991);

David Quentin Voigt, *American Baseball: From the Commissioners to the Continental Expansion* (University Park: Pennsylvania State University Press, 1983).

BASKETBALL

College Ball. In the 1930s college basketball *was* the dominant form of organized basketball. The Depression had sunk the professional American Basketball League (ABL), which had been formed in the 1920s, but it actually revived the college game, which was played mostly in gymnasiums and armories. Those lean years inspired new promotions, one of which was the college doubleheader, such as the games played at Madison Square Garden, the

The New York Rens, the best team in basketball during the mid 1930s

brainchild of sportswriter Ned Irish, who later founded the New York Knickerbockers. Irish brought in big-name universities, mostly from eastern cities. The first intersectional games on 29 December 1934 brought 16,188 fans into the Garden. The games introduced young talent, helped spread the popularity of basketball, and made lots of money. Other cities followed suit in their hometown arenas. On the West Coast, at Stanford, Hank Luisetti was revolutionizing the game with his one-handed jump shot and other innovations. Play became faster with the elimination of the center jump after every basket. Even a reformulated ABL in 1933 could not compete with collegiate basketball. The Depression added another twist in the absence of a well-organized professional league. While there was not enough money to support players full-time, semipro leagues prospered. When college stars graduated they could still play ball on company-run clubs, such as Henry Clothiers (Wichita), Diamond DX Oilers (Tulsa), and Healey Motors (Kansas City); the opportunity allowed young men to pursue business careers while continuing to play basketball.

The Celtics Live. The original Boston Celtics had been the elite professional basketball team of the 1920s,

winning as much as 90 percent of their games. Several of the veterans teamed up with younger players to form a new squad in 1931 as part of the new ABL. Few professional teams managed to survive the turmoil of the 1930s, but the Celtics and the Brooklyn Visitations were two teams that helped keep the professional game from dying out entirely. Abe Saperstein's Globetrotters, based in Chicago but called "Harlem" because of its all-black squad, could also be a match for any other professional team.

Rens and Sphas. The best professional teams, however, were ethnic — one Jewish, the other black. The South Philadelphia Hebrew Association basketball team (Sphas) team, called the Sphas, boasted all-Jewish players under Coach Eddie Gottlieb and star Harry Litwack. The team won seven titles in thirteen years and dominated the independent clubs they regularly faced. The Sphas played on the ballroom floor of the plush Broadwood Hotel, which featured dancing after the game. The New York Rens, with only seven players, were basketball's best team between 1932 and 1936. Their home court was the Renaissance Casino ballroom in Harlem, which is how the team got its name. While barnstorming

New York, predecessors of the Harlem Globetrotters, 1930. Standing, from left: Abe Saperstein, Toots Wright, Fat Long, Inman Jackson, and Kid Oliver. Runt Pullins is seated.

The Philadelphia Sphas, mid 1930s. Manager and coach Eddie Gottlieb is in tie; clockwise from him: Red Rosen, Inky Lautman, Gil Fitch, Red Wolfe, Moe Goldman, Cy Kaselman, and Shikey Gotthoffer.

during the Depression years, they faced prejudice and racism; but they played white teams, including the Celtics, regularly and usually beat them. The Rens' record for those years was 473–49, including a winning streak of 88 games. They demonstrated precision, teamwork, and stamina, preferring to let other teams call time-outs. The team included six-footers, like Wee Willie Smith, and two-sport professionals like Bill Yancey, Eyre Saitch, and Fats Jenkins, who was only five feet six inches tall. After team founder Bob Douglas was forced to introduce young players in 1939, his new team won the World Professional Tournament that season.

The NBL. Eastern cities dominated basketball, but one league that proved to be a strong link in the chain that became organized professional basketball was the Midwest Industrial League, which included company teams such as Goodyear, Firestone, and General Electric. Located in the Ohio-Indiana region, these teams felt capable of competing with professional clubs. Indeed, Goodyear won the first league championship, and Firestone the next two. In 1937–1938 thirteen teams joined to form the National Basketball League (NBL). Franchise problems would deplete the league, which included such teams as the Oshkosh All-Stars and the Kankakee Gallagher Trojans — and later eastern teams such as the Syracuse Nationals and the Rochester Royals. But the league survived because it recognized the virtues of the college sport, recruited the best college players, and fashioned its rules along college lines. NBL teams were the seedlings of the future National Basketball Association (NBA). Ironically, the great professional teams in the eastern cities all but died out, but the NBL lasted for more than ten years, before the postwar rise of the competing Basketball Association of America, with which it would merge to form the NBA in 1949–1950.

Sources:

Arthur Ashe, *A Hard Road to Glory: A History of the African American Athlete, 1919–1945*, revised edition (New York: Amistad, 1993);

Zander Hollander, ed., *The Pro Basketball Encyclopedia* (Los Angeles: Corwin Books, 1977);

John D. McCallum, *College Basketball, U.S.A., Since 1892* (New York: Stein & Day, 1978).

AMERICA'S QUEEN OF BOWLING

Never Too Late. America's greatest woman bowler in the 1930s was thirty-five before she even bowled her first game in 1923 — but Colorado's Floretta Doty McCutcheon kept getting better and better at it. By 1927 she was beginning to secure her reputation with a series of high-scoring games and exhibitions, and on 18 December she defeated world champion Jimmy Smith in a challenge match, making sports headlines across the country. When she went on tour for the Brunswick Corporation a year later, she was already something of a legend. She told women that they could begin bowling at almost any age and in any physical shape.

Role Model. Throughout the 1930s she continued to bowl professionally; she also gave free lessons at bowling alleys across the country and through the Mrs. McCutcheon School of Bowling, sponsored by local newspapers. She toured from 1930 until her retirement in 1938, organizing leagues and teaching classes for high school and college students. She saw bowling as one sport in which men and women could compete equally.

Outstanding Numbers. McCutcheon bowled ten 300 games and 75 games between 279–299. In 1930 she bowled 245 or better for twelve consecutive games. In 1932 she bowled 260 or better for five consecutive games and 248 or better for twelve consecutive games. In 1931 she bowled a total of 813 in three games and eight years

Floretta McCutcheon

BOXING

The Next Most Popular Sport. Boxing was America's second most popular sport, next to baseball, in the 1930s, though much of the attraction had a lot to do with the heavy gambling that accompanied the bouts. But if a fight were going to be a sensational one — even in the lean years of the Depression — fans tried to scrape up good money to see it. The Depression did hurt gate receipts, but radio also cut into profits as more and more Americans tuned in to ringside coverage. The career of Joe Louis paralleled the rise of boxing on the wireless and contributed significantly to the popularity of other sports reported over the new medium.

Revolving Champions. With the retirement of Gene Tunney the heavyweight title remained vacant from August 1928 to June 1930, while a series of elimination bouts to determine the new champion were fought. Max Schmeling won the championship when Jack Sharkey was disqualified for a foul in the finals of the elimination tournament. In the next seven years the title changed hands four times: Jack Sharkey beat Schmeling in 1932; Primo Carnera beat Sharkey in 1933; Max Baer beat Carnera in 1934; and James J. Braddock beat Baer in 1935. Joe Louis took the title from Braddock in June 1937 and retained the championship until he retired in 1949.

Would-Be Heavyweights. The best of the light heavyweights gave up their titles to compete as heavyweights. Maxey Rosenbloom was a skillful fighter, but he lacked a punch. He made up in experience for what he lacked in power. A veteran of 285 bouts between 1925 and 1939, Rosenbloom held the title from 1930 to 1934, when he was outpointed by Bob Olin. In 1935 Olin lost a punishing fifteen-round decision to John Henry Lewis, who defended twice before vacating the title in 1938 for a chance at Joe Louis. Lewis was knocked out in the first round. Melio Bettina won the elimination tournament to determine a successor to Lewis in February 1939 and held the title for seven months before he was outpointed by Billy Conn, regarded as one of the best light heavyweights in history. He promptly resigned to prepare for a fight with Louis in which he acquitted himself well before the champ knocked him out in the thirteenth round. That 1941 match, the first of two championship fights between Louis and Conn, was considered one the most credible challenges to Louis's title.

Middleweights. In 1931 Mickey Walker resigned the middleweight championship he had held since 1926, claiming he could no longer make the 160-pound weight limit; the next month, fighting at 169 pounds, he fought a fifteen-round draw with heavyweight contender Jack Sharkey, and in the next year he won four of six heavyweight fights, all against legitimate contenders. In a confusing tournament to determine Walker's successor, Gorilla Jones was recognized as the National Boxing Association (NBA) champion, and Ben Jeby was recognized as

later bowled 827 in three games. Her bowling average over the span of the decade was 201 in 8,076 games. She continued as a master teacher until her midsixties and as a bowler into her seventies. Though none of her accomplishments was ever officially sanctioned by the Women's International Bowling Congress, she reaped many honors and awards, which recognized her remarkable achievements, not only as a great bowler but also for almost single-handedly helping to popularize further what was fast becoming America's most participatory sport.

Source:
Janet Woolum, *Outstanding Women Athletes* (Phoenix: Oryx Press, 1992).

Primo Carnera and Joe Louis before their heavyweight boxing match on 25 June 1935

lightweight Poncho Villa in 1925 had caused the Filipino fighter's death, took the title from Corbett with a first-round knockout in June 1933. Eleven months later in a well-promoted match, Barney Ross, who had given up his lightweight championship to campaign as a welterweight, took the title in a fifteen-round decision. That was the first of three fifteen-round fights between Ross and McLarnin; in September 1934 McLarnin regained his title, but in May 1935 Ross took the title and held on to it for the next three years, while McLarnin retired after three more fights against other contenders. In May 1938 Ross was defeated by Henry Armstrong, who was also the reigning featherweight champ and who won the lightweight championship in August. Armstrong held the welterweight title for two years.

Lightweights. Among the lightweights, the stars of the division were Tony Canzoneri, Lou Ambers, Ross, and Armstrong. When in 1935 Ross vacated the title he won from Canzoneri in 1933, Canzoneri regained the championship in a hard fifteen-round match with top contender Ambers, but in a 1936 rematch Ambers prevailed. Armstrong took his title in 1938 before 18,340 fans at Madison Square Garden, but Ambers won a rematch in August 1939 with a fifteen-round decision.

Below the Belt. Early in the decade the heavyweight crown was tainted by many scandals. Max Schmeling of Germany won the title in 1930 on a questionable below-the-belt punch from Jack Sharkey. Sharkey won on points in a long, uneventful rematch two years later. Sportswriters quipped that Schmeling had won the title lying down and lost it standing up. The Italian Primo Carnera, a boxer of questionable skills, became the next heavyweight champion in June 1933, due largely to his underworld connections (gangster Owney Madden owned him). All of Carnera's fights leading up to the heavyweight match were fixed, and some believed Sharkey took a fall, though most boxing writers turned their heads to the fraud. In June 1934 Max Baer dropped Carnera to the floor eleven times in eleven rounds to put the title in legitimate hands, finally.

Emergence of Joe Louis. Joe Louis, a black fighter from Detroit, won twelve of his fights in 1934, his first year as a professional, knocking out ten of his opponents. He was the most exciting heavyweight boxer of the day. Jim Braddock, a boxer, in the words of sports historian John Kieran, with "a broken past and a dreary future . . . a washed-up fighter on his way out," upset Baer in June 1935 and sat on his title for two years. Louis, Baer, and Schmeling all vied for the opportunity to challenge Braddock. Louis won fight after fight and got to meet Carnera, who had at least learned a little during his spotted career. He outweighed Louis considerably; but Louis brought him down in the sixth round in June 1935. Baer was also sitting down, bruised and dazed, when he took the count in the fourth round in his fight with Louis in September 1935. Schmeling knocked out an over-

the title holder in New York. Jones was disqualified for a foul in the eleventh round of a fight against Frenchman Marcel Thil in Paris, and although Thil defeated the British and German champions in due course, he was stripped of his title by the NBA for inactivity. Ben Jeby then emerged as champion by the end of 1932, though he was recognized in the United States alone. In a volatile division, Lou Brouillard (1933), Vince Dundee (1933), Teddy Yarosz (1934), Babe Risko (1935), Freddy Steele (1936), Al Hostack (1938, 1939), and Solly Krieger (1938) were all heirs to Jeby's suspect crown. Fred Apostoli, one of the strongest fighters in the division during the 1930s, further complicated matters. He had beaten Thil in 1937, when the Frenchman was regarded as champion outside the United States. Apostoli also beat Steele in 1937 in an overweight match, and, when Steele refused a rematch for the championship, the New York Commission awarded Apostoli its version of the championship. Apostoli was knocked out by Ceferino Garcia in 1939 for the New York title.

Welterweights. Tommy Freeman (1930), Young Jack Thompson (1931), Lou Brouillard (1931), Jackie Fields (1932), and Young Corbett III (1933) all held the welterweight championship in a division that lacked excitement until Jimmy McLarnin and Barney Ross arrived at the top. Hard-hitting McLarnin, whose punishment of

Max Schmeling being pounded by Joe Louis during their second fight, on 22 June 1937; Louis knocked Schmeling out in the first round.

confident and undertrained Louis in twelve rounds in June 1936, but he never got a title match with Braddock.

Second Louis-Schmeling. After defeating Jack Sharkey (August 1936), Louis earned a match with an aging Braddock, who finally realized that his career was slipping away. Though Braddock knocked Louis down for a two count, Louis put him away easily in the eighth round of the championship fight in Chicago on 22 June 1937. Schmeling, who once employed a Jewish manager but now had joined the Nazi Party, finally agreed to meet Louis after two years. The grudge match occurred on 23 June 1938, and it was clearly over from the minute it started. Louis flattened Schmeling three times in two minutes and four seconds before eighty thousand fans at Yankee Stadium. Wrote James P. Dawson of *The New York Times* — in a few carefully chosen words — "The German ex-champion threw exactly two punches. That is how completely the Bomber established his mastery in this second struggle with the Black Uhlan."

Sources:

Sam Andre and Nat Fleisher, *A Pictorial History of Boxing*, revised edition (Secaucus, N.J.: Citadel, 1987);

Allison Danzig and Peter Brandwein, eds., *The Greatest Sport Stories from the New York Times* (New York: Barnes, 1951).

FOOTBALL

Reform Efforts. Reformers in the 1930s hoped to deemphasize intercollegiate football. They wanted fewer games, and they wanted coaches to be educators and counselors rather than taskmasters. After the death of a

Yale player in 1931, reformers were alarmed that the number of fatalities had almost tripled from 1930 to 1931. But the public was indifferent. A 1931 report of the Carnegie Foundation called for reforms in college football, just as it had done ten years earlier. The report lamented what the foundation felt were corrupting influences (alumni dollars, massive press coverage) that were turning football into a quasi-professional sport rather than a purely collegiate one. At the same time the report cited positive growth in such programs as Notre Dame's and hesitated making any clear-cut recommendations. The report expressed hope that the Depression would do the job of retrenching athletic programs, which, it suggested, students had begun to tire of anyway in favor of intramurals.

Chicago Drops Football. University of Chicago president Robert M. Hutchins (founder of the Great Books program) became convinced that America needed more brains than brawn. He "retired" legendary coach Amos Alonzo Stagg after the 1932 season and began deemphasizing the football program, first by refusing to recruit new players. Once a national powerhouse under Stagg, Chicago sank to the bottom of the Big Ten and eventually abandoned the football program altogether after 1939. In 1937 Notre Dame, the bellwether of college football, dropped the University of Pittsburgh, coached by Jock Sutherland, from its schedule, since Pitt was considered to be a de facto professional team, having paid its players and trained them rigorously. Pitt soon reformed itself, and Sutherland moved to the NFL.

The Game Moves Forward. Football's offensive formations had not really progressed beyond the single wing in the 1920s. There were only a handful of plays to call, and players played both offense and defense. But individual players and astute coaches pioneered a new era of play in the 1930s. Sammy Baugh, quarterback at Texas Christian University, showed just how devastating a passing attack could be. Few coaches or quarterbacks believed in the merits of the forward pass, but Baugh proved them wrong by upsetting a superior Santa Clara team and then beating Marquette in the Cotton Bowl in his senior year in 1936. He brought the pass attack to the NFL when he joined the Washington Redskins in 1937, leading the team to the Eastern Division title and then defeating the Chicago Bears with three touchdown passes, of 55, 78, and 33 yards. He broke all the passing records up to that time, and football was never quite the same. Don Hutson, as an all-American at Alabama and a standout for the Green Bay Packers (from 1935 to 1945), ushered in the era of the wide receiver. No one could keep up with the speedy Hutson, and for years no one matched his ability to catch on the run.

The NFL Stabilizes. At the start of the decade the team with the best record was considered the NFL champion. Teams included the Providence Steam Rollers, the Cleveland Indians, and the Frankford Yellow Jackets. Most fans considered college football the real game. But

Professional football quarterbacks Sammy Baugh, Benny Friedman, and Sid Luckman

by mid decade there were two solid five-team divisions, each promising team rivalries and each featuring young, dynamic players who would become bona fide stars. Starting in 1933 a championship game was played between the Eastern and Western Division winners, and in 1938 the first Pro Bowl took place, pitting league all-stars against the league champion New York Giants. More than anything else, the NFL was laying the groundwork to showcase a more offensive game, as the run-oriented single wing gave way to the T-formation. Coach George Halas of the Chicago Bears drafted Columbia's Sid Luckman in 1939 with the sole intent of making him the NFL's first T-formation quarterback. A rule permitting the ball to be thrown forward anywhere behind the line of scrimmage (rather than just five yards out) assured that the passing game would be here to stay.

Great College Coaching. The golden age football star Red Grange retired in 1935, convinced that college football could never compete with professional football, whose players, he said, ate, drank, and slept the game. Nonetheless, fans flocked in large numbers to big college events, even as the Depression affected attendance and retarded athletic programs. Knute Rockne, who died in 1931, was still college football's greatest coach as the decade began. His final team — the 1930 Notre Dame

eleven — was 10–0 and scored 265 points while yielding only 74. USC dominated the Rose Bowl in Pasadena, California, which generally pitted the best western team against the best team from the East. Other great coaches included Fritz Crisler at Minnesota and Princeton; Dick Harlow at Harvard; and Northwestern's Lynn Waldorf, who was elected by the American Football Coaches Association as the first College Football Coach of the Year in 1935. Amos Alonzo Stagg wound up at the College of the Pacific, where he finished a career that comprised 314 victories.

Decade of Bowl Games. The big college football game or team rivalry (Notre Dame–Army; the Princeton-Harvard-Yale series) always provided ample excitement during the regular season. In 1935 Texas Christian, 10–0 and led by passing great Sammy Baugh, lost 20–14 to Southern Methodist, also 10–0, in the year's big game. Rivals Pittsburgh and Fordham, both undefeated, met early in the season and played to a 0–0 tie in a much-anticipated game in 1937. Such games whetted fans' appetites for more football. In 1934 Arch Ward, sports editor of the *Chicago Tribune*, devised the idea of a football all-star game in which the best college players would meet the NFL Chicago Bears. In the 1930s college and pro teams were more evenly matched, and in that first all-star game they played each other to a 0–0 tie. The Rose Bowl was the most significant postseason matchup, but beginning in 1935 other postseason bowl games, including long-forgotten ones like the Ice Bowl, the Rhumba Bowl, and the Tobacco Bowl, proliferated. The following is a list of some of the inaugural bowl games of the 1930s:

Orange Bowl, Miami — Bucknell, 26 vs. Miami, 0 (1935)

Sugar Bowl, New Orleans — Tulane, 20 vs. Temple, 14 (1935)

Sun Bowl, El Paso — Hardin Simmons, 15 vs. New Mexico State, 14 (1936)

Cotton Bowl, Dallas — Texas Christian, 16 vs. Marquette, 6 (1937)

North-South (Shrine All-Stars), Baltimore — South, 7 vs. North, 0 (1932)

Blue-Gray Game, Montgomery, Alabama — Blue, 7 vs. Gray, 0 (1938).

Sources:

Tim Cohane, *Great College Football Coaches of the Twenties and Thirties* (New Rochelle, N.Y.: Arlington House, 1973);

Will McDonough and others, *75 Seasons: The Complete Story of the National Football League, 1920–1995* (Atlanta: Turner Publishing, 1995);

Murray Sperber, *Shake Down the Thunder: The Creation of Notre Dame Football* (New York: Holt, 1993).

GOLF

Significant Developments. The Depression caused many country clubs to close, but New Deal programs such as the WPA saw to the building of nearly two hundred public golf courses. Enthusiasm for the sport dwindled a little, as smaller crowds came out to see the major tournaments. Still, golfing got better. Equipment — both golf clubs and golf balls — improved. The move from hickory shafts to steel ones provided longer drives. Golfer Gene Sarazen invented the sand wedge in his Florida garage in 1930. More-meticulous attention was paid to groundskeeping and landscaping. Built for Bobby Jones, the Augusta National, one of the most challenging golf courses in the world, opened in Augusta, Georgia, in 1934 and became the home of the Masters Tournament. The new event would be limited to sixty-five or so of the very best golfers in the world. The miniature-golf craze would die out by the end of the decade, but in 1930 the first national open miniature-golf tournament was held in Chattanooga, Tennessee.

Searching for Bobby Jones. From the day Bobby Jones retired (after winning the Grand Slam in 1930), people kept hoping another golfer with skill and charisma might come along who could assume the mantle of his greatness. No one, however, was able to fill his golf shoes. Twenty-year-old Gene Sarazen thrilled golf fans by coming from behind to win the 1932 U.S. Open by playing

Mr. and Mrs. Gene Sarazen in 1932. She is holding his trophy for winning the British Open Golf Championship; he is holding his trophy for winning the U.S. Open.

his last twenty-eight holes in a hundred strokes. In 1935 he double-eagled in the Masters to force Craig Wood into a playoff, which Sarazen won the next day. His career was marked by inconsistency but also by longevity and proficiency. In 1934 Stanford's Lawson Little Jr. burst onto the scene, capturing both the British and Amateur titles two years in a row. But even winning the double-double did not endear the stoic Little to fans. Ralph Guldahl also won two consecutive U.S. Opens in 1937 and 1938, but he played too methodically and emotionlessly. By the end of the decade a host of talented young golfers appeared, including Sam Snead and Byron Nelson, who won the Masters in 1937 and earned well-deserved comparisons with golden-age hero Jones.

Jockey Earle Sande atop 1930 Triple Crown winner Gallant Fox

What Price Pro? There was not much money to be made in professional golf, especially during the height of the Depression. Paul Runyon was the big moneymaker in 1934, but he figured that when his expenses were deducted from his earnings he netted about $2. Of the thirty-three or so Professional Golfers' Association (PGA) tournaments in 1935, gross winnings totaled $135,000. Big winner Johnny Revolta won less than $10,000, while more than two hundred professional golfers split the rest. Since amateurs regularly competed with — and often defeated — professionals, the gallery seemed indifferent to status. Women golfers remained amateur, although many of them could hit in the low 70s. Fans saw veteran Glenna Collett defeat seventeen-year-old Patty Berg ("the darling of the Minneapolis galleries") for her sixth national championship in 1935. Virginia Van Wie won three consecutive amateur titles between 1932 and 1934. One major disappointment for Americans was the loss of the biennial Walker Cup to Great Britain in 1938; Americans had won it every other time it was contested since its inauguration in 1922.

Sources:
John M. Gross and the editors of *Golf Magazine*, *The Encyclopedia of Golf*, updated and revised (New York: Harper & Row, 1979);

Herbert Warren Wind, ed., *The Complete Golfer* (New York: Simon & Schuster, 1954).

HORSE RACING

Gaining Popularity. For many years it was a toss-up in America whether horse racing or boxing was America's second most favorite spectator sport. Horse racing's popularity steadily grew as boxing became more crooked and baseball more predictable. Bigger payouts helped increase interest too, though the track was also a good place to get one's pocket picked. Fans who bet on Head Play in the 1933 Kentucky Derby might have thought they were robbed by Broker's Tip jockey Don Meade, who allegedly fouled the favorite's jockey, Herb Fisher. Both riders fought through the stretch and in the jockey room afterward, but the foul was disallowed. Man O' War's day had come and gone, but his scions — Battleship and War Admiral — would step into winner's circles in the 1930s.

The Fox. Gallant Fox, a three-year-old ridden by jockey Earl Sande, burst out of the starting gate at the beginning of the decade and looked as though he would never stop. He won the Triple Crown in 1930, including a tough race in the Belmont Stakes against his chief competitor, Whichone. Gallant Fox also won the Dwyer and the Arlington Classic, and by the time he had won the Lawrence Realization Stakes in September he was the top-winning racehorse. He was, however, finally defeated by an obscure thoroughbred named Jim Dandy at Saratoga Springs in August in the mud.

Seabiscuit by Three Lengths. The race of the decade took place at Pimlico on 1 November 1938, and when it was over no one had seen anything like it. War Admiral, son of Man O' War, had been the Triple Crown winner the previous year, undefeated in eight starts, and was the one-to-four favorite. Seabiscuit, cast-off son of Man O' War's son Hard Tack, was described, at best, as "phlegmatic" by most racing writers. The horse had started eighty-three races already. Under the whip Seabiscuit burst out to a full-length lead. War Admiral gave it all he could and bounded forward, leading by a nose going into the homestretch. But Seabiscuit put everything he could into the drive and pulled away. "Through the last eighth of a mile," wrote the *Chicago Tribune*, "it was a procession."

The Great Gray Gelding. Harness racing was almost as popular as horse racing in the 1930s, due largely in part to Greyhound, who up until that time was the fastest trotter in history. He won the celebrated Hambletonian (the most famous harness-racing event in North America) and elsewhere set a record for the mile at 1 minute 55.25 seconds, which remains close to contemporary records.

Source:
Arch Ward, ed., *The Greatest Sports Stories from the* Chicago Tribune (New York: Barnes, 1953).

ICE HOCKEY

Getting More American. Nine out of ten hockey players were Canadians in the 1930s, but National Hockey League (NHL) teams in Boston first and New York, Chicago, and Detroit later were helping to increase the sport's popularity and give universal recognition to the organized league. The New York Rangers had become the first American Division team to win the Stanley Cup in 1928. They came in first place in 1930, only to be eliminated in four games by the Montreal Maroons. The Chicago Black Hawks won the Stanley Cup in 1934 behind the goaltending of an ailing Charlie Gardiner (who died two months later) and the playmaking of Mush March. In 1938, with the veteran Marsh and American-born players such as Alex Levinsky, Carl Voss, and goalie Mike Karakas (who played the final game with a broken toe), the Black Hawks, who had the sixth-best — or third-worst — record in league play, captured their second Stanley Cup.

More Offense. For too long hockey had been a defensive game. There was call for a much more open style of play. A big rule change came in 1930 when forward passing was finally permitted in all zones. Scoring got

Howie Morenz, "The Stratford Streak," circa 1935

another big boost during the 1933–1934 season when the league mandated that only three players (including the goalie) could occupy the defensive zone. The penalty shot was introduced and modified over the next couple of years. As the game became faster and more offensive, it also grew more violent. As George Strickler described one game in the *Chicago Tribune*, "fist fights developed and several times sticks came crashing down on unprotected scalps." In 1933 Toronto's Ace Bailey nearly died after being hit over the head by Boston's Eddie Shore, who received a suspension. After getting his nose broken for a third time, goalie Clint Benedict designed a leather mask, which he wore infrequently. Protective gear of any kind was considered cowardly.

A New Era. Franchises came and went in the 1930s, dropping from ten to eight, then finally to seven teams playing a forty-eight-game schedule. Amateur hockey got going about the same time in the United States. But with the improved offense and concentration of teams, players were becoming faster skaters and more-adept stick handlers. Many future Hall of Famers began playing in the 1930s: Syl Apps, Frank Boucher, Eddie Shore, Earl Seibert, Babe Siebert, Art Coulter, Charlie Conacher, Dave Schriner, Toe Blake, and goalie Tiny Thompson.

The Stratford Streak. The biggest star of them all was the Montreal Canadiens' "Stratford Streak," Howie Morenz. Morenz had been a young star in the 1920s, but three of his best seasons came in the early 1930s, when he won two consecutive Hart Trophies as the league's most valuable player. In 1936 his trade in midseason to the Rangers (from Chicago) prompted John Kieran to imagine "Morenz going out in a New York uniform to annoy

HOCKEY'S LONGEST GAME

The record for the longest hockey game ever played was set and broken in the 1930s. Both were Stanley Cup games, and both went into the sixth overtime. In 1933 the Bruins and the Leafs went 0–0 for an additional one hour, forty-four minutes and forty-six seconds until Toronto scored a goal. Three years later an even longer game was played between the Detroit Red Wings and the Montreal Maroons in the first round. One reason for the tight games was that teams often relied on their old habit of playing more-defensive hockey in a championship series. Games were long and slow, with few penalties, few shots on goal, and few risks. After the 1933 game the league wanted to cut overtime games short by using a coin toss or playing without goalies, but the fans protested. In 1936 it was sudden death — or nothing. The sixth overtime had nearly elapsed when Red Wing rookie Mud Bruneteau beat Lionel Conacher. The game had begun a little past 8:30 P.M. and finished just before 2:30 A.M. The teams had played 176 minutes of hockey, and the fans had sat for almost six hours. The next night Detroit goalie Norm Smith shut out the Maroons again and did not give up a goal until twelve minutes into the third and final game of the series — still a playoff shutout record. The Red Wings went on to clinch the Stanley Cup.

THE STRANGE CASE OF HELENE MAYER

Her mother was Christian; her father a Jewish physician. She herself was an image of Aryan womanhood. But Helene Mayer did not consider herself a Jew. The Nazis, however, considered anyone of mixed parentage to be Jewish. Mayer found herself caught between two worlds. She had won a gold medal in the foils for Germany in the 1928 Olympics and was the world champion in 1929 and 1931, the year her father died. She traveled to Los Angeles for the 1932 games but did not fare well there. She remained in the United States to study at the University of Southern California and later taught German at Mills College. Between 1933 and 1935 she was the American fencing champion. The Germans initially refused to invite her to the 1936 Berlin games but relented under IOC pressure. She was a significantly good token and a useful propagandistic tool for the Nazis to prove that they placed no restrictions on Jewish athletes. Mayer was more than willing to play for her homeland, where her mother and brothers still lived, even though the fencing club in her native Offenbach had revoked her membership. American Jews, led by Rabbi Stephen Wise, pleaded with her not to play. Mayer accused Wise of interfering and returned to Germany. She won the silver medal in a close competition with Ilona Schacherer-Elek, a Hungarian Jew, who won the gold solely on points. The Nazi press ironically blamed Mayer's defeat on "Jewish judges." At the medal ceremonies Mayer gave a stiff-armed "Heil, Hitler."

the Habitants, the team with which he soared to fame in hockey." But Morenz was on the decline by then. He returned to the Canadiens in 1937 and played just as hard and furiously — the way he lived. He was badly injured in a game and languished in a hospital bed with a broken leg. He suffered a nervous breakdown and died there two months later of heart failure at the age of thirty-four. Roger Kahn wrote in 1956, "It was always speed with Howie Morenz, and in the end it was speed that killed him."

Sources:

Zander Hollander and Ed Bock, eds., *The Complete Encyclopedia of Ice Hockey*, revised edition (Englewood Cliffs, N.J.: Prentice-Hall, 1974);

Roger Kahn, "The Life and Death of Howie Morenz," in *Games We Used to Play* (New York: Ticknor & Fields, 1992).

NAZI OLYMPICS

Germany Shows the World. Fascism had swept through Germany, Italy, and into Spain by 1936. Jews had been stripped of their citizenship and civil rights under the Nuremberg Laws. It was clear, even to the uninitiated, that Germany was preparing for war. Yet the predominant feeling in the United States was one of noninvolvement in European affairs. A few voices urged boycott of the games, but their efforts were repelled by an Olympic committee willing to overlook anything but the most overt kinds of anti-Semitism on the condition that Germany abide by Olympic guidelines and practices. Germany, to whom the games had been promised in 1931 before the rise of Hitler, would take the opportunity to show the world its sweeping accomplishments and display its Aryan ethic, which promised superior athletic demonstrations as expressions of German vitality and will.

German Deception. Germany put its best face forward, made new friends, acted as gracious hosts, and even "proved" that it treated its Jewish population humanely. Most observers were easy dupes (with the exception of such journalists as William Shirer, Paul Gallico, and Westbrook Pegler), appeasers, or, worse, willing accomplices. Many visitors were sadly ingenuous and unfazed by German arrogance and paganism. Eleanor Holm was

Jesse Owens on Broadway in New York City after winning four gold medals in the 1936 Olympics

charmed by the likes of Hermann Goering. Arthur Daley of *The New York Times* wrote of Hitler: "There can be no doubt that he was proud of this moment of the climax of two years' preparation and endeavor. For once pride in an achievement showed in his bearing." Only the International Olympic Committee president Count Henri de Baillet-Latour, no admirer of Jews, had the courage to confront Hitler about anti-Jewish slogans he saw plastered along German highways. Baillet-Latour argued heatedly with Hitler and demanded removal of the signs, threatening to suspend all the games unless Hitler complied with his orders. The signs came down, and conciliatory gestures were even made toward some German Jewish athletes. The Nazi propaganda machine, desperate not to lose the prestigious games, whirled on.

Source:
Richard D. Mandell, *The Nazi Olympics* (New York: Macmillan, 1971).

OLYMPICS

American Olympics. The Depression was, in part, a result of lack of confidence in the American system. The popular song "Brother, Can You Spare a Dime" was written to protest the attack by fellow American troops on World War I veterans camped in Washington, D.C. The Olympics Games, scheduled to take place in the

United States in 1932, actually helped stimulate the economy as well as revive the national spirit.

1932 Winter Games. The 1932 Winter Games in Lake Placid, New York, were the first games broadcast on radio and the first Winter Games in which the United States captured more medals than any other nation: six gold, three silver, two bronze. Seventeen countries participated. Canada won the ice hockey tournament for the fourth game running. Speed skating was a big American event, with Jack Shea winning the 1500-meter race and Irving Jaffee taking the 5000-meter. The United States also commanded the bobsled races with its speed-enhancing, iron V-shaped runners, which were barred from international competition following the Olympics. Karl Schafer of Austria and Sonja Henie of Norway, who continued to dominate figure skating through the decade, won their first and second Olympic gold medals, respectively.

1932 Summer Games. In the 1932 Summer Games in Los Angeles, California, Mildred "Babe" Didrikson, destined to become the greatest woman athlete of the twentieth century, broke world records — some her own — in three events. She won a gold medal in the javelin throw and the 80-meter hurdles, and a silver medal (after an illegal headfirst dive) in the high jump. Lillian Copeland won the gold in the discus throw. American women won

The 1932 U.S. Olympic four-man bobsled team: Jay O'Brien, Eddie Eagan, Clifford Gray, and Billy Fiske. Eight years later only Eagan was still alive.

half of all the medals in track-and-field events. American men were just as spectacular. In a controversial heat Finland's Lauri Lehtinen and the American Ralph Hill tied in the 5000-meter run. Americans beat out Americans in other races, some of which were sweeps. Eddie Tolan bested his friend Ralph Metcalfe and set a world record in the 100-meter. Tolan was also the winner by a big margin in the 200-meter. Bill Carr outran rival Ben Eastman for the gold medal in the 400-meter run. Other significant American victories were the 400-meter relay, anchored by Frank Wykoff; George Saling in the 110-meter hurdles; Ed Gordon (an African American) in the long jump; Helene Madison in the 100- and 400-meter freestyle; Eleanor Holm in the 100-meter backstroke; and Clarence "Buster" Crabbe in the 400-meter freestyle. Japanese men surprised everyone by winning eleven of the eighteen total swimming medals.

1936 Winter Games. The 1936 Winter Games in Garmisch-Partenkirchen, Germany, were uneventful from an American standpoint. The United States won only one gold medal, in the two-man bobsled. In other respects it was both ominous and fascinating. The Ger-

mans invited Rudi Ball, the Jewish hockey star of the 1932 bronze-medal-winning team, to play in the 1936 games. Ball returned from exile in France. Karl Schafer and Sonja Henie, with whom Hitler became infatuated, again won gold medals in figure skating. As the games were under way, the Rhineland crisis was unfolding. German remilitarization had begun.

1936 Summer Games. What the "master race" termed the American or black "Auxiliaries" — America's black athletes — ruled the 1936 Summer Games, winning eight gold, three silver, and two bronze medals. Blacks won the following events:

Jesse Owens — 100-meter dash

Jesse Owens — 200-meter dash

Archie Williams — 400-meter run

John Woodruff — 800-meter run

Cornelius Johnson — high jump

Jesse Owens — long jump.

In addition Owens and Ralph Metcalfe were on the winning 400-meter team.

Helen Stephens, winner of the women's 100-meter dash in the 1936 Olympics, with Adolf Hitler

Two Myths Dispelled. Owens was not snubbed by Adolf Hitler, who had congratulated two German victors and one from Finland on the first day of the events. It was Cornelius Johnson, the black high jump gold medal winner, whom Hitler ignored by leaving the stadium shortly after Johnson's victory. Hitler was later told to shake everyone's hand or no one's, so he opted to wait until the end of the games to hold a celebration for German victors. Also, the German Lutz Long, who matched Owens in the high jump every step of the way until his last jump, which Owens beat by seven inches, did not, as the popular story went, give Owens the special bit of coaching Owens needed to win the event. Long, nonetheless, agreed to be photographed with Owens, shook his hand, and showed him courtesy, friendship, and respect.

Symbolic Victories. American men also won gold medals in the 110-meter hurdles, 400-meter hurdles, discus throw, and pole vault. Glenn Morris won the decathlon. A controversy, never resolved, accompanied the American victory in the 400-meter relay race, as the track team's only Jewish stars, Sam Stoller and Marty Glickman — world-class runners both — were scratched from the race in favor of Owens and Foy Draper, whom the U.S. track coach had known at the University of Southern California. The 1500-meter race was won in world-record time by New Zealand's Jack Lovelock, defeating Glenn Cunningham, who also broke the world record. Helen Stephens was the female star of the Olympic Games. She won the 100-meter dash against her old rival Stanislawa Walasiewicz (whose name was shortened to

Stella Walsh by reporters) and anchored the 400-meter team relay, which the Americans won when the German team dropped the baton. Canoeing and basketball joined the Olympic program for the first time in 1936; Americans won the latter sport. Japan again dominated the swimming contests, though Jack Medica won a gold in the 400-meter freestyle and Adolf Kiefer did the same in the 100-meter backstroke. Both American men's and women's diving teams took home most of the gold, but Germany captured more medals (101) than any other nation (the United States was second with 57), giving Hitler the symbolic victory he sought. As to his larger claims of Aryan superiority, the games were a failure. Hitler had put on a great show, but anti-Semitism, which had resumed after the close of the Winter Games and intensified after the Summer Games, reached its dark apotheosis in the years to come.

Political Olympics. Germany spared no expense in bringing the Winter and Summer Olympics to the world. It had always been the case that the games could be used for nationalistic as well as propagandistic purposes. Germany took it to the extreme. The 1936 games were a turning point in the history of the Olympics in more ways than one, though. Avery Brundage and other hard-liners who vigorously opposed the boycott of the 1936 games con-

Prizefighting, in one form or another (usually melodrama), was the most prevalent theme of sports movies during the decade:

1930 — *Hold Everything:* Comedian turns prizefighter; features French heavyweight champion Georges Carpentier

1931 — *The Champ:* Washed-up boxer Wallace Beery and his adoring son

The Iron Man: From the W. R. Burnett novel; gold digger Jean Harlow eggs on prizefighter husband Lew Ayres

1932 — *The Crowd Roars:* Racetrack driver dissuades younger brother from taking up the sport

Horse Feathers: Crooked college football, with the Marx Brothers on the gridiron

1934 — *Death on the Diamond*

1935 — *Alibi Ike:* From the Ring Lardner story; travails of a middling pitcher

1936 — *Cain and Mabel:* Prizefighter falls in love with showgirl

1937 — *The Kid Comes Back:* Tenderfoot turns prizefighter with the help of a former champ; features light heavyweight champ Maxey Rosenbloom

Kid Galahad: Trainer does too good a job of turning a bellhop into a fighter

1938 — *Campus Confessions:* film debut of Hank Luisetti, and the end of his film career

The Crowd Roars: Young boxer gets mixed up with gangsters

Hold That Co-Ed: Girl dresses up as boy to play football, win the game, and save the governor's hide

1939 — *Ex Champ:* Twist on *The Champ*, only retired fighter, now a doorman, has a reckless and thoughtless son

Golden Boy: From the Clifford Odets play; man must decide between boxing and playing the violin

Indianapolis Speedway: Remake of *The Crowd Roars*.

solidated their power in the organization; supporters of the boycott were voted out. Athletes were expected to follow orders without regard for their feelings or individual concerns; moral and political issues were not to interfere with or impede Olympic sport, which took on a neoreligious significance to men such as Brundage. The 1936 games were no doubt on the minds of U.S. president Jimmy Carter and the U.S. Olympic Committee when in 1980 they decided to boycott the Summer Games in Moscow as a protest against the Soviet invasion of Afghanistan.

Sources:

Alan Guttman, *The Olympics: A History of the Modern Games* (Urbana: University of Illinois Press, 1992);

Bernard Postal, Jesse Silver, and Roy Silver, *Encyclopedia of Jews in Sport* (New York: Bloch Publishing, 1965);

David Wallenchinsky, *The Complete Book of the Olympics* (New York: Viking, 1984).

SOCCER

An Immigrant Game. As the decade began, few Americans had any interest in soccer. Professional and amateur teams vied for the National Challenge Cup. Ethnic and regional leagues, such as the German American Football Association and Fall River Football Club, were the most vital sources for soccer in the 1930s, and U.S. teams were composed largely of immigrants from Scotland and England. As these newcomers sought to become more assimilated into the culture, however, they opted to play baseball and American football.

World Cup Play. The 1936 Olympics helped make U.S. soccer more competitive, but it did little to change the image of the game in American eyes. When the first World Cup took place in Montevideo, Uruguay, in 1930, it received scant notice in the sports pages, although the United States defeated Belgium and Paraguay and advanced to the semifinals. It faced a true world-class Argentine team in the next round and suffered several heartbreaking injuries (including one to their goalkeeper) before losing 7–1.

The College Game. Intercollegiate soccer broadened sharply and geographically. The Middle Atlantic League was created in 1932 with Ivy League schools among its members. Swarthmore College was the dominant team. More teams joined the league for the 1933–1934 season, and a New England Intercollegiate League was formed. More than twenty new teams were added by the end of the decade, though many of them would be forced to disband in the war years ahead.

Source:

Michael L. LaBlanc and Richard Henshaw, *The World Encyclopedia of Soccer* (Detroit: Visible Ink Press, 1994).

The Age of Reason and Skepticism. The golden age of sports had been something of a golden age of sportswriters also: Ring Lardner, Grantland Rice, Damon Runyon, W. O. McGeehan, Paul Gallico, and Heywood Broun were colorful scribes, many of whom went on to other fields of literary endeavor. These writers, who still considered themselves reporters first, had been given a great deal of leeway and freedom in terms of style and content. An "Aw Nuts" group wrote cynical, witty prose, while a "Gee Whiz" group was more romantic and celebratory. They came to dominate sports journalism in the 1930s. A few writers, however, began to look at heroes as ordinary human beings and at sports more critically. While writers were still treated well by the clubs they were covering, the journalists did not feel they were obliged to report only good news. As a result sportswriting grew more objective and analytical.

A New Style of Writing. Sportswriting developed into a journalistic craft that needed to be fit into nine-inch columns of space. Writers had to be aware of certain reader expectations, possess a necessary technical knowledge of games (and language), and have an understanding of the growing science of statistics. The Depression also forced writers to acquire expertise in all sports, since many newspapers could no longer afford the luxury of hiring a variety of specialists. Because reporters were professionals, they demanded professionalism (at least in practice) in the sports they covered. As a result the focus of the sports page began slowly to turn away from college and rank amateur athletics to the more professional game. Dealing with emerging black athletes remained problematic. Writers could be patronizing, particularly when it came to instructing black athletes how they ought to behave.

The Best Writers. Many of the older sportswriters continued to write in the 1930s, and several who began in the 1930s, such as Red Smith, Arthur Daley, and Shirley Povich, lasted well into the 1970s and even the 1980s. Grantland Rice was still considered to be the dean of American sportswriters. There were many fine young writers, and not all of them were situated in Chicago and New York. Chet Smith of the *Pittsburgh Press* and Bill Leiser of the *San Francisco Chronicle* were two outstanding columnists. Not all of them were Caucasian either. Sam Lacy of the *Baltimore Afro American* and Wendell Smith of the *Pittsburgh Courier* were first-rate sportswriters. The best of the new breed of writers was Frank Graham of the *New York Journal-American*, who perfected the conversation and mood piece that was widely imitated during the decade.

Sources:
Stanley Frank, *Sports Extra* (New York: Barnes, 1944);

Stanley Woodward and Frank Graham Jr., *Sportswriter* (Garden City, N.Y.: Doubleday, 1967).

Don Budge, U.S. national tennis champion, 1938

TENNIS

After Tilden. In the 1920s both Bill Tilden and the French tennis star Suzanne Lenglen were largely responsible for the upsurge in popularity of lawn tennis in America and Europe in the following decade. It became increasingly clear, also, in the 1930s that this resurgence of interest and the financial benefits (in the form of "expenses") that accompanied it made it more and more difficult to distinguish between pure amateurs and professional players, who were mainly supposed to be involved in coaching. There were many disputes and irregularities regarding the issue, and by 1939 three other American Wimbledon champions (Ellsworth Vines, Don Budge, and Bobby Riggs) followed Tilden's lead and turned pro after winning a big event — a trend that would be almost routine after the war.

Tennis for Everyone. Tennis was still not a sport for the everyman in the 1930s. The Italian Championships, won first by Tilden, began in 1930, and two Swedish indoor tennis events begun in 1936 reflected the game's growing international and often aristocratic flavor. Still, the United States Lawn Tennis Association (USLTA) took steps to make tennis a lifetime sport for all types of people and particularly to encourage young people to play. A Junior Davis Cup program for boys and a Junior Wightman Cup program for girls were instituted in 1935 and 1938 respectively. African Americans, however, were not welcome in USLTA and continued to play in their separate American Tennis Association (ATA).

The State of the Game. The U.S., British, Australian, and French tournaments were generally recognized now as the major tennis events in world play. Britain's Fred Perry had won them all between 1933 and 1935, but Donald Budge of the United States captured all four titles (the Grand Slam) in a single year — 1938 — the most outstanding athletic accomplishment of that year, especially considering that tennis had beome a faster sport when the standard pressure of the ball was increased. Women's tennis changed in several ways: plunging necklines, Bermuda shorts, and culottes appeared on the courts; women now almost regularly served overhead; and Alice Marble introduced the power-serve volley and wore her shorts even shorter than her opponents.

Budge and Moody Again. Tennis was one of the few sports not to experience a dramatic drop in attendance during the Depression. Record numbers came to Forest Hills and Madison Square Garden to see professional matches featuring Tilden, Vines Perry, and Budge, who beat both Vines and Perry in his debut. After dominating American women's tennis from the early 1920s to the early 1930s, Helen Wills Moody made a remarkable comeback at Wimbledon in 1935. Budge was easily the most exciting male tennis star of the era. A fast and overwhelming baseline player, Budge had a devastating backhand. His five-set match against Baron Gottfried von Cramm at Wimbledon in 1937 was tennis at its apex. Von Cramm was unable to hold a 4–1 lead in the final

set, and Budge took him to 6–6. He then broke von Cramm's serve and went on to win his seventh match point with a wicked ground shot on von Cramm's return of service. As a result of that victory, the United States went on to win its first Davis Cup in ten years, with Budge shining once more. Australia, though, would claim the cup in 1939. That same year Jimmy McDaniel won the first of his four ATA titles.

Sources:

Arthur Ashe, *A Hard Road to Glory: A History of the African-American Athlete* (New York: Warner, 1988);

Allison Danzig and Peter Schwed, eds., *The Fireside Book of Tennis* (New York: Simon & Schuster, 1972);

Max Robinson and Jack Kramer, eds., *The Encyclopedia of Tennis: 100 Years of Great Players and Events* (New York: Viking, 1974).

TRACK AND FIELD

American Competition. No one could match the Finnish miler Paavo Nurmi in the 1920s, but in the 1930s attention turned to U.S. athletes in track. George Venzke burst onto the scene in 1932, breaking Nurmi's mile record of 4:12 (shared with Joie Ray) in the Milrose Games. Venzke bettered his own record of 4:11.2 a little more than a week later, coming in at 4:10. By 1934, though, Venzke was regularly coming in second to the great Kansas runner Glenn Cunningham and third when Princeton's Bill Bonthron participated in the races. In the Princeton Invitation Meet, Cunningham put on one of his greatest shows ever, outdistancing Bonthron and Venzke and clocking 4:06.7 in the mile. Two weeks later at the AAU National Championships in Milwaukee it was Bonthron's turn, though this race, like most of the later Cunningham-Bonthron matches, would be neck and neck. Future races between the two stars would draw record crowds. Bonthron retired early, and rising stars, such as Archie San Romani and Wisconsin's Chuck Fenske, eventually got the better of Cunningham near the end of the decade; but because of these great contests of the 1930s — and "Galloping Glenn" in particular — track grew enormously in popularity nationwide.

Integration for the Sake of Sport. Of all athletic contests in the decade, track and field accomplished more in the way of integration than any other sport. The reason predominantly white colleges sought out black athletes,

of course, was largely that they knew they could not win without them. Black colleges continued to have their own programs, clubs, and meets, but those were rarely officially sanctioned. White colleges, particularly those in the Midwest, made great efforts to recruit African Americans to become part of their athletic programs. Jesse Owens at Ohio State, Eddie Tolan of Michigan, and Ralph Metcalfe at Marquette were two such outstanding runners and stars of the 1932 Olympics. Though blacks were forced to bear the indignities of racism at these same colleges and national athletic events, the decade heralded their excellence in almost all areas of track and field.

HEADLINE MAKERS

MILDRED "BABE" DIDRIKSON

1911-1956

TRACK & FIELD STAR

Greatest Woman Athlete. Most observers generally agree that Babe Didrikson Zaharias was the finest woman athlete of all time, which was exactly what she always wanted to be. There was nothing she could not do short of winning the Kentucky Derby (as one sportswriter said) — and the 1930s were only the beginning of her extraordinary, though tragically short, career. Born in Port Arthur, Texas, she earned the nickname "Babe" because as a schoolgirl she could hit home runs like Babe Ruth. She played on every sports team in high school and became a high-school basketball star. She played for an AAU-sanctioned insurance-company team in Dallas — the Golden Cyclones — and led the team to a national championship in 1931, while reaching the finals in 1930 and 1932 as well. She made all-American three times. Since few sportswriters followed women's sports, not many people knew about Babe at first.

One-Woman Team. Didrikson competed for her company (she was a clerk-typist) in AAU track-and-field meets in Dallas and Jersey City. Her second-place finish in the 1930 broad jump beat a world record, and the next

year she threw a baseball 296 feet. In 1932, at the AAU Nationals/Olympic tryouts in Evanston, Illinois, in about two and a half hours Babe won five events (shot put, javelin, long jump, baseball throw, and 80-meter hurdles, setting a world record in the hurdles and javelin); tied one (the high jump, another world record); and finished fourth in the discus. She won the title for her company single-handedly, scoring eight points higher than her nearest competition, a team of twenty-two women from the University of Illinois. People knew about Babe Didrikson now.

Olympic Hero. At the 1932 Olympics Didrikson won gold medals in the javelin and 80-meter hurdles, again breaking her own world record in both events. She might have won another gold medal in the high jump, but her "western roll" style of diving over the bar was ruled illegal, even though she had been using it all along. Although she broke her own world record of 5 feet, 5 inches, as did Jean Shiley (with whom she also tied at the qualifying matches in Evanston), Didrikson was awarded the silver and Shiley the gold. Babe was named American Woman Athlete of the Year by the Associated Press in 1932, an honor she would win five more times in her career.

Professional. Because her name and picture were used for an automobile advertisement, the AAU suspended Babe in 1932. She turned professional. In the 1930s she played vaudeville, toured with the Babe Didrikson's All-Americans basketball team, and pitched for the Philadelphia Athletics and the House of David team. The AAU soon reinstated her, to their own benefit, hers, and the public's.

Taking Up Golf. Though she always thought of herself as feminine, Didrikson experienced stereotypical comments due to her masculine physique. Furthermore, women's sports were only just beginning to be taken seriously. Having played all sports, Didrikson knew something about golf and often seriously considered taking up the sport. Sportswriter Grantland Rice always believed that Didrikson ("Grant's girl," she was sometimes called) could become great at golf, a sport in which she could compete with men one-on-one, as she had with Rice and his newspaper pals. She was winning amateur events in 1934 and 1935 but was again disqualified because of her prior professional status. She did a series of exhibitions with Gene Sarazen in 1936, waiting patiently for opportunities for professional women golfers. In the meantime, she married wrestler George Zaharias.

In the 1940s and 1950s she would win countless amateur and professional titles and help to found the Ladies' Professional Golf Association. She died of cancer at the age of forty-four.

Source:
Mildred Babe Zaharias and Harry Paxton, *This Life I've Led: My Autobiography* (New York: Barnes, 1955).

Lou Gehrig

1903-1941

Baseball Player

Young Athlete. The only surviving child of German immigrants, young Lou Gehrig was an outstanding all-around athlete at the High School of Commerce in New York City. He continued his athletic prowess at Columbia University and became a baseball star there as a pitcher and right fielder. Since he played in the minors at Hartford (under an alias) he lost one year of eligibility at Columbia. In 1923 Yankee scout Paul Krichell signed him to a contract, and Gehrig spent two years in the minors (though he played a few games each year with the parent club), honing his skills as a first baseman.

Larrupin' Lou. Gehrig batted .295 and .313 in his first two major-league seasons, and by 1927 he had developed into one of the best players in the game, outhitting Babe Ruth in most categories. His 47 home runs were second to Ruth's 60 that year. Gehrig won the most valuable player (MVP) and led the Yankees to a sweep of the Pirates in the World Series. By the 1930s he was on his way to achieving recognition as the finest first baseman ever to play baseball, a remarkable feat in that he was playing in the era of Jimmie Foxx (who probably edged Gehrig in most categories) and Hank Greeberg. He

played hurt a lot throughout his career and never took a day off, thus earning his moniker, "The Iron Horse."

Hall of Fame Numbers. By 1931, with Ruth on the decline, Gehrig became the symbol (and captain) of the New York Yankees. In 1931 he hit 46 homers, knocked in 184 runs, and scored 163. Yet he did not win a Triple Crown until 1934. He was awarded as MVP for a second time in 1936. On 3 June 1932 he hit four home runs in one game, something neither Ruth nor any other American League ballplayer had ever accomplished. He finished his career with a .340 batting average, 493 home runs, 1,990 runs batted in, 1,188 runs scored, 535 doubles, 162 triples, and 1,508 bases on balls. Even more remarkable was his 2,130-consecutive-game playing streak. For all his greatness, he played the first part of his career in the shadow of Babe Ruth and the latter in the shadow of young Joe DiMaggio.

Streak Ends. Gehrig's consecutive-game playing streak began on 31 May 1925 and ended on 2 May 1939. Wrote James P. Dawson in *The New York Times*, "A deafening cheer resounded as Lou walked to the dugout, doffed his cap and disappeared in a corner of the bench." Though he was only thirty-five years old, there were definite signs that all was not well with him. He had contracted a rare muscle disease that in layman's terms now bears his name. On 4 July 1939 the Yankees honored him on "Lou Gehrig Day" at Yankee Stadium. It was there before a crowd of 61,000 fans that he announced, "Fans, for the past two weeks you have been reading about a bad break I got. Yet today I consider myself the luckiest man on the face of the earth. . . ." He died on 2 June 1941, the day of the nineteenth game of DiMaggio's 56-game hitting streak. Fans lined up outside Christ Episcopal Church for the viewing of the man sportswriter Frank Graham aptly called "A Quiet Hero."

Sources:
Tom Meany, *Baseball's Greatest Players* (New York: Barnes, 1953);

Ray Robinson, *Iron Horse: Lou Gehrig in His Time* (New York: Norton, 1990).

Hank Luisetti

1916-

Basketball Star

Basketball Youth. Born bowlegged, young Angelo Joseph "Hank" Luisetti of San Francisco had to wear leg braces. It did not stop him from playing schoolyard basketball. Shorter than most other kids, Luisetti compensated by learning to shoot with one hand from farther out. He played high-school basketball and earned a scholarship to Stanford.

The Modern Game. Basketball began rather primitively at the turn of the century as a passing game. By the beginning of the 1930s national individual scoring leaders averaged about 10 points a game, and most players still used a two-hand set shot. The game was still evolving into its modern form. Luisetti helped. He had many natural abilities: he could pass behind his back; he moved well around the court; and he carved out defensive as well as offensive strategies as he played. Though he was recognized as an offensive star because of the national attention his unorthodox shooting style attracted, Luisetti was very much an all-around player.

Leading Stanford. Luisetti led Stanford to three Pacific Coast Conference championships between 1936 and 1938. He could shoot from nearly every position on the court and run and shoot. He was named all-American three years in a row, and twice he was Collegiate Player of the Year. His 15 points were the difference in his eastern debut at Madison Square Garden — a stunning Stanford 45–31 upset over Long Island University, which had won forty-three consecutive games. In one game he brought Stanford from behind by scoring 14 points in five minutes. Encouraged by his teammates, Luisetti scored 50 points in a single game against Duquesne in his senior year, though he left the game with three minutes still to play. When he graduated he was the all-time college scoring champion with 1,596 points and a 16.5 points-per-game average.

Amateur Afterlife. After a role in a Hollywood movie cost him his amateur status for a time, Luisetti broke another scoring record in the AAU national tournament in 1939–1940. He later played for the Phillips 66 Oilers but suffered numerous injuries and ailments, which put an end to his playing career. He became a successful basketball coach and was voted second place in the Associated Press's poll of the best basketball player of the half-century. Luisetti had revolutionized the game for the second half-century, and in 1959 he was voted to basketball's Hall of Fame.

Source:
Sandy Padwe, *Basketball's Hall of Fame* (Englewood Cliffs, N.J.: Prentice-Hall, 1970).

HELEN WILLS MOODY

1905-

TENNIS CHAMPION

Golden Age Carryover. Even when she was not playing tennis or playing hurt, Helen Wills Moody was America's greatest female tennis player in the 1920s and 1930s. Between 1923 and 1938 she won eight Wimbledon titles (a record until 1990), seven

U.S. National titles, and four French titles. Though an aggressive baseline player, she won numerous doubles and mixed-doubles matches. Many of her great victories came in the 1920s, but she also suffered her toughest defeat in 1926, losing to Suzanne Lenglen in Cannes. It is still a hotly debated issue as to who was the better player of the era — Lenglen or Moody. Between 1927 and 1933 she won 180 consecutive singles matches, without having lost a set in any of them. She had, after all, vowed after her loss to Lenglen never to lose again.

Little Miss Poker Face. Wills played with cold, hard determination. Bill Tilden found her an emotionless, ruthless, self-centered champion. The press generally portrayed her as more genteel and refined, in keeping with the public's Victorian image of a game that few people considered to be a "real sport." Wills remained devoted to her amateur status. Though she never wore shorts, she was still unconventional in her shirt sleeves and knee-length skirts, without stockings. She might have won more titles at Forest Hills in the 1930s but for nagging injuries and personal differences with the USLTA.

Comeback. Moody was the Wimbledon queen for most of the 1930s. Her fiercest rival was Helen Jacobs, a formidable player who could never get the better of Moody. In 1933 an injured Moody was forced to default to Jacobs in the finals at Forest Hills; but in 1935 Jacobs, leading 5–2 at match point, was subject to one of the grandest comebacks in tennis history. Moody, well past her prime, fought back with lobs and aces and unsettled her younger opponent to win her seventh Wimbledon title. Three years later Moody won her eighth and last Wimbledon title. After 1939 she all but retired from serious tournament tennis.

Source:
Larry Engleman, *The Goddess and the American Girl: The Story of Suzanne Lenglen and Helen Wills* (New York: Oxford University Press, 1988).

BRONKO NAGURSKI

1908-

FOOTBALL PLAYER

Man and Myth. Few athletes in the 1930s possessed as many golden age qualities as Chicago Bears running back Bronko Nagurski. Son of Ukrainian immigrants, Nagurski moved to northern Minnesota as a young boy and played on a winless high-school team that often had to travel one hundred miles away to play a game. He was unheralded when he entered the University of Minnesota in 1926, but by the end of his college career he was on most all-American teams as either a fullback or a tackle, or both. He was possessed of extraordinary strength. He blocked punts, led interference, and ran over defensive backs, dragging players with him into the end zone. In a game against a superior Wisconsin team, he forced a fumble and then scored the game's only touchdown. He became a folk hero, and tales soon arose about his knocking down walls, pulling fenders off cars, or pointing with a plow to give directions.

Teaming Up with Grange. In 1930 Nagurski joined George Halas's Chicago Bears, a team that featured such greats as Bill Hewitt and Red Grange. Nagurski continued to play fullback and tackle and was an occasional quick passer. One coach said that to stop Nagurski you had to shoot him before he left the locker room. In the 1932 championship game against Portsmouth, he threw a jump pass to Red Grange more than five yards behind the line of scrimmage, a controversial play at the time that prompted an important NFL rule change the following year. Playing for the Bears between 1930 and 1937 (and 1943), Nagurski rushed for 4,301 yards in 872 carries for an average of almost 5 yards a carry (in an age when statistics were hardly scientific). He may have played harder and tougher and been more intimidating than any player before him.

Life After Football. Nagurski retired in 1937 after a contract dispute with Halas. Nagurski had become a professional wrestler in 1934. He toured the country until 1960, demonstrating his "flying block" maneuver and lending credibility to what was obviously becoming a rigged sport. In 1943 he filled the manpower shortage caused by the war by returning to the Bears as a tackle and scoring the go-ahead touchdown in the title game against the Redskins.

JESSE OWENS

1913-1980

TRACK & FIELD/OLYMPIC HERO

Hard Times. Personal difficulties, racial discrimination, and challenges to his status as an athlete plagued James Cleveland Owens throughout his career, but on the track and field he put them aside to perform unequaled feats of athletic prowess. In the early 1930s he was the nation's most promising high school star. At Cleveland East Technical High School in 1932, when he was nineteen, he ran the 100-yard dash in 9.4 seconds, tying the world record; long jumped 24 feet, 11.25 inches; and ran 220 yards in 20.7 seconds. He broke the world indoor broad-jump record in 1933. Yet no colleges were interested in him. He enrolled at Ohio State (known then for its discriminatory practices against blacks). To earn his scholarship he operated a freight elevator in the State Office Building

after attending classes and working out with the track team.

Great Day. In a single day in 1935 — in the space of forty-five minutes — racing against other amateurs at the AAU nationals in Ann Arbor, Michigan, Owens broke five world records and tied one. Three of those records were still standing almost twenty years later. He matched his own 9.4 seconds in the 100-yard dash; he set world records in the 220-yard dash (20.3 seconds), the 220-yard low hurdles (22.6 seconds), and the long jump (26 feet, 8.25 inches). He also set a world record for the 200-meter portion in a longer race and then bettered it in another portion.

Hitler's Nemesis. His performance at the 1936 Summer Olympics, at which Adolf Hitler's attempt to prove the physical superiority of the Aryan race was challenged by the stunning success of black athletes on the U.S. team, was charged with political as well as athletic significance. Owens's triumph at Berlin began with the 100-meter race, in which he equaled a world record with a time of 10.3 seconds. The next day Owens had difficulty qualifying for the long jump, barely making the finals on his last jump after two defaults; but he eventually won the event with a jump of 26 feet, 5 5/16 inches, an Olympic record. He then won the 200-meter race in 20.7 seconds, another Olympic record. He was a last-minute fill-in, perhaps because he had become such a crowd pleaser, to lead off the 400-meter relay, which the U.S. team won easily, earning Owens his fourth gold medal.

Lasting Fame. Along with Joe Louis, Jesse Owens led the way during the 1930s to greater parity and respect for African American athletes in the world of sports. Few writers patronized him or thought of racially charged nicknames to describe him. Full equality was not something that happened overnight, though. Southern papers would not print his picture. In an era in which white runners like Venzke, Bonthron, and Cunningham got most of the press coverage, Owens was still "the colored runner" of the group. But his fame and prowess outlasted them all.

Source:
Jesse Owens, *Jesse: The Man Who Outran Hitler* (New York: Fawcett Gold Medal Books, 1978).

SATCHEL PAIGE

1906-1982

BASEBALL PLAYER

Born Thirty Years Too Early. Leroy Robert "Satchel" Paige was the greatest pitcher of the 1930s. White and black players of the era alike attested to that fact. No player since Babe Ruth was a bigger box-office draw, and Paige was every bit a showman, a man who would clear the field and pitch to batters with no one behind him. Yet, because of the racist policy of baseball, Paige had to wait until he was forty-two years old, in 1948, to become the first African American to pitch in the big leagues, though he frequently played with and against white players in off-season barnstorming tours, including such admirers as Joe DiMaggio and Dizzy Dean.

Pitching Everywhere. Paige was known widely not only for his durability and blazing, buzzing "Bee Ball" but also because he pitched wherever he could draw an audience throughout the year. He began his career in 1929 in semipro ball with the Mobile Tigers and played for Chattanooga, Birmingham, Baltimore, Nashville, and Cleveland before hooking up in 1932 with the Pittsburgh Crawfords, the greatest black team of the era. Seeking more money, he played for an integrated semipro team in Bismarck, North Dakota, in 1935 and was briefly banned from the Negro National League for breaking his contract, but he returned to the Crawfords the next year. He pitched for dictator Rafael Trujillo's ball club, Trujillo's Stars, in the Dominican Republic in 1937 and then headed to the Mexico League in 1938. However, he developed arm trouble and returned home.

Don't Look Back. Paige signed on with the Kansas City Monarchs in 1939 and gradually rehabilitated his arm. For the next eight years he dominated Negro League baseball, winning in 1942 three of four straight victories in the first Negro Leagues World Series since 1927. By 1948, the year after Jackie Robinson had become the first black to play Major League Baseball, the Negro Leagues were all but dead, and Paige was recruited to pitch for Bill Veeck's Cleveland Indians. His major-league career had some shining moments (he made the All-Star team at age forty-six for the Saint Louis Browns in 1951), but it was more a testimony to what ought to have been. Paige later pitched three innings for the Kansas City A's in 1965 when he was fifty-nine years old. He rounded out his long career by playing for the Indianapolis Clowns, the last of the old barnstorming clubs. In 1971 he was belatedly elected to Baseball's Hall of Fame.

Sources:

Dick Clark and Larry Lester, eds., *The Negro Leagues Book* (Cleveland: SABR, 1994);

Leroy Satchel Paige, as told to David Lipman, *Maybe I'll Pitch Forever* (Garden City, N.Y.: Doubleday, 1962).

PEOPLE IN THE NEWS

Henry Armstrong won the world lightweight championship on 17 August 1938 to add to his welterweight and featherweight titles; he was thus the first man to hold championships in three different weight divisions at once.

James "Cool Papa" Bell of the Pittsburgh Crawfords in the Negro Leagues from 1933-1937, called the fastest base runner in the history of baseball, stole 175 bases in 1933.

Middle-distance runner **Bill Bonthron,** one of the great milers of the 1930s, won the title Amateur Athlete of the Year in 1934, the same year he set a world record in the 1500-meter.

In 1935 **Frank Boucher,** center for the New York Rangers hockey team, won his seventh Lady Byng Memorial Trophy in eight years as the league's most gentlemanly player.

On 13 June 1935 **James J. Braddock,** a 10–1 underdog, defeated Max Baer for the heavyweight title in a fif-teen-round decision before 35,000 fans at the Long Island City Bowl.

In 1937 and 1938 **Don Budge** won the U.S. Open and Wimbledon tennis championships; he led America to two Davis Cups those same years.

In 1933 and 1935–1938 **Glenn Cunningham** won the United States Championship in the mile run, repeatedly breaking the world record.

From 1933 to 1936 **Dizzy Dean** (baseball) won 102 Major League Baseball games, including 31 in 1934, when he was named most valuable player in the National League; his career ended in 1937 when he broke his toe in the All-Star Game.

New York Yankees catcher **Bill Dickey** hit over .300 every year except one throughout the 1930s.

Joe DiMaggio led the American League in home runs in 1937 and batting average (.381) in 1939, the year of his first MVP award. In the four years he played in the

1930s, he had already, as sportswriter Jimmy Cannon observed, made a reservation in Cooperstown.

Philadelphia Athletics power hitter **Jimmie Foxx** won the Triple Crown in 1934; he hit 58 home runs in 1932 and 48 in 1933, along with 163 RBI and a .356 batting average.

Former second baseman **Frankie Frisch** managed the Saint Louis Cardinals from 1933 to 1938, winning the world championship in 1934.

Josh Gibson won Negro Leagues home run titles in 1932, 1934, 1936, 1938, and 1939; he hit .440 in 1938, and once, during a Negro Leagues Day game in the decade, hit the ball completely out of Yankee Stadium.

New York Yankee pitcher **Lefty Gomez** led the American League in strikeouts, ERs, and wins in 1934 and again in 1937; he started four All-Star games through 1937 and won six World Series games without a loss.

Detroit Tiger first baseman **Hank Greenberg** was American League MVP in 1935; he challenged Babe Ruth's record with 58 home runs in 1938.

In 1930, when the average American League ERA was 4.97, Philadelphia Athletics pitcher **Lefty Grove** led the league with a 2.95 ERA, 209 strikeouts, and 28 wins, against only 5 losses.

Ralph Guldahl was National Open golf champion in 1937 and 1938, Masters winner in 1939, and Western Open Golf victor from 1936 to 1938.

Chicago Cubs catcher **Gabby Hartnett** was the best backstop in the National League in the 1930s; in 1938 he hit the "homer in the gloamin'" (the twilight) that broke a 5–5 tie with the Pirates and put the Cubs in the World Series, which they lost in four games.

In 1938 **Mel Hein**, center (and linebacker) for the New York Giants between 1931 and 1945, became the first and only offensive lineman to win the National Football League Most Valuable Player award; an all-pro for eight consecutive years, he perfected the art of dropping back to protect the quarterback.

Edward A. Hennig won the AAU Indian club swinging championship in 1904 and tied in 1911; he then came back to win again in 1933, 1936, 1937, and 1939, as well as seven times between 1940 and 1951.

Eleanor Holm, gold medal winner in the 100-meter backstroke at the 1932 Olympic Games, went into show business and married Billy Rose, former husband of Fanny Brice.

Carl Hubbell, screwball pitcher for the New York Giants, struck out "Murderers' Row" (Ruth, Gehrig, Foxx, Simmons, and Cronin) consecutively in the 1934 All-Star Game; in 1933 he pitched 46 scoreless innings and was voted National League Most Valuable Player, an award he won again in 1936.

Helen Jacobs was U.S. Open women's tennis champion from 1932 to 1935. She had a devastating chop shot but never beat her rival Helen Wills.

Irving Jaffee, winner of 1932 Olympic gold medals in the 5,000- and 10,000-meter speed skating events, had to pawn his medals during the Depression and was never able to recover them.

Howard Harding Jones, head football coach at the University of Southern California, won twenty-five consecutive games between 1931 and 1933 and led his team to Rose Bowl victories in 1930, 1932, 1933, and 1939.

Bob Kiphuth, Yale University swimming coach for thirty-five years, led his team to 447 victories and only 10 defeats, with a winning streak (163) that lasted from 1926 to 1937.

Philadelphia Phillies outfielder **Chuck Klein**, *Sporting News* National League player of the year in 1931 and 1932, was named the league's MVP in 1932 and won the Triple Crown in 1933, when he led the league in four other categories.

Elmer Layden, Notre Dame head coach and one of its legendary "Four Horsemen," won 40, lost 11, tied 2 games from 1934 to 1939 and helped restore the Fighting Irish to the greatness of the Rockne years.

Buck Leonard, first baseman for the Homestead Grays of the Negro Leagues, perennial East-West All-Star, and third-highest-paid player behind Josh Gibson and Satchel Paige, hit .492 in 1939.

Helene Madison won three gold medals in the 1932 Summer Games, setting an Olympic record in the 100-meter freestyle and a world record in the 400-meter freestyle; she was the first woman to swim 100 yards in less than a minute.

In 1938 **Alice Marble**, U.S. Open tennis champion in 1936, 1938, and 1939, defeated Nancye Wynne of Australia in the shortest women's final on record (twenty-two minutes); Marble was ranked number one in the world between 1936 and 1940 and was the Wimbledon champ in 1939.

New York Yankee manager **Joe McCarthy** led his team to World Series championships in 1932 and 1936–1939.

Byron Nelson won the Masters golf tournament in 1937 and the U.S. Open title in 1939.

New York Giants right fielder **Mel Ott** led the league in home runs in 1932, 1934, 1936–1938 (and once more in 1942).

Race car driver **Floyd Roberts** won the Indianapolis 500 with a record-breaking 117.200 mph in 1938, the best finish for the decade and a record until 1948.

Gene Sarazen won each of the four major golf tournaments at least once in the 1930s.

Defenseman **Eddie Shore** of the Boston Bruins was named the National Hockey League MVP in 1933, 1935, 1936, 1938, and he made the league's all-star starting team seven times.

Helen Stephens, known as the "Missouri Express" and "the world's fastest woman," was a track star of the 1936 Olympics; her gold-medal-winning 11.5 in the 100-meter was unequaled until 1948 and remained a world record until Wilma Rudolph broke it in 1960.

Eddie Tolan set world and Olympic records for the 100-yard dash at 10.3 seconds and an Olympic record for the 200-meter dash at 21.2 seconds in the 1932 Olympics.

Virginia Van Wie won U.S. amateur golf titles in 1932, 1933, and 1934, the year she was named Associated Press Female Athlete of the Year.

H. Ellworth Vines was U.S. Men's Open Singles champion, 1931 and 1932.

Glenn Scobey "Pop" Warner finished his 1933–1938 coaching career at Temple University in Philadelphia; he first coached in 1895 at Georgia and then in the late 1920s and early 1930s at Stanford; his lifetime record was 313 wins, 106 losses, and 32 ties.

Kenny Washington lettered in baseball, track, football, and boxing at UCLA between 1936 and 1939; he was Pacific Coast League collegiate batting champion in 1938 and national leader in football for total offense in 1939; in a player poll to determine college all-stars he received the vote of all 103 players who ever opposed him, but, presumably because he was black, he was not named in any of the national all-star polls.

Orfa Washington, called "the black Alice Marble," won eight American Tennis Association titles between 1929 and 1937.

Byron "Whizzer" White, all-American halfback at the University of Colorado, was the first-round draft pick of Pittsburgh football Pirates in 1938; he led the NFL in rushing as a rookie and then studied as a Rhodes Scholar at Oxford the next year; he played two seasons with the Detroit Lions before retiring to pursue a career in law; in 1962 he was named to the U.S. Supreme Court.

AWARDS

1930

Major League Baseball World Series — Philadelphia Athletics (AL), 4 vs. Saint Louis Cardinals (NL), 2

National Football League Championship — Green Bay Packers (best record)

Rose Bowl, Collegiate Football — Southern California, 47 vs. Pittsburgh, 14

National Hockey League Stanley Cup — Montreal Canadiens, 2 vs. Boston Bruins, O

Kentucky Derby, Horse Racing — Gallant Fox (Earl Sande, jockey)

U.S. Open Golf Tournament — Bobby Jones

U.S. National Tennis Tournament — John Doeg; Betty Nuthall

James E. Sullivan Memorial Trophy (inaugural year), Amateur Athlete of the Year — Bobby Jones (Golf)

1931

Major League Baseball World Series — Saint Louis Cardinals (NL), 4 vs. Philadelphia Athletics (AL), 3

National Football League Championship — Green Bay Packers (best record)

Rose Bowl, Collegiate Football — Alabama, 24 vs. Washington State, 0

National Hockey League Stanley Cup — Montreal Canadiens, 3 vs. Chicago Black Hawks, 2

Kentucky Derby, Horse Racing — Twenty Grand (Charles Kurtsinger, jockey)

U.S. Open Golf Tournament — William Burke

U.S. National Tennis Tournament — H. Ellsworth Vines; Helen Wills Moody

James E. Sullivan Memorial Trophy, Amateur Athlete of the Year — Barney Berlinger (Track)

Associated Press Athletes of the Year (inaugural year) — Pepper Martin (Baseball); Helene Madison (Swimming)

1932

Major League Baseball World Series — New York Yankees (AL), 4 vs. Chicago Cubs (NL), 0

National Football League Championship — Chicago Bears, 9 vs. Portsmouth Spartans, 0 (first-place playoff)

Rose Bowl, Collegiate Football — Southern California, 21 vs. Tulane, 12

National Hockey League Stanley Cup — Toronto Maple Leafs, 3 vs. New York Rangers, 0

Kentucky Derby, Horse Racing — Burgoo King (Eugene James, jockey)

U.S. Open Golf Tournament — Gene Sarazen

U.S. National Tennis Tournament — H. Ellsworth Vines; Helen Jacobs

James E. Sullivan Memorial Trophy, Amateur Athlete of the Year — Jim Bausch (Track)

Associated Press Athletes of the Year — Gene Sarazen (Golf); Babe Didrikson (Track)

1933

Major League Baseball World Series — New York Giants (NL), 4 vs. Washington Senators (AL), 1

National Football League Championship — Chicago Bears (West), 23 vs. New York Giants (East), 21

Rose Bowl, Collegiate Football — Southern California, 35 vs. Pittsburgh, 0

National Hockey League Stanley Cup — New York Rangers, 3 vs. Toronto Maple Leafs, 1

Kentucky Derby, Horse Racing — Brokers Tip (Donald Meade, jockey)

U.S. Open Golf Tournament — John Goodman

U.S. National Tennis Tournament — Fred Perry; Helen Jacobs

James E. Sullivan Memorial Trophy, Amateur Athlete of the Year — Glenn Cunningham (Track)

Associated Press Athletes of the Year — Carl Hubbell (Baseball); Helen Jacobs (Tennis)

1934

Major League Baseball World Series — Saint Louis Cardinals (NL), 4 vs. Detroit Tigers (AL), 3

National Football League Championship — New York Giants (East), 30 vs. Chicago Bears (West), 13

Rose Bowl, Collegiate Football — Columbia, 7 vs. Stanford, 0

National Hockey League Stanley Cup — Chicago Black Hawks, 3 vs. Detroit Red Wings, 1

Kentucky Derby, Horse Racing — Cavalcade (Mack Garner, jockey)

U.S. Open Golf Tournament — Olin Dutra

Masters Golf Tournament (inaugural year) — Horton Smith

U.S. Open Tennis Tournament — Fred Perry; Helen Jacobs

James E. Sullivan Memorial Trophy, Amateur Athlete of the Year — Bill Bonthron (Track)

Associated Press Athletes of the Year — Dizzy Dean (Baseball); Virginia Van Wie (Golf)

1935

Major League Baseball World Series — Detroit Tigers (AL), 4 vs. Chicago Cubs (NL), 2

National Football League Championship — Detroit Lions (West), 26 vs. New York Giants (East), 7

Heisman Trophy, Collegiate Football (inaugural year) — Jay Berwanger (Chicago)

Rose Bowl, Collegiate Football — Alabama, 29 vs. Stanford, 13

National Hockey League Stanley Cup — Montreal Maroons, 3 vs. Toronto Maple Leafs, 0

Kentucky Derby, Horse Racing — Omaha (Willie Saunders, jockey)

U.S. Open Golf Tournament — Sam Parks

Masters Golf Tournament — Gene Sarazen

U.S. National Tennis Tournament — Wilmer Allison; Helen Jacobs

John E. Sullivan Memorial Trophy, Amateur Athlete of the Year — Lawson Little Jr. (Golf)

Associated Press Athletes of the Year — Joe Louis (Boxing); Helen Wills Moody (Tennis)

1936

Major League Baseball World Series — New York Yankees (AL), 4 vs. New York Giants (NL), 2

National Football League Championship — Green Bay Packers (West), 21 vs. Boston Redskins (East), 6

Heisman Trophy, Collegiate Football — Larry Kelley (Yale)

Rose Bowl, Collegiate Football — Stanford, 7 vs. Southern Methodist, 0

National League Hockey Stanley Cup — Detroit Red Wings, 3 vs. Toronto Maple Leafs, 1

Kentucky Derby, Horse Racing — Bold Venture (Ira Hanford, jockey)

U.S. Open Golf Tournament — Tony Manero

Masters Golf Tournament — Horton Smith

U.S. National Tennis Tournament — Fred Perry; Alice Marble

James E. Sullivan Memorial Trophy, Amateur Athlete of the Year — Glenn Morris (Track)

Associated Press Athletes of the Year — Jesse Owens (Track and Field); Helen Stephens (Track)

1937

Major League Baseball World Series — New York Yankees (AL), 4 vs. New York Giants (NL), 1

National Football League Championship — Washington Redskins (East), 28 vs. Chicago Bears (West), 21

Heisman Trophy, Collegiate Football — Clinton Frank (Yale)

Rose Bowl, Collegiate Football — Pittsburgh, 21 vs. Washington, 0

National Hockey League Stanley Cup — Detroit Red Wings, 3 vs. New York Rangers, 2

Kentucky Derby, Horse Racing — War Admiral (Charles Kurtsinger, jockey)

U.S. Open Golf Tournament — Ralph Guldahl

Masters Golf Tournament — Byron Nelson

U.S. National Tennis Tournament — Don Budge; Anita Lizana

James E. Sullivan Memorial Trophy, Amateur Athlete of the Year — Don Budge (Tennis)

Associated Press Athletes of the Year — Don Budge (Tennis); Katherine Rawls (Swimming)

1938

Major League Baseball World Series — New York Yankees (AL), 4 vs. Chicago Cubs (NL), 0

National Football League Championship — New York Giants (East), 23 vs. Green Bay Packers (West), 17

Heisman Trophy, Collegiate Football — David O'Brien (Texas Christian)

Rose Bowl, Collegiate Football — California, 13 vs. Alabama, 0

National Hockey League Stanley Cup — Chicago Black Hawks, 3 vs. Toronto Maple Leafs, 1

Kentucky Derby, Horse Racing — Lawrin (Eddie Arcaro, jockey)

U.S. Open Golf Tournament — Ralph Guldahl

Masters Golf Tournament — Henry Picard

U.S. National Tennis Tournament — Don Budge; Alice Marble

James E. Sullivan Memorial Trophy, Amateur Athlete of the Year — Don Lash (Track)

Associated Press Athletes of the Year — Don Budge (Tennis); Patty Berg (Golf)

1939

Major League Baseball World Series — New York Yankees (AL), 4 vs. Cincinnati Reds, 0

National Football League Championship — Green Bay Packers (West), 27 vs. New York Giants (East), 0

Heisman Trophy, Collegiate Football — Nile Kinnick (Iowa)

Rose Bowl, Collegiate Football — Southern California, 7 vs. Duke, 3

National Collegiate Athletic Association Basketball (inaugural year) — Oregon, 46 vs. Ohio State, 33

National Hockey League Stanley Cup — Boston Bruins, 4 vs. Toronto Maple Leafs, 1

Kentucky Derby, Horse Racing — Johnstown (Jimmy Stout, jockey)

U.S. Open Golf Tournament — Byron Nelson

Masters Golf Tournament — Ralph Guldahl

U.S. National Tennis Tournament — Bobby Riggs; Alice Marble

James E. Sullivan Memorial Trophy, Amateur Athlete of the Year — Joe Burk (Rowing)

Associated Press Athletes of the Year — Nile Kinnick (Football); Alice Marble (Tennis)

DEATHS

Heywood Broun, 51, sportswriter and noted critic and columnist. Spent most-fruitful years covering sports for the *New York Herald Tribune*, 1911–1921, 18 December 1939.

Dennis "Dan" Brouthers, 74, great Hall of Fame first baseman of the 1880s, 2 August 1932.

Joe Carr, 58, National Football League president since its inception, 20 May 1939.

Frank Cavanaugh, 57, "The Iron Major," football player and coach, most prominently at Fordham, 29 August 1933.

Jack Chesboro, 57, Hall of Fame pitcher, won forty-one games in 1904, 6 November 1931.

Charles Comiskey, 72, the "Old Roman," onetime ballplayer and first owner of the Chicago White Sox, 28 November 1939.

James J. Corbett, 67, "Gentleman Jim," the first man to win the heavyweight crown under the Marquis of Queensberry rules; he beat John L. Sullivan in a famous fight in 1892, 18 February 1933.

Edward H. "Ted" Coy, 47, all-American Yale fullback, who was one of the early power runners and an all-around player, 8 September 1935.

Charles Dryden, 74, one of the most famous and influential sportswriters of the twentieth century; his stories ran on the front page of such newspapers as the *Philadelphia North American* and the *Chicago Tribune*, 11 February 1931.

Amelia Earhart, 40, pioneer aviator, presumed dead after disappearing during flight over Howland Island in the Pacific, 2 July 1937.

Andrew "Rube" Foster, 51, the father of black baseball; founder and president of the Negro National League, owner of the Chicago American Giants, and onetime pitcher, 9 December 1930.

Charlie Gardiner, 29, Chicago Black Hawk goalie and two-time Vezina Trophy winner, 13 June 1934.

William "Kid" Gleason, 67, manager of the 1919 Chicago Black Sox who never overcame the hurt and betrayal of his players, 2 January 1933.

Ned Hanlon, 80, manager of the old Baltimore Orioles, the most exciting and provocative team of the 1890s, 14 April 1937.

John W. Heisman, 67, football star at Brown and Penn and later coach who built Georgia Tech into a national power. Award to the nation's most outstanding football player named for him, 3 October 1936.

Nathaniel G. Herreshoff, 90, shipbuilder, credited with designing every America's Cup defending yacht for twenty-seven years, 2 June 1938.

Ring Lardner, 48, well-known American short-story writer, as well as noted Chicago sportswriter in the early 1910s and author of the epistolary baseball novel *You Know Me Al* as well as other baseball stories, 25 September 1933.

Suzanne Lenglen, 39, French tennis star and six-time Wimbledon champion; one of the greatest women ever to play the game, 4 July 1938

Sir Thomas Lipton, 81, British tea merchant who unsuccessfully tried five times to wrest America's Cup from the United States, 2 October 1931.

John McGraw, 61, "Little Napoleon," the fiesty New York Giants manager who won ten pennants, 25 February 1934.

William A. Muldoon, 88, noted health enthusiast, trainer, and wrestling champion; he set many standards and guidelines as chairman of the New York State Athletic Commission, 3 June 1933.

Knute Rockne, 43, Notre Dame football coach and the player who, as an end receiver, revolutionized the forward pass; he was killed in a plane crash in a desolate Kansas wheat field, 31 March 1931.

Wilbert "Uncle Robbie" Robinson, 70, manager of the National League Brooklyn team, called the Robins for him, 1914–1931, which won pennants in 1916 and 1920, 8 August 1934.

Alber "Babe" Siebert, outstanding left-winger turned superb defenseman, killed in a drowning accident in the prime of his career, 25 August 1939.

Matthias Sindelar, considered the finest Austrian soccer player of his day; he disappeared fleeing the Nazis and was presumed dead, 1939.

Edward Stratemeyer, 68, founder of syndicate producing popular children's books, including the *Baseball Joe* and Buck and Larry series, 10 May 1930.

Henry L. Williams, 61, Yale football and track star and later coach at Army and Minnesota, who compiled a .788 winning percentage, 14 June 1931.

PUBLICATIONS

Donald Budge, *Budge on Tennis* (New York: Prentice-Hall, 1939);

Mickey Cochrane, *Baseball: The Fan's Game* (New York: Funk & Wagnalls, 1939);

Allison Danzig, *The Racquet Game* (New York: Macmillan, 1930);

Elmer Dawson (Edward Stratemeyer), *The Buck and Larry Series* (New York: Grosset & Dunlap); *Buck's Home Run Drive* (1931); *Buck's Winning Hit* (1930); *Larry's Fadeaway* (1930); *Larry's Speedball* (1932); *The Pick-up Nine* (1930);

Eddie Egan, *Fighting for Fun: The Scrapbook of Eddie Egan* (New York: Macmillan, 1932);

Paul Gallico, *A Farewell to Sport* (New York: Knopf, 1938);

Reed Harris, *King Football* (New York: Vanguard, 1932);

William Inglis, *Champions Off Guard* (New York: Vanguard, 1932);

Helen Hull Jacobs, *Beyond the Game: An Autobiography* (Philadelphia: Lippincott, 1936);

John Kieran, *The Story of the Olympic Games: 776 B.C.–1936 A.D.* (New York: Stokes, 1936);

Ring Lardner, *Lose With a Smile* (New York: Scribners, 1933);

Lou Little and Robert Harron, *How to Watch Football* (New York: Whittlesey House/McGraw-Hill, 1935);

Herbert Manchester, *Four Centuries of Sport in America: 1490–1890* (New York: Derrydale Press, 1932);

H. B. Martin, *Fifty Years of American Golf* (New York: Dodd, Mead, 1936);

Helen Wills Moody, *Fifteen-Thirty: The Story of a Tennis Player* (New York: Scribners, 1937);

Juda P. Phelps and Robert Wood, *Hold 'em Girls* (New York: Putnam, 1936);

Grantland Rice and Harford Powel, eds., *The Omnibus of Sport* (New York: Harper, 1932);

Jim Tully, *The Bruiser* (New York: Greenberg, 1936);

John R. Tunis, "The Amateur Sports Racket," *New Republic* (28 May 1930): 34–36; (18 June 1930): 120–122;

Tunis, *American Girl* (New York: Brewer & Warren, 1930);

Gene Tunney, *A Man Must Fight* (Boston: Houghton Mifflin, 1932);

Henry Van Dyke, *Travel Diary of an Angler* (New York: Derrydale Press, 1930);

Hazel Hotchkiss Wightman, *Better Tennis* (Boston: Houghton Mifflin, 1933);

Barry Wood, *What Price Football?* (Boston: Houghton Mifflin, 1932);

The American Golfer, periodical;

American Lawn Tennis, periodical;

Baseball, periodical;

The Blood Horse, periodical;

Ring, periodical;

The Sporting News, periodical.

GENERAL REFERENCES

GENERAL

Mary Kupiec Cayton, Elliott J. Gorn, and Peter T. Williams, eds., *Encyclopedia of American Social History*, 3 volumes (New York: Scribners, 1993);

Chronicle of the Twentieth Century (Mount Kisco, N.Y.: Chronicle, 1987);

John Patrick Diggins, *The Proud Decades* (New York: Norton, 1988);

John W. Dodds, *Everyday Life in Twentieth Century America* (New York: Putnam, 1965);

Paul Johnson, *Modern Times: From the Twenties to the Nineties*, revised edition (New York: HarperCollins, 1991);

Charles D. Lowery and John F. Marszalek, eds., *Encyclopedia of African-American Civil Rights: From Emancipation to the Present* (Westport, Conn.: Greenwood Press, 1992);

Iwan W. Morgan and Neil A. Wynn, *America's Century: Perspectives on U.S. History Since 1900* (New York: Holmes & Meier, 1993);

Michael Downey Rice, *Prentice-Hall Dictionary of Business, Finance, and Law* (Englewood Cliffs, N.J.: Prentice-Hall, 1983);

Barbara Sicherman and Carol Hurd Green, with Ilene Kantrov and Hariette Walker, eds., *Notable American Women: The Modern Period, A Biographical Dictionary* (Cambridge, Mass.: Harvard University Press, 1980);

Time Lines on File (New York: Facts On File, 1988);

James Trager, *The People's Chronology*, revised edition (New York: Holt, Rinehart & Winston, 1994);

Claire Walter, *Winners: The Blue Ribbon Encyclopedia of Awards* (New York: Facts On File, 1982);

Leigh Carol Yuster and others, eds., *Ulrich's International Periodicals Directory: A Classified Guide to Current Periodicals, Foreign and Domestic, 1986–1987*, twenty-fifth edition, 2 volumes (New York & London: Bowker, 1986).

ARTS

Charles C. Alexander, *Here the Country Lies* (Bloomington: Indiana University Press, 1980);

H. Harvard Arnason, *History of Modern Art: Painting, Sculpture, Photography*, third edition (Englewood Cliffs, N.J.: Prentice-Hall, 1986);

Tino Balio, *Grand Design: Hollywood as a Modern Business Enterprise 1930–1939*, volume 5 of *History of the American Cinema*, edited by Charles Harpole (New York: Scribners, 1993);

Whitney Balliett, *American Musicians: Fifty Portraits in Jazz* (New York: Oxford University Press, 1986);

John Baxter, *Hollywood in the Thirties* (London: Tantivy Press, 1968);

Stephen Becker, *Comic Art in America* (New York: Simon & Schuster, 1959);

Thomas Hart Benton, *An American in Art* (Lawrence: University Press of Kansas, 1969);

Andrew Bergman, *We're in the Money: Depression America and Its Films* (New York: New York University Press, 1971);

Harold Bloom, ed., *Twentieth-Century American Literature* (New York: Chelsea House, 1987);

Malcolm Bradbury, *The Modern American Novel*, revised edition (New York: Viking, 1992);

Oscar G. Brockett and Robert Findlay, *Century of Innovation: A History of European and American Drama Since the Late Nineteenth Century* (New York: Simon & Schuster, 1991);

Lorraine Brown and John O'Connor, *Free, Adult, Uncensored: The Living History of the Federal Theatre Project* (Washington, D.C.: New Republic Books, 1978);

Patrick Carr, ed., *The Illustrated History of Country Music* (Garden City, N.Y.: Doubleday, 1980);

Samuel B. Charters and Leonard Kunstadt, *Jazz: A History of the New York Scene* (Garden City, N.Y.: Doubleday, 1962);

Gilbert Chase, *America's Music: From the Pilgrims to the Present,* revised third edition (Urbana & Chicago: University of Illinois Press, 1987);

Harold Clurman, *The Fervent Years: The Story of the Group Theatre and the Thirties* (New York: Harcourt Brace Jovanovich, 1975);

Malcolm Cowley, *The Dream of the Golden Mountain* (New York: Viking, 1964);

Cowley, *A Second Flowering* (New York: Viking, 1973);

Thomas Cripps, *Slow Fade to Black: The Negro in American Film, 1900–1942* (New York: Oxford University Press, 1977);

Dorothy Nyren Curley, Maurice Kramer, and Elaine Fialka Kramer, eds., *Modern American Literature: A Library of Literary Criticism* (New York: Ungar, 1969);

Francis Davis, *The History of the Blues: The Roots, the Music, the People from Charley Patton to Robert Cray* (New York: Hyperion, 1995);

Agnes de Mille, *America Dances* (New York: Macmillan, 1980);

John Dizikes, *Opera in America: A Cultural History* (New Haven: Yale University Press, 1993);

Leonard Feather, *The Book of Jazz* (New York: Bonanza Books, 1965);

Hallie Flanagan, *Arena: The Story of the Federal Theatre* (New York: Duell, Sloan & Pearce, 1940);

Rusty E. Frank, *Tap! The Greatest Tap Dance Stars and Their Stories, 1900–1955* (New York: Morris, 1990);

Joseph Freeman, *An American Testament* (New York: Farrar, Straus & Giroux, 1973);

Wolfgang Fuchs and Reinhold Reitberger, *Comics: Anatomy of a Mass Medium* (Boston: Little, Brown, 1970);

Lois G. Gordon and Alan Gordon, *American Chronicle: Six Decades in American Life* (New York: Atheneum, 1987);

Leslie Halliwell, *Halliwell's Film Guide* (New York: Harper & Row, 1990);

John Tasker Howard and George Kent Bellows, *A Short History of Music in America* (New York: Crowell, 1957);

H. W. Janson, *History of Art,* fifth edition (New York: Abrams, 1995);

Ephraim Katz, *The Film Encyclopedia,* revised edition (New York: HarperPerennial, 1994);

Barry Dean Kernfield, *The Blackwell Guide to Recorded Jazz* (Oxford, U.K., & Cambridge, Mass.: Blackwell, 1991);

David Madden, ed., *Tough Guy Writers of the Thirties* (Carbondale: Southern Illinois University Press, 1968);

Bill C. Malone, *Country Music U.S.A.: A Fifty Year History* (Austin: University of Texas Press, 1968);

Joseph H. Mazo, *Prime Movers: The Makers of Modern Dance in America* (New York: Morrow, 1977);

John McCarty, *Hollywood Gangland* (New York: St. Martin's Press, 1993);

Don McDonagh, *The Complete Guide to Modern Dance* (Garden City, N.Y.: Doubleday, 1976);

Richard D. McKinzie, *The New Deal for Artists* (Princeton: Princeton University Press, 1973);

Barbara Melosh, *Engendering Culture: Manhood and Womanhood in New Deal Public Art and Theater* (Washington, D.C.: Smithsonian Institution Press, 1991);

Beaumont Newhall, *The History of Photography* (Boston: Little, Brown, 1982);

Paul Oliver, Max Harrison, and William Bolcom, *The New Grove Gospel, Blues and Jazz* (New York: Norton, 1986);

Richard H. Pells, *Radical Visions and American Dreams: Culture and Social Thought in the Depression Years* (Middletown, Conn.: Wesleyan University Press, 1973);

Frederic Ramsey Jr. and Charles Edward Smith, eds., *Jazzmen* (New York: Harcourt, Brace, 1939);

Nikos Sangos, *Concepts of Modern Art* (New York: Thames & Hudson, 1994);

Russell Sanjek, *American Popular Music and Its Business, Volume III: From 1900 to 1984* (New York: Oxford University Press, 1988);

Thomas Schatz, *The Genius of the System* (New York: Pantheon, 1988);

Ted Sennett, *Hollywood's Golden Year, 1939* (New York: St. Martin's Press, 1989);

Sennett, *This Fabulous Century: The Thirties* (New York: Time-Life Books, 1969);

Wendy Smith, *Real Life: The Group Theatre and America, 1931–1940* (New York: Knopf, 1990);

Eileen Southern, *The Music of Black Americans: A History* (New York: Norton, 1983);

Marshall W. Stearns, *The Story of Jazz* (New York: Oxford University Press, 1956);

William Stott, *Documentary Expression and Thirties America* (Chicago: University of Chicago Press, 1973);

David W. Stowe, *Swing Changes* (Cambridge, Mass.: Harvard University Press, 1994);

John Warthen Struble, *The History of American Classical Music* (New York: Facts On File, 1995);

Nicholas E. Tawa, *Serenading the Reluctant Eagle: American Musical Life, 1925–1945* (New York: Schirmer, 1984);

Nick Tosches, *Country: Living Legends and Dying Metaphors in America's Biggest Music* (London: Secker & Warburg, 1985);

Katrina vanden Heuvel, ed., *The Nation, 1865–1990* (New York: Thunder's Mouth Press, 1990);

Martin Williams, *The Jazz Tradition* (New York: Oxford University Press, 1993).

BUSINESS AND THE ECONOMY

Irving Bernstein, *Turbulent Years: A History of the American Worker, 1933–1941* (Boston: Houghton Mifflin, 1970);

John Brooks, *The Autobiography of American Business* (Garden City, N.Y.: Doubleday, 1974);

Brooks, *Telephone: The First Hundred Years* (New York: Harper & Row, 1975);

Stuart Bruchey, *Enterprise: The Dynamic Economy of a Free People* (Cambridge, Mass.: Harvard University Press, 1990);

Keith L. Bryant Jr. and Henry C. Dethloff, *A History of American Business*, second edition (Englewood Cliffs, N.J.: Prentice Hall, 1990);

Bryant Jr., ed., *Encyclopedia of American Business History and Biography: Railroads in the Age of Regulation, 1900–1980* (New York & Oxford: Facts On File, 1988);

Ron Chernow, *The House of Morgan: An American Banking Dynasty and the Rise of Modern Finance* (New York: Simon & Schuster, 1990);

Edward F. Denison, *The Sources of Economic Growth in the United States and the Alternatives Before Us* (New York: Committee for Economic Development, 1962);

John M. Dobson, *A History of American Enterprise* (Englewood Cliffs, N.J.: Prentice Hall, 1988);

John Kenneth Galbraith, *Economic Development* (Cambridge, Mass.: Harvard University Press, 1964);

John A. Garraty, *The Great Depression* (New York: Harcourt Brace Jovanovich, 1986);

George Gilder, *The Spirit of Enterprise* (New York: Simon & Schuster, 1984);

Charles E. Gilland Jr., ed., *Readings in Business Responsibility* (Braintree, Mass.: Mark, 1969);

James R. Green, *The World of the Worker: Labor in Twentieth-Century America* (New York: Hill & Wang, 1980);

Robert Heilbroner and Aaron Singer, *The Economic Transformation of America* (New York: Harcourt Brace Jovanovich, 1977);

Harry Hurt III, *Texas Rich: The Hunt Dynasty from the Early Oil Days through the Silver Crash* (New York: Norton, 1981);

William Keylor, *The Twentieth-Century World: An International History* (New York: Oxford University Press, 1984);

Charles P. Kindleberger, *The World in Depression, 1929–1939* (Berkeley: University of California Press, 1986);

William M. Leary, ed., *Encyclopedia of American Business History and Biography: The Airline Industry* (New York: Facts On File, 1992);

Chester H. Liebs, *Main Street to Miracle Mile: American Roadside Architecture* (Boston: Little, Brown, 1985);

Ann R. Markusen, *The Rise of the Gunbelt: The Military Remapping of Industrial America* (New York: Oxford University Press, 1991);

Iwan W. Morgan, *Deficit Government: Taxing and Spending in Modern America* (Chicago: Dee, 1995);

Cabell Phillips, *From the Crash to the Blitz, 1929–1939* (New York: Macmillan, 1969);

Glenn Porter, ed., *Encyclopedia of American Economic History: Studies of the Principal Movements and Ideas*, 3 volumes (New York: Scribners, 1980);

Joseph C. Pusateri, *A History of American Business* (Arlington Heights, Ill.: Davidson, 1984);

John B. Rae, *The American Automobile: A Brief History* (Chicago & London: University of Chicago Press, 1965);

Sidney Ratner, James H. Soltow, and Richard Sylla, *The Evolution of the American Economy* (New York: Basic Books, 1979);

Graham Robinson, *Pictorial History of the Automobile* (New York: Smith, 1987);

Larry Schweikart, ed., *Encyclopedia of American Business History and Biography: Banking and Finance, 1913–1989* (New York & Oxford: Facts On File, 1990);

Bruce E. Seely, ed., *Encyclopedia of American Business History and Biography: Iron and Steel in the Twentieth Century* (New York & Oxford: Facts On File, 1994);

Herbert Alexander Simon, *The New Science of Management Decision* (New York: Harper & Row, 1960);

Joan Hoff Wilson, *Herbert Hoover: Forgotten Progressive* (Boston: Little, Brown, 1975);

Daniel Yergin, *The Prize: The Epic Quest for Oil, Money and Power* (New York: Simon & Schuster, 1992).

EDUCATION

Richard J. Altenbaugh, *Education for Struggle: The American Labor Colleges of the 1920s and 1930s* (Philadelphia: Temple University Press, 1990);

James D. Anderson, *The Education of Blacks in the South, 1860–1935* (Chapel Hill: University of North Carolina Press, 1988);

Philippe Aries, *Centuries of Childhood* (New York: Knopf, 1962);

David L. Bachelor, *Educational Reform in New Mexico: Tireman, San José, and Nambé* (Albuquerque: University of New Mexico Press, 1991);

Leslie Lee Chisholm, *The Work of the Modern High School* (New York: Macmillan, 1953);

Burton R. Clark, *The Distinctive College: Antioch, Reed and Swarthmore* (Chicago: Aldine, 1970);

Columbia University Teachers College, *Are Liberal Arts Colleges Becoming Professional Schools?* (New York: Columbia University Teachers College, 1958);

James B. Conant, *Citadel of Learning* (New Haven: Yale University Press, 1956);

Conant, *The Revolutionary Transformation of the American High School* (Cambridge, Mass.: Harvard University Press, 1959);

Lawrence A. Cremin, *The Transformation of The School: Progressivism in American Education, 1876–1957* (New York: Knopf, 1961);

William Clyde De Vane, *The American University in the Twentieth Century* (Baton Rouge: Louisiana State University Press, 1957);

Martin Duberman, *Black Mountain: An Exploration in Community* (New York: Dutton, 1972);

William Edward Eaton, *The American Federation of Teachers, 1916–1961: A History of the Movement* (Carbondale: Southern Illinois University Press, 1975);

Vincent P. Franklin, *The Education of Black Philadelphia: The Social and Educational History of a Minority Community, 1900–1950* (Philadelphia: University of Pennsylvania Press, 1979);

Myles Horton, with Judith Kohl and Herbert Kohl, *The Long Haul* (New York: Doubleday, 1990);

Robert M. Hutchins, *Conflict in Education in a Democratic Society* (New York: Harper, 1953);

Hutchins, *Some Observations on American Education* (Cambridge: Cambridge University Press, 1956);

Robert W. Iversen, *The Communists and the Schools* (New York: Harcourt, Brace, 1959);

Russell Kirk, *Academic Freedom* (Chicago: Regnery, 1955);

Mary Knapp and Herbert Knapp, *One Potato, Two Potato . . . : The Secret Education of American Children* (New York: Norton, 1976);

Edward A. Krug, *The Shaping of the American High School, Volume 2, 1920–1941* (Madison: University of Wisconsin Press, 1972);

John Francis Latimer, *What's Happened to Our High Schools* (Washington, D.C.: Public Affairs Press, 1958);

Gordon C. Lee, *An Introduction to Education in America* (New York: Holt, 1957);

Fritz Machlup, *The Production and Distribution of Knowledge in the United States* (Princeton, N.J.: Princeton University Press, 1962);

Majorie Murphy, *Blackboard Unions: The AFT and the NEA, 1900–1980* (Ithaca, N.Y.: Cornell University Press, 1990);

Iona Archibald Opie, *The Lore and Language of Schoolchildren* (Oxford: Clarendon Press, 1959);

Philip W. Perdew, *The American Secondary School in Action* (Boston: Allyn & Bacon, 1959);

Jean Piaget, *Play, Dreams and Imitation in Childhood* (New York: Norton, 1962);

Hyman G. Rickover, *Education and Freedom* (New York: Dutton, 1959);

Peter M. Rutkoff and William B. Scott, *New School: A History of the New School for Social Research* (New York: Free Press, 1986);

Wilbur Schramm, J. Lyle, and I. de Sola Pool, *The People Look at Educational Television* (Stanford, Calif.: Stanford University Press, 1963);

Schramm, ed., *The Eighth Art* (New York: Holt, Rinehart & Winston, 1962);

Harvard Sitkoff, *A New Deal For Blacks: The Emergence of Civil Rights as a National Issue, Volume 1: The Depression Decade* (New York: Oxford University Press, 1978);

David Tyack, Robert Lowe, and Elisabeth Hansot, *Public Schools in Hard Times: The Great Depression and Recent Years* (Cambridge, Mass.: Harvard University Press, 1984);

James M. Wallace, *Liberal Journalism and American Education, 1914–1941* (New Brunswick, N.J.: Rutgers University Press, 1991);

Robert Westbrook, *John Dewey and American Democracy* (Ithaca, N.Y.: Cornell University Press, 1991);

Julia Wrigley, *Class Politics and Public Schools: Chicago, 1900–1950* (New Brunswick, N.J.: Rutgers University Press, 1982).

FASHION

Michael Batterberry and Ariane Batterberry, *Mirror, Mirror: A Social History of Fashion* (New York: Holt, Rinehart & Winston, 1977);

Helen L. Brockman, *The Theory of Fashion Design* (New York: Wiley, 1965);

The Changing American Woman: Two Hundred Years of American Fashion (New York: Fairchild, 1976);

Mila Contini, *Fashion: From Ancient Egypt to the Present Day* (New York: Odyssey, 1965);

Maryanne Dolan, *Vintage Clothing, 1880–1960: Identification and Value Guide* (Florence, Ala.: Books Americana, 1984);

Elizabeth Ewing, *History of Twentieth Century Fashion*, revised and updated edition (London: Batsford, 1992; Lanham, Md.: Barnes & Noble, 1992);

James J. Flink, *The Automobile Age* (Cambridge, Mass. & London: MIT Press, 1988);

Jane Gaines and Charlotte Herzog, eds., *Fabrications: Costume and the Female Body* (New York: Routledge, 1990);

Sandra Ley, *Fashion for Everyone: The Story of Ready-to-Wear, 1870–1970s* (New York: Scribners, 1975);

Chester H. Liebs, *Main Street to Miracle Mile: American Roadside Architecture* (Boston: Little, Brown, 1985);

Valerie Lloyd, *The Art of Vogue Photographic Covers: Fifty Years of Fashion and Design* (New York: Harmony, 1986);

Lloyd, *McDowell's Directory of Twentieth Century Fashion* (Englewood Cliffs, N.J.: Prentice-Hall, 1985);

Virginia McAlester and Lee McAlester, *A Field Guide to American Houses* (New York: Knopf, 1992);

Barbara Melosh, *Engendering Culture: Manhood and Womanhood in New Deal Public Art and Theater* (Washington, D.C. & London: Smithsonian Institution Press, 1991);

Caroline Rennolds Milbank, *New York Fashion: The Evolution of American Style* (New York: Abrams, 1989);

Meyric R. Rogers, *American Interior Design: The Traditions and Development of Domestic Design from Colonial Times to the Present* (New York: Norton, 1947);

Mary Shaw Ryan, *Clothing: A Study in Human Behavior* (New York: Holt, Rinehart & Winston, 1966);

Stephen W. Sears, *The Automobile in America* (New York: American Heritage Publishing, 1977);

Donald Stowell and Erin Wertenberger, *A Century of Fashion 1865–1965* (Chicago: Encyclopaedia Britannica, 1987);

Jane Trahey, *The Mode in Costume* (New York: Scribners, 1958);

Trahey, ed., *Harper's Bazaar: One Hundred Years of the American Female* (New York: Random House, 1967);

Anne V. Tyrrell, *Changing Trends in Fashion: Patterns of the Twentieth Century, 1900–1970* (London: Batsford, 1986);

Marcus Whiffen and Frederick Koeper, *American Architecture 1607–1976* (Cambridge, Mass.: MIT Press, 1981);

Barry James Wood, *Show Windows: Seventy-five Years of the Art of Display* (New York: Congdon & Weed, 1982).

GOVERNMENT AND POLITICS

Kristi Andersen, *The Creation of a Democratic Majority, 1928–1936* (Chicago: University of Chicago Press, 1979);

William J. Barber, *From New Era to New Deal: Herbert Hoover, the Economists, and American Economic Policy, 1921–1933* (Cambridge & New York: Cambridge University Press, 1985);

Harry Elmer Barnes, *Perpetual War for Perpetual Peace: A Critical Examination of the Foreign Policy of Franklin Delano Roosevelt* (New York: Greenwood Press, 1969);

Irving Bernstein, *Turbulent Years: A History of the American Worker, 1933–1941* (Boston: Houghton Mifflin, 1970);

Alan Brinkley, *Voices of Protest: Huey Long, Father Coughlin, and the Great Depression* (New York: Knopf, 1982);

David Brody, *Workers in Industrial America* (New York: Oxford University Press, 1980);

Bert Cochran, *Labor and Communism: The Conflict That Shaped the Unions* (Princeton: Princeton University Press, 1977);

Wayne S. Cole, *Roosevelt and the Isolationists, 1932–1945* (Lincoln: University of Nebraska Press, 1983);

Paul K. Conkin, *F.D.R. and the Origin of the Welfare State* (New York: Crowell, 1967); republished as *The New Deal* (New York: Crowell, 1969);

Robert A. Dallek, *Franklin D. Roosevelt and American Foreign Policy, 1932–1945* (New York: Oxford University Press, 1981);

Martha Derthick, *Policymaking for Social Security* (Washington, D.C.: Brookings Institution, 1979);

Robert A. Divine, *The Illusion of Neutrality* (Chicago: University of Chicago Press, 1962);

Henry L. Feingold, *The Politics of Rescue: The Roosevelt Administration and the Holocaust, 1938–1945*, expanded and updated edition (New York: Holocaust Library, 1980);

Steve Fraser and Gary Gerstle, eds., *The Rise and Fall of the New Deal Order, 1930–1980* (Princeton: Princeton University Press, 1989);

Frank Freidel, *FDR: Launching the New Deal* (Boston: Little, Brown, 1973);

Eric F. Goldman, *A Rendezvous with Destiny: A History of Modern American Reform*, revised and abridged edition (New York: Vintage, 1956);

Otis L. Graham Jr., *An Encore for Reform: The Old Progressives and the New Deal* (New York: Oxford University Press, 1967);

Ellis W. Hawley, *The New Deal and the Problem of Monopoly* (Princeton: Princeton University Press, 1966);

Robert F. Himmelberg, *The Origins of the National Recovery Administration* (New York: Fordham University Press, 1976);

Joan Hoff-Wilson, *Herbert Hoover, Forgotten Progressive* (Boston: Little, Brown, 1975);

Richard Hofstadter, *The American Political Tradition and the Men Who Made It* (New York: Knopf, 1948);

Preston Hubbard, *Origins of the TVA* (Nashville: Vanderbilt University Press, 1961);

Manfred Jonas, *Isolationism in America, 1935–1941* (Ithaca, N.Y.: Cornell University Press, 1966);

William R. Keylor, *The Twentieth-Century World: An International History,* revised edition (New York: Oxford University Press, 1992);

David E. Kyvig, ed., *FDR's America* (Saint Charles, Mo.: Forum Press, 1976);

Walter LaFeber and others, *The American Century* (New York: McGraw-Hill, 1990);

John H. Leek, *Government and Labor in the United States* (New York: Rhinehart, 1952);

William E. Leuchtenburg, *Franklin D. Roosevelt and the New Deal, 1932–1940* (New York: Harper & Row, 1963);

Leuchtenburg, *New Deal and Global War* (New York: Time-Life Books, 1964);

Haskell Lookstein, *Were We Our Brothers Keepers? The Public Response of American Jews to the Holocaust, 1938–1944* (New York: Hartmore House, 1985);

Samuel Lubell, *The Future of American Politics,* third edition (New York: Harper & Row, 1965);

Thomas J. McCraw, *TVA and the Power Fight: 1933–1939* (Philadelphia: Lippincott, 1971);

Raymond Moley, *The First New Deal* (New York: Harcourt, Brace & World, 1966);

Arnold A. Offner, *American Appeasement: United States Foreign Policy and Germany, 1933–1938* (New York: Norton, 1976);

James T. Patterson, *Congressional Conservatism and the New Deal* (Lexington: Organization of American Historians/University of Kentucky Press, 1967);

Geoffrey Perrett, *Days of Sadness, Years of Triumph: The American People, 1939–1945* (Madison: University of Wisconsin Press, 1985);

Cabell Phillips, *From Crash to the Blitz, 1929–1939* (New York: Macmillan, 1969);

Elliot A. Rosen, *Hoover, Roosevelt, and the Brains Trust: From Depression to New Deal* (New York: Columbia University Press, 1977);

Arthur M. Schlesinger Jr., *The Age of Roosevelt,* 3 volumes (Boston: Houghton Mifflin, 1956–1960);

Schlesinger Jr., ed., *History of American Presidential Elections, 1789–1968,* 3 volumes (New York: Chelsea House/McGraw-Hill, 1971);

Schlesinger Jr., ed., *History of U.S. Political Parties* (New York: Chelsea House, 1973);

James L. Sundquist, *Dynamics of the Party System: Alignment and Realignment of Political Parties in the United States,* revised edition (Washington, D.C.: Brookings Institution, 1983);

Rexford G. Tugwell, *The Brains Trust* (New York: Viking, 1968);

T. H. Watkins, *The Great Depression* (Boston: Little, Brown, 1993);

Dixon Wecter, *The Age of the Great Depression, 1929–1941* (New York: Macmillan, 1948);

Michael M. Weinstein, *Recovery and Redistribution under the NIRA* (New York: North-Holland Publishing, 1980);

William Appleman Williams, *The Contours of American History* (Chicago: Quadrangle Books, 1966);

John E. Wiltz, *From Isolation to War, 1931–1941* (New York: Crowell, 1968);

Edwin Witte, *The Development of the Social Security Act* (Madison: University of Wisconsin Press, 1962).

LAW

Henry J. Abraham, *Justices and Presidents: A Political History of Appointments to the Supreme Court* (New York: Oxford University Press, 1985);

Irving Bernstein, *Turbulent Years: A History of the American Worker, 1933–1941* (Boston: Houghton Mifflin, 1970);

Dan T. Carter, *Scottsboro: A Tragedy of the American South* (Baton Rouge: Louisiana State University Press, 1969);

Robert F. Cushman, *Leading Constitutional Decisions* (Englewood Cliffs, N.J.: Prentice-Hall, 1977);

Gerald T. Dunne, *Hugo Black and the Judicial Revolution* (New York: Simon & Schuster, 1977);

Steven R. Fox, *Blood and Power: Organized Crime in the Twentieth Century* (New York: Morrow, 1989);

J. C. Furnas, *The Life and Times of the Late Demon Rum* (New York: Putnam, 1965);

G. Russell Girardin, *Dillinger: The Untold Story* (Bloomington: Indiana University Press, 1994);

Kermit L. Hall, *The Magic Mirror: Law in American History* (New York: Oxford University Press, 1989);

Hall, ed., *The Oxford Companion to the Supreme Court* (New York: Oxford University Press, 1992);

Maureen Harrison and Steve Gilbert, eds., *Landmark Decisions of the United States Supreme Court II* (Beverly Hills: Excellent Books, 1992);

John W. Johnson, *American Legal Culture, 1908–1940* (Westport, Conn.: Greenwood Press, 1981);

Alfred H. Kelly, Winfred A. Harbison, and Herman Belz, *The American Constitution: Its Origins and Development — Volume II*, seventh edition (New York: Norton, 1991);

William E. Leuchtenburg, *Franklin Roosevelt and the New Deal* (New York: Harper & Row, 1963);

Jethro K. Lieberman, *The Enduring Constitution: A Bicentennial Perspective* (New York: West, 1987);

Alpheus Thomas Mason, *The Supreme Court from Taft to Burger* (Baton Rouge: Louisiana State University Press, 1979);

Robert G. McCloskey, *The American Supreme Court* (Chicago: University of Chicago Press, 1960);

Robert S. McElvaine, *The Great Depression: America, 1929–1941* (New York: Times Books, 1984);

Robert Morris, ed., *Encyclopedia of American History*, sixth edition (New York: Harper & Row, 1982);

Jay Robert Nash, *Bloodletters and Badmen* (New York: Evans, 1973);

Richard L. Pacelle Jr., *The Transformation of the Supreme Court's Agenda* (Boulder, Colo.: Westview Press, 1991);

Richard Gid Powers, *G-Men, Hoover's FBI In American Popular Culture* (Carbondale: Southern Illinois University Press, 1983);

Arthur M. Schlesinger, *The Politics of Upheaval* (Boston: Houghton Mifflin, 1960);

Bernard Schwartz, *The American Heritage History of the Law in America* (New York: McGraw-Hill, 1974);

Bernard Schwartz, *The Law in America, A History* (New York: McGraw-Hill, 1974);

Jordan A. Schwartz, *The New Dealers: Power Politics in the Age of Roosevelt* (New York: Knopf, 1993);

Page Smith, *Redeeming the Time: A People's History of the 1920s and the New Deal*, 8 volumes (New York: Penguin, 1987);

Robert Stevens, *Legal Education in America from the 1850's to the 1980's* (Chapel Hill: University of North Carolina Press, 1983);

The Supreme Court of the United States — Its Beginnings and Its Justices, 1790–1991 (Washington, D.C.: Commission on the Bicentennial of the United States, 1992);

John Toland, *The Dillinger Days* (New York: Random House, 1963);

Treaties and Alliances of the World (New York: Scribners, 1968);

Sanford J. Ungar, *FBI* (Boston: Atlantic Monthly Press/Little, Brown, 1976).

LIFESTYLES AND SOCIAL TRENDS

Michael Barone, *Our Country: The Shaping of America from Roosevelt to Reagan* (New York: Free Press, 1990);

Mary Kupiec Cayton, Elliott J. Gorn, and Peter W. Williams, eds., *Encyclopedia of American Social History*, 3 volumes (New York: Scribners, 1993);

William Chafe, *The American Woman: Her Changing Social, Economic, and Political Roles, 1920–1970* (New York: Oxford University Press, 1972);

Lizabeth Cohen, *Making a New Deal: Industrial Workers in Chicago, 1919–1939* (Cambridge & New York: Cambridge University Press, 1990);

Peter G. Filene, *Him/Her/Self: Sex Roles in Modern America* (New York: Harcourt Brace Jovanovich, 1974);

John Hope Franklin and Isidore Starr, *The Negro in Twentieth Century America* (New York: Random House, 1967);

Estelle B. Freedman and John D'Emilio, *Intimate Matters: A History of Sexuality in America* (New York: Harper & Row, 1988);

James N. Gregory, *American Exodus: The Dust Bowl Migration and Okie Culture in California* (New York: Oxford University Press, 1989);

Steven Mintz and Susan Kellogg, *Domestic Revolutions: A Social History of American Family Life* (New York: Free Press, 1988);

John Modell, *Into One's Own: From Youth to Adulthood in the United States, 1920–1975* (Berkeley: University of California Press, 1989);

Cabell Phillips, *From Crash to the Blitz, 1929–1939* (New York: Macmillan, 1969);

Rosalind Rosenberg, *Divided Lives: American Women in the Twentieth Century* (New York: Hill & Wang, 1992);

Warren Susman, *Culture as History: The Transformation of American Society in the Twentieth Century* (New York: Pantheon, 1985);

Studs Terkel, *Hard Times: An Oral History of the Great Depression* (New York: Random House, 1970);

Susan Ware, *Holding Their Own: American Women in the 1930s* (Boston: Twayne, 1982).

MEDIA

Daniel Aaron, *Writers on the Left* (New York: Harcourt, Brace & World, 1961);

Erik Barnouw, *The Golden Web: A History of Broadcasting in the United States, Volume II, 1933 To 1953* (New York: Oxford University Press, 1968);

Barnouw, *A Tower in Babel: A History of Broadcasting in the United States, Volume I, To 1933* (New York: Oxford University Press, 1966);

Charles O. Bennett, *Facts Without Opinion: First Fifty Years of the Audit Bureau of Circulation* (Chicago: ABC, 1965);

Mike Benton, *The Comic Book in America: An Illustrated History,* revised edition (Dallas: Taylor, 1993);

Thomas L. Bonn, *Under Cover: An Illustrated History of American Mass Market Paperbacks* (New York: Penguin, 1982);

Robert Campbell, *The Golden Years of Broadcasting: A Celebration of the First Fifty Years of Radio and TV on NBC* (New York: Scribners, 1972);

John Diggins, *Up from Communism: Conservative Odysseys in American Intellectual History* (New York: Harper & Row, 1975);

John Dunning, *Tune in Yesterday: The Ultimate Encyclopedia of Old-Time Radio 1925–1976* (Englewood Cliffs, N.J.: Prentice-Hall, 1976);

Michael Emery and Edwin Emery, *The Press and America: An Interpretive History of the Mass Media* (Englewood Cliffs, N.J.: Prentice Hall, 1992);

Walter B. Emery, *National and International Systems of Broadcasting: Their History, Operation, and Control* (East Lansing: Michigan State University Press, 1969);

George Everson, *The Story of Television: The Life of Philo T. Farnsworth* (New York: Norton, 1949);

Tony Goodstone, ed., *The Pulps: Fifty Years of American Popular Culture* (New York: Chelsea House, 1970);

Ron Goulart, *Cheap Thrills: An Informal History of the Pulp Magazines* (New Rochelle, N.Y.: Arlington House, 1972);

Goulart, *The Dime Detectives* (New York: Mysterious Press, 1988);

Goulart, *The Hardboiled Dicks* (New York: Pocket Books, 1967);

Goulart, ed., *The Encyclopedia of American Comics* (New York & Oxford: Facts On File, 1990);

John Grant, *Encyclopedia of Walt Disney's Animated Characters,* revised edition (New York: Hyperion, 1993);

Sydney W. Head and Christopher H. Sterling, *Broadcasting in America: A Survey of Television, Radio, and New Technologies,* fourth edition (Boston: Houghton Mifflin, 1982);

Amy Janello and Brennon Jones, *The American Magazine* (New York: Abrams, 1991);

Norman M. Klein, *Seven Minutes: The Life and Death of the American Animated Cartoon* (London & New York: Verso, 1993);

Daniel J. Leab, *A Union of Individuals: The Formation of the American Newspaper Guild, 1933–1936* (New York: Columbia University Press, 1970);

Laurence W. Lichty and Malachi Topping, *American Broadcasting: A Source Book on the History of Radio and Television* (New York: Hastings House, 1975);

J. Fred MacDonald, *Don't Touch That Dial: Radio Programming in American Life from 1920 to 1960* (Chicago: G. K. Hall, 1979);

Leonard Maltin, *Of Mice and Magic: A History of American Animated Cartoons,* revised edition (New York: New American Library, 1987);

Richard Marschall, *America's Great Comic-Strip Artists* (New York: Abbeville, 1989);

Alexander McNeil, *Total Television: A Comprehensive Guide to Programming from 1948–1980* (New York: Penguin, 1980);

Frank Luther Mott, *A History of American Magazines,* 5 volumes (Cambridge, Mass.: Harvard University Press, 1938–1968);

Max D. Paglin, ed., *A Legislative History of the Communications Act of 1934* (New York: Oxford University Press, 1989);

Richard Pells, *Radical Visions and American Dreams: Culture and Social Thought in the Depression Years* (Middletown, Conn.: Wesleyan University Press, 1973);

Cabell Phillips, *From the Crash to the Blitz, 1929–1939* (New York: Macmillan, 1969);

Steve Schneider, *That's All Folks! The Art of Warner Bros. Animation* (New York: Holt, 1988);

Piet Schreuders, *Paperbacks, U.S.A.: A Graphic History, 1939–1959,* translated by Josh Pachter (San Diego: Blue Dolphin, 1981);

Lee Server, *Danger Is My Business: An Illustrated History of the Fabulous Pulp Magazines* (San Francisco: Chronicle, 1993);

Christopher Sterling, ed., *Broadcasting and Mass Media: A Survey Bibliography* (Philadelphia: Temple University Press, 1974);

Sterling, ed., *The History of Broadcasting: Radio to Television,* 32 volumes (New York: New York Times/Arno, 1972);

Sterling, ed., *Telecommunications,* 34 volumes (New York: New York Times/Arno, 1974);

Alan Wald, *The New York Intellectuals: The Rise and Decline of the Anti-Stalinist Left from the 1930s to the 1980s* (Chapel Hill: University of North Carolina Press, 1987).

MEDICINE AND HEALTH

Leonard Berkowitz, *Aggression: A Psychological Analysis* (New York: McGraw-Hill, 1962);

James Bordley and A. McGehee Harvey, *Two Centuries of American Medicine, 1776–1976* (Philadelphia: Saunders, 1976);

Allan M. Brandt, *No Magic Bullet: A Social History of Venereal Disease in the United States Since 1880* (New York: Oxford University Press, 1985);

The Cambridge World History of Human Disease (New York: Cambridge University Press, 1993);

Rick J. Carlson, *The End of Medicine* (New York: Wiley, 1975);

Frederic Fox Cartwright, *Disease and History* (New York: Crowell, 1972);

James H. Cassedy, *Medicine in America: A Short History* (Baltimore: Johns Hopkins University Press, 1991);

Companion Encyclopedia of the History of Medicine (London: Routledge, 1993);

Bernard Dixon, *Beyond the Magic Bullet* (New York: Harper & Row, 1978);

John Patrick Dolan, *Health and Society: A Documentary History of Medicine* (New York: Seabury, 1978);

John Duffy, *The Healers: The Rise of the Medical Establishment* (New York: McGraw-Hill, 1976);

Martin Duke, *The Development of Medical Techniques and Treatments: From Leeches to Heart Surgery* (Madison, Conn.: International Universities Press, 1991);

Abraham Holtzman, *The Townsend Movement: A Political Study* (New York: Bookman, 1963);

Michael B. Katz, *In the Shadow of the Poorhouse: A Social History of Welfare in America* (New York: Basic Books, 1986);

Esmond R. Long, *A History of Pathology* (New York: Dover, 1965);

Albert S. Lyons, *Medicine: An Illustrated History* (New York: Abrams, 1978);

Geoffrey Marks and William K. Beatty, *The Story of Medicine in America* (New York: Scribners, 1973);

Sherwin B. Nuland, *Doctors: The Biography of Medicine* (New York: Knopf, 1988);

John R. Paul, *A History of Poliomyelitis* (New Haven & London: Yale University Press, 1971);

Sheila M. Rothman, *Living in the Shadow of Death* (New York: Basic Books, 1994);

David Shakow and David Rapaport, *The Influence of Freud on American Psychology* (Cleveland: Meridian Books, 1964);

Edward Shorter, *The Health Century* (New York: Doubleday, 1987);

Jane S. Smith, *Patenting the Sun: Polio and the Salk Vaccine* (New York: Morrow, 1990);

Theodore L. Sourkes, *Nobel Prize Winners in Medicine and Physiology: 1901–1965* (London: Abelard-Schuman, 1966);

Paul Starr, *The Social Transformation of American Medicine* (New York: Basic Books, 1982);

Rosemary Stevens, *American Medicine and the Public Interest* (New Haven: Yale University Press, 1971);

Elliot S. Valenstein, *Great and Desperate Cures* (New York: Basic Books, 1986);

James Harvey Young, *The Medical Messiahs* (Princeton: Princeton University Press, 1967).

RELIGION

Sydney E. Ahlstrom, *A Religious History of the American People*, 2 volumes (Garden City, N.Y.: Doubleday, 1975);

Catherine Albanese, *America, Religions and Religious* (Belmont, Calif.: Wadsworth, 1981);

Nancy T. Ammerman, *Bible Believers: Fundamentalists in the Modern World* (New Brunswick, N.J.: Rutgers University Press, 1987);

Yehuda Bauer, *American Jewry and the Holocaust: The American Joint Distribution Committee, 1939–1945* (Detroit: Wayne State University Press, 1981);

Bernham P. Beckwith, *The Decline of U.S. Religious Faith, 1912–1984* (Palo Alto, Calif.: Beckwith, 1985);

Robert N. Bellah and Frederick E. Greenspahn, eds., *Uncivil Religion: Irreligious Hostility in America* (New York: Crossroads, 1987);

Robert Benne, *Defining America: A Christian Critique of the American Dream* (Philadelphia: Fortress Press, 1974);

David H. Bennett, *Demagogues in the Depression: American Radicals and the Union Party, 1933–1936* (New Brunswick, N.J.: Rutgers University Press, 1969);

John C. Bennett, *Christians and the State* (New York: Scribners, 1958);

Gregory D. Black, *Hollywood Censored: Morality Codes, Catholics, and the Movies* (New York: Cambridge University Press, 1994);

Charles Samuel Braden, *These Also Believe: A Study of Modern American Cults and Minority Religious Movements* (New York: Macmillan, 1950);

Jerald C. Brauer, *Protestantism in America: A Narrative History* (Philadelphia: Westminster, 1953);

Alan Brinkley, *Voices of Protest: Huey Long, Father Coughlin and the Great Depression* (New York: Knopf, 1982);

Kenneth E. Burnham, *God Comes to America: Father Devine and the Peace Mission Movement* (Philadelphia: Imperial Press, 1982);

Jackson W. Carroll, *Beyond Establishment: Protestant Identity in a Post-Protestant Age* (Louisville, Ky.: Westminster/John Knox, 1993);

Samuel McCrea Cavert, *The American Churches in the Ecumenical Movement, 1900–1968* (New York: Association Press, 1968);

Mickey Crews, *The Church of God: A Social History* (Knoxville: University of Tennessee Press, 1990);

Jay P. Dolan, *The American Catholic Experience: A History from Colonial Times to the Present* (Garden City, N.Y.: Doubleday, 1985);

Tom Driberg, *The Mystery of Moral Re-Armament: A Study of Frank Buchman and His Movement* (New York: Knopf, 1965);

Robert F. Drinan, *Religion, the Courts, and Public Policy* (New York: McGraw-Hill, 1963);

John L. Eighmy, *Churches in Cultural Captivity: A History of the Social Attitudes of Southern Baptists* (Knoxville: University of Tennessee Press, 1987);

Henry L. Feingold, *A Time for Searching: Entering the Mainstream, 1920–1945* (Baltimore: Johns Hopkins University Press, 1992);

Roger Finke and Rodney Strunk, *The Churching of America, 1779–1990: Winners and Losers in Our Religious Economy* (New Brunswick, N.J.: Rutgers University Press, 1992);

George Q. Flynn, *American Catholics and the Roosevelt Presidency, 1932–1936* (Lexington: University Press of Kentucky, 1968);

Flynn, *Roosevelt and Romanism: Catholics and American Diplomacy, 1937–1945* (Westport, Conn.: Greenwood Press, 1976);

Saul S. Friedman, *No Haven for the Oppressed: United States Policy toward Jewish Refugees, 1938–1945* (Detroit: Wayne State University Press, 1973);

James J. Hennesey, *American Catholics: A History of the Roman Catholic Community in the United States* (New York: Oxford University Press, 1981);

Arthur Hertzberg, *The Jews in America: Four Centuries of an Uneasy Encounter — A History* (New York: Simon & Schuster, 1989);

Darryl Hudson, *The Ecumenical Movement in World Affairs* (London: Weidenfeld & Nicolson, 1969);

Winthrop S. Hudson, *Religion in America: An Historical Account of the Development of American Religious Life* (New York: Scribners, 1981);

William R. Hutchinson, *The Modernist Impulse in American Protestantism* (Cambridge, Mass.: Harvard University Press, 1976);

Donald G. Jones and Russell E. Richey, eds., *American Civil Religion* (San Francisco: Mellen Research University Press, 1990);

Samuel C. Kincheloe, *Research Memorandum on Religion in the Depression* (Westport, Conn.: Greenwood Press, 1970);

Charles H. Lippy, *Being Religious, American Style: A History of Popular Religiosity in the United States* (Westport, Conn.: Greenwood Press, 1994);

Edward L. Long, *The Christian Response to the Atomic Crisis* (Philadelphia: Westminster, 1950);

David W. Lotz, ed., *Altered Landscapes: Christianity in America, 1935–1985* (Grand Rapids, Mich.: Eerdmans, 1989);

Martin E. Marty, *Pilgrims in Their Own Land: Five Hundred Years of Religion in America* (Boston: Little, Brown, 1984);

Donald B. Meyer, *The Protestant Search for Political Realism, 1919–1941* (Berkeley & Los Angeles: University of California Press, 1960);

Constance Ashton Myers, *The Prophet's Army: Trotskyists in America, 1928–1941* (Westport, Conn.: Greenwood Press, 1977);

John K. Nelson, *Peace Prophets: American Pacifist Thought, 1919–1945* (Chapel Hill: University of North Carolina Press, 1967);

Frederick A. Norwood, *The Story of American Methodism: A History of the United Methodists and Their Relations* (Nashville: Abingdon, 1974);

Leo Pfeiffer, *Church, State, and Freedom,* second edition (Boston: Beacon, 1967);

Mel Piehl, *Breaking Bread: The Catholic Worker and the Origins of Catholic Radicalism in America* (Philadelphia: Temple University Press, 1982);

A. James Reichley, *Religion in American Public Life* (Washington, D.C.: Brookings Institution, 1985);

Russell E. Richey, *American Civil Religion* (New York: Harper & Row, 1974);

Robert W. Ross, *So It Was True: The American Protestant Press and the Nazi Persecution of the Jews* (Minneapolis: University of Minnesota Press, 1980);

Ralph Lord Roy, *Apostles of Discord: A Study of Organized Bigotry and Disruption on the Fringes of Protestantism* (Boston: Beacon, 1953);

Roy, *Communism and the Churches* (New York: Harcourt, Brace, 1960);

Howard M. Sachar, *A History of the Jews in America* (New York: Knopf, 1992);

James M. Skinner, *The Cross and the Cinema: The Legion of Decency and the National Catholic Office for Motion Pictures, 1933–1970* (Westport, Conn.: Praeger, 1993);

Charles J. Tull, *Father Coughlin and the New Deal* (Syracuse, N.Y.: Syracuse University Press, 1965);

Joseph Tussman, ed., *The Supreme Court on Church and State* (New York: Oxford University Press, 1962);

Robert Weisbrot, *Father Devine and the Struggle for Racial Equality* (Urbana: University of Illinois Press, 1983).

SCIENCE AND TECHNOLOGY

Garland Allen, *Life Science in the Twentieth Century* (Cambridge: Cambridge University Press, 1978);

Erik Barnouw, *The Golden Web: A History of Broadcasting in the United States, Volume II, 1933 to 1953* (New York: Oxford University Press, 1968);

Barnouw, *A Tower in Babel: A History of Broadcasting in the United States, Volume I, to 1933* (New York: Oxford University Press, 1966);

Roger Billstein, *Flight in America* (Baltimore: Johns Hopkins University Press, 1985);

Carnegie Library of Pittsburgh, Science and Technology Department, *Science and Technology Desk Reference* (Detroit: Gale Research, 1993);

William Chandler, *The Myth of TVA: Conservation and Development in the Tennessee Valley, 1933–1983* (Cambridge, Mass.: Ballinger, 1984);

Joseph J. Corn, *The Winged Gospel: America's Romance with Aviation, 1900–1950* (New York: Oxford University Press, 1983);

Corn, ed., *Imagining Tomorrow* (Cambridge, Mass.: MIT Press, 1987);

Hamilton Cravens, *The Truimph of Evolution: American Scientists and the Heredity-Environment Controversy, 1900–1941* (Philadelphia: University of Pennsylvania Press, 1978);

Carl N. Degler, *In Search of Human Nature: The Decline and Revival of Darwinism in American Social Thought* (New York: Oxford University Press, 1991);

Harold Dick and Douglas Robinson, *The Golden Age of the Great Passenger Airships* (Washington, D.C.: Smithsonian Institution Press, 1985);

George H. Douglas, *All Aboard! The Railroad in American Life* (New York: Paragon House, 1992);

Laura Fermi, *Illustrious Immigrants: The Intellectual Migration from Europe* (Chicago: University of Chicago Press, 1968);

Donald Fleming and Bernard Bailyn, eds., *The Intellectual Migration* (Cambridge, Mass.: Harvard University Press, 1969);

Charles Coulston Gillespie, ed., *Dictionary of Scientific Biography*, 18 volumes (New York: Scribners, 1970–1990);

Stephen B. Goddard, *Getting There: The Epic Struggle Between Road and Rail in the American Century* (New York: Basic Books, 1992);

David A. Hounshell and John Kenly Smith Jr., *Science and Corporate Strategy: Du Pont R&D, 1902–1980* (Cambridge & New York: Cambridge University Press, 1988);

G. Kass-Simon and Patricia Farnes, eds., *Women of Science* (Bloomington: University of Indiana Press, 1990);

Daniel J. Kevles, *In the Name of Eugenics: Genetics and the Uses of Human Heredity* (New York: Knopf, 1985);

Kevles, *The Physicists: The History of a Scientific Community in Modern America* (New York: Knopf, 1978);

Stefan Kühl, *The Nazi Connection: Eugenics, American Racism, and German National Socialism* (New York: Oxford University Press, 1993);

Peter J. Kuznick, *Beyond the Laboratory: Scientists as Political Activists in 1930s America* (Chicago: University of Chicago Press, 1987);

Anthony O. Lewis, ed., *Of Men and Machines* (London: Dutton, 1963);

Ernst Mayr, *The Growth of Biological Thought: Diversity, Evolution, and Inheritance* (Cambridge, Mass.: Harvard University Press, 1982);

Mayr and William B. Provine, *The Evolutionary Synthesis: Perspectives on the Unification of Biology* (Cambridge, Mass.: Harvard University Press, 1980);

McGraw-Hill Encyclopedia of Science and Technology, fourth edition, 14 volumes (New York: McGraw-Hill, 1977);

Lewis Mumford, *The Myth of the Machine: The Pentagon of Power* (New York: Harcourt Brace Jovanovich, 1964);

David Nye, *American Technological Sublime* (Cambridge, Mass.: MIT Press, 1994);

George P. Oslin, *The Story of Telecommunications* (Macon, Ga.: Mercer University Press, 1992);

Carroll W. Pursell, ed., *Technology in America* (Washington, D.C.: USIA Forum Series, 1979);

Ronald Rainger, Keith Benson, and Jane Maienschen, eds., *The American Development of Biology* (Philadelphia: University of Pennsylvania Press, 1988);

Margaret W. Rossiter, *Women Scientists in America: Struggles and Strategies to 1940* (Baltimore: Johns Hopkins University Press, 1982);

Daniel L. Schodek, *Landmarks in American Civil Engineering* (Cambridge, Mass.: MIT Press, 1987);

C. P. Snow, *The Two Cultures and the Scientific Revolution* (New York: Cambridge University Press, 1961);

J. E. Stevens, *Hoover Dam: An American Adventure* (Norman: University of Oklahoma Press, 1988);

Arnold Thackray and others, *Chemistry in America, 1876–1976* (Hingham, Mass.: Kluwer Academic Publishers, 1985).

SPORTS

Charles C. Alexander, *Our Game: An American Baseball History* (New York: Holt, 1991);

Sam Andre and Nat Fleisher, *A Pictorial History of Boxing,* revised edition (Secaucus, N.J.: Citadel Press, 1987);

Arthur Ashe, *A Hard Road to Glory: A History of the African American Athlete, 1919–1945,* revised edition (New York: Amistad, 1993);

Ashe, *A Hard Road to Glory: A History of the African-American Athlete Since 1946* (New York: Warner, 1988);

William J. Baker and John M. Carrol, eds., *Sports in Modern America* (Saint Louis: River City, 1981);

Jim Benagh, *Incredible Olympic Feats* (New York: McGraw-Hill, 1976);

Edwin H. Cady, *The Big Game: College Sports and American Life* (Knoxville: University of Tennessee Press, 1978);

Roger Caillois, *Man, Play, and Games* (London: Thames & Hudson, 1962);

Erich Camper, *Encyclopedia of the Olympic Games* (New York: McGraw-Hill, 1972);

Dick Clark and Larry Lester, eds., *The Negro Leagues Book* (Cleveland: Society for American Baseball Research, 1994);

Tim Cohane, *Great College Football Coaches of the Twenties and Thirties* (New Rochelle, N.Y.: Arlington House, 1973);

Allison Danzig and Peter Schwed, eds., *The Fireside Book of Tennis* (New York: Simon & Schuster, 1972);

John Durant, *Highlights of the Olympics* (New York: Hastings House, 1965);

Ellen W. Gerber and others, *The American Woman in Sport* (Reading, Mass.: Addison-Wesley, 1974);

Elliott J. Gorn, *The Manly Art* (Ithaca, N.Y.: Cornell University Press, 1986);

Will Grimsley, *Golf: Its History, People and Events* (Englewood Cliffs, N.J.: Prentice-Hall, 1966);

Grimsley, *Tennis: Its History, People and Events* (Englewood Cliffs, N.J.: Prentice-Hall, 1971);

John M. Gross and the editors of *Golf Magazine, The Encyclopedia of Golf,* revised edition (New York: Harper & Row, 1979);

Allen Guttman, *The Olympics: A History of the Modern Games* (Urbana: University of Illinois Press, 1992);

Guttman, *A Whole New Ball Game: An Interpretation of American Sports* (Chapel Hill: University of North Carolina Press, 1988);

Dorothy V. Harris, ed., *Women and Sports* (University Park: Pennsylvania State University Press, 1972);

Robert J. Higgs, *Sports: A Reference Guide* (Westport, Conn.: Greenwood Press, 1982);

Zander Hollander, ed., *The Pro Basketball Encyclopedia* (Los Angeles: Corwin Books, 1977);

Hollander and Ed Bock, eds., *The Complete Encyclopedia of Ice Hockey,* revised edition (Englewood Cliffs, N.J.: Prentice-Hall, 1974);

Neil D. Isaacs, *All the Moves: A History of College Basketball* (Philadelphia: Lippincott, 1975);

Bill James, *The Bill James Historical Baseball Abstract* (New York: Villard, 1986);

Roger Kahn, *The Boys of Summer* (New York: Harper & Row, 1972);

Ivan N. Kaye, *Good Clean Violence: A History of College Football* (Philadelphia: Lippincott, 1973);

Michael L. LaBlanc and Richard Henshaw, *The World Encyclopedia of Soccer* (Detroit: Visible Ink Press, 1994);

Richard D. Mandel, *The Nazi Olympics* (New York: Macmillan, 1971);

Mandel, *Sport: A Cultural History* (New York: Columbia University Press, 1984);

John D. McCallum, *College Basketball, U.S.A., Since 1892* (New York: Stein & Day, 1978);

Will McDonough and others, *75 Seasons: The Complete Story of the National Football League, 1920–1995* (Atlanta: Turner, 1995);

Tom Meany, *Baseball's Greatest Players* (New York: Barnes, 1953);

Robert Mechicoff and Steven Estes, *A History and Philosophy of Sport and Physical Education* (Dubuque, Iowa: Brown, 1993);

James A. Michener, *Sports in America* (New York: Random House, 1976);

Jack Olsen, *The Black Athlete: A Shameful Story* (New York: Time-Life Books, 1968);

Sandy Padwe, *Basketball's Hall of Fame* (Englewood Cliffs, N.J.: Prentice-Hall, 1970);

Robert W. Peterson, *Only the Ball Was White* (Englewood Cliffs, N.J.: Prentice-Hall, 1970);

Bernard Postal, Jesse Silver, and Roy Silver, *Encyclopedia of Jews in Sport* (New York: Bloch, 1965);

Benjamin G. Rader, *American Sports: From the Age of Folk Games to the Age of Spectators* (Englewood Cliffs, N.J.: Prentice-Hall, 1983);

Steven A. Riess, ed., *The American Sporting Experience* (New York: Leisure Press, 1984);

Max Robinson and Jack Kramer, eds., *The Encyclopedia of Tennis: One Hundred Years of Great Players and Events* (New York: Viking, 1974);

Leverett T. Smith Jr., *The American Dream and the National Game* (Bowling Green, Ohio: Bowling Green State University Popular Press, 1975);

Betty Spears and Richard A. Swanson, *History of Sport and Physical Education,* third edition (Dubuque, Iowa: Brown, 1983);

Murray Sperber, *Shake Down the Thunder: The Creation of Notre Dame Football* (New York: Holt, 1993);

John Thorn and Pete Palmer, eds., *Total Baseball,* second edition (New York: Warner, 1991);

Jules Tygel, *Baseball's Great Experiment* (New York: Oxford University Press, 1983);

David Quentin Voigt, *America Through Baseball* (Chicago: Nelson-Hall, 1976);

Voigt, *American Baseball: From the Commissioners to the Continental Expansion* (University Park: Pennsylvania State University Press, 1983);

David Wallenchinsky, *The Complete Book of the Olympics* (New York: Viking, 1984);

Janet Woolum, *Outstanding Women Athletes: Who They Are and How They Influenced Sports in America* (Phoenix: Oryx Press, 1992);

Earle F. Zeigler, ed., *A History of Physical Education and Sport in the United States and Canada* (Champaign, Ill.: Stipes, 1975).

CONTRIBUTORS

ARTS	LAURA BROWDER *Richmond, Virginia* DAVID MCLEAN *Boston, Massachusetts*
BUSINESS AND THE ECONOMY	VICTOR BONDI *University of Massachusetts — Boston* ROBERT BATCHELOR *Sacremento, California*
EDUCATION	VICTOR BONDI *University of Massachusetts — Boston*
FASHION	JANE GERHARD *Brown University*
GOVERNMENT AND POLITICS	JOHN LOUIS RECCHIUTI *Michigan Technological University*
LAW AND JUSTICE	JACK BENGE *Santa Barbara, California*
LIFESTYLES AND SOCIAL TRENDS	MARGO HORN *Los Altos, California* ROBERT BATCHELOR *Sacremento, California*
MEDIA	VICTOR BONDI *University of Massachusetts — Boston* DARREN HARRIS-FAIN *Bruccoli Clark Layman, Inc.* JAMES W. HIPP *Bruccoli Clark Layman, Inc.*
MEDICINE AND HEALTH	JOAN D. LAXSON *Boston, Massachusetts*
RELIGION	JOHN SCOTT WILSON *University of South Carolina*
SCIENCE AND TECHNOLOGY	GUILLAUME DESYON *Albright College*
SPORTS	RICHARD ORODENKER *Wyncote, Pennsylvania*

INDEX OF PHOTOGRAPHS

INDEX

Alex Maury, Sportsman (Gordon) 54
Alexander, Franz 410–411
Alexander the Great 422
Alford, L. B. 413
Alfred W. McCann Laboratories, New York City 425
Alger, Horatio 130–131
Algren, Nelson 34, 43, 53
Ali, Bardu 78
Alibi Ike (movie) 523
Alison's House (Glaspell) 88
Alka-Seltzer 383
All Brides Are Beautiful (Bell) 35
"All I Need Is You" (Fitzgerald) 78
"All of Me" (Simons and Marks) 28
All Quiet on the Western Front 26, 45, 87
All Saints Episcopal Church, Atlanta 207
All-Story 359
All the King's Men (Warren) 249
Allegheny coal strike 99
Allen, Fred 353–354
Allen, Freeman 421
Allen, Gracie 29–30, 353–354
Allen, Henry J. 247
Alley Oop (Hamlin) 341, 349
Allgood, Sara 40
Allison, Wilmer 533
Allport, Frank 421
Almanac Singers 81
Alphonso XIII of Spain 448
Aluminum City, New Kensington, Penn. 202
Aluminum Company of America 137
Alvarez, C. W. 413
Alvin Theater, New York City 27, 30, 33, 35, 37, 42
Always the Young Strangers (Sandburg) 84
Amana Society of Iowa 82
Amateur Athletic Union (AAU) 505–507, 525–526, 528–529
Amateur Athletic Union Indian club swinging championship 531
Amazing Stories 360
Ambers, Lou 503, 513
America 362
America First Party 253
"America Today — Changing West I" (Benton) 76
America's Cup (sailing) 498, 500, 502, 535
American Abstract Artists (AAA) 48

American Academy of Arts and Letters 85
American Academy of Dermatology and Syphilology 406
American Academy of Ophthalmology and Otolaryngology 425
American Airlines 95, 477, 480
American Anthropological Association 483
American Association for Cancer Research 424
American Association for the Study and Prevention of Infant Mortality 428
American Association of Applied Psychologists 387
American Association of Medical Jurisprudence 427
American Association of University Women 175
American Austin (automobile company) 189
American Ballet Caravan 45, 50
American Ballet Company 50
American Bankers Association 118, 147
American Bar Association (ABA) 275, 299, 343
— Canon 35 343
American Basketball League (ABL) 509–510
American Birth Control League 316
American Board of Internal Medicine 407
American Board of Missions to Jews 459
American Board of Obstetrics and Gynecology 401, 407
American Board of Pediatrics 407
American Board of Surgery 407
American Chemical Society 422
American Civil Liberties Union (ACLU) 285, 295, 315, 455
American Civil War 70, 103, 150, 167, 169, 223, 239, 426, 441
American College of Physicians 420, 427
American College of Surgeons 422, 423, 425, 427
American Congress on Internal Medicine 427
American Defense Society 156
American Dental Association 426
American Document (Graham) 45, 49–50

American Economic Association 137, 176
American Embassy, Paris 426
American Eugenics Society 471
American Exodus (Lange) 81
American Expeditionary Force 421–422
American Fashion Critics Award (Coty) 203
American Federation of Labor (AFL) 95, 101–103, 125, 132–133, 154, 213, 231–232, 335, 337, 362, 364
American Federation of Musicians 354
American Federation of Teachers (AFT) 142, 146, 156–157, 159–160, 171
American Fiction Guild 372
American Film Institute 69
American Folksong (Guthrie) 81
American Football Coaches Association, College Football Coach of the Year Award 515
American Foreign Policy in the Making, 1932–1940 (Beard) 167
American Friends Service Committee 159, 459
American Geographical Society 427
American Gothic (Wood) 26, 47
American Gynecological Society 424, 428
American Historical Association 166
American Historical Association, Commission on the Social Studies in the Schools 166–167, 170
"American Historical Epic" (Benton) 75
American Holiday (Humphrey) 45, 49
American Hospital Association 390, 392
American Institute for Psychoanalysis 410
American Institute of Architects Gold Medal 206
American Institute of Electrical Engineers 468
American Institute of Homeopathy 427
American Institute of Mining and Metallical Engineers 468
American Institute of Public Opinion 342, 406, 464

American Interplanetary Society 462

American Jewish Congress 439

The American Jewish World 85

The American Jitters (Wilson) 52

American Journal of Surgery 422

American Journal of the Diseases of Childhood 382

American Laboratory Theatre 71

American Landscape (Sheeler) 46

American Laryngological Association 425

American League 499, 508–509, 527, 530–534
— Most Valuable Player Award 530–531

American League Against War and Fascism 457

American League for Peace and Freedom 441, 457

American Legion 141, 152, 155–156, 289

American Liberty League (ALL) 118, 234–235, 240, 248, 277

American Lutheran Church 432, 441

American Lyric (Graham) 50

American Medical Association (AMA) 317, 386–387, 390–391, 394, 399, 401, 403–404, 407, 409, 411, 420, 424
— Council of Medical Education 401
— Distinguished Service Award 420

American Men of Science 493

American Mercury 362

American Microchemical Society 470

American Museum of Natural History, New York City, 484, 494

American Newspaper Guild (ANG) 89, 341, 362–364

American Newspaper Publishers Association (ANPA) 363–364, 376–378

American Oriental Society 176

American Peoples School, Gladden, Missouri 152

American Physical Society 469, 481

American Polar Society 464

American Political Science Association 166

American Provincials (Graham) 50

American Psychiatric Association 423, 426

American Psychopathological Association 422

American Public Health Association 420, 424

American Red Cross 137, 168, 203, 249, 271, 309, 397, 421, 422, 424, 426–427
— Bureau of Refugees 332

American Review 362, 372

American Relief Administration 245, 370

American Relief Committee 245

American Saga (Weidman) 49

American Sanatorium Association 422

American School of the Air 140, 356

American Social Hygiene Association 405

American Socialist Quarterly 362

American Society of Brewing Chemists 470

American Society of Civil Engineers 468

American Society of Composers, Authors, and Publishers (ASCAP) 344, 354

American Society of Electrical Engineers 494

American Society of Mechanical Engineers 468

American Spectator 358

American Surgical Association 426

American Teacher 175

American Telephone and Telegraph (AT&T) 104, 328, 366

American Tennis Association (ATA) 525, 532

American Therapeutic Society 427

American Tobacco Company 115

An American Tragedy 27

American Union Against Militarism 455

American Unitarian Association 455

The American Way (Kaufman and Hart) 42

American Weekly 374

Americana 362

America's Hour of Decision (Frank) 172

America's Town Meeting of the Air 356

Ames, Jessie Daniel 336

Amherst College 150, 177

Ammann, Othmar H. 463, 473

Amos 'n' Andy 352–354

Anarchism 134, 294, 299, 337, 346, 361, 448

Ancient and Mystical Order of the Rosae Crucis 460

"And the Angels Sing" (Elman and Mercer) 41

And to Think That I Saw It on Mulberry Street (Dr. Seuss) 38

Anders, Glenn 27

Anders, James Meschter 421

Anderson, Carl David 463, 469, 488, 492

Anderson, Carl Thomas 340

Anderson, Judith 205

Anderson, Marian 68, 250, 308

Anderson, Maxwell 35, 38, 42, 88

Anderson, O. A. 464

Anderson, Paul Y. 376

Anderson, Queen Candace 66

Anderson, Sherwood 29, 43, 52, 77, 82–83, 294, 361

Andre, Fabian 28

Andrew Jackson (M. James) 88

Andrew Todd McClintock Foundation 423

Andrews, Charles McLean 88

Anesthesiology 382–386, 395–396, 417, 421

Angel 58

Angels With Dirty Faces 58, 438

Anglo-Saxon Federation 156

Anna Christie 26

Anna Karenina 34

Annals of Surgery 426

Annenberg, Max 365

Annenberg, Moses 342, 344, 365–366

Annenberg, Walter 366

Another Thin Man 58

Anslinger, Harry J. 268

Anson, Cap 508

Antheil, George 68

Anthony, Benjamin Harris 376

Anthony, Daniel Reed Jr. 376

Anthony Adverse 87

Anthropology 361, 423, 462, 482–484, 494

Anti-Imperialist League 285

Anti-Saloon League 445–446, 451

Antibiotics 387, 394, 402, 405

Antioch College 155

Anvil 362

Anything Goes 33

Apollo Theater, New York City 33

Apostoli, Fred 513

Appalachian Spring (Graham) 50

Apparel Arts 340, 351
Appeal 362
Apple Mary 342
Appleton, John Howard 176
Appointment in Samarra (O'Hara) 32
Apps, Syl 518
Aquacade 505
Arbuckle, Roscoe Conkling "Fatty" 89
Arcaro, Eddie 506, 534
Archaeology 422, 494
Architects' Collaborative 202
Architectural Record 183–184, 206
Architecture 180, 182, 185–186, 193–196, 198–199, 201–202, 204–207, 463, 467, 479
Archive of American Folk Song 63
Arden, Dale 57
Arden, Elizabeth 203
"Are You Having Any Fun" 42
Argosy 359
Arlen, Harold 28, 31, 41, 79
Arlington Classic (horse race) 518
Arliss, George 87
Armistice Day 40
Armory Show 47
Armstrong, Charles 413
Armstrong, Edwin Howard 342, 366–367, 474
Armstrong, Henry 503, 513, 530
Armstrong, Herbert W. 433–434
Armstrong, Louis 45, 60, 79, 354
Arnaz, Desi 42
Arnheim, Gus 28
Arnold, Harold D. 493
Arnold, Henry H. "Hap" 487
Arnold, Matthew 153
Arodin, Sidney 28
Arrowsmith (Lewis) 55
Art deco 180, 185, 189, 192–193, 200
Art Front (Davis) 47
Art Institute of Chicago 327
The Art of Living (Peale) 433
Arthur, Jean 35, 37, 39, 41
The Artist's Mother (Whistler) 86
Artists' Congress 47
Arvin, Newton 83
As I Lay Dying (Faulkner) 26, 77
As Thousands Cheer (Berlin and Hart) 31
"As Time Goes By" (Hupfield) 28
Asbury Park [N.J.] *Daily Press* 377
Asch, Nathan 52, 82
Asch, Sholem 41
Ashcroft, Peggy 38

Ashford, Bailey Kelly 421
Ashhurst, Astley Paston Cooper 421
Ashton, William Easterly 421
Ashwander v. Tennessee Valley Authority 95
Asimov, Isaac 360
Asquith, Anthony 39
Associated Press (AP) 241, 265, 336, 368, 373, 375–378, 501, 528
— American Woman Athlete of the Year 526
— Athlete of the Year Awards 533–534
— Female Athlete of the Year Award 532
Association Against the Prohibition Amendment (AAPA) 321
Association for the Advancement of Psychoanalysis 410
Association for the Study of Negro Life and History 168
Association of Catholic Trade Unionists 435
Association of National Advertisers 352
Association of Southern Women for the Prevention of Lynching (ASWPL) 336
Astaire, Adele 27–28, 86
Astaire, Fred 27–28, 30, 34–35, 37, 59
Astor, Mary 296
Astor, Vincent 358
Astounding Science-Fiction 340, 359–360
Astronomical Computing Bureau 463
Astronomy 463, 468, 482, 490–491, 493–494
"A-Tisket, A-Tasket" (Fitzgerald) 39, 78
Atlanta Constitution 374, 379
Atlanta Georgian 378
Atlanta Journal 376
Atlanta University 306, 334
— School of Education 170
Atlantic [Iowa] *News-Telegraph* 375
Atomic bomb 217, 489–490
Atomic physics 466–469
Atwood, Charles Edwin 421
Auburn (automobile company) 182, 189
Augusta National Golf Course 500, 516
Augustine, D. L. 413
Auschwitz concentration camp 107

Austin, Louis 493
Austin, Mary 89
Auto racing 501, 504–506, 523, 531
Automobiles 46, 97, 104–105, 109, 112–113, 132, 136–137, 157, 180–183, 185, 187–189, 196, 198–199, 202, 206, 232, 277, 323, 326, 328, 336, 342, 353, 372, 448, 504, 526
Autry, Gene 29, 62
Avery, Oswald T. 413, 420
Avery, Sewell 118
Avery, Tex 348
Aviation 57, 96, 307, 408, 425, 462, 477, 480, 485–486, 491, 493, 504, 535
Awake and Sing! (Odets) 34, 71
The Awful Truth 37, 60, 87
Aycock, L. W. 414
Aydelotte, Frank 155
Ayres, Lew 26, 58, 523

B

B movies 57, 59
B. F. Goodrich company 462
Babbitt, Irving 176–177, 362
Babe Didrikson All-American Basketball team 526
Babes in Arms 38, 69
Babes in Toyland 32
Babies' Hospital, New York City 426
Babson, Roger 158
"Baby Take a Bow" (Temple) 32
Bach, Johann Sebastian 85
Bachelor Born 40
Bacon, Lloyd 30, 39
Bad Girl 87
Baer, Max 500–501, 512–513, 525, 530
Baer, W. S. 414
Baetjer, Frederick Henry 421
Baez, Joan 81
Bagley, William C. 164
Bailey, Ace 500, 518
Bailey, C. Weston 143
Bailey, Josiah 267
Bailey, Mildred 65
Baillet-Latour, Count Henri de 520
Bainter, Fay 87
Baird Television Company 525
Bakelite Corporation 466
Baker, Elbert H. 376
Baker, Newton D. 254

Berg, Patty 517, 534
Bergdorf Goodman 202–203
Bergen, Edgar 343, 353–354
Bergeron-Findeisen theory 472
Berkeley, Busby 34, 58
Berkeley Laboratory 469
Berkman, Alexander 337
Berkshire Music Festival, Lenox, Mass. 33
Berle, Adolf A. Jr. 115, 223–224
Berle, Milton 28
Berlin, Irving 29, 31, 34–35, 38, 40, 79
Berlinger, Barney 532
Bernard, Felix 32
Bernheim, Alice R. 414
Berwanger, Jay 501, 533
Besant, Annie 459
"Bess, You Is My Woman Now" (G. Gershwin) 35
Best and Company 203
Beth David Hospital, New York City 416
Bethe, Hans 468
Bethlehem Steel 137
Bethune, Albertus 167–168
Bethune, Mary McLeod 167–168, 215, 223, 230, 250, 252, 305, 319
Bethune-Cookman College, Jacksonville, Fla. 167–168
Better Homes and Gardens 379
Bettina, Melio 512
Betty Crocker 355
Beyond Desire (Anderson) 29
"Beyond the Blue Horizon" (Whiting and Harling) 26
Bible 163, 432
Bible Institute for Home and Foreign Missions (Moody Bible Institute) 167
Bicycling 505
Biddle, George 70
Big Boy restaurants 186
The Big Broadcast 29
The Big House 26
Big Little Books 349
The Big Money (Dos Passos) 35, 53
The Big Parade 89
The Big Rock Candy Mountain (Stegner) 39, 53
Big Sister 354
The Big Sleep (Chandler) 41, 54, 78, 346
The Big Trail 26
Big White Fog (Ward) 51
Bigard, Albany "Barney" 28
A Bill of Divorcement 29

Billings, Warren 294–295
Billy Rose's Crazy Quilt 28
Billy the Kid 40, 45, 68
Biltmore Theater, New York City 26, 36–37
Biograph Theater, Chicago 292
Biography 30
Birchall, Frederick T. 375
Bird, Caroline 329
Bird, Richard 297
Birdsall, Frank R. 372
Birdseye Frosted Foods 302, 321
Birth control 261, 305–306, 316–317, 330, 386–387, 389, 391–392, 432
Bismarck Club 509
Bismarck [N.D.] *Tribune* 37
Bituminous Coal Conservation Act of 1935 95
Black, Hugo 141, 261, 289–290
Black, Walter J. 372
Black, William Henry 176
Black, Winifred (Annie Laurie) 376
Black Mask 359–360, 369–370
Black Monday 280–281
Black Mountain College 154–155, 202
Black Shipping Line 334
Black Shirts 318
Black Spring (Miller) 35
Blackstone School 451
Blaik, Red 507
Blair, John Henry 110
Blake, Eubie 27, 60
Blake, Joseph Augustus 421
Blake, Toe 518
Blakeslee, Albert Francis 490
Blakeslee, Howard W. 375
Blalock, Alfred 414
Blanc, Mel 38
Blanchard, Frank Le Roy 376
Blanchard, Phyllis 330
Blanton, Thomas L. 167
Bliss, Eleanor A. 394
Bliss, Sidney 414
Blitzstein, Marc 44, 67–68, 71
Bloch, Ernest 38
Bloch, Robert 360
Blonde Venus 29
Blondell, Joan 30
Blondie (Young) 340–341, 346, 348
Blood banks 390
Bloodgood, Joseph Colt 421
Bloom, William 191
Bloor, Ella Reeve "Mother" 331–332

Bloor, Richard 331
Blue Cross and Blue Shield 384, 388, 390, 392, 403
"Blue Hawaii" (Robin and Rainger) 38
"Blue Moon" (Rodgers and Hart) 32
Blue Ridge Assembly of the Protestant Church, Black Mountain, N.C. 154
Blue Ridge Mountains 305
Blue Ridge Parkway 476
Blue Shirts 149
Blue Sky Boys 61–62
Blue-Gray Game (football) 516
Bluebird (race car) 504
Blum, Léon 243
Blume, Peter 44, 47
Boas, Franz 483–484
Bob Jones College 433
Bob Wills and His Texas Playboys 62
Bobbitt, Franklin 164
Boeing Aircraft 477
Bogart, Humphrey 35, 58
Bogen, Emil 414
Bogen, Harry 86
Bohn, R. B. 146
Bohr, Niels 469, 489
Boifeuillet, John Theodore 376
Boland, Mary 34–35
Bold Venture (racehorse) 534
Boldt, O'Brien 372
Boleslawski, Richard 35
Bolger, Ray 36, 41
"Boll Weevil" (Ledbetter) 63
Bolshevik Revolution of 1917 155, 213
Bolshevism 393
Bolton, Guy 33
Bond, Horace Mann 144, 150, 168–170
Bond, Julian 170
Bondi, Beulah 37
Bonfils, Frederick G. 373
Bonhoeffer, Dietrich 439–440
Boni, Charles 360
Boni Paper Books 360
Bonibooks 360
Bonnano, Joseph 270
Bonneville Dam, Utah 315
Bonneville Salt Flats, Utah 501
Bonthron, Bill 500, 522, 525–526, 529–530, 533
Bonus Army 211, 221–222, 259, 271, 303, 322
Bonus Loan Bill 258

Bonwit Teller 206
Book Digest 372
The Book of American Negro Poetry (J. Johnson) 89
Booth, Evangeline 458
Booth, Philip 42
Booth, Shirley 42
Booth, Gen. William 458
Booth Theater, New York City 37, 40
Borah, William E. 236, 239, 242, 252, 290
Borden company 328
Boretz, Allen 38
Born to Dance 35
Born to Win (Guthrie) 81
Borzage, Frank 30, 37, 39, 87
Bose, John 367
Boston Braves 502, 509
Boston Bruins 499–500, 518–519, 532, 534
Boston Celtics 510–511
Boston Memorial Hospital 418
Boston News Bureau Co. 376
Boston Psychopathic Hospital 411
Boston Redskins 502, 533
Boston Symphony 28
Boston University 79, 176, 457
— School of Medicine 427
Boswell, Connie 78
Boswell, Peyton 376
Boswell Sisters 29
Both Your Houses (Anderson) 88
Bottom Dogs (Dahlberg) 26, 53
Boucher, Frank 518, 530
Boulanger, Nadia 68
Boulder Dam. *See* Hoover Dam.
Bound For Glory (Guthrie) 81
"Bourgeois Blues" (Ledbetter) 64
Bourke-White, Margaret 43, 359
Bowdoin College 369
Bowen, Clarence Winthrop 376
Bowling 505, 511
Boxing 363, 499–504, 512–513, 517, 523, 525, 530, 532–533
Boy Meets Girl (Bella and Spewack) 35
Boyd, Ernest 358
Boyer, Charles 37, 41
Boyle, Paul 414
Boynton, Frank David 176
Boys' Town 87, 438
Bracken, Eddie 42
Brackett, Leigh 78
Braddock, James J. 501–502, 512–514, 530
Bradford, Roark 26, 432

Bradshaw, Tony 78
Brady, Alice 29, 87
Brain Trust 115–116, 223
Brancusi, Constantin 48
Brand, Max 26
Brande, Dorothea 372
Brandeis, Louis D. 114–116, 262, 290, 293, 322
Brandt, Karl 154
Branstein, Richard 83
Brave New World (Huxley) 467
"Breadline Blues" (Smith) 63
Brecher, Leo 33
Brecht, Arnold 154
Breen, Joseph I. 443
Breen Office 443–444
Bremer, Edward 288
Brennan, Walter 87
Brent, George 39
"B'rer Rabbit Ball" (Lardner) 508
Bretton Woods Conference (1944) 119
Breuer, Marcel 199, 202
Brewer, E. D. 415
Brewster, Rev. W. Herbert 66
Brezhnev, Leonid 126
Brice, Fanny 28, 33, 353, 531
Brickner, Walter M. 422
The Bride of Frankenstein 34
The Bridge (Crane) 74
Bridges, Calvin 493
Bridges, Harry 94
Bridgewater, Ernest R. 480
Bridgman, P. W. 490
Brieger, Hedwig 172
Brier, Royce 375
Briggs, Thomas H. 163–164
Brigham, Carl 169
Brigham Young University 368
Bright Ambush (Wurdemann) 88
Bright Eyes 32
Brill, Marty 498
Bringing Up Baby 39
Bringing Up Father (McManus) 348
Brisbane, Arthur 365
British Amateur Golf Tournament 501
British Broadcasting Corporation (BBC) 352, 356, 525
British College of Obstetricians and Gynecologists 424
British Museum 427
British Open Golf Tournament 498
British Order of St. Michael and St. George 421

Britten, Florence 330
Broadacre City (Wright) 182, 194–195
Broadcast Music Incorporated (BMI) 344
Broadhurst, Jean 414
Broadhurst Theater, New York City 31, 42
Broadway Tabernacle Church (Skyscraper Church) 460
Broadway Theater, New York City 27–28
Broadwood Hotel, Philadelphia 510
Broderick, Helen 28
Brodie, Edward E. 376
Brodie, Maurice 414
Broker's Tip (racehorse) 499, 517, 533
Bromerg, J. Edgar 71
Bromfield, Louis 85
Bromley, Dorothy 330
Bronfenbrenner, J. 414
Brookings, Robert Somers 136
Brookings Institution 136
Brooklyn College of Pharmacy 423
Brooklyn Dodgers 502, 505, 525
Brooklyn Eagle 356, 374, 377
Brooklyn Robins 535
Brooklyn Visitations 510
Brooks, Van Wyck 36, 85, 88
Brookwood Labor College 142, 152–155
Broomzy, Big Bill 68
"Brother, Can You Spare a Dime" 520
Brother Rat 37
Brotherhood of Sleeping Car Porters 335
Brouillard, Lou 513
Broun, Heywood 89, 363–364, 372, 524, 535
Brousseau, Kate 422
Brouthers, Dennis "Dan" 535
Browder and Ford for Peace, Jobs and Socialism (McKenney) 82
Browder, Earl 56, 82, 233
Brown, Clarence 26, 34, 76
Brown, Elmer E. 176
Brown, Lawrason 422
Brown, Lew 38–39
Brown, Ray 79
Brown, Samuel 319
Brown, Sterling 150
Brown, William Montgomery 459
Brown Brothers Harriman 115
Brown University 176, 292, 535

Chicago Municipal Court 298

Chicago Poems (Sandburg) 83

Chicago Post-Graduate Medical School 423

Chicago Psychoanalytic Institute 410

Chicago Stadium 140

Chicago Symphony 327

Chicago Times 379

Chicago Times-Herald 379

Chicago Tribune 158, 269, 346, 363, 374–375, 378–379, 499, 515, 518, 535

Chicago Tribune Building 207

Chicago White Sox 286, 499, 535

Chicago World's Fair (1893). *See* Columbian Exposition, Chicago.

Chicago World's Fair (1933). *See* Century of Progress Exposition, Chicago

Chick Webb band 78

Child abuse 410

Child Health Day (1 May 1939) 388

Child labor laws 78, 116–117, 216, 230, 249, 261, 337, 363

Children Discover Arithmetic: An Introduction to Structural Arithmetic (Stern) 173

Children Discover Reading (C. Stern and T. Stern) 173

Children of Darkness (Mayer) 26

The Children's Hour (Hellman) 33

Childs, John L. 163

China Clipper 305

Christ Church, Methodist, New York City 434

Christ Episcopal Church, New York City 527

Christian, Charlie 80

Christian, Eugene 422

Christian Action 448

Christian Century 362, 440, 445

Christian Church (Disciples of Christ) 437, 456

Christian Front Against Communism 440, 453

Christian Herald 459

Christian Social Response 448

Christianity 53, 129, 233, 315, 362, 384, 427–428, 433, 435–441, 443–445, 448–450, 453, 455–457, 459, 519

Christmas Seals 397

The Chrysanthemum and the Sword: Patterns of Japanese Culture (Benedict) 483

Chrysler Building, New York City 98, 180, 193

Chrysler Corporation 103, 149, 181, 183, 185, 187, 189, 464–465

Church, Ellen 135, 302

Church, George 36

Church of God, Cleveland, Tenn. 460

Church of the Messiah, New York City 455

Churchill, Frank E. 31, 37

Churchill, Winston 246, 251

Churchill Downs 500

Churchman, John Woolman 422

The Churchman 440

Cierva, Juan de la 491

Cimarron (movie) 87

Cimarron (Ferber) 26

Cincinnati Evening Post 379

Cincinnati Railway Terminal 196

Cincinnati Reds 448, 500, 502–503, 525, 534

The Circle 379

"Ciribiribin (They're So in Love)" (Pestalozza, James, and Lawrence) 41

Citizen Kane 51

Citizens' Committee on Public Expenditures 158

Citizenship schools 152

City College of New York 156, 227, 251, 329, 334, 458

City Lights 27

City National Bank, Chicago 158

City Streets 58

Civic Repertory Theater, New York City 34

Civil Aeronautics Act of 1938 350

Civil rights 44, 118, 150, 152–153, 156, 168, 170–171, 250, 252, 264, 305–307, 319, 333–336, 361, 445, 519

Civil War. *See* American Civil War and Spanish Civil War.

Civil Works Emergency Relief Act of 1934 93, 213

Claire, Ina 26, 30, 36, 86

Clampitt, Bob 348

Clapp, Cornelia 493

Clare, Sidney 32

Clark, Bobby 26

Clark, G. W. 417

Clark, John Bates 176

Clark, L. Pierce 422

Clark University 176–177, 484

Clarke, Mae 27

Clarke, Selah Merrill 376

Classic Landscape (Sheeler) 46

Clayton, Lew 27

Clayton Anti-Trust Act of 1914 95, 115

Cleopatra 45, 58

Cleveland, Grover 255, 508

Cleveland East Technical High School 529

Cleveland Indians 514, 530

Clifford, Gordon 28

Clift, Montgomery 35

Cline, Edward 29

Clinical Medicine & Surgery 397

Clinton, Larry 38

The Cloisters, New York City 40

Cloos, Hans 472

Clurman, Harold 71

Cobb, Lee J. 38, 71

Cobb, Ty 508

Coca, Imogene 27

Coca-Cola Company 115, 304

Cochet, Henri 505

Cochrane, Mickey 501, 509

Cody, Frank 158

Coffey, Robert Calvin 422

Coffin, Henry Sloane 435

Coffin, Howard Earle 136

Coffin, Robert P. Tristram 88

Coffin, William Sloane 136

Cohan, George M. 31

Cohen, Benjamin V. 290–291

Cohen, Ella 331

Cohen, Elliot 362

Cohen, John Sanford 376

Cohen, Lester 56

Cohen, Louis 331

Cohn, Fannia 134

Cohn, Leopold 459

Coit Tower, San Francisco 98

Colbert, Claudette 32, 41, 60, 87

Cold Morning Sky (Zaturenska) 88

Cold virus 382, 401–402, 414, 422

Cold War 118, 450, 458

Colgate, Gilbert 136

Colgate Sports Newsreel 505

Colgate-Palmolive-Peet Company 136

Collected Poems (Frost) 88

Collected Verse (Hillyer) 88

College All-Star Game of 1934 507

College of Physicians and Surgeons of Chicago 427

College of the Pacific 515

Collett, Glenna 501, 517

Collier, Constance 30

Collier, John Jr. 81

Collier, William Jr. 27

Dana, Henry Wadsworth Longfellow 166
Dana Hall School 332
Dance Fools Dance 76
Dance Repertory Theatre 49
Dangerous 87
Daniels, Bebe 30
Daniels, Josephus 434
Dante Alighieri 240
Danton's Death 72
Danville Advocate 373
Danzig, Allison 506
"Dare Progressive Education Be Progressive?" (Counts) 140, 163, 170
Dare, Yvette 328
Daring Young Man (Saroyan) 32
Dark Victory 41
Darrow, Charles B. 336
Darrow, Clarence 285, 296, 298
Dart, Harry Grant 377
Dartmouth College 79, 177, 522
— Medical School 424
Darwin, Charles 471
Darwinism 55
Dashing (perfume) 201
Da Silva, Howard 71
Daughters of the American Revolution (DAR) 141, 155–156, 250, 308
David Copperfield (movie) 34
Davidson, Donald 44, 54
Davies, John V. 493
Davis Cup (tennis) 502, 525, 530
Davis, A. B. 422
Davis, Allison 150
Davis, Bette 39, 41, 58, 76, 87, 186
Davis, F. B. 146
Davis, Hallowell 414
Davis, Harold L. 88
Davis, Herman S. 493
Davis, James E. 315
Davis, Jerome 160
Davis, Jimmie 62
Davis, John W. 234
Davis, Maxine 328
Davis, Norbert 370
Davis, Oscar King 377
Davis, Pauline A. 414
Davis, Phil 349
Davis, Stuart 45, 47–48, 70, 323
Davis, William Stearns 176
Davisson, Clinton J. 492
Dawes, Charles C. 158
Dawes, Charles Gates 237, 373
The Dawn Patrol 26, 39
Day, Clarence 42

Day, Doris 36
Day, Dorothy 336, 341, 433, 440, 444, 448, 453
Day, Edmund E. 166–167
Day, Holman Francis 377
Dawson, James P. 514, 527
The Day 376
A Day at the Races 37
"Day by Day" (Day) 453
The Day of the Locust (West) 41, 53, 82
Days Without End (O'Neill) 33
Daytona Normal and Industrial Institute, Florida 168
DC Comics 349
Dead End 58
Dean, Dizzy 500, 505, 509, 530, 533
Dean, Paul "Daffy" 509
The Death and Birth of David Markand: An American Story (Frank) 32
Death in the Afternoon (Hemingway) 29
Death on the Diamond 523
Death Valley Days 340, 355
DeBakey, Michael 386
DeBeck, Billy 348–349
Debs, Eugene V. 83, 298, 331
Decca records 79
"Declaration of Policy" (Fletcher) 238
Dee, Frances 27
"Deep Purple" (De Rose and Parish) 32
Deep Song (Graham) 50
Defenders of the Christian Faith 440
De Forest, Lee 342, 366
de Havilland, Olivia 39, 41
DeJonge v. *Oregon* 293
de Kooning, Willem 41, 46, 48, 70, 154
Del Rio, Dolores 30
Del Ruth, Roy 35
De Lange, Eddie 32, 41
Delano, Jack 82
Delaware College 170
Dell, Floyd 360
Dell Publishing Company 372
"De-Lovely" (Porter) 37
DeMille, Cecil B. 58
Democratic National Committee 252, 326, 333
Democratic National Convention (1932) 223, 250, 253

Democratic National Convention (1936) 235, 237, 239–240
Democratic Party 108, 115, 118, 155, 210–211, 214, 216, 218, 222–223, 234–241, 245–248, 250–255, 263, 277, 282, 284, 287, 316, 319, 323, 325–326, 333, 426, 436, 446–447, 451, 453, 456, 477
Dempster, Arthur Jeffrey 469
Deng Xiaoping 126
Denishawn dance company 49
Dennett, Tyler 88
Dennis, Alfred Lewis Pinneo 176
Dennis, Frederick Shepard 423
Density 21.5 (Varèse) 68
Denver Post 373, 509
DePauw University 166
Dern, George Henry 254
De Rose, Peter 32
De Rothschild, Pauline 201
Des Moines Register 343
Des Moines Register & Tribune 375
Desegregation 140, 149–150, 170, 335, 505
Design for Living 31, 58
De Silver, Margaret 73
De Soto 189, 464
Destinn, Emmy 66
Destry Rides Again (Brand) 26, 41
Detective Comics 343–344, 350
Detective Picture Stories 343
Detroit Automobile Show 206
Detroit Free Press 374
Detroit Lions 532–533
Detroit Red Wings 501, 519, 533–534
Detroit Tigers 500–501, 531, 533
Detroit Unemployed Council 303
Detroit-Edison 109
Father Devine (George Baker) 336, 437, 454
Dewey, John 140, 143, 153, 163–164, 166, 322, 345–346, 442
Dewey, Melvil 176
Dewey, Richard Smith 423
Dewey, Stoddard 377
Dewey, Thomas E. 261, 270
Dewey decimal system 176
Dewson, Mary Williams "Molly" 325–326, 332–333
Diabetes 386, 393, 402, 414–415
The Dial 361
Diamond, David 68
Diamond DX Oilers, Tulsa, Okla. 510
Diamond Lil (West) 84

Diamond-T company 464
Dibble, Bernard 373
Dick Tracy (Gould) 340, 349, 369
Dickey, Bill 509, 530
Dickey, James 362
Dickie Dare (Caniff) 341, 349
Dickinson, L. J. 237
"Did You Ever See a Dream Walking?" (Revel and Gordon) 31
Didrikson, Mildred "Babe" 499, 505–506, 520, 526–527, 533
Dies, Martin 235, 262, 307
Dieterle, William 34, 37, 41
Dietrich, Marlene 27, 29, 41, 58, 186, 192, 201
Dietz, David 375
Digges, Dudley 40
Dilantin 386, 417
Dill, D. B. 414
Dill-Crozier Act 94
Dillard University 169
Dilles, John 57
Dilling, Elizabeth 156
Dillinger, John 58, 189, 260, 269, 292, 297
Dillion, Read 115
Dillon, Arthur 207
Dillon, George 88
DiMaggio, Joe 504, 506, 509, 527, 530
Dime Detective 359–360
The Dinah Shore Show 344
Dinkelberg, Frederick 207
Dinner at Eight 30
Dionne, Elzire 317
Dionne, Oliva 317
Dionne quintuplets 304, 317
Diphtheria 389, 402, 405
"The Dipsy Doodle" (Clinton) 38
Dirac, P. A. M. 463, 469
Dirks, Rudolph 348, 373
Dishonored 27
The Disinherited (Conroy) 31, 53
Disney, Walt 347
Disraeli 87
District of Columbia Court of Appeals 298
Distinguished Flying Cross 463
Distinguished Service Cross 421
Distinguished Service Medal 421
Ditmars, Isaac E. 207
Ditmars, R. L. 414
The Divorcee 87
Dix, Dorothy (Elizabeth Meriwether Gilmer) 373
Dixiecrats 235
Dixon, Joseph M. 254

Dixon, Maynard 81
Dixon, Mort 28
"Do-Re-Mi" (Guthrie) 81
Dobel (automobile company) 189
Doc Savage Magazine 341, 359
Dochez, Alphonse Raymond 401, 414
Doctor Jekyll and Mr. Hyde (movie) 58, 87
Dodsworth 35
Doheny, Edward 258
Doisy, Edward Adelbert 387, 415, 470
Dollar, Robert 136
Dollar steamship company 136
Domagk, Gerhard 394, 419
Don Winslow of the Navy (Martinek) 349
Donaldson, Walter 26–28
Donat, Robert 41, 87
Doolin, C. Elmer 135
Doolittle, Rev. Moses 65
Doorway to Hell 58
Doran, James M. 320
Doraty, Ken 499
Dorrance, Arthur C. 146
Dorsey, Jimmy 26, 28, 40, 64
Dorsey, Thomas "Georgia Tom" 65–66
Dorsey, Tommy 28, 40, 45, 64, 354
Dorsey House of Music 65
Dos Passos, John 26, 29, 35, 39, 43, 45, 52–53, 56, 73, 130, 243, 306, 346, 351–352, 361
Doty, Alvah Hunt 423
Double Indemnity (Cain) 35, 54
Doubleday, Abner 508
Douglas, Bob 511
Douglas, Donald W. 477, 492
Douglas, John 423
Douglas, Lewis 115, 135
Douglas, Lloyd C. 432
Douglas, Melvyn 35
Douglas, William O. 262, 275
Douglas Aircraft Company 95, 477, 486, 492
Douglass, Andrew Ellicott 462
Douglass, Frederick 52, 70
Douglass Film Company 59
Dove, Arthur 47
Dow Chemical 470
Dow Jones Industrial Average 92
Dow Jones and Co. 376
Dowell, Saxie 41
Dowling, Eddie 40
Dowman, Charles Edward 423
Down Beat 78–79

Downey, Sheridan 241
Downing, F. B. 480
Doyle, Sir Arthur Conan 369
Dracula (movie) 27, 58
Drag 84
Dragstedt, L. R. 415
Drake, W. A. 27
Draper, Foy 522
Draper, George 415
Draper, John William 423
Drayton, Grace Gebbie 377
"Dreadful Memories" (Jackson) 63
"Dream a Little Dream of Me" (Andre, Schwandt, and Kahn) 28
The Dream Life of Balso Snell (West) 27
Dreams of a Rarebit Fiend (McCay) 378
Dreiser, Theodore 43, 52–53, 56, 358, 361
Dresser, Louise 26
Dressler, Marie 87, 89
Dreyer, George Peter 423
Dreyfus Affair 294
Dreyfuss, Henry 199
Drifting (perfume) 201
Drinker, Philip 415
Drinkwater, John 467
Drug abuse 443
Drums Along the Mohawk 35, 41, 45, 69
Drury, Wells 377
Dryden, Charles 535
Du Barry Was a Lady 42
Du Bois, W. E. B. 144, 149–150, 169, 333–334
Dubin, Al 29–30, 32, 34
Dubinsky, David 124–125, 134
Dubinsky, Jacob 124
Dubos, René Jules 387, 413, 415
Duck Soup 30
Duel, Arthur Baldwin 423
Duffy, Edmund 374–375
Duffy, James O. G. 377
Duke, Vernon 27
Duke University 382, 534
Dumbarton Oaks Conference (1944) 246
DuMont, Allen B. 373
Dumont, Hap 509
Dunaway, Faye 77
Duncan, Isadora 49
Duncan, Robert 154
Dundee, Vince 513
Dunford, Uncle Alec 63
Dunham, Theodore Jr. 468

Erie Railroad 280
Erie Railroad v. *Tompkins* 279–280, 290
Erskine, John 85
Esquire 73, 304, 341, 351–352
Essentialism 164
The Eternal City (Blume) 44
Ethan Frome (Wharton) 90
Ethel Barrymore Theater, New York City 30–31, 36, 42
Ethical Culture Society 176, 331, 459
Ethyl Corporation 135
Etting, Ruth 28
Eugenics movement 471, 484
Evangelical and Reform Church 433, 441
Evangelical Lutheran Joint Synod of Ohio 432, 441
Evangelical Lutheran Synod of Iowa 432, 441
Evangelical Synod of North America 433, 441
Evans, Madge 40
Evans, Walker 43, 81
Evergood, Philip 47
Every Day's a Holiday 84
Everybody's Welcome 28
"Everything I Have Is Yours" (Lane and Adamson) 31
Evian Conference (1938) 440
Evipan 385
Evocations (Ruggles) 68
Ewell, Tom 36
Ewing, Buck 508
Ex Champ 523
The Executioner Waits (Herbst) 32, 53
Executive Order 8802 335
Executive Order 9066 (Lange) 82
Executive Order 9981 335
Experimenting with Numbers: Structural Arithmetic for Kindergarten (C. Stern and T. Stern) 173
Explorer II 464
Export-Import Bank of Washington, D.C. 93, 213
Expressionism 43, 47

F

Fabian socialism 166
A Fable (Faulkner) 78
"Facetious Fragments" (King) 377
Facts Forum 129
Fadiman, Clifton 362
Fain, Sammy 28, 38–39, 42

Fair Labor Standards Act of 1938 96, 117, 216, 231, 249, 262, 291
Fairbanks, Douglas Jr. 26, 37, 41, 58, 70, 76, 85
Faisal, King of Saudi Arabia 126
Falk, Lee 57, 349
Fall, Albert B. 298
The Fall of the City (MacLeish) 343
Fall River Football Club 523
Fallingwater, Bear Run, Penn. 185, 195, 205
Family Circle 340, 358
Famous Funnies 349
Fantasia 348
Fantus, Bernard 415
Fard, W. D. 432
Farley, Edward 34
Farley, James A. 240, 249, 252
Farm Bureau Federation 107
Farm Credit Act of 1933 93, 211
Farm Mortgage Refinancing Act of 1934 93, 213
Farm unions 322
Farmer Boy (Wilder) 52
Farmer-Labor Party 210, 231, 236, 238, 241, 252, 254
Farmers' Holiday Association 225, 231, 254
Farnsworth, Philo 357, 368–369, 371
Farnsworth Radio and Television Corporation 368
Farouk I of Egypt 126
Farrell, James 104
Farrell, James T. 29, 32, 34–35, 39, 43, 44, 53
Fascism 44, 50, 58, 68, 71, 73, 116, 118, 154, 157, 159–160, 202, 218, 233–235, 242–243, 262, 322–323, 355–356, 361–362, 373, 437, 439, 448, 450, 453, 457, 466, 506, 519
Fashion Is Spinach (Hawes) 202–203
The Fathers (Tate) 39
Faulkner, Estelle Oldham 77
Faulkner, William 26–27, 29, 35, 43–45, 54, 57, 77–78, 346, 352, 443
Fauvism 46
Faye, Alice 39
Fayette High School, Orchard, Iowa 173
Fazikas, J. F. 416
"F. D. R. Jones" (Rome) 39
Fechner, Robert 175–176, 228

Federal Council of Churches 383, 432, 439
Federal Council of Churches of Christ 433, 440
Federal Economy Act of 1932 303, 324
Federal Emergency Relief Act of 1933 93, 212, 251
Federal Farm Bankruptcy Act of 1934 94, 214, 260, 304
Federal Income Tax Act of 1913 246
Federal Securities Act of 1933. *See* Truth-In-Securites Act of 1933
Fédération Aéronautique Internationale 485
Federation for Social Service 458
Federation of American Zionists 458
Federation of Women's Clubs 149
Feinberg, S. M. 415
Feingold, Gustave A. 175
Feldman, Al 39
Feller, Bobby 506, 509
Fellowship of Reconciliation (FOR) 444, 455
Feminism 250, 254, 325, 337, 386, 410, 483, 486, 493
Fenske, Chuck 526
Fer-de-lance (Stout) 32
Ferber, Edna 26, 30, 36
Fermi, Enrico 469, 492
Ferno, John (Fernhout) 73
Ferrer, José 37, 42
Ferry, N. S. 415
Fess, Simeon Davison 254
Fessenden, Reginald 493
Fewkes, J. Walter 493
Fewkes, John M. 158
Fibber McGee and Molly 342, 354
Fiction House 343
Fiddle-Dee-Dee 90
Field, Betty 38
Field and Stream 370
Fields, Dorothy 34–35
Fields, Jackie 513
Fields, W. C. 29–30, 32, 34, 84
Fife, George Buchanan 377
Filene, Edward A. 136, 172
Filene's department store 99, 115
Filer, Henry 158
Filling Station (ballet) 45, 50
Fillum Fables (Gould) 369
Filsinger, Ernest 74
The Finger Points 58
Finger, Bill 344, 350
Finkelman, Isidore 415

A Free Soul 87

Free Synagogue, New York 439, 458

Freeland, Thornton 30

Freeman, Douglas S. 88

Freeman, Mary E. Wilkins 89

Freeman, Tommy 513

Freeman, Walter 415

Freemen's Hospital, Washington, D.C. 319

Freer, Otto "Tiger" 423

Freer surgical instruments 423

Freidel, Frank 237

Freleng, Friz 348

Fremont [Nebr.] *Tribune* 374

French Army 422

French Ministry of Public Health 409

Frenkel-Brunswik, Else 405

Freud, Sigmund 404–405, 410, 426

Freudianism 386, 390, 404–405, 410–411

Freund, Jules 417

Frick, Henry 337

Frisch, Frankie 498, 509, 531

Fritos Corn Chips 135

Fritzi Ritz (Bushmiller) 341

Froebel, Friedrich 205

From Death to Morning (Wolfe) 34

From Flushing to Calvary (Dahlberg) 29

From the Deep Woods to Civilization (Eastman) 423

From the Gayety and Sadness of the American Scene (Harris) 30

Froman, Jane 33

Frontier Nursing Service 399

Frost, Robert 88–89

Frost, Wade Hampton 420, 423

Fruit of Islam 432

Fuchs, Daniel 32, 37

The Fugitive 54

Fuller, Buckminster 154

Fuller, Charles 432, 437

Fulton, John Farquhar 415

Fulton, John Samuel 423

Functionalism 185, 193–194, 199, 201

Fundamentalism 315, 362, 433, 437, 440, 450, 454–455

Funnies on Parade 349

Funny Pages 343

Funny Picture Stories 343

A Further Range (Frost) 88

Furthman, Jules 78

Fury 35, 58

Fusion Party 213, 247, 287

Futurism 361

G

Gable, Clark 32, 34–35, 41, 60, 70, 76, 87, 190, 444

Gaillard, Slim 39

Gallant Fox (racehorse) 498, 517–518, 532

Gallatin, A. E. 48

Gallico, Paul 499, 507, 519, 524

Gallup, George Horace 342, 464

Gallup polls 122, 306, 448, 464

Galton, Sir Francis 471

Gamble, James Norris 337

Gandhi, Mohandas K. 445

Gannett, Lewis 206

Garbo, Greta 26, 29–30, 34–35, 69, 76, 186, 192, 205

Garcia, Ceferino 513

Gardiner, Charlie 518, 535

Gardner (automobile) 189

Gardner, Cyril 26

Gardner, Erle Stanley 29, 369

Garfield, James A. 423

Garfield, John 34, 71

Garfield, Jules 38

Garfield, Sidney 415

Garland, Joe 41

Garland, Judy 41, 69

Garner, John Nance 237

Garner, Mack 500, 533

Garrett, Betty 82

The Garrick Gaieties 27

Garson, Greer 41

Garvey, Marcus 51, 334

Gas (Hopper) 47

Gashouse Gang 500, 509

Gaskill, Clarence 29

Gass, Gilbert 207

Gates, Fanny 493

Gates, Rev. J. M. 65

Gaxton, William 29, 33

Gay, Frederick Parker 423

Gay Divorce 30

Gaynor, Janet 37

Gebhardt, L. P. 413

Geddes, Norman Bel 199, 328

Geer, Will 81

Gehrig, Lou 499, 503–506, 508–509, 527, 531

Gehringer, Charlie 509

Gelert, Lawrence 49

Gellhorn, Martha 52, 73

General Assembly of the Northern Presbyterian Church 436

General Broadcasting System 481

General Convention of Christian Churches 432, 441

General Council of Congregational and Christian Churches 432, 441

General Electric (GE) 115, 121, 130, 135, 220, 302, 328, 355, 474, 511

General Foods 92, 234, 302

General Houses 467

General Motors (GM) 95–96, 103–104, 118, 120–121,133, 154, 160, 181–183, 185, 187–189, 220, 232, 234, 306, 327–328. 462S-464

General Theory of Employment, Interest, and Money (Keynes) 118

Genetics 471

Gentleman's Quarterly (GQ) 340

George V of Great Britain 317

George VI of Great Britain 370

George, Henry 336

George, Walter 241

George Washington Battalion 243

George Washington Bridge, New York–New Jersey 98, 180, 463, 473

George Washington University 425 — Medical School 385

George Westinghouse Bridge, Pennsylvania 463

George White's Scandals 42

George-Deen Act 142

Georgetown University 352 — School of Medicine 412

Georgia Institute of Technology 535

"Georgia on My Mind" (Carmichael and Gorrell)) 26

Georgia Supreme Court 297

Gerling, Henry J. 147

German American Football Association 523

German Confessing Church 439

German measles 402

German-American Bund 234, 308

Gernsback, Hugo 360

Gershwin, George 26–27, 29, 35, 37–39, 45, 61, 67–68, 79, 89

Gershwin, Ira 26–27, 29, 35, 37–39, 72, 79, 88

Gertie the Dinosaur (McCay) 378

Gervasi, Frank 356

Gestring, Marjorie 506

Gettysburg Memorial 184

Geva, Tamara 36

Grant, Cary 29–30, 37, 39, 41, 60, 70, 84

Granz, Norman 79

The Grapes of Wrath (Steinbeck) 39, 41, 43, 53, 81, 86, 108, 437

Graves, Bibb 285–286

Graves, Frank P. 175

Graves, William Phillips 424

Gray, Carl Raymond 136

Gray, Harold 340, 349

Gray, James Martin 459

Great Books Program 514

Great Depression

— and World War II 219, 244

— causes 104–105, 117–118, 131, 210, 309, 314, 322, 520

— economic effects 44, 97, 103, 144–147, 149, 150, 154, 159, 168–169, 173, 203–204, 210, 218–220, 224, 229, 245, 250, 309, 384, 389–390, 392, 394, 403, 405–407, 410, 412, 467, 481

— effect on advertising 183

— effect on agriculture 92, 106, 225, 309, 313–315

— effect on architecture 194, 196

— effect on art 43, 45, 48, 56, 61, 79

— effect on automobile industry 97, 180–182, 187, 189

— effect on banking 104, 111–112, 227–228

— effect on birth rate 316

— effect on business 97, 104, 106, 129, 131, 143, 158, 164, 321

— effect on child labor 312–313, 315, 317, 328, 330

— effect on construction 98, 195, 436

— effect on consumers 316

— effect on crime rates 267–268, 272

— effect on education 140, 142–147, 149, 151–152, 154–156, 158, 160, 162, 164–165, 169–172, 174, 309, 329

— effect on employment 104, 109, 149, 156, 249, 309, 311, 315, 318–319, 324, 328

— effect on family life 71, 97, 309–310, 312, 315–317, 329

— effect on fashion 180, 186, 189, 191, 203–204

— effect on foreign policy 235, 242

— effect on foreign trade 104

— effect on gender roles 97, 133, 311, 313, 316, 323, 325, 329

— effect on government policy 106, 212, 218, 222, 237, 241, 245

— effect on health 149, 310–312, 315, 384, 389–390, 392, 394, 397, 403, 405

— effect on Hoover policies 43, 92, 98–99, 104–107, 112–113, 115–116, 118, 210–211, 218, 220–222, 227, 237, 242, 245, 248, 251, 258–259, 271–272, 309, 352, 398, 452

— effect on immigration 310

— effect on labor 56, 133, 159, 276

— effect on literature 43–45, 52–54, 82, 346

— effect on manufacturing 104

— effect on mass media 45, 61, 345, 347, 350–352, 358–363, 365, 367, 370–372

— effect on migration 315

— effect on movie industry 28, 43–45, 57–59, 69, 76, 312, 347, 443

— effect on music 63–66, 79–80

— effect on oil industry 119, 129

— effect on race relations 311, 318

— effect on scientific research 466, 490

— effect on senior citizens 309

— effect on sports 504, 507–510, 512, 514–517, 524–525, 531

— effect on theater 71–72

— effect on transportation 186, 196, 474

— international effects 86, 221–222, 242

— political effects 113, 163, 167, 216, 218, 233, 236, 312, 329, 361, 398

— psychological effects 43, 248, 310–311, 322, 330, 345, 404, 479

— religious effects 319, 436, 441, 453–455, 457, 459

— riots, strikes, and demonstrations 98–99, 109, 125, 270

— sociological effects 405, 412

Great Smoky Mountains National Park 196

The Great Society (Wallace) 137

Great Society programs 229

"The Great Speckled Bird" (Acuff) 61

The Great Ziegfeld 35, 87

Greater Salem Baptist Church Choir, Chicago 65

Green, Bud 38–39

Green, John 28–29

Green, Mitzie 26

Green, Paul 28, 71–72

Green, William 124–125

Green Bay Packers 503, 514, 532–534

Green Grow the Lilacs (Riggs) 28, 43

Green Hills of Africa (Hemingway) 54

The Green Hornet 355

Green Pastures (Connelly) 26, 43, 88, 432

Greenbaum, Isadore 308

Greenberg, Hank 509, 527, 531

Greenburg, Clement 362

Greener, Richard 150

Greenlaw, Edwin 176

Greenlee, W. A. "Gus" 508

Greenough, Robert Battey 424

Greenwich Village, New York City 312, 360

Grey, Zane 89

Greyhound (racehorse) 501, 518

Grier, Jimmy 32

Griffin, D. S. 415

Griffin, Rush 297

Griffis, Stanton 373

Griffith, D. W. 26

Griffith, Edward H. 76

Griffith, William 377

Grinell College 493

Grofe, Ferde 29

Grollman, Arthur 415

Gropius, Walter 45, 183, 185, 194, 199, 201–202

Gross, Robert E. 415

Grosz, George 45, 75

Groton School 250

Group f/46 81

Group Health Association of Washington 409

Group Theatre 31, 34, 71

Grove, Lefty 499, 531

Grover Cleveland (Nevins) 88

Gruelle, John 377

Gruenberg, Louis 66

Guaranty Safe Deposit Company 321

Guggenheim, Daniel 490, 493

Guggenheim, Murry 136

Guggenheim, Solomon R. 48

Guggenheim Aeronautical Laboratory 486

Guggenheim Award 491

Guggenheim family 477

Guggenheim Fellowships 74, 82

Guggenheim Museum 185

The Guiding Light 343
Guild Theater, New York City 27–31, 36, 42
Guinan, Mary Louise Cecelia "Texas" 89
Gulbrandsen, Lars 415
Guldahl, Ralph 516, 531, 534
The Gumps (Smith) 379
Gunga Din (movie) 41, 70
Gunnison, Herbert Foster 377
Gurko, Leo 329
Guston, Philip 70
Gutenberg, Beno 472
Guthrie, Arlo 81
Guthrie, Clyde Graeme 424
Guthrie, Woodrow Wilson "Woody" 36, 40, 44, 63–64, 80–81, 355
Guttzeit, C. W. 146
Gymnastics 505
"The Gypsy in Me" 33

H

Haffron, Daniel 415
Hagen, O. J. 415
Hagen, Uta 42
Hagen, Walter 498
Hagerty house, Cohasset, Massachusetts 202
Haggerty, Melvin Everett 424
Hague, Frank 252
The Hague Tribunal 292
Hahn, Otto 469
Hahnemann Medical College 421
Haines Normal and Industrial Institute 167
Hairbreadth Harry (Kahles) 377
Halas, George 515, 529
Hale, George Ellery 493
Haley, Jack 41
Hall, Alexander 82
Hall, Edwin Herbert 493
Hall, Jon 37
Hallenbeck, Earl 207
Halsted, William S. 427
Hamann, Carl August 424
Hambletonian Stakes (horse race) 501, 518
Hamilton, Margaret 41
Hamilton Fish (Nevins) 88
Hamilton Standard Company 492
Hamilton v. *Regents of the University of California* 260
Hamlin, V. T. 341, 349
Hamm, William 289
Hammer, Armand 125–127

Hammer, Julius 126
Hammerstein, Oscar II 30, 34, 36, 43
Hammett, Dashiell 26–27, 32, 53–54, 58, 73, 341, 351, 359–360, 369–370
Hammett, F. S. 416
Hammond, John 68
Hammond, Laurens 33
Hammond organs 33
Hampton, Lionel 80
Hanford, Ira 534
Hanlon, Ned 535
Hanna, Mark 114
Hansel and Gretel (opera) 66
Hansen, Alvin 105
Hanson, Howard 40, 66, 68
Hanson, John 379
The Happy Family (Levy) 425
Harbach, Otto 32, 34
"Harbor Lights" (Kennedy and Williams) 38
Harbord, James Guthrie 373
Harburg, E. Y. 27–28, 31, 41
Hard Tack (racehorse) 518
Hard To Get 39
"Hard Traveling" (Guthrie) 80
Harden, Rosemary 203
Hardin Simmons University 516
Harding, George Tryon Jr. 424
Harding, Warren G. 245, 292, 424, 443
Hardwicke, Cedric 40
Hardy, Oliver 30, 32
Harlan County, Kentucky, coal miners' strike 43, 56, 63, 92, 109–111, 361
Harlan Miners Speak (Dos Passos) 56
Harlem Committee for Better Schools 159
Harlem Globetrotters 510
Harlem Liberator 362
Harlem Opera House, New York City 78
Harling, W. Franke 26
Harlow, Dick 515
Harlow, Jean 26–27, 30, 58, 523
Harms, H. P. 415
Harold F. Pitcairn and Associates 492
Harper and Brothers 52
Harper's Weekly 377
Harriman, W. Averell 246, 358
Harris, Frank 89
Harris, Louis Israel 424
Harris, Roy 30, 33, 42, 68

Harris Teachers College 170
Harrison, Patrick 141, 147
Harrison, W. T. 413
Hart, Lorenz 26, 32, 34–35, 38, 42, 72, 79
Hart, Merwin K. 156
Hart, Moss 27, 31, 37, 42, 88
Hartley, Marsden 47
Hartman, Grace 37
Hartnett, Gabby 531
Harvard University 63–64, 79, 150, 170, 172, 175–176, 185, 202, 250, 290, 333, 413–414, 417, 419, 427, 490, 515
— Graduate Center 202
— Graduate School of Design 201
— Harvard College 29
— Infantile Paralysis Commission 414
— Law School 272, 290, 487
— Medical School 382, 411, 414–416, 418, 424, 426–427
— Peabody Museum 493
— School of Architecture 183, 194
Haskell, Douglas 206
Haskell, Miriam 192
Hass, G. M. 417
Hassam, Childe 89
Hassler, William C. 424
Hastie, William H. 261, 307, 336
Hatch Act of 1939 262
Hathaway, Henry 34
Hattie Carnegie, Inc. 200
Hauptmann, Bruno Richard 261, 278–279
Haviland, Clarence Floyd 424
"Having a Wonderful Time" (Kober) 38
Hawaii Clipper 425
Hawes, Elizabeth 186, 191, 202–203
Hawes, Inc. 203
Hawks, Frank 485
Hawks, Howard 26–27, 32, 39, 41, 60, 76, 78
Haworth, Norman 470
Hay, Ian 40
Hay, John 244
Hayden, Charles 136
Hayden, Oliver M. 480
Haydon, Julie 40
Hayes, Ellen Amanda 493
Hayes, Helen 32, 87, 205
Hayes, Patrick Joseph 460
Haynes, Edith 416
Hays, Lee 81
Hays, Will H. 33, 443

Hays Office 33, 443

Hayworth Building, Chicago 207

He Upset the World (Barton) 432

Head, Gay 330

Head Play (racehorse) 517

Healey Motors basketball team, Kansas City 510

Hearst, William Randolph 146, 155–156, 237, 345, 364–365, 371

Hearst Newspapers 155–157, 167, 274, 337, 345, 364–365, 372–374, 376, 378

Heart disease 384, 386, 389, 393, 402, 405, 416–418

"Heartaches" (Hoffman) 28

Heartbreak House (Shaw) 72

The Heat's On 84

"Heaven Can Wait" (Van Heusen and De Lange) 41

Hebrew Union College 458

Hechler, Herbert LeRoy 306

Hefferan, Helen 158

Heflin, Van 36, 42

Hegenberger, Albert F. 492

Heidi 70

"Heigh-Ho" (Churchill and Mose) 37

Heimann, Eduard 154

Hein, Mel 531

Heinlein, Robert A. 346, 359–360

Heinz 328

Heisman, John W. 535

Heisman Trophy 501, 533–535

Helen Retires (Antheil) 68

Helion, Jean 48

"Hell Hound on My Trail" (Johnson) 38, 64

Hellman, Lillian 33, 42, 44, 58, 73, 243

Hell's Angels 26

Hellzapoppin' (Johnson) 40, 72

Helvering v. *Davis* 282

Hemingway, Ernest 29, 37, 54, 73, 78, 243, 306, 341, 351–352

Henderson, Caroline 225, 313

Henderson, Fletcher 64, 80

Henderson, Marjorie Lyman "Marge" 342

Henie, Sonja 201, 505, 520–521

Hennig, Edward A. 531

Henri, Robert 47

Henry (Anderson) 340

Henry Clothiers basketball team, Wichita 510

Henry Miller's Theater, New York City 33, 40

Hepburn, Katharine 29–30, 36, 39, 42, 87, 182–184, 186, 191, 204

Herbert Jacobs House, Madison, Wisc. 195

Herbst, Josephine 31–32, 41, 44, 52–53

Herbuveaux, Jules 79

Here Come the Clowns (Barry) 40

Herndon, Angelo 297

Heroes For Sale 58

Herreshoff, Nathaniel G. 535

Herrick, James B. 420

Herriman, George 348

Hersholt, Jean 29

Herty, Charles Holmes 373

Hess, Victor Franz 492

Heyman, Edward 28–29, 31–32

Heymans, Corneille 419

Heyward, DuBose 35, 60, 72

Heyward, George 72

Hibben, John Grier 176

Hickman, William Edward 426

Hickok, Lorena 336

Hicks, Granville 156, 361

Hickson, William J. 298

High School of Commerce, New York City 527

High Tor (Anderson) 38

Highland Park Shopping Village, Dallas 180

Highlander Folk School 152, 155

Hill, Abram 52

Hill, Billy 62

Hill, George 26, 146

Hill, Ralph 521

Hiller, Howard 39

Hiller, Wendy 39

Hillman, Sidney 124

Hillquit, Morris 136

Hillyer, Robert 88

Hilton, James 360

Himwich, H. E. 416

Hindemith, Paul 28, 45, 68

Hindenburg 356, 465, 479–480

Hines, Earl 45, 64

Hippodrome, New York City 35

His Wife's Mother 89

Hispanic Americans 174

History is Made at Night 37

A History of American Magazines (Mott) 89

History of Communication 47

Hitchcock, B. S. 417

Hitchcock, Albert Spear 493

Hitchcock, Henry-Russell 180

"Hitler was a Liberal" (Facts Forum) 129

Hitler, Adolf 72, 129, 182, 202, 216–217, 233, 235, 244, 250, 307, 347, 356, 361, 370–372, 408, 410, 439–440, 450, 453, 455, 458, 484, 501, 506, 519–522, 529

Hitler-Stalin Pact (1939) 157, 160, 219, 233, 243–234, 361–362, 441

Hitz, William 298

Hockey 498–503, 506, 518–521, 530, 532–534

Hockey Hall of Fame 518

Hocutt, Thomas 212

Hodes, H. L. 416

Hodgson, "Red" 34

Hoffman, Al 28, 32

Hofmann, Hans 45, 48

Hofstadter Joint Legislative Committee, New York State 286

Hold Everything 523

Hold That Co-Ed 523

Holiday 39

Holiday, Billie 65, 78

Hollander, Frederick 36

Hollick-Kenyon, Herbert 464

Hollingshead, Richard M. Jr. 181, 206

Holliway, Harrison 373

Holloway, Sterling 27

Hollywood Hotel 355

Holm, Eleanor 502, 505, 519, 521, 531

Holm, Hanya 49

Holman, Alfred 377

Holmes, John Haynes 445, 455

Holmes, Oliver Wendell 259, 290, 298

Holmes, Phillips 27

Holocaust 441

Holth, Baard 464

Holy Cross College 176

Homans, John 426

Home Building & Loan Assn. v. *Blaisdell* 293

Home Loan Act of 1932 93, 211

Home Owners Loan Act of 1934 214

Home Owners' Refinancing Act 1933 213

Homer, Winslow 47

Homestead (Benton) 33

Homestead Act of 1862 52, 94

Homestead Grays 508, 531

Homestead steel strike of 1892 337

Homosexuality 33, 74–75, 84, 325, 330

Leale, Charles Augustus 425
Learned, William S. 164
Leave It to Me 40
Leavenworth Prison 273
Leavenworth [Michigan] *Times* 376
Le Corbusier 467
Ledbetter, Huddie "Leadbelly" 36, 43, 63–64, 81
Lederer, Emil 154, 176
Lee, Gypsy Rose 243
Lee, Higginson and Company 112
Lee, Ivy Ledbetter 136
Lee, Russell 81
Leef, Charles 107
Lefkowitz, Abraham 157
Left Front 362
Léger, Fernand 48
Legion of Decency 438, 443–444
Legion of Honor 421
Lehman, Herbert 253, 290
Lehman Brothers 99, 113, 115
Lehtinen, Lauri 521
Leibowitz, Samuel 285
Leidy, Joseph 425
Leigh, Janet 82
Leigh, Vivien 41, 70, 87, 193
Leinster, Murray 360
Leiser, Bill 524
Lemare, Jules 28
Lemke, William 241, 413, 434, 452–453, 457
Lemmon, Jack 82
Lenglen, Suzanne 505, 524, 528, 535
Lenin, Vladimir Ilyich 31, 47, 125–126
Lennox, W. G. 416
Lent, J. P. 464
Pope Leo XIII 456
Leonard, Buck 531
Leonard, Robert Z. 35
Leopold, Nathan 298
Leopold-Loeb murder trial 298
Leprosy 423
LeRoy, Mervyn 26, 29–30, 37
Lescaze, William 180
Leser, Tina 191
Leslie, Amy 377
Leslie, Edgar 34
Letchworth Village, N.Y. 425
"Let's Dance" 79
"Let's Face the Music" (Berlin) 35
"Let's Fall in Love" (Arlen and Koehler) 31
Leukemia 416
Levin, Meyer 31, 37
Levine, Philip 411, 416

Levine, Sam 38
Levinsky, Alex 518
Levy, Irwin 415
Levy, John 425
Levy, Lucian 366
Levy, Melvin P. 56
Lew Leslie's Blackbirds of 1930 27
Lewin, Afred 405
Lewis, Ed "Strangler" 500
Lewis, Gladys Adelina 85
Lewis, Grace Hegger 85
Lewis, Harvey Spencer 460
Lewis, James H. 237
Lewis, John Henry 512
Lewis, John L. 96, 101–103, 111, 120, 124–125, 132–133, 231–232, 298, 307, 336
Lewis, Myrta 132
Lewis, Ross A. 375
Lewis, Sinclair 34, 37, 43–44, 51, 55, 85, 88, 154, 352
Lewis, Wyndham 75
Lewisohn, Adolph 136
Libbey High School, Toledo, Ohio 159
Liberal Party of New York 171
The Liberator 361
Liberty 373
Liberty at the Crossroads 342
Liberty Deferred 52
Lichty, John Alden 425
Lieberman, H. S. 416
Liebowitz, Samuel 274
Life 76, 190, 328, 343, 358–359, 377–378
Life Can Be Beautiful 347, 354
The Life of Emile Zola 37, 87
Life With Father (Lindsay and Course) 42, 72
Liggett, Walter William 377
Light in August (Faulkner) 29, 43, 54, 77
Lightnin' 26
Lights Out 355
Li'l Abner 342, 346, 349, 367–369
Lilienthal, David 487
Lilly, Beatrice G. 30
Limited Editions Club 85
Lincoln, Abraham 45, 69–70, 83, 223, 422, 425
Lincoln, Mary Todd 425
Lincoln (automobile) 59, 183
Lincoln College, Pennsylvania 150
Lincoln Memorial, Washington, D.C. 250, 308
Lincoln Tunnel, Hudson River 98, 183

Lincoln University 169–170
Lindbergh, Anne Morrow 259, 278, 477
Lindbergh, Charles A. 259, 278–279, 373, 385, 477, 485–486, 506, 408–409
Lindbergh, Charles A. Jr. 261
Lindbergh kidnapping trial 342
Lindbergh Law of 1934 260, 263, 266, 273
Lindemann, Erlich 416
Lindsay, Howard 33, 42, 72
Lindsay, Vachel 73–74, 89
Lindsey, Ben B. 297
Lingle, Alfred "Jake" 269
Lippmann, Walter 245
Lipton, Sir Thomas 498, 535
Lister, Joseph 423
Literary Digest 239, 241, 342, 370, 377
Little, Charles S. 425
Little, Lawson Jr. 498, 501, 516, 533
Little Bohemia Lodge, near Rhinelander, Wisc. 269, 292
Little Caesar 26, 58
The Little Colonel 70
The Little Foxes (Hellman) 42, 44
Little House in the Big Woods (Wilder) 29, 52
Little House on the Prairie (Wilder) 52
Little League baseball 503
"Little Man, You've Had a Busy Day" (Wayne, Sigler, and Hoffman) 32
Little Miss Broadway 70
Little Miss Marker 70
Little Nemo in Slumberland (McCay) 348, 378
Little Orphan Annie 340, 346, 349
The Little Princess 70
Little Town on the Prairie (Wilder) 52
"Little White Lies" 27
Little Women 30
Litwack, Harry 510
Liveright, Horace B. 85, 89
Lives of a Bengal Lancer 34
Living Newspapers 44, 49, 51–52
The Living Wage (Ryan) 456
Livingood, Jack 491
Lizana, Anita 534
Llewellyn, Karl 275
Lloyd, Frank 34, 87
Lloyd, Nelson McAllister 378
Lloyd, Wray 418

Lobingier, Andrew Stewart 425
Lochner, Louis P. 375
Lochner v. *New York* 298
Locke, Alain 150
Lockhart, Gene 31
Lockwood, Margaret 41
Loeb, Howard Scott 466
Loeb, James 136
Loeb, Leo 420
Loeb, Richard 298
Loeb Classical Library 136
Loesser, Frank 38, 41
Loewi, Otto 419
Logan, Rayford 150, 319
Lomax, Alan 36, 43, 61, 63, 81
Lomax, John Avery 36, 61, 63
Lombard, Carole 32, 35, 60, 201
Lombardo, Guy 64
London Economic Conference (1933) 213
London Naval Treaty of 1930 210
Londos, Jim 500
The Lone Ranger 340, 355
Miss Lonelyhearts (West) 31
Lonergan, Lenore 42
Long Island City Bowl 501, 530
Long Island Daily Press 364
Long Island University 528
The Long Winter (Wilder) 52
Long, Huey P. 117, 133, 215, 219, 232, 248–249, 253, 261, 304, 355, 413, 434, 452, 457
Long, Jimmy 29
Long, Lutz 522
Long, Perrin H. 394
Long, Ray 377
Long and Bliss 385
Longacre Theater, New York City 34, 40
Longan, George Baker 373
Look 343, 359
Look Homeward, Angel (Wolfe) 90
"(Lookie, Lookie, Lookie) Here Comes Cookie" (Gordon) 34
Lord and Taylor 126, 181, 191, 203–204, 206
Lord, Heal the Child (Benton) 33
Lord's Prayer 328
Lorentz, Pare 44, 81, 108
Lorimer, William 254
Loring, Eugene 40
Los Angeles 478–480
Los Angeles County Superior Court 296
Los Angeles Examiner 159
Los Angeles Hospital 417

Los Angeles Institute of Family Relations 422
Los Angeles Times 298, 320
Lost Horizon (Hilton) 37, 360
The Lost Patrol 32
Lou Gehrig's disease 527
The Loud Red Patrick (McKenney) 83
Louis, Jean 201
Louis, Joe 501–502, 504, 506, 512–514, 529, 533
Louisiana Constitution 248
The Louisiana Educator 377
Louisiana Purchase Exposition, Saint Louis (1903–1904) 326, 378
Louisville Bank v. *Radford* 281
Louisville Courier-Journal 373, 378
Love Affair 41
"Love for Sale" 27
"Love is Sweeping the Country" 29
"Love Is the Sweetest Thing" (Noble) 31
"Love Letters in the Sand" (Coots, Kenny and Kenny) 28
Love on the Run 76
Love Songs (Teasdale) 90
"Love Thy Neighbor" (Revel and Gordon) 32
"Love Walked In" (Gershwin and Gershwin) 39
Love, Robertus 377
Lovecraft, H. P. 346, 359–360, 378
Lovelock, Jack 502, 522
Lovett, Robert Morss 442
Low Company (Fuchs) 37
Lowden, Frank 239
Lowe, Frederick Rollins 378
Lowe, Ruth 41
Lowell, A. Lawrence 175
Lowell Observatory 468
Lowry, Raymond 159
Loy, Myrna 30, 35, 58, 60
Loyalism 306, 448–449
Lubitsch, Ernst 29, 31, 58, 69
Luce, Claire 30
Luce, Clare Boothe 36, 42
Luce, Henry 340–341, 343, 345, 358–359
Luciano, "Lucky" 269–270
Luciano-Costello crime empire 287
Lucius, Reuben 373
Lucke, Baldwin 416
Luckman, Sid 515
Ludlow, Louis 271
Ludlow proposal 262, 271
Ludwig, David Keith 135

Lugosi, Bela 27
Luisetti, Hank 502, 505, 510, 523, 527–528
Lukas, Paul 35
"Lullaby of Broadway" (Warren and Dubin) 34
Lumber (Colman) 27
Lumpkin, Grace 29
Lumsford, Bascom Lamar 63
Lundy, John 417
Lunt, Alfred 31
Lust for Life (Stone) 32
The Lutheran Hour 432
Lutheran Synod of Buffalo 432, 441
Lyceum Theater, New York Theater 38
Lyman, Lauren D. 375
Lynd, Helen 147, 187, 311, 436
Lynd, Robert 147, 187, 311, 436
Lyon, Ben 26
Lyster, Brigadier-General Theodore Charles 425

M

M 33
Ma Perkins 354
MacArthur, Gen. Douglas 129, 211, 222, 271
Macauley, Charles Raymond 374, 378
Macbeth (Shakespeare) 51
MacDonald, A. B. 374
Macdonald, Dwight 362
MacDonald, Jeanette 35
MacDonald-Wright, Stanton 47
MacGuire, C. J. 425
Machen, J. Gresham 460
Mack, Cecil 27
Mack, Connie 499, 504, 508
Mack, Julian 290
Macklin, Madge T. 417
MacLeish, Archibald 44, 73, 88, 343
MacLennan, Frank Pitts 378
MacLeod, Norman 41
MacMurray, Fred 39
Macon 478–479
Macon Telegraph 377
MacVeagh, Franklin 136
Macy's department store 57, 99, 183, 191, 193, 321
Macy, Anne Mansfield Sullivan 176
Macy, R. H. 191
Madame X 89

Mädchen Gymnasium, Breslau, Germany 172
Madden, Owney 513
Madeline (Bemelmans) 41
Madison Avenue Presbyterian Church, New York City 460
Madison Square Garden, New York City 227, 308, 439, 448, 458, 499, 503, 509, 513, 525, 528
Madison, Helene 521, 531, 533
Maher, Stephen John 425
Mahier, Edith 71
Maier, Walter A. 432
Mailer, Norman 362
Main, Marjorie 36
Major Bowes' Amateur Hour 354
Major League Baseball World Series 499–500, 502–503, 504, 509, 527, 531–534
Make Way for Tomorrow 37
Mako, Gene 503
Malaria 398
Malden, Karl 38, 71
Malneck, Matt 36
The Maltese Falcon (Hammett) 26, 53–54
Maltz, Albert 39
Mamoulian, Rouben 30, 58
Man Against Himself (K. Menninger) 411
Man at the Crossroads Looking with Hope and High Vision to the Choosing of a New and Better Future (Rivera) 31, 47
Man O' War (racehorse) 502, 503, 517–518
Man of Aran 32
The Man of Bronze (Robeson) 39
The Man on the Flying Trapeze 34
Man, the Unknown (Carrel) 408
A Man to Remember 59
The Man Who Came to Dinner (Hart) 42, 72, 205
The Man with the Blue Guitar (Stevens) 38
Manasses, Carolyn 330
Mandelbaum, M. J. 417
Mandrake the Magician (Davis) 349
Manero, Tony 534
Mann, Thomas 45
Manning, William Thomas 86, 439, 458
Man's Castle 30
Mansfield Theater, New York City 26
Manual of Modern Surgery (Da Costa) 422

Maple Leafs Gardens, Toronto, Canada 498
Maranzano, Salvatore 270
Marble Collegiate Church, New York City 433, 459
Marble, Alice 525, 531–532, 534
Marbury v. Madison 235
March of Dimes 399–400, 417
The March of Time 355
March, Fredric 26, 31, 34, 37, 42, 87
March, Mush 518
Marching! Marching! (Weatherwax) 34, 53
Marconi, Guglielmo 366
Marden, Charles Carroll 176
Margin for Error (Luce) 42
Marijuana Traffic Act of 1937 307
Marin, John 47
Marine, David 417
Marionettes (Faulkner) 77
Markham, Edwin 86
Marks, Gerald 28
Marlowe, Christopher 51
Marmon (automobile company) 189
Marquand, John Phillips 37, 41, 88
Marquette University 422, 514, 516, 526
Marquis of Queensberry boxing rules 535
Marsh, Clarence S. 175
Marsh, Reginald 47, 70, 75
Marshall, E. Kennerly Jr. 394
Marshall, George 41
Marshall, George Preston 502
Marshall, Herbert 29, 34
Marshall Field 190, 203
Marshall Plan 119
Martin, D. D. 374
Martin, Fletcher 71
Martin, Glenn L. 492
Martin, Herbert S. 313
Martin, Homer S. 120
Martin, Mary 40, 205
Martin, Pepper 509, 533
Martin, Roberta 65
Martin, Sallie 65
Martin Beck Theater, New York City 27, 28, 35, 38
Martin Brothers 63
Martinek, Frank V. 349
Martino, Bohuslav 68
Martyn, Thomas John Cardel 341, 343
Marvel Comics 344
Marvin, Frank 62

Marx, Karl 153, 334
Marx Brothers 27, 29–30, 34, 37, 346, 507, 523
Marxism 47, 56, 156, 164, 167, 362, 455–456
Marxist Quarterly 362
Mary Lincoln: Wife and Widow (Sandburg) 84
Mary Worth 342
Maryland State Board of Health 423
Marymount College 458
Mason, Walt 378
Masonic Temple, Atlanta 207
Masque Theater, New York City 32
Massachusetts General Hospital 393, 395, 414, 426–427
Massachusetts Institute of Technology (MIT) 129, 481, 488, 490–491
Massachusetts State Industrial School for Girls 332
Massachusetts Suffrage Association 332
Masseria, Joe 270
The Masses 360–361
Massey, Raymond 37, 40
Massie, Thomas 296, 426
Masson, Thomas Lansing 378
Masters, Edgar Lee 355
Masters, Frankie 41
Masters Golf Tournament 500, 516, 531, 533–534
Matas, Rudolph 420
Maternal mortality 331, 386–387, 400–401
Mathematical Review 494
Mathematische Grundlagen der Quantenmechanik (Von Neumann) 489
Mather, Stephen Tyng 136
Mathewson, Christy 508
Matthew, William D. 494
Matthews, J. B. 444
Maurer, Martin 197
Maurin, Peter 336, 453
Max, L. W. 417
Maxine Elliott's Theater, New York City 33
Maxwell, Elsa 86
Maxwell House Showboat 353
Mayer, Edwin Justus 26
Mayer, Emil 425
Mayer, Helene 519
Mayer, Karl 154
Mayo, Archie 27, 35

Mexican Americans 193, 303, 311, 315
Mexico League baseball 530
Meyer, Eugene 341
Miami News 375
Miami Tribune 365
Michelson, Albert 488, 494
Michigan state militia 121
Michigan State University 171
Mickey Mouse (Gottfredson) 340
Middle Atlantic League (soccer) 523
Middle West Utilities Company 31, 130
Middleton, Ray 32
Midgley, Thomas Jr. 135, 462, 470
Midland 362
Midway Gardens, Chicago 205
Midwest Industrial League (basketball) 511
Mies van der Rohe, Ludwig 199
"Migrant Mother" (Lange) 82
Mike Mulligan and His Steam Shovel (Burton) 41
Milburn, John George 298
Mildred Pierce (Cain) 76
Milestone, Lewis 26, 39, 87
Milgron, Sally 181
Milhaud, Darius 68
The Militant 362
Millard House, Pasadena, Calif. 205
Millard, Harry 76
Millay, Edna St. Vincent 44
Miller, B. D. 146
Miller, C. P. 411
Miller, Caroline 88
Miller, Frank Ebenezer 425
Miller, Glenn 26, 40–41, 64
Miller, Henry 27, 35, 41
Miller, Kelly 318
Miller, Marilyn 27, 31
Miller, Nathan 234
Miller, Richard 417
Millikan, Robert A. 417, 463, 486, 488
Million Dollar Legs 29
Mills, Irving 28–29, 31–32, 39
Mills Brothers 29, 60
Mills College 519
Mills Report of 1907 508
Milrose Games 525
Milwaukee Journal 207, 375, 378
Milwaukee News 364
Min and Bill 87, 89
The Mind of Primitive Man (Boas) 484

"Mine Rescue" (Martin) 71
The Miners — A Drama of the Non-Union Coal Fields of West Virginia 153
Miniature golf 516, 525
Miniature Photography (Simon) 86
"Minnie the Moocher" (Calloway, Mills, and Gaskill) 29
Minot, George R. 385, 389, 418, 419
Minotaure 48
Miranda, Carmen 42, 201
Miscellany 362
Mississippi 34
Missouri ex. rel. Gaines v. *Canada* 142, 150, 307
Missouri State Capitol mural (Benton) 75
Missouri Valley College 176
Mr. Deeds Goes to Town 35, 87
Mister Gilfeather (Capp) 368
Mr. Home, Sweet Home (Dart) 377
"Mr. Paganini" (Fitzgerald) 78
Mr. Smith Goes to Washington 41, 70
Mitchell, Arthur L. 213
Mitchell, Charles E. 112, 228
Mitchell, Margaret 35, 70, 85, 88, 444
Mitchell, Thomas 37, 87
Mitchell, Verne Beatrice 505
Mitchell, William N. 274, 283
Mitchell's Christian Singers 68
Mobile Register 376
Mobile Tigers 530
Modern dance 43, 49
Modern Language Association (MLA) 63
Modern Merchandising Bureau, New York 193
Modern Monthly 360–361
Modern Quarterly 361–362
Modern Times 35, 467
Modernism 43–47, 49–50, 52–54, 68, 74–76, 77, 82–83, 198–200, 362, 441, 445, 454–455, 467
Moffitt, John C. 37, 51
Moley, Raymond 112, 115, 223, 358
Molotov, V. M. 246
Mommie Dearest (C. Crawford) 77
Monahan, Michael 378
Monkey Business 27
Monks, John Jr. 37
Monopoly 305, 312, 317, 336
Monroe, Harriet 83, 89
Monroe Brothers 61–62

Montana State College 225
Montefiore Hospital, New York 417
Monteil, Germaine 191
Montessori teaching method 173
Montgomery, Helen Barrett 460
Montgomery, Little Brother 64
Montgomery, Olen 284
Montgomery Ward 118
Montreal Canadiens 498, 518–519, 532
Montreal Maroons 501, 503, 518–519, 533
Mood (automobile company) 189
"Mood Indigo" 28
Moodie, Leroy 494
Moody Bible Institute 459
Moody, Helen Wills 499, 501, 505, 525, 528, 532–533
Moon Mullins 373
"The Moon of Manakoora" (Newman and Loesser) 38
"Moon Over Miami" (Burke and Leslie) 34
Mooney, Thomas 262, 294–295
Mooney v. *Holohan* 295
"Moonlight and Shadows" (Hollander and Robin) 36
"Moonlight Serenade" (Miller and Parish) 41
Moonshine and Honeysuckle 355
Moore, Anne 494
Moore, Don 341, 349
Moore, Douglas 68
Moore, Marjorie B. 417
Moore, Ray 349
Moore, Victor 29, 33, 37
Moral Man and Immoral Society (Niebuhr) 444
Moral Re-Armament (MRA) 450
Moran, "Bugs" 269
Moran, Jackie 39
More, Paul Elmer 89, 177
More Fun 349
Morehead v. *New York ex. rel. Tipaldo* 95
Morehouse, Frederick Cook 378
Morenz, Howie 498, 518–519
Morgan, Arthur 487
Morgan, Frank 41
Morgan, Harcourt 487
Morgan, Helen 28, 35
Morgan, J. P. 95, 107, 112, 118, 130–131
Morgan, Thomas Hunt 384, 389, 417, 419, 472
Morgan financial group 107

Morgan Stanley (investment firm) 95

Morganthau, Hans Jr. 135

Morgenstern, Oskar 489

Morley, Felix 375

Mormons 82

The Morning Freiheit 378

Morning Glory 87

Morosco Theater, New York City 36, 40

Morris, Glenn 522, 534

Morris, Roger Sylvester 417, 425

Morrisett, Lloyd N. 164

Morrison, Herb 356

Morro Castle 304

Morrow, William 90

Morse, Charles Wyman 137

Morse code 366

Mort, Paul 147

Mortimer, Frederick Craig 378

Morton, William T. G. 395–396

Moscow Art Theatre 71

Mose, Larry 37

Mosely, Rev. W. M. 65

Moses, Anna Mary Robertson "Grandma" 42

Mosquitoes (Faulkner) 77

"The Most Beautiful Girl in the World" (Rodgers and Hart) 35

Moten, Bennie 64

Motherwell, Robert 46

Motion Picture Association of America (MPAA) 443

Motion Picture Producers and Distributors of America (MPPDA) 33, 84, 443

Mott, Frank Luther 89

Mount Holyoke College 249, 493

Mt. Sinai Hospital, New York City 418, 421, 425

Mount Wilson Observatory 468

Mourning Becomes Electra (O'Neill) 29, 43, 72

"Move on Up a Little Higher" (Brewster) 66

Movietone 370

Mowrer, Edgar Ansel 356, 375

Mudd, Stuard 415

Mudge, W. A. 462

Muhammad, Elijah (Elijah Poole) 304, 432

Muhammad, Farad (W. D. Fard) 304

Muir, Malcolm 358

Mulatto (Hughes) 31

Muldoon, William A. 535

Mumford, Lewis 322–323, 466–467

Muncie [Ind.] *Post-Democrat* 376

Mundelein, George William Cardinal 459

Muni, Paul 27, 29, 34, 37, 42, 45, 87

Munich Pact of 1938 216, 244, 347, 356

Munroe, Charles 494

Munsey, Frank 359

Muralism 44, 47, 70, 75

Murder in the Cathedral (Eliot) 51

Murder, Inc. 270

Murphy, Dudley 60

Murphy, Frank 121, 158, 235, 253, 365

Murphy, George 32

Murphy, Gerald 73

Murphy, William P. 385, 389, 417, 418, 419

Murray v. *Maryland* 141, 150

Murray, Donald 141, 150

Murray, John 38

Murray, John Courtney 435

Murray, William H. "Alfalfa Bill" 92, 237

Murrow, Edward R. 343, 356, 371

Muscle Shoals plant, Ala. 93, 131

Muse, Clarence 28, 60

Museum of Living Art 48

Museum of Modern Art, New York City 42, 48, 180, 184

Museum of Non-objective Art 48

Music Box Theater, New York City 27, 29–31, 36, 39, 42

Music for Radio 68

"The Music Goes 'Round and 'Round" 34, 79

Music in the Air 30

Mussolini, Benito 72, 217, 235, 347, 355–356, 362, 370, 376, 408–409, 455, 506

Muste, A. J. 154

Mutiny on the Bounty 34, 87

Mutt and Jeff (Fisher) 348

Mutual Broadcasting Network 342, 432, 437

My America (Adamic) 52

"My Baby Just Cares for Me" (Kahn and Donaldson) 26

"My Day" (E. Roosevelt) 215, 250

My Experiences in the World War (Pershing) 88

"My Funny Valentine" (Rodgers and Hart) 38

"My Heart Belongs to Daddy" (Porter) 40

My Heart's in the Highlands (Saroyan) 42

My Life and Loves (Harris) 89

My Little Chickadee 84

My Man Godfrey 35

My Sister Eileen (McKenney) 82–83

My Way of Life (J. Crawford) 77

Mydans, Carl 81

Myers, Richard 31

Myra Breckenridge 85

Myrt and Marge 354

Mystery Men Comics 344

N

Nags Head, N.C. 196

Nagurski, Bronko 528–529

Nambé Community School 173–174

Nancy (Bushmiller) 341

Napoleon I 86, 370

Nash, Charles 189

Nash, Frank "Jelly" 273, 288, 298

Nash, Ogden 27

Nash Motors 183, 198

Natchez Trace Parkway 476

Nathan, George Jean 358, 370

Nation 89, 158, 163, 312, 362, 411

Nation of Islam 304

National Advisory Council on Radio in Education 383

National Amateur Athletic Union (AAU) 500

National Association for the Advancement of Colored People (NAACP) 89, 150, 168, 170, 212, 215, 217, 264–266, 285, 306–307, 319, 334, 336, 362

National Association for the Study of Epilepsy 422

National Association of Broadcasters 344

National Association of Colored Women (NACW) 168

National Association of Manufacturers (NAM) 104, 118

National Association of Teachers in Colored Schools 168

National Baptist Convention of America 65, 437

National Baptist Convention of the United States 437

National Barn Dance (WLS, Chicago) 61, 67

National Baseball Congress 509

National Basketball Association (NBA) 511

National Basketball League (NBL) 511

National Biscuit Company 79

National Board of Fire Underwriters 143

National Book Award 78

National Boxing Association (NBA) 512–513

National Broadcasting Corporation (NBC) 38, 66, 340, 343–344, 352, 354–355, 357, 370, 454, 459, 481, 504

— Blue network 340, 342, 355

— Red network 345, 355

— Symphony 38, 40, 343

National Bulk Carrier 135

National Cancer Institute 386

National Cash Register 328

National Catholic Welfare Conference 456

National Challenge Cup (soccer) 523

National City Bank 112–113, 228

National Collegiate Athletic Association (NCAA) 501, 503, 507, 534

National Commission on Prisons and Prison Labor (NCPPL) 337

National Committee for Economy in Government 143

National Committee for Mental Hygiene 427

National Committee for the Defense of Political Prisoners (NCDPP) 56

National Committee on Federal Legislation for Birth Control, Inc. 391

National Committee to Aid Striking Miners Fighting Starvation 56

National Conference on Problems of the Negro and Negro Youth 319

National Consumers' League 290, 332, 337

National Convention of Gospel Choirs and Choruses 65

National Council of Congregational Churches of the United States 441

National Council of Methodist Youth 434

National Council of Negro Women (NCNW) 168, 252, 305, 337

National Council of Teachers of English 151

National Economic League 143

National Education Association (NEA) 146–147, 155–157, 159–160, 175

National Education Association Journal 159

National Electrical Manufacturers Association 135

National Farmers' Union 255

National Football League (NFL) 230, 499–501, 503–505, 507, 514–515, 529, 532–535

— Most Valuable Player Award 531

National Foreign Trade Council 377

National Foundation for Infantile Paralysis 387, 389, 399–400

National Gallery of Art, Washington, D.C. 182, 196

National Geographic 76

National Geographic Society 464, 485

— Gold Medal 463

National Health Conference (1938) 390

National Health Survey 399

National Hockey League (NHL) 500–501, 503, 518–519

— Most Valuable Player Award 518, 532

— Stanley Cup 499, 502–503, 518–519, 532–534

National Housing Act of 1934 213

National Housing Act of 1937 216

National Industrial Recovery Act of 1933 93, 99, 110, 117, 120, 125, 132, 211, 214, 230–231, 249, 251, 259, 260, 276–277, 281, 289, 293, 304, 476

National Institute of Health 382, 413

National Invitational Tournament (basketball) 502

National Labor Relations Act of 1935 (Wagner Act) 94, 99, 102, 110, 117, 120, 182, 215, 230, 231, 235, 251–252, 277, 280, 282, 293, 305, 350

National Labor Relations Board v. *Fansteel Metallurgical Co.* 262, 277

National Labor Relations Board v. *Jones & Laughlin Steel Corp.* 277, 282

National League (baseball) 499, 508, 531–535

— Most Valuable Player Award 530–531

National Medal of Science 487

National Open Golf Championships 531

National Park Service 136

National Periodical Publications 349

The National Radio Pulpit 434

National Recovery Act 280

National Republic 156, 362

National Shore Line, Cape Cod, Massachusetts 196

National Socialist Party 371

National Survey of School Finance 140, 147

National Theater, New York City 27, 42

National Tuberculosis Association 397, 419

National Union for Social Justice 232–233, 452–453

National Urban League 168

The National Vesper Hour 454

National Woman's Christian Temperance Union 424

Nationalism 36, 97, 118, 323, 448–449, 484

Native Americans 45, 70, 89, 174, 197, 423, 462, 484

Native Son (play) 72

Naturalism 53–54

The Nature of the Chemical Bond and the Structure of Molecules and Crystals (Pauling) 490

Natwick, Mildred 36

The Nazarene (Asch) 41

Nazimova, Alla 29

Nazism 33, 48, 86, 107, 116, 153–154, 167, 173, 176, 213, 218, 234, 242–243, 262, 307–308, 323, 372, 390, 394, 404, 410, 433, 437–441, 458, 469, 471, 494, 501, 514, 519–520, 536

NBC University of the Air 356

Neal, Claude 265–266

Near v. *Minnesota* 293, 340

Nearing, Scott 153

Nebbia v. *New York* 264, 293

Neddermayer, Seth 469

Negri, Pola 86

New York Flower Hospital and Medical College 254

New York Gallery 47

New York Giants (baseball) 498–499, 502, 508, 531, 533–535

New York Giants (football) 503, 515, 531, 533–534

New York Globe 369

New York Herald 377–378

New York Herald Tribune 373–375, 377, 500, 535

New York Journal 373

New York Journal-American 524

New York Knickerbockers 510

New York Law School 227

New York Local #5 of the AFT 156–157, 159–160, 171

New York Metropolitan Sewerage Commission 426

New York Mirror 365

New York Morning Telegraph 379

New York Morning World 378

New York Neurological Institute 418

New York Philharmonic 38, 86, 354

New York Pollution Commission 426

New York Polyclinic Medical School and Hospital 424

New York Port Authority 463

New York Post 82, 372

New York Psychiatric Society 422

New York Psychoanalytic Institute 410

New York Rangers 518, 530, 533–534

New York Rens 510–511

New York School of Fine and Applied Arts 90, 204

New York State Athletic Commission 535

New York State Board of Regents 427

New York State Conservation Commission 426

New York State Department of Health 159, 412

New York State Economic Council 156

New York State Industrial Commission (renamed "Board") 249

New York State Narcotic Commission 425

New York State prison reform program 274

New York State Rapp-Coudert Committee 156

New York State Senate 250

New York State Teachers Association 176

New York Stock Exchange 103, 207, 228, 298

New York Sun 376, 379

New York Supreme Court 286

New York Teachers Guild 157

The New York Times 50, 52, 66, 68, 180, 195, 203, 220, 223, 236, 313, 320, 373–379, 514, 520, 527

New York Triborough Bridge system 196

New York Tribune 377–378

New York University 176, 414, 417, 423

— Law School 247

New York World 348, 373, 377

New York World-Telegram 82, 372, 375

New York World's Fair, 1939 *See* World of Tomorrow Exposition, New York

New York Yacht Club 502

New York Yankees 502–503, 508–509, 527, 530–531, 533–534

New York Zoological Park 414

The New Yorker 27, 42, 82, 202, 374, 508

The New Yorkers 27

The New Ziegfeld Follies 33

New, Clarence Herbert 378

Newark Call Printing and Publishing Company 379

Newark Ledger 364

Newark News 378

Newbery Honor 52

Newhouse, Edward 32

Newlon, Jesse H. 151, 163, 166

Newman, Alfred 38

Newman, Pauline 134

Newspaper Enterprise Association 379

Newsweek 192, 341, 343, 358

"The Next Great Plague To Go" (Parran) 406

Nezelof, Pierre 86

Niagra Movement (Du Bois) 334

"Nice Work If You Can Get It" (I. Gershwin and G. Gershwin) 38

Nicholas Brothers 60

Nichols, Red 26, 80

Nicholson, Samuel Edgar 337

Nicholson, Seth Barnes 468

Niebuhr, Reinhold 152, 437, 444–445, 455

Niebuhr, Richard 433, 455

Nieman, Lucius W. 378

Nieuwland, Julius 494

Night After Night 84

A Night at the Opera 34

"The Night Is Young and You're So Beautiful" (Suesse, Rose, and Kahal) 36

Night Rider (Warren) 41

Night riders 108

Nightwood (Barnes) 35

Nine Power Treaty of 1922 244

Nineteen Eighty-Four (Orwell) 467

1919 (Dos Passos) 29, 53

Ninotchka (Lubitsch) 69

Nipkow, Paul 481

Nitti, Francesco 373

Nitti, Francesco Saverio 373

Nitti, Frank 269

Niven, David 39

Nixon, Richard 126

Nixon v. *Condon* 264

No More Ladies 76

No Star Is Lost (Farrell) 39

Nobel, Alfred 468

Nobel Peace Prize 126, 246, 252–254, 303, 408, 459

Nobel Prize for chemistry 489, 492

Nobel Prize for literature 54–55, 78, 85, 88

Nobel Prize for medicine or physiology 382, 384–385, 389, 394, 408, 410, 414–415, 417–419

Nobel Prize for physics 470, 488, 492, 494

Noble, Alfred 468

Noble, Ray 31–32, 39–40

Noble Prize 468

Noether, Emmy 494

Noguchi, Isamu 48

Nolan, Bob 32, 36

Norell, Norman 201

Norman v. *Baltimore & Ohio Railroad* 281

Norris, Charles 426

Norris, Charles Gilman 86

Norris, Clarence 284, 286

Norris, Frank 53

Norris, George 242, 282

Norris–La Guardia Act of 1932 92, 211, 247, 259

Norris v. *Alabama* 211, 285

North American Airlines 477

North American News Alliance 73

PA 203
Pacelli, Eugenio Cardinal 434, 459
Pacific Coast Borax Company 136
Pacific Coast Conference (basketball championships) 528
Pacific Coast League (baseball) 506, 532
Pacific Coast Lines 96
Pacifica (Stackpole) 327
Packard Motor Company 182–183, 189, 492
Page, Kirby 444
Paige, Satchel 505, 508–509, 529–531
Paine, Mary 494
Palace Theater, New York City 28
Pale Horse, Pale Rider (Porter) 41
Paley, William S. 345, 347, 370
Palmer, A. Mitchell 291
Palmer, Roland G. 373
Palomar Ballroom, Los Angeles 35, 79
Palooka, Joe 340
Pan Am Airlines 96, 305, 477, 492
Pan-African Movement 334
Pan-American Postal Congress 377
Panama Pacific International Exposition, San Francisco (1915) 326
Panama Refining Company v. *Ryan* (Hot Oil Cases) 277
Panay 216, 244, 253
Papyrus 378
"Paramount Problems of the United States" (National Economic League) 143
Paramount Studios 58, 84, 373
Parents 330
Paris Exposition 425
Parish, Mitchell 31–32, 41
Park, William H. 414, 420
Park Avenue Baptist Church, New York City 454
Park Central Hotel, New York City 78
Parker, Bonnie 58, 189, 260
Parker, Dorothy 45, 57, 73, 243
Parker, George B. 375
Parker, John J. 258, 297
Parker, William Belmont 378
Parker Brothers 336
Parkhurst, Charles 460
Park-In Theaters 206
Parkinson, Donald 193
Parkinson, John 193
Parks, Sam 533
Parnis, Mollie 191

Parran, Thomas Jr. 402, 405–406, 412, 420
Parson Weems' Fable (Wood) 47
Parson's School of Fine and Applied Arts, New York 202
Parsons, F. A. 90
Parsons, Louella 355
Parsons, Payn Bigelow 426
Partisan Review 55, 312, 360, 362
Partridge, Edward Lasell 426
Pasteur Institute, Paris 394
"Pastures of Plenty" (Guthrie) 81
Patman, Wright 271
Patou, Jean 180
Patterns of Culture (Benedict) 483
Patterson, Haywood 284–286
Patterson, J. D. 426
Patterson, Joseph Medill 373
Patton, Charlie 64
Paul Whitman and His Orchestra 29
Pauling, Linus 490
Pavlova, Anna 49
Paxton, Tom 81
Payne Fund 443
Peace Mission movement 336, 454
Peale, Rev. Norman Vincent 129, 433
Pearl, Jack 353
Pearl Harbor bombing 118, 244, 246, 309, 323
Pecora, Ferdinand 107, 112–113, 227–228
Pecora Investigation 107, 113, 118, 227–228
Peder Victorious (Rolvaag) 90
Pedlar's Progress (Shephard) 88
Peer, Ralph 61
Peerless (automobile company) 189
Pegler, Westbrook 519
Pelley, William 234
Pembroke (Freeman) 89
Pendergast, Thomas 253
Penguin Books 360
Penicillin 387, 394
"Pennies From Heaven" (Johnston and Burke) 36
Pennington, Ann 27–28
Pennsylvania AC 522
Pennsylvania Railroad 425, 475
Pennsylvania State College 164, 169, 207, 329, 535
Pennsylvania Turnpike 476
Penthouse 30
The People 153
The People, Yes (Sandburg) 36, 45, 83

The People's Choice (Agar) 88
Peoples Gas, Light and Coke 130
People's World 81
Pepper, Charles Melville 378
Pepper, O. H. P. 417
Pepperdine, George 141
Pepperdine College 141
Pepsi-Cola Company 76
Percy, Julian 150
Perey, Marguerite 469
Perkins, Frances (Secretary of Labor) 249–250, 303, 325, 333
Perkins, Francis (social worker) 115
Perkins, Frank (entertainer) 32
Perkins, Osgood 36
Perkins, Roger Griswold 426
Perkins Institution for the Blind in Massachusetts 176
Perlon 465
Permanent Court of International Justice 292
Perry, Frank 77
Perry, Fred 525, 533–534
Perry, George W. 499
Perry, Ralph Barton 88
Perry v. *U.S.* 281
Persephone (Benton) 41
Pershing, John J. 88
Pesotta, Rose 134
Pestalozza, A. 41
Peter Ibbetson (Taylor) 66
Peter, Paul and Mary 81
Peters, C. F. 351
Peters, Charles C. 164
Petillo, Kelly 501
Petrified Forest 35, 45, 58
Pevsner, Antoine 193
Pew, J. Howard 118
Pfahler, G. E. 417
Pfiffner, J. J. 418
The Phantom 57, 349
The Phantom of the Opera 89
Phelps, Martha Austin 494
Philadelphia Athletics 504, 508, 526, 531–532
Philadelphia Board of Public Education 150
Philadelphia Bulletin 378
Philadelphia Court House 196
Philadelphia Inquirer 342, 344, 365
Philadelphia Institute for Medical Research 418
The Philadelphia Negro (Du Bois) 333
Philadelphia North American 535
Philadelphia Phillies (baseball) 500, 508, 531

S

Saarinen, Eliel 180
Sabin, Albert B. 390, 400, 418
Sabin, Charles 321
Sabin, Florence R. 418
Sabin, Pauline 321
Sabin's Women's Organization for National Prohibition Reform 321
Sacco, Nicola 29, 35, 299, 332, 361
Sachs, Julius 177
Sacramento Bee 375, 378
Sadie Hawkins Day 368
Sadler, Lena Kellogg 426
St. Denis, Ruth 49
St. John's College 141
Saint Louis 441
Saint Louis Browns 508, 530
Saint Louis Cardinals 498, 500, 508–509, 531–533
Saint Louis Post-Dispatch 374–375, 378
Saint Louis Star-Times 207
Saint Louis World's Fair (1903–1904). *See* Louisian Purchase Exposition
St. Moritz Hotel, New York City 320
St. Nicholas Magazine 379
St. Olaf College 177
Saint Petersburg Institute of Technology 371
St. Valentine's Day Massacre, Chicago 298
St. Vincent's Hospital, New York City 425
Saitch, Eyre 511
Saling, George 521
Salk, Jonas 126, 400
Salomon, Albert 154
Salut au Monde 44, 49
Salvation Army 458
Sam, Guillaume 214
Samba 40
Sampson, Edgar 36
Sampson, Flem 110
San Diego, I Love You (McKenney) 83
San Diego State Normal School 494
San Diego World's Fair. *See* California Pacific International Exposition, San Diego
San Francisco 35
San Francisco Chronicle 375, 524
San Francisco Examiner 376

San Francisco News 296
San Francisco Seals 506
San Francisco World's Fair (1915). *See* Panama Pacific Internation Exposition 326
San Francisco World's Fair (1939). *See* Golden Gate International Exposition
San José Demonstration and Experimental School, Bernalillo County, N. M. 173–174
San Quentin Prison 295
San Romani, Archie 526
Sanabria Company 481
Sanctuary (Faulkner) 27, 77, 443
Sandburg, Carl 36, 45, 83–84, 355
Sande, Earl 498, 517, 532
Sandison, George Henry 378
Sandrich, Mark 34–35, 37
Sanford, Edward T. 299
Sanger, Margaret 316, 387, 391–392
Santee Dakota tribe 423
Saperstein, Abe 510
Saratoga Springs (horse race) 518
Sarazen, Gene 516, 527, 531, 533
Sargent, Fred W. 158
Sargent, John 427
Sarnoff, David 345, 357, 367–368, 372–373
Saroyan, William 32, 42
Sartoris (Faulkner) 77
Satterthwaite, Thomas Edward 426
Saturday Evening Post 77, 190, 239, 340, 342, 358, 370, 378
Saturday Review of Literature 55
Saunders, Willie 533
Savannah Evening Press 379
Savannah Press 379
Save the Children 433
The Savoy, New York City 78
Sawyer, W. A. 418
"Say It Isn't So" (Berlin) 29
Sayre, Joel 78
Scarface 27
Scarlet fever 414, 418
"Scatterbrain" (Keene, Bean, Masters, and Burke) 41
Schacherer-Elek, Ilona 519
Schafer, Karl 520–521
Schall, Thomas D. 255
Schappes, Morris 156
Schechter Poultry Corp. 231, 260, 264, 277, 281–282, 293
Schechter Poultry Corp. v. *United States* 260, 264, 277, 281–282, 293

Scherhag, Richard 472
Schettler, O. H. 419
Schick, Jacob 135, 137
Schick Dry Shaver, Inc. 135, 303
Schiff, Mortimer 86
Schiffman, Frank 33
Schildkraut, Joseph 87
Schlink, Fred J. 321
Schmeling, Max 499, 501–502, 504, 506, 512–514
Schmelkes, Franz C. 418
Schmitt, Bernadotte E. 88
Schneiderman, Rose 134
Schoedsack, Ernest 30
Schoeffer, Anna 278
Schoenberg, Arnold 45, 68
School and Society (Dewey) 163
School for Scandal Overture (Barber) 31
School Mathematics Study Group 173
Schrembs, Bishop Joseph 86
Schriner, Dave 518
Schroeder, C. R. 414
Schroeder, E. F. 417
Schultz, Dutch 261, 270
Schultz, E. W. 413
Schunzel, Reinhold 76
Schwab, Charles M. 137, 146
Schwandt, Wilbur 28
Schwartz, Delmore 40, 362
Schwartzkopf, Norman 278
Schwartzman, Gregory 418
Science 484
Scientific American 471, 491
Scopes, J. T. 298
Scopes Monkey trial 141, 298
Scotia Seminary (Barber-Scotia College) 167–168
Scott, Charles Frederick 378
Scott, Myrtle 65
Scott, Randolph 35
Scottsboro Boys 258–259, 284–286
"Scottsboro Boys" (Ledbetter) 64
Scottsboro Defense Committee 285
Scribner, Arthur H. 90
Scribner, Charles 90
Scripps, Robert Paine 378
Scripps-Howard newspaper chain 364, 374, 375, 378
Scripps-McRae newspapers 378
Scudder, Wallace McIlvaine 378
Seabiscuit (racehorse) 503, 518
Seaborg, Glenn Theodore 491
Seabury, Samuel 286–287, 298

Sisler, George 508
Sisters of the Blessed Sacrament for Indians and Colored People 433
Sit-down strikes 120–122
60 Minutes 76
Skippy 27, 87
Slavery 54, 60, 70, 82, 167, 333, 435, 441, 443
Sleeping sickness 402, 414, 418, 423
Slesinger, Tess 32, 53
Slezak, Walter 30
A Slight Case of Murder (O'Connor) 39
Slim, Memphis 64
Sloan, Alfred P. 118, 187
Sloan, J. N. W. 374
Sloan, John 360
Sloane, Everett 35
Sloanism 187
Slowe, Lucy 337
Small, Albion 170
Small, Samuel White 379
Smart, David A. 351
Smart Set 340, 361
Smelt Workers Union 71
Smiles 27
Smith, Alfred E. 118, 195, 234, 237, 245, 249, 255, 333, 437, 439–440, 446, 451, 456, 458
Smith, Arthur Donaldson 427
Smith, Bessie 33, 64, 68
Smith, Charles Morton 427
Smith, Chet 524
Smith, Clark Ashton 360
Smith, David 48
Smith, E. E. "Doc" 360
Smith, Eleanor 462
Smith, Ellison "Cotton Ed" 241, 267
Smith, Frances Stanton 379
Smith, George 86
Smith, Rev. Gerald L. K. 253, 413, 434, 440, 456–457
Smith, Henry Justin 363
Smith, Henry Lester 158
Smith, Hoke 255
Smith, Horton 500, 534
Smith, J. M. Powis 432
Smith, Jimmy 511
Smith, Joseph L. 237
Smith, Kathryn Elizabeth "Kate" 28–29, 40, 354
Smith, M. I. 418
Smith, Margaret C. 418
Smith, Nora 177
Smith, Norm 519

Smith, Ormond Gerald 379
Smith, Red 524
Smith, Richard B. 32
Smith, Robert E. 434
Smith, Robert H. 305
Smith, Ruby 68
Smith, Seymour Wemyss 379
Smith, Slim 63
Smith, Sydney 379
Smith, Theobald 420
Smith, Thorne 360
Smith, Wee Willie 511
Smith, Wendell 524
Smith, Wendy 71
Smith, Willie Mae Ford 65
Smith, Willis Warren 206
Smith College 493
Smithsonian Institution 61
Smoke and Steel (Sandburg) 83
"Smoke Gets in Your Eyes" (Kern and Harbach) 32
Smoky Mountain Boys 61
Smoot-Hawley Tariff Act of 1930 92, 94, 106–107, 210, 221
Smyth, Conn 498
Snead, Sam 516
Snedden, David 164
Snook, Neta 485
Snow, Hank 62
Snow White 343, 348
Snow White and the Seven Dwarfs 37
Snuffy Smith (Lasswell) 349
Soap operas 45, 342–343, 354
Soccer 523, 536
"The Social Creed of the Churches" 457
Social Darwinism 99, 114, 128–129
Social Frontier 146, 163, 170–171
Social Gospel 457
Social Justice 453, 457
Social reconstructionism 140, 144, 154, 156, 160, 163–164, 167, 170
Social security 412
Social Security Act of 1935 95–96, 117–118, 214–215, 219, 223, 229, 233, 235, 240, 251–252, 282, 305, 310, 321–322, 333, 385–386, 387, 390, 399, 413, 465
— Aid to Dependent Children 229
The Social Triumph of the Ancient Church (Case) 459
Socialism 44, 55, 73, 83, 103, 145, 152–153, 156, 163, 172, 194, 218, 220, 234–235, 242–243, 253–254, 294, 322–323, 329, 331, 334, 360–362, 393, 398,

403, 436, 442, 445, 455–456, 466, 493
Socialist Labor Party 126, 331, 362
Socialist Party 83, 124, 136, 314, 331, 362, 444, 455, 457
Socialist Party of America 234, 253
Socialized medicine 390, 393, 399, 403, 409, 424
Society for the Suppression of Vice 85
Society of Friends (Quakers) 166, 245, 337, 459
Sociology 61, 63, 114, 147, 154, 168–170, 172, 187, 249, 272, 311, 318, 332–333
Sockman, Rev. Ralph W. 434
Soconyland Sketches 355
Soglow, Otto 373
Soil Conservation Act of 1935 214
Soil Conservation and Domestic Allotment Act (1936) 109, 227
Sokoloff, Nikolas 61
Soldier Field, Chicago 500
Soldier's Pay (Faulkner) 77
Solf and Wichards 202
"Solitude" (Ellington, De Lange, and Mills) 32
Solitude of the Soul (Taft) 90
Solomon, Erich 340
Solow, Herbert 362
"Some Day My Prince Will Come" (Churchill and Mose) 37
Somebody in Boots (Algren) 34, 53
"Somewhere Over the Rainbow" 41
Sonata for Clarinet (Cage) 69
Sonata No. 1 for piano and orchestra (Ives) 42
Sondergaard, Gale 87
Song of Surrender (McKenney) 83
Songs of Protest (Gelert) 49
Sons of the Desert 30
Sons of the Pioneers 62
"Sophisticated Lady" (Ellington, Mills and Parish) 31
Sorrells, John 374
Soule, George 322
The Souls of Black Folks (Du Bois) 334
The Sound and the Fury (Faulkner) 77
Sousa, John Philip 90
"South American Way" (Miranda) 42
"South of the Border (Down Mexico Way)" (Carr) 41

Tomoka Mission, Daytona, Fla. 168

Tompkins, Harry 279–280

Tone, Franchot 28, 34, 39, 71, 76, 78

Too Many Girls 42

"Too Marvelous For Words" (Whiting and Mercer) 38

Too True to Be Good (Shaw) 30

Top Hat 34, 59

Topeka Institute of Psychoanalysis 411

Topics of the Times 378

Topper (Smith) 37, 360

Toronto Maple Leafs 498–500, 502, 518–519, 533–534

Torrio, Johnny 269

Tortilla Flat (Steinbeck) 34

Tosca (Puccini) 66

Toscanini, Arturo 38, 68, 86, 343, 354

"The Touch of Your Hand" (Kern and Harbach) 32

Tower Hill School 164

Town Hall, New York City 42, 85

Townsend Plan 233, 241, 412–413, 452, 457

Townsend Weekly 413

Townsend, Francis Everett 219, 233, 412–413, 434, 452, 457

Track and field 499, 501, 504–505, 507, 521–522, 525–526, 529, 532–534, 536

Tracy, Spencer 30, 35, 37, 87

Trade Agreements Act of 1934 214

Trade Union Unity League (TUUL) 303

Trade unions 141, 337, 363–364

Tragic America (Dreiser) 52

"Traitors in the Pulpit" (Facts Forum) 129

Trans-World Airlines (TWA) 477

Transatlantic (Antheil) 68

Transbay Bridge, San Francisco 136, 182, 327, 474

Transcontinental Airlines 462

Traylor, Melvin A. 255

Treasure Island (movie) 32

Treasure Island, San Francisco Bay 327

Tremaine, F. Orlin 360

Trenton Times 377

Tresca, Carlo 73, 362

Trevor, Claire 41, 69

Triangle Publications 366

Trigère, Paula 201

Trilling, Lionel 153, 361–362

Trio-Quartet-Quintet 80

Tripartite Pact 244

Triple-A Plowed Under 36, 51

Triple Crown (baseball) 527, 531

Triple Crown (horse racing) 517–518

Troland, Leonard Thompson 427, 494

Tropic of Cancer (Miller) 27

Tropic of Capricorn (Miller) 41

Trotsky, Leon 361–362

Trotskyism 73, 243, 329

Trouble in Paradise 29

The Trouble With Women (McKenney) 83

Trout, Robert 356

True and False 354

Truett, Rev. George W. 433

Trujillo, Rafael 530

Trujillo's Stars 530

Truman, Harry S 168, 246, 335, 413

Trumbo, Dalton 41, 57

Trumpler, R. J. 491

Truth-in-Securities Act of 1933 213, 259, 291

Tryon Park, N.Y. 40

Tubb, Ernest 62

Tuberculosis 389–390, 396–397, 400, 402–403, 405, 417–419, 422–423, 425, 428

Tubular chair (Breuer) 199

Tucker, Gilbert Milligan 379

Tudor Style architecture 199

Tufts, James A. 177

Tufts College 491

Tugwell, Rexford Guy 115, 156, 223–225

Tulane University 248, 414, 516, 533

"Tumbling Tumbleweeds" (Nolan) 32

Tunis, John R. 504, 507

Tunney, Gene 363, 512

Turck, Fenton Benedict 427

Turing, Alan Mathison 491

Turk, Roy 28

Turner, Frederick Jackson 88, 166, 177

Turner, John P. 150

Turner, Lana 37

Turpentine 51

Tuskegee Institute 168

Tuskegee Machine (Washington) 334

Tuskegee Syphilis Study 384

Tuttle, Frank 29

TV Guide 366

Twain, Mark 75

Twentieth Century 32, 60

20th Century–Fox 31, 58, 78, 87, 370

Twenty Grand (racehorse) 532

Twenty Thousand Years In Sing Sing (Lawes) 273

Two Appositions (Cowell) 68

Tydings, Millard 241

Typhoid fever 389, 402, 405, 415, 418–419, 423

Typhus 126

U

Ulysses (Joyce) 31

Uncle Tom's Children (Wright) 39, 44, 53–54

"Undecided" (Shavers and Robin) 41

Unemployed Teachers Association (UTA) 159

Unger, Leon 417

Union for Social Justice 336

"Union Maid" (Guthrie) 80

Union Pacific Railroad 136, 298

Union Party 233, 241, 253, 434, 452–453, 457

Union Theological Seminary, New York City 433, 435, 439, 441, 445, 454, 457

United Airlines 135, 302, 477

United Artists 58

United Auto Workers (UAW) 96, 120–121, 134, 154, 160, 215, 261, 277, 306–307

United Cloth Hat and Cap Makers Union 331

United Farmers' League 332

United Features Syndicate 368, 373

United Jewish Appeal 459

United Mine Workers (UMW) 71, 92, 101, 109–111, 132–133, 136, 231, 298, 331, 336

United Nations 129, 168, 246
— Relief and Rehabilitation Administration 247

United Office Building, Niagra Falls, N.Y. 207

United Palestine Appeal 459

United Press Association 379

United Rubber Workers of America 95

United States
— Agricultural Adjustment Administration (AAA) 93, 107–109, 225–226, 235, 248, 319
— Aircraft Board 136
— Army 162, 168–169, 211, 222, 228, 247, 289
— Army Air Corps 464, 492
— Army General Hospital No. 9, Lakewood, New Jersey 427
— Army Medical Reserve Corps 428
— Army Signal Corps 366
— Atomic Energy Commission 488, 490
— Board for Rehabilitation of Disabled Soldiers 425
— Bureau of the Budget 135
— Bureau of Chemistry 426
— Bureau of Entomology 491
— Bureau of Indian Affairs 423
— Bureau of Labor Statistics 120, 363
— Bureau of Mines 120
— Bureau of Prisons 273
— Census Bureau 387, 390, 396
— Children's Bureau 254, 312, 337, 384, 386–387, 400
— Circuit Court of Appeals 296, 305, 386, 391, 409
— Civil Aeronautics Authority (CAA) 96
— Civil Service Commission 249
— Civil Works Administration (CWA) 93, 118, 213, 228, 304, 325, 398
— Civilian Conservation Corps (CCC) 118, 140, 160–162, 175–176, 212, 228, 230, 249, 319, 398
— Commodity Credit Corporation 304
— Congress 28, 92–96, 108, 112–113, 117, 120, 129, 140, 142, 147, 156, 171, 175, 181, 196, 210–217, 219, 221–222, 224–225, 227–228, 230, 233, 236, 238, 241, 243–244, 246–248, 250, 252–254, 258–260, 262–267, 269, 271, 273–274, 276–277, 279–284, 289, 293, 298, 302–304, 306–308, 320–322, 332, 336, 342, 347, 350–351, 376, 385, 387–388, 390–391, 394, 399, 413, 425–426, 433, 447, 462, 471, 476, 479, 487, 506
— Congressional Advisory Committee on Education 175

— Constitution 94–95, 109, 116, 156, 166, 210, 212–216, 227, 230–231, 234–235, 237, 248, 251, 258–259, 262–264, 267, 271–273, 277, 279–285, 291, 293, 297, 319, 321, 340, 427, 433, 445, 447, 451–452, 455
— Council of National Defense 130
— Council on Negro Affairs 168
— Court of Appeals 325
— Custom House building, New York City 207
— Declaration of Independence 45, 50, 239, 355
— Department of Agriculture 96, 217, 224, 253, 491
— Department of Commerce 463
— Department of Justice 272, 283, 409
— Department of Justice Bureau of Investigation 272–273, 291
— Department of Labor 249, 303, 311
— Department of State 129, 243, 246, 258, 268, 291
— Department of the Interior 36, 252, 336
— Department of the Treasury 71, 112, 222, 245–246, 271–272
— Department of the Treasury Bureau of Narcotics 268
— Department of War 175, 474
— District Court, New York 31
— Electoral College 211
— Emergency Relief Administration 390, 398
— Fair Employment Practices Committee 335
— Farm Credit Administration (FCA) 107, 227
— Farm Resettlement Administration (FRA) 314
— Farm Security Administration (FSA) 43, 108–109, 215, 314, 316, 390, 403
— Farm Service Administration 81–82
— Federal Bureau of Investigation (FBI) 168, 189, 206, 260–261, 263, 268–269, 272–274, 288–289, 291–292, 297–298, 371
— Federal Communications Commission (FCC) 214, 342, 344, 346–347, 350–351, 354, 356, 367, 373, 464

— Federal Deposit Insurance Corporation (FDIC) 113, 213, 228, 273
— Federal Emergency Relief Administration (FERA) 81, 161, 212, 224, 228, 252, 304, 314, 319
— Federal Farm Board (FFB) 107, 115, 225
— Federal Housing Administration (FHA) 213, 227, 319
— Federal Power Commission 350
— Federal Radio Commission 321, 350
— Federal Reserve Board 228
— Federal Reserve System 95, 98, 104, 113, 115, 117, 137, 235, 452
— Federal Resettlement Agency (FRA) 81–82
— Federal Surplus Relief Corporation 304
— Federal Works Agency (FWA) 217
— Food and Drug Administration (FDA) 394–395
— Forest Service 162
— Home Owners Loan Corporation (HOLC) 93, 213, 227
— House of Representatives —
— House Judiciary Committee 262, 271
— House Labor Committee 254
— House Un-American Activities Committee (HUAC) 51, 156, 168, 216, 235, 262, 307
— Housing Authority (USHA) 216, 227, 307
— Internal Revenue Service (IRS) 269
— Interstate Commerce Commission 94, 350, 464, 474–475
— Interstate Commerce Commission 350
— Labor Relations Board 117
— Liberty Bonds 485
— Library of Congress 61, 63, 81
— Marines 214, 374
— Medical Corps 424
— Medical Reserve Corps 422, 424
— Merchant Marines 243
— Military Academy (West Point) 86, 504, 507, 515, 536
— National Academy of Sciences 488, 490–491
— National Advisory Committee on Aeronautics (NACA) 477

Waddington, C. H. 472
Wadsworth, Frank 494
Wagenen, James van 494
Wagner, Honus 508
Wagner, Sen. Robert F. Sr. 251, 259, 264, 266, 276, 404, 439, 458
Wagner, Robert F. Jr. 251
Wagner Health Bill 388, 390, 399, 404
Wagner Labor Relations Act. *See* National Labor Relations Act of 1935
Wagner-Hatfield Bill 341, 356
Wagner-Steagall Housing Act of 1937 251
Wainwright Building, St. Louis 205
Wait, Henry Heileman 494
Waiting for Lefty (Odets) 34, 44, 71
Waiting For Nothing (Kromer) 34
Waksman, Selman 397
Walasiewicz, Stanislawa 506, 522
Waldman, Bernard 193
Waldorf, Lynn 515
Waldorf-Astoria Hotel, New York City 195
Walgreen, Charles R. 137, 156, 427
Walgreen Drug Stores 137, 427
Walk Together Chillun (Wilson) 51
Walker, Adelaide 56
Walker, Charles 56
Walker, James "Jimmy" 195, 211, 258, 286–287, 297–298
Walker, Lapsley Greene 379
Walker, Mickey 512
Walker, Stanley 374
Walker, William Henry 379
Walker Cup (golf) 517
"Walkin' Blues" (Johnson) 36, 68
Wall Street, New York City 94–95, 105, 112, 116, 159, 185, 203, 218, 228–229, 410, 451
Wall Street Journal 376
Wallace, Henry A. 115, 225, 253
Wallas, Graham 137
Waller, Thomas "Fats" 38
Waller, Willard 329
Wallgren, Abian Anders "Wally" 374
Walsh, Edmund A. 352
Walsh, Raoul 26
Walsh, Stella. *See* Walasiewicz, Stanislawa.
Walsh-Healey Public Contracts Act of 1936 261

Walt Disney Studios 31, 37, 340, 342–343, 347–348, 399
War Admiral (racehorse) 503, 517–518, 534
The War of Independence (Van Tyne) 88
War of the Worlds (Welles) 307, 343, 347, 357
War Resisters' League 455
Warburg, Felix 137
Warburg, Otto 419
Ward, Arch 499, 515
Ward, Harry F. 437, 441, 445, 455, 457–458
Ward, Helen 65
Ward, Lester Frank 114
Ward, Theodore 51
Ward Singers 65
Ware, Dan 331
Ware, Lucien 331
Warga, Mary E. 418
Warner, Glenn Scobey "Pops" 532
Warner, Jack 58
Warner Bros. 31, 38, 58, 76, 87, 273, 348
Warren, George F. 255
Warren, Harry 28–30, 32, 34, 39
Warren, Howard Crosby 494
Warren, John C. 395
Warren, Robert Penn 41, 44, 54, 75, 249, 362
Wartime rationing 132
Wash Tubbs (Crane) 348
Washington, Booker T. 167, 169, 334
Washington, George 327, 379
Washington, Henry Stephens 495
Washington, Kenny 532
Washington, Ned 29
Washington, Orfa 532
Washington Cathedral 207
Washington Daily News 375
Washington Naval Treaty of 1922 210, 214
Washington Park, Illinois 504
Washington Post 341, 375
Washington Redskins 514, 529, 534
Washington Senators 499, 533
Washington State University 532
Washington University 79, 136, 414
Wassermann, August 405
Watch Tower Bible and Tract Society of Pennsylvania 432
Waters, Ethel 27, 31, 60
Waters, R. M. 418

Waters, Walter W. 271
Watson, Goodwin 151
The Way of All Flesh (Butler) 360
The Way Things Are and Other Stories (Maltz) 39
"The Way You Look Tonight" (Fields) 35
Waymack, William Wesley 375
Wayne, John 26, 41, 69, 129
Wayne, Mabel 26, 32
Waynesburg University 525
Weatherwax, Clara 34, 53
Weaver, Robert C. 150, 319
The Web and the Rock (Wolfe) 41
Webb, Chick 36, 45, 64–65, 78
Webb, Clifton 31, 205
Webb, F. D. 374
Weber, Max 47
Webster, L. T. 418
The Weekly People 362
Weems, Charles 284, 286
Wegener, Alfred 472
Weidman, Doris 49
Weidman, Jerome 32, 86
Weighing Cotton (Benton) 41
Weill, Kurt 68
Weintraub, William H. 351
Weird Tales 359–360, 377–378
Weisberger, David 414
Weisenburg, Theodore 427
Weismann, August 471
Weiss, Carl 249
Weiss, Mendy 268
Weiss, Soma 418
Weissmuller, Johnny 32, 56, 505
Welch, William Henry 427
Welch Medical Library, Johns Hopkins Medical School 427
Weldman, Charles 49
Weldon, Frank 31
Welles, Orson 45, 51, 71, 307, 343, 346–347, 355, 357
Welles, Sumner 246, 253
Wellesley College 332, 493
Wellman, Walter 379, 495
Wellman, William A. 27, 37
Wells, D. B. 418
Wells, H. G. 307, 343, 357
Wells, Horace 395
"We're in the Money" (Dubin and Warren) 30
"We're Off to See the Wizard" 41
Werner, Charles G. 375
Wersing, Martin 435
Wertheimer, Max 154, 173, 405
Wescot, Marcy 42

West, Mae 30, 60, 84, 146, 354, 443

West, Nathanael 27, 31–32, 41, 45, 53, 82

West Airlines 462

West Coast Hotel v. *Parrish* 96, 261, 282

Western Auto Supply 141

Western Conference outdoor track-and-field meet 501

Western Electric 104

Western Open Golf championships 531

Western Reserve University Medical School 424

Western Society of Engineers 468

Western Union 365, 465

Westinghouse, George 493

Westinghouse 220, 327–328, 372

Westley, Helen 28

Westminster Theological Seminary 460

Weston Electrical Instruments 30

Wettling, Louis Eugene 495

Whale, James 27, 34–35, 58

Wharton, Edith 90

What Every Woman Knows 32

What Price Coal? 153

What to Listen for in Music (Copland) 68

Whatever Happened to Baby Jane? 76

What's in It for Me? (Weidman) 86

Wheaton College 202

Wheeler, Burton 228

Wheeler, Burton K. 242, 282, 293

"When I Grow Too Old to Dream" (Romberg and Hammerstein) 34

"When I Take My Sugar to Tea" (Fain, Kahal, and Connor) 28

"When It's Sleepy Time down South" (L. Rene, O. Rene, and Muse) 28

"When the Moon Comes over the Mountain" (Smith) 28

Where Life Is Better: An Unsentimental American Journey (Rorty) 52

"Which Side Are You On?" (Reece) 64

Whichone (racehorse) 518

Whipple, George Hoyt 385, 389, 418, 419

"Whistle While You Work" (Churchill and Mose) 37

Whistler, James Abbott McNeill 86

Whitaker, L. R. 418

White, Andrew 284–286

White, Byron "Whizzer" 532

White, George 237, 264

White, Roy 284

White, Walter F. 264–266, 307, 319, 336

White, William Allen 239, 247

"White Angel Breadline" (Lange) 81

White Haven Sanitarium 423

White House Conference on Children in a Democracy 388

White House Conference on the Emergency Needs of Women 304

White Knights 149

The White Steed (Carroll) 42

Whiteman, Paul 354

Whiting, Richard A. 26, 29, 32, 38

Whitman Publishing 341, 349

Whitman, Walt 44, 48–49

Whitney, Gertrude Vanderbilt 28

Whitney, Leon F. 471

Whitney, Mrs. Harry Payne 86

Whitney Museum of American Art, New York City 28, 86

WHO (radio station, Des Moines, Iowa) 353

"Who's Afraid of the Big Bad Wolf?" 31, 348

Why Not Have A Baby? 373

Why Women Cry, or, Wenches with Wrenches (Hawe) 203

Wickersham, George W. 272

Wickford Point (Marquand) 41

Wiener, Alexander 411, 416

Wiener, Norbert 491

Wiernik, Peter 379

Wiggin, Kate Douglas 70

Wigner, Eugene Paul 469

Wilberforce University 333

Wilbur, Ray Lyman 476

Wilcox, Ansley 299

Wilcox, Reynold Webb 427

Wild Boys of the Road 58

Wilde, Oscar 86

Wilder, Laura Ingalls 29, 52

Wilder, Thornton 40, 85, 88

"Wildwood Flower" (Carter Family) 61

Wiley, Harvey 425

Wiley, Louis B. 379

Wilkerson, Doxey A. 151

Wilkie, John Elbert 379

Wilkins, R. W. 418

Wille, Phantasie and Werkgestaltung (Stern) 173

Willebrandt, Mabel Walker 283

William H. Spencer High School, Columbus, Ga. 140

Williams, Alfred Brockenbrough 379

Williams, Archie 521

Williams, Aubrey 162

Williams, Cootie 80

Williams, Esther 505

Williams, Eugene 284

Williams, Frankwood Earle 427

Williams, Henry L. 536

Williams, Herbert Upham 427

Williams, Hope 27, 30

Williams, Hugh 34, 38

Williams, Ira 480

Williams, Joe 509

Williams, John Whitridge 428

Williams, Linsly Rudd 419, 428

Williams, Mary Lou 39

Williams, Robert R. 419

Williams, Roger J. 463, 470

Williams, Ted 506

Williamsburg, Virginia 196

Williamson, Jack 360

Willis, Henry Parker 137

Willkie, Wendell L. 133, 487

"Willow Weep for Me" (Ronell) 29

Wills, Helen 531

Willy-Overland (automobile company) 180, 189

Wilmington Star News 372

Wilson, Bill 305, 434

Wilson, Edmund 52, 54, 361

Wilson, Frank 51

Wilson, Hack 498, 508

Wilson, M. L. 225

Wilson, Rev. Clarence True 447

Wilson, Teddy 80

Wilson, Woodrow 214, 221, 250, 254, 283, 292, 294, 298

Wimbledon tennis championships 501, 502, 505–506, 524–525, 528, 530–531, 535

Winchell, Walter 341, 355, 371

Winner Take Nothing (Hemingway) 54

Winrod, Rev. Gerald B. 440

Winter Garden Theater, New York City 33

"Winter Wonderland" (Bernard and Smith) 32

Winterset (Anderson) 35

Wintrobe, M. M. 419

Wirt, William A. 164, 177

Wisconsin General Hospital 418

Wisconsin News 365